The Complete Book Of
Doo-Wop

Dr. Anthony J. Gribin
Dr. Matthew M. Schiff

Published by

krause publications

700 East State St., Iola, WI 54990-0001
715-445-2214
www.krause.com

Please, call or write us for our free catalog of antiques and collectibles publications. To place an
order or receive our free catalog, call 800-258-0929. For editorial comment and further information,
use our regular business telephone at (715) 445-2214

Library of Congress Catalog Number: 99-68104
ISBN: 0-87341-829-8

Printed in the United States of America

Dedication

To Doris Tauber Gribin, who brought music into the lives of many people.

Acknowledgments

As you read the pages ahead, you'll understand that this book has been a labor of love throughout. That doesn't mean, though, that it's been easy. Just fun. There are a whole slew of people who made it both easier and more fun, and whose contributions made this work more interesting and complete.

First, thanks to those who contributed directly. Bob Bosco, Ron Italiano, Nay Nasser, Steve Propes, Bob Pruter and Gordon Skadberg took the time to compose and contribute original essays which are included here. And to George Moonoogian, Ed Engel and Bob Diskin, who allowed previously written material to be interwoven. And to Sandy Marrone and Bill Himmelman, who contributed most of the sheet music covers and pictures, respectively, that illustrate the book.

Less direct contributions were made by many people in many different ways. Information to fill in the blanks, interesting stories about the era, leads to make contact with other aficionados or "moguls," help with managing the computer, donation of audiotapes with some interesting songs, locating some hard-to-find periodicals or books were all desperately needed at some point in time. People who came through for us were Bob Belniak, Alan Blowstein, Trevor Churchill, Donn Fileti, Doug Friedman, Marv Goldberg, Jesse and Sara Gribin, Della Griffin, Neil Hirsch, Herb Johnson, William Martin, Don Mennie, P.J. Noce, Tony Oetjin, Lou Rallo, Don K. Reed, Harvey Robbins, Steven Roberts, Andy Rosetta, William Martin, Ernie Sierra, Val Shively, Robert L. Snyder, Lou Sylvani, Chris Towns, Hy Weiss, and Jerry Zwecher. Thanks.

Foreword

A small group of neighborhood boys from Pittsburgh gathers at the same place every Saturday afternoon, right on the corner where we used to "loaf." The group of multi-racial friends hi-five and begin their usual game of pick-up basketball, while their fully equipped music system blares these broken syllables of what they call music today.

I hum my own tune as I strut my way down to the corner just as I have every Saturday since the late '50s. The group always takes a break to shout "Hey Mr. Bassman." I lower my sunglasses and shake my head. Even though I want to ask them what they like about their music, I just say, "What's up, fellas?"

They always say things to each other like, "You really think that Freddy Johnson sang on this corner back then?" Then someone answers, "Nah. There was no such thing as a boom box back then, so they had no beat."

I lean against the fence along the court, remembering what it was like on that same corner in 1961. My friends and I got together, too, but we didn't play ball and listen to thumping from a boom box. We sang about whatever was on our minds and put harmony to it, and we were on that corner on days other than Saturdays. We skipped school to be on the corner; that was our domain.

Once the memories start coming back, I get comfortable against the fence and hum "Blue Moon." That always brings back a lot of fond moments on that corner. I light my Newport cigarette; afterall, I need something to calm me since so much as changed in the last forty years. I flick my cigarette and my smirk turns into a smile because even though technology has changed music today, nothing can change a memory, especially a time when music had meaning to it. To me, memories are glimpses of a legendary time—the days of that doo-wop street-corner sound.

This book by Gribin and Schiff also takes me back to those times I sang on the corner.

My friends and I, coming from a ghetto area in Pittsburgh, didn't have much to do, so we hooked everything from church to our paper routes just to sing on the street corner—our corner. We listened to and mimicked already-established groups like the Eldorados, Moonglows and Frankie Lymon and the Teenagers. It was like we wandered into our own world when we were on our own corner.

Jimmy Beaumont and the Skyliners and the Del Vikings were already making Pittsburgh known for that distinct doo-wop sound, but it didn't matter because we just needed our street corner fix. Plus, our style was different: we sang the old standards almost as a tribute to the barber shop quartets which began the whole harmonious chain.

But there was one day I wasn't loafing, only because I needed a haircut. I got small finger rolls put in—back then the 'do was called a marcel. I went back to the corner and just like we snapped our fingers, we had our name. We were the Marcels: me, the youngest, along with Ronald "Bingo" Mundy, the first tenor; Gene Bricker, the second tenor; Dick Knauss, the baritone; and lead singer Cornelius Harp.

So we were an established group—on our street corner, at least. We would listen to the simple radio, that only one of us owned, to hear the 1961 hits like Ben E. King's "Spanish Harlem." Although Pittsburgh wasn't recognized as one of the popular doo-wop cities, and most of the hits were coming from the New York-based groups, we felt no pressure because singing doo-wop was a part of us.

Before we knew it, the moon would creep out and the streetlights would automatically come on. Most of the white teens would sit on a friend's porch and talk about the girl next door while hearing the Four Preps over the static on their radio. The black kids played stick ball and scattered to a nearby park while humming the sounds of the Dells. But not the Marcels. We were one of the first integrated doo-wop groups, and we were proud. We'd just stand under the streetlight because to us, it was a spotlight. We didn't need an audience. Our self-satisfaction was all the applause we needed.

The doo-wop sound was mere syllables to songs with a different melody, and we used our own doo-wop style to perfect the standards. We were different races and cultures combining talents into a certain sound. While we stood under the spotlight and sang "Blue Moon," using our finger snapping as instruments, we did more than hear a distinct sound. We felt those syllables create our very own version of a song that distinguished a doo-wop sound, and months later, "Blue Moon" was the number-one hit.

The sound was more than those shoo-wops and dip-dados in harmony that made songs popular. It was even more than the dialect and word phrasing combinations that created a Pittsburgh success. It was young people basking in the simplicity of youth, ignoring a culture distinction and focusing on a musical expression of the time. That sound carried a sense of longevity and depicted a sense of time—standing under a streetlight singing under a blue moon.

Now when I lean against the fence near my old corner, lighting a cigarette, I hear jumbled sounds with no meaning coming from a boom box. The neighborhood boys can't hear that harmonious sound that will live on, because it is a part of me.

They finish the pick-up game, but in a few days it will be forgotten. I am sure next week they will argue about who won this week. But I have 40 years of that doo-wop sound to reminisce about, and that moment in time will never change or be forgotten. Rock 'n' roll may be here to stay, but doo-wop never went away.

Freddy Johnson

Freddy Johnson, The Marcels

Contents

Chapter 1

G.R.A.B. A. T.U.S.H.

(Group Rhythm And Blues And Teen Urban Streetcorner Harmony)

What do the following ten songs have in common?

"Crying In The Chapel" by Sonny Til & the Orioles (1953)

"Gee" by the Crows (1953)

"Only You" by the Platters (1955)

"Why Do Fools Fall In Love" by Frankie Lymon & the Teenagers (1956)

"In The Still Of The Night" by the Five Satins (1956)

"The Closer You Are" by Earl Lewis & the Channels (1956)

"Maybe" by the Chantels (1958)

"I Wonder Why" by Dion & the Belmonts (1958)

"My True Story" by the Jive Five (1961)

"You Belong To Me" by the Duprees (1962)

First, all of them are fairly well-known, even among those who are not oldies' fans. If you've picked up this book, if you're over thirty, or even if you can still fog a mirror, chances are you've heard of most of them. Another thing they have in common is that all of the artists are, in effect, groups that sing in harmony. Another is that they were all first released in the 1950s or early 1960s. Another is that the members of these groups were relatively young (early teens to early twenties) when these songs were issued. These commonalities not only define a type of music, but a socio-logical, historical and geographical phenomenon as well. What to call it?

Believe it or not, the answer to this question is not easy. The music comes from the barbershop quartets of the early part of the century, it comes from the jive, jazz and pop groups of the 1930s, it comes from the rhythm & blues, gospel and "race" music of the 1940s, and is intertwined with the rock 'n' roll of the 1950s. As a result, it has a little bit of a lot of things in it. We've chosen to call it "doo-wop," but arguments can be (and have strenuously been) made for other titles.

One problem with the term "doo-wop" is that it was not used as a title during the main part of the so-called "Doo-Wop Era" (the late 1940s to the early 1960s). In the 1950s, the music was simply called "rock 'n' roll" by the white community, as was the music of Fats Domino, Gene Vincent and Fabian, or "rhythm & blues" by the black community, as was the output of Chuck Berry, Ivory Joe Hunter and LaVerne Baker. Back then, everyone lumped single artists and vocal groups together. The reason is probably that most of the above artists catered to young people, and music was either the mainstream music geared to adults, or was for young people (rock 'n' roll or rhythm & blues).

These days we kind of expect young people to have their own music, but back then it was revolutionary. The following interchange between WCBS-FM (New York) deejay Don K. Reed and Arlene Smith, lead singer of the Chantels, is instructive[1]:

Don: That term, 'doo-wop,' how do you feel about it? Some people have told me they're not crazy about it... ...From my perspective as a youngster growing up listening to this music...I never heard that term, at all. Doo-wop was never there, as far as I know.

Arlene: It sounds like [someone said] 'we're gonna go do our doo-wops today'...on the way to rehearsal, and it stuck. 'Cause it was really rhythm and blues.

Don: And when I went to a show at the old Brooklyn Paramount with Alan Freed, I saw everybody. It wasn't just groups. It was...the Chantels...Charlie Gracie...the Everly Brothers...Bill Haley...the Flamingos. It was rock 'n' roll...Do you think that the labeling of what we do here in 'The Doo-wop Shop'...[accurately portrays the music]...to somebody, perhaps, who did not grow up in that era and now hears...the groups referred to as 'doo-wops' and the Buddy Hollys and the Frankie Avalons referred to as rock 'n' roll?

Arlene: No! No, you know it doesn't. It really doesn't. It's divided it. What was rhythm and blues became rock 'n' roll became doo-wop.

So how can one use the term "doo-wop" when it was only applied after the fact? Well, it wasn't quite after the fact because it was literally within the music. The sound "doo-wop" could be heard as part of the background chanting in the recordings which make up the genre. It was one of the most commonly used "fillers" during and even before the era began. It can be heard in "My Gal Sal" by the Charioteers in 1939 and in "Low Down Gal Blues" by the Lewis Bronzeville Five in 1940. The string "doo doo doo doo-wop" is used repeatedly in the famous song "Just A Sittin' And A Rockin'" by the Delta Rhythm Boys in 1946. In the early 1950s, it was used by most of the "big" rhythm and blues groups; it can again be found at the end of "Wagon Wheels" by the Ravens from 1951; it appears in "Let The Boogie Woo-gie Roll," recorded by the Clyde McPhatter Drifters in 1953; it frequents the background of "Over The Rain-bow" by the Checkers in 1954; it is used by the Flamin-gos in "I'm Yours" in 1955.

---

1. From Don K. Reed's "Doo-wop Shop," April 14, 1996.

"Doo-wop" has put in guest appearances in some of the most prominent songs of the middle 1950s as well, showing up in "Most Of All" by the Moonglows (1955), "When You Dance" by the Turbans (1955), "A Thousand Miles Away" by the Heartbeats (1956) and "Teardrops" by Lee Andrews and the Hearts (1957). Tons of other examples exist. Calling the music "doo-wop" therefore, becomes pure unmitigated onomatopoeia, a word we were sure we'd never need or see again after high school. Onomatopoeia , as our English teachers would gleefully remind us, is a word that sounds like what it defines.

Oddly enough, proof exists of this phenomenon. In 1976, a fellow by the name of Bill Newell reported, "The origin of the word Doo-wopp, comes from my friend John Fletcher, of Gresham, Oregon.[2] One night, some ten years ago [which would place it roughly in 1966], we were playing some records [at] midnight and getting down. I'd been trying to get him into group sounds and blues for a few months. We'd previously met in Korea and he was into jazz. After playing a lot of oldies, he said: 'Why don't you play something else? All you play is that doo-woppy shit.' I said, 'What?' and he said, 'Those records, all they do is go doo-wopp, doo-wopp.' I laughed and thought, Wow, that's kinda true (for an untrained ear) but it's a good name for them.[3] So from then on, group sounds, '50s, oldies, etc. became 'doo-wopps.' I used the term in my dealings and tapes with other collectors and it stuck. The moniker was a natural. Thanks John."[4]

Newell began to work with deejay Gus Gossert, then working at a station in San Francisco. The term caught on and was appropriated by Gossert, who brought it east to New York with him in 1969 when he went to work for WCBS-FM. There, it caught on in a big way. While Newell's friend's usage is clearly onomatopoetic, it is not, as Newell thought, the first time the term was used.

The homonym "Du-Whop" is found as the title of a 1958 song by the Chessmen, even though, as used, it seems to refer to a dance. "Doo-wop," with its current meaning was found in the print media as early as 1961. Referring to "Blue Moon" by the Marcels, an article by one Chuck Davis in the Chicago Defender[5] told of "a real doo-wop, like those of many years ago, [that] is making the scene but big in Chi-town..." So the phrase, while not exactly native to the era, has had at least 39 years to grow on us.

Over the years, "Doo-Wop" has been used in the name of many radio shows (e.g. "The Doo-Wop Shop" on CBS-FM, New York), in the title of periodicals (e.g.

"Doo-Wop Retrorock Review"), in the names of multi-group retrospective shows (e.g. "The Royal New York Doo-Wop Show") and on numerous record albums (e.g. "Doo Wop Uptempo" on Rhino, "Harlem: The Doo-Wop Era" on Collectables and "Twenty Great Doo Wop Recordings" on Cascade) and compact discs ("A Lighter Shade Of Doo Wop" on Relic, "Hard Core Doo-Wop" on Specialty and "Starlight Serenade: 1950's Doo-Wop Groups 'Acappella'" on Starlight). When you describe music as "doo-wop," people know what you mean, making communication easier. It has become common usage. Too common, perhaps.

The rap against the phrase is that over the last twenty-five or so years, the term "doo-wop" has been overused and thus cheapened. By putting it in the title of almost every revival show which is partially comprised of singing groups from the '50s, the term has been associated with single artists like Chuck Berry or Leslie Gore, non-doo-wop groups like the Motown Supremes/Temptations, pastiche groups like Sha Na Na and Flash Cadillac, and thus has had its meaning diluted. It has, they say, become almost synonymous with "oldies," rather than connoting the vocal group harmonic music of the 1950s (plus and minus a few years).

Another criticism of the use of the term is that many of the groups that used a lot of "doo-wops" in the background of their songs (among other clearly heard discrete syllables like "boom boom boom" and "doe doe doe") didn't really come along until almost midway in this musical era (i.e. mid-1950s) and are more allied to rock 'n' roll than the earlier music from which doo-wop evolved (and which some die-hard fans revere). If "doo-wop" backgrounds weren't in common usage during the formative 1946-1952 period, why lump the musics together? Diehards would prefer the term "rhythm & blues" to describe this early music, and they prefer that "doo-wop" be reserved for uptempo tunes with lots of nonsense syllables. Some right-wing diehards would go as far as to completely banish the word "doo-wop" from the lexicon.[6] They would like it to doo-wop off the face of the earth, so to speak.

"Rhythm & Blues" is a term that dates back to the 1940s. Billboard published its Pop Charts for many years before it kept track of "race" music. In 1942, Billboard published a second chart that it called the "Harlem Hit Parade" through February 1945 and the "Race" chart from that point through mid-1949. Thereafter, its name was changed to the "Rhythm & Blues" chart. While the chart was named in 1949, "rhythm and blues" was used to describe bluesy music to which rhythm had been added at least since the end of World War II. "Rhythm and Blues" is thus a post-hoc term, just like "doo-wop."[7]

Another big problem with using "Rhythm & Blues" to describe what we call doo-wop is that, for the most

2. Heretofore, Gresham, Oregon has not been often mentioned as the birthplace of doo-wop.
3. Luckily for us, he shortened it to doo-wopp.
4. Newell, Bill. "Gus Gossert: His early years." From *Out Of The Past*, Issue #4, p. 16.
5. Davis, Chuck. "Platters," *Chicago Defender*, March 18, 1961.

6. Notice that there were three hyphenated words in this sentence. We're very proud of this.
7. It just hocced its post earlier than did "doo-wop."

part, the term is not nearly specific enough. If one looks at Billboard's early R&B charts, it's apparent that only a fraction of the recordings on these charts are by groups. Most of what was called R&B was by single artists with or without strong instrumental backing. Of the Top 40 R&B hits of the 1940s (actually 1942-1949), only two offer vocal group harmony. Of the Top 40 R&B hits of the 1950s, only twelve are by vocal groups. Of the 44 "Top Rhythm And Blues Artist Before 1952" that were identified by Lee Cotton, only eight were groups.[8] Apparently, Louis Jordan's Tympani Five, Cecil Gant and Wynonie Harris are much more integral to the term "Rhythm & Blues" and to the R&B charts than are the Ravens, Orioles and Dominoes (the holy trinity of early R&B groups). The R&B charts are dominated by instrument-heavy, single artist sounds, while the music we're trying to name is primarily vocal, with instruments being secondary. So while "Rhythm & Blues" only implies the presence of a group occasionally, "doo-wop" always does.

Lynn McCutcheon, in his 1971 treatise called Rhythm & Blues[9] (probably the first analytical treatment of the subject), divided the era into three stages: Pioneer, Rock 'n' Roll and Soul. Without getting into disagreements now over his classification system, the fact that he includes "Soul" in "Rhythm & Blues" makes our point that the term is overly general. Fortunately or not, R&B has been used to describe almost any and all music recorded by African-Americans since World War II. The Clovers and Drifters are R&B, but so are the Jackson Five, the (Detroit) Temptations, Sly & the Family Stone and Boyz 2 Men. A term which is this general and includes so many different types of music under its umbrella, is not a useful tool for describing our music.

Further, whatever R&B meant in the 1950s bears no resemblance to the music that bears its name today. A look at an average large record store, such as Sam Goody's, will demonstrate that the artists who appear on the R&B racks are not even close to the doo-wop music created in the 1950s. In contrast, a doo-wop is a doo-wop is a doo-wop. So to use "rhythm and blues" as a term one must qualify it many ways. "Vocal group rhythm and blues of the 1950s" is quite accurate but awfully unwieldy. It sure wouldn't fit on a license plate, while "DOO-WOP" and DU-WHOP" can and have.

Brian Stilwell, writing for Echoes Of The Past, agreed with the parsimony theory. "As the term is used today...[today equates to 1990]...any group sound from the late forties, like the Ravens, on through the early sixties sounds of the Earls or Duprees is now put under the Doo-Wop heading. However, if my memory serves me correctly, this is an expansion of the original meaning. When I first started hearing the term Doo-Wop used in the late fifties and early sixties, it was primarily used to describe the white group sound of that time. But slowly over the years, the black group sound of the mid-fifties and even the heavy R&B sound of the late forties and early fifties have been placed under the Doo-Wop label instead of rhythm and blues."[10] Thus, the term "rhythm and blues" had was supplanted over the years, perhaps for the sake of simplicity, with "doo-wop."

A third candidate for the title is "vocal group harmony" which ably describes part of what doo-wop is but contains no time reference. The Five Satins and Moonglows offer vocal group harmony, but so do the Andrews Sisters, Four Seasons, the Beach Boys, the Beatles and the Mamas and the Papas. To pin it down more, one needs to add a time reference, such as "vocal group harmony of the 1950s." Unfortunately, this is also a bit unwieldy—which brings us to "GRAB A TUSH," the title of this chapter. Perhaps, in this age of soundbytes, an acronym does make sense, conveying a great deal of information in a short, upbeat, peppy phrase. There are options as well. "BUSH" could be substituted for "TUSH," as in "Black Urban Streetcorner Harmony, or the connective "A" could be replaced by "ANY," as in "And New York" or by "MY," as in "Meets Young." Actually, "doo-wop" is beginning to sound better and better.

At one time, adopting a less frivolous approach, we thought about combining the two leading candidates, "doo-wop" and "rhythm and blues." Since "doo-wop" is easily used as an adjective (e.g. doo-wop music and doo-wop groups), it can be used to modify the noun "rhythm and blues." Thus the title becomes "doo-wop rhythm and blues" (DWR&B). By using doo-wop as a descriptor, one that easily connotes groupness, it differentiates our music from single artist and instrumental rhythm and blues.

In a way, DWR&B made some sense to us for a while. The group vocal music created in 1948, 1955 and 1961 has many shared characteristics, but some differences as well. The Cardinals, Four Buddies, Larks and Dominoes, groups that began life around 1951, created music that was quite rhythm and bluesy with a few doo-wop characteristics thrown in. The songs of the Channels, Belmonts and Jesters have a "doo-woppy" feel, with some rhythm and bluesy characteristics. The term DWR&B allowed for these combinations.

An additional reason to choose a hybrid title was to get past some of the political implications of choosing one or the other. While the politics of doo-wop has its own chapter, for now suffice it to say that people who dabble in the music use "doo-wop," while dyed-in-the-wool enthusiasts/ hobbyists will only use "rhythm and blues." By choosing DWR&B, we were hoping to get past that hurdle.

8. Cotton, Lee. Shake Rattle & Roll: The Golden Age of American Rock 'n' Roll, Vol. 1, 1952-1955. Pierian Press, 1989.

9. McCutcheon, Lynn Ellis. Rhythm and Blues. Arlington, VA: Beatty, 1971.

10. Stilwell, Brian. "What's In A Name?" Echoes Of The Past, Issue #14, Fall 1990, p. 20.

Not so fast, title-bereft authors! Our publisher pointed out that using "Doo-Wop Rhythm and Blues" in the title would be misread as "Doo-Wop and Rhythm and Blues." Since our book only deals with a small portion of the totality of R&B music, we would be misrepresenting our work. Oh well...For the joint purposes of brevity and our own sanity, we'll use "doo-wop" in the title and as the primary descriptor of the music in the rest of the book.

That being settled, how then do we spell it?[11] For the first syllable, we can choose "Do," "Doo" or "Du." "Do" could be mispronounced as "Doe," and "Du" sounds too French and high-class for such an American-born music, so we're resigned to "Doo" (even though it's something we'd prefer not to step in). For the last syllable, we have to choose between "Wopp," "Whop" and "Wop." "Wopp" always looks like there are too many "p's" (i.e. it is "missppelled"), and as for "Whop," we'd prefer to get the "h" out of there. "Doo-Wop" it is then, but we do (or doo) realize that the term has its shortcomings.

While naming and spelling "Doo-Wop" are issues not quite as compelling as world peace or pollution, they do evoke emotional responses in those close to the music. Val Shively, a record collector who has had a mail-order business and/or store for around thirty years[12], described how he was smitten.[13] He started collecting records in 1956 and was leading a happy life enjoying all sorts of rock 'n' roll sounds, like Chuck Berry and Little Richard. He even went to school to be an accountant. His life was going along swimmingly, until the bottom fell out in 1962. That's when he heard Gerry Blavat ("The Geator with the Heater") playing all those doo-wops. He (Val) had been listening to "whiter" stations, and Blavat's show reached him at the core of his very being, and it changed him. All of a sudden he needed money to buy all those group sounds that he just had to have. He sold Berry and Penniman for a pittance. He was hooked. And there are plenty more poor souls where he came from. After a while, one develops a "doo-wopcentric" view of the universe.[14] So don't ever ask us why we wrote a book on doo-wop. We couldn't not.

These are the kinds of stories one hears about when one trods about within the doo-wop world. And we've been trodding and plodding for quite a while now. These burning issues we've uncovered for this book are really the fault of a previous book, called *Doo-Wop: The Forgotten Third of Rock 'N' Roll*. That one came about because between early 1990 and the summer of 1992, we didn't have much important stuff to do besides making a living and raising our families. So we wrote a book on doo-wop.

As we began to gather information for that first book, we began to realize that we were in virgin territory; that no man had been there before. There were a few excellent books that focused on parts of the doo-wop scene, but none that attempted to define and describe the whole doo-wop era in its entirety. Now, if you're a real guy, that kind of thing is a motivator, a real turn-on. Another thing we realized is how much we didn't know about the subject. Although we loved the music since our teenage years, our knowledge of it was scant compared to some of the people we met along the way. In a way, as a later chapter on the political side of the music will explain, our naivete was an advantage because we could remain somewhat objective. So we had the motivation and objectivity. All we had to do was put in the hours.

We learned about our subject as we were writing the book and even after it was finished. In the summer of 1992, the book came out and, though not quite a best seller, was well-received among people who love the music. We also found ourselves in demand (meaning we didn't have to beg too much) as guests on many of the radio shows which support the doo-wop genre. We first guested on Harvey Holiday's show on WOGL (a CBS affiliate) in Philadelphia, and eventually landed a guest appearance on Don K. Reed's "Doo-Wop Shop" on CBS-FM in New York. We even became minor celebrities (perhaps an overstatement) within our nuclear families.

Being guests on roughly a dozen radio programs put us in contact with disc jockeys and collectors who knew more about the music than we did and/or were as passionate about it. Many of the disc jockeys, amateur or professional, started out as record collectors and fans. Many have been involved in the music through the era itself and through the various revivals which have popped up every few years since the late fifties. Lengthy involvement like this brought not only knowledge but strongly held views about the music business in general and the doo-wop community in particular. In time, we began to see ourselves not so

---

11. If you think this is an easy question either, you're terribly naive. Even the experts (we hope they're experts, anyway) who contributed articles to be included in this book don't agree on the spelling. Bob Pruter spells it "Doowop" (no space, no hyphen), Steve Propes and Bob Bosco use "Doo Wop" (no hyphen), Ed Engel and these authors prefer "Doo-Wop," Ronnie Italiano's Clifton Music has printed T-shirts and other memorabilia with "Doowopp University" on them (no hyphen, no space, extra p), and the senior author of this book has a New Jersey license plate with "Du-Whop" on it (to be accurate, the reported hyphen is really a tiny little picture of the State of New Jersey).

12. It's called "R&B Records" and is located in Upper Darby, Pennsylvania.

13. Phone conversation, Jan. 15, 1997.

14. doo-wopcen'trism, n. [from Amer. doo-wop, great music, and center, and -ism.] the emotional attitude that vocal group rhythm and blues, created between the late 1940s and early 1960s, is superior to all other musics, and is the standard by which all others are measured. Amen.
-Websters Unabridged Dictionary (not).

much as experts (the more you know, the more you know you don't know), but as chroniclers of those with expert knowledge or experience in the field. Almost as John Watson, M.D. did for Sherlock Holmes (except perhaps not quite as ineptly as Watson). These contacts helped to alter our views significantly.

The upshot of this major exposure to the real world of doo-wop is that we've decided to exercise a woman's prerogative (we're not sure which woman yet) and change our minds about significant parts of the theses put forth in the first book. It's not that we necessarily think that anything put forth in that book was wrong (being guys we wouldn't admit it anyway), just incomplete.

The first book was made up of roughly 120 pages of text and about 480 pages of discography. The discography was, as of the date of publication, the most complete listing of doo-wop recordings around, alphabetized by group. Due to the balance of allotted space, however, the book probably appealed more to the record collector who, in effect, was getting a checklist of records (among other things), than to the non-collector who just liked the music and wanted to learn more about it. This latter group might have bought the book, but eighty percent of what they bought was filler for them. Because the discography took up so much space, there were aspects of the subject that we wanted to include, but couldn't. After all, you don't publish a list of half the doo-wop songs ever recorded; it's all or none. So this time we've decided to focus on the story of the music.

The difference between the first book and this one is primarily a matter of depth. The more we've learned about the genre, the more we've wanted to delve deeper into the music and its concomitants. We've dug deeper in several ways. First, we've gone further back in time to examine the precursors of the doo-wop sound and have also decided that the "birth" of doo-wop occurred earlier than we thought it had. This decision opened up our minds, hearts and ears (and perhaps a few other essential organs) to a whole untapped body of music that was created between 1946 and 1951. We remarked on this earlier music in the first book, but didn't pay that much attention to it.

We've also looked deeper into the output of the more well-known groups. For each hit that a given group had, there are probably at least two other songs that are just as good, but for reasons out of their control, never attained recognition. Taking the Solitaires as an example, "Walking Along" is known to most people who like doo-wop, so is "The Angels Sang." Looking a little bit deeper into the group, one finds a series of unbelievably beautiful ballads, such as "Please Remember My Heart," "Blue Valentine," "Wonder Why" and "I Don't Stand A Ghost Of A Chance," as well as catchy jump tunes like "I Really Love You So (Honey Babe)" and "Later For You Baby." If you haven't heard these, you're in for a real treat.

Another way to look deeper into the music is to examine the output of the more obscure groups. To everyone except real aficionados, groups like the Orchids, Gems, Four Buddies and Castelles won't conjure up many memories because they didn't chart and weren't played much over the airwaves in the 1950s, and are rarely heard, even today. As you listen to their music, however, you begin to realize that many of their recordings were as good as those that became hits. One big problem with the music business in the 1950s was that it was not a pure Darwinian process; that is, the cream didn't necessarily rise to the top. Connections, musical politics, money and luck determined which songs were heard on the airwaves and bought, rather than raw talent or beauty in the music.

Even a group that had a hit frequently disappeared as quickly as it arrived. The follow-up releases, often better because the group had some experience, went nowhere fast. The label owner may not have been able to put the next record out quickly enough, or couldn't reach (afford?) the deejays, with a net result that the groups returned to obscurity. So some good records went unheard or stayed "in the can" (were unreleased). This is really a gift to us in the 1990s, however. If you've just dabbled heretofore in doo-wop, you have an unbelievable treat in store for you. There are thousands of beautiful songs, most of which you've probably not heard, waiting just around the (street) corner. As a preview, peruse our Top 1,000 songs in a later chapter.

A further difference between the first book and this one is that we've looked into the politics and geographical influences that inhere in the music. These are subjects not usually associated with the supposedly innocent music of the 1950s. Besides the "Teenage Menace" chapter, which looks into the sociology of the music, and the "Indies Vs. the Establishment" chapter, which examines business aspects, there are new chapters on "Doo-wopolitics" and "Doo-wogeography." Although the "heartland" of doo-wop today is clearly centered along the New York City to Philadelphia corridor, it wasn't always so. And although the music, when first sung, seemed to have nothing to do with politics, the intervening years have spawned factions and frictions that have sometimes detracted from the innocence of the music and even limited its popularity.

Added to the original (but expanded) "Idiosyncrasies of Doo-wop" chapter are "High School Confidential" and "Songstories" that sometimes take a poke at the attitudes of the era of the 1950s, sometimes deliver a message and sometimes offer no redeeming value whatsoever. Generally these chapters will be fun to read and were even more fun to write.

Some chapters from the first book were revised and presented again here. The chapter on the "Teenage Menace" looks at the birth of the teen generation. Youngsters may have been too young to write about their experiences, but they weren't too young to sing about them. The body of doo-wop songs that emerged from the early 1950s onward really represent the first utterances of the modern collective teen generation and gives us our first clues as to what they were feeling and thinking.

The "Death Knell" Chapter from the first book has been renamed "God Digs Doo-Wops, Man" (for reasons that will become apparent after you've read it), has been revised and expanded, and now takes a deeper look at the important players in the post-doo-wop era. We were gently chided by a writer who calls himself "Squire" a few years ago, in an excellent article about Times Square Records.[15] "The definitive work on Doo-Wop [he means *The Forgotten Third*...] devotes a paltry three sentences to this famous institution [he means Times Square Records]." Squire, we've seen the light.

The "Doo-Wop In The Bucket" chapter is also enlarged to include the views of others and, in summary, deals with the tenet that doo-wop gets no respect. Chapters dealing with nonsense syllables, bass singers, lead singers, the white group sound and the girl group sound have been added.

Additionally, there are puzzles and quizzes strategically placed throughout the book to keep the reader on his/her/their toes.[16] Some of them are difficult, and the rest of them are even harder. Toward the end, we give a sort of "final exam" in the form of the Doo-Wop Aptitude Test, or DWAT. Get a good night's sleep before you take this one.

We've tried to make the book inclusive in the sense that the opinions and experiences of others appear. Among the people who have directly or indirectly contributed articles or have allowed their stories to be retold are Bob Bosco, Bob Diskin, Ed Engel, Ronnie Italiano, George Moonoogian, Nay Nasser, Steve Propes, Robert Pruter, Val Shively and Gordon Skadberg. If the reader has any doo-wop or rhythm and blues periodicals or CDs, we'll lay even money that you have something written by at least one of these guys. They're pros.

At various times, the book will be both presumptuous and irreverent. The irreverent stuff will be in footnotes, sidebars or italics. The presumptuous stuff you won't have any trouble distinguishing. As for whatever stuff is in between, you're on your own. And now that we've decided what to call it (doo-wop) and how to spell it (doo-wop), we may as well move on to discuss it (doo-wop).

---

15. Squire. "Off The Wall: A Collector's Memories of Times Square Records." *Echoes Of The Past*, Issue #29, Autumn 1994, p. 4.

16. Just keep off ours.

Chapter 2

No Respect

Once upon a time we were young. Teen-aged young. Those were the times when we began to figure out who we were, to assert ourselves, to tell the world that we were here. We had our own opinions that were, we thought, original; we were sure that our parents knew less than us; we wanted to run our own lives. We were almost adults and wanted to be treated as adults, except for the responsibility part.

For some reason, most of us look back fondly on those years, even if they really weren't so great as we lived through them. We tend to forget the humiliations, or at least seem to be able to laugh at them. And the triumphs, few as they may have been, are remembered as though they were grand slams in the ninth of the seventh of the World Series. We know we can't go back there, but we love to revisit those times in our minds. We think back to the friends, the girlfriends or guy-friends, the school days and the summers. Seeing old movies, television shows or photographs helps us to go back, but the best link is given aurally, by music. For some reason, maybe because "oldies" are so accessible these days on radio and CDs, music provides a time machine, with which we can shed forty or so years.

The music of our memories is doo-wop for many of us. That music easily reminds us of the male or female bonding activities of our generation. The by-now-proverbial candy store hangouts, the schoolyard stickball and basketball courts, the drag strips and pool halls, the bowling alleys and back stairs of schools. We cherish our friendships back then, marvel at our feelings of invincibility and regret what we lost because of our insecurities. The lyrics of the songs we loved were as innocent as we were, or vice versa. Those lyrics easily bring back memories of our first love and first object of lust. The second object too, and the third. In so many ways, doo-wop music helps us retrace the journey of our lives, as we went from being children to being adults.

The "oldies" phenomenon was born toward the end of the doo-wop era, around 1960, and has been a presence in the music scene ever since. Younger people know many of the songs and dance to the sound at clubs with names like "At The Hop" or "Yakety Yak Cafe." Since doo-wop music is readily available, especially on radio, one might think that books on doo-wop would also be easy to obtain.[1] Not even close. Looking for one such book led us to the conclusion that there were none, and led to our first effort, titled *Doo-Wop: The Forgotten Third of Rock 'n' Roll*, which came out in 1992. We quickly learned that doo-wop was consistently overlooked and underrated. We also found socio-cultural reasons for separating doo-wop and rhythm and blues from the larger body of rock 'n' roll.

When we began research for our first book in 1990, there were no (meaning zero) books written about doo-wop music. There were a few obscure books on rhythm and blues, a few album and CD covers that used the term doo-wop, a few fanzines that did the same, and that's about it. A fellow by the name of John Rockwell wrote an article on doo-wop for the New Grove Dictionary of American Music, a revered and oft-consulted reference work spanning thousands of pages in four huge (very heavy) volumes. The amount of space allotted to the subject we revere is one-quarter of one page. Is there no end to injustice? Further, Mr. Rockwell made an unfortunate error, citing "There's A Moon Out Again" by the Capris in 1961 as a song representative of the era. The correct citation was "There's A Moon Out Tonight," the former being the flip of their 1980s hit, "Morse Code of Love." A rather auspicious beginning, nicht wahr?

We aren't alone in sensing the dearth of material on doo-wop in the print medium. Robert Santelli, at one time a music critic for the *Asbury Park Press*,[2] once wrote, "Page through any rock-history book and, chances are, doo-wop is given scant attention. There is no good reason why this offshoot of '50s rock 'n' roll that featured intricate rhythm and blues-flavored harmonies and urban street corner sensibility gets shortchanged, other that its rather short-lived popularity (it was all but dead as a pop vocal form by 1963) and its limited influence on future rock 'n' roll."[3] Rock critic Dave Marsh, ex-contributor to *Rolling Stone* magazine and author of *The Heart of Rock and Soul: The 1001 Greatest Singles Ever Made*, apparently concurs. He wrote, "Some of the most beautiful records ever made (though you'd be hard-pressed to find it out in previous histories) are the sound of willful young men learning to unify themselves in three- and four- or five-part harmony: That is the special glory of doo-wop, and restoring that music to its central place in the early chapters of the story provides one of the great lost truths of rock and soul."[4] Apparently the flood of books on doo-wop music has not yet crested.

Musical tributes to doo-wop abound, issued by labels such as Ace (London, England), Classic Artists (Los Angeles, CA), Clifton (Clifton, NJ), Collectables (Nar-

---

1. Yeah, right!

2. He is, as of November 1996, director of education for the Rock 'n' Roll Hall of Fame in Cleveland, Ohio.

3. Santelli, Robert. "Rhino Records remembers doo-wop." Asbury Park Press, Asbury Park, N.J.: Feb. 9, 1990, p.12.

4. Marsh, Dave. *The Heart of Rock and Soul: The 1001 Greatest Singles Ever Made*. New York: New American Library, 1989.

berth, PA), Crystal Ball (Little Neck, NY), Relic (Hackensack, NJ) and Rhino (San Francisco, CA). Most of these have excellent liner notes. And while books on doo-wop and rhythm & blues are scarce, they can be found. Phil Groia's book, titled, *They All Sang on the Corner*, is a fascinating chronicle of the intertwined careers and destinies of many of New York's doo-wop groups. Lynn McCutcheon's *Rhythm and Blues* was an analytical study of rhythm and blues and soul styles, with the intention of comparing and contrasting their similarities and differences. And *Du-Wop*, by Johnny Keyes, the lead of the erstwhile Magnificents (who sang "Up On The Mountain"), told the story of the trials and tribulations of being a member of a group in those times. Jim McGowan, leader of the Four Fellows, does a wonderful job of retelling the formation and career of his pop-styled R&B group in *Here Today, Here To Stay*. First released in 1983 and quite obscure (and unknown to these authors), it has been republished with an additional introduction in 1997.

In the early 1990s, Jay Warner contributed *American Singing Groups: A History 1940-1990*, which presented biographical essays on most of the important groups that performed before, during and after the doo-wop era. It is an invaluable resource for anyone in the field. Todd Baptista added *Group Harmony: Behind the Rhythm and the Blues* in 1996, which offers longer and more detailed biographies of eleven important groups from the 1950s. It, too, is worth having, but Warner's is essential.

Unfortunately, with the exception of the Warner book, all of the above have had limited circulation and thus are fairly difficult to find. Along the same lines are a dozen or so periodicals (really fanzines) that were sold to doo-wop buffs and which were outside[5] the mainstream media. Usually these magazines started out with lofty goals, spat out a bunch of issues, and then faded into oblivion. Examples are *Bim Bam Boom*, (14 issues between 1971 and 1974), *Record Exchanger* (31 issues between 1969 and 1983) and *Record Collector's Monthly* (51 issues between 1982 and 1993). There is one mainstream periodical, *Goldmine*, that puts out occasional issues devoted to the doo-wop genre. Almost always, the articles present the history of individual groups, labels or other significant figures. Rarely, if ever, can one find an analytical treatment of the subject. Nothing has been done to place doo-wop in its proper sociological, psychological or musical perspective. Even since the publication in 1992 of our first book on the subject, very little of significance has emerged, and absolutely nothing of an analytical nature. The world is just about crying out for something in this vein.

Aside from the scarcity of written material, doo-wop gets lost in the statistics of musical charts. Not only does the importance of doo-wop depend on which chart one views, but on the way the chart is viewed. In the material that we analyzed for our earlier book, the penetration of doo-wop varied from around 3% to around 30%, depending on how we looked at and analyzed the data.

For example, if we look to see how popular the doo-wop genre was since the beginning of the rock 'n' roll era, the numbers are disappointing. According to the *Billboard* charts from 1955 to 1988, only 2% of the top 100 records and 3% of the top 100 artists fall into the doo-wop category.[6] Of *Billboard's* top 1,000 singles between 1955 and 1987, only 3.8% were doo-wops[7], as were only 4.4% of those which made the "Top 40" during those same years.[8] This rather broad longitudinal view implies that doo-wop was really a "doo-wop in the bucket."

But suppose we narrow our focus to look only at the doo-wop era, that is, the years during which the music flourished. From *Billboard*, 15.4% of the number-one hits between 1955 and 1963 were doo-wops[9], and, according to the Norm N. Nite Almanac, 19.7% of the most popular songs from 1954 to 1963 were our kind of music.[10] These numbers are much more encouraging.

The numbers get even better if we look at the penetration of doo-wops on the oldies scene. Oldies stations usually run annual or biennial polls of their listeners to see what they want to hear. It's a great gimmick, for it makes listeners feel like their preferences count and also gives the radio station feedback to revise their play lists. We reviewed data from polls taken by oldies stations in ten cities. In New York, 31.8% of the songs appearing on a Top 500 survey were doo-wops. The respective numbers for the other cities were 25.7% of 400 in Houston, 22.8% of 500 in Philadelphia, 22% of 300 in Los Angeles, 18% of 500 in Boston, 14.5% of 400 in St. Louis, 13.8% of 500 in Cincinnati, 12.2% of 500 in Chicago, and 11.2% of 500 in Tampa and Kansas City.[11] The average of these numbers (although this average is not a real good statistic), is 18%, meaning that roughly one in five songs cherished by oldies fans comes from the doo-wop stable. Considering that doo-wop was not a significant force in its heyday, and that the genre was competing with Elvis Presley, the Beatles, the Motown sound and even Michael Jackson in the minds of oldies fans, this is a pretty good performance.

Actually, we can get even higher than one in five if we narrow our focus even further. Suppose we concentrate on the larger urban areas where doo-wop was born and thrived. People from most southern states were listening to rockabilly, but the guys and gals from New York, Philly and L.A. were into the doo-wop sound. Many local hits in these cities were local hits by local groups.

If we try to focus on those adults who grew up in the doo-wop era and came from urban areas, the percent of

---

5. Way outside, like a wild pitch.

6. Whitburn, Joel. *The Billboard Book of Top 40 Hits.* New York: Watson-Guptill, 1989.

7. Ibid.

8. ibidibid.

9. Ibidibidibid.

10. Norm N. *Rock on Almanac.* New York: Harper & Row, 1989.

11. More detailed information about the surveys and radio stations can be found in *Doo-Wop: The Forgotten Third...*

doo-wop penetration increases. Looking at the WCBS-FM (New York) Top 500 poll for 1989, we see that doo-wop gets a lot more respect. Doo-wop songs occupied 7 of the top 10 places, 46% of the top 100, and 31.8% of the top 500. The numbers from the same survey taken in the 1990s didn't change much. Doo-wops made up 28.8% of the Top 500 in 1991, 31.4% in 1993-94 and 28.8% in 1995-96. It appears, from these statistics, that doo-wop is appreciated more today than it was during the era, at least among certain populations.

Another way that doo-wop gets overlooked, is that it has been "gypped" by the timing of the rock 'n' roll explosion, which occurred in 1955. Many people start histories of the rock 'n' roll era in 1955, which coincides with the emergence of "Rock Around The Clock" from the film "The Blackboard Jungle" and the arrival of Elvis Presley. Unfortunately, that date hides from view a myriad of doo-wop rhythm & blues masterpieces that came earlier.[12] Rhythm and blues-flavored doo-wop came before rock 'n' roll and may well have helped to create it.

If doo-wop was around before rock 'n' roll became popular, then it should at least be seen as an important part of rhythm & blues, which was around in name since World War II, shouldn't it? One woulda thunk that if the early doo-wop material was not popular among whites, and therefore made virtually no showing on the pop charts, that at least they would've made inroads on the rhythm & blues charts, which reflected what blacks were listening to and buying. Not so. The table presented below displays the percent of top singles and top artists that were group harmony efforts, by five-year span. Data are from a book by Big Al Pavlow.[13] Interestingly, the three time periods below correspond roughly to what we have labeled pre-doo-wop, paleo-doo-wop and classical doo-wop in our chapter on Evolution, elsewhere in this book. As can be seen, the overwhelming majority of hits were produced by single artists or instrumental groups, although both the percent of Top Records and Top Artists increased as the years wore on.

The Contribution of Groups

Years	Percent of Top Records performed by groups	Percent of Top Artists that were groups
1943-1949	11.4	7.9
1950-1954	20.9	19.0
1955-1959	30.4	42.0

12. Some examples are the Orioles "It's Too Soon To Know" (1948) and "What Are You Doing New Year's Eve?" (1949), the Ravens "Count Every Star" (1950), the Five Keys "Glory of Love" (1951), the Clovers "Fool, Fool, Fool" (1951), the Vocaleers "Be True" (1952), the Clovers "One Mint Julep" (1952), the Harptones "Sunday Kind Of Love" (1953), the Spaniels "Baby It's You" (1953), the Chords "Sh-Boom" (1954) and the Diablos "The Wind" (1954).

13. Pavlow, Big Al. *The R & B Book: A Disc-History of Rhythm & Blues.* Providence, R.I.: Music House Publishing, 1983.

As for books dealing with rhythm and blues, they tend to gloss over the group material, going from Wynonie Harris to Louis Jordan to Ray Charles. Rhythm and blues writers would rather leave doo-wop to the rock 'n' rollers, but that brings us back to the beginning, because rock 'n' rollers overlook doo-wop. To add to the confusion, Osborne Enterprises put out a series of price guides for 45 r.p.m. records that, in effect, classified the record as rock 'n' roll or rhythm and blues depending upon the race of the singing group. *The Blues, R&B and Soul Price Guide* lists black groups almost exclusively, while *Rockin' Records: Buyers-Sellers Reference Book and Price Guide* list only white groups! *Honkers and Shouters: The Golden Years of Rhythm & Blues* by Arnold Shaw makes almost no mention of white groups, while *Goldmine's Rock 'n' Roll 45 RPM Record Price Guide* leaves out many important black groups. We guess if you're black, you can't sing rock 'n' roll and if you're white, you can't sing rhythm and blues.

The way out of this situation is to insist that the music, and not skin color, be the point of reference. "Gloria" is doo-wop, whether sung by the Cadillacs or Channels, both black, or by the Passions or Vito & the Salutations, both white. Dion and the Belmonts' music is closer in style to their black doo-wopping counterparts than it is to that of Presley, Berry or Penniman. That doo-wop needs to be an entity in its own right was a major theme of our first book.

By now this will not come as a surprise, but doo-wop groups never received much adulation compared to the single artists of their day. With a few exceptions like Benny Goodman and Frank Sinatra, artists were not idolized to the degree they were post-Presley. Record companies believed that the songs were more important than the artists who sang them. Stores often carried several renditions of the same popular song. A prime example was that in the summer of 1953, "Crying In The Chapel" was available in six flavors,[14] four of which were in the Top 10 at the same time! When rock 'n' roll arrived, teens went gaga over individuals, like Presley, Gene Vincent, Carl Perkins, Fats Domino, Chuck Berry and Ray Charles. The first time that groups came to be idolized and swooned over was with the British Invasion and the Beatles.

Statistics from the Rock and Roll Hall of Fame clearly show disrespect for groups that sang doo-wop. Of 94 performers admitted between 1986 and 1997, only eight bear any relation to doo-wop music. Five were groups, beginning with the Coasters in 1987, and followed by the Drifters in 1988, the Platters in 1990, Frankie Lymon and the Teenagers in 1993 and the Shirelles in 1996. Three others, namely Clyde McPhatter (1987), Dion (1989) and Hank Ballard (1990) were let in without their respective groups, the Dominoes/Drifters, Belmonts/Del Satins and

14. The Orioles on Jubilee, June Valli on RCA, Darrell Glenn on Valley, and Rex Allen, Ella Fitzgerald and Sister Rosetta Tharpe on Decca.

Royals/Midnighters.[15] All three of these "single artists" made their best and most famous music fronting vocal groups, and yet these groups were omitted.

The Rock and Roll Hall of Fame has another category for inductees which ostensibly treats the doo-wop years with more respect. Of 21 inductees in the "Non-Performer" category, 12 were involved with doo-wop. Alan Freed and Dick Clark are in; record label nabobs Leonard Chess (Chess/Checker), Ahmet Ertegun and Jerry Wexler (Atlantic/Atco), Syd Nathan (King/Federal/DeLuxe), Ralph Bass (King/Federal) are in; composers Jerry Lieber and Mike Stoller, Gerry Goffin and Carole King, and Doc Pomus are in; and producers Phil Spector and Johnny Otis are in. It strikes us as odd that the big fish from the doo-wop era represent 57% of those honored as non-performers, while when it comes to artists, only 8.5% are doo-woppers. It's tantamount to saying that the music was loved and has stayed popular through the years despite the groups that sang it. A third category, celebrating "Early Influences" on rock 'n' roll, lists only the Orioles and Ink Spots among 24 named artists, which comes to 8.3%. What happened to the Ravens, Five Keys, Larks and Dominoes, not to mention some of earlier groups like the Mills Brothers, Delta and Deep Rhythm Boys and Golden Gate Quartet? When Freed coined the term "rock 'n' roll" in the early 1950s, his shows featured a high percentage of vocal groups. If groups were there in the beginning, why haven't they been recognized as artists, or at least as "early influences?" A little bit bizarre, more than a little bit disrespectful and, from our point of view, way off the mark.

Another reason doo-wop hasn't been adequately documented is that its name has been pretty slippery. When popular, it was seen as part of rock 'n' roll or rhythm and blues. After 1960, it was often put under " '50s music" or "oldies." Although it has been found in print as early as 1961 (see Chapter 1), it was not in common usage until the very late 1960s. Even the spelling was up in the air for awhile, being called doo-wap, do-wop, doo-wopp, doowhop and any other combination that sounded right. It makes one wonder what group vocal music of that era would have come to had Freed coined the term "doo-wop" instead of, or in addition to, rock 'n' roll. Setting it apart from single artist forms would likely have given it more popularity. It's tough to muster enthusiasm for something you don't categorize separately, have no name for, and can't spell.

Ironically, despite the disrespect shown it, the genre refuses to die. It's been revived numerous times, the first time beginning with the Oldies But Goodies and Golden Oldies album series in the early 1960s. These albums became so popular that they propelled many of the songs contained in them to greater popularity than they received when first issued. Songs like "In The Still Of The Night" by the Five Satins and "Earth Angel" by the Penguins became super-hits and to this day usually place at or near the top of most oldies surveys. Later in the 1960s, another revival was sparked by a deejay named Gus Gossert and a showman by the name of Richard Nader. And so it goes.

Early in the 1970s, oldies began to populate the radio dial. Norm N. Nite, with his "Nite Train Show" on WCBS-FM (New York) was one of the forerunners. His heir-apparent, Don K. Reed, still has that show, renamed "The Doo-Wop Shop," after more than twenty years on the air. All through the last couple of decades, oldies revival concerts have appeared frequently and are usually well-attended. It seems that there is more work around for the old groups than there was when their records were on the charts. They're certainly getting paid more than they did in the "good old days." The Earls, Cadillacs, Drifters, Cleftones and Channels keep on truckin' even though some of them have no more than one original member. They still make sure that the vocals sound like they used to. And that's what counts.

The groups on the oldies concert "circuit" tend to come from the mid-1950s on. Unfortunately, most of the groups that were around in the late 1940s and early 1950s, the ones that are revered by die-hard doo-wop and rhythm & blues fans, still beget anonymity today. As Goldberg and Redmond[16] point out, the groups that are overlooked include the Orioles before 1953 (when "Crying In The Chapel" became a hit), the early Five Keys (before they sang in pop style) and the Ravens (the grand daddy of all the groups). Obviously, there's more gospel to be spread.

As for the "no respect" issue, we've come to a few conclusions after studying it for six years. With the possible exception of the New York-New Jersey metropolitan area, the group medium was not as popular as the single artist medium both before and during the heyday of rock 'n' roll. With the passage of time, however, interest in groups has grown relative to the single artist sound, so that retro-concerts from that era are weighted toward the group sound. The reasons aren't quite clear, but probably involve love of the harmony, the bonding that the group sound represents, the romanticism or nostalgia, or perhaps identifying with the underdog.

It does leave us doo-wop and rhythm & blues fanatics in the curious position of being out of touch with reality. While most of us loved the sounds of Chuck Berry, Fats Domino and yes, even Elvis Presley during the '50s, today many of us have narrowed our focus to the point of excluding all non-group music. We collect, listen to and love music by vocal harmony groups exclusively. We attend concerts where groups abound and avoid them when groups are absent. We have become historical revisionists. All's right with the world.

---

15. Jackie Wilson and Marvin Gaye, both admitted in 1987, were omitted from our discussion because although they started their careers as members of groups (Dominoes and Rainbows, respectively), their primary success came as single artists.

16. Goldberg, Marv, and Redmond, Mike. "The Clovers." *Record Exchanger*, Issue #15, p. 5, June 1973.

Chapter 3

Websterizing Doo-Wop

Defining doo-wop can be approached on a number of different levels. Primarily, perhaps, doo-wop is a music that was around between the late 1940s and the early 1960s. It is a music that conveys more naiveté, innocence and raw feeling than any other kind. Other musics may require more musical expertise, but none are sung with more heart than doo-wop. Others may offer more political or social messages, such as folk and soul, but none can help conjure up innocent love as doo-wop can.

On another level, it is a hobby that may include other genres from the 1950s, such as classic cars and grade-B movies. On this level, it is a "guy" thing. Women can enjoy the music, but don't seem to drool over it the way men do. Women will say that a '57 Chevy is nice; a guy will want to own it. Men get this way about their hobbies and their sports. Men don't just want their team to win. They need their team to win. If the team loses, they're morose and inconsolable for awhile. They're passionate about things and "stuff," but not necessarily about people. Leave the relationship stuff and the need to communicate to the fairer sex; guys want their gadgets and their beer. And often their doo-wop.

On a third but related level, doo-wop is fodder for the record collector. The fifties didn't invent collections, but it's the first period of time when teens had enough money to spend on amassing things, whether those things be stamps, coins, baseball cards, or 45 r.p.m. records. Many of the people who are closely associated with the doo-wop culture grew into it through the hobby of record collecting. To them, the music didn't necessarily represent romance or fast cars, but completing a set of records on the Timely, Chance or (yellow) Atlantic labels. Those who saw collecting as a purely business venture left the music behind. For a certain portion of the collectors, however, their love of vinyl grew into a love of what was embedded in the vinyl that has stayed with them over the years.

On a fourth level, doo-wop represents an effort, psychologically, to glorify one's own past, to give it meaning or to put it in perspective. More than forty years after the middle of the doo-wop era (looking backward from 1999), men (and some women) in their fifties are looking back fondly on the years when they grew up. Their memories are intricately bound to music that was created back then by groups of kids who, like themselves, were in their early teens to early twenties. Kids whose lives, like their own, were ordinary, everyman's lives. There were few rousing success stories tied to doo-wop. Even Frankie Lymon's rags-to-riches saga ended badly. There were just the struggles, the hopes and dreams, the triumphs and failures of a myriad of underdogs. The childhood and the teenage years, the buddies and the girlfriends, the schoolyards and school teachers, the cockiness and the frailty; all gone and unreclaimable, yet still there to be touched through the music.

No matter what level doo-wop is viewed from, it is certainly a genre that has its own characteristics. Most of these are hard to miss, and if not unique, are rarely employed outside of doo-wop. One would think that a definition is easy to come by. It is not. Even though doo-wop has been around close to fifty years, deejays or those who write the liner notes for CDs or record albums seem to assume that people know what it means. Occasionally, in musical dictionaries or encyclopedias, broad definitions will appear. If our music is to be taken seriously as a genre, we need to Websterize it; that is, define it in a rigorous manner.

To begin, we note that doo-wop is only a style of vocal group music. Although we and other writers get lax and use the terms "doo-wop groups" and "doo-wop songs," these phrases are misleading. Songs, of and by themselves, are neither doo-wop nor not doo-wop. Songs can be rendered in doo-wop style, or in some other (by definition inferior) style. Similarly, singing groups are neither doo-wop nor not doo-wop. Groups can sing in the doo-wop style, or some other style such as soul. A doo-wop record occurs when a vocal group sings a song in doo-wop style.

Also, in case we forgot to mention it, doo-wop music has to have a group. There must be a group singing on the record. Single artists can be included only if they are backed by a group, whether or not the group is mentioned on the label. Often, featured single artists, like Dion, backed by a group like the Del Satins, will offer a sound that has the same characteristics as that of more conventional groups. Other examples are Bobby Day, Thurston Harris and Nathaniel Mayer backed respectively by the Satellites, Sharps and Fabulous Twilights. One frequent difference between these single artist doo-wops and other doo-wop efforts is that in the former, the lead singer stands out more. That is, the volume of the lead, relative to his/her group, is greater. While we can't give our approval to the single artist route because it goes against the "group-ness" of the music, we realize that it is only a marketing strategy on the part of the record company.

Given these qualifications, doo-wop music comes down to a style of music which usually meets five criteria. They are 1) vocal group harmony, 2) a wide range of voice parts (usually from bass to falsetto), 3) nonsense syllables, 4) a simple beat and light instrumentation, and 5) simple music and lyrics. Each of these will be discussed in turn. Later chapters on nonsense syllables, bass singers and leads will go into greater detail.

Group Harmony

Doo-wop music is offered by vocal groups that sing in harmony. If a group sings the same notes at the same time (i.e. singing in unison), it is not doo-wop. Doo-wop offers a wide range of voices, from bass up to high tenor or falsetto. These differing voices combine in vocal harmony and can be heard behind the voice of the lead vocalist. In a five-person group, the second tenor and baritone usually blend into one sound, with a high tenor or falsetto singing on top, and the bass resounding underneath. This paradigm of harmony, or something quite similar, is always found in doo-wop renditions. This is a necessary, though not sufficient, condition for a given sample of music to be classified as doo-wop.

The harmonizers do not often lead throughout the song, as is the case in barbershop style, but there are exceptions. Occasionally group harmonizers will alternate with a tenor as lead voice. Earl Lewis and the Channels do this frequently.

In the late 1940s and early 1950s, signal groups such as the Ravens, Five Keys and Four Buddies helped the music change direction from jazz and pop and blues to doo-wop with a rhythm & blues flavor. "Blow harmonies," so-called because the sounds that resulted, like "ha-oo" or "ah-hoo" were the result of blowing air out of the mouth, replaced humming as the predominant background support. As the 1950s progressed, background harmonies became more ornate syllabically, but not necessarily musically more complicated.

A device commonly used by vocal groups was that of progressive entrances, wherein one voice enters at a time until full harmony is reached. Other names for this technique are "chiming up," "chiming down," "bell-tone" and "pyramid," the choice of name usually describing the order in which the voices enter. Examples of progressive entrances can be found at least as far back as the 1940s, as in "Blueberry Hill" by Steve Gibson and the Redcaps. Doo-wop examples occur in "Bermuda Shorts" by the Delroys, "Memories of Love" by Lenny Dean & the Rockin' Chairs, and "Bong, Bong (I Love You Madly)" by Vince Castro backed by the Tonettes. The presence of this technique is almost a guarantor of the doo-wop style.

Wide Range of Voice Parts

Most often, the lead singer is a tenor, sometimes a high tenor, like Maithe Marshall of the Ravens, sometimes a young high tenor ("castrato") like Frankie Lymon of the Teenagers, or sometimes a regular tenor like Nick Santo of the Capris. Sometimes groups feature baritone or bass leads, examples of which are "Bim Bam Boom" by the El Dorados and "Zing Went The Strings Of My Heart" by the Coasters. Bass leads are more common in uptempo songs while falsetto leads are found more often in ballads. Double leads can be found occasionally. Sonny Til of

the Orioles, a tenor, often yielded to George Nelson, a baritone, in the bridge of the group's songs.

A technique derived from gospel, called "melisma" was used frequently by leads in the mid-1950s. This device, wherein syllables are added to fit the meter of the song, became a trademark for Tony Williams, the lead voice of the Platters. For Tony, "Only You" became "O-o-only You."

One signature of the doo-wop rhythm & blues sound is the presence of a bass part. The bass often provides the introduction to the song, as in "Fine, Fine Frame" by the Continentals, and/or punctuates the song between verses, as in the song "Dorothy" by the Hi-Fives. A bass can also commonly be heard under the lead, either blending with the background harmonizers or running separately from both lead and harmony. The more accomplished bassmen were given more freedom to "do their thing" behind the melody. Examples of "free bassing" can be found in "All Night Long" by the Du Mauriers, "Never Let You Go" by the Five Discs and "I Wonder Why" by Dion and the Belmonts. Sometimes a bass will dramatically talk his way through the channel, creating a "talking bridge," as in "Little Darling" by the Diamonds (which covered the Gladiolas' version). The bass may also provide a percussive beat to the song, as if taking the place of a stand-up bass instrument. The first of the great bassmen was Jimmy Ricks of the Ravens, who would frequently sing lead. He is important as an influence on the doo-wop style, as well as a contributor to the earlier pop-jazz style of the 1940s.

Opposite the bass voice on the scale is the high-pitched falsetto. Prototypes of this voice are found in the operatic high tenors of Maithe Marshall and Joe Van Loan of the Ravens (neither of whom sang in doo-wop style). By and after the mid-1950s, falsetto leads were plentiful, as in "Florence" by the Paragons, "Dee I" by the Rocketones and "Hey You" by the Imaginations. Falsettos were kind of a jack-of-all-trades, being used to echo the lead voice, as in "Dear Lord" by the Continentals or as a trail-off by the lead at the end of the song, as in "Tell Me Why" by Norman Fox and the Rob Roys and "Since I Don't Have You" by the Skyliners.

While the range of voices in male groups is wide, it is much narrower in female groups, being more uniformly high. A lower register female voice has to substitute for a male bass, but some mixed groups kept a guy around for his deep voice. Steve Caldwell, of the otherwise all-female Orlons, is an example. Falsetto is rarely used. In mixed groups, a high-pitched (soprano) female voice equates to the male high tenor/falsetto, as in "To Know Him Is To Love Him" by the Teddy Bears. When groups that featured the Frankie Lymon-type sound try to make a comeback, a female lead is usually enlisted because the mature male voice is virtually incapable of warbling in a high pre-pubescent register.

Nonsense Syllables

Another signature of the doo-wop rhythm & blues sound is the presence of nonsense syllables. Examples are "doo-wop," "boom buh boom buh boom" and "diddle liddle lit." The syllables are expressed by both the bass voice and harmony parts of the group. The presence of these syllables makes it quite likely that the musical selection belongs within the province of the doo-wop genre. In ballads, the choice of syllables is more restrained, as in "doe-doe-doe" or "doo-wah." In uptempo tunes, the range of the syllables is greater and they are delivered with more gusto.

Nonsense syllables trace their roots to the music of African-Americans. They can be found in West African chants going back hundreds of years, and appear in the bop and jazz stylings of the first half of the 20th century. They were used by the early jazz singers, like Satchmo and Crosby, who improvised by "scatting" their syllables. The use of nonsense syllables in doo-wop differs in that there are predictable patterns of them repeated throughout the song. It is likely that they entered, and thus helped to form the doo-wop style, on the streetcorner. In a cappella renditions, they were used to replace the instrumental bass, just as hand-claps and finger-snaps replaced drums. Naturally appealing to the ear, it's easy to see how they caught on around the turn of the decade in 1950. By 1954, they were found in abundance, as in "Gee" by the Crows, "Goodnight, Sweetheart, Goodnight" by the Spaniels, "Hearts Of Stone" by the Jewels and Charms, and "Oop Shoop" by Shirley Gunter and the Queens. Catchy and imitable, they soon became essential to the doo-wop mystique.

Sometimes nonsense syllable became almost the whole song. "Vadunt-Un-Va-Da-Song" by the Ramblers in 1954, is both the song's title and an accurate summation of its lyrics. Other songs dominated by nonsense syllables are "Rubber Biscuit" by the Chips in 1956, and "Harmony Of Love" by the Five Dollars in 1955.

Beat and Instrumentation

Rhythm on the streetcorners was provided by snapping fingers and clapping hands. As a result, the beat behind doo-wop songs is both simple and heavy. There is an emphasis on the second and fourth beats, producing a pattern that we associate with generic rock 'n' roll.

The streetcorners relied on voices, not instruments, to produce the doo-wop sound. So when the singers moved from outside the candy store to the recording studios, instrumentation took a back seat. This provides a major difference between pure doo-wop and other forms of rock 'n' roll that were around at the same time. Rockabilly and the rhythm and blues "honkers" relied heavily on instrumentation by piano, guitar, stand-up bass, sax and drums. These instruments can be heard in many doo-wop arrangements, but they recede into the background.

The exception to the above statements occurs in the middle of the song. This "break" (or "bridge" or "channel") is most notably occupied by a saxophone, which wails on for a few bars before the singers reenter. Jimmy Wright, working as the house musician for the Gee/Rama label group and King Curtis, on Atlantic, were the most prolific and famous of the saxmen. These brief instrumental incursions into an otherwise vocal milieu is descended from the solos that occurred in the swing band music of Duke Ellington, Count Basie, and their contemporaries in the 1930s. Guitars also appeared in doo-wop bridges, especially on the smaller labels that couldn't afford big ticket musicians.

Simple Music and Lyrics

Most doo-wop songs are melodically simple. Many depended on basic four-chord progressions, which produced a host of sound-alike songs. Even remakes of the old standards, like "Over The Rainbow," "Stormy Weather" and "A Sunday Kind Of Love" tended to flatten out the original melody line. Leroy Kirkland, R&B impresario, added, "Of the early records, I could play about three or four dozen of them, and every now and then you'd find one with a different chord structure. That's why I said it was pretty hard to write all of these ideas around the same chord changes. I used to go to sleep at night and, really, try to dream of something new to do with these same chord progressions."[1] Ed Ward also remarked that it was "a real testimony to the inventiveness of the harmony group singers that those changes could be rung so many ways and so successfully so much of the time."[2]

Actually, lyrics written earlier in the era, before teenagers got into the act, could be quite sophisticated, as in "I'd Rather Have You Under The Moon (Than Anyone Under The Sun)" by the Orioles. Around 1954, when youthful singers started to compose their own material, the rules changed. Doo-wop lyrics are often moon-June simple and dialectical, but are usually still able to convey genuine emotions like sadness, tenderness and love. Sometimes the words are just trite, in an obvious attempt to sound "cool,"[3] and other times the words don't make much sense.[4] Those looking for Cole Porterish lyrics will be sorely disappointed, but this is part of the cachet of innocence that permeates doo-wop.

Vernon Green, lead singer of the Medallions, whispered "sweet words of pismotality" and spoke of "the pulpitudes of love." Well Vernon, we kind of know what

1. " 'Music, Maestro, Please,' Leroy Kirkland." Big Town Review, Issue #2, April-May 1972, p. 41.
2. Ward, Ed, et al.. Rock Of Ages: The Rolling Stone History Of Rock & Roll. New York: Summit Books, 1986.
3. Witness the Indigos, in "Woo Woo Pretty Girl" from 1958: "One, two, three, look at me, Four, five, six, she's the coolest of chicks, Seven, eight, nine, she's as fi-hine as wine."
4. "You see my dear, ding dong is here to stay, yes..." says the bass of the Quintones in "Ding Dong" from 1958.

you meant, without really knowing what you meant. We could feel the tenderness and sincerity that you surely intended. Who cared if our vocabulary suffered?

The music is rife with pairs like "kiss you" and "miss you," "don't hurt me" and "don't desert me," "I'll never let you go" and "because I love you so," and the inimitable "by my side" and "to be my guide/bride." For the most part, both the words and melodies of the doo-wop genre touch the emotions while leaving the intellect unscathed. Exceptions are found in some of the songs of the early part of the era, and in the old standards that were doo-wopped up.

Ideally, a song done in doo-wop style will contain all of the above characteristics. Realistically, there are exceptions and varying degrees of conformity. Exceptions occur because some songs, considered by most to be in doo-wop style, don't contain the falsetto voice, while others had bass lines that blended with the harmony and didn't stand out. Other songs witnessed voices echoing the lead in words rather than by using nonsense syllables. A song may be rendered in doo-wop style by degrees.

A related problem of classification occurs with the vocal groups themselves. Many groups came and went during the doo-wop era and didn't exist outside of it (e.g. Paragons and Bop Chords). Virtually all of their output fits comfortably in the doo-wop style. Others sang some songs in doo-wop style and some that are better characterized as soft rock, popular music, or even gospel. Sometimes groups grew into the doo-wop genre from an earlier style, or started singing doo-wop and moved on to other types of music (e.g. the Four Seasons, Dells, and Little Anthony and the Imperials). We shouldn't let these classification problems bother us much. The genre is pretty easy to define and, most importantly, we know one when we hear one.

Chapter 4

Making Sense of Nonsense

In most books, if the authors told you they were about to talk nonsense, you would not be happy. In a book on doo-wop, however, nonsense, in syllabic form, is just what the doctor ordered. Nonsense syllables, by definition, are syllables that don't have any meaning or make any sense.[1] And yet as meaningless as they are, they are quite important to the doo-wop signature. Of all the characteristics of this style, none is more integral than the presence of nonsense syllables. Not to say that they occur in each and every song which is classified as doo-wop, but they do occur in most. Before the doo-wop era, nonsense syllables were rarely found, and after the era they were scarce to nonexistent. But during the period of the late 1940s to the early 1960s, they flowed through group vocal music like fine wine, whatever that means. In fact, the genre was named for the king of these syllables, "doo-wop."[2][3]

Nonsense syllables that occurred in group vocal music before the doo-wop era served a different purpose. As early as the 1920s, the phrase, "Oom-clanka-lanka" was found in vocal group recordings and was repeated sporadically through the 1930s and 1940s (e.g. "Sleep On, Mother" by the Silver Leaf Quartette in 1928).[4] Beginning in the 1930s, the Mills Brothers (e.g. "Tiger Rag" and "Bugle Call Rag" both from 1932, "Jungle Fever" in 1934), Four Blackbirds ("Black-Eyed Susan Brown" in 1935), Four Vagabonds ("Gee I Wish" from 1945) and others used their voices to imitate instruments such as horns[5], woodwinds and the stand-up bass (a fuller treatment of this can be found in the chapter on bass singers). Nonsense syllables were used to create these sounds of the "human orchestra." "Wah wah wah" or "wop wop wop," sung by background harmonizers, muted by cupping the hands and varying the distance from the microphone, produced a sound remarkably like a real trombone. Groups and their record companies took pride in the ability to mimic instruments, especially if it fooled the listener into thinking that real instruments were present.

Nonsense syllables were also used for jazz styling, either for scat singing (usually by single artists like Ella Fitzgerald), or as a substitute for a horn riff (like "doo-doo-

doo-doo-wop" as in "Just Sittin' And A Rockin' " by the Delta Rhythm Boys in 1946). The Ravens used the string "doo doot doo" in a jazzy rather than doo-wop style in the background of "You Don't Have To Drop A Heart To Break It" and "There's No Use Pretending," both from 1951.

Nonsense syllables can be, and have been, used by either the bass, the harmonizers (usually a second tenor and a baritone) or both. They can be uttered as simple monosyllables like "boom" or "doe" or can be strung together in complex strings ("oop-shoop-ching-a-ling"). They can be "blow harmonies" and contain vowels only ("ooh" or "ah") or they can offer both vowels and consonants ("bon" or "bome"). All have appeared at various times in the doo-wop era, and the order in which they appeared is relatively predictable.

Beginning in the 1940s, background harmonizers regularly blew only vowels such as "ooh," "oh" and "ah." The Orioles, one of the earliest and most important groups of the era, would have Sonny Til up front, two guys backing him up singing "oh-oh-oh" and a false tenor singing "ooh." This combination can be heard in "Forgive And Forget" from 1949 and "At Night" from 1950. In the late 1940s, Jimmy Ricks of the Ravens used the jazzy "doot doot doot" or "doot dee doot doot" strings with regularity in songs like "Tea For Two," "Always," "Lilacs In The Rain" and "I'm Gonna Paper All My Walls With Your Love Letters."

The changeover from pop, jazz and blues styles of the forties to the doo-wop style was an evolutionary process rather than a revolutionary one (as when the Beatles arrived and changed music almost overnight). Evolution implies gradual and sometimes seemingly trivial changes. An argument can be made that the changeover to the doo-wop style occurred when bass singers used "doo" instead of "doot" and when background singers used syllables such as "doo," "boom" and "doe" in place of vowel sounds like "ooh." These changes happened gradually in the period 1946 to 1951. Some isolated recordings by fairly well-known groups that featured the modern style were "Lullabye" by the Ravens in 1946, "That's My Desire" by the Bachelors in 1947, "Little Jane" by the Four Tunes in 1948, "Until Now" by the Rhythm Masters in 1949, and "Hesitating Fool" recorded by the Striders in 1949. Jimmy Ricks, bass of the Ravens, exerted enormous influence. When he made his foray into the world of doo-wop-styled nonsense syllables with "Count Every Star" in 1950, you can be sure that it was heard clearly by all contemporary groups. "The Masquerade Is Over" by the Blenders, recorded in October of 1950 clearly features a doo-wop bass part. The Four Buddies employed a "doe doe doe" bass line in almost all of their songs, starting with their first recording session in

---

1. Sort of like some people.
2. By this point in the book, this should not come as a big surprise.
3. Please note that the main purposes of endnotes in this book are to offer references and to make cheap jokes easier to deliver. This practice has little redeeming educational or intellectual value and is against editorial advice.
4. Moonoogian, G. A.. "Wax Fax." *Record Collector's Monthly*, Issue #45, December 1989, p. 12.
5. This may be the source of the term "male sax organ."

December of 1950. The Larks also began recording in 1950, but started by using nonsense syllables to imitate instruments. By 1951 their bass, David McNeil, employed the "doe doe doe" bass and their harmonizers used nonsense syllables. By 1954, however, they were a pop group that rarely used these devices. As a general guideline, most groups used "doo" and "doe" before they employed other syllables like "bome," "bon" or "dit." You've got to crawl before you walk.

By 1952, the horse was out of the barn. Nonsense syllables were used frequently in group harmony efforts by both background and bass singers. They were found in arrangements of songs from all over the country, implying that cross-fertilization was occurring. Examples are "It Won't Be Very Long" by the Imperials, "This Is The Real Thing Now" by the Billy Dawn Quartet (aka Four Dukes), "My Inspiration" by the Five Crowns, "Night Has Come" by Billy Austin & the Hearts and "The Shrine Of St. Cecilia" by the Royals.[6] Young singers used them more freely and frequently, but even veteran groups like the Drifters and Dominos would use "doo-wop doo-wop doo-wop" in the background of their jump tunes (e.g. "Let The Boogie Woogie Roll" by the Drifters in 1953).

Nonsense syllables soon became an essential part of the doo-wop character. Commonly, they are heard in the background, serving to accentuate or punctuate the lyrics. Once in a while, they become the focus of the song, as in "Blue Moon" and "Heartaches" by the Marcels, "Mope-Itty Mope" by the Bosstones, "Rang Tang Ding Dong" by the Cellos or "Ala-Men-Sa-Aye" by the Quotations. In rare instances, they actually are the song. In "Rubber Biscuit" by the Chips, the "Vadunt-Un-Va-Da Song" by the Ramblers, "Harmony Of Love" by the Five Dollars, "Hi-Oom" by the Saucers and "Street-corner Symphony" by the Belmonts, nonsense syllables make up all or almost all of the vocal utterances.

From a marketing perspective, it seems like it would be a good idea to tell the buying public what they're getting if they buy a certain record, like the mood of the song, for example. In doo-wop, however, composers often graced records with titles made up of only nonsense syllables. In doo-wop, this was done so often that it is almost not remarkable, except for the fact that it does occur so often. By our count[7], there are roughly 400 doo-wop songs whose titles are composed of nonsense syllables alone. And that is not counting songs where there are real honest-to-goodness words anywhere in the title like "Oo-Wee Baby" by the Ivy-Tones or "Bong Bong (I Love You Madly)" by Vince Castro (with the Tonettes). Whatta world.

Using titles made up entirely of nonsense syllables is not found to any degree in other musical genres. One can only take a guess at the origins of this idiosyncratic practice. In the 1953-1954 period, the immense popularity of songs like "Gee" by the Crows and "Sh-Boom" by the Chords may have spurred imitation. Another possibility is that many of the nonsense-syllable-only titles, being uptempo "B" sides for ballads, may have been considered throwaways. Or there may have been the intention to advertise subtly to their intended teenaged audience. Record company execs may have been saying, "Hey kids, you'll like this one!" True to form, the titles were fairly reliable predictors of the songs lyrics.

To make wieldy our lofty discussion of nonsense syllables in the titles of doo-wop songs, we have grouped them into "families," the first of which is the estimable "Ding Dong" family. These syllables may parallel the tendency of doo-wop songs to dwell on bells as a subject matter.[8] At least eleven groups, by our count, had the good sense to record songs with the reductionist "Ding Dong" as a title. The most well-known of these was by the Echoes in 1957. Almost invariably, whenever a "Ding" appears, a "Dong" is not far behind.[9] The only exceptions to this rule occurred with "Ring A Ling A Ding" by Richie Thompson & the Jesters, "Ding-A-Ling-A-Ling" by the Troys and "Sha-Bee-Dah-Ah-Ding" by the Four Vanns.

Several commercially successful records came from this family. "Rama Lama Ding Dong," was a big hit for the Edsels in 1961, reaching number 21 on Billboard's pop charts. The song was originally released in 1958 as "Lama Rama Ding Dong," but it met with little success at that time. Another big song from this family was "Ka Ding Dong" by the G-Clefs, which reached number 24 on the pop charts in 1956, and was covered by the Diamonds, the mother of all cover groups. Many of the songs in this family have long and mellifluous titles such as "Shang Lang A Ding Dong" by the Charades, "Shanga Langa Ding Dong" by the Cameos (note the subtle differences), "Giddy-Up And Ding Dong" by the Continentals, "Giddy-Up-A-Ding-Dong" by the Playmates, "Ding Ding Dong" by the Jivetones (extra "Ding" for emphasis), "Ding Dong Doo" by the Frontiers and the infamous "Ding-A-Ling-A-Ling Ding Dong" by Dicky Dell & the Bing Bongs.

A second family is the Ching/Chop clan. One song contains both, namely "Chop, Chop, Ching-A-Ling" by the Roamers, but as a rule, Ching and Chop make separate appearances. We have "Ching Ching" by Gloria Wood & the Afterbeats, "Ching Chong" by the Pips, "Ching-A-Ling" by the Accents, "Ching-A-Ling Baby" by the Rocky Fellers and "Ching Bam Bah" by the Velveteens (which is readily available at the local Chinese restaurant). Representing the Chop side of this family are "Chop Chop" by Ferris & the Wheels and the Chimes, "Chop Chop Chop" by the Candy Makers, "Chop Chop Boom" by the Dandeliers and the Savoys and "Chickie Chop Chop" by the Flints and the Newports.

With "Sh-Boom" as a headliner, the "Boom" family is a colorful one. Aside from the Chords' "Sh-Boom," which reached number two on Billboard's Rhythm &

---

6. In "Shrine," one can hear the syllables "whoa-oh whoa oh" used by these Royals about one year before the Buccaneers employed it and two years before the Solitaires used it regularly on their ballads.

7. Gribin & Schiff.

8. Teens must have found them quite ap-peal-ing.

9. A person should always know where his dong is.

Blues charts, others to achieve notoriety were "Bim Bam Boom" by the El Dorados in 1956 and "Shtiggy Boom" by Patti Anne (Mesner with the Flames) in 1955. A fairly complete list, alphabetized by title, follows.

Group Name	Song	Year	Label
El Dorados	Bim Bam Boom	1956	Vee Jay 211
Cardinals	Bim Bam Boom	N/A	Atlantic EP only
Hearts (Lee Andrews & the)	Boom	1959	United Artists 162
Fascinations	Boom Bada Boom	1960	Sure 106
Barons	Boom Boom	1955	Imperial 5343
Five Keys	Boom Boom	1957	Capitol 3786
Jiveleers	Boom Chic-A-Boom	1960	Cousins 1/2
Starlites (Kenny Esquire & the)	Boom Chica Boom	1957	Ember 1021
Creslyns	Boom Chip-A-Boom	1963	Beltone 2036
Pastels	Boom De De Boom	1956	United 196
El Dorados	Boom Diddle Boom	1957	Vee Jay 263
Charms	Boom Diddy Boom Boom	1956	Chart 623
Love Bugs	Boom Diddy Wawa Baby	1955	Federal 12216
Cashmeres	Boom Mag-Azeno Vip Vay	1955	Mercury 70617
Astro Jets	Boom-A-Lay	1961	Imperial 5760
Tidal Waves	Booma Shooma Rock	1961	Tide 0020
Storey Sisters	Cha Cha Boom	1958	Baton 255
Del-Rhythmetts	Chic-A-Boomer	1958	J-V-B 5000
Danderliers	Chop Chop Boom	1955	States 147/B&F 1344 (61)
Savoys	Chop Chop Boom	1955	Combo 90
Tokays	Fatty-Boom Bi Laddy	1952	Bonnie 102
Gadabouts	Go Boom Boom	1955	Mercury 70581
Jaye Sisters	Pitter Patter Boom Boom	1958	Atlantic 1171
Four Blues	Re Bop-De-Boom	1950	Apollo 1145
Thunderbirds	Rock Boom Boom	1955	G.G. 518
Chords	Sh-Boom	1954	Cat 104
Sh-Booms	Sh-Boom	1961	Atco 6213
Popular Five	Sh-Boom	1967	Rae-Cox 1001
Crowns (Arthur Lee Maye & the)	Sh-Boom	N/A	Dig 149 (unrel.)
Sapphires	Sh-Boom	N/A	Ravin' 100
Decades (Brother Zee & the)	Sha-Boom Bang	1962	Ramco 3725
Creators	Shoom Ba Boom	1963	Philips 40060
Houston, Joe (& group)	Shtiggy Boom	1955	RPM 426
Nuggets	Shtiggy Boom	1955	Capitol 3052
Patti Anne (Mesner with the Flames)	Shtiggy Boom	1955	Aladdin 3280
Castells	Stiki De Boom Boom	1961	Era 3064
Dories	Stompin' Sh-Boom	1962	Dore 629
Savoys	Yacka Hoom Boom	1955	Combo 75
Supremes	Zip Boom	1985	Murray Hill LP 000083
Cadillacs	Zoom Boom Zing	1959	Jubilee LP 1089

"La" appears often in a number of musical genres[10], but in doo-wop it is title-fodder. It can appear in titles up to five times. "La La" was a minor hit for the Cobras in 1964 and is in our Top 1,000. Two "la's" also show up in "La La" by the Five Knights, "Ooh-La-La" by Skip & the Echotones and the Hollywood Flames, "Oo La La" by Dave Joseph (& group), "Ooh La La" by Bobby Long & His Cherrios, "Tra-La-La" by the Majors and "Sha La La" by the Prophets and the Shirelles. There are three in "La La La" by the Co-Eds and the Del-tones, four in "Tra La La La La" by the Viriations and five in "La La La La La" by the Blendells.

A couple of other families of syllables, namely the "Z" and "Y" families, tend to be alliterative. We guess nothing goes as well with one z-word as another z-word. The "Z" family is actually quite prolific because

---

10. e.g. La Traviata and Volare.

there are a lot of "Zooms" out there, either used singly, as in "Zoom" by the Cadillacs, et al., or in triplets like "Zoom Zoom Zoom" by the Collegians et al. An extensive list, alphabetized by title, follows.

Group Name	Song	Year	Label
Diamond, Ronnie (& group)	Zig Zag	1958	Imperial 5554
Counts (Bobby Comstock & the)	Zig Zag	1959	Triumph 602
Del-Rays (Detroit Jr. & the)	Zig Zag	1964	CJ 636
G-Clefs	Zing Zang Zoo	1957	Paris 506
Dells	Zing Zing Zing	1955	Vee Jay 166
Pitch Pikes	Zing Zong	1957	Mercury 71099
Commodores (Darrell Glenn & the)	Zinga-Zingo	1957	RPM 488
Diamonds	Zip Zip	1957	Mercury 71165
Jivetones	Zip Zip	N/A	Apt (unreleased)
Empires	Zippety Zip	1957	Amp-3 132
Pearls	Zippety Zippety Zoom	1956	Onyx 503
Chords	Zippety Zum	1954	Cat 109
Cadillacs	Zoom	1956	Josie 792
Historians (Barbaroso & the)	Zoom	1957	Jade 110
Cuff Linx	Zoom	1958	Dooto 438
Starlighters	Zoom	1960	Hi-Q 5016
Unique Echos	Zoom	1961	Southern Sound 108
Crescents	Zoom	1985	Relic LP 5053
Heartspinners (Dino & the)	Zoom	N/A	Robin Hood 141
Cadillacs	Zoom Boom Zing	1954	Josie 759 (unreleased)
Collegians	Zoom Zoom Zoom	1957	Winley 224
Dreamlovers	Zoom Zoom Zoom	1961	Heritage 107
Enchords	Zoom Zoom Zoom	1961	Laurie 3089
Craftys	Zoom Zoom Zoom	1962	Elmor 310
Schaefer, Freddy (& group)	Zoom Zoom Zoom	1962	King 5621
Reminiscents	Zoom Zoom Zoom	1963	Day 1000
Charts	Zoop	1957	Everlast 5001/ Everlast 5026 (1963)/ Lost Nite173 (1981)
Delstars	Zoop Bop	1964	Mellomood 1001
Keynotes	Zup Zup	1956	Apollo 498

The only member of the "Y" family to achieve popularity was "Yakity Yak" by the Coasters (and Markeys).[11] Other family members include "Ya Ya" by Frankie Gee (& group), the Revlons, Shepherd Sisters and Videls, "Yum Yum" by the La Salles, Lamplighters and Swinging Earls, "Yum Yummy" by the Pearls, "Yo Yo Yo Yo Yo" by Little Caesar & the Romans, "Yibby-Yah" by the Caprisians, "Yodee Yakee" by the Drifters and "Yadi-Yadi-Yum-Dum" by the Rivingtons.

The "Ting-A-Ling" family brings us back to bells. And just as "ding" begets "dong," so does "ting" beget "a-ling," one way or another. The only exception to this important rule is "Ting Tang Tagalu" by Jerry McCain (& group). The Clovers, Poka-Dotts and Nicky & the Nobles recorded the reductionist "Ting-A-Ling." Other somewhat more inventive groups added suffixes to arrive at "Ting Aling Ting Toy" by Lenny Dell & the Demensions (note the brazen absence of hyphens) and "Ting-A-Ling-Ling" by the Sweethearts. Prefixes were enlisted to get "Ring-A-Ting-A-Ling" by the Creations, "Ring Ting-A-Ling" by the Dials, "A-Ting-A-Ling" by the Metrotones and the mellifluous "Ring Dang Doo Ting A Ling" by the Bell Hops.

Ironically, there aren't many titles related to the name of the genre, i.e. doo-wop. There are a few, and some groups get close to the correct spelling, but none hit it on the head. There is "Du Wap" by the Chimes, "Du Whop" by the Chessmen, "Do Whop-A-Do" by the Five Daps and "Shu-Wop" (originally called "New Way") by the Dandeliers. Considering that there are more songs with "zoom" and/or "boom" in titles, it's surprising that the genre didn't end up being "zoom boom" music, or some such thing. "Doo-Wop" is, however, one of the most commonly used nonsense syllable strings, even though it is too shy to appear in song titles.

We have just scratched the surface of songs that are composed entirely of nonsense syllables. We all know that you can't judge a book by its cover, so if there are so many nonsense syllables on the outside of doo-wop songs, imagine how many are on the inside!

---

11. "Y" you ask? We have no idea.

Below are two quizzes to see whether you've been paying attention. The first is for the general population, the second is for that select group of human beings willing to put their egos on the line. Good luck. Answers can be found in the Appendix.

Quiz #1: Testing Your Mettle

Directions: For each string of nonsense syllables, name the song and group.

1) "Oh-ooooh,
   N-dot n-dot n-dot n-dot,
   Dih-li-li-li wah wah wah..."
2) "Bome bome bome,
   Where's everybody runnin'..."
3) "Boom boom boom,
   Bang bang bang..."
4) "Tra la la la la la la la la la,
   La la la la la la la la la la..."
5) "Sha duh dah duh,
   Sha duh dah duh dah duh... (4 times)
   Ah, dyip dyip dyip dyip dyip dyip dyip dyip,
   Bum mum mum mum mum mum..."
6) "Bah dah bah dah boom tee-ay-tee-ay..."
7) "Dom dom dom dom dom,
   Dom dee doobie,
   Dom, wah wah wah wah-ah..."
8) "Lang lang lang lang lang,
   Zoom zoom zoom,
   Bop bop bop bop..."
9) "Ding dong ding dong,
   Ka ding dong, ding dong, ding..."
10) "Sunday to Monday, Tuesday to Wednesday,
    Thursday to Friday, Saturday to Sunday..."
    (although technically not nonsense syllables, these words are repeated in the background to serve the same purpose)
11) "Bon, bon, nim-a-nim-a-nim-ah,
    Rid-i-dah, rib-i-dah, rib-i-dib-i-dib-i-dah,
    Doo-bop doo-bah, rip-ay,
    Bon, bon nim-a-nim-a-nim-ay..."
12) "Bop, bah doe, bah doe, bah doe,
    Bah doe bop, bah doe..."
13) "Hello, hello again,
    My friends I hope that we will meet again,
    Ling-a-ling-a-ling ling-a-ling-a-ling..."
14) "Slowly, yeah-p yeah-p,
    Really slow slow buh dum mum,
    To the sea, sea, look-a-the sea..."
15) "Bom bom, bom bom, bom bom, a nim-mim-mim-mim..."
16) "Koo-bah koo-bah koo-bah..."
17) "Gow gow hoo-oo,
    Gow gow wanna dib-a-doo,
    Chick'n hon-a-chick-a-chick hole-a-hubba..."
18) "Hi low 'n' a swing ding,
    A ricky fing your helty one a hubba..."

Quiz #2: For Experts Only!

Directions: For each string of nonsense syllables, name the song and group.

19) "Al a men saigon yay itzkee boom,
    Tiddly hi tiddly ho tiddly rama bomp,
    Nicka nacka nicka nacka daddio,
    Whoa oh oh..."
20) "Doo lang doo lang doo lang..."

1) "Bow wow wow,
   Dit it, di di dit,
   Dit di dit, yeah-p yeah-p..."
2) "Dom dom doobie,
   An' dom dom dee doobie doobie..."
3) "R-r-r-r-r-r-r-r-r-r-r-r-r-r-r-r (trill for 1.5 seconds),
   Mmh-aaht mmh-aaht sh'bow,
   Yeah bawn bawn bawn..."
4) "Flip flip zoo wah,
   Flip flip zoo wah..."
5) "Buh-buh-buh-buh-buh-buh-buh-buh (by the bass),
   Doo dee wop, bom bom dee waddy waddy...(by the harmony part)"
6) "Doo dat duh datta datta, (3 times)
   Whoa, whoa..."
7) "Diddly doo-wop, doo-wop-doo-wop, (3 times)
   Ah oh ho ho ho ho..."
8) "Oop oop oop oop oop,
   Dee ooh ooh-ooh-ooh..."
9) "Doo buh bop bop whoa doo bop duh boppa boppa, (3 times)
   Whop! Ugh!"
10) "Doo-doo dee-dee, doo-doo dee-dee,
    Bop-bop, doo-doo dee-dee..."
11) "Yeah, boom di di di, di di dip-i-dip,
    Dum di dip dim dip dip dup dup..."
12) "Sahm-in a vicky..." (4 times)
13) "Doo-wop doo waddy waddy,
    Ring a ling a ling a ling shoot shoot shoot..."
14) "Dun duh dun duh dun doo-dee wah,
    Dun duh dun duh dun, oh..."
15) "Bom, bom, bom, bom dee-doo-bee..." (2 times)
16) "Dom doobee dom, whoa oh,
    Doobee doobee dom doobee dom whoa oh..."
17) "Nin nin nin-eh,
    Nin nin nin ni-neh,
    Nin nin nin-eh,
    Nin nin ni-neh..."
18) "Bum muh mum muh mum,
    Bum muh mum muh mum,
    Mum muh mum muh mum,
    Mum mum mum mum..."
19) "Doo-wah,
    Doo-wop sha-wa-wa, doo-wah..."
20) "Bome bome bome,
    Zoom-a-lang zoom-a-lang zoom bop bop,
    Well zoom-a-lang zoom-a-lang zoom bop bop..."

Chapter 5

Getting To First Bass

"Mr. Bassman, you've got that certain something,
Mr. Bassman, you set that music thumping,
To you it's easy, when you go 1, 2, 3 buh buh buh buh bon..."

What Johnny Cymbal[1] really meant by "that certain something" was that the presence of a distinct bass is a large part of what sets doo-wop apart from other musics such as Motown and Surf music. What he implied by "you set that music thumping" is that the bass voice in doo-wop often provides a rhythm for the other voices. Later in the song, Johnny asserts:

"It don't[2] mean a thing,
When the lead is singing,
Or when he goes aye yi yi yi yi yi..."

Here, he's making a judgment as to the relative contributions of the bass, lead and falsetto voices and crowns Mr. Bassman as "the hidden King of Rock 'n' Roll." Whether we agree with his assessment (after all, Johnny was born in Ochitree, Scotland, which is a far cry from Harlem[3]), there's little doubt that the bass voice part played a large role in the both the distinctiveness and popularity of the doo-wop style.

Not that low-register voices were absent in earlier musical eras. In the early 1930s, the Mills Brothers regularly used kazoos to imitate musical instruments in order to "accompany" their vocal arrangements. According to legend, the kazoos were forgotten one day, so the group improvised and replaced the kazoos with only their voices and cupped hands.[4] This substitution so pleased their audience that it was firmly incorporated into their act and the human "orchestra" was born. Among the "instruments" in this orchestra were various members of the horn family (with the exception of Lena) and a stand-up bass "played" by John Mills Jr. (beginning, on record, with "Tiger Rag" in 1932).

The imitated bass sounded real, as did the human horns. The Mills Brothers used this technique so often (e.g. "Bugle Call Rag" and "Dirt Dishin' Daisy," both from 1932) and were so convincing with it that the Brunswick record label printed a caveat on their discs stating, "No musical instruments or mechanical devices used on this recording other than one guitar." This gimmick was utilized from the early 1930s well into the 1940s by many groups like the Boswell Sisters

("All About Crazy People" from 1932), the Four Vagabonds ("Roseann of Charing Cross" from 1943) and the Golden Gate Quartet ("The General Jumped At Dawn" from 1945). Of all musical instruments, the stand-up bass was the easiest to imitate. The only requirements were a relatively low register voice and the ability to say "boom" (the "oo" as in "look") at the right times. So of all the human "instruments," the bass found its way most often into recordings and likely evolved, over the next twenty or so years, into the riffing bass of the doo-wop era.[5]

Another early use of the bass voice was in a "talking bridge," the bridge being the middle of a song between choruses. The first of these is commonly attributed[6][7] to the Mills Brothers in "Rockin' Chair," recorded in May 1932. However, at least one prior example exists[8] performed by one Jimmy Harrison (with an unnamed vocal group) fronting the Fletcher Henderson Orchestra, and recorded on Oct. 3, 1930 for Columbia. The man who took this technique to the bank, however, was bassman Orville "Hoppy" Jones of the Ink Spots. Beginning in 1939 with, "If I Didn't Care," Jones' talking bridge solos graced hit after hit ballad. After several choruses of Bill Kenny's ethereal tenor, the group would provide a humming background and Jones would deliver a strong and emotional message of love and/or longing. Kenny would then reassert himself for the last chorus. These talking bridge solos retained their popularity well into the 1950s, as in "Someday You'll Want Me To Want You" by the Drifters, "My Prayer Tonight" by the Checkers and even "Little Darling" by the (white) Diamonds.

The Ink Spots' hits firmly established the practice of utilizing a second lead in vocal group ballads. Recordings in the late 1940s by the Orioles (with George Nelson doing an emotional second lead behind Sonny Til) and the Ravens (operatic tenors Maithe Marshall and Joe Van Loan backing up bass Jimmy Ricks or vice versa) were continuations of this tradition. The Spots also brought the bass voice into the spotlight which eased the way for the emergence of the bass lead in the mid 1940s.

In 1946, the Ravens were formed. Originally led by tenor Ollie Jones, the remarkably deep and mellifluous

---

1. "Mr. Bassman" by Johnny Cymbal...
2. Bad grammar, Johnny!
3. "Goldmine's Second Annual One-Hit Wonders: Johnny Cymbal." *Goldmine*. Dec. 1, 1989, p.18.
4. Grendysa, Peter, Moonoogian, George, and Whitesell, Rick. "The Mills Brothers ...Four Boys and A Guitar." *Record Exchanger*, Issue #24, p. 5.

5. Howard B. Daniel, bass of the Billy Williams' Charioteers, uses his voice to portray a rolling tuba in "Ride, Red, Ride" from 1942.
6. Ibid.
7. Warner, Jay. *American Singing Groups: A History 1940-1990*. New York: Billboard Books, 1992.
8. Bill Olb on Ronnie Italiano's "R&B Party" radio show, 3/16/94.

voice of their bass, Jimmy Ricks, propelled him to the foreground. In counterpoint to the operatic tenor lead of Maithe Marshall (who replaced Ollie Jones later in 1946) and Joe Van Loan (who replaced Marshall in 1951), Ricks frequently led the jazz-pop Ravens on both ballad and uptempo sides. Influenced by Hoppy Jones of the Ink Spots, John Mills Jr. of the Mills Brothers and Lee Gaines of the Delta Rhythm Boys, Ricks' leads paved the way for the next generation of bass singers. Ricks really had no peers. No bass before him led their group with such frequency, and none had a greater influence on their contemporaries. His sophisticated jazzy, rhythm & blues phrasing opened the playing field to groups that sounded "black." Earlier African-American vocal groups like the Mills Brothers and Ink Spots sounded fairly "white" and aimed for a white audience. Ricks and the Ravens changed that.

Ricks almost singlehandedly popularized the bass lead, paving the way for the likes of Bobby Nunn (Robins, Coasters), Bill Brown (Dominoes, Checkers), Bill Pinkney (Drifters), Norris "Bunky" Mack (Swallows), Will "Dub" Jones (Cadets, Jacks), Bob Kornegay (Du Droppers) and Gerald Gregory (Spaniels). In the 1950s, some of them made the big time with recordings like "Sixty Minute Man" (Brown), which held the number-one position on the R&B charts for 14 weeks, "White Christmas" (Pinkney), which held number one for two weeks, and "It Ain't The Meat" (Mack). None, however, could match Ricks for a smooth, romantic delivery on ballads.

Bass leads were regularly issued in the early 1950s (the period we've labeled paleo-doo-wop) by vocal groups that were past their teen-age years. The basses who sang lead were almost always mature men. Occasional forays into this area by more youthful bassmen fell flat, e.g. "The Draw" from 1961 by Sherman Garnes of the Teenagers. Youthful bassmen couldn't convey the mature strength and sexual innuendo that were necessary to put over lyrics that were often filled with double entendres. They were better suited to the innocent lyrics and phrasings of mid- to late-1950s songs. On the other hand, the more mature bassmen were not at all at home with the riffing style of their younger counterparts.

What happened next in the evolution of bass singing is clear, though exactly when and by whom is not. Sometime between the early 1940s and the early 1950s, short staccato riffs (strings of nonsense syllables) by a bass could be heard in rhythm & blues ballads, either underneath the melody or punctuating choruses. We've called this style a "punctuating" bass because the vocalizations offered are short and short-lived (i.e. "doe doe doe") and may repeat at the end of each line or chorus (as a comma or period might punctuate a sentence). Early examples of these sounds, as in "Comin' In On A Wing And A Prayer" by both the Golden Gate Quartet and the Four Vagabonds, resemble the earlier style of imitating instruments. Somewhat later examples are found in "Lullaby" (1946) by the Ravens, "That's My Desire" (1948) and "Yesterday's

Roses" (1949) by the Bachelors, "Until Now" by the Rhythm Masters (1949) and from Jimmy Ricks and his Ravens again in "Once In A While" (1948), "Tea For Two" (1949), "Count Every Star" (1950) and "Please Believe Me" (1950). In these post-war songs, utterances by the bass can be heard, if one listens carefully. By 1950, these utterances can clearly be heard as punctuations. They are also heard in more songs. Group by group, song by song, imitating the instrumental bass gave way to short strings of nonsense syllables that had a sound all their own.

The Four Buddies began their recording career at the end of 1950. In December of that year, they waxed "Just To See You Smile Again" and "I Will Wait," two classic paleo-doo-wop ballads. With Leon Harrison out front and the group blowing harmony behind him ("oo"), William "Tommy" Carter can be clearly heard underneath singing "doe doe doe" punctuating the end of many lines. This became a fairly fixed pattern for a series of beautiful mournful ballads between 1950 and 1953 on the Savoy label. Carter can be counted as one of the first true 1950s-style bassmen.

Another pioneer was a bassman for the Blenders. Not their regular, moderately famous bass James De Loach, but his stand-in, Ray Johnson.[9] The Blenders, who recorded from 1949-1953 were a Ravens sound-alike group. Ollie Jones founded the group in 1948 with the help of his friend Jimmy Ricks, who "owed him one" for kicking him out of the Ravens in favor of a higher-voiced Maithe Marshall. They issued a series of recordings on National and Decca beginning in 1949 that copied the Ravens pop-jazz style with frequent bass leads. In late 1950, De Loach became ill and was replaced by Ray Johnson, who not only sang bass with the Beavers on Coral, but played a stand-up bass instrument as well. Lo and behold, the only two of the groups' early recordings to feature a doo-wop bass stemmed from the Oct. 4, 1950 session when Johnson pinch hit (and reached bass). "What About Tonight," released in November of 1950, contained hints of the doo-wop style, and "I'm Afraid The Masquerade Is Over," released in January 1951, contained repetitive and clearly doo-wop bass punctuations. When De Loach returned in mid-1951, the group returned to its doot-doot-dooting pop-jazz style. Johnson became a post-Blender, as well as a post-Beaver, and went on to sing with the Marshall Brothers and Dominos.

If one follows the recordings of the Larks on the Apollo label, and listens carefully to the ministrations of their bass, David McNeil, one can almost see the evolution of bass singing taking place.[10] Their first

9. The talking bridges of Hoppy Jones of the Spots clearly sounded ethnic, but in a folksy, non-threatening way.
10. Goldberg, Marv, and Redmond, Mike. "Yesterday's Memories: The Blenders." *DISCoveries*, May 1989, p.110-111.

recordings from late 1950 were gospel numbers, "Shad-rack" and "Honey In The Rock." Both are uptempo and feature syllabic strings by McNeil such as "boom-mum-mum…," which are clearly older-styled attempts to mimic an instrumental bass. In "Coffee, Cigarettes And Tears," recorded in December 1950, one hears "doot doot doot" and "wah wah wah" in the bridges, which again clearly aim at imitating instruments. A month later, January 1951, saw the recording of "Hopefully Yours," a ballad in the Orioles style, which has the background singing "oo-oo…" and the bass blending with that background. Also recorded in that session was "It's Breaking My Heart," which features "boom-mum-mum…" by McNeil. Done in a regular, insistent kind of way, it's almost as if the bass part is breaking away from imitating an instrument and beginning to use a doo-wop riffing style. "When I Leave These Prison Walls," from the same session, also has McNeil uttering "boh boh boh" in a style that borders on doo-wop. "My Reverie" and "Let's Say A Prayer," both ballads from the winter of 1951, feature a beginning doo-wop-styled bass chanting "boom boom boom." Then, two months later in March of 1951, McNeil sounded totally doo-wop in style, riffing with "doo doo doo" to punctuate lines in the great ballad, "What's The Matter." The Larks' bass part continued in the doo-wop idiom with the ballads, "My Lost Love" from October 1951 and "In My Lonely Room" and "I Live True To You" from February 1952. (In 1952, the first Larks group disbanded, to be replaced with a second, more pop-sounding group in 1954, a group which abandoned doo-wop bass riffing.)

In the late 1940s, the presence of these punctuating bass riffs was more the exception than the rule. That is, there are more Ravens, Orioles, Four Tunes and Four Knights songs without bass riffs than with them. Gradually, as the 1950s unfolded, it became more and more common to hear a distinct bass voice punctuate the melody. In and after 1953, the bass was supposed to stand out more. Not only did the bassman punctuate the lyrics, but he often provided an introduction to the song and ran under the melody line for most of the song as well. Witness the "Hooly bop a gow" bass intro to "I Promise To Remember" by Sherman Garnes of Frankie Lymon and the Teenagers in 1956. After his famous introduction, Sherman can clearly be heard riffing underneath Frankie and the boys. Another example is found in "Little Girl Of Mine" by the Cleftones, in which bass Warren Corbin can be heard singing "Yeah" as a deep punctuation and also riffing under the harmonizers. If you listen to the backgrounds of these mid-1950s jump tunes, especially on a compact disc where digitized recording lends clarity to each voice, the bass usually has his own agenda and can be heard separate from the harmony (second tenor and baritone).

As opposed to leads by the bass, this "riffing" style is what most people associate with the doo-wop idiom. It should be noted that it wasn't that these youthful bassmen couldn't sing lead. They just weren't supposed to, given the newer and more youthful style of the music. The singing abilities of the better ones are apparent by listening to their riffing. The recordings of one of the greatest riffers of them all, Leroy McNeil of the Nutmegs, will convince the reader of this.

Basses of the mid- to late-1950s were sometimes used in a comedic or novelty role. In "Peekaboo" by the Cadillacs, their bass Bobby Phillips haunts and taunts his audience; in "Rang Tang Ding Dong (I Am Japanese)," Alvin Williams, bass of the Cellos, plays the part of a big shot who can mesmerize the ladies; and in "Charlie Brown" by the Coasters, Will "Dub" Jones, posing as poor Charlie cries, "Why is everybody always picking on me?"

With the entry of white groups to the doo-wop arena in the late 1950s came the birth of the "power" bass, wherein the bass voice almost or actually took over the song. One of the first examples of this is "I Wonder Why," the first issue by Dion and the Belmonts (1958):

"Dun dun dun,
Duh dun duh dun dun,
Duh duh dun dun dun,
Duh dun, duh duh duh duh duh duh duh…"[11]

says their bass, Carlo Mastrangelo, and away they go. Or similarly…

"Nnn-dot nnn-dot nnn-dot nnn-dot,
Dil lil lil lil wah wah wah…"

in "I Remember" by the Five Discs in 1958. This same group recidivated in 1961, with the infamous bass introduction "Never Let You Go":

"Bon, bon, nim-a-nim-a-nim-ah,
Rib-i-dah, rib-i-dah, rib-i-dib-i-dib-i-dah,
Doo-bop doo-bah, rip-ay,
Bon, bon, nim-a-nim-a-nim-ay…"

These power bassmen stood out from their groups more than their counterparts of the mid-1950s. The latter might provide an intro to the song, but then would join the background harmonizers (for the most part) and let the lead take over. Power bassmen would keep coming at you throughout the song. Works of the Marcels, such as "Blue Moon" and "Heartaches" are prime examples. Fred Johnson, their bass, just took over. He owned those songs, despite a capable lead by Cornelius Harp and excellent background harmonies.

In sum, the doo-wop era saw the bass voice used in a number of different ways. The bass lead was offered by mature bassmen[12] beginning in 1946 and continued on a regular basis through the mid-1950s. The punctuation style of bass began in the late 1940s and became commonplace by the early 1950s. Origi-

---

11. This is reminiscent of the "ontogeny recapitulates phylogeny" stuff from High School biology. Here, the evolution of the bass voice within one singing group, the Larks, seems to imitate the way bass voices evolved generally through the doo-wop era.

12. Can an aging bass be called "Old Man Riffer?"

nally used by adult bassmen, it was picked up by the teen bassmen as the first real doo-wop bass style. Punctuation continued throughout the doo-wop era and, in fact, was the only distinct bass contribution in less doo-woppy tunes of the era (as in "You Belong To Me" by the Duprees in 1962 and "Til Then" by the Classics in 1963). The more youthful riffing style emerged in the early to mid-1950s and is most representative of the doo-wop era, even to the present day. Bassmen often assumed a comic role (Coasters) or novelty role (Cellos, Eternals). Power basswork began to emerge in the late 1950s and is an exaggeration of the riffing style.

The style in which a bassman sang (or talked) is an excellent clue as to his age and/or the musical era that he emerged from. Talking bass bridges or imitation of the instrumental bass imply that the singer is anchored in the 1940s or earlier. A bass lead usually points to a man well out of his teens by 1955, while riffing and power bassing imply teenagehood. This results in two distinct bass camps; those who riff and rarely lead and those who lead and rarely riff. One camp isn't better than the other, just different.

In March of 1995, Ronnie Italiano, deejay host of "The R&B Party" (on WNYE in Brooklyn, N.Y.) ran a contest to see who was top banana in bassland. He picked ten bassmen on his own, limiting the menu to those guys who sang both harmony and lead parts (thus eliminating riffers like Charles Moffit of the Velours and Fred Johnson of the Marcels). He then played sample songs and asked the first ten callers from his audience to rate them by choosing a number between 80 and 100 (the range was limited because he was afraid some voters would "low ball" some entrants). The nominees and scores were:

Norris "Bunky" Mack	(Swallows)	927
Will "Dub" Jones	(Cadets, Jacks)	934
Steve Gibson	(Red Caps)	956
David McNeil	(Larks, Dominoes)	972
Bill Brown	(Dominoes, Checkers)	975
Lee Gaines	(Delta Rhythm Boys)	979
Bobby Nunn	(Robins, Coasters)	983
Tommy Evans	(Ravens, Drifters)	989
Jimmy Ricks	(Ravens)	996
Gerald Gregory	(Spaniels)	997

The results surprised even Mr. Italiano. He had a hard time believing that Jimmy Ricks didn't win, even though he held Gerald Gregory in high esteem.[13] These results are questionable, however, because of the methodology, (i.e. choice of songs to represent each singer, bias toward the still active Mr. Gregory, range restriction of scores, limiting the number of votes, etc.). Other noteworthy bass leads

---

13. Apparently a bass injustice occurred.

not placed in nomination in this contest were Bill Pinckney (Drifters), Bob Karnegay (Du Droppers) and Harold Winley (Clovers).

Since the above selection of bassmen covered primarily bass leads, we've assembled our nominations for the ten best riffers and power basses, presented in alphabetical order:

Fred Barksdale/Pat Gaston	Solitaires
Sherman Garnes	Teenagers
Gerald Gregory	Spaniels
Andrew Johnson/John Russell/ Charles Di Bella	Five Discs
Fred Johnson	Marcels
Carlo Mastrangelo	Dion & the Belmonts
Leroy McNeil	Nutmegs
Charles Moffet	Velours
Wally Roker	Heartbeats
Alex Miranda	Eternals

Very often with riffers, it was the entire group that determined the style and contribution of the bassman. In both the Solitaires and Five Discs, more than one man sang bass and each is mentioned above. Of all the bassmen, Gerald Gregory of the Spaniels is the only one to appear on both lists, bridging the gap between two generations of bassmen and displaying a versatility not often seen.

We offer the following lists so that the reader may seek out further examples of (primarily) the riffing and power styles of bass. The first list contains songs in which the bass part is exemplary within songs that are quite well-known. The second list contains another bunch of great bass performances in less well-known songs (although many readers will be familiar with all of them).

Well-Known Songs with Great Bass Parts

Blue Moon (or Heartaches)	Marcels
Book Of Love	Monotones
Can I Come Over Tonight	Velours
Get A Job	Silhouettes
I Wonder Why	Dion & the Belmonts
Nag	Halos
Papa Oom-Mow-Mow	Rivingtons
Pretty Little Angel Eyes	Curtis Lee (backed by the Halos)
Rip Van Winkle	Devotions
Rockin' In The Jungle (or Babalu's Wedding Day)	Eternals
Unchained Melody	Vito & the Salutations
Up On The Mountain	Magnificents
Village Of Love	Nathaniel Mayer and the Fabulous Twilights
Walking Along	Solitaires

Less Well-Known Songs with Great Bass Parts

All Nite Long	Du Mauriers
Bermuda Shorts	Delroys
Donna Lee	Demilles
Go Back Where You Came From	Summits
Heartbeat	Whirlwinds
I Really Love You So (Honey Babe)	Solitaires
I Remember (or Never Let You Go)	Five Discs
Lamplight	Deltas
Let Me Tell You	Nutmegs
Long Tall Sally	Barbara Green (& group)
Mope-Itty Mope	Bosstones
Roaches	Temptations
The Clock	Contenders
Vowels Of Love	Poets

By the way, what do the above-listed songs of the Contenders, Delroys, Summits and Temptations have in common? (!oot gniffir eht seod dna dael sgnis namssab ehT)

As a measure of whether you know your bass riffs, see how you fare on the following quizzes. Sherman Garnes, bass of the Teenagers, provided a bass introduction to most of his group's hits. The first quiz dares you to match the Shermanism with the song.

Quiz #3: Shermania

1. Hey, tum-bah tuh tum-bah tuh tum-bah, duh duh...
2. Boo doo doo doo doo doo wah...
3. Doe doe doe...
4. Dum a-num a-num a-num a-num a-num a-num a-num...
5. Hooly boppa cow boppa cow boppa cow cow...
6. Comb a letta sadie boom...
7. Boo doo doo doo doo wah...
8. Doo bop shuh-doo, boom buh boom boom boom...
9. Shuh doobie doobie doobie...
10. Bay bay bay bay-bome, doobie doo-wop...

a. Who Can Explain
b. Teenage Love
c. I Promise To Remember
d. Share
e. Paper Castles
f. ABC's Of Love
g. I Want You To Be My Girl
h. Please Be Mine
i. Why Do Fools Fall In Love
j. Love Is A Clown

For the second quiz, see if you can match the bassman to his group, and then both to another member of that group. Answers to both quizzes can be found in the Appendix.

Quiz #4: Running The Basses

A) Jimmy Ricks	1) Vito & the Salutations	a) Eddie Rich
B) Wally Roker	2) Willows	b) Gerhart Thrasher
C) Gerald Gregory	3) Five Discs	c) Billy Ward
D) Will "Dub" Jones	4) Robins	d) Joe Stubbs
E) Norris "Bunky" Mack	5) Cleftones	e) Freddie Milano
F) Sherman Garnes	6) Platters	f) Eugene Pitt
G) Fred Johnson	7) Ravens	g) Grady Chapman
H) Carlo Mastrangelo	8) Jive Five	h) Vernon Seavers
I) Bobby Nunn	9) Frankie Lymon/Teenagers	i) Ron "Bingo" Mundy
J) Raymond Edwards	10) Halos	j) Joe Barsalona
K) Herb Reed	11) Drifters	k) Berman Patterson
L) Bill Brown	12) Dion & the Belmonts	l) Billy Horton
M) Norman Johnson	13) Falcons	m) Ralph Martin
N) Arthur Crier	14) Silhouettes	n) Willis Jackson
O) Lenny Citrin	15) Cadets	o) David Lynch
P) John Steele	16) Marcels	p) Al Cleveland
Q) Willie Schofield	17) Heartbeats	q) Aaron Collins
R) Warren Corbin	18) Dominoes	r) Randy Silverman
S) Bill Pinkney	19) Spaniels	s) Warren Suttles
T) Charles Di Bella	20) Swallows	t) Joe Negroni

Chapter 6

Getting The Lead Out

Earlier, we described the characteristics that a song should possess to be classified within the doo-wop style. Nowhere in that list is the type of lead voice specified. In fact, it's possible that a song could be considered doo-wop in style without a single discernible lead. Some doo-wop renditions contain dual leads and many groups alternated their lead singers depending upon the type of material to be tackled. The Cadets/Jacks are an example of this. Aaron Collins fronted the group most of the time on ballads, while Dub Jones led on uptempo numbers.

There's no denying that many great voices have graced doo-wop recordings. Clyde McPhatter, Tony Williams and Willie Winfield come to mind as exemplars and there are many others. But great lead singers do not a doo-wop make. Nonsense syllables maybe, or bass riffing, or an ethereal falsetto behind the lead, but not the lead him- or herself. Does a great lead add to listening pleasure? Yes and no. It's surely a pleasure to hear Clyde wail or Willie croon, but some of the best doo-wops were fronted by guys with gravel-pit voices. Witness the entire Paragons vs. Jesters album. Adam Jackson (Jesters) and Mack Starr (aka Julius McMichael of the Paragons) could stay on the melody most of the time, and their feeling for the music and their delivery were mesmerizing, but they sure ain't winnin' no voice contests.

Another problem with lead singers that had excellent voices in their own right is that all too often they went AWOL like dirty rats. A more polite way to say this is that they obeyed the Peter Principle, which states that people rise to their level of incompetence.[1] For groups that sang doo-wop, this means that many of the best leads left their groups of origin for greener pastures. In effect, they were promoted out of their groups to go for solo careers. Clyde McPhatter, Jackie Wilson, Frankie Lymon, (Little) Anthony Gourdine and Dion (DiMucci) are some of the more notable examples. Sometimes it was the singer himself who felt he wasn't getting a big enough piece of the pie; sometimes the singer was searching for more artistic latitude or career growth, and sometimes his manager or record company executive thought he was more viable as a single artist. To be fair, this phenomenon was never limited to the doo-wop era or genre. Earlier in the 20th century, Billy Murray left the

American Quartet, Crosby left the Rhythm Boys and Connee Boswell left the Boswell Sisters for solo careers. After the doo-wop era, Frankie Valli left the Four Seasons, Diana Ross left the Supremes and Michael Jackson left the Jackson Five to follow their stars.

The desertion of a group's lead voice was quite a blow to the remaining members, especially since most groups grew out of neighborhoods and were conglomerations of friends. However, the very "groupness" of the style buffered the loss. Buffered, because again, the doo-wop style depends more on the presence of other characteristics than on the quality or particular approach of their lead voice. The Dominoes survived and flourished despite the loss of not just one, but two, exceptional leads (Clyde McPhatter and Jackie Wilson) and the Drifters produced lead-independent hit after hit in both rhythm and blues and pop-rock styles. Listening to Don K. Reed's Doo-Wop Shop over a number of years, one is impressed by the resilience of the groups that sing professionally today. They persevere, even thrive, despite quite a high rate of turnover. In some ways the lead voice is the easiest role to replace because his or her voice part is less intertwined with those of the other group members. Thus, when Fred Parris of the Five Satins went into the army, his place as lead singer was taken over by Bill Baker. Maryland Pierce did the same for Rudy West of the Five Keys. Even when the lead was a standout, the sound of the group as a whole remained fairly constant.

One can examine lead singing by looking at the vocal characteristics of the lead him- or herself or by viewing the relationship of the lead voice to the other voice parts in the doo-wop ensemble. Jean-Charles Marion took the latter point of view.[2] Marion catalogued non-standard types of leads, that is, leads other than the normal tenor leads. His first category is that of harmonizing leads, where two or more voices sang lead in harmony. Two harmonizers led in "I'm Sorry (I Did You Wrong)" by the Royal Holidays[3] and "Be Sure My Love" by the Dubs. Triple harmonizing leads were offered frequently by the Earl Lewis & the Channels, as in "The Closer You Are" and "That's My Desire" and by the Sixteens in "Teenage Promise" and "My Special Guy." Frequently, when harmonizing leads occurred in the choruses, a single tenor carried the ball in the bridge (e.g. Earl Lewis for the Channels). In "So Fine" by the Fiestas, however, the entire group was out front (in harmony) for the whole song.

1. Peter, Lawrence. *The Peter Principle*. New York: William Morrow, 1969. In business, if you're a standout performer in the mail room you'll get promoted to a better job. If you excel at this other job, you'll be promoted again. Eventually, you get kicked upstairs to a position where you don't excel any more and, in fact, may be relatively incompetent. It's at this level that you'll stay for the remainder of your career.

2. Marion, Jean-Charles. "The Aesthetics Of Lead Vocals." *Record Exchanger*, Issue #8, 1971, p. 16.
3. Most examples cited here are those offered by Jean-Charles Marion.

Another category isolated by Marion is the alternating (or push-pull) lead, where two singers alternated lines as if they were completing each others' sentences. An example of this style is "I Cried" by the Velvets. There are some recordings where dual leads carried the main choruses, with this alternating lead style being utilized in the bridge. Examples of this type can be found in "The Wedding" and "The Honeymoon" by the Solitaires and "See You Next Year" by the Cleftones.

Related to the practice of alternating leads is the echo effect, wherein a tenor (usually in falsetto) repeated the words uttered by the lead singer. Thus there were two voices clearly heard, one after the other, but here the uttered words were identical (rather than different in the alternating lead style). Famous examples of falsetto echoing are found in "Close Your Eyes" by the Five Keys, "Dear Lord" by the Continentals and "Love Is A Vow" by the Melloharps.

Marion also paid attention to double leads, where one voice handled the choruses and a second voice led in the bridge. This practice hearkens back at least as far as the beginning of the era, when Jimmy Ricks and Maithe Marshall of the Ravens shared the spotlight and Sonny Til regularly gave way to George Nelson in the middle of songs by the Orioles. Marion's examples from the 1950s were "I Want To Know" by the Ladders, "So Strange" by the Jesters and "My Mother's Eyes" by the Softones.

In sum, Marion listed (A) harmonizing leads (dual or triple), (B) alternating leads (or push-pull), (C) the echo effect and (D) double leads (two voices leading at separate times). For Marion, the recording that offers the largest number of unusual effects is "Moonlight" by the Vanguards which featured "a standard lead, tenor falsetto lead, echo effect by both bass and tenor, and ends with the now familiar bass to second tenor pyramid finale." Quite a performance, guys.

In addition to the relationship of the lead voice to other voices, the style of lead may also be examined. There are many different types of leads and lead voices and they often offer clues as to the date of a particular recording and the provenance of the group itself. As a guideline for listening to the music, we offer below the following categorization of styles of lead voice, with examples and descriptions. They appear in rough temporal order. In general, it can be noted that the styles of lead voices changed as the doo-wop era evolved.

Aside from the innate talents of the lead singer and the quality of his/her voice, there were other factors which influenced the style of lead. First, the age of the group members played a part. Frankie Lymon didn't attempt to sound bluesy, and adult lead singers did not feel compelled to sing in Frankie's schoolboy style. Also, the intended audience affected the lead singers phrasing, which in turn affected the style of lead. Early leads by members of the Five Keys (Rudy West or Dickie Smith) were intended for a black audience and sounded bluesy with a little gospel thrown in, but songs released by them after 1954, when they left Aladdin and signed with Capitol, were clearly aimed at broader audience (white as well as black) and offered pop-styled leads. Related to the audience factor is the material offered the group. A blues would evoke a lead style much different from a song that emanated from Tin Pan Alley or from the schoolyards of Harlem. This becomes kind of circular, however, for the type of material recorded by a group would in turn be affected by their age and their intended audience.

Operatic

Time Frame: Mid-1930s to late 1940s

Examples: Billy Williams (Charioteers), Bill Kenny (Ink Spots), Maithe Marshall and Joe Van Loan (Ravens)

Notes: High-register male voice anchored in the pre-doo-wop era. Affected and formal delivery geared to adult audience. First used by Williams but made famous by Kenny, in a string of hits beginning in 1939 with "If I Didn't Care."

Jazzy

Time Frame: Late 1940s

Examples: Jimmy Ricks (Ravens), Ormand Wilson (Basin Street Boys)

Notes: Romantic, adult, sophisticated.

Romantic

Time Frame: Late 1940s through late 1950s

Examples: Sonny Til (Orioles), Willie Winfield (Harptones), later Eugene Mumford (Dominos)

Notes: Til set the standard for romantic leads as a matinee idol on the chitlin circuit.

Gospel

Time Frame: Early 1950s through late 1950s

Examples: Clyde McPhatter (Dominos, Drifters), Jackie Wilson (Dominos), David Baughan (Checkers), early Eugene Mumford (Larks)

Notes: Wailing, crying, living, dying. Melismatic, emotional and, at times, ethereal. Call and response common between lead and background. Aimed at black audience.

Bluesy

Time Frame: Early 1950s through late 1950s (eventually transitioned to soul)

Examples: Early Rudy West (Five Keys), Junior Denby (Swallows), Bobby Lester and Harvey Fuqua (Moonglows), Solly McElroy (Flamingos)

Notes: Moonglows and Flamingos influenced by Chicago blues. Denby sounds like he's sitting on a barroom stool. Rudy West borderline blues and gospel.

Sweet/Cute

Time Frame: Early 1950s to mid-1950s

Examples: Eddie Rich (Swallows), Ray Wooten (Mellomoods), Joe Duncan (Vocaleers), George Grant (Castelles)

Notes: Young teens trying to sound romantic and adult-like, before Frankie Lymon made it legitimate for a kid to sound like a kid. Thus, precursor to Schoolboy style lead. Typified by early Bobby Robinson Red Robin groups.

Pop

Time Frame: Mid- to late 1950s

Examples: Tony Williams (Platters), later Rudy West (Five Keys), Nate Nelson (Flamingos)

Notes: Generally refers to "blaccent"-free leads with good voices that would sell to a white audience. The material these leads were given was generally geared for adults, although teens liked it too.

New York Style

Time Frame: 1953 to early 1960s

Examples: Sonny Norton (Crows), Herman Dunham and Milton Love (Solitaires), Earl Carroll (Cadillacs), Earl Lewis (Channels)

Notes: Pleading leads doing slow ballads, with heavy background, lots of riffing bass and falsetto. Dialectic and slangy.

Stylized

Time Frame: 1954 to early 1960s

Examples: James "Shep" Sheppard (Heartbeats, Limelites), Anthony Gourdine (Little Anthony and the Imperials), later Lee Andrews (Hearts)

Notes: Sounded as if they were acting out the lyrics as they sang them. Stilted yet effective way of sounding out the words.

Schoolboy

Time Frame: 1956 to end of era in 1960s

Examples: Frankie Lymon (Teenagers), Lewis Lymon (Teenchords), Pearl McKinnon (Kodaks)

Notes: Kids with high tenor voices, singing like kids. Earlier youngsters sang rather mournful ballads with adult themes and lyrics (see Sweet/Cute). This generation offered upbeat, uptempo songs with simple lyrics.

Gang

Time Frame: 1956 through 1959

Examples: Mack Starr (Paragons), Adam Jackson (Jesters), Ernest Harriston (Bopchords)

Notes: These guys get the job done without smoothness. Sound romantic yet you might prefer not to turn your back on them. Primarily a New York phenomenon.

Rock 'n' Roll

Time Frame: 1955 through the end of the era

Examples: Kripp Johnson (Dell Vikings), Herb Cox (Cleftones), Johnny Maestro (Crests), Norman Fox (Robroys)

Notes: More or less blaccent-free leads in a delivery that was aimed at a white teen audience. Heavy beat with greater reliance on instruments.

West Coast

Time Frame: mid-1950s through late 1950s

Examples: Jesse Belvin (Cliques), Cleve Duncan (Penguins), Arthur Lee Maye (Crowns)

Notes: Generally laid-back vocal style compared to East Coasters. Short on diction, long on feeling.

White

Time Frame: 1958 through end of the era

Examples: Dion DiMucci (Belmonts), Jimmy Beaumont (Skyliners), Jimmy Gallagher (Passions), Larry Chance (Earls), Joey Canzano (Duprees)

Notes: Just as almost all black leads grew up with gospel, learning and practicing the art of melisma (many notes per syllable), many white singers grew up listening to opera or crooners like Crosby, Como and Bennett. Crooners avoid melisma, holding their notes for longer periods of time. White leads sound like they're being paid by the minute to hold their notes. Less "soulful" than black leads.

Soul

Time Frame: 1958 into and through the 1960s

Examples: Jerry Butler and Curtis Mayfield (Impressions), Johnny Funches (Dells), Pookie Hudson (Spaniels), Millard Edwards (Sheppards), Tommy Bullock (Fiestas)

Notes: Frequent use of melismas, conveyance of feeling, suffering. Gospel-influenced delivery. Early examples still anchored in the innocent love of the doo-wop era, later ones become socio-political statements.

Falsetto

Time Frame: 1950 through the end of the era

Examples: Nolan Strong (Diablos), Julius McMichael (Paragons), Al Banks (Turbans), Earl Lewis (Channels)

Notes: Falsetto is primarily a technique that has been used by lead singers for part or all of the song (e.g. Little Joe Cook of the Thrillers on "Peanuts" and "Lilly Lou"), by lead singers who sing as tenors for most of the song but then use the false tenor to trail off at the end of the song (e.g. Norman Fox of the Robroys in "Tell Me Why"), by second leads usually during the bridge (Al Crump of the Heartbeats on "Tormented"), as an echo to the lead (in "Dear Lord" by the Continentals), or by a first tenor behind the lead during choruses (Billy Taylor of the Castelles on "Marcella"). Singers have used falsetto leads throughout the entire doo-wop era; from Buddy Bailey of the Clovers in "Yes Sir, That's My Baby" in 1950 to Julius McMichael of the Paragons on "Florence" in 1957 to Frank Mancuso of the Imaginations on the white-style doo-wop "Hey You" from 1961. Thus, falsetto crosses both time and color boundaries throughout the doo-wop years.

Use of more than one falsetto is even found occasionally. "Alone" by the Universals (1957) has a falsetto lead with a falsetto tenor behind the lead, as does "House Of Love" (1958) by Henry Hall and the Five Bellaires and "Queen Of The Angels" by the Orients (1964), while "Plan For Love," an early effort by the Flamingos, features shrill double falsettos backing up the lead tenor.

Falsetto has always been a staple of African-American vocal music and probably entered the doo-wop arena through its use in gospel music and as a substitute for the operatic-style high tenor lead of the 1940s.

10th	Lee Andrews	(Lee Andrews & the Hearts)	919 points
9th	Maithe Marshall	(Ravens)	944
8th	Sonny Til	(Orioles)	962
7th	James Shepard	(Heartbeats, Limelights)	963
6th	Bobby Lester	(Moonglows)	966.9 (go figure!)
5th	Rudy West	(Five Keys)	976
4th	Clyde McPhatter	(Dominos, Drifters)	979
1st (tie)	Solly McElroy	(Flamingos, Moroccos)	993
1st (tie)	Eugene Mumford	(Larks, Dominos)	993
1st (tie)	Willie Winfield	(Harptones)	993

Charles Keil[4] adds, "Falsetto singing comes directly from Africa, where it is considered to be the very essence of masculine expression."

As far as preferences in lead styles, one man's meat is another man's poison. Those not deeply committed to the music will be more comfortable with the Rock 'n' Roll, Pop and perhaps Schoolboy styles than they will with the Operatic, Gospel or Bluesy lead styles. Ronnie Italiano, deejay of a show catering to those deeply involved in the music, ran a contest to get at the best lead singer of all time. Ten leads were nominated by calls to his radio show, naming a singer and one song on which he sang lead. When two votes were received for a singer, he was "in" for the final ten. When two votes were recorded for one song, the song was "in." Those leads nominated, in order of nomination, were Clyde McPhatter, Eugene Mumford, Willie Winfield, James Shepard, Rudy West, Solly McElroy, Sonny Til, Maithe Marshall, Bobby Lester and Lee Andrews.[5] Each week, for five weeks, the ten chosen singers were presented in pairs for a vote. Number ten was paired against number nine, etc. Phoned-in ratings were limited by Italiano to between 80 and 100, since allowing a full range had resulted in "low-balling" in a previous contest. Ten ratings for each singer were tallied. The results are shown at the top of the page.

A run-off was held on Feb. 15, 1995. Solly McElroy, who unfortunately languished and died of cancer during the time these playoffs were held, finished third with a total of 985. Mumford and Winfield again tied, however, with 989 points. In the second run-off three weeks later, Willie Winfield edged out Gene Mumford, 995 to 993, although Italiano admitted to eliminating some outlying scores from both sides. Apparently politics has insinuated itself into the very pinnacle of the doo-wop world!

The reader may have noticed that all of the nominees in the above contest were black. Among those people really rabid about the music, it is generally held that black leads were better than white leads. Most would admit, however, that what they like is the black "style" of singing more than the white style, and that voice quality is less of an issue. The white sound, which is discussed at length in a later chapter, also has its adherents. One of these is Ed Engel, who wrote an article titled, "Top 20 White Lead Singers."[6] Here are his choices, in alphabetical order:

1) Nicky Addeo (Darchaes)

2) Jimmy Beaumont (Skyliners)

3) Jay Black (Americans)

4) Larry Chance (Earls)

5) Eddie Delmar (Bob Knight Four)

6) Dion DiMucci (Belmonts)

7) Teddy Graybill (Stardrifts & Concords)

8) Jordan (Fascinations)

9) Richard Kelly (Ovations)

10) Mike Lasman (Utopians)

11) Dennis Lowell (Explorers)

12) Johnny Maestro (Crests)

13) Anthony Maresca (Sophomores & Twilights & Dynamics)

14) Carlo Mastrangelo (Belmonts)

15) Tony Passalacqua (Fascinators)

16) Vito Picone (Elegants)

17) Joe Prolia (Fabulous Four & Four J's)

18) Dominic Safuto (Randy and the Rainbows)

19) Nick Santamaria (Capris)

20) Jay Siegel (Tokens)

There you have it folks. The favorite lead singers of all time, coming to you in black and white. For the stout of heart, the following quiz is offered. Match the lead singer with his group and with another member of that group. Answers can be found in the Appendix.

---

4. Keil, Charles. *Urban Blues.* Chicago: University of Chicago Press, 1966.
5. Note that his audience chose to omit some well-known leads like Fred Parris, (Little) Anthony Gourdine, Dion DiMucci and Johnny Maestro. Refer to the chapter on Doo-Wopolitics for a lengthier treatment.

6. Engel, Ed. "Top 20 White Lead Singers." *Echoes Of The Past*, Issue #4, Summer 1988, p.22.

Quiz #5: One Thing Leads To Another

A) James Shepherd	1) Rays	a) Alexander Sharp
B) Joe Villa	2) Harptones	b) Mitch Margo
C) Tony Williams	3) Spaniels	c) Buzzy Willis
D) Jimmy Beaumont	4) Duprees	d) Pat De Prisco
E) Sonny Til	5) Tokens	e) Earl Wade
F) Junior Denby	6) Flamingos	f) Zola Taylor
G) Earl Carroll	7) Chimes	g) Robert Del Din
H) Willie Winfield	8) Earls	h) Albert Crump
I) Bobby Lester	9) Capris	i) Wes Forbes
J) Margo Silvia	10) Solitaires	j) Zeke Carey
K) Fred Parris	11) Tune Weavers	k) Bob Gaudio
L) Solly McElroy	12) Platters	l) Davey Jones
M) Milton Love	13) Five Satins	m) Eddie Rich
N) Larry Chance	14) Orioles	n) Gilbert Lopez
O) Nick Santo	15) Moonglows	o) Janet Vogel
P) Lenny Coco	16) Heartbeats	p) Joe Santollo
Q) James "Pookie" Hudson	17) Swallows	q) Raoul Cita
R) Jay Siegel	18) Cadillacs	r) Mike Minicelli
S) Hal Miller	19) Royal Teens	s) Harvey Fuqua
T) Joey Vann	20) Skyliners	t) Ernest Warren

Chapter 7

Evolution

Part I: The Primordial Musical Ooze

Did doo-wop evolve from earlier, lesser and inferior types of music, or was it just serendipitously placed here on earth, by divine intervention, for our listening pleasure? Tough call, but let's go with the evolution theory. The problem is, where do we begin? We know evolution only began once, hasn't stopped since, and hopefully won't end, but where do we place our viewing window? On one hand, it would make sense to begin our search in the 1940s, for that is when the characteristics of doo-wop, as we know it, began to emerge. On the other hand, since vocal group harmony has been around since the inception of recorded sound, we may as well begin there, in the late 1800s. Our intention is not to rewrite the history of music, but to attempt to give an overview of the events that relate to the formation and evolution of the doo-wop style.

One problem in looking for the antecedents of doo-wop is that, because of the large number of musics that fed into it, almost any and all twentieth-century non-classical music is in some way related. Doo-wop was born out of the confluence of gospel, popular music, barbershop, jazz, blues and rhythm and blues. Each one of these musics, in turn, had its own set of ancestors. For example, the nonsense syllables found in doo-wop can be traced to groups like the Mills Brothers imitating instruments in the 1930s. This in turn is related to the advent of the big-band sound in the 1920s, which contained the horn and rhythm sections that groups like the Mills imitated. Background harmonies found in doo-wop can be traced to black gospel, which in turn comes from the combination of white church music and Negro field chants, which came from Europe and Africa respectively. The rhythm in doo-wop can be traced backward through post-war rhythm and blues to jazz, boogie-woogie and swing. The AAB format of many uptempo doo-wops that evoke the feel of R&B comes from the blues of the inner city, which in turn conjures up the earlier country bluesmen of the Mississippi Delta. The pop-doo-wop style of the Platters is descended from the formal ballad style of the Ink Spots, which in turn can be heard in the barbershop quartet singing in the early years of this century. It seems that the further back we look, the more complicated it gets. Of course.

The social and political realities of the times must also be taken into account. For example, the further back in time we go, the slower music (and everything else) changed or evolved. There were no radios or television sets in the 1890s, and the recording of music had just begun (on tinfoil cylinders in 1877, on wax-covered cardboard cylinders in 1886, and on flat discs in 1887[1]). By far the most important medium for the performance of music was live entertainment. Even in the early 1900s, only a small percentage of the American population had machines on which to play cylinders or records. People heard their music at minstrel shows, concerts and houses of worship. Theoretically, if one was born in Nebraska in 1860 and didn't travel much (most didn't), one more or less heard the same Nebraska music from birth to death.[2] Contrast that with someone born in 1960, or even 1910. Faster evolution of musical styles didn't occur until the 1930s, when radio became commonplace and made it possible to reach much larger numbers of people much more quickly.

Another fact of life that is inseparable from musical evolution is segregation. Whites and blacks lived parallel, unequal lives in the years before the doo-wop era. Communication between the races and cross-fertilization of their musics was more difficult the further back in time we go, but was helped by the tendency of musicians to be more liberal and affiliative than the society as a whole, and by radio. Blacks and whites found it difficult to sing together (there are exceptions), couldn't dance together in public, but could certainly listen to each other over the ether.

The Early Groups

Given the above parameters, a reasonable way to begin our study of the complex route to the doo-wop genre is by looking at early singing groups. Many quartets were among the first artists to record in the 1890s and the early part of the twentieth century. Groups with names like the Peerless Quartet, the American Quartet, the Haydn (spelled Hayden after 1910) Quartet and Heidelberg Quartet[3] recorded songs that we know today as standards such as "In The Good Old Summer Time" (1903, Haydn), "Take Me Out To The Ball Game" (1908, Haydn), "Let Me Call You Sweetheart" (1911, Peerless), "Oh You Beautiful Doll" (1911, American) and "By The Beautiful Sea" (1914, Heidelberg).

---

1. Walsh, Jim. "Polk Miller and His 'Old South' Quartet." *Hobbies*, p. 34, January 1960.
2. Which was almost as bad as having to live in Nebraska from birth to death.
3. Walsh, Jim. "A Directory of Pioneer recording Groups." *Hobbies*, p. 32, October 1962.

Unfortunately, while many of these songs have remained close to us, the artists and their singing styles have not. A fellow by the name of Billy Murray was the Bing Crosby or Elvis Presley of his era, recording as a solo artist, in duets with the top male and female singers of his day, and as lead of the Haydn, American and Heidelberg Quartets at various times. He was nothing if not prolific, controversial and regaled. And yet today, not one in a hundred will know his name. The closest most of us can come to his style of singing is through the legend of Al Jolson, who has become the most famous of the early singers, though Murray preceded and outsold him. These early quartet sounds are foreign to our ears at the end of the twentieth century, presenting the sound of barbershop but with deliveries that are formal and very dramatic, and with musical accompaniment that sounds tinny by today's standards. Back then, however, it was state of the art, and had a great deal of influence on the boys and girls that would form the quartets of the twenties and thirties.

Black groups were there at the beginning also, although you won't find their recordings on the Charts of the day, which were derived from cylinder, record and sheet music sales.[4] Few blacks had the funds to purchase these luxuries with any frequency or in any great numbers. With a small market, few black groups were recorded, and few copies were pressed when they were. "These groups toured the country singing both religious and secular harmony songs on the professional stage. One of the most popular Black group was the Standard Quartette of Chicago. This group was composed of four singers whose last names we know to have been Williams, DeMoss, Scott and Cattrell. It was this group, while on a visit to Washington, D.C. in early 1894, that went the honor of being the very first Black vocal group ever to make a commercial sound recording! Their efforts were released by the Columbia Phonograph Company as cylinders, and at least 20 were known to have been issued. Sadly, none are presently known to exist."[5]

The first black group to record on the flat disc format (records, as we know them) was the Dinwiddie Quartet from Philadelphia, who recorded spirituals and jubilees for the Monarch label (which was part of the Victor Recording Company) beginning in October, 1902. Keeping in mind the earlier caveat about social realities, "...Race-conscious Victor saw fit to dub them the Dinwiddie Colored Quartet on the label, thus making any buyer quite aware of what he or she was purchasing, since 'blackface' white quartets were also very popular. In fact, what seems to be a very over-zealous recording engineer on Monarch #1714 ["Down On The Old Camp Ground"], announces (before the group begins to sing)

'...this is an authentic Coon Shout by the Dinwiddie Colored Quartet.' "[6]It should be noted that gender was also telegraphed by the recording company, as in the "That Girl" Quartet, the Columbia Mixed Quartet (two ladies, two gentlemen) or the Edison Male Quartet.

Jim Walsh, *the* expert on early recordings, reports on what is probably the first integrated group to record. A fellow by the name of Polk Miller, a druggist by trade who fought for the South in the Civil War, recorded on cylinder in 1910 with His "Old South" Quartet. Miller, who was 65 at the time of these recordings, apparently rounded up four black men who worked on his father's plantation before the War. "All [Miller's]...records were issued by Edison in March 1910. The set consisted of four Amberoles, playing four minutes each, and three Standard two-minute cylinders. Miller sings in four, and the other three are by the quartet alone."[7] Some reviews of these issues in a periodical titled *The New Phonogram*, and quoted by Walsh read: "Amberole #389, 'The Bonnie Blue Flag'— Polk Miller and Quartet. One of the most popular war songs of the South, surpassing in popularity even the world famous 'Dixie' in the days from '61 to '65. It was sung by Miller around army campfires and he now sings it at Confederate Veterans reunions. Banjo accompaniment. ...Amberole #390, 'Laughing Song'—Quartet. It takes a genuine Southern Negro to sing this song, which is typical of the happy darkey nature. The laughter is natural and contagious. Guitar accompaniment."[8] White lead singer, black harmonizers, a precious few years before Norman Fox & the Rob Roys, Paul Himmelstein & the Heartbreakers, Mike Lasman & the Utopians, Vic Donna & the Parakeets and Jerry Dorn with the Hurricanes.[9]

The 1920s

Singing groups maintained their barbershop style through the 1920s, with the Shannon Four, the Revelers (which counted three ex-Shannons among its four singers) and the Peerless Quartet being among the most popular groups. This decade also witnessed the birth and growth of the non-military[10] big bands, which were central to the American music scene from the mid-1920s through World War II. Though individual singers and singing groups might accompany these bands (e.g. Bing Crosby with Paul Whiteman's band), the mainstay of the music was instrumentation. Singing groups took a back seat, most of the time. Occasionally black groups like the Norfolk Jazz Quartet sprang up, mixing uptempo spirituals ("Jubilees") with more secular fare.

Another relevant musical development of the 1920s was the emergence of classic blues, initially sung by

4. Whitburn, Joel. *Pop Memories, 1890-1954.* Menomenee Falls, Wis.: Record Research Inc., 1986.
5. Moonoogian, G.A. "Wax Fax." *Record Collector's Monthly,* Issue #49, p. 7, May-June, 1991.

6. Ibid
7. Walsh, Jim. "Polk Miller and His 'Old South' Quartet." *Hobbies,* p. 34, January 1960.
8. Ibid.
9. All of these are black groups fronted by a white lead from the 1950s.
10. Believe it or not, John Phillips Sousa and his band was a top artist in the early years of the 20th century.

women like Mamie Smith ("Crazy Blues," 1920), Bessie Smith ("Down Hearted Blues," 1923) and Ethel Waters ("Am I Blue," 1929). These songs and artists were popular among both black and whites, as evidenced by their presence on the Pop charts, and established classic blues as a black-white fusion music, setting the stage for the evolution of jazz in the 1930s.

Jazz, as difficult to define as it is easy to recognize, began to differentiate itself in terms of its rhythm ("swing"), structure (central melody punctuated by individual solos) and language (scat singing using nonsense syllables) in the late 1920s. Instrumentally, Louis Armstrong led the way, and vocally the trail was blazed by none other than Bing Crosby and the Boswell Sisters.

While classic blues was received well by white audiences in the early 1920s, the reception was short lived. According to Big Al Pavlow,[11] when record companies started using the phrase "race" as a descriptor of the blues to merchandise their records, and when country blues (meaning individual singers accompanying themselves on an instrument) by male artists joined the urban blues (meaning singers backed by large ensembles) in the mid 1920s, the paths of blues/race and jazz began to diverge. "From 1926 to the mid-forties, race and jazz would maintain their separate identities, with an occasional common ground like boogie-woogie. Black popular music was thus divided into these two main categories. Jazz entered the pop world and prospered. Its early innovators became legends, and its contemporary artists were commercially and critically well received, while all that was race was ignored. Where jazz sought out and thrived on musical elements that existed outside of black culture and experience, race turned inward to explore that culture. Jazz became complicated and sophisticated. Race remained simple and funky. Jazz had a mixed audience, race did not."[12]

The 1930s

The important groups to emerge in the late 1920s and early 1930s were in the pop vein, jazz vein or both. The Rhythm Boys, who were comprised of Bing Crosby, Al Rinker and Harry Barris, sang for Paul Whiteman's Orchestra in the late 1920s, listing the imitation of instruments, jiving (talking and kidding around while singing), and scatting among their weapons. The Boswell Sisters, a trio from New Orleans, took over their place as the premier jazz vocal group in 1931 when the Rhythm Boys went on to solo careers. The Boswells combined unusual jazzy vocal arrangements with exceptional harmony, and backed themselves with the best jazz musicians around. They charted twenty times in the 1930s and were by far the most important female group of their era.

Other noteworthy groups with a jazz-jive flavor in their recordings from this time period were the Three Keys and the Spirits of Rhythm. Jiving, where members dialogue with each other before or after stanzas can be heard in "Jig Time" by the Keys in 1932 and "Dr. Watson and Mr. Holmes" by the Spirits in 1934. Electronic (as opposed to mechanical) recording of music made these uptempo jump numbers come alive, and they seem quite modern, even by today's standards.

Also emerging in 1931 were the Mills Brothers, from Piqua, Ohio. Beginning with "Tiger Rag" in 1931, they placed 71 songs on the Pop charts, five of which reached number one ("Tiger Rag," "Dinah," "Paper Doll," "You Always Hurt The One You Love" and "Glow Worm"), and five of which reached number two. The group sang in a pop/barbershop style that was smooth and easy to listen to while throwing in elements of jazz (especially early in their career). The Mills were one of the first groups that recorded (certainly the first successful group) to use the talking bass solo in the bridge of a song, and were one of the first groups to mimic instruments, although the gimmick has its roots in the 19th century.[13]

While the Rhythm Boys and Boswells mimicked various instruments in jazzy vocal conversations with the instruments that accompanied them, the Mills set out to imitate a whole orchestra. One brother played guitar and "boom boomed" to sound like a stand-up bass, thus creating a rhythm section, while the other three took on the parts of horns. Their innovations moved the music one step closer to the style that would later be called doo-wop. Perhaps more importantly, they were the first African-American group to make significant inroads with white listening audiences. While black artists such as Ethel Waters, Louis Armstrong and Billie Holiday sold to white audiences as well as black, the Mills Brothers were the first group to attain widespread popularity with white audiences. A measure of this is that they had their own 15-minute prime time show, twice weekly, on the mainstream CBS radio network in the early 1930s.[14] While they weren't the first black vocal group to be nationally syndicated (that honor goes to the Southernaires Quartet in 1929[15]), their popularity helped break the ice for those that came after. By being successful African-American artists, they became essential role models for the youths that would grace the group recordings of the early to mid-1950s.

---

11. Pavlow, Big Al. *The R & B Book: A Disc-History of Rhythm & Blues.* Providence, R.I.: Music House Publishing, 1983.

12. Ibid.

13. "The imitation horn effect predates the Mills Brothers by many years. A programme for a performance given in Indianapolis in the year 1894, by the Bell Quartette (Black) included among the selections: 'Imitation of Caliope' and 'Imitation of Band.' The Mills Brothers' utterly convincing human orchestra far outstripped all prior efforts of this kind." From the liner notes to *The Human Orchestra: Rhythm Quartets in the Thirties*, Clanka Lanka Records, by Doug Seroff and Ray Funk.

14. Whitesell, Rick. "The Early Days of Radio and Vintage Vocal Groups." *Record Exchanger*, Issue #19, 1975, p. 11.

15. Ibid.

The Ink Spots came on the scene in 1935 as a jazz-jive group but didn't achieve success until 1939 with the beautiful ballad "If I Didn't Care." The long series of hits that followed utilized the same formula; that is, the silky falsetto tenor lead of Bill Kenny, solid and smooth background harmony, and a talking bass recitation in the bridge. This latter characteristic, though used by the Mills and other groups before them, was honed to perfection by the bass of the Ink Spots, Orville "Hoppy" Jones, and laid the groundwork for the reverence of bass singers that would last three decades. The group made the Pop charts 46 times and hit the number one slot on six occasions ("Address Unknown," "We Three," "I'm Making Believe," "Into Each Life Some Rain Must Fall," "The Gypsy," and "To Each His Own"). The Ink Spots were less pop-oriented than the Mills, and let their "color" come through in their sound. Listening to Hoppy Jones, it's clear that he's not Caucasian, while the Mills are accent-free. Perhaps for this reason, the Ink Spots are seen as more of a direct link to the doo-wop era than are the Mills. And by the choice of their name, they were one of the first to display "black pride." Other groups like the Brown Dots and Ravens would follow suit in the 1940s.

The Ink Spots, like the Mills, had their own 15-minute radio show twice a week. Interestingly, their show was on the "Blue Network" (NBC) in the 1937-1938 time frame, which was before they hit the big time in 1939 with "If I Didn't Care." They also "appeared on nearly all of the major variety programs of the 1940s and early 1950s, as featured guests. This is another example of the general scheme by which the early black groups achieved and maintained their success. Following a well-received program series, the groups confined themselves thereafter to occasional guest spots on variety shows; this served the two-fold purpose of preventing over-exposure of an act to the public, and it served as a fine springboard for new releases a group had recorded."[16]

A third group which made its mark on the charts was the Andrews Sisters, who first recorded in 1937. While more on this group can be found in the chapter dealing with female artists, suffice it to say that they charted almost 100 times from 1938 to 1951, and sang a wide range of material in a pop music style peppered with jazz. Ironically, they were the first all-female group to make the R&B charts and, like the Mills and Inks, they had multi-racial appeal and therefore influence.

Aside from these three seminal groups, other important groups that emerged in the 1930s were the Charioteers (who first recorded in 1935), Golden Gate Quartet (1935), and Cats & the Fiddle (1939). Actually, "emerged" is not that great a word to use here. None of these groups made the Pop charts in the 1930s and before 1942, when Billboard began keeping track of who was buying what in urban black communities, no widespread measuring stick was available. Records either made the Pop charts or they made no charts. So while blacks may have been buying the "race" records, it's difficult to know which groups and songs were being bought. Even when Billboard unveiled the "Harlem Hit Parade" in 1942, only ten songs per week made the charts, as opposed to twenty-five on the Pop charts of that year. We can know what the top ten songs were, but have a more difficult time discovering the second tier. Al Pavlow made note of "Representative Race and Jazz Records" by year beginning with 1920. In the 1930s, only the big guys appear: "Tiger Rag" by the Mills in 1931 and four by the Ink Spots in 1939.[17] However, there were other measures of success for the groups of this era, namely appearances on radio and films.

The Charioteers, featuring a great lead singer in Billy Williams, reached the R&B charts seven times, beginning in 1940. Their style was predominantly pop, occasionally pop-gospel, and they did much backup work for the likes of Bing Crosby, Frank Sinatra and Pearl Bailey. They also were regulars on Crosby's radio show in the mid-1930s and had their own 15-minute prime-time radio show on the Mutual network, which gave them a wide audience.[18] The Golden Gate Quartet began recording in 1937, with a style that was mostly pop-gospel with some jazz/jive wrinkles. It was almost as if they took the innovations of the Mills Brothers, such as using only a guitar and imitating instruments, and applied them to the singing of spirituals. They appeared in the film "A Song Is Born" in 1948 with Benny Goodman, Danny Kaye and Louis Armstrong. The Cats & the Fiddle were on the cutting edge of vocal jazz from their first recording in 1939, as were the Boswells before them. They appeared in a couple of movies called "Goin' Places" and "Jeepers Creepers" in the late 1930s and, although they didn't make noise on the charts, were one of the most innovative groups of the era.

Running on a parallel track to the pop groups were the rhythm, or "jive" vocal groups. Early Mills Brothers and Ink Spots recordings were often in this vein, which featured lots of scat singing, jive talk, witty lyrics, and imitation of instruments within uptempo arrangements. "Doodle deedle dot doo day" and "rah cha cha cha" can be heard in "Dixie Rhythm" by the Four Blackbirds and "Buh dah duh lah dot, buh dah duh lah dot" rocks out at you from "Minute And Hour Blues" by the Five Breezes, which pretty much qualifies as a rock 'n' roll song in 1939. Jive talk occurred mostly during instrumental (real or imitated) breaks and would typically be shouted like "solid," "swing it boys," "slap that bass" or "oh you dawg!" "Kickin' The Gong Around" by Rollin Smith's

---

16. Ibid junior.

17. Pavlow, Big Al. *The R&B Book: A Disc-History of Rhythm & Blues*. If one is wondering what did appear on these lists, the 280 entries for the years 1931-1939 were comprised of Big Band sounds, urban and country blues, with an occasional gospel number thrown in for good measure.

18. Whitesell article.

Rascals contains references to "Smokey Joe" twenty years before the Robins had a hit with the Lieber and Stoller-penned "Smoky Joe's Cafe." Even groups like the Golden Gate Quartet and Norfolk Jazz Quartet recorded in this jazz-jive idiom in the 1930s. Most of these imitated horns and stand-up bass regularly.

The style was taken to its logical extreme in 1937 by Leon Rene, best known as a composer and founder of the West Coast's Exclusive record label. He put together two vocal quartets that he managed at the time, the Five Jones Boys and the aforementioned Four Blackbirds, to form the Jones Boys Sing Band.[19] Extrapolating the Mills technique of sounding like instruments, the Sing Band aimed at duplicating the sound of an entire orchestra, featuring trumpet, trombone and sax sections. They appeared on radio and in a Bing Crosby film called "Double Or Nothing"(1937) in which they provided instrumental accompaniment.[20]

The 1940s

From 1940 to 1946, vocal group music was either pop, jazz, gospel, blues, or some combination thereof. There were white pop-jazz groups that were attached to some of the big bands of the day, like the Modernaires with Glenn Miller's Orchestra and the Pied Pipers with Tommy Dorsey's Band. Then there were the black gospel groups like the Soul Stirrers and Pilgrim Travelers that enjoyed almost total anonymity in the white community and charts. Other groups that began their careers in this era were the Deep River Boys (gospel-pop, first recording in 1940), Delta Rhythm Boys (pop-gospel, 1941), Four Vagabonds (pop-jazz, 1942), Five Red Caps (jazz-pop-blues, 1943), Coleman Brothers (gospel-pop, 1944), Brown Dots (pop-jazz, 1945), Four Tunes (pop-jazz, 1946) and Four Knights (pop-gospel, 1946). Each of these groups carved out a slightly different niche for themselves. The Deltas appeared in the most films, fifteen, of any vocal group and featured the first super-bass, Lee Gaines; the Four Vagabonds became known for their skill at emulating instruments and appeared regularly on Blue network radio; the Red Caps were the bluesiest of the above groups; and the Brown Dots were Ink Spots imitators in name and sound. Each gained a reasonable amount of popular acclaim, but the major innovations were done by the Mills Brothers and Ink Spots in the previous decade. The next major change awaited the Ravens. It should be noted that despite the popularity of the Mills and the Inks, groups still made up only a fairly small percentage of chart hits. Don Heckman, in a 1970 article titled "The Forties" for the *Record Exchanger*,[21] mentions only the Ravens

Golden Gate Quartet.

and says that their style "obviously lay in earlier groups like the Ink Spots and Mills Brothers," in an article that mentions roughly 100 artists.

Just how close were we to the doo-wop style at the beginning of 1946? In effect, it didn't exist yet, judging by the criteria set forth in an earlier chapter. The characteristic of group harmony was certainly there, and had been since the turn of the century. Other qualities are absent, or used in much different ways. The bass part often separated from the harmony, but it was used to imitate an instrumental bass (e.g. Mills Brothers, Four Vagabonds)

Coleman Brothers.

19. Grendysa, Peter. "R&B Music on Recycled Shellac: Leon Rene's Exclusive Label." *Record Collector's Monthly*, Issue #6, P. 1, February 1983.

20. From the liner notes to *The Human Orchestra: Rhythm Quartets in the Thirties*, Clanka Lanka Records, by Doug Seroff and Ray Funk.

21. Heckman, Don. "The Forties." *Record Exchanger*, Issue #3, June 1970, p. 13.

Four Knights.

Four Tunes.

or to perform a talking recitation (Ink Spots). Falsetto wasn't used to run above the lead; rather it was the lead (Ink Spots). Nonsense syllables were present but they were used in scat singing (Boswells, Cats & the Fiddle) or to imitate instruments. They were not used, as in doo-wop, to punctuate stanzas or as riffs running under the melody. The beat was still either light as in pop, syncopated as in jazz, or heavy as in the big band sound. The simple, insistent rhythm of a doo-wop ballad wasn't around yet. Lyrics were still pop-oriented and fairly sophisticated. The somewhat salacious, double-entendre style that are exemplified by the Dominoes' "Sixty Minute Man" in 1951 were reserved for the blues style which, before the late 1940s, wasn't being used by many groups (but was used extensively by single artists). And the simple teen-age four-chord melodies hadn't arrived yet. So, in 1946, we had pop-jazz, jazz-pop, single artist blues and gospel, but nary a doo-wop in sight.

It was also at this juncture in time that the term "rhythm and blues" began to gain wider acceptance, replacing terms like "ebony," "sepia" and "race" as a catchall phrase to describe music produced by blacks for blacks. The official stamp was placed on this term by *Billboard* magazine, in 1949, when "R&B" was used as the new title for its "Race" charts. The scene was now set for the emergence of the new sound. But don't get excited, nothing dramatic happened, no quantum leaps were in the offing. Doo-wop emerged slowly, from the ever-changing primordial musical ooze.

If the reader has an inclination to pursue the pre-doo-wop group sounds of the 1930s and 1940s, 100 recommended and representative songs are listed in the Appendix.

Part II: The Birth of Doo-Wop

Before 1946, African-American singing groups tried to "cross over" to white markets by sounding white. Beginning in 1946 with the Ravens, however, many groups stopped trying to hide their ethnicity, with the result that the music sounded more raw and rhythmic. In fact, two main fonts of African-American music, R&B and gospel, began to help shape and define the new sound. The group singers maturing in the late 1940s and early 1950s combined the earlier pop-jazz style with the gospel heritage that they were exposed to in church and the R&B of the streets, to produce new and exciting sounds that would motivate and enthrall the next generation of teen-agers.

The post-war era also saw the birth and growth of a large number of independent record companies which not

Ravens.

Orioles.

only tolerated rhythm and blues, as the major record companies did, but were devoted to its existence. Thus legendary labels like King, Jubilee, Savoy, Chess, Aladdin and Atlantic were born at the right place at the right time to help complete the building blocks for a new music.

But the birth of doo-wop would not be an easy one. In May of 1946, the B-side of the first release by a new group on the Hub label titled "Lullaby," began with a simple guitar introduction, as had a legion of Ink Spots' (and their imitators') records before it. Their lead opened the song with "Goodnight, my love..." in tenor, lower and less smooth than Bill Kenny of the Spots would've done it. In the background, the harmonizers produced "ooh-ooh" in a nondistinctive way, while a piano tinkled innocently throughout the first verse. By the second verse, however, the harmonizers became emboldened, chanting "doo doo doot" not only at greater volume, but stridently and with rhythm. And at the end of this verse something remarkable happened.

The bass of this new group, which was called the Ravens, showed up. And boy did he show up. He clearly separated from his groupmates to utter, and we quote, "doo doo doo doo doo doo," as a punctuation to the last line of the second verse. A few more punctuations were heard before the bridge, less loud this time. The bass, whose name was Jimmy Ricks, sang second lead in the bridge and introduced the world to the quality of his voice, but then faded into the background for the remainder of the song. "Lullaby" gave us, if only for part of one song, the insistent rhythm of the doo-wop genre, nonsense syllables by background harmonizers and a distinct punctuating bass. Ironically, just as quickly as the new style appeared, it disappeared again.

The Ravens were formed in New York City by bass Jimmy Ricks and baritone Warren Suttles, who were waiting tables at the time, by adding second tenor Leonard Puzey and lead first tenor Ollie Jones who they met while looking for work at the Evans Booking Agency. They first appeared in the spring of 1946 at the Club Baron on West 132nd St. and Lenox Ave. in Harlem.[22] After recording six sides for the Hub label (of which "Lullaby" was the most doo-woppy) Ricks, who was apparently not just the bass but the boss as well (and as they say in sports, the "franchise"), replaced Jones with falsetto (operatic) tenor lead Maithe Marshall. The group then left Hub to join Jerry Blaine's National label. With a new lead singer, new producers and arrangers, the groups' sound changed significantly.

The Ravens now sang in the pop-jazz style of earlier groups like the Three Keys and the Spirits of Rhythm, but added a blues interpretation to the material that hadn't been done before. What made the group special was Ricks. He was, quite simply, unique, doing things better and lower and different than any bass before him. Oth-

22. Belniak, Bob. "Remembering Jimmy Ricks 1924-1974." *Echoes of the Past*, Issue #8, Summer 1989, p. 17.

ers, like Lee Gaines of the Delta Rhythm Boys, had done bass leads, but no one did them so frequently or in such a bluesy, sensuous manner. Ricks led the Ravens on the bluesy, jazzy, uptempo sides, and commonly did his basso profundo contrasting second lead in the bridge of Maithe Marshall-led ballads. Marshall was replaced in 1951 by Joe Van Loan, whose voice was similar. Both Ricks and the Ravens' background harmonizers used nonsense syllables, but they were almost always "doot doo doot doots" done in a jazz idiom. The way this group combined jazz, pop and blues made the relatively new term "rhythm and blues" come to life. Further, their choice of name not only set the precedent for the assumption of bird names by flocks of groups in the 1950s[23] but, because Ravens are black, a statement of pride was being made as well. They were an enormous influence of the next generation of young singers.

The Orioles were just as important as the Ravens, but in a different way. They were the first to lay down the form of a doo-wop ballad. They were invariably led by Sonny Til (nee Erlington Tilghman), a second tenor who possessed a sweetly romantic, yet strong voice which was clearly ethnic. They then regularly assigned the second lead duties to baritone George Nelson, whose voice was rough yet emotional at the same time. Think of Louis Armstrong singing with a great deal of feeling and you have George Nelson to a tee. To that they added a falsettoed first tenor, Alexander Sharp, who often separated from the harmony to float above Til's lead. The bass part was done capably by Johnny Reed, though he sang with the harmony as opposed to distinct from it. Put them all together and, in 1948, when they hit the ground running with "It's Too Soon To Know," the full compliment of doo-wop characteristics was right around the corner. "It's Too Soon..." had the overall feel of what we now call a doo-wop ballad and in a way, marked the beginning of the doo-wop era. An interesting sidelight is that the song crossed over to number thirteen on the Pop charts, despite its ethnic style. Things were looking up.

The influence of the Ravens and Orioles on later groups cannot be emphasized enough. In 1997, reviewing an article from Stormy Weather from 1971[24], which reviewed some Billboard blurbs from 1951, this conclusion is unshakeable. The Ravens and the Orioles were it, and since the same conclusions were drawn in 1951, this is not just revisionist twaddle. "The Four Buddies 'I Will Wait' [is a] ballad loaded with clichés... done appealingly by a new group with a style set somewhere between the Ravens and Orioles (from Billboard 1/13/51)." "The Dominoes 'Chicken Blues' [is]

a Raven's-type approach to a medium blues falls short on material; the bass lead is not Ricky (from Billboard 1/20/51)." "Vocal groups have taken command in the R&B field. Never before in the history of the specialty field have so many groups developed and taken so deep a root both on wax and in personal appearances. The development of the vocal group in this field dates back a few years to the successes originally achieved by the Ravens and Orioles. With these groups still potent box office attractions in the R&B market, almost a dozen others have sprung up, most of them in the last six months...(from Billboard 9/22/51)."

The only ingredients missing from the Orioles' songs to complete the doo-wop recipe were nonsense syllables and a bass that sang separate from the harmonizers. These were the puzzle pieces that the Ravens teased us with in "Lullaby" in 1946, and then took away again. It was typical, in these last years of the 1940s, to have some, but not all, of the characteristics of doo-wop. The Rhythm Masters, on "Until Now," in 1949, give us a falsetto over the lead and a bass under it, but not the doo-wop form. "That's My Desire" by the Bachelors (with a pre-Ravens Joe Van Loan), recorded in 1947, has a doo-wop bass that falls out of the harmony part. "Yesterday's Roses" by the same group in 1949 has a doo-wop feel, a bass that can be heard with but under the harmonizers throughout, but no nonsense syllables. "Don't You Ever Mind Them" by the Melody Masters, recorded in 1947, sounds like the Orioles before the Orioles. "Tea For Two" by the Ravens in 1949 has a doo-wop bass intro by Ricks within a jazzy arrangement. Clearly, by 1947 or 1948, doo-wop characteristics were common enough to signal that the dawn of a new musical era was just around the corner. We prefer to label these songs, which meet some but not all of the criteria, as pre-doo-wop, though we realize the decision is arbitrary. This is opposed to songs from the 1950-1954 time frame, many of which contain just about all the requirements for doo-wop status.

It all seemed to come together in 1950. In April, the Ravens put out an unusual song for them, called "Count Every Star." Out front was tenor Louis Heyward, which freed Ricks and Marshall up to do other things. Ricks did a doo-wop bass intro to the song, and Marshall can be heard in falsetto on the top, and the background voices use a "bome bome bome" nonsense string. The same emerging form can be heard in "Please Believe Me," recorded in 1950, but not released until the 1990s. It is perhaps not coincidental that Heyward led on this song as well, freeing up both top and bottom voices from that duty. The form, feeling and rhythm were appropriate to a new style. The Ravens had regained the path they had found and lost four years before. Doo-wop was born.

It didn't take long for other groups to put out songs in full-fledged doo-wop style. At the end of 1950, the Blenders released "I'm Afraid The Masquerade Is Over" and the Four Buddies issued "Just

---

23. There were earlier examples of bird names being used, e.g. the Four Blackbirds in the 1930s, but for some reason, avian appellation did not run amok back then.

24. "The Ravens." Stormy Weather, Issue #3, January 1971, p. 4.

Larks.

Five Keys.

Clovers.

Swallows.

To See You Smile Again," both of which sport a doo-wop style. The Four Buddies were, in fact, the first group to sing in doo-wop style regularly, right from the beginning of their recording career. "I Will Wait," "Why At A Time Like This," "Sweet Slumber" and "My Summer's Gone," all from 1951, have all the requirements; 1951 also saw the Larks enter the fray with "Hopefully Yours," "When I Leave These Prison Walls" and the magnificent "My Reverie." The

Dominoes, Clovers, Swallows, Five Keys and Cardinals all produced doo-wop flavored music (and all made the R&B charts) by the time 1951 drew to a close. There was no going back.

It's tempting to get into the game of trying to name the first doo-wop record. If pinned to the wall, we'd have to say that the doo-wop era began in 1948 with the Orioles, but that "Lullaby" or "Count Every Star" (take your pick), both by the Ravens, was the first full-

Dominoes.

Five Royales.

Cardinals.

fledged doo-wop song. Jim Dawson and Steve Propes took on that kind of task in their book, *What Was The First Rock 'n' Roll Record.*[25] They narrowed it down to a mere fifty songs that were issued between 1944 and 1956, which made for interesting reading. They never came up with the answer, which, we guess, was the point. We know that parts of the doo-wop signature were around in the late 1940s, we know that the Ravens and Orioles were the most important catalysts of the early sound, and we know that by 1950, the doo-wop era was upon us. We'd prefer not to get any more specific than that.[26]

Paleo Doo-wop (1948-1954)

While the proto-paleo-doo-wop songs between 1948 and 1950 were only partially doo-wop in style, after this time the full compliment of doo-wop characteristics was commonly found. Between 1951 and 1954, not only did pioneering groups like the Four

25. Dawson, Jim, and Propes, Steve. *What Was the First Rock 'n' Roll Record?* Boston: Faber and Faber, 1992.
26. Besides, the less specific we are, the less flak we'll get.

Crows.

Buddies and Larks emerge, but better-known groups like the Harptones, Crows, Clovers, Dominoes, Drifters, Five Keys, Flamingos, Moonglows and Lee Andrews and the Hearts began their careers as well. Each group put its own slant on the music they recorded. The influence of R&B can be heard in the Clovers' "One Mint Julep," the Dominoes' "Sixty Minute Man" and the Drifters' "Money Honey." "Heavenly Father" by the Castelles and

Chords.

Drifters.

Midnighters.

Du Droppers.

Spiders.

Rainbows.

Five Crowns.

Diablos.

"The Bells Of St. Mary's" by Lee Andrews and the Hearts have more of a gospel feel. And the influence of black popular vocal group harmony can be found in "Foolishly" by the Three Chuckles and "Only You" by the Platters.

As the doo-wop era dawned, blow harmonies and nonsense syllables were used by harmonizers, falsetto appeared more frequently over the lead and choruses were punctuated by bassmen. Lead singers in paleo-doo-wop brought their musical baggage, in the form of the style they cut their teeth on, to the recording sessions. Gospel can be heard in the style of Clyde McPhatter (Dominoes, Drifters), Little David Baughan (Checkers, Drifters) and Gene Mumford (while singing with the Larks). More of a blues orientation can be heard in the early works of Bobby Lester (Moonglows), Solly McElroy (Flamingos) and Rudy West (Five Keys). Melisma was employed frequently, especially in ballads. To cite but one example, the melismatic background nonsense string "Whoa-oh, whoa-oh" was used by the Royals in 1952 in "The Shrine Of St. Cecelia" and by the Buccaneers

in "In The Mission Of St. Augustine" in 1953, before being used often by the Solitaires a few years later.

After the standard set by the Orioles, slow tunes usually featured little instrumentation aside from guitar accompaniment, allowing the voices to occupy center stage.

In uptempo numbers, the subject matter was often suggestive, as it had been in single artist rhythm and blues. "Laundromat Blues" and "Baby Don't Do It" by the Five Royales are for mature audiences only. The AAB lyric pattern found in twelve-bar blues was also common (e.g. "Can't Do Sixty No More" by the Du-Droppers). As the 1950s progressed, double-entendres dropped out and innocence dropped in. Instrumentation on these numbers was also allied to single artist R&B, with a predominance of piano, drums and horns. Paleo-doo-wop jumps contained the rock 'n' roll beat before that phrase was in widespread usage. Some prominent examples of paleo-doo-wop, taken from our list of the 1, 000 Best Doo-wop Songs (found elsewhere in this book), are listed below. They are roughly divided into ballads and uptempo numbers, and were chosen for their representativeness.

Group	Song	Tempo	Year
Cadillacs	Gloria	slow	1954
Cardinals	Under A Blanket Of Blue	slow	1951
Castelles	Over a Cup Of Coffee	slow	1954
Chords	Sh-Boom	fast	1954
Clovers	Blue Velvet	slow	1952
Crows	Gee	fast	1954
Diablos	The Wind	slow	1954
Dominoes	Sixty Minute Man	fast	1951
Drifters	Money Honey	fast	1954
Flamingos	Jump Children	fast	1954
Harptones	A Sunday Kind Of Love	slow	1953
Jewels	Hearts Of Stone	fast	1954
Larks	My Reverie	slow	1951
Medallions (Vernon Green &)	Buick '59	fast	1954
Midnighters	Sexy Ways	fast	1954
Moonglows	Secret Love	slow	1954
Orioles	It's Too Soon To Know	slow	1948
Ravens	Count Every Star	slow	1950
Rivileers	A Thousand Stars	slow	1954
Swallows	It Ain't The Meat	fast	1951

Classical Doo-Wop (1955-1959)

As the 1950s wore on, the number of group records released by both major and independent record companies increased dramatically in relation to efforts by single artists. Apparently, as early groups like the Dominoes, Four Buddies, Orioles, and Clovers met with success of the charts, teen-agers got the idea that singing wasn't such a bad way to get ahead. Idol worship was pursued closely by imitation, with the semi-realistic goals of making some money, commanding some respect and impressing the ladies. Anyone with a modicum of talent soon gravitated to this new musical art form, which led to a virtual explosion of groups. These singers were unsophisticated musically and influenced as much by what they heard last night on the stoop on the next block, as they were by the older more experienced groups that they heard over the radio. Pre-era rhythm and blues, gospel, black pop music, swing and jazz became much less of a factor in their singing, although many of the emerging harmonizers had experience with gospel music as youths. As a result, the younger sound, which we call "classical doo-wop" evolved quickly from 1954 to 1955.

In classical doo-wop, lead singers didn't possess the sophistication or smoothness found so often in older paleo-doo-wop singers. The operatic tenor was replaced with falsetto leads in many arrangements. Falsetto was also employed regularly to "run above" the harmony in ballads, and became almost de rigeur as a trail-off of the melody in jump tunes. Bass emerged from the harmonizers to stand alone "under" the melody. They also began to punctuate choruses on a regular basis. Nonsense syllables appeared in almost every song, sometimes employed by the harmonizers and other times expressed by the bass. Riffs were more subdued in ballads than they were in jump tunes.

Cleftones.

Danleers.

Dubs.

Del Vikings.

Fi-Tones.

Five Satins.

Little Anthony and the Imperials.

G-Clefs.

Monotones.

Nutmegs.

Rays.

Pastels.

Pearls.

Shields.

Shells.

Velours.

Most of the groups that emerged in this 1955-1959 period were comprised of teen-agers, and the words of their songs dwelt on the topic of youthful idealized love. The bawdy, suggestive lyrics of the paleo doo-wop years were hard to find. Some of the earlier groups, like the Coasters, Clovers, and Robins put out "story" records in an attempt to maintain their audience. Songs like "Charlie Brown," "Love Potion #9" and "Smoky Joe's Café" resulted.

The melodies of this period were simple by Tin Pan Alley standards, often employing only four chords. Slow songs like this earned the moniker "rockaballad." Background beats were pronounced, but instrumentation was light except for the bridge. Despite the limitations on form, groups showed surprising creativity and produced a bevy of beautiful ballads and catchy jump tunes. The rap that songs of this era all sound alike is no more valid than asserting that all symphonies are alike. To a neophyte both are true, but with repeated listening, the individuality of these musical works emerges. After you've been involved for a while, Earl Lewis (Channels) sounds quite different than Earl Carroll (Cadillacs) sounds quite different than Little Anthony (Imperials).[27]

As the classical era unfolded, substyles began to emerge, corresponding to slightly differing teen-age audiences. One audience was young teens, a second was made up of older and tougher teens, and a third of white teens who "crossed over" to black-sounding music. These slight differences in audience led to substyles that we have titled "schoolboy doo-wop," "gang doo-wop," "pop doo-wop," and the white group sound (which, in *Doo-wop: The Forgotten Third*...was called italo-doo-wop). Songs representative of the classical sound follow.

27. And all sound quite different from Beethoven and Mozart.

Group	Song	Tempo	Year
Cleftones	Little Girl Of Mine	fast	1956
Cuff Links	Guided Missiles	slow	1957
Del Vikings	Whispering Bells	fast	1957
Du Mauriers	All Night Long	fast	1957
Dells	Oh What A Night	slow	1956
Dubs	Don't Ask Me To Be Lonely	slow	1957
El Dorados	At My Front Door	fast	1955
Five Satins	In The Still Of The Night	slow	1956
Flamingos	Lovers Never Say Goodbye	slow	1958
Harmonaires	Lorraine	slow	1957
Heartbeats	Crazy For You	slow	1955
Monotones	Book Of Love	fast	1958
Nutmegs	Ship Of Love	slow	1955
Rays	Silhouettes	slow	1957

Group	Song	Tempo	Year
Rob Roys (Norman Fox & the)	Tell Me Why	fast	1957
Shells	Baby Oh Baby	slow	1960
Silhouettes	Get A Job	fast	1957
Turbans	When You Dance	medium	1955
Valentines	Woo Woo Train	fast	1955
Willows	Church Bells May Ring	fast	1956

Schoolboy Doo-Wop

In 1956, "schoolboy doo-wop" emerged as a subcategory within the classical doo-wop era. As boys around the age of thirteen heard the "older guys" singing their doo-wops, they, of course, formed their own groups and tried to do it themselves. While groups comprised of young teens, like Ray "Buddy" Wooten and his Mello-Moods, were around since the early 1950s, they sang adult themes, geared themselves to adult audiences and sounded teenage-youthful, as opposed to child-youthful. "Where Are You," backed with "How Could You," were beautiful and serious ballads about the sadness of being ditched by a woman, and were a far cry from the innocent love proclaimed by the Teenagers and Teenchords a few years later. Even the difference in the names of the groups seems to tell the story. A second youthful group of this type was Philadelphia's Castelles, led by George

Lewis Lymon and the Teenchords.

Grant, who put out a string of beautiful ballads with adult themes, such as "Over A Cup Of Coffee," "My Girl Awaits Me," "This Silver Ring" and "Heavenly Father."

Authentic schoolboy doo-wops hit the airwaves in early 1956, led by "Why Do Fools Fall In Love" by Frankie Lymon & the Teenagers, although the Leslie Martin-led Schoolboys, with the two-sided goodie "Please Say You Want Me/Shirley" and the Cubs, with "I Hear Wedding Bells" on Savoy preceded them by a few short months. The defining characteristic of this substyle is the youthful high tenor lead (or "castrato") of a male or female in early teen-age years. Frankie Lymon (fronting the Teenagers) was the most well-known singer in this category and perhaps in the entire doo-wop era. He, with his Teenagers, met with the most commercial success as well. Many good lead singers, like Frankie's brother Lewis (with his Teenchords) and Leslie Martin (Schoolboys) followed in Frankie's footsteps, but never quite filled his shoes. Words and music in this substyle were even more simple and predictable than was the average classical doo-wop offering. The appeal lay in the catchiness of the tunes and the novelty of the sound.

Another interesting feature of schoolboy leads is that they were often schoolgirl leads. Very few people, excepting the parents of the singers, could tell the gender of the singer from the record.[28] If you were a betting man (or woman), "male" was your best shot, but some distaff

Frankie Lymon and the Teenagers.

28. Alan Fredericks, subbing for Don K. Reed on "The Doo-Wop Shop" one night in 1997, mentioned that it was almost as if record producers all found the same yound boy to use on all songs of this subgenre.

Schoolboys.

Ronnie & the Hi-Lites.

leads were notable. The most noteworthy was Pearl McKinnon, who fronted the Kodaks on many memorable tunes beginning with "Little Boy And Girl/Teenager's Dream" in 1957. Some others were Pat Cordel, who belted out "Darling Come Back" in 1956 while fronting the

Crescents (a group that would evolve into the Elegants), June Bateman, who led the otherwise male Marquis on "Bohemian Daddy" in 1956, and Little Clydie (King), who fronted a male group called the Teens in 1956. Representative songs follow:

Group	Song	Tempo	Year
Desires	Let It Please Be You	slow	1960
Elchords	Peppermint Stick	fast	1957
Heartbreakers (Paul Himmelstein & the)	Without A Cause	fast	1957
Hemlocks (Little Bobby Rivera & the)	Cora Lee	fast	1957
Kodaks	Little Boy And Girl	fast	1957
Schoolboys	Please Say You Want Me	slow	1957
Students	I'm So Young	slow	1958
Teenagers (Frankie Lymon & the)	Paper Castles	slow	1957
Teenchords (Louis Lymon & the)	Honey Honey	fast	1957
Tops (Little Jimmy Rivers & the)	Puppy Love	fast	1961

Gang Doo-Wop

Doo-wop evolved in urban areas and, as we know, urban areas foster toughness, bravado and a competitive spirit. Social life centered around teen-age gangs and clubs whose members hung out on the streets, playgrounds, and parks. Singing groups, which often developed within these gangs or clubs, would engage in "singing rumbles,"[29] or talent contests which were held at local parks or community centers. As one might imagine, the audience was usually quite partisan and enthusiastic at these events. These sing-offs were stepping stones to

the recording studio, either because someone attached

---

29. This tradition of groups singing off against one another goes at least as far back as the 1930s. Doug Seroff and Ray Funk note that (the Five Aces of Rhythm, who were formed in 1935) performed regularly at the Cabin Inn, and barnstormed from club to club (in Chicago), engaging in 'Battles of Rhythm' with other swing groups." From the liner notes to *The Human Orchestra: Rhythm Quartets in the Thirties*, Clanka Lanka Records.

Paragons.

Channels.

to a record label attended the fray, or because a winning group "won" a chance to record for a given label.

The prototype album, "The Paragons Meet The Jesters," is a figurative extension of these singing rumbles. The album cover features two tough-looking teens sporting the latest in gangwear. These tough-sounding groups often came from Harlem, on the island of Manhattan in New York City. Phil Groia, an expert on these groups, further narrows down their turf to between 115th and 119th streets, and between Fifth and Eighth avenues (e.g., the Matadors, Jesters, Bop Chords, and Love Notes). To be fair, singers imitating juvenile-delinquent types could also be found in Brooklyn and the Bronx. We didn't want to leave them out.

In the days before equality of the sexes and health consciousness and ecology, guys had to talk brashly and appear cocky, even if they weren't the fighting type. They also spit a lot. This posturing and braggadocio found its way into songs which we have labeled "gang doo-wop." Lead singers in this category sounded tough even when they sang.[30] They seemed street smart and cracked wise musically when they could. Thus, Adam Jackson of the Jesters, in "Oh Baby" sang "Oh-oh-oh baby, don't try to get away from me, (repeat), I'm yours pretty baby, and I guess I'll always be…"[31] [32]Or consider the lead of the

Paragon's soliloquy in "Hey Little Schoolgirl." "Hey, pretty little girl walkin' down the street, Looks so fine, dressed so neat, Hey-ey, little girl, will you be mine, I'm gonna love you all the time..."[33] These guys honed in on their women and pounced. The may have been teddy bears inside, but if they were, you'd never know it.

The harmonies[34] in the gang doo-wop style were intricate, using much bass and falsetto. Falsetto leads were common as well. The end products were rough-sounding with pounding beats driving catchy melodies. Representative songs follow on the next page.

The White Group Sound and Other Stuff

Before 1958, more than ninety percent of the participants in the doo-wop movement were African-Ameri-

30. "L7s" need not apply. L7s are squares, aka nerds; to form the square, one makes an "L" with the forefinger and thumb of the left hand, then a "7" with the same fingers of the right, then brings them together.
31. What a lucky girl.
32. "Oh Baby," Harlan Jackson, Paul Winley (Ninny-Ethel-Byrd, 1958), BMI.
33. "Hey, Little Schoolgirl," Reese palmer, Paul Winley (Cranford Music Corp., 1957), BMI.
34. Perhaps we should say "hormonies?"

Group	Song	Tempo	Year
Bop Chords	When I Woke Up This Morning	fast	1957
Cadillacs	Speedoo	fast	1955
Channels	That's My Desire	slow	1957
Charts	Zoop	fast	1957
Continentals	Dear Lord	slow	1956
Jesters	I'm Falling In Love	fast	1957
Love Notes	United	slow	1957
Matadors	Vengeance	slow	1958
Paragons	The Vows Of Love	slow	1957
Whirlers	Tonight And Forever	fast	1957

can. In 1958, that changed, as white groups entered the arena in large numbers. Their sound was different than what had come before, and the White Group Sound (WGS) became a third separate subcategory of the classical doo-wop era (though the WGS lasted past the end of the classical era). The saga of their journey on the road to doo-wop heaven is chronicled in the chapter titled, "People of Pallor," later in this book. If the reader is so disposed, he or she might branch off to that chapter now, returning to this spot upon its completion.

A couple of descriptors are important to mention, though they were not quite subcategories. "Novelty doo-wop" broke away from the omnipresent theme of love lost and gained. Some offered us fantasies like "Stranded In The Jungle" by the Cadets, "Rockin' In The Jungle" by the Eternals, "Rang Tang Ding Dong" by the Cellos, and "Love Potion Number 9" by the Clovers. Others described rebelliousness, like "Charlie Brown" and "Yakety Yak" by the Coasters; fads, as in "Bermuda Shorts" by the Delroys or "Short Shorts" by the Royal Teens; or even comic book or cult figures, as in "The Lone Teen Ranger" by Jerry Landis and group (aka Paul Simon), "Big Boy Pete" by the Olympics or "Alley Oop" by Dante & the Evergreens. These songs were always jump tunes.

Another descriptor is "pseudo-doo-wop" which, as the name implies, is not really doo-wop at all. The term pertains to those recordings, done by single artists or duos, that closely resemble doo-wop, except for the fact that no group sings on the record. "Angel Baby" by Rosie & the Originals, "Love You So" by Ron Holden & the Thunderbirds, and more recently "Looking For An Echo" by Kenny Vance and the Planetones are single artist recordings, despite the fact that groups are named on the label. The lyrics and melody of these songs is simple, the beat heavy, creating doo-wop style rockaballads. Yet, sadly, each recording is groupless. Other pseudo doo-wop songs that didn't list groups on the label were "Confidential" by Sonny Knight and "A Teenage Prayer" by Gloria Mann. Many songs by duos such as Marvin & Johnny, Johnny & Joe, Robert & Johnny, and Don and Juan also sound doo-woppy. We prefer to call them "duo-wop," not doo-wop.

Pop Doo-Wop

Sometimes a group would be recorded in a style that obviously came straight from the streets. At other times, the style would be molded by the record company execs that hired them. These record company people had all the leverage. They could record the group or send them packing. If the label owner said jump, most of them jumped. So if they were channeled into a sound that was smoother and less noisy than the usual doo-wop sound, they obeyed.

Delroys.

Coasters.

Royal Teens.

Cellos.

Looking for commercial success, many label owners turned to the "prep" sound of the Four Lads, Preps, Aces and Freshmen. These groups were influenced by the pop groups of the 1940s, like the Ink Spots, Mills Brothers, Modernaires, and Pied Pipers. They harmonized well, but met few other doo-wop criteria.

Many record producers tried to amalgamate this preppy sound with the more teen-oriented classical

doo-wop style in order to sell more records. The strategies that evolved to broaden their market appeal included (a) "cover" records, which are discussed in the chapter dealing with record companies, (b) softening the typical doo-wop sound so that it would appeal to a wider range of age groups, and (c) jazzing up the adult-oriented "old standards" so that they would appeal to youngsters. We have called the outgrowth of these collective strategies "pop doo-wop."

Most often, the arrangers would mute or eliminate doo-wop characteristics so that it would appeal to an older, more conservative audience. Falsetto was used rarely, except as a trail-off, bass singers blended with the harmonizers rather than standing alone and nonsense syllables were simpler, softer and less common. Songs ended up being somewhere between doo-wop and prep styles. As an example, the Fleetwoods allowed a tenor to riff "Dom Dom, Dom Doo Dom, Doo Doo Bee Doo (repeat until you die)," which softened the sound and made it hypnotic. In general, these songs had more melody and better lyrics than the average doo-wop fare, and the beat assumed less importance. Other groups to have success with the pop doo-wop style were the Avalons ("My Heart's Desire"), Fidelities ("The Things I Love"), the late-1950s Platters ("Twilight Time"), Skyliners ("This I Swear") and Duprees ("You Belong To Me"). Pop doo-wop songs spent much time on the charts in the late 1950s and early 1960s.

Another route to pop doo-wop was the remaking of old "standards" by adding doo-wop characteristics. Some examples are "Pennies From Heaven" and "I'll Be Seeing You" by the Skyliners, "Have You Heard" by the Duprees and "I'm In The Mood For Love" by the Chimes.[35] The common thread among these songs was a smoother, manufactured sound, with the goal of

35. Not all remakes of old songs were done in a pop doo-wop manner. Records such as "Over The Rainbow" by David Campanella and the Delchords, "Them There Eyes" by Lewis Lymon and the Teenchords and "That's My Desire" by the Channels were done in straight classical doo-wop style.

Olympics

Group	Song	Tempo	Year
Avalons	My Heart's Desire	slow	1958
Castells	So This Is Love	slow	1962
Duprees	My Own True Love	slow	1962
Echoes	Baby Blue	medium	1961
Fidelitys	The Things I Love	slow	1958
Fleetwoods	Come Softly To Me	medium	1959
Jaguars	The Way You Look Tonight	slow	1956
Platters	My Prayer	slow	1955
Skyliners	Pennies From Heaven	fast	1960
Tymes	So Much In Love	slow	1963

reaching a wider audience. In general, there was a relatively large number of white groups in this subcategory. Examples shown above.

Classical doo-wop began when white teen-agers began to gravitate to music performed by (predominantly) black artists. These artists were almost all teen-agers themselves and were musically unsophisticated. The fruit of their labors was the rockaballad, simple and emotional paeans to love. By 1960, this formula had just about run its course. The next generation of teens wanted something different. They wanted their own music. Classical doo-wop began to fade from the pop and R&B charts.

A look at the dances of the day is a good indicator of the change in sentiments. In the 1950s, teens danced to the lindy, stroll and grind. The teens of the 1960s preferred fast dances, where the partners were not in contact with one another. The twist was an enormous hit twice for Chubby Checker (backed by the Dreamlovers) and once for Joey Dee & the Starlighters ("Peppermint Twist"). The twist was followed by the pony and hucklebuck (Chubby Checker), the swim (Bobby Freeman), the mashed potatoes (Dee Dee Sharp) and the monkey (Smokey Robinson & the Miracles, Major Lance). Slow dances retained the same principle: get as close as you can.

Another fly in the doo-wop ointment was the "payola" scandal of the late 1950s. "Payola," the practice of deejays getting money from record company people to have their songs played, was not illegal at the time, just unethical. But it brought an end to the careers of a host of "personality deejays," the best known of whom was Alan Freed. It was replaced by jockeys with less-flamboyant antics and deliveries who played what the station manager told them to play. Thus was born the "Top-40" format, which was started in the Midwest by Todd Storz in the mid-1950s. The effect of this programming was to bar the door to the smaller independent record labels that didn't have much money for public relations. If you couldn't publicize your new recordings, you were not going to get them played on the air, and you would have big problems—like going out of business-type problems. And with the small labels that supported classical doo-wop folding in droves, that didn't leave the groups with a very rosy future in the entertainment world.

Another factor in the demise of classical doo-wop was the growth of idol worship among teens. Around 1959, a wave of clean-cut, pretty-boy artists hit the music industry. Frankie Avalon, Fabian, Bobby Rydell, Bobby Darin, Freddie "Boom Boom" Cannon, Tommy Sands, Sal Mineo, Tab Hunter, Bobby Vee, and Bobby Vinton emerged in the 1958-1959 time frame and began to hit the charts. In addition, guys like Clyde McPhatter, Neil Sedaka, Dion, and Johnny Maestro left doo-wop groups to try it on their own (and were successful).

Skyliners.

Although some of the new teen idols could actually sing well, all were manufactured. Record companies sold them like products to drooling teens, knowing that parents could accept this wave of artists more readily than they could the first wave of rock 'n' rollers, who were more easily seen as delinquent types. The group sound, and the (mostly) black artists who produced it, were the odd men out.

What allowed the success of these handsome singers was the increasing role played by television in a teen-ager's life. Teens, who had once inherited hand-me-down radios from their parents, began to inherit TVs. And Dick Clark's strategy of putting "American Bandstand" on in the afternoon, when adults would yield the family television without much problem, really helped. Black doo-wop artists were much less appealing to a white teen audience around 1960.

With the exception of a few record companies (like Atlantic and Vee Jay), many of the small independent record companies that stoked the fires of doo-wop went out of business. The artists, now in their twenties, had to stop kidding themselves about making it big and get real jobs to support themselves and/or their families. Only a few very talented individuals were able to continue to make a living in music. Harvey Fuqua, one of the lead singers of the Moonglows, became a record producer for Motown, and Teddy Randazzo did the same for United Artists. The fat lady was about to sing some doo-wop when...

Neo-Doo Wop (1960-1963)

...fate intervened to give doo-wop a second life. Record albums (playing at 33 r.p.m.) were the latest fashion in music, supplanting 45s and putting the last nail in the coffin for 78s. Non-major labels began to put out compilation albums consisting of the best of the classical doo-wop period. Because of Art Laboe's "Oldies But Goodies" series of albums, songs such as "In The Still Of The Night," "Earth Angel," "Tonight, Tonight" and "Heaven And Paradise" became more popular than when first issued in the mid-1950s.

These compilation albums sold well, not only to those who lived through the era, but to youngsters achieving their teenagehood in the 1960-1963 period. Thus, the youth-friendly music of the doo-wop era began a comeback. A fellow by the name of Irving "Slim" Rose, owner of the Times Square record store (housed in the 42nd Street subway station in New York) began reissuing classical doo-wop songs on a number of small labels and, with a buy-sell-trade approach to record collecting, developed a cult following. Most teens who liked doo-wop and who grew up in New York City in the early 1960s, remember Times Square Records. By reissuing and trading in hard-to-find records and by putting out unreleased material by well-known groups, Slim helped in the resuscitation process.

Around the same time, a second generation of personality deejays like Murray "the K" Kaufman, Alan Fredericks and "Cousin" Bruce Morrow hit the airwaves and introduced the next generation of teens to doo-wop music. While some of the music from the 1950s was still played, a slightly different style of doo-wop emerged between 1960 and 1963. This "neo-doo-wop" sound was provided by a new set of groups which included the Marcels, Earls, Tokens, Angels and Chiffons.

Neo-doo-wop kept some of the characteristics of classical doo-wop, and changed others. Melody lines were still simple, lyrics still spoke of innocent love. But as record producers sought to figure out new ways to sell a style that seemed to be growing hackneyed, many doo-wop characteristics were exaggerated. More nonsense syllables appeared, and they played more of a role in the song. Vocal bass parts became more prominent and often took over the song. Falsetto leads increased in number and instrumentation played more of a role.

As an example, regard the two bass riffs below:

"Bon Bon Bon,[36] "Bon Buh Buh Bon,
Buh Bon Buh Bon Bon,Buh Bon Buh Bon Bon,
Buh Buh Bon Bon Bon,Buh Buh Bon Bon Bon,
Buh Bon Buh Bon Bon Bon..."[37] Ka Dang A Dang Dang,
Ka Ding A Dong Ding..."[38]

The sample on the left is from "Zoom Zoom Zoom," a classical doo-wop effort by the Collegians in 1956. The sample on the right comes from "Blue Moon," by the Marcels in 1961. The Marcels took this "standard" ballad from 1935, put it in a peppy uptempo format, and added a liberal dose of bass singer doing nonsense riffs. Pure and optimal neo-doo-wop. Not only did the riffs punctuate choruses, as they had in "Zoom," they threw it at you immediately at the opening of the song. It appears as though they lifted the core of the bass riff used by the Collegians and added a few Ka Dangs and Ding Dongs to create a new sound. Those readers familiar with both songs know also that the "Zoom" riffs were delivered in a relaxed "cool" fashion, while those from "Moon" oozed strength and enthusiasm. These differences are indicative of the great strides made during the neo-doo-wop years.

As with the classical doo-wop era, neo-doo-wop

---

36. The pronunciation of the nonsense syllable "bon" is difficult to convey, though anyone who's heard these songs can do it. It's not pronounced like the ice cream "bon bon." The "n" is not pronounced, which one achieves by not allowing one's tongue to touch the palate. A related syllable is "bome," as in "home." The difference is, when stringing many of them together, whether the "m" is heard or not. If it's not heard, the syllable is "bon"; if heard, it's "bome." (Try it.)

37. "Zoom Zoom Zoom," Donald Hayes, Harlan Jackson (Selma Music, 1957), BMI.

38. "Blue Moon," Lorenz Hart, Richard Rodgers (Robbins Music Corp., 1934), ASCAP.

Cupids.

Jarmels.

Kac-Ties.

Edsels.

Volumes.

had subcategories that emerged within it. The White Group Sound, that emerged in classical doo-wop, continued through the neo-doo-wop years and played a significant role on the charts. "Distaff doo-wop," i.e. doo-wop sung by female groups, emerged with the Chantels and Bobbettes in 1957, but really didn't make much of an impression on the music scene until 1960. It is dealt with in depth in the chapter titled, "Group Her-mony." Also in that chapter will be found the story of "Tin Pan Alley doo-wop," another product of the 1960s.

In short, many talented and creative songwriting teams, like Carole King and Jerry Goffin, Jeff Barry and Ellie Greenwich, Barry Mann and Cynthia Weil, and young producers like Phil Spector and members of the Tokens, put out doo-wop songs painstakingly created under very controlled production practices. The groups they recorded, like the Chiffons, Crystals,

Marcels.

Paradons.

Stereos.

Ronettes, and Randy & the Rainbows, allowed their sound to be molded to fit the producers whims, unlike the groups of the 1950s, who were recorded as is. The results were more complicated melodies, sophisticated lyrics, heavily instrumented records that charted often. Many of the groups employed by these Tin Pan Alley types, unlike the groups from earlier eras, were female. Some of the better non-distaff Tin Pan Alley doo-wop efforts were "Picture In My Wallet" by Darryl & the Oxfords, "Denise" and "Why Do Kids Grow Up" by Randy & the Rainbows, and "Tonight I Fell In Love" and "The Lion Sleeps Tonight" by the Tokens. Readers curious about either distaff or Tin Pan Alley doo-wop are encouraged to take a side journey to the aforementioned chapter now. Representative songs from the neo-doo-wop era follow on the next page.

Group	Song	Tempo	Year
Blue Jays	Lover's Island	slow	1961
Candles (Rochell & the)	Once Upon A Time	slow	1960
Chandler, Gene (with the Dukays)	Duke Of Earl	medium	1961
Corsairs	Smoky Places	medium	1961
Demensions	Over The Rainbow	slow	1962
Devotions	Rip Van Winkle	fast	1961
DiMucci, Dion (with the Del Satins)	The Wanderer	fast	1961
Dreamlovers	When We Get Married	slow	1961
Drifters	Sweets For My Sweet	medium	1961
Excellents	Coney Island Baby	slow	1962
Jive Five	Never Never	slow	1961
Lee, Curtis (with the Halos)	Pretty Little Angel Eyes	fast	1961
Marcels	Heartaches	fast	1961
Paradons	Diamonds And Pearls	slow	1960
Quotations	Imagination	fast	1961
Reflections	(Just Like) Romeo & Juliet	fast	1964
Regents	Barbara Ann	fast	1961
Rivingtons	Papa-Oom-Mow-Mow	fast	1962
Shells	Baby Oh Baby	slow	1960
Stereos	I Really Love You	fast	1961

Ironically, neo-doo-wop held within it the seeds of its own demise. By exaggerating nonsense syllables, bass and falsetto, some records exhibited ridicule for the style. Pastiche songs such as "Papa-Oom-Mow-Mow" by the Rivingtons, "Surfer Bird" by the Trashmen and "Mr. Bassman" by Johnny Cymbal (with Ronnie Bright, an ex-Valentine, in the starring role) seemed to relegate the doo-wop style to no more than a novelty. When this happens, it's usually time to get out of town.

By contrast, the music also cross-fertilized with other types of music, so that the clearly doo-wop characteristics of nonsense syllables, bass and falsetto blended with pop or soul and lost their own identity. Thus was born the pop-doo-wop music of the Duprees and Chimes, the Motown and soul sounds, and the girl group sounds of the early to mid-1960s. As an example, the Four Seasons were quite successful with falsetto and harmony, but without the wide range of voices, the nonsense syllables or the distinct bass voice that characterized doo-wop.

Evolution is irrepressible, and by 1963 doo-wop was ready for the history books. Starting in 1962, fewer songs with doo-wop characteristics were heard over the ether. Instruments such as lead guitar and bass guitar, replacing falsetto and bass voices, made their way into the new musics. The wide range of voices found in doo-wop was gone, replaced often by singing in unison. Background singers, when present in the new musics emanating from Detroit, Philadelphia, California or Liverpool, responded to their lead singer with words, rather than nonsense syllables.

Some groups made a smooth transition from doo-wop to another type of music. The Tokens had a doo-wop standard in "Tonight I Fell In Love," while their later work featured heavier instrumentation and pop styling. The Beach Boys started their career singing "surf doo-wop"[39]

at the tail end of the era, but made their mark in later years. Many stars that fall under the Motown umbrella cut their teeth in the doo-wop era before moving on. The Four Tops started as the Four Aims, the Supremes sang as the Primettes, Gene Chandler started with the Dukays ("Duke Of Earl"), and both Jerry Butler and Curtis Mayfield started out with the ("For Your Precious Love") Impressions.

With surf music, the Philadelphia sound, and the British Invasion, the evolution that took place was a solely musical one. In the case of Motown, soul and folk music, however, political and social factors played a large part. As the 1960s progressed, African-Americans began to exert a greater influence in the social and political arenas. The conservative views of Dwight Eisenhower were replaced with the liberalism of John F. Kennedy. The change in culture supported a change in music. Social strife and political statements found their way into song. The innocence and innocent lyrics of the doo-wop years faded. The soul music that evolved was sung in higher voice registers, with frequent falsettoes and melisma. The bass took a back seat and nonsense syllables disappeared. The music grew emotionally closer to its gospel beginnings.

As amplification of instruments got better, lead, bass and rhythm guitars assumed more importance in popular music. Stereophonic sound, allowing heretofore undreamed of sound effects, gave an added boost to instrumentation. The Beatles started a trend, which we take for granted but was new back then, for groups to be self-contained. That is, they played their own instruments so that musicians did not need to be hired. Most members of doo-wop groups were not musically skilled and were at a loss in this new musical world.

---

39. Consider the bass line from "Surfin'," "bon bon dit dit it dit it, bon bon dit dit it."

Compared to the new sounds available by 1963, the doo-wop sound reeked of old age. Competing for the ears of 13-year-olds with the likes of the Beatles, Stones, Beach Boys, Orlons, Supremes, Temptations, Four Tops, etc., was a losing battle. Kids prefer their own music, just like we did. The vacuum created when doo-wop withered was quickly and capably filled. Over the years, isolated doo-wop efforts were noteworthy hits, such as "Whenever A Teenager Cries" by Reperata and the Delrons, "May I" by Bill Deal and the Rondells, "Morse Code of Love" by the Capris, "For The Longest Time" by Billy Joel and group, and "In The Still Of The Night" by Boyz 2 Men. Doo-wop ballads were even issued by post-era groups like Cannibal and the Headhunters ("Show You How To Make Love To Me" as the flip of their hit rocker, "Land Of A Thousand Dances") and the Orlons ("Heart Darling Angel"), but overall the game was all over.

At least doo-wop had the distinction of fading from the public eye more than once. It lived twice and died twice. In the early 1950s, it became popular because it appealed to the newly awakened teen-age generation. At that time, doo-wop was new and different, which fit into a teen-ager's need to appear new and different. As it began to wane in the late 1950s, it was resuscitated for a new run in the early 1960s with slightly altered characteristics. Then a host of new genres overwhelmed it and sent it packing.

As a summary of this chapter, and for the sake of clarity, the table which follows offers a synopsis of the most important characteristics of the doo-wop style for the various periods discussed in this chapter. While the entries in the table are generalizations, it should be possible for the reader to trace the evolution of nonsense syllables; for example, before, through, and after the doo-wop era.

Doo-Wop Characteristics in Different Time Periods

	Pre-doo-wop (before 1948)	Paleo-doo-wop (1948-54)	Classical doo-wop (1955-59)	Neo-doo-wop (1960-63)	Post-doo-owop (after1963)
Nonsense Syllables	not present or used in different ways	emergence of blow harmonies & simple patterns of non. sylls.	more complex patterns in almost every song	subdued in some cases and more complex patterns in others	words replace non. sylls. as background responses
Harmony Part	humming, very much in background	given more voice may alternate with lead	given even more voice,	same as classical	recedes into background
Falsetto	occasionally present, but has operatic quality	present more often, occasionally leads, operatic quality	almost always present, frequently leads, almost always used as trail-off	not always present, but more frequently leads when present, used less as trail-off	diminished presence, almost never leads or used as trail-off
Bass	frequent bass leads and talking bridges, but not between stanzas, not distinct from harmony under lead	begins to separate from harmony, begins to punctuate stanzas	frequently introduces song, almost always seperate from harmony, by punctuating or riffing	same as classical, but sometimes used in exaggerated ways	used less as a separate voice throughout
Beat	allied with jazz, r&b or other earlier styles	very little jazz influence, more allied with r&b	beat heavy & distinct (on 2nd & 4th beats), allied with rock 'n' roll	same as classical except for pop doo-wop where beat is softer	remains heavy in most new musics
Instrumentation	heavier than standard doo-wop fare	less present than before, honky-tonk piano or organ typical	instruments unimportant except during break in middle of song	instruments re-emerging	instruments much more important
Melody	blues or jazz progressions	melodies begin to simplify	simple melodies & four-chord structures common	more variation than in classical	significantly more variation in melodies
Lyrics	often lascivious in R&B, else mature love themes	still lascivious, but innocent love themes begin to take over	almost exclusively innocent love, almost no politicizing or social commentary	lyrics remain innocent	most lyrics still deal with love, but social commentary & politicizing appears

Chapter 8

Doo-Wopuzzles

Test your knowledge on the following two crosswords. The first centers around the early groups, the second focuses on groups from the classical era, and the third concentrates on the names of songs. See how well you can do. The answers can be found in the back of the book.

Name That Tune

ACROSS

4 Marvelows (1965)
8 Ray & the Darchaes (1962)
9 Spaniels (1955)
10 Rocketones (1957)
11 Chimes (1963)
14 Rocketones (1957)
15 Angels (1961)
16 Five Discs (1961)
18 Colonairs (1957)
20 Versatones (1958)
21 Turks (1955)
22 Cobras (1964)
24 A-Tones (1961)
26 Halos (1961)
28 Earls (1963)
29 Bobbettes (1957)
31 Hollywood Flames (1954)

34 Five Discs (1959)
36 Bopchords (1957)
37 Chantels (1958)
38 Frankie Lymon & the Teenagers (1956)
39 Laddins (1957)

DOWN

1 Emotions (1962)
2 Cadillacs (1956)
3 Fiestas (1958)
4 Hollywood Flames (1953)
5 Jesters (1958)
6 Bonnevilles (1960)
7 Charts (1957)
12 Four Deuces (1955)
13 Lee Andrews & the Hearts (1959)

15 Arthur Lee Maye & the Crowns (1955)
16 Universals (1957)
17 Sheppard Sisters (1957)
19 Five Emeralds (1954)
20 Avons (1957)
21 Medallions (1955)
23 Premiers (1960)
25 Nutmegs (1963)
27 Drifters (1955)
30 Vel-Tones (1960)
32 Crows (1953)
33 Aquatones (1958)
35 Tru-Tones (1957)
36 Maurice Williams & the Zodiacs (1960)

The Early Groups
Name That Group (No "Brothers," No "Sisters")

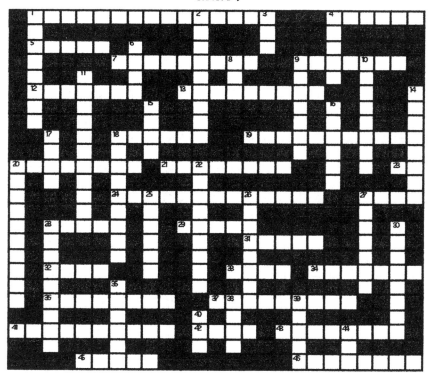

ACROSS

1 "Just A-Sittin And A-Rockin" (1945)
4 _____ Marshall, second first tenor of the Ravens
5 _____ Macs
7 "Wheel Of Fortune" (1952)

9 "Get Away Mr. Satan, Get Away" (1946)
12 "Crying In The Chapel" (1953)
13 "Golden Teardrops" (1953)
18 Lee Andrews and the
19 "Swing Low, Sweet Chariot" (1939)

20 "I'm Afraid The Masquerade Is Over" (1951)
21 "The Glory Of Love" (1951)
23 _____ Stafford, of the Pied Pipers
24 "Runaround" (1953)
27 Ricks' voice part
28 _____ Street Boys

29 _____ Jones, first first tenor of the Ravens
31 "Gee"
32 Billy _____, founder of the Dominoes
33 _____ River Boys
34 "Boogie Woogie Bugle Boy" (1941)
36 "A Beggar For Your Kisses" (1952)
37 "Over A Cup Of Coffee" (1954)
41 _____ Fiddle
42 Four _____
43 "Money Honey" (1953)
45 Four _____
46 "Eternally" (1951)

27 "I'd Rather Be Wrong Than Blue" (1950)
28 "For Sentimental Reasons" (1945)
30 "Shout, Sister, Shout" (1931)
35 _____ Gate Quartet
38 "The Naughty Lady Of Shady Lane" (1954)
39 "My Reverie" (1951)
40 Joe _____ Loan, third first tenor of the Ravens
44 Sonny _____ of the Orioles

DOWN

1 "Sixty Minute Man" (1951)
2 "Sincerely" (1954)
3 _____ Cooke, of the Soul Stirrers
4 "Jungle Fever" (1934)
6 Five Red _____
8 First initials of the Andrews Sisters
9 "One Mint Julep" (1952)
10 "They Call The Wind Mariah" (1950)
11 "Just To See You Smile Again" (1951)
14 "If I Didn't Care" (1939)
15 _____ Silvertones
16 Five _____
17 _____ Pipers
18 "A Sunday Kind Of Love" (1953)
20 "Dear Ruth" (1953)
22 "Be True" (1952)
25 "Count Every Star" (1950)
26 "Ghost Of My Baby" (1953)

Chapter 9

People of Pallor

Until 1958, artists of the Caucasian persuasion made almost no contribution to doo-wop music. White jive-jazz and pop jazz artists, such as the Boswell Sisters, Andrews Sisters, and Bing Crosby and the Rhythm Boys, did influence and perhaps create[1] jazz vocal group stylings in the 1930s, but whatever effect they had on black music happened way before the dawning of the doo-wop era. And groups like the Ames Brothers and Four Aces produced a body of vocal group music that sounded white, but it was preppy, pop and for adults The doo-wop genre was born in the late 1940s from a combination of earlier black styles such as gospel, black vocal group harmony and urban blues. While whites predominated in managerial roles, as record company executives, and even as deejays, the artists themselves were almost all African-American.

Doo-wop began with the Ravens, Orioles and the like; black groups that were singing primarily for black audiences. Early on, there were few white groups performing because there was very little white interest in rhythm and blues. What is a little surprising is that between 1954 and 1957, when the white teen-age audience began to buy records by black artists, and when recordings by black artists "crossed over" to the pop charts (as "Gee" by the Crows did), that white groups didn't immediately spring up.

One obvious reason is that since the primary white idol was an individual by the name of Elvis Presley, many whites aspired to be single artists (especially rockabilly artists), rather than members of singing groups. Young blacks reaching teen years in the early 1950s had plenty of group role models, including the most famous of all groups, the Mills Brothers and Ink Spots. By 1954, they also had been exposed to a large number of singing groups that had already left pop behind for rhythm and blues and doo-wop arrangements (e.g. the Dominoes, Four Buddies, Swallows, Cardinals, etc.). White youngsters, on the other hand, had few group role models except in the realm of pop/barbershop styling, as in the efforts of the Ames Brothers, Four Aces and Four Freshmen.

While there were surely a few white teens that listened to the pre-1954 black groups, most didn't hear the early black group harmony sound until the schoolboy doo-wop groups hit the ground running in early 1956. It probably didn't take long for these teens to be bitten by the bug to sing, but forming groups, developing a repertoire, going through the usual first gigs at local high schools and making contact with someone to record them took a lot longer.

Another reason for the invisibility of white groups was that white teens were probably, on average, more protected and less free to hang out in the streets than their black counterparts. Also, whites and blacks, for the most part, lived separately and there was slower cross-fertilization of musical ideas and styles between blacks and whites than there was among blacks. Many black kids saw and heard black kids singing, some singing very well, every day of their lives—in the schoolyard, on the corner while walking home from school, or even in the hallway of the building in which they lived. White kids rarely heard or saw black groups, and the white groups they heard were fewer in number and probably less experienced, especially in the early to mid-1950s.

Finally, on average, music was more a part of a black teen-ager's childhood, especially through the church, than it was for a white teen. That's not to say that white boys didn't attend church services and sing in choirs, but the Latin-based hymnal music of the Catholic church is a much further cry from doo-wop music than is the melismatic, call and response, gospel that young blacks heard and participated in. The same can be said for opera music, which was heard in the homes of many Italian-American youth of the 1950s. Mario Lanza had a great set of pipes, but he was a long way from doo-wop.

A look at the charts confirms the paucity of white groups sounds. The R&B charts are unnecessary until 1956 because no white group sounds (WGS) appeared. As for the pop charts, the Three Chuckles were the first to appear in November 1954 with "Runaround." This is the first white group effort that has any trace of doo-wop or rhythm and blues in it. According to Jean-Charles Marion[2], "Their sound was as close to early Orioles as any white group ever got." Seems like quite a compliment, but he continues, "The Orioles, incidentally, recorded a superior version of 'Runaround' on Jubilee Records." Oh well. The group followed up its hit with a non-charting, but equally pleasing, ballad called, "Foolishly," rendered in the same soft style. It was the only white group to appear at Alan Freed's first show at the Brooklyn Paramount. The lead of the Three Chuckles was Teddy Randazzo, a talented young man with matinee-idol good looks, who later went on to write and produce records. The next white group effort to chart was "Black Denim Trousers" by the Cheers from September of 1955, which is really neither doo-wop nor R&B, but rather a rock 'n' roll novelty song. This group is most famous for containing Bert Convy, who later made a name for himself as a game-show host.

1. Friedwald, Will. *Jazz Singing*. London: Quartet Books, 1990.

2. Marion, Jean-Charles. "Early White Arrivals." *Record Exchanger*, Issue #23, p. 26.

In 1956 came the Diamonds, a white group out of Canada, that every true fan of doo-wop music loves to hate, because they covered so many records by black groups and usually outsold them. They are the Pat Boone of group singing (which is not so good).[3] In effect, the Diamonds bleached, sanitized and defiled some of the best records of the era. Their label Mercury was a "major" and had the resources to crank out a cover version within a couple of weeks, and get them distributed and played faster than the smaller independent record companies from which the original songs emerged. This commercial approach worked, as they charted five times in 1956, including covers of the Teenager's "Why Do Fools Fall In Love," the Willows' "Church Bells May Ring," the Clovers' "Love, Love, Love," and the G-Clefs' "Ka-Ding-Dong." They had four more chart hits in 1957, including covers of the Gladiolas' "Little Darlin'," and the Rays' "Silhouettes." They really pulled the wool over everyone's eyes because the four songs mentioned last also appeared on the R&B charts, meaning that blacks were listening and buying, as well as whites. Truth be told, they weren't bad technically, just mismatched to the type of music they were singing.

Hearing their covers today provides amusement. They sing "walking along..." rather than "walkin' along..." when covering the Solitaires, and "My baby, oh honey, my sweetheart, oh poochie..." at the end of "Little Girl Of Mine" (originally by the Cleftones). Now a romantic lead like James "Pookie" Hudson of the Spaniels might get away with singing "oh poochie," but the Diamonds' lead, David Somerville, could not. Their popularity is really a commentary on the times. Rock 'n' roll, rhythm and blues, and doo-wop were new to most teens, especially white teens. The white bread sound of the Diamonds was still progressive compared to the stuff their parents listened to by Doris Day, Perry Como, and even Lawrence Welk. The Diamonds were much less of a stretch for their tastes, and didn't meet with that much opposition from parents because they were white and elocuted well. Parents could accept the Diamonds a lot quicker than they could the Drifters, El Dorados, or Moonglows. In a way, however, they were deliciously subversive; by being parent-friendly, they allowed millions of teens to hear music that would soon whet their appetites for more exciting stuff, while avoiding most parental objections. The best of their covers was of the Gladiolas' "Little Darlin'" which reached #2 on both R&B and Pop charts. This recording at least had some punch to it, with a good talking bass bridge that improved on the

Three Chuckles.

Diamonds.

---

3. Pat Boone covered many R&B sides, including "Ain't That A Shame," "At My Front Door" and "I'll Be Home." Otis Williams & the Charms also successfully covered black-group records, but they aren't despised quite as much, probably because they are black. The purist roots for the underdog, no matter what. For more on this subject, see the chapter on Doo-Wopolitics.

original. In the 1950s, they were politically correct and sold a ton of records. In the 1990s, they are politically incorrect, but then hindsight is 20-20.

Three other white group sounds (WGS) hit the pop charts in 1956. One was "Priscilla" by Eddie Cooley & the Dimples, which had a rockabilly lilt to it despite being by a black group (that sounded lily white and

Neons.

Three Friends.

Danny and the Juniors.

Mello-Kings.

made it to #20 on the pop charts). A second was called "City Of Angels," a preppy ballad by the Highlights (#20 pop) and the third was a cover of (the Cadets') "Stranded In The Jungle" by the Gadabouts (#39 pop). In 1957, the only white group to chart besides the Diamonds was Danny & the Juniors, who hit with "At The Hop" in December of 1957. This was a landmark record, remaining at number one for seven weeks on the pop charts and five weeks on the R&B charts. Kind of slim pickins Caucasian-wise, when it came to doo-wop. The music was more pop-rock than doo-wop or rhythm and blues.

In a way, the WGS action was more interesting off the charts. The Teardrops, a little-known group that recorded for Josie, had a couple of nice sides including, "The Stars Are Out Tonight" in 1954. Their sound is actually very close to that exhibited by black groups recording at that time. The Neons, a group coached by none other than Raoul Cita of the Harptones, released "Angel Face" in 1956. While the song didn't hit nationally, it made most of the local charts. Pat Cordel & the Crescents had a peppy white schoolgirl doo-wop song called "Darling Come Back" in 1956. These Crescents, without Pat Cordel, became Vito Piccone's Elegants a year and a half later. The Three Friends copied the style of the Three Chuckles and issued "Blanche," which was a big hit in the New York City area, but failed to chart nationally. The Mello-Kings first released "Tonite Tonite" in 1957, a record destined to achieve much more popularity as an oldie than it did originally. And the Chuck Alaimo Quartet issued a nice ballad called "How I Love You," also in 1957.

Integrated groups also began to arise in the mid-1950s. Don Julian and the Meadowlarks (in 1954, one of the first, if not the first), the Jaguars (1955) and the Dell Vikings (1956) emerged early, but had black lead singers and sounded black. The Crests, (New York) Heart-

Crests.

Heartbreakers.

breakers[4] and Rob Roys all were mixed groups that emerged in 1957, fronted by white lead singers (Johnny Maestro, Paul Himmelstein, and Norman Fox, respectively). The Crests especially were influential in doo-wop circles. Maestro's strong clear tenor belted out the melody in front of catchy backgrounds beginning with "Sweetest One" and "My Juanita" in 1957, "Pretty Little Angel," "I Thank The Moon" and "Sixteen Candles" (#2 pop, #4 R&B) in 1958, "Six Nights A Week" (#17 R&B, #28 pop) and "The Angels Listened In" (#14 R&B, #22 pop) in 1959, and "Step By Step" (#14 pop), "Trouble In Paradise" (#20 pop) and "Isn't It Amazing" in 1960. Norman Fox's distinctive nasal voice graced one of the quintessential doo-wops "Tell Me Why," as well as perky follow-ups like "Dance Girl Dance," "Pizza Pie," and the romantic "Dream Girl." The group didn't chart nationally, but are perennial New York favorites to this day. Himmelstein led the Heartbreakers with a clear, powerful, schoolboy-type voice. "Without A Cause," "1, 2, I Love You" and "Come Back My Love" (the Wrens tune) were good recordings, but made no noise commercially.

The white pop sound during these years was alive and well. Beginning with the Ames Brothers in the late 1940s and continuing with the Four...Aces, Coins, Esquires, Freshmen, Lads, Preps Voices, as well as the Crew Cuts and Playmates in the 1950s, this all-American pop-music style that contained traces of barbershop, black pop harmony of the 1940s and even show music, remained popular through the late 1950s. "Love Is A Many Splendored Thing" by the Four Aces (1955), "Graduation Day" by the Rover Boys and Four Freshmen (1956) and "Standing On The Corner" by the Four Lads (1956) received lots of "four-play" on the airwaves. Nice, but not doo-wop.

And then came 1958. In January, the Diamonds hit the charts (#4 pop, #5 R&B) with "The Stroll," an original song that became the first rock-'n'-roll group dance, akin to folk or country-line dancing. It was made popular by repeated exposure on Dick Clark's "American Bandstand," a show which became a model for teen-age life in the 1950s. In February, the novelty "Short Shorts" by the Royal Teens hit the charts (#2 R&B, #3 pop) and March saw Danny & the Juniors' recording of "Rock And Roll Is Here To Stay" (#16 R&B, #19 pop) become, along with the songs of Chuck Berry (e.g. "Roll Over Beethoven" and "Sweet Little Sixteen"), an anthem for the new generation. March also witnessed "So Tough" by the Casuals, a pop-rocker (#6 R&B, #42 pop).

Also in March, a Brooklyn group called the Bay Bops recorded "Joanie," which reached number 58 on the *Cash Box Top 60* for the week of May 17th. According to Bob Diskin[5], "Joanie" did even better in selected smaller

---

4. There was an earlier black group from the Washington D.C. area by the same name. Led by Robert Evans, they recorded a song called "Heartbreaker" for RCA, which the Crows would later score with.

5. Diskin, Bob. "Brooklyn's Bay Bops Launch White-Group Harmony and Pave the Way for '60s Doo-wop Hitmakers." *Record Collector's Monthly,* Issue #33, Nov.-Dec. 1985.

markets (e.g. #5 on a station in Troy, N.Y.), and was on the charts before Dion & the Belmonts released "I Wonder Why." More than any of the efforts by white groups before them, the Bay Bops represented the new white group sound that seemed to emerge simultaneously from the boroughs of Brooklyn and the Bronx in New York City. Diskin remarks on the abundance of streetcorner groups in these boroughs and the cross-borough fertilization[6] of ideas that occurred in these times.

And then, in the late Spring of 1958, was heard:

"Dun dun dun,
Duh dun duh dun dun,
Duh dun duh dun dun,
Duh dun, duh duh duh duh duh duh duh..."[7]

It was a new sound, and a distinctive one—unlike the Harptones, the Heartbeats, the Cadillacs, or the Drifters before them. It was the first release on the newly formed Laurie label called "I Wonder Why" by Dion & the Belmonts, an unknown white singing group. In fact, both Dion and the group of three Belmonts, Carlo Mastangelo, Fred Milano, and Angelo D'Aleo, had grown up near each other in the Bronx and had separately recorded unsuccessfully in 1957. According to Ralph Newman[8], Dion was paired with the Belmonts, rather than a studio group, because he knew them from the neighborhood and would be more comfortable when recording. "I Wonder Why" was an outstanding recording, and had influence way beyond its success on the pop charts (staying for ten weeks and reaching number 22). In a nutshell, this recording enthralled, influenced, and encouraged a whole generation of white kids. It helped pave the way for other recordings by white teen groups and helped many non-singers to appreciate the vocal group sound.

Ed Ward agrees. "The group had a real flair for arrangements—what attracted me to them instantly was their first Biggie, "I Wonder Why" (1958), with the voices chiming in one at a time. I almost ruined my vocal cords trying to sing all three parts at once, and trying to imitate Dion's teen-age nasality... I think every kid in my school [Eastchester, N.Y.] idolized Dion and the Belmonts when the group was hot."[9]

By influencing so many other groups, "I Wonder Why" helped establish the sub-category that we and others call the "White Group Sound."[10] In their *Encyclopedia Of Rock*, Hardy and Laing[11] have separate listings for "Doo-wop" and "Doo-wop, White." The lat-

ter is defined as "The interpretation by white vocal groups of the black harmony sound [that] became a craze in the U.S. during the late Fifties and reached epidemic proportions between 1961 and 1963." The style was created by "white groups whose love of black harmony brought an honest authenticity to their performances."

Stephen M. Bennett, in an introduction to *White & Still All Right!* by Edward R. Engel[12], commented, " 'I Wonder Why'...introduced the catchy, bouncing bass which was to become the most distinctive element of all white group R&R harmony which was to follow." Thus, in 1958, was born the "power bass," which became a signal part of the doo-wop style through the end of the era.[13] While earlier bassmen often provided an introduction to songs, could be heard separate from the harmony part and often exuded nonsense syllable "riffs," "I Wonder Why" featured such a prominent bass part that it almost took over the song. The Belmonts were joined by the Five Discs ("I Remember" and "Never Let You Go"), the Quotations ("Imagination") and Regents ("Barbara Ann") in using the power bass to reach the charts. Many other groups, white and black, used it less successfully in the late 1950s and early 1960s. Ironically, the group which hit the most pay dirt with power bassing was the Marcels ("Blue Moon," "Heartaches"), originally an integrated group but Caucasian-free for most of their career. At minimum, these bassmen wanted to wake you up a little. At most, they were shooting you with vocal machine guns.

Bennett continued, "There were several additional elements which characterized this emerging sound. To begin with, it was a young sound, much less mature in nature than its black counterpart. The lead typically sang as if his voice were undergoing pubescent changes, and you would almost expect his voice to crack halfway through the song!" The effect of tenors singing at or near the top of their ranges produced a "sweet" sound, as in Dion DiMucci on "When You Wish Upon A Star" and Vito Piccone on "Little Star."

Back to Bennett..."The lyrics tended to underscore the youth element as well, dealing, as they did, with teenage love in its most innocent sense—the hope of getting a date, a dance or merely a look from a girl were common subjects." The character of the lyrics was directly related to the youthfulness of the artists and the fact that in the 1950s, young people were actually innocent by today's standards. Whites, perhaps slightly more than their black contemporaries, but not by much. As Bennett points out, the white group lyric often described "hoping" for a date, while their black counterparts sang about making time. Even in "Gee" by the

6. Euphemism for "borrowing," which is a euphemism for "stealing."
7. From "I Wonder Why" by Dion & the Belmonts.
8. Newman, Ralph. "The Laurie Story." *Time Barrier Express*, Issue #22, March-April 1977, p.15.
9. Ward, Ed. "Italo-American Rock." In Miller, Jim, Ed., *The Rolling Stone Illustrated History Of Rock & Roll*, New York: Rolling Stone Press, 1980.
10. In *Doo-wop: The Forgotten Third...*, we called this category "Italo-doo-wop." It was changed to "White Group Sound" to be more inclusive.

11. Hardy, Phil & Laing, Dave. *Encyclopedia Of Rock*. New York: Schirmer Books, 1988.
12. Engel, Edward R. *White And Still All Right!* Scarsdale, N.Y.: Crackerjack Press, 1977.
13. See the chapter titled, "Getting To First Bass."

Crows, a relatively innocuous hit song that crossed over to the (white) pop charts, Daniel "Sonny" Norton pleads, "Hold me pretty baby, never let me go..."

Another difference is in the way the lead singer modulated his voice. Black leads frequently used melisma, that is they hit more than one note per syllable, thus seeming to move around the melody. White singers tended to hold their notes, as if being paid by the minute. Believe it or not, this makes perfect sense. Black kids were brought up hearing preachers and bluesmen singing emotionally, while white kids (who were often Italian) heard opera singers and crooners like Mario Lanza and Frank Sinatra. A kid raised on the Soul Stirrers and Pilgrim Travelers is going to sound a lot different that a kid raised on Caruso or Como.

Bennett concludes, "With an eye toward commercial success, the background harmony usually revolved around some attention-getting device, be it a repetitive chant (ra-ta-ta), chiming on successive notes (blong-blong-blong-blong) or the like, and all these elements appear in abundance." The two examples that Bennett uses are from "Little Star" by the Elegants (1958) and "This Is My Love" by the Passions (1960). These "attention-getters" were really nonsense syllables used more

Elegants.

Mystics.

Dion and the Belmonts.

regularly and often, in greater variety (not just "doe doe doe"), and with more oomph[14] than before. Their use continued into the neo-doo-wop years of the early 1960s, by groups like the Earls and Randy and the Rainbows.

The floodgates opened. The Belmonts, after pioneering a power bass presence, were retooled to appeal to a wider teen market. The result was a sweeter and more innocent sound which is easy to listen to, but lacked the innovation and drive of "I Wonder Why." These syrupy Dion & the Belmonts produced songs like "No One Knows" (#12 R&B, #19 pop, in 1958), "Don't Pity Me" (#40 pop, in 1959), "A Teenager In Love" (#5 pop, in 1959), "Where Or When" (#3 pop, #19 R&B, in 1960), (a very capable rendition of) "That's My Desire" (1960) and "When You Wish Upon A Star" (#30 pop, in 1960). The year 1958 also brought first recordings by the Elegants, Five Discs, Capris, Fascinators and Selections. The Elegants release of "Little Star" was only a few months behind "I Wonder Why." It was a big record, reaching #1 on both the R&B (for four weeks) and pop (one week) charts in August. The flip, "Getting Dizzy," was also a great uptempo tune with a driving beat and a heavier doo-wop

---

14. Pardon the technical language.

Passions.

Capris.

Fascinators.

feel. The sequels to their first record, "Goodnight" and "Little Boy Blue" had the soft sound of "Little Star," but neither had quite the same potential and neither charted. According to Vito Piccone[15], the group was on the road too long and gave scant attention to following up "Little Star." In an age of one-hit wonders, by

15. Engel, Edward R. *White & Still All Right!*

the time they recorded a sequel, they were cold.

The Five Discs never achieved widespread fame, never charted nationally, but are considered by many of those who know their doo-wops as the prototype of the white group sound, despite the fact that they were an integrated group. Beginning in 1958 with "I Remember" and continuing with "Adios," "My Baby Loves Me" and "Never Let You Go," all in 1961, this group combined ultimate power basswork with the straining tenor lead and intricate background harmonies. Through the years, the group utilized the services of three bassmen (Andrew Johnson, John Russell, and Charles DiBella) who filled each others' shoes without missing a step. The Capris first issued "There's A Moon Out Tonight" in 1958 on the Planet label, but it went nowhere. The song was resuscitated in 1961 when the music entered its neo-doo-wop phase and became an enormous hit, reaching #3 pop and #11 R&B. They had a good follow-up in 1961 called "Where I Fell In Love," but they are perhaps best known for their 1982 recording of "Morse Code Of Love" for the Ambient Sound label that most doo-wop lovers can sing in their sleep. On recent CBS-FM (New York) polls of the "Top 101 Doo-Wops," taken in 1992 and 1994, "Morse Code" came in at number four and five respectively, far surpassing any other doo-wop recorded after the era. The Fascinators, a great group that achieved only local prominence, were known for their melodic songs and great leads by Tony Passalacqua. They gave us "Chapel Bells," "Oh Rosemarie," "Who Do You Think You Are" and "Wonder Who." The Selections were a no-hit wonder that pleased doo-wop aficionados with "Guardian Angel," which has since become a doo-wop "standard."

By now, four somewhat separate sub-styles of white group sound existed side by side (by side by side). The first was a rock 'n' roll-oriented sound represented by Danny & the Juniors. The second was the hard doo-wop style usually featuring a power bass that came on the scene with "I Wonder Why." The third was a soft doo-wop sound represented by "Little Star," "There's A Moon Out Tonight" and "Chapel Bells," and the last was an amal-

Knockouts.

Impalas.

Safaris.

gamation of doo-wop and pop music which we've labeled "pop doo-wop." Some groups used one of these four styles exclusively, other groups used several, a few used two on the same release (e.g. "Little Star/Getting Dizzy").

The Mystics and Passions, both espousing soft doo-wop arrangements, both from Brooklyn[16], emerged in 1959. The Mystics scored big with "Hushabye" and followed it up with "Don't Take The Stars" and "All Through

16. See chapter on Doo-wogeography.

The Night," two soft sweet songs in the same style as "Hushabye" (which was written for them by Doc Pomus in an attempt to emulate "Little Star" by the Elegants). The Passions issued "Just To Be With You," "This Is My Love," and "Gloria" (one of the two highly regarded white versions), all sweet ballads, and "I Only Want You," a great uptempo number, despite the presence of violins. Other white groups having hits in 1959 were the Bell Notes, with "I've Had It," a pleasant four-chord uptempo with a country twang to it, the Impalas (who were four white guys with a black lead that produced a white sound) scored with "Sorry, I Ran All The Way Home," the Eternals, a Latino group with the white sound who issued "Rockin' In The Jungle" and "Babalu's Wedding Day," and the Skyliners. The Skyliners from Pittsburgh had a pleasing sound which combined doo-wop with pop (i.e., pop doo-wop) and utilized a female voice (Janet Vogel) as part of the background harmony that gave their records a Modernaires-type feeling. They scored often with classics like "Since I Don't Have You," "This I Swear," "It Happened Today," "Lonely Way" and "Pennies From Heaven." The Fireflies displayed a similar pop doo-wop style on two pretty ballads, "You Were Mine" and "I Can't Say Goodbye." The Fleetwoods, so soft they made the Skyliners sound like a hard-rock group, also began a string of hits in this year with "Come Softly To Me," "Mr. Blue," and "Runaround."

The year 1960 was an off year, producing charting debuts by Dante & the Evergreens, with their novelty glorifying "Alley Oop" (#15 pop), the Innocents with "Honest I Do" (#28 pop), the Demensions with a pop version of "Over The Rainbow" (#16 pop), and the Safaris with one of those "longing-from-afar" rockaballads called "Image Of A Girl" (#6 pop). The next year, 1961, saw the debuts of the Chimes, with a remake of the old standard "Once In A While," which was the next development in the "popping" up of the doo-wop sound to make it appeal to a wider audience. While the Skyliners and Fireflies before them used falsetto and nonsense syllables liberally, if not extensively, the Chimes didn't. The tight harmony, wide range of voices, including a distinct bass, was present, but the doo-wopishness rating was way down. The Classics, with "Til Then" in 1963 and the Duprees with "You Belong To Me," "My Own True Love" (both from 1962), "Why Don't You Believe Me" and "Have You Heard" (from 1963) continued down this path. This sound appealed to adults and to those young people who had tired of the more raucous sound offered by some of the neo-doo-wop groups like the Regents and Earls. The Echoes offered "Baby Blue," a soft and sweet mid-tempo number that was a cross between "Hushabye" and "Mr. Blue."

The Regents used a power bass style and entered the charts with their smash "Barbara Ann" and followed it up in with "Runaround" and "Liar," all in 1961. The Earls released their first record in April of 1961, an uptempo remake of the Harptones' "Life Is But A Dream," which was a local New York hit, but was invisible nationally. Their innovative style of utilizing long chains of nonsense syllables to catch attention (such as "da-duh da-duh bop bop duh shoo bop duh bop bop"), was established with this song. The style was used capably and repeatedly in songs like "Lookin' For My Baby" ("ron ron, ron-day-doe, ron-day-doe chicky wah wah") from 1961, "Remember Then" ("oop-shoo shanga langa jinga bop") from 1962 and "Never" ("oop-shoop jinga linga chop chop") from 1963. They had softer sides in 1963 with "Eyes" and "I Believe" (which always places near the top on oldies surveys). Of the white groups that began recording after 1960, they are one of the most prominent and certainly the most distinctive.

Also releasing their first record in 1961 was the Dovells, a Philadelphia group with a style that is best described as rock 'n' roll, with a little doo-wop thrown in every once in a while. They made some peppy, danceable music in the early sixties and were the link between Danny & the Juniors and the Orlons in Philly. Nino & the Ebbtides covered "Those Oldies But Goodies" by a black group, Little Caesar & the Romans, in 1961, and promptly followed it with "Juke Box Saturday Night." In both of these tunes, they pay homage to the music of yore, which in 1961 wasn't very yore at all. These two successful releases kind of made them the kings of the "retro-song." If you're going to do

Devotions.

Belmonts.

something, you may as well be the best.

Dion DiMucci and the Belmonts split up in 1960 and soon began recording separately. In a way, their output was ironic. Together, they precipitated the WGS in 1958 with the hard-hitting "I Wonder Why," but followed it with a string of soft -type ballads—pleasant, but uncomfortably nice. Separately, they both turned back to uptempo numbers with more of a doo-wop flavor. Dion's first solo recording (actually he was backed by the Del Satins[17] on almost all of his post-Belmon-

---

17. The Del Satins weren't mentioned on the labels of Dion's recordings. They had their own hit in 1962 with "Teardrops Follow Me."

Regents.

Del Satins.

tian recordings in the doo-wop vein) was "Lonely Teenager," still in a "cutesy" groove. He then cut "Runaround Sue," with the great "Hey, hey, hum-duh-hey-duh-hey-duh-hey, hey…" hook. It caught on and reached #1 pop (#4 R&B) in the fall of 1961. The formula was used again and again to reach the charts with "The Wanderer" (which reached #2 pop in January 1962), "Lovers Who Wander" (#3 pop, #16 R&B, in 1962), "Little Diane" (#8 pop, 1962), "Love Came To Me" (#10 pop, #24 R&B, 1962), "Ruby Baby" (#2 pop, #5 R&B, 1963), "Donna The Prima Donna" (#6 pop, #17 R&B, 1963), "Drip Drop" (#6, 1963), with a few others thrown in for good measure.

The Belmonts also came out with more doo-woppy sound including "I Need Someone" and a decent copy of the Rob Roys' "Tell Me Why" (which reached #18 pop) in 1961, and "Come On Little Angel" (#28 pop) and "Diddle-De-Dum" in 1962. It leaves one wondering what would have happened to the course of doo-wop and even rock 'n' roll if they had stayed in the "I Wonder Why" bag in 1958 instead of changing over to a sweet sound. They were good looking, talented and white, and might have been the first supergroup.

The Tokens had two big hits in 1961 which were worlds apart from each other. In April, they scored with "Tonight I Fell In Love," with the hook "dom doobie dom whoa-oh," seemingly putting the group on the path to power bassdom. Something changed their minds, however; for in November, they reached number one on the pop charts (#7 R&B) with the falsetto-led "The Lion Sleeps Tonight," a song done by the Weavers and other folk groups as "Wimoweh," a Zulu tribal folk song from Africa. This combination of folk music and doo-wop is virtually unique and presaged Paul Simon's "Graceland" album thirty years later. The Tokens also created and produced Randy & the Rainbows in their image and issued "Denise" in 1963, a pleasing paean to a girl containing the hook, "oh Denise, doobie doo." Apparently the Tokens were big on "doobies." Figuratively that is.

Tokens.

Nino and the Ebbtides.

Other decent white groups emerged as the doo-wop era drew to a close. The Excellents were a Bronx group that sang about a Brooklyn girl in Bronx style. Although this is a generalization that doesn't hold true all the time, Brooklyn groups patterned themselves after the Mystics and Passions, both of which were successful, and ended up with a sweeter, more melodic sound. Bronx groups tended to use

Randy and the Rainbows.

Dovells.

more power bass (Dion & Belmonts, Regents, Excellents, Earls, Selections) and use more falsetto. That Brooklyn girl was "Coney Island Baby," and she was backed by a power bass version of the Cleftones' "You Baby You." The Devotions featured a booming bass in "Rip Van Winkle," a semi-novelty that was first released in 1961. Obscurity discovered the song quickly but, according to the group's founder Ray Sanchez,[18] it was revived in 1962 by Roulette's "Golden Oldies" LP series and again in 1964 by a Pittsburgh deejay who kept playing the song over and over. The third time was the charm and it became a national hit, reaching #36 on the pop charts. The Reflections also had a hit that year with another semi-novelty, "(Just Like) Romeo And Juliet." By this point in time, only songs that had a compelling hook could get through the wall of new sounds and make the charts. In a way, the WGS, along with the girl groups that were popular from roughly 1960-1963, were the last bastions of the doo-wop sound. And by 1964, the fat lady had sung.

White vocal groups sporting a preppy-pop style, like the Ames Brothers, Four Aces, etc., began to make the Pop charts in the late 1940s and continued to chart until the early 1960s. They really had an impact on the

18. From an interview on Don K. Reed's Doo-Wop Shop, July 21, 1996.

charts from the early 1950s through 1958, with a peak in 1954. On the other hand, white groups that sang in doo-wop style were nowhere to be found on the charts before the mid-1950s, but then attained and maintained popularity through 1963, the tail end of the era. It's almost as if the prep style made way for the doo-wop style after 1958. This type of comparison cannot be made using the R&B charts because while white doo-wop sounds regularly made it to these charts, white pop sounds did not.

As a conclusion to the story of the WGS, we've listed below recommended recordings, grouped by substyle (rock 'n' roll, powerbass, soft doo-wop, pop-doo-wop). While most songs fit clearly and cleanly into one or another of the four sub-styles, there are some songs that straddle two or more categories. Instead of being obsessive-compulsive and describing the straddle, we've chosen to dump the song into the category that fits best. Fifteen songs are listed for each substyle. Note that groups with female leads are left out because they play a part on the chapter on that particular subject (e.g. Pat Cordel & the Crescents, Kathy Young & the Innocents, Jamies). Mixed groups, like the Rob Roys, Crests and Impalas, are similarly omitted.

Substyle	Group	Song	Year
Powerbass	Arrogants	Mirror Mirror	1963
	DeMilles	Donna Lee	1964
	Devotions	Rip Van Winkle	1961
	Dion & the Belmonts	I Wonder Why	1958
	Earls	Remember Then	1962
	Encounters	Don't Stop	1965
	Eternals	Babalu's Wedding Day	1959
	Excellents	You Baby You	1962
	Five Discs	Adios	1961
	Four J's	Here I Am Broken Hearted	1964
	Quotations	Ala-Men-Sa-Aye	1961
	Selections	Guardian Angel	1958
	Tokens	Tonight I Fell In Love	1961
	Treblechords	Theresa	1959
	Vito & the Salutations	Unchained Melody	1963
Soft Doo-Wop	Bob Knight Four	Good Goodbye	1961
	Caslons	Anniversary Of Love	1961
	Chaperones	Cruise To The Moon	1960
	Dennis & the Explorers	Vision Of Love	1960
	Echoes	Baby Blue	1961
	Elegants	Little Star	1958
	Emotions	Echo	1962
	Fascinators	Who Do You Think You Are	1959
	Fleetwoods	Come Softly To Me	1959
	Imaginations	Hey You	1961
	Mello-Kings	Tonite Tonite	1957
	Mystics	Hushabye	1959
	Passions	I Only Want You	1960
	Randy & the Rainbows	Denise	1963
	Safaris	Image Of A Girl	1960
Pop Doo-Wop	Castells	So This Is Love	1962
	Chimes	Once In A While	1960
	Classics	Til Then	1963
	Demensions	Over The Rainbow	1960
	Dion and the Belmonts	Where Or When	1960
	Duprees	My Own True Love	1962
	Duprees	You Belong To Me	1962
	Fireflies	You Were Mine	1959
	Roommates	Band Of Gold	1961
	Skyliners	Lonely Way	1959
	Skyliners	This I Swear	1959
	Tempos	See You in September	1959
	Temptations	Barbara	1960
	Three Chuckles	Runaround	1954
	Three Friends	Blanche	1956
Rock 'n' Roll	Bell Notes	I've Had It	1959
	Original Casuals	So Tough	1958
	Danny & the Juniors	At The Hop	1957
	Danny & the Juniors	Rock and Roll Is Here To Stay	1957
	Del Satins	Teardrops Follow Me	1962
	Diamonds	The Stroll	1957
	Dion (w. Del Satins)	Runaround Sue	1961
	Dovells	Bristol Stomp	1961
	Dovells	No No No	1961
	Nino & the Ebbtides	Juke Box Saturday Night	1961
	Nicky & the Nobles	Poor Rock 'n' Roll	1957
	Reflections	Just Like Romeo And Juliet	1964
	Regents	Barbara Ann	1961

Rockin' Chairs	Memories Of Love	1959
Royal Teens	Short Shorts	1957

As a postscript to this chapter, we are including an article graciously submitted by Ed Engel and Bob Diskin. For those of you not familiar with these folks, they are probably two of the most knowledgeable people on this planet about the White Group Sound. Both have written extensively on the subject. Engel is the owner of Crystal Ball Records which, over the years, has put out more than 50 albums and 100 45s (most by white

groups), and Diskin manages many groups still singing today like the Five Discs, the Blue Sonnets and the Quotations. Most important, they are doo-wopcentrists.

Their article is dated March 1, 1989. It is full of opinions, rather than facts, but the opinions and the reasoning and ideas behind them are quite interesting. The way the article was written, it seems almost like these guys were thinking aloud. Let them share their thoughts with us...

The White Group "Sound"
(The First and Last Record of the Pre-Beatles Era)

by Edward Engel and Bob Diskin

I would like to try and discover the first white group style doo-wop and the last. I'm sure every reader has their own opinions and I'd love for them to share them with me. I will use the words 'style' and 'sound,' rather than white-group doo-wop because this sound could appear in a Black or Hispanic vocal group as well.

Disc jockeys like Alan Freed, who had the courage to play the early "true" sounds of R&B, paved the way for the "White Style Sound." With the arrival of this sound, no longer was it necessary to clutter the air waves with cover versions of great tunes with the likes of the Crew Cuts, Gail Storm or Pat Boone. Now, for the first time, white urban youths were able to emulate the Heartbeats, Flamingos, and Harptones and form a sound of their own, one that was more to their liking. Group R&B, which started in late 1952 and by 1954-55 began to arrive with hits like "Earth Angel," took almost four years to perfect by white groups. This white "sound" was short-lived. It lasted from 1958 to 1963-64 when the Beatles invaded the United States and changed our music forever.

On to the discussion. To compare records, many things must be taken into consideration. I will try to examine records that are considered classics by collectors, as well as the ones that achieved success on the national (Billboard) charts.

Surveys or charts can sometimes be misleading. Consider the following. A group that hits the charts in June 1958 may have been singing their song for over a year before they even had a recording contract. Once the group recorded, the record company could have taken three months after the session before the record was released. It usually took another three months for the record to receive enough air play and exposure to even dent the national charts. A record may have been #1 in New York for two or three weeks, but never charted higher than 75 or 80 nationally. So two categories for the first true white style sound are possible: (a) the first actual white style record and (b) the first successful white style record that had an impact on the music scene. The same is true for the last white style record. Also, the time period 1954-

1964 must be invoked, otherwise records from the late 1970s or early 1980s would have to be considered, like "Morse Code Of Love" by the Capris and Manhattan Transfer, or Billy Joel's "Longest Time."

The first white group to be considered would be the Teardrops on Josie, who recorded "The Stars Are Out Tonight" in 1954. This group, although white, had a black style and sound, and therefore would not qualify. The black style vs. white sound issue brings up a heated phone conversation with my colleague, Bobby Diskin.

It is his interpretation that "style" and "sound" should not be mixed up. He feels that some white groups sing in a black style with a white sound. An example of this was "Ding Dong" by the (white) Echos on Gee in 1957. The first record in this category to achieve monster success was "Tonight Tonight" by the Mello-Kings, which charted in August 1957.

This brings up the question of "You Baby You" by Herbie Cox and the Cleftones. If the Echos and Teardrops were white groups with a black style or sound, then the Cleftones were a black group with a white sound or style. So their 1955-56 entries "You Baby You" and "Little Girl Of Mine" should qualify, but with an asterisk.

Next let's take a quick look at "My Juanita" by Johnny Maestro and the Crests in July 1957. Although Johnny is white, the group and their sound isn't, so it does not qualify. Neil Sedaka and the Tokens had a minor hit on Melba in 1956 with "While I Dream," backed with "I Lost My Baby," but can you call this a doo-wop? It does not qualify.

The little boy ("kiddy") lead made famous by Frankie Lymon in 1956 has no white or black sound, it just has a "kiddy" sound. Therefore, songs like "Please Say You Want Me" (1956) or "Carol" (1957) by the Schoolboys don't qualify. Pat Cordel and the Crescents, a group that eventually evolved into the Elegants, copied the Lymon style. Since they didn't achieve success, despite the fact that "Darling Come Back" (backed with "My Tears") was released on three different labels, it doesn't qualify.

The Diamonds on Mercury had success on the charts in 1956 with their cover versions of "Ka-Ding-Dong" and "Church Bells May Ring," but since these were covers and the Diamonds were a cover group, they do not qualify. In 1957, "At The Hop" by Danny and the Juniors was on the charts for 21 weeks and reached #1. I feel, however, that this is a rock 'n' roll record, rather than a doo-wop. Though it changed the music scene, it does not qualify. Of course, if you flip it over, "Sometimes" is a very strong candidate for the first white-style doo-wop record, and definitely the first with impact.

As far as the first successful white group record is concerned, I think everyone is in harmony with the choice of "I Wonder Why" by Dion and the Belmonts, which reached the charts on May 10, 1958, stayed on for 13 weeks and reached #22 nationally. Next came "Little Star" by the Elegants, which charted first on July 12, 1958, stayed for 19 weeks and reached #1 in the nation. In between these two entries, once again, we have Danny and the Juniors with "Dottie," which spent six weeks on the charts, beginning on June 14, 1958, and reached #41. Let's also keep in mind "Joanie" by the Brooklyn-based Bay Bops, which charted, and the original Planet label release of "There's A Moon Out Tonight" by the Capris (which didn't chart until 1961, two labels later). "You" by the Aquatones also charted, beginning on April 19, 1958, reaching a high of #21 with a stay of 12 weeks. As we round out the year 1958 we see a strong entry by the Royal Teens in "Believe Me," which charted for 15 weeks beginning on Nov. 1, 1958 and reached #26. Naturally, their entry at the beginning of 1958 (Jan. 18th), titled "Short Shorts," was a novelty hit rather than a doo-wop. Even though it reached #3 in the nation and lasted 16 weeks, it does not qualify.

In 1958, record after record with the white-style sound started to flood the markets in the New York area and all over the country. It would be impossible to try and name all these releases, but a few are worthy of mention. The Hi Fives released "My Friend" and "How Can I Win" in January 1958 on Decca, and by August had two additional releases. For the hard core collector, the Planet label gave us an obscure release by Tony and the Daydreams called "I'll Never Tell." There were so many records issued, many of which aren't applicable. For example, "Chapel Bells" by the Fascinators on Capitol and "I Remember" by the Five Discs on Emge, Vik or Rust were great classics, but fall under the black style.

I guess it's time to give my choice for the first white group record. The first true doo-wop, from a collectors standpoint, was probably a local hit in 1957: either "Franny Franny" by Nino and the Ebb Tides on Acme or "We Went Away," backed with "Tag Along," which was the first release by Dion and the Belmonts on Mohawk. My choice for the first white style sound to make a dent in the world of music on a national basis, came in June of 1956 with "Angel Face" by the Neons on the Tetra label.

Now let's set up rules for what records qualify for the honor of being the last release with a white doo-wop sound or style in the pre-Beatles era. As before, let's get all the "don't qualifies" out of the way before I announce my winner. I hope most of you who started this article are still with me. Groups like Jay and the Americans, the Happenings and the Four Seasons cannot be considered doo-wop, although each covered older songs or made an effort in the group harmony field.

A few groups immediately come to mind. The Duprees had that smooth sound, much like the Skyliners. But as sweet as the sound was, or as great as Jimmy Beaumont's lead was, their tunes were not doo-wop. Thus, songs by the Duprees, like "Why Don't You Believe Me," which charted beginning on Aug. 24, 1963 (seven weeks on the chart, reaching #37), the giant hit "Have You Heard," which reached the chart on Nov. 9, 1963 (10 weeks, reaching #18), and even the later release of "It's No Sin," which reached on Jan. 25, 1964 (five weeks, reaching #74) don't qualify. As for the Skyliners, they did chart on July 7, 1965 with "The Loser," which reached #72 and stayed five weeks, but the title of their disc pretty much tells the story.

"Wait A Minute" by Tim Tam and the Turn Ons charted on March 5, 1966, reached #76 and stayed five weeks, and "Be My Girl" by the 4-Evers hit the charts on May 30, 1964, stayed for four weeks and reached #75. Both sound too much like the Four Seasons and do not qualify. The Raindrops, a four-person group which featured the writing team of Jeff Barry and Ellie Greenwich, charted with their cover version of "Book Of Love," staying for seven weeks and reaching #62. We can't allow this to qualify, not so much because it is a cover record, but because Jeff and Ellie represent a different time period than we are dissecting. Their period involves the Ronettes, Phil Spector and all those artists that flourished on the Red Bird label during the British Invasion, while our sound died.

Probably a strong contender, if not for the fact that it was a girl group, would be "Whenever A Teenager Cries" by Reperata and the Del Rons, which charted on Jan. 9, 1965, and was written by Ernie Maresca in his usual doo-wop style. The record that immediately comes to the minds of most collectors and many can truly say is their choice, would be "Rip Van Winkle" by the Devotions. This was first released on Roulette 4541, charted on Feb. 8, 1964, and spent ten wonderful weeks on the charts, eventually reaching #36. A doo-wop in the true fashion. Unfortunately, we have to put an asterisk next to this record because Roulette released it two years earlier, in 1962 on Roulette 4406, and it also came out in 1961 on the very rare Delta label.

The year 1963 brought tremendous success to Vito and the Salutations, with their doo-wop version of "Unchained Melody," which was a strong chart climber. They also had follow-ups known mostly to collectors like "Walkin" on Apt in 1965 and "Hello Dolly" on Rust in 1966. Although the Salutations were a white group, their style of singing was geared to the black sound, and does not qualify. The same is true of the 1963 release of "Gloria" by Nicky Addeo and the Darchaes on Savoy.

The year 1963 also gave us pure collectables, such as "I Lost My Baby" by the Darvels on the Eddies label and a Billboard charter by the Tokens called "Hear The Bells," which reached #94 on Aug. 24, 1963 showing that it had little impact. Another one released around the same time that had little influence was "Please Don't Cheat On Me" by the Roommates on Philips. There are so many more, but again, I'm looking for some national impact.

On June 22, 1963, the Classics released "Til Then," reaching #20 in a nine-week stay. This could be the winner by one week, but due to the impact of a higher chart number and eight more weeks on the charts, the prize for the last white-style doo-wop of this era with impact goes to the Rust recording stars, Randy and the Rainbows, who hit with "Denise." It hit the charts on June 15, 1963, stayed for 17 weeks and reached #10 nationally. Hats off to the boys from Maspeth, Queens, New York, and their writer Neil Levinson.

Although their sound comes close to a Four-Seasons' flavor, I feel that unlike the 4-Evers, they have enough group harmony to allow them the victory. They also nicked the charts on Dec. 14, 1963 with their follow-up, "Why Do Kids Grow Up," which stayed for two weeks and reached #97, but the lack of impact makes us revert to their titanic smash "Denise."

We've also narrowed down the possibilities for the last record in this style and era which didn't chart or even become a local hit. These choices would be different depending on which collector and which part of the country was involved, but for me, I would like to name a few 1964 releases which are my favorites.

Year	Label	Group	Song
1964	Ember	Barries	Tonight, Tonight/Mary Ann
1964	Old Town	Crowns	Possibilities
1964	Kapp	Boyfriends (5 Discs)	Let's Fall In Love
1964	United Sound Ass. 175	Delcades	Two To Fall In Love
1964	Mala 475	Del-Satins	Two Broken Hearts
1964	Mala 480	Nino/Ebb Tides	Linda Lou Garrett
1964	Laurie 3247	Demilles	Cry And Be On Your Way
1964	Sunny 22	Riffs	Little Girl
1964	Coral	Del-Airs	Arlene
1964	Raven 8004	Jumpin Tones	I Had A Dream
1964	Raven 8005	Jumpin Tones	Grandma's Hearing Aid
1964	Swing 100	4-Winds (Tokens)	Remember Last Summer
1964	Jamie 1267	4 J's	Here I Am Broken Hearted
1964	Jamie 1274	4 J's	My Love Possessed
1964	Epic 9747	Barons	Remember Rita

(Note: the group's earlier release, Epic 9586, "Pledge Of A Fool," was re-released on Epic 10093 in October 1966)

Year	Label	Group	Song
1964	Barry 108	Nicky & the Nacks	The Night
1964	Epic 9697	Concords	Should I Cry/It's Our Wedding Day
1964	Congress 233	Squires	Joyce
1964	T.A. 101	Stage Hands	Hello Dolly
1964	Guyden 2116	Newports	Tears/Disillusioned Love
1964	Josie 916	Ovations	Who Needs Love
1964	Josie 920	Styles	School Bells To Chapel Bells

(This group was also known as the Vels, who recorded "In Laws" earlier on the Amy label, which was produced by Jerry Landis aka Paul Simon)

Year	Label	Group	Song
1964	Blast 216	Velons	Shelly
1964	Roulette 4556	Devotions	Sunday Kind Of Love
1964	Roulette 4580	Devotions	Snow White
1964	Mercury 72283	Epics	The Bells Are Ringing
1964	Smash 2045	Billy & the Essentials	Babalu's Wedding Day
1964	Atlantic 2228	Four Casts (aka Lydells)	Stormy Weather
1964	West Side 1020	Darnell/Dreams	The Day Before Yesterday

Here are a few from beyond our time frame:

Year	Label	Group	Song
1965	Coral 62453	Goldbugs	Stop That Wedding
1965	Coral 62456	4 Directions	Tonight We Love
1965	Rust 5097	Bon-Airs	The Shrine Of St. Cecilia
1965	Lawn 253	Denotations	Nena/Lone Stranger
1965	Laurie 3298	Elegants	Wake Up
1965	Delsey 303	Robin Hood & His Merri Men	Mary Ann/We Had A Quarrel
1965	General American 720	Velvet Satins	Angel Adorable
1965	ABC 10737	Anthony & the Sophomores	Gee
1965	Old Town 1182	Earls	Remember Me Baby

In this article, I embarked on a project that entered waters never before sailed. These are my opinions, and your input would be greatly appreciated. All correspondence can get to me via the authors.

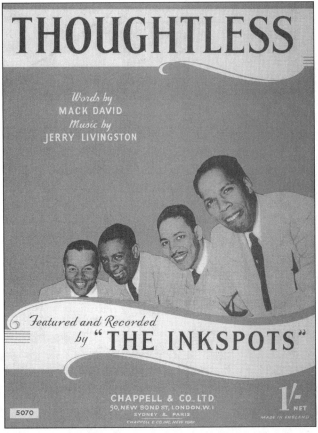

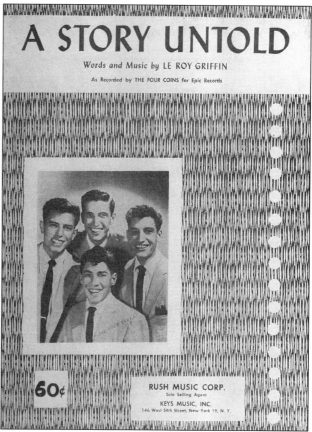

90 •

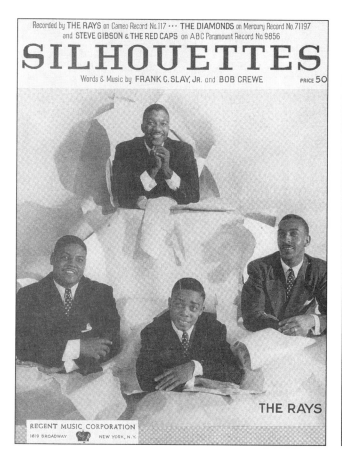

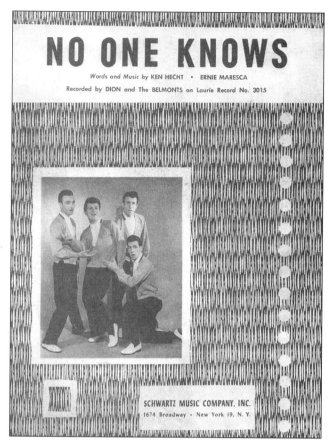

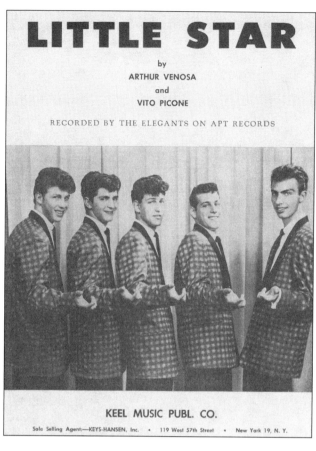

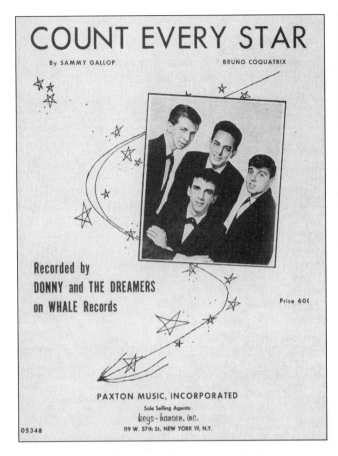

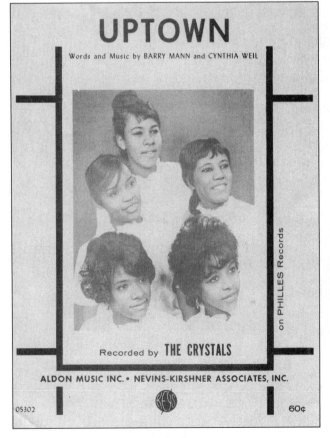

Chapter 10

Group Her-mony

Did feminism and the women's liberation movement start in the 1960s with Betty Friedan, Gloria Steinem and the quest for equal rights? Nope. Did it start with the Helen Reddy opus "I Am Woman?" No way. How about with the Chantels and Shirelles in the late 1950s? Hell no. Where it did start is with Shirley Gunter and the Queens in 1954 or maybe Della Griffin and the Enchanters in 1951, or with Ella Fitzgerald and the Ink Spots in the 1940s, or even with the Johnson, Boswell and Andrews Sisters in the 1920s and 1930s. It depends on your perspective.

At various times and in various ways, directly and indirectly, this book makes the point that music is intertwined with the sociological issues of the times. Teen-agers coming of age as a group, the "haves" using and abusing the "have-nots," and the black-white issue are some of the factors that gave the doo-wop era its character. The place of women in society in the 1940s and 1950s is another.

The truth is that women weren't much of a factor in the doo-wop movement.[1] Guys hung out; girls didn't, weren't allowed to. The "primordial ooze" from which doo-wop groups formed was the neighborhood peer group that played ball together, sat on the stoops together, commented on passerby girls together. When girl groups formed, they usually did so in their school, under the tutelage of some choral teacher who liked real music. Now, if you're not allowed to hang out on the streets after school and in the evening, how are you going to sing doo-wops? In this way, young ladies, if and because they were young ladies, were at a distinct cultural disadvantage.

Additionally, there was a belief on the part of record company executives that groups made up exclusively of women wouldn't sell. In theory, this was because since women bought most of the records, they would be more likely to buy one with a male or male group at the helm.[2] With female groups, it was almost as if there was a quota system operating. As with black male groups, where only the Mills Brothers and Ink Spots "crossed over" to popularity with white audiences, so it was with distaff groups. There was room for a few, like the Andrews and McGuire Sisters, but few others made it big. It may also have been the chauvinistic idea that women belonged in the home. Though group vocal music was a male thing, the realm of single artists was different. Ella (Fitzgerald), Lady Day (Billie Holiday), Lena Horne, Sarah Vaughan,

Savannah Churchill, LaVerne Baker, Ruth Brown and others made the big time. These were women of the world, the kind you wouldn't necessarily want to bring home to mom and dad. But the female groups were innocent, and innocence didn't necessarily sell.

Another reason for the paucity of interest in the female-group sound is that there was too much uniformity in group members' voices. Unlike male groups of the doo-wop era, which usually featured a wide range of voice parts (bass to falsetto), voices in female groups displayed less diversity. Which equated to boring. Female leads fronting male groups, which offered a wider range, fared much better (e.g. Ella Fitzgerald with the Ink Spots, Savannah Churchill with the Four Tunes and Striders).

Since this essay is primarily concerned with group singing, the plight of female single artists will be put aside. What's left are females in groups in three categories: (a) groups with all female members, (b) female leads fronting a male groups and (c) groups with a female member(s) in a supporting role. The second category has many variations. Sometimes the unions between female lead and male group were one-time events, sometimes they were occasional (as with Ella Fitzgerald and the Ink Spots), and frequently they were the way the group was intended to function (such as Pearl McKinnon & the Kodaks). All three categories have existed for a good part of the twentieth century.

The Early Years

Although all-female groups recorded on both disc and cylinder in the early 1900s (e.g. the Olive Meade Quartet, Manhattan Ladies Quartet and Columbia Ladies Quartet, all around the year 1912), male groups dominated the charts.[3] The only exception was the "That Girl" Quartet, that placed the evergreen[4] "Put Your Arms Around Me, Honey" and three other songs on the charts between 1911 and 1913. They were the only all-female group to chart before the Boswell Sisters, an all-white female group, began recording in 1931. Along with Bing Crosby's Rhythm Boys, the Boswells virtually invented vocal group jazz stylings that would set the pace for groups for decades to come (and which predated the jive-jazz style of the Mills Brothers). Between the years 1931 and 1938, they placed twenty songs on the pop charts and were an enormous influence on later female artists like Ella Fitzgerald and the Andrews Sisters. In comparing the

---

1. Using the word "movement" lends an air of importance to whatever you're describing.
2. This same conclusion was reached by George Moonoogian in his "Wax Fax" column in *Record Collector's Monthly*, Issue #36, Dec.-Jan./1986/87, p.7.

---

3. Whitburn, Joel. *Pop Memories, 1890-1954*. Menomonee Falls, Wis.: Record Research Inc., 1986.
4. "Evergreen" is often used by music writers to denote an old standard that yew might pine fir.

Boswells and Mills, Will Friedwald[5] quipped: "The Bozzies supplemented their sumptuous singing with the finest instrumental soloists; the Millses just cupped their hands in front of their faces and blew. And who would you rather hear: Bunny Berigan or some bozo trying to sound like a trumpet, even if he does it well?"[6]

The Johnson Sisters, from the Chicago area, began singing barbershop harmonies in the late 1920s and invaded the previously all-male barbershop world, the SPEBSQSA (Society for the Preservation and Encouragement of Barbershop Quartet Singing in America) by 1939. They paved the way for thousands of female groups (that, when organized, called themselves the "Sweet Adelines") that would follow in their footsteps. Their careers firmly anchored in the 1930s, both the Boswells and Johnsons took the male part in some of their songs. For example, in "Sweet Kitty Dooley" by the Johnsons, the girls sing the part of a swain vowing his love to his lass ("Sweet Kitty Dooley I love you..."). The Boswells take similar roles in "When I Take My Sugar To Tea" and "Million Dollar Baby."

The first of the modern female groups, the Andrews Sisters, changed this practice. Beginning in 1937, the Andrews Sisters placed more than 100 songs on the pop charts in a little less than a decade and a half. Their material ranged from ethnic music, to bouncy patriotic tunes like "Boogie Woogie Bugle Boy," to joint efforts with an obscure crooner named Bing Crosby, to slightly naughty jump tunes like "Don't Sit Under The Apple Tree With Anyone Else But Me." Overall though, they had both feet firmly planted in the pop style. They were photogenic and appeared in more than twenty movies, many with a patriotic theme. Most important perhaps, they broke the ice for female groups by making it big in show business, in the same way as the Mills Brothers and Ink Spots paved the way for later black male groups. Despite being lily-white, the Andrews also must have reached a black audience, for they appeared on the Rhythm & Blues charts three times in the mid-1940s. Two of these efforts were shared with Bing (on "Pistol Packin' Mama" and "Don't Fence Me In,"), but the third, "Rum And Coca Cola" ironically made them the first all-female group to score on the R&B charts (January 1945). Contemporary to Andrews Sisters were the Merry Macs (who first recorded in 1938), the Pied Pipers (1938, containing a young Jo Stafford), the Modernaires (1945) and Skylarks (1946). All of these groups contained one female member (usually the lead voice) but their pop and/or big band styles leave them outside the scope of this book.

5. Friedwald, Will. *Jazz Singing*. London: Quartet Books, 1991.
6. Before we take Friedwald too seriously, witness a comment on the tendency for jazz vocal groups to be white: "The black gift for vocal harmony for some reason rarely surfaced in jazz, as we shall see; instead, it realized itself in such unfortunate forms as doo-wop..." Did someone use the word "bozo?"

The 1940s witnessed the beginning of a style wherein strong female leads would join forces with male groups and hit the R&B charts fairly often. In some cases, the male group was given the opportunity to co-lead the song, as in "Cow Cow Boogie" by Ella Fitzgerald and the Ink Spots in 1944, or Little Esther with the Robins in "Double Crossin' Blues" in 1950. More commonly, a group was provided behind a female lead to produce a fuller sound. Ella Fitzgerald thus recorded songs backed by the Four Keys,[7] Ink Spots, Delta Rhythm Boys, Andy Love Quintet, Song Spinners and even the Ray Charles Singers. Savannah Churchill made a career for herself between the mid-1940s and early 1950s fronting three groups: the Sentimentalists (aka Four Tunes), the Striders and the Five Kings. Fitzgerald's efforts were in the pop-jazz field rather than within the scope of rhythm and blues, but Miss Churchill's output was honest-to-goodness late-40s R&B music. By hitting the R&B charts (and in the 1940s they were the only thrushes that did), they influenced the next generation of R&B songstresses.

1948-1954

What happened next is, to use a musical term, weird. Women in groups (actually single female artists also) virtually disappeared from the Rhythm & Blues charts for just about six years. From July of 1948, when Savannah Churchill backed by the Four Tunes made the chart with "I Want To Cry," to October of 1954, when "Oop Shoop" by Shirley Gunter & the Queens hit, only three records featuring women appeared on the R&B chart (compared to 98 male group records for the same span of time). Two of these were pop efforts by Ella Fitzgerald backed by groups, and only one, "Double Crossin' Blues," by the Robins with Little Esther (February, 1950) resembled rhythm and blues. It's not as if group R&B wasn't big then. This was the golden age of the Ravens and Orioles, Dominos and Clovers, Swallows and Four Buddies and Larks. This was the period of time in which group rhythm and blues and doo-wop were born.

Does the reader remember the age-old philosophical question, "If a tree falls in the forest but there is no one around to hear it fall, does it still make a noise?" Well, if very little was heard from females in the R&B group world, does that mean they weren't recording? The answer is probably "sort of," though we'd prefer to hedge on the question. Though few of the "thrush-hooks-up-with-male-group" recordings achieved widespread popularity (i.e didn't make the charts), they were at least fairly plentiful. Little Esther, in addition to hitting the charts with the Robins, also did "Other Lips, Other Arms" and "Heart to Heart" in 1951 with Clyde McPhatter and the Dominoes. Savannah Churchill put out such wonderful efforts as "Let's Call A Spade A Spade" (1947, Five Kings), "Can Anyone Explain" (1950, Four

7. The Four Keys were really the 1930s male jazz-jive group, The Three Keys, with the addition of a guitar player.

The Ten Best R&B Songs: Female Lead with Male Group (1948-54)

Artists	Song	Year	Label
Ella Fitzgerald/Delta Rhythm Boys	Paper Moon	1945	Decca 23425
Savannah Churchill/Sentimentalists	I Want To Be Loved (But Only By You)	1946	Manor 1046
Ella Fitzgerald/Andy Love Quartet	That's My Desire	1947	Decca 23866
Savannah Churchill/Five Kings	Let's Call A Spade A Spade	1947	Manor 1061
Savannah Churchill/Four Tunes	Time Out For Tears	1948	Manor 1116
Little Esther/Robins	Double Crossin' Blues	1950	Savoy 731
Ruth Brown/Delta Rhythm Boys	Sentimental Journey	1950	Atlantic 905
Dinah Washington/Ravens	Out in the Cold Again	1951	Mercury 8257
Little Esther/Dominos	Heart To Heart	1951	Federal 12036
Viola Watkins/Crows	Seven Lonely Days	1953	Rama 3

Tunes) and "Once There Lived A Fool" (1950, Striders). Ruth Brown hooked up with the Delta Rhythm Boys for the unbelievable "Sentimental Journey" and "It's All In Your Mind" in 1950, and Ann Nichols combined with the Bluebirds for "Those Magic Words," also in 1950. The immortal Dinah Washington and the Ravens crossed paths for the first R&B version of "Out In the Cold Again" in 1951, the Four Jacks gave cameo appearances to Lil Greenwood, Shirley Haven and Cora Williams for unremarkable blues-type recordings in 1952, and the Crows (of "Gee" fame) made their debut backing up one Viola Watkins on "Seven Lonely Days." For the readers' information, the ten best of female-male group collaborations is offered above. Most are late 1940s rhythm and blues or pop-jazz efforts that do not contain doo-wop characteristics. They should be contrasted with the lists offered later in the chapter.

Where are all of those all-female R&B groups, you ask? Well, Della Griffin and the Enchanters recorded "How Could You/Today Is Your Birthday" and "I've Lost/Housewife Blues" in the 1951-1952 period. With a few personnel changes, this group became the Dell Tones on Brunswick and the Dell-Tones on Rainbow and recorded a few more sides. This later group included a talented but undeveloped Gloria Lynne as second lead. According to Louie Sylvani[8], Vicki Burgess, who later sang with the Charmers and Joytones, auditioned for this group and didn't make it. Ms. Griffin, still active with a new version of her Enchanters, loved music, singing and groups like Sonny Til and the Orioles, and just decided, with a friend of hers, to put a group together.[9] No historical or feminist intent, no sense of destiny, no angst—just a youthful "can do" attitude. Though totally unheard of[10], and without fanfare or notice, this makes the Enchanters the leading candidate for first all-female rhythm and blues group.[11] A runner-up for the title was Lydia Larson and the River Rovers,[12] who recorded two songs (one of which was actually released on Apollo) in September of 1951 and made the Enchanters seem like a household name. The obscurity of these groups raises the question of whether they were capable of influencing any other young females. If they weren't heard by many people, they probably didn't. And that's about all she wrote (or sang) for these years for all-female R&B groups, believe it or not.

1954-1957

There have been many books written about the "Girl Group Sound" that became a big player in the early 1960s with the likes of the Crystals, Chiffons, Ronettes, Shangri-Las, and the Motownette sounds of the Marvelettes and Supremes. Seemingly without fail, they take the Chantels as the beginning of this era, sometimes throwing the Bobbettes' "Mr. Lee" a bone because it preceded the Chantels' August 1957 debut record, "He's Gone/The Plea," by two months. All books then segue to the Shirelles and then leave the 1950s behind. Alan Betrock[13] begins the girl group story with the Chantels and Shirelles and includes no mention of earlier groups. Even the Bobbettes are omitted. Charlotte Greig's[14] work is only slightly better. Groups like the Miller Sisters, Three Tons of Joy, and Shirley Gunter

---

8. Phone conversation on 11/26/96.
9. From an interview with Della Griffin by Don K. Reed on the Doo-Wop Shop, Nov. 17, 1996.
10. So unheard of, in fact, that we could be making them up. But we're not.

11. Another group called the Sugartones also recorded "Today Is Your Birthday" around the same time on the Onyx label. It is not clear which version came out first. This group was comprised of a female lead and male background singers, so they are not in competition for the first female group honors.
12. Fileti, Donn. Liner notes from Relic record album 5077: The Golden Groups-Part 47, The Best of Apollo Records, Vol. 1.
13. Betrock, Alan. *Girl Groups: The Story of a Sound*, 1982, Delilah Books, New York.
14. Greig, Charlotte. *Will You Still Love Me Tomorrow?: Girl Groups from the 50s on...*, 1989, Virago Press, London.

and the Queens are mentioned in passing, as being influences on Arlene Smith, lead singer of the Chantels. The pop-styled Chordettes are discussed briefly as well. The best treatment of the early years of the three books examined was offered by Gillian Garr[15]. Even though her scope is wider because she looks over a longer period of time at both groups and single artists, she steps through early single artists and some of the early girl pop groups of the 1950s. Omitted, unfortunately, were Savannah Churchill and her backup groups, Little Esther and her collaborative efforts, and the Hearts and Deltairs, two of the favorites of purists. And all of these early singers are given short shrift.

While it can be argued that the thrush-with-male-group material of the early years should be ignored because it is more rhythm and bluesy than doo-wop, and that the Enchanters' and River Rovers' stuff can be overlooked because you need a microscope to find it, it's hard to understand overlooking the contribution of females to the group material from 1954 to the summer of 1957, a period of time which can be referred to as the pre-Chantellian years[16]. True, there's not an overabundance of material, but there is some, and a lot of it is very, very good. Starting with the all-female groups, there's Shirley Gunter and the Queens, the (West Coast) Dreamers, Etta James and the Peaches, the Cookies, Miller Sisters, Deltairs, Joytones, Rosebuds and, of course, the Hearts. And if you're in a good mood and grit your teeth a little, you can even throw in the Bonnie Sisters, Chordettes, Shepherd Sisters, and the Poni-Tails.

If you take a pass on the Enchanters and River Rovers because of their obscurity, then Shirley Gunter and the Queens qualifies as the first all-female R&B group. They made the charts with "Oop Shoop" (which is probably the first all-female 100% doo-wop recording) near the end of 1954, and followed it up with other great tunes such as the infectious "You're Mine" and a mellow ballad called "What Difference Does It Make?" Ms. Gunter was the sister of Coaster/Flair member Cornel Gunter, and the clique that her group belonged to included Richard Berry and Etta James.

The Dreamers didn't have any big hits, but had modest success on the West Coast when they backed up Richard Berry on "Bye Bye/At Last" in 1954. They are more famous because they later changed names to the Blossoms and reorganized their personnel to include one Darlene Love, who became the lynch pin for 1960s' groups like the Crystals and Bobb B. Soxx and the Blue Jeans. Etta James prefaced her three-decade solo career by recording a monster number one (for four weeks) hit called "The Wallflower" with a

female group called the Peaches in February, 1955.

Miss James was also involved in the Richard Berry clique, who provided the male voice on this record. The record was also called "Dance With Me Henry," a reference and tribute to Hank Ballard, whose "Annie" records piqued the interest of many teens.

The Hearts were arguably the premier female group[17] of the 1954-57 era. Their first release on Baton, "Lonely Nights," made the R&B charts and is considered by purists as the best female group R&B recording ever. The appeal of the record is the plaintive lead fronting strong harmony and a hook in the bridge where their bass, Louise Murray,[18] seductively invites, "Please come home, you great big lump of sugar." In fact, Ms. Murray's voice gave the group a wider range of voices than other all-female groups of the era, thus helping them to stand out. Although the group is also known for featuring Justine[19] "Baby" Washington, who had a healthy solo career beginning in 1957, she didn't sing lead on "Lonely Nights." Some other members in a shuffling line-up included Joyce James, Joyce Peterson, and Johnnie Richardson. Other masterpieces by the group, such as "All My Love Belongs To You" and "He Drives Me Crazy," though not charting, helped assure a place in history for the Hearts.

The Cookies, a female trio featuring Earl-Jean McCrea, later evolved into the Raeletts, the back-up group for Ray Charles. In March of 1956, the Cookies hit the R&B charts with a song called "In Paradise." A later version of the group, with Earl-Jean still on lead scored big hits on both the R&B and pop charts with "Chains" (December 1962) and "Don't Say Nothin' Bad (About My Baby)" (March, 1963). The Miller Sisters never had any big hits, but made up for it by being prolific, issuing roughly twenty singles from 1955 through the early 1960s. The Joytones were a Harlem trio that had a great version of "My Foolish Heart" and a few other nice releases in 1956, all of which went nowhere. A similar fate met "Collegian" by the Copasetics in 1956 and the Rosebuds' pretty release "Dearest Darling" in 1957. The Deltairs were an East Coast group that had a local hit called "Lullaby Of The Bells." It never charted, but has always rivaled the Hearts' "Lonely Nights" in the Hearts and Deltairs of doo-wop lovers. The flip of "Lullaby," titled, "It's You Dear," has the distinction of featuring an extremely rare female bass lead.

The Bonnie Sisters, Poni-Tails, and Chordettes, though not strictly in the realm of doo-wop or rhythm and blues, were the more acceptable of the string of female white pop groups that appeared on the charts in the mid-1950s. The Bonnies covered "Cry Baby" by

15. Garr, Gillian G. *She's A Rebel: The History of Women in Rock & Roll*, 1992, Seal Press, Seattle, WA.
16. The end of these years is marked by the release of "Mr. Lee" by Bobbettes and, a few months later, "He's Gone/The Plea" by the Chantels. "Pre-Chantellian" is used because it sounds a lot better than "pre-Bobbetian."
17. The group sometimes included a guy by the name of Rex Garvin, but Rex wasn't assertive in the vocal sense and is tough to hear separately. We've left the group in the all-female category.
18. If a female bass gets a job in law enforcement, what is her title? She-riff.
19. She sometimes went under the name of Jeanette "Baby" Washington.

Hearts.

Six Teens.

Deltairs.

Chordettes.

the Scarlets (aka Five Satins) and (Pop) charted with it in 1956. The Poni-Tails began recording in January of 1957 and had one national pop hit in the summer of 1958 called "Born Too Late." The Chordettes had a string of pop hits from 1954 through 1961 beginning with "Mr. Sandman." Sporting a barbershop style, the Chordettes made both the pop (peaking at number two) and R&B (number three) charts with the nonsense syllable-laden "Lollipop" in 1958. Other, more adult-oriented female pop groups appeared on the pop charts regularly, not only using up the quota for records with a female sound, but covering male groups as well. Thus, the Fontane Sisters hit number one on the pop charts (for three weeks) by covering the Jewels/Charms "Hearts of Stone" in 1954, and the McGuire Sisters stayed at number one on the pop charts for ten weeks with a 1955 cover of the Moonglows' "Sincerely." The McGuires also covered "Goodnight, Sweetheart, Goodnight" by the Spaniels, which appeared on both the pop and R&B charts in 1954. The Lennon Sisters, DeJohn, and Decastro Sisters

were other groups of this ilk. Listed below are the ten best doo-wop songs recorded by groups with all female members in the years 1954-1957. Pop oriented groups are omitted. Compared to the hundreds (perhaps thousands) of all-male groups that began recording in this time frame, it is scary how few all-female groups cut wax. And with all due respect to the Hearts,

The Ten Best Doo-Wop Songs: Groups with All Females (1954-1957)

Artist	Song	Year	Label
Shirley Gunter & the Queens	Oop-Shoop	1954	Flair 1050
Etta James & the Peaches	The Wallflower	1955	Modern 947
Hearts	Lonely Nights	1955	Baton 208
Bonnie Sisters	Cry Baby	1956	Rainbow 328
Cookies	In Paradise	1956	Atlantic 1084
Hearts	He Drives Me Crazy	1956	Baton 228
Joytones	My Foolish Heart	1957	Rama 215
Deltairs	Lullabye Of The Bells	1957	Ivy 101
Rosebuds	Dearest Darling	1957	Gee 1033
Shepherd Sisters	Alone	1957	Lance 125

Queens, etc., the quality of the overall body of female group recordings just doesn't cut the mustard.[20] The road to liberation, even in doo-wop, is apparently a long and hard one.

While the pickin's are fairly slim when it comes to all-female groups in the 1954-57 period, they're only slightly better when it comes to females fronting male groups—great quality, so-so quantity. Nineteen fifty-four saw the debut of Lillian Leach and the Mellows, the Capris and the Charmers. Between 1955 and 1956, the Sensations, Six Teens, and Chestnuts emerged. The Tuneweavers and Kodaks began recording in 1957. Also in this period were records issued by the union of a female single artist and an available local male (usually studio) group. And a few groups featuring non-leading female members has some hits.

Lillian Leach and the Mellows may qualify as the most talented group to ever record and yet never chart. From 1954 to 1957, led by Leach's crystal-clear voice and backed by solid male harmony, this group turned out a series of ethereal ballads. "How Sentimental Can I Be" was followed by "Smoke From Your Cigarette" (their signature), was followed by "Yesterday's Memories," "My Darling" and "Moon Of Silver." One after another, one more beautiful than the other. Anyone not impressed with this group should retire from the doo-wop arena pronto.

The Capris, a male group fronted by 14-year-old Renee Hinton, hailed from Philadelphia and were representative of that city's high-tenor harmony style. Their masterpiece was their first release (1954) titled, "God Only Knows." The male Charmers (who recorded for the Central label) featured one Vicki Burgess on lead for two releases in 1954 that are treasured by doo-wop aficionados, "The Beating Of My Heart" and "Tony My Darling." Vicki's real name was "Lucille" and, as a friend of Clyde McPhatter and his family, she was the inspiration for the Drifters' 1954 song by that name.[21] Ms. Burgess later recorded with the all-girl Joytones in 1956.

The Sensations featured the strong and perky voice of Yvonne Mills Baker. They recorded the old standard "Yes Sir, That's My Baby" in November 1955 and charted with it (R&B) three months later. They had another R&B charter with "Please Mr. Disc Jockey" in 1956, shot blanks for a few years and came back in the early 1960s with "Music, Music, Music" (R&B chart) and "Let Me In" (both R&B and pop charts). Another fairly successful group was the Six Teens from the West Coast, featuring three girls and three guys. The Trudy Williams-led "A Casual Look" made both the R&B and pop charts in June 1956. Several other songs by the group were notable, namely "Teenage Promise" and "Arrow Of Love," but they couldn't recidivate on the charts.

The year 1956 also saw the debut of Chestnuts featuring Ruby Whittaker from New Haven, CT. A few nice ballads like "Love Is True" and "Forever I Vow" had little commercial success and then Ruby left the group. In this same year, a couple of one-record (no-hit) groups offered the female equivalent of schoolboy doo-wop leads. "Darling Come Back" by Pat Cordel and the Crescents (who evolved into Vito Piccone & the Elegants sans Pat) combined a shrill lead by Pat with a background that's not quite in synch with her to produce an uptempo doo-wop that somehow compels one to listen and sing along, as does the infectious "Bohemian Daddy" by the Marquis featuring lead June Bateman.

The Kodaks, one of two other important female-led groups to make their debut in 1957, really epitomized this "schoolgirl" doo-wop sound. They featured the clear, youthful voice of Pearl McKinnon and put out a series of doo-wop classics including "Little Boy And Girl," "Oh Gee Oh Gosh," "Runaround Baby" and "Teenager's Dream." Though popular in and around the New York City area, the Kodaks never charted nationally. Pearl's voice, of all the high-tenor ("Schoolboy") leads

---

20. It's like Podunk U. trying to field a football team against Penn State. Podunk draws from a pool of a couple of hundred applicants, Penn State from tens of thousands. It's not that women couldn't sing, it's just that most of them weren't singing doo-wop.

---

21. Interview with Vicki Burgess on Ronnie Italiano's "R&B Party" on Dec. 11, 1996.

Kodaks.

Tune Weavers.

that followed Frankie Lymon, most resembled the master's in quality. The other important group in 1957 was the Tune Weavers from Boston, featuring the smooth and sweet lead voice of Margo Sylvia. "Happy Happy Birthday Baby" hit top ten on both pop and R&B charts and has been a perennial "oldie" dedication song.

The practice of a female thrush being backed with a male group for one-offs or a few records continued into this period. Donna Hightower recorded "Dog Gone It," while backed by the Jacks (of "Why Don't You Write Me Fame"). Ann Cole backed by the Suburbans actually hit the R&B charts twice with "Are You Satisfied" (January 1956) and "In The Chapel" (January 1957). And Ruth McFadden recorded three great songs with a trio of groups from Hy Weiss' Old Town label; "Darling Listen To The Words Of This Song"[22] in late 1955 with the Supremes, "Two In Love (With One Heart)" in February 1956 with the Royaltones, and "School Boy" later in 1956 backed by the Harptones.

In addition to all-female groups and female leads over male groups, women were occasionally found in groups in supporting roles. The prime example of this practice is Zola Taylor of the Platters. She joined the group in early 1955, right before the group made the switch from the "indie" Federal label to Mercury (a major record company), so she was there for all of their big hits in the latter half of the decade. In the late

22. Ms. McFadden told an interesting story about how she came to record this song on Ronnie I's "R&B Party," which aired on Nov. 20, 1996. Having won four amateur shows in a row at the Apollo Theatre, she was given a prize of a connection with a record company executive, who turned out to be Hy Weiss of Old Town Records. When she got to the studio, Weiss told her to just sit there and observe, seemingly not having a lot of faith in his ward's abilities. The Supremes, an all-male studio group for Old Town, was recording "Darling, Listen To The Words Of This Song" within Ruth's earshot. "They wanted it done a certain way. They wanted 'Dah ah ahrling, I lay the whole ni-ight through.' And you know he [the lead] was a little older and he wasn't comfortable doing that kind of kid-ish thing. So he would sort of sing through it...They did it about ten times and I'm like, 'Why can't that guy just go Dah-ah-ahr...' and we're giggling...and he said, 'Who's that kid over there?' And he said, 'She came down from the Apollo...and let her show this guy how to do it.' So then they decided after a while he's not going to do it so let Ruth do it..." And the rest is her-story.

The Twenty Best Doo-Wop Songs: Groups with Female Leads (1954-57)

Artists	Song	Year	Label
Capris	God Only Knows	1954	Gotham 7304
Charmers	The Beating Of My Heart	1954	Central 1002
Mellows (Lillian Leach & the)	How Sentimental Can I Be		1954 Jay-Dee 793
Cole, Ann (with the Suburbans)	Are You Satisfied	1955	Baton 218
Mellows (Lillian Leach & the)	Yesterday's Memories	1955	Jay-Dee 807
Mellows (Lillian Leach & the)	Smoke From Your Cigarette		1955 Jay-Dee 797
Chestnuts	Love Is True	1956	Davis 447
Crescents (Pat Cordel & the)	Darling Come Back	1956	Club 1011
Marquis	Bohemian Daddy	1956	Onyx 505
McFadden, Ruth (w. the Supremes)	Darling, Listen To The Words Of This Song	1956	Old Town 1017
McFadden, Ruth (w. the Royaltones)	Two In Love (With One Heart)	1956	Old Town 1020
McFadden, Ruth (w. the Harptones)	School Boy	1956	Old Town 1030
Mellows (Lillian Leach & the)	My Darling	1956	Celeste 3002
Sensations	Yes Sir, That's My Baby	1956	Atco 6056
Sensations	Please Mr. Disc Jockey	1956	Atco 6067
Six Teens	A Casual Look	1956	Flip 315
Kodaks	Teenager's Dream	1957	Fury 1007
Kodaks	Little Boy And Girl	1957	Fury 1007
Kodaks	Oh Gee Oh Gosh	1957	Fury 1015
Tune Weavers	Happy Happy Birthday Baby	1957	Casa Grande 4037

fall of 1956, the El Venos from Pittsburgh put out "Now We're Together/Geraldine," which featured one Ann Mae Jackson as group member and part-time lead. In June of 1957, the Lovenotes made the R&B charts with a song called "United," which featured the voice of Lucy Cedeno. Lucy also went under the name Lucy Rivera to record "Make Me Queen Again" with a male group in 1959 and later married Gary "U.S." Bonds. Some other successful groups that had female non-lead members were the Skyliners (Janet Vogel) and Fleetwoods (Barbara Ellis and Gretchen Christopher), both of which began recording in early 1959.

1958-1964

A big problem in trying to deal with distaff groups in a book on doo-wop is that the songs they offered weren't too doo-woppy to begin with. First, female groups usually didn't offer much of a contrasting lower voice as was common among male groups. Although the Hearts on Baton were an exception, the breadth of voices is still not what obtains with males. Sometimes this problem was solved by having a male sing the bass line, as in "What A Guy" by the Raindrops in 1963 or, as mentioned previously, having a female lead backed by a male group, as with Baby Washington on "The Time" in 1959 or Barbara Lewis on "Hello Stranger" in 1963. Second, arrangements of most songs by distaff groups usually omitted nonsense syllables. The first Shirelles outing, "I Met Him On A Sunday" ("doo ron, day ronday ronday boppa doo ron")

and the Chiffons "He's So Fine" ("doo-lang, doo-lang doo-lang") were notable exceptions.

If a group didn't have a bass, thus having a restricted voice range, and didn't use nonsense syllables can we, by our own definition of the doo-wop style, call their material "doo-wop?" Also, how then do we distinguish them from female pop groups of the era, like the McGuires or the Chordettes? If certain female groups like the Chiffons and Cookies fall just within the boundaries of doo-wop and rhythm and blues, how do we know which groups fall just outside of these boundaries? Where are these boundaries? Since many distaff groups became popular at the end of the doo-wop era, shouldn't some of them have one foot in the era and one foot in another musical style (like the Philadelphia sound or the Motown sound)?[23]

While the questions are good, the answers are arbitrary. Listed below are all of the songs by distaff groups that made Billboard's R&B and/or Pop charts from the release of the Bobbettes' "Mr. Lee" to the end of the era. Included are all-female groups and groups with a female sound even though they may include male members (e.g. "Down The Aisle Of Love" by the Quin-Tones). We've included some groups, like the Teddy Bears and Chordettes ("Lollipop" only) because they made it onto the R&B charts and thus had some influence on doo-wop and rhythm and blues artists. In other cases, like Patti LaBelle & the Blue-Belles and Gladys

---

23. We sure ask a lot of questions, don't we?

Bobbettes.

Chantels.

Shirelles.

Knight & the Pips, we've included their earlier works which fit the genre and omitted their later stuff which doesn't. Some groups were left out altogether because they are identified with a different type of music, like pop (McGuires, Fontanes, Lennons omitted), soul/Motown (Supremes, Ruby & the Romantics and most Marvelettes omitted) and kitsch (Shangri-Las omitted). We'll begin in 1957, the year that Mr. Lee was given musical life by his Bobbettes. Following the entries below, "P" stands for Pop charts,[24] "R" for Rhythm and Blues charts[25] and numbers for peak position achieved.

24. Whitburn, Joel. *The Billboard Book of Top 40 Hits*. New York: Watson-Guptill, 1989.
25. Whitburn, Joel. *Top R&B Singles, 1942-1988*. Menomonee Falls, Wis.: Record Research Inc., 1988.

Year	Date First Charted	Artist	Song	Chart/ Hi Position
1957	8/12	Bobbettes	Mr. Lee	R1/P6
	9/16	Tune Weavers	Happy, Happy Birthday Baby	R4/P5
1958	1/27	Chantels	Maybe	R2/P15
	3/17	Chordettes	Lollipop	P2/R3
	4/7	Chantels	Every Night (I Pray)	R16/P39
	5/5	Aquatones	You	R11/P21

Year	Date First Charted	Artist	Song	Chart/ Hi Position
	7/14	Chantels	I Love You So	R14
	7/28	Poni-Tails	Born Too Late	P7/R11
	9/8	Quin-Tones	Down The Aisle Of Love	R5/P18
	10/13	Teddy Bears	To Know Him Is To Love Him	P1/R10
1959	1/5	Baby Washington (& group)	The Time	R22
	6/22	Baby Washington (& group)	The Bells	R20
	8/31	Chantels (w. Richard Barrett)	Summer's Love	R29
1960	10/10	Shirelles	Tonight's The Night	R14/P39
	10/24	Kathy Young & the Innocents	A Thousand Stars	P3/R6
	12/12	Shirelles	Will You Love Me Tomorrow	P1/R2
1961	2/6	Shirelles	Dedicated To The One I Love	R2/P3
	3/6	Cathy Jean & the Roommates	Please Love Me Forever	P12
	5/1	Shirelles	Mama Said	R2/P4
	5/29	Gladys Knight & the Pips	Every Beat Of My Heart	R1/P6
	6/5	Baby Washington (& group)	Nobody Cares (About Me)	R17/P60
	6/12	Starlets	Better Tell Him No	R24/P38
	8/14	Sensations	Music, Music, Music	R12/P54
	8/28	Shirelles	A Thing Of The Past	R26
	9/11	Chantels	Look In My Eyes	R6/P18
	10/2	Paris Sisters	I Love How You Love Me	P5
	10/23	Shirelles	Big John	R2/P21
	11/27	Crystals	There's No Othe (Like My Baby)	R5/P20
	12/4	Angels	'Til	P14
	12/11	Chantels	Well, I Told You	P29
	12/25	Gladys Knight & the Pips	Letter Full Of Tears	R3/P19
1962	1/6	Shirelles	Baby It's You	R3/P8
	1/13	Ikettes	I'm Blue (The Gong-Gong Song)	R3/P19
	2/3	Sensations	Let Me In	R2/P4
	3/3	Paris Sisters	He Knows I Love Him Too Much	P34
	3/31	Shirelles	Soldier Boy	P1/R3
	4/7	Angels	Cry Baby Cry	P38
	4/28	Crystals	Uptown	P13/R18
	5/12	Blue-Belles (aka Starlets)	I Sold My Heart To The Junkman	R13/P15
	7/7	Shirelles	Welcome Home Baby	R20/P22
	7/14	Claudine Clark & the Spinners	Party Lights	R3
	10/6	Crystals	He's A Rebel	P1/R2
	10/6	Shirelles	Stop The Music	P36
	11/10	Sherrys	Pop Pop Pop-Pie	R25/ P35
	12/1	Cookies	Chains	R6
	12/8	Bobb B. Soxx & the Blue Jeans	Zip-A-Dee Doo-Dah	R7/P8
	12/15	Exciters	Tell Him	P6/R5
	12/15	Shirelles	Everybody Loves A Lover	R15/P19
1963	1/19	Crystals	He's Sure The Boy I Love	P11/R18
	3/2	Chiffons	He' So Fine	R1/P1
	3/23	Bobb B. Soxx & the Blue Jeans	Why Do Lovers Break Each Other's Heart?	P38
	3/30	Cookies	Don't Say Nothin' Ba (About My Baby)	R3
	4/13	Shirelles	Foolish Little Girl	P4/R9
	5/11	Crystals	Da Doo Ron Ron (When He Walked Me Home)	P3/R5
	5/25	Barbara Lewis (with the Dells)	Hello Stranger	R1/P2
	6/8	Chiffons	One Fine Day	P5/R6
	6/8	Raindrops	What A Guy	R25
	6/22	Essex	Easier Said Than Done	P1/R1
	7/13	Shirelles	Don't Say Goodnight And Mean Goodbye	P26
	8/10	Angels	My Boyfriend's Back	P1/R2
	8/31	Crystals	Then He Kissed Me	P6/R8
	8/31	Patti LaBelle & the Bluebelles	Down The Aisle (Wedding Song)	R14/P37

Year	Date First Charted	Artist	Song	Chart/ Hi Position
	8/31	Raindrops	The Kind Of Boy You Can't Forget	P17/R27
	9/7	Jaynetts	Sally, Go 'Round The Roses	P2/R4
	9/7	Chiffons	A Love So Fine	R40/P40
	9/7	Shirelles	What Does A Girl Do?	R53
	9/14	Essex	A Walkin' Miracle	R11/P12
	10/5	Pixies Three	Birthday Three	P40
	10/19	Shirelles	It's A Mad, Mad, Mad, Mad World	R92
	11/2	Shirelles	31 Flavors	R97
	11/9	Angels	I Adore Him	P25
	11/9	Four Pennies	When The Boy's Happy, The Girl's Happy	R95
	11/16	Chiffons	I Have A Boyfriend	R36/P36
	11/16	Essex	She's Got Everything	R56
	11/23	Charmettes	Please Don't Kiss Me Again	R100
	11/30	Cookies	Girls Grow Up Faster Than Boys	R33
	12/7	Murmaids	Popsicles And Icicles	P3
	12/7	Secrets	The Boy Next Door	P18
1964	1/11	Shirelles	Tonight You're Gonna Fall In Love With Me	R57
	1/14	Patti LaBelle & the Bluebelles	You'll Never Walk Alone	R34/P34
	2/1	Crystals	Little Boy	R92
	3/14	Raindrops	Book Of Love	R62
	3/21	Shirelles	Sha-La-La	R69
	5/2	Dixie Cups	Chapel Of Love	R1/P1
	6/20	Jelly Beans	I Wanna Love Him So Bad	R9/P9
	6/20	Patti & the Emblems	Mixed-up, Shook-up Girl	R37/P37
	7/18	Dixie Cups	People Say	R12/P12
	7/18	Shirelles	Thank You Baby	R63
	8/1	Chiffons	Sailor Boy	R81
	8/1	Crystals	All Grown Up	R98
	9/26	Jelly Beans	Baby Be Mine	R51
	10/10	Jewels	Opportunity	R64
	10/24	Dixie Cups	You Should Have Seen The Way He Looked At Me	R39/P39
	10/31	Shirelles	Maybe Tonight	R88
	12/19	Dixie Cups	Little Bell	R51
	12/26	Shirelles	Are You Still My Baby	R91
1965	1/30	Ad Libs	The Boys From New York City	R6/P8
	4/15	Dixie Cups	Iko Iko	R20/P20

Although the above chart represents most of the best of the female sound during the post-Chantellian years, some of the good ones never made it to pay dirt. Some of the better ones that sailed in uncharted waters were "So They Say" by Nancy Lee & the Tempo-Tones (1957), "I Met Him On A Sunday" by the Shirelles (one of the greatest female doo-wops) and "Oh What A Baby" by the Tonettes (1958), "Sweet As A Flower" by Miriam Grate & the Dovers and "Make Me Queen Again" by Lucy Rivera & group (1959), "Lover's Prayer" by the Clickettes (1960), "You Can Come (If You Want To)" by the Carousels and "Stop What You're Doing" by the Viscaynes (1961), "Forever" by the Marvelettes, "442 Glenwood Avenue" by the Pixies 3, "Long Tall Sally" by Barbara Green & group (1963) and "Whenever A Teenager Cries" by Reperata & the Delrons (1964). All of these can be found in the Top 1,000 presented elsewhere in this book.

The charts yield some interesting conclusions. The first is that the "girl group sound" (GGS) didn't really start with the Chantels, as many books on the subject purport. The first release by the Chantels was in August of 1957 ("He's Gone/The Plea"), and they didn't chart until their second release "Maybe" hit in January of 1958. This record, though a classic, didn't lead to an avalanche of girl-group hits. Quite the contrary, according to the charts. Eight records featuring the GGS charted in 1958, but only three in 1959 and three in 1960 made the charts. It seems difficult then, to see the Chantels as the originators of the GGS. In a way, it was more of the same kind of thing that happened in the 1954-57 period; that is, a girl group would have a hit now and then and then fade away.

Since the rise in the number of GGS records really began in 1961, the best candidate for the originator of the sound is the Shirelles. Starting in October of 1960, and continuing through the end of 1964, the group had an almost uninterrupted string of chart appearances. Although beginning their recording career in 1958 with "I Met Him On A Sunday" and first releasing "Dedicated To

Angels.

Patti LaBelle and the Blue Belles.

Chiffons.

The One I Love" in 1959, the Shirelles made their first Top 40 appearance at the end of 1960 with "Tonight's The Night," which reached #14 R&B and #39 Pop.

Next came "Will You Love Me Tomorrow," which first charted in December of 1960 and stuck around on the charts for the next three months, hitting #1 Pop and #2 R&B. February of 1961 saw a reissue of "Dedicated..." go to #2 R&B and #3 Pop. "Mama Said" followed in May and reached #2 R&B and #4 Pop. These are impressive songs and chart positions, in case no one noticed. Then came "A Thing Of The Past" in August of 1961 (only #26 R&B) and "Big John" in October (#2 R&B, #21 Pop) before two more blockbusters: "Baby It's You" in January of 1962 (#3 R&B, #8 Pop) and "Soldier Boy" in March (#1 Pop, #3 R&B). These eight high-penetration records in a seventeen-month span seem to qualify the Shirelles as the precipitators of the GGS. Though they charted eleven more times through October of 1964, none of their issues reached the heights as before.

A second conclusion that can be gleaned from the above chart is that since 1963 was the halcyon time for the GGS, and since the Shirelles had shot their proverbial wad by this time, there must be another factor(s) accounting for this peak. That factor is Tin Pan Alley or, what we labeled in our first book, "Tin Pan Alley doo-wop." "Tin Pan Alley" was a term that dates back to around 1900.[26] Union Square in New York City was then the center of the songwriting industry and in the summer one could hear a cacophony of

Dixie Cups.

Jelly Beans.

sounds emanating from the windows of nearby buildings. When heard altogether, the tinkling pianos, some out of tune, resembled the sound of pots and tin pans rattling; hence the term "Tin Pan Alley."

Before and through the doo-wop era, Tin Pan Alley was centered around the Brill Building in New York. The composers, lyricists and record company representatives housed there turned out mainstream popular music aimed at white audiences. The Tin Pan Alley crowd was allied with ASCAP (American Society of Composers Authors & Publishers) and the major record companies (such as RCA Victor, Decca and Capitol), rather than BMI (Broadcast Music Incorporated) and the maverick smaller independent labels ("indies"). The latter group, historically, was more closely linked to black and hillbilly artists and music.

Beginning in the late 1950s, a new group of young songwriters entered the job market. These young men and women were exposed to early and mid-1950s doo-wop, rhythm and blues and rock 'n' roll, yet often had studied music theory and classical music while growing up. Not unreasonably, they developed their

own ideas about what the "modern" music of the early 1960s should sound like. For Tin Pan Alley, these ideas were new and radical. The songwriting teams of Gerry Goffin and Carole King, Barry Mann and Cynthia Weil, Jeff Barry and Ellie Greenwich, and producers like Phil Spector and the Tokens became hitmakers.

The GGS creations usually blended the doo-wop characteristics of tight harmony, bass and nonsense syllables with more complex melodies, more instrumentation (e.g., Spector's "Wall of Sound") and painstaking production practices. The songs were upbeat, the voices young, strong and innocent, and the melodies hummable. Although this cadre of music people also produced male groups (e.g. Tokens, Randy & the Rainbows), their main squeezes, so to speak, were distaff groups.[27] The GGS was put on the map by 1963.

In a way, these GGS creations foretold the way music would be created in later eras; it was produced, rather than simply recorded. The male doo-wop groups of the 1950s were allowed to do their thing. Instrumental accompaniment was added, but the sound was basically a street sound. The GGS records, after 1960, were carefully planned to sound

26. Shepherd, John. *Tin Pan Alley*. London: Routledge & Kegan Paul, 1982.

27. Squeezettes, perhaps?

a certain way. In a way, the sounds of many of these groups are interchangeable, though quite pleasing. The Chiffons sound like the Crystals sound like the Blossoms sound like Bobb B. Soxx & the Blue Jeans sound like the Jelly Beans. The subject matter was "music of celebration—of simple joy, of innocence, of sex, of life itself, at times—but most often it was a celebration of The Boy. The Boy is the central mythic figure in the lyrics of girl-group rock. He is shadowy: the boy who'll love walking in the rain, the fine fine boy, the leader of the pack, the angel baby. He is irresistible—and almost never macho. He is sensitive. He must be pursued. How to reach him?"[28]

The GGS took over the charts from 1962 to1964.

---

28. Marcus, Greil. "The Girl Groups." In Miller, Jim, Ed. *The Rolling Stone Illustrated History of Rock & Roll*, New York: Rolling Stone Press, 1980.

A look at the R&B charts shows that 15% of group doo-wop records that charted in 1961 were by all female groups or had a female lead (4 of 26). This increased to 22% in 1962 (11 of 49), then to 55% in 1963 (11 of 20), 60% in 1963 (24 of 40) and 57% in 1964 (16 of 28). The percent drops off drastically after 1964 because the female groups that charted did not sing in doo-wop style (e.g. Supremes, Shangri-Las). So the lady doo-woppers had their day in the sun, as the gentlemen doo-woppers had before them. They exited the stage gracefully, leaving it open to other musical styles. Or maybe they were yanked off.

Chapter 11

Some Idiosyncrasies of Doo-Wop

The bands called Strawberry Alarm Clock, Moby Grape, Electric Prunes and Iron Butterfly hail from the late 1960s and early 1970s, the psychedelic era of rock. Putting together words that have nothing to do with one another is a signpost of Woodstock-Generation music makers. In a similar way, the doo-wop era produced a whole slew of idiosyncrasies, some dealing with the choice of group name, others with songs chosen to record, and still others with the subject matter and titles of those songs.

As an example, doo-wop groups had a penchant for telling us, in their names, how many members they had. The Five Discs, the Four Fellows and the Three Friends are examples. In the songography presented in the back of this book, there are 121 different "Five" groups, 145 different "Fours" and 28 different "Threes." If all groups are included, that is, different editions of groups called the Four Fellows are counted separately, there are 136 "Fives," 180 "Fours" and 30 "Threes."

Another general quirk of doo-wop is that groups incorporated the suffix "-tones" or the word "Tones" in their name whenever they could. A staggering 229 groups did this and the figure burgeons to 275 when different groups with the same names, e.g. Mello-Tones (1) and Mello-Tones (2) are counted separately.

A third general characteristic is the use of the adjectives "Original" and "Fabulous" as introductions to the group name, as in the "Original Drifters" and the "Fabulous Flames." The careers of most doo-wop groups were short. "Fabulous" would often be used if and when the group tried to make a comeback well after the demand for its services had waned.[1] "Original" was often used to distinguish a group from other groups which had taken the identical name, or from splinter groups started by a departing group member (e.g., Original Cadillacs, Original Drifters). It is no wonder that confusion surrounds group identity when there are so many groups going by identical names (e.g., there are 18 groups calling themselves the "Dreamers," 15 that go by the name "Continentals," and seven groups going by the name "Accents," etc.).

The Choice of Group Name

Since most birds are natural-born singers, it's not surprising that singing groups chose to incorporate an avian into their name. As pointed out by G. A. Moonoogian,[2] this practice dates at least back to the Blackbirds of Harmony in 1926. Other groups, with names such as the Seven Musical Magpies, the Whipporwill Four, the Four Blackbirds, the Four Blue Birds and the Dixie Hummingbirds, recorded from roughly 1930 through the 1940s. This practice reached its beak (sorry, couldn't resist) beginning in the late 1940s. The heightened affinity for bird doo-woppings no doubt started with the Ravens and Orioles, who first recorded in 1946 and 1948 respectively. For these groups, the names made sense. Birds sing, ravens are black, the "Ravens" is an excellent choice for a black singing group (as was the "Ink Spots"). The Oriole is the state bird of Maryland, and Sonny Til and his friends came from Baltimore. Again, good choice. After them, however, many groups just jumped on the bandwagon and the logic behind their choice of names was for the birds. By our count, more than 40 additional groups chose a fine feathered friend to represent them. That's enough for a decent-size aviary.

Interestingly, while the Orioles are quickly connected with the state of Maryland because of the baseball team, the Baltimore Orioles, can the reader make any other connections between singing groups and states?[3] Well, the all-time champs are the Cardinals, because that bird is the state avian of seven states, namely Illinois, Indiana, Kentucky, North Carolina, Ohio, Virginia, and West Virginia. Ironically, Missouri, home of the St. Louis (baseball) Cardinals, is not on the list. The runners-up, in the group-state connection are the Meadowlarks, since that bird is the state bird of six mostly Western states, namely Kansas, Montana, Nebraska, North Dakota, and Wyoming. Other doo-wop group names that have been appropriated by states, without paying royalties, are the Bluebirds, Larks, Pelicans, Pheasants, Quails, Robins, and Wrens. A fairly complete list of bird-group names follow, in order of the first year they recorded.

Group Name	Year First Recorded
Ravens	1946
Orioles	1948
Bluebirds (The Four)	1949
Robins	1949
Cardinals	1951
Larks	1951
Skylarks	1951
Swallows	1951
Blue Jays	1953
Crows	1953

1. Actually, after they had stopped being fabulous.
2. *Record Collector Monthly*, Issue #51, July-Aug. 1992, p. 23.

3. Has anyone ever questioned why states have a "State Bird?" Why not a "State Hamster" or "State Invertebrate?"

Group Name	Year First Recorded
Flamingos	1953
Parrots	1953
Sparrows	1953
Swans	1953
Whipoorwills	1953
Buzzards (Big John & the)	1954
Eagles	1954
Feathers	1954
Hawks	1954
Parakeets	1954
Peacocks	1954
Pelicans	1954
Penguins	1954
Quails	1954
Starlings	1954
Wrens	1954
Birdies (Robert Byrd & His)	1956
Jay Birds	1956
Jayhawks	1956
Night Owls	1956
Drakes	1957
Ospreys	1957
Bobolinks	1958
Nighthawks	1958
Jays	1959
Doves	1960
Birds	1961
Nightingales	1961
Chicks (Kell Osborne & the)	1962
Hummingbirds	1962
Pheasants	1963
Ladybirds	1964
Whooping Cranes	1966
Warblers	1973
Five Vultures	1973
Owls	N/A

It had been commonly held[4] that the love of doo-wop singers for living things stopped with birds. Not even close. Young men chose to name themselves after mammals (especially felines, bears and horses), invertebrates, fictional animals and yes, even insects. A zoography follows:

Style of Animal	Group Name
Mammals:	
Felines:	Bengals (Bobby & the)/Five Cats/Jaguars/Leopards/Lions/Panthers (Charles Watson & the)/Tabbys/Tigers/Wildcats
Bears:	Bears/Bear Cats/Cubs/Honey Bears
Horses:	Chippendales/Colts/Mustangs
Miscellaneous:	Anteaters (Chuck Harrod & the)/Beavers/Dolphins/Ermines/Fawns/Foxes/Gazelles/Hound Dogs/Impalas/Jackals/Stags

Style of Animal	Group Name
Invertebrates:	Cobras/King Cobras/Neons/Reptiles (Johnny Cole & the)/ Sharks/Stingrays
Fictional/Prehistoric:	Dragons/Dyna-Prehistoric:Sores
Insects:	
Flying, non-biting:	American Beetles/Butterflys/Lady Bugs
Flying, biting:	Bees/Honey Bees/Fleas/Mosquitos
Crawling & hopping:	Crickets/Grasshoppers/Roaches/Spiders/Termites

Many groups preferred to name themselves after non-moving living things, such as flowers. This trend was started by the Carnations in 1952, and the Blue Belles and Orchids in 1953.[5] A list of groups follows:

Group Name	Year First Recorded
Carnations	1952
Blue Belles	1953
Orchids	1953
Daffodils	1955
Laurels	1955
Marigolds	1955
Blossoms	1957
Dahlias	1957
Gladiolas	1957
Hollyhocks	1957
Rosebuds	1957
Roses	1958
Goldenrods	1959
Tigre Lillies	1959
Lavenders	1960
Azaleas	1963
Bouquets	1963
Daisies	1964
Astors	1965

Aside from living things, doo-wop groups also had an affinity for dead ones like precious stones and gems. Here, the first groups to emerge were the Diamonds in 1952, and the Rubies, Crystals, and Jewels in 1953. As the trend continued, 17 gem-type names were used, representing more than 60 doo-wop groups when all were counted; that is, Rubies (1) and Rubies (2), etc. These sparkling monikers were:

Group Name	Year First Recorded
Diamonds	1952
Crystals	1953
Jewels	1953
Rubies	1953
Blue Diamonds	1954
Emeralds	1954
Gems	1954
Opals	1954
Ivories	1956

---

4. By who we're not sure.

5. Were the session producers for these groups called "floral arrangers"?

Group Name	Year First Recorded
Pearls	1956
Garnets	1957
Zircons	1957
Jades	1958
Sapphires	1958
Blue Crystals	1959
Fabulous Pearls	1959
Ivorys	1962

The tendency to name a group after the name of a car or car model was more than a trend; it became practically an obsession. Although there were several groups with car names before 1954, it was more by accident than intention. For example, although Checker was the name of a car company, the singing group called the "Checkers" was named after the game, to take advantage of the success of another "game" group, the Dominoes. In 1954, the Cadillacs began recording and, as the list below demonstrates, many other groups followed in their dust. Esther Navarro, manager of the Cadillacs, said that the name was chosen because all the good bird names were already taken and a member of the group suggested "Cadillacs" after seeing one pass by the window. Cadillacs' member Charles Brooks had another version, stating that they named the group as they did to impress the ladies. There have been worse reasons.

Cars were always an expression and reflection of the male ego, so the idea to name your group after a car that you had or desired was compelling. As the first important car group, the Cadillacs took the most prestigious name available at the time. In the early to mid-1950s, the Cadillac was considered the best car around. Lincolns and Chrysler Imperials were not as popular, the company that produced Packards was in decline, and the foreign showboats such as Jaguars, Mercedes and BMWs had not as yet made significant penetrations into the American market. This was in an age when American-made products were considered the best and anything "made in Japan" was met with derision. Paralleling the state of affairs in the marketplace, doo-wop groups chose to use the names of General Motors cars more frequently than either Chrysler or Ford products. Among cars produced abroad, British vehicles were the most popular and were also chosen most often as names for doo-wop groups. A complete listing follows.

Category	Name of Car	Group Name
General Motors:		
	Chevrolet:	Belairs/Chevelles/Chevies/ Corvairs/Corvettes/El Caminos/Impalas/Stingrays
	Pontiac:	Bonnevilles/Catalinas/ Tempests
	Oldsmobile:	Deltas/Holidays/Starfires
	Buick:	Centurys/Electras/Invictas/ Rivieras/Skylarks/ Specials/Wildcats

Category	Name of Car	Group Name
	Cadillac:	Caddys/Cadillacs/De Villes/ El Dorados/Fleetwoods
Chrysler:		
	Plymouth:	Belvederes/Furys/Satellites/ Savoys/Valiants
	Dodge:	Coronets/Rams/Royals
	Chrysler:	Chryslers/Imperials/New Yorkers/Newports/Windsors
Ford:		
	Ford:	Fairlanes/Falcons/Galaxies/ Mustangs/Thunderbirds/ T-Birds
	Mercury:	Mercurys/Meteors/Monarchs/ Montereys
	Lincoln:	Continentals/Lincolns
	Edsel:	Edsels
American Motors:		
	Nash:	Metropolitans
	Rambler:	Ambassadors/Ramblers/ Rebels/Matadors
Misc. American:		
	Studebaker:	Avantis/Hawks/ Studebaker "7"
	Packard:	Packards
	Checker:	Checkers
	Jeep:	Cherokees
	Shelby:	Cobras
Foreign:		
	(British:)	Bentleys/Healeys/Jaguars/ Phaetons/Rovers/ Sunbeams/Triumphs
	(French:)	Renaults
	(German:)	Merceedees (misspelled)
	(Italian:)	Fiats/Spiders

While there is no doubt that doo-wop groups often took their names from car models, it is conceivable that the reverse is also true. This is because car models introduced after the doo-wop era quite frequently have names that were used earlier in time by doo-wop groups. Astros (van), Blazers (all-purpose), Cavaliers, Celebrities, Citations and Suburbans (all-purpose) are all newer model Chevrolets and names of doo-wop groups. Challengers, Chargers, Darts, Diplomats, Lancers and Shadows are all names of more recent Dodge models and names of doo-wop groups. Escorts, Explorers (all-purpose), Fiestas and Tempos are newer Fords and names of doo-wop groups. Were marketing executives from Detroit hanging around on the street corners or is this phenomenon just a coincidence?

Another possibility presents itself when we examine the names of professional baseball teams. Almost half of them, or 13 out of 28, share names with doo-wop groups. There were doo-wop groups called the Angels, Astros, Blue Jays, Cardinals, Cubs, Dodgers, Mariners, Orioles, (Swinging) Phillies, Pirates, Royals, Tigers and (Hong Kong) White Sox. It just may be that some names are testosterone-friendly, that is, they attract men. Since baseball, cars and doo-wop form a cluster of interests that appeal especially to males, it is not surprising that these activities share labels.

Lest anyone think that doo-woppers were not capable of cerebral activity, many chose to name themselves after games of skill. In fact, after a long and hard practice, they were particularly gamy. There were the Checkers, Dominoes and a whole host of chess-related groups like the Chessmen, Kings, Queens, Bishops, Knights, Pawns, Castle Kings, and finally, the Checkmates.

But the man-boys of the 1950s were also geographically aware. Groups named themselves after countries from the four corners of the globe (if that is how many corners the world has). Here are five continents worth of guys that helped put doo-wop music on the map, so to speak:

Area	Group Name
Asia:	Orientals/Orients/Saigons
North America:	Canadian Meteors (Buddy Burke & the) /U.S. Four
Middle East:	Arabian Knights (Haji Baba & the)/ Arabians/Egyptians/Moroccans/ Moroccos/Persians/Persianettes/ Tunisians (Terry & the)
Europe:	Belgianettes/Bohemians/Danes/ Francettes/Gypsies/Parisians/ Romans/Scotties/Venetians (Nick Marco & the)
Caribbean:	Bermudas/Caribbeans/Carribeans/ Carribians/Cubans/Martineques/ Trinidads
South America:	Ecuadors/Equadors

In what may be an illustration of wishful thinking, many groups named themselves after action-oriented heroes, adventurous or historical characters, and even political leaders, royalty and religious leaders. Grandiosity is nine-tenths of the law. Most of these titles were macho guy-type names, before being macho was politically incorrect. A list by category follows:

Category	Group Name
Men on the Move:	Gypsies/Nomads/Phantoms/Ramblers/Roamers/Rovers/ Runarounds/Runaways/Trailblazers/Travelers/Voyagers/ Wanderers
Men of Action or War:	Conquerors/Gallant Men/Generals/ Headhunters (Cannibal & the)/Lancers/Majors/ Raiders/Rebels/Renegades/ Swordsmen
Men of the Sea:	Buccaneers/Corsairs/Gondoliers/ Mariners/Pirates/Whalers/ Yachtsmen/Yeomen
World History Guys:	Caesars/Crusaders/Explorers/Gladiators/Historians (Barbaroso& the)/ Neanderthals (Dave Meadows &the)/Pagans/Romans (Little Caesar & the)/Spartans/Trojans/ Victorians/Vikings

Category	Group Name
American History Guys:	Alamos (Sam Houston & the)/ Colonials/Deputees (Peter Marshall & the)/Minute Men/Pilgrims/ Pioneers/Posse (Marshall Laws & the)/Ravels (Sheriff & the)/Red Coats
Native Americans:	Cherokees/Mohawks/Seminoles
Spanish Culture:	Aztecs/Don Juans/Entertainers (Cortez & the)/Matadors/Toreadors
Fictional Men:	Aladdins/Casanovas/Gallahads/ Merrymen (Robin Hood & His)/Vampires
Royalty (General):	Caliphs/Egyptian Kings/Maharajahs/ Pharaohs/Rajahs/Sheiks/Sultans/ Tribunes
Royalty (Headwear for):	Coronets/Crowns/Tiaras
British/Upper Crust:	Anglos (Linda Martell & the)/Aristocrats/Duchesses/Dukes/Earls/ Gentlemen/Gentrys/Kings/ Knights/Lords/Monarchs/ Noblemen/Nobles/Parliaments/ Queens/Red Coats/Saxons/ Squires/Viscounts/Windsors
European Upper Crust:	Barons/Chancellors/Contessas/ Counts/Czars of Rhythm/Dons/ Emperors/Marquis
Leaders (General):	Champions/Champs/Imperials/ Leaders/Legends/ Majestics/Masters/Regals/Regents/ Royals/Titans/Tyrants (Terry & the)/Victors
Leaders (Business):	Bossmen/Executives/Millionaires/ V.I.P.s
Leaders (Religious):	Bishops/Creators/Disciples/Idols/ Lords/Mystics/Prophets/Saints
Leaders (Political):	Ambassadors/Consuls/Diplomats/ Premiers/Presidents/Senators/ Viceroys

Regardless of what they fantasized being, doo-wop singers were just schoolboys at heart. Actually, more than just schoolboys. The were Adolescents (Little Willie & the), Boyfriends, Boys, Four Teens, Girlfriends, Juveniles, Kids, Seventeens, Six Teens, Sixteens, Teenagers, Teenchords, Teens, Threeteens, Tots (Barry & the), Young Lads, Young Ones and Youngsters.

They were the kind of kids that went to school with a pack of cigarettes rolled up in their shirt sleeves. Perhaps that's why many groups were named after either their brand of smoke or their school affiliation. There were singing groups named the Belairs, Chesterfields, Du Mauriers, Dunhills, Kents, Kool (Gents), Newports, Salems and Winstons. There were also groups called the Academics, Class Cutters (Herbie & the), Class-Notes, Classmates, Classmen, Co-Eds, Collegians, Collegiates, Fraternity Brothers, Fraternity Men, Graduates, High School Chanters, Juniors, Minors, Notations, Notetorials, Note Makers, Pledges, Scholars, Schoolboys,

Schoolgirls, Schoolmates, Semesters, Seniors, Sophomores (Anthony & the) and Students. Rah rah rah.

Doo-Wop Songs Recorded Most Often

As part of the rock 'n' roll explosion, doo-wop groups recorded music that was lyrically and melodically quite different from what had come before. It is ironic, therefore, that the three songs most recorded by doo-wop groups had their roots in earlier eras. These three are "Over The Rainbow," written by Harold Arlen and E. Y. Harburg in 1939, "A Sunday Kind Of Love," written by Barbara Belle, Louis Prima, Anita Leonard and Stan Rhodes in 1946, and "Gloria," the provenance of which is discussed in another chapter.

"Over The Rainbow" was first recorded by Judy Garland for the movie "The Wizard of Oz" in 1939 (winning an Oscar that year for Best Song). It was initially recorded by doo-wop groups in 1954 (Castelles and Checkers) and then repeatedly throughout the doo-wop era. Sometimes the title was lengthened to "Somewhere Over The Rainbow," the lyrics simplified to fit the doo-wop style, and was usually rendered as a ballad. The most well-known doo-wop versions are by David Campanella (son of Roy Campanella, M.V.P. catcher for the erstwhile Brooklyn Dodgers) & the Delchords in 1959 and by the Demensions in 1960. The latter spent nine weeks on the *Billboard* charts, reaching number 16 in August 1960. Thirty-nine versions are listed below.

Group Name	Year	Label
Checkers	1954	King 4719
Castelles	1954	Grand 118
Dominos	1955	King 1502
Moroccos ("Somewhere...")	1956	United 193/B&F 193 (1960)
Del Vikings ("Somewhere...")	1957	Luniverse 106
Echoes	1957	Specialty 601
Mondellos (Yul McClay & the)	1957	Rhythm 105
Satisfiers	1957	Coral 61788
Chanters (Bud Johnson & the)	1958	DeLuxe 6177
Hi-Liters	1958	Hico 2433/Zircon 1006
Buddies (Little Butchie Saunders & the)	1959	Angle Tone 535
Delchords (David Campanella & the) ("Somewhere...")	1959	Kane 25593
Emjays	1959	Paris 538
Imperials (Little Anthony & the)	1959	End LP 303/End EP 204 (1959)
Baysiders	1960	Everest 19366
Demensions	1960	Mohawk 116/Coral 65559 (1966)
Delrons	1961	Forum 700
Guys (Little Sammy Rozzi & the)	1962	Pelham 722
Original Checkers	1962	King 5592
Tones (Little Sammy & the)	1962	Pelham 722/Jaclyn 1161
Vibrations	1962	Checker 1002
Darchaes (Nicky Addeo & the)	1964	Selsom 104
Lytations (a capella)	1964	Times Square 107
Young Ones (a capella)	1964	Times Square 104

Group Name	Year	Label
Aztecs (Billy Thorpe & the)	1965	GNP Crescendo 34
Blue Belles (Patti LaBelle & the)	1965	Atlantic 2318
Five Fashions	1965	Catamount 103
Mustangs	1965	Vest 8005
Hamiltons (Alexander & the)	1966	Warner Bros. 5844
Portraits	1968	Sidewalk 935
Admirations	1972	Kelway 108
Kac-Ties (a capella)	1975	Kape 702/Relic LP 108
Image	1982	Clifton 68
Deja-Vu	1984	Starlight 22
Mystics	1987	Collectables LP 5043
Marcels	N/A	Monogram 113
Monarchs	N/A	Reegal 512
Remainders	N/A	Vico 1
Ricquettes (Danny Skeene & the)	N/A	Valex 105/106

"A Sunday Kind Of Love" was first recorded by Jo Stafford for Capitol records in 1947. Paleo-doo-wop ballad versions were released in 1953; the great Harptones' rendition on Bruce and one by Bobby Hall & the Kings on the Jax label. In 1957, the Del Vikings put out an up-tempo arrangement that caught on and made the song a doo-wop standard (especially for a cappella groups) even though no rendition has ever charted in the *Billboard Top 40*. Since then, renditions have been roughly equally divided into slow and up-tempo numbers. Twenty-seven versions are listed.

Group Name	Year	Label
Harptones	1953	Bruce 101/Raven 8001 (1962)
Kings	1953	Jax 320 (Bobby Hall & the)
Del Vikings	1957	Mercury 30112
Highlanders	1957	Ray's 36
Sentimentals	1957	Mint 802
Lambert, Rudy	1958	Rhythm 128 (with the Lyrics)
Gothics	1959	Dynamic 101
Winters, David	1959	Addison 15004 (& group)
High Seas	1960	D-M-G 1001/D-M-G 4000
Heard, Lonnie	1961	Arliss 1008 (bb the Halos)
Marcels	1961	Colpix LP 416
Mystics	1961	Laurie 3104
Regents	1961	Gee LP 706/Forum Circle LP
Persians	1962	RTO 100
Rapid-Tones	1962	Rapid 1002 (Willie Winfield & the)
Roommates	1962	Cameo 233
Camelots	1963	AAnko 1004
El Sierros	1963	Yussels 7702
Timetones	1963	Times Square 26
Devotions	1964	Roulette 4556
Excellons	1964	Bobby 601/Old Timer 601 1964)
Five Shadows	1965	Mellomood 011/012
Bees (Honey & the)	1968	Arctic 158
Emery's	1977	Clifton 19
Blue Moons	N/A	Jaguar 1001

Group Name	Year	Label
Earls	N/A	Harvey 100
Statics (Lynn & the)	N/A	Mantis 101
Themes	N/A	Ideal

While the third most-recorded song, "Gloria," is discussed in detail elsewhere, the story of how Esther Navarro penned a modern version which was based on Leon Rene's earlier version points out another recurrent theme in doo-wop; the practice of "borrowing" parts of songs. Groups practiced in close proximity to each other, some singers practiced with more than one group, many singers had relationships that crossed over and through group lines. Record executives, group managers and even composers worked in close proximity to each other, they often took advantage of the naivete of the group members and the failure to copyright. The practice of borrowing was tolerated, if not accepted. In this way, "I Wonder Why," the song that established Dion & the Belmonts in 1958, was partly borrowed from "I Don't Know" by the Casanovas in 1956 and "Now I'm Telling You" by the Legends, also in 1958. What goes around comes around, because "I Wonder Why" itself was transparently copied by Dino & the Diplomats in their 1961 song, "I Can't Believe." We can't either, Dino.

In the same way, most of "I Do Love You" by Tex & the Chex in 1961 was more closely "borrowed" from "My Darling To You" by the Bop Chords in 1957; and "Dreams Come True" by the Earls in 1974 is an exact, though up-tempo, replica of "Teenager's Dream" by the Kodaks in 1957.

Incidentally, other "standards" popularized in previous eras were also favorites with the doo-wop set. The songography in this book contains 15 versions of "The White Cliffs Of Dover" (written by Nat Burton and Walter Kent in 1941) emanating from World War II, and "Stormy Weather" (Harold Arlen and Ted Koehler in 1933), and 17 versions of "Blue Moon" (written by Richard Rogers and Lorenz Hart in 1934).

The Subject Matter of Doo-Wop Songs

Detectives glean information from clues, garbologists deduce much about the way a family lives by examining their refuse, and much can be inferred about the doo-wop generation by examining the subjects of their songs. To begin, doo-woppers were wild about jungles. This trend is easily traced to the novelty song, "Stranded In The Jungle," which was released in 1956 by the Jayhawks, Cadets, and Gadabouts. Edgar Rice Burroughs' Tarzan, played in movies by fine specimens of manhood Buster Crabbe and Johnny Weissmuller, enjoyed widespread popularity, and television shows such as "Ramar Of The Jungle" entertained the adolescents of the 1950s. Songs with "Jungle" in the title soon proliferated. Songs without the word "Jungle," but conveying similar messages, also were heard, as in "Dancin' In The Congo" (by the Chandeliers in 1958) and "Tarzan's Date" (by the Chuck-A-Lucks in 1961), "The Lion Sleeps Tonight" (by the Tokens in 1961), "Bongo Stomp" (by Little Joey & the Flips in 1962), and "(Native Girl) Elephant Walk" (by Donald Jenkins & the Delighters in 1963). Six "Jungle" songs made our Top 1,000, namely "Stranded In The Jungle" (by both the Jayhawks and Cadets), "Rockin' In The Jungle" (Eternals), "Bongo Stomp," "(Native Girl) Elephant Walk," and "The Lion Sleeps Tonight." The complete list of "Jungle" songs includes:

Group Name	Song	Year	Label
Cadets	Stranded In The Jungle	1956	Modern 994
Gadabouts	Stranded In The Jungle	1956	Mercury 70898
Jayhawks	Stranded In The Jungle	1956	Flash 109
Five Quails	Jungle Baby	1957	Mercury 71154
Flips (Kip Tyler & the)	Jungle Hop	1958	Challenge 59008
Raiders	Walking Through The Jungle	1958	Brunswick 55090
Shadows	Jungle Fever	1958	Del-Fi 4109
Starlettes	Jungle Love	1958	Checker 895
Channels	Jungle Lights	1959	Mercury 71501
Eternals	Rockin' In The Jungle	1959	Hollywood 68/ Musictone 1111 (1961)
Fabulous Pearls	Jungle Bunny	1959	Dooto 448
Individuals	Jungle Superman	1959	Show Time 595/ Show Time 598 (1959)/Red Fox 105
Playboys	Jungle Fever	1959	Rik 572
Dyna-Sores	Jungle Walk	1960	Rendezvous 120
Passions	Jungle Drums	1960	Audicon 106
Romancers	Jumpin' Jungle	1960	Palette 5067
Vibrations	Stranded In The Jungle	1960	Checker 982
Concepts	In The Jungle	1961	Apache 1515/ Musictone 1109 (1961)
Five Cashmeres	Walkin' Through The Jungle	1961	Golden Leaf 108
Cap-Tans (Wailing Bethea & the)	Rockin' In The Jungle	1962	Hawkeye 0430
Casanovas	Deep In The Heart Of The Jungle	1962	Planet 1027
Legends	Jungle Lullabye	1962	Caldwell 410
Mystics (Ed Gates & the)	In The Jungle	1962	Robins Nest 2

Group Name	Song	Year	Label
Grand Prees	Jungle Fever	1963	Candi 1020
Apostles	Stranded In The Jungle	1966	A-Square 401
Velvet Angels	Jungle Fever (a capella)	1972	Relic LP 5004
Starlites	Bop Diddle In The Jungle	N/A	Claremont 959

Another passion of the doo-wop generation was exotic women.[6] The foreign women who were celebrated most often in song were Spanish-speaking. While Spanish maidens were regaled in other musical eras, as in "In A Little Spanish Town" from 1926, "Lady Of Spain" from 1931 and "The Rain In Spain" from 1956, they were omnipresent in the doo-wop years.

They were addressed as "senorita" if the swain did not know her, and usually had the name "Juanita" if he did. She was almost invariably from south of the border, down Mexico way. Other Spanish-speaking countries were only occasionally visited. The Mexican senorita represented well the idealized version of love so prominent in songs of the doo-wop era. Infatuation and chauvinism are common themes in these songs. A selected list of songs of this type follows.

6. This should not shock the reader to any large extent.

Group Name	Song	Year	Label
Diablos	Adios My Desert Love	1954	Fortune 509/510
Penguins	Hey Senorita	1954	Dootone 348/Power 7023 (1954)
Rivileers (Gene Pearson & the)	Hey, Chiquita	1954	Baton 200
Dootones	Ay, Si, Si	1955	Dootone 366
Robins	Smokey Joe's Cafe	1955	Spark 122/Atco 6059 (1956)
Swans (Paul Lewis & the)	Little Senorita	1955	Fortune 813
Champions	Mexico Bound	1956	Chart 611
Coasters	Down In Mexico	1956	Atco 6064
Echoes	ye Senorita	1956	Combo 128
Four Wheels	Adios, My Pretty Baby	1956	Spin-It 108
Royaltones	Latin Love	1956	Old Town 1028
Belvin, Jesse (& group)	Senorita	1957	Modern 1013
Crests	My Juanita	1957	Joyce 103/Musictone 1106 (1962)
Magic Tones	Spanish Love Song	1957	Howfum 101
Rocketones	Mexico	1957	Melba 113
Five Discs	Adios	1958	Callo 202
Holidays	Never Go To Mexico	1958	Music City 818
Bell Notes	Old Spanish Town	1959	Time 1010
Impressions	Senorita I Love You	1959	Abner 1025
Kappas	Sweet Juanita	1959	Wonder 1012
Royal Holidays	Down In Cuba	1959	Herald 536
Wonders	Hey Senorita	1959	Ember 1051
Caronators	Senorita	1960	Clock 1045/Clock 227
Mastertones (Scotty & Bobo & the)	Mamacita Mia	1960	Band Box 238
Skyliners	Lorraine From Spain	1960	Calico 114
Blue Chips	Adios, Adios	1961	RCA 7935
Catalinas	Hey Senorita	1961	Zebra 101
Schoolboys (Professor Hamilton & the)	Juanita Of Mexico	1961	Contour 0001
Swinging Hearts	My Spanish Love	1961	620 1002
Drifters	Mexican Divorce	1962	Atlantic 2134
Locomotions	Adios My Love	1962	Gone 5142
Wanderers	Run Run Senorita	1962	United Artists 570
Delighters (Donald & the)	Adios My Secret Love	1963	Cortland 112
Magnatones	Adios My Desert Love	1963	Fortune 555
Nutmegs	Down In Mexico	1963	Times Square 27
Serenaders	Adios My Love	1963	Riverside 4549
Travelers	Spanish Moon	1963	Princess 52/Vault 911
Visuals	My Juanita	1963	Poplar 117
Hollywood Flames	Dance Senorita	1965	Symbol 211
Kents	My Juanita	1965	Relic 1013
Valids	Hey Senorita	1966	Amber 853
Tokays	Hey Senorita	1967	Brute 001
Heartspinners(Dino & the)	Hey Senorita	1973	Bim Bam Boom 119
Heartspinners (Dino & the)	Mexico	N/A	Starlight 11
Jades	Hey Senorita	N/A	Adona 1445
Royal Ravens	Grand Spanish Lady	N/A	Mah's 0015

A second group of exotic women that were exalted by the doo-wop generation came from the Orient. Usually the orient-ation was Chinese, but Japanese ("Fuji Womma") and Korean ("Ichi-Bon Tami Dachi") settings appear. Most often the maiden spoke Chinese, frequently called Hong Kong home, and was duly servile and obedient. Sometimes, the damsel can be heard speaking "Chinese" in the background, except it really sounded like a male in falsetto muttering gibberish (e.g., "Hong Kong" by the Quinns and "My Chinese Girl" by the Five Discs). These efforts symbolized the ultimate in male-domination fantasies. Males in these Oriental odysseys were often wise or had special powers, as in "Ling Ting Tong" by the Five Keys or "Rang Tang Ding Dong" by the Cellos. A selected list follows.

Group Name	Song	Year	Label
Five Keys	Ling Ting Tong	1954	Capitol 2945
Rovers	Ichi-Bon Tami Dachi	1954	Music City 750/Capitol 3078 (1955)
Charms	Ling Ting Tong	1955	DeLuxe 6076
Rays	Moo Goo Gai Pan	1955	Chess 1613
Blue Jays	Ling Ting Tong	1956	Dig EP 778
Downbeats	China Doll	1956	Gee 1019
El Dorados	Chop Ling Soon	1956	Vee Jay 197
Hi-Fives	Hong Kong	1956	Flair-X 3000
Ray-O-Vacs	Hong Kong	1956	Kaiser 389
Cellos	Rang Tang Ding Dong	1957	Apollo 510
Glad Rags	My China Doll	1957	Excello 2121
Three Friends	Chinese Tea Room	1957	Lido 504
Columbus	China Girl	1958	Esta 290/Ransom 101 (1958)/ Paradise 109 (1958)
Hy-Tones	Chinese Boogie	1958	Hy-Tone 120
Peppers	Yoko Hoko Homa	1958	Jane 105
Premiers	China Doll	1958	Cindy 3008
Quinns	Hong Kong	1958	Cyclone 111
Five Discs	My Chinese Girl	1959	Dwain 6072/Dwain 803 (1959)/ Mello Mood 1002 (1964)
Quarter Notes	Suki-Yaki-Rocki	1959	Whizz 715
Revels	Foo Man Choo	1959	Norgolde 104
Four Steps (Benny Williams & the)	Mamie Wong	1961	N/A
Lincolns	Sukiyaki Rocki	1961	Bud 113
Masquins (Tony & the)	Fuji Womma	1961	Ruthie 1000
Tellers (Artie Banks & the)	Oriental Baby	1961	Imperial 5788
Tabbys	Hong Kong Baby	1963	Metro 2
Bermudas	Chu Sen Ling	1964	Era 3125
Q's (Bruce Clark & the)	Went To Chinatown	1964	Hull 762
Channels	Old Chinatown	1965	Groove 0061
Pixies	Geisha Girl	1965	Autumn 12
Royaltones	Hong Kong Jelly Wong	1985	Murray Hill LP 000083
Fabulous Persians	Ling Ting Tong	N/A	Bobby-O 3123
Master Four	Love From The Far East	N/A	Tay-Ster 6012

Although the country was at peace for most of the doo-wop era, the Korean War and World War II were not yet forgotten. Phil Groia's book on the New York doo-wop groups notes that many group members left their singing careers in midstream to join the service, voluntarily or involuntarily. Being before Vietnam, the 1950s were years of unabashed patriotism. The songs written by and for doo-wop groups often reflected this patriotism by addressing soldiers and sailors in song as buddies or loved ones. This was nothing new in the twentieth century. George M. Cohan's "Over There" and Irving Berlin's "Oh! How I Hate To Get Up In The Morning" stemmed from World War I, and "Praise The Lord And Pass The Ammunition," (recorded by the Southern Sons in 1942) "(There'll Be Bluebirds Over) The White Cliffs Of Dover," (1941, recorded by Lee Andrews and the Hearts and the Checkers in 1954), "Boogie Woogie Bugle Boy" (Andrews Sisters, 1941), "Comin' In On A Wing And A Prayer" (Four Vagabonds, 1943) came out of the World War II era.

Ironically, a couple of the best records of this type, "Good Goodbye" by the Bob Knight Four (1961) and

Group Name	Song	Year	Label
Marshalls (Bill Cook & the)	A Soldier's Prayer	1951	Savoy 828
Question Marks	Another Soldier Gone	1954	Swing Time 346
Violinaires	Another Soldier Gone	1954	Drummond 4000
Four Fellows	Soldier Boy	1955	Glory 234
Williams, Mel (& group)	Soldier Boy	1955	Federal 12236
Five Echoes	Soldier Boy	1956	Vee Jay 190
Stags	Sailor Boy	1958	M&S 502
Tassels	To A Soldier Boy	1959	Madison 117/ Amy 946 (1966)
Interludes	White Sailor Hat	1960	Valley 107
Cavaliers (Little Bernie & the)	Lonely Soldier	1962	Jove 100
Debelaires	So Long, My Sailor	1962	Lectra 502
Dootones	Sailor Boy	1962	Dooto 471
Hallmarks	My Little Sailor Boy	1962	Dot 16418
Illusions	Lonely Soldier	1962	Mali 104/ Sheraton104/ Northeast 801
Shirelles	Soldier Boy	1962	Scepter 1228
Shondelles	Don't Cry My Soldier Boy	1962	King 5597
Soldier Boys	I'm Your Soldier Boy	1962	Scepter 1230
Montells	Soldier Boy, I'm Sorry	1963	Golden Crest 582
Chiffons	Sailor Boy	1964	Laurie 3262
Kisses (Candy & the)	Soldier Baby (Of Mine)	1965	Cameo 355
Shirelles	(Mama) My Soldier Boy	1965	Scepter 12123 Is Coming Home
Chantels	Soul Of A Soldier	1966	Verve 10387
Echoes	Soldier Boy	N/A	4 Hits EP 11
Marie, Elena (& group)	Soldier Boy	N/A	Gee Bee 01

"Pray For Me" by the Four Pharaohs (1957), don't mention a soldier or sailor in the title.[7] A partial list of soldier/sailor songs follows. Roughly three-quarters address soldiers, the remaining quarter address sailors, and an inordinate number of these songs are rendered by distaff groups.

Few people realize that doo-woppers were also amateur campanologists; that is, they loved bells of any sort. Especially favored in titles of songs were chapel bells, church bells, wedding bells (do we detect a trend?) and school bells. There are "The Bells Of St. Mary's" (by the Drifters, Lee Andrews & the Hearts, and Tokens), "The Bells Of Rosa Rita" (Admirations), "The Bells Of Love" (Pearls, Mint Juleps, Terri & the Velveteens), "The Bells Of My Heart" (Fascinators), and "The Bells Of Joy" (Angelo & the Initials). The bells whisper (so say the Del Vikings and a slew of others), ring out (L' Cap-Tans and Van Dykes) and even whistle (School Belles). There are well more than 100 songs with "Bells"

in the title contained in the songography of *Doo-Wop: The Forgotten Third...*, and many appear in our Top 1,000 (e.g. "The Bells Of Rosa Rita" by the Admirations, "Whispering Bells" by the Del Vikings, "Lullaby Of The Bells" by the Deltairs, "Chapel Bells" by the Fascinators, "Wedding Bells" by Tiny Tim & the Hits and "Church Bells May Ring" by the Willows).

Of course, the doo-wop generation had a serious side as well. Many songs were written and sung about characters, real and fabled. Those who gravitated to doo-wop evidently had quite an interest in both American history and American literature. "Christopher Columbus" was recorded by the Paramounts, "George Washington" by the Toppers, "The Ballad Of Betsy Ross" by the Bachelors, "Paul Revere" and "The Ride Of Paul Revere" by the Furness Brothers and Terracetones, respectively (the American Revolution must have been a particular favorite), "Pony Express Riders" by Shadoe & the Highbrows and "A Prayer at Gettysburg" by the Velvitones. The works of the American novelist Washington Irving were celebrated by no less than five groups in "Rip Van Winkle" (Devotions, Nutmegs, and Adventurers), and in "The Legend Of Sleepy Hollow" (Monotones and Carnations). Herman Melville's "Billy Budd" was offered by the Montereys.

---

7. "Good Goodbye" contains, "Uncle Sam is calling me, From way way beyond the sea, Grab your coat and grab your pack, You know you'll be coming back..." "Pray For Me" pleads, "Pray for me, so I'll return safe and free."

Other doo-wop groups took us on a tour of "recorded" history. "Adam And Eve" was offered by the Mystics, "The King Tut Rock" by Kenny & the Socialites, "Romeo And Juliet" by the Reflections and Starlets, "Cleopatra" by Bobby Sanders & the Performers, Precisions and Bobby Capri & the Velvet Satins, "Come Back Cleopatra" by the Top Notes, "Caesar Haircut" by Tammy James & group (the aforementioned six records may also imply a latent interest in Shakespeare), "Casanova" by Erlene & the Girlfriends and "Napoleon Bonaparte" by the Top Notes.

Detectives of the era were celebrated, as in "Mr. Moto" by Nino & the Ebbtides, "Charlie Chan" by the Eventuals and "Dick Tracy" by the Chants. Television shows and personalities were regaled in "Our Miss Brooks" by the Goofers, "Mr. Dillon, Mr. Dillon" by the Fiestas (the show was "Gunsmoke"), "Steve Allen" by the Emperors, "Clarabel" by Vince Anthony & the Bluenotes ("The Howdy Doody Show") and "Mister Magoo" by the Kodoks.

Teens of the fifties loved cowboys, monsters, and comic strips, and all of these interests were well-reflected in song. There was "The Masked Man (Hi-Yo Silver)" by Eddy Bell & the Bell- Aires, "The Lone Stranger" by the Majestics and Del Counts, "The Lone Teen Ranger" by Jerry Landis (& group), "Dodge City" and "Western Mov-ies" by the Olympics, "Wyatt Earp" by the Marquees and "Billy The Kid" by the Raves. Monsters crept into "Dead Man's Stroll" by the Revels, "Frankenstein's Den" by the Hollywood Flames, "Frankenstein's Party" by the Swinging Phillies, "Miss Frankenstein" by George Jackson & the Uniques, "You Can Get Him-Frankenstein" by the Castle Kings, "The Mummy's Ball" by the Verdicts and "Screamin' At Dracula's Ball" by the Duponts. "Popeye" was performed by the Dreams and Enchantments and "Popeye The Sailor Man" by the Gaylads. "Superman Lover" was released by Andy & the Marglows, "Jungle Superman" by the Individuals and "He's My Superman" by the Sweethearts. The story of "Alley Oop" was recounted by Dante & the Evergreens, the Hollywood Argyles and the Dyna-Sores.

Perhaps reflecting the innocence of the times, nursery rhymes were also accorded inordinate attention by doo-wop lyricists. Old MacDonald, Humpty Dumpty, Mary Had A Little Lamb and Hickory Dickory Dock were favored subjects. Other songs that had nursery rhyme subjects, but not titles (such as "Little Star" by the Elegants, which is related to "Twinkle Twinkle Little Star" and "Great Big Eyes" by the Rivieras, which is derived from "Goldilocks") are not included in the following list:

Group Name	Song	Year	Label
Five Keys	Old MacDonald Had A Farm	1952	Aladdin 3118
Bradford Boys	Little Boy Blue	1955	Rainbow 307
Bonnie Sisters	Little Bo Peep	1956	Rainbow 336
Errico, Ray (with the Honeytones)	Humpty Dumpty Rock	1956	Masquerade 56003
Five Stars	Humpty Dumpty	1956	Atco 6065
Jumpin' Jacks (Danny Lamego & the)	Hickory Dickory Rock	1956	Andrea 101
Shaweez (Big Boy Myles & the)	Hickory Dickory Dock	1956	Specialty 590
Orlandos	Old MacDonald	1957	Cindy 3006
Chargers	Old MacDonald	1958	RCA 7301
Emperors	Nursery Rhyme	1958	3-J 121
Gems	Nursery Rhymes	1958	Win 701
Ricardos	Mary's Little Lamb	1958	Star-X 512
Schoolmates (Colleen & the)	Mairzy Doats	1958	Coral 62024
Bluedots	Mary Had A Rock 'n' Roll Lamb	1959	Hurricane 104
Elegants	Little Boy Blue	1959	Hull 732
Five Sparks	Little Bo Peep	1959	Jimbo 1
Ideals (Johnny Brantley & the)	Mary's Lamb Checker 979 (1961)	1959	Checker 920/
Isley Brothers	Rockin' MacDonald	1959	Mark-X 8000
Troupers	Peter, Peter, Pumpkin Eater	1959	Red Top 118
Lions	Hickory Dickory	1960	Imperial 5678
Magnatones	MacDonald's Rock	1960	Cedargrove 313/ Time108 (1960)
Emblems	Poor Humpty Dumpty	1962	Bay Front 107
Rock-A-Byes (Baby Jane & the)	Hickory Dickory Dock	1962	Spokane 4001
Selectones (Jay Jay & the)	Humpty Dumpty	1962	Guest 6201/6202
Aladdins	Simple Simon	1963	Witch 111
La Donna, Marie (& group)	Georgie Porgie	1963	Gateway 730
Nobletones	Rock And Roll Nursery Rhymes	1973	Vintage 1014
Kingsmen	Humpty Dumpty	N/A	Arnold 2106

We hope you've enjoyed the tour of the foibles of the doo-wop generation. To see whether you've been paying attention, see if you can solve the following puzzle. Hidden below are the names of 45 bird groups. See how many you can find. The solution can be found in the Appendix.

For The Birds

S	H	B	S	D	C	Q	S	W	O	R	R	A	P	S	C	B	B	K	S
P	K	B	U	E	R	R	H	A	W	K	S	O	C	H	I	L	F	L	S
P	H	N	C	Z	L	A	O	J	A	Y	S	A	I	R	U	O	A	D	S
U	E	E	I	W	Z	O	K	W	O	F	N	C	D	E	U	N	R	K	R
S	X	N	A	L	H	A	I	E	S	Z	K	I	J	R	I	I	W	A	S
E	S	W	G	S	O	O	R	R	S	S	E	A	B	D	B	A	V	I	K
L	G	A	B	U	A	B	O	D	O	S	Y	L	R	Y	H	E	W	Z	Y
A	N	R	S	K	I	N	O	P	S	S	U	A	D	Y	N	W	R	U	L
G	I	B	N	Z	G	N	T	B	I	E	C	A	A	S	Y	I	E	S	A
N	L	L	A	F	G	E	S	S	B	N	L	J	I	S	D	C	N	E	R
I	R	E	W	B	A	S	S	I	N	F	G	J	S	S	N	Q	S	V	K
T	A	R	S	G	Y	R	R	I	S	N	L	C	A	T	L	I	Q	O	S
H	T	S	L	E	E	D	G	T	S	P	I	A	R	Y	O	I	B	D	Y
G	S	E	R	H	S	H	E	N	B	U	E	G	M	A	B	R	A	O	B
I	S	P	T	L	T	E	A	I	O	H	M	A	H	I	N	I	R	U	R
N	S	A	S	H	K	C	R	R	S	L	W	O	C	T	N	E	R	A	Q
O	E	K	A	A	I	D	L	A	R	K	S	F	W	O	O	G	S	D	P
F	V	W	R	L	S	S	W	A	L	L	O	W	S	L	C	W	O	Y	S
T	K	A	E	W	H	I	P	O	O	R	W	I	L	L	S	K	L	S	J
S	P	P	I	L	S	D	R	I	B	G	N	I	M	M	U	H	S	S	W

BIRDIES	FLAMINGOS	NIGHTINGALES	RAVENS
BIRDS	FOUR BLUEBIRDS	ORIOLES	ROBINS
BLUE JAYS	HAWKS	OSPREYS	SKYLARKS
BOBOLINKS	HUMMINGBIRDS	OWLS	SPARROWS
BUZZARDS	JAY BIRDS	PARAKEETS	STARLINGS
CARDINALS	JAYHAWKS	PARROTS	SWALLOWS
CHICKS	JAYS	PEACOCKS	SWANS
CROWS	LADYBIRDS	PELICANS	WARBLERS
DOVES	LARKS	PENGUINS	WHIPOORWILLS
DRAKES	NIGHT OWLS	PHEASANTS	WHOOPING CRANES
EAGLES	NIGHTHAWKS	QUAILS	WRENS
FEATHERS			

Chapter 12

Doo-Wogeography

This chapter will trace the geographical patterns of the groups that made the music we've come to love. Here, we are concerned mostly with the geographical patterns and much less with the sociological or financial reasons for said patterns (because those have or will be dealt with elsewhere). The discussion will deal with the period 1930 to 1954, by which time distinct and separate "sounds" emerged. To describe and trace these separate regional sounds, "guest authors" were invited to contribute their views. But first things first...

Without a doubt, the hub of doo-wop activity in the 1990s is the New York to New Jersey to Philadelphia axis. There are more oldies record stores in this area, more concerts, and more impassioned fans than anywhere else in the country. That is not to say that Chicago, Los Angeles and even Pittsburgh and New England have ignored the doo-wop calling, but the center of the doo-wop world resides somewhere along the New Jersey Turnpike (which for non-northeasterners, connects New York to Philadelphia). It would make sense and achieve parsimony then, if it turned out that the doo-wop sound was born and bred in this fertile musical plain, symbolized so poignantly by the Statue of Liberty, the Nathan's hot dog, and the smell of oil refineries. That's not the way it worked out, though, and, given our obligation to provide nothing but the truthful course of events, it shall be told like it is, or was.

First, a few guidelines about influence. In order for a group to be influenced by other singers, those influencing singers had to be heard. This could happen in two ways. The influences could either grow up in the same neighborhood or city as an influencing group and hear their output directly, or they could hear them as a result of their making a record (radio play or record sales). This may seem trivial, but barring the local influence theory, the influencers not only had to record, they had to be reasonably popular. The higher they made it on the charts, the more times their records were played or bought, the more they could be heard, the more they could influence.

So a recording date for a particular record merely carves in stone how much influence a group has incorporated into their music. A release date only indicates the date after which a group could, emphasis on could, influence others. No influence will occur unless the record receives good air play.

The importance of neighborhood influence cannot be overestimated. When Frankie Lymon & the Teenagers hit it big in 1956, there were a whole host of groups that followed with the schoolboy style. And quickly. And all from the same area of the United States, within a 15-mile radius of Sugar Hill (upper Manhattan in New York City). The groups, among others, were Louis Lymon & the Teenchords, Schoolboys, Desires, Elchords, and Bobby Rivera & the Hemlocks. The similarity of the sound and the geographical proximity imply that many young kids heard of or saw the Teenagers directly. While it is true that the success of the Teenagers also brought ambitious label owners out of the woodwork looking for copy groups, the place they looked, and the place where they struck paydirt, was in the Teenagers' back yard.

Further, information traveled much more slowly back then. When doo-wop was coalescing in the late forties, there was no television to speak of and no computers. It took roughly fifteen years (1948-1963) for doo-wop to run its full course. Given the way information (and, of course, music) spreads in the current age, doo-wop could have evolved into and out of existence in a year or two in the 1990s. The longevity of the doo-wop genre relative to today's musical styles may account for the undying loyalty of its fans. One feels closer to a music that one has spent one's entire youth with, than one does to a music that has only been around for a few haircuts.

1930-1945: The Pre-doo-wop Years

Given this introduction, the groups from the 1930-1945 era that had an influence on the formation of the doo-wop style were the Mills Brothers (who first recorded in 1931), Boswell Sisters (1931), the Ink Spots (1935), Charioteers (1935), Golden Gate Quartet (1937), Andrews Sisters (1937), Cats & the Fiddle (1939), Deep River Boys (1940), Delta Rhythm Boys (1941), Four Vagabonds (1942), Five Redcaps (1943), Coleman Brothers (1944), and Brown Dots (1945).

An examination of the Billboard Rhythm & Blues and Pop charts of the era yields some interesting data. As reported in "Joel Whitburn's Top R&B Singles, 1942-1988," the *Billboard's* record charts began as the "Harlem Hit Parade," which tallied record sales in large Eastern cities. These charts only reported roughly ten songs per week, so that the total number of records is fairly small. And though the period of our interest is from 1930-1945, the charts only existed from 1942 on.

With these qualifications, data show that between 1942 and 1945, 30 group records made the charts. Of these, 13 were by the Ink Spots (5 of which were with Ella Fitzgerald), 5 by the Mills Brothers, 4 by the Five Red Caps, 3 by the Andrews Sisters, and one each by the Four Vagabonds, Ella Fitzgerald with the Four Keys, Ella with the Delta Rhythm Boys, the Royal Harmony Quartet and the Southern Sons. These last two groups leaned toward gospel and they both charted with the same topical, World War II song, "Praise The Lord And Pass The Ammunition."

Influential Groups: 1930-1945

On the pop charts, as presented in "Joel Whitburn's Pop Memories, 1890-1954," the names of the groups are familiar. Since these charts cover the full range of years (1930-1945) and present somewhere between 20 and 30 songs per week, the totals are much greater. The Andrews Sisters made the pop charts 51 times between 1930 and 1945, the Mills Brothers had 36 chart hits, the Ink Spots 34 and the Boswell Sisters 20. The only other "race" groups to make the pop charts for these years were the Four Vagabonds (three times), Charioteers and Five Red Caps (once each).

Although most of these groups came to the big cities to record, the places where the groups were formed were frequently more rural. The geographical birthplaces for the groups mentioned above can be found in the map above. Note that there is not much of a pattern to the scatter. The Midwest is well-represented and there are contributions from the New York area, Virginia, as well as the West Coast. Many of the groups were outgrowths of family musical traditions (Mills, Boswells, Andrews and Colemans) and quite a few formed through college choral groups (Deltas, Deeps and Charioteers).

1946-1951: The Coalescence of the Doo-Wop Era

The most important rhythm and blues groups that emerged during the years following the second World War (in temporal order) were the Four Tunes (who first recorded in 1946), Four Knights (1946), Ravens (1946), Dozier Boys (1948), Orioles (1948), Blenders (1949),

Robins (1949), Dominoes (1950), Clovers (1950), Four Buddies (1950), Cap-Tans (1950), Hollywood Flames (1950), Five Keys (1951), Five Royales (1951), Swallows (1951), Vocaleers (1951), Cardinals (1951), and Larks (1951). In general, these groups had a less pop-oriented sound than those of the earlier era.

Fifty-six group records made *Billboard's* R&B charts for the years 1946-1951. Of these, 13 were by "old timers," namely the Mills Brothers (6), Ink Spots (6), and Charioteers (1). Of the 43 remaining, the Ravens placed 10, the Orioles 7, the Four Tunes (aka Sentimentalists), Herb Lance & the Classics and the Dominoes 3 apiece, the Robins, Clovers, Jubilaires and Larks 2 apiece. Groups placing one each on the charts were the Andy Love Quartet (with Ella Fitzgerald), the Dixieaires, the Four Jacks, the Shadows, the Five Blind Boys, Four Buddies, Swallows, Five Keys and Cardinals.

On *Billboard's* Pop Charts, stalwarts like the Andrews Sisters, Mills Brothers and Ink Spots continued to sell well, with 39, 14, and 12 chart hits respectively. By comparison, the newer, up-and-coming, "blacker" sounding groups had difficulty penetrating the white pop charts. From 1946-1951, the Four Knights and the Billy Williams Quartet placed three songs each, and the Four Tunes, Orioles, Ravens, and Dominoes placed one each.

A look at the map on the next page reveals a coalescing of the breeding grounds for groups along the Eastern seaboard. There are a few outliers, especially on the West coast, but most of the influential groups of

Influential Groups: 1946-1951

the era are from the New York metropolitan area, the Baltimore-Washington D.C. area and the Virginia-North Carolina area. These groups virtually all report being influenced by the Mills Brothers and Ink Spots and were generally younger when they hit the charts than were the groups from the 1930-1945 era. The trend toward youth in rhythm and blues vocal group members (that culminated with schoolboy doo-wop in the mid-1950s) began in this period.

Since the members were younger on average, the groups tended to form in high school (Clovers, Swallows, and Five Keys) rather than college, and/or form in the local neighborhoods (Orioles, Cardinals, and Vocaleers). It is during this period that "singing on the streetcorners," a pastime inextricably linked with the doo-wop era, began in earnest. Most of these groups came from urban areas with no shortage of streetcorners. While most of the young singers began singing in their local church, the North Carolina groups, the Four Knights, Larks and "5" Royales, began as actual gospel groups.

1952-1953: A New Trend Emerges

During the 1930-1945 period, the singing groups that presaged the doo-wop style came from all over the country. There were groups from the large metropolitan centers such as New York and Chicago, but also groups from more rural areas of Virginia, Ohio and Indiana. Then the 1946-1951 period saw a concentration of emerging groups from the Atlantic seaboard, from the Carolinas, through Baltimore and D.C., up to New York.

The trend that appeared in the years 1952 and 1953 was a further concentration of the emergence of (what by now can clearly be called) doo-wop groups into the larger metropolitan areas of New York, Chicago, and Los Angeles. These years witnessed the first recordings by eminent New York groups like the Checkers, Crows, Drifters, Five Crowns, Harptones, and Willows; Chicago super groups like the Moonglows (who began to form in Louisville and became complete in Chicago), Flamingos, and Spaniels (actually nearby Gary, Indiana); and outstanding Los Angeles groups like the Flairs and Platters. The first groups of significance to come out of Philadelphia also first recorded in 1953, but the Baltimore-D.C. area, which was such an important player in the 1946-1951 era (if not the most important), was rather quiet. This geographical trend is displayed in the map below.

The reason for this concentration of groups may lie with the centralization of the recording industry. The independent record companies, especially the larger ones, were concentrated in New York, Chicago, and Los Angeles. In the early years, the record companies would send representatives with tape recorders out to the hinterlands. As soon as the word got out that records were being cut in the big cities, the talent went to the companies, rather than the other way around. Thus Harvey Fuqua and Bobby Lester went from Louisville to Chicago and Dean Barlow came to New York from Detroit to find fortune and fame.

Further, the general migration of black families from the South to the Northern urban areas to find work, also resulted in the establishment of night clubs and radio programs catering to their tastes. This exposed local youth to the prospect of becoming famous through singing. There are numerous stories of groups of young singers seeking out, chasing, and even pestering record company personnel to audition them. With talented locals

Groups Emerging in 1952 & 1953

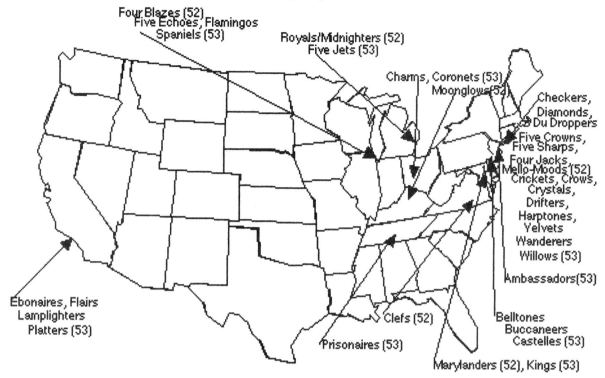

Four Blazes (52)
Five Echoes, Flamingos
Spaniels (53)

Royals/Midnighters (52)
Five Jets (53)

Charms, Coronets (53)
Moonglows (52)

Checkers,
Diamonds,
Du Droppers
Five Crowns,
Five Sharps,
Four Jacks,
Mello-Moods (52)
Crickets, Crows,
Crystals,
Drifters,
Harptones,
Velvets
Wanderers
Willows (53)

Ambassadors (53)

Ebonaires, Flairs
Lamplighters
Platters (53)

Clefs (52)

Prisonaires (53)

Belltones
Buccaneers
Castelles (53)

Marylanders (52), Kings (53)

offering group sounds that were fresh and new, there was little incentive to look elsewhere for artists.

While these groups began recording in 1952 or 1953, very few of them had chart hits this early. For example, of the 37 group records that made *Billboard's* R&B Charts in this time frame, only nine were by these groups. The Du Droppers and Four Blazes charted twice, and the Coronets, Crickets, Drifters, Royals, and Spaniels each charted once.

Geographical Styles: 1954

The tendency of groups to concentrate in the larger cities continued into 1954. New York, Los Angeles, Chicago and Philadelphia, taken together, produced an immense number of singing groups that recorded for the first time in this year. The year 1954 produced the Cadillacs, Chords, Solitaires, and Valentines from New York, the El Dorados and Five Chances from Chicago, the Capris and Lee Andrews & the Hearts from Philadelphia, and Penguins and Vernon Green & the Medallions from Los Angeles.

The concentration of talent and sheer numbers of singers in these four cities resulted in the emergence of different styles. In effect, the singers in each town knew each other, often played ball with each other, and competed against one another. They were frequently friends and sometimes rivals. The black cultures of Harlem and Sugar Hill, South and West Philly, the South Side of Chicago and South L.A. produced inbred styles that became quite distinct from one another. For a few years, these styles became more and more discernible.

Wrens.

Valentines.

Heartbeats.

Cadillacs.

Harptones.

Solitaires.

Moonglows.

El Dorados.

Flamingos.

Magnificents.

Dells.

Platters.

Penguins.

Hollywood Flames.

Jayhawks.

Cadets.

Castelles.

Flairs.

Lee Andrew/Hearts.

Blue Notes.

Little Joe and the Thrillers.

Silhouettes.

The differences in the way groups sang in Los Angeles, Chicago, Philadelphia, and New York lasted for quite a few years. Since most deejays and record companies were geographically nepotistic, giving an edge to local groups and sounds, teen-agers actually heard slightly different doo-wop music, depending upon where they grew up. Philly teens heard more shrill tenors, Chicago kids heard more mournful ballads and bluesier jumps, Los Angelenos grew up on looser harmonies, and New Yorkers heard more schoolboy and gang sounds. A Philadelphia youngster grew up loving the Capris, Billy and the Essentials, and the Four J's, groups not well-known outside that city. The Orchids, Five Chances, and Delighters were fairly successful in Chicago, but conundrums to New Yorkers. The Fascinators, Ladders, and Legends were legends in New York, but not elsewhere. And the Native Boys, Premiers, and Squires had West Coast hits, but their success was geographically limited.

To compensate, somewhat, for not having grown up in different areas of the country simultaneously, we've solicited help. First, we sought out knowledgeable people who grew up in each of the four major areas under discussion, namely New York, Philadelphia, Chicago, and Los Angeles, and asked them to describe their music. Their task was to tell us about the rhythm and blues and/or doo-wop created in their fair cities, to help us to distinguish it from music created elsewhere, and to give us a set of 50 representative songs.

1954: The Emergence of Geographical Styles

In addition, we've recruited two others to report on the Baltimore-Washington D.C. sound and on the Southern sound. The Capitol area was very important in the late 1940s and early 1950s, providing us with a whole host of beautiful, mournful ballads by groups like the Orioles, Cardinals, Swallows, and Four Buddies. These are the groups that developed and bequeathed to us the form of the R&B ballad that evolved into the "rockaballad" format in the mid-1950s (when the backbeat got stronger).

The "southern" sound is an amalgamation of sounds that come from a variety of places like Nashville, the shore area of Virginia, and even Texas. As such, it's hard to characterize in one dimension. The overall sound is less sophisticated than the big cities, there's often more guitar, and the lead often has a southern twang. This "rockabilly meets doo-wop" approach provides an interesting contrast to the Big Four. The reader will note in all six essays, that although the styles of the writers differ, in each case the author's passion for the sound comes through in their writing.

Please be a little bit wary though, because unlike the present reader and current authors, they're not perfect. Or rather, because they grew up in different places listening to different doo-wop records, their opinions may not be the same as ours. Aside from a few big records that made a nationwide impact, many of the songs that scored in one city went unnoticed in others. So if their opinions seem very different from

what the reader expects, it probably had to do with "filters" like "doo-wop-colored glasses" or even "Philadelphia-colored glasses."

An extreme example of this effect was reported by Peter Brown, an author and writer for the Copley News Service.[1] Peter grew up in New Mexico and Texas, and his exposure to rhythm and blues was through the cover records of Gail Storm, Pat Boone, and the Crew Cuts. He never heard black versions of his favorites songs, despite listening to local radio stations and frequenting local record stores. When he heard the real McCoy as an adult, he was floored. Peter maintained that he and his friends would certainly have bought the originals had they had the opportunity to do so. With these warnings, let us present our guest doo-wogeographers.

Bob Bosco, representing Philadelphia, has been a prolific contributor to fanzines past and present, including *Record Collector's Monthly* and the still-published *Echoes Of The Past*. Steve Propes, a denizen of Los Angeles, is an author of many books on our music (including *Those Oldies But Goodies*, *What Was The First Rock And Roll Record*, and his latest (*L.A. R&B Vocal Groups and Duets, 1945-1965*), has also contributed to fanzines and has worked as a deejay. Bob Pruter has written a few books himself (*Doo-Wop: The Chicago Scene and*

---

1. Phone conversation of Feb. 19, 1997. Peter called to interview us for an article he was doing on doo-wop. Turnabout is fair play.

Chicago Soul), as well articles on the subject, and serves as R&B editor for *Goldmine* magazine. Ron Italiano, aside from being the President of the United In Group Harmony Association, has deejayed, written, talked about, produced, and recorded the music for many years, and appears in many other places in this text. Ron speaks to the New York sound. Nay Nasser, covering the Capitol area, has been a deejay both there and in New England, and has written extensively for rhythm and blues periodicals such as *Echoes of the Past*. Gordon Skadberg, also a deejay, has recently annotated two CDs on Southern Doo-Wop (among others) for Ace Records. These guys are all heavyweights in the rhythm and blues and doo-wop field. In fact, if we gathered all the books, articles and liner notes that these guys have written, laid the pages end to end in a straight line...we'd get a lot of funny looks. Enjoy.

My Name is Nay and I Played the Groups in Baltimore

by Nay Nasser

As a longtime collector of the group sound, I have long recognized and appreciated the subtle distinctions between groups from different areas of the country. My roots and initial influence (my "sound buds") came from New York, but career moves to the West Coast, Philadelphia and Baltimore enabled me to develop insight and appreciation for the distinctive sounds and styles of these areas.

While residing five years in Baltimore, I hosted a radio show which I named "Echoes of the Past." This weekly three-hour excursion into the roots of group harmony provided the opportunity to not only share my music, but to learn how the Baltimore-Washington D.C. region differed in group harmony.

Several social and economic factors merged to create the Baltimore/D.C. group sound. As early as 1950, both Baltimore and the District were becoming predominantly black urban centers. The exodus from the agricultural South to the industrialized North produced a talent base that blended the Gospel and Blues with secular influences indigenous to the Mid-Atlantic region Much like other cities, the streetcorners of Baltimore and Washington were the spawning ground for local talent. However, the lack of local record labels, at least in the early 1950s, forced groups to bus up to New York City in search of fame and fortune. Some of the local groups who were able to secure a recording contract in New York City were: the Orioles (from Baltimore, with Jubilee), the Clovers (D.C., Atlantic), the Cardinals (Baltimore, Atlantic), the Rainbows (D.C., Red Robin), the Plants (Baltimore, J.&S.), the Four Buddies (Baltimore, Savoy) and the Marylanders (Baltimore, Jubilee). The Swallows from Baltimore signed with King Records in Cincinnati, while the District's Five Blue Notes recorded for the Chicago-based Sabre label.

What this region lacked in major record labels, it more than made up for with its answer to New York's

Apollo Theater. Both Washington's Howard Theater and Baltimore's Royal Theater were major stops on the so-called "Chitlin Circuit" and were primary venues to showcase local and regional talent. Unlike New York, which produced large numbers of white, as well as black vocal groups, the Mid-Atlantic region was a much more prolific environment for black vocal groups. This is a personal observation, but the black groups were more numerous and arguably better.

Some other influences that forged this distinctive group sound were Lillian Claiborne and Max Silverman, both white business owners/entrepreneurs operating in black urban environments. Claiborne was a Washington record store proprietor and owner of D. C. Records. She was the District's answer to Detroit's Devora Brown of Fortune Records. Silverman owned the Quality Record Shop in Washington and was a purveyor of local talent. To this day, you can still find "Waxie Maxie" record shops throughout the region.

Like other urban centers, the disc jockeys of Baltimore and Washington were major factors in promoting and influencing the sound. Some of the more prominent deejays were: Jack Gale, Buddy Deane, Mary Dee, Hot Rod Hulbert, and Fat Daddy from Baltimore, and Billy Fox and Al Jefferson from D.C.

The 1960s signaled the emergence of numerous local record labels in both the District and Baltimore. Although few national hits resulted, a number of labels produced gems for local collectors of group sounds. In Washington, there was Rumble, Start, Monument, Bale, PAC, D.C. Shrine, Winn, and Norwood, while Baltimore had YRS, Little D, Wedge, Monumental, Lookie, Century, Chesapeake, Marshall, Jalo, Jay Wing, Jett, Don But, and Bay Sound.

This fertile metropolitan area produced some of the finest vocal groups and sounds that this country has put to wax. The group records from 1951-1956 emanating from this region are generally characterized by a bluesy, melancholy mood on the ballads, while the uptempo sides do not generally have the sax break that shows up regularly on the New York sound. Early efforts by the Orioles, Clovers, and Swallows seem to fit these generalizations. Once you get to 1957 and later, the Baltimore/Washington groups tend to sound much like their New York counterparts, at least stylistically.

I will attempt to list my favorite 50 vocal group records by groups from this region. My favorite group sounds come primarily from the 1957-1963 era. If you expect to see a lot of national hits or well-known group records, you've come to the wrong place.

Thanks to all my friends in the Baltimore/D.C. area for making me feel welcome, training me and, most importantly, letting me return home.

Baltimore/D.C. Artists on Non-Local Labels

1. Swallows: Beside You/You Left Me (1952), King 4225
2. Orioles: Crying In The Chapel/Don't You Think I Ought To Know (1953), Jubilee 5122

3. Four Buddies: My Mother's Eyes/Ooh-Ow (1953), Savoy 888

4. Magic-Tones: When I Kneel Down To Pray/Good Home "Googa Mooga" (1953), King 4665

5. Ramblers: Vadunt-Un-Va-Da Song/Please Bring Yourself Back (1954), M.G.M. 11850

6. Cardinals: The Door Is Still Open/Misirlou (1955), Atlantic 1054

7. Rainbows: Mary Lee/Evening (1955), Red Robin 134

8. Clovers: Devil Or Angel/Hey Doll Baby (1956), Atlantic 1083

9. Sonnets: Why Should We Break Up/Please Won't You Call Me (1956), Herald 477

10. Plants: Dear I Swear/It's You (1957), J&S 1602

11. Bachelors: After/You Know You Know (1957), Poplar 101

12. Sam Hawkins: King Of Fools/The Watchamacallit (1958), Gone 5042

13. Starlighters: I Cried/You're The One To Blame (1959), End 1049

14. Cruisers: Crying Over You/Don't Tease Me (1960), V-Tone 214

15. Twylights: Darling Let's Fall In Love/I'm Gonna Try (1961), Rock'n 102

16. Van McCoy: That's How Much You Mean To Me/I Wantcha Back (1961), Rock'n 100

17. George Jackson & the Unisons: Watching The Rainbow/Miss Frankenstein (1962), Lescay 3006

18. Trueleers: Waiting For You/Forget About Him (1962), Checker 1026

19. Van Dykes: Stupidity/King Of Fools (1962), Atlantic 2161

20. Billy Stewart: Wedding Bells/True Fine Lovin' (1962), Chess 1835

21. Connie Christmas: What A Night What A Morning/Big Chief (1962), Checker 1015

22. Freddy Owens: Bye Bye Baby/What Kind Of Heart (1962), Bethlehem 3036

23. Paramounts: Shedding Teardrops/In A Dream (1963), Ember 1099

24. Belairs: Where Are You/Tell Me Why (1963), X-Tra 113

25. Brenda & the Tabulations: Dry Your Eyes/The Wash (1967), Dionn 500

Local and Regional Groups on Local and Regional Labels

26. Twilighters: Please Tell Me You're Mine/Wondering (1953), Marshall 702

27. Kings: Angel/Come On Little Baby (1958), Jalo 203

28. Little "D" & the Delighters: Oh My Darling/A Love So Fine (1958), Little "D" 1010

29. Coolbreezers: The Greatest Love Of All/Eda Weda Bug (1958), Bale 101

30. Truetones: Honey Honey/Whirlwind (1958), Monument 4501

31. Kings: Surrender/Hold Me (1959), Jay Wing 5805

32. Napoleon Tyce: Sitting Here/Paper Doll (1960), Norwood 105

33. Gales: I Love You/Squeeze Me (1960), Winn 916

34. Kenny Hamber: Tears In My Eyes/Do The Hully Gully (1960), Spar 101

35. Kings: I Want To Know/Bump-I-Dy Bump (1960), Lookie 18

36. Marvells: For Sentimental Reasons/Come Back (1961), Winn 1916

37. Goldentones: I'm So Lonely/If I Had The Wings Of An Angel (1961), Y.R.S. 1001

38. The Kid: Sleep Tight/True Love (1961), Rumble 1347

39. Curly Bridges & Motley Crew: A Prayer Of Love/Yeah Let's Fly (1961), D.C. 0436

40. Senators: Wedding Bells/I Shouldn't Care (1962), Winn 1917

41. Tippie & the Clovermen: Please Mr. Sun/Gimme Gimme Gimme (1962), Stenton 7001

42. Goldentones: Without You/Journey Bells (1962), Y.R.S. 1002

43. Satisfactions: We Will Walk Together/Oh Why (1962), Chesapeake 610 44. Four Jewels: Johnny Jealousy/Someone Special, (1963), Start 638

45. Little Hooks & the Kings: Count Your Blessings/How To Start A Romance (1963), Century 1300

46. Vic Marcel: Come Back To These Arms/That's My Girl (1963), Don But 17349

47. Veltones: I Want To Know/My Dear (1964), Wedge 1013

48. Larks: Love You So/Love Me True (1965), Jett 3001

49. Ebbtides: Come On And Cry/Straightaway (1965), Monumental 520

50. Bleu Lights: Forever/They Don't Know My Heart (1968), Bay Sound 67003

New York City Rhythm & Blues Vocal Groups

by Ronnie I.

Before talking about the roots of R&B vocal groups in the New York City area, I must first lay the foundation. The birth of R&B vocal group harmony should be credited to the South. Most of the members of the pioneer groups, who settled in New York City during the late 1940s and early 1950s migrated from Washington, D.C., Baltimore, Virginia, the Carolinas, and Georgia. Included in this category are members of legendary groups like the Ravens, Dominoes, and Larks.

The release of "It's Too Soon To Know," by the Orioles out of Baltimore, in 1948, marked the beginning of pure rhythm and blues four-part ballad harmony. The Orioles, consisting of Sonny Til, George Nelson, Alexander Sharp, Johnny Reed, and guitarist Tommy

Gaither, were the innovators of the R&B vocal group sound, a sound that influenced thousands of black youngsters in urban areas throughout the country.

New York City had become a mecca for R&B music, with all the major record companies setting up their main offices there. New York had the record companies, the recording studios, the R&B nightclubs, and the most prestigious of all the concert halls on the "Chitlin' Circuit," the Apollo Theater. Thus the "Big Apple" became a magnet for talented black singers looking to find that proverbial "pot of gold."

Even established groups had to travel from their homes to New York City, to record in their company's recording studio. Groups such as the Five Keys, from Newport News, VA, and the Five Royales, from Winston-Salem, NC, were just two of many groups to visit New York's Beltone Recording Studio, at 4 West 31st St. Beltone was the studio used to record the Keys and Royales, as well as for many other great R&B groups. Don't look for Beltone today, though, for it no longer exists.

Now that I've stressed the importance and impact of non-New York groups on the pioneer vocal group scene, let's get into the New York City area (which includes New York City, New Jersey, and Connecticut) home-born, home-bred, and honest-to-goodness R&B vocal groups.

The Apollo Theater became a showcase for R&B artists and groups by the early 1950s. It provided a major route for the R&B gospel to be spread. Its location was naturally ideal for Harlem youngsters, who frequented the Apollo, to see their heroes in such groups as the Orioles, Ravens, Five Keys, Dominoes, Cardinals, Four Buddies, Larks, Five Royales, etc.

Teen-agers began to congregate on street corners, in hallways and alleys, to imitate those Apollo Theater celebrities, whose recordings were so accessible in local record stores. The easiest way for a youngster to gain prestige in his neighborhood, become popular with the girls, and possibly make a little money while having fun, was to be discovered by a representative of one of the local independent record companies. The rapidly growing marketability of vocal groups resulted in frequent contract-signing by many of these "street-corner troubadours."

The Red Robin record label was one of New York City's first major independent black labels, a pioneer of the New York sound. Mr. Bobby Robinson founded Red Robin in 1951, introducing the Mello-Moods, Velvets, and Vocaleers, as well as Fred Parris' first group, the Scarlets from New Haven, CT. Robinson entered the music scene in 1946 with Bobby's Record Shop, one of Harlem's first retail record stores. Other Robinson-owned labels that produced local R&B group hits were Whirling Disc, Fury and Fire. Among his stable of stars were local teen-age groups like Earl Lewis and the Channels, Lewis Lymon and the Teenchords, Pearl McKinnon and the Kodaks, and Jackie and the Starlights. Robinson's first #1 hit record came in 1959, with Wilbert Harrison's "Kansas City."

Other pioneer independent record companies from the early 1950s that developed the New York sound were Bruce, which had the Harptones; Old Town, which had the Solitaires; Rama with the Crows; Rainbow with the Five Crowns; Allen with the Five Willows; Baton with the Rivileers; Jay-Dee with the Crickets; and Josie with the Cadillacs. The years 1951 through 1954 were the era of pure R&B vocal harmony in New York City. It was an age of innocence, when the arrangements were simple and stressed the vocals, as opposed to the instruments. Real-life stories of women, liquor, lack of money and jobs, were some of the every-day problems put on wax.

Enter Alan Freed in 1954, who came from Cleveland to the New York radio scene, and who brought an end to the age of R&B vocal harmony innocence. Freed, always the opportunist, took advantage of the country's most prestigious, powerful and influential radio region; the New York City metropolitan area. Freed called it "rock 'n' roll" instead of "rhythm and blues." He was the major force in repackaging black groups for white audiences, by effecting the beat in their recordings (rock 'n' roll was here to stay). This closed the door on pioneer groups such as the Ravens, Orioles, Dominoes, Larks, Clovers, etc., unless they incorporated the rock 'n' roll-style beat into their music.

Freed's greed for money and power finally took its toll on him with the Payola scandal in 1959. His heavy drinking also hastened his downfall and eventually contributed to his death. Freed was once quoted during an interview on the "Ted Steel Hour" as saying, "Rock 'n' roll is just a fad. It will soon pass and teen-agers will turn their energy towards better music." To be fair, however, Freed was unintentionally instrumental in the success of many of our legendary groups, including the Moonglows and Flamingos.

The years 1954 and 1955 brought a change to the New York sound, from simplicity to complexity, from pure to enhanced, from meager to generous, and from "race" music to music accepted by whites. At this time, the New York City area was involved in a musical expansion. The vocal group sound had achieved eminence. Small independent record companies were springing up everywhere, with groups continually getting opportunities to record. What once was an adult market turned into a market for teen-agers, with the youngsters monopolizing both the recording field and the buying practices.

The years between 1955 and 1959 were the most successful and popular period for vocal group harmony in New York. Major pop labels started to turn their attention to these upstart teen-age vocal groups. MGM, RCA, Decca, Capitol, and Mercury could no longer ignore the rock 'n' roll and R&B market. After the previous success of labels like Atlantic, Aladdin and King, many, many smaller independent companies were gradually making a large impact on the lucrative record-buying market.

Some New York labels and their New York groups during this period were Apollo with the Keynotes, Vocaltones and Cellos, Atlas with the Fi-Tones and Parakeets,

Coed with the Crests and Rivieras, Cub with the Wanderers, Ember/Herald with the Five Satins, Nutmegs and Mello-Kings, End with the Chantels and Imperials, Everlast with the Charts, Gee with the Cleftones and Teenagers, Glory with the Four Fellows, Gone with the Dubs and Channels, Holiday with the Bop-Chords, Hull with the Heartbeats and Avons, Johnson with the Shells, Joyce with the Gaytunes, Crescents and Crests, J&S with the Climbers and Hearts, Melba with the Willows, Onyx with the Velours, Rama with the Wrens and Valentines, Winley with the Paragons and Jesters, as well as the aforementioned Bobby Robinson-owned labels, Whirlin' Disc and Fury. With these groups and their recording companies enjoying vast success on the R&B and Rock 'n' Roll charts, New York was the musical center of the world during this period.

The end of 1955 brought us what is now considered the most distinctive form of the New York sound. Enter 12-year old Frankie Lymon and the Teenagers, a kiddie lead with an adolescent group anchored by a "forced" bass voice (a youngster trying to sound more mature). Frankie Lymon was the best, and the first to gain popularity. Other local groups that enjoyed success with the New York kiddie sound in the mid-1950s were Lewis Lymon and the Teenchords and Pearl McKinnon and the Kodaks on Fury, the Schoolboys on Okeh and the Cubs on Savoy.

The late 1950s brought the less complicated harmonies of the white group sound to New York. Two of the premier groups were Dion and the Belmonts from the Bronx and Vito Piccone and the Elegants from Staten Island. Although the Mello-Kings from Mt. Vernon were already on the scene, they didn't have the recognizable "white sound."

By the early 1960s, with the vocal group sound quickly losing its popularity, a slow transition period started. New York City was no longer the king-pin of the recording industry. Many of the major recording companies had set up their main headquarters in California. Soul music was starting to make an impact on the music scene. New York's most prominent group during this period was the Jive Five from Brooklyn, featuring Eugene Pitt, a throwback to the groups of the 1950s, with some soul added in. While I'm on the subject of Brooklyn, let me mention two more pioneer groups that did not record for New York labels, but that were important to the foundation of the New York sound. These were the Strangers and Hurricanes, both of which were auditioned by and recorded for the King label out of Cincinnati.

The hobby of collecting vocal group records gained serious credibility in New York in the 1960s, spearheaded by Slim Rose and his Times Square Record Shop. Some thirty-odd years later, the hobby still thrives, perhaps on a smaller scale. The music survives, also perhaps on a smaller scale. The New York City metropolitan area is once again the mecca for vocal group harmony music. In addition, there are small pockets of people enjoying the music in other parts of the country, especially in California and Florida, where there are many who transferred from New York. However, in the New York City area, it remains a part of life, it is a religion.

In the beginning, New York didn't have its own sound, instead being influenced by the R&B feel of the Orioles, the gospel wailings of the Dominoes and the pop sound of the Ravens. In the 1950s, New York developed its own sound, being more polished than the high-tenor sound of Philadelphia or the bluesy sound of Chicago. Lead singers were sweet tenors, and the songs had a lot more bass riffs and introductions. The New York sound "keyed" or leaned on the bass, which was used not as a lead, but to keep the tempo. The falsetto lead was also more present in New York in the 1950s than anywhere else, as in the songs of the Paragons, Jesters, Charts, Ladders, Mello-Harps and Legends, before it was taken over by the California groups in the 1960s. And of course, the kiddie sound was a New York original.

Much of the credit for the survival, preservation and exposure of vocal group harmony music should go to the United In Group Harmony Association of Northern New Jersey, minutes from New York City. UGHA was formed in 1976 to achieve the above goals, and now boasts a worldwide membership of 2,000 plus. The organization holds meeting-shows-socials on the last Friday or Saturday of every month (over 225 over the last 20 years) in North Bergen, NJ, a stone's throw away from the Lincoln Tunnel. UGHA is responsible for the reformation of many of the pioneer R&B groups, who frequently entertain at shows or the annual Hall of Fame bash held in New York City to honor the legendary groups. Against all odds, UGHA has survived for a longer span of time than the music it was designed to represent. The organization receives no funding, instead depending on support from those who love the music. Like you and me.

Ronnie I's Top 50 New York City Metropolitan Area Group Records

1. Diamonds: A Beggar For Your Kisses (1952), Atlantic 981
2. Harptones: I'll Never Tell (1953), Bruce 101
3. Crickets: For You I Have Eyes (1953), MGM 11507
4. Mello-Moods: Call On Me (1953), Prestige 799
5. Vocaleers: Is It A Dream (1953), Red Robin 114
6. Velvets: I (1953), Red Robin 122
7. Rivileers: Eternal Love (1954), Baton 205
8. Master-Tones: Tell Me (1954), Bruce 111
9. Coins: Blue, Can't Get No Place With You (1954), Gee 10
10. Mellows: How Sentimental Can I Be (1954), Jay-Dee 793
11. Teardrops: The Stars Are Out Tonight (1954), Josie 766

12. Strangers: Blue Flowers (1954), King 4709

13. Solitaires: Wonder Why (1954), Old Town 1000

14. Solitaires: Please Remember My Heart (1954), Old Town 1006

15. Crows: Miss You (1954), Rama 30

16. Wrens: Beggin For Love (1954), Rama 53

17. Fi-Tones Quintette: It Wasn't A Lie (1955), Atlas 1051

18. Five Crowns: God Bless You (1955), Gee 1011

19. Concords: Candlelight (1955), Harlem 2328

20. Nutmegs: Ship Of Love (1955), Herald 459

21. Heartbeats: Crazy For You (1955), Hull 711

22. Cadillacs: Window Lady (1955), Josie 778

23. Twilighters: Little Did I Dream (1955), MGM 55011

24. Harptones: Life Is But A Dream (1955), Paradise 101

25. Harptones: My Success (It All Depends On You) (1955), Paradise 103

26. Four Fellows: Loving You Darling (1956), Glory 250

27. Bop-Chords: Castle In The Sky (1956), Holiday 2601

28. Heartbeats: Your Way (1956), Hull 716

29. Heartbeats: A Thousand Miles Away (1956), Hull 720

30. Solitaires: Nothing Like A Little Love (1956), Old Town 1032

31. Velours: My Love Come Back (1956), Onyx 501

32. Valentines: Woo Woo Train (1956), Rama 196

33. Continentals: Dear Lord (1956), Whirlin' Disc 101

34. Love Letters: Walking The Streets Alone (1957), Acme 714

35. Sunbeams: Please Say You'll Be Mine (1957), Acme 109

36. Dubs: Don't Ask Me To Be Lonely (1957), Gone 5002

37. Avons: Baby (1957), Hull 722

38. Legends: The Legend Of Love (1957), Hull 727

39. Gaytunes: I Love You (1957), Joyce 101

40. Crests: Sweetest One (1957), Joyce 103

41. Hurricanes: Priceless (1957), King 5042

42. Keytones: Seven Wonders Of The World (1957), Old Town 1041

43. Velours: This Could Be The Night (1957), Onyx 515

44. Heartbeats: Everybody's Somebody's Fool (1957), Rama 231

45. Matadors: Vengeance (1957), Sue 700

46. Paragons: Let's Start All Over Again (1957), Winley 220

47. Jesters: Please Let Me Love You (1957), Winley 221

48. Du Mauriers: All Night Long (1958), Fury 1011

49. Channels: My Love Will Never Die (1959), Fury 1021

50. Sonics: This Broken Heart (1959), Harvard 801

Chicago Doowop

by Robert Pruter

Chicago will always be overshadowed by the five boroughs of New York as a cultural seed-bed for doowop groups. The Metropolitan area was such a colossus from its two natural advantages—being the center of the recording industry and possessing an urban population of some eight million. No city could match New York's production of countless numbers of African-American, Puerto Rican, Italian-American, and Jewish teen-agers during the 1950s who stood on the street corners to create the rock 'n' roll harmony sounds we today call doowop. New York was the world center of doowop music.

Yet as one of the hinterland cities, Chicago's contribution to doowop was considerable. When one hears a typical New York doowop group, one thinks of the music as a style of early rock 'n' roll—the Cadillacs, Frankie Lymon and the Teenagers, and innumerable greasy groups such as the Paragons, Channels, and Charts come to mind. But upon hearing many a Chicago group, one hears something a bit different. A touch of gospel, a touch of blues, and an earthier feeling overall, so that one senses that what is being heard is not a rock 'n' roll, but a proto-soul recording.

The Chicago groups—unlike many groups in the South, notably the Larks and the Five Royales—were not simply gospel groups who merely secularized their lyrics with rhythm and blues themes. Rather, they were streetcorner groups like those in New York, but because they came straight up the Mississippi from the deep South—the heart of the deep gospel and blues sounds—their take on doowop is a bit more flavored by blues and gospel influences.

Chicago groups were not at first streetcorner groups. In the early 1950s, many of them, such as the Flamingos, Five Chances, and Five Echoes, sang in clubs. The first record company in the Windy City to make an impact on the doowop scene was Chance, which pioneered recordings by the three previously mentioned groups, as well as those by the Moonglows (not counting a wretched effort in Cleveland). The groups at Chance reflected the type of material vocal groups were recording all over the country at the time. They did not typecast themselves as just balladeers or jump specialists. They tackled the whole gamut of rhythm and blues, recording blues, ballads, jumps, and Tin Pan Alley standards.

What Chance produced during its four years of existence, however, hardly ranks with the big labels in Chicago, both in quantity and quality. To those looking for rock 'n' roll in doowop, most Chance recordings sound too deep and bluesy, the exceptions being the Flamingos' "Golden Teardrops" and the Moonglows' "Secret Love."

The next label complex to make an impact in Chicago was the Parrot/Blue Lake complex, owned by Al Benson, who cut some fabulous sides on the Flamingos (notably "I'm Yours," which used the "doowop" vocal riff), the Orchids (notably the subtle "You Said You Loved Me"), and the Five Chances (notably "All I Want," a deep and soulful classic). Parrot went out of business in 1955 just as rock 'n' roll was making its presence felt on the national landscape. Most of the company's vocal group releases featured a deep rhythm and blues sound that reflected the early 1950s period, but by 1954 and 1955, with the Flamingos and Orchids gaining steam, Benson was beginning to create genuine rock 'n' roll. The Flamingos' subsequent success at Chess and later at End recording as rock 'n' roll stars, and the emergence of Orchids sides in later rock 'n' roll anthologies, demonstrates vividly that Parrot served as a midwife in the birth of rock 'n' roll. Yet the Flamingos and the Orchids recordings could never be mistaken for New York sides; they were a bit too deep.

By 1955, the club scene had died for Chicago doowop groups, who were now being presented on large theater stages as part of teen packaged revues, reflecting changes nationwide.

Another great Chicago label complex, United/States, was practically moribund in its last years, 1955-57, but during that time the company came out with some great doowop records by Danderliers, Moroccos, and others. The Danderliers recordings were most typical of the Chicago approach to doowop, in which such ballads as "My Autumn Love" and "May God Be With You" have a spiritual feel to them. These recordings are not yet proto-soul, but one can hear a bit of the flavor of soul.

Chess Records, with its connection to Alan Freed, made one of the more substantial impacts with doowop groups during the golden age of rock 'n' roll in the late 1950s, particularly with recordings by the Moonglows ("Sincerely") and the Flamingos ("I'll Be Home"). Both groups became better known for their ballads, which crossed over onto the pop charts. Typical of most Chicago groups, the Moonglows and the Flamingos both made jump sides that sounded more like r&b than rock 'n' roll.

Vee Jay was the city's other major label in the late 1950s, and put out notable recordings by the El Dorados ("At My Front Door"), Dells ("Oh What A Nite"), Spaniels ("Goodnite Sweetheart, Goodnite"), and Magnificents ("Up On The Mountain"), among others. The spiritual side of Chicago doowop is particularly evident in certain Spaniels' recordings, notably, "You Gave Me Peace Of Mind" and "I Lost You," in which lead vocals by James "Pookie" Hudson conveyed deep emotion. Hudson had a "soul" voice long before the birth of soul.

The years 1959 to 1963 have long been unfairly denigrated by popular music critics, who saw the era as one of no-talent pretty boy Bobbys who crooned to early adolescent girls. Yet the era was a rich and vibrant transitional one for African-American music. The soul era was coming on and the older sounds of rhythm and blues and rock 'n' roll, such as doowop and saxophone instrumentals, were fading. Chicago in particular made a major contribution during this time. Its record companies opportunistically came out with vocal group music that seemed to partake of the past, yet looked forward to the future. Doowop vocal techniques were much in evidence on the recordings, yet there was something more gospelly, more urgent, in the sound of the vocals, and that would be the sound of soul in the coming years.

Ironically, while New York was looking backward by experiencing a doowop revival period with belated recordings by the Shells, Capris, and Edsels hitting the charts—a revival that within a few years sank into degeneracy with the a capella craze—Chicago was looking forward by creating new sounds. Chicago producer Bill Sheppard was making an impact with such groups as the Sheppards ("Tragic") and Dukays ("Duke Of Earl"), whose recordings are classic examples of transitional r&b, representing proto-soul and neo-doowop both at once. While one still heard doowop nonsense syllables in these transitional groups, the records incorporated more instrumentation and the groups sang with more intense funkier vocal stylings that in later years would inform soul music.

Witch/Cortland was the one label complex in Chicago that seemed dedicated to recording nothing but transitional r&b, with such groups as Donald Jenkins and the Delighters ("Elephant Walk"), the Blenders ("Daughter"), and Versalettes ("Shining Armor"). Many of the Witch/Cortland releases may have sounded dated during the 1962-64 period, but that datedness was hardly noticed because of the crazy quilt of sounds—some looking backwards and some looking forward—of the period. It made for an exciting mixture on the charts.

When one looks at such Chicago groups as the Dukays, Sheppards, Daylighters, Donald Jenkins and the Delighters, and the Vibrations, they are the artists who redeemed the early 1960s from the onslaught of the pretty boys by creating a marvelous transitional style of r&b distinctive to the period. They were thus both the last doowop groups and the first soul groups to come out of Chicago. Thus, this brief look at Chicago doowop yields two conclusions. First, its doowop groups tended to sound more soulful and obviously pre-scienced the soul era. Secondly, because of the greater gospel flavor of its groups, the city naturally emerged in the forefront in the development of transitional vocal group music that bridged the doowop and the soul eras.

Robert Pruter's Top 50 Chicago Group Records

1. Coronets: Nadine (1953), Chess 1549
2. Flamingos: Golden Teardrops (1953), Chance 1145
3. Spaniels: Baby It's You (1953), Vee Jay 101
4. Moonglows: Sincerely (1954), Chess 1581
5. Spaniels: Goodnite Sweetheart, Goodnite (1954), Vee Jay 107
6. Danderliers: My Autumn Love (1955), States 147
7. Dells: Dreams of Contentment (1955), Vee Jay 166
8. El Dorados: At My Front Door (1955), Vee Jay 147
9. El Dorados: I Began To Realize (1955), Vee Jay 165
10. Five Chances: All I Want (1955), Blue Lake 115
11. Five Notes: Park Your Love (1955), Chess 1614
12. Five Notes: Show Me The Way (1955),
13. Flamingos: I'm Yours (1955), Parrot 812

14. Orchids: Newly Wed (1955), Parrot 815
15. Orchids: You're Everything To Me (1955), Parrot 815
16. Orchids: You Said You Loved Me (1955), Parrot 819
17. Orchids: You Have Two (I Have None) (1955), Vee Jay (rel. 1993)
18. Spaniels: You Painted Pictures (1955), Vee Jay 154
19. Moonglows: Most of All (1955), Chess 1589
20. Danderliers: May God Be With You (1956), States 152
21. Dells (1956): Oh What A Nite, Vee Jay 204
22. Flamingos: I'll Be Home (1956), Checker 830
23. Flamingos: A Kiss From Your Lips (1956), Checker 837
24. Kool Gents: I Can't Help Myself (1956), Vee Jay 207
25. Magnificents: Up On The Mountain (1956), Vee Jay 183
26. Moonglows: We Go Together (1956), Chess 1619
27. Spaniels: You Gave Me Peace of Mind (1956), Vee Jay 229
28. Gems: Til the Day I Die (1957), Drexel 915
29. Spaniels: Everyone's Laughing (1957), Vee Jay 246
30. Spaniels: I Lost You (1957), Vee Jay 264
31. Spaniels: Here Is Why I Love You (1958), Vee Jay 290
32. Bel Aires: My Yearbook (1958), Decca 30631
33. Magnificents: Don't Leave Me (1958), Vee Jay 281
34. Dells: Dry Your Eyes (1959), Vee Jay 324
35. Bo Diddley: I'm Sorry (1959), Checker 914
36. Bo Diddley: You Know I Love You (1959), (released 1990)
37. Moonglows: Twelve Months of the Year (1959), Chess 1725
38. Sheppards: Island of Love (1959), Apex 7750
39. Faith Taylor and the Sweet Teens: I Need Him To Love Me (1959)
40. Spaniels: I Know (1960)
41. Sheppards: Tragic (1961 Apex version), Apex 7762
42. Sheppards: Queen of Hearts (1961), Constellation LP 4
43. Sheppards: Forgotten (1961), Constellation LP 4
44. Swinging Hearts: Please Say It Isn't So (1961), Lucky Four 1011
45. Vibrations: Oh Cindy (1961), Checker 1002
46. Dukays: Night Owl (1961), Nat 4002
47. Gene Chandler (Dukays): Duke of Earl (1961), Vee Jay 416
48. Daylighters: Whisper of the Wind (1962), Tip Top 2007
49. Uniques: Silvery Moon (1962), Lucky Four 1024
50. Donald and the Delighters: (Native Girl) Elephant Walk (1963), Cortland 109

Los Angeles Rhythm and Blues Vocal Groups

by Steve Propes

The modern L.A. rhythm-and-blues or, if you prefer, doo-wop, scene came into being in 1949 or 1950 with the first releases by several groups. There were the Robins, the Hollywood Flames and the Barons, the unit that first joined the voices of Jesse Belvin and Marvin Phillips. Out of that duet came "Dream Girl" by Jesse and Marvin, which begat "Earth Angel" by the Penguins. From Jesse and Marvin came "Cherry Pie" by Marvin and Johnny. And that's just for starters (but what a start)! The motivator, the originator, the setter of the L.A. style, Jesse Belvin with his erstwhile partner Phillips were too busy creating a sound to notice the profound impact they were having.

Meanwhile, the Robins were a combination of the A-Sharp Trio out of the Bay Area and Bobby Nunn out of the Barrelhouse in Watts, courtesy of Johnny Otis, who had already paid some important dues on Central Avenue. It was years later that the Coasters emerged from this effort, just like Bobby Day and his "Rockin' Robin" flew the Flames' coop. Also from the Barrelhouse stable came Big Jay McNeely, who employed the voices of Belvin and Phillips on the emergency call-out, "All That Wine Is Gone." The Flames responded by advising "Go And Get Some More" under the moniker of the Question Marks.

The same generation also brought about the Lamplighters, whose raunchy "Ride, Jockey Ride" brought us the talents of Thurston Harris with a backup group that would evolve into the Sharps ("Six Months, Three Weeks, Two Days And An Hour") and the Rivingtons ("Papa Oom Mow Mow" and "The Bird's The Word").

At about the same time, Dolphin's Of Hollywood Record Shop at Vernon and Central began making important noises. In 1953, the first truly teen-aged vocal group, the Flairs, emerged from Jefferson H.S. They first visited Dolphin's and never returned. Featuring the lead voices of Richard Berry and Cornel Gunter, they put down "She Wants To Rock" for the Modern/RPM combine, which milked these harmonies to great effect. If you don't believe me, listen to the duet harmonies in "This Is The Night For Love."

Meanwhile, Dolphin's continued on with records from dozens of creative minds. Thus came "Emily" and "I'm A Fool" by the Turks, "Hey Now" by the Voices (a Bobby Day alter ego group) and "Fare Thee Well" by the Hollywood Flames, on labels like Cash, Money and Recorded In Hollywood (from...where else...Dolphin's Of Hollywood). Jesse Belvin was always anxious to sell a song, "Earth Angel" being a case in point. Belvin's "Beware" could've been the national breakthrough for a label with bigger ambitions. His lack of big sales on Dolphin's Cash label for "So Fine" by the Sheiks, "Girl Of My Dreams" by the Cliques or "Tell Me" by the Gassers (all alter ego groups of Belvin's) is perplexing. Face it, Jesse Belvin redesigned the L.A. doo-wop landscape, as did his friend and Jeff High classmate, Richard Berry.

Belvin finally proved his hitmaking ability with the powerful "Goodnight My Love" for Modern, a label with national reach. He was just starting to make a mark globally for RCA Victor when he died in 1960. His shoes were so big, RCA had to sign Sam Cooke to attempt to fill them.

The mid- to late 1950s were still the age of the indie. Some companies paid royalties, but others thought that term referred to some king in a distant land. Other indies competed with Dolphin's, like black-owned Combo (Jake Porter), Dootone (Dootsie Williams), and Flash Records. National labels based in L.A., like Modern, Specialty, and Aladdin, also recorded their share of local talent.

Flash Records operated several retail record shops beginning in the 1930s. The group which brought the label the greatest success was the Jayhawks. Their early talking doo-wop, "Counting My Teardrops" (with the famous ringing phone in the spoken bridge) was followed by the original rendition of "Stranded In The Jungle," a local hit taken nationally by the Cadets.

All Dootsie Williams did was take a label that did hired-gun recording for up-and-coming songwriter/singers and put together the elements of doo-wop's most durable classic, "Earth Angel" by the Penguins. It was created when Jesse Belvin, Gaynel Hodge and Curtiss Williams, the Penguins lead, were messing around writing songs for the Hollywood Flames and other units. Now we're getting into neighborhoods and high schools. Jefferson High, right off of Central, produced Belvin, Richard Berry and the rest of the Flairs, and Gaynel Hodge, who sang with the Flames, Turks, and Platters. He created the Platters because his brother Alex needed a group, too. The Platters' first efforts were in the background, behind Big Jay McNeely on "Nervous Man Nervous" and Joe Houston on "Shtiggy Boom."

Oh yeah, another group came to life when Cornel's sister, Shirley Gunter, decided to invent something we now know as the girl group. She and three teen-aged friends (no, one of them was not Zola Taylor of the Platters), called themselves the Queens, and hit with the national girl group nonsense lyric sensation called "Oop Shoop." Waste no more time, put these girls in the Pioneers wing of the Rock And Roll Hall Of Fame.

Fremont High was giving us stars, too. Integrated, as were most schools at the time (sadly, no more), Fremont gave the sound two important multi-racial groups, Don Julian & the Meadowlarks, who hit big with "Heaven And Paradise" for Dootone, and the Jaguars, who did the same with the moving "The Way You Look Tonight." As with all of these groups, their place at El Monte Legion Stadium was forever guaranteed by the fans of the real sound. The Calvanes did a word-jazz thing called "Crazy Over You" for Dootsie. Later came the Marathons and a host of other doo-woppers from this school. Story goes that Richard Berry attended Fremont until he found they assigned homework.

After leaving the Flairs, Richard put together the Dreamers, L.A.'s second girl group, and gave the recording industry perhaps the world's busiest session-backing group for decades to come in the Blossoms. Out of this group came Darlene Love, Clydie King, Gloria Jones and some really finely tuned voices. Richard then hooked up with the Robins, courtesy of Leiber and Stoller, to put the menace to their "Riot In Cell Block #9." From that local hit, came the style that turned the Robins into the Coasters. As is often the case with fast stardom, great talent and youthful ambition, the Flairs disappeared as quickly as they arrived, Richard taking up with his Dreamers, Cornel ending up with the Coasters and Young Jesse taking "Mary Lou" on the road as a single.

At the same time, Modern needed a utility vocal group badly, and they pulled this one off by creating the Cadets/Jacks, an outfit that was drawn from a gospel group. As the balladeering Jacks, they hit quickly with "Why Don't You Write Me," a song that was "borrowed" unceremoniously from the Feathers. Under the name the Cadets, the same guys broke up the charts with a manic version of "Stranded In the Jungle," a Jayhawks' original, with "great googly moo" added by Prentice Moreland. The Jacks kept crooning, the Cadets kept rocking and Modern Records kept raking in the cash until that imprint went into hibernation in 1957. Sisters of Jacks/Cadets' member Aaron Collins were Rosie and Betty, the Teen-Queens, whose "Eddie My Love" best suited the adolescent age of angst.

Meanwhile, Buck Ram put his Vegas touch on more than a handful of neighborhood groups. He had the Flairs, the Teen Queens, the Penguins, the Fortunes and, with most success, the Platters. They took their sound straight to the top and didn't leave for a good decade with songs like "Only You," "Twilight Time" and "Smoke Gets In Your Eyes."

Leon Rene, a black songwriter who began recording in the 1930s (or perhaps before), kept churning out hits with voices like Bobby Day and the Satellites ("Rockin' Robin") and Eugene Church ("Pretty Girls Everywhere"), as well as big ticket rarities by the Intervals ("Here's That Rainy Day"), a group that would evolve into the Fifth Dimension.

Bob Keane, who got his biggest payday with Ritchie Valens, released discs by the Valiants ("This Is The Nite"), before they met Lou Adler who dubbed them the Untouchables ("Poor Boy Needs A Preacher"), who lent them to Phil Spector who called them the Alley Cats ("Puddin N Tain"). The names these guys used, from the Sabres to the Electras, are still being recalled and documented. They might be the record holders in this area, renaming themselves at every session. What they often had in common was the haunting lead of Billy Jones, aka Billy Storm, who several producers attempted to mold into the next Johnny Mathis.

Watts was part of the picture because we know that Vernon Green & the Medallions went to Jordan High. Vernon came out here from Denver and, as if he couldn't shake traveling from his blood, debuted with the classic "Buick '59," recorded at Brinson's garage. It was recorded on the same date with the Penguins, who put down the intended A side, "Hey Senorita," and then "Earth Angel" for Dootsie Williams. But good as "Buick 59" was, what others have retained over the years were "those sweet words of pismotology," that Green invented in "The Letter." Donald Woods later appropriated the Medallions, when he needed a backing group for his Vel-Aires, and came up with the outrageous "Death Of An Angel."

Another classic, "Nite Owl" by Tony Allen & the Chimes on Specialty, came out one release before labelmate Little Richard's debut with "Tutti Frutti," and thus lost national momentum. On the same label, Arthur Lee Maye dusted "Gloria" with Richard Berry, Darlene Love fronted the Echoes on "Over the Rainbow" and Eugene Church and Jesse Belvin revived the Cliques on "Open Up Your Heart."

Other neighborhoods contributed, too. East L.A. and the El Monte Legion Stadium scene produced Little Julian Herrera & the Tigers, the Storytellers, and various other integrated and Hispanic acts. Orange County was another scene altogether. Richard Berry performed there for years, and one night he sang with the Rhythm Rockers, a Filipino group and band. Out of that mix came America's most-loved party song, "Louie Louie," little more than a sea chantey.

In L.A., the suburbs can reach over mountains and across the high desert. Out of the euphemistically named "Inland Empire," really steel mills and biker gangs, from San Bernardino and Fontana, came groups like the Jewels ("Hearts Of Stone"), the Metallics ("Need Your Love"), the Pentagons ("To Be Loved") and the Rollers ("Continental Walk"). Out of the country and western center of Bakersfield came the Paradons ("Diamonds And Pearls") and the Colts ("Adorable").

From Pasadena, came the Squires with "Sindy," and from the Squires came the rockinest doo-wop duet, Don & Dewey. From Compton came the Olympics, whose hits like "Western Movies" in 1958 to "Good Lovin'" in the mid-1960s, made them second only to the Coasters in the novelty genre. Also from Compton were Charles McCullough & the Silks, who put down "My Girl" and "Zorro" for Dootsie Williams, and the Utopians, who became powerful hitmakers under another name. From Venice came Leon Peels & the Blue Jays. From Long Beach came the Velveteers, and from San Pedro by way of Fremont High came M&M and the Peanuts.

Deejays got in on the scene with labels like Johnny Otis' Dig, Hunter Hancock's Swingin' and Magnum, Huggy Boy's Caddy and Canton (after his hometown, Canton, Ohio, not China), Zeke Manners' Loma, Rudy Harvey's Dynamic and Titanic, as well as Art Laboe's Starla and Original Sound (which exists to this day). Dig started the ball rolling with classics by Little Julian Herrera ("Those Lonely Lonely Nights"), Arthur Lee Maye & the Crowns ("This Is The Night For Love"), Julie Stevens & the Premiers ("Blue Mood") and the Gladiators ("Girl of My Heart").

On Caddy, came several by the Jeanette Baker-lead Dots ("I Confess") and the Twilighters with Charles Wright ("Eternally"). On Starla was an Herrera classic ("I Remember Linda"), while on Original Sound came the Hitmakers ("Chapel Of Love") and the Jaguars with Richard Berry and Tony Allen on falsetto ("Thinking of You"). And on Swingin' came at least one powerful hit by Rochell & the Candles ("Once Upon a Time").

George Motola had his own style. An old time song plugger and label owner of the "dis and dat" school, Motola found or invented groups and group names like the Capris, Shields, Cyclones, Youngsters, Saxons and Senders. To cover the Slades on "You Cheated," he brought in Frankie Ervin as lead, and backed him with Belvin, Johnny "Guitar" Watson, Buster Williams and Eugene Church, to create the Shields, and national success. Later Shields groups would use Charles Wright or Tony Allen as leads.

Life is complicated enough, but trust that George would confuse and confound everyone by his re-use of tracks and his multiple renaming of groups. In his vaults, were more tracks than the Union Pacific, and he used them to advantage often, creating groups like the Swallows, Guides, Senders and the group backing Bobby Sanders, for just one track. The Hollywood Saxons took Motola's approach, giving us hits like "Diamonds" off of the Senders' "Spinning." Also out of this scene came the Uptones, with their hit "No More."

Several originators showed up with hits in the 1960s. Don Julian created a Larks group to hit with "The Jerk," Charles Wright's 103rd Street Rhythm Band had a hand in inventing what we now know as funk, Al Wilson came out of the Rollers, while the Rivingtons, Darlene Love and even Frank Zappa's Ruben & the Jets came out of this musical environment.

The L.A. groups had a simplicity and feeling, an unpolished sincerity and earnestness. Many of these acts, especially the Central Avenue groups like the Lamplighters, early Platters, Turks, Penguins, Flairs and the various Jesse Belvin groups like the Cliques and Gassers, often practiced together and developed songs together. Gaynel Hodge of the early Platters and Turks would laughingly refer to this style as "ice cream changes." Whatever it was, it told a story that teens and record buyers of all ages, races and hometowns could identify with, love, and spend their few record-buying pennies on. When you listen to Vernon Green make up lyrics like "pismotology" on "The Letter" or Julian Herrera singing about remembering Linda, you somehow knew that the experience was real and the motivation was to communicate this feeling. New York had the more polished "doo-wop" style, Chicago had a bluesier sound, but for true feeling and sincerity with a lyric, a vocal, a spoken bridge, it was for that ingredient that you came to Los Angeles.

These were also the days where recording a record wasn't such a major problem, and in some sense that's not changed. A teen can still walk into a studio with a few bucks and walk out with the finished product. But back then, deejays like Huggy Boy and Hunter Hancock would be accessible to put the paean out over the air and on the streets. If it reached and spoke to the teen ear, then it sold, not that the groups ever got rich or even made any serious money. That's an altogether different issue.

This L.A. sound stayed around for a good 15 years, shut down only by the transformation brought by the British Invasion and, more powerfully, by the Watts Riots in August of 1965. After that event, the link between Central Avenue/Watts and the recording industry in Hollywood and other more affluent neighborhoods, if not broken, certainly frayed. It also charged the music with a touch of anger, a harder edge, and a need to give out a social or political message sans love making, drinking wine, or fast cars, subjects that marked the earlier era.

That's not to say that certain groups didn't keep on. Some did, but their world had changed. Some records got through and some were hits. Mentioned were just the bigger groups and more major songs. Research on the more obscure and songs groups continues apace. You'll be surprised at what history will be revealed.

Steve Propes' Top 50 L.A. Group Records
(arranged roughly by year)

1. Robins with Little Esther: Double Crossin' Blues (1950), Savoy 731
2. Hollywood Flames: Young Girl (1950), Recorded In Hollywood 165
3. Three Dots & A Dash with Jesse Belvin: All That Wine Is Gone (1951), Imperial 5115
4. Platters: Give Thanks (1953), Federal 12153
5. Lamplighters: Be Bop Wino (1953), Federal 12152
6. Flairs: She Wants To Rock (1953), Flair 1012
7. Hollywood Flames: I Know (1953), Swing Time 345
8. Robins: Riot In Cell Block #9 (1954), Spark 103
9. Penguins: Earth Angel (1954), Dootone 348
10. Medallions: The Letter (1954), Dootone 347
11. Jewels: Hearts Of Stone (1954), R&B 1301
12. Flairs: This Is the Night For Love (1954), Flair 1044
13. Shirley Gunter & the Queens: Oop Shoop (1954), Flair 1050
14. Donald Woods & the Vel Aires: Death Of An Angel (1955), Flip 306
15. Tony Allen & the Chimes: Nite Owl (1955), Specialty 560
16. Squires: Sindy (1955), Mambo 105
17. Turks: Emily (1955), Money 211
18. Sheiks: Sentimental Heart (1955), Federal 12237
19. Jaguars: The Way You Look Tonight (1956), Aardell 0011
20. Jayhawks: Counting My Teardrops (1956), Flash 105
21. Twilighters: Eternally (1956), Cholly 712
22. Dots: I Confess (1956), Caddy 101
23. Cadets: Stranded In The Jungle (1956), Modern 994
24. Velveteers: Tell Me You're Mine (1956), Spitfire 15
25. Native Boys: Oh Let Me Dream (1956), Combo 120
26. Cliques: Girl In My Dreams (1956), Modern 987
27. Premiers: My Darling (1956), Dig 113
28. Six Teens: A Casual Look (1956), Flip 315
29. Jesse Belvin: Beware (1956), Cash 1056
30. Richard Berry & Pharoahs: Take the Key (1956), Flip 318
31. Little Julian Herrera & the Tigers: I Remember Linda (1957), Starla 6
32. Eugene Church: Open Up Your Heart (1957), Specialty 604
33. Valiants: This Is the Night (1957), Keen 34004
34. Sharps: Six Months Three Weeks Two Days & An Hour (1957), Tag 2200
35. Jerry Stone & the Four Dots: It's Heaven (1958), Freedom 44002
36. Shields: You Cheated (1958), Tender 513
37. Storytellers: You Played Me A Fool (1959), Stack 500
38. Jaguars: Thinking Of You (1959), Original Sound 06
39. Pentagons: To Be Loved (1960), Fleet International 100
40. Gallahads: Lonely Guy (1960), Donna 1322
41. Elgins: Uncle Sam's Man (1961), Flip 353
42. Little Sammy: Can You Love Me (1961), Shade 1002
43. Blue Jays: Lover's Island (1961), Milestone 2008
44. Atlantics: Boo Hoo Hoo (1961), Linda 103
45. Charles McCullough & the Silks: My Girl (1961), Dooto 462
46. Utopians: Along My Lonely Way (1962), Imperial 5876
47. Intervals: Here's That Rainy Day (1962), Class 304
48. Metallics: Need Your Love (1962), Baronet 2
49. Rivingtons: Cherry (1963), Liberty 55610
50. MM & the Peanuts: Open Up Your Eyes (1964), Money 101

Blazing Boulevards

By Robert Bosco

The neat street-beat singers of Philadelphia The 1950s.

An era of cold war and hot blondes. On the one paw you had Marilyn, Jayne, and Mamie, on the other you had Kruschev, DeGaul, and Eisenhower. Whatta crew.

A perfect backdrop, as it were, for the rapid rise of a relatively new form of music. Some called it streetcorner harmony. Others, doo wop. These days, classic urban harmony is the politically correct euphemism, particularly among researchers, raconteurs, and those in the know. Doo wop, when you get down to it, is a pejorative, pure and simple.

Whatever the case, outside of New York City, this experimental group vocalizing was no more rampant anywhere than in Philadelphia. So let's venture back, boarding the same sorry public trans our fearless fivesomes used back in the day. Presently, a true-blue Philadelphian might blanch as it's painfully obvious each precinct exists in marked contrast from the days of yore. In fact, there's just no use soft soaping what is. These wards are veritable war zones; the crack vials glisten like diamonds alongside the graffiti, the abandoned houses, and the endless mounds of litter. So hold onto your seats, leave the wife and kids at home, reach for your Tech-9, and check your wallet. Away we go...

West Philadelphia, for starters, was a hotbed of singing talent. Early in 1952, George Grant, Octavius Anthony, Frank Vance, Ron Everett, and Billy Taylor coalesced as the Castelles, opened their mouths, and presto, the so-called Philadelphia Sound became part of R & B lexicon, as if such a sound ever existed. Replete with the sparkling high tenor lead vocals of Grant, along with the soaring silver tenor of Anthony, who framed both Grant and the group, the Castelles emitted an ethereal sound which captured the hearts and minds of local teens. Though largely unappreciated by the rest of the hemisphere, their chirpings on Herb Slotkin's Grand Label, situated in the rear of Slotkin's downscale furniture store squatting on Lancaster Avenue, have evolved into a populist parable, underscoring all the teen-age insecurities and mores of the period. Beginning with "My Girl Awaits Me" (1953), they were on an 18-month roll which included such eloquent offerings as "Over A Cup of Coffee," "Marcella," and this writer's fave, "This Silver Ring." Classics, all.

They prepped the public for such similar-sounding outfits as the Dreamers (with estimable lead Kent Peeler), the Dreams (lead, George Tinley), the Belltones (Irv Natson, Estelle Powell, Fred Walker), who may lurk just outside the confines of W. Philadelphia and who later emerged as Little Joe's Thrillers ("Peanuts"), the Angels (Sonny Gordon doing lead chores), and the odd-sounding Capris, whose lead shrieking by Rene Hinton advanced run-of-the-mill weepers like "It's A Miracle" into the realm of hydraulic suction. Except for Tinley's Dreams, who waxed eloquently for Savoy Records in Newark, N.J., all these conglomerations recorded for Philadelphia labels, thus assuring their trek to oblivion.

A shame, really. Such etchings as "Darlene" (Dreams), "Tears In My Eyes" (Dreamers), "Estelle" (Belltones, one of the top potboilers of all time), and "God Only Knows" (Capris), all issued around 1954, languished virtually unnoticed. The Capris' track, to be fair, engendered action in scattered markets, and curiously embraced a new audience eight years down the road. This go-around, white teen-agers eagerly scarfed up the disc after it was re-issued by Lost Nite records and pushed to the max by deejay Jerry Blavat. Incredibly, as I write this piece, it is now leaking from the cut-rate speakers of my chintzy hi-fi, directly from Blavat's Friday afternoon soiree. Airing over WSSJ-AM, this is exactly where Mr. Blavat embarked over three and a half decades ago (when it was called WCAM). Thus, Blavat, you may have noticed, remains an AM disc jockey in an FM world. Go figure. Meantime, the evergreen sounds as plaintive and haunting as ever, one of the melodies which hooked this writer back in 1959 when he first heard it at scurvy Slim Rose's Time Square Records, a grope and hope operation for the ages. Unfortunately, the Capris' catalog of ensuing efforts was spotty, with such blather as "My Weakness" and "It Was Moonglow," both of which are virtually unlistenable, so their evaporation from the airwaves may have some justification.

Incidentally, the Castelles, their elan and perspicacity notwithstanding, were only not the best group in city, they may have not been the best group on their own label. That title arguably belongs to the rough, tough Cherokees, who sound nothing like any tribe anywhere. Lead Russell Carter, with his West Philly homeboys George Pounds, Melvin Storey, Tommy Lee, and Karl English at his elbow, crooned "Rainbow of Love" and "Please Tell Me So," as though their lives depended on it, which they probably did. As if those two waxings weren't enough, in the early '60s, Lost Nite dished out the unparalleled "Brenda/By the Candlelight" from their '54 sessions, and both surpass "Rainbow..." and "Love..." by a city block. As Louis Silvani hypothesized in his tome, *Collecting Rare Records*, "Wimps these guys ain't." Amen.

Traveling on the Market Street Subway, we switch trains at City Hall, and venture up a couple of miles to North Philadelphia. Here, such assemblages as the Majors, Blue Notes, Bosstones, Parliaments and this writer's pick to click, the Re-Vels, ruled the schoolyards and bathrooms. For my money, it's the Re-Vels who are hands down the best all-around confab ever to emerge from this city. Dreamlovers? They were only together about seven years and had numerous personnel switches. Besides, they were a '60s' outfit. Blue Notes? No one in these parts is exactly sure what the connection was between Harold Melvin's aggregation, who produced all those soul explosions in the 1970s, with such real-deal luminaries as Roosevelt Brody and Franklin Peaker and bass Jesse Gillis, dudes who peopled the Blue Note roster in their Josie days, with such first-rate product as "Retribution Blues," "If You Love Me," and the startling "He Was Mine" (Lost). Peaker's top notes will chip the edges right off your champagne glasses. By all accounts, Melvin was recruited around 1960, and was aboard from "My Hero" (Val-ue) until they shot through the stratosphere in the early '70s, with hit after hit , like "The Love I Lost," for one.

In and of themselves, the Re-Vels, from the moment they uttered that immortal opening phrase on their Atlas coupling, "Love My Baby" (1954), "North Philly's got fine girls, Germantown, ooh...," made their decade hajj through R & B music a remarkable one. After "My Lost Love," the underside to "Love..." went nowhere for the fledgling New York concern, they persevered, issuing such breathtakers as "You Lied to Me" (1955), "Dream My Darling Dream" (1956), and "So In Love" (1956), all for the dinky Sound/Teen complex on 13th & Locust Streets in Center City, Philadelphia. Each sunk promptly without a trace, and today are highly sought-after, garnering hundreds of dollars apiece when they show up on dealer bid-lists, and a bargain at that. Even the "B" sides were superb.

Trudging onward, Henry Colclough, Big John Jones, Billy Jackson, Walt Miller, and Sam Hart contacted the Chicago-based Checker/Chess entity, who sprung the catchy "False Alarm" on an unsuspecting public in 1957. Although it garnered considerable airplay as an oldie well into the '90s, it received a frosty reception from those few who managed to hear it way back when.

Finally, by 1959, they struck paydirt. Their dizzy "Dead Man's Stroll," re-named "Midnight Stroll" solely for the benefit of finicky jocks, served up by Norgolde Records, was a gutsy departure from their weeper/jump syndrome. An hypnotic chant with graveyard undertones, it caught record buyers unawares, creeping up the pop chart and embedding itself in the top 40 for months. It engendered fluky follow-ups like "Tweedly Dee" and "Two Little Monkeys" for Norgolde and Laurie subsid, Andie, respectively. Collectors then, as well as today, opted for their more conventional flipsides, which kept current the unique Re-Vel harmonics. There were one or two less than exemplary releases for Norgolde, when Henry Colclough ventured to Atlantic Records, concocting a take-off on a Shirelles' ditty which had 'hit' written all over it. A court order instigated by Scepter Records erased that notion in two heartbeats. Billy Jackson, for his part, produced the Tymes ("So In Love") on most of their hitmakers, then scurried to greener pastures, transferring to New York City to do A&R work for Columbia and later Arista. The other fellas assumed ordinary day jobs, you know, like policeman and carpet installer, while one even entered the ministry. The Re-Vels, this city's pluckiest entry into the R & B field, were history. Soon thereafter, Teen, Sound, Norgolde, and Andi were geography. Hey, at least the fellas didn't have to face the indignity of the British Invasion, which loomed on the horizon.

Back down the Broad Street Subway to South Philadelphia. Exit at Snyder Avenue. Here we have such dauntless posses as the Keystoners, Turbans, Buccaneers, Sensations, Silhouettes, and Mohawks, but all of them were presaged and perhaps influenced by the legendary Ford Brothers and the Mystery Quartette.

On balance, the Ford Brothers, with their weekly appearances on the Parisian Taylor Kiddie Hour radio show broadcast live from 15th & South Streets, influenced all the singing groups in the first half of the 1950s in Philadelphia. They cloned themselves into the Keystoners ("Magic Kiss," G & M), but at the same time influenced the Turbans, Blue Notes, Castelles, as well as a plethora of other performers like Kenny Gamble, Leon Huff, and Herb Johnson ("Guilty," Len), and Frank Peaker, all of whom were to make their mark in pop music in the decades to come. The Mystery Quartette, however, deserves mention in this monologue because in 1950, they presaged EVERYBODY in this city in more ways than one. First of all, they were probably the first integrated quartet anywhere, even edging out Arthur Godfrey's corny Mariners by a few months.

They worked regularly, appearing nightly at the Little Rathskeller in Center City, just up the street from the renowned Pep's and the Showboat, and issued two (some theorize three), ultra-rare records for the local Essex Label. One, "Mommy's Boy," is so scarce that only six known 78s exist of the 1950 release. The other, "Go Tell Your Troubles to Somebody Else," exists in the singular only. That's correct: one copy. Moreover, all their sides are extraordinary. By 1953, a confluence of inept management, no new recordings, and serious threats from mob wiseguys, zapped our gang from South Philadelphia. So they discarded their glow-in-the-dark-masks, matching bop ties and guitar, and rotated back to the real world. As far as can be determined, only tenor Frank "Skeets" Squillace is still among the living. An act a decade ahead of its time, Maxie Rosenbloom tried to sign them up, until he received a dead fish in the mail.

Another flock from South Philadelphia, 10th & Bainbridge Streets to be precise, who cannot be ignored, was the Silhouettes. Out of the gate as the Thunderbirds, lead vocalist Bill Horton, Earl Beale, Ray Edwards, and Joe Jenkins broke in as penniless gospel singers. Jenkins was drafted, was replaced by Rick Lewis, and the group approached local disc jockey and impresario Kae Williams with a new jingle they had composed and which virtually no one would listen to, titled "Get A Job." The fellas got a grip, morphed into the Silhouettes, and Williams, for his part, likewise smartened up when orders for more than 100,000 copies of "Get A Job" poured in after an appearance on "Bandstand."

An unsavory deal was struck with Al Silver, owner of Herald/Ember Records in NYC, and the platter moved more than a million and a half units, a bonanza for an urban harmony etching at that time. Were Horton and his cronies reclining in their Barca Loungers, ticking off royalties? Get real. It wasn't until the early '90s when they regained their precious copyright. Only then did emoluments began to trickle in. It was a tad too late for Horton, though. The years of toiling at heavy construction took their toll; he quietly passed away in early 1995 when his heart gave out. Raymond Edwards, their booming bassman, cashed in his chips in March 1997 at the age of 72. Neither of them can be accused of living large.

There were a number of would-be successors to "...Job," the best of which was "Bing Bong," even a couple of albums, but all vanished without a trace. These gentlemen, regrettably, became one of the supreme one-hit wonders of all-time.

Nonetheless, "Get A Job" thrives. It found its way on to the musical score of such cinematic send-ups as "American Graffiti" (1974), "Nightbreaker," "Stand By Me" (1988), and "Trading Places" (1983), none of which, happy to report, was shot in the Phillipines. There were probably others. The Silhouettes have been the subject of not one, but two, alleged rockumentaries.

And while we're at it, where do you think Sha Na Na acquired their handle? From Neil Diamond? Hardly. From the opening passage of "Get A Job," natch.

We'd be remiss with our scrutiny of South Philly without at least recognizing the Sensations (Yvonne Baker, Alphonso Howell) and their three smart, chart records. Starting in 1956 with such boo-hooers as "Please Mr. Disc Jockey" and "My Debut to Love" for Atlantic's Atco division, they labored in obscurity until a resurrected group hit the motherload with the bouncy "Let Me In" during 1962. This time it was Argo who raked in the profits; Atco simply conceded too early in the game and missed the boat. Tough noogies. In this biz, they eat their young.

Finally, back up to City Hall, after hopping the rickety Rt. 13 subway-surface tram, we exit at 49th Street in Southwest Philadelphia, the home of Philadelphia's most famous congregation, Lee Andrews' Hearts. Arthur Thompson, Butch Curry, Wendell Calhoun, Roy Calhoun, and Ted Weems got together in 1952, hit some chords, and began an odyssey which would last for decades. Mr. Thompson got wise to himself, opted to utilize his two middle names, and christened the group Lee Andrews & Hearts. They quickly logged on with Eddie Heller's Rainbow label out of NYC, and out came three unremarkable but highly sought-after singles in rapid succession, the best of which was "The Bells of St. Mary." They made a blip or two on the R & B charts, received merely fair reviews, but showed plenty of promise.

A few additional, less crude diskings for Ivan Ballen's Gotham label, a local outlet, followed and helped round out their sound, while lollipops like "Bluebird of Happiness" and "Lonely Room" demonstrated they were on their way. What was lacking was some first-rate promotion, a foreign language to the thrifty Ballen. Unlike many wannabe moguls, he certainly had a clue, but wasn't exactly wearing out his pockets in support of the boys. Inevitably, as the years rolled by, other blokes shuffled in and out of the line-up, yet the Hearts' managed to maintain the integrity of their unique vocal blend.

Jocko Henderson's invisible Main Line Records was the next stopover. Out popped "Long Lonely Nights," and a nanosecond later Williams realized he was way out of his league, so he threw in with Leonard and Phil Chess, our old goombahs at Chess/Checker in Chicago, and the rest was history. With Chess, and later with United Artists, they sold thousands of records, gracing the charts regularly from 1956 to 1959, when their career flourished. All through the 1960s, they had issuings for such under-sized labels as Swan, Parkway, Gowen, Guyden, Chancellor, and Lost Nite; some found buyers, others didn't. By then, no one wanted to hear the real stuff anyway. Nevertheless, the mellifluous sound of Andrews, accompanied by an ever-changing array of Hearts, was omnipresent. Even through the advent of the British Invasion, Motown, Stax/Volt, Phil Spector, and pulsating distaff confabs like the Supremes, Vandellas, and Ronettes, they were selling sophisticated items like "Cold Gray Dawn" for Lost Nite as late as 1968. For personal drop-ins and pocket change, they were on the college circuit, doing three to four gigs a week to pay the bills. By 1970, the jig was up and they knew it. These days, Mr. Andrews performs, though more sporadically than in the old days, looking and sounding as cool as ever. He may not be as thin and smooth as in those thrilling days of yesteryear, but who is? Incidentally, are Lee and the fellas receiving their proper royalties via regular monthly installments? Let's not get crazy.

Arthur Thompson and the Hearts? Naaaaahh...

Sure, we've omitted some lesser known posses, like the Spiedels (Crosley), Skylighters (Emjay), Hide-a-ways (Ronni, MGM), Troopers, Guytones (Deluxe), Students, Jimmy & Sparrows, Angels, Gainors, Ivytones, Furness Brothers, and Philly's top 50's female brood, the Sharmeers, but nobody ever heard of them but their mothers. Even the Rays, whose charming lullaby, "Silhouettes," put Cameo on the map, never mind firm financial footing, but it's believed three of the four members were from New York.

On balance, the so-called Philadelphia sound, the one with all the high-tenor high jinx, was a short-lived phenomenon. It lasted about two to three years, and by 1956, it was confined, basically, to six square blocks in West Philly, virtually forgotten elsewhere. Sure, you had gatherings like the enigmatic Marquis or the Castros still reinventing this stuff, but by and large, it was a retro thang by then. Still, the Dreamlovers in the early '60s, not to mention the ubiquitous Turbans, as well as the Bluenotes, revived the style from time to time, whenever it suited their purpose. Above all, by 1957, the groups had more or less homogenized themselves, and those distinctive high-pitched wailings were yesterday's news.

And so were the singers who sang them.

Bosco's Phab Philly Phifty

1. Mystery Quartette: Mommy's Boy (1950), Essex 706
2. Mystery Quartette: Go Tell Your Troubles to Somebody Else (1950), Essex 713
3. Castelles: My Girl Awaits Me (1953), Grand 101
4. Capris: God Only Knows (1953), Gotham 7304
5. Belltones: Estelle (1953), Grand 102
6. Buccaneers: The Stars Will Remember (1953), Rama 21
7. Doris Browne & group: Until the End of Time (1953), Gotham 296
8. Dreams: Darlene (1954), Savoy 1130
9. Castelles: This Silver Ring (1954), Grand 103
10. Castelles: Do You Remember (1954), Grand 105
11. Cherokees: Rainbow of Love (1954), Grand 106
12. Eddie Carter Quartet: Take Everything But You (1954), Grand 107
13. Castelles: Over A Cup of Coffee (1954), Grand 109
14. Cherokees: Please Tell Me So (1954), Grand 110
15. Castelles: Marcella (1954), Grand 114
16. Angels: Wedding Bells (1954), Grand 115

17. Angels: Lovely Way to Spend An Evening (1954), Grand 121
18. Re-Vels: My Lost Love (1954), Atlas 1035
19. Hide-A-Ways: Cherie (1954), MGM 55004
20. Lee Andrews & the Hearts: Maybe You'll Be There (1954), Rainbow 252
21. Lee Andrews & the Hearts: White Cliffs of Dover (1954), Rainbow 256
22. Lee Andrews & the Hearts: Bells of St. Mary (1954), Rainbow 259
23. Dreams: Under the Willow (1954), Savoy 1140
24. Skylighters: How Foolish Am I (1954?), Emjay 6152
25. Marquis: The Rain/The Bells (1955), Grand 141
26. Hide-A-Ways: Can't Help Loving That Girl of Mine (1955), Ronni 1000
27. Dreamers: Melba (1955), Rollin' 5
28. Dreams: I'll Be Faithful (1955), Savoy 1157
29. Re-Vels: You Lied to Me (1955), Sound 129
30. Re-Vels: Dream My Darling Dream (1955), Sound 135
31. Ebbtides: What Is Your Name Dear? (1956), Teen 121
32. Re-Vels: So In Love (1956), Teen 122
33. Turbans: I'm Nobody's (1956), Herald 478
34. Guytones: Hunky Dory (1957), DeLuxe 6159
35. Re-Vels: False Alarm (1957), Chess 1708
36. Universals: Again (1957), Mark-X 7004
37. Cameos: Merry Christmas (1957), Cameo 123
38. Slip & Dell & group: Don't Take A Chance (1962?), Modern Artists 101
39. Sharmeers: A Schoolgirl In Love (1958), Red Top 109
40. Silhouettes: Get A Job (1958), Junior 391
41. Fabulairs: While Walking (1958), Main Line 103
42. Castros: Darling I Fell For You (1959), Lasso 501
43. Castros: Is It Right (1959), Lasso 502
44. Everglades: Sitting In the Chapel (1961), BPV 112577
45. Lee Andrews & the Masters: I'm Sorry Pillow (1962), Parkway 860
46. Orlons: Mr. Twenty-One (1962), Cameo 211
47. Butlers: Lovable Girl (1963), Guyden 2081
48. No Names: Love (1963), Guyden 2114
49. 4 J's: Here I Am Broken Hearted (1963), Jamie 1267
48. Billy & the Essentials: The Actor (1965), Cameo 344
50. Uptites: Girl of the Night (1965), RaSel

Southern R 'n' B Vocal Groups

by Gordon Skadberg

The genre of R 'n' B vocal group music had its beginnings in large United States cities such as Baltimore, New York, Chicago and Los Angeles. However, it wasn't long before this young art form spread throughout the country, especially to its roots in the South. The result was quite different from the R 'n' B beginnings in Baltimore, the street corner feel of New York, the bluesy vocals of Chicago, and the dreamy mood of Los Angeles. Instead, a unique sound of gospel-flavored harmonies, country lyrics, and somewhat raw vocal stylings was created; the southern sound of vocal group harmony.

Imperial Records was the first major label to widely introduce southern R 'n' B vocal group music into the new marketplace. Although based in California, their connection to the South was deeply rooted in New Orleans with their marquee recording artist whose name was Fats Domino. In the early 1950s, Imperial issued many records by groups such as the Hawks, Bees, Barons, Spiders, Kidds and Dukes. Most of them were recorded in New Orleans, so the result was a distinct "New Orleans touch" to southern vocal group harmony.

Excello Records in Nashville, Tennessee, introduced their "flower" groups, the Gladiolas and Marigolds (and later the Hollyhocks on Nasco), in the mid-1950s. Their Nashville recordings had a unique southern R 'n' B flavor often punctuated with a calypso beat. This sound was also captured by other Excello vocal groups such as the Peacheroos, Rhythm Casters, Five Chums, King Crooners and Gladrags.

Duke and Peacock Records were the major contributors to southern R 'n' B vocal group music in Texas. Best known for "Pledging My Love" by Johnny Ace and an extensive gospel repertoire, these two sister labels also recorded a variety of groups such as the Tempo Toppers (featuring Little Richard), Scamps and Clefs on Peacock, and the Sultans, El Torros and Capistranos on Duke. Their records are fine examples of Texas-influenced R 'n' B vocal group harmony.

Numerous other labels also produced/issued southern R 'n' B vocal group records in the 1950s. These labels were based in the South (e.g. Ace, Sun and Chart), as well as in other parts of the country (e.g. Chess and King). In addition, many short-lived southern labels (e.g. Harlem, Hart, Hi-Po, OJ and Vulcan) released obscure sides which have made this musical art form all the richer. Taken in its entirety, all these recordings, from labels large and small, represent the southern sound of vocal group harmony.

The following is a list of 50 recordings of southern R 'n' B vocal groups in approximate chronological order. It is intended to represent (with some personal favorites thrown in) the musical output of the vocal groups that produced the southern R 'n' B harmony sound of the 1950s.

1. Bobby Mitchell & the Toppers: One Friday Morning (1953), Imperial 5250
2. Prisonaires: Just Walking In The Rain (1953), Sun 186
3. Prisonaires: My God Is Real (1953), Sun 189
4. Varieteers: If You And I Could Be Sweethearts (1953), Hickory 1014
5. Hawks: Candy Girl (1954), Imperial 5266
6. Pelicans: Chimes (1954), Imperial 5307

7. Bees: Toy Bell (1954), Imperial 5314

8. Tempo Toppers: Rice, Red Beans, And Turnip Greens (1954), Peacock 1628

9. Clefs: I'll Be Waiting (1954), Peacock 1643

10. Hawketts: Mardi Gras Mambo (1955), Chess 1591

11. Marigolds: Rollin' Stone (1955), Excello 2057

12. Thunderbirds: Love Is A Problem (1955), G.G. 518

13. Kidds: Are You Forgetting Me (1955), Imperial 5335

14. Barons: Eternally Yours (1955), Imperial 5343

15. Jewels: Hearts Can Be Broken (1955), Imperial 5351

16. Spiders: Bells In My Heart (1955), Imperial 5354

17. Barons: My Dear, My Love (1955), Imperial 5359

18. Spiders: Witchcraft (1955), Imperial 5366

19. Scamps: Waterproof (1955), Peacock 1655

20. Sharptones: Made To Love (1955), Post 2009

21. Five Tinos: Sitting By My Window (1955), Sun 222

22. Five Owls: Pleading To You (1955), Vulcan 1025

23. Kool Toppers: Cause I Love You (1955), Beverly 702

24. Evergreens: Very Truly Yours (1955), Chart 605

25. Dukes: Teardrop Eyes (1956), Imperial 5401

26. Dukes: Cotton Pickin' Hands (1956), Imperial 5415

27. Majestics: Nitey Nite (1956), Marlin 802

28. Esquires: Only The Angels Know (1956), Hi-Po 1003

29. Trutones: Magic (1957), Chart 634

30. Supremes: Just For You And I (1957), Ace 534

31. El Torros: Dance With Me (1957), Duke 175

32. Sultans: If I Could Tell (1957), Duke 178

33. Gladiolas: Little Darling (1957), Excello 2101

34. Gladiolas: Hey Little Girl (1957), Excello 2120

35. Five Chums: Give Me The Power (1957), Excello 2123

36. Hollyhocks: Don't Say Tomorrow (1957), Nasco 6001

37. Rockin Dukes: Angel And A Rose (1957), OJ 1007

38. Uniques: Somewhere (1957) Peacock 1677

39. Five Royales: Dedicated To The One I Love (1957), King 5098

40. Capistranos: Now Darling (1958), Duke 179

41. Sensational Dellos: Lost Love (1958), Mida 109

42. Chester McDowell & group: I Wonder Why (1959), Duke 302

43. King Crooners: Now That She's Gone (1959), Excello 2168

44. King Crooners: Won't You Let Me Know (1959), Excello 2168

45. King Crooners: She's Mine All Mine (1959), Hart 1002

46. Berrycups: Hurt By A Letter (1959), Khoury's 710

47. Lyrics: Oh Please Love Me (1959), Wildcat 0028

48. Huey Smith & group: Dearest Darling (1959), Ace 571

49. El Torros: What's The Matter (1960), Duke 321

50. Royal Jesters: My Angel Of Love (1960), Harlem 105

In addition to these major sources of the sound, secondary geographical styles did exist. We've already visited the Baltimore-D.C. sound, which was a big player from 1946 to 1951, but which seemed to fold into the Philadelphia and New York sounds by 1954. New York also absorbed the sounds of its neighbors, Connecticut and New Jersey. Most of the Connecticut groups came out of New Haven,[2] like the Nutmegs, Scarlets/Five Satins, Four Haven Knights, Chestnuts, Academics and Hi-Lites. All of these groups, with the exception of the Academics (who had a good white group sound) produced melodic ballads with heavy backbeats and many doo-wop characteristics. Probably because of cross-fertilization, the groups have as many things in common with New York groups as they have with each other, so it is hard to justify establishing a "Connecticut Sound."

Groups from New Jersey met a similar fate. The Avons, Kodaks, Monotones, Fiestas, Keytones, Ambassadors and Gentlemen all came from cities in Northern Jersey, a stone's throw away from New York. Most also recorded for labels that were headquartered in New York (as did Connecticut groups), making it even tougher to distinguish a "New Jersey Sound" from a New York one.

Detroit was to Chicago as Connecticut and New Jersey were to New York. Detroit was a real player, spawning the Royals/Midnighters, Diablos, Pearls, Falcons and Don Juans. The sound of these groups was basically bluesy, which some have described as proto-soul, and Nolan Strong of the Diablos is thought to be a harbinger of the Motown sound. Great music, but very akin from what was coming out of Chicago at around the same time (the mid-1950s).

The Boston area had a bunch of groups, like the G-Clefs from Roxbury, the Love-Notes, the Jamies and, of course the Tune Weavers. It's tough to get a separate description of the Boston sound though, except that it's pretty rock 'n' rollish and not overly streetcornerish. New Orleans, the "Fertile Crescent" for other musical styles, was infertile for the vocal group genre, with the exception of the Spiders, an almost-supergroup that had a few chart successes in the mid-1950s. Pittsburgh had some big-name groups, like the Dell Vikings, Skyliners and Marcels and a few minor ones, like the El Capris and Capitols. Aside from often having a big bass part, the songs are pretty hard to characterize.[3]

As an epilogue, it must be reported that the differences between the four major locations narrowed, by degrees, as the 1950s drew to a close. The passage of time allowed for cross-fertilization of one geographi-

2. For more information, consult: Lepri, Paul. *The New Haven Sound: 1946-1976*. New Haven, CT.: by the author, 1977.

3. Robert Pruter, however, disagrees. In a phone interview conducted on Feb. 10, 1997, he sees the Pittsburgh sound as "romantic music, reminiscent of early '60s teen dances, with a slightly white doo-wop sound." The big bass sound of the Marcels and Dell Vikings is, he feels, atypical.

cal style with another. The styles never quite merged, but fewer and fewer groups adhered to the original sound of their city. Instead they evolved, to a generic doo-wop style which probably fell closest to the New York sound or to other musics, like Chicago soul or Philadelphia rock 'n' roll.

In case some of you think that New York City was the only place that was conducive to the formation of doo-wop and rhythm and blues groups, here is little quiz that proves otherwise. Below can be found 25 groups, 25 cities or towns (some of them certifiably dinky) and 25 states. To solve, connect the group with the city/town and state from whence they came. Answers are given in the Appendix. Any reader supplying zip codes will be given extra credit (and strange glances).

Quiz #6: Stating The Facts

A) Blue Jays	1) Arlington	a) CA
B) Carnations	2) Asbury Park	b) CT
C) Chandeliers	3) Atlanta	c) DC
D) Clefs	4) Baltimore	d) FL
E) Clovers	5) Bridgeport	e) GA
F) Corsairs	6) Chicago	f) IL
G) Crescendos	7) Detroit	g) IN
H) Darchaes (Ray & the)	8) Gary	h) KS
I) Delta Rhythm Boys	9) Kansas City	i) KY
J) Diablos	10) La Grange	j) MA
K) Fleetwoods	11) Lancaster	k) MD
L) Four Vagabonds	12) Langston	l) MI
M) G-Clefs	13) Louisville	m) MO
N) Gladiolas/Zodiacs	14) Miami	n) NC
O) Majestics	15) Mt. Vernon	o) NE
P) Marcels	16) Nashville	p) NJ
Q) Mello-Kings	17) Odessa	q) NY
R) Moonglows	18) Olympia	r) OH
S) Orioles	19) Omaha	s) OK
T) Pips	20) Pittsburgh	t) PA
U) Sheppards	21) Roxbury	u) SC
V) Spaniels	22) St. Louis	v) TN
W) Stereos	23) Steubenville	w) TX
X) Sultans	24) Venice	x) VA
Y) Velvets	25) Washington	y) WA

Chapter 13

Doo-Wopolitics

One of the major tenets of this book is that doo-wop music, despite its continued popularity, has not been accorded appropriate respect in relation to other musics. Unfortunately, one of the reasons for the continuation of this travesty is that there is no united front presented by those who love the music. Sometimes groups even work at cross-purposes, in effect shooting themselves in the foot or other body part.

In the 1990s, a person hungry for doo-wop can get his or her music from one of two different delivery systems which represent two disparate schools of thought or factions. These systems are driven by both idealism and economics. The two systems cater to different types of people, although there is some overlap among their adherents. In general, both systems can do an excellent job of delivering "product." This chapter will take a look at how these systems work and interact.

Our discussion centers mainly around the greater[1] New York metropolitan area, for that is where most of the influential players in the doo-wop world ply their trade. New York City is where WCBS-FM, the most powerful (influence AND wattage) oldies station in the country broadcasts; New Jersey is home to the United In Group Harmony Association; the metropolitan area hosts more concerts than anywhere else and is home to more of the singers than other locales. Other geographic regions that support doo-wop, such as Los Angeles, Boston, the Miami area and Philadelphia, while having their own particular doo-wopolitics, nonetheless are affected by what goes on in and around New York.

The first delivery system centers around the aforementioned WCBS-FM (New York, 101.1), its doo-wop deejays, its listening audience (many of whom consider doo-wop as their favorite type of music) and the more popular and visible of the currently active groups singing doo-wop. CBS got into the oldies business in the early 1970s, at a time when rock 'n' roll was old enough for many people to crave the music of days past. Gus Gossert, who many credit with initiating a doo-wop revival in the late 1960s, came to CBS and became the first of its deejays to specialize in doo-wop music. Unfortunately, he was arrested, convicted, and incarcerated for drug possession in 1972, which was a serious downer for his career in radio. The last few years of Gossert's life were shrouded in mystery and he was found murdered in Knoxville, Tennessee in August 1976. The murder remains unsolved to this day.

Gossert was replaced by Norm N. Nite (nee: Norman Derma) as the CBS doo-wop specialist, who started his "Nite Train Show" in 1972.[2] Norm started the trend of having singing groups do jingles to use as advertisements for the show. These jingles had the melodies of doo-wop songs and new lyrics, like "Norm N. Nite, he's all right, Norm N. Nite, outta sight." Norm published *Rock On* in 1974, an encyclopedia of recording artists (pop and rock 'n' roll) which included information about their careers and most of their hit records. Although only major doo-wop groups were included, it was still a milestone, being one of the few easily accessible sources where a lover of doo-wop (who, in 1974, was roughly 30 years old) could find information on his/her favorite groups.

In 1975, Norm departed CBS to have a go on WNBC, and then to return to his native Cincinnati to write more books (*Rock On, Vol. 2*, *Rock On, Vol. 3* and the *Rock On Almanac*). Don K. Reed, a career deejay who moved over to CBS from a smaller station on Long Island (N.Y.), took over the helm. Twenty-five years later, he's still there, reminding sports fans of the Pipp-Gehrig story. He renamed the show "The Doo-Wop Shop" and over the years has carved out an identity as probably the world's most popular doo-wop deejay. While not quite as well-known as the mayor of New York, surely more people listen to him. Reed's show airs on Sunday nights from 7-12 p.m. Other deejays on this station do play doo-wops, but their commitment is more toward generalized oldies. Two other important players at CBS are deejay Bobby Jay, who sang bass with the Laddins during the Classical Doo-Wop era and who remains actively involved in the doo-wop business today when not on the air, and Joe McCoy, the program director at CBS for the last number of years.

CBS-FM is a commercial radio station. It pays the salaries of its employees by getting sponsors to pay for on-air advertising. If the music aired doesn't attract listeners, then the Arbitron ratings go down. If the ratings go down, then either sponsors disappear or pay less for a given amount of advertising time. Either way, it's no good, and heads roll. For most of the 1990s, however, CBS-FM (New York) has been the top-rated station among 35- to 54-year olds, the population that sponsors covet for their buying power. Apparently guys like McCoy, Reed and Jay have been doing their jobs well.

As a business, CBS has to give the audience what it wants to hear. If Presidents Clinton, Bush, Reagan, and Carter formed a doo-wop group, they would make the news. CBS-FM or any commercial radio station should and would play the hell out of their records, regardless of

---

1. This is not necessarily a value judgment.

2. Not to be confused with Alan Frederick's "Night Train Show," which preceded Nite's show by around 15 years.

the quality of the music. That's not to imply that the "Presidentones" (Bill Clinton: lead; Jimmy Carter: first tenor/falsetto; Gerald Ford: second tenor; George Bush: second tenor; Ronald Reagan: bass) would suck eggs, but, to a commercial radio station, it just wouldn't matter.

The "Doo-Wop Shop" attracts people who enjoy the music. Doo-wop is the music that most of these listeners grew up with and it brings back fond memories of their own youths. It is an emotional/visceral response to the music that draws them; doo-wop, for them, is not an intellectual pursuit. The music is used, repeatedly, to refresh memories of their own lives, creating a sort of "musical

songs are dimmed because these songs are not heard. Over time, listeners who are (a) reminded of the popular songs by frequent play and (b) inattentive to the less popular songs that they have not heard in a while, become even more narrow in liking the well-known songs.

Evidence for this is found in a survey conducted in early 1993 by Don K. Reed. He asked Doo-Wop Shop listeners to call in with their two favorite doo-wop songs. The results were tabulated and titled the "Top 101 Doo-Wop Songs of All Time." The distribution of songs by year is shown in the chart below.

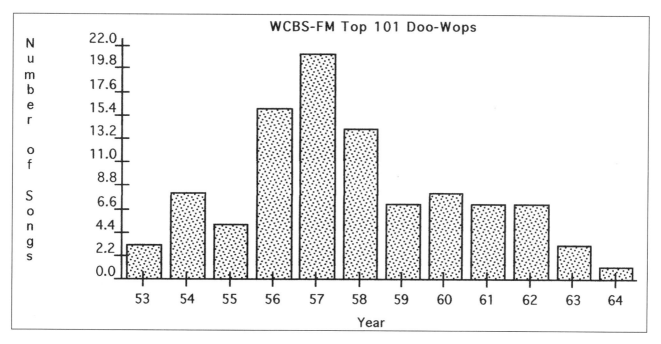

scrapbook." Often fans will associate particular events or people (old flames in particular) with a song that was popular at the time. For these reasons, this group of fans can be called "Nostalgics," because fond memories play an important role in their choice of songs. The more popular the song, generally reflected by local or national chart penetration, the more memories it evokes.

"Nostalgics" strongly identify with the more popular songs of the doo-wop era. This is how songs like "In The Still Of The Night" and "Earth Angel," which were popular in the mid-fifties and even more popular during the "Oldies But Goodies" revival of 1960, invariably run one-two in the eyes of the CBS-FM audience, year after year (as measured by this station's yearly "Top 500" survey and their recent "Top 101 Doo-Wop Songs Of All Time" survey).

At one time or another, just about everyone who listens to the "Doo-Wop Shop" danced with their honey to these songs, or at least fantasized doing so.[3] As a result, Nostalgics love hearing the same songs over and over because of the pleasant memories they evoke. If a station plays mostly the well-known songs of the era, this helps to reinforce memories of these songs. Conversely, memories of the less popular

As seen in the chart, the expected bimodal curve, with peaks representing classical the and neo-doo-wop eras is found. Heading the survey, as usual, are "In The Still Of The Night" and "Earth Angel," in that order. Less expected perhaps is the finding that 41% of these songs (41/101) charted on the Billboard Top 40. Remembering back to the discussion in the first chapter

3. Interestingly, a 1970 oldies poll conducted by *Stormy Weather* magazine, in issue #4, March-April 1971, has these two songs, in the same order, running one and two, in its Top Twenty All-Time Favorite Oldies But Goodies. A sidelight of this poll was that nine of the Top Ten Male Groups were in the doo-wop or R&B vein. The exception came in at the number-one position: the Beatles. The Chantels and Shirelles came in tied for the Top Female Group. An article by Harold Doezar titled, "Oldies Scene-'59" (*Time Barrier Express*, Issue #2, p. 14), reports on a survey conducted over the air by Alan Fredericks on his Night Train Oldies Show of June 28, 1959 on WHOM. "Earth Angel" came in number one, beating out number two "In The Still…" and number three "Tonite, Tonite." Plus ca change…

about the obscurity of doo-wop, this 41% figure supports the notion that CBS listeners, or Nostalgics, as we are calling them, like the more popular songs.

The CBS affiliate in Philadelphia, also an oldies station, is WOGL (98FM, 1210AM). Harvey Holiday, the doo-wop deejay with a Sunday night show, also caters to an audience of Nostalgics. Harvey did a similar survey with similar results, which are displayed by year below.

Holiday's "Top 98 Doo-Wops of 1992" resulted in a bimodal distribution similar to the Don K. Reed Survey, except that the first (classical doo-wop) peak occurs in

Marcels, were counted as black.) In surveys that polled only doo-wop fans (the Nostalgics), the numbers decreased but were still higher than expected. Thirty-five percent of Don K. Reed's "Top 101 Doo-Wops" and 26% of Harvey Holidays "Top 98 Doo-Wops" were performed by white groups.

This could simply reflect prejudice, but is more likely to reflect the fact that since most of today's audience for doo-wop is white, white groups allow Nostalgics to better identify with their own youth. Either way it is unfortunate, because it seems as if blacks get further and

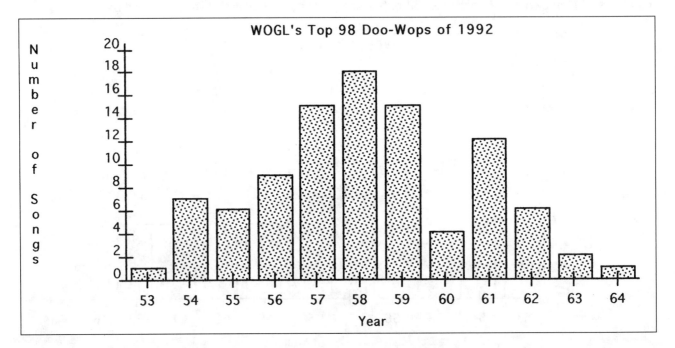

1958 rather than 1957, and the second (neo-doo-wop) peak occurs in 1961 rather than 1960. This may mean that doo-wop hit Philadelphia slightly later in time than it hit New York or that Philadelphians are just a little bit slower on the uptake than the rest of us. Philadelphian doo-woppers voted for songs that made the Billboard national Top 40 charts an amazing 50% of the time (49/98), confirming the hypothesis that listeners to a CBS affiliate attracts those that like the more popular songs.

Another characteristic of the population of Nostalgic listeners is that they also seem to like doo-wops sung by white groups such as the Earls, Duprees, Capris, Chimes etc. This proclivity is quite noticeable because of the groups that sang doo-wop in the paleo- and classical doo-wop eras, approximately 90 percent were black. The 1991 CBS-FM survey that yielded the "Top 500 Oldies of All Time" (discussed earlier), which polled all CBS listeners, and not just doo-wop fans, reported that roughly 30 percent of the Top 500 were doo-wop songs. Of these doo-wop songs, 42% were performed by white groups, as opposed to the 10% expected by history. (To get this percentage, mixed groups with white leads, such as the Crests and Rob Roys, were counted as white, while mixed groups with black leads, like the Dell Vikings and

further removed from the music that they created. Minorities are scarce at concerts and appear to rarely call to request a record or talk on New York metropolitan area doo-wop radio shows. Blacks may have less fond memories of the era and the music, perhaps associating them both with exploitation and being ripped off by the white establishment. Or perhaps blacks, seemingly always the creators of new trends in American music, e.g. ragtime, jazz, doo-wop, have simply moved on to newer things, such as rap and hip hop.

Nostalgics are also quite tolerant of the practice of borrowing the material of other groups. If Earl Lewis & the Channels sing "Shout" (a big hit for the Isley Brothers), an audience made up of Nostalgics would likely be pleased. Nostalgics who go to see the Channels want to remember the era, and if a song is borrowed, that's just fine. This practice is not universally accepted. Don K. Reed, while interviewing Lewis Lymon, commented, "Sometimes groups don't even do their own songs. If you come to see the Teenchords, I would assume you want to see them do their [own] hits."[4] Still, for Nostalgics, the most important criterion for acceptance is

4. From the "Doo-Wop Shop," April 18, 1993.

familiarity, because that is the link between the music and the memories.

On the other hand, for people subscribing to the second delivery system, familiarity often breeds contempt. This system, much smaller than the CBS-Nostalgic alliance, centers around a bunch of small radio stations, many of them emanating from colleges and universities, and a New Jersey-based organization called the "United In Group Harmony Association" (UGHA). Founded in 1976 by Ronnie Italiano (Ronnie I), the UGHA has a membership of roughly 2,000 people, almost all of whom are very serious about their music. We call this group of individuals the "Purists."

According to Christine Vitale, Ronnie Italiano's onetime coworker, "Through monthly meetings/shows, concerts, literature, radio and even television, UGHA provides in-depth insight of urban harmony culture. UGHA is also responsible for reuniting many groups, making it possible for many of them to return to the performance circuit. UGHA shows provide a more thorough and accurate representation of R&B/doo-wopp history than commercial productions by presenting groups based not on their 'marquee value' or the number of hits they had, but by their ability to emulate the sound of their recordings."[5] Whether or not all these statements are accurate, it's clear that Purists approach their music with quite a bit of enthusiasm.

A large percentage of doo-wop Purists got into the music as kids through the hobby of record collecting. Many people had copies of "Why Do Fools Fall In Love" by the Teenagers and "Only You" by the Platters, which reduced their importance in the eyes of the record collector cum Purist. But how many kids on the block had a copy of "If I Can't Have You" by the Flamingos on Chance, "Just To See You Smile Again" by the Four Buddies on Savoy, or "Skylark" by the Clovers on Atlantic? These were records worth putting on your want list, worth saving your dimes for, worth thinking about, talking about and having. Rarity was the driving force behind record collecting. The driving force of the hobby turned into the driving force of listening as these collectors matured. The scarcer the record, the more interesting it was to them. Just as many Nostalgics believe "the more popular the better," many Purists subscribe to "the rarer the better." Neither of these beliefs is necessarily accurate, but together they create a natural antagonism between some Purists and some Nostalgics.

While the Nostalgics were being exposed to the more popular recordings of any given group, the Purists were collecting, and therefore learning, about the group's rarer recordings. They thus learned about groups in depth. Nostalgics heard "Walking Along" by the Solitaires and loved it (who wouldn't?), but because it was the only one of the group's recordings that made it commercially (and at that it was covered by the Diamonds who had more commercial success), that was the only one they heard. Collector-Purists, however, were seeking out, to own and thus to listen to and appreciate, classics like "Blue Valentine," "Please Remember My Heart," and "I Don't Stand A Ghost Of A Chance." Purists learned about groups in depth and amassed a body of knowledge about the doo-wop genre in the process.

Music acceptable to these Purists is delivered over the airwaves by shows staffed by part-time deejays that love the doo-wop and/or group rhythm and blues sound. The central program among this group for many years was Ronnie I's "R & B Party," which was aired on WNYE-FM, New York (91.5).[6] This is the New York City Board of Education station, and the R & B Party was sandwiched between shows that cater to Russian immigrants and French-speaking populations. Financial support for the show came partly from the Board of Education, partly from the UGHA (of which Ronnie I is the president), Clifton Music (a record store which Ronnie owns) and donations from faithful listeners. Other shows that cater to the Purist population are aired on college radio stations[7] in the New York metropolitan area.

All of the deejays on these shows say they do it for love, not money. All, to our knowledge, are volunteers. All have other, probably less rewarding, full-time jobs. Most of the deejays and most of the listeners are linked together by the UGHA. The music aired over these stations is not programmed as much by economics as it is at CBS-FM. These Purist deejays play what they like and what their loyal fans want to hear. While some make a living from the music, no one seems to be getting rich. The choice of music is governed by their taste, not ratings. And the taste of these record collectors who became Purists and deejays or listeners is not the same as the taste of those that listen exclusively to CBS-FM. In fact, the Purists have developed an unofficial set of principles or rules that have become almost a "Purist Manifesto." Just as the most orthodox members of a religious group are more critical of members of their own flock that they consider not pious enough than they are of members of other sects, so the Purists look down on the Nostalgics.

The Purists see themselves as the conservators or preservationists of the rhythm and blues vocal group genre. They see the music as being undervalued, ignored and watered down, and their goal is to preserve it in its original form. They resist and resent any attempt to commercialize the music to make it more palatable for the masses. They feel an obligation to teach people about the provenance and history of the music, and to convert new aficionados to the cause. The music is to

---

5. From the *Program to the 3rd Annual United in Group Harmony Association Hall of Fame Awards Ceremony*, held March 27, 1993 at the Symphony Space Performing Arts Center, New York, N.Y.

6. Past tense, because as of the fall of 1998, his show was off the air. See postscript at end of this chapter.

7. Specifics about some of these programs can be found in a footnote in the Recidivism chapter.

be taken seriously, not lightly. It is to be appreciated and understood and not used as a tool just to make money. Nostalgia or entertainment value of the music, while not ignored, is not the primary focus. And injustices perpetrated by the recording industry on these mostly black groups that created their music need to be talked about, exposed, and, if possible, redressed.

Tudor and Tudor[8] generalize the cult characteristics of the Purists: "...we have found that one of the most maddening things about loving minority musical styles is the frustration we feel when we try to share that love with others who are both ignorant of the form and apathetic toward it ('I don't know and I don't care'). In addition, there is the equally disheartening feeling—when that favorite minority musical style either changes into another form of expression which becomes more popular than the original while still being imitative [as when the white group sound eclipsed the black paleo-doo-wop sound of the early 1950s], or when it gets raped by enterprising producers and performers who then try to pass it off as theirs alone [as when the Drifters of the late 1950s drifted away from their original gospel-bluesy style and began putting out popular music like "Save The Last Dance For Me"]. The circle becomes complete and the frustrations compounded when we try to convince others that this more 'popular' music is but a pale imitation of the originals."

Marty Gottlieb points out the paradoxical nature of this do-goodism: "The difference in racial makeup between the organization and most of the groups it idolizes is striking: the largest number of the U.G.H.A.'s members are blue-collar, suburban [white] men between 45 and 60 years old, who by many accounts are Reagan Democrats who don't share, and in fact are hostile to, broad social agendas endorsed overwhelmingly by the black community."[9] In effect, the same people who idolize these black singers don't socialize with blacks and are likely to vote against social programs that help blacks. The difference may be explained by the underdog sentiments of the Purist camp; that is, they see themselves, and the black singers they revere, as allied against the oppressive corporate giants of the recording industry. Or it may be that they identify with the hard work and hard lives that many of these singers went through, seeing it as similar to their own struggle through life, and that the social programs that they vote against are for the "lazy" or "welfare" blacks, and thus don't deserve their support.

Gottlieb describes the reverence in which these singers are held: "To have been in a black group, no matter how insignificant, is to be royalty at [U.G.H.A.]. Ask Eugene Tompkins...When he was a sophomore at Morris High School in the South Bronx in 1956, he was a member of the Limelighters, who cut a single record featuring

a quickly forgotten flop, 'Cabin Hideaway.' Twenty-one years later, he found himself at an association festival, and when word passed of his presence, he was called to the stage, where he received an ovation. Association members recited to him the lyrics of 'Cabin Hideaway'."[10]

The bulk of the music that is played on the Purist radio shows and presented at UGHA Collectors Shows are from the 1950s, but pre- and post-World War II group harmonic music also gets some exposure. Very little neo-doo-wop, very little white doo-wop and very little distaff doo-wop has been tolerated by Purists. According to the gospel of a few years ago, female groups sing harmony, but not well. Ronnie I maintained that the best female group can't compare to a mediocre male group. White groups just can't sing as well as the black groups, and have sold out to the establishment to make a buck. Recently, the party line has been revised.

Italiano, who both creates attitudes in his listeners and, in turn, reflects their attitudes, is the pacesetter. Within the last few years he remarried, and his wife's best friend Amy Ortiz is the (very capable) lead singer of the reformed Chantels, so that his position on distaff harmony has softened considerably. In addition to bringing harmony into his own home, so to speak, it has also righted a bias that was unfair and undeserved. Italiano's bark has always been worse than his bite, philosophically speaking. Within the last few years, he has put on separate concerts with all white groups and all female (or at least female-led) groups, featuring the likes of Della Griffin (of the Enchanters), Vicki Burgess (Charmers/Joytones) and Ruth McFadden (Supremes/Harptones/Royaltones) and, of course, the Chantels. He has recently even issued several CDs with the double-entendre titles, "Ladies First," featuring female leads (i.e. Sandra Italiano, Amy Ortiz and others) fronting male groups.

The concerts staged by those catering to Purist tastes differ drastically from those produced for Nostalgics. Concerts for Nostalgics are big productions. They are held in places like Radio City Music Hall (New York City), Westbury Music Fair and the Garden State Arts Center (suburban New York and New Jersey, respectively). These places can hold thousands and are often filled. Usually eight to ten well-known (in the sense of having had at least one big hit) groups appear and sing anywhere from three to five songs. Percentage-wise, the groups are disproportionately white and they sing the songs that made them popular. If one were to attend this type of concert regularly to follow a particular group, it is likely that you would hear the same songs performed from show to show. The acts vary their material less than at concerts for Purists.

Concerts for Purists, on the other hand, are frequently produced by the UGHA and are held in smaller, less well-known and in some cases less ritzy locales. Shows that draw more than a few hundred

8. Tudor, Dean, and Tudor, Nancy. *Black Music.* Littleton, Colorado: Libraries United Inc., 1979.
9. Gottlieb, Martin. "On the White Side of Crossover Dreams." *New York Times*, Feb. 14, 1993, p. 6.

10. Gottlieb, Martin. "The Durability of Doo-Wop." *New York Times*, Jan. 17, 1993, Sec. 2, p. 1.

people are considered successful. The names of many of the groups would often be unrecognizable to the Nostalgic; purists take pride in unearthing and/or reuniting some of the more arcane groups of yore. One gets his or her money's worth, however, as groups sing from five to ten songs each and the concerts usually last in excess of three hours. Even the groups that have had a hit record are encouraged by the audience to dig deep into their repertoires to revive less well-known material. And it goes without saying that a group must sing only its own material; poaching on another group's turf invites ridicule.[11]The Purist craves depth and diversity. The Purists give their allegiance to an era and to a group, while Nostalgics are loyal to songs that evoke memories. At concerts for Nostalgics, groups never get past their popular material, while concerts run by Purists don't welcome the presence of groups that have achieved some financial success, like the Five Satins, Cleftones and Earls. To the Purists, you're either fer us or agin us.

Many of the beliefs of the Purists emerged in a survey recently conducted among doo-wop cognoscenti. The Relic Rack, an oldies record store (and not to be confused with Gries and Fileti's Relic Records which puts out albums and CDs), ran a poll of knowledgeable UGHA members in 1992. Eighty-four people selected their fifteen favorite vintage harmony groups and ranked them from one to fifteen. Points were assigned and tabulated, and a rank order of 152 groups, in order of their popularity was obtained. The top twenty groups were:

1) Five Keys
2) Flamingos
3) Orioles
4) Moonglows
5) Solitaires
6) Harptones
7) Dominoes
8) Ravens
9) Clovers
10) Spaniels
11) Cadillacs
12) Heartbeats
13) Swallows
14) Larks
15) Drifters (1953-1958)
16) Cardinals
17) Frankie Lymon & the Teenagers
18) Diablos
19) Castelles
20) Robins

There are many interesting and revealing things about this survey. First, of the top twenty groups, all but six were known for singing in the Paleo-doo-wop style. Five groups were known best for classical doo-wop (Solitaires, Spaniels, Cadillacs, Heartbeats, & Teenagers) and one group, the Ravens, was primarily pre-doo-wop. Overall, 10% of the 152 groups were pre-paleo-doo-wop by our definition (that is, they made their biggest impact in the years before doo-wop existed), 39% made their biggest impact in the paleo-doo-wop years (1951-1954), 41% in the classical doo-

wop years (1955-1959) and 10% in the neo-doo-wop years (1960-1963). This is a unimodal (one peak) distribution that contrasts with the bimodal distribution found in most surveys of doo-wop popularity. This shows where the heart of the Purist lies, namely in the early fifties. Understandably, the Purists feel that CBS-FM concentrates on the music of the classical and neo-doo-wop eras and ignores these earlier groups to which they are so devoted. One reason for this, as yet unverified, is that Purists are four or five years older on average than Nostalgics, had their adolescence four or five years earlier, and gravitated to music that came out four or five years earlier.

Second, the first white group to appear on the list, the Skyliners, only achieved 52nd place. This fact, when compared to the white-black ratio on shows like the "Doo-Wop Shop," which approximates one third of the plays, makes it obvious why the blood of Purists boil when talking about CBS. Further, the first female group to show up, the Chantels, appears in 99th place. Overall, just 5% of the 152 groups mentioned were white, and only 2% have female voices playing an important role.

Donn Fileti explains the white-black thing: "Among longtime fans of R&B vocal group harmony, there's an unwritten pecking order and established hierarchy. The classic, pioneer black groups of the early-to-mid fifties are at the top: the Orioles, Five Keys, Ravens, or Flamingos; the black groups closely identified with the mid-to-late fifties- the Spaniels, Solitaires, Harptones, of Dells- are in the middle, and those African American groups from the late fifties and early sixties the Del Vikings, Channels, Charts, or Dreamlovers-come close behind. At the very bottom (to some avid doo-wop fans, not even worthy of serious consideration) are the white groups; those Johnny and Vito-come latelys to the world of R&B/R&R vocal group harmony.

It's tough to mount a reasoned or complicated defense of the white group, many of whom were very young, Italian-American, and New York City born and bred. With a very few exceptions (Dion and Johnny Maestro come to mind immediately), their lead singers just couldn't cut it compared with Pookie of the Spaniels or Willie of the Harptones. At best, many were blatantly commercial mimics of their black peers, offering a watered-down, highly artificial interpretation of the complex harmonies of the better R&B groups."[12]

Not only do purists give white groups a hard time, they can be impossible to please. Paul Bennett, in reviewing Roulette reissue of the somewhat famous "Teenage Party" LP, was one tough audience for what most consider sacrosanct tunes. In reviewing "You Baby You" by the Cleftones, he writes "...The group vocal lead-in is not too good. The first bridge is vocalized with guitar support while the second features a sax but the initial notes are off key. The group exhibits great difficulty

11. This only applies to groups that recorded during the doo-wop era. Newly formed groups have more latitude, but are encouraged to sing songs that aren't done by existing groups.

12. Fileti, Donn. Liner notes from the CD titled, *A Lighter Shade of Doo-Wop*, Relic Records, August 1993.

getting into and out of the bridges. Not a professional attempt. Fair."[13] On "I Love You So" by the Crows, Bennett states, "...The group is very secondary except for the second tenor who wails in the background. The second bridge is by the bass and is not very good, although the tenor tries to remedy the situation. The first bridge features the first tenor with the second tenor in support.[14] The fade is fair. The group seems as if it were cut off short. I like the song but not by the Crows in this case. A decent effort at best."[15] Whew!

Other evidence for the taste differences between the two camps can be found in the Purists choice of admittees to the United In Group Harmony Hall Of Fame. (The name "Doo-Wop Hall of Fame" cannot be used because an organization by that name already exists.[16] This organization, headed by Harvey Robbins, held an inaugural concert in Providence, Rhode Island, in May 1993. Unfortunately, as of early 1997, for financial reasons this group has not been able to find a home for its hall, and so no groups have been admitted or announced. According to the groups that appeared at its one concert, such as the Drifters and the Jive Five, the organization will honor and sponsor groups that will appeal to Nostalgics.) In the first eight years, 1991-1998, 44 groups have been voted in by the UGHA membership and 12 have been appointed as honorary inductees (Delta Rhythm Boys, Ink Spots, Mills Brothers, etc.) by the founder and president of UGHA, Ronnie Italiano. A complete list of the inductees can be found in Chapter 20. Including the honorary inductees, all groups are black, 11 are from the pre-paleo doo-wop years (almost all of the honorary inductees), 17 made their mark in the paleo-doo-wop era, 27 in the classical doo-wop era and not surprisingly, if it weren't for the Jive Five, the neo-doo-wop era would've run up a goose egg.

A look at the flagship radio programs, Reed's "Doo-Wop Shop" and Italiano's "R&B Party" points out further differences between the two factions. The non-musical time on the "Doo-Wop Shop" is almost entirely devoted to commercials (with occasional sports and weather updates, community service notices and "Doo-Wop Shop" jingles). This is as it should be, CBS-FM is a commercial radio station, and the bills have to be paid. Reed is a pleasant, likable and professional deejay. He avoids doo-wopolitics and controversy whenever possible. Even though Italiano likes his listeners to think there's a war out there, Don is above it, even to the extent of playing music emanating from Ronnie I's Clifton label and interviewing groups associated with the UGHA. Bobby Jay, who works for CBS, similarly stays out of the fray, often visiting UGHA

events and occasionally getting on stage to sing.

Reed goes about his business without fanfare and without a lot of kibitzing around and about the music. He is also constrained by the format of an "oldies" station. For example, CBS-FM sometimes runs "50s" and "60s" weekends (whereon only songs for the given decade can be played), in roughly equal numbers, at various times during the year. This practice is clearly prejudicial against pre-paleo-, paleo-, and even classical doo-wop, because the majority of doo-wop appeared in the '50s, not the '60s. For "60s" weekends, Reed really has to hustle to find appropriate material.

Every two years or so, Reed runs a contest to let people vote for the "Top 101 Doo-Wop Songs of All Time," by calling in with their top two or three picks. Three different lists, from 1992, 1994, and 1996 were examined and compared.[17] First, there's an enormous amount of correspondence among the lists. Of the 101 songs that made the 1992 list, 69 also made the 1994 list and 63 made the 1996 list. Of the 101 songs that made the 1994 list, 75 also made the 1996 list. All of the Top 20 from 1992 and 1994 made both of the other lists, and 19 of the Top 20 from 1996 made the other two lists. Only two songs on each list were performed by female groups and 35% on average were performed by white groups. "In The Still Of The Night" by the Five Satins topped all three polls (just as it always tops CBS's Top 500 list) and "Earth Angel" by the Penguins finished second twice and third once. In 1996, 19 of the 101 were performed by nine of the Purists' favorite groups (Five Keys, Flamingos, Moonglows, Harptones, Dominoes, Cadillacs, Heartbeats, Teenagers, and Diablos). The average recording date of the three surveys was 1957.87 for the 1992 poll, 1958.32 for the 1994 poll and 1958.33 for the 1996 poll. The modal (most popular) year for all three was 1957. The songs preferred by Reed's listeners are consistently classical doo-wops performed by male groups that are more white than one would expect by chance.

On the "R&B Party," by contrast, there were no commercials because the show was on a public radio station, although Ronnie "slipped in" plugs for U.G.H.A. and Clifton music. The time between records was filled with facts about the records and editorializing by Ronnie I. Calls from the audience were taken and reported by his helper (at one time Christine Vitale, then Tony "Tony O" Oetjin), and Ronnie commented on the callers' opinions (or just said hello) as he saw fit. Many of his listeners apparently liked this format, because they kept calling up week after week to express their opinions. This provided a way for the audience to feel like they

13. Bennett, Paul M. "Album Alley." *Bim Bam Boom*, Issue #8, December 1972, p. 46.
14. This is beginning to sound like an Abbott and Costello routine.
15. Bennett, Paul M. "Album Alley."
16. Actually, the name is "Doo-Wop Hall of Fame of America."

17. Single artist recordings, such as "Angel Baby" by Rosie and the Originals and "Looking For An Echo" by Kenny Vance and the Planetones were excluded from statistics. "Morse Code Of Love" from 1982 was excluded from calculation of the average year because, as an outlier, it would unduly affect the result.

were participating and that their opinions were at least given air. The show provided a vocal bulletin board also, so that friends in the doo-wop world could say hello to one another, wish each other happy birthday, etc. More and more as the years pass, the show also served to broadcast news of the death of performers. Those who tuned in were made to feel like they belonged to a club, and an elitist one (devoted to "Purism") at that. On the "Doo-Wop Shop," deaths are announced and requests taken (at the approximate rate of one per half-hour) but "clubbiness" is absent.

Italiano, unlike Reed, is not reticent. He takes any and every opportunity to tell you what he thinks and what he feels about any topic even remotely related to doo-wop. He has even "lobbied" (filibustered is more like it) for groups that he would prefer to see voted into the UGHA Hall of Fame. He asked members to vote for the Larks and Cardinals in 1993 and played quite a few of their records. The authors don't recall him offering time for an opposing view to be heard. This pushed groups like the Five Satins and Cleftones out of the running for induction that year. His disdain for fair play even bothered his co-host at the time, Chris Vitale, although he managed to convince enough members so that the Larks and Cardinals were voted in. Although shading the limits of objectivity—no, let's face it, throwing objectivity out the window and watching it splat on the ground—one can often see the method in his madness. Thermon Ruth of the Larks and Ernie Lee Warren and Donald Johnson of the Cardinals were still alive, available and willing to appear on stage at the UGHA Hall of Fame show. To be blunt, Italiano wanted these guys on stage before they died. To this day, he's very proud of getting Herb Kenny of the Ink Spots and Cleo Perry of the Inspirators up on the UGHA stage shortly before their deaths.

In December of 1986, right after performing at the 100th U.G.H.A. meeting-show, Charles Moffit, the legendary bass of the Velours, was murdered in the elevator of his apartment building. Italiano seems to have ample reason to hurry the appearances of these singers along; Joe Duncan of the Vocaleers and Harmon Bethea of the Cap-Tans took ill just before they were scheduled to appear at early 1993 UGHA events. The performers are aging, and in a short while there will be very few left. Italiano isn't saintly, however. He began to play and seemingly revere Tony Williams, the great lead of the Platters, only after he died. Before Williams' death, Italiano was, at best, neutral to the Platters works.

What are his motives? Surely not just monetary, because encouraging people to vote for the Five Satins, Cleftones or even the Belmonts (over his dead body) would have made more financial sense. It is likely that his idealism endears him to the Purists. A transcript of part of one of his shows[18] illustrates his style, his beliefs and his passion:

---

18. From "The R&B Party," April 14, 1993.

Ron: We bring back some great memories of the '50s. We're helping to try to keep that sound alive…although it's difficult at times. You know we're talkin' about the show [Collector's Show #10, held the previous weekend] and it was the holiday [Easter] weekend. We didn't have the greatest turnout, right Chris? It makes me think I may discontinue the Collector's Shows and just concentrate on the Pioneer and Vintage Shows and bring people like the Five Pennies once in a while…because we lost a lot of money on the U.G.H.A…We can't afford to lose that kind of money.

Chris: The turnout…it was very disappointing.

Ron: And it was the holidays and it was dumb, really, on my part to have it then but…you don't even get all the U.G.H.A. members there [at the concerts]. You get the people who pay their ten bucks to come to a meeting and see 18 a capella groups…but [not to see]…this history being made. They'll sit at a bar [at the back of Schuetzen Park, a meeting hall], be noisy all night, but they won't come to one of these shows…a lot of them. You notice that?

Chris: Oh, I definitely notice. You have the people who just frequent the meeting shows and then others who only come out for the Collector's Show. You don't really get that many for both.

Ron: Can you imagine if we had a major station in New York City playing things like "Mr. Moon" [by the Five Pennies]. Why shouldn't "Mr. Moon" be played? It's a beautiful song. Or all those beautiful Ravens [songs] that are never played on major radio.

Chris: Well, it's true. Our poor ticket sales for a lot of the shows that we do…we have to attribute to the fact that the major New York City radio station [that] plays oldies does not play the groups we like to book, and if they did, we'd have no problem selling tickets.

Ron: [Facetiously] What if I booked Lenny Cocco & the Chimes and Larry Chance & the Earls?

Chris: Then you, too, would sell tickets.

Ron: We would sell a lot because that's all they play, but I'd rather not do anything.

Chris: [Sarcastically] Think of all the money you could make Ronnie.

Ron: Yeah. Right!

Chris: But think about what you'd be doing to this music. You gotta follow your heart.

Ron: I know. So you guys [the audience] gotta remember one thing. I have to get my frustrations off somehow, and bitchin' and complainin' all the time is how I get my, you know, get this away, so bear with me. I know a lot of them say, 'There he goes again,' but how else [voice clearly emotional] am I gonna do this. You want me to stop it, discontinue it, and get aggravated? I have to get this stuff off of me. You don't want me to give it all to Christine [calming down, lightening up] all the time. You guys have to take a share too. You guys love the music like Christine does. You guys gotta take your share of my verbal abuse and my frustrations [laughs]. That's pretty good, right [referring to his harangue]?

And the audience (that stays tuned) did seem to take his "verbal abuse," and appeared to love it, because they kept coming back for more—and sometimes goaded him on to more editorializing. Somewhere, under the surface abrasiveness, was a nice guy trying to advance a cause. Notice that in the dialogue he bemoaned losing money, criticized himself for choosing a poor date, chastised UGHA members for not attending enough shows (and sometimes being too noisy when they do), lambasted CBS-FM for not playing enough obscure ("Mr. Moon") and early (Ravens) music, and for being too commercial, and took a slap at white doo-woppers. He then went on to sort of apologize, or at least explain why he needed to vent his frustrations. And at the end, the listener is left liking him.

A numerical and sadistical analysis of the songs played by Reed and Italiano was performed on data from the first four months of 1993. Fourteen of Reed's 17 shows in this time frame, representing 56 hours of music (his "Interview Hour" was not included), were included in the analysis. Sixteen of Italiano's shows, representing 32 hours of music, were analyzed. Some of the conclusions yielded by the data were:

a) The sample of songs used was 366 for Italiano and 940 for Reed, implying that Reed played more songs per hour than did his counterpart (16.8 to 11.4). Italiano used his show as a sort of clubhouse, and this left less time for music.

b) 7.6% of the songs played by Italiano were from before 1950; none of the 940 songs played by Reed fall in this category. The weighted average of the years of the songs played Italiano was 1955.03, compared to 1958.37 for the songs played by Reed. On average, Italiano played songs that are more than three years older than the ones played by Reed.

c) Italiano played obscure music, as compared to Reed. As a basis of comparison, we used our Top 500 from our earlier work, *Doo-Wop: The Forgotten Third of Rock 'n' Roll*. While one can argue with our choices, it is clear that our list represents most of the most popular and well-known doo-wops ever recorded. Reed played 41.1% of Top 500 songs, while Italiano only played 2.5%. It is clear that the Purists pooh-pooh the popular pap.

For example, on Reed's Top 101 Doo-Wops survey for 1996, the Cadillacs' "Speedoo" (#62) and "Gloria" (#8) both placed. In a phone survey conducted by Italiano on his radio show (April, 1995), his listeners' three favorite Cadillacs' songs, in order, were "The Girl I Love," "You Are" and "Window Lady." "Gloria" and "Speedoo" didn't even make the list.[19] "Why Do Fools Fall In Love," by Frankie Lymon and the Teenagers, came in at #27 on Reed's list, yet wasn't in the top five favorite Teenagers' songs on Italiano's poll. "Share,"

by the same group, was #17 on Reed's list and was second to "Paper Castles" with Italiano's audience.

d) Reed played a much larger percentage of white groups than did Italiano, 25.6% to 4.1%, and a larger percentage of female groups (or female leads), 6.8% to 4.1%. Italiano, who used to disdain female groups, had an attitude adjustment since his remarriage in 1996.

In summary, Italiano played more older, more obscure, blacker and male music than did Reed—and was more vocal and controversial about the differences. Is this controversy stirred up by Purists good or bad for doo-wop music? On one hand, it's probably irrelevant. Purists regularly snipe at the establishment, but their audience is small. Members of the establishment allied with Nostalgics have generally chosen the higher road. That is, they just don't react to the barbs and continue playing the songs they were playing.

On the other hand, the differences between these two camps prevents a united front to common problems. Unfortunately, if one projects into the future, the picture is not a pretty one. First, because the Purists seem to look down their nose at anyone who doesn't support the music that they do, they are unlikely to attract much positive attention to their cause. As they age, they will continue to be an insular, small, select club of geezers that say they want to pass their music on, but are unable to attract enough younger people who want to learn about it. They will repel many members of the younger set, just as complaining, crotchety old people do.

The Nostalgics will age also, but they will be able to hear less and less of their music on the airwaves. Stations like CBS-FM, which must follow the dollar, will eventually be attracted to the next generation, as their economic clout grows in turn. Thus, with the dawn of the 21st century, oldies stations will be playing music from the 1970s and 1980s. Doo-wop will be just as easy to find as music from the 1930s and 1940s is today. If one knocks CBS-FM for this shift, one must also knock the market economy which is the basis of our political system. If someone or something is going to help stem the march into obscurity of doo-wop and group rhythm and blues, some things have to change. Toward the goal of preserving the music, we have come up with a set of suggestions.

FOR CBS-FM (and similar oldies stations): The parent corporation of CBS-FM has no reason to push doo-wop music over other kinds of oldies unless it makes them more money. According to their own ingenious and inexpensive market research, however, in the form of the "Top 500 Oldies of All Time," it should make them more money. Doo-wop music, year after year, occupies 30% of the Top 500 Oldies surveys, including more than half of the top ten. It would seem that expanding the air time allotted to doo-wop would be a sound financial decision. As of the year 2000, only four hours per week (the "Doo-Wop Shop") is strictly dedicated to doo-wop music.

---

19. Maybe they were on a date.

FOR THE "PURISTS": Cut the holier-than-thou stuff. You can preserve the music and teach about it without turning up your noses at those who know less. It's like college students being critical of the grade-school students because they don't know as much. Purists should encourage those new to the doo-wop or vintage rhythm-and-blues genres to tune into the Nostalgic type of music. They should say, "When you want to learn more, come to us." As they say, you have to learn how to crawl before you can walk. Even Chris Vitale, a Purist through and through, admitted to having trouble appreciating some of the early groups (like the Cardinals) until after she studied them for awhile. Donn Fileti notes[20] that songs by white groups are a lot more accessible and understandable to novice listeners than those recorded by benchmark groups like the Orioles and Clovers. The niche for the Purist lies with their greater expertise and knowledge. They do not necessarily have better taste than the rest of us. They should teach without belittling those who know less.

FOR CBS-FM: Listen to what the Purists are saying and educate your audience. Add a structured, regular weekly program designed to examine the antecedents of doo-wop, different styles that make up the group harmony sound, and even touch on the sociocultural issues of the 1950s. Bruce Morrow does this in spots, so does Bobby Jay (other CBS-FM deejays), but neither does it specifically for doo-wop. Hire someone to design, write and organize these musical shows in consultation with people knowledgeable about the music. Number the shows, like Italiano does. This will make tapes of the shows attractive to collectors and give you more credibility as an oldies radio station. It will also make the music more understandable to younger people who want to learn about it. Air the show once a week and see what kind of response ensues. Some possible topics for these shows are:

1) How was doo-wop born from gospel, post-war R&B and black popular music?
2) Who were the famous single artists who started as members of doo-wop groups?
3) Tracing the history of the nonsense syllable in doo-wop music.
4) The emergence of the novelty song in doo-wop music.
5) How and when did white doo-wop groups emerge?
6) How did falsetto become a part of the music?
7) Trace the history of the (fill in a city) sound in doo-wop music.
8) What were the geographical differences in the doo-wop style?
9) Look at the history of the (fill in a name) record label.
10) Look at the career of the (fill in the name of a

singing group) and the lives of its members.

FOR THE "PURISTS": Don't discard the term "doo-wop." It's the only term that describes a significant portion of your music that is instantly recognizable by young people as well as by baby boomers. By the time any other phrase like "classic rhythm and blues" or "vintage harmony" becomes as well-known, we will all have doo-wopped off the face of the earth.

Ronnie Italiano, on an April 1993 show, held a mock burial for the term "doo-wop." In 1996, he ran comic spots on his "R&B Party," urging people to "chump the 'D' word," which we assume meant not to use it. While it is true that "doo-wop" is overused and misused, the place of the Purist (as the expert) is to teach and point out the mistakes, not to take your proverbial ball (or records) and go home. "Angel Baby" by Rosie Hamlin & the Originals is NOT doo-wop because there is no group singing behind Rosie. Don & Juan's "What's Your Name?," a record with the right "feel" for doo-wop is still not. Doo-wop requires at least three voices. Nostalgics are not born knowing this stuff. They need to be taught.

What if the Eskimos, who have many different words for what non-Eskimos call snow, said, "Those warm-weather guys are really butchering the word 'snow.' They call sleet 'snow,' they call hail 'snow,' they call wet (good packing) snow 'snow,' and they call dry snow (bad for snowballs) 'snow.' Those guys are mindless dolts. We'll teach them a lesson! We'll stop using the word 'snow.' Instead, all us Eskimos will call it 'frebbish' instead." For the Eskimos, this would be silly, because non-Eskimos wouldn't care what Eskimos called their cold stuff. Burying doo-wop has the same effect.

And yes, we know that doo-wop will not suffice for the Purist who also is interested in material recorded before the doo-wop era. Vintage group harmony could be used, or early group vocal harmony or early group rhythm and blues. The musics of the Mills Brothers, Ravens, Five Keys, Harptones, Solitaires, Teenagers, Belmonts, and Marcels are so dissimilar that one name, be it "doo-wop" or "vintage group harmony" will not describe them all adequately. The authors feel that even the term "doo-wop" is too all-encompassing; that is why we have made an attempt to come up with eras and subcategories. If one says "gang doo-wop" or "school boy doo-wop" the music the term connotes is instantly understood by anyone even vaguely familiar with the music. Description, communication and ultimately understanding are made easier by specificity. (How's that for a high fallutin' sentence?)

FOR THE NOSTALGICS: Choose one group from among the Five Keys, Flamingos, Harptones, Moonglows, Orioles, and Solitaires. Study the group by purchasing one or several records or CDs that contain not just their greatest hits (so that you won't know all the songs). If possible get one with extensive liner notes. Listen to all the songs all the way through several times. Think about the music; how is it like the doo-wop music you usually listen to, how does it differ. Can you start to pick out the different voices? Now you will begin to

---

20. Fileti, Donn. Liner notes from the CD titled, *A Lighter Shade of Doo-Wop*, Relic Records, August 1993.

understand how the Purist enjoys his/her music.

As a matter of fact, you, too, can become a Purist. The test is: If you can't name 10 doo-wop groups in 60 seconds, your are a Nostalgic. If you can, but you struggle, you have elevated yourself to the level of "Dabbler." If you can name ten groups easily but any of them are white or female or made their mark after 1960, you are an "Aficionado." Only if the groups that pour off your tongue are all black and male can you even think of being a Purist.

FOR THE "DOO-WOP RECORD/CD PRODUCERS": Make sure that the liner notes are extensive. Most Nostalgics have few other ways of learning about the music in depth. Also, while it is wonderful to see the performers of the era that we treasure return to the stage after a gap of 30-35 years (more in some cases), there may be other ways to preserve this era for future generations. If Babe Ruth were alive today (he'd be 105 years old as of 2000), it might be interesting to watch him (try to) swing a bat, but it would be a lot more rewarding to hear him talk about his experiences. Likewise, although it's a treat to see guys our age still able to hit the harmony, recordings should be made of their recollections of their careers in music. Further, the advent of the CD would allow multimedia products, such as pictures plus music or music plus narration. At one time doo-wop enthusiasts resisted the CD era because the sound was too clear for ears trained on vinyl, but most of us now realize that it adds to the doo-wop cause (increased length of play, digitizing previously unreleased masters, making voices more distinct). We may as well use it in new ways as well.

FOR ALL DOO-WOP LOVERS: Work toward the establishment of a Center for the Study of Doo-wop Vocal Group Harmony. This center would not necessarily be to honor the living members of old groups, or new groups performing currently under original names as do existing halls of fame. The purpose of the center would simply be for the study and preservation of the music.

The center would be housed in a location that makes sense for doo-wop, such as New York City, northern New Jersey or Philadelphia. It would contain complete sets of all the extinct and current doo-wop periodicals, relevant books and the liner notes from all available record albums and CDs. Photographs could be collected and displayed, and their quality improved through with the use of CD-ROM technology (just as aural CD technology has improved sound quality). Old movies and performances on tape featuring singing groups could be either shown, available for rent, or both. The latest in equipment would be used to store music and information thereon for the benefit of future generations.

Discovering funding for a study center may not be that difficult. Since the story of doo-wop is inextricably mingled with the history of minorities in the larger Northeastern cities, one would think that urban political leaders would try to help with seed money. Further, there are quite a number of people left over from the doo-wop years that are enormously successful (e.g. Ahmet Ertegun, Harvey Fuqua, Teddy Randazzo) and might be interested in helping to preserve the music that gave them their start. Grants and fund-raising could be supplemented by admission fees and the use of volunteer staff.

If the center is to run smoothly, it would have to be non-partisan. That is, it should not be dominated or run by either camp previously discussed. Instead, historians and career managers should run it with input from Purists, Nostalgics, columnists and authors, deejays and record collectors, and even computer and media experts. The center should be a place where music can be heard, films and photographs seen, and stories of the doo-wop era are available for reading. The atmosphere should be uptempo, and the mood one of harmony. It should be a place that people from the doo-wop generation will want to visit, and bring their children and grandchildren along. In this way will the music cross the generations.

FOR THE DOO-WOP AUDIENCE: Speak up! Listen to radio stations that play doo-wop and let the station know what your favorite subcategories, groups and songs are. Call up CBS-FM. Call up these stations, whether they're mainstream, big-time oldies factories like WCBS-FM in New York or one of the smaller college outfits and let them know you're out there. If doo-wopolitics annoys you and/or turns you away from the station, or if you kind of enjoy the controversies, let them know. Write to the Rock 'n' Roll Hall of Fame in Cleveland and let officials know who you think they should be inducting.

POSTSCRIPT: There is flux in the world of our music. Ronnie I's "R&B Party" went off the air recently, the victim of politics in the world of public radio. He lost one of his two hours to a Russian-language broadcast first, then was ousted by a French-language broadcast at the end of August 1998. A travesty, n'est pas? He's hopeful that he'll find another station for his show and is working on obtaining funding for a hall of fame site somewhere in New York City or Northern New Jersey.

Meanwhile, he has brought protégés of his (the Variations and a bevy of female leads that produced a "Ladies First" CD) up to Don K. Reed's "Doo-wop Shop" twice in November of 1988 (the 8th and 22nd). It may just be that the battle between the purists and nostalgics is at least partly for show. And that would be good for all of us.

To add salt to the wounds, Don K. Reed's "Doo-Wop Shop" was cut from five hours to four, 8 p.m. to 12 a.m. on Sunday nights. The walls are beginning to close in, folks.

Chapter 14

The Teen-age Menace

One can make a strong argument that doo-wop vocal group harmony in particular, or rock 'n' roll in general, could not have emerged at any earlier point in time. While the right combination of previous musics (gospel, rhythm and blues and pop), technology, radio deejays and recording industry may have been necessary conditions to produce the new music, they were not sufficient conditions. The existence of a separate, musically challenged, teenage generation provided the missing piece of the puzzle.

Before the 1950s, teen-agers were treated like young adults. Most boys were obliged to work as soon as they were physically able, weren't expected to attend college, and were programmed to work full-time or join the armed forces after high school graduation. Young women were prepared to marry and start families after graduation. If they hadn't a willing beau, they worked at a job (not a career) until they found one to settle down with. There was no women's liberation, no postponing work by going to college (for most) and no free rides. Kids watched their dads work hard and long, usually six days per week, and watched their moms raise lots of kids and take care of the house. Sometimes, especially in the 1940s, youngsters saw their fathers go off to war. Some didn't come back. With life getting pretty serious after high school, the earlier teen-age years assumed somewhat of a serious air as well.

Societal norms were different, too. Teen-agers who talked back got their mouths washed out with soap or got hit. Getting hit wasn't considered abusive back in the 1940s; parents subscribed to "spare the rod, spoil the child." There was less divorce to distract parents from discipline, more respect for and contact with grandparents, and less teen sex. That's not to say that teens didn't cut up once in a while, or didn't have fun. Their antics were just less in-your-face and more within limits accepted by parents than is the case today. Parents had the control, and teens had little choice but to obey, more or less. This control extended to mode of dress, to where you went on Saturday night, and to what music you listened to. The music of the 1940s was overwhelmingly created for adults. Teens liked the more lively variations of this music, but it was adult music nonetheless.

The birth of a teen generation was an evolutionary process; that is, it happened gradually over time. The end of World War II began a period of prosperity in the United States. Young soldiers returned from the European or Pacific theater and started families, creating a sex boom which created what is now referred to as the "baby boom." The Korean War put a crimp in an otherwise peaceful decade but, luckily, it was resolved within a few years. Teens went to college in greater numbers, preferring that to work or soldiering. The country was booming economically as well, allowing teen-agers to keep and spend some of the money they made at after-school jobs.

Parents raised their children according to Dr. Benjamin Spock, who espoused a more lenient approach to child rearing than was popular before. While ostensibly creating psychologically healthier children, it also resulted in offspring that were more assertive, and perhaps more demanding, than their parents were comfortable with. Due to economic prosperity, kids weren't forced to work as much, and many children were given an "allowance." This lent economic clout to their opinions. Led by emotions fueled by hormones, teens fought more and more stridently and often to borrow the family car, wear pegged pants and listen to music they found appealing. In effect, they were fighting to carve out their own identities in relation to their peers and parents. Teens were no longer little adults.

Further, since they weren't working as much, they were "hanging out" more. Peer group contact and pressure both increased, and supported the newly carved-out values about music and dress. In general, life was a lot less serious for the average teen-ager in 1954 than it had been in 1944. College pranks, drag racing, fraternity hazing and drinking, Volkswagon-stuffing, goldfish-swallowing, toga parties and panty raids all became part of the lexicon in the 1950s. As parents scoffed at news of these types of antics, teens gobbled it up, providing a fairly good definition of the "generation gap."

Teens had the motives and they had the opportunities, all they needed was the music. At first, white teens had to look for the music. Where they found it was in the black musical culture of the early 1950s. They listened to rhythm and blues on radio stations that played it, and they went to concerts where it was featured. News of a hot new station playing cool music got around your English class real fast and, since you recently got a new transistor radio for your 16th birthday or inherited your Dad's Phillips when the family got a new "hi-fi," it didn't take you long to glom onto that spot on the dial. Alan Freed, and others like him, became your deities.

After awhile, the music found the teens. The audiences of youth-oriented radio programs grew, increasing the popularity and influence of the deejays. The deejays put on concerts which exposed more teens to more talent and made them want to buy records. The record companies obliged by farming talent, and recording and distributing their work. Rock 'n' roll in general, and doo-wop in particular, became one and the same with teenagedom—which further empowered teens to stand up for their music in the face of parental disdain; which, just incidentally, along with similar battles over dress, pastimes, speech patterns and beliefs, changed society forever.

Black teens didn't have the same problem. They didn't have to find the music because it was all around them. Black families depended heavily on local radio stations, as opposed to the national network affiliates that whites preferred. On these stations, purer strains of blues, gospel and rhythm and blues could be heard, before these sounds were blended with whiter sounds to produce music acceptable to the larger and more affluent white audience. These radio stations brought the black culture, including the new music, into the homes of many black teens of the 1950s. Others would get their music from the church, or from neighborhood "jams," which took place on the porch or nearby street corner. In fact, for many black teens, singing on the corner or in the local rec center was a participatory activity, in much the same way sports were. Successful singers became idols, just as athletes like Jackie Robinson, Don Newcombe and Larry Doby did.

One occurrence which sped up the acceptance of black music among white teens was the coining of the term "rock 'n' roll" by Alan Freed in the early 1950s. "Rock 'n' roll" gave teens a name to put on the music that stirred their loins. The music wasn't new, and neither was the moniker, but using the moniker to describe the music was.[1] Nelson George asserted that the new term hid the fact that the music was "black," allowing whites to espouse it and feel comfortable with it. Heretofore, rhythm and blues was music for blacks, but rock 'n' roll was for everyone who was youthful. The record industry now had a large and eager new market to sell to: white teen-agers.

White teens gravitated to the new music, of which doo-wop vocal group harmony was a large part, in droves. The word "cats" came into usage to describe white teens that dug black music. Ed Ward described these cats as "poor white kids who lived in slum neighborhoods with blacks and worked side by side with them at various bottom-of-the-barrel jobs. Although few of them thought of the blacks as their equals and most were happy to be segregated from them in movie theaters and at school, the cats somehow related more to black culture than to hillbilly culture, yearning for the sophistication they heard in rhythm and blues songs. Being cats meant they could stand out in a world that offered them precious little in the way of a chance to be somebody."[2]

The songwriting team of Jerry Lieber and Mike Stoller, whose music scored the Broadway hit, "Smoky Joe's Café," were primary examples of cats. They grew up in integrated neighborhoods in the Los Angeles area and were part of the rock 'n' roll explosion as it unfolded. Other talented youngsters made their way up the ladder by being black or white cats that cut their teeth as members of singing groups, usually as lead singers. The list of these singers includes Clyde McPhatter (Dominoes and Drifters), Jackie Wilson

(Dominoes), Marvin Gaye (Rainbows and Moonglows), Dion DiMucci (Belmonts), Bobby Darin (Rinky Dinks and Ding Dongs), Carole King (Palisades), Wilson Pickett (Falcons), Frankie Lymon (Teenagers), Teddy Randazzo (Three Chuckles), Jimmy Jones (Pretenders), Eddie Floyd (Falcons), Neil Sedaka (Tokens), Gene Pitney (Embers), Diana Ross (Primettes), Ben E. King (Five Crowns and Drifters), Phil Spector (Teddy Bears and Spector's Three), Dee Clark (Kool Gents), Billy Stewart (Rainbows), Paul Simon (Tico & the Triumphs, Jerry Landis & group), Bobby Freeman (Romancers), Ernie K-Doe (Blue Diamonds), Van McCoy (Starlighters), Robert John (Bobby & the Consoles) and Brook Benton (Sandmen). The first eight names on this list even made it all the way to the Rock 'n' Roll Hall of Fame.

The culture was changing, and changing fast. By the mid- to late-1950s rock 'n' roll, which included group vocal music, ruled the airwaves. It was the medium of flirting, courting, humping, petting, and loving at teen dances, now called "sock hops." Uptempo numbers, fodder for the jitterbug and lindy, were just appetizers. The main events were the slow numbers, often doo-wop efforts. Though the dances were still chaperoned by adults, the romance that these songs offered virtually eliminated the distance between partners on the dance floor. It can be argued that the musical revolution for teens in the 1950s allowed closeness while dancing, which in turn led to the sexual revolution of the 1960s.

Changes such as these scared parents, and rightly so. It wasn't just the music that was changing. Compared to what they knew from their own childhoods, their own children, the teens of the 1950s, were more private, sullen, clannish, defensive, and disrespectful. They dressed according to whimsical fads, had their own slang and listened to raucous music with unintelligible lyrics sung by delinquent types. The music was the easiest to blame because it was all over the media (radio, television and records). Parents read about riots at concerts, listened to romance-inducing plaints by the artists and saw Elvis Presley wiggle on the Ed Sullivan Show. There was little reason to be reassured. These days we know that teens eventually grow out of their recalcitrance (they would probably say the same of us), but in the 1950s the generation gap was new, and the future less certain.

The trouble was, there was some basis for their fears. Juvenile delinquency was an indirect and unwanted result of the new teen freedom. Integration was progressing, though slowly and painfully. Parents were afraid that their children would be influenced by the bad kids or would mix with children of other races. Because many of the artists across the spectrum of rock 'n' roll were black or hoodlum-lookalikes or both, the music was to be defamed. Unfortunately for parents, one other quality of the emerging teen character was oppositional behavior. The more parents put down the music, the more teens valued it.

Parents didn't go down without a fight. Various media attacked the music at various times for reasons which were always variations of perverting the morals

---

1. "Rock 'n' roll" was used in black music as a polite substitute for having sexual intercourse since the 1920s.
2. Ward, Ed, et al. *Rock of Ages: The Rolling Stone History of Rock & Roll.* New York: Summit Books, 1986.

Bobby Darin.

Marvin Gaye.

Jimmy Jones.

Neil Sedaka.

Frankie Lymon.

Teddy Randazzo.

Ben E. King.

Wilson Pickett.

Gene Pitney.

Clyde McPhatter.

"Rogue's Gallery"

Artists who deserted groups to find fortune and fame as single artists

of young folk. For example, Peter Potter, host of Los Angeles' "Juke Box Jury" on CBS-TV, often took pot(ter) shots at the music. He called rhythm and blues "obscene and of lewd intonation, and certainly not fit for radio broadcast."[3] Continuing, he felt that "the artist and repertoire men [talent developers for record companies] are responsible for inculcating poor listening tastes of today's teen-agers."[4] Guess he didn't like it. A guest of his, a famous satirist Stan Freberg, "hope[d] this puts an end to rhythm and blues."[5] Maybe not.

In New York, some pretty influential deejays got together and agreed not to play records with lascivious content. Hal Jackson from WLIB, Tommy "Dr. Jive" Smalls from WWRL and Jack Walker from WOV, among others, banned records like "Such A Night" by Clyde McPhatter and the Drifters. Similar actions were taken in many other cities, to no avail. Teens kept requesting records like the "Annie" series, "Peppermint Stick" and the like, and buying them, too. The train was on track, and moving downhill.

Today, these lyrics would not even get a raised eyebrow, but in the 1950s, they were titillating. Suggestive lyrics, as well as those dealing with drinking and cheating, were always a part of rhythm and blues, and straight blues before that. But this music was heard only by the black population, which tolerated and encouraged "slice of life" music. A problem arose only when white teen-agers got interested in the music. That's when the parents of these innocents got their backs up. *Billboard* and *Cash Box*, leading the recording industry, played a big part in eliminating suggestivity by editorial comments. While some record company execs, radio stations personnel and distributors were against lewd lyrics on ethical grounds, the rest realized that if they wanted their records played, they had better cut it out. You didn't have to hit them over the head too hard.

The print media were venomous when someone connected with the new music stepped out of line. A headline in *The Miami Herald* read, "Booze, Broads and Bribes" the day after an annual deejays convention.[6] *The New York Times* regularly went after Alan Freed for antics that occurred during or after his concerts. Ed Sullivan even kept Elvis from shaking his booty on his show for a while because of bad press, but he eventually relented when beaten in the ratings by a Presley-loving Steve Allen. Even morality has a price. And then the meetings of the Harris Congressional Subcommittee received lots of news coverage as it went after the practice of payola and the payolees. It seemed as though if the establishment couldn't eradicate the music itself, at least it could put a hurtin' on the messengers, who happened to be disc jockeys.

The net-net of the backlash was a draw. Lewd lyrics were all but gone from the music by roughly 1955, but rock 'n' roll, doo-wop, rhythm and blues, or whatever you'd prefer to call it, was here to stay. The parental backlash had worked, bringing economic pressure to bear on record industry people to eliminate suggestivity. But the same economics demanded the production of the new musical sound. Controversality was further buried when young teens themselves began to record in the mid-1950s. They brought with them the innocence of youth and left behind the "blues" approach of some of the earlier, more mature groups.

Steve Propes, in *Those Oldies But Goodies: A Guide To 50's Record Collecting*, identified some topics of the new rock 'n' roll: sex/virility, partying/night life, fast cars, drinking, money problems and crime/punishment.[7] While these topics were new to the music of the white world, they were old hat in black circles, being a part of earlier rhythm & blues and blues genres. And while records with these topics did titillate and sell (e.g. "Work With Me Annie" by the Midnighters and "Sixty Minute Man" by the Dominoes), they were swamped by the sales of a myriad of songs sporting innocent and non-controversial lyrics (e.g. "Gee" by the Crows). If any conclusion can be drawn from the subject matter of the songs, it is that the music reflected the changing social climate, including the new phenomena of "teen-agers," the "generation gap" and *Playboy* magazine. Very few teens took on evil ways by listening to the music.

Actually, the lyrics that sold from 1955 on, dwelt on idealistic love, with a capital "L." Bawdy and sensationalistic themes were left behind with paleo-doo-wop. Artists from the classical doo-wop period were almost always teen-agers or men in their early 20s. They were innocent and sang innocent. Subthemes that recur under the banner of love include attraction (wanting someone from afar), celebration (regaling in love), insecurity (fear of losing that love), rejection (getting dumped or cheated on), revenge, remorse (sorry for cheating), and begging for forgiveness. As a rough guess, the lyrics of 90% of the slow songs of the doo-wop era fall into one or more of these categories. It could be higher. The "Book of Love" below, taken from *Doo-wop: The Forgotten Third...* shows how different songs focus on different parts of the love process.

The Book of Love

Our musical protagonist dreams of a girl...
   "Girl In My Dreams" by the Cliques,

Loves her from afar...
   "Image Of A Girl" by the Safaris,

Is afraid to approach her but dares to..
   "Please Say You Want Me" by the Schoolboys,

Thinks she's fine...
   "So Fine" by the Fiestas,

Dates her...

3. Gart, Galen. *The History of Rhythm & Blues*, Vol. 4 (1954). Milford, NH: Big Nickel Publications, 1990.
4. Ibid.
5. Double ibid.
6. Smith, Wes. *The Pied Pipers of Rock 'n' Roll*. Marietta, GA: Longstreet Press, 1989, p. 211.

7. Propes, Steve. *Those Oldies But Goodies: A Guide To 50s Record Collecting*. New York: MacMillan, 1973.

"Saturday Night At The Movies" by the Drifters,

Proclaims his undying adulation of her...
"Sunday Kind Of Love" by the Harptones,
Revels in her beauty...   "Love Doll" by the Scarlets,

Asserts that she meets every need that he has...
"The Way You Look Tonight" by the Jaguars,

Anticipates graduation day so they may wed...
"When We Get Married" by the Dreamlovers,

Disdains parental warnings that they're young...
"Not Too Young To Fall In Love" by the Teenchords,

A break-up occurs...
"Tears On My Pillow" by Little Anthony & the Imperials,

Because he was cruel to her...
"Sorry, I Ran All The Way Home" by the Impalas

Or cheated on her...
"Little Darlin" by the Gladiolas,

Or took her for granted or deceived her...
"Come Back My Love" by the Wrens,

He begs abjectly for forgiveness...
"Down On My Knees" by the Heartbeats,

And promises atonement...
"I'm Sorry" by the Platters,

Occasionally she dumps him permanently...
"I Met Him On A Sunday" by the Shirelles,

He then mourns his loss but keeps hoping...
"Long Lonely Nights" by Lee Andrews & Hearts,

That if he waits long enough she will return...
"In My Lonely Room" by the Four Haven Knights,

And the story of their love replays in his mind...
"The Book Of Love" by the Monotones.

These themes also predominate for uptempo sides, but the faster numbers often lack the serious approach and tenderness of the ballads. One also finds braggadocio ("Speedoo" by the Cadillacs) , humor ("Along Came Jones" by the Coasters), lasciviousness ("Honey Love" by the Drifters), chauvinism ("Hot Dog Dooly Wah" by the Pyramids), teen-age rebellion ("Charlie Brown" by the Coasters), and cockiness ("Hey, Little School Girl" by the Paragons) on occasion.

Some indication of the degree to which romance dominated the music is found in the vast number of "name songs," wherein the title of the song targets a particular (usually) damsel. It's understandable that girls with names like Mary, Sue and Sally have songs named after them, but doo-woppers didn't stop at popular monikers. We therefore find songs pleading to Annie Mae (Arrows), Flossie Mae (Saucers), Lillie Mae (Cupids), Lilly Maebelle (Valentines), Lula Mae (Barons), Molly Mae (Crests), Sally Mae (Corvairs) and Verdie Mae (Twilights), as well as Annabelle Lee (Coeds), Barbra Lee (Orioles), Carol Lee (Martels), Coralee (Hemlocks), Donna Lee (Demilles), Jerri Lee (Flamingos), Lola Lee (Five Trojans), Mary Lee (Rainbows), Wanna Lee (Vocal Tones). If not for love, how to explain this phenomenon?

More practical, in the business sense, efforts resulted in a slew of "Honey Darling Baby" titles that appealed to a wider record-buying audience. Thus we have "Honey Baby" (Blue Diamonds), "Honey Bun" (Colts), "Honey Love" (Drifters), "My Love" (Arcades), "Oh My Love" (Chiffons), "Love Doll" (Scarlets), "Doll Baby" (Paragons), "My Baby Dearest Darling" (Charms), "Dearest Darling" (Castroes), "My Darling" (Aquatones), "Oh My Darling" (Capris), and "Always My Darling" (Cadillacs), which are only drops in the bucket of love.

The music proves to be a good reflection of the teen subculture of the 1950s. And although the title of this chapter is "The Teen-age Menace," the word "menace" is best taken with a degree of salt. Compared to the teenagers of earlier generations, kids of the 1950s were badasses, but only in a relative sense. They drag-raced their cars, joined gangs on occasion, spiked the punch at dances, got girls pregnant and dropped out of school to marry them, and "called the English teacher Daddio."[8] But they didn't do crack, didn't have rap sheets and didn't commit suicide, like 90% of today's youth.[9]

Even the singers were relatively innocent. In that mall-free, video arcadeless society, the singers were relegated to local candy stores, bowling alleys or pool halls. They sung at these venues, or looked for some proverbial "echo" on subway platforms, back stairwells or bathrooms. They weren't studious, they weren't "nerdy," and they were fairly social. They were kids who loved the music and enjoyed singing it with their buddies. Singing in the neighborhood earned them respect; actually recording accorded sainthood. "Recording artist" was up there with "star athlete" in the neighborhood pecking order. Except star athletes had lots of talent. Neighborhood singers needed tunefulness, not virtuosity. The groupness of the music hid most of the vocal flaws. Even lead singers could be rough if they could stick to the melody. And it sure was a way to attract the girls, too. As Kenny Vance sang, "...and the girls would gather round us, and our heads would really swell."[10]

So this dreaded teen-age "menace" turns out to be one bunch of innocent kids, mostly black, creating a new and exciting music that another bunch of innocent kids, mostly white, thoroughly enjoyed. Somehow, it was tied up with the sociological factors that emerged in the late 1940s and early 1950s like the generation gap, race relations and the birth of the coming of age of the modern teen-ager.

The primary job of these teens, singer and audience alike, was to lay down precedents for coming generations of young people. They set themselves apart from their parents with new musics, new modes of dress and ever-evolving slang. Yet this first generation was truly innocent, free of the existential, political and racial issues, drugs and alienation that succeeding generations of young people would have to face. They achieved freedom, however, and not many chose to give it back.

8. From "Charlie Brown" by the Coasters.
9. Just kidding, Moms and Dads.
10. "Looking For An Echo," Kenny Vance (Warner Brothers Music Corp., 1975), ASCAP.

Chapter 15

High School Confidential

Mathematics

"One, you're my only one,
Two, I belong to you,
Three, you belong to me,
Four, oh oh
Five, it's great to be alive,
Six, our hearts had to mix,
Seven, we'll go to heaven still in love."

-Keynotes in "Seven Wonders Of The World" from 1957. Apparently our singer had a numerological lapse in the middle. Is this a prime example of 4-getfulness?

"Two lips pressed together,
Rapture's in the air..."
[And later]
"The evening breeze blows tenderly,
As two lips softly part..."

-lead of the Fascinators, in "My Beauty, My Own," in describing kissing his baby. It appears that an error in math may have occurred, because four lips, not two, are needed for this maneuver. Or, perhaps, each participant chose to contribute only one lip to the buss. The Universals, in "Think," find themselves in a similar situation, viz.:

"Think, before we kiss, (2X),
Think before you kiss,
Another tender lip, oh please,
Think, before you kiss."

-and witness the Vocaltones in "My Version Of Love":

"Two lips would kiss,
Feeling love's sweet bliss,
Enjoying nature's ecstasy,
My version of love..."

-Now it is possible that there were quite a few one-lipped people around in the '50s, or there may have been another math error made. By contrast, the Ink Spots' "To Each His Own" (1946) features much more accurate lip-counting; viz: "Two lips must insist on two more to be kissed." Underestimation of raw numbers of facial features in not limited to lips in the doo-wop genre. Witness "Lend Me Your Ear" by the Originals (1960).

English Grammar

"I gave you my house,
I gave you my home,
I gave you everything I ever owned,
I gave you my heart,
Gave you my hand,
I even went as far as to gave you my name."

-Earl Lewis (of Earl Lewis and the Channels) in "Bye Bye Baby" during a "tense interchange" with his ex-girl.

"A means all of my love,
E is forever,
I means that there is,
Only one love,
That's you [U]."

-lyrics of a song that is called "The Vowels of Love," right? Wrong. It's called "The Vows of Love" and was recorded by the Paragons in 1958. There is a song called "The Vowels of Love," by the Poets (also 1958), whose philandering lead chants...

"A is for Arlene, I love you so much,
E is for Edna, I thrill at your touch,
I is for Inez, I think about you so,
O is for Odessa,
But you [U] are my love."

-(what a lucky girl)

"Let me whisper sweet words of pismotality,
And discuss the pulpitudes of love,
And put them together and what do you have...
Matrimony."

-Vernon Green of Vernon Green and the Medallions in the 1954 classic, "The Letter." Some of the best doo-wop minds (no, this is not a null set) have studied these words. Most of the collective brain power has been focused on "pismotality"; "pulpitudes" has been given short shrift. The entire stanza is reminiscent of a single algebraic equation with two unknowns.

"Our romance could be so cool,
As you are to me."

-Eugene Mumford, of the Larks in "My Reverie" from 1951. Note the usage of the word "cool." This is one of a myriad of examples of words appearing in the black culture years before they attain popular usage among people of pallor. Dances that Chubby Checker made famous in song in 1960 were mentioned in songs recorded much earlier by the Drifters. "The Twist" appears in the lyrics of "Let The Boogie Woogie Roll," recorded in 1953, and "The Hucklebuck" is mentioned in the words of "What'cha Gonna Do," from 1955.

"I wish that I had the wings of a peasant,

I'd fly away and tear the stars down from heaven."

> -Leon Harrison of the Four Buddies, from "Just To Make You Smile Again" (1950). Leon may have meant to say "pheasant," although as birds go, pheasants leave something to be desired in the flying department. Alternatively, he may have meant what he said; that is, people back then may have traveled by peasant (especially less affluent ones).

Religion

Not only were there vows and vowels of love, there were Commandments as well. Harvey (Fuqua) and the Moonglows, in "The Ten Commandments Of Love" (1958), espouse:

1. "Thou shalt never love another"
2. "Stand by me all the while"
3. "Take happiness with the heartaches"
4. "Go through life wearing a smile"
5. "Thou shall always have faith in me in everything I say and do"
6. "Love me with all your heart and soul until our life on earth is through"
7. "Come to me when I am lonely"
8. "Kiss me when you hold me tight"
9. "Treat me sweet and gentle"
10. "And always do what's right"

> -When the song was issued on 78 r.p.m., the ninth Commandment was "Treat me sweet and gentle..." At this point an error of enormous magnitude, commandment-wise, occurred, because after the background singers said "Ten," the lead only added to the ninth commandment by singing "...when we say goodnight." In effect, there was no 10th commandment. That meant, that if you paid $.79 for the record, that your true cost was an inflated 8.8 cents per Commandment instead of the expected 7.9 cents. In a subsequent rendition (which is featured above), the situation was rectified.

> We can't help noticing that the content of the Commandments is a little one-sided. If she goes for that deal, there's this bridge in Brooklyn that we can part with for a price.

"Together we stand,
Divided we fall,
Together in love,
Or no love at all."

> -Love Notes, in "United" from 1957. Perhaps the Moonglows could take a (love) note or two from these lines.

"Don't you tempt me with your whims,
I'm too busy singin' hymns."

> -lead of the Coleman Brothers, singing to the devil, in "Get Away, Mr. Satan, Get Away" from 1945.

"I do live to adore them,
I love, love and implore them..."

> -Tony Passalacqua of the Fascinators in "Chapel Bells" (1958). The fact that Tony was pleading with a bunch of bells doesn't bode well for his state of mind. Also, this is the first, and probably the only time, the word "implore" is to be found in a doo-wop song.

History

"Why not cut classes,
Smoke again in the hall,
Fight in Korea,
A regular ball,
Bring back the fifties..."

> -Robert Klein, in his parody "The Fabulous Fifties," the only song, to our knowledge, in which Senator Joe McCarthy's name appears in song (in falsetto, twice).

Home Economics

"I need someone...to cook my food, make my bed,
I need someone...to clean my shoes and hold my head."

> -Bill Witt, lead of the Rocketones, who's going back to his "home town" of "Mexico" to find a woman. That's good, because he'd never get away with that stuff living in America.

"The boys in the jungle had me on the run,
When something heavy hit me, like an atomic bomb,
When I woke up and my head started to clear,
I had a strange feeling I was with cookin' gear,
I smelt something cookin' and I looked to see,
That's when I found out they was a-cookin' me,
Great googa mooga, let me outta here..."

> -lead of the Cadets in "Stranded In The Jungle" (1956). He was right to leave, rather than sit around and "stew."

Horticulture

Not many groups took a horticultural view of love. The Del Rios, in "Vines of Love" (1958), were an exception:

"I'm giving you, giving you, the Vines of Love,
And with this ring placed on your hand,
I swear by stars above,
That I'll always love you,
Cherish til death do us part...
Wear this ring, around your finger,
As for your thoughts,
They'll no longer linger,
We'll be united,
Together we'll always be..."

> Picture this. They're standing at the altar and he produces not only a ring, which she expects and wants, but the Vines of Love as well. She knows what the ring is for, but the Vines? Where does she put them? How often do they

need watering? And what about those thoughts that he says won't linger any more? Maybe they should linger.

Anatomy

"Peppermint Stick will eat my dick."

-Little Butchie Saunders, 14-year-old lead of the Elchords, in a line that promptly got his record banned from the airwaves. This only managed to provide the teen-agers of 1957 with such an enormous amount of titillation that they made this song one of the first underground classics.

"Once I had a heart,
Yes it's true,
But now it's gone,
From me to you...
...Now you have two and I have none."

-Gilbert Warren, lead singer of the Orchids on "Happiness" (1955) who was not only mathematically correct, but who was probably the world's first singing heart transplant donor. He was not the last, however. The lead of the (female) Crystals ("I Do Believe") and the lead of the Shytones ("Just For You") underwent similar open-heart surgery in 1957 and 1960 respectively.

Science

"Am I the fire, or just another flame?"

-Sonny Til, of Sonny Til and the Orioles in "It's Too Soon To Know" (1948).

"Darling you are the flame not the spark."

-Master-Tones in "Tell Me" (1954).

"One is the fire, the other the flame." [both of them are you]

-Sonny Wright, lead of the Diamonds in "Two Loves Have I" (1953).

"One is the flame, one is the spark." [both of them are you]

-the Colonials, in "Two Loves Have I" (continuing the hot debate in a 1956 uptempo remake of the Diamonds song).

"It's a fire, it's a raging flame."

-Jesse Belvin, of the Cliques, in "Girl In My Dreams" from 1956.

"You are my match and my flame."

-Storytellers, in "Please Remember My Love" from 1990.

French

"Darling je vous aime beaucoup, Jenny say poss [je ne sais pas] what to do."

-the lead of the Chateaus, in "Darling Je Vous Aime Beaucoup" (1956).

"Cherie, live, live and love me,
My little tender morsel of feminine pulchritude,
In all your magnificent splendor..."

-the lead of the Chateaus, again, in "Darling Je Vous Aime Beaucoup." When your on a roll, you're on a roll.

Love

"My head is spinning,
My heart is turning around,
I'm walking in a daze,
Tell me baby, where can I be found?"

-Five Discs, in "I Remember" (maybe not) from 1958.

"Yes dear, they are playing our songs,
And they will always remain our songs...
Each time you hear them,
I hope you too will cherish the wonderful memories that our love once knew,
For these songs are just a symbol of the love I had for you."

-Carl (Little Caesar) Burnett, of Little Caesar & the Romans to his first love, hopefully with a straight face.

"Great jumpin' catfish, baby, kiss me again."

-Ray Pollard, the lead of the Wanderers, who was presumably talking to his girlfriend.

"My car is warm and comfortable,
I bought it just for you,
Won't you come and sit right down,
Enjoy its comfort too."

-Roger Hayes of the Collegians, with an offer that's hard to refuse.

"Love doll, I'll be by your side,
Love doll, from you I'll never hide."

-from "Love Doll" by the Scarlets in 1955.

"I want you baby by my side,
For your love I'll never never hide."

-from "Careless Love" by Rudy & the Tradewinds

Group in tuxedos.

Group in togas.

in 1962. One can imagine a young lady running and telling her friends how her new swain promised not to hide from her. Apparently, back then not hiding from your baby was paying her quite a compliment.

"I said I loved you,
You started laughing...
Now everyone's laughing at me...
Next time I'll play it cool,
And they'll not be laughing at me."

> -Pookie Hudson of the Spaniels in "Everyone's Laughing," a painfully accurate description of the agony of being humiliated when you're a teen-ager.

"I would fight 10,000 dragons,
Just to be by your side..."

> -lead of the Five Satins in "A Night To Remember" from 1958. That's an awful lot of dragons.

"I've got a girl named Rama Lama Lama Lama Ding Dong."

> -George Jones Jr. of the Edsels, from "Rama Lama Ding Dong" in 1958, who must have been willing to risk strange glances and enormous engraving costs at the jewelry store when he bought his baby trinkets.

"Don't make love by the garden gate,
'Cause love is blind but the neighbors ain't."

> -from the song "Nosy Neighbors" by the Larktones (1958).

"We had a quarrel last night,
Yeah we both thought we were right,
You fought well for your side,
And I won for my pride,
Yes a victory, when I won a broken heart..."

> -Gene Pitney backed by the Embers from 1958. Who said the lyrics of the doo-wop era weren't good?

"I'm looking over,
A four-leaf clover,

That I overlooked before."

> -lead Little Bobby Rivera of the Hemlocks at the beginning of his paean to his love, "Coralee." Had Bobby fallen in love with a Mary or a Sue, he would've sold a lot more records.

"You are my only love,
You're as pretty as a turtle dove."

> -lead of the Romans in "You Are My Only Love" in 1958. Apparently it wasn't enough for his baby to be his turtle dove, she also had to be as fetching. ("Oh Mary, you have such a noble beak")

Loneliness

"I am like a blind man without its [sic] cane,
I am like a violin with one string,
I am like a rainbow minus its colors,
Yes my darling, I am like the sky without a star."

> -lead of the No Names in "Love" from 1964. That's one lonely guy.

"Darling, days gone by,
You haven't called,
Weeks gone by,
The phone haven't [sic] rung,
Darling, could it be that you don't love me,
Please, darling, please
Don't say no."

> -Quintones, in "The Lonely Telephone" from 1954. Which side is this guy on, anyway? Unless he's using reverse psychology.

"Please come home, you great big lump of sugar."

> -Louise Murray, bass of the Hearts, in "Lonely Nights" (1955).

Infidelity

"She's cheatin' on me,
And I'm beatin' on she."

> -lead singer of Newark, New Jersey's Ambassadors (not of good will), as he commits physical abuse, emotional intimidation and grammatical impropriety in one fell swoop. This 1953 song, titled "Willa Bea," is backed by "Darling I'm Sorry."

"Oh pretty baby I played your game,
I found out you just a divin' dame,
I bought you a great big gold locket,
Oh little girl get out of my pocket."

> -Truetones (1958)

"He was just like a brother,
She was pledged to be my wife,
But they married each other,
And made a mess of my life."

> -understatement by the lead of the Gentlemen ("Story Of A Love Gone Cold" from 1954) whose problem may have been that he was too much of one. Apparently, he was not alone in his grief. The lead of the Cool-

breezers suffered a similar fate in 1957 in the song "My Brother":

"My brother, my brother, I love you through and
  through,
But you ruined my life,
When you took my wife,
My brother, oh how could you?"

"There she goes, my old gal,
And there he goes, my old pal,
And here am I, broken-hearted,
The last time that we said goodbye,
It broke my heart in two,
It's not enough I lost her love,
I had to lose him too..."

> -lead of the Four J's, proving that you don't have to be related to steal your best friend's girl. Reminds us of the old Henny Youngman line, "My best friend ran off with my wife...Gee, I'm gonna miss that guy."

Speaking of infidelity, a guy from the Souvenirs had to deal with ten (count 'em ten) rivals in "Double Dealin' Baby" from 1957:

"I saw you kissin' on Jim,
Huggin' on Jack,
Ridin' around in John's Cadillac,
Lovin' on Slim,
Squeezin' on Moe,
Slippin' my money to a cat named Joe,
  You're my double dealin' baby (3X)
  But I want you to deal with me...
I saw you lookin' at James,
Flirtin' with Lee,
Winkin' your eyes at every man you see,
Callin' to Paul,
Writin' to Pete,
Makin' everything sound so awful sweet,
  You're my double dealin' baby (3X)
  But I want you to deal with me...
Heard you slip in last night,
A quarter to one,
Tellin' some joker you had so much fun,
Wakin' me up,
Squeezin' me tight,
Tellin' me 'Daddy everything's all right'..."

> Quite a handful, wasn't she. By the way, that unnamed 'joker' from the last verse may be number 11. In 1951, the Larks noted a similar situation with a car analogy in "Little Side Car":

"You're a good little car baby,
Too many drivers at the wheel..."

"I hate your walk, I hate your talk, I hate everything
  about you,
If I had my way, they'd put you away, it's a better
  world without you.
I hate you, I hate you, wo wo wo wo wo, I hate you."

> -J.B. of J.B. and the Sha La La, being a little more than assertive in "I Hate Your Guts."

Doo-Wop After Death

"The first kiss you gave me,
The first day we met,
I'll remember darling,
Long after I'm dead."

> -the perhaps overly sincere lead singer of the El Vireos, from "First Kiss" (1959).

"Now I'm gettin' old and hey brother I'm gettin'
  ready to die,
But there's one request that I must make before I hit
  the sky,
And that request is something no man in his right
  mind could not deny,
'Cause when they put me six feet under I'm takin' a
  great big pizza pie."

> -lead Norman Fox of Norman Fox & the Rob Roys in "Pizza Pie." In this stanza, Norman takes us to places we've never been before. Note that even though the third line is grammatically wacky, we know exactly what he's saying. Further, this is the only doo-wop song, in fact the only known recorded song, to deal with the sensitive topic of planning one's menu after death. Is this the opposite of a slice of life?

"Her Kisses were warm as ever,
Which made me realize,
New loves may come and go,
But an old love never really dies."

> -David Baughan, lead singer of the Checkers, trying to make sense of a dream wherein he had one last lusty evening with his deceased lover, in "Ghost Of My Baby" from 1953.

"Way up in the sky,
There's a girl I love,
She kicked the bucket,
She died..."

> -says Lincoln, of Lincoln Fig and the Dates, in a burst of warm sentimentality from "Way Up" in 1958. He continues, with what must be the doo-wop version of a death wish:

"Some day,
I hope to find her up there,
So we can resume,
Our love affair."

Le Derriere Mot

"I've got a girl that I'm just simply wild about,
Folks think that I'm a lucky boy,
Everywhere we go people rave about,
This little bundle of joy,
She's got freckles on her butt, she is nice,
When she's in my arms she's paradise,

She was born in Hackensack,
She made a fortune on her...face,
She's got freckles on her butt, she is nice,
She drinks til she gets plastered,
She gets drunker than...my brother,
She's got freckles on her butt, she is nice..."

-the Four Vagabonds, in "The Freckle Song" from 1947.

"A little bit of soap will wash away your lipstick on my face,
A little bit of soap will never, never never ever erase,
The pain in my heart and my ass,
As I go through the lonely hills,
A little bit of soap will never wash away my tears..."

-lead Nathaniel West, of the Jarmels, who was dumped by his girl and apparently landed on his...hillocks.

"Am I assing too much,
When I ask you to pity me?"

-Earl "Speedo" Carroll in "Sympathy" by the Cadillacs (1955). Either he meant to say "asking" or he was inquiring as to whether he was using the correct amount of a certain body part (what a lot of cheek!).

"You're out on the town,
With somebody new,
I'm home all alone,
And I'm feelin' blue,
You said to me,
'Oh let's make amends,
I know that we're through,
But we can still be friends,'
So I said to you,
And I'm very sure,
'Up yours, up yours, up yours...' "

-Tino, of Tino and the Revlons, being assertive with his ex in "Up Yours."

Chapter 16

The Technology of the Doo-Wop Era

The decade of the 1950s witnessed enormous growth in the music industry. As the decade unfolded, more and more teen-agers gravitated to the music that has been called rock 'n' roll, rhythm and blues and doo-wop. This was the first time that teen-agers had music that was all their own, and they took to it with a vengeance, the way teens will. They wanted not only a specific kind of music, but they wanted a lot of it. They demanded records, lots of records, and hi-fis to play them on. They wanted radio programming, and not the stodgy kind that their parents liked. These demands, in our capitalistic society, quickly produced responses on the part of the music and radio industries.

In the next few chapters, we will examine the ways in which supply matched demand. First, we'll look at the way a post-World War II explosion in technology helped hasten the spread of rock 'n' roll. We'll then turn to the "personality deejays," who both helped to create the enormous demand for the new music, and then, conveniently, helped to supply it. Finally, we'll investigate the growth of small independent record labels (called "indies") that competed with the large well-established record companies (called "majors"), to deliver the music into the waiting hands of the teen-age generation. Before we begin, we'll take a brief tour of the history of recorded music.

The Alleged History of Recorded Music

In ancient times, the only way to preserve oral music was to pass melody and lyrics down from parents to children, from mouth to mouth (poor people passed it down from hand to mouth). But let's face it, how many songs could parents remember all the words to? And their children, that the songs were passed down to, had similar limits. There was no "Top 40" radio back then to drum the lyrics into their heads. Every once in awhile a child would ask, "Please sing 'Old Ezekiel Loved His Goat' for me, would yer pa? I ferget some of them words." Usually the parent (Ezekiel) would accede to the request, if he weren't busy with his goat.

The passing down of songs from generation to generation was somewhat enhanced by the invention of sheet music (not to be confused with sheep music, popularized by herders in the paleotrapezoidal era). The music and lyrics of songs now were available to the general population. There were some glitches with this system of distribution, however: (a) many people didn't have pianos or other musical instruments (everybody theoretically had access to the old comb and tissue paper kazoo, but little sheet music was written for this instrument), (b) many people who owned non-kazoo instruments could not read music, and (c) most people not only didn't have musical instruments and couldn't read music, they couldn't read words, either, making their purchase of sheet music rather unlikely.

Which brings us to the dawn of recorded music. The first way that music could be stored and played back was on the Edison "Wax Cylinder," invented in 1887. Edison made a big mistake in choosing to name it as he did. Because of the name, some people at first mistook it for a candle and tried to light it (this is where the phrase "hot wax" came from). Not only did lighting the cylinder destroy the recorded song, it also left the purchaser without light to read by, because the things didn't burn very well. Others, again because of the name, mistook them for suppositories, with results too unfortunate to report here. It took several years for the real and accurate purpose of the product to be known.

The first attempt to develop a record that played music took the shape of a narrow piece of grooved vinyl that was brittle and roughly 100 yards long. The inventor, whose name has been lost to history, shaped a small needle so that it would fit in the groove, attached a wire to it and connected the wire to an amplifier. He then placed the needle in the groove at the beginning of the plastic strip and ran down along its side at the steady rate of 78 feet per minute. The sound was exquisite, but as the inventor's strength ebbed, the tempo of the song would appear to get slower. Further, after playing a few hundred of these "records," this inventor developed a game leg, dampening somewhat the listening pleasure of his audience and increasing his need for orthopedic surgery. After a while, unable to improve upon his design, he retired from the field of play, so to speak.

The first improvement on this design was made when another inventor proposed the step-saving process of bending the 100-yard vinyl strip in circles, creating a disc roughly one foot in diameter. This flat circular object was placed on one's lap, and the needle put in the groove as before. The record player, the one whose lap the disc was on, would then make a steady churning movement, creating beautiful recorded sound. The best record players were found to be from Wisconsin, the state whose economy fosters the strongest and most talented churners. Even these players eventually flagged, however, and a new player needed to be called up from the farm (this is where the baseball term "farm team" came from). Also, because the discs were played from the inside out, yelps were often heard as the song ended, as the needle flew off the outside edge of the disc and impaled itself in the thigh area of a surprised record player. These painful experiences led the recording industry to adopt a more humane "outside-in" policy for future recording forms.

Finally, around the time of World War I came the 78 r.p.m. (revolutions per minute) record as we know it today. It was invented by a man named Emile Berliner, who figured out that it was easier to make the disc revolve on a turntable than to make the arm of the player person turn repeatedly. This meant less and less elbow surgery, as one by one the Wisconsin churners, discouraged by the lack of demand for their services, returned to careers in butter and cheese. By adopting the "outside-in" theory, Berliner created the "ouchless" record. If Berliner were alive today, many people would be eager to ask him questions, such as, "Why 78?" "Why not 77 or 79?" "Why not a round number like 100?" "Why make things difficult, Emile?"[1]

Unencumbered by the unfortunate misperceptions surrounding the wax cylinder, the 78 r.p.m. record soon became the global medium for the spread of music. This is cataloged, as most of us know, in *The Guiness Book of World Records*. The 78-r.p.m. format remained the primary medium of musical transcription until the post-World War II era.

The Modern Era

Before World War II, the primary way for entertainment to reach the population was through the medium of radio. Television had been invented but was not yet available—audiotapes, CDs and VCRs were not even on the drawing board. A typical family had one radio, a big and bulky plug-in Stromberg-Carlson or Motorola, which was situated in a common area of the house like the living room so that everyone would be able to listen. When decisions about which program to tune in had to be made, most often it was parents or other elders who made them, youngsters having little say. What changed everything was the advent of the transistor.

Transistors are tiny electronic devices, invented in the late 1940s, that replaced vacuum tubes. Gradually radios became smaller, portable, less expensive, and delivered better sound by the 1950s. The reduced prices of radios allowed families to own more than one. At times teens, earning money or getting an allowance, would purchase the battery-driven portable themselves. Others would inherit the old family radio when Mom and Dad brought a new one into the house. Since the 1950s

was also the decade during which TVs proliferated, often a teen-ager would inherit a radio because Mom and Dad didn't listen to it any more, preferring instead the novelty of the new visual medium.

The advent of television indirectly conspired to spread the music in another way, as well. As television populated more and more homes, fewer and fewer people turned to the radio for their news and entertainment. Fewer people meant less sponsors and much lower advertising revenue, which spelled potential disaster. Either the owners of radio stations found new listeners or they went out of business. Not coincidentally, this all happened at a time when teens were inheriting or buying radios in larger numbers. In the evenings, especially, when parents would be gathered in front of the wondrous new television, teens would have unimpeded access to a radio somewhere else in the home. The inclusion of earphones with small transistor radios helped teens make their choices privately. Radios with earphones replaced teddy bears as nocturnal companions for many a young teen.

The problem was that teens didn't necessarily want to hear the same things their parents did. Many talk shows, news programs and farm reports bit the dust. What did attract these youngsters was the new rock 'n' roll. The more a disc jockey on a given station played their music, the more the station and the disc jockey were listened to. Reverence was even bestowed on the more outlandish of those deejays. Kids will be kids. Thus was born a bevy of personality deejays whose flamboyant or provocative behavior was tolerated by program directors because antics equated to bucks.

While radio and television helped the cause of doo-wop music, the record industry was not exactly sitting around, rotating on their turntables either. The 78-r.p.m. phonograph record was the primary medium available for music between WWI and the late 1940s. In May of 1948, Columbia Records came out with the 33 1/2 r.p.m. record, which eventually was called "long playing," "LP" or simply "album." This format offered better sound and could record roughly ten times the amount of music as 78s. The needle on the players for 33s was much finer, the grooves on the records much thinner, and the resultant sound better with wider range.

Not to be outdone, the Radio Corporation of America (RCA) produced the 45 r.p.m. format in March of 1949. These 45s had roughly the capacity of the old 78s but produced better sound. While 78s were made of shellac (with lamp black added so that the disc appeared black) that was brittle, the newer 45s were made from some combination of vinyl (polyvinyl chloride) and shellac, creating a less fragile product.[2] When you're hawking a product that teens must handle, resistance to breakage is a definite plus. By January of 1950, RCA reported that "nine months after the introduction of the 45, sales

---

1. Peter Grendysa, in an article titled "Variable-speed Turntable Makes Old 78s Sing on Key Every Time (*Record Collector's Monthly*, Issue #9, May 1983, p. 1)," tells us that before 1930 records were made at anywhere between 70 and 100 revolutions per minute. Must've been an economy move since you could Charleston or fox trot to the same record depending on the speed at which you played it.

---

2. Cook, Warren Blob. "Paper and Plastic-Part One." *Record Exchanger*, Issue #15, 1973, p. 10.

have jumped to a rate of over 20,000,000 a year. Forty-five players, it stated, are selling at the rate of 65,000 per month."[3] Before the year was out, the major record companies stopped squabbling and adopted three-speed catalogs (33, 45 and 78).

By the middle of 1954, 45s totally replaced 78s as disc jockey promotional copies. "The smaller discs used less vinyl, were smaller and thus fit more easily in jukeboxes, in addition to being hardier. In terms of sales, it depended on the type of music. Spirituals and down home blues sold better on 78s, doo-wop releases better on 45s. By 1956, the 45 r.p.m. format began to assert itself over 78s, and by 1958 78s were just about history.[4]" In addition, the availability of light, portable record players that would play up to 10 records on a spindle made 45s honored guests at teen parties and dances. The LP format wasn't much of a player in the doo-wop or rhythm & blues market until the late 1950s, partly because at $3, it was a bit pricey for teen budgets.

In today's market, albums (or CDs) are produced and single songs are released afterwards. In the 1950s, the reverse was true; that is, an album would not be released unless and until a group had enough cuts to comprise one. For many groups, their whole recording career may be made up of only one or two recording sessions, with two ballads and two jumps per session, so that not many had enough decent sides to qualify. Even for those that had enough recordings, albums weren't much of a factor in spreading doo-wop until the "Oldies But Goodies" series began around 1960. Before that, 45s held sway.

The use of audiotapes was spreading during the 1950s, but out of view of the public. Originally developed by the Germans in 1935, tape recording soon replaced the older medium of wire recording to duplicate sounds. In the 1950s, tape recordings replaced 16-inch records to distribute network broadcasts to affiliates across the country. The tapes reproduced sound more faithfully, were lighter, and an awful lot less breakable than records. It was not until the 1960s, however, that eight-track cartridges and cassettes became available to the public.

The technology of the "hardware" of sound delivery, namely record players, also grew rapidly in the 1950s. Most families had old players, left over from bygone years, that only played 78s. New purchases could include consoles that played all three speeds in "Hi-Fidelity," a box-like portable player with the fat spindle for 45s that could be the centerpiece at teen parties or,

if one waited until the latter part of the decade, players featuring "Stereophonic Sound."

The compact disc, or CD[5], though not a part of the doo-wop era directly, has inadvertently played a part in making the sound more accessible to more people; 1983, its first year, saw 380 releases on CD and 1984 had 1,155.[6] Thus began an inexorable pattern of growth that soon overran and extinguished records as we knew them, even though it was hard to see it coming. In its January 1983 issue, *Record Collector's Monthly* reported that Sony, Hitachi and Magnavox were coming out with CD players, retailing at $1,000.[7] In the same issue, an editorial finds it "inconceivable that reissues in the digital format will ever duplicate this vast array of analog 'software' [e.g. records]. Since record buyers with any sense of history (this must surely include all serious record collectors) would always need analog playback equipment to maintain archival access, the motivation to 'buy digital' is greatly diminished."[8] So much for soothsaying.

Well, the prices did come down over the years, of both the equipment and the CDs themselves. The absence of background noise, their resistance to wear and breakage, and their increased capacity all made them preferable to older formats, including tape. CDs were able to hold roughly 70 minutes of music, at least double the capacity of an LP. During the end of the doo-wop era when albums prevailed, it was common to get one or two hits and ten "fillers." In the 1980s and after, one CD easily held the entire career output of most groups. More prolific groups could be dealt with using "boxed sets." The beauty of having the luxury of the extra room is that alternate takes and previously unreleased material finally saw the light of day. Compilations of different groups, when they include 25 or so selections, are really impressive.

While CDs make it easy today for middle-aged lovers of the music to acquire it, doo-wop gained its popularity in a simpler time, when family and transistor radios ruled. With teens on the speaker ends of those radios, the microphone ends were occupied by a bunch of wild and crazy guys that almost literally sold us the music, though it wasn't really such a hard sell. It is to those purveyors of the music, the "personality deejays," to whom we now turn.

---

3. *Billboard*, Dec. 31, 1949.

4. Gart, Galen. "Sales Figures Show 78s Slipping Away By 1956, Production Curtailments Follow." *Record Collector's Monthly*, Issue #31, June-July 1985, p. 1.

5. Invented by an ancient Greek Olympian, it was called the "compact discus" back then.

6. "Record & Tape Sales Net $4.3 Billion in '84," *Record Collector's Monthly*, Issue #30, May 1985, p. 5.

7. "Digital Players Revive Record Industry," *Record Collector's Monthly*, Issue #5, January 1983, p. 1.

8. Mennie, Don. "Digital Audio: Aural Triumph; Archival Disaster." *Record Collector's Monthly*, Issue #5, January 1983, p. 2.

Chapter 17

The Personality Deejays

Black vocal groups, like the Mills Brothers and Ink Spots, regularly found their way onto radio as early as the 1930s. Some even had syndicated slots on the national "Red" (NBC-R), "Blue" (NBC-B), Mutual (MBS) and Columbia (CBS) networks. Rhythm and blues after World War II was also on the radio, but usually on second-tier stations. The difference was in the intended audience. R&B was music by blacks for blacks; there were few white listeners. The deejays that played this music sounded black, whether they were or not, in order to maintain credibility with their audience and sell the offerings of their advertisers. Some of these men took the high road, serving the community as role models and teachers, and others were less altruistic.[1]

Economics governed what type of music was heard. Those spinning platters in rural areas played country music, rhythm and blues and eventually rockabilly and country and western. Deejays in the cities played rhythm and blues, both single artists and groups. They played what their audiences wanted to hear, for that's what sold products. And selling products kept them on the air. At the turn of the decade, around 1950, things were kind of at equilibrium. Blacks listened to music by blacks, whites listened to music by whites, everything was fairly predictable. Then something happened.

Alan Freed didn't necessarily cause what happened. But he was certainly at the right place at the right time to exert an enormous influence over what occurred. What happened was teen-agers entered the mix, seeking out music that felt good to them. Music that their parents neither liked nor approved of. Not just black kids, for the way society was back then, that would've been a non-event to white society. But white kids! That was something to notice.

Although these "cats" (white kids that liked music by blacks) were undoubtedly popping up all over the country, the first noteworthy news item came out of Cleveland, and guess who was in the center of the controversy? Once in the limelight, Freed found a way to stay there, through good times and bad, for almost a decade. On March 21, 1952, Freed produced and hosted a concert/dance called "Moon Dog's Coronation Ball" in the Cleveland Arena, selling out all 10,000 seats. Fortunately or unfortunately, roughly double that number got in. There was a lot of dancing in the aisles, a reasonable amount of drinking and one reported stabbing over a girl or a seat. Fire and police officials called off the concert halfway through. Needless to say, the Cleveland newspapers teed off on the event, calling it a "riot." All the

negative publicity was great for the cause, however, making Freed into a cult figure from just another deejay spinning tunes for cats, and attracting the attention of whatever as-yet unconverted teens still existed. Nothing did, does and will attract a youngster quite as much as an adult telling them to stay away. Freed followed the first "fiasco" with sold-out concerts in Akron (July 1952), Cleveland (July 1953) and Newark (May 1954).

Freed parlayed his notoriety into a career. He really was the first of the new breed of personality deejays. He banged telephone books to the beat of the song, howled like a "Moon Dog," shouted "Go! Go! Go!" above the music. If you're a teen, how could you hate this stuff? He broke the ice, set the style and pace, got the glory, and eventually paid for it. He did more for the music than anyone else of his era.

Whatever music Freed happened to favor was going to be popular. According to legend, he coined the term rock 'n' roll and, luckily for us, what he meant by rock 'n' roll included a lot of vocal group singing. It would've been better if he'd been even more disposed toward groups on a percentage basis, or had given the group sound its own separate name, but we have to take what we get. By putting them in his concerts, Freed helped to establish the careers of many of the most popular groups of the era, such as the Platters, Flamingos, Moonglows, Frankie Lymon and the Teenagers, and the Three Chuckles.

What made Freed so audacious was that he was attracting white teen-agers like flies. Audiences at his first three concerts in 1952 and 1953 were roughly one-third white which, incidentally, spurred fears that black youths would adversely influence white. After that, concerts spread geographically and in numbers. Audiences changed from being mostly black to mostly white, except for those held at "chitlin circuit" theaters in black urban neighborhoods, like Apollo in New York, the Howard in Washington, D.C., the Uptown in Philadelphia and the Royal in Baltimore.

Middle-class white kids were definitely in on most of the action, however. An R&B song in 1952, which made it to the number-one spot on the *Billboard* charts sold an average of 250,000 copies. By 1953, that average jumped to about 1,000,000 records, with the implication that white teens were making up the difference.[2]

What these kids were drawn to was the excitement of it all, the newness of the music, and the feeling of wanting to be in on something that had never quite happened

1. Smith, Wes. *The Pied Pipers of Rock 'n' Roll.* Marietta, GA: Longstreet Press, 1989.

2. Jackson, John A. *Big Beat Heat: Alan Freed and the Early Years of Rock & Roll.* New York: Schirmer Books, 1991.

before. *The New York Times*, in May 1960, reported: "Going to one of Alan Freed's musicales has always been something like having an aisle seat for the San Francisco earthquake. His favorite art form has caused riots in Boston, been banned in New Haven and broken all marks for drawing customers to the Brooklyn Paramount."[3]

Jeff Greenfield[4] described the group singing that one saw at a Freed concert: "Four or five singers, outlandishly dressed, in flaming red tux jackets, purple pants, yellow shirts with velvet ties—this in a time when charcoal gray was a bit daring. There are always two mikes—one for the lead singer, one for the rest of the group, including (always) a bass singer who supplies the doo-bobba, doo-bobba doo line, one falsetto to surround the reedy lead voice with logistical support in the form of descants.

The steps. They defy description. In a tribute to symmetry, the guy on the left puts out his left hand, the guy on the right puts out his right hand, and the guy in the middle puts out both hands. Fingers snap and wave, legs flash out and up, in mirror-image perfection. Now the hands switch, the feet shuffle in tempo. The tenor sax break begins. The singers spin completely around; they do splits. They gesture with the words.

> 'You know'—(the singers) point out
> 'In my heart'—point to the heart
> 'I pray'—hands together in prayer
> 'We'll never part'—hands separate, heads shake no'."

After Freed came to New Jersey for a one-off and sold out the Newark Armory in May of 1954, someone at the popular WINS in New York City figured that maybe Freed had earned his ticket to the big time. Freed came to WINS in September of that year for $75,000 per year, and a share of the syndication purse, an enormous package for the time. He started out in a late time slot, 11 p.m. to 2 a.m., and then added a show between 7-9 p.m., making him more accessible to teens. Everything was bigger in New York; the salaries, the audience and the concert halls.

His first concert in New York was held before 16,000 fans at the St. Nicholas Arena on Jan 14th (and 15th), 1955. Called the "Rock 'n' Roll Jubilee Ball," it featured the Clovers, Drifters, Harptones, and Moonglows. The Times reported on the "...solid mass that stood for five hours to see the spectacular r&b show put on by Freed and company. Seen from above, the enthusiastic teeners seemed to be jelled into one swaying body with thousands of heads. That they adored Freed was evident from the uproarious welcome with which they greeted his appearance. The enthusiasm of the audience was transferred to the performers, who reacted to the frenzy with tremendous performances. A finale that lasted about half an hour was rocked in the atmosphere of a revival meeting."[5] Finally, "...the entire troupe

returned to the stage for a closing that was without parallel. Singers and instrumentalists danced, dancers and singers grabbed instruments and instrumentalists and dancers sang. Alan Freed and his lovely wife, Jackie, jitterbugged and the kids went wild."[6] And that's why he got paid the big bucks.

Freed's most famous venue, the Brooklyn Paramount, was visited first on April 12, 1955 and returned to on Sept. 2, 1955. The second show featured the Moonglows, Harptones, and an unknown guy by the name of Tony Bennett. It netted more than $100,000, a big take for that time. Big pay days occurred often. "Take, for example, his 'Easter Jubilee of Stars,' which played the Brooklyn Paramount in April 1956. This blockbuster show brought in $240,000 in 10 days, breaking all existing records. Police had to halt traffic on the streets around the theater because of the huge lines of ticket-seekers. The admission charge, originally set at $1.25, was raised to $2 after a few days, which of course didn't thin down the crowds any! The lucky ones who got inside had a choice of six to seven complete shows every day..."[7] "I remember packing a lunch and leaving my house in the Bronx at 5:30 in the morning for the long ride to the theater. The doors opened at 9:30 A.M. and of course I had to be one of the first ones there. I waited in line for the doors to open and ran for a front-row seat. The movie went on at 10 a.m. and the first stage show started at 11:30. The prices then were mornings $.90, afternoons $1.25 and in the evening $1.50... ...The movie that was shown in between shows had to be omitted in order to cater to the big crowds that were trying to get in. I remember leaving after the 4th show and seeing a line around the block."[8]

Freed loved instrumentals with wild sax solos, but he loved vocal groups as much, and did much to put their talents in the public eye. In his 10-day 1956 Easter show at the Brooklyn Paramount, he featured the Teenagers with Frankie Lymon, the Flamingos, the Platters, the Valentines, the Willows, the Cleftones and the Royal-Tones.[9] Not a bad lineup.

Freed wasn't the only deejay to make it big, only the first. New York, having the most fans and being home to trade publications like Billboard and Cash Box, fostered the most intense competition. Many of the New York deejays became household names. The strongest competitors among deejays who played doo-wop in the New York arena were Tommy "Dr. Jive" Smalls, Peter Tripp and Douglas "Jocko" Henderson.

"Dr. Jive" had the most popular program in the afterschool slot with a show on WWRL, and brought a

3. "Rock 'n' Roll Pied Piper: Alan Freed." *New York Times*, May 20, 1960, p. 62.
4. Greenfield, Jeff. *No Peace, No Place*. Garden City, NY: Doubleday & Co., 1973.

5. Gart, Galen. *The History of Rhythm & Blues*, Vol. 5 (1955). Milford, N.H.: Big Nickel Publications, 1990.
6. Ibid.
7. Grendysa, Pete. "Sneakin' Back." *Bim Bam Boom*, Issue #5, April-May 1972, p. 39.
8. Farlekus, Mike. "Memory Lane." *Bim Bam Boom*, Issue #7, September 1972, p. 14.
9. Ibid.

rhythm and blues (and doo-wop) review to the Ed Sullivan "Toast of the Town" show. He later bought Small's Paradise, a landmark Harlem night club previously owned by one Edwin Smalls (no relation), and capitalized on the name to showcase premier doo-wop and rhythm and blues acts. He put on his first show at the Apollo at Easter time in 1956, featuring acts like the Solitaires, Fi-Tones, Moonglows, Schoolboys, Teen Queens, Charlie and Ray, Dean Barlow, Brook Benton, and the Buddy Griffin Orchestra.[10] Unlike Freed, Smalls catered less to the white crowd, and featured, almost exclusively, acts that were black. Thus, he could present the Ravens, Chips and Bop Chords, and omit Cirino & the Bowties, Buddy Knox and Charlie Gracie. Smalls was also the most popular of the emcees at the Apollo theater, and was second only to Freed in number of concerts in New York.

The "Top 40" format was the innovation of WHB in Kansas City.[11] WMGM in New York not only adopted its format in 1956, but appropriated one of its deejays, Peter Tripp, to try out that format in the 5-8 p.m. slot. Tripp promptly popularized it, despite being on a station that played mostly pop and carried New York Yankee baseball games. Tripp nicknamed himself "the curly-headed kid in the third row" and put on the first record countdown show which was based on actual record sales. Freed also had a countdown show, but it was subjective, based on listener requests and his own preferences. Tripp's only subjectivity showed up in "extras," inserted between countdown entries.

"Jocko" Henderson (on WLIB in New York and WHAT in Philadelphia) gave the world his famous rhyming patter (e.g., great gugga mugga shugga bugga) that was the forerunner of modern rap music. His first concert was on April 17, 1957 at the Loew's State in Manhattan, and featured the Jive Bombers, Clovers, Teenchords, Paragons, Heartbeats and, believe it or not, the (white) Diamonds, who at the time had a big hit with the Gladiolas' "Little Darlin'."[12] He later had a series of his "Rocket Ship" shows at the Apollo, and even had a doo-wop song dedicated to him, called "Jocko Sent Me" by Ben White & the Darchaes.

Other players on the New York scene were Phil "Dr. Jive" Gordon on WLIB, Willie "The Mayor of Harlem" Bryant and Ray Carroll on WHOM, Jack "The Pear Shaped Talker" Walker on WOV (who did public relations for Atlantic Records on the side), Hal Jackson on WLIB, Joe Bostic on WBNX and Alan Fredericks, with his "Night Train Show" on WGBB, WHOM and WADO. WLIB was far and away the most popular station in the black community during the doo-wop years. WOV offered the rather unexpected combination of rhythm and blues and Italian music which may have something to do with influ-

ence of black music on Italian youth who eventually developed a distinct white group sound in the late 1950s. Italian programming was mostly during the day with rhythm and blues programming at night after 8 p.m.[13]

Although the politics of race did not seem to be much a part of the doo-wop era, the issues were always brewing beneath the surface. Willie Bryant was a talented light-skinned black who never quite made it to the big time as an actor, orchestra leader, dancer, and comedian. He seemed to gravitate to the R&B scene as deejay and emcee at the Apollo Theater only after other avenues were closed to him. Ted Fox, in Showtime At The Apollo, interviewed Leonard Reed, one of Bryant's dance partners, who stated: 'But they knew he was part Negro, and downtown they wouldn't let him work. Willie was made to stay in Harlem. ...But Willie was Negro, and he never did get the chance. The white man only lets a few Negroes through. At the time, there was no room for five; maybe one or two.'[14] Bryant was honored by then New York Mayor Vincent Impellitteri by being appointed Harlem's "Locality Mayor" in 1952. He later called a protest meeting in Harlem to censure Freed for trying to sound black. One big objection was to the syndication of Freed's radio shows which, he felt, would take jobs away from blacks. Today his actions would be seen as politically correct; in the 1950s they were ineffectual.

The competition among these deejays was ultimately about audience share. In sheer numbers, over all audiences, Freed usually won. He was more charismatic than the other white deejays and could attract more of the white teen audience than the black deejays. For the same reasons his concerts usually outgrossed those put on by Dr. Jive and Jocko, though the competition was fierce. Since New York was the center of the doo-wop world, all the new songs were filtered through this capitalistic system governed by this group of deejays. Teen-agers "voted" with their radio dials and allowance money.

These types of "elections" went on in most large metropolitan areas. Usually white males who sounded black, hep, or black and hep, became enormously popular throughout the area reached by their stations. Buffalo had George "Hound Dog" Lorenz on WKBW and WBLK, Boston had "Symphony Sid" Torin and Ken Malden on WEZE, Pittsburgh had Porky (Platter Pushin' Papa) Chedwick on WAMO, New Haven had Carl Loucks on WELI, Milwaukee had Chuck Dunaway on WRIT and WMIL. In Chicago,[15] black deejays held sway. The most popular station for R&B in Chicago was WGES, where Al Benson ("The Mayor of

10. Ibid.
11. Baer, Jon. "Peter Tripp & 50's N.Y. Radio." Record Exchanger, Issue #23, 1977, p. 22.
12. Farlekus, Mike. "Memory Lane." Bim Bam Boom, Issue #7, September 1972, p. 14.
13. Gart, Galen. The History of Rhythm & Blues, Vol. 5 (1955). Milford, N.H.: Big Nickel Publications, 1990.
14. Fox, Ted. Showtime At the Apollo. New York: Holt, Rinehart & Winston, 1983.
15. Chicago information from: Pruter, Robert. Doo-wop: The Chicago Scene. Chicago: University of Illinois Press, 1996.

Bronzeville") reigned as king. Richard Stamz ("The Crown Prince of Disc Jockeys") and Sam Evans were other popular deejays on WGES, WSBC had Jack L. Cooper, McKie Fitzhugh worked at WGES, WHFC and WOPA, Herb "Kool Gent" Kent at WBEE. Los Angeles forerunners were Hunter Hancock, who worked for a series of stations beginning with KFVD in the 1940s, Art LeBoe on KGFJ and Dick "Huggie Boy" Hugg on KRKD. And, as in New York, the spoils of victory included night club work, production of Revues and multi-act shows at chitlin circuit locales, sock hops, group sponsorship and idol-worship.

Initially the impact of deejays centered around the radio dials and concert arenas. Before long, they began to get into other media, like "composing" music, movies, and television. Not surprisingly, Freed was in the forefront in all of them. Under the guise of making the songs more visible, Freed was one of the first deejays to put his name as composer on songs written by others. According to John Jackson in Big Beat Heat, Freed put his name on songs of groups he managed, such as "Sincerely" by the Moonglows and "Nadine" by the Coronets. As with the "payola" issue and the underpayment of group members for their labors, claiming composer credits has been judged harshly in historical perspective. Whether legal or not, whether effective or not, whether seen as fostered by our capitalistic system or not, these actions are clearly unethical. Since Freed was the poster boy for the music, these practices have made him a "bad guy" to many over the years, in spite of his having made significant positive contributions to our culture.

As the medium of television grew in importance, the radio deejays tried their hand there as well. The after-school and Saturday afternoon slots were the most popular. Teens now had the chance to not only hear the music they loved, but to see glamorous, personable and nimble-footed peers dance to it. Many teens lived their lives vicariously through these shows. Freed was the first, but far from the most successful. His first show in Cleveland in 1950, called "Request Review," was a failure. He tried again in 1957 with a show that featured mostly black artists and vocal groups, but he ran afoul politically. According to Wes Smith, one of the show's first guests, Frankie Lymon, had the cheek to dance with a white girl in front of the cameras.[16] John Jackson reported that so much pressure was exerted by the show's sponsors and the Southern white audience that the show was canceled after four outings.[17] This is another instance where Freed got involved in the racial politics of the day. This time, however, we'd judge him politically correct retrospectively.

Of course, the king of teen music shows on television was and is "American Bandstand," hosted by Dick

Clark. "Bandstand" welcomed doo-wop acts, but was more "white-oriented" than Freed's show, which made it more acceptable to the white teen population. The show made its national debut in August 1957, after ABC picked it up from its Philadelphia affiliate. Clark's clean-cut good looks and his personable manner made him and his show a success. Within a year, it became far and away the most popular show of its ilk and the only one that was national. The only competition for "Bandstand" was local market shows hosted by Freed, Clay Cole and "Jocko" Henderson.

The movies were an enormous part of our culture in the 1950s. The subject of teen-age rebellion was dealt with as it happened. The year 1953 saw the appearance of "The Wild One" starring Marlon Brando, which forever doomed nice teen-agers to only riding their motorcycles over their parents' dead bodies. "The Blackboard Jungle" was released in the spring of 1955. This film, about delinquency, teen-age life and inner city schools, scared the pants off of many parents. It also contained "Rock Around The Clock" by Bill Haley and the Comets, which quickly became a teen anthem and signature for the whole rock 'n' roll movement. These movies, along with "Rebel Without A Cause" featuring James Dean, both incited teen-age rebellion and the parental backlash against it.

The movies that were produced by the personality deejays were a lot less controversial (and less successful) than the ones mentioned above. Basically they sought to showcase the new music and the artists who sang it. Willie Bryant emceed two full-length feature films in 1955, called "The Rock 'n' Roll Revue" and "The Rhythm & Blues Revue," which showcased all-black talent. Geared for a black audience, few whites knew of their existence. Freed released two better-known movies in 1956. The first, titled "Rock Around the Clock," featured the Platters, Bill Haley & the Comets and Freed himself. The second, "Rock, Rock, Rock," welcomed Frankie Lymon & the Teenagers, the Moonglows, the Flamingos, Chuck Berry, the Three Chuckles, Cirino and the Bowties, and the Johnny Burnette Trio. Another 1956 film was "The Girl Can't Help It," featuring some legitimate actors (Edmund O'Brien, Tom Ewell and Jayne Mansfield) with a legitimate script that allowed for incidental appearances by Little Richard, Fats Domino, Gene Vincent, Eddie Cochran and the Platters. And, of course, Elvis made his film debut in September of 1956 with "Love Me Tender."

Syndication of radio shows was another area pioneered by Freed. While at WJW in Cleveland, Freed's show was leased to ten other stations, which grew to more than 50 after he moved to WINS in New York. Other deejays like Hunter Hancock in Los Angeles, Zenas "Daddy" Sears in Atlanta and Tommy Smalls in New York also had their shows syndicated as early as 1954. Ironically, these R&B jocks succeeded where pop music deejays had failed in earlier efforts. Their charisma, the adulation and fanaticism of the teen-age audience, and the fact that the shows went to teen-ori-

16. Smith, Wes. The Pied Pipers of Rock 'n' Roll. Marietta, GA: Longstreet Press, 1989.

17. Jackson, John A. Big Beat Heat: Alan Freed and the Early Years of Rock & Roll. New York: Schirmer Books, 1991.

ented independent (as opposed to network) radio stations accounts for this success.

These deejays were the right people for the times. They loved rhythm & blues and/or rock 'n' roll, and had personalities that teens found charismatic. They created or used the latest slang, employed humor frequently and were usually anti-establishment. Often they were cynical and sarcastic, taking pokes at adult values. Some were even lewd, but the majority kept their shows clean, in keeping with the music they played. The appeal of the music and the teen-oriented delivery made these personality deejays winners. The audiences grew by leaps and bounds.

The good times came to an end in the late 1950s, perhaps because of excesses, perhaps because adults needed a scapegoat for their fears brought on by the rebellion of their children. In May of 1958, Freed's show in Boston supposedly set off a riot. The press came down hard on Freed, and this became the first step in his eventual fall from grace. In 1959, the practice of "payola" (pay for play) came under the scrutiny of the Harris Commission. By this time, many factions had axes to grind. Parents were scared and angry about what they felt was the seduction of their children by these deejays. Radio station owners weren't getting a slice of the pie and wanted to be seen as upstanding members of their communities. Record companies tired of paying out so much money to get their records on the air. Payola, though not illegal at the time, was unethical enough to result in the creation of new industry standards for doing business. More subtle ways to get records noticed, like promotional campaigns, record giveaways and expense account lunches became acceptable business practice. The choice of the "play list," or which records were played on any given show, was left in the hands of program directors who owed their livelihoods to the station owners and not the deejays. The spontaneity associated with the personality deejays ended.

The personality deejays were casualties of these revisions. Some tried to tough it out, like Alan Freed and Tommy "Dr. Jive" Smalls, but were ruined in the process. Some cooperated, like Dick Clark, and were able to stay in the industry. Peter Tripp, though he only added extra records to an untampered-with Top 40, didn't survive the notoriety. Yet these men had achieved a lot in a few short years, converting millions of teen-agers to the cause of the new music. A job well done.

Those of you who have not slept through this chapter should do pretty well on the following quiz. Just match the nickname with the deejay's real name.

Quiz #7: Dee Jay Du Jour

1) Dr. Jive (on WLIB)
2) The curly-headed kid in the third row
3) Daddy
4) The Mayor of Harlem
5) Kool Gent
6) Platter Pushin' Papa
7) The Pear-shaped Talker
8) Hound Dog
9) The curly-headed kid in the second row
10) The Crown Prince of disc jockeys
11) Dr. Jive (on WWRL)
12) Moon Dog
13) Huggie Boy
14) Symphony Sid
15) Jocko
16) Cat man on a back fence
17) The Mayor of Bronzville
18) Wide-eyed Italian
19) The geeter with the heater
20) Swingin' Slim

a) Dick Hugg
b) Tommy Smalls
c) Richard Stamz
d) Peter Tripp
e) Sidney Torin
f) Jerry Blavat
g) Herb Kent
h) Alan Freed
i) Danny Styles
j) Willie Bryant
k) Al Benson
l) Zenas Sears
m) Porky Chedwick
n) Dick Biondi
o) Irving Rosensweig
p) Jack Walker
q) Gus Gossert
r) Phil Gordon
s) George Lorenz
t) Douglas Henderson

Chapter 18

Indies Versus the Establishment

Before the birth of doo-wop music, the recording industry was dominated by a small number of major record companies (called "majors"). In the late 1940s, these behemoths were Capitol, Columbia, Decca, Mercury, MGM and RCA. They sold the most records, took in the most in terms of revenues, and had the most influence on which kinds of music was recorded and played. Because they were in business to make money, they catered to the people that spent the most money on records, namely the white population. As a result, minority musics, including Latin, Polish, Yiddish, country music and "race" music received little attention. If they couldn't make much money with a given music, it was largely ignored.

The powers-that-be within these corporations found it easy to overlook the vocal group rhythm & blues of the late 1940s and early 1950s because, in terms of sheer numbers, it wasn't of much consequence. In a way, they made the market, for if the majors ignored a given music for long enough, it would eventually fade away, or at least stay permanently linked to a limited market.

Rhythm & blues was largely overlooked because the people for whom the music held appeal, namely blacks, didn't buy many records in comparison to white people. The overhead expenses involved in discovering talent, hiring backup musicians and other professionals, and then selling the record to radio stations and record stores, often outweighed their anticipated profits. And then there was the racial issue. The 1940s and early 1950s were still times of segregation of schools and stages. Music by blacks, if it sounded black, was foreign to most white ears, and thus went unpurchased. If the music sounded "white enough," it would have a chance to penetrate the white pop charts, as in the works of Nat "King" Cole on Capitol, and Ella Fitzgerald, the Mills Brothers and the Ink Spots on Decca. When the majors occasionally made forays into rhythm and blues music, it was done mainly through subsidiaries like RCA's Bluebird label and Columbia's Okeh label.

The rock 'n' roll explosion caught these majors with their pants down, so to speak. Rock 'n' roll, of which doo-wop was a part, didn't go away as other musics had. Okeh, for example, which was a significant source of black music between the 1920s and 1940s, was revived so that Columbia could compete in the profitable teen market in the 1950s. RCA, at the same time, and for the same reasons, established the "X" and Groove labels in the early to mid-1950s. By the mid-1950s, the majors were playing catch-up. They had ignored the growth of a set of new musics, collectively called "rock 'n' roll" and had allowed a whole new set of record companies and artists to gain footholds in the industry.

The same oversight that record companies committed was also made by ASCAP (American Society of Composers, Authors, and Publishers). ASCAP was formed in 1914 to protect the rights of composers. The organization keeps track of which songs are played/sold, in what medium, and how many times. The radio and television stations, record companies and live shows that use a composer's work, then pay royalties to ASCAP which are passed on to composers. Again, perhaps for economic reasons, for many years ASCAP kept out composers of race or hillbilly music. To protect these "small-timers," a parallel organization, called BMI (Broadcast Music Incorporated), was established in 1940. BMI was itself a small-timer, until the rock 'n' roll explosion hit the big time in the mid-1950s. All of a sudden, the music and composers it represented were in enormous demand.

With the major record companies and ASCAP tending to the needs of the majority audience, the remaining market segments had always been serviced by small independent record companies ("indies"). Because the market for rhythm and blues was small, the number of records pressed and sold were small, the revenues were small and the record companies were small. They were usually "mom and pop" operations, with the owners often being involved in finding the talent, producing the recordings and selling the product. In order to survive, the operators had to be hard working and versatile. Often they were passionate about vocal group rhythm and blues and doo-wop. Many of them were typical of the American success story and were themselves minorities, being women (e.g., Vivian Bracken of Vee Jay and Bess Berman of Apollo), blacks (Bobby Robinson of Whirlin' Disc and Paul Winley of Winley Records) and Jews (George Goldner of Gee and Leonard and Philip Chess of Chess).

Operating on a shoestring both helped and hurt these fledgling companies. Overhead was low, real low. Often their offices were located in the poorer neighborhoods where talent was located, making it easy to "farm the land." The image of a group singing their hearts out on the sidewalk below the window of a record company executive, hoping to attract his or her interest, was more than just fable. If the record people were patient and tireless, had a modicum of musical taste and business sense, they made out all right.

On the other hand, not having a large bankroll often put companies in difficult situations. Putting out records, with the inherent costs of production and pressing, wasn't cheap. If the label had a run of non-selling records, that was often enough to put them under. Ironically, even a hit would put the label in jeopardy. Ed

Ward remarked, "The whole economic structure of a record company is based on distributor payments, and in order to get major distributors...a label had to offer them attractive terms, such as allowing them to return unsold records for credit and letting them hold on to wares for up to 90 days without paying a cent. Meanwhile, the label would need money to keep pressing and shipping records, and if a record got hot, that could mean a huge sum. Of course, many distributors were less than honest about sales figures, and during the 1950s, some even pressed and sold bootleg or counterfeit copies, sending the legitimate records back, especially but not solely to indies. By the time the big profits started rolling in, a label owner could very well have sold everything he owned to amass the capital to keep pressing- literally starving his company to death with success."[1] Profit margins were usually not large, so that each decision assumed enormous importance.

The way out for these small companies was to peddle something of value. A record that was taking off was sometimes sold to a better capitalized record concern, like Imperial or Dot. These larger companies could push the record with more financial zeal. If an artist under contract got hot, his/her/their body of works had a street value, especially if the artist was no longer under contract. Even fledgling artists became commodities, as when Elvis Presley was sold to RCA by Sam Philips (of Sun Records) for $40,000 in 1955. For Sam, a bird in the hand was worth two in the bush. Except that time, there was a whole aviary in that bush.

The home bases of these labels were most often poorer areas within urban centers like Chicago, Los Angeles and New York. The label owners, producers and talent usually all knew each other, producing subcultures wherein all members were not necessarily equal. Label owners held most of the cards and sometimes played them to the detriment of the artists. Group members might be robbed of composer credits, under the guise of making the song well-known. Or the group might be paid a small fee (like $50 a man for a session), but have to give up their rights to any royalties generated by the records they participated in. Johnny Keyes[2] described the way groups were mistreated on tours by being underpaid or not paid at all. The groups were so anxious to make it that they'd put up with anything just to record or tour, and the record label owners knew that groups were plentiful and, with some exceptions, interchangeable. It was as if most of the label owners belonged to the same fraternity, having similar business practices, and sharing the successes and failures. Hy Weiss, co-owner of the Old Town label, reported discussing songs and arrangements with the Bermans, of Apollo, and George Goldner of Gee, in the early to mid-1950s.[3]

Charms.

Although much has been written about the way label owners profited at the expense of the artists, the label owners themselves were involved in an economic contest. Everything boiled down to survival of the fittest, supply and demand, Dun and Bradstreet. There was a lot of money to be made in the years that vocal group music hit the big time, but there was also a lot of competition. Labels would put out records that were, in effect, voted on by the public. Those indies that won a good share of these "elections," like Atlantic Records, flourished artistically and monetarily. Others, whose owners had less taste musically, less business sense or lousy timing went out of business. And the major record companies didn't take their usurping lying down.

The first thing the majors did was begin to "cover" the hits put out by the smaller indies. The campaign began in 1954 and lasted through 1957. The major would hire a (usually) white vocal group to duplicate the sound of a successful record put out by a black group. If the whole arrangement was duplicated note for note, it was called a "copy." Since two almost identical records were competing for the same buying population, this strategy obviously diminished the income or the original record company and artists. It was a great strategy, because the majors had the wherewithal to cover a record in a couple of weeks, with no costs associated with the finding of talent or material. Their facilities and musical resources assured top quality. In no time, a white version of a song could be beating a black version on the white-oriented pop charts. And, back then, the pop charts were where the money was.

Covering was almost a foolproof method. If the records by black artists that were chosen were already making some noise, it was fairly certain that a white cover would be well-received. Imagine hearing 10 new recordings and being able to choose which ones to release. Anyone with a modicum of musical taste could pick out the catchiest of the lot. In this way, the Crew Cuts covered "Sh-Boom" by the Chords (for Mercury), the McGuire Sisters covered

1. Ward, Ed, et al. *Rock of Ages: The Rolling Stone History of Rock & Roll*. New York: Summit Books, 1986.
2. Keyes, Johnny. *Du-Wop*. Chicago: Vesti Press, 1987.

3. Phone interview conducted on Oct. 16, 1996.

Pat Boone.

"Sincerely" by the Moonglows (for Coral/Decca) and the Diamonds covered "Walkin' Along" by the Solitaires and "Little Darling" by the Gladiolas (both for Mercury). The above-mentioned McGuire Sisters record hit number one nationally in early 1955.

The Dot label became infamous for this strategy. Under its aegis, the Fontaine Sisters issued "Adorable" by the Drifters (who themselves covered the original by the Colts), and Pat Boone kept busy covering "Gee Whitakers" by the Five Keys, "At My Front Door" by the El Dorados, "I'll Be Home" by the Flamingos and "Two Hearts" by Otis Williams and the Charms. "Two Hearts" was a popular target; even Frank Sinatra and Doris Day got into the action, both covering it in 1955.

Although the cover strategy at first consisted mostly of white artists reissuing material by black artists, black groups soon began to cover one another. Otis Williams and the Charms did this often, covering such records as "Hearts Of Stone" by the Jewels and "Ling Ting Tong" by the Five Keys. Also in this category are the Cadets version of the Jayhawks' "Stranded In The Jungle" and Frankie Lymon and the Teenagers' issue of Jimmy Castor and the Juniors' record of "I Promise To Remember."

Covering was somewhat related to the practice of releasing different versions of songs to hit different markets. What covering and marketing segmentation have in common is the attempt on the part of record companies to make as much money as they could. Thus the Moonglows did up an R&B version of Doris Day's "Secret Love" and the Orioles scored with a song that was origi-

Crew-Cuts.

nally a country and western hit for Darrell Glenn, "Crying In The Chapel." In each of these cases, there was little competition between the differing versions.

It's interesting to take a look at who was hurt and helped by the practice of covering. If you were a composer, covering wasn't so bad. It probably meant that the song you wrote would tickle the fancy of more people and you would get higher record sales, sheet music sales, more airplay and higher royalties. The same was true of publishing houses. The more the merrier.[4]

---

4. One exception to this was created when record companies started "giveaway" programs. To better market their songs, some labels would give one disc free of charge for every three or four bought. Copyright laws required ($.02 per disk) royalties be paid on the number sold, not shipped. In this example, the publisher would lose one fourth of the expected royalties. Several men (Syd Nathan, head of King/Federal, and Herman Lubinsky of Savoy) fought this practice by refusing to allow other record companies to use their songs. This forced them to file papers with the copyright office before releasing a cover, which slowed them up and forced them to pay royalties on the number shipped. This effectively ended giveaway programs.

The people who were hurt were the record companies that produced the original versions. They put money and time into "research and development" of records that were then stolen by others. So less of their records were sold and played on the air, and they made less money. The same is true for the artists on original versions. The original label would rather sell 500,000 of a given song, than have the song sell 1,000,000 if its version only sold 400,000 of that total. Ironically, this created factions within the music and recording industries; composers and publishers who benefited from covers, versus artists and labels who were hurt.

Distinction was made back then between covers and "copies," which not only reproduced the song, but the exact arrangement of the song. In 1951, the courts stated that although the Copyright Act of 1909 protected the song (and thus the composer), the arrangement was not protected. In 1955, Laverne Baker went public, stating that she lost $15,000 in royalties to exact copies of her smash "Tweedle Dee" sung by Georgia Gibbs and Vicki Young. As a result of Baker's complaint, Alan Freed banned copies from being played on his station, WINS in New York. Other stations joined the cause and soon instances of copying decreased sharply. Covering was still considered ethical, however.

Covers and copies differ from "remakes," which are harmless. What makes a remake a remake, and not a cover, is time. If the original record has had its run on the charts and rolled off into the sunset, remaking the song doesn't hurt anyone while helping the composer and publisher. In fact, a remake theoretically might revive interest in the original version. Remakes occurred thousands of times during the 1950s, because groups had a penchant for giving a new twist to old standards, like "Zing Went The Strings Of My Heart" by the Coasters in 1958 and Gabriel & the Angels in 1961, or "I Don't Stand A Ghost of A Chance" by the Five Keys in 1951 and the Solitaires in 1955. Groups also established a new set of "standards" for the doo-wop years with songs like "Gloria" and "Zoom Zoom Zoom," which were revisited often by groups during the era.

By 1955, the major record companies were hurting in the fields of vocal group harmony and rock 'n' roll. Of the Top 30 rhythm and blues hits of 1954, only two came from the majors, while Atlantic, the biggest of the indies, placed 11 records on that list alone. Concurrently, they were beginning to lose ground to the indies on the pop charts, where "crossover" hits were becoming more and more common. Examples are "White Christmas" by the Drifters for Atlantic, "Sincerely" by the Moonglows on Chess, "Earth Angel" by the Penguins on Dootone and "Hearts Of Stone" by the Charms on DeLuxe.

Aside from covers, the majors tried to find or develop their own artists. This strategy worked well when it came to rockabilly. RCA ended up with Elvis, Decca/Coral with Bill Haley and Capitol had Gene Vincent, giving the majors a huge part of the business. With doo-wop rhythm & blues the numbers weren't too impressive. For example, of the records listed in the songography in the back of this book, only about nine percent of the songs were released by major labels (Columbia, RCA, Decca, Mercury, Capitol & MGM) or any of their subsidiaries. The remaining 91 percent were released by the indies. The three most prolific indies, Gee/Rama, King/Federal and Atlantic, released more records than all the majors combined (roughly 11%).

While sometimes the majors would buy out the contract of a group from its label (e.g. the Five Keys going to Capitol from Aladdin and the Platters going to Mercury from Federal), the majors were minors when it came to doo-wop. Nonetheless, the entry of the majors into the fray resulted in more competition and meant that the pie was being sliced into smaller pieces. This unfortunately spelled doom for many of the less successful indies.

The more successful of the indies are discussed below, grouped by area of the country. Subsidiaries were plentiful, because if you approached a deejay with too many records on the same label, they wouldn't all get played. Better to spread the talent around on a number of labels. Sometimes different subsidiaries represented different groupings of owners for business purposes and sometimes a subsid cropped up to give a wayward relative something to do.

Beginning our tour in the Midwest, we find three big indie labels that reflected the rhythm & blues side of doo-wop, because Chicago was host to the expatriate Mississippi Delta Blues sound. This bluesy approach to music found its way into most of the individual and group sounds of the area. These three big diskeries were the Chess and Vee Jay consortiums out of Chicago, and the King/Federal complex in Cincinnati.

Phil and Leonard Chess immigrated from Poland in 1928 and ran a popular Chicago nightclub called the Macamba Lounge, which put them in contact with local talent. They first tried their hand at the recording business in the 1940s with the Aristocrat label, but when it flagged they changed its name to Chess in 1948. Conversant with black artists and their music, they were very successful in the blues and R&B fields, and had their first big vocal group hit with "Sincerely" by the Moonglows in 1955. The Chess brothers developed a close relationship with Alan Freed, giving at least tacit approval to his "co-composing" the Moonglows "Sincerely" and Chuck Berry's "Maybelline," and producing the first rock 'n' roll soundtrack for Freed's 1956 film, "Rock Rock Rock."[5]

By the late 1950s, the Chess brothers had started two other important labels, Checker and Argo, bought out others like Al Benson's Parrot and Blue Lake labels, Joe Liebowitz's Monarch and Leo Egalnick's Premium, owned several radio stations and Arc Publishing, a big player in the R&B field. Big groups that had hits for them included the Students, Monotones and Tuneweavers, in addition to the aforementioned Flamingos and Moonglows.

Chess' big rival in Chicago was the Vee Jay label,

5. Featuring the Moonglows and Flamingos.

with its Falcon and Abner subsids. The three principals in Vee Jay were Vivian Carter Bracken, her brother Calvin Carter and her husband James Bracken. Bracken and Vivian Carter owned "Vivian's Record Shop," which grew into Vee Jay in 1953, and the Brackens relationship concurrently grew from a business partnership into a marriage. Calvin Carter, a musician by trade, became the A&R man for the label. Vee Jay was one of the first big indies to be owned by blacks, and this allowed them access to talent in the black communities of Gary, Indiana and Chicago.

While Chess entered the fray earlier with blues performers, the Carter-Brackens hit the ground running in 1953 with groups like the Spaniels, El Dorados, Magnificents, Dukays, Dells and Sheppards, all of which scored more than once for them. Like Chess, Vee Jay became a conglomerate, buying the Chance and Sabre labels from Art Sheridan and Steve Chandler, and Ping Records from Frank Evans, forming their own subsidiaries and running Conrad Publishing. Great with talent, they were less skilled at finances and they closed their doors in 1966, despite having groups like the Dells, Four Seasons and Jerry Butler and the Impressions in their stable.

In nearby Cincinnati, Syd Nathan started King Records in 1945. Nathan's had success with many types of music including hillbilly, blues, single artist rhythm and blues and doo-wop. He added the Federal and Queen labels and bought DeLuxe from David and Jules Braun in 1949 and Rockin' from Andy Razaf and Henry Stone in 1953. The Platters, Swallows, Dominoes, Midnighters, and Otis Williams and the Charms all scored for him. Nathan had a reputation for being cunning and bold, coming out with "Annie Had A Baby" as an answer record to "Work With Me Annie" by the Midnighters. He passed away in 1968.

If the Midwest contributed the sound of the blues, New York chipped in with a bunch of different group styles, including gospel, urban R&B, gang doo-wop, schoolboy doo-wop and the white group sound.

New York was the most influential player in the doo-wop vocal group sound, and the most influential of its labels was Atlantic Records. Atlantic was created in 1947 by Ahmet Ertegun, who was the jazz-buff son of a Turkish diplomat, and Herb Abramson, the jazz-buff-dentist A&R (Artist and Repertoire) man for National Records. They had uncanny musical taste, good business sense, and treated their artists fairly. First came the Cardinals and Clovers, the latter having a string of number-one hits in the early 1950s. Then Ertegun sought out Clyde McPhatter after he was dismissed by Billy Ward and melded him into a gospel group called the Thrasher Wonders to form the Drifters, a group which produced hits, with and without Clyde, for a dozen years. The Chords, Coasters, Bobbettes and Sensations followed.

Atlantic was a primary target of cover records by the major record labels. In 1954, seven of their bigger hits, including "Sh-Boom" by the Chords and "Honey Love" and "Such A Night" by the Drifters were covered 18 times by different artists. Diversification paid off for them, however, because they made money on all those versions through their publishing arm. Atlantic survived and flourished because they were perfectionists about their products, hiring only the best session musicians (like saxman King Curtis) and producers (like Jesse Stone). Jerry Wexler joined the label in 1953 and Atlantic, with its reputation for producing hits, continued to attract talent.

The Cat (after white "cats" who loved R&B) and Atco subsidiaries were added in 1954 and 1955 respectively. The West Coast Spark label was bought in 1955, and brought with it the Robins, who were reformed into the Coasters, and Jerry Lieber and Mike Stoller, who went on to write all those famous "playlet" records for those Coasters (such as "Along Came Jones" and "Yakety Yak"). The work of Lieber, Stoller and the Coasters forms the nucleus for the magnificent Broadway musical, "Smoky Joe's Café" in the 1990s.

If Atlantic had a rival in New York, it was probably the bevy of labels presided over by George Goldner. Goldner began his odyssey in the early 1950s, first forming the Tico label to produce Latin music, and then Rama in 1953, which focused on rhythm and blues. Rama issued the first crossover smash, when "Gee" by the Crows made it big on the pop charts. Goldner then established the Gee label, in honor of the record, as well as Gone, End, Juanita, Roulette, Mark-X, Goldisc, and a few others. He believed in starting new labels to exploit new niches in the market.

Where Atlantic created sophisticated group sounds to cater to a sophisticated audience, Goldner's labels catered to teenage tastes. He hired Richard Barrett, a member of the Valentines, to find talent and produce records. Barrett's contacts and musical taste and Goldner's business sense resulted in recordings by the Chantels, Cleftones, Crows, Dubs, Flamingos, Harptones, Heartbeats, Little Anthony & the Imperials, Frankie Lymon & the Teenagers, Valentines and Wrens. Goldner went on to form the Red Bird label with Lieber and Stoller in the early 1960s, a label that produced the distaff sound of the Dixie Cups, Shangri-Las and Ad Libs. Goldner passed away in 1970, at the age of 52.

Another major group sound to come out of New York was gang doo-wop, which came from the hearts and minds of two Harlem-based sources, the Robinson brothers and Paul Winley. In the late 1940s, Bobby Robinson opened a record store in the middle of Harlem that was so well known, that successful white record men, such as the Bihari Brothers (Modern/RPM), the Mesners (Aladdin) and the Chess Brothers (Chess) would come to him for advice about what was hot. After a while, he figured that he may as well be the one profiting from his own counsel. He formed Red Robin with his brother Danny, Fire, Fury, Enjoy and Fling himself, and Whirlin' Disc with Jerry Blaine of National Records. After leaving Red Robin, Danny Robinson started Everlast, Cee Jay, Vest and Holiday, fonts of the gang doo-wop sound. Together, the Robinsons invented the sound of New York with early groups like the Vocaleers, Velvets and Scarlets, the gang doo-wop sound with Earl Lewis and the Channels, Continentals, Bop Chords, Charts and Love

Notes, while adding to the schoolboy doo-wop sound with the Kodaks and Lewis Lymon and the Teenchords.

The other big contributor to the gang doo-wop cause was Paul Winley[6] with his Winley, Porwin and Cyclone labels. Winley had a hand in producing and/or writing almost every song on his labels. His gift for composition, and the talents of Dave "Baby" Cortez, with whom he worked closely, produced gang-doo-wop masterpieces. The Winley banner, started in 1955, was home to the magnum opus, "The Paragons Meet The Jesters," arguably the most famous doo-wop album ever made. In a few short years, Winley unearthed local street talent and turned out gems by the Collegians, Quinns, Duponts, as well as the Paragons/Jesters.

The record world was a small one around 1950. Everyone knew one another, partnerships formed and reformed. Jubilee Records, home to many of the hits of Sonny Til and the Orioles, was started in 1947 in New York by Jerry Blaine and Herb Abramson. Abramson would later go on to be a founding father in Atlantic. Blaine subsequently formed Whirlin' Disc with Bobby Robinson, and was once in the record distribution business with Sam Weiss, a founder of the Old Town label. Blaine's daughter married the son of a founder of Herald Records (Jack Braverman). And so it goes. Blaine, who made his mark earlier as a band leader and record distributor, formed the Josie (aka Jo-Z) label in 1954, which featured the Cadillacs. Other labels that Blaine had a hand in were Todd, Chex, Le Cam and Port.

Another important label group centered around a guy named Al Silver. Silver, in a series of partnerships with his brother in-law Jack Braverman, Fred Mendelsohn and Jack Angel, started Herald and Ember Records, and added the Natural banner. His good ear for the music resulted in a series of classical doo-wop hits in the period 1955-1956 which retain their appeal to this day. Among them were "Paradise Hill" by the Embers, "Story Untold" and "Ship Of Love" by the Nutmegs, and "In the Still Of The Nite" by the Five Satins within the period 1955-1956. Other groups that had hits for him were the Mello Kings, Silhouettes, Turbans and Maurice Williams and the Zodiacs—an impressive catalog.

Two other important influences in New York were the Bermans and the Weiss brothers. Bess and Ike Berman started Apollo Records as a gospel label in the mid-1940s.[7] Bess Berman managed Mahalia Jackson and was a close personal friend to the great gospel chanteuse. In the early 1950s, Apollo diversified, launching the careers of the Larks, Little Anthony Gourdine (who was with the Chesters at the time), the Opals and the Cellos. Other labels under the Bermans' purview were Doe, Timely, Lloyds and Luna.

Sam and Hy Weiss formed Old Town Records in 1954. Sam left Jerry Blaine at Cosnat, a record distributing business and, with Hy, went on to record major works by the Solitaires, Harptones, Royaltones, Keytones, Clefftones, Earls and Fiestas. Related labels were Paradise, Whiz and Munich.

The sound of white groups was produced and sold by the Laurie complex of labels, headed by Allen Sussel, Gene and Bob Schwartz, Elliot Greenberg and Ernie Maresca. Sussel was central to this group, naming the Laurie, Andie and Jamie[8] labels for his children. Mohawk, Emge and Rust were other related labels. Maresca was another big player, being a performer ("Shout! Shout!" with the Del Satins), a prolific songwriter for Dion ("Runaround Sue," "The Wanderer," etc.), and a record producer (for the Belmonts and Five Discs). The white group sounds of the Dion & the Belmonts, Del Satins, Five Discs, Randy and the Rainbows, Vito and the Salutations and Mystics (plus the Jarmels and Chiffons who were and are black) passed through their doors.

West-Coast labels produced a rhythm and bluesy group sound that featured loose harmony and lots of emotion. The main banners were Modern, Aladdin and Dootone, and all were located in Los Angeles. The Modern complex of labels, started in the mid-1940s, was run by the Bihari brothers who were involved in many parts of the recording business. Jules, Joe, Lester and Saul Bihari not only owned a whole host of labels (Modern, RPM, Flair, Crown, Kent, Meteor, Rhythm & Blues), but a publishing company, a jukebox business and a record pressing plant as well. They started by unearthing local Los Angeles artists such as the Cadets/Jacks, Shirley Gunter & the Queens, Arthur Lee Maye & the Crowns and the Teen Queens. Working for the Biharis on the record distribution end was Lester Sill, who gave Lieber, Stoller and Phil Spector their starts in the business. Sill later went on to partner Spector in Philles Records ("Phil-" for Spector, "-les" for Sill).

Eddie, Leo and Ida Mesner founded Philo Records in 1945, but changed its name to Aladdin within a few years. They initially recorded single artist rhythm and blues, and added groups as the 1950s unfolded. They hit paydirt by signing the Five Keys after seeing them at one of their performances at New York's Apollo Theatre. They launched a subsidiary, called Lamp, in 1954, after they lured Jesse Stone away from Atlantic to head it up. Subsids named Score and 7-11 were soon added to the roster. Aside from the Keys, who produced some of the best group music ever waxed while with the Mesners, the Jayhawks, Robins and Thurston Harris & the Sharps passed through their doors.

Finally, Dootone/Dooto was founded by Dootsie Williams in 1954. Williams was black and was networked into the Watts community in L.A. One of his

---

6. Winley began as a singer with a group called the Rockets (Paul Winley & the Rockets). His brother, Harold, sang bass on most of the Clovers hits.
7. Their partners were Hy Siegel and Sam Schneider, but Ms. Berman ran the show.

---

8. This Philadelphia-based label was formed with Harold Lipsius and Harry Finfer, and was not part of the Laurie network.

first forays was "Earth Angel" by the Penguins, a monster hit despite a successful cover by the Crew Cuts. Although his commercial success peaked with "Earth Angel," Dootsie gave the world a series of beautiful ballads by groups like the Cuff Links, Don Julian & the Meadowlarks, and Vernon Green & the Medallions.

Advances in technology, spearheaded by cheaper and more portable radios, television, and better recording and playback equipment helped to foster the growth of doo-wop rhythm & blues. The music became easier to listen to, buy and play. Concurrently, the men and women spinning the records made it more attractive and available to an eager teen-age audience through old media like radio and movies and newer ones like television and rock concerts. In parallel, the small independent record companies grew to meet the demand for more artists and more records. Taken together, these industries gave the teen-age generation something they had never had before and would never relinquish: their own music.

For your entertainment, or consternation, or both, we've included two matching quizzes. In the first, the reader (that's you) is asked to match the "parent" with its "offspring" or subsidiary, and also with a person who was central to the operation of the parent label. In the second quiz (which is slightly more difficult), a label must be matched with its home state and also with a significant group that sang for the label. Though hard work, we think you'll find that it's a label of love. Answers can be found in the Appendix.

Quiz #8: Label Babies

Parent Label	Key Person	Subsidiary
A) Chess	1) Jerry Blaine	a) Ember
B) Rama	2) Danny Robinson	b) RPM
C) Old Town	3) Eddie Mesner	c) Everlast
D) King	4) Al Silver	d) Back Beat
E) Atlantic	5) Vivian Carter Bracken	e) Lamp
F) Herald	6) Randy Wood	f) Parkway
G) Vee Jay	7) Allen Sussel	g) Fire
H) Aladdin	8) Joe Bihari	h) Checker
I) Apollo	9) Paul Winley	i) Hamilton
J) Red Robin	10) Jack Kapp	j) Rust
K) Modern	11) Bess Berman	k) Josie
L) Jubilee	12) Larry Newton	l) Federal
M) Holiday	13) Bobby Robinson	m) Abner
N) Peacock	14) Ahmet Ertegun	n) Coral
O) Cameo	15) George Goldner	o) Paradise
P) Dot	16) Syd Nathan	p) Apt
Q) Laurie	17) Hy Weiss	q) Cyclone
R) Winley	18) Don Robey	r) Gee
S) Decca	19) Leonard Chess	s) Lloyds
T) ABC-Paramount	20) Bernie Lowe	t) Atco

Quiz #9: The State Of The Label

Label	Home State	Key Group
A) Savoy	1) Illinois	a) Rays
B) Herald	2) Alabama	b) Hurricanes
C) Chess	3) Tennessee	c) Diablos
D) Dootone	4) Texas	d) Tuneweavers
E) Cameo	5) North Carolina	e) Coolbreezers
F) King	6) Connecticut	f) Fleetwoods
G) Nasco	7) Missouri	g) Majestics
H) Fortune	8) California	h) Alan and the Flames
I) Standord	9) Virginia	i) Maurice Williams/Zodiacs
J) Back Beat	10) Colorado	j) Moonglows
K) Casa Grande	11) Pennsylvania	k) Five Sheiks
L) Dolton	12) New Jersey	l) Penguins
M) Ef-N-De	13) Washington, D.C.	m) Swans
N) Marlin	14) Washingon	n) Four Chevelles
O) Astro	15) South Carolina	o) Five Satins
P) Bale	16) Ohio	p) Crescendos
Q) Ballad	17) Florida	q) Starlets
R) Band Box	18) Massachusetts	r) Nutmegs
S) Cole	19) New York	s) Norman Fox/Rob Roys
T) Colonial	20) Michigan	t) Jive Bombers

Chapter 19

The Street Corner Singers

In the Beginning

Contrary to legend, most groups did not start singing on the street corners, but they did end up singing there eventually. Most singers, in interviews, report their first experience with music was either through the church or at home, and usually before the onset of adolescence. At best, there was an uneasy truce between the church and the group music produced when youthful enthusiasm and rebelliousness was appended to gospel training. Sometimes there was no truce at all.

Hank Ballard (of the Midnighters) recalled, "'...I was a runaway at 14, man... That part of the family was heavy into religion. They used to beat me if they caught me humming the blues in the house. They couldn't understand. I was not allowed to sing anything but gospel. I had to get out of that.' After the eighth grade, he dropped out of school and returned to Detroit to live with another set of relatives."[1]

The family of Eugene Pitt (lead singer of the Jive Five), as related by Wayne Stierle, was a lot more supportive: "Pitt came from a family of nine girls and five boys, and, as he says, 'We had two complete gospel groups right there.' In fact, they did have two gospel units, and the kids were trained very seriously by Eugene's father, who would see to it that everybody practiced. Pitt's father did not approve of Eugene singing anything other than gospel, but naturally, Eugene was listening to the radio, and could not miss what was going on in '50s music. Pitt's father, who had been a member of a gospel group, no doubt understood what his talented son was feeling, and when Eugene finally sang in an r&b group, his father provided important help."[2] Another Eugene, Eugene Mumford, lead singer of the Larks, also began his singing career in a family gospel group called the Mumford Brothers.

These group singers were teen-agers, and often young ones at that. Schoolboy doo-woppers with high tenor leads started notoriously young; Richard Lanham recorded with the Tempo-Tones at age 12; the Schoolboys, Desires and Bobbettes formed and were active in junior high school. Frankie Lymon of the Teenagers was 13 when his group first recorded, and Cathy Jean of the Roomates was 14. Other classical doo-wop artists such as Gaynel Hodge of the Turks was 16 when he recorded, as was Joe "Speedo" Frazier of the Impalas; Herb Cox of the Cleftones was a mature 17. It was the norm for groups to form in high school (or before), and many of those that eventually recorded did so during their high school years. While many of the paleo-doo-wop artists were "old men" of 20-30 by the mid-1950s, the classical doo-wop explosion was fueled, driven and supported by high schoolers.

Bruce Pollock, author of *When Rock Was Young*, sets the scene well. "Those four chords would usher in an age of harmony. In almost any ethnic neighborhood in the early 1950s, especially in the East, in housing project and candy store and school yard, wherever baseball cards were being flipped or traded and pennies pitched, there was that sound caterwauling in courtyards, cascading down the sides of buildings from the rooftop, sinuously drifting out of open basement windows. It was to be heard on the street corners under lamplight or moonlight, or under boardwalks or elevated train lines in the summer, or inside hallways and under stairwells in the winter—an urban, rattling, reckless sound, blending with the sirens and the traffic. In threes and fours and fives, hardly ever twos, they gathered in minigangs, basketball teams, sidewalk social clubs, their heads close together, hands behind their backs, the odd finger sings bass, to serenade the urban passing throng, city girls, and the very moon of love. Most of these serenades would never be preserved. Most of these singers would never leave the street. But in their dreaming voices, their ceaseless quest for harmony, lay the seeds of the future."[3]

In many ways, the kids who created the doo-wop genre were very similar to teens of any era. They were carefree, hedonistic and sometimes irresponsible. They were naive and gullible and ignorant of the larger world around them. They knew it all, felt invincible, yet lived with a whole host of secretly held insecurities. They hung out with the guys or gals, told white lies to their parents and laughed about the furtive pranks and adventures they got away with. They thought incessantly about the opposite gender, learned about love and sex by trial and error, and were usually awkward and shy in social situations because they were deathly afraid of humiliation.

By the time these young people were ready to sing on the corner, they had already formed groups. Each of the between four and six members knew their voice part and their roles within the group, just as they would know their position on a softball field. Singing on the streets was meant to impress; it was a social thing that helped establish a group's turf, to pull rank on friends not in the group, and to show off for the ladies. At night, outdoor locales were often used as the apartments and hallways were off limits because of sleep-

1. Pollock, Bruce. *When Rock Was Young*. New York: Holt, Reinhardt and Winston, 1981.
2. Stierle, Wayne. "The Jive Five: A True New York Story." *Goldmine*, Aug. 12, 1988.
3. Pollock, Bruce. *When Rock Was Young*.

ing younger sibs. More serious practices were often held at indoor locales geared to deliver echo, nirvana for the doo-wop singer. According to Johnny Keyes, lead singer of the Magnificents, in Du-Wop: "...The men's room of any office building had the best echo in the world, as far as the '50s' Du-Wop Group was concerned. And, the boy's bathroom in high school was used for something other than smoking cigarettes and washing your hands. This area furnished the best echo chamber for singing slow songs with 'woooo' in the background. All of that tile and porcelain was tailor-made for singing."[4] Subway stations and the back stairwells of schools were coveted for similar reasons.

Most of the time the singing group was synonymous with the peer group; they were really one and the same. Charlie Horner and Steve Applebaum, in a story about the Castelles, wrote: "Picture five young boys, not yet in their teens, living in the same neighborhood, playing basketball together, fighting together, going to school together, and raising hell together. On summer evenings, they would sit on the steps...and harmonize."[5] Fred Parris, of the Five Satins, adds: "We were just ordinary chums in school. We went to Hillhouse High School together."[6] Groups were formed gradually, starting with a dream in one guy's head. As people were enlisted, they formed or became a new peer group and soon were tight friends. If a member couldn't or didn't get along, he left or was asked to leave. The group that remained became even tighter.

In Watts, a black section of Los Angeles that was to become famous (or infamous) in another generation for different reasons, friendships and singing groups were one and the same. "We used to sit around [Alex and Gaynel Hodge's] living room and harmonize. Back then I wanted to be a part of the music, part of the fun at parties. It wasn't about being a star,"[7] explained Al Frazier (of the Lamplighters and Rivingtons). Harry Weinger, writing about the early days of the Platters, continues: "The Hodge house on East 56th Street was a favorite hangout. Gaynel was sweet on Zola Taylor, then a student at Jordan Junior High. She [Ms. Taylor] reminisced, 'Jesse Belvin and Gaynel used to fight over me but my boyfriend was Carl Gardner. He's the one mama approved of. I had a piano but the Hodges lived closer to everyone else, so we'd all go to there to sing- Richard Berry, Etta James, the Hollywood Flames, the Robins, Bobby Day, the Queens. And when the recording companies signed us up we all sang on each other's records.' "[8] What an unbelievable collection of talented young people gathered in that house. They had it all; they had youth, they had friends and they had their music. It doesn't get much better than that!

Almost all of the groups were formed in industrial urban areas, particularly in the big cities. The cornfields of Nebraska didn't give good echo. In urban neighborhoods, doo-wop groups were often formed from within street gangs. Johnny Keyes reports about his experience in Chicago in the early 1950s: "There were very little gang problems in the '50s, by today's standards. Gangs seldom killed anything but time. One reason may be the fact that street kids competed on more than one level. It's true that there was a lot of fighting over territorial rights, or the capital offense of talking to the wrong girl. That one would get you hurt seriously, sometimes mortally. But, in addition to the combat, they would compete on the softball diamond or the street corner. Every gang had within its ranks a softball team and a singing Group, made up of six or seven cats. It was similar to belonging to a club within a club, a fraternity within a fraternity."[9]

(Little) Anthony Gourdine (of the Imperials) had no choice but to join a gang. "They weren't social clubs," Anthony says, "they were real gangs. If you were hanging out with the guys on the street, you automatically were part of the gang. I was in the Chaplains. I was what you call a part-time Chaplain. I didn't give my all to it. I was the type of guy that was too busy singing, too interested in that. But when I need it, like in school, when I needed the protection of a gang, I did cling close to them...I didn't want to be in any gang. But where I lived it was a thing you fell right into."[10]

Doo-wop groups, like gangs and fraternities, had codes of ethics that were uniquely their own. "There were several unwritten laws for vocal groups of the '50s, and among these was the understandable, although strange, practice of contributors to 'style' or background being listed as co-writers of the tune itself. Another law was that the writer of a song became the lead singer on that song," wrote Wayne Stierle.[11] Another unwritten part of the code was that singers were allowed to traverse hostile territory with impunity. Keyes explains that, "a group singer, who for some reason found himself 'visiting' out of his neighborhood, was seldom attacked by the gangs that inevitably surrounded him as he was leaving the girl's house. Escaping is hard to do, so you're trapped. A Group singer would be allowed to go on his way if he identified himself and was believed, or was recognized as belonging to another gang...the gang would invite the alleged Group singer to 'hit a tune' with a couple of the fellas...to weed out impostors. ...if they called a tune and you were not a Group singer or were no good at improvisation, you better be good at running because

4. Keyes, Johnny. *Du-Wop*. Chicago: Vesti Press, 1987.
5. Horner, Charlie, and Applebaum, Steve. "The Castelles." *Bim Bam Boom*, Vol.2, No. 6, 1974.
6. Jones, Wayne. "The Five Satins featuring Fred Parris." *Goldmine*, May 1979.
7. Weinger, Harry. "The Platters' Glory Days." *Goldmine*, Feb. 21, 1992.
8. Ibid.

9. Keyes, Johnny. *Du-Wop*.
10. Pollock, Bruce. *When Rock Was Young*.
11. Stierle, Wayne. "The Monotones: They Wrote the Book of Love." *Goldmine*, Aug. 12, 1988.

there was going to be trouble. It was either 'hit a tune' or get hit in the head."[12]

Sometimes you didn't get a chance to explain yourself. William "Pete" Johnson, a member of a group called the Romancers from Philadelphia, was talking to another guy's girl at a party. The jealous boyfriend "called him out" and shot him five times in front of witnesses. The rest of the Romancers drafted another lead singer and, out of respect for Will, changed their name to the Dreamlovers ("When We Get Married").[13]

The singing groups formed almost as naturally as non-singing peer groups did. Once formed, the group became the most important influence in the life of any of the members. Singing in a group was similar to being a gifted athlete; it was accorded respect and status on the block, in the neighborhood and the school. Girls were even more attracted to the singers than they were to the jocks because the singers were a lot more romantic. The following interchange took place between Larry Chance of the Earls (LC) and Don K. Reed (DKR) on the latter's show:

LC: It was an easy way to get girls. I'll tell you, we just sang on the street corner and had all the ladies...

DKR: You' re not the first person who said that.

LC: You' re a teen-ager. What's important in life? The girls. The girls came easy when you sang.[14]

As did competence in sports, singing offered the dream of escape from the poverty, prejudice and a lack of education that many doo-wop singers had to endure. In an article about the Crows, Jeff Beckman and Hank Feigenbaum report that "...[they] were just five ordinary black kids growing up on 142nd Street between 7th and Lenox Avenues facing the harsh realities of life in the Harlem of the late 1940s and early 1950s. The expectations and aspirations of people born in this ghetto were few. Whether through faults of their own or through the influences of their environment, education was usually neglected, probably in many instances because it was no guarantee that the door would not be closed in their face when the time came to look for a job. Whatever the reason, without an education the vicious circle was unbroken, and most blacks found themselves relegated to occupations that required long hours, many of them spent at hard, manual labor."[15]

Candice Van Ellison, in *Harlem on My Mind*, presented shocking statistics about the problems in education of the teen-age population from which doo-wop singers emerged: "In [Harlem's] one high school, Benjamin Franklin, the 1966 senior class contained approx-

imately 2,000 seniors, 1,000 June graduates, and 38 graduating academic diplomas."[16] And Little Anthony Gourdine, of the Imperials, was also "...a kid who never had anything and never went anywhere, and I was used to it. I didn't have the kind of education I wanted because I didn't finish high school. I really didn't know where I was going, all I could do was sing."[17]

Singing doo-wop was a clear-cut way to emulate one's idols. Homer Dunn, lead singer of the Rivieras, was "captivated...by singing combos with names like the Swallows and the Dominoes and he'd breathe in every note. He listened for songs by his favorite group, Sonny Til and the Orioles. Sonny was not yet getting the lead singer recognition but Homer Dunn knew his name."[18] Paleo-doo-wop singers were the idols of the younger and as yet unrecorded classical doo-wop generation.

Bobby Jay (actually Robert Jeffers of the Laddins) told a similar story of idol-worship to Don K. Reed in 1990:[19]

BJ: I started singing in 1955 and in 1956, in the month of January, when I heard a record called 'Why Do Fools Fall In Love.' I decided from then on that I was going to be a singer and aspire to a professional career as a singer.

DKR: When you heard the song 'Why Do Fools Fall In Love,' did you envision yourself as the next Frankie Lymon?

BJ: No, I envisioned myself as the next Sherman Garnes.

DKR: At that point, you knew you were a bass?

BJ: When I heard Sherman, because at the time that the Teenagers were starting and that record came out, my voice was in the transitional stage. Prior to that I was a first tenor. I'm still a frustrated first tenor. I still break out into falsetto every chance I get but when I heard [sings the opening bass part to 'Why Do Fools Fall In Love'], I said I got to be a bass singer. I lived vicariously through Sherman Garnes, followed everything Sherman did. I achieved a lot of what Sherman did except his height. I never got tall."

DKR: When the hormones cut loose you were a bass?

BJ: Absolutely!

Getting the same people together repeatedly for practice was often close to impossible and sometimes even comical. Carl Hatton, in letters to Will Anderson, described the instability in membership endured by the ("Long Tall Girl") Carnations: "'As the years went by, things were a little rough on some of the guys, living in the ghetto. As a result, in 1957, Harvey, Arthur and I

12. Keyes, Johnny, *Du-Wop*.
13. Jancik, Wayne. "The Dreamlovers: Keeping the Dream Alive." *Goldmine*, Dec. 28, 1990.
14. From an interview on "Don K. Reed's 'Doo Wop Shop'"(audiotape), WCBS-FM Radio, New York, May 19, 1991.
15. Beckman, Jeff, and Feigenbaum, Hank. "Gee, It's the Crows." *Big Town Review*, Vol. 1, No.2, 1972.
16. Schoener, Allon (ed.). *Harlem on My Mind: Cultural Capitol of Black America 1900-1968*. New York: Random House, 1968.
17. Turco, Art. "Interview: 'Little' Anthony Gourdine." *Record Exchanger*, April 1973.
18. Aita, Frank. "The Rivieras." *Record Exchanger*, Vol. 4, No. 3.
19. From an interview on Don K. Reed's "Doo Wop Shop"(audiotape), WCBS-FM Radio, New York, June 24, 1990.

joined the Army. While in the Army, we sang with several members of the Eldorados. When our two-year enlistment was up, in 1959, Harvey and I got out, but Arthur liked it so much he stayed in. By 1959, Arthur's younger brother, Tommy Blackwell, was old enough to "hang out," and since he had a good bass voice, took his brother's place in the group. Also, while we were in the service, Allen had joined another group, so we needed an additional voice. That's when Edward Kennedy [not the future senator] joined us. At this time, with several personnel changes, we decided to change our name to 'the Teardrops.' "[20]

The changes within the Solitaires, however, makes the Carnations seem stable by comparison. Paraphrasing an article by Marv Goldberg and Mike Redmond[21], the original members in 1954 were Winston "Buzzy" Willis (second tenor), Pat Gaston (bass), Eddie "California" Jones (lead), Rudy "Angel" Morgan (baritone) and Nick Anderson (first tenor). Alvin "Bobby" Baylor came over from the Hi-Lites to replace "California" when the Solitaires got a recording contract. Bobby "Schubie" Williams and Monte Owens (both from the Mello-Moods) replaced Rudy and Nick, who didn't show up for rehearsals. Herman Curtis (aka Herman Dunham of the Vocaleers) joined as lead to make a sextet. In 1955, Curtis joined the Air Force, and Milton Love (from the Concords) took his place as lead. In 1956, Pat Gaston joined the Air Force and was replaced by Freddy Barksdale (although Wally Roker from the Heartbeats sometimes stood in for him). Bobby Williams left to do some jazz singing with Charlie Mingus and subsequently died in 1961. In 1960, Buzzy Willis and Bobby Baylor both went into the Army and were replaced by Cecil Holmes and Reggie Barnes (both from the Fi-Tones). Roland Martinez (of the Cadillacs) joined the group for occasional appearances. Milton Love went into the Army in 1961, and Harriet "Toni" Williams (who sung with the Harptones and married Reggie Barnes) joined. Cathy Miller eventually replaced Williams, Cecil Holmes (from the Cavaliers Quartet and Fi-Tones) joined, and Herman Curtis rejoined briefly before going on to the Vocaleers. Got all that? *They All Sang on the Corner*, by Phil Groia, also does a great job of sorting out the complex patterns of seemingly interchangeable memberships that plagued many of the early New York groups.

Once the group members stabilized, they refined their repertoire. Often there would be standard songs that they "had" to sing, such as "Gloria" or "Lily Maebelle." Each city, borough or neighborhood had its own set of requisite numbers, but a good portion of any group's material was original and was written by group members. Most of the guys would have a contribution to make to each new song, especially when it involved

the voice part they themselves sang. With repeated practice the groups would improve, the amount of improvement depending on their cohesiveness, work ethic and talent. They would enter "battle of the groups" contests held at local schools, churches and parks. The best groups would end up singing on the stage of the Apollo and other chitlin circuit locales. Eventually, the cream rose to the top.

Some were fortunate to hook up with musically talented people like Raoul Cita, Phil Spector or Al Browne ("Mr. New York Sound"), who would help them refine their talent. Browne, who worked with groups like the Crests, Crescents, Gaytunes and Eddie & the Starlights, in an interview with Don K. Reed, described how he would try to help a group: "Well, when you're arranging, you have to think of the group you're working with. Sometimes you have a good group and sometimes not so good. You have to work it out. If the tenor isn't doin' right you give it to the baritone...You try to get the voices as close as possible...And sometimes when they can't harmonize, then you let the instruments do something in the background."[22] Phil Spector backed the Ducanes on the four-chord "I'm So Happy" with 15 musicians (which is almost four musicians per chord) and a professional screamer for the bridge, according to member Eddie Brian.[23]

Once established and with repertoire, a group was ripe for discovery. For some, it was easy because someone in the music business tripped over them, as when Bobby Robinson found the Mello-Moods singing on a stoop in the Harlem River Projects, or when the engineer at a recording studio liked the sound of the (Lenny Cocco) Chimes so much he had them wait until he returned with an executive from Tag records. Others had the tubes greased for them because a group member knew someone of importance in the music business. Goldberg and Redmond describe the way the Solitaires hit paydirt: "Fortunately, Buzzy [Willis, of the Solitaires] knew the great DJ, promoter, and manager, Hal Jackson. Buzz and Hal's son, Jackie, had grown up together, and Buzzy worked as unofficial program librarian for Hal's show at WLIB in Harlem's Hotel Teresa. Hal made arrangements for Buzzy to meet Hy Weiss of Old Town Records."[24]

For most groups it was much more difficult, sometimes requiring that some member of the group, literally or figuratively, pursue someone in the music business. Fred Parris and his buddies "used to stand around singing on the street corners and I wanted to make a record.

20. Anderson, Will. "The Carnations." *Bim Bam Boom*, Issue 8, December 1972.
21. Goldberg, Marv, and Redmond, Mike. "The Life and Times of the Solitaires." *Record Exchanger*, Issue #15, Fall 1973, p. 4.

22. From an interview on "Don K. Reed's Doo Wop Shop'": (audiotape), WCBS-FM Radio, New York, July 29, 1990.
23. Mennie, Don. "Ducanes Chart With 'I'm So Happy,' Phil Spector Discovers Doo-wop." *Record Collector's Monthly*, Issue #39, December 1987-January 1988.
24. Goldberg, Marv and Redmond, Mike. "The Life and Times of the Solitaires." *Record Exchanger*, Issue #15, Fall 1973, p.4.

So, I decided to go to New York and pound the pavement. I really didn't know where to go and was unaware that the downtown area was the place to go to make a record. So, I went to Harlem because that was the only section of New York City that I knew at the time. I met Bobby Robinson from Red Robin Records, and we recorded our first record..."[25] In Philadelphia, Marcia Vance reports that Danny (Rapp) and the Juniors "used to sing outside [Johnny Madera's] window, hoping to attract his attention (a la The Teenagers and Richie Barrett). They got his ear but the wrong way for he used to yell at them to 'shut up- you're waking my kids.' The boys didn't give up and apparently Johnny listened to them because one day he came downstairs and said that they were pretty good. He took them to see a local disc jockey named Larry Brown and Larry's partner, Artie Singer of Singular Records."[26]

Lee Andrews and the Hearts were persistent and cunning. According to Andrews, "We went down to [Kae Williams'] radio show after school one day [in 1954]. He allowed kids to come in and dance in another studio, while listening to the music he was playing. We had contrived an idea, where all of us would go down, under the guise of dancing. When he came in to talk to the kids, as he always did, we would tell him what great singers we were. We were very persistent and he said, 'Well, after I get off the air, I'd like to hear you.' When he finished his show, we went into yet another studio and we sang for him."[27] Williams liked their sound enough to both manage and record the group.

Even persistence was sometimes not enough. As told to Richard Dunne by group member Paul Albano,[28] the talent of the Five Discs was appreciated by record companies but they were denied contracts in the beginning of their career because they were an integrated group. All-white or all-black was all right, but interracial was a no-no, probably because the label figured that no one would book them on a tour. They finally were signed on Emge and went on to record for other labels, but their concert tours were relegated to the northeast portion of the country. A great many other groups, not being resourceful or lucky, not having contacts and not possessed of great talent, retained their amateur status until the time when they eventually broke up.

Making the Big Time

Hooking up with someone in the music business, which most of the time meant that the group would eventually record, must have been an unbelievable event for those teen-agers. And they were, for the most part, teen-agers with all the naivete, idealism, and all the feelings of cockiness and indestructibility that goes along with that time of life. For most, what they imagined was in store for them had to be infinitely better than what really lay ahead.

As mentioned earlier, recording practices were often primitive by today's standards. Bobby Robinson, referring to the Mello-Moods, recounts that he "...had them come down to rehearse in the record shop. I didn't have anyplace else. They'd come down at night at about eleven, and we'd lock the doors and rehearse right in there. We worked out the whole idea right there in the record shop. We worked until about one, two or three nights a week until I got it just the way I wanted it. No musicians had ever heard it and when we got to the studio they just listened to the group put it down. I said just accompany what you hear. The musicians got their instruments together and the group got in the middle of the floor and started singing just the way we had worked it out."[29] Head arrangements, unthinkable today in an era of layering tracks and digitalized sound, were the order of the day. They were more the rule than the exception with the doo-wop sound and lent a wonderful air of spontaneity to the product.

Bobby Jay, as told to Jeff Tamarkin, described the Laddins' record "Did It" as having "a certain street charm but it was crudely done, recorded in a store in Harlem under the crudest of circumstances."[30] Herb Cox, of the Cleftones, recalled the situation in detail: "A hallmark of the early days of the rock era was its uninhibited spontaneity, but a recording session with Jimmy Wright's hard-honking band was downright unabashed disorganization. There was almost no structure to the session, except for our vocals, which we had practiced and refined. There was nothing in the way of written charts or arrangements. A lead sheet would be developed right on the spot to identify the changes and chord progressions for the musicians. The band members had a sixth sense to 'feel' the music, as well as the other musicians.

The studio had all the ambiance of a production line. Groups would queue up as if they were in a dentist's waiting room. Any night you might find four or five acts lined up awaiting their turn to record. The emphasis was on getting out the best product in the shortest possible period of time. Time was money, and the independent labels such as Gee just didn't have the resources the major labels had. Therefore, creativity and productivity were the order of the day. The sessions were usually all-night affairs..."[31]

After recording and releasing a record, a group

25. Jones, Wayne. "The Five Satins Featuring Fred Parris." *Goldmine*, May 1979.
26. Vance, Marcia. "Danny & the Juniors." *Bim Bam Boom*, Vol. 2, No. 6, 1974.
27. Horner, Charlie. "Lee Andrews and the Hearts." *Goldmine*, Dec. 28, 1990.
28. Dunne, Richard W. "The Five Discs." *Goldmine*, Feb. 8, 1991.

29. Turco, Art et al. "An Interview With Bobby Robinson." *Record Exchanger*, Issue #10, May 1972, p. 4.
30. Tamarkin, Jeff. "The Laddins: A New York Story." *Goldmine*, April 6, 1990.
31. Cox, Herb, and West, Steve. "The Heart and Soul of the Cleftones." *Goldmine*, Feb. 21, 1992.

would walk on air. Odds are that the group members, their girlfriends and friends would be calling all the local disc jockeys with requests for their song. Eddie Brian, of the Ducanes, recalled that so many fans of theirs called Murray "the K" to request "Little Did I Know," which was the B-side of their hit "I'm So Happy," that it became Kaufman's record of the week.[32] Sometimes the group's manager or label owner would invest money in his proteges to hire a choreographer, as when Esther Navarro hired "Cholly" Atkins (from the well-known dance team of Coles & Atkins) to devise dance routines for her Cadillacs. Her investment paid off well because fans went wild over the group's elegant footwork. Atkins later worked with the Solitaires and the Motown Temptations.

Dancing, rather than harmonizing, was sometimes the strong point of a group. Robert Pruter quotes Reggie Smith, of the Five Chances, on their practices. "We used to rehearse eight hours a day dancing and the next day would rehearse singing eight hours a day. We learned a lot of dance steps from different shows we were on...."[33] Later in the same article, Wesley Spraggins from the (Chicago West Side) Ideals commented that "the Five Chances...were one of the first to have great choreography."[34] This is high praise for a group that did not have professional coaching. The Laddins of New York were another group known for their self-taught dance routines.

Sometimes the label owner would see that they got an advance to buy outfits so they would look impressive on stage. They were professionals now. Usually the duds were tuxedos of varying color and style that gave each group a different look. "Nolan Strong and the Diablos wore purple satin jackets with yellow shirts, ties and pants...the Moroccos [wore] red tuxedos with gold cummerbunds, black shirts and white ties...Bobby Charles wore a white suit, red shirt and white tie..."[35] reported Peter Grendysa about a 1956 concert in Detroit. Take a hike, Pierre Cardin.

Novelty groups such as Little Caesar & the Romans needed no haberdasher; they sported togas, sandals and wreaths around their heads. David Ceasar Johnson (Little Caesar) reported that once an overstimulated bunch of followers "jumped up and ripped our nightgowns right off."[36] Fortunately, the group was given to wearing undergarments.

The groups that recorded became heroes in their neighborhoods, schools, families and, most notably,

with the ladies. Johnny Keyes describes the motivations behind singing against other groups to a hometown audience: "You sing two of the five songs you know and you're not setting the world on fire. But everybody's there in the audience, friends from school, a couple of buddies from the neighborhood and, most importantly, girls are there. They're right in front and poised, ready to scream hysterically. Screaming girls motivated Du-Wop Groups at this stage of the game, because money hasn't entered into it yet. There had to be certain inducements besides sounding better than the other singing Groups on the show or who could win the trophies. Screaming girls were the main inducement. If they liked what you were doing, they would scream and pull on your clothes, organize fan clubs, invite you to dinners (at their homes), buy your record when and if you record one and pay to see you perform if your record is hot enough to get you booked. These girls made a guy pay for the ticket to see you, bought your autographed souvenir programs at the big concerts and would occasionally visit your hotel room to inspire you to put on a better show the next time you step on stage. Yes, they were in the front, paying attention. And that was enough to keep some serious adrenaline flowing."[37]

Joey Dee, of the Starlighters, commented on the between-show activity while doing the "Murray the K Christmas Show" at the Brooklyn Fox. "You'd hang out in the dressing room playing cards or trying to talk to some pretty chicks out the window. There was heavy security at the theater, but we'd be yelling out the window to them and they'd be yelling to us, and we'd get a phone number or something. There were a lot of parties."[38]

Singing professionally was hard and sometimes anxiety-provoking. Herb Cox, lead of the Cleftones, recalled: "[Our] first big show was Alan Freed at the Paramount. The very first time we were very scared to see the amount of people coming out to see the show. After overcoming that, it was the nine to eleven shows a day...That was the norm for the Apollo Theater, too."[39]

"You try to remain calm, but are soon tapping your feet nervously...The make-up people dust you off, which causes the hairs on your neck to stiffen. There are dance steps and words to remember...the studio floor was covered with masking tape, leaving little chance for error...What if the record skips?...To tell the truth, I was in a state of panic, not so much for the performance itself because we were lip-synching, but because of the interview [Dick] Clark would do after-

32. Mennie, Don. "Ducanes Chart With 'I'm So Happy,' Phil Spector Discovers Doo-wop." *Record Collector's Monthly*, Issue #39, December 1987-January 1988.

33. Pruter, Robert. "The Five Chances and Their World of Chicago R & B." *Goldmine*, April 6, 1990.

34. Ibid.

35. Grendysa, Peter. "The Diablos." *Goldmine*, Jan. 3, 1986.

36. Gagnon, Rick & Gnerre, Dave. "Little Caesar & the Romans: Still Singin' Those Oldies But Goodies." *Goldmine*, Aug. 12, 1988.

37. Keyes, Johnny. *Du-Wop*. Chicago: Vesti Press, 1987.

38. Pollock, Bruce. When Rock Was Young. New York: Holt, Reinhardt and Winston, 1981.

39. From an interview on "Don K. Reed's 'Doo Wop Shop'" (audiotape), WCBS-FM Radio, New York, July 8, 1990.

ward." Those are some of the anxiety-ridden thoughts of Jeff Leonard, Johnny Smith and Fred Gerace, members of Little Joey & the Flips, immediately prior to their appearance on "American Bandstand."[40]

In addition to stage fright, another hazard of the trade was a restive or disappointed audience. Ted Weems, of Lee Andrews & the Hearts, once recounted a story about playing the Royal Theater in Baltimore. "If they didn't like you, they threw these little miniature whiskey bottles at you," said Weems.[41] "Frankie Lymon got bottles! He'd be singing and the bottles were whistling through the air! That was a hard place."[42] Luckily for the Hearts, they pleased the audience and avoided the barrage, and luckily for Frankie the audience preferred their libations in small packages. Herb Cox, of the Cleftones, supports this view of Baltimore audiences. "There was only one place in the world that we wanted to be less than Korea in 1956; that was the Royal Theater. The crowds in Baltimore were absolutely aggressive and antagonistic toward their guests. Among other expressions of ugly deportment, the Royal audiences often threw bottles at the performers on stage."[43] As with Lee Andrews & the Hearts, the Cleftones were greeted warmly so that no incoming missiles were reported. Apparently, the groups upon whom the bottles were bestowed were either too embarrassed or too concussed to tell about the incident.

Additionally, the black groups of the 1950s had to endure segregation and openly expressed prejudice, especially in the South. As Charlie Horner remarked, "Traveling in the South during the 1950s presented problems for black entertainers. Since much of the South was segregated, it was often difficult to get food or lodging. [Lee Andrews &] The Hearts would often stock up on crackers and sodas from gas station vending machines, since they didn't know when they'd find a restaurant that served blacks on the open road. Once at their destination they had to find a hotel or boarding house in the black section of town.

While the entire Jackie Wilson Tour was black, many whites attended the concerts. Inside the concert arenas, the audiences were segregated: The blacks were on one side and the whites on the other. Even being cautious, black entertainers were at risk. In Birmingham, Curry and Calhoun [members of Lee Andrews & the Hearts] were walking across the street when a white policeman threw them against the wall and pointed a gun at their heads for jaywalking."[44]

The Bobbettes, just teen-agers and young ones at that, experienced things on a southern tour that no kids should have to face. Reather Turner, an original member, recalled, "One night, the Ku Klux Klan was outside the bus. We had no experience with the Ku Klux Klan. We were five girls from Spanish Harlem...We were on this bus, and we were being noisy, as usual. They were pushing our heads down so we wouldn't make so much noise. We were yelling, 'What's wrong? Why do they have those masks on, what's happening?' And everybody was saying 'Shhh! Be quiet, be quiet!' The tour manager was outside, telling them that we were entertainers. And that was the first time I ever saw a KKK, or knew anything about them.

We didn't know anything about [segregation], and you don't know unless you really experience it. I tell my kids now that they don't really understand. All they know is what they read in books, and they don't really believe that. We experienced seeing dogs set loose on black people...We even saw a guy hanging from a tree once. We were on the tour bus and we stopped to go to the bathroom. And the guy was out there in the field hanging from the tree."[45]

For many groups, the adulation was the only positive reinforcement they ever got. This was because many of the singers made little money out of what they did. The label owners, concert promoters and agents sometimes soaked up what money there was to be had. The singers were led down the proverbial garden path. Not that they could be blamed, for they were really just kids with no understanding of business practices. For example, Nate Nelson, lead of the Flamingos, argued that he should have gotten a good part of the credit for composing "I'll Be Home," a solid hit for the group. Instead, the writing credits were given to disc jockey Fats Washington and a record distributor named Stan Lewis. "Leonard Chess came to me," said Nelson, and "all he had was the first line and the first line melody. I took the thing home and worked on it...I wrote the entire second verse, the bridge, the melody for the bridge, and the third verse. But I didn't know anything about copyrighting."[46]

Groups trusted their contact in the music business. After all, didn't their contact find them and/or give them the break the group needed? Why would he try to help and then take them to the cleaners? There was very little reason to be suspicious of motives. If a label owner told a group that his own name would be listed as composer (instead of theirs) so that the disc jockeys would recognize the name (and therefore hold the record in higher regard), they believed it. If the group was told that it was standard practice to pay the talent by the session, rather than by the number of records sold (e.g., royal-

40. Bosco, Robert. "Joey/Flips From Bandstand to Obscurity." *Record Collector's Monthly*, Issue #50, November-December 1991.

41. Horner, Charlie. "Lee Andrews and the Hearts." *Goldmine*, Dec. 28, 1990.

42. Ibid.

43. Cox, Herb, and West, Steve. "The Heart and Soul of the Cleftones." *Goldmine*, Feb. 21, 1992.

44. Horner, Charlie. "Lee Andrews and the Hearts." *Goldmine*, Dec. 28, 1990.

45. Garvey, Dennis. "The Bobbettes: Mister Lee's Star Pupils." *Goldmine*, Feb. 21, 1992.

46. Pruter, Robert. "The Flamingos: The Chicago Years." *Goldmine*, April 6, 1990.

ties), they believed it. When the group was told that their money would come from the tours they would be sent on until their names became well-known, they believed it. And signed on the dotted line when asked.

Peter Grendysa pointed out that the groups, especially those without professional representation, could sign contracts that allowed the record company to pay studio and promotional costs out of the artist's share of royalties. This gave the record company close to a free ride. The contract could also cede to the owner of the record company the rights to an artist's original songs. If a group signed without looking, they were assuring financial suicide. Grendysa does note, however, that many record companies, such as Atlantic records, were more ethical, and were quite fair with their artists.[47]

Hank Ballard (of the Midnighters) was deceived by his record company when it came to "...maintaining a piece of the publishing rights. 'The company I was with said there's no such thing,' he laughs today. 'King Records, ...if you asked for publishing rights, they'd give you your contract back. I didn't know there was so much money involved in publishing...On my early tunes I didn't even have a BMI contract. I got it later, but they didn't even tell me I had to apply for it.' "[48]

Hank's manager did him dirty, too. " '...He tied us up in a contract where he was getting 50 percent of our money. We didn't know a...thing about it. When we found out, we took him to court and got out of that contract...' ...In those days, the manager's job seemed more secretarial than anything else. If the caller on the other end of the line was willing to pay the price, the manager would accept the date, take his cut, and let the chips fall where they might. Such niceties as career-planning and longevity, routing, and proper accommodations were unheard of. Besides, what did it matter if the next gig was 500 or 700 miles away?...Thus were the acts encouraged to spend their nights on the road. This attitude toward black performers prevailed until Berry Gordy, at Motown, put some structure and guidance into the business and made the artists feel a bit more secure, esteemed as human beings with a life-span of more than six months to a year."[49]

These rip-offs happened to a large percentage of doo-wop groups. It happened to the Willows: "Although 'Church Bells' was a million seller for The Willows (selling even bigger than The Diamonds' version), the guys never got paid for it (writer royalties) because Morty Craft claimed bankruptcy. The Willows took him to court—won their case—but were only awarded $200! Split between the five of them! And on

a million seller!"[50] This was confirmed on the phone by Tony Middleton, the group's lead singer.[51] It happened to the Pipes also, according to group member Louis Candys: "Although 'Be Fair' did well locally, the Pipes received only a few dollars (and no songwriting royalties) for their effort. Most of the money was lavished on 'sessions and traveling.' "[52]

It happened to the Quin-Tones, according to member Phyllis Carr. "People may not believe this, but we've yet to receive royalties on that record ['Down The Aisle Of Love']. Never, not ever, did we get anything! I don't know what 800,000 copies would bring. I didn't even know till recently that many were sold. It's all so frustrating, so, so frustrating. We were just kids, too young, didn't know nothin'. We didn't know we had any recourse."[53]

Ralph Newman reports on a whole host of shady practices experienced by Tony Passalacqua and his group, the Fascinators. "Tony maintains that out of all the records, he received a statement for only one of them, in the amount of $6; that was for one of the records of himself as a single artist, and the Fascinators never received a dime. He also recalls that the lack of royalties did not extend merely to recordings, and that most of the acts were doing the big rock shows for free to push their records. In addition, he feels that payola was very much a reality and an overwhelming factor in determining whether or not you had a hit. Apparently, for instance, it was standard practice for a group to have to pay to appear on the major television shows, instead of the reverse! During the later days, when the rules were tightened and it was mandatory for checks to be issued to acts per union scale, the acts had to surrender a check before the performance which was larger than the one which they would receive after!"[54] This kind of transaction was substantiated by Mike Zero of Randy and the Rainbows. "We did the 'Clay Cole Show' in New York about four times. They'd give you the check. You'd sign it. Thank you. And back to them. You want to be on TV, so you did what you had to do."[55] The Bay Bops (according to group members)[56] and Little Joey & the Flips (according to their co-manager Sy Kaplan)[57] had the same experience on "American Bandstand" in 1958 and 1962, respectively. Apparently

47. Grendysa, Peter. "Fifties (50s) R & B Stars Helped Cheat Themselves By Signing Poorly Negotiated Contracts" *Record Collector's Monthly*, Issue #17, February 1984.

48. Pollock, Bruce. *When Rock Was Young*. New York: Holt, Reinhardt and Winston, 1981.

49. Ibid.

50. Vance, Marcia, and Groia, Phil. "The Willows." *Bim Bam Boom*, Vol. 1, No. 6, 1972.

51. Phone interview conducted on Feb. 24, 1992.

52. Whitesell, Rick "The Pipes." *Goldmine*, April 1979.

53. Jancik, Wayne. "Down the Aisle With the Quin-Tones." *Goldmine*, Dec. 28, 1990.

54. Newman, Ralph. "Tony Passalacqua and the Fascinators." *Bim Bam Boom*, Vol. 1, No. 7, 1972.

55. Garvey, Dennis. "Randy and the Rainbows: What's in a Name?" *Goldmine*, Feb. 8, 1991.

56. Diskin, Bobby. "Brooklyn's Bay Bops Launch White-Group Harmony and Pave the Way for '60s Doowop Hitmakers." *Record Collector's Monthly*, Issue #33, November-December 1985.

that was standard operating procedure back then.

As a matter of fact, most doo-wop groups interviewed on radio or in print report similar treatment. The record men were greedy, the singers naive, and the rules of the game loose. Some groups did make money, especially those with real talent, such as the Moonglows, and those associated with the larger (and in some ways more legitimate) record companies. It is sadly ironic that many of the small independent record companies, which practically gave birth to the whole genre of doo-wop rhythm & blues music, ended up being the villains by legally shortchanging the singers.

Another part of this irony is that many more of the groups could have survived and even prospered if they could have avoided the unfair deals into which they entered. Those that should have made the most money were the singers who were also the composers of the songs their group sang. Examples of these prototype singer-songwriters were Curtis Williams of the Penguins, who co-wrote "Earth Angel," Fred Parris of the Five Satins who wrote "In The Still Of The Nite," and James Sheppard of the Heartbeats who wrote "A Thousand Miles Away." These people would have received so-called "mechanical rights" royalties as a performer and "performance rights" royalties as a composer. They would have been paid for the number of records that were sold (roughly one million in the case of the above three examples), for the number of albums sold which contained their song (for example, all three songs were on the Oldies But Goodies album series), and for radio plays both at the time the song was popular, for years thereafter for replays on "oldies" stations and for plays of versions by other artists over the years. We have tried to come up with a conservative estimate for how much money should have been made on a million seller by a singer-songwriter on the number of records sold. Please note that these are only estimates.

For the sale of the 45:

(a) (1,000,000 records sold)—10 percent giveaways/returns = 900,000 records
(b) 900,000 records x $.98/record = $882,000 gross sales
(c) $882,000 x .02 royalty rate = $17,640
(d) $17,640—$5,000 (production/distribution costs) = $12,640
(e) $12,640/four group members = $3,160 per man

For album sales:

(a) (500,000 albums sold)—10 percent giveaways/returns = 450,000 albums
(b) 450,000 albums x $3.98/album = $1,791,000 gross sales
(c) $1,791,000 x .03 royalty rate = $53,730

(d) $53,730—$6,000 (production/distribution costs) = $47,730
(e) $47,730/12 cuts per "Oldies But Goodies" album = $3,978
(f) $3,978/four group members = $994 per man

By our calculations, $4,154 was due each member of a four-member group for records sold. Thirty-five years ago, $4,154 was a year's salary for the average person. In today's dollars, an equivalent sum might be more than $40,000. The figures for composer's royalties for radio plays, both at the time the song was popular, and throughout the years as an "oldie but goodie" are much more elusive. For the really popular songs such as "In The Still Of The Nite," there would be dozens of versions recorded over the years and released both as singles and as album cuts. All of these versions would have added to the coffers of the composers and, of course, the publishers as well. The royalties over the 30 or so years since the doo-wop era would have meant a small fortune for the composers of a really popular doo-wop song.

For example, in a phone interview a BMI representative reported that "In The Still Of The Nite" was played 1,307,815 times between the time it came out in 1956 and the end of 1991. This figure is for the United States and Canada and includes both radio and television "plays" for all versions of the song. If we conservatively estimate $.08 per play as an average rate of remuneration over the years (it was less in the 1950s and more in recent years), the revenue would equate to 1,307,815 plays multiplied by $.08/play, or $104,625. Of this amount, one-half goes to the publisher and the remaining half to the composer(s). In the case of "In The Still Of The Nite" that would mean more than $52,000 to Fred Parris over the years (he was the lone composer). This figure does not include royalties for foreign plays, jukeboxes plays, live performances, bonuses for frequent plays or premiums for multiple hits by one composer. The actual bottom line is likely to be a great deal higher than $52,000. Writing and recording a hit record paid well, that is, if you could arrange to get paid what was due you!

Of those who did make money and achieve fame, some just couldn't handle it. Timmy Lymon said that his talented brother Frankie "made a lot of money (probably not a million dollars by the age of 13 as the legend goes), which went, in part, for a Saratoga Springs home for his mother. Frankie never complained of being ripped off by companies, managers, or lawyers."[58] Frankie, unfortunately, was one of the ones who couldn't handle success, and he started using heroin. In the aforementioned article, Timmy Lymon believes Frankie's drug problem stemmed from "a combination of the urban ghetto struggle, plus some personal hang-ups."[59] Louie Lymon, in the same article, blames "super-stardom, attained before

57. Bosco, Robert. "Joey/Flips From Bandstand to Obscurity." Record Collector's Monthly, Issue #50, November-December 1991.

58. Sicurelli, Joe. "(I Found Out Why) The Lymon Brothers." Big Town Review, Vol. 1, No. 3, July-August 1972.

59. Ibid.

maturity" and "Frankie's desire to please and be accepted by the adults he was exposed to."[60] Frankie died in 1968 in a friend's apartment in Harlem. He was 26. Clyde McPhatter, one of the few singers of that era with talent greater than Frankie's, ended up on a similar road. He drank himself to death at the age of 40. Jimi Hendrix, Janice Joplin, Jim Morrison, move over.

Sometimes the sudden fame led group members to make decisions, such as quitting school, which they would regret in later life. Vito Piccone (of the Elegants) recalled, "The next thing we knew we were on top of the world. I was in my last year of high school at the time, so I left to go on [tour]. Frankie left, he was a junior; Jimmy had graduated, Carmen had quit. We never really thought about any kind of financial situation at that point. We were just enjoying ourselves."[61]

The road to glory taken by these youngsters had a lot of potholes. Most of the groups were little fish in a big pond. The best part was the adulation and notoriety they received after having recorded. Seeing the name of their group on the marquee of the Apollo or Brooklyn Paramount had to be a thrill. They were also given the illusion of wealth in the form of fancy clothes and fancier talk. The money didn't come through for most, and those that made money often had problems as a result of it. A group was seen and treated as special as long as their records were on the charts; when their run was over and they were no longer seen as a meal ticket by their managers, they were discarded.

The End of the Dream

The way the members of a group handled the end of their career probably paralleled a general paradigm of grieving for any significant loss. In the beginning, when news of their records not charting and their labels not being overeager to record them again began to come in, there was probably a good deal of "denial." That is, the group members refused to or couldn't see that the end was in sight and continued to have dreams of stardom. They pretended the bad news wasn't there. When it was no longer possible to hold onto these dreams, i.e. denial was no longer possible, anger and frustration set in.

Group members may have looked to blame their label, their manager or even each other for the lack of success. There may have been a "bargaining" stage, in which the members hoped for just one more hit, so they could go out as winners. When this didn't work, depression set in. Group members saw things as hopeless, both in terms of their careers in music and in terms of other parts of their lives. They also might see themselves as helpless to do anything about it. The final stage of grief was reaching "acceptance," wherein they were at peace with what happened to them, they accepted the bad times with the good, and got on with the rest of their lives.

Unfortunately, not everyone made it through to the last stage. Some got stuck in the stage of anger and walked around with a chip on their shoulders. Others became stuck in depression and couldn't get themselves started on the rest of their lives. Alcohol and drugs were easy paths to follow for those that were bitter or hopeless. Luckily, it seems from the articles written about the doo-wop groups that most members eventually reached the stage of acceptance and went on to lead productive lives in other spheres. It's a biased sample, however. The less fortunate ones aren't around to be interviewed.

The bottom-line reason for abandoning a career as a doo-wop singer was financial. As a rule, the 16-year-olds who started singing weren't very materialistic. They didn't have to be because, as minors, their parents provided food, clothing and shelter. After graduation from high school (or quitting it), however, the situation changed. Parents might be willing to provide for a short time while the singer had a go at his career, but they became impatient quickly if progress was not in evidence. Eventually they ran out of patience and the singer had to get a "real" job.

Love also had a way of sobering up a fellow. A 16-year-old girlfriend tolerated a lack of ambition, very rarely even thought about it. A 21-year-old wife had a lot less tolerance, and the infant son or daughter you helped bring into the world provided a strong motivation to get a legitimate job with a predictable income. Emil Stucchio, lead singer of the Classics, put it this way: "We stayed together but that was our last record. From then [1966] on we went under different agents and tried different styles...The group never really broke up but when nothing is happening there is no need to get together. We went for three years with nothing happening and, when you have a family, you have to look elsewhere for money. I became a cop."[62]

Sometimes, egos got in the way. Danny Zipfel, talented lead singer of the Bay Bops, practically forced the group's demise by telling them he wanted to claim songwriting credits on a collection of material written by all members of the group. This came at a time when the group was beginning to experience success. "Joanie" was a local hit for them and they made numerous appearances on national television shows, including those of Dick Clark and Steve Allen. According to the group's founder, Barney Zarzana, it was as much the feeling of betrayal as it was the issue of royalties which led the group to, in effect, tell Danny to get lost.[63]

Lucius McGill, an original member of the El Rays (soon to become the Dells), dropped out of the group in favor of a job with the U.S. Postal Service. McGill said, "I just didn't have that feeling for show business. The thrill and excitement of having a lot of young people screaming at you, it just wasn't for me. I needed a job, we all did."[64]

60. Ibiddy bobbidy boo.
61. Pollock, Bruce. *When Rock Was Young*.
62. Flam, Steve. "The Classics." *Bim Bam Boom*, Vol. 1, No. 6, 1972.
63. Diskin, Bobby. "Brooklyn's Bay Bops Launch White-Group Harmony and Pave the Way for '60s Doowop Hitmakers." *Record Collector's Monthly*, Issue #33, November-December 1985.

Sometimes a shift in priorities prematurely ended the career of a group. According to Margo Sylvia of the Tune Weavers, "My son was eight months old when we went on the road. By the time we came back, he was about a year-and-a-half, and he didn't know who I was. That hurt me to my heart. You know, it became very detrimental to our home life. The money was not really worth it when I thought about going home to kids who saw me and thought, 'Who is that lady over there?' "[65] For the (Chicago) Pastels, their manager, Leona Lee (who was a teacher at one member's school), quit because her husband complained that he didn't see enough of her. The group, having lost their contact in "the business," never recorded again.[66]

Not many doo-wop rhythm & blues groups were able to make a living out of singing. Either because of the monetary practices by which the singers were shortchanged or because of the lack of demand for their product in the years 1959-1960 and again after 1963, the pickings were slim. Most groups were one-hit (or no-hit) wonders, and when the hits stopped, they would be dropped from their label. The more successful groups followed a hit immediately with another release. If there was too much of a gap between records, the group would be forgotten by the disc jockeys and the public. That was exactly the problem that befell the Elegants. "That much touring was probably our downfall. We were on the road so long we didn't know we should have come back to New York and recorded the follow-up to 'Little Star.' We never really prepared for a second hit. We had a manager, but he wasn't really experienced either, to say the least. He was on the road making money, we were making money, and that's what he thought we should be doing. Nobody remembered that it all started in the studio.[67]

Release decisions, however, were out of the hands of the group itself and squarely in the lap of a sometimes inept label owner. With talent, good material and rapid-fire releases, groups like the Platters and Drifters enjoyed relatively long careers. Some, such as the Dells and Little Anthony & the Imperials, were even able to make the transition to other styles of music, but most groups just disbanded.

Sometimes the monetary aspects of singing created rifts that destroyed the sound of a group or the group itself. Peter Grendysa reports that the Del Vikings were split into two groups when their manager had group members, who were under 18 when they signed with the Fee Bee label, sign with Mercury (because as minors their old contract was null and void). This left the rest of the group still on Fee Bee. The rift occurred in May 1957,

just after "Come Go With Me" had a successful run on the charts. Grendysa continues, "Attempting to unravel the tangled web of personnel changes and comings and goings of the Del Vikings from this point on could break the heart of the corporate lawyer. Suffice to say, the Del Vikings as a discrete entity ceased to exist with this initial breakup. Clarence Quick and Kripp Johnson orbited around each other for the next 30 years, occasionally even singing together."[68]

The reason the Hurricanes broke up was financial but the story is rather unique. As told by Marv Goldberg, "…In 1959, the group got to do a year-long tour of Canada with a troupe that contained country singers and a belly dancer. All they received was enough weekly allowance to pay the hotel bills and eat. They were told that the rest of the money was being held back, to be paid at the end of the tour in one lump sum. However, before the tour ended, the promoter ran off with the belly dancer, leaving the rest of the acts stranded. This was the last straw, and the group disbanded."[69]

As it became clear that the group members couldn't make a living through singing, some of the groups parted amicably, and some burst apart from dissension. When things go wrong, it's easy to look for someone to blame for the lack of success. "People just don't get along. They used to fight like cats and dogs. They were just too close to each other," said Buck Ram, manager of the Platters.[70] The (West Coast) Pearls were a group that parted amicably. "By early 1961, various forces were tugging at the group. The members had families," Elsie Pierre admitted. "This was a pretty unhappy time for us because we'd been together for four years and we were very close friends, and we felt that we had a good sound. But I guess we were just in the wrong place at the wrong time."[71] So the groups broke up, and the members went their separate ways to live their lives as adults. But that's not the end of the story.

Recidivism for Fun and Profit

Time was kind to some of the singers and hard on others. Over the years, almost all had jobs outside of the music business to support themselves and their families. Many died over the years; the articles written on the groups describe more losses than one would expect considering their ages. Joey Hall, of Little Joey & the Flips, was a diabetic and had a reputation for not eating right and forgetting his medicine. The co-manager of the group, Sy Kaplan, said that he died from insulin shock in

64. Pruter, Robert. "The Early Dells" *Record Collector's Monthly,* Issue #50, November-December 1991.
65. Garvey, Dennis. "The Tune Weavers: One-Hit Wonderfuls." *Goldmine,* Feb. 8, 1991.
66. Pruter, Robert. "Pastels' Promise Eclipsed By Manager's Marital Problems." *Record Collector's Monthly,* Issue #45, December 1989.
67. Pollock, Bruce. *When Rock Was Young.*

68. Grendysa, Peter, "The Coming and Going of the Del Vikings." *Goldmine,* Feb. 21, 1992.
69. Goldberg, Marv. "Toppers, Hurricanes, Memos Are Same Brooklyn R&B Group on Wax." *Record Collector's Monthly,* Issue #43, March-April 1989.
70. Wasserman, Steve. "Buck Ram and the Platters." *Bim Bam Boom,* Vol. 1, No. 6, 1972.
71. Heather, Bruce, and Dawson, Jim. "The Pearls: Anatomy of a Doo-Wop Group." *Goldmine,* Feb. 8, 1991.

1974, at the age of 32.[72] Nolan Strong of the Diablos died of unknown causes at the age of 43. Jesse Belvin was killed at the age of 27 in a head-on car crash caused by, it is thought, a heroin-addicted chauffeur who was driving recklessly. Jannie Pought, a member of the Bobbettes, was 35 when she was stabbed to death while walking down the street in Jersey City, New Jersey. And everyone knows Frankie Lymon and Clyde McPhatter died young.

Even putting aside these early deaths, many of the people from the doo-wop era are still dying too young. A singer who was 18 in the very beginning of the era, say 1950, was born in 1932, making him or her 67 years of age in 1999. One who was 18 in 1963 was born in 1945 and would be 54 years old in 1999. People between 54 and 67 shouldn't be dying as often, and yet the losses mount: Kripp Johnson (lead, Del Vikings at 57), Bobby Day (fronting the Satellites and other groups, at 56), Margo Sylvia (lead, Tuneweavers, at 55) and Richard Blandon (lead, Dubs, at 57) have all died in the early 90s. Since then, Jimmy Weston (Danleers), Jimmy Keyes (Chords), Bill Baker (Five Satins), Solly McElroy (Flamingos), Sugar Grier (Joytones/Harptones), Adam Jackson (Jesters), Johnny Funches (Dells), Rudy West (Five Keys), Don Julian (Meadowlarks), Chuck Carbo (Spiders), Johnny Moore (Drifters) and many others have passed on as well. One can only speculate on the reasons for these premature deaths. Alcohol and drugs are often associated with the entertainment industry. Success as a youth, followed by anonymity thereafter, may have been hard to countenance for some, and may have led them to substance abuse. Perhaps poverty during the formative years, with concomitantly poor access to health care, may have played a part.

Some of the singers never left the music business or, if they did, didn't leave it for long. Lenny Cocco has been particularly persistent. He's had a "Chimes" group from 1957 to 1965, then again from 1970 to 1973, and yet again from the early 1980s to the present. Many members of the Chicago groups like the El Dorados, Kool Gents and Moroccos have managed to keep their hands in the business, if only on a sporadic basis. Richard Lanham (who fronted the Tempo-Tones) has worked with jazz artists and new and reconstituted doo-wop groups, and has done off-Broadway theater in the United States and abroad. Bobby Jay (original bass of the Laddins) has spent almost 30 years as a disc jockey, and has put doo-wop groups such as the Laddins and Desires back together. He sings bass for the Teenagers, Joel and the Dymensions and any other group that will have him. He often dances while he sings, does occasional repertory theater and helps produce record albums in his spare time.

It seems that most others that left the business jump at any reasonable chance to reenter. Many who are interviewed describe singing as being in their blood and look back fondly on the years in which they sang, despite the financial hardships. Considering that most of the original singers are at least in their early 50s, they have probably reached the age when their children are grown and on their own. They have time on their hands, especially in the evenings after their day jobs and don't have to be asked a second time to rejoin their old group or even a new one. Even for the groups of lesser stature, there seems to be enough work at local clubs to keep most groups' calendars pretty full.

These men came back to singing for the music and for the thrill of performing, but the prospect of renewed male bonding may be the strongest motivation of all. On Don K. Reed's "Doo-Wop Shop" on CBS-FM, New York, on Sunday evenings, the 11 p.m. to 12 a.m. slot is usually reserved for interviews with doo-wop groups that are currently performing. Regardless of their ages, the interaction among the group members is almost always the same. These grown men kid each other and even demean each other in a playful way. The interactions are full of gallows humor and pot shots at one another that (one can tell) have been repeated a hundred times. This banter is the verbal equivalent of giving a friend a punch in the arm. It conveys the apparent attempt to injure while saying "just kidding." This type of male-male exchange was once the fodder of the search for identity when these men were boys. Now the exchanges are fun because the venom is gone and there's no longer anything to prove.

Even men who love their wives and children cannot have this kind of relationship with them. Nor can their wives easily understand what lies behind the apparent cruelty of the verbal sparring. In truth, it is not cruel. It conveys loyalty (without intimacy) and understanding (without verbalization), things that men generally have a much more difficult time putting into words than do women. Mock ridicule is the perfect medium for men to be able to show caring to other men, receive it in return, and yet not seem to do so. It feels good and it's fun. That's why these guys keep coming back to singing. They get the same feelings as others do from poker games, Monday Night Football or bowling leagues, but singing allows more nights out, a fairly strong sense of accomplishment, and the chance to make a few bucks as well.

Although the oldies revival is usually pegged at 1969, the year of "The Gossert" and the first of Richard Nader's oldies concerts, the revival in doo-wop, at least on the East Coast, still seems to be heading toward a crescendo in the 1990s. An oldies concert in July 1990 put on by Nader featured 15 doo-wop groups, attracted 15,000 people and went on for six hours. DeLauro and Lanz's Annual Royal New York Doo-Wop Show put on at the famous Radio City Music Hall in New York City regularly attracts thousands of people. The services of doo-wop groups are more in demand than ever. Some of the groups ironically make more money than they did during the doo-wop era. It's not a totally rosy picture though. Tony Middleton noted that he couldn't get rich through concert appearances although he enjoyed

72. Bosco, Robert. "Joey/Flips From Bandstand to Obscurity." *Record Collector's Monthly*, Issue #50, November-December 1991.

doing them. The group might get paid $1,500-2,000, which seems like a lot. However, after getting suits cleaned, arranging for transportation and paying your backup musicians $100 apiece for the evening, there isn't that much left to split among five guys.[73]

For many of the singers, there are other perquisites, such as being able to relive their youth for a short while. A 40-year perspective makes the good times better and the bad times easier to take. It is also nice for group members to see each other again and catch up on old times. In many ways the concerts serve the function of high school reunions for the group singers. And, at roughly 60 years of age, it must be nice to see that your talent and the efforts that you made are recognized and appreciated by so many people, even if this recognition comes a few years late.

Things aren't perfect in doo-wop land. Group conflicts still occur, just as they did during the months and years that the groups were forming. Guys drop out, others replace them, the rest of the group gets closer. In 1990, Randy & the Rainbows split into two factions, each group purporting to be the real thing. Vito Balsamo, personable ex-lead singer of Vito & the Salutations, has to call his act "The Vito Balsamo Group" because somehow, someway, sometime and for some reason, he legally lost the right to use the group's original name. Fortunately, there are groups that still get along, and better represent the group bonding that originally was so much a part of the doo-wop genre. " 'A difference between the Bobbettes and

their contemporaries is their close togetherness,' Turner [Reather Turner, group member then and now] explains. 'We aren't just business partners, we're friends. Everybody knows that the rest of us are there for them, no matter what. Even though there were hard times, we stuck together. Most groups are just in it for the money, just business partners. They don't see each other when they're not singing. Our kids all call us 'Aunt Emma,' 'Aunt Laura' and 'Aunt Reather.'

Another reason we stuck together is that we were never 'Emma and the Bobbettes' or 'Laura and the Bobbettes' or 'Reather and the Bobbettes.' Whoever sounded best singing a song, sang it. We were never a leader and a group. That's why a lot of groups broke up. Someone will take that leader and leave the rest of the group behind. That couldn't happen with us. We've always been very loyal to each other. Nobody could ever break us up."[74]

In other words, doo-wop was about friendship, about loyalty and about caring. And that's why so many people still love it.

To add a little spice to your life, try the following quiz. Match the real name of the singer to their nickname and to the group(s) they sang with. Note that some singers had the same nickname, and more than one singer may have sung with the same group. Answers appear in the Appendix.

73. Phone interview conducted on Feb. 24, 1992.

74. Garvey, Dennis. "The Bobbettes: Mister Lee's Star Pupils." *Goldmine*, Feb. 21, 1992.

Quiz #10: Pookie, Bunky & Baby

A) Terry Clinton	1) Pookie	a) Clovers
B) Harold Wright	2) Bunky	b) Solitaires
C) Will Jones	3) Baby	c) Desires
D) Bobby Williams	4) Bootsie	d) Diamonds
E) Herman Denby	5) Buddy	e) Hearts
F) David Johnson	6) Bingo	f) Orioles
G) Ray Wooten	7) Buzzy	g) Crows
H) William White	8) Bounce	h) Del Vikings
I) Ron Mundy	9) Bobby	i) Marcels
J) Earlington Tilghman	10) Speedo	j) Swallows
K) Corinthian Johnson	11) Schubie	k) Mello-Moods
L) Earl Carroll	12) California	l) Spaniels
M) Harriet Williams	13) Sonny	m) Pastels
N) Difosco Ervin	14) Little Caesar	n) Cadets
O) Winston Willis	15) Cookie	o) Harptones
P) Eddie Jones	16) Big Dee	p) Romans
Q) Vicki Burgess	17) Bobby Day	q) Cupcakes
R) Norris Mack	18) Lucille	r) Demens
S) Justine Washington	19) Dub	s) Cadillacs
T) John Bailey	20) Junior	t) Joytones
U) Robert Byrd	21) Kripp	u) Satellites
V) Daniel Norton	22) Toni	
W) James Hudson		
X) Alvin Baylor		
Y) Gerald Gregory		

Chapter 20

"God Digs Doo-wops, Man..."[1]

In *Doo-wop: The Forgotten Third...*, we included a chapter called "The Death Knell," which proposed that doo-wop died twice. Once in the late 1950s, and once again in 1963 or thereabouts. We now think that "died" may have been too strong a word. "Waned" is more like it. And as we all know, things that "wane" are almost obligated to "wax," and vice versa. In fact, doo-wop, like a bad cold, refuses to go away. It was being revived even before it died, or waned.

One reason for its longevity is the tendency for the music to attract wackos (or is it whackos?) like us. There's really no serious money to be made. We know of no multi-millionaire doo-wop groups, no doo-wop producers or record-company types who are asked to give advice to presidents or who drive Rolls-Royces. And yet, from the early 1960s on, the music has attracted people committed (perhaps they should be) to keeping it alive.

A good place to start with the story of the post-doo-wopian doo-wop era is with a guy went by the unlikely name of Irving "Slim" Rose. Pied piper and guru types with the nickname "Slim" are rare, but that's exactly what this man turned out to be. Without trying or intending to, we should add. First of all, the store that he owned was a hole in the wall, downstairs in the concourse of the Times Square subway station at 42nd Street in New York City. Not exactly the Ritz. "Once inside the store, I found it hard to believe what my eyes were seeing. There were hundreds of group records hanging on the walls, thousands more on tables, and countless others stacked on shelves behind the front counter. There were pictures of groups hung helter-skelter on the walls along with various lists indicating the records for which credit towards the purchase of new records would be given, or for which cash would be paid. After taking in this whole scene in a glance, my first thought was: what the hell kind of record store am I in?"[2]

Many people have written about Slim, and everyone is consistent in not denying that Slim was out to make a buck.[3] A huckster at heart, Slim advertised on Alan Frederick's Night Train show on WHOM from the late 1950s to 1961. He and Fredericks then parted ways, and Slim became a deejay and sponsor concurrently on some small New York radio stations, such as WBNX, WWRL, WNJR and WHBI through 1965.[4] Once, after the only known (at that time) version of

"Stormy Weather" by the Five Sharps was broken, according to legend by his pet raccoon[5] Teddy, Slim offered $25, then $50, for a copy. He kept raising his finder's reward in steps up to $500, to no avail, but it did garner him an awful lot of publicity in the bargain.

Slim's taste in music was restricted to groups in general, and leaned toward schoolboy doo-wops or four-chord uptempos in particular. A sample "Top 100" list, courtesy of Bob Becker and the Record Exchanger, is provided below.[6] Slim had his hand on the pulse of the doo-wop generation; almost all of the records referred to above made our Top 1,000. His taste, far from sophisticated, attracted young people who liked the peppy sounds of jump tunes laden with lots of bass, falsetto and idealistic, youth-oriented lyrics. These fans were invariably white, and unsophisticated musically. They hadn't yet experienced and didn't appreciate the earlier pre- and paleo-doo-wop sounds of the Ravens, Orioles and Dominoes. That would come later for many of them.

So Slim had teen-agers like Jared Weinstein and Jerry Green working for him in the store, and teen-agers like Donn Fileti and Wayne Stierle entering into business deals with him, and teen-agers like Louie Sylvani buying records from his "Wall." These names may not mean anything to the reader, but all of them became involved in the post-doo-wop era as record store owners, record producers and label owners, writers, or some combination thereof. Weinstein and Green ended up in Philadelphia with a store called the Record Museum and a record label called Lost Nite. Green later founded Collectable Records, today a major source of doo-wop reissues. Fileti joined with Eddie Gries, who owned the Relic Rack in Hackensack, to found Relic Records, another major reissue label. Fileti is also one of the most eloquent and prolific annotators of doo-wop albums around. Stierle has written extensively for rhythm and blues periodicals, started Candlelite Records and put groups like the Shells back together to record. Sylvani took over the helm of Times Square Records and published a book on identifying rare records and counterfeits. Working for Slim and/or hanging around his store must have provided invaluable learning experience for these guys.

The heritage of Slim, even aside from his "progeny," is pretty impressive. With Stierle, Rose was responsible

---

1. Attributed to Robert Charles ("Gus") Gossert III (1943-1976).
2. Feigenbaum, Hank. "The Good Old Days." *Big Town Review*, Issue #1, Feb.-March 1972.
3. Confused by our syntax? So are we.
4. Squire. "Off the Wall: A Collector's Memories of Times Square Records." *Echoes of the Past*, Issue #29, Autumn 1994, p. 4.
5. Yes, raccoon.
6. Becker, Bob. "Signs of the Times." *Record Exchanger*, Issue # 26, 1978.

TIMES SQUARE RECORDS

TOP 100 - IN SALES

For The Month of Jan. 1961

$1.00 Each Record - Minimum Mail Order $3. - Money In Advance Sent With Order

```
1958....1.   I Remember..........................5 Discs
1958....2.   Lama Rama Ding Dong.................Edsels
1959....3.   The Bells Of Rosa Rita.............Admirations
1958....4.   Peppermint Stick...................Elchords
1959....5.   There's A Moon Out Tonight.........Capris
1958....6.   Dorothy............................Hi-Fives
1957....7.   I Really Love You..................Channels
1957....8.   Flames In My Heart.................Channels
1957....9.   Picture Of Love....................Continentals
1958....10.  Every Day Of The Week..............Students
1958....11.  Life Can Be Beautiful..............Cineramas
1958....12.  I See A Star.......................Roulettes
1957....13.  No, No, No.........................Chanters
1957....14.  Row Your Boat......................Chanters
1957....15.  Fine Little Kisses.................Chanters
1957....16.  My, My Darling.....................Chanters
1957....17.  Lamplight..........................Deltas
1958....18.  Ding Ding Dong.....................Jive-Tones
1957....19.  Don't Ask Me.......................Dubs
1956....20.  If You Love Me.....................Bluenotes
1959....21.  Let It Please Be You...............Desires
1959....22.  Guardian Angel.....................Selections
1954....23.  Gloria.............................Cadillacs
1957....24.  Bermuda Shorts.....................Delroys
1958....25.  Wait Up............................Cameos
1958....26.  Bong Bong..........................Vince Castro
1957....27.  Mexico.............................Rocketones
1957....28.  Baby Oh Baby.......................Shells
1957....29.  The Way You Look Tonight...........Jaguars
1957....30.  The Bells Are Ringing..............Van Dykes
1959....31.  Bad Girl...........................Miracles
1958....32.  Bye, Bye Baby......................Channels
1957....33.  Please Say You Want Me.............Schoolboys
1955....34.  Mary Lee...........................Rainbows
1957....35.  Sweetest One.......................Crests
1957....36.  Can I Come Over Tonight............Velours
1954....37.  Smoke From Your Cigarette..........Mellows
1958....38.  Lullaby Of The Bells...............Deltairs
1958....39.  Ankle Bracelet.....................Pyramids
1957....40.  When I Woke Up This Morning........Bop-chords
1959....41.  There Goes My Baby.................Drifters
1956....42.  Pretty Little Girl.................Monarchs
1956....43.  Up On The Mountain.................Magnificents
1956....44.  Dear Lord..........................Continentals
1958....45.  This Is My Love....................Emjays
1957....46.  United.............................Love-notes
1957....47.  Counting The Stars.................Ladders
1958....48.  Chapel Of Dreams...................Dubs
1957....49.  Desiree............................Charts
1958....50.  Teenagers Dream....................Kodaks
```

(continued on other side)

```
1957....51.  Gleam In Your Eyes.................Channels
1959....52.  Shout..............................Isely Bros.
1960....53.  Zu-Zu..............................Bonnevilles
1956....54.  The Angels Sang....................Solitaires
1954....55.  God Only Knows.....................Capris
1957....56.  Coralee............................Hemlocks
1959....57.  Dedicated To The One I Love........Shirrells
1956....58.  The Closer You Are.................Channels
1957....59.  Tell Me Why........................Rob-roys
1957....60.  Could This Be Magic................Dubs
1960....61.  My Hero............................Bluenotes
1956....62.  People Are Talking.................Heartbeats
1957....63.  Let's Go For A Ride................Collegians
1958....64.  I Love You So......................Chantels
1956....65.  Devil Or Angel.....................Clovers
1957....66.  Been So Long.......................Pastels
1958....67.  Hong Kong..........................Quinns
1958....68.  Two People In The World............Little Anthony & Imperials
1958....69.  One Summer Night...................Danleers
1959....70.  To Make A Long Story Short.........Eddie & The Starlites
1955....71.  Crazy For You......................Heartbeats
1958....72.  Way Up.............................
1958....73.  Book Of Love.......................Lincoln Fig & The Dates
1956....74.  A Thousand Miles Away..............Heartbeats
1956....75.  Little Girl Of Mine................Cleftones
1958....76.  Sunday Kind Of Love................Sentimentals
1956....77.  We Go Together.....................Moonglows
1957....78.  That's My Desire...................Channels
1954....79.  Bells of St. Marys.................Lee Andrew & The Hearts
1956....80.  On Your Radio......................Richard Lanham and The Tempo-tones
1958....81.  Tres...............................Cubs
1958....82.  Kathleen...........................Spaniels
1957....83.  Teenage Love.......................Frankie Lymon & The Teenagers
1958....84.  Legend Of Sleepy Hollow............Monotones
1954....85.  The Wind...........................Diablos
1957....86.  Ding-A-Ling-A-Ling.................Troys
1955....87.  You Came To Me.....................Duvals
1957....88.  Li'l Darlin........................Gladiolas
1954....89.  Paradise Hill......................Embers
1958....90.  This Is The Night..................Valiants
1957....91.  You I Adore........................Youngtones
1957....92.  Why Do You Make Me Cry.............Cubs
1959....93.  Lovers Never Say Goodbye...........Flamingos
1957....94.  Be My Girl.........................Videls
1958....95.  Gumma, Gumma.......................Mello-harps
1959....96.  Baby...............................Jeanie & Her Boy Friends
1958....97.  Trickle, Trickle...................Videos
1956....98.  Ship Of Love.......................Nutmegs
1957....99.  School Bells.......................Nicky & The Nobles
1957....100. I Put A Spell On You...............Screamin' Jay Hawkins
```

RECORDS THAT COULD HIT THE "TOP HUNDRED" NATION WIDE

```
The Bells Of Rosa Rita..............Admirations  - Mercury
I Remember..........................5 Discs      - Rust
Chapel Bells........................Fascinators  - Capitol
Lama Rama Ding Dong.................Edsels        - Dub
The Bells Are Ringing..............Van Dykes      - King
```

RECORDS EXPECTED IN SOON

```
Bila...................................Versatones
Miss Annie.............................Plurals
Sunday Kind Of Love.......45/single.....Del-vikings
Doom-Lang..............................Tokens
Dreams of Contentment..................Dells
Tell The World.........................Dells
Shomblar...............................Ravels
Moonlight..............................Vanguards
```

TIMES SQUARE RECORDS
(First Subway Level)
1475 Broadway - 42nd St.   New York, N.Y.
(beneath Walgreen's Drug Store)
Tel: BRyant 9-3458

for finding tapes of rehearsals by the Nutmegs. Rose issued them, and with that issue, gave us the new genre of "a cappella" singing. "It is very important to understand that there were no 'a cappella groups' in the '50s. Up until the point that this music was christened 'a cappella,' any group that sang on the corner, in an alley, in the subway, or anywhere, without music, was simply a group that was singing. There were groups, but there were no 'acappella groups.' Not only that, 'a cappella' was not a 'style,' but merely the way groups practiced in order to fine-tune their sound. But all that changed in the early sixties, when the 'art form' received its name; it also received its legitimate status."[7]

In a way, Slim is reminiscent of an Inspector Clouseau type of character who bungles, but for whom things turn out okay in the end. This was true when "Stormy Weather" was unintentionally broken and resulted in a lot of publicity. "Finally it happened. Slim turned to the dictionary to see what a definition of 'no music' would be. There in the dictionary he found '...a cappella, without instruments, chapel like.' But none of us liked it. It looked foreign, it was foreign, and hardly

seemed to fit the 1950's harmony. With no fanfare, Slim simply changed the spelling, which made it look Italian, but Brooklyn-Italian, not Italy-Italian. That was exactly when 'acappella,' as we know it today, came into being."[8] Move over Peter Sellers.

Another gift of Slim and his minions came as a result of Slim, Fileti, Stierle and the other "wunderkinder" nagging, cajoling and otherwise pressuring record companies into reissuing songs from the 1950s. The result was that "Rama Lama Ding Dong" by the Edsels, "Baby Oh Baby" by the Shells, and "There's A Moon Out Tonight" by the Capris became more popular the second time around than they were when first issued. Not bad work for kids. And that's aside from Slim's label called, appropriately, "Times Square," which helped start and fuel the neo-doo-wop sound in the early 1960s. By reviving many songs from the previous decade, Slim, along with Art Laboe with his "Oldies But Goodies" albums and the Roulette "Golden Oldies" series really helped to create a love of oldies that endures today. Slim's store, Times Square Records, also set the style for record shops that specialize in oldies. Its architecture could be called "early

---

7. Stierle, Wayne. "Just Something I Remember." *Harmony Tymes*, #3, Winter 1987.

8. Ibid.

hole-in-the-wall." Clifton Music, the Relic Rack, Whirlin' Disc Records and Downstairs Records in the New York metropolitan area, along with those that popped up in other large urban areas, can all trace their provenance to Times Square Records.

Inadvertently, as always, Slim may have catalyzed and accelerated the hobby of record collecting. Before the 1950s, people collected stuff, but it was adult stuff like stamps, coins and campaign buttons. Even the names of the hobbies were serious, like philately and numismatics. With the peace that followed World War II, and the affluence that peace brought, came the teen-age menace. This generation not only set trends in music and dress, but it had money to put wherever its mouth was. Baseball cards were one of the first things to be collected, records weren't far behind. In the beginning, baseball cards were amassed for the fun of it; for bragging rights, or to be the "first on your block," or just to feel good about completing something you started. Very few card-carrying kids back then thought they would make a fortune out of it. Slim, with his capitalistic approach to the hobby, taught many a youngster painful lessons in economics and gave many of them pie-in-the-sky dreams of getting rich quick. Stories of finding that old warehouse that housed unsold stacks of rare records, or buying valuable disks in a three-for-a-dollar bin, or traveling down south to hunt down collections, or of the "one that got away" were recounted often in rhythm and blues periodicals. Back then, it was capitalism for fun and profit for those young kids. And good old Slim planted the seeds, for better or worse.

Between 1963-1969, things quieted down in the doo-wop arena. The neo-doo-wop sound represented by Times Square Records, Tin Pan Alley and Distaff Doo-wop was virtually snuffed out by the invasion of other musics. Doo-wopeople either suffered in silence or were, for the moment, confused, distracted and, please forgive us for saying it, even tempted by these insidious upstarts. According to Stephen Bennett, "In 1969, the appreciation of vocal group harmony was at its lowest ebb. The flow of records bearing this sound, which had been reduced to a trickle after 1964, was now reduced to the most erratic drippings. Most black groups had moved on to either a 'Motown' or 'Memphis' soul sound. White groups were either doing a Rascals-Vanilla Fudge bit, or 'bubblegum' music. A vast majority of the older groups, black or white, had simply ceased to record."[9]

One good thing that happened in this time frame was the inception of the "Time Capsule Show" on WFUV in New York (Fordham University). The founders were young people again, two college students named Tom Luciani and Joe Marchesani, and they began broadcasting on March 28, 1963. The show, though now called the "R&B Group Harmony Review" and hosted by Dan Romanello and Neil Hirsch, is still going strong. While preceded by professional deejays like Jocko, Alan Freed and Alan Fredericks, and guys out to make a buck like Slim, this was the first radio show by doo-wop purists for doo-wop purists. In the 1990s, this type of show, often associated with educational institutions, is one of the most important ways that the sound is kept alive.

By 1969, doo-wopressure was apparently building up inside a generation of young people who had cut their teeth on the music but were thwarted by its unavailability, aside from a well-established sprinkling of record stores catering to their tastes. What happened was a revival. A second revival if you consider the neo-doo-wop era as the first; a first revival if you don't (we don't). A bunch of things seemed to happen concurrently. Concerts popped up catering to the old sounds, the music was again heard on mainstream radio and periodicals paying homage to the sound began publication. As before, there were young men at the helm.

In 1969, a 26-year-old named Robert Charles "Gus" Gossert III came to New York via Knoxville, Honolulu and San Francisco and started broadcasting vocal group sounds on a major New York radio station, WCBS-FM. According to Bill Schwartz, publisher of Time Barrier Express, "Gus Gossert was the major driving force in what we call 'the revival.' In the late sixties, the oldies scene was so far underground it wasn't funny—just a smoldering ember being kept going for a few hard-core collectors and by the 'Time Capsule Show.' The appearance of Gus Gossert fanned that smoldering ember into a raging fire. Doo-wopps were bigger than they had been in years. Many records that weren't even heard of in the fifties and early sixties were finally receiving recognition and many young people just born in the late fifties and too young to have known the music were being turned on for the first time by shows at the Academy of Music. Even Madison Square Garden shows were selling out."[10]

Arlene Coletti, co-editor of From Out of the Past, recalled his radio show in the fanzine's first issue (that memorialized Gossert). "I can remember so many things about Gus, starting with the insane things he did on his radio show. One of the funniest things was waiting to see what time he'd show up at the station. He was supposed to begin at 5:00, but you wouldn't hear him sometimes until 6:00-6:30. Until then, you'd hear songs and commercials, but no Gus. For any other disc-jockey to try that would be unthinkable, but with Gus' charm, charisma and personality, it was not only accepted, but laughed with—not laughed at."[11] He also hosted a burping contest and noisily ate pizza while on the air. Not even news in the 1990s, but unusual for that period in time. Considering that Gossert was also program director at the time, one can imagine how station management viewed these antics.

9. Bennett, Stephen. "My Radio, Gus Gossert & Me." *From Out of the Past*, Issue #1, Sept.-Oct. 1976, p.14.

10. Schwartz, Bill. Editorial. *Time Barrier Express*, Issue #20, Nov.-Dec. 1976, p.3.

11. Coletti, Arlene. The Editor's Viewpoint. *From Out of the Past*, Issue #1, Sept.-Oct. 1976, p.3.

Gus Gossert.

Stan Krause[12] describes Gossert as enthusiastic and charismatic, but not really knowledgeable about the music he played. Apparently Krause and the ever present Wayne Stierle provided technical support to Gossert, in the form of records and information about them. His ability to make listeners enthuse about the music hearkened back to the 1950s and the era of the personality deejays. He attracted quite a following and

inspired others to get involved in vocal group music. He would say cool things like, "It's 5:37 with your curly-headed Gossert" and closed his show with, "...and don't forget, God digs doo-wops, man..."

Unfortunately, "The Gossert,"[13] as the reverent refer to him, also had a dark side. Besides showing up late for his time slots, he had frequent run-ins with authority figures at the stations he worked for, and more than likely had a problem with drugs, alcohol or both. Interviewed by Stormy Weather's Lenny Goldberg in the Fall of 1970,[14] Gossert was wordy, preachy and manic, proselytizing and full of himself. His "underground" attitude at a basically mainstream station couldn't last despite his success in the ratings. The next issue of Stormy Weather, from January of 1971, announced his termination from WCBS. Apparently Gossert delivered the bad news over the airwaves personally at 9:45 p.m. on Sunday, Oct. 18, 1970.[15]

In the spring of 1971, he was hired by WPIX to do his "Oldies" show[16] on Saturday and Sunday nights, but was soon fired from there as well. By 1973, he was convicted of importing drugs[17] into the United States and spent two years in jail. Gossert, a 1966 graduate of the University of Tennessee with a major in political science, soon got a job as a part-time deejay for WOKI-FM in Oak Ridge, Tennessee, a far cry from the Big Apple. On Aug. 10, 1976, he was found murdered, lying by a roadside in Knoxville, Tennessee, three bullets in his head.[18] He was 33 years old.

Like Slim, Gossert was another unlikely pied piper. The key to his ability to attract adherents, aside from his personality, was probably his anti-authority stance, which was "cool" in 1969 (as it might be among teens today). As mentioned before, *From Out of the Past* memorialized him in its first issue and *Time Barrier Express* put out a "Gus Gossert Memorial Issue" in 1976, which included paeans by Krause, Ronnie Italiano and Ferdie Gonzales. Krause went on to produce records and issue them on his Catamount label, Italiano attributes his deejaying career to Gossert (along with arranger/record man Al Browne), and Gonzales became one of the most respected discographers of the group R&B and doo-wop sounds. Gossert also popular-

---

12. Krause, Stan. "Gus Gossert-The Man." *Time Barrier Express*, Issue #20, Nov.-Dec. 1976, p. 5.

13. Actually, Gossert referred to himself as "the Gossert," as in advertisements like "Tell them the Gossert sent you and get a special discount..." Apparently, with time, he went from being "the Gossert" to "THE Gossert."

14. Goldberg, Lenny. "Oldies DJ: Gus Gossert." *Stormy Weather*, Issue #2, Oct./Nov. 1970, p.5.

15. Letters to the Editor. *Stormy Weather*, Issue #3, January 1971.

16. Which featured single artists such as Elvis and Fats Domino sprinkled in among the groups.

17. Or gold, depending on who you read.

18. "OR Disc Jockey Found Fatally Shot in His Car," *Knoxville Sentinel*, Aug. 11, 1976.

1.	I'm So Young	Students	Note	1958
2.	The Stars	Ocapellos	General	1966
3.	Share	Teenagers	Gee	1956
4.	My Vow To You	Students	Note	1958
5.	There Goes My Love	Fantastics	RCA	1959
6.	Memories Of El Monte	Penguins	Original Sound	1963
7.	Since You've Been Gone	Diablos	Fortune	1958
8.	I'm In The Mood For Love	King Pleasure	UA	1959
9.	Chapel Bells	Fascinators	Capitol	1958
10.	Please Be My Love Tonight	Charades	Ava	1963
11.	I'll Never Tell	Harptones	Bruce	1953
12.	The Verdict	Five Keys	Capitol	1955
13.	Don't Say Goodnight	Valentines	Rama	1957
14.	Deep In My Heart	Shells	Johnson	1962
15.	A Sunday Kind Of Love	Harptones	Bruce	1953
16.	Be Sure My Love	Dubs	Gone	1958
17.	Who Do You Think You Are	Fascinators	Capitol	1959
18.	The Bells Of Rosa Rita	Admirations	Mercury	1959
19.	Bring Back Those Doo-Wopps	Bagdads	Double Shot	1963
20.	You Told Another Lie	Youngsters	Leslie	1958
21.	The Shrine Of St. Cecilia	Harptones	Rama	1957
22.	Hello	Nutmegs	Times Square	1962
23.	Can I Come Over	Youngtones	X-tra	1960
24.	I'm Just A Dancing Partner	Platters	Mercury	1955
25.	Pizza Pie	Rob Roys	Capitol	1959
26.	Every Day Of The Week	Students	Note	1958
27.	My Memories Of You	Harptones	Bruce	1954
28.	I'd Like To Thank You Mr. D.J.	Charms	Deluxe	1956
29.	My Juanita	Crests	Joyce	1957
30.	Soft Shadows	Monotones	Argo	1958
31.	String Around My Heart	Cleftones	Gee	1956
32.	Down In Mexico	Nutmegs	Times Square	1962
33.	Chapel Of Dreams	Dubs	Gone	1958
34.	Love Will Make Your Mind...	Penguins	Dootone	1954
35.	Close Your Eyes	Five Keys	Capitol	1955
36.	The Wind	Diablos	Fortune	1954
37.	Poor Rock 'n' Roll	Nobles	Klik	1957
38.	Mommy And Daddy	Students	Red Top	1958
39.	Letter To A Schoolgirl	Delacardos	Elgey	1959
40.	My Hero	Bluenotes	Value	1960

ized the term "doo-wop," which had been around before, but was not in such widespread usage. The success of the concert series that began late in 1969 and continued for years is, in part, attributable to Gossert. He seemed to get everyone's juices flowing again. He attracted a close inner circle, and his ratings implied that he had wider appeal as well. Not a bad legacy, but it leaves one wondering what Gossert could've achieved, or what the music would've become, if he had been a little more conservative in his personality and habits. Outgrowths of what Gossert began, such as the show "Grease," the films "American Graffiti" and "American Hot Wax," and television's "Happy Days" brought "oldies" music to younger generations; the

exposure and influence could have been broader and deeper had Gossert not self-destructed.

Gossert's taste in the music, like Slim's, was not sophisticated and didn't reach back to the sounds of the early 1950s. His favorite 40 songs, as gleaned by Ronnie Italiano from conversations he had with people who knew Gossert, are listed above.[19]

Almost concurrent with Gossert's ascendance, concerts kicked in. First was Richard Nader's "Rock & Roll Revisited" series which began in 1969. Nader, from a

---

19. Italiano, Ronnie. "Gus Gossert's Top 40 All-Time Favorite Doo-Wopps." *Time Barrier Express*, Issue #20, Nov.-Dec. 1976, p.16.

small town outside Pittsburgh, grew up listening to Porky Chedwick, that area's answer to Alan Freed. Some dee-jay work at local stations and Armed Forces Radio led to him becoming a booking agent on his release from the army.[20] On Oct. 18, 1969, the first of the revival concerts was staged, at Madison Square Garden in New York, and featured Bill Haley and the Comets, Chuck Berry, the Platters, Coasters, Shirelles, Jimmy Clanton and Sha Na Na. His second show, one month later, brought back Haley, and added Jackie Wilson, the Penguins, Johnny and Joe, the Mello-Kings, Gary "U.S." Bonds, the Capris, Spaniels, Shep and the Limelites (his last performance) and Bobby Comstock's Band. In the ten years between 1969 and 1979, Nader produced 25 concerts at the Garden under the rock 'n' roll umbrella. The Five Satins appeared in 11 of these shindigs, which may play a part in why their "In The Still Of The Nite" still comes out at the top of most oldie and doo-wop popularity contests after all these years (Chuck Berry was second with 10 appearances).

Nader's concerts covered the breadth of rock 'n' roll, including single artists and rock 'n' rollers, as well as groups. Larry Marshak, editor of *Rock* magazine at the time, began to put on his first of many concerts on April 18, 1970 at the Academy of Music Theater (New York). It was hosted by Alan Fredericks (of the original "Night Train Show") and featured all groups, the majority of them from the New York[21] area. In passing, both Marshak[22] and Nader (in a 1995 interview on Don K. Reed's Doo-wop Shop) credit Gossert with the success of the revival.

Interestingly, in the same 1972 issue of *Bim Bam Boom* (Issue #4) that featured the article lauding Marshak's activities, Tom Luciani, aforementioned co-founder of the "Time Capsule Show" on WFUV, waxed cynical. "There is a renewed interest in the music of the fifties, as evidenced by the many 'Rock and Roll Revival' shows in various cities, and the jumping on the oldies bandwagon of many radio stations. Even this magazine can be considered a significant manifestation of the trend. I prefer to think of the movement not so much as a revival (in the sense the music died and has been reborn), but as an emergence from the underground (where the music still existed, but was appreciated by a minority of listeners). In any event, I am disturbed by the thought that perhaps too much of a good thing can destroy it or, if you will, familiarity breeds contempt. An occasional revival show, say every three months, is great. But what do we have now? One show is scarcely offstage when the radio is blaring advertisements for the next one. Oldies groups are appearing all over the place at clubs, bars, discotheques, etc.."[23]

Apparently Luciani's predictions that the music would die (or kill itself) because of overexposure never came true. Oldies concerts have appeared regularly over the years and it doesn't seem like many fans have been turned off. Guys like Nader, Anthony DeLauro and Dick Fox have put on multi-group shows over the years, with names like "The Royal New York Doo-Wop Show" or "The Doo-Wop Extravaganza" to keep the sound alive. Combining the hobbies of old cars and fifties music has produced festivals like "Lead East" in New Jersey. These efforts may have driven away some purists (who prefer the less known groups), but that's about it. (Thank goodness.)

One big reason for the heightened interest in revival concerts was that they were one of the only ways that people who loved the doo-wop sound could hear their music. It certainly wasn't being played on the radio much outside of New York. The old groups had either disbanded or abandoned the doo-wop sound in favor of other genres, like soul or rock. There were a few groups with original approaches that achieved recognition in the seventies, like the doo-wop/soul/gospel Persuasions and the pop/jazz/doo-wop Manhattan Transfer, but they were about all she wrote. Pastiche groups also emerged in the 1970s, like Sha Na Na and Flash Cadillac, but they only whet one's appetite for the real thing. Other groups, like the Spinners, Main Ingredient and Stylistics, sang beautifully, but not in the style to which we had been accustomed.

Another medium for the revival was the appearance of periodicals dealing with some combination of record collecting and doo-wop, or rhythm and blues. Often the magazines contained group biographies, or individual label discographies, and were peppered with information of interest to doo-wop and R&B fans. Frequently they were attached to or owned by a reissue label or people who made money by brokering record auctions or sales. Considering that most were issued at irregular intervals and eventually folded, no one was getting wealthy. *The Record Exchanger* began publication in 1969 and lasted until 1983. Out of Anaheim, California, *RE* produced 31 issues, and was put out by Art and Ellen Turco, owners of Vintage Records, a reissue label. *Stormy Weather* began publication in 1970 in Brooklyn, New York, and ended its run, 10 issues later, in Oakland, California in 1976. It was the first of a number of periodicals to be named after a famous doo-wop or R&B song. *SW* was named after the famous rarity by the Five Sharps (the tale of which appears in our Songstories chapter).

Bim Bam Boom (taken from a song by the El Dorados) began publication in 1971 and ended three years later, but did manage to put out 14 issues. With its home in the Bronx, *BBB* was very closely associated with the staff of the aforementioned WFUV-FM out of Fordham University, and eventually was linked with reissues on the Bim Bam Boom label. Its first issue lists contributions by Tom Luciani and Joe Marchesani, who founded the "Time Capsule Show,"

20. Newman, Ralph M. "The Rock & Roll Revival: A Portrait of Richard Nader." *Bim Bam Boom*, Issue #10, p. 34.
21. Flam, Steve. "Rock & Roll Revival." *Bim Bam Boom*, Issue #4, Feb.-March 1972, p. 34.
22. Ibid.
23. Luciani, Tom. "Time Capsule." *Bim Bam Boom*, Issue #4, Feb.-March 1972, p. 17.

Record Exchanger Cover V2#3 (Orioles).

Big Town Review Cover V1#1 (Arthur Lee Maye).

Bim Bam Boom Cover V1#1 (Cleftones).

Time Barrier Express Cover #22 (Films).

Story Untold Cover V1#4 (Four Fellows).

Harmony Tymes Cover #1 (Crests).

Wayne Stierle and Lou Silvani, who started with Slim Rose, and Stan Krause, linked to "The Gossert." It's a small world out there.

The next entry was *Big Town Review* out of Flushing, New York. Advertised as "The Magazine That Begins Where Others Leave Off," it appeared three times in 1972, and then left off. The *50s Revisited* spat out two issues in 1973 and then ceased publication, as did *Remember Then* (from a song by the Earls) in 1974. Both emanated from Brooklyn. *Time Barrier Express* also began in 1974, and managed to last for 27 issues through 1980. Its stated goal, taken from the editorial of its first issue was, "...With your support, *Time Barrier Express*, along with the newly formed Rhythm 'n Blues and Rock 'n Roll Society Inc., also Times Square Records, *Bim Bam Boom*, *Remember Then* and many others, will give the great Doo-Wop sounds the proper backing and exposure they need, not only to save them from extinction but to become a new 'now sound' making the pop charts, being around for all people to enjoy, and taking their rightful place in the world of music. And don't say it can't happen."[24]

The one-per-year trend continued for a while. *Yesterday's Memories* (named for a song by Lillian Leach and the Mellows), out of New York, N.Y., published 12 issues between 1975 and 1977. *From Out Of The Past*, another New York magazine, appeared four times between 1976 and 1977. *Story Untold* (named for the Nutmegs nugget) appeared 10 times from 1977 to 1986, was published in Jackson Heights, N.Y., and was associated with another reissue label, Arcade Records. *Harmony Tymes*, published in Clifton, N.J., appeared three times in the 1980-1987 time span, and was associated with labels emanating from Clifton Music, such as Clifton, U.G.H.A. and Ronnie. *Record Collector's Monthly*, a tabloid based in Mendham, N.J., appeared an amazing 53 times between 1982 and 1993. There is one magazine that is still publishing, and even seems to come out four times a year, thanks to its publisher Bob Belniak. *Echoes Of The Past*, out of Agawam, Mass., has come out 47 times (as of spring 1999) since its inception in 1987. Keep it up Bob. Please!

Actually, the "Revival" with a capital "R" really never went away, and certainly as far as print media is concerned. As existing fanzines folded, others periodically[25] unfolded to take their place. They were invariably started by enthusiasts who were businessmen or businessmen who were enthusiasts. Over time, these well-intentioned and often naive people eventually realized that the amount of labor they injected wasn't worth the cash they extracted. Initially on a publication schedule like one issue every two months, the time between issues grew as their motivation sapped, until eventually the project was abandoned. And yet another generation of motivated people, with the hopes of making a buck doing

24. OK, we won't, but we're tempted.
25. Pun intended.

something they enjoy, seemed to always be waiting in the wings. The 1990s has seen the advent of a series of newsletters hoping to be the equivalent of *Bim Bam Boom* and the *Record Exchanger* of 20 years ago. *The Doo Wop Retrorock Revue* began publication in August 1992 and was a medium for advertising the exploits of WCBS-FM (New York) as well as providing useful information about groups. The Story Untold Music Alliance, out of Princeton, N.J., has published a newsletter since 1992. Even the left coast got into the act beginning in the summer of 1989 with *Echo Echo Echo* (after the song by the Emotions), published by the Southern California Doo-Wop Society and spotlighting local concerts.

Another common avenue for information about doo-wop comes from established periodicals designed for wider, and often younger, audiences. *Goldmine* magazine (Iola, WI), a successful magazine in tabloid format oriented to record collectors in general, often features stories on the doo-wop sound. Published since 1974, and sporting a circulation of around 30,000, it has even devoted several entire editions to the vocal group sound of the 1950s. *DISCoveries* magazine often features stories about vocal harmony groups as well.

The Internet is also proving a useful tool for disseminating information about the music. For example, Jean-Charles Marion has published more than a dozen "issues" (as of late 1999) of an online fanzine titled *Doo-wop Nation*. Subject matter experts Marv Goldberg and Jim Dunn & Nikki Gustafson post information about groups and records. U.G.H.A. publicizes its concerts and provides information about groups, WCBS-FM and the Rock & Roll Hall of Fame have their own sites, as do a bevy of proprietary record labels and stores. Some of them are provided below to get the reader started but, as with any subject on the net, search engines and hot links allow the easy discovery of more information. All that follow need to be preceded by "http://" in order to connect.

J.C. Marion	home.earthlink.net/~jaymar41/ index.htmlU.G.H.A.doowop. bayside.net/
Dunn/Gustafson	members.aol.com/Wawawaooh/ index.htm
Marv Goldberg	members.aol.com/marvy42/ marvshow.html
WCBS-FM (N.Y.)	www.wcbsfm.com/
R&R Hall of Fame	www.rockhall.com/

As regards radio programming, the Revival has never really gone away. When Gossert was banished from its airwaves in the early 1970s, WCBS-FM didn't throw out the baby with the bathwater. In early July of 1972, it switched over from a contemporary rock to an all-oldies format with a high percentage of doo-wop recordings. It soon acquired the services of one Norm N. Nite to deejay and host "The Nite Train Show," a Sunday-night program which played doo-wops exclusively (and became a competitor to Gossert's WPIX show). Nite's path was quite similar to that of Richard

Nader. Starting in Freed's backyard, Cleveland, Ohio[26], Nite worked his way around the area's low-power radio stations while attending high school and college. He took an intellectual approach to his subject and orchestrated an annotated record album titled "Rock & Roll: Evolution or Revolution" in the mid-1960s, as well as producing thematic radio programs called "The Honor Roll of Hits," which he aired on his Midwest shows. Nite's show was successful and paved the way for his successor, Don K. Reed, in New York, as well as a myriad of doo-wop disc jockeys in just about all urban areas from coast to coast.

Reed, after paying some deejay dues at WPAC and WLIR on Long Island (New York), took over the doo-wopotentate spot when Nite left to go to WNBC in 1975. Called "The Doo-Wop Shop," his show was soon expanded to five hours (7 p.m. to midnight) on Sunday night and began to feature guest groups, beginning with an a cappella group from Chicago called Stormy Weather.[27] Usually on in the last hour of the show, this slot includes interviews with group members, live a cappella singing and/or recorded music by the groups. While Nite had groups doing jingles for his show by changing the lyrics to recognizable doo-wops (e.g. "Norm N. Nite, he's all right, Norm N. Nite, outta sight..."), Reed expanded the practice over the years. Still going strong in late 1999, the personable Reed and his show has served as the model for most other shows that focus on doo-wop music.

Other WCBS personnel in New York also occasionally wave the doo-wop banner. Bobby Jay, credible because he sang bass with the Laddins in the 1950s, continues to riff whenever and with whomever he can. He often subs for Reed, as does Alan Fredericks, erstwhile host of the original "Night Train Show" 40 or so years ago. In fact, each large urban area seems to develop its own cadre of addicted souls who are involved in the music in some manner. Thus, Philadelphia has Harvey Holiday, that city's equivalent of Don K. Reed, who hosts a Sunday night doo-wop show on the local CBS affiliate, WCAU. And then there is Charlie Horner, a knowledgeable purist who, up until the end of 1995, had a 20-year run with his "Classic Urban Harmony Show" on WXPN, and Gerry Blavat, "The Geeter With The Heater," who's been playing doo-wops for longer than he'd probably like to admit. Boston has Walter "Little Walter" DeVenne who broadcasts on the CBS affiliate when he's not remixing and editing albums for Relic Records (among others).

---

26. The paths are all the more similar because the authors, being New Yorkers, are thus geographically cockeyed, and disposed to see states like Pennsylvania and Ohio as interchangeable.

27. Mennie, Don. "Don K. Reed Has Made a Home for Doo-Wop on NY Radio With Live and Recorded Music Drawn From Five Decades." *Record Collector's Monthly*, Issue 53, Sept.-Oct. 1993.

As of 1997, there are also a plethora of doo-wop-heavy shows on smaller radio stations, many emanating from college campuses. Most of these shows cater to those who are really into the music, a group that we have labeled the "Purists" (see the chapter titled "Doo-Wopolitics"). In the New York metropolitan area in 1999, this type of show can be found at Fordham[28], Hofstra[29] and Rutgers[30] universities among others. You can bet that whoever does this, doesn't do it for the money.

In a way, Purists created the neo-doo-wop era around 1960. And while the 1969 revival was begun by guys more interested in show business than doo-wop, like Gossert and Nader, it was certainly fueled by Purists working behind the scenes. Since then, the Purists have served that same function, namely to keep the "Revival" from stopping, to keep the music alive. The most important organization for purists is clearly the United in Group Harmony Association (U.G.H.A.) and the most influential person is its President, Ronnie Italiano. In a way, they are one and the same. Italiano, who is called "Ronnie I" by just about everyone, began as a record collector and took over Clifton (New Jersey) Music in January 1972. Later that year, he leased the rights to "Go Back Where You Came From" by the Summits (an old Slim Rose favorite) from Wayne Stierle and it became the first release on his Clifton label. In September of 1975, Italiano became a deejay, starting his "Ronnie I Just For You Show" on WHBI-FM, a small New Jersey station. In 1998, he completed a 10-plus-year run on WNYE-FM, a strong station owned and operated by the New York City Board of Education. In 1976, he started U.G.H.A.

U.G.H.A.'s mission is to promote and preserve rhythm and blues music. The term "doo-wop" is out of favor with Purists as of 1995. The organization, which has more than 2,000 members, sponsors meeting-shows once per month, where Ronnie I shares the latest relevant news with his audience before the acts come on, and occasional "collectors' shows," which feature some big name groups. For these latter shows, groups such as the El Dorados, Spaniels or Calvanes are flown in, expenses paid for by U.G.H.A. Groups are reformed by Italiano around one or two original members, like the Castelles or Robins. A cappella groups abound at the shows, and often do double duty, backing up original singers who are missing part or most of their group (e.g. the Nutmeg-less Harold Jaynes or Supreme-less Ruth McFadden). Unhappy with the acceptance of R&B groups by the Rock and Roll Hall of

Fame, Italiano founded a Rhythm and Blues Hall of Fame which has inducted 63 groups up through 1999. A list of recipients can be found below. Italiano takes pride in unearthing missing members or heretofore unreconstituted groups and showcasing them at the shows. He and a handful of other members serve as an information clearinghouse for all things related to the music. The Doo-Wop Society of Southern California, though smaller than U.G.H.A., serves many of the same functions for the West Coast.

United In Group Harmony Association Hall of Fame Inductees

1991: Cadillacs
Clovers
Harptones
Heartbeats/Shep & the Limelites
Orioles
Ravens
Teenagers (Frankie Lymon & the)
Honorary Award: Delta Rhythm Boys
Literary Award: Phil Groia
Industry Award: Ahmet Ertegun (Atlantic Records)

1992: Channels
Five Keys
Flamingos
Moonglows
Solitaires
Spaniels
Honorary Award: Ink Spots
Humanitarian Award: Marcia Vance

1993: Cardinals
Dominoes
(pre-1959) Drifters
Dubs
Larks
Honorary Award: Mills Brothers
Industry Award: Bobby Robinson
Literary Award: Rick Whitesell
Special Awards: Deborah Chesler, Clio Perry, Glenny T.

1994: Dells
Jive Five
Nutmegs
Platters
Swallows
Honorary Award: Deep River Boys, Golden Gate Quartet

1995: Chantels
Five Satins
Lee Andrews & the Hearts
Mellows
Robins
Honorary Award: Swan Silvertones, Dixie Hummingbirds

1996: Castelles

28. WFUV-FM, 90.7, "The Rhythm and Blues Group Harmony Review," hosted by Dan Romanello and Neil Hirsch, Sat. 3-6 p.m.

29. WRHU-FM, 88.7 (Hempstead, N.Y.), "The Rhythm & Blues Serenade," hosted by Frank Gengaro and Gordon Skadberg, Sunday, 4-6 p.m.

30. WRSU-FM, 88.7 (New Brunswick, N.J.), "The Big Beat Show," hosted by Bill Swank and Lou Rallo, Thursday 7-8 p.m.

Chords
Del Vikings
El Dorados
Jesters
Vocaleers
Honorary Award: Harmonizing Four

1997: Diablos
Little Anthony & the Imperials
Paragons
Valentines
Velours
Honorary Award: Four Vagabonds, Hollywood
Flames

1998: Cleftones
Crows
Four Fellows
Penguins
Wrens
Honorary Award: Four Buddies, Jubilaires

1999: Crickets
Five Royales

Jacks/Cadets
Mello-Moods
Spiders
Honorary Award: Fairfield Four, Four Knights

Perhaps the most essential medium for perpetuating (or is it perpetrating) the doo-wop sound is the production of records and, in the 1990s, CDs. For the most part, the important players are those that reissued the old sound to those who couldn't find, afford or didn't know about originals. In the 1960s and 1970s, many of these reissues were 45s, but the retro nature of the genre makes it more conducive to compilations on vinyl album and CD. The CD, especially, with the ability to hold 25 songs, has made vocal group harmony more available to more people than ever before. With larger capacity, the CD era has brought about the inclusion of out-takes of many songs, and the first-time release of songs recorded in the doo-wop era but kept in the "can," usually for financial reasons. A list of some great songs that were recorded during the doo-wop years, but went unreleased until considerably after the era, is given below. All were good enough to become hits.

Group	Song	Era	Tempo	Date Rec.	Date Rel.	Label
5 Bell-Aires	House Of Love	C	F	1960	1990	Relic LP 5085
Bees	Darling Please	P	S	1954	1987	Imperial 17232
Bees	Sunny Side Of The Street	P	F	1955	1987	Imperial 17232
Cadillacs	Party For Two	C	F	1954	1983	Murray Hill 61285
Channels	Gloria	C	S	1956	1971	Channel 1000
Chantels	So Real	C	S	1957	1987	Murray Hill 000385
Clefftones	Little Girl (I Love You Madly)	C	F	1955	1985	Murray Hill 000083
Clefftones	Gloria	P	S	1955	1985	Murray Hill 000083
Clouds	Say You Love Me	C	S	1954	1960s	Broadcast/Parrot
Drifters	Three Thirty Three	P	F	1954	1971	Atco LP 375
Fiestas	Things We Can't Forget	C	F	1959	1993	Old Town/Ace
Flamingos	If I Could Love You	P	S	1956	1976	Chess LP 702
Hummers	Gee What A Girl	C	F	1956	1993	Old Town/Ace CD 470
Imaginations	The Mystery Of You	N	S	1962	1985	Relic LP 5058
Jacks	Away	C	S	1955	1984	Relic LP 5023
Kool Gents	Just Like A Fool	C	S	1956	1990s	Vee Jay LP 1019
Larks	All I Want For Christmas	P	S	1951	1988	Relic LP 8014
Ravens	It's The Talk Of The Town	P	S	1950	1972	National 9158
Solitaires	Come Back And Give Me Your Hand	C	S	1956	1984	Murray Hill 000059
Spiders	Love's All I'm Puttin' Down	P	F	1954	1992	Bear CD 15673
Swallows	In The Palm Of My Hand	P	S	1958	1992	Federal 12328
Vocal Teens	Be A Slave	C	M	1960	1972	Downstairs 101

The first of the important reissue labels was Relic Records, run by Eddie Gries and Donn Fileti. Beginning in 1964, they have released approximately 100 45 r.p.m. singles, 125 vinyl albums and roughly 150 CDs documenting the doo-wop and R&B sound, organized both by group and by record label. Their innovative "Golden Groups" series, highlighting such obscure labels as Timely, Luna, Jay Dee and Atlas/Angletone, as well as some of the more well-known ones like Apollo, Winley and Herald/Ember, is quite simply outstanding. These recordings were just not available before Relic got into

the act. The liner notes by Fileti, group by group and label by label, has given us a window to the past, and are worth the price of the CD or album alone. Incidentally, the Relic Rack in Hackensack, which was sold by Gries and Fileti to George Lavatelli in 1978, is thought to be the oldest still-operating oldies store in the country.[31]

Collectables, started by Jerry Green in 1980, has become one of the biggest players in doo-wop by issuing

---

31. We'll probably get lots of cards and letters about this one.

CDs and CD sets that focus on individual groups such as the Five Keys, Orioles and Flamingos, providing an in-depth view of their repertoires. Greene has also teamed up with CBS-FM to put out a series of CDs for neophytes. Rhino records operates in a similar vein, doing CDs on individual groups like Shep & the Limelites, Marcels and Harptones, and has put out two "Doo-Wop Box Sets," which contain four CDs each and which are expertly annotated and packaged by Bob Hyde.

Ace Records, the most important player from England, has issued both group compilations (Solitaires, Fiestas, Earls) and label compilations (e.g. four volumes on Hy Weiss' Old Town label). They also recently issued "Voices of America," a CD that explores vocal group harmony from the 1930s to the 1990s.[32] Bear Family Records from Germany got into the act, releasing individual CDs and box sets on groups like the Spiders and Orioles. Series like Dynamite Doo-Wops, Explosive Group Sounds, Dynamite Group Sounds have filled the gaps and made even obscure groups on obscure labels from obscure places available to the doo-wopublic. Even the omnipresent Wayne Stierle is still around, putting out compilation CDs with titles such as "Doo-Wop Jive" and "Doo-Wop Party."

Ed Engel has carved out a niche in the "White Group Sound" and has put out over a hundred records in that sub-genre on his Crystal Ball label out of Little Neck (Queens), New York. Bruce Patch, the originator of Classic Artist Records has taken a different approach by finding original artists and providing them with new material which remains true to the doo-wop era.[33] Beginning in 1988, Margo Sylvia (of the Tune Weavers), Don Julian (Meadowlarks), Johnny Staton (Feathers), Vernon Green (Medallions), Leon Peels (Blue Jays), Jimmy Beaumont (Skyliners), George Grant (Castelles), Richard Blandon (Dubs) and Herb Cox (Cleftones) all waxed new songs for Patch, many written by the talented Dave Antrell. The heritage of the independent record labels of the 1950s, and the fervor and zeal of Slim's entourage in the early 1960s is alive and well today.

Most of the CDs referred to above are available in the larger record/CD store chains such as Sam Goody, CD World and Coconuts. The larger urban areas that have many adherents and collectors of the genre, still can support the "mom and pop" type record store, which will sell records as well as CDs. While the flow of good doo-wops is not as heavy as it once was, many newer issues can recall the same feelings within us. Some of the better songs released after the end of the doo-wop era are listed below.

32. Coincidentally, this was annotated by the present authors.

33. Propes, Steve. "Classic (Doo-Wop) Artists Get the Green Light in LA." *Record Collector's Monthly*, Issue #50, Nov.-Dec. 1991, p. 14. Also see: Arslanian, Jim. "Bruce Patch, the 'Classic' Guy." *Echoes of the Past*, Issue #11, Spring 1990, p. 14.

Group	Song	Era	Tempo	Year	Label
Blue Emotions	Doo-Wop All Night Long	N	F	1982	Ambient Sound 38346
Bon-Aires	Cherry	C	S	1976	Flamingo 1000
Capris	Morse Code Of Love	N	F	1982	Ambient Sound 02697
Arthur Lee Maye & gp.	Moonlight	C	S	1985	Antrell 102
Arthur Lee Maye & gp.	I'm In Love	C	F	1985	Antrell 102
Crystalaires	Teenage Ding Dong Bells	N	F	1990	Crystal Ball 159
Dahills	She's An Angel	C	F	1978	Crystal Ball 107
Dell Vikings	My Heart	N	F	1991	BVM 002
Dubs	Where Do We Go From Here	N	S	1973	Clifton 2
Emotions	Keep On Keepin' On	N	M	1990s	Crystal Ball
Exodus	M & M	C	F	1971	Wand 11248
Fabulous Dudes	Betty Blue Moon	N	F	1994	Presence Rec.
Billy Joel & gp.	For The Longest Time	N	F	1984	Columbia 04400
Jaynells	One In A Million Girls	N	S	1984	Angela 101
Jaynells	Hollywood Actor	N	F	1984	Angela 102
Rob Roys (Norman Fox & the)	Rainy Day Bells	C	F	1982	Back Beat 500
Storytellers	Please Remember My Love	N	S	1990	Classic Artists 118
Tuneweavers (Margo Sylvia &)	Come Back To Me	N	S	1989	Classic Artists 104

When the spate of periodicals began in 1969, one would have thought that books on the subject would follow. They didn't. A dearth of books led to the writing of the first tome by these authors (*Doo-Wop: The Forgotten Third of Rock 'n' Roll* published in 1992), and is discussed elsewhere. The earliest relevant book was *Rhythm & Blues* by Lynn McCutcheon in 1971, which provided an overview of the field with some philosophy thrown in. A good effort and worth reading, but it was published by an obscure book house and was not widely available. In 1973-1974, Steve Propes put out two books for hobbyists titled *Those Oldies But Good-*

ies: A Guide to 50s Record Collecting and Golden Oldies: A Guide To 60s Record Collecting. While mainly geared to collectors, some interesting information about vocal groups and the doo-wop era can be found. In 1974, Rock On by Norm N. Nite came out. Arranged alphabetically by artist, this encyclopedia provided biographical data on many groups, but they were interspersed among all artists that had hits (primarily) in the 1950s. One could find the Drifters, Teenagers and Moonglows (and Frank Sinatra and Elvis), but not the Bop Chords, Norman Fox & the Rob Roys, and Students. Nicely formatted, the book was a great tease to anyone interested in doo-wop or rhythm and blues.

Arnold Shaw's Honkers and Shouters: The Golden Years of Rhythm & Blues came out in 1978 and, like Charlie Gillett's The Sound of the City: The Rise of Rock and Roll in 1983, and Ed Ward et al.'s Rock of Ages: The Rolling Stone History of Rock & Roll in 1986, gave doo-wop and vocal group rhythm and blues only a small part to play in the stories they told. Doo-wop wasn't ignored, just underemphasized.

Ed Engel published his own White and Still All Right in 1980, a compilation of white-group biographies which was fun to read. Ed tried to restore balance to the tendency of some Purists to ignore anything recorded by white artists (see chapter on Doo-Wopolitics). Phil Groia came out with They All Sang on the Corner in 1983, and to this day it remains a masterpiece. Looking mostly at the groups that evolved in Harlem and Sugar Hill (Manhattan, New York) through an enormous number of first person interviews, the book really gives a flavor for what the times, places and people were like. The only criticism, itself flattery, is that when we finished it, we were hungry for more.

There wasn't a lot more to be had. In 1987, Johnny Keyes told of the trials and tribulations of his group, the Magnificents, in Du-Wop, and in 1989, Dave Marsh came out with The Heart of Rock and Soul: The 1,001 Greatest Singles Ever Made. Of the 1,001 songs, several hundred were of the doo-wop persuasion and Marsh makes the stories interesting. The importance of disc jockeys in the early years were examined in Wes Smith's The Pied Pipers of Rock 'n' Roll in 1989, and Alan Freed was microscopically examined by John Jackson's Big Beat Heat in 1991. Both offer a refreshing change and see the music and the performers from a different perspective.

Jay Warner's 1992 book, American Singing Groups, is a valuable source of information because, by decade, it details the stories of almost all the important vocal groups that sang doo-wop and rhythm and blues. Assembled largely from secondary sources like the aforementioned periodicals, it allows the reader to cross-reference between groups, and also includes useful discographies in many instances. Robert Pruter, a man synonymous with Chicago rhythm and blues, came out with Doowop: The Chicago Scene in 1996. It offers, through an impressive array of first-person interviews, the intricate stories of the groups and labels that emanated from that part of the world. It is to Chicago what Phil Groia's book is to New York.

Also in 1996 came Todd Baptista's book Group Harmony: Behind the Rhythm and the Blues, which offered an in-depth look at 11 important purveyors of the doo-wop sound, including the El Dorados, Solitaires and Harptones. Going to press in 2000 is a book by Steve Propes and Galen Gart, titled L.A. R&B Vocal Groups and Duets, 1945-1965, which discusses what the title says it will. Both of these authors are real pros and their book provides us with the complete story of the L.A. sound.

The current work and its predecessor Doo-Wop..., have attempted to take a broad-band approach to the music that is called doo-wop or vocal group rhythm and blues, an approach that no other authors seem to have taken. We've carved out a niche, one that had to be scratched.

So there you have it folks. The music being kept alive by small record stores, hucksters, small specialized record companies, a cappella singers, radio stations on shoestring budgets, concerts for nostalgics, obscure and esoteric periodicals, organizations for purists, a book here and there, and small slices of time on mainstream radio. Art Mariano, writing for Big Town Review in 1972[34], cautioned that any attempt to bring back doo-wop music would "be frustrating and ultimately fruitless" because doo-wop arose out of a need that young people of the 1950s had, but that the youth of today do not have. A better goal, he avers, is to preserve the music, so that there's enough of it for us to enjoy and so that it can be appreciated and understood by those who follow along in our footsteps. Sounds like good advice to us.

34. Mariano, Art. "The Torn Corner." Big Town Review, Issue #3, July-August, 1972, p. 43.

Chapter 21

Songstories

1) The Gloria-fication of Doo-Wop

Of all the songs recorded in the doo-wop era, "Gloria" has the most interesting history. The original "Gloria" was penned by Leon Rene in the late 1940s. Rene's inspiration for the song was apparently his assistant, whose name was Gloria Kort. George Moonoogian discovered this in the Oct. 23, 1948 issue of *Cash Box*, which reported that Ms. Kort "laughed when confronted with the rumor..."[1]

Ferdie Gonzalez and Art Turco[2] help to make sense of the subsequent events. The song was first recorded by Johnny Moore's Three Blazers for Rene's Exclusive record label. Next, the Mills Brothers hit the charts with the same version for Decca in November 1948. The song told the story of a guy (the singer) who used to toy with women's affections until he met our protagonist, Gloria. He duly fell in love with her, but she wasn't buying. The lyrics, as recorded by Gonzales and Turco, were:

"Gloria, it's not Marie, it's Gloria
It's not Cherie, it's Gloria
She's in your every dream

You like to play the game of kiss and runaway
But now you find it's not that way
Somehow you've changed it seems

Wasn't Madeline your first love
It was just hello goodbye
Wasn't Caroline your last love
It's a shame you made her cry

What a fool you are
You gave your heart to Gloria
You're not so smart cause Gloria
Is not in love with you

What a fool you are
She's not in love with you"[3]

Now most people don't realize how brilliant these lyrics were. Not only did Mr. Rene tell you who it is, he tells you who it's not! No one had ever done that before! Think of the musical legacy he would have left had he continued in this vein, viz.:

"Gloria, it's not Tom, it's Gloria
It's not his Mom, it's Gloria..."

The outer limits of how many people it's not was never really tested.

Anyway, skip to 1954, when the Cadillacs put out the first doo-wop version of "Gloria," written ostensibly by one Esther Navarro, the group's manager. Navarro wrote the song after one of her protégés, a singer named Gloria "Little Miss Muffet" Smith. Somehow, Navarro took elements of the older song and blended them into a doo-wop format to resurrect the belle Gloria. Navarro's lyrics were:

"Gloria, it's not Marie
Gloria, it's not Cherie
Gloria, but she's not in love with me

Can't you see, it's not Marie
It's Gloria, it's not Cherie
It's Gloria, but she's not in love with me

Yes, maybe she loves me, but who am I to know
And, maybe she loves me, but who am I to know

Gloria, it's not Marie
It's Gloria, it's not Cherie
It's Gloria, but she's not in love with me"[4]

The commonalities between the two versions are (1) the plot of the lyrics, i.e., Gloria not returning the love of a suitor, and (2) three lines, namely "It's not Marie," "It's not Cherie" and "She's not in love with me (you)." The melodies differ and Rene's lyrics are much more sophisticated, as befitting a song geared for adult audiences. Navarro's lyrics are simpler and more repetitive. Additionally, Rene's tale is recounted in second person (e.g., "What a fool you are") while Navarro's is told in first person (e.g., "Who am I to know"). Whether the "borrowing" that Navarro did was accidental or purposeful will never be truly known. Gonzalez and Turco sense that she knew what she was doing because her name did not appear on the first pressing but did on subsequent ones. Apparently when no one raised a fuss, she figured it was all right to take credit.

Ms. Navarro apparently played by her own rules. According to Bobby Thomas, a member of the Vibranaires who recorded the well-respected "Doll Face" (and now singing with the 1990s version of the Orioles), it was his group that Navarro saw from a window and summoned, with the intention of making them the "Cadillacs." He and his buddies went home to New Jersey, only to learn that Speedo and his group impressed Navarro to the point that she used them instead. Speedo's Cadillacs went on to fame and fortune, while the Vibranaires were left only with an interesting story to tell their grandchildren.[5]

Whether "Gloria" was stolen by design or not, Navarro and the Cadillacs left the legacy of a doo-wop

---

1. Moonoogian, George. "Wax Fax." *Record Collector's Monthly*, Issue #30, May 1985.
2. Gonzalez, Ferdie and Turco, Art. "It's Not Cherie..." *Record Exchanger*, June 1973.
3. "Gloria," Leon Rene (Rene Leon Publications, 1946), ASCAP.

4. "Gloria," Esther Navarro (Benell Music, 1954), BMI.

Esther Navarro.

Cadillacs.

masterpiece, one that quickly became a street corner "standard." "Gloria," along with "Sunday Kind Of Love," became fodder for would-be doo-woppers to strut their stuff. You had to be able to sing these two songs to get respect on the street.

As the doo-wop era unfolded, the name "Gloria," despite being difficult to rhyme with (except perhaps

5. The story can be found in: Italiano, Ronnie. "The Nicky Addeo Story, Part One." *Story Untold*, Issue #1 , January 1978, p. 30. It was substantiated in a conversation between Thomas and Italiano on Italiano's show of April 20, 1994.

with "eu-" and "dysphoria," "trattoria" and "I wanna see more a ya"), attracted songwriters like flies. The Passions, Vito & the Salutations, Darchaes and Earl Lewis & the Channels, among others, recorded the Cadillacs version. Other groups such as the Five Thrills, the Five Chances, the Chariots, Arthur Lee Maye & the Crowns and the Hi-Lites put out entirely different songs by the same name. The Frankie Grier Quartet put out "Oh Gloria," the Windsors recorded "My Gloria" and the New Yorkers Five produced "Gloria, My Darling." Van Morrison wrote the G-L-O-R-I-A "Gloria" in 1965 (not a doo-wop version) for his group Them, and the Shadows of Knight had an eight-week run on the *Billboard* charts with a garage band version of it in 1966. Finally, Laura Branigan visited the charts for 22 weeks (three of them at number two) with a neurotic, manipulative "Gloria" in 1982 (again, not doo-wop). A list of "Gloria" songs done in pre-doo-wop or doo-wop style follows.

Group Name	Year	Label
Johnny Moore's Three Blazers	1946	Exclusive 703
Four Gabriels	1948	World Records Inc. 2505
Mills Brothers	1948	Decca 24509
Cadillacs	1954	Josie 765/Lana 119 (1964)
Five Thrills	1954	Parrot 800
New Yorkers 5 ("...My Darling")	1955	Danice 801
Clefftones	1955	Old Town/Murray Hill LP 000083 (1983)
Crowns (Arthur Lee Maye & the)	1956	Specialty 573
Five Chances	1956	States 156
Wallace, Jerry (& group)	1956	Mercury 70812
Clark, Dee (with the Kool Gents)	1957	Falcon 1002/Vee Jay 355(1960)
Grier Quartet (The Frankie Grier Quartet) ("Oh...")	1958	Swan 4019

Group Name	Year	Label
Windsors (Lee Scott & the) ("My...")	1958	Back Beat 506
Chariots	1959	Time 1006/Brent
Passions	1960	Audicon 106
Chapelaires	1961	Hac 102
Blue Knights (Steve Colt & the)	1962	Fleetwood 4550
Escorts	1962	Coral 62302
Hi-Lites	1962	Julia 1105
Love Notes	1964	Wilshire 203
Parrish, Troy (& group)	1962	Baronet 10
Salutations (Vito & the)	1962	Rayna 5009/Red Boy 5009(1962)
Youngones (a capella)	1962	Times Square 28
Darchaes (Nicky Addeo & the)	1963	Savoy 200/Earls 1533
Del-Lourds	1963	Solar 1003
Vandells (Johnny Greco & the)	1963	Far-Mel 1
Five Sharks	1964	Old Timer 604/Siamese 404 (1965)
Ubans	1964	Radiant 102
Good Guys (Doug Robertson & the)	1965	Jerden 767
Savoys (a capella)	1965	Catamount 105
Sultans	1965	Ascot 2228
DiMucci, Dion (& group)	1969	Warner Bros. ?????
Channels (Earl Lewis & the)	1971	Channel 1000 (recorded in 1956)
Lanterns (a capella)	1973	Baron 110

As a footnote, the *Record Exchanger* reported in an issue subsequent to the Gonzales/Turco article, "We were surprised by the mail received on the Gloria feature. In fact, the most mail ever received on a single column was on this feature." Gloriaphilia run amok.

2) Rhythm and Bruise

The lyrics of the doo-wop era almost always portray innocent love between innocent young people. On the surface, and by reputation, there is no violence, no abuse, and no sexual power plays in the words. Unfortunately, not quite true. The words of some songs hearken back to a rougher, less sheltered era of music, namely urban rhythm and blues. Further, in the 1950s the rules for how women and men treated each other were different than today, and much less egalitarian. Hitting one's spouse/girlfriend was far from unheard of and, if not applauded, not terribly sanctioned either. Witness the lyrics from "Willa Bea" by the Ambassadors (1953) in a situation where his girlfriend cheats on him:

"Well I got a gal named Willa,
She's gonna make me kill her,
Every time I see Miss Willa Bea she's always cheatin'
     on me...

She tells me that I tickle her,
She's gonna make me cripple her,
That gal Willa's gonna make me kill her,
'Cause she's always always cheatin' on me...

And I'm beatin' on she,
Yes beatin' on she,
'Cause she's cheatin' on me,
Goin' upside of her head,

I'm gonna blackin' her eyes,
'Cause she's cheatin' on me..."

Notice that the thought of just telling her to get lost never enters the guy's head. It's almost as if that her being unfaithful has given him license to beat her up. Further, it is Willa who is making him do it. (The flip side of this 45 contains the song "Darling, I'm Sorry." Ironically, this pattern of abuse and apology is characteristic of real-life wife batterers.)

These lyrics demonstrate that "gangsta" rap wasn't the first music to carry violent and antisocial messages to teens. Gangsta rap has been publicized, however, while songs like "Willa Bea" fortunately were not. There are other examples. In "I'm Gonna Do That Woman In" by the Sparrows (1953), the bass lead proclaims:

"I'm gonna bust her lip,
Swell her eye,
Beat her so much, it be paralyzed,
Knock her out on the floor,
Bring her to and beat her some more..."

He sees himself retaliating for the things she did to him despite the fact that he "tried like a dog to keep her by my side." She stole his money and even stole "the clothes I'm livin' in."

The Orbits in "Knock Her Down" (1959) propose that you "knock her down to the ground" when "your baby roams around all night." The Jayhawks, in "Don't Mind Dyin'" (1956), assert to their beloved that "if you do me wrong," or "if you misuse me" then "you don't mind dyin'." The Rocketeers (1953) confide that they're "Gonna Feed My Baby Poison" (in a stew) because she done them wrong. The "5" Royales state that "[My baby] told me a lie, now she don't live no more" in "What's That" from 1954. The song title refers to what (or who) is under the singer's bed.

Threats were sometimes used to keep women in line. The Charts, judging by most of their output, an innocent-love and teen-oriented group, take their turn at abuse in "All Because Of Love" from 1957. Joe Grier, their lead, warns his baby not to stray, using the experience of a friend to give warning:

"I had a friend in love until,
She put him down and then he killed her,
I tell you this my darling stay true,
Or the same thing will happen to you..."

Even rape (or something real close to it) is portrayed in "It Won't Take Long" by the Native Boys in 1954:

"It was early one morning, half past three,
I told my little girl why don't you come with me,
Because it won't take long, baby it won't take long...

Well she scratched and kicked, called me names,
Said that's all right baby, that's how I like you dames...

Well she scratched and kicked, came on strong,
Said that's all right baby, it won't take long..."

The ladies can play rough too. The Mellows' "I'm Gonna Pick Your Teeth With An Ice Pick" has a spritely Caribbean lilt to it, containing lyrics that are both artful and humorous, if somewhat intimidating. Their male lead exclaims:

"Mercy on me, my old lady,
Sure will be mad as all sin,
It's after four, oh man, the door,
I sure afraid to open,
Hello my little honey bunny,
Why do you look at me so funny,
I'm a Johnny Brown on the way,
Tell me how did you spend the day..."

If he thought this light patter would divert her, he was sorely mistaken. Lillian Leach, the female lead of the group, calmly rejoins:

"I gonna pick your teeth with this ice pick,
I done tole you 'bout this before,
I gonna pick you teeth with this ice pick,
You won't come home late any more.

When reminded that the neighbors might overhear, she replies, "...but I now talking here with you, and I tell you what I gonna do." Then she brings up the dreaded ice pick again, refusing to be distracted from her message. Then, in a domestic playlet, they exchange:

He: "My sugar plum"
She: "Don't think I dumb, sweet talk won't be of no use,
    You better weigh each word you say,
    I done heard every excuse"
He: "Now, I went with my large committee,
    To visit a friend who was sickly"

She: "Well, I tell you what's really true,
They gonna soon have to visit you"

When the truth finally comes out, that he was playing poker, won, and had the good sense to buy his wife a "diamond choker," she forgives him. He is then once more reminded, nicely this time, to be on time or face her wrath, in the form of an ice pick.

The side of the man cuckolded is portrayed in "Time Takes Care Of Everything" by the Ravens. Not only does the guy have to spring for an enormous feed bill and a fur, he foots the bill for some major reconstructive surgery, only to learn that she's not faithful.

"You're a square city block, and you're dumb too,
And then I helped you, you turned to somebody new,
Well time takes care of everything, and time will
    take care of you...

You never had a decent meal til you hit my door,
With me you ate three squares, and sometimes more,
Bought you a mink coat instead of that gunny sack,
Then you turned around and cheat behind my back...

Well I bought you some new teeth baby,
Then I fixed your nose,[6]
Uncrossed your eyes,
And lord in heaven knows..."

The lesson, if there is one, seems to be that whatever goes around, comes around (or is it vice versa?). Or maybe it's nice guys (and gals) finish last.

3) Let's Get Serious

OK, here's a quiz. Here are some lyrics as written on the sheet music provided by Windswept Pacific Entertainment Co. of Beverly Hills, CA. Your task is to name the song.

"Ba, ba her wa da her da wa da her wa-doo,
Her wa da her da wa ja ja er wa do oo,
Ah wa da ah da wa ma jig er wa da oo,
Ah wa da her ba wa da jig er ma a oo,
Her wa da her da wa da her da wa da oo,
Her wa da her da wa ja ja er wa da oo,
Ah wa da her da wa ma jig er wa da oo,
Ah wa da her ba wa da jig er ma a oo,
Her wa da her da wa da her da wa da,
Do that again! (to the chorus)"

Not familiar at all, you maintain. OK, now try these:

"Gow gow hoo-oo,
Gow gow wanna dib-a-doo,
Chick'n hon-a-chick-a-chick hole-a-hubba,
Hell fried chuck-a-lucka wanna jubba,
Hi-low 'n-ay wanna dubba hubba,
Day down sum wanna jigga-wah,
Dell rown ay wanna lubba hubba,

---

6. In 1946, the Melody Masters, in "Wig Blues," plead "Give me back that glass eye, them false teeth and that blond wig, and let your big head go bald..." Wonder if it's the same gal.

Mull an a mound chicka lubba hubba,
Fay down ah wanna dip-a-zip-a-dip-a,
Mm-mh, do that again! (interjected by the bass)"

Mm-mh you say yourself, that's beginning to sound a lot like "Rubber Biscuit" by the Chips, recorded in 1956, the ne plus ultra among examples of the creative use of nonsense syllables. Well you are correct and obviously possess a first-rate mind. Of course, the first set of lyrics are from "Rubber Biscuit" also, but it's obvious that the official transcriber used by the sheet music company was either insensitive or out to lunch. The second set was taken from the record itself by no less than one of the current authors.

According to Phil Groia in "They All Sang On The Corner,"[7] these lyrics were inspired by neighborhood "callin' cades" and were refined by lead singer Charles "Kenrod" Johnson while marching around the campus of the Warwick School for Delinquents in upstate New York (he was not there to compose music). The tune was later "covered" by the Blues Brothers (Dan Aykroyd and John Belushi) in 1979. The actual lyrics are presented to allow those so disposed to sing along, but please do not hold the authors responsible for their accuracy. In the second stanza, "Kenrod" ejaculated:

"Gow gow lubba 'n a-blubba lubba,
Ow rown hibb'n 'n a-hibba-lu,
How low lubbin 'n a-blubba-lubba,
Hell fried ricky ticky hubba lubba,
Dull ow de moun'chicky hubba lubba
Wen down trucka lucka wanna do-uh,
How low a zippin 'n a-hubba-lu,
Hell fried ricky ticky blubba-lu,
How low duh woody woody pecka pecka..."[8]

"Rubber Biscuit" has a rival named "Shombalor," performed in 1959 by Sheriff and the Ravels (pronounced Ra-vels in the U.S. of A. and Rah-vels in the U.K.). The author-transcribed, sing-along-if-you-wish lyrics follow:

"Shombalor, shombalor,
Checkin'out 'n'a rick faw checkin' 'n a shombalor,
Hey bitch on a move out good now,
Check in on a countdown please,
Hey bay jing the puck you need now,
Check in on a captain's knees 'n' a
Hi low 'n' a swing ding,
A ricky fing your helty one a hubba,
Hey bitch on a sum an a jigga wah,
Hi low 'n' a pick a ma play now,

"Shombalor, shombalor,
Checkin'out 'n' a rick faw checkin' 'n a shombalor,
Hey bitch on a wine-o bine-o,

Retag a frankenstein-o,
Hey bitch an a came to dine 'n' a,
Checkin' an a stole my wine 'n' a,
Hayj an a bing-dee-bown-dee-bown,
A lay a tippin 'n'a skip a one a hubba,
Hey bitch an a sum an a jigga wah,
Hi low 'n' a pick a ma play now..."[9]

This song is even more cryptic than "Rubber Biscuit" because it's a tease. At least with "R.B." you know that the lyric has no meaning and little redeeming value. It is consistently vacuous and puerile from beginning to end. "Shombalor," on the other hand, seems like it's trying to say something, but never quite does. You can tell that it's another "callin' cade" song because it's well-sprinkled with "hubbas," has something to do with being in the army and marching, but little else. Perhaps that's the idea; it's a puzzle posed to eager young army guys to ponder on while their bodies are being pounded into the ground at the whim of their kind-hearted platoon leaders.

If "Rubber Biscuit" and "Shombalor" represent the ravings of strange individuals, what do we call it when two people agree to talk nonsense to each other. Witness the interchange between bass and lead tenor of the Concepts, in their magnum opus "Jungle" from 1961:

Lead:"Umma summa gomma romma momma"
Bass:"Jigga megga nooga mooga"
Lead:"Jimmy somma lomma jomma"
Bass:"Nogga megga mooga mooga"
Lead:"Neeky momma lomma jomma gomma?"
Bass:"Jigga mooga megga mooga"
Lead:"Tooken meedy momma lomma momma"
Bass:"Mahga mooga mooga mooga"
Lead:"Moogie momma, moogie momma"
Bass:"Chuckah mooga mahga mooga"
Lead:"Somma romma jomma jomma"

After years of cryptographic and etymological[10] study, the meaning of this conversation has been unearthed. It is the obvious that the bass mooga mahga mooga mooga, while the lead, to the contrary, momma lomma jomma gomma. And quite often. If we can recall these words in times of strife, many people will feel sorry for us.

4) Paragons of Beauty

The 1950s was not only an age of innocence, it was as age of idealism. Almost always, the subjects of doo-wop songs were beautiful, desirable girls or women. They are almost always revered, idolized, put on pedestals. Rarely were they flawed, or rather, rarely were the flawed ones found in song.

There were exceptions, as in "Bony Maronie" and "Short Fat Fannie" by Larry Williams, "Long Tall Sally" by Little Richard and "Fat Fat Fat Mommio" by the

7. Groia, Phil. *They All Sang On The Corner*. Port Jefferson, N.Y.: Phillie Dee Enterprises,1983.
8. "Rubber Biscuit," Nat Epps, Charles Johnson, Shedreck Lincoln, Samuel Strain (Adam R. Levy & Father Enterprises, 1956), BMI.
9. "Shombalor," written by Elmer Sheriff and Aki Aleong, BMI.
10. This means either the study of words or the study of insects.

Chalets. Note that even these morphologically challenged ladies were revered by their respective singers. Once in a while, however, a woman with particularly noteworthy features escaped adulation. In "Bim Bam Boom" by the Eldorados, the lead (Pirkle Lee Moses in real life) describes his assignation with a siren:

> "She was a foxy little mama with great big hips,
> Pretty long hair and pretty red lips,
> Five foot two with eyes of blue,
> And knew exactly what to do..."

Poor Pirkle. Unfortunately for him, James Maddox, bass of his singing group, just happened to be watching the entire meeting as it unfolded. According to this second, unbiased view:

> "This cat is wrong, I had a ringside seat,
> She had great big ears and funny little feet,
> Six foot two, dress polka-dot blue,
> And she looked like somethin' from the Brookville Zoo..."

Also, there was the guy from the Eternals who went on a "Blind Date" (1961). He had a terrible time. Afterward he vows, "Never again will I go on a blind date, one of these days I might meet up with a monster like her." Noticing her shape, he remarks, "She don't dance, she just rolls."

And then there's the aforementioned Jimmy Ricks of the Ravens who, in "Time Takes Care Of Everything," had to buy his baby some new teeth, fix her nose and uncross her eyes. She couldn't have been much to look at before he began his crusade. If he was living with her at the time, he may have invented the term "home improvement project."

So although for the most part the women of the doo-wop era were Paragons of beauty, there were some Jesters thrown in as well.

5) A Little Help From Ones' Friends

Winning and watching over one's baby was a difficult job in the doo-wop era, sometimes requiring a team effort. Not only do some singers want the help of naturally occurring topographical features, celestial bodies, meteorological phenomena and small birds, but they want to be able to call them Mister. In "Please Mr. Sun" by Tippie & the Clovermen (1962) a whole team of experts is called in to give Tippie an edge with his honey:

> "Talk to her please Mr. Sun,
> And speak to her Mr. Robin,
> And take her under your branches, Mr. Tree,
>
> Babble to her, Mr. Brook,
> And kiss her for me, Mrs. Raindrop,
> And Mr. Moonlight, put in a word for me..."

The lead singer of the Emotions adopts a similar strategy when he has to leave his baby in "Mr. Night" in 1961:

> "While I'm gone, don't let her forget how much I love her...
> Oh Mr. Night, keep her Mr. Night,

> When you send her off to bed,
> Lay your hand upon her head,
> Soothe her gently so it seems,
> That I am there in all her dreams,

Apparently it occurs to this singer that Mr. Night may not be enough. Sensibly, he calls in Mr. Star, who should be able to coordinate with Mr. Night:

> Oh Mr. Star, twinkle Mr. Star,
> Shine so bright from up above,
> To remind her of our love,
> Look at her so tenderly,
> So she can't help but think of me,

By this time, he must be thinking he's on a roll so he calls in a few other guys to help watch over his baby while he's away (where he went is a mister-y).

> Watch her Mr. Dawning,
> Keep her warm, Mr. Sun,
> Wake her, Mr. Morning,
> To let her know that she's the only one,
>
> Oh Mr. Wind, wild Mr. Wind,
> When she's in your company,
> Kiss her softly just for me,
> On her lips, her eyes, her face,
> Til I come to take your place,
>
> Thank you Mr. Night, Mr. Star, Mr. Dawning,
> Hold her Mr. Wind, Mr. Sun, Mr. Morning...

Anthropomorphism seems to be this guy's strong suit. He enlisted all the help he could possibly get (except perhaps for "Don't let our love go down the drain, Mr. Sewer"), but at least he was polite and courteous about it. He overlooked one problem, however. What if his baby prefers the ministrations of ("wild") Mr. Wind to him? What if she tells him to blow?

6) Decisions, Decisions...

Many people think that guys had it easy during the doo-wop era. What these people don't realize is that because the Women's Movement had not yet occurred, guys were the ones who had to make all the decisions. This placed an enormous burden on the average male psyche. In 1960, Mr. Lee (backed by a group called the Cherokees) told his sad tale in "The Decision," which came out on the Winter label. The message must have struck a chord in the hearts of others similarly afflicted, for within a few short weeks the song was covered by the Enchanters on the Sharp label. Mr. Lee told us:

> "I have a decision, that I must now make...
>
> Yes darling,
> I have a decision that I must now make,
> I don't know how it will turn out,
> Or whose heart it will break,[11]

---

11. This line makes it clear that Mr. Lee is beginning to suffer.

No, you didn't know,
For you were too busy being true,
And yet all the while my darling,
I did nothing but lie to you,[12]

When I first met you dear,
I had just lost my love,
And I was hurt, alone and bewildered,[13]
And God sent you from above,

But now she has come back to me,
And with me she will always be,
And yet deep in my heart I know,
You are also a part of me,

Yes, your tender ways,
The little things that you do,
And just being your sweet, kind self,
Has made me love you too,[14]

But why should I tell you,
That our love can still be,
When I know I wasn't meant for you,
And darling, you weren't meant for me,[15]

Yes, if I were to say goodbye,
Oh, it would make you cry,
But then you would find someone new,
And fall in love the way I fell in love with you,
Now you know my darling,
The misery that I'm going through,
But, it's a decision that must be made,[16]

For I know, oh yes I know,
Darling, I can't love two [I can't have you]...[17]

These fellows were not alone in their distress. Kenny, of Kenny and the Socialites, reported a similar dilemma even as early as 1958 in "I'll Have To Decide":

"I had a girl friend,
And Audrey was her name,[18]
But now things aren't the same,
And I'll have to decide,
Which one will be my bride,[19]

I really loved her,

The best girl a guy ever had,[20]
But now I feel pretty bad,
And I'll have to decide,[21]

She couldn't go out on Saturday night,
So I went to the party alone,[22]
I tried not to look at any other girls,
But I couldn't keep my eyes off of Joan,[23]

I'm sorry, but the tears won't help me now,
I must be strong somehow,[24]
And I'll have to decide,

(Spoken recitation by the bass:)
Many hearts have been broken,
This way because of jealousy,
It can happen to anyone,
Beggar or king,
I pray it won't happen to me.[25]

As the lyrics of both of these songs portray, the men of the 1950s were up to making those tough emotional decisions. Or almost up to making them, anyway. Maybe not.

In some instances, the strain was too much. Take a look at the quandary the lead of the Four Peaks finds himself in on "Sitting On The Porch":

Sitting on the porch,
Hour after hour,
Gazing at the girls,
And looking at the flowers,[26]

But I don't know which one,
Of them I'll like the best,
I'll have to put them to a test,[27]

The girl in the red,
The flowers are blue,
Which one of them,
I choose will be true...

And later...

Heaven only knows,
Which one I like the best,
The flower or the girl,[28]

---

12. It's really amazing how honest he's capable of being.
13. The pain you felt is obvious, Mr. Lee.
14. He obviously has deep deep feelings for both women. There is much love in his heart.
15. Here is where he puts her needs (that is, those of his second woman) before his own.
16. Despite what on the surface is philandering, one can easily see through this to recognize the emotional depth of our protagonist.
17. While Mr. Lee will only admit that he 'can't love two' without telling us which one he would like to have, the Enchanters' lead knows that he 'can't have you' which implies that at least he has made 'The Decision.'
18. Perhaps the same Audrey that was regaled on the flip side of "Tell Me Why" by Norman Fox & the Rob-Roys in 1957?

19. You can tell this young man is sincere. He not only feels compelled to choose between dating two young ladies, but is committed to marrying the one he eventually chooses.
20. These lines convey the depth of his feelings for Audrey.
21. Maybe they're not so deep.
22. It's really Audrey's fault that he's in this pickle.
23. It sounds like he didn't keep his hands off her either.
24. This shows the strength of his conviction, whatever it is.
25. Considering he's a bass, this is a very emotional and empathic commentary. (We understand that he and Audrey are an item these days.)
26. So far, no problem.
27. One assumes he's choosing between two girls, right?
28. Most guys would not have much of a problem with this decision.

I have not made my test,
Tell me who to choose to rid me of my blues,
You guess the rest..."

This guy is either shell-shocked, burnt by women frequently or he's just been sitting on that porch for too long. By the way, though recorded in the late 1950s, this song wasn't released until the early 1980s. Too sensitive a topic, we suppose.

7) Babalu, Babalina

Every walk of life has its celebrities, from pin-up guys and gals to the captain of the local school's football team. One of the celebrated heroes of the doo-wop age was the female protagonist of a song called "Babalu's Wedding Day" which was written by Carlos (Charlie) Girona, William Martin, and Alex Miranda, who were the lead singer, manager and bassman respectively of a group called the Eternals. "Babalu" was the groups' second release, a worthy follow-up to "Rockin' In The Jungle," which made it to number 78 on the *Billboard* pop charts in the summer of 1959. "Babalu" was released in the fall of 1959 on the Hollywood label and never charted, but it has always been a favorite of those who are into their doo-wops. It's an uptempo rocker with a Caribbean-accented lead and a resounding bass. If you don't like this song, you probably don't like doo-wop.

Over the years, "Babalu" has attracted the attention of music analysts. Dave Marsh, in *The Heart of Rock and Soul*,[29] counts it as one of his 1,001 favorite songs of the rock 'n' roll era (number 410 to be exact). The story, according to Marsh, is that "The announcement that Babalu (apparently a household name in whatever universe this song is situated) is finally getting hitched sends an entire society into frantic activity. Some laugh. Some sigh. We learn that he met his fiancée, Hoskie Bopalena, at a Milwaukee Braves baseball game. Then, it seems, Babalu misses the ceremony because his cheapskate friend refused to lend him a dime to call for a ride. So he goes to work with a trained monkey, who steals all the cash and runs away as soon as work is over. That's it."

Dave, Dave, Dave, what do you mean "That's it?" You missed the most important part, the part about her being a professional athlete, as well as a doo-wop personality (like Arthur Lee Maye of the Crowns). Witness the lyrics:

"He met his woman at a baseball game,
Played second base with the Milwaukee Braves,
Huskie Babalina was her name,
Asked her for an autograph and made a date..."

Babalu was some operator. Not only did he cop her John Hancock, but he used it as an excuse to ask her out. Quite a coup, Babalu!

This same endearing Huskie was the answer to a trivia question in a quiz presented by *Goldmine* in the summer of 1989.[30] The question, as posed, was "In the song 'Babalu's Wedding Day,' by the Eternals. What is the name of the girl he meets at a baseball game and then marries?"[31] The question was answered correctly by almost all the entrants. The problem was that there was almost no agreement on the spelling of the poor girl's name. *Goldmine* reported no less than 85 different versions, which are listed below.

Oske Babalena	Osski Bobalena	Bopalena
Oski Babalena	Oskie Bapalina	Babalina
Oskee Babalena	Oskie Boppa Lena	Bobalina
Oski Bobolina	Osca Boop-a-Lena	Babalena
Osky Bopalina	Oskie-Bob-A-Lena	Ah-Skee Boppa-Lena
Oski Bablina	Oskipoplina	Auski Bop-A-Lina
Oskey Bobolena	Oski Bopaleena	Auskie-Boppa-Lena
Oskee Bopalena	Osca Babellina	Aussie Bop A Lena
Oski Bobalena	Oskee-Bopalena	Auhskibablina
Osky Bopalena	Oskeebobaleena	Askee Babalina
Oski Bobbalina	Osski Bobalena	Ausky Bobalena
Oskie Papa Lena	Oske Babalena	Awskie Bopaleena
Oskie Bobalena	Os-Ke-Bop-A-Lena	Oukie Bopalenie
Oskie Bobalina	Oska-Bop-A-Le-Bah	Hey Skinny Boba leena
Oski Babalina	Oschibobalina	Skinny Babalena
Oskey Bopalena	Oshkie Bobalina	Rocky Babalina
Oskie Barbalena	Husky Babalina	Moski Bop-A-Lena
Oscy Bapa-Lena	Husky Babalena	Moe-Skee-Bop-A-Leena
Oskie Bopalina	Huski Babalena	Baska Lee Baba Lene
Oscar Pop-A-Lena	Husky Bobalina	Boski Babalina
Oisky Bop-A-Lena	Husky Bop-A-Lena	Bosky Babalina
Oski Bablina	Usky Babalina	Boski Bobalena
Oske Bop A Leena	Uskey Bubalena	Boss-Kee-Bop-A-Lena
Oscie Bobbalena	Huskey Bubaleena	Bossky Bop A Lina
Osky Bopalena	Huskey Bab A Linia	Honey Bobalina
O-Ske-Bop-A-Lena	Huskiy Bopa Lena	
Oski Bopalena	Husky Babolina	
Oscie Bobba Lena	Hosky Babalina	
Oskey Bobalena	Hosky Bobalina	
Oski Baabalina	Uskey Papalina	

Since Dave Marsh, usually a cracker-jack reporter, overlooked the most significant part of the story, and *Goldmine* jumped to conclusions about the marital state of the Babalu-Babalina coalition,[32] we decided to do some actual research in the area of doo-wop historical fiction by calling a few of the principals. Ernie Sierra,[33] founder of the Eternals, reported that the group first billed itself as the Orbits and, in those first days of space exploration, imagined their pictures on the record sleeve in the shape of planets. For some

29. Marsh, Dave. *The Heart of Rock & Soul: The 1,001 Greatest Singles Ever Made.* New York: New American Library, 1989.

30. *Goldmine*, June 30, 1989.

31. Dear *Goldmine*: Can we really state that he actually married her? His intentions were good but his finances weren't. At last look, he was trying to hustle some change so he could get to the church.

32. Sort of like "Dewey Beats Truman."

33. Phone interview conducted on May 14, 1996.

Eternals.

unrecalled reason, they couldn't use that name (perhaps because there was at least one other Orbits group already in existence). Their manager's wife picked the name Eternals out of the Bible, taking it as a sign that the group would stay together forever.

Sierra recalls those days fondly. He, Charlie Girona, Freddy "Pineapple" Hodge, Arnie Torres and Alex Miranda used to play stickball and softball together in the Fort Apache area of the Bronx (around Southern Boulevard and Freeman Street). A girl, whose real name he can't recall (and who later was fictionalized as Huskie), used to hang around with the guys and play with them (softball that is). He recalls her as "a tom-boy type, pretty tough, attractive, with great shoulders and great cheeks." (Anatomical location of said cheeks unspecified.)

When Freddy Hodge was about to be married, Charlie Girona wrote a song for him. "Babalu's Wedding Day" was the result. We can assume that Freddy was fictionalized as Babalu, and the unnamed tom-boy became the professional athlete Babalina. Sierra assures us that there was no actual relationship between Freddy and Huskie. William Martin, the group's manager, reported that he added the monkey and the organ grinder that (believe it or not) appear in the lyrics "so that the song would appeal to the children."[34] This simian, though not apparently crucial to the story of the Babalina and her swain, seems to provide continuity between the group's first hit and its sequel. "Rockin' In the Jungle" offers Tar-

zan, Jane, Boy and (you guessed it) Cheetah, who is a full-fledged chimpanzee-style monkey.

We can take pride in knowing, however, that the correct spelling of the lady's name has finally been unearthed. Dave Marsh addressed her as "Hoskie Bopalena," while *Goldmine* called her Oskee Babalina and offered their readers 84 alternate spellings! Not one of these "experts" correctly spelled her entire name.[35] In a second exclusive interview with William Martin,[36] in which he read directly from the original lead sheet, the spelling of her name has finally come to light. It is "Huskie Babalina." At long last. Mr. Martin also assured us that the wedding did actually occur, as witnessed by a sequel, which he himself wrote, called "Babalu II."[37] Mr. Martin, we would all rest easier if you could produce the marriage certificate.

8) Man of the Hour

"Listen here girls,
I'm tellin' you now,
Come up and see ol' Dan,
I rock 'em, roll 'em all night long,
I'm a sixty minute man..."

So says Dan, the protagonist (and we do mean "pro") of "Sixty Minute Man," a song written by Billy Ward and Rose Marks and released by Ward's Dominoes in early 1951. The song was remarkable in several ways. It spent 30 weeks on the R&B charts, an amazing 14 of which were at #1. Both of these are milestones for a doo-wop/rhythm & blues group release. And it actually crossed over to the white pop charts, which was unheard of at the time, in spite of (rather, because of) its ribald lyrics.

Dan, an organized kind of guy, lays out his agenda:

"There'll be fifteen minutes of kissin',
Til you holler 'please don't stop,'
There'll be fifteen minutes of teasin',
Fifteen minutes of pleasin',
And fifteen minutes of blowin' my top..."

Apparently a big believer in customer satisfaction, there are no "slam-bam-thank-you-ma'ams" for this buckaroo. A legendary kind of guy, Dan's history deserved thorough research, which was indeed carried out by George Moonoogian in his "Wax Fax" column for a periodical titled *Record Collector's Monthly*.[38] George was gracious enough to allow us to quote virtually all of his article. Editorial comments that occur in the middle of quoted segments appear in brackets ([ ]).

"The turn of the century was already ripe with stories, poems and songs dealing with unfaithful lovers and clandestine liaisons, 'Frankie and Johnny' being one of the most popular. In fact, the 'back-door-man'

---

34. Phone interview conducted on May 14, 1996.

35. Nah nah nah naaaah nah.
36. Phone interview conducted on May 20, 1996.
37. Available in 1996, on CD.
38. *Record Collector's Monthly*, Issue #50, Nov./Dec. 1991.

was the plague of jealous husbands everywhere. *The New Dictionary of American Slang* defines this term as: '...A married woman's lover. Originated in Negro use, often featured in blues songs...'

My initial research uncovered a gem of vocal-group harmony from 1937 that just about said it all. It is called 'Dan, The Back Door Man' and sung by an obscure black harmony group billed as The Four Southerners. Released as Decca #7291 in their Sepia Series, it was quickly lost and forgotten, as were many fine vocal harmony items from this period. Aside from the fact the group sang exceptionally tight harmony, they also sang simulated instrument harmony on the record, making it truly unique. Today I know that just two copies of this record exist for certain.

A few years later, I was pleasantly surprised when I happened on a copy of 'Dan, The Back Door Man' by Georgia White, also a blues singer in Decca's Sepia Series of the 1930s. This record, however, carried the number 7269, which means it preceded the Four Southerners' version by 21 releases, making their version a cover!

The lyrics of this ditty are pure, subtle, double-entendre:

'Take your time, we've got all night,
Take it easy, 'cause I'm Dan, the Back Door Man,

Shake it easy, now that's right,
Can't you take it, it won't bite [chorus],

Now baby, you've got it,
Give me a chance, to gaze in your eyes,
Now baby you've caught it,
This is romance, and what a door prize!

Kiss me baby, call it square,
Someday maybe, you'll play fair [chorus]...'

Just these lyrics alone let us know that by the time the Dominoes got to it, 'Lovin' Dan, the sixty-minute back door man,' had been popular for at least two decades on wax. However, further research brought me even further back in black music in the exploits of the infamous Dan.

[Take a look at this] sheet music cover, for it is from 1921, and features a song about a Black Pullman porter. While the music and lyrics appear to be by white authors, and the song's success attributed to Eddie Cantor in blackface, there can be no doubt as to the song's origins in Black folklore. 'Dapper Dan, The Ladies Man From Dixieland' set the standard for all the Dans to follow later on:

Dapper Dan was a Pull-Man porter

On a train that ran thru Dixie
Ev'ry one knew Dapper Dan
Knew him for a ladies' man
Never cared to settle down
Had a girl in every town...

While the song goes on to mention all the girls he has in 'Alabam', Georgia, 'Caroline', Louisville, New Orleans, etc., it is the final chorus lines that strike a note with a certain 'sixty-minute Dan' some 30 years later:

'Now I ain't handsome, I ain't sweet,
But I've got a brand of lovin' that can't be beat,
I'm the ladies' man, Dapper Dan from Dixie-land...

I won't let no gal run my life,
'Cause if I lose them all, I still got my wife,
I'm the ladies' man, Dapper Dan from Dixie-land...'

Don't go away, there's more! Back in October of 1930, the great Bessie Smith sang about an unfaithful lover named—you guessed it—Dan! Her "Hustlin' Dan" (Columbia #14554-D) was just another page in the ongoing saga of Dans in black music, which finally hit its peak with the Dominoes' "Sixty-Minute Man" in 1951, and all the offshoots it produced.

However, the record find that really made me sit up and take notice was [on the] Gennett label...Released in December of 1923, "Dancing Dan" was a bit more tame than the other mentioned. What really got my attention though was the name of the group that recorded the song, the Black Dominoes! Was this a deja-vu from almost 30 years earlier? The record turns out to be a jazz band with vocal. Further research told me it was cut in New York, and that two of the band members were Harry Gluck and Miff Mole... Dan, old buddy, whether you're dancin', lovin', sixty-minuting, hustling, or back-dooring it—good luck, guy. You've brought us a hell of a lot of good musical fun!"

The above-quoted "Wax Fax" column was written in 1991, and was actually a follow-up article to several others by Mr. Moonoogian on the same subject. While it was written to update the reader on newly uncovered predecessors to "Sixty Minute Man," the story from 1951 on is covered better by his 1981 article for *It Will Stand* magazine, which was dedicated to the preservation of Beach Music.[39] This music, which is basically danceable, rhythm and blues party music[40] that has an epicenter in the Carolina beach areas, counts "Sixty Minute Man" as one of its all-time favorites. The story continues:

"As with all successful songs, it also wasn't long before the cover versions cropped up. Nathan [Syd Nathan, owner of the King/Federal record complex] had a liking for crossing R&B and Country artists and also recorded the song with the York Brothers as King #970. The C&W field proved quite viable as a version by Roberta Lee and Hardrock Gunter soon appeared on Decca. However, the original version by the Dominoes held strong, and has remained the best version to this day. Members of the original Dominoes group that created this classic recording were: Clyde McPhatter, first tenor; Charlie White, second tenor;

39. Moonoogian, George & Chris Beachley. "Lovin' Dan: A Look Thirty Years Later. Does He Have 59 To Go?" *It Will Stand*, Vol. 3, No. 20, 1981.
40. Beachley, Chris, "Beach Music: What Is It and Where Did It Come From?," *DISCoveries*, May-June 1988, p. 103.

Joe Lamont, baritone; Bill Brown, bass; and Billy Ward, pianist, composer and leader.

One of the first offshoots of the song was recorded later that year [1951] by Ric Harper for the Abbey label. His song was titled 'I'm A Sixty Minute Rocket Man' and made use of the new song craze devoted to the 'Rocket 88'automobile [an Oldsmobile, 'Rocket 88'was a huge R&B hit for Jackie Brenston, a member of Ike Turner's troupe, in 1951]. His lyrics mention several other popular R&B songs of the time [which appear in boldface below], while his double-entendre lyrics put the car image to good use:

'...Hey little girl, I'm waiting just for you,
It's no use to masquerade,
If you're lookin' for a man, that'll thrill you too,
I know I can make the grade...

...I'm a **Sixty Minute Man** in my **Rocket 88**,
Dig that **Castle Rock** tonight,
Better come along baby, before it's too late,
If you want to make things right...

...If the **Little Car Blues** has got you down,
And the taxi cabs make you wait,
Just tell me baby, when you're ready tonight,
And I swear I won't be late...'

It was generally assumed that Billy Ward composed the song, 'Sixty Minute Man,' by himself, although Rose Marks, the manager of the group, appeared as co-author on the label credits. In early 1952, another cover version of the song appeared. It was on the Citation label by a new group that called themselves the Jive-Bombers. Actually the group featured a holdover from the famous Palmer Brothers of the 1930s and '40s, Clarence Palmer, whose raspy-voiced leads were a trademark. The Jive-Bombers'1952 release was unique in that it credited William 'Pee Wee,' Tinney a member of the group, as the author of 'Sixty Minute Man.' Whether any lawsuits were ever issued is dubious since the record slipped quietly into the obscurity it still achieves today!"

The Dominoes' record clearly had enormous influence. Not only did it lionize the reputation of "Dan" in music annals, but it opened up the door for uptempo R&B tunes with off-color lyrics dealing with male virility. By crossing over to the white Pop charts, it kind of broke the ice. One of the more ingenious treatments was offered by the Swallows on King in 1952 with their song "It Ain't The Meat (It's The Motion)." In it, bassman Norris "Bunky" Mack proclaims:

"It ain't the meat, it's the motion,
That makes your daddy wanna rock,
It ain't the meat it's the motion,
It's the movement that gives it the sock..."

In effect, Bunky is saying that quality, not quantity, is what counts or it's not what you say, but how you say it, or you can't judge a book by its cover. Bunky was a deep kind of guy, R&B-wise.

Back to Mr. Moonoogian... "One of the on-going fads in the R&B and Country music fields was to 'answer 'popular hit records. 'Sixty Minute Man' was no exception and in 1952, 'I Can't Do Sixty No More,' by the Du-Droppers appeared. Its purpose was fully stated in the title... 'Lovin' Dan' just wasn't up to his game any more:

'...Yes, I love you baby, but I can't do sixty no more,
Just a short thirty minutes is all I can afford...'

The song stirred some local attention in the R&B field and was eventually even recorded by the Dominoes with David McNeil as the 'worn out' Sixty Minute Man but not released until almost three years later!"

It must be noted that "Sixty Minute Man" established another unit of measurement for male virility. Ordinarily, the benchmark for male bragging rights was expressed in inches. Hereafter, or Danafter, longevity was considered the ultimate yardstick. Thus we find the Du-Droppers rather effete hero apologizing for giving his baby the short end of the stick, so to speak. The ultimate in longevity, an all-nighter, is offered by the Majors in their 1952 song, "Come On Up To My Room":

"I've got no clock to tell me when to stop,
I've got a sign on the door so nobody will knock,
You don't have to worry, everything's okay,
We'll have a good time going 'til the break of day..."

Notice how the Majors deride Dan for going by the clock. Give him a break guys; he's probably got more than one assignation and probably hates to keep them waiting. Besides, isn't the whole idea to "make time?" Anyway, George Moonoogian continues the tale of other guys "...who would try to usurp Dan's title, and in 1952 Federal records released 'The Last of the Good Rockin' Men' by the Four Jacks. Backed by members of the Johnny Otis rhythm section, this quartet belted out a tune whose melody and theme were very familiar:

'I'm a good rockin' man you see,
Me and good rockin' can't you see,
I've got something strong and tan,
I'm the last of the good rockin' men...'

The melody itself was a carbon-copy of the Dominoes' original, complete with a bass lead and a high, floating tenor voice. The record, while good, faired poorly sales-wise and remains a coveted collector's piece today.

At this point, the 'Sixty Minute Man' fad seemed to cool off for a while. No doubt that old Dan was somewhere trying to get his act together again. While Dan was biding his time other artists slipped in and tried to squelch his fame. The first was in the form of a song by a group called the Imperials, who recorded for the Great Lakes label. Their rendition of 'Life of Ease' spelled out the situation in a tradeoff of verses between the lead tenor and the bass:

Tenor:'...Just let me alone, let me be,
At this pace you're killing me,
Baby, baby, can't you see,
I can't all night, it's too much for me,
I want a life of ease...'

Bass:'...You don't need Dapper Dan, the Sixty Minute Man,
And some of the fellas you know,
'Cause when I get you rockin' all night long,
You holler, 'Daddy, darling, don't let me go!' '

It didn't take Dan long to return, for in 1954 he burst back upon the recording scene in the form of 'Don't Stop Dan' on the King label, sung by the Checkers. This group boasted the fine bass lead of one Bill Brown, the same Bill Brown that had led the Dominoes' 'Sixty Minute Man' success three years earlier. Bill had left the Dominoes to form his own group back in 1952, and the Checkers had enjoyed some mild hits since that time. Hit or not, 'Don't Stop Dan' ranks today as a top Beach favorite...'Lovin' Dan' is right back in the old groove again on this item offering to teach his 'little baby'...'Dan's Sixty Minute Plan'...The chorus, replete with female voice interjections, begs old Dan not to stop for he's '...got 59 minutes to go!'

Well, the news was out. If 'Lovin' Dan' could wow the gals with his 'Sixty Minute Plan,' then it was only logical that someone else would devise a new method of his own. The method finally did appear in a 1955 gem by the Robins called 'Hatchet Man.' This double-entendre ditty, penned by songwriters Lieber and Stoller, left very little to the imagination as to what the new 'method' would be. It was spelled out quite clearly by bass-lead, Bobby Nunn:

'I've been swingin' so long,
They call me the Hatchet Man,
You can find me in the forest,
With my hatchet in my hand...

I've chopped my way,
From Maine to Tennessee,
You've got to learn how to chop,
If you want to get along with me...

Now if you've got sixty minutes,
Call up Lovin' Dan,
But if you want some choppin',
Call up the Hatchet Man...

Now Lovin' Dan may knock you out,
But the Hatchet Man will make you jump and shout...'

Needless to say, with lyrics like these the record received very few airplays in an R&B world now becoming more prominent with white, 'POP,' airwaves listeners. The record quickly sank into the obscurity that makes it a collector's item today.

Let's face it...if old Dan was going to survive in the oncoming mid-50s, teen-oriented recording field, he was going to have to clean up his act—King records found one way to do it. It simply avoided any mention of 'Dan, the Sixty Minute Man' in the lyrics to a Cathy Ryan tune called '24 Hours A Day.' However, writers Rudy Toombs and Henry Glover pirated the 'Sixty Minute Man' melody almost note for note![41]

Modern records and the Cadets went a step further and released the old Dominoes' classic as 'Dancin' Dan' in 1956. No more was Dan the 'Lovin' Man' but now was relegated to do his 'rockin' and rollin' all night long' on the dance floor! The 'powers that were' back then simply didn't want any young, innocent, easily influenced teen-ager reading any other meanings into Dan's actions, so 'Lovin' Dan' went the Arthur Murray Way! He was only following the earlier lead of Hank Ballard's 'Henry,' who, too, now 'danced' and contracted 'flat feet' rather than risking unwanted parenthood or social disease while 'working' with his 'Annie.'

One obscure offshoot of the 'Sixty Minute Man' craze surfaced in the late 1950s. Actually it had been recorded earlier, but remained unreleased. It is called 'Don't Knock,' and was recorded sometime in the 1954-55 period by the Spiders but was first issued on their later Imperial LP. The lyrics tell of a woman who's 'too old,' 'unfriendly, 'and who... 'ain't puttin' down nothin.' Lead Chuck Carbo goes on to demand:

'I want good, good lovin,
I'm a Sixty Minute Man,
I want a frantic babe,
Who can raise some sand...'

And so the long saga of old 'Lovin' Dan' and his offshoot-trend buddies seemed at an end. With the exception of a rather odd version released as 'Summer's Comin' On' by Bob Marley in 1960, all subsequent versions have been reworkings of the 1951 hit classic."

And so Dan has been carved in the annals of R&B history, much in the same way that Gloria was over the years. Dan could make her a happy woman. Problem is, knowing the way she was, she wouldn't give him the time of day. Or night.

9) Stormy Whether

The song "Stormy Weather" was written in 1933 by Ted Koehler (lyrics) and Harold Arlen (music) and has been recorded often since, becoming hits for, among others, Ethel Waters, Guy Lombardo and Duke Ellington in 1933, and Lena Horne in 1943. In fact, it would become the trademark song for both Ms. Waters and Ms. Horne. Little did Ted and Harold know, however, that their song would create stormy weather in the atmosphere of the doo-wop world. Many articles have been written about the song in magazines catering to the doo-wop aficionado. We've culled, quoted and editorialized these articles to present the whole story, conflicts and all. Editorial comments that occur in the middle of quotes appear in brackets ([ ]). The first leg of the story is taken up by Ralph Newman in a 1974

41. Mark Zucker, in "The Saga Of Lovin' Dan" (*Time Barrier Express*, Issue #2, October 1974, p.32) cites the song "My Baby's 3-D", written by Billy Ward and recorded by the Dominoes, which also keeps the melody of "Sixty Minute Man" but changes the subject and words.

article for *Bim Bam Boom* (Issue #13, p. 34) titled "Clear Skies At Last! The Five Sharps Revisited."

"The continuing saga of R&B's most sought-after record has taken another unique turn, and, as in the story's initial stage, a radio show was involved. Several months ago, New York's Tom Luciani was playing [on Fordham University radio station WFUV on 'The Time Capsule Show'] the *Bim Bam Boom* reissue of this legendary master and it was overheard by Robert Ward, another original 'Sharp.' [Previous information about the group had come from original member Clarence Bassett in an interview granted to Billy Vera in *Bim Bam Boom*, Issue #6, p. 33, July 1972 titled "Tracked Down and Identified: The Five Sharps." Bassett's recollections and Ward's differ on several facts, but since Bassett sang with two more successful groups after the Five Sharps, his memories might be less clearly defined than Ward's.] This was the first time Ward had heard that record in two decades and he called the station in total disbelief. Yes, Ward was informed, this was indeed the original master and he was referred to this publication for further information; a meeting was arranged and much to our surprise, he arrived with yet another original member, Tommy Duckett. Here then is the definitive Five Sharps' story:

Amazing point: As far as the singing parts on the record are concerned, all that is heard is a quartet! The group was composed of Ronald Cuffey, lead; Clarence Bassett, first tenor; Robert Ward, second tenor and Mickey Owens, bass; the fifth member, although very capable of singing, did not do so in the case of the Five Sharps and is heard playing the piano. In fact, Tom Duckett was a piano player for many of the groups indigenous to...[Jamaica, Queens in New York City such as the] (Cleftones, Rivileers, etc.); he was never a member of any of these groups but merely helped them with their work and his first actual participation as a member of any group was with the Sharps.

None of the group had made any previous recordings although all had participated in several street-corner conglomerations. Bobby Ward, a member of the Rivileers' brother group 'The Bencholeers'(they sang in the park) joined with Ronald Cuffey in the latter's garage and began dabbling in songs. Eventually, Cuffey's cousin, Mickey Owens, was invited to join, as was Tom Duckett, who would be most helpful with his musical guidance. Known as 'Mr. Music' in the housing projects was Clarence Bassett, who worked in the city [to those from the city, this means the Borough of Manhattan] and probably had more contact with the outside world than most residents of the area; the group endeavored to recruit him and succeeded.

How was the name Five Sharps selected? Says Bobby Ward: 'You sharp'—that was the slang going around at the time. We thought we were sharp—so you know where the rest is coming from...The newly formed group continued to rehearse in Cuffey's garage and such original tunes as 'Duck Butt Dottie' and 'Sleepy Cowboy' emerged from those sessions. They followed the by-now

classic pattern of singing at local school affairs and on the streets and were, somewhere in the process, heard by an independent record producer named Oscar Porter; he took an interest in the group and was soon to tell them that Jubilee would cut a record with them. A dream come true! The Five Sharps recording for the same company as the Orioles and the Ravens!

The session was held in Harlem's Sugar Hill district and was an all-day affair. Only two sides were cut: the group's original composition of 'Sleepy Cowboy' and an old standard selected by the label, 'Stormy Weather.' The only instrumentation is Tommy Duckett's distinctive piano and, to the best of the group's recollection, some conga drum playing by Johnny Hall, a member of a group called the Kings who were recording there that day also. Oscar Porter had rehearsed them furiously and made all kinds of promises; he and Jubilee were never heard from again. Additionally, as it now turns out, Porter had inserted his name as sole writer on 'Cowboy.'

The Five Sharps remember hearing their record on the radio exactly twice—once played by Dr. Jive [deejay Tommy Smalls] and once by Hal Jackson in return for a visit to the studio by the group. They never made any personal appearances and were reduced to buying a copy of the record for each of themselves since they weren't given any by the company. Bobby Ward relates that the record was selling so poorly that his local store had moved it to a special shelf away from the other records; in fact, he recalls that store, Triboro Records, telling him: 'If you guys don't take these records out of here, we're gonna throw 'em away.'(!!!!!!)

As might be expected, this experience thoroughly demoralized the group and ego forces began to come into play. Ward and Duckett were being pressured by their families to leave the business, and Bassett and Cuffey were on to bigger things; they eventually became two of the Videos whose 'Trickle Trickle' was somewhat of a hit. Cuffey subsequently died and Bassett spent the ensuing years as a member of [Shep &] the Limelites, the Flamingos and most recently, Creative Funk.

We discussed with the two Sharps some of the questions which had arisen about their mysterious group. Firstly, they do recall that William Shepherd (Shep) did sing with them for a very brief time[42]; he was at the time a member of a group called the Starlites (no recordings) and was soon to join the Heartbeats [Bassett maintains that Shep was never in the Five Sharps. It may be a matter of semantics.] Julius Brown-McMichael [who would become lead of the Paragons] did not sing with the group— he apparently wanted to but was not allowed because he did not meet their standards of singing. [Bassett has him as a member who dropped out to join the Paragons.] They speculate that he is known under the two different names because he was born an orphan and might have assumed one or both of them.

---

42. For a Heartbeat, perhaps?

Finally, the ultimate question: Did they ever see a copy of the record as a 45? 'No' they replied emphatically—it was the label's policy to test market records first as 78s and if they sold, 45 pressings might follow. The ghetto areas where R&B records were selling in the early 50s were not abounding with 45 record players, at that time a luxury, and only the more popular records were being pressed, in limited quantities, at the new speed. [Bassett remembers seeing a 45.] What happened to their personal copies of the record: They broke a long time ago, as 78s will in the company of young children. When asked whether any of their ex-girlfriends, friends or relatives might still have a copy, Robert Ward and Tommy Duckett replied, almost in unison: 'Nobody liked that record, nobody bought it. As far as we know, there were only five copies of that record bought, and they were by the Five Sharps!' Have fun collectors."

Now one woulda thunk that a record made by a group that would never record again and that sold poorly at best would be quite un-newsworthy. It would have been, except for the fact that a copy of the record showed up. What's so special about that? Well, only one copy showed up. The story is picked up by Sal Mondrone, Steve Flam and Ralph M. Newman in a story called "The End of a Legend," again for *Bim Bam Boom* in July 1972 (Issue #6, p.33).

"Among serious collectors of Rhythm & Blues records, it can be safely said that the record they would most like to own is Jubilee 5104, 'Stormy Weather' by the Five Sharps. This one disc has been the subject of countless stories and endless conjecture as to its history. It has been written about in virtually every publication in the field and a group of Brooklyn collectors went so far as to name an entire magazine after it [titled 'Stormy Weather,' a total of 10 issues between 1970 and 1976]. Over the last decade, the stories have persisted, the collectors have searched, but not a single copy of the record materialized. Until now...

...During the early '60s, Irving 'Slim' Rose was doing a weekly radio show on WBNX devoted to the spinning of rare R&B sides. In 1961, Bill Pensebini found a copy of an obscure, deep rhythm and blues version of the standard 'Stormy Weather' in Benny's Record Store on Fulton Street in Brooklyn, New York..." At this point, we are going to switch horses and let Louie Sylvani pick up the story in his "From the Square" column in the first issue of *Bim Bam Boom* from August-September of 1971 (p. 9). Notice that there are discrepancies in the accounts of what transpired.

"Bill Pensibini, a collector and regular customer [of Slim's], was back tracking one of Slim's connections, a warehouse in Jersey. Slim had already made a deal with the guy and Bill went to see what Slim had missed. The day turned out successful. Bill found about 15 assorted script Oriole records and a few copies of "I Miss You So" on red plastic. He wanted $8 for each copy, which was a little high at the time. Along with a pile of 78s was this odd record by the Five Sharps on a pink and blue Jubilee label #5104.

All the guys met down at TIMES [Times Square Records, which Slim owned] on Saturday and Bill was raving about this record by the Five Sharps. I was beginning to collect at this time and was a good customer of Slim. Bill gave Slim the record to play on the radio. Slim had the intention of reissuing it after he got everybody hungry for it. He played the flip side, 'Sleepy Little Cowboy,' and I really did not expect much with a title like that. After the introduction, I flipped. It sounded on the order of 'Ghost of a Chance' by the Solitaires. It had a high tenor background with a Five Crown's type lead. In the middle of the record, the tenor does a solo and on top of him another lead comes in. Right then and there I knew I had to have it. I didn't get the chance to hear the main side until some time later. I offered Bill $10 for the record, at that time a very high price. He told me I would have to wait until Slim played it. All you New Yorkers who remember the old Times Square Records must recall Teddy, Slim's pet raccoon. I never had anything against raccoons until that fateful day. The stupid animal sat on my future copy of 'Stormy Weather' and broke it. Bill found out about it and had an argument with Slim. Slim told him not to worry, saying he would get a replacement..."

Here, a moment to get up close and personal with Bill, again through Louie's eyes, but in a different article, this one appearing in the first issue of Time Barrier Express in September, 1974 (p. 9). "William (Billy) Pensabene [note that this is the third variation of spelling for this name], who is noted for his eccentricity, was the odd one of the group. We'd be looking for records by the Crows and he'd be coming out with 'Hey look what I found! The Marshall Brothers on Savoy.'...Billy was also the first human who ever completed the Orioles in a span of less than a year. He had things on red plastic that to this day I think I was having hallucinations...

The last thing we remember him discovering was a record called 'Stormy Weather,' it was sung by a group that none of us had ever heard of, the Five Sharps...He liked the other side better saying that the tenor reminded him of the Solitaires' 'Ghost Of A Chance.' I immediately found out about it and offered to buy it. After some arm-twisting persuasion, he sold it to me for five dollars (top price in those days) except that Slim came in and wanted to play the record on his radio show on WBNX. The following week I came down to pick up my record and there was Billy foaming from the mouth. I asked him what happened and he said that Slim cracked the record under his arm. I have my suspicions of who really cracked it; it was that dang raccoon. Slim probably figured that we might string the animal up if he told us the truth but he said don't worry, I'll get another copy..."

Back to the Mondrone, Flam and Newman article..."Slim, feeling extremely badly about having broken Bill's record, immediately announced on the air that he would pay $25 for a copy of this record. It was Slim's intention to quickly obtain a replacement copy in this fashion, but, to his surprise, he got no response! The logical thing to do, of course, was to raise the offer, which he did, but to no avail. This led to a series of events which ended in 'Stormy Weather' being on the top of Slim's want list, for an incredible $500 credit! Even more incredible was the fact that not one copy of the record turned up.

The most serious collectors began to doubt that the record ever existed, although this was not logical. A label such as Jubilee did not customarily skip release numbers, and those records which were released at the time were pressed in both 78 and 45. Released before and after 5104 were found as 45s, so where were the copies of 5104? [Recall Bobby Ward's comment on the Triboro Records store!] As far as 78s were concerned, Jubilee certainly released more than one. Where were they? No possible source was left untouched by collectors, yet the elusive record remained unfound. Slim felt that he had to exploit this situation to the fullest, and he approached Jerry Blaine, owner of Jubilee Records, for the right to release it on his own Times Square label. He was told that Jubilee had no master to give him because approximately 80 masters, including this one, were destroyed in a fire. (Jerry Blaine now maintains that these masters were actually destroyed by water damage rather than by fire.) Not to be outdone, however, they joined forces and formed a new group called 'The Five Sharps.' This group released 'Stormy Weather'/'Mammy Jammy' on Jubilee 5478, and the label copy showed the word 're-issue,' which would imply that this was indeed the original recording. Before this fraud became apparent, the record sold quite well, but word soon spread among collectors that this was not THE 'Stormy Weather.'

At this point, a rumor began to circulate that a Brooklyn collector named John Dunn had found a cracked 78 copy. As it turned out, this was not merely a rumor, for he actually found a cracked pink and blue 78 at Pioneer Music Shop on Stone Avenue in Brooklyn. John now relates that he found it among several other cracked 78s and did not consider it worth very much. So little did he think of it, in fact, that he did not take it with him immediately, but returned to purchase it several days later for 50 cents!!! He took it to a studio and had a dub cut, and filed the 78 in his collection, never to be played again. As word spread of John's find, his mailbox was practically never empty. John 'Stormy Weather' Dunn his mail would read, but he refused to play more than half of the dub for anyone, much less sell the original record, in spite of numerous offers. He did this, of course, out of the fear that someone would tape and bootleg it, and the record remained in his collection for nine years, until March 1972.

At this point, after lengthy negotiations, *Bim Bam Boom* obtained the record in the condition in which it was originally found. (The dub was obtained at the same time to be kept as a 'safety' in the event that anything should ever happen to the only original copy now known to exist.) The original record was now played for the second and last time, and this time only to create what was to become a master tape. An engineer named Ralph Berliner spent in excess of 50 hours on the technical restoration of the sound, part of which involved the splicing out of more than 190 'clicks'! At this point the record and dub lie, heavily insured, in a safety deposit box at a branch of the Chemical Bank New York Trust Company. Will the record ever be put on public display? Will it ever be played on the radio? Will the record be released to the public?"

Do bears poop in the woods? The answer to all these questions is, of course, yes, as readers of *Bim Bam Boom* found out in the next issue. Not coincidentally, it was released on the *Bim Bam Boom* label for a price of $2. If Dunn thought to dub the original and eventually techno-fix it, one might wonder why Slim Rose, generally a good businessman, didn't do the same thing. Lou Sylvani tells us (*Bim Bam Boom*, Issue #1) that he "...hung the label of 'Stormy Weather' in the window and eventually someone came along and paid $20 for the label," although as of July 1977, *Time Barrier Express* assures us that the remains of Slim's copy "are now in the hands of Relic Rack's Eddie Gries."

We're not quite done yet. In 1978, a short article appeared in *The Record Exchanger* (Issue #26, p. 21) with the title "Rarest Record Sells for $3,866." The report goes, "In our auction...we offered the world's rarest record for sale, the only known copy of 'Stormy Weather' pictured above. (Of the other two copies that have been found, one is cracked [this must be Dunn's] and the other completely destroyed [Bill's]...)

Quite a few years ago, an East Coast radio station invited listeners to come in for a free handful of 78s. This happened to be one of them. The fellow that got it didn't realize what he had. Years later, when he moved to California, the records came with him. One day he brought his records to Rowe's Rare Records in San Jose. When Gary Rowe realized what he had, he called *Record Exchanger* to discuss a sale...

The record was listed with $1,000 as a minimum bid. Interest in it was high, even with the minimum. Prior to this, the highest price paid for a record was $800 ('Can't Help Loving That Girl Of Mine' by the Hideaways). Phone inquiries came from across the country. One bidder, perhaps with the intention of being able to say he participated, offered $1,000, another tried $1,111.11, and the bids covered the full range of amounts to the highest bid of $3,866.

The record was won by two customers who, to avoid bidding against each other, joined forces on this one. Dave Hall and Gordon Wrubel are coin dealers by trade, but as record collectors they are now co-owners of the world's rarest record."

So there you have the story of "Stormy Weather," doo-wop intrigue at the highest levels. There were undervalued artists, frustrated record collectors, journalists cum businessmen (or vice versa) and the pot of gold at the end of the rainbow. Sounds like great fodder for a Hollywood movie. The dastardly raccoon could even be cast in a sympathetic light to show humanity. It might even be a "record breaking" film.

10) Annie-versary of Love

Earlier, we discussed the careers of Gloria, Dan and Babalina, for differing reasons infamous characters in the world of doo-wop and rhythm and blues. There's another pair equally infamous, both apart and together. Of course we're talking about "Annie," who is fictional, and "Henry," who is both real and fictional. George Moonoogian tells the story in an article titled "Oh, That Annie!" for the *Record Exchanger* (Issue #23, p. 20) in 1977. Editorial comments in the middle of George's article appear in brackets ([ ]).

"When a collector approached the subject of answer records, which he is almost certain to do the more involved in collecting he gets, there is one series of recordings that stands supreme. These records all have one basic theme in common, and that is that they are all about Rhythm and Blues' most famous, or infamous, little girl, Annie! Shackled with a reputation of dubious sorts, Miss Annie (last name unknown!) was the major subject of an R&B gossiping campaign via record wax that spanned many years.[43]

Miss Annie of R&B fame was the fictional brainchild of one Henry 'Hank' Ballard, newly acquired lead singer of a Detroit-based group known as the Royals [Charles Sutton, lead and tenor; Henry Booth, lead and tenor; Lawson Smith, baritone; Sonny Woods, bass; Alonzo Tucker, guitar player[44]]. Formed in early 1952, the Royals had featured the smooth, ballad voice of Charles Sutton on most recordings but, with the exception of 'Moonrise,' which sold well locally, they had not approached anything which resembled a hit. [Four songs by the Royals, "Every Beat Of My Heart," "A Love In My Heart," "Moonrise" and "Starting From Tonight" made our Top 1,000, and in 1953 they issued a beautiful rendition of "The Shrine Of St. Cecilia," several years before the more famous version by the Harptones.] The merging of Hank Ballard with the group in1953 brought about a rather abrupt change in both their style and material. Many factors could be cited here as to why this occurred, one of them most likely being their awareness that tempos and styles were experiencing a transition at this time. A look at the top R&B group hits of the past year told them so. One of the top groups at this time was the 5 Royales who recorded for Apollo. They had scored high on the R&B charts again and again with such items as 'Baby, Don't Do It,' 'Too Much Lovin',' and 'Laundromat Blues.' Their format was mostly up-tempo, blues-oriented and, frankly, suggestive or double-entendre material. It is no wonder that Hank's first lead with the Royals was on a song penned by him and the group's guitarist, Alonzo Tucker, called 'Get It,' which incorporated all of the aforementioned techniques.

In only a few short months, February of 1954 to be exact, the Royals knew their efforts had met with success. The release of 'Work With Me Annie' was to begin a Rhythm and Blues legend that has yet to be matched.[45] Miss Annie took the R&B field by storm, so much so that DJs refused to air the record on some stations because of the content of the lyrics. Despite this, the record sold very well and remained on the charts for most of the year. Only one thing now needed to be done. A new style and new material warranted a new group name. This, and the fact that Federal-King had just placed the 5 Royals under contract, sped their decision. But what should they be called? Certainly the name Royals suggested a smooth, ballad-oriented group, but what name fit a partying, risqué, blues-belting quintet? And so, the Midnighters were born!"

Pete Grendysa, in a "Sneakin' Back" column for *Big Town Review* (Issue #3, p. 48, July-August 1972) tells the ironic story of the "Royal" name. In early 1953, the Royals went on a tour impersonating the 5 Royales, who were riding high at the time. A lawsuit was filed, an injunction was slapped (we're told that's what you do with an injunction) and someone "ceased and desisted." While the lawyers worked it out, the Royals released "Work With Me Annie" in February of 1954, which became an enormous smash. Now the Royals didn't want to be associated with the 5 Royales, the group they had tried to impersonate, and changed their name to the Midnighters. From idols to riff raff in one year. Further, the 5 Royales then joined the Royals/Midnighters on the King/Federal label complex after having contract disputes with Apollo. And when a group from Detroit began to use the newly available "Royals" moniker, King/Federal forced the group to transmogrify into the "Royal Jokers."

"Federal records knew they had a good thing going, and subsequent releases by the Midnighters proved this point. They were true to their new-found format and pursued poor Annie's questionable lifestyle with their next two theme-oriented releases, 'Give It Up' and 'Sexy

---

43. In an interview given to Drew Williamson (*Record Collector's Monthly*, Issue #36, p. 1, Dec. 1986-Jan. 1987), Hank Ballard said that he chose the name for commercial purposes, but that there was a real Annie who was an old girlfriend of his from Kentucky. In another interview, granted to Bob Belniak (*Echoes Of The Past*, Issue #2, Winter 1987, p.8), Hank claimed that, "Her name was Dorothy Butler and she was from Chicago. I saw her just a couple of months ago. I was picking weeds in front of my house, man, and she pulled up in a car and got out and said hello. I almost flipped. We talked for quite awhile and laughed about the old times. We are still friends."

44. For more information, consult Goldberg, Marvin, "The Midnighters," *Big Town Review*, Issue #3, p. 46, July-August 1972.

45. In an interview granted to Lynn McCutcheon, Sonny Woods maintained that "Work With Me Annie" was thrown together by the group on a train trip to Cincinatti for a recording session. "The group needed some material for the session and hastily threw this song together." McCutcheon, Lynn. "Interview: Sonny Woods." *Record Exchanger*, Issue #4, Aug-Sep. 1970, p. 20.

Ways,' the latter setting the stage for their first true answer to Annie's problem. [Both "Work With Me Annie" and "Sexy Ways" are on our Top1,000 list.] 'Annie Had A Baby' left nothing to the imagination. By now everyone had heard of her various affairs, including the radio DJs who absolutely refused to air the record. In fact, Federal records reissued the opposite side 'She's The One' a few months later, coupled with an overdubbed version of 'Moonrise' just to have this cut aired!

Now the door was opened! Answer records flew out on the market as fast as the rival companies could press them. Annie was scorned, defended, idolized, praised, accused and confused in an awesome array of songs. Hazel McCollum [backed by the El Dorados] took Annie's part to answer back that it was all a lie ["Annie's Answer"]. The Midnights, borrowing on a now famous name, stated that Annie had created a major hoax, or humbug ["Annie Pulled A Humbug"]. Linda Hayes even went so far as to offer her services to Annie's lover, while assuring everyone that her name wasn't Annie ["My Name Ain't Annie"]. The Midnighters themselves had their own answer-to-the-answer in 'Annie's Aunt Fannie,' which told of an omnipresent relative who inadvertently postponed most of Annie's social activities. Of all the answers, one of the rarest was done by Danny Taylor on the Bruce label. Danny wasn't shy and he stated emphatically that 'I'm The Father Of Annie's Baby!'

One of the major rumors that filtered around at this time was that the Midnighters had cut a demo-record with the eye-catching title of 'Annie Had A Miscarriage,' a subject not yet released from the mid-50's taboos. Whether this item ever existed or not is still speculation, but the rumor has it that, despite its monetary possibilities, it was too much for even the Federal record executives, and they miscarried it before it had a chance. [This is not surprising in an era when television shows such as "I Love Lucy" could not use the word "pregnant."]

Throughout the remainder of the 50's, records related to Miss Annie continued to appear. However, another chapter was unfolding in this R&B soap opera roughly about the same time. Modern records had released a record by Etta James called 'The Wallflower.' It was later issued under the title of 'Roll (or Dance) With Me Henry,' which comprised its major lyrics. There could be only one Henry that anyone could be talking about at this time, and he sang lead for the Midnighters! Etta even released a similar item called 'Hey, Henry!,' and a new fad was born!

Not to be outdone, the Midnighters told of the painful problem their lead singer had. Thus, 'Henry's Got Flat Feet' kept the answer craze alive. Later efforts such as Young Jesse's 'Here Comes Henry' and the unavoidable 'Annie Met Henry,' done by both the Champions and Cadets [the only group to explore both Dan and Annie], only served to reinforce this tradition. [Just as happened with the "Dan" series, where Dan gave up sex for dancing in the mid-1950s, Henry met the same fate. As the intended audience for the music changed from blacks to innocent white teen-agers, the lyrics had to be cleaned up. Not that white kids wouldn't have drooled over these songs, but deejays wouldn't play tunes with lascivious lyrics for fear of censure by sponsors.[46] Without airplay, few would sell, few were made, and Henry and Dan had to give up romancin' for dancin'.']

Although the major Annie craze died down completely about two years later, related recordings periodically turn up. Little Junior Parker's 'Annie Get Your Yo-Yo' and Little Richard's 'Annie's Back' served to remind us that the young lady is still alive and well. For all the commotion that she caused, Annie and her friends stand out as a very unique chapter in the history of Rhythm and Blues."

Although answer records have come and gone over the years, Annie and Henry had the longest run and were certainly the most titillating. In an era in which kids memorized the page numbers of the good parts of "Peyton Place" and "Lady Chatterley's Lover," and records like "Honey Love" and "Such A Night" by the Drifters were considered obscene, one can only imagine how many teen-agers giggled and raised their eyebrows upon hearing Annie's predicament. Heady stuff, in the 1950s.

11) POW-OOD: A Backward Glance At Our Music

There must be an anatomical location within the human brain devoted[47] to "oldies." The importance of this intercranial site varies with the person, like intelligence level does, but it's there in all of us nonetheless. In some, it is a prominent area (near the lateral hippopotamus) and helps us to see the world through oldies-colored glasses. In others, it is a scrawny and shriveled patch that relegates those afflicted, to living life in a forward-thinking manner. It's not conjecture any longer, it's plain fact.

While actual proof will have to await pathological analyses pursuant to autopsies of rabid doo-wop and rhythm and blues fanatics, there is plenty of indirect evidence. How else can one explain the fact that so many songs, sung by so many groups and individuals, have been devoted to looking back at our music. Why else, when the doo-wop era ended around 1964, would lovers put out retrospective songs before this end? Thus, in 1961, spake Little Caesar and the Romans, giving us a retro-anthem with "Those Oldies But Goodies." And Nino and the Ebb Tides, also in 1961 with "Juke Box Saturday Night," were waxing nostalgic about the music roughly two years before it actually went away. How can this behavior be explained by anything else but destiny governed by brain chemistry?

In a serious vein, these songs actually helped to fuel the birth of neo-doo-wop. Along with the "Oldies

---

46. A good treatment of records banned in the 1950s can be found in Grendysa, Pete, "Sneakin' Back," *Bim Bam Boom*, Issue #11, p. 41, 1973.

47. Perhaps "dedicated" would be a better choice of words.

But Goodies" series of albums on the Original Sound label, they played an important part in reminding young people of the songs they danced to several years previously, and whetted the appetites of a new group of teens for some really good music.

Over the years, "oldies" have been regaled in different ways. Sometimes songs with their original melodies have been woven together to become part of one song, while at other times the names of songs, groups or individual performers are just mentioned in the lyrics. Much of the time the emphasis is on the group sound, but there are songs that celebrate the broader field of rock 'n' roll as well.[48]

Some songs even concentrate on dead performers, to the exclusion of live ones. For example, Johnny Cymbal, the man who gave us "Mr. Bassman," remembered the Big Bopper, Eddie Cochran, Buddy Holly and Richie Valens, in a ditty called "Teenage Heaven" (1963 on Kapp 524). This is much in the same vein as Rick Nelson's "Garden Party" (1972 on Decca 75391) and "Rock And Roll Heaven" by the Righteous Brothers (1974 on Haven 7002). In "Very Precious Oldies" by the Five Satins (1973 on Kirshner 4251) "Clyde, Frankie and Sam" (McPhatter, Lymon and Cooke, respectively) are mentioned, along with "Dinah and John" (Washington and Lennon, we suppose). Unfortunately, or fortunately, there are no dead groups,[49] so that these songs are of limited interest to us.

Actually, the first of the "retro" songs, "Those Oldies But Goodies (Remind Me Of You)" by Little Caesar and the Romans (March, 1961 on Del Fi 4158), contains no references to any other songs or performers, individual or group, living or dead. It's just a plaintive rockaballad that strongly makes the point that true love cannot exist in this world without our music. It says, ever so subtly of course, that those who ignore the history of doo-wop are destined to long for it. They came right back with "Memories Of Those Oldies But Goodies" in August of 1961 (Del Fi 4166) which interwove snippets[50] of "Stranded In The Jungle" (Jayhawks/Cadets) done as a ballad (!), "A Thousand Miles Away" (Heartbeats), "Oh What A Night" (Dells), "Story Untold" (Nutmegs), "Heaven And Paradise" (Don Julian and the Meadowlarks), "White Cliffs Of Dover" (take your pick), "Glory Of Love" (Velvetones/Five Keys), "Donna" (Richie Valens), "Love You So" (Ron Holden and the Thunderbirds) and, of course, the Holy Trinity of doo-wops "In The Still Of The Night," "Earth Angel" and "Tonight, Tonight." They even threw in their own hit, "Those Oldies But Goodies." Nice work boys.

Nino and the Ebb Tides were runners-up in the category of "King of the Retro Groups." Their "Juke Box Saturday Night," in 1961 on Madison 166, was one of the first to contain imitations of original doo-wops, namely "Book Of Love" and "Get A Job." Nino and the boys also covered the Romans' "Oldies But Goodies" hit, and did fairly well with it on the East Coast. Also in 1961, came "Those Oldies But Goodies Are Dedicated To You" by Sonny Knight[51] & group (on Original Sound[52] 18) which featured songs by Little Anthony and the Imperials ("Tears On My Pillow" and "Two People In The World"), the Flamingos ("Lovers Never Say Goodbye"), the Harptones ("My Memories Of You") and the Skyliners ("Since I Don't Have You").

In 1962, the Lydells, who had a hit with "Wizard Of Love" on Master 251 in 1961, entered the fray with "Book Of Songs" in 1962 (SCA 18001). The group does a take-off on the Monotones' "Book Of Love" and refers to "Blue Moon" (Marcels), "Bristol Stomp" (Dovells), "Duke Of Earl" (Gene Chandler backed by the Dukays), "Mope-Itty Mope" (Boss-Tones), "A Little Bit Of Soap" (Jarmels), "Don't Pity Me" (Dion and the Belmonts), and a bevy of girl groups singing "Mr. Lee" (Bobbettes), "I Met Him On A Sunday" (Shirelles) and "Cry Baby Cry" (Angels).

The year 1963 produced at least three more good entries. Anthony and the Sophomores (Mercury 72103) gave us the bouncy "Play Those Oldies, Mr. Dee Jay," which featured "Tears On My Pillow" and the Holy Trinity. The Penguins produced "Memories Of El Monte,"[53] also on the Original Sound label (#27), which paid kudos to "You Cheated" (Shields), "A Thousand Miles Away" (Heartbeats), "The Letter" (Vernon Green and the Medallions), "Night Owl" (Tony Allen and the Champs), as well as "In The Still Of The Night" and "Earth Angel." Less well-known, but equally retro, was "Our Songs Of Love" by the Love Notes (Wilshire 200) who revisited "You Cheated" (Shields), "Little Star" (Elegants), "This I Swear" (Skyliners), "A Thousand Miles Away" (Heartbeats) and even "Those Oldies But Goodies" (guess who?).

The Bagdads gave us a nugget in 1968 with "Bring Back Those Doo-Wopps" (Double Shot 133) which celebrated "One Summer Night" (Danleers), "Over The Mountain" (Robert and Johnny), "Goodnight, Sweetheart, Goodnight" (Spaniels) and, of course, "In The Still Of The Night" and "Earth Angel." In 1972, the Five Discs added "Rock And Roll Revival" (Laurie 3601) which featured groups like the Angels, Mello-Kings, Dovells, Monotones and Crests, as well as single artist types like Sam Cooke, Buddy Holly and Bobby Freeman. The aforementioned "Very Precious Oldies" by the

---

48. We are not the first to write about "retro" songs. We recognize: Abend, Richard F. "Memories of Those Oldies but Goodies." *Story Untold*, Issue #2, March-April 1978, p. 18.

49. There are groups that have no members who are still living, but we're not sure if this equates to a dead group.

50. Please forgive the technical language.

51. Sonny Knight had a hit with "Confidential," which is in doo-wop style, but is without a group. It's kind of a "uni-wop."

52. This is the label that first issued "Oldies But Goodies" albums in 1959.

53. This song refers to the El Monte Legion Stadium outside Los Angeles where rock 'n' roll shows were held regularly in the 1950s.

Five Satins (1973), listed "Devil Or Angel" (Clovers), "Only You" (Platters), "Little Girl Of Mine" (Cleftones), "Get A Job" (Silhouettes), as well as their own "In The Still..." and assorted single artists (living and dead).

These same Five Satins tried again with "Memories Of Days Gone By" (1982 on Electra) which included "Sixteen Candles" (Crests), "Only You" (Platters), "A Thousand Miles Away" (Heartbeats), "Tears On My Pillow" (Little Anthony and the Imperials), "Since I Don't Have You" (Skyliners), "Earth Angel" and "In The Still..." The Satins also mentioned deejays Alan Freed, Bruce Morrow and Don K. Reed. Then a group called the Toreadors put out a retro-record with the title "Do You Remember" on both sides. One side celebrated slow songs, i.e. "Story Untold" (Nutmegs), "Most of All" and "Sincerely" (Moonglows), "You Send Me" (Sam Cooke), "You Cheated" (Shields), "A Thousand Miles Away" (Heartbeats), "Glory Of Love" (Five Keys), "Earth Angel" (Penguins), "Cherry Pie" (Marvin & Johnny) and "Goodnight My Love" (Jesse Belvin). The flip commemorated the jumps "Church Bells May Ring" (Willows), "Gee" (Crows), "I'm Not A Juvenile Delinquent" (Teenagers)[54], "Rama Lama Ding Dong" (Edsels), "Blue Moon" (Marcels), "Little Girl Of Mine" (Cleftones) and "Now You Know" (Channels).[55]

With the formula already old, the Belmonts found a way to make it fresh again, with their "Streetcorner Symphony," issued in 1972 on their "Cigars, Acappella, Candy album. They start off with the words to "Sunday

Kind Of Love," namely "I'm through with my new love, I loved her through and through, I'm searching for a new love, can that new love be you..." and then launch into a series of eleven songs, identifiable only by their non-sense syllable hooks. They are "Sincerely" (Moonglows), "In The Still..." (Five Satins), "Darling Lorraine" (Knockouts), "Please Say You Want Me" (Schoolboys), "Come Softly To Me" (Fleetwoods), "Come Go With Me" (Del Vikings), "You Baby You" (Cleftones), "I Wonder Why" (Dion and the Belmonts), "Gee" (Crows), "You Belong To Me" (Duprees), "Teenager In Love" (Dion and the Belmonts), and "Little Girl Of Mine" (Cleftones). They then trail off with "Little Darling" done more in the style of the Diamonds (with the talking bass) than the Gladiolas. An entirely loveable, hummable, memorable effort. Finally, in 1991, the Del Vikings helped us reminisce with "Rock and Roll Remembered" (BVM 002).

Our list is not a complete one, but it does contain most of the better ones.[56] Hints of past musical glory can be found often in post-era group harmony efforts, as if to fulfill a biological destiny. Even Kenny Vance and the Planetones, in "Looking For An Echo" (itself a tale of nostalgia), recounted, "We'd sing songs by the Moonglows, the Harptones and the Dells..." The real truth is that many of us really loved that music, and we wish we could have it back again. Sincerely.

---

54. A rather strange choice!
55. Ditto.

56. A list of "tribute" records that partially overlaps ours can be found in Stidom, Larry. "Record Report." *Echoes of the Past*, Issue # 23, Spring 1993, p. 20.

Chapter 22

The Best 1,000 Doo-Wop Songs

In Doo-Wop: The Forgotten Third of Rock 'n' Roll, released in 1992, a "Best 500" was presented. The selection was obviously a subjective process, but we would bet that most of those songs would be chosen by most people if they were given a similar task. In a way, those 500 could be seen as a "primer" for the doo-wop era, representing the most popular and most widely known doo-wop groups and songs.

In the time since we researched that first book, we've had the chance to learn more about the music. What we've learned, for example, that doo-wop began before we originally thought it had and that much of the "good stuff" never got a lot of air play, has been a prime motivation in writing the current book. What's relevant here, though, is that the old "Best 500" was nowhere nearly adequate to describe the way we now see the doo-wop era.

For example, the "Best 500" omits most of the good paleo-doo-wop songs from the late 1940s through the early 1950s. It omits cardinal records by obscure (to many) groups like the Four Pharaohs, Orchids, and King Krooners. It omits songs by well respected but rhythm and bluesy groups like the Checkers, Cardinals, and "5" Royales. It omits songs such as "Please Remember My Heart," "Blue Valentine," and "Wonder Why" by the Solitaires, which go "deeper" into this group's repertoire than do the more popular "Walking Along" and "The Angels Sang." All of these situations are corrected to a large extent with our "Best 1,000." (The way we're going, we may end up with a "Best 2,000" shortly after the year 2000.)

The toughest decisions revolved around the degree to which the early groups would be included. Our criterion was the extent to which their songs displayed some characteristics of doo-wop. Thus the Ravens, Orioles, and Dominos are included, but the Mills Brothers and Ink Spots were not, although they were precursors of the doo-wop genre. With the exception of the Ravens and Orioles, no other groups from before 1950 appear. While groups like the Cabineers, Striders, and Bachelors offered some doo-wop characteristics in their songs in the late 1940s, we arbitrarily decided to relegate these recordings to a pre-doo-wop category. We had to make a cut-off somewhere. These marginal groups and songs are discussed in the chapter on Evolution, and a list of recommended recordings can be found in the Appendix.

While not everyone, especially not every "purist," will agree with the set of selected songs, it is hoped that most will abide it. The original 500 songs are almost identical to those appearing in Doo-wop: The Forgotten Third...[1] By adding the new 500, the reader can compare the more with the less popular, the more with the less well-known. There is not an implication that the first 500 were of better quality than the second 500. If any inference can be drawn at all, it is that the second 500 songs were much less accessible to teens of the doo-wop era and thus achieved less popularity.

A comparison of the first "Best 500" with the second "Best 500" is presented in the figure below:

The black rectangles represent the original Top 500, and the gray ones represent the 500 songs that were added to make a "Top 1,000." On average, the gray rectangles are more to the left on the chart, and imply that the second 500 are, on average, earlier recordings. The average of the release years for the first 500 is 1958.212 versus 1956.198 for the second 500. Thus, songs from the second 500 are, on average, more than two years older than those from the first 500. The mean release date for songs for the entire Top 1,000 is 1957.205.

In terms of other variables, the first 500 has more of the Girl Group Sound and more of the White Group Sound than the second 500. The figures are given in the table below. Overall, these statistics define the second 500 as earlier, blacker and more male than the first.

1. There is one exception. "I Laughed" by the Highlands was dropped because we learned that it existed only as a demo (i.e., has never been released). It was replaced by "Dear I Swear" by the Plants. The authors apologize to those collectors trying to find all 500 songs on the original list.

First "Best 500"	Second "Best 500"	Top 1,000
All-Female group 17 (3.4%)	9 (1.8%)	26 (2.6%)
Female lead 23 (4.6%)	17 (3.4%)	40 (4.0%)
Total GGS 40 (8.0%)	26 (5.2%)	66 (6.6%)
White Group Sound 104 (20.8%)	47 (9.4%)	151 (15.1%)

It is hoped that our learning process can result in learning by others through exposure to this "doo-wop in depth." For those readers not familiar with the early works of groups like the Five Keys, Flamingos and Moonglows, you really have something wonderful to look forward to. Perhaps the list can function as a "need list."

Please note that songs that were recorded during the doo-wop era but unreleased until later (after 1965) are not included in our list. Neither are songs that were recorded after the doo-wop era. Separate lists for these songs appear in another part of this book as recommended listening.

This list is for the personal use and pleasure of authorized readers only. It may not be copied, distributed for profit or taken in vain; if you choose, however, it may be memorized at your own risk.

Key

(N) after a song title means that it is "New," that is, from the second 500 songs. The absence of the parenthetic N means that the selection is from the original Best 500, published in 1992.

C= Classical Doo-Wop EraN= Neo-Doo-Wop EraP= Paleo-Woo-Wop Era

S= Slow TempoM= Medium TempoF= Fast Tempo

D= Distaff Doo-WopI= Italo-Doo-WopG= Gang Doo-Wop

SB= Schoolboy Doo-WopPOP= Pop Doo-WopNOV= Novelty Song

TPA= Tin Pan Alley Doo-Wop

Pricing

In parentheses after each listing is a dollar value. This reflects the current (Year 2000) market value for a near mint copy of the original black-vinyl pressing on the listed label. "Near mint" means "it looks as if you went to a record store yesterday and bought it brand new." Some of the below records have never been seen in near-mint condition by today's collectors! To determine the value for a used copy, reduce the values by at least half, and for a well-used copy, reduce it by 75 percent or more. Colored (usually red) wax versions of the below records often exist; those command a premium over the black vinyl pressings in almost all cases.

Also, the values reflect the cost of a 45 rpm version of the record. If a record was only issued on 78, that value is listed with an asterisk (*) after the price. In general, for records issued before 1955, the value of a 78 will be less than that of a 45; if issued in 1955, it'll be about the same; and if issued after 1955, the 78 will be worth more than the 45. Several of the listings below only appeared as album tracks; the number and value listed is for the LP.

Because of the rarity of many of the below originals, some have been counterfeited or reproduced. The prime time for this was the 1970s, but "repros," as they are called, are still being sold today. If in doubt about a rare record that seems too good to be true, consult an expert before plunking down hundreds or thousands of dollars.

The pricing comes from Goldmine book editor and research director Tim Neely, who has put together the Standard Catalog Of American Records and the Goldmine Price Guide To 45 RPM Records, among other price guides.

Academics

Something Cool (N)	C	F	I	1958	Elmont 1001/1002 ($60)

Ad Libs

The Boy From New York City	N	F		1965	Blue Cat 102 ($15)

Adelphis

Kathleen (N)	C	F	I	1958	Rim 2020 ($100)

Admirations

The Bells Of Rosa Rita	C	S		1959	Mercury 71521 ($40)

Alaimo, Chuck (Chuck Alaimo Quartet)

How I Love You	C	S		1957	MGM 12508 ($15)

Alley Cats

Puddin' 'n Tain (N)	N	F		1962	Philles 108 ($25)

Ambassadors

Darling I'm Sorry (N)	P	S		1954	Timely 1001 ($400)

Angels (A)

Wedding Bells (Are Ringing In My Ears)	P	S		1954	Grand 115 ($400)

Angels (B) (female)

Til	N	S	D/TPA	1961	Caprice 107 ($20)
My Boyfriend's Back	N	F	D	1963	Smash 1834 ($16)

Angels (C) (Gabriel & the)

Zing Went The Strings Of My Heart	N	F		1961	Amy 823 ($40)

Aquatones

You	C	S	D	1958	Fargo 1001 ($25)

Arrogants

Mirror Mirror (N)	N	F	I	1963	Lute 6226 ($30)

Astros (Pepe & the)

Judy My Love (Judy Mi Amor)	N	F		1961	Swami 553/554 ($50)

Audios (Cell Foster & the)

I Prayed For You (N)	C	S		1956	Ultra 105 ($400)

Avalons

My Heart's Desire (N)	C	S		1958	Unart 2007 ($120)

Avons

Our Love Will Never End (N)	C	F		1956	Hull 717 ($200)
Baby	C	S		1957	Hull 722 ($150)

Bachelors (Dean Barlow & the)

Baby (N)	C	F		1955	Earl 102 ($1,000)

Baltineers

Moments Like This	P	S		1956	Teenage 1000 ($300)
Tears In My Eyes (N)	C	S		1956	Teenage 1002 ($300)

Bel-Larks

A Million And One Dreams	N	S		1963	Ransom 5001 ($500)

Bell Notes

I've Had It	C	F	I	1959	Time 1004 ($30)

Belmonts

Diddle De-Dum	N	F	I	1962	Sabina 507 ($20)

Belmonts (Dion & the)

No One Knows	C	S	I	1958	Laurie 3015 ($50)
Don't Pity Me	C	S	I	1958	Laurie 3021 ($25)
I Wonder Why	C	F	I	1958	Laurie 3013 ($60)
A Teenager In Love	C	F	I	1959	Laurie 3027 ($25)
Where Or When	C	S	I	1960	Laurie 3044 ($25)

Belvin, Jesse (& group)

Goodnight My Love	C	S		1956	Modern 1005 ($40)

Bing Bongs (Dicky Dell & the)

Ding-A-Ling					
A-Ling Ding Dong (N)	C	F		1958	Dragon 10205 ($150)

Bishops

The Wedding (N)	N	S		1961	Bridges 1105 ($150)

Blenders

The Masquerade Is Over (N)	P	S		1950	Decca 27403 ($400)
I'd Be A Fool Again (N)	P	S		1952	Decca 28092 ($300)

Blue Belles (Patti LaBelle & the)

You'll Never Walk Alone	N	S	D	1963	Nicetown 5020 ($15)/Parkway 896 (63) ($12)

Blue Jays

Let's Make Love	N	S		1961	Milestone 2010 ($20)
Lover's Island	N	S		1961	Milestone 2008 ($40)

Blue Jeans (Bob B. Soxx & the)

Why Do Lovers Break Each Other's Hearts	N	F	D/TPA	1963	Philles 110 ($20)

Blue Notes

If You Love Me	N	S		1956	Josie 800 ($200)/Port 70021 (61) ($60)
My Hero	N	S		1960	Val-Ue 213 ($80)/Red Top 135 (63) ($30)
Blue Star	N	S		1961	20th Century 1213 ($15)

Bobbettes

Mr. Lee	C	F	D	1957	Atlantic 1144 ($25)

Bonnevilles

Zu Zu	C	S		1960	Munich 103 ($300)/Barry 104 (62) ($50)
Lorraine	C	S		1960	Munich 103 ($300)/Barry 104 (62) ($50)

Bonnie Sisters

Cry Baby (N)	C	F	D	1956	Rainbow 328 ($20)

Bop Chords

I Really Love You	C	F	G	1957	Holiday 2603 ($200)
Castle In The Sky	C	F	G	1957	Holiday 2601 ($200)
When I Woke Up This Morning	C	F	G	1957	Holiday 2603 ($200)
So Why	C	S	G	1957	Holiday 2608 ($300)
My Darling To You (N)	C	S	G	1957	Holiday 2601 ($200)

Bosstones

Mope-Itty Mope	N	F	NOV	1959	Boss 401 ($100)/V-Tone 208 (60) ($60)

Buccaneers

Dear Ruth (N)	P	S		1953	Southern 101 ($4,000)/Rainbow 211 (53) ($800)

C-Notes (aka C-Tones)

On Your Mark	C	F		1957	Everlast 5005 ($50)

Cabineers

Each Time (N)	P	S		1951	Prestige 904 ($200)

Cadets

Stranded In The Jungle (N)	C	F	NOV	1956	Modern 994 ($40)
Fools Rush In (N)	C	F		1956	Modern 1006 ($40)

Cadillacs

Gloria	P	S		1954	Josie 765 ($700)
I Wonder Why (N)	P	S		1954	Josie 765 ($700)
Wishing Well (N)	P	S		1954	Josie 769 ($500)
Down The Road	P	F		1955	Josie 778 ($200)
Speedoo	P	F		1955	Josie 785 ($60)
Sympathy (N)	P	S		1955	Josie 773 ($100)
You Are	P	S		1956	Josie 792 ($50)
The Girl I Love (N)	P	F		1956	Josie 805 ($100)
Zoom	P	F		1956	Josie 792 ($50)
My Girl Friend	P	F		1957	Josie 820 ($50)

Calvanes

Don't Take Your Love From Me (N)	C	S		1955	Dootone 371 ($200)

Camelots (aka Cupids/aka Harps)

Don't Leave Me Baby	C	S		1964	Crimson 1001 ($30)

Candles (Rochelle & the)

Once Upon A Time	N	S		1960	Swingin' 623 ($20)
Each Night (N)	N	S		1962	Challenge 9158 ($40)

Cap-Tans

With All My Love (N)	P	S		1950	Dot 15114 ($100)
I'm So Crazy For Love (N)	P	S		1950	Dot 15114 ($100)

Capistranos (John Littleton &)

Now Darling (N)	C	S		1958	Duke 179 ($80)

Capris (A)

God Only Knows (N)	P	S		1954	Gotham 7304 ($600)/ 20th Century 7304 (57) ($20)
It Was Moonglow (N)	P	S		1954	Gotham 7306 ($200)

Capris (B)

There's A Moon Out Tonight	N	S	I	1958	Planet 1010/1011 ($1,200)/Old Town 1094 ($30)
Where I Fell In Love (N)	N	S	I	1961	Old Town 1099 ($30)

Carollons (Lonnie & the)

Chapel Of Tears	N	S		1960	Mohawk 108 ($150)/Streetcorner 101 (73) ($5)

Cardinals

Shouldn't I Know (N)	P	S		1951	Atlantic 938 ($100*)
Wheel Of Fortune (N)	P	S		1952	Atlantic 952 ($600)
You Are My Only Love (N)	P	S		1953	Atlantic 995 ($400)
Under A Blanket Of Blue (N)	P	S		1954	Atlantic 1025 ($200)
The Door Is Still Open (N)	P	S		1955	Atlantic 1054 ($80)
Off Shore (N)	P	S		1956	Atlantic 1090 ($50)

Carnations (aka Startones)

Long Tall Girl	C	F		1961	Lescay 3002 ($100)

Carousels

You Can Come (If You Want To)	N	S	D	1961	Gone 5118 ($50)

Caslons

Anniversary Of Love	N	F	I	1961	Seeco 6078 ($20)

Castelles

My Girl Awaits Me	P	S		1953	Grand 101 ($2,000)
Over A Cup Of Coffee	P	S		1954	Grand 109 ($2,000)
This Silver Ring (N)	P	S		1954	Grand 103 ($2,000)
Do You Remember	P	S		1954	Grand 105 ($1,500)
Heavenly Father (N)	P	S		1955	Grand 122 ($7,000)

Castells

So This Is Love	N	S	POP	1962	Era 3073 ($20)

Castro, Vince (with the Tonettes)

Bong Bong (I Love You Madly)	C	F		1958	Doe 102 ($40)/Apt 25007 (58) ($12)

Castroes

Dearest Darling	C	S		1959	Grand 2002 ($150)

Cavaliers

Dance Dance Dance	C	F		1958	Apt 25004 ($40)
The Magic Age Of Sixteen	N	S		1963	Music World 101 ($30)

Cellos

You Took My Love (N)	C	S		1957	Apollo 510 ($80)
Rang Tang Ding Dong (I Am The Japanese Sandman)	N	F	G	1957	Apollo 510 ($80)

Chalets

Fat Fat Fat Mommio	C	F		1961	Tru-Lite 1001 ($50)/Dart 1026 (61) ($25)/ Musicnote 1001 ($20)

Chandeliers (aka Chandeliers Quintet)

Blueberry Sweet	C	F		1958	Angle Tone 521 ($200)
Chandler, Gene (with the Dukays)					
Duke Of Earl	N	M		1961	Vee Jay 416 ($25)

Channels (Earl Lewis & the)

Now You Know (I Love You So) (N)	C	S	G	1956	Whirlin' Disc 100 ($250)/Port 70014 (59) ($25)
The Closer You Are	C	S	G	1956	Whirlin' Disc 100 ($250)/Port 70014 (59) ($25)
I Really Love You So (N)	C	S	G	1956	Whirlin' Disc 107 ($200)/Port 70023 (60) ($25)
The Gleam In Your Eyes	C	S	G	1956	Whirlin' Disc 102 ($200)/Port 70017 (60) ($25)
That's My Desire	C	S	G	1957	Gone 5012 ($60)
Bye Bye Baby	C	F	G	1957	Fury 1021 ($50)/Fury 1071 (58) ($40)
My Love Will Never Die	C	S	G	1957	Fury 1021 ($50)/Fury 1071 (58) ($40)

Chantels

He's Gone	C	S	D	1957	End 1001 ($80)
Maybe	C	S	D	1958	End 1005 ($80)
Look In My Eyes	C	S	D	1961	Carlton 555 ($20)

Chanters

My My Darling (N)	C	F	SB	1958	DeLuxe 6162 ($50)
Angel Darling (N)	C	S	SB	1958	DeLuxe 6172 ($50)
No No No	C	F	SB	1958	DeLuxe 6191 ($40)

Chaperones

Cruise To The Moon	N	S	I	1960	Josie 880 ($25)

Charades

Please Be My Love Tonight (N)	N	S		1963	Ava 154 ($30)

Chariots

Gloria	C	S		1959	Time 1006 ($40)

Charles, Jimmy (with the Revelettes)

A Million To One	N	S		1960	Promo 1002 ($15)

Charms (Otis Williams & the)

Two Hearts (N)	C	F	1954	DeLuxe 6065 ($50)
My Baby Dearest Darling (N)	C	F	1954	DeLuxe 6056 ($200)
Ivory Tower (N)	C	S	1956	DeLuxe 6093 ($30)
Gumdrop (N)	C	F	1956	DeLuxe 6090 ($30)
One Night Only (N)	C	F	1956	DeLuxe 6095 ($30)

Charts

Why Do You Cry (N)	C	S		1957	Everlast 5002 ($80)/Lost Nite 180 (60s) ($6)
Desiree	C	S	G	1957	Everlast 5001 ($80)/Everlast 5026 (63) ($25)/Lost Nite 173 (60s) ($6)
You're The Reason (N)	C	S		1957	Everlast 5006 ($60)/Lost Nite 186 (60s) ($6)
Dance Girl	C	F	G	1957	Everlast 5002 ($80)/Lost Nite 180 (60s) ($6)
Zoop	C	F	G	1957	Everlast 5001 ($80)/Everlast 5026 (63) ($25)/Lost Nite 173 (60s) ($6)

Checkers

Nights Curtains (N)	P	S	1952	King 4581 ($1,000)
Ghost Of My Baby (N)	P	S	1953	King 4626 ($800)
White Cliffs Of Dover	P	F	1954	King 4675 ($400)

Chesters

The Fires Burn No More	C	S	1958	Apollo 521 ($60)

Chestnuts

Love Is True	C	S	1956	Davis 447 ($150)

Chevrons

Lullabye	C	F	1959	Brent 7007 ($50)

Chex (Tex & the)

I Do Love You	N	S	1961	Atlantic 2116 ($60)

Chiffons

One Fine Day	N	F	D/TPA	1963	Laurie 3179 ($20)
Oh My Lover (N)	N	F	D	1963	Laurie 3162 ($20)
He's So Fine	N	F	D/TPA	1963	Laurie 3152 ($20)
I Have A Boyfriend	N	F	D/TPA	1963	Laurie 3212 ($12)

Chimes

Once In A While	N	S	POP/I	1960	Tag 444 ($50)/Musicnote 1101 (61) ($25)
I'm In The Mood For Love	N	S	POP/I	1961	Tag 445 ($25)

Chips

Rubber Biscuit	C	F	1956	Josie 803 ($100)
Oh, My Darlin' (N)	C	S	1956	Josie 803 ($100)

Chords

Sh-Boom	P	F	1954	Cat 104 ($120)

Clark, Dee (bb the Kool Gents)

Just Like A Fool (N)	C	S	1960	Vee Jay LP 1019 ($50)/Charly LP 1113 ($12)/Solid Smoke LP 8026 ($10)

Classic IV

Island Of Paradise	N	S	1962	Twist 1001 ($100)

Classics

Till Then	N	S	I	1963	Musicnote 1116 ($30)

Clefs

We Three (N)	P	S	1952	Chess 1521 ($400)

Cleftones

Can't We Be Sweethearts?	C	F	1956	Gee 1016 ($40)
String Around My Heart (N)	C	F	1956	Gee 1025 ($40)
Little Girl Of Mine	C	F	1956	Gee 1011 ($40)
You Baby You	C	F	1956	Gee 1000 ($60)
See You Next Year	C	S	1957	Gee 1038 ($40)
Why You Do Me Like You Do	C	F	1957	Gee 1031 ($40)
Heart And Soul	N	M	1961	Gee 1064 ($25)

Click-Ettes

Lover's Prayer	N	S	D	1960	Dice 96/97 ($150)

Cliques

Girl In My Dreams	C	S	1956	Modern 987 ($50)

Clovers

Yes Sir, That's My Baby (N)	P	S	1950	Rainbow 11-122 ($400*)
Skylark (N)	P	S	1951	Atlantic 934 ($1,000)
Needless (N)	P	S	1951	Atlantic 944 ($250)

Fool, Fool, Fool (N)	P	F		1951	Atlantic 944 ($250)
One Mint Julep	P	F		1952	Atlantic 963 ($100)
I Played The Fool (N)	P	S		1952	Atlantic 977 ($250)
Blue Velvet	P	S		1955	Atlantic 1052 ($60)
Devil or Angel	P	S		1956	Atlantic 1083 ($200)
Love Potion No. 9	C	F	NOV	1959	United Artists 180 ($25)

Clusters

Darling Can't You Tell	C	F		1958	Tee Gee 102 ($300)/End 1115 (62) ($40)

Coasters

Young Blood (N)	C	F		1957	Atco 6087 ($70)
Searchin'	C	M		1957	Atco 6087 ($70)
Yakety Yak	C	F	NOV	1958	Atco 6116 ($25)
Poison Ivy (N)	C	F	N	1959	Atco 6146 ($20)
Charlie Brown	C	F	NOV	1959	Atco 6132 ($25)
Along Came Jones (N)	C	F	N	1959	Atco 6141 ($20)

Coasters

Down In Mexico (N)	C	F		1956	Atco 6064 ($80)

Cobras

La La	N	F		1964	Casino 1309 ($60)/Swan 4176 (64) ($25)

Coins

Blue, Can't Get No Place With You (N)	C	F		1954	Gee 10 ($2,000)

Collegians

Zoom Zoom Zoom	C	F	G	1957	Winley 224 ($50)
Heavenly Night (N)	C	S	SB	1958	X-Tra 108 ($400)Times Square 11 (63) ($10)
Let's Go For A Ride	C	F	G	1958	X-Tra 108 ($400)/Times Square 11 (63) ($10)

Colts

Adorable (N)	C	F		1955	Vita 112 ($150)/Mambo 112 (55) ($400)

Columbus Pharaohs

Give Me Your Love (N)	C	S		1957	Esta 290 ($1,000)

Concords

Candlelight (N)	P	S		1954	Harlem 2328 ($600)

Consorts

Please Be Mine (N)	N	F	I	1961	Cousins 1004 ($400)/Apt 25066 (62) ($120)

Contenders

The Clock	N	F		1963	Java 101 ($100)

Continentals

Dear Lord	C	S	G	1956	Whirlin' Disc 101 ($200)/Port 70018 (59) ($30)
You're An Angel (N)	C	S		1956	Rama 190 ($1,500)
Picture Of Love	C	F	G	1956	Whirlin' Disc 105 ($200)/Port 70024 (59) ($30)
Fine Fine Frame	C	F	G	1956	Whirlin' Disc 101 ($200)/Port 70018 (59) ($30)
Soft And Sweet (N)	C	S		1956	Whirlin' Disc 105 ($200)/Port 70024 (59) ($30)

Convincers

Rejected Love (N)	N	S		1962	Movin' 100 ($400)

Cookies

Chains	N	F	D	1962	Dimension 1002 ($20)
Don't Say Nothin' Bad (About My Baby)	N	F	D	1963	Dimension 1008 ($20)

Copasetics

Collegian (N)	C	F	D	1956	Premium 409 ($200)

Cordells

The Beat Of My Heart (N)	N	F		1961	Bargain 5004 ($50)

Cordovans

Come On Baby	C	F	SB	1960	Johnson 731 ($25)

Coronets

Nadine (N)	P	S		1953	Chess 1549 ($200)

Corsairs

Smoky Places	N	M		1961	Tuff 1808 ($25)/Chess 1808 (61) ($15)

Corvairs

True True Love	N	F		1962	Comet 2145 ($30)

Cosmic Rays

Daddy's Gonna Tell You No Lies (N)	C	F		1960	Saturn 401 ($2,000)

Crescendos

Oh Julie	C	S		1957	Nasco 6005 ($25)/Tap 7027 (62) ($15)

Crescents (A) (Pat Cordel & the)

Darling Come Back (N)	C	F		1956	Club 1101 ($1,500)/Michelle M 503(59) ($150)/Victory 1001 (63) ($80)

Crescents (B)

Everybody Knew But Me	C	S		1957	Joyce 102 ($250)

Crests

Sweetest One	C	S		1957	Joyce 103 ($300)/Musictone 1106 (62) ($20)
No One To Love	C	S		1957	Joyce 105 ($300)/Times Square 2 (62) ($20)
My Juanita	N	F		1957	Joyce 103 ($300)/Musictone 1106 (62) ($20)
Sixteen Candles	C	S		1958	Coed 506 ($30)
The Angels Listened In	C	F		1959	Coed 515 ($30)

Trouble In Paradise (N)	C	F		1960	Coed 531 ($25)
Step By Step	N	F		1960	Coed 525 ($25)
Crickets (Dean Barlow & the)					
You're Mine (N)	P	S		1953	MGM 11428 ($250)
Your Love (N)	P	S		1954	Jay-Dee 785 ($200)
Criterions (Tygh & the)					
To Be Mine	C	S		1963	Flite 101 ($120)
Crowns (Arthur Lee Maye & the)					
I Wanna Love (N)	C	F		1954	Modern 944 ($600)
Truly (N)	C	S		1955	RPM 424 ($200)
Love Me Always (N)	C	S		1955	RPM 429 ($120)
Gloria (N)	C	S		1956	Specialty 573 ($60)
This Is The Night For Love (N)	C	S		1956	Dig 124 ($250)
Crows					
I Love You So	P	S		1954	Rama 5 ($70)
Gee	P	F		1954	Rama 5 ($70)
Miss You (N)	P	S		1954	Rama 30 ($400)
Untrue (N)	P	S		1954	Rama 29 ($200)
Baby Doll (N)	C	F		1955	Rama 50 ($400)
Crystals					
There's No Other (Like My Baby)	N	S	D/TPA	1961	Philles 100 ($40)
Da Doo Ron Ron	N	F	D/TPA	1963	Philles 112 ($30)
Cuff Links					
Guided Missiles	C	S		1957	Dooto 409 ($80)
Cupids					
Brenda	N	S		1962	KC 115 ($40)/Aanko 1002 (63) ($100)
Danderliers					
My Autumn Love (N)	C	S		1955	States 147 ($400)/B&F 150 (61) ($20)
Danleers					
I Really Love You (N)	C	S		1958	Mercury 71356 ($20)
One Summer Night	C	S		1958	Amp-3 2115 ($40)/Mercury 71322 (58) ($20)
Darchaes (Ray & the)					
Carol	N	S		1962	Aljon 1249/1250 ($120)
Debonaires					
Darling	C	F		1957	Herald 509 ($60)
We'll Wait	N	S		1960	Gee 1054 ($25)
Decoys					
It's Gonna Be Allright (N)	N	F		1963	Times Square 8 ($10)
Del Satins					
Teardrops Follow Me (N)	N	F	I	1962	Laurie 3132 ($25)
Delighters (Donald Jenkins & the)					
(Native Girl) Elephant Walk (N)	N	F		1963	Cortland 109 ($25)
Dell Vikings					
Come Go With Me	C	F		1957	Fee Bee 205 ($500)/Dot 15538 (57) ($30)/Dot 16092 ($20)
Whispering Bells	C	F		1957	Fee Bee 214 ($400)/Dot 15592 (57) ($30)
When I Come Home (N)	C	S		1957	Dot 15636 ($30)
A Sunday Kind Of Love	C	F		1957	Mercury 30112 ($20)
I'm Spinning (N)	C	F		1957	Dot 15636 ($30)
Dells					
Tell The World (N)	C	S		1955	Vee Jay 134 ($2,000)
Oh What A Night	C	S		1956	Vee Jay 204 ($120)
Time Makes You Change (N)	C	F		1957	Vee Jay 258 ($40)
Why Do You Have To Go (N)	C	S		1957	Vee Jay 236 ($40)
Dry Your Eyes (N)	C	S		1959	Vee Jay 324 ($40)
Delmonicos					
World's Biggest Fool (N)	N	S	I	1964	Musictone 6122 ($30)
Delrons (Reparata & the)					
Whenever A Teenager Cries	N	S	D	1964	World Artists 1036 ($10)
Tommy (N)	N	S	D	1965	World Artists 1051 ($10)
Delroys					
Bermuda Shorts	C	F	NOV	1957	Apollo 514 ($25)
Deltairs					
Lullabye Of The Bells	C	S	D	1957	Ivy 101 ($150)
Deltas					
Lamplight	C	F		1957	Gone 5010 ($3,000)
Demens					
Take Me As I Am (N)	C	S		1957	Teenage 1006 ($200)
Demensions					
Over The Rainbow	N	S		1962	Mohawk 116 ($50)
Demilles					
Donna Lee	N	F	I	1964	Laurie 3230 ($30)
Desires					

Hey, Lena	C	F	SB	1959	Hull 730 ($80)
Let It Be You	C	S	SB	1959	Hull 730 ($80)
I Wanna Rendezvous With You	C	F	SB	1960	Hull 733 ($80)
Devotions					
Rip Van Winkle	N	F	NOV	1961	Delta 1001 ($150)/Roulette 4406 (61) ($40)/Roulette 4541 ($20)
Diablos					
The Wind	P	S		1954	Fortune 511 ($100)
Diablos (featuring Nolan Strong)					
Adios My Desert Love (N)	C	S		1954	Fortune 509/510 ($100)
Hold Me Until Eternity (N)	C	S		1955	Fortune 514 ($100)
Diablos (Nolan Strong & the)					
Can't We Talk This Over (N)	C	S		1957	Fortune 525 ($80)
If I Could Be With You Tonight (N)	C	F		1959	Fortune 532 ($40)
Diamonds					
A Beggar For Your Kisses (N)	P	S		1952	Atlantic 981 ($1,500)
Two Loves Have I (N)	P	S		1953	Atlantic 1003 ($600)
Cherry (N)	P	S		1953	Atlantic 1017 ($600)
Dimples (Eddie Cooley & the)					
Priscilla	C	F		1956	Royal Roost 621 ($25)
DiMucci, Dion (with the Del Satins)					
Runaround Sue	N	F	I	1961	Laurie 3110 ($25)
Lovers Who Wander	N	F	I	1962	Laurie 3123 ($20)
Donna The Prima Donna (N)	N	F	I	1963	Columbia 42852 ($20)
Diplomats (Dino & the)					
I Can't Believe (N)	N	F		1961	Laurie 3103 ($30)
Hushabye My Love (N)	N	F		1961	Vida 0100/0101 ($30)
Dodgers					
Drip Drop (N)	P	S		1955	Aladdin 3271 ($500)
Dominoes					
Do Something For Me (N)	P	S		1950	Federal 12001 ($800)
Harbor Lights (N)	P	S		1951	Federal 12010 ($300*)
Sixty Minute Man (N)	P	F		1951	Federal 12022 ($500)
Have Mercy Baby (N)	P	F		1952	Federal 12068 ($250)
The Bells (N)	P	S		1952	Federal 12114 ($200)
I'd Be Satisfied (N)	P	S		1952	Federal 12105 ($180)
When The Swallows Come Back To Capistrano (N)	P	S		1952	Federal 12059 ($400)
These Foolish Things (N)	P	S		1953	Federal 12129 ($300)
Star Dust (n)	P	S		1957	Liberty 55071 ($25)
Deep Purple (N)	P	S		1957	Liberty 55099 ($25)
Don Juans					
Girl Of My Dreams (N)	C	S		1959	Onezy 101 ($2,000)
Dorn, Jerry (with the Hurricanes)					
Wishing Well	P	S		1956	King 4932 ($80)
Dovells					
No No No (N)	N	F		1961	Parkway 819 ($20)
Dovers (Miriam Grate & the)					
Sweet As A Flower	C	S		1959	Davis 465 ($40)
Devil You May Be (N)	C	S		1961	New Horizon 501 ($30)
Dream Kings					
More Than Yesterday, Less Than Tomorrow (N)	C	S		1957	Checker 858 ($150)
Dreamers					
Tears In My Eyes (N)	C	S		1955	Grand 131 ($300)
Dreamlovers					
When We Get Married	N	S		1961	Heritage 102 ($20)
Drifters (A)					
I'm The Caring Kind (N)	P	S		1950	Coral 65037 ($300)
Drifters (B)					
Money Honey	P	F		1953	Atlantic 1006 ($80)
Honey Love	P	F		1954	Atlantic 1029 ($50)
The Way I Feel (N)	P	S		1953	Atlantic 1006 ($80)
Adorable	P	S		1955	Atlantic 1078 ($40)
White Christmas (N)	P	F		1954	Atlantic 1048 ($60)
Someday You'll Want Me To Want You (N)	P	S		1954	Atlantic 1043 ($40)
Warm Your Heart (N)	P	S		1954	Atlantic 1029 ($50)
Such A Night (N)	P	F		1954	Atlantic 1019 ($70)
Ruby Baby	P	F		1956	Atlantic 1089 ($30)
What'Cha Gonna Do (N)	P	F		1955	Atlantic 1055 ($50)
Your Promise To Be Mine (N)	P	S		1956	Atlantic 1089 ($30)
There Goes My Baby	N	M		1959	Atlantic 2025 ($25)
This Magic Moment	N	M		1960	Atlantic 2050 ($20)
Save The Last Dance For Me	N	M	TPA	1960	Atlantic 2071 ($20)

Let The Boogie Woogie Roll (N)	P	F		1960	Atlantic 2060 ($20)
Du Mauriers					
All Night Long	C	F		1957	Fury 1011 ($100)
Dubs					
Could This Be Magic	C	S		1957	Gone 5011 ($60)/Musictone 1141 (61) ($25)
Don't Ask Me (To Be Lonely)	C	S		1957	Johnson 102 ($1,500)/Gone 5002 ($100)
Chapel Of Dreams	C	S		1958	Gone5046 ($60)/Gone 5069 (59) ($40)
Beside My Love (N)	C	S		1958	Gone 5020 ($60)
Is There A Love For Me (N)	C	S		1958	Gone 5046 ($60)
Duprees					
My Own True Love	N	S	POP	1962	Coed 571 ($20)
You Belong To Me	N	S	POP	1962	Coed 569 ($20)
Have You Heard (N)	N	S	POP	1963	Coed 585 ($15)
Why Don't You Believe Me	N	S	POP	1963	Coed 584 ($30)
Earls					
Lookin' For My Baby	N	F	I	1961	Rome 102 ($40)/Clifton 39 (74) ($5)
Life Is But A Dream	N	F	I	1961	Rome 101 ($100)
Remember Then	N	F	I	1962	Old Town 1130 ($40)
Eyes	N	F	I	1962	Old Town 1141 ($20)
Never (N)	N	F	I	1963	Old Town 1133 ($25)
I Believe	N	S	I	1964	Old Town 1149 ($25)/Barry 1021 ($40)
Ebb Tides (Nino & the)					
Jukebox Saturday Night	N	F	I	1961	Madison 166 ($30)
Ebonaires					
Love Call (N)	C	S		1959	Lena 1001 ($200)
Echoes (A)					
Ding Dong (N)	C	F		1957	Gee 1028 ($60)
Echoes (B)					
Baby Blue	N	F	POP	1961	SRG 101 ($200)/Seg-Way 103 (61) ($25)
Edsels					
What Brought Us Together	N	S		1960	Tammy 1010 ($50)
Rama Lama Ding Dong	C	F		1961	Dub 2843 ($70)/Twin 600 (61) ($25)
Shake Shake Sherry	N	F		1962	Capitol 4675 ($20)
El Capris					
Oh, But She Did (N)	C	F		1956	Bullseye 102 ($200)/Argyle 1010 (61) ($30)
El Domingoes					
Lucky Me, I'm In Love	N	F		1962	Chelsea 1009 ($200)/Candlelite 418 (62) ($25)
El Dorados					
Baby I Need You (N)	P	S		1954	Vee Jay 115 ($80)
I'll Be Forever Loving You	C	F		1955	Vee Jay 165 ($60)
I Began To Realize (N)	P	S		1955	Vee Jay 165 ($60)
At My Front Door	C	F		1955	Vee Jay 147 ($70)
Bim Bam Boom	C	F		1956	Vee Jay 211 ($80)
There In The Night (N)	P	S		1956	Vee Jay 211 ($80)
Elchords					
Peppermint Stick	C	F	SB	1957	Good 544 ($80)/Musictone 1107 (59) ($20)
Elegants					
Little Star	C	M	I	1958	Apt 25005 ($50)
Goodnight (N)		S	I	1958	Apt 25017 ($30)
Little Boy Blue (Is Blue No More) (N)	C	F		1959	Hull 732 ($100)
Elgins					
Here In Your Arms (N)	N	S		1964	Congress 225 ($40)
Embers					
Solitaire (N)	C	S		1961	Empress 101 ($30)
Emblems (Patty & the)					
Mixed Up, Shook Up Girl (N)	N	F	D	1964	Herald 590 ($20)
Emotions					
Echo	N	M	I	1962	Kapp 490 ($20)
Encounters					
Don't Stop Now	N	F	I	1965	Swan 4205 ($150)
Ermines					
I'm So Used To You Now (N)	C	F		1956	Loma 703 ($150)
Essentials (Billy & the)					
Maybe You'll Be There	N	F		1962	Jamie 1239 ($30)
Essex					
Easier Said Than Done (N)	N	F		1963	Roulette 4494 ($15)
A Walkin' Miracle (N)	N	F		1963	Roulette 4515 ($15)
Eternals					
Rockin' In The Jungle	C	F	NOV	1959	Hollywood 68/69 ($60)/Musictone 1111 (61) ($12)
Babalu's Wedding Day	C	F	NOV	1959	Hollywood 70/71 ($50)/Musictone 1110 (59) ($12)
My Girl (N)	C	S		1959	Hollywood 70/71 ($50)
Evergreens (Dante & the)					
Alley Oop	N	F	NOV	1960	Madison 130 ($20)

Excellents
Coney Island Baby	N	S		1962	Blast 205 ($30)

Explorers (Dennis & the)
Vision Of Love (N)	N	S		1960	Coral 62147 ($60)

Extremes
Come Next Spring	C	S		1958	Everlast 5013 ($150)

Fabulaires
While Walking	C	F		1957	East West 103 ($300)/Main Line 103 (58) ($200)

Fabulous Pearl Devines
You've Been Gone (N)	C	F		1959	Alco 101 ($400)

Fabulous Twilights (Nathaniel Mayer & the)
Village Of Love	N	F		1962	Fortune 545 ($20)/ United Artists 449 ($25)

Falcons
You're So Fine	C	F		1959	Flick 001 ($400)/Unart 2103 (59) ($30)/United Artists 2013X ($20)

Fantastics
There Goes My Love (N)	C	S		1959	RCA 7572 ($40)

Fascinators (A)
My Beauty, My Own (N)	P	S		1954	Your Copy 1136 ($1,000)

Fascinators (B)
Chapel Bells	C	S	I	1958	Capitol 4053 ($150)/Capitol 4544 (61) ($80)
Wonder Who (N)	C	F	I	1958	Capitol 4053 ($150)/Capitol 4544 (61) ($80)
Oh Rose Marie	C	F	I	1959	Capitol 4247 ($200)
Who Do You Think You Are (N)	C	S	I	1959	Capitol 4137 ($200)

Fashions
I'm Dreaming Of You	C	F		1959	V-Tone 202 ($50)

Feathers
Johnny, Darling	P	S		1954	Aladdin 3267 ($200)

Fi-Dells
What Is Love	N	S		1961	Imperial 5780 ($25)

Fi-Tones
My Faith	C	S		1957	Old Town 1042 ($400)
Foolish Dreams (N)	C	S		1957	Atlas 1050 ($400)

Fi-Tones Quintette
It Wasn't A Lie (N)	C	S		1955	Atlas 1051 ($100)

Fidelitys
The Things I Love	C	S		1958	Baton 252 ($25)

Fiestas
Last Night I Dreamed (N)	C	S		1958	Old Town 1062 ($50)
So Fine	C	F		1958	Old Town 1062 ($50)
The Hobo's Prayer (N)	C	S		1961	Old Town 1111 ($40)

Fireflies
You Were Mine	N	S		1959	Ribbon 6901 ($30)
I Can't Say Goodbye	C	S		1959	Ribbon 6904 ($25)

Five Blue Notes
The Beat Of Our Hearts (N)	P	S		1954	Sabre 108 ($2,500)

Five Chances
All I Want (N)	P	S		1955	Blue Lake 115 ($800)
Gloria (N)	C	S		1956	States 156 ($800)

Five Crowns
Lullaby Of The Bells (N)	P	S		1952	Old Town 792 ($400*)
You Came To Me (N)	P	S		1955	Riviera 990 ($4,000)/Rainbow 335 (56) ($200)

Five Discs
I Remember	C	F	I	1958	Emge 1004 ($400)/Vik 0327 (58) ($80)/Rust 5027 (61) ($25)
Adios (N)	N	F		1961	Calo 202 ($150)
Never Let You Go	N	F	I	1961	Cheer 1000 ($50)
My Baby Loves Me (N)	N	S		1961	Calo 202 ($150)
That Was The Time (N)	N	S		1962	Cheer 1000 ($50)

Five Dollars
Harmony Of Love (N)	C	S		1955	Fortune 821 ($100)/Fraternity 821 (58) ($40)
That's The Way It Goes (N)	C	S		1960	Fortune 854 ($50)

Five Embers
Please Come Home (N)	P	S		1954	Gem 224 ($800)

Five Emeralds
I'll Beg (N)	P	S		1954	S-R-C 106 ($1,000)
Darling (N)	P	S		1954	S-R-C 107 ($1,200)

Five Keys
With A Broken Heart (N)	P	S		1951	Aladdin 3085 ($200*)
Glory Of Love (N)	P	S		1951	Aladdin 3099 ($1,000)
Red Sails In The Sunset (N)	P	S		1952	Aladdin 3127 ($6,000)
Mistakes (N)	P	S		1952	Aladdin 3131 ($1,200)

These Foolish Things (N)	P	S		1953	Aladdin 3190 ($4,000)
Deep In My Heart (N)	P	S		1954	Aladdin 3245 ($800)
Ling Ting Tong	P	F		1954	Capitol 2945 ($40)
The Verdict (N)	P	S		1955	Capitol 3127 ($40)
Close Your Eyes (N)	P	S		1955	Capitol 3032 ($40)
Out Of Sight, Out Of Mind	P	S		1956	Capitol 3502 ($30)
Wisdom Of A Fool	P	S		1956	Capitol 3597 ($30)

Five Notes

You Are So Beautiful (N)	C	S		1955	Jen D 4185 ($500)/Josie 784 (55) ($80)
Show Me The Way (N)	C	S		1956	Chess 1614 ($150)

Five Royales

Give Me One More Chance (N)	P	S		1951	Apollo 434 ($100*)
My Wants For Love (N)	P	S		1956	King 4901 ($50)
Dedicated To The One I Love (N)	P	S		1957	King 5098 ($40)

Five Satins

Wonderful Girl	C	S		1956	Ember 1008 ($40)
I Remember (In The Still Of The Night)	C	S		1956	Standord 200 ($2,000)/Ember 1005 (56) ($50)
Oh Happy Day	C	S		1957	Ember 1014 ($40)
To The Aisle	C	S		1957	Ember 1019 ($40)
Our Anniversary (N)	C	S		1957	Ember 1025 ($40)
Wishing Ring (N)	N	S		1961	Ember 1070 ($25)

Five Sharps

Stormy Weather	P	S		1952	Jubilee 5104 ($10,000+*)

Flairs

This Is The Night For Love (N)	P	S		1954	Flair 1044 ($400)

Flairs (Cornel Gunter & the)

She Loves To Rock (N)	C	F		1956	ABC 9698 ($40)

Flamingos

Golden Teardrops	P	S		1953	Chance 1145 ($1,000)/Vee Jay 384 (61) ($25)
If I Can't Have You (N)	P	S		1953	Chance 1133 ($800)
Someday Someway (N)	P	F		1953	Chance 1133 ($800)
Dream Of A Lifetime (N)	P	S		1954	Parrot 808 ($800)
Jump Children (N)	P	F		1954	Chance 1162 ($600)
I'll Be Home	P	S		1956	Checker 830 ($80)
A Kiss From Your Lips	P	S		1956	Checker 837 ($80)
Lovers Never Say Goodbye	C	S		1958	End 1035 ($40)
I Only Have Eyes For You	C	S		1959	End 1046 ($30)
Nobody Loves Me Like You Do (N)	N	F		1960	End 1068 ($25)
Mio Amore (N)	C	S		1960	End 1065 ($25)

Fleetwoods

Come Softly To Me	N	M	POP	1959	Dolphin 1 ($25)/Liberty 55188 (59) ($25)/Liberty 77188 (59) ($50)
Mr. Blue	N	M	POP	1959	Dolton 5 ($20)

Flips (Little Joey & the)

Bongo Stomp	N	F		1962	Joy 262 ($15)

Four Bars

If I Give My Heart To You (N)	P	S		1954	Josie 768 ($300)

Four Buddies

Simply Say Goodbye (N)	P	S		1951	Savoy 823 ($250)
I Will Wait (N)	P	S		1951	Savoy 769 ($500)
Just To See You Smile Again (N)	P	S		1951	Savoy 769 ($500)
Why At A Time Like This (N)	P	S		1951	Savoy 789 ($250)
You're Part Of Me	P	S		1952	Savoy 845 ($250)

Four Deuces

W-P-L-J (N)	P	F		1955	Music City 790 ($150)

Four Dots (Jerry Stone & the)

Pleading For Your Love	C	S		1959	Freedom 44005 ($100)

Four Fellows

Angels Say (N)	P	S		1955	Glory 236 ($60)
In The Rain (N)	P	S		1955	Glory 236 ($60)
Soldier Boy	P	S		1955	Glory 234 ($60)
You Don't Know Me (N)	P	S		1956	Glory 248 ($60)
Darling You (N)	P	S		1956	Glory 242 ($80)
Give Me Back My Broken Heart (N)	P	S		1957	Glory 250 ($60)

Four Flames

Tabarin (N)	P	S		1951	Fidelity 3001 ($300*)

Four Haven Knights

In My Lonely Room	C	F		1956	Atlas 1066 ($150)/Josie 824 (57) ($30)/Angletone 1066 (58) ($50)
Just To Be In Love (N)	C	S		1957	Atlas 1092 ($150)/Angletone 1092 (58) ($50)

Four J's

Here I Am Broken Hearted	N	F		1964	Jamie 1267 ($25)

G-Clefs

Daria My Darling (N)	C	F	1956	Pilgrim 715 ($30)
'Cause You're Mine	C	F	1956	Pilgrim 720 ($30)
Ka Ding Dong	C	F	1956	Pilgrim 715 ($30)
Symbol Of Love	C	S	1957	Paris 502 ($30)

Gardenias

Flaming Love (N)	C	F	1956	Federal 12284 ($120)

Gay Knights

The Loudness Of My Heart (N)	C	S	1958	Pet 801 ($40)

Gaytunes

I Love You	C		1957	Joyce 101 ($200)
Plea In The Moonlight	C	F	1958	Joyce 106 ($8)

Gazelles

Honest (N)	C	S	1956	Gotham 315 ($300)

Gems

You're Tired Of Love (N)	P	S	1954	Drexel 904 ($300)
'Deed I Do (N)	P	S	1954	Drexel 901 ($500)

Genies

Who's That Knockin'	C	F	1959	Shad 5002 ($20)

Gentlemen

Don't Leave Me Baby	C	F	1954	Apollo 470 ($100)

Gladiators

Girl Of My Heart (N)	C	S	1957	Dig 135 ($300)

Gladiolas

Little Darlin'	C	F	1957	Excello 2101 ($75)

Goldentones

The Meaning Of Love (N)	C	S	1955	Jay Dee 806 ($80)/Beacon 560 (61) ($25)

Greco, Johnny (& group)

Rocket Ride (N)	N	F	1963	Pageant 602 ($150)

Greene, Barbara (& group)

Long Tall Sally (N)	N	F	1963	Atco 6250 ($40)

Guytones

This Is Love (N)	C	F	1957	DeLuxe 6159 ($80)

Halos

Nag	N	F	1961	7 Arts 709 ($20)

Harmonaires

Come Back (N)	C	F	1957	Holiday 2602 ($300)
Lorraine	C	S	1957	Holiday 2602 ($300)

Harptones

A Sunday Kind Of Love	P	S	1953	Bruce 101 ($3,000)/Relic 1022 (73) ($5)
Since I Fell For You (N)	P	S	1954	Bruce 113 ($80)
Life Is But A Dream	P	S	1954	Paradise 101 ($150)
Loving A Girl Like You (N)	P	S	1954	Bruce 123 ($60)
My Memories Of You	P	S	1954	Bruce 102 ($200)/Relic 1023 (73) ($5)
Three Wishes	P	S	1956	Rama 203 ($80)
On Sunday Afternoon	P	S	1956	Rama 214 ($80)
That's The Way It Goes	P	S	1956	Rama 203 ($80)
The Shrine Of St. Cecilia (N)	P	S	1957	Rama 221 ($80)
Cry Like I Cried (N)	P	S	1957	Gee 1045 ($60)

Harris, Thurston (with the Sharps)

Little Bitty Pretty One	C	F	1957	Aladdin 3398 ($40)

Heart Beats Quintet (aka Heartbeats)

Tormented (N)	C	S	1955	Network 71200 ($300)/Candlelite 437 (76) ($5)

Heartbeats

Your Way	C	S	1956	Hull 716 ($200)/Gee 1061 (61) ($20)
Rock 'n' Rollin' 'n' Rhythm 'n' Blues-n' (N)	C	F	1956	Hull 711 ($300)
Darling How Long	C	S	1956	Hull 713 ($200)/Gee 1062 (61) ($20)
Oh Baby Don't (N)	C	F	1956	Hull 720 ($250)/Rama 216 (57) ($80)
People Are Talking	C	S	1956	Hull 716 ($200)/Gee 1061 (61) ($20)
Crazy For You	C	S	1956	Hull 711 ($300)
A Thousand Miles Away	C	S	1956	Hull 720 ($250)/Rama 216 (57) ($80)
Down On My Knees (N)	C	S	1958	Roulette 4054 ($30)

Heartbreakers (A)

Heartbreaker (N)	P	S	1951	RCA 47-4327 ($600)

Heartbreakers (B)

Without A Cause (N)	C	F	1957	Vik 0261 ($150)

Hearts (A) (Lee Andrews & the)

Maybe You'll Be There	P	S	1954	Rainbow 252 ($400)
Bluebird Of Happiness (N)	P	S	1956	Gotham 318 ($200)
Lonely Room (N)	C	S	1956	Gotham 320 ($300)
Long Lonely Nights	P	S	1957	Grand 157 ($12)/Main Line 102 (57) ($400)/Chess 1665 ($40)
The Clock (N)	C	F	1957	Grand 157 ($12)/Main Line 102 ($400)/Chess 1665 ($40)

The Girl Around The Corner (N)	C	F		1957	Grand 156 ($12)/Main Line 105 ($12)/Argo 1000 ($50)/Chess 1675 ($20)
Teardrops	P	S		1957	Grand 156 ($12)/Main Line 105 (57) ($12)/Argo 1000 ($50)/Chess 1675 ($20)
Why Do I	P	S		1958	United Artists 136 ($20)
Try The Impossible	P	S		1958	Casino 452 ($600)/United Artists 123 (58) ($25)
I'm Sorry Pillow	P	S		1963	Parkway 860 ($15)
Hearts (B) (female)					
Lonely Nights (N)	C	S	D	1955	Baton 208 ($50)
He Drives Me Crazy (N)	C	F	D	1956	Baton 228 ($25)
Hemlocks (Little Bobby Rivera & the)					
Cora Lee	C	F	SB	1957	Fury 1004 ($100)
Hi-Fives					
Dorothy	C	F		1958	Decca 30657 ($50)
Hi-Lites (A) (Ronnie & the)					
I Wish That We Were Married	N	S		1962	Joy 260 ($25)
Hi-Lites (B)					
Gloria (N)	N	S		1962	Julia 1105 ($120)
Pretty Face (N)	N	S		1962	Dandee LP 206 ($2,000)
Hide-A-Ways					
Can't Help Loving That Girl Of Mine	P	S		1954	Ronni 1000 ($6,000)
Highlands					
I Laughed	N	F		1961	
Hits (Tiny Tim & the)					
Wedding Bells	C	S		1958	Roulette 4123 ($50)
Hollywood Flames					
Peggy (N)	P	S		1954	Lucky 006 ($600)
Buzz Buzz Buzz	C	F		1957	Ebb 119 ($30)/Mona Lee 135 ($25)
Just For You (N)	C	S		1959	Ebb 153 ($30)
Hornets					
Crying Over You (N)	C	S		1957	Flash 125 ($250)
Hurricanes					
Dear Mother (N)	C	S		1956	King 4947 ($120)
Maybe It's All For The Best (N)	C	S		1956	King 4867 ($200)
Priceless (N)	C	S		1957	King 5042 ($100)
Fallen Angel (N)	C	S		1957	King 5018 ($100)
Imaginations					
Hey You	N	S		1961	Music Makers 108 ($50)/Duel 507 (61) ($20)/Bo Marc 301 ($40)
The Search Is Over (N)	N	S		1961	Music Makers 103 ($50)
Impalas					
Sorry (I Ran All The Way Home)	C	F		1959	Cub 9022 ($20)
Imperials (A)					
My Darling (N)	P	S		1952	Savoy 1104 ($200)/Buzzy 1 (62) ($20)
Imperials (B) (Little Anthony & the)					
Two People In The World	C	S	SB	1958	End 1027 ($40)
So Much (N)	C	S		1958	End 1036 ($25)
Tears On My Pillow	C	S	SB	1958	End 1027 ($40)
When You Wish Upon A Star	C	S		1959	End 1039 ($25)
Shimmy, Shimmy Ko-Ko-Bop (N)	C	M		1959	End 1060 ($30)
Traveling Stranger	C	F		1961	End 1091 ($15)
Impressions (Jerry Butler & the)					
For Your Precious Love	N	S		1958	Vee Jay 280 ($8.000)/Falcon 1013 (58) ($60)/Abner 1013 (58) ($40)
Initials (Angelo & the)					
Bells Of Joy (N)	C	S		1959	Dee 1001 ($200)/Sherry 667 ($50)
Ivy-Tones					
Oo-Wee Baby	C	F		1958	Red Top 105 ($20)
Jacks					
Why Don't You Write Me	P	S		1955	RPM 428 ($200)
Why Did I Fall In Love (N)	C	S		1956	RPM 458 ($60)
Jaguars					
The Way You Look Tonight	P	S	POP	1956	Aardell 0011 ($250)
Jamies					
Summertime, Summertime	C	F		1958	Epic 9281 ($12)
Jayhawks					
Stranded In The Jungle	C	F	NOV	1956	Flash 109 ($50)
Jaytones					
Oh Darling	C	F		1958	Timely 1003/1004 ($1,500)
Jelly Beans					
I Wanna Love Him So Bad	N	F	D/TPA	1964	Red Bird 10-003 ($20)
Jesters					
Please Let Me Love You	C	S	G	1957	Winley 221 ($50)

Love No One But You (N)	C	S	G	1957	Winley 218 ($50)
I'm Falling In Love	C	F	G	1957	Winley 221 ($50)
So Strange	C	S	G	1957	Winley 218 ($50)
Now That You're Gone (N)	C	S	G	1958	Cyclone 5011 ($50)
I Laughed	C	F	G	1958	Cyclone 5011 ($50)
Oh Baby	C	F	G	1958	Winley 225 ($40)

Jets

Heaven Above Me (N)	C	F		1956	Gee 1020 ($2,000)

Jewels

Hearts Of Stone	P	F		1954	R&B 1301 ($200)

Jive Bombers

Bad Boy (N)	P	S		1957	Savoy 1508 ($20)

Jive Five

My True Story	N	S		1961	Beltone 1006 ($30)/Relic 1026 (75) ($5)
Never, Never (N)	N	S		1961	Beltone 1014 ($20)/Relic 1030 (78) ($5)
These Golden Rings (n)	N	S		1962	Beltone 2029 ($20)/Relic 1029 (77) ($5)
What Time Is It	N	S		1962	Beltone 2024 ($20)/Relic 1028 (76) ($5)

Johnson, Herb (bb the Cruisers)

Have You Heard (N)	N	M		1960	Len 1007 ($30)

Joytones

My Foolish Heart (N)	C	S	D	1956	Rama 215 ($500)

Juniors (A) (Jimmy Castor & the)

Somebody Mentioned Your Name (N)	C	S	SB	1957	Atomic 100 ($500)

Juniors (B) (Danny & the)

Sometimes When I'm All Alone	C	S		1957	Singular 711 ($1,200)/ABC 9871 (57) ($30)
Rock And Roll Is Here To Stay	C	F	I	1957	ABC 9888 ($30)
At The Hop	C	F	I	1957	Singular 711 ($1,200)/ABC 9871 (57) ($30)

Kac-Ties

Happy Birthday	C	S		1963	Kape 501 ($15)

Keynotes

Zup Zup (Ooh You Dance So Nice) (N)	C	F		1956	Apollo 498 ($100)
Really Wish You Were Here (N)	C	F		1956	Apollo 493 ($120)
In The Evening (N)	C	F		1956	Apollo 503 ($80)
One Little Kiss (N)	C	S		1957	Apollo 513 ($80)

Keystoners

Sleep And Dream (N)	C	F		1961	Riff 202 ($200)

Keytones

Seven Wonders Of The World	C	S		1957	Old Town 1041 ($100)

King Crooners

Won't You Let Me Know You (N)	C	F		1959	Excello 2168 ($40)
She's Mine All Mine (N)	C	F		1959	Hart 1002 ($400)

Knight, Bob (The Bob Knight Four)

Good Goodbye	C	S		1961	Laurel 1020 ($25)/Taurus 100 (61) ($25)

Knockouts

Darling Lorraine	C	S		1959	Shad 5013 ($25)

Kodaks (aka Kodoks)

Teenager's Dream	C	S	SB	1957	Fury 1007 ($80)
Little Boy And Girl	C	F	SB	1957	Fury 1007 ($80)
Oh Gee Oh Gosh	C	F	SB	1957	Fury 1015 ($60)
Runaround Baby	C	F	SB	1960	Fury 1020 ($60)

Kool Gents

This Is The Night (N)	C	S		1956	Vee Jay 173 ($200)

Kuf-Linx

So Tough	C	F	G	1958	Challenge 1013 ($40)/ Challenge 59002 (58) ($25)

Ladders

Counting The Stars	C	F		1957	Holiday 2611 ($300)

Laddins

Did It	C	F		1957	Central 2602 ($700)/ Times Square 3 (61) ($15)
Yes, Oh Baby Yes	C	F		1959	Grey Cliff 721 ($30)

Lamplighters

I Used To Cry Mercy, Mercy (N)	P	F		1954	Federal 12176 ($150)

Larks (A)

Hopefully Yours (N)	P	S		1951	Apollo 1180 ($4,000)
My Reverie (N)	P	S		1951	Apollo 1184 ($2,000)
In My Lonely Room (N)	P	S		1952	Apollo 1190 ($2,500)
Darlin'	P	S		1952	Apollo 437 ($1,000)
If It's A Crime (N)	P	S		1954	Lloyds 110 ($800)

Larks (B) (with Don Julian)

There Is A Girl	N	F		1961	Sheryl 338 ($25)

Leaders

Stormy Weather (N)	P	S		1955	Glory 235 ($60)

Lee, Curtis (with the Halos)
Pretty Little Angel Eyes	N	F		1961	Dunes 2007 ($25)

Legends
I'll Never Fall In Love Again	C	F		1957	Melba 109 ($150)
The Legend Of Love (N)	C	S		1958	Hull 727 ($100)

Lexingtons (Joey & the)
Bobbie (N)	N	F		1963	Dunes 2029 ($100)

Limelighters
Cabin Hideaway (N)	C	F		1956	Josie 795 ($150)

Limelights (Shep & the)
Daddy's Home	C	S		1961	Hull 740 ($40)
Three Steps To The Altar	C	S		1962	Hull 747 ($20)/Roulette 102 ($5)
Our Anniversary (N)	C	S		1962	Hull 748 ($20)

Lollypops
Believe In Me (N)	C	F		1958	Universal Int'l 7420 ($4,000)/ Holland 7420 (58) ($3,000)

Love Notes
Tonight	C	F		1957	Holiday 2605 ($60)
United	C	S	G	1957	Holiday 2605 ($60)

Ly-Dells
Wizard Of Love	N	F		1961	Master 251 ($60)

Lyrics
Let's Be Sweethearts Again	N	S		1961	Fernwood 129 ($800)/ Fleetwood 233 (61) ($400)
You And Your Fellow (N)	N	F		1961	Fernwood 129 ($800)/ Fleetwood 233 (61) ($400)

Maestro, Johnny (& group)
What A Surprise (N)	C	S		1961	Coed 549 ($25)

Magnificent Four
The Closer You Are	N	F		1961	Whale 506 ($80)/Blast 210 (63) ($40)

Magnificents
Up On The Mountain	P	F		1956	Vee Jay 183 ($75)
Don't Leave Me	C	F		1958	Vee Jay 281 ($100)

Majestics
Nitey Nite (N)	C	S		1956	Marlin 802 ($1,000)

Majors (A)
Laughing On The Outside, Crying On The Inside (N)	P	S		1951	Derby 779 ($600)

Majors (B)
A Wonderful Dream	N	F		1962	Imperial 5855 ($15)

Marcels
Heartaches	N	F		1961	Colpix 612 ($25)
Blue Moon	N	F		1961	Colpix 186 ($30)
Goodbye To Love	N	S		1961	Colpix 186 ($30)

Marquis
Bohemian Daddy	C	F		1956	Onyx 505 ($2,000)/Relic 505 (64) ($8)

Marvelettes
Forever	N	S	D	1963	Tamla 54077 ($15)

Marvelows
I Do (N)	N	F		1965	ABC 10629 ($15)

Marvels (aka Dubs)
I Won't Have You Breaking My Heart (N)	C	S		1956	ABC 9771 ($500)

Marylanders
I'm A Sentimental Fool (N)	P	S		1952	Jubilee 5079 ($400)
Make Me Thrill Again (N)	P	S		1952	Jubilee 5091 ($400)

Master-Tones
Tell Me (N)	P	S		1954	Bruce 111 ($500)

Masters (Rick & the)
I Don't Want Your Love (N)	N	F		1963	Cameo 247 ($50)

Matadors
Vengeance (Will Be Mine)	C	S	G	1958	Sue 700 ($100)

McFadden, Ruth (bb the Royaltones)
Two In Love (N)	C	S		1956	Old Town 1020 ($100)

Meadowlarks (Don Julian & the)
Always And Always	P	S		1955	Dootone 367 ($75)
This Must Be Paradise	C	S		1955	Dootone 372 ($60)
Heaven And Paradise	P	S		1955	Dootone 359 ($300)

Medallions (Vernon Green & the)
The Letter (N)	P	S		1954	Dootone 347 ($200)
Buick '59	P	F		1954	Dootone 347 ($200)

Mello-Harps
Love Is A Vow (N)	C	S		1955	Do-Re-Mi 203 ($8,000)

Mello-Kings
Tonight Tonight	C	S		1957	Herald 502 ($50)

Mello-Moods

Where Are You? (Now That I Need You) (N)	P	S		1952	Red Robin 105 ($5,000)
How Could You	P	S		1952	Red Robin 105 ($5,000)

Mellows (Lillian Leach & the)

How Sentimental Can I Be? (N)	P	S		1954	Jay-Dee 793 ($200)
Smoke From Your Cigarette	P	S		1955	Jay-Dee 797 ($200)
Yesterday's Memories (N)	P	S		1955	Jay-Dee 807 ($200)
My Darling (N)	P	S		1956	Celeste 3002 ($120)

Mellows (Lillian Lee & the)

Moon Of Silver (N)	P	S		1956	Candlelight 1011 ($150)

Metronomes

I Love My Girl	C	S		1957	Cadence 1310 ($100)

Midnighters (aka Royals)

Work With Me Annie (N)	P	F		1953	Federal 12169 ($100)
Sexy Ways (N)	P	F		1954	Federal 12185 ($80)
Partners For Life (N)	C	S		1956	Federal 12251 ($60)

Monarchs

Always Be Faithful	C	F		1956	Neil 103 ($120)
In My Younger Days (N)	C	F		1956	Neil 101 ($150)/Melba 101 (56) ($80)
Pretty Little Girl	C	F		1956	Neil 101 ($150)/Melba 101 (56) ($80)

Moniques

I'm With You All The Way	C	F		1963	Centaur 105 ($25)

Monotones

Book Of Love	C	F		1958	Mascot 124 ($700)/Argo 5290 (58) ($30)

Montclairs

Give Me A Chance (N)	C	S		1956	Premium 404 ($400)

Moonglows

Secret Love	P	S		1954	Chance 1152 ($1,000)/Vee Jay 423 (62) ($25)
Sincerely	P	S		1954	Chess 1581 ($60)
Most Of All	P	S		1955	Chess 1589 ($60)
In My Diary	P	S		1955	Chess 1611 ($60)
Seesaw	P	F		1956	Chess 1629 ($50)
When I'm With You (N)	P	S		1956	Chess 1629 ($50)
We Go Together	P	S		1956	Chess 1619 ($50)

Moonglows (Bobby Lester & the)

Penny Arcade (N)	P	S		1962	Chess 1811 ($25)

Moonglows (Harvey & the)

Ten Commandments Of Love	C	S		1958	Chess 1705 ($30)

Mystics

Don't Take The Stars (n)	C	F	I	1959	Laurie 3038 ($25)
Hushabye	C	M	I	1959	Laurie 3028 ($30)
White Cliffs Of Dover	C	F	I	1960	Laurie 3058 ($25)
All Through The Night (N)	C	S	I	1960	Laurie 3047 ($25)

Native Boys

Strange Love	C	F		1956	Combo 113 ($60)

Neons

Angel Face (N)	C	F	I	1956	Tetra 4444 ($80)

New Yorkers 5

Gloria, My Darling (N)	C	S		1955	Danice 801 ($400)

Nobles (Nicky & the)

Poor Rock & Roll	C	F	I	1958	Kilk 305 ($200)/Times Square 1 (62) ($25)/Lost Nite 153 (60s) ($6)

Note-Torials

My Valerie (N)	C	?		1959	Impala 201 ($1,000)/Sunbeam 119 ($200)

Nutmegs

Ship Of Love	C	S		1955	Herald 459 ($40)
Story Untold	C	S		1955	Herald 452 ($70)
Whispering Sorrows (N)	C	S		1955	Herald 466 ($50)
A Love So True (N)	C	S		1956	Herald 492 ($40)
Shifting Sands	C	F		1957	Relic 1006 ($10)
My Story (N)	C	S		1959	Herald 538 ($40)
Hello (N)	C	S		1963	Times Square 6 ($25)/Relic 531 (65) ($10)
Down In Mexico (N)	C	F		1963	Times Square 27 ($20)
Let Me Tell You	C	F		1963	Times Square 6 ($25)/Relic 531 (65) ($10)
Down To Earth (N)	C	S		1963	Times Square 19 ($20)

Olympics

Western Movies (N)	C	F	NOV	1958	Demon 1508 ($30)
Dance By The Light of The Moon	N	F	POP	1960	Arvee 5020 ($20)

Opals (aka Crystals)

My Heart's Desire (N)	P	S		1954	Apollo 462 ($200)
Come To Me Darling	P	S		1954	Luna 100/101 ($400)

Orchids

Newly Wed (N)	C	S		1955	Parrot 815 ($500)

You're Everything To Me (N)	C	S		1955	Parrot 815 ($500)
You Said You Loved Me (N)	C	S		1955	Parrot 819 ($300)
Orients					
Queen Of The Angels	N	S	SB	1964	Laurie 3232 ($40)
Orioles (Sonny Til & the)					
It's Too Soon To Know	P	S		1948	It's A Natural 5000 ($150*)/ Jubilee 5000 (48) ($4,000)
What Are You Doing New Year's Eve	P	S		1949	Jubilee 5017 ($800)
A Kiss And A Rose (N)	P	S		1949	Jubilee 5009 ($80*)
Please Give My Heart A Break (N)	P	S		1949	Jubilee 5002 ($80*)
Tell Me So (N)	P	S		1949	Jubilee 5005 ($2,000)
I'd Rather Have You Under The Moon (N)	P	S		1950	Jubilee 5031 ($70*)
At Night (N)	P	S		1950	Jubilee 5025 ($1,000)
I Miss You So (N)	P	S		1951	Jubilee 5051 ($800)
I Cover The Waterfront (N)	P	S		1953	Jubilee 5120 ($400)
Crying In The Chapel	P	S		1953	Jubilee 5122 ($80)/Lana 109 (64) ($8)
Oxfords (Darrell & the)					
Picture In My Wallet	N	S	TPA	1959	Roulette 4174 ($30)
Packards					
Dream Of Love (N)	C	S		1956	Paradise 105 ($400)
Paradons					
Diamonds And Pearls	N	S		1960	Milestone 2003 ($50)
Paragons					
Florence	C	S	G	1957	Winley 215 ($50)
Stick With Me Baby	C	F	G	1957	Winley 220 ($50)
Hey, Little School Girl	C	F	G	1957	Winley 215 ($50)
Let's Start All Over Again	C	S	G	1957	Winley 220 ($50)
The Vows Of Love (N)	C	S	G	1958	Winley 227 ($40)
So You Will Know (N)	C	S	G	1958	Winley 228 ($30)/Times Square 9 (63) ($20)
Twilight (N)	C	S	G	1958	Winley 227 ($40)
Passions					
Just To Be With You	C	S	I	1959	Audicon 102 ($40)
I Only Want You	C	F	I	1960	Audicon 105 ($30)
This Is My Love (N)	C	S		1960	Audicon 105 ($30)
Pastels					
So Far Away (N)	P	S		1958	Argo 5314 ($25)
Been So Long	P	S		1958	Mascot 123 ($300)/Argo 5287 (57) ($25)
Pearls					
Let's You And I Go Steady	C	F		1956	Onyx 503 ($60)/Relic 513 (64) ($8)
Your Cheating Heart (N)	C	F		1957	Onyx 510 ($60)
Penguins					
Hey Senorita	P	F		1954	Dootone 348 ($150)/Power 7023 (54) ($8)
Earth Angel	P	S		1954	Dootone 348 ($150)/Power 7023 (54) ($8)
My Troubles Are Not At End (N)	C	S		1956	Mercury 70799 ($50)
Pentagons					
To Be Loved (Forever)	N	S		1960	Fleet Int'l 100 ($200)/Donna 1337 (61) ($30)
Perfections					
Hey Girl	C	F		1959	Lost Nite 111 ($50)
Personalities					
Woe Woe Baby	C	F		1957	Safari 1002 ($200)
Yours To Command (N)	C	S	SB	1957	Safari 1002 ($200)
Phillips, Phil (with the Twilights)					
Sea Of Love	N	S		1959	Khoury's 711 ($1,500)/Mercury 71465 (59) ($25)
Pips					
Every Beat Of My Heart (N)	C	S		1961	Huntom 2510 ($500)/Vee Jay 386 (61) ($20)/Fury 1050 ($25)
Pixies Three					
Birthday Party	N	F	D	1963	Mercury 72130 ($15)
442 Glenwood Avenue	N	F	D	1963	Mercury 72208 ($15)
Platters					
I'll Cry When You're Gone (N)	P	S		1953	Federal 12164 ($1,000)
Voo-Vee-Ah-Bee (N)	P	F		1954	Federal 12198 ($200)
The Great Pretender	P	S	POP	1955	Mercury 70753 ($40)
Only You (And You Alone)	P	S	POP	1955	Mercury 70633 ($50)
Heaven On Earth (N)	P	S		1956	Mercury 70893 ($40)
(You've Got) The Magic Touch (N)	P	S		1956	Mercury 70819 ($40)
On My Word Of Honor (N)	P	S		1956	Mercury 71011 ($30)
You'll Never Never Know (N)	P	S		1956	Mercury 70948 ($30)
My Prayer	P	S	POP	1956	Mercury 70893 ($40)
My Dream	P	S	POP	1957	Mercury 71093 ($30)
Twilight Time	P	S	POP	1958	Mercury 71289 ($25)
Smoke Gets In Your Eyes	P	S	POP	1958	Mercury 71383 ($30)/Mercury 10001 (58) ($50)
Poets					

Vowels Of Love (N)	C	F		1958	Pull 129 ($150)/Flash 129 (58) ($60)
Poni-Tails					
Born Too Late	C	S	D	1958	ABC 9934 ($25)
Precisions					
Eight Reasons Why (I Love You)	N	S		1962	Highland 300 ($400)
Premiers (A)					
My Darling (N)	C	S		1956	Dig 113 ($250)
Is This A Dream? (N)	C	S		1957	Gone 5009 ($300)
Premiers (B)					
Help (N)	C	F		1960	Palm 301 ($300)
Prisonaires					
Just Walkin' In The Rain (N)	P	S		1953	Sun 186 ($500)
Pyramids (A)					
And I Need You (N)	C	S		1955	Federal 12233 ($400)
Pyramids (B)					
Hot Dog Dooly Wah	C	F		1958	Shell 711 ($50)
Ankle Bracelet	C	S		1958	Shell 711 ($50)
Queens (Shirley Gunter & the)					
Oop-Shoop	P	F	D	1954	Flair 1050 ($30)
You're Mine	P	F	D	1955	Flair 1060 ($30)
Quin-Tones					
Down The Aisle Of Love	C	S		1958	Red Top 108 ($120)/Hunt 321 (58) ($50)
Quinns					
Hong Kong	C	F		1958	Cyclone 111 ($150)
Oh Starlight	C	S		1958	Cyclone 111 ($150)
Quotations					
Imagination	N	F		1961	Verve 10245 ($30)
Ala-Men-Sa-Aye	N	F		1961	Verve 10245 ($30)
Rainbows (A)					
Mary Lee (N)	C	F		1955	Red Robin 134 ($600)/Pilgrim 703 (56) ($50)/Fire 1012 (60) ($20)
Stay (N)	C	S		1956	Pilgrim 711 ($200)
They Say (N)	C	S		1957	Rama 209 ($600)
Rainbows (B) (Randy & the)					
Denise	N	F	I/TPA	1963	Rust 5059 ($30)
Raindrops (A)					
(I Found) Heaven In Love (N)	C	S		1956	Spin-It 104 ($200)
Raindrops (B)					
The Kind Of Boy You Can't Forget	N	F	TPA	1963	Jubilee 5455 ($20)
Ramblers (A)					
Vadunt-Un-Va-Da Song	P	S		1954	MGM 11850 ($300)
Ramblers (B)					
Come On Back (N)	C	F		1963	Trumpet 102 ($400)
Ravels (Sheriff & the)					
Shombalor (N)	C	F		1959	Vee Jay 306 ($40)
Ravens					
Lullabye (N)	P	S		1946	Hub 3030 ($120*)
September Song (N)	P	S		1948	National 9053 ($300*)
Until The Real Thing Comes Along (N)	P	S		1948	National 9045 ($300*)
Once In A While (N)	P	S		1948	National 9053 ($300*)
Count Every Star (N)	P	S		1950	National 9111 ($3,000)
Time Takes Care Of Everything (N)	P	S		1950	Columbia 39050 ($250*)/Columbia 6-903 (50) ($700)
You Foolish Thing (N)	P	S		1951	Columbia 39408 ($2,000)
Don't Mention My Name (N)	P	S		1953	Mercury 70060 ($200)
Rays					
Silhouettes	C	S		1957	XYZ 102 ($200)/Cameo 117 (57) ($25)
Re-Vels					
False Alarm	C	F		1958	Chess 1708 ($150)
Reflections					
(Just Like) Romeo & Juliet	N	F		1964	Golden World 8/9 ($20)
Regan, Tommy (backed by the Marcels)					
I'll Never Stop Loving You (N)	N	F		1964	Colpix 725 ($100)
Regents					
Barbara Ann	N	F	I	1961	Cousins 1002 ($1,200)/Gee 1065 (61) ($25)
Runaround	N	F	I	1961	Gee 1071 ($25)
Revalons					
Dreams Are For Fools (N)	C	F		1958	Pet 802 ($120)
Rhythm Aces					
I Wonder Why (N)	P	S		1954	Vee Jay 124 ($200)
Rialtos					
Let Me In (N)	N	F		1962	CB 5009 ($300)
Riffs					

Little Girl (N)	N	F		1964	Sunny 22 ($200)
Rivera, Lucy (& group)					
Make Me Queen Again	N	S		1959	End 1041 ($20)
Rivieras					
Moonlight Cocktails (N)	C	S		1960	Coed 529 ($25)
Count Every Star	N	S		1958	Coed 503 ($50)
Rivileers					
A Thousand Stars	P	S		1954	Baton 200 ($200)/Baton 241 (57) ($40)
					Dark 241 ($25)
Rivingtons					
Papa Oom-Mow-Mow	N	F	NOV	1962	Liberty 55427 ($25)/Wand 11253 (73) ($5)
Rob Roys (Norman Fox & the)					
Dream Girl	C	S		1958	Hammer 544 ($30)/Capitol 4128 (59) ($700)
Robins					
Smoky Joe's Café	P	F	NOV	1955	Spark 122 ($340)/Atco 6059 (56) ($50)
Rocketones					
Dee I (N)	C	S		1957	Melba 113 ($50)
Mexico	C	F		1957	Melba 113 ($50)
Rockin' Chairs (Lenny Dean & the)					
A Kiss Is A Kiss	C	F		1959	Recorte 402 ($100)
Please Mary Lou (N)	C	F		1959	Recorte 404 ($50)
Memories Of Love	C	F		1959	Recorte 412 ($50)
Romans (Little Caesar & the)					
Those Oldies But Goodies (Remind Me Of You)	N	S		1961	Del-Fi 4158 ($30)
Roomates					
Band Of Gold	N	S		1961	Valmor 010 ($20)
Roomates (Cathy Jean & the)					
Please Love Me Forever	N	S		1960	Valmor 007 ($25)
Rosebuds					
Dearest Darling	C	S	D	1957	Gee 1033 ($50)
Roulettes					
I See A Star	C	S		1958	Champ 102 ($80)
Royals (A) (aka Midnighters)					
Every Beat Of My Heart (N)	P	S		1952	Federal 12064 ($1,500)/
					Federal 12064AA ($3,000)
A Love Of My Heart (N)	P	S		1952	Federal 12098 ($800)
Moonrise (N)	P	S		1952	Federal 12088 ($2,000)
Starting From Tonight (N)	P	S		1952	Federal 12077 ($2,500)
Royals (B) (Richie & the)					
And When I'm Near You (N)	N	F		1961	Rello 1 ($80)
Royaltones					
Crazy Love (N)	C	F		1956	Old Town 1018 ($100)
Royal Teens					
Believe Me	C	F	I/POP	1959	Capitol 4261 ($30)
Safaris					
Image Of A Girl	C	S	I	1960	Eldo 101 ($25)
Salutations (Vito & the)					
Unchained Melody	N	F	I	1963	Herald 583 ($30)
Scarlets					
Dear One	P	S		1954	Red Robin 128 ($500)/Event 4287 (55) ($40)
Love Doll	C	S		1955	Red Robin 133 ($500)
Schoolboys					
Please Say You Want Me	C	S	SB	1957	Okeh 7076 ($30)
Shirley	C	F	SB	1957	Okeh 7076 ($30)
Angel Of Love	C	S	SB	1958	Juanita 103 ($150)
Scott Brothers					
Part Of You (N)	C	F		1959	Skyline 502 ($25)
Selections					
Guardian Angel	C	F	I	1958	Antone 101 ($250)/Mona Lee 129 ($60)
Senors					
May I Have This Dance	N	M	SB	1962	Sue 756 ($50)
Sensations					
Please Mr. Disc Jockey	P	S		1956	Atco 6067 ($40)
My Debut To Love	P	S		1957	Atco 6090 ($40)
Let Me In	N	F		1961	Argo 5405 ($20)
Serenaders					
I Wrote A Letter (N)	C	F		1957	Chock Full O' Hits 101 ($300)/MGM 12623 ($80)
Sharps					
Love Me My Darling (N)	P	S		1954	Two Mikes 101 ($500*)
Shells					
Baby Oh Baby	C	S		1957	Johnson 104 ($40)
What's In An Angel's Eyes (N)	C	S		1957	Johnson 104 ($40)
Sippin' Soda (N)	C	S		1958	End 1022 ($150)/Gone 5103 (61) ($25)

Shepherd Sisters

Alone (N)	C	F	D/POP	1957	Lance 125 ($25)

Sheppards

Sherry (N)	C	S		1956	United 198 ($250)
Island Of Love	C	S		1959	Apex 7750 ($40)

Shields

You Cheated	C	S		1958	Tender 513 ($150)/Dot 15805 (58) ($25)

Shirelles

I Met Him On A Sunday	C	F	D	1958	Tiara 6112 ($800)/Decca 30588 (58) ($25)/Decca 25506 (60s) ($15)
Dedicated To The One I Love	N	S	D	1959	Scepter 1203 ($40)
Tonight's The Night	N	M	D	1960	Scepter 1208 ($30)
Will You Love Me Tomorrow	N	M	D	1960	Scepter 1211 ($30)
Mama Said (N)	N	F	D	1961	Scepter 1217 ($20)
Baby It's You	N	S	D	1961	Scepter 1227 ($20)
Soldier Boy	N	S	D	1962	Scepter 1228 ($15)

Showmen

It Will Stand	N	F	1961	Minit 632 ($30)/Imperial 66033 (64) ($12)/Liberty 56166 (70) ($6)

Silhouettes

I Sold My Heart To The Junkman (N)	C	S	1958	Ace 632 ($20)/Junior 396 (58) ($100)
Get A Job	C	F	1957	Junior 391 ($800)/Ember 1029 ($30)
Bing Bong	C	F	1958	Ember 1037 ($20)

Silva-Tones

Chi Wa Wa (That's All I Want From You)	C	S	1957	Monarch 528 ($50)/Argo 5281 (57) ($30)

Sinceres

Please Don't Cheat On Me (N)	N	F	1961	Richie 545 ($600)

Six Teens

A Casual Look	C	S	1956	Flip 315 ($20)

Skarlettones

Do You Remember (N)	C	F	1959	Ember 1053 ($120)

Skyliners

Lonely Way (N)	C	F		1959	Calico 109 ($30)
This I Swear	N	S	POP	1959	Calico 106 ($30)
It Happened Today	C	F	POP	1959	Calico 109 ($30)
Since I Don't Have You	N	S	POP	1959	Calico 103/104 ($50)/Original Sound 35 (63) ($15)
Pennies From Heaven	C	F	POP	1960	Calico 117 ($25)/Original Sound 36 (63) ($15)

Solitaires

South Of The Border	C	M	1954	Old Town 1006/1007 ($700)
Please Remember My Heart (N)	C	S	1954	Old Town 1006/1007 ($700)
Blue Valentine (N)	C	S	1954	Old Town 1000 ($400)
Wonder Why (N)	C	S	1954	Old Town 1000 ($400)
Later For You Baby (N)	C	F	1955	Old Town 1015 ($100)
I Don't Stand A Ghost Of A Chance (N)	C	S	1955	Old Town 1010 ($500)
Nothing Like A Little Love (N)	C	S	1956	Old Town 1032 ($200)
You've Sinned (N)	C	S	1956	Old Town 1026 ($300)
I Really Love You So (Honey Babe) (N)	C	F	1957	Old Town 1044 ($400)
The Angels Sang	P	S	1956	Old Town 1026 ($100)
Walkin' Along	C	F	1957	Old Town 1034 ($75)/Argo 5316 (58) ($30)

Sophomores (Anthony & the)

Play Those Oldies Mr. D.J. (N)	N	F	1963	Mercury 72103 ($60)
Embraceable You	C	S	1963	Grand 163 ($60)

Souvenirs

Double Dealing Baby (N)	P	F	1957	Dooto LP 224 ($100)

Spaniels

The Bells Ring Out (N)	P	S	1953	Vee Jay 103 ($300)
Baby It's You (N)	P	S	1953	Vee Jay 101 ($800)/Chance 1141 (53) ($500)
Goodnight Sweetheart Goodnight	P	S	1954	Vee Jay 107 ($300)
Let's Make Up (N)	C	S	1954	Vee Jay 116 ($100)
You Painted Pictures (N)	C	S	1955	Vee Jay 154 ($60)
You Gave Me Peace Of Mind (N)	C	S	1956	Vee Jay 229 ($60)
Everyone's Laughing (N)	C	M	1957	Vee Jay 246 ($60)
Stormy Weather (N)	C	F	1958	Vee Jay 290 ($60)

Spectors Three

I Really Do (N)	N	M	1960	Trey 3001 ($25)

Spiders

I Didn't Want To Do It (N)	P	F	1954	Imperial 5265 ($100)/Imperial 5618 (59) ($30)
I'm Slippin' In (N)	P	F	1954	Imperial 5291 ($250)
Witchcraft (N)	P	F	1955	Imperial 5366 ($100)
That's My Desire (N)	P	S	1957	Imperial 5423 ($30)

Spinners (Claudine Clark & the)

Party Lights	N	F		1962	Chancellor 1113 ($20)
Squires					
Dreamy Eyes	C	S		1957	Aladdin 3360 ($80)
Starlites					
Missing You (n)	C	S		1957	Peak 5000 ($200)
Starlites (Eddie & the)					
To Make A Long Story Short (N)	C	S		1959	Scepter 1202 ($60)
Come On Home (N)	N	S		1963	Aljon 1260/1261 ($30)
Stereos					
I Really Love You	N	F		1961	Cub 9095 ($25)
Strangers					
My Friends (N)	P	S		1954	King 4697 ($400)
Hoping You'll Understand (N)	P	S		1954	King 4728 ($400)
Blue Flowers (N)	P	S		1954	King 4709 ($500)
Students					
I'm So Young	C	S	SB	1958	Note 10012 ($500)/Argo 5386 (61) ($20)/Checker 902 ($40)
Every Day Of The Week	C	F	SB	1958	Note 10012 ($500)/Argo 5386 (61) ($20)/Checker 902 ($40)
Summits					
Go Back Where You Came From (N)	N	F		1961	Times Square 422 ($25)
Sunbeams					
Please Say You'll Be Mine (N)	C	S		1957	Acme 109 ($3,000)
Superiors					
Lost Love	C	S		1957	Atco 6106 ($70)/Main Line 104 (58) ($600)
Supremes (A)					
Could This Be You (N)	P	S		1956	Kitten 6969 ($500)
Supremes (B) (Ruth McFadden & the)					
Darling, Listen To The Words Of This Song	P	S		1956	Old Town 1014 ($50)
Supremes (C)					
Just For You And I (N)	C	S		1957	Ace 534 ($80)
Swallows					
Since You've Been Away (N)	P	S		1951	King 4466 ($300*)
Eternally (N)	P	S		1951	King 4501 ($800)
Will You Be Mine (N)	P	S		1951	King 4458 ($1,500)
It Ain't The Meat (N)	P	F		1951	King 4501 ($800)
Dearest (N)	P	S		1951	King 4458 ($1,500)
Beside You (N)	P	S		1952	King 4525 ($400)
Please Baby Please (N)	P	M		1952	King 4579 ($800)
Swans					
My True Love (N)	P	S		1953	Rainbow 233 ($1,500)
Swinging Hearts					
How Can I Love You (N)	N	S		1961	620 1002 ($200)/NRM 1002 (61) ($300)
Teardrops					
The Stars Are Out Tonight (N)	C	S		1954	Josie 766 ($200)/Port 70019 (60) ($25)
Techniques					
Hey! Little Girl	C	S	POP	1957	Stars 551 ($40)/Roulette 4030 ($25)
Teddy Bears					
To Know Him Is To Love Him	C	S	TPA	1958	Dore 503 ($30)
Teenagers (Frankie Lymon & the)					
ABC's Of Love (N)	C	F	SB	1956	Gee 1022 ($30)
I'm Not A Know It All (N)	C	S	SB	1956	Gee 1012 ($50)
Share	C	S	SB	1956	Gee 1022 ($30)
Why Do Fools Fall In Love	C	F	SB	1956	Gee 1002 ($80)
I Promise To Remember	C	F	SB	1956	Gee 1018 ($30)
Out In The Cold Again (N)	C	S	SB	1957	Gee 1036 ($30)
Paper Castles (N)	C	F	SB	1957	Gee 1036 ($30)
I Want You To Be My Girl	C	F	SB	1956	Gee 1012 ($50)
Teenage Love	C	F	SB	1957	Gee 1032 ($30)
Teenchords (Lewis Lymon & the)					
I'm Not Too Young To Fall In Love	C	F	SB	1957	Fury 1006 ($80)
Please Tell The Angels	C	S	SB	1957	Fury 1003 ($80)
Honey Honey	C	F	SB	1957	Fury 1003 ($80)
I'm So Happy (Tra-La-La-La)	C	F	SB	1957	Fury 1000 ($200)
Tempo-Tones (Nancy Lee & the)					
So They Say	C	S		1957	Acme 711 ($80)
Tempo-Tones (with Richard Lanham)					
Get Yourself Another Fool	C	S		1957	Acme 713 ($150)
Temptations (A)					
Standing Alone (N)	C	F		1958	King 5118 ($300)
Roach's Rock (N)	C	F		1958	King 5118 ($300)
Temptations (B)					
Barbara	C	F	POP	1960	Goldisc 3001 ($30)

Three Chuckles (with Teddy Randazzo)

Runaround	P	S	POP	1954	Boulevard 100 ($80)/X 0066 (54) ($25)
Foolishly	P	S	POP	1955	X 0095 ($25)

Three Friends

Blanche	C	S	I/POP	1956	Lido 500 ($60)/Relic 1021 (73) ($8)

Thrillers (Little Joe & the)

Peanuts	C	F	SB	1957	Okeh 7088 ($20)

Timetones (aka Time-Tones)

I've Got A Feeling (N)	N	S		1961	Atco 6201 ($25)
(Times Square Productions) Pretty Pretty Girl	C	F		1961	Atco 6201 ($25) (Times Square)
Here In My Heart	C			1961	Times Square 421 ($30)/Relic 538 (65) ($10)

Tokens (A)

Doom Lang (N)	C	F		1957	Gary 1006 ($100)/ Musictone 1113 (59) ($20)

Tokens (B)

The Lion Sleeps Tonight	N	M	TPA	1961	RCA 7954 ($25)
Tonight I Fell In Love	N	F	TPA	1961	Warwick 615 ($30)

Tonettes

Oh What A Baby	C	F	D	1958	Doe 101 ($80)/ABC 9905 (58) ($20)

Tops (Little Jimmy Rivers & the)

Puppy Love	C	F	SB	1961	Len 1011 ($30)/Swan 4091 (61) ($20)/V-Tone 102 ($150)

Treble Chords

Theresa	C	F		1959	Decca 31015 ($100)

Tremaines

Jingle Jingle	C	F		1958	Cash 100/101 ($400)/Val 100/101 (58) ($250)/Old Town 1051 ($50)

Tru-Tones

Magic (N)	C	F		1957	Chart 634 ($800)

Tune Weavers

Happy Happy Birthday Baby ($25)	C	S		1957	Casa Grande 4037 ($150)/Checker 872 (57)

Turbans

When You Dance	C	F		1955	Herald 458 ($50)
Valley Of Love (N)	C	S		1957	Herald 495 ($30)
Congratulations	C	S		1957	Herald 510 ($25)

Turks

Emily (N)	P	S		1955	Money 211 ($60)

Tuxedos

Yes It's True (N)	C	S		1960	Forte 1414 ($150)

Twlighters

Little Did I Dream (N)	P	S		1955	MGM 55011 ($200)

Tymes

So Much In Love	N	M	POP	1963	Parkway 871A ($25)/Parkway 871C (63) ($15)
Somewhere (N)	N	S		1963	Parkway 891 ($15)

Tyson, Roy (& group)

Oh What A Night For Love (N)	C	F	SB	1963	Double L 723 ($80)

Uniques (A)

I'm So Unhappy	N	S		1960	Bliss 1004 ($500)/Pride 1018 (61) ($200)/Gone 5113 ($200)

Uniques (B)

Do You Remember	N	S		1959	Flippin' 202 ($60)

Universals

Again	C	S		1957	Mark-X 7004 ($200)

Utopians (Mike & the)

Erlene (N)	C	F		1958	Cee Jay 574 ($300)

Vacels (Ricky & the)

Lorraine	N	S		1962	Express 711 ($30)

Val-Chords

Candy Store Love	C	F	SB	1957	Gametime 104 ($300)

Valentines

Lily Maebelle (N)	C	F		1955	Rama 171 ($150)
Woo Woo Train	C	F		1955	Rama 196 ($100)
Don't Say Goodnight (N)	C	S		1957	Rama 228 ($150)
Nature's Creation	C	S		1956	Rama 208 ($100)

Valiants

This Is The Night (N)	C	S		1957	Keen 34004 ($30)

Valrays

Yo Me Pregunto (N)	N	F		1963	Parkway 904 ($20)

Van Dykes

Come On, Baby (N)	C	S		1958	Decca 30762 ($40)

Vanguards

Moonlight (N)	C	S		1958	Ivy 103 ($100)

Velours
My Love Come Back (N)	C	S		1956	Onyx 501 ($200)/Relic 503 (64) ($15)
This Could Be The Night (N)	C	S		1957	Onyx 515 ($120)/Relic 516 (64) ($15)
Can I Come Over Tonight	C	S		1957	Onyx 512 ($200)/Gone 5092 (60) ($20)/Relic 504 (64) ($15)

Vel-Tones
Now	C	F		1960	Zara 901 ($80)/Lost Nite 103 (61) ($100)

Velvetones
The Glory Of Love (N)	C	S		1957	Aladdin 3372 ($200)/ Imperial 5878 (62) ($25)

Velvets (A)
I (N)	P	S		1953	Red Robin 122 ($150)/Pilgrim 706 (55) ($50)/Event 4285 (70s) ($8)

Velvets (B)
Tonight (Could Be The Night)	N	F		1961	Monument 441 ($30)

Videls
Mr. Lonely (N)	N	S		1960	JDS 5004 ($30)

Videos
Trickle Trickle	C	F		1958	Casino 102 ($50)

Viscaynes
Stop What You're Doing (N)	C	S		1961	Tropo 101 ($150)

Vocaleers
Be True	P	S		1952	Red Robin 113 ($600)
I Walk Alone (N)	P	S		1953	Red Robin 119 ($400)
Is It A Dream	P	S		1952	Red Robin 114 ($300)

Voices
Two Things I Love (N)	P	F		1955	Cash 1011 ($60)

Volumes
I Love You	N	F		1962	Chex 1002 ($40)

Voxpoppers
Wishing For Your Love (N)	C	S	POP	1958	Amp-3 1004 ($40)/Mercury 71282 (58) ($20)

Wanderers (A)
Thinking Of You (N)	C	S		1957	Onyx 518 ($60)

Wanderers (B) (Tony Allen & the)
If Love Was Money (N)	C	F		1961	Kent 356 ($15)

Wheels
My Heart's Desire	C	S		1956	Premium 405 ($60)

Whirlers
Magic Mirror	C	S	G	1956	Whirlin' Disc 108 ($80)/ Port 70025 (60) ($20)

Whispers
Fool Heart (N)	P	S		1954	Gotham 309 ($200)

Willows
Church Bells May Ring	C	F		1956	Melba 102 ($80)

Wrens
Beggin' For Love (N)	P	S		1955	Rama 53 ($1,500)/Rama 65 (55) ($150)
C'est La Vie (N)	C	S		1956	Rama 194 ($400)
Come Back My Love	P	F		1955	Rama 65 ($400)

Youngsters
Shattered Dreams (N)	C	F		1956	Empire 104 ($100)

Zodiacs (Maurice Williams & the)
Stay	C	F		1960	Herald 552 ($20)

Chapter 23

Doo-Wop Aptitude Test

The Doo-Wop Aptitude Test is scored like a Scholastic Aptitude Test (S.A.T.). The range of scores is between 200 and 800, the latter being a perfect score. For each of the 200 questions in the D.W.A.T., each correct answer receives 3 points. The number of points earned (# of correct answers times 3 is added to 200 to attain the final score).

The questions are arranged in four blocks of 50 questions. The first 50 are, on average, the easiest; questions 51-100 are the second easiest, etc. By the time you get to questions 151-200, you're in expert territory, so watch out! It is suggested, especially for those whose doo-wop rhythm and blues elevators don't go all the way to the top, that you can read the book before you attempt the dreaded D.W.A.T. Or, you could take a "pre-test," then read the book, then take it again. In any case, you'll need a good night's sleep before the test, so get to bed early. And eat a good breakfast.

Answers are found in the Appendix I.

1. All of the following are underrated paleo-doo-wop groups except the...
   a. Marylanders
   b. Swallows
   c. Four Buddies
   d. Heartbeats

2. The lead singer of the Four Lovers was...
   a. Neil Sedaka
   b. Wilson Pickett
   c. Frankie Valli
   d. Fabian Forte

3. The Paragons took their name from the Paragon Oil Company. What other famous Brooklyn group got their name from a nationwide oil company?
   a. Essos
   b. Mobils
   c. Shells
   d. Citgoes

4. Gene Mumford sand lead for which of the following?
   a. Billy Ward and His Dominoes
   b. Larks
   c. Serenaders
   d. All of the above

5. The Cadets had the most popular version of "Stranded in the Jungle." Who did the original version?
   a. Hollywood Flames
   b. Feathers
   c. Jayhawks
   d. Robins

6. All of the following Robinsons were New York City record label owners except...
   a. Danny
   b. Jackie
   c. Bobby
   d. Tommy

7. Which nonsense syllable strings are found in "Never" by the Earls?
   a. "Oop oop jinga linga bop bop..."
   b. "Loppa lotta lips" and "Choppa tow tips"
   c. "Oop shoop jinga linga chop chop..."
   d. All of the above

8. Which of the following labels helped develop prototypes of the "soul" sound?
   a. Vee Jay
   b. Laurie
   c. Gee
   d. Dootone

9. Which song was the first hit by Frankie Lymon and the Teenagers?
   a. I Promise To Remember
   b. Oh Gee Oh Gosh
   c. The ABCs Of Love
   d. Why Do Fools Fall In Love

10. Famous songs with "Jungle" in the titles were recorded by all but which of the following groups?
    a. Jayhawks
    b. Cellos
    c. Eternals
    d. Cadets

11. All of the following groups were in the Vee Jay stable except...
    a. Midnighters
    b. Dells
    c. Spaniels
    d. Magnificents

12. All of the following male groups were known for cover records except...
    a. Otis Williams and the Charms
    b. Crew Cuts
    c. Diamonds
    d. Gladiolas

13. The following are all groups with a "white group sound" except the...
    a. Elegants
    b. Sunbeams
    c. Mystics
    d. Bay Bops

14. "My My Darling" and "Stars In The Sky" were recorded by which group?
    a. Charms
    b. Chanters
    c. Chalets
    d. Charts

15. All of the following female groups were infamous for cover records except the...
    a. McGuire Sisters
    b. Fontane Sisters
    c. Shepherd Sisters
    d. Chordettes

16. Sonny Til was the lead singer of the Orioles. What was his real name?
    a. Sonny Til
    b. Tillington Earlghman
    c. Earlington Tilghman
    d. Early Wynn

17. Find the "lemon" among the Lymons:
    a. Lewis
    b. Lester
    c. Frankie
    d. Timmy

18. All of the following were gang doo-wop groups except the...
    a. Charts
    b. Continentals
    c. Matadors
    d. Chords

19. Which of the following songs, on which Johnny Maestro sang lead, is not done in doo-wop style?
    a. The Worst That Could Happen
    b. What A Surprise
    c. Sixteen Candles
    d. Sweetest One

20. The Fleetwoods' 1960 version of "Runaround" was a remake of which of the following group's hit?
    a. Four Aces
    b. Hilltoppers
    c. Three Chuckles
    d. Four Esquires

21. Which of the following did *not* have a reputation for being a novelty group?
    a. Robins
    b. Jacks
    c. Cellos
    d. Coasters

22. "A Sunday Kind Of Love" was recorded in the doo-wop era by all but which of the following groups?
    a. Harptones
    b. Orioles
    c. Marcels
    d. Del Vikings

23. What color is represented by the Ebonaires, Ravens and Ink Spots?
    a. Black
    b. Blue
    c. Red
    d. Violet

24. "A Thousand Stars" was a hit for which of the following?
    a. Elegants
    b. Channels
    c. Heartbeats
    d. Rivileers

25. Which song was recorded least often in the doo-wop era?
    a. A Sunday Kind Of Love
    b. In The Still Of The Night
    c. Gloria
    d. Over The Rainbow

26. Which of the following was *not* done by the (female) Angels?
    a. Til
    b. I Met Him On A Sunday
    c. My Boyfriend's Back
    d. Cry Baby Cry

27. Jessie Belvin was a member of the...
    a. Moonglows
    b. Crowns
    c. Cliques
    d. Feathers

28. All of the following aided in reviving the doo-wop sound *except*...
    a. Dave Marsh
    b. Irving Rose
    c. Donn Fileti and Eddie Gries
    d. Art Laboe

29. Which group never had a female member?
    a. Crests
    b. Skyliners
    c. Heartbeats
    d. Cleftones

30. "A Wonderful Dream" was a hit for which of the following groups?
    a. Majors
    b. Earls
    c. Flairs
    d. Ravens

31. Which of the following did not lead to the demise of the doo-wop sound?
    a. Payola
    b. The development of CDs
    c. Increased use of instruments
    d. Folk music

32. What were the names of the three people involved in the love triangle in "My True Story" by the Jive Five?
    a. Sue, Earl and Lorraine
    b. Mary, Sue and Bobby
    c. Earline, Bobbie and Tony
    d. Patti, Maxine and Laverne

33. "Bong Bong (I Love You Madly)" was a semi-hit for which of the following groups?
    a. Tony Vincent, backed by the Castros
    b. Vince Castro, backed by the Tonettes
    c. Tony Castro, backed by the Variations
    d. Vince Anthony, backed by the Castros

34. Ellie Greenwich's writing partner for many Tin Pan Alley doo-wop songs was...
    a. Paul Simon
    b. Jeff Barry
    c. Len Barry
    d. Jay Siegel

35. Which group had a famous song with "Sunday" in the title?
    a. Heartbeats
    b. Cleftones
    c. Harptones
    d. Clovers

36. Which of the following women was never a doo-wop lead singer?
    a. Zola Taylor
    b. Arlene Smith
    c. Darlene Love
    d. Jo Stafford

37. The following were all post doo-wop-era groups *except*...
    a. Four Lovers
    b. Jay and the Americans
    c. Diana Ross and the Supremes
    d. Four Seasons

38. What does SPEBSQSA stand for?
    a. Who knows?
    b. Who cares?
    c. Society for the Preservation and Encouragement of Barbershop Quartet Singing in America
    d. What?

39. "Heaven And Paradise" was a big hit for...
    a. Fred Parris and the Five Satins
    b. Vernon Green and the Medallions
    c. Don Julian and the Meadowlarks
    d. Julian Herrara and the Tigers

40. The groups that made "Crying In The Chapel" a rhythm and blues standard was the...
    a. Dominoes
    b. Clovers
    c. Drifters
    d. Orioles

41. All of the following are doo-wop groups *and* fodder for jewelry except the...
    a. Pearls
    b. Diamonds
    c. Emeralds
    d. Aquamarines

42. Ronnie and the Relatives achieved fame as...
    a. Ronnie and the "I"s
    b. Ronnie and the Highlights
    c. Ronnie and the Daytonas
    d. the Ronettes

43. Which of the following singers was *not* a schoolboy doo-wop lead?
    a. Frankie Lymon
    b. Leslie Martin
    c. Sherman Garnes
    d. Louis Lymon

44. Which of the following was not a song recorded by the Chiffons?
    a. He's So Fine
    b. A Love So Fine
    c. One Fine Day
    d. Fine Fine Frame

45. Which instruments are featured in the opening of the Diamonds' version of "Little Darlin'?"
    a. Piano and bongo drum
    b. Castanets and a cowbell
    c. Tamborine and banjo
    d. Saxophone and stand-up bass

46. Which one of the following people was a major Tin Pan Alley doo-wop songwriter?
    a. Teddy Randazzo
    b. Harvey Fuqua
    c. Jerome Kern
    d. Carole King

47. Which group was *not* integrated?
    a. Don Julian and the Meadowlarks
    b. Norman Fox and the Rob Roys
    c. Herb Cox and the Cleftones
    d. Johnny Maestro and the Crests

48. A big hit for Nathaniel Mayer and the Fabulous Twilights was…
    a. The Quiet Village
    b. Bongo Stomp
    c. Village Of Love
    d. In The Jungle

49. Alan Freed's movie "Rock Rock Rock" featured which of the following?
    a. Jesse Belvin
    b. Dion
    c. Teddy Randazzo
    d. Johnny Maestro

50. All of the following are prominent paleo-doo-wop groups except the…
    a. Nutmegs
    b. Clovers
    c. Larks
    d. Chords

51. The Crows recorded "Heartbreaker" in 1954. Which group recorded it first?
    a. Heartbreakers
    b. Hearts
    c. Heartbeats
    d. Heartspinners

52. Maurice Williams was the lead singer of both the…
    a. Dominoes and Larks
    b. Gladiolas and Zodiacs
    c. Mello-Moods and Solitaires
    d. Paragons and Jesters

53. Later standout recordings by the Flamingos include all but which of the following?
    a. Mio Amore
    b. In My Diary
    c. I Only Have Eyes For You
    d. Lovers Never Say Goodbye

54. Who was the female voice on the Clusters' recording of "Darling Can't You Tell?"
    a. Shirley Alston Reeves
    b. Arlene Smith
    c. Ruth McFadden
    d. Gloria Steinem

55. For "Little Bitty Pretty One," Thurston Harris was backed by the…
    a. Halos
    b. Dreamlovers
    c. Sharps
    d. Marcels

56. Which group did *not* sing a famous doo-wop song about Mexico?
    a. Moonglows
    b. Rocketones
    c. Coasters
    d. Nutmegs

57. Supposedly, the rarest record is a ballad called "Stormy Weather" by the Five Sharps on Jubilee. Which group redid this sing uptempo?
    a. Earls
    b. Harptones
    c. Moonglows
    d. Spaniels

58. The Moonglows had hits with all of the following except…
    a. The Ten Commandments Of Love
    b. Most Of All
    c. Out Of Sight, Out Of Mind
    d. Sincerely

59. Which of the following was *not* a hit for the Coasters?
    a. Poison Ivy
    b. Searchin'
    c. Yakety Yak
    d. Short Shorts

60. Justine "Baby" Washington sang for which of the following groups?
    a. Hearts
    b. Kidneys
    c. Deltairs
    d. Cookies

61. The bass of the Marcels is…
    a. Fred Johnson
    b. Gerald Gregory
    c. Norris "Bunky" Mack
    d. Willis Jackson

62. Which label was not headquartered in Chicago?
    a. King
    b. Chance
    c. Chess
    d. Vee Jay

63. "A Thousand Stars" by Kathy Young and the innocents was a remake of a 1954 hit by a group from Queens, New York, called the…
    a. Heartbeats
    b. Rivileers
    c. Cleftones
    d. Videos

64. Barbara Custis, sister of lead Eddie Custis of the "Lost Love" Superiors, also sang with the group and later married another famous Philadelphia lead singer. Name him.
    a. Al Banks
    b. Len Barry
    c. George Grant
    d. Lee Andrews

65. "Over The Rainbow" was not recorded in the doo-wop era by which of the following groups?
    a. Baysiders
    b. Moroccos
    c. Demensions
    d. Passions

66. Which group backed up Curtis Lee on "Pretty Little Angel Eyes?"
    a. Marcels
    b. Halos
    c. Olympics
    d. Johnson Brothers

67. Who was the lead singer of the Cardinals?
    a. Junior Denby
    b. Ernie Lee Warren
    c. Billy Dawn Smith
    d. Arthur Lee Maye

68. Which is not currently (in 1997) an active record label?
    a. Earth Angel
    b. Classic Artists
    c. Crystal Ball
    d. Relic

69. "Born Too Late" was a hit for the…
    a. Aquatones
    b. Bonnie Sisters
    c. Poni-Tails
    d. Six Teens

70. Sonny Knight was a solo artist who had a hit with "Confidential." Sonny Norton was the lead of the Crows, the group that had "Gee." Sonny Wright sang lead for which of the following groups?
    a. Larks, Dominos and Serenaders
    b. Bachelors, Montereys and Buddies
    c. Diamonds, Regals and Metronomes
    d. Cadillacs, Channels and Ladders

71. Lucy Rivera, who sang with the Love Notes on their hit "United," later married a rock 'n' roller, changing her name to Laurie Anderson. Who is he?
    a. Tommy Sands
    b. Jose Feliciano
    c. Gary "U.S." Bonds
    d. Chris Montez

72. Which one of the following Brooklyn groups with a white group sound was *not* all-white?
    a. Classics
    b. Passions
    c. Mystics
    d. Impalas

73. In "La La" by the Cobras, how many times does the lead singer say "la?"
    a. 24
    b. 48
    c. 96
    d. 192

74. Boyz 2 Men had a hit with "In The Still Of The Night" in the 1990s. Who did the original version?
    a. Penquins
    b. Orioles
    c. Five Satins
    d. Nutmegs

75. Below are the names of four doo-wop songs. Which one is *not* also the name of a doo-wop periodical?
    a. Bim Bam Boom
    b. Story Untold
    c. Those Oldies But Goodies
    d. Stormy Weather

76. Which one of the following groups sang about a "Sailor Boy?"
    a. Chiffons
    b. Shirelles
    c. Shondelles
    d. Chantels

77. Classics by the Harptones include all but...
    a. White Cliffs Of Dover
    b. Sunday Kind Of Love
    c. My Memories Of You
    d. That's The Way It Goes

78. "Zing Went The Strings Of My Heart" by Gabriel & the Angels," "Bongo Stomp" by Little Joey & the Flips and "True True Love" by the Corvairs all have which of the following nonsense syllable phrase?
    a. Babadoowah
    b. Ungowa
    c. Ding-aling-aling-ding-dong
    d. Bopagowa

79. "Tonight (Could Be The Night)" was a hit for the...
    a. Turbans
    b. Love Notes
    c. Velvets
    d. Mello-Kings

80. "Coney Island Baby" by the Excellents and "Echo" by the Emotions are both examples of...
    a. the White Group Sound
    b. Tin Pan Alley Doo-Wop
    c. Schoolboy Doo-Wop
    d. Gang Doo-Wop

81. Which of these early classics was *not* redone by the Platters?
    a. Smoke Gets In Your Eyes
    b. Harbor Lights
    c. My Prayer
    d. Moon Over Miami

82. Ernie Maresca, a songwriter-producer-artist who was involved in much of the music of Dion and the Belmonts, the Five Discs and the Del Satins, is associated with which of the following labels?
    a. Old Town
    b. Savoy
    c. Crystal Ball
    d. Laurie

83. Which of the following was *not* a release by Lewis Lymon and the Teenchords?
    a. I'm Not Too Young To Fall In Love
    b. Honey, Honey
    c. Oh Gee Oh Gosh
    d. I'm So Happy

84. Which of the following was not a hit for the Platters?
    a. My Prayer
    b. Harbor Lights
    c. To Each His Own
    d. My Heart's Desire

85. "Blue Moon" by the Marcels was a big hit in 1961. Its flip, "Goodbye To Love," was first recorded in the 1950s by which group?
    a. Charms
    b. Chanters
    c. Channels
    d. Chantels

86. Swingin' Slim Rose owned the famous Times Square Record shop. What was his real name?
    a. Slim Roscoe
    b. Slim Fell
    c. Benjamin Booker
    d. Irving Rosenweig

87. The WMGM disc jockey who was called the "curly-headed kid in the third row" was
    a. Peter Tripp
    b. Gus Gossert
    c. Alan Fredericks
    d. Paul Sherman

88. Which song was a hit for the Falcons?
    a. So Fine
    b. He's So Fine
    c. She's So Fine
    d. You're So Fine

89. The Ink Spots had a hit with "My Prayer" in 1939. It was later revived successfully by the...
    a. Five Keys
    b. Platters
    c. Fidelities
    d. Flamingos

90. Nate Bouknight was the lead of the Shells, a group that recorded...
    a. Baby Oh Baby
    b. A Thousand Stars
    c. You Cheated
    d. Can I Come Over Tonight

91. Sonia Rivera currently sings lead with the Valentinos. In the early '60s, she led a group that recorded "Bad Boy," an answer record to "Bad Girl" by Smoky Robinson and the Miracles. Name the group.
    a. Hemlocks
    b. Clickettes
    c. Gleems
    d. Marquis

92. Which group sang back-up on "Memories Of Love" by Lenny Dean and the Rockin' Chairs?
    a. Nino and the Ebbtides
    b. Del Satins
    c. Bonnevilles
    d. Bell Notes

93. The Chantels had a hit with "I Love You So" in 1958. Which group recorded it first?
    a. Clovers
    b. Cliques
    c. Crows
    d. Drifters

94. Which of the following groups did not have a female member at one time?
    a. Cleftones
    b. Skyliners
    c. Classics
    d. Chestnuts

95. "Down The Aisle Of Love" was a hit for the...
    a. Dixie Cups
    b. Patti LaBelle and the Blue-Belles
    c. Quin-Tones
    d. Dreamlovers

96. Tony Middleton was the lead singer of the…
    a. Bop Chords
    b. Ladders
    c. Jesters
    d. Willows

97. The lead singer of the Chiffons was…
    a. Judy Craig
    b. Arlene Smith
    c. Anita Humes
    d. Shirley Alston

98. Lenny Cocco was the lead singer of the…
    a. Classics
    b. Duprees
    c. Fi-Tones
    d. Chimes

99. Who sang lead on the Ravens famous recording of "Count Every Star?'
    a. Maithe Marshall
    b. Louis Heyward
    c. Joe Van Loan
    d. Jimmy Ricks

100. "Tonight I Fell In Love" was a hit for the…
    a. Mello-Moods
    b. Mello-Kings
    c. Tokens
    d. Teenagers

101. The Dells started out as the…
    a. El Rays
    b. El Dorados
    c. El Vireos
    d. El Torros

102. Lee Andrews and the Hearts did a fine job on a ballad called "Maybe You'll Be There" in 1954. Another Philadelphia group, Billy and the Essentials, did another version in 1962. What was different about it?
    a. It had the same melody with different words
    b. It had the same words with a different melody
    c. It was an entirely different sing
    d. It was done uptempo

103. The New York sound was sent over the ether by all but which of the following dee jays?
    a. Hunter Hancock
    b. Willie Bryant
    c. Jocko Henderson
    d. Tommy Smalls

104. "When You Wish Upon A Star," recorded by Dion & the Belmonts was written for which of he following movies?
    a. Cinderella
    b. Sleeping Beauty
    c. The Lion King
    d. Pinocchio

105. What was the first black female singing group to sell more than a million records worldwide?
    a. Hearts
    b. Bobbettes
    c. Chantels
    d. Shirelles

106. All of the following are both doo-wop groups and nicknames of Big Ten Conference teams except the…
    a. Buckeyes
    b. Spartans
    c. Wildcats
    d. Wolverines

107. Which group backed Dee Dee Sharp on her 1962 smash called "Mashed Potatoes?"
    a. Chantels
    b. Dreamlovers
    c. Orlons
    d. Shirelles

108. A complete listing of R&B harmony groups was written by…
    a. George Moonoogian
    b. Val Shively
    c. Ferdie Gonzalez
    d. Peter Grendysa

109. All of the following were great bass singers from the classical doo-wop years except…
    a. Jimmy Ricks
    b. Sherman Garnes
    c. Wally Roker
    d. Gerald Gregory

110. Carole King wrote Tin Pan Alley doo-wops most often with
    a. Little Eva
    b. Harvey Fuqua
    c. Barry Mann
    d. Gerry Goffin

111. A major book on the doo-wop sound in New York City was written by…
    a. Steve Propes
    b. Phil Groia
    c. Charlie Horner
    d. Bill Pruter

112. Which "moon song" was not done by the Orioles?
    a. Moonlight
    b. Moonglow
    c. I'd Rather have You Under The Moon
    d. In The Chapel In The Moonlight

113. Which of the following labels was not based in Chicago?
    a. Abner
    b. Chance
    c. Blue Lake
    d. Fortune

114. "Blue Moon" by the Marcels was a neo-doo-wop nugget written by…
    a. Simon and Garfunkel
    b. Rodgers and Hart
    c. Rodgers and Hammerstein
    d. Baskin and Robbins

115. "I Promise To Remember" by Frankie Lymon and the Teenagers was first recorded by which of the following?
    a. Louis Lymon and the Teenchords
    b. Pearl McKinnon and the Kodaks
    c. Little Jimmy Rivers and the Tops
    d. Jimmy Castor and the Juniors

116. The home of the Mercury, a major record label was…
    a. New York
    b. Chicago
    c. Los Angeles
    d. Philadelphia

117. The Solitaires waxed all but which of the following?
    a. Red Sails In The Sunset
    b. Blue Valentine
    c. The Wedding
    d. I Don't Stand A Ghost Of A Chance

118. The primary lead of the jazz-jive Rhythm Boys from the 1930s was…
    a. Frank Sinatra
    b. Rudy Vallee
    c. Mel Torme
    d. Bing Crosby

119. All of the following are names of doo-wop groups and represent the names of exotic countries except…
    a. Ecuadors
    b. Mozambiques
    c. Tunisians
    d. Moroccos

120. Songs celebrating a young lady's 16th birthday were recorded by all but which of the following?
    a. Colts
    b. Turbans
    c. Crests
    d. Tropicals

121. The following were all pre-doo-wop groups *except* the...
    a. Four Vagabonds
    b. Basin Street Boys
    c. Harptones
    d. Striders

122. The Savoy record label emanated from which New Jersey City?
    a. Jersey City
    b. Cherry Hill
    c. Morristown
    d. Newark

123. The Flamingos recorded for all of the following labels *except*...
    a. End
    b. Vee Jay
    c. Checker
    d. Chance

124. "Wheel Of Fortune" by Kay Starr was performed in doo-wop style by which of the following?
    a. Orioles
    b. Clovers
    c. Four Buddies
    d. Cardinals

125. Frankie Ervin is singing lead on "You Cheated" by the Shields. Who sang the ethereal falsetto part?
    a. Eugene Church
    b. Arthur Lee Maye
    c. Jesse Belvin
    d. Bobby Day

126. What happened on Aug. 5, 1957?
    a. Dick Clark's "American Bandstand" went on the air nationally
    b. Alan Freed held his first New York concert
    c. Sputnik was launched
    d. Elvis was drafted

127. All of the following would be equally at home singing doo-wop *and* looking pretty in a garden except the...
    a. Orchids
    b. Mums
    c. Gladiolas
    d. Roses

128. "Till Then" was a monster hit for Emil Stucchio's Classics in 1963. It was first done by a group in 1944. That group was the...
    a. Ink Spots
    b. Andrews Sisters
    c. Mills Brothers
    d. Charioteers

129. Al Silvers, head of the Herald/Ember group, recorded all of the following groups except the...
    a. Turbans
    b. Swallows
    c. Mello-Kings
    d. Five Satins

130. All of the following labels emanated from the Big Apple except...
    a. Ember
    b. Old Town
    c. Everlast
    d. RPM

131. Who provided the background to Robert Klein's pseudo-sarcastic, semi-sincere paean to the doo-wop era called "Fabulous '50s?"
    a. Mystics
    b. Halos
    c. Dreamlovers
    d. Klein himself, doing voiceovers

132. The Midnighters' "Annie" story included all but which of the following?
    a. Work With Me Annie
    b. Annie Is My Baby
    c. Annie Had A Baby
    d. Annie's Aunt Fanny

133. The Harptones recorded for all of the following labels *except*...
    a. Warwick
    b. Bruce
    c. Paradise
    d. Chess

134. Which one of the following alcohol songs was *not* done by a doo-wop or rhythm and blues group?
    a. Rye And Whiskey
    b. WPLJ (White Port And Lemon Juice)
    c. One Mint Julep
    d. Nip Sip

135. The one that is not both a doo-wop group and a major league baseball team is the...
    a. Dodgers
    b. Tigers
    c. Astros
    d. Athletics

136. The Imaginations backed up which female lead?
    a. Kathy Young
    b. Darlene Day
    c. Nancy Lee
    d. Ruth McFadden

137. Tony Orlando, of Tony Orlando and Dawn fame, sang with which of the following?
    a. Five Chances on Blue Lake ("All I Want")
    b. Five Discs on Emge ("I Remember")
    c. Five Gents on Veiking ("Baby Doll")
    d. Five Satins on Ember ("A Night To Remember")

138. The man who taught the Cadillacs to dance was...
    a. Fred Astaire
    b. Cholly Atkins
    c. Chevy Chase
    d. Bill "Bojangles" Robinson

139. Paul Winley owned all of the following labels except...
    a. Winley
    b. Porwin
    c. Cyclone
    d. Whirlin' Disc

140. All of the following cities became the basis for the names of doo-wop groups except...
    a. Paris (Parisians)
    b. Tangiers (Tangiers)
    c. Algiers (Algerians)
    d. Rome (Romans)

141. Which of the following was *not* done by the Platters?
    a. The Things I Love
    b. My Prayer
    c. Voo-Vee-Ah-Bee
    d. The Great pretender

142. The world-traveling Coasters sang all but which of the following?
    a. "China Doll"
    b. "Down In Mexico"
    c. "Brazil"
    d. "Little Egypt"

143. In total, how many male singers were there in the Orlons, (Baby Washington's) Hearts, Spector's Three and Fleetwoods?
    a. 4
    b. 5
    c. 6
    d. 7

144. Which label complex was responsible for songs that introduced dances like the "Mashed Potatoes," "Watusi" and "Bristol Stomp?"
    a. Cameo/Parkway
    b. King/Federal/DeLuxe
    c. Atlantic/Atco
    d. Aladdin/Lamp

145. The one that is *not* both a doo-wop group and a professional basketball team (past or present) is the...
    a. Warriors
    b. Royals
    c. Hawks
    d. Rockets

146. Which of the following was *not* a hit for the Clovers?
    a. Fool, Fool, Fool
    b. One Mint Julep
    c. Devil or Angel
    d. Ghost Of My Baby

147. Sly Stone, of Sly and the Family Stone, first sang with the...
    a. Little Jimmy Rivers and the Tops
    b. Premiers
    c. Chines
    d. Viscaynes

148. The major biography of Alan Freed was written by...
    a. Jeff Kreiter
    b. John Jackson
    c. Don Mennie
    d. Steve Propes

149. Early standout recordings by the Flamingos include all but which of the following?
    a. Dream Of A Lifetime
    b. Jump Children
    c. Golden Teardrops
    d. Secret Love

150. In total, how many female singers were the in the Kodaks, Tuneweavers, Fleetwoods and Platters?
    a. 4
    b. 5
    c. 6
    d. 7

151. Which group backed Nancy Lee on "So They Say?"
    a. Love Notes
    b. Sunbeams
    c. Tempo-Tones
    d. Ebb Tides

152. Who is playing piano in the background of the Supremes' 1957 recording of "Just For You And I?"
    a. Liberace
    b. Dave "Baby" Cortez
    c. Jesse Stone
    d. Huey "Piano" Smith

153. Which of the following was *not* a female group?
    a. Angels on Smash
    b. Hearts on Baton
    c. Crystals on DeLuxe
    d. Crystals on Philles

154. "You'll Never Walk Alone" by Patti LaBelle and the Bluebelles comes from which Broadway show?
    a. Rent
    b. Oklahoma
    c. Hair
    d. Carousel

155. Who was the lead singer of the Globetrotters, who released "Rainy Day Bells" in 1970 (it was also recorded by Norman Fox & the Rob Roys)?
    a. Arthur Lee Maye (of the Crowns)
    b. Bill Baker (of the Five Satins)
    c. Willie Winfield (of the Harptones)
    d. J.R. Bailey (of the Cadillacs)

156. The Cobras, who recorded "La La," were a combination of a Philadelphia group called the Cherokees and a lead who was a member of another famous Philadelphia group. Who was he?
    a. Billy Carlucci (of the Essentials)
    b. Billy Taylor (of the Castelles)
    c. George Tindley (of the Dreams)
    d. Bill Horton (of the Silhouettes)

157. The man who said, "let me whisper sweet words of pismotality" in the song "The Letter" was...
    a. Don Julian of the Meadowlarks
    b. David "Little Caesar" Johnson of the Romans
    c. Cleve Duncan of the Penguins
    d. Vernon Green of the Medallions

158. The original lead singer of the Flamingos was...
    a. Solly McElroy
    b. Nate Nelson
    c. Johnny Carter
    d. Zeke Carey

159. Mike Lasman was the white lead singer of a black group called Mike and the Utopians that recorded an uptempo classic called "Erlene." What group did Lasman move on to join?
    a. Parakeets
    b. Impalas
    c. Accents
    d. Boss Tones

160. All of the following have personnel that intermingled with the Hollywood Flames *except* the...
    a. Four Flames
    b. Bobby Day and the Satellites
    c. Flairs
    d. Tangiers

161. Which was the first all-female group to score a hit on the Billboard Rhythm & Blues charts?
    a. Shirley Gunter & the Queens
    b. Della Griffin & the Enchanters
    c. The Andrews Sisters
    d. Lydia Larson & the River Rovers

162. The Edsels are to Youngstown, Ohio as the Five Satins are to...
    a. Pittsburgh, PA
    b. Boston, MA
    c. New Haven, CT
    d. Philadelphia, PA

163. The Wheels are to the Federals as the Cadets are to the...
    a. Flairs
    b. Crowns
    c. Jayhawks
    d. Jacks

164. Lamont Dozier of the famous Motown Holland-Dozier-Holland songwriting team sang with which Detroit group?
    a. Fortunes
    b. Diablos
    c. Romeos
    d. Royals

165. Michael Eisner, head of the Disney Corporation, is the nephew of which famous independent record company exec from the 1950s?
    a. Sam Goldner of Rama/Gee
    b. Ike (and Bess) Berman of Apollo
    c. Jerry Blaine of Jubilee
    d. Herb Abramson of Atlantic

166. Johnny Greco was backed by which of the following groups on his hit "Rocket Ride?"
    a. Marcels
    b. Dovells
    c. Rick and the Masters
    d. Dreamlovers

167. "The Shrine Of St. Cecilia" was a major hit for the Harptones. Which of the following groups recorded it in the 1940s?
    a. Andrews Sisters
    b. Golden Gate Quartet
    c. Swan Silvertones
    d. Barrett Sisters

168. Which of the following is not on the famous "Paragons Meet The Jesters" vinyl album?
    a. "Please Let Me Love You" by the Jesters
    b. "Let's Start All Over Again" by the Paragons
    c. "The Wind" by the Jesters
    d. "The Vows Of Love" by the Paragons

169. Which group did Jewel Akens, who later had a big hit with "The Birds And The Bees," sing with?
    a. Premiers
    b. Hollywood Saxons
    c. Little Julian Herrara and the Tigers
    d. Jerry Stone with the Four Dots

170. The second lead of the Orioles, behind Sonny Til, had an emotional delivery and a gravel-pit type of voice. Name him.
    a. George Nelson
    b. Harmon Bethea
    c. Alexander Sharp
    d. Robert Evans

171. "I Love You" was a hit in 1962 for a Detroit group whose lead singer's name was Eddie Union. What was the name of the group?
    a. The Diablos
    b. The Volumes
    c. The Don Juans
    d. The Midnighters

172. Pearl McKinnon is to the Kodaks as Lillian Leach is to the…
    a. Supremes
    b. Mellows
    c. Tempo-Tones
    d. Sentimentalists

173. Little Joe and the Thrillers recorded "Peanut" and "Lilly Lou" among others. After Little Joe booked, what name did the Thrillers record under?
    a. Field Brothers
    b. Scott Brothers
    c. Marshall Brothers
    d. Madison Brothers

174. The Kool Gents, the group that spun off Delecta "Dee" Clark, were so named because…
    a. They saw themselves as genuinely "cool gents"
    b. They were named by their manager, a Chicago dee jay named Herb "Kool Gent" Kent
    c. They all smoked Kool cigarettes
    d. They picked the name out of a hat

175. One of the co-writers of "I Don't Stand A Ghost Of A Chance," recorded by the Five Keys and Solitaires, among others, was…
    a. Dick Haymes
    b. Bing Crosby
    c. Nat King Cole
    d. Billy Williams

176. The Classmates sang often about school events or topics. Which was not one of their releases?
    a. "Homework"
    b. "Graduation"
    c. "School Days"
    d. "Who's Gonna Take You To The Prom"

177. Gerald Gregory is to Pookie Hudson as Fred Johnson is to…
    a. Kripp Johnson
    b. Clarence Quick
    c. Cornelius Harp
    d. Jimmy Beaumont

178. Who was the bass of the Nutmegs?
    a. Leroy Griffin
    b. James "Sonny" Griffin
    c. Leroy McNeil
    d. Leroy Gomez

179. Bruce Patch, owner-operator of Classic Artist records, once sang with the…
    a. Premiers
    b. Storytellers
    c. El Sierros
    d. C-Quins

180. Which group sang "Mr. Moto?"
    a. Mystics
    b. Belmonts
    c. Nino & the Ebbtides
    d. Fantastics

181. Songs about a woman named Cherry were recorded by all but which of the following groups?
    a. Cleftones
    b. Diamonds
    c. Rivingtons
    d. Jive Bombers

182. The Spiders, featuring Chick and Chuck Carbo, had several R&B hits including "Witchcraft" in 1955. Where were they from?
    a. St. Louis
    b. Nashville
    c. Memphis
    d. New Orleans

183. Which of the following groups did not record a song with "Hong Kong" in the title?
    a. Tabbys
    b. Quinns
    c. Hi-Fives
    d. Sparrows

184. Dean Barlow sang with all of the following groups except the…
    a. Montereys
    b. Crickets
    c. Bachelors
    d. Wrens

185. The first song by a quintet called the Heartbeats was…
    a. Crazy For You
    b. Tormented
    c. Your Way
    d. A Thousand Miles Away

186. In 1962, a guy named Jerry Landis (backed by a group) recorded a song titled "Lone Teen Ranger." Who was that man (in real life)?
    a. Art Garfunkel
    b. Neil Sedaka
    c. Paul Simon
    d. Wilson Pickett

187. For which group did the jazz artist George Benson sing?
    a. Uniques
    b. Del Prados
    c. Altairs
    d. El Domingos

188. The group that backed Paul Anka on "I Confess" was the…
    a. Jacks
    b. Sharps
    c. Penguins
    d. Cliques

189. The Ravens classic, "Count Every Star," was successfully redone in 1958 by the…
    a. Rivingtons
    b. Rivileers
    c. Rivieras
    d. Robins

190. Which of the following singers was not a lead singer of the Five Keys?
    a. Lowman Pauling
    a. Rudy West
    c. Dickie Smith
    d. Maryland Pierce

191. The Rivingtons, who had a hit with "Papa-Oom-Mow-Mow" in 1962, were also variations of all the groups below *except* the...
    a. Lamplighters
    b. Sharps
    c. Tenderfoots
    d. Shields

192. "Good Goodbye" was a semi-hit in 1961 for a Brooklyn group by the name of the...
    a. Fascinators
    b. Passions
    c. Bob Knight Four
    d. Clusters

193. Of the following hits by the Moonglows, which was the first to be released?
    a. Sincerely
    b. Secret Love
    c. Most Of All
    d. In My Diary

194. The Carnations are known for their 1961 hit called...
    a. Who Do You Think You Are
    b. A Wonderful Dream
    c. Long Tall Girl
    d. Hey You

195. Fred Johnson is to the Marcels as Wally Roker is to the...
    a. Heartbeats
    b. Devotions
    c. Channels
    d. Cadillacs

196. All of the following sang about guys named Johnny *except*...
    a. Antwinetts
    b. Four Jewels
    c. Bonnie Sisters
    d. Bobbettes

197. "The Fires Burn No More" was originally recorded by...
    a. Nicky Addeo and the Darchaes
    b. Little Anthony and the Imperials
    c. Lee Andrews and the Hearts
    d. The Chesters

198. Which of the following groups did not have a famous song with "Blue" in the title?
    a. Clovers
    b. Cardinals
    c. Escorts
    d. Echoes

199. Eddie Custis, lead of the "Lost Love" Superiors, later sang with two other famous groups. Name them.
    a. Commodores, Persuasions
    b. Spinners, O'Jays
    c. Huey "Piano" Smith & the Clowns, Chairmen of the Board
    d. Beatles, Stones

200. Who was the boy mentioned in "Blanche" by the Three Friends?
    a. Artie
    b. Bobby
    c. Johnny
    d. Billy

Appendix I

Solutions to Puzzles, Quizzes & D.W.A.T.

Chapter 4

Quiz #1: Testing Your Mettle

1) "I Remember" by the Five Discs
2) "Babalu's Wedding Day" by the Eternals
3) "Who's That Knocking" by the Genies
4) "I'm So Happy" by Lewis Lymon and the Teenchords
5) "Get A Job" by the Silhouettes
6) "Guardian Angel" by the Selections
7) "Come Go With Me" by the Dell Vikings
8) "When I Woke Up This Morning" by the Bop Chords
9) "Ka-Ding-Dong" by the G-Clefs
10) "Every Day Of The Week" by the Students
11) "Never Let You Go" by the Five Discs
12) "Sincerely" by the Moonglows
13) "Church Bells May Ring" by the Willows
14) "Unchained Melody" by Vito and the Salutations
15) "Unchained Melody" by Vito and the Salutations
16) "Sorry I Ran All The Way Home" by the Impalas
17) "Rubber Biscuit" by the Chips
18) "Shombalor" by Sheriff and the Ravels
19) "Ala-Men-Sa-Aye" by the Quotations
20) "He's So Fine" by the Chiffons

Quiz #2: For Experts Only!

1) "Pretty Little Girl" by the Monarchs
2) "Darling" by the Debonaires
3) "Counting The Stars" by the Ladders
4) "Always Be Faithful" by the Monarchs
5) "Let Me Tell You" by the Nutmegs
6) "Lamplight" by the Deltas
7) "Laughing Love" by the Native Boys
8) "Diamonds And Pearls" by the Paradons
9) "I'll Be Forever Loving You" by the El Dorados
10) "Mexico" by the Rocketones
11) "Dorothy" by the Hi-Fives
12) "Smoky Places" by the Corsiars
13) "Hey Girl" by the Perfections
14) "Don't Leave Me" by the Magnificents
15) "Oo-Wee Baby" by the Ivy-Tones
16) "Tonight I Fell In Love" by the Tokens
17) "The Closer You Are" by the Magnificent Four
18) "Walking Along" by the Solitaires
19) "Magic" by the Tru-tones
20) "Bobby" by Joey and the Lexingtons

Chapter 5

Quiz 3: Shermania

1-i, 2-d, 3-h, 4-a, 5-c, 6-b, 7-e, 8-f, 9-j, 10-g.

Quiz 4: Running the Basses

A-7-s, B-17-h, C-19-n, D-15-q, E-20-a, F-9-t, G-16-i, H-12-e, I-4-g, J-14-l,
K-6-o, L-18-c, M-8-f, N-10-p, O-1-r, P-2-m, Q-13-d, R-5-k, S-11-b, T-3-j

Chapter 6

Quiz #5: One Thing Leads to Another

A-16-h, B-19-k, C-12-f, D-20-o, E-14-a, F-17-m, G-18-e, H-2-q, I-15-s,
J-11-n, K-13-i, L-6-j, M-10-c, N-8-g, O-9-r, P-7-d, Q-3-t, R-5-b, S-1-l, T-4-p

Chapter 12

Quiz #6: Stating The Facts

A-24-a, B-5-b, C-9-h, D-1-x, E-25-c, F-10-n, G-16-v, H-2-p, I-12-s, J-7-l,
K-18-y, L-22-m, M-21-j, N-11-u, O-14-d, P-20-t, Q-21-j, R-13-i, S-4-k,
T-3-e, U-6-f, V-8-g, W-23-r, X-19-o, Y-17-w

Chapter 8

Name That Tune

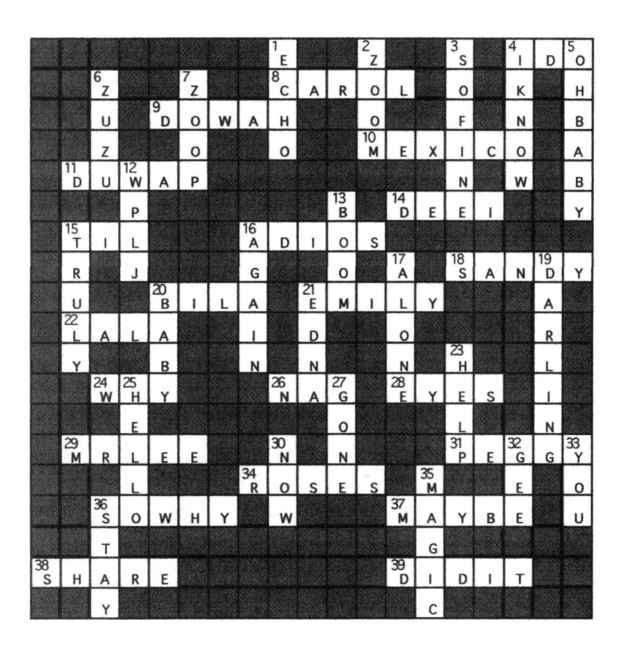

The Early Groups
Name That Group (No "Brothers," No "Sisters")

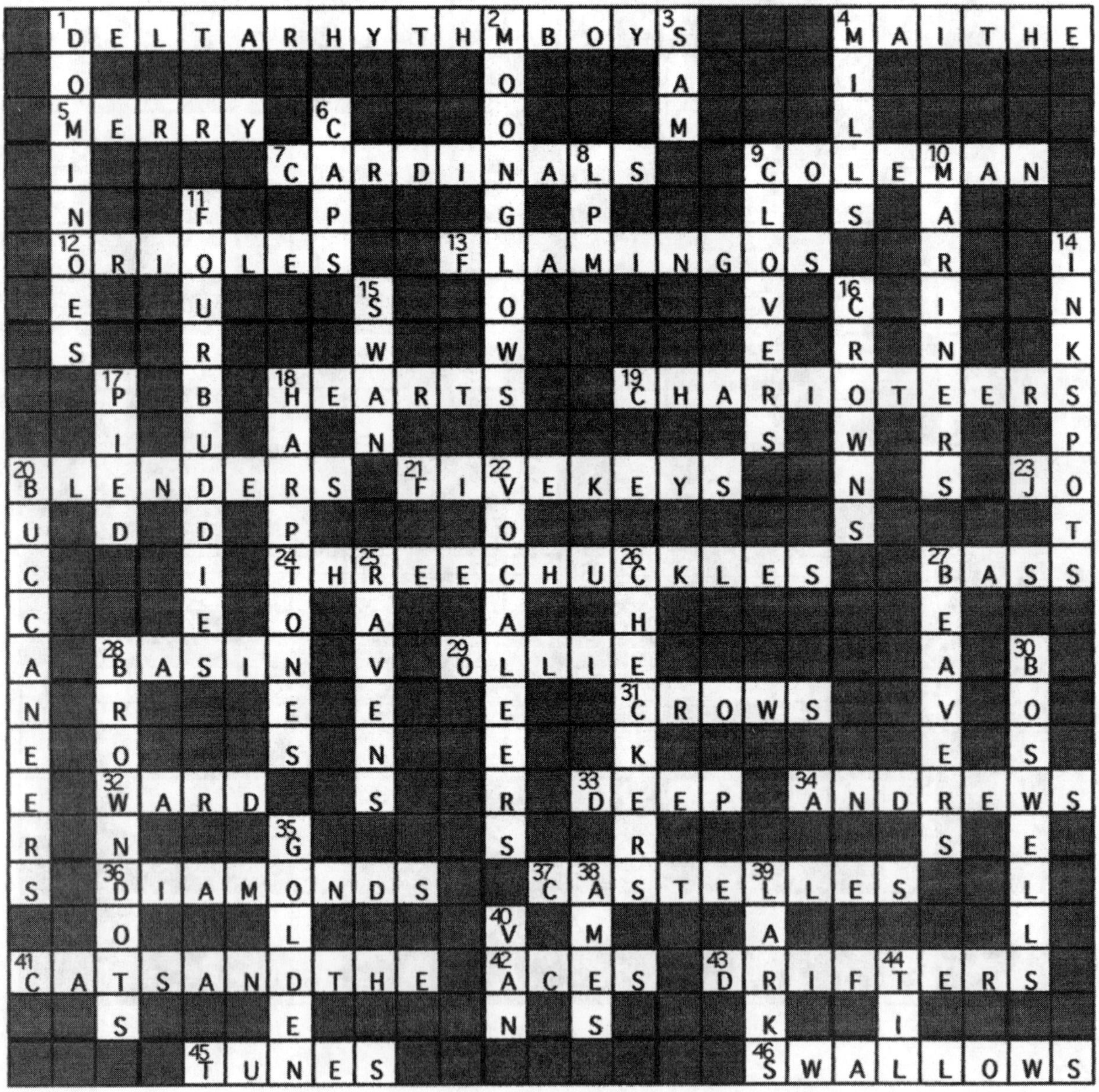

Across and down answers filled in the solution grid:

- 1. DELTARHYTHMBOYS
- 4. MAITHE
- 5. MERRY
- 6. C
- 7. CARDINALS
- 9. COLEMAN
- 12. ORIOLES
- 13. FLAMINGOS
- 16. C
- 18. HEARTS
- 19. CHARIOTEERS
- 20. BLENDERS
- 21. FIVEKEYS
- 24. THREECHUCKLES
- 27. BASS
- 28. BASIN
- 29. OLLIE
- 31. CROWS
- 32. WARD
- 33. DEEP
- 34. ANDREWS
- 36. DIAMONDS
- 37. CASTELLES
- 41. CATSANDTHE
- 42. ACES
- 43. DRIFTERS
- 45. TUNES
- 46. SWALLOWS

Down answers (reading vertically): DOMINOES, MINERS, SAM, MILLER, MOONGLOWS, ALPS, LIGHTS, COLVERS, MAN, INKSPOTS, FURIES, BUDDICANEERS, PILGRIMS, HEARTSPAN, BLUEDIAMONDS, FLOWS, CRINAWS, CROWNS, JOTS, BEAVERS, BOSS, WINGS, GOLDENTEES, VMS, RAVENS, VOLUMES, CANS, DAKS, TITE, BELLS

Chapter 17

Quiz # 7: Dee Jay Du Jour

1-b, 2-d, 3-k, 4-i, 5-f, 6-l, 7-o, 8-r, 9-p, 10-c, 11-q, 12-g, 13-a, 14-e, 15-s, 16-h, 17-j, 18-m, 19-e, 20-n

Chapter 18

Quiz #8: Label Babies

A-19-h, B-15-r, C-17-o, D-16-l, E-14-t, F-4-a, G-5-m, H-3-e, I-11-s, J-13-g, K-8-b, L-1-k, M-2-c, N-18-d, O-20-f, P-6-i, Q-7-j, R-9-q, S-10-n, T-12-p

Quiz #9: The State of the Label

A-12-t, B-19-r, C-1-j, D-8-l, E-11-a, F-16-b, G-3-p, H-20-c, I-6-o, J-4-s, K-18-d, L-14-f, M-9-k, N-17-g, O-2-q, P-13-e, Q-7-m, R-10-n, S-15-i, T-5-h

Chapter 19

Quiz #10: Pookie, Bunky & Baby

A-15-q, B-13-d, C-19-n, D-11-b, E-20-j, F-14-p, G-5-k, H-4-c, I-6-i, J-13-f, K-21-h, L-10-s, M-22-o, N-16-m, O-7-b, P-12-r, Q-18-t, R-2-j, S-3-e, T-5-a, U-17-u, V-13-g, W-1-l, X-9-b, Y-8-l

Chapter 23:

Doo-Wop Aptitude Test answers

1. d	35. c	69. c	103. a	137. c	171. b
2. c	36. d	70. c	104. d	138. b	172. b
3. c	37. a	71. c	105. b	139. d	173. d
4. d	38. c	72. d	106. d	140. c	174. b
5. c	39. c	73. c	107. c	141. a	175. b
6. b	40. d	74. c	108. c	142. a	176. c
7. d	41. d	75. c	109. a	143. b	177. c
8. a	42. d	76. a	110. d	144. a	178. c
9. d	43. c	77. a	111. b	145. a	179. d
10. b	44. d	78. d	112. b	146. d	180. c
11. a	45. b	79. c	113. d	147. d	181. a
12. d	46. d	80. a	114. b	148. b	182. d
13. b	47. c	81. d	115. d	149. d	183. d
14. b	48. c	82. d	116. b	150. c	184. d
15. c	49. c	83. c	117. a	151. c	185. b
16. c	50. a	84. d	118. d	152. d	186. c
17. b	51. a	85. d	119. b	153. c	187. c
18. d	52. b	86. d	120. b	154. d	188. b
19. a	53. b	87. a	121. c	155. d	189. c
20. c	54. b	88. d	122. d	156. b	190. a
21. b	55. c	89. b	123. b	157. d	191. d
22. b	56. a	90. a	124. d	158. a	192. c
23. a	57. d	91. c	125. c	159. c	193. b
24. d	58. c	92. a	126. a	160. c	194. c
25. b	59. d	93. c	127. b	161. c	195. a
26. b	60. a	94. c	128. c	162. c	196. c
27. c	61. a	95. c	129. b	163. c	197. d
28. a	62. a	96. d	130. d	164. c	198. c
29. c	63. b	97. a	131. d	165. c	199. c
30. a	64. d	98. d	132. b	166. c	200. d
31. b	65. d	99. b	133. d	167. a	
32. a	66. b	100. c	134. a	168. c	
33. b	67. b	101. a	135. d	169. d	
34. b	68. a	102. d	136. b	170. a	

Appendix II

100 Recommended Pre-Doo-Wop Recordings

Artists	Song	Year	Label
Crosby, Bing (with the Rhythm Boys and Gus Arnheim's Orchestra)	Them There Eyes	1930	Victor 22580
Boswell Sisters	When I Took My Sugar To Tea	1931	Brunswick 6083
Mills Brothers	Tiger Rag	1931	Brunswick 6197
Mills Brothers	Rockin' Chair	1932	Brunswick 6287
Rollin Smith's Rascals	Kickin' The Gong Around	1932	
Three Keys	Wah Dee-Dah	1932	Brunswick 6423
Mills Brothers	Jungle Fever	1934	Brunswick 6785
Boswell Sisters	The Object of My Affection	1935	Brunswick 7348
Boswell Sisters	Alexander's Ragtime Band	1935	Brunswick 7412
Four Blackbirds	Black-Eyed Susan Brown	1935	Vocalion
Ink Spots	Swinging On The Strings	1935	RCA 24851
Ink Spots	If I Didn't Care	1939	Decca 2236
Cats and the Fiddle	I Miss You So	1940	Bluebird 8429
Five Breezes	Minute And Hour Blues	1940	Bluebird 8590
Golden Gate Quartet	Stormy Weather	1940	Bluebird 8579
Ink Spots	Java Jive	1940	Decca 3432
Pied Pipers (with Frank Sinatra)	I'll Never Smile Again	1940	Victor 26628
Andrew Sisters	The Shrine Of St. Cecelia	1941	Decca 4097
Andrew Sisters	Boogie Woogie Bugle Boy	1941	Decca 3598
Ink Spots	I Don't Want To Set The World On Fire	1941	Decca 3987
Modernaires (with the Glenn Miller Orchestra)	Chattanooga Choo Choo	1941	
Andrews Sisters	Don't Sit Under The Apple Tree	1942	Decca 18312
Four Vagabonds	Rose Ann Of Charing Cross	1943	Bluebird 300811
Mills Brothers	Paper Doll	1943	Decca 18318
Song Spinners	Comin' In On A Wing And A Prayer	1943	Decca18553
Southern Sons	Praise The Lord and Pass The Ammunition	1943	
Fitzgerald, Ella (with The Ink Spots)	I'm Beginning To See The Light	1944	Decca 23399
Five Red Caps	I've Learned A Lesson I'll Never Forget	1944	Beacon 7120
Merry Macs	Mairzy Doats	1944	Decca 18588
Mills Brothers	Till Then	1944	Decca 18599
Brown Dots	For Sentimental Reasons	1945	Manor 1009
Four Dots	As Strange As It Seems	1945	Castle 2006
Basin Street Boys	I Sold My Heart To The Junkman	1946	Exclusive 225
Cats 'N' Jammer Three	I Cover The Waterfront	1946	Mercury 2003
Charioteers	You Make Me Feel So Young	1946	Columbia 37074
Churchill, Savannah (bb the Sentimentalists)	I Want To Be Loved But Only By You	1946	Manor 1046
Coleman Brothers	Go Away Mr. Satan, Get Away	1946	Decca 8673
Delta Rhythm Boys	Just A-Sittin' And A-Rockin'	1946	Decca 18739
Four Knights	Funny How You Get Along Without Me	1946	Decca 18739
Four Tunes (aka Sentimentalists)	I'd Rather Be Safe Than Sorry	1946	Manor 1049
Deep River Boys	Jealous	1947	RCA Victor 20-2157
Fitzgerald, Ella (with the Andy Love Quartet)	That's My Desire	1947	Decca 23866
Four Vagabonds	The Gang That Sang Heart Of My Heart	1947	Apollo 1076
Four Vagabonds	P.S. I Love You	1947	Apollo 1057
Johnson, Bill (& His Musical Notes)	Dream Of A Lifetime	1947	RCA 20-2498
Melody Masters	Don't You Ever Mind Them	1947	Apollo 383
Scamps	I'll Never Smile Again	1947	Modern 561

Artists	Song	Year	Label
Velvetones	It's Written All Over Your Face	1947	Sonora 3010
Churchill, Savannah (bb the Four Tunes)	The Best Of Friends	1948	Columbia 30146
Deep River Boys	Recess In Heaven	1948	RCA Victor 20-3203
Four Blues	It Takes A Long Tall Brown Skinned Gal	1948	Apollo 398
Master Keys	Don't Cry Darling	1948	Abbey 2017
Radars	You Belong To Me	1948	Abbey 3025
Beavers	If You See Tears In My Eyes	1949	Coral 65018
Blenders	I Can Dream Can't I	1949	National 9092
Cabineers	Whirlpool	1949	Abbey 3003
Charioteers	A Kiss And A Rose	1949	Columbia 38438
Delta Rhythm Boys	Fantastic	1949	Musicraft 597
Four Jacks	I Challenge Your Kiss	1949	Allen 21000
James Quintet	Bewildered	1949	Coral 60018
Johnson, Bill (& His Musical Notes)	I Love You More Each Day	1949	King
Red Caps (Steve Gibson & the)	Blueberry Hill	1949	Mercury 8146
Rhythm Masters	Until Now	1949	Bennett 401
Skyscrapers (Browley Guy & the)	That Gal Of Mine	1949	Miracle 137
Striders	Hesitating Fool	1949	Apollo 480
Tom Cats	Honey I'm Yours	1949	Capitol 15415
Bachelors	Yesterday's Roses	1950	Mercury 8159
Bachelors	Hereafter	1950	Mercury 8159
Balladeers	I Never Knew I Loved You	1950	Jubilee 5024
Brown, Ruth (bb the Delta Rhythm Boys)	Sentimental Journey	1950	Jubilee 5024
Cap-Tans	I'm So Crazy For Love	1950	Dot 1009
Cap-Tans	With All My Love	1950	Dot 1018
Churchill, Savannah (bb the Striders)	Once There Lived A Fool	1950	Regal 3309
Dozier Boys	Pretty Eyes	1950	Chess 1436
Drifters	I'm The Caring Kind	1950	Coral 65037
Four Blues	As Long As I Live	1950	Apollo 1160
Jubilaires	A Dream Is A Wish Your Heart Makes	1950	Capitol 845
Nichols, Ann (with the Bluebirds)	Let Me Know	1950	Sittin' In With 552
Palmer Brothers	Brown Boy	1950	Coral
Rivals	Don't Say You're Sorry Again	1950	Apollo 1166
Shadows	I'd Rather Be Wrong Than Blue	1950	Lee 202
Songmasters	What Do Your Tears Really Mean	1950	
Striders	Cool Saturday Night	1950	Apollo 1159
Whispers	I've Got No Name	1950	Apollo 1156
Cabineers	Each Time	1951	Prestige 904
James Quintet	A Neighborhood Affair (recorded in 1941)	1951	Decca 43218
King Odom Four	Teardrops Of Angels	1951	Derby
Majors	Laughing On The Outside, Crying On The Inside	1951	Derby 779
Mariners	They Call The Wind Mariah	1951	Columbia 39568
Sugartones	Today Is Your Birthday	1951	Onyx 2007
Varieteers	I'll Try To Forget I Loved You	1951	MGM 10888
Williams, Billy (Quartet)	You Made Me Love You	1951	MGM 10967
Comets (Herb Kenny & The)	When The Lights Go On Again	1952	Federal 12083
Starr, Kay (bb the Lancers)	I Waited A Little Too Long)	1952	Capitol

Appendix III

Geographical Data on Groups

Group	Year	City or Area	State	Comments
Academics	1956	New Haven	CT	Hillhouse H.S.
Ad Libs	1965	Newark	NJ	
Adelphis	1958	NYC (Brooklyn)	NY	Ft. Greene
Admirations	1959	NYC (Brooklyn)	NY	Liberty Ave. & Elderts Lane
Aladdins	1955	San Diego	CA	
Alaimo, Chuck (Chuck Alaimo Quartet)	1957	Buffalo	NY	
Altairs	1960	Pittsburgh	PA	Hill District/Herron Hill J.H.S.
Ambassadors	1953	Newark	NJ	Central Ward
Angels (female)	1960	Orange	NJ	
Angels (Gabriel & the)	1959	Philadelphia	PA	
Angels (male) (grand)	1954	Philadelphia	PA	
Aquatones	1958	Valley Stream	NY	Long Island
Arrogants	1960	NYC (Brooklyn)	NY	South Brooklyn
Arrows (Joe Lyons & the) (Hitmaker)	1956	Washington	DC	
Astros (Pepe & the) (Swami)	1961	NYC (Brooklyn)	NY	
Audios (Cell Foster & the)	1956	San Diego	CA	
Avalons	1956	Norfolk	VA	
Avons	1956	Englewood	NJ	Englewood H.S.
Aztecs (Jose & the)	1955	Washington	DC	
Bachelors (Dean Barlow)	1955	NYC (Bronx)	NY	
Baltineers	1956	Baltimore	MD	
Barries	1962	New Haven	CT	
Basin Street Boys	1946	Philadelphia	PA	Formed in Philadelphia, then went to L.A.
Bay Bops	1958	NYC (Brooklyn)	NY	Sheepshead Bay
Bees	1954	NYC	NY	
Bel-Larks (Ransom)	1963	Syracuse	NY	
Bell Notes	1959	East Meadow	NY	Long Island
Belltones (Grand)	1953	Philadelphia	PA	West Philadelphia
Belmonts (Dion & the)	1957	NYC (Bronx)	NY	Belmont Ave.
Belvin, Jesse (and group)	1951	Los Angeles	CA	
Bing Bongs (Dicky Dell & the) (Dragon)	1958	NYC (Brooklyn)	NY	
Bishops (Bridges)	1961	Pasadena	CA	
Blenders	1949	NYC (Manhattan)	NY	
Blue Belles (Patti LaBelle & the)	1962	Philadelphia	PA	West Philadelphia
Blue Jays (Milestone)	1961	Venice	CA	
Blue Jeans (Bob B. Soxx & the)	1962	Los Angeles	CA	
Blue Notes	1958	Philadelphia	PA	North Philadelphia
Bobbettes	1957	NYC (Manhattan)	NY	Harlem/P.S. 109
Bonnevilles	1959	Hempstead	NY	
Bonnie Sisters	1956	NYC (Manhattan)	NY	Bellevue Hospital (nurses)
Bop Chords	1957	NYC (Manhattan)	NY	Harlem (115th St. & Lenox Ave.)/Mrs. Martin's
Bosstones	1959	Philadelphia	PA	
Brown Dots	1945	NYC (Manhattan)	NY	
Buccaneers	1953	Philadelphia	PA	Logan St. section of N. Phila.
Butlers	1963	Philadelphia	PA	
C-Notes (aka C-Tones)	1957	NYC (Queens)	NY	Astoria
Cadets/Jacks	1955	Los Angeles	CA	
Cadillacs	1954	NYC (Manhattan)	NY	Harlem (7th & 8th Aves.Near 131st St.)/P.S. 43
Calvanes	1955	Los Angeles	CA	Fremont H.S.
Cameos (Johnson)	1960	Orange	NJ	
Camerons	1960	NYC (Bronx)	NY	
Candles (Rochelle & the)	1960	Los Angeles	CA	

Group	Year	City or Area	State	Comments
Cap-Tans	1950	Washington	DC	
Capistranos (Duke)	1958	?	TX	
Capitols (Mickey Tolliver)	1957	Pittsburgh	PA	Tioga St.
Capris (black)	1954	Philadelphia	PA	West & South Phila.
Capris (white)	1958	NYC (Queens)	NY	Ozone Park
Carallons (Lonnie & the)	1960	NYC (Brooklyn)	NY	Bedford-Stuyvesant
Cardinals	1951	Baltimore	MD	Corner of Gay St. & Forest
Carnations (aka Startones)	1961	Bridgeport	CT	Yellow Mill River Area/Watersville School
Carousels (Gone)	1961	Cleveland	OH	
Carter, Eddie (The Eddie Carter Quartet)	1953	Philadelphia	PA	
Casanovas	1955	High Point & Winston	NC	
Cashmeres (Herald)	1956	Philadelphia	PA	
Caslons	1961	NYC (Brooklyn)	NY	Marine Park/James Madison H.S.
Castelles	1953	Philadelphia	PA	West Phila. (49th & Brown)/
Sulzberger J.H.S. Castells	1961	Santa Rosa	CA	
Castro, Vince (with the Tonettes)	1958	NYC (Bronx)	NY	South Bronx
Castroes (Grand)	1959	Philadelphia	PA	
Casuals (Back Beat)	1957	Dallas	TX	
Cats & the Fiddle	1939	Chicago	IL	
Cavaliers (Apt)	1955	NYC	NY	
Cellos	1957	NYC (Manhattan)	NY	Downtown/
Charles Evans Hughes H.S. Chalets	1961	NYC (Brooklyn)	NY	Bushwick section
Champs (Tony Allen & the)	1955	Los Angeles	CA	
Chandeliers (aka Chandeliers Quintet)	1958	Kansas City	KS	
Chandler, Gene (with the Dukays)	1961	Chicago	IL	South Side (Englewood area)
Channels (Earl Lewis & the)	1956	NYC (Manhattan)	NY	Harlem (115th to 116th Sts.)
Chantels	1957	NYC (Bronx)	NY	St. Anthony Padua School
Chanters (DeLuxe)	1958	NYC (Queens)	NY	Ozone Park/John Adams H.S.
Chaperones	1960	Nassau County	NY	Long Island
Charades	1958	Tulare	CA	
Charioteers	1935	Ohio	OH	Wilberforce University
Chariots (Time)	1959	NYC	NY	
Charles, Jimmy (with the Revelettes)	1960	Paterson	NJ	
Charmers (119th St. & St. Nicholas)	1954	NYC (Manhattan)	NY	Harlem
Charms	1953	Cincinatti	OH	
Charts	1957	NYC (Manhattan)	NY	Harlem (115th St.)
Checkers	1952	NYC	NY	
Cherokees	1954	Philadelphia	PA	West Phila.
Chessmen	1964	NYC	NY	166th St.
Chesters	1958	NYC (Brooklyn)	NY	Boys H.S.
Chestnuts (Davis)	1956	New Haven	CT	
Chevrons	1959	NYC (Manhattan)	NY	
Chex (Tex & the)	1961	NYC (Brooklyn)	NY	Brownsville
Chiffons	1960	NYC (Bronx)	NY	James Monroe H.S.
Chimes (Specialty)	1955	Los Angeles	CA	South Central L.A.
Chimes (Tag)	1957	NYC (Brooklyn)	NY	
Chips	1956	NYC (Brooklyn)	NY	Bedford-Stuyvesant (Bergen St., Classon Ave., Clifton Pl.)
Chords	1954	NYC (Bronx)	NY	P.S. 99 & Morris H.S.
Classic IV (Twist)	1962	Philadelphia	PA	
Classics (Stucchio)	1959	NYC (Brooklyn)	NY	Garfield Pl.
Clefs	1952	Arlington	VA	
Cleftones	1956	NYC (Queens)	NY	Jamaica/Jamaica H.S.
Click-Ettes	1958	Philadelphia	PA	
Click-Ettes	1958	NYC (Bronx)	NY	
Climbers	1957	NYC (Bronx)	NY	
Cliques	1956	Los Angeles	CA	Jefferson H.S.
Clovers	1950	Washington	DC	Armstrong H.S.
Clusters	1958	NYC (Brooklyn)	NY	Bushwick section
Coasters	1956	Los Angeles	CA	

Group	Year	City or Area	State	Comments
Cobras (Casino)	1964	Philadelphia	PA	West Philadelphia
Coeds (Old Town)	1956	NYC (Manhattan)	NY	Harlem
Coins	1954	NYC	NY	
Coleman Brothers	1944	Montclair	NJ	
Collegians (Winley)	1957	NYC (Manhattan)	NY	Harlem (Park Ave. around 123rd St.)
Colonairs	1957	NYC	NY	
Colonials (Bill "Bass" Gordon & the)	1954	NYC	NY	
Colts	1955	Bakersfield	CA	
Columbus Pharaohs	1957	Columbus	OH	
Concords	1954	NYC (Manhattan)	NY	Seward Park H.S.
Consorts (Cousins)	1961	NYC (Bronx)	NY	Theodore Roosevelt H.S.
Contenders	1959	Upper Darby	PA	69th & Market St.
Continental Five	1959	Petersburg	VA	
Continentals	1956	NYC (Brooklyn)	NY	
Convincers (Movin')	1962	?	?	
Cookies (Dimension)	1962	NYC (Brooklyn)	NY	
Copesetics	1956	NYC (Manhattan)	NY	Harlem (East 135th St.)
Cordells (Bargain)	1961	?	NJ	
Cordovans	1960	NYC	NY	
Coronets	1953	Cleveland	OH	Thomas Edison H.S.
Corsairs	1961	La Grange	NC	
Corvairs (Comet)	1961	NYC	NY	
Cosmic Rays (Saturn)	1960	Chicago	IL	
Counts	1954	Indianapolis	IN	
Creations (Meridian)	1956	Indianapolis	IN	
Crescendos	1957	Nashville	TN	
Crescents	1957	NYC (Brooklyn)	NY	
Crescents (Pat Cordel & the)	1956	NYC (Staten Island)	NY	
Crestones (Jimmy & the)	1964	NYC (Bronx)	NY	Fordham Rd.
Crests	1957	NYC (Manhattan)	NY	Lower East Side
Crickets	1953	NYC (Bronx)	NY	Morisania section, Forest House Community Center
Criterions (Tygh & the)	1963	?	?	
Crowns (Arthur Lee Maye & the)	1954	Los Angeles	CA	Jefferson H.S.
Crows	1953	NYC (Manhattan)	NY	Harlem (142nd St. between 7th & Lenox Aves.)
Cruisers (with Herb Johnson)	1960	Washington	DC	Northeast DC
Crystals	1953	NYC (Manhattan)	NY	Amsterdam & St. Nicholas Aves. in the 140s
Crystals (female)	1961	NYC (Brooklyn)	NY	Mixed areas
Cues	1954	NYC (Manhattan)	NY	
Cuff Links	1957	Sacramento	CA	Fort McClellan
Cupids	1962	NYC (Brooklyn)	NY	Coney Island/Lincoln H.S.
Danderliers	1955	Chicago	IL	South Side (Cottage Grove between 60th & 68th Sts.)
Danleers	1958	NYC (Brooklyn)	NY	
Darchaes (Ray & the)	1962	Asbury Park	NJ	Asbury Park H.S.
Debonaires	1956	Atlanta	GA	
Decoys	1963	NYC (Bronx)	NY	Melrose section
Deep River Boys	1940	Hampton	VA	Hampton Institute
Del Satins	1961	NYC (Manhattan)	NY	Lenox Hill Neighborhood House
Delcos	1962	Mishawaka	IN	
Delighters (Donald Jenkins & the)	1963	Chicago	IL	
Dell Vikings	1956	Pittsburgh	PA	U.S. Air Force Base
Dells	1955	Harvey	IL	Chicago suburb/Thornton Township H.S.
Delmonicos	1963	NYC (Manhattan)	NY	East Harlem (116th St.)
Delrons (Reperata & the)	1964	NYC (Brooklyn)	NY	St. Brendan's H.S.
Delroys	1957	NYC (Queens)	NY	Long Island City (Queensbridge Housing Projects)/Long Island City
Delta Rhythm Boys	1941	Oklahoma	OK	Langston University
Deltairs	1957	NYC (Queens)	NY	Jamaica
Deltas (Gone)	1957	NYC (Brooklyn)	NY	

Group	Year	City or Area	State	Comments
Demens	1957	NYC (Manhattan)	NY	61st St. & Columbus Ave.
Demensions	1960	NYC (Bronx)	NY	Christopher Columbus H.S.
Demilles (featuring Carlo Mastrangelo)	1964	NYC (Bronx)	NY	
Desires	1958	NYC (Manhattan)	NY	Harlem (118th St. Youth Center)
Devotions	1961	NYC (Queens)	NY	Astoria
Diablos	1954	Detroit	MI	Central H.S.
Diadems	1961	Pittsburg	PA	Homestead area
Diamonds (black)	1952	NYC (Manhattan)	NY	Harlem (134th St. between 7th & 8th Aves.)
Dimples (Eddie Cooley & the)	1956	NYC (Brooklyn)	NY	Ft. Greene
DiMucci, Dion (with the Del Satins)	1960	NYC	NY	Del Satins from Manhattan, Dion from the Bronx
Diplomats (Dino & the)	1961	NYC (Manhattan)	NY	Sugar Hill
Dodgers (Aladdin)	1955	NYC	NY	
Dominoes	1950	NYC	NY	
Don Juans	1956	Detroit	MI	
Dovells	1961	Philadelphia	PA	Overbrook Section/Overbrook H.S.
Dovers (Miriam Grate & the)	1955	NYC (Manhattan)	NY	Sugar Hill
Dozier Boys	1948	Chicago	IL	
Dream Kings (Checker)	1957	Chicago	IL	
Dreamers (Grand)	1954	Philadelphia	PA	
Dreamlovers	1960	Philadelphia	PA	Northeast H.S.
Dreams (Savoy)	1954	Philadelphia	PA	West Philadelphia
Drifters	1953	NYC (Manhattan)	NY	Harlem
Drifters (Coral)	1950	Los Angeles	CA	
Du Droppers	1952	NYC (Manhattan)	NY	Harlem (149th St. & 7th Ave.)
Du Mauriers	1957	NYC (Brooklyn)	NY	
Dubs	1957	NYC (Manhattan)	NY	Harlem
Dukes (Specialty)	1954	Pasadena	CA	
Duprees	1962	Jersey City	NJ	
Duvals	1958	NYC (Bronx)	NY	
Dynamics (Herald)	1961	Philadelphia	PA	South Philadelphia
Earls	1961	NYC (Bronx)	NY	
Earls (Parrot)	1954	Chicago	IL	
Ebb Tides (Nino & the)	1957	NYC (Bronx)	NY	
Ebbtides	1957	Philadelphia	PA	
Ebonaires	1953	NYC (Manhattan)	NY	Harlem (Amsterdam in the 140s)
Echoes (white)	1961	NYC (Brooklyn)	NY	
Edsels	1958	Campbell	OH	Near Youngstown
El Capris	1956	Pittsburgh	PA	Hill District/Francis St.
El Domingoes	1962	NYC (Brooklyn)	NY	
El Dorados	1954	Chicago	IL	South Side/Englewood H.S.
El Venos	1956	Pittsburgh	PA	
Elchords	1957	NYC (Manhattan)	NY	Sugar Hill
Elegants	1958	NYC (Staten Island)	NY	
Elgins	1958	Los Angeles	CA	Crenshaw neighborhood
Embers (Valmor)	1960	NYC (Bronx)	NY	
Emblems (Patty & the) (Herald)	1964	Philadelphia	PA	
Emotions	1961	NYC (Brooklyn)	NY	
Empires	1954	NYC (Manhattan)	NY	Harlem
Encounters	1963	NYC (Brooklyn)	NY	Bushwick
Ermines	1955	Los Angeles	CA	Jefferson H.S.
Essentials (Billy & the)?	1962	Philadelphia	PA	West Philadelphia
Essex	1963	Camp Lejune	NC	U.S. Marine Corps
Eternals	1959	NYC (Bronx)	NY	Freeman St. areas
Evergreens (Dante &)	1960	Los Angeles	CA	
Excellents	1962	NYC (Bronx)	NY	Columbus H.S. and Clinton H.S.
Explorers (Dennis & the) (Coral)	1960	NYC	NY	
Extremes (Everlast)	1958	NYC (Staten Island)	NY	
Fabulaires	1957	Philadelphia	PA	
Fabulous Twilights (Nathaniel Mayer & the)	1961	Detroit	MI	

Group	Year	City or Area	State	Comments
Falcons	1956	Detroit	MI	
Fantastics	1959	NYC (Brooklyn)	NY	
Fascinators	1958	NYC (Brooklyn)	NY	
Fascinators (Your Copy)	1954	Detroit	MI	
Fashions (V-Tone)	1959	Philadelphia	PA	
Feathers	1954	Los Angeles	CA	South-Central L.A. (East 29th St.)
Fi-Dells (Imperial)	1961	?	?	
Fi-Tones	1955	NYC (Brooklyn)	NY	Boys H.S.
Fidelitys (Baton)	1958	NYC	NY	
Fiestas	1958	Newark	NJ	
Fireflies	1958	NYC	NY	
Five Blue Notes	1954	Washington	DC	
Five Chances	1954	Chicago	IL	South Side/Fesenthal Grade School/DuSable H.S.
Five Crowns	1952	NYC (Manhattan)	NY	Harlem (115th St. between 7th & 8th Aves.) /Wadleigh J.H.S.
Five Discs	1958	NYC (Brooklyn)	NY	Bedford-Stuyvesant/J.H.S.
Five Dollars	1955	Detroit	MI	
Five Dukes	1955	Providence	RI	
Five Echoes	1953	Chicago	IL	South Side (35th-39th Sts.)
Five Embers	1954	Central City	KY	
Five Emeralds	1954	Detroit	MI	
Five Jets	1953	Detroit	MI	
Five Keys	1951	Newport News	VA	Huntington H.S.
Five Notes (Jen D)	1955	Philadelphia	PA	
Five Owls	1955	Birmingham	AL	
Five Redcaps	1943	Los Angeles	CA	Migrated to L.A. from other parts of the country
Five Royales	1951	Winston-Salem	NC	
Five Satins/Scarlets	1954	New Haven	CT	Hillhouse H.S.
Five Scamps	1954	Kansas City	KS	
Five Sharps	1952	NYC (Queens)	NY	Jamaica H.S.
Five Thrills	1953	Chicago	IL	South Side
Flairs	1953	Los Angeles	CA	Jefferson H.S.
Flamingos	1953	Chicago	IL	35th & 36th & Lake Park
Fleetwoods	1959	Olympia	WA	Olympia H.S.
Flips (Little Joey & the)	1960	Upper Darby	PA	Philadelphia suburb
Four Bars	1954	Washington	DC	
Four Blackbirds (Vocalion)		Los Angeles	CA	Jefferson H.S.
Four Blazes	1952	Chicago	IL	
Four Blues	1941	Philadelphia	PA	
Four Buddies	1950	Baltimore	MD	Frederick Douglas H.S.
Four Buddies (Club 51)	1956	Chicago	IL	
Four Dates	1958	Philadelphia	PA	South Philadelphia
Four Deuces	1955	Salinas	CA	
Four Dots (Jerry Stone & the)	1958	Los Angeles	CA	South L.A.
Four Fellows	1954	NYC (Brooklyn)	NY	
Four Flames	1951	Los Angeles	CA	
Four Haven Nights	1956	New Haven	CT	
Four J's	1958	Philadelphia	PA	South Philadelphia
Four Jacks (Federal)	1952	Los Angeles	CA	
Four Jewels	1961	Washington	DC	
Four Knights	1946	Charlotte	NC	
Four Lovers	1956	Newark	NJ	
Four Tunes	1946	NYC	NY	
Four Vagabonds	1942	St. Louis	MO	Vashon H.S.
G-Clefs	1956	Roxbury	MA	
Gardenias	1956	?	?	
Gay Knights	1958	NYC	NY	
Gay Larks	1955	San Francisco	CA	

Group	Year	City or Area	State	Comments
Gaytunes	1957	NYC (Brooklyn)	NY	Bedford-Stuyvesant/Alexander Hamilton & Boys H.S.
Gazelles	1956	Philadelphia	PA	North Philadelphia
Gems	1954	Evanston	IL	Chicago suburb
Genies	1959	Long Beach	NY	Long Island
Gentlemen	1954	Newark	NJ	Avon Ave.
Gladiators	1957	Los Angeles	CA	South L.A.
Gladiolas/Zodiacs	1957	Lancaster	SC	Barr Street H.S.
Golden Gate Quartet	1937	Norfolk	VA	Washington H.S.
Goldentones (Jay-Dee)	1955	NYC (Brooklyn)	NY	
Greco, Johnny (bb Rick & the Masters)	1963	Philadelphia	PA	South Philadelphia
Green, Barbara (& group) (Atco)	1963	?	?	
Guytones (DeLuxe)	1957	Philadelphia	PA	
Halos	1961	NYC (Bronx)	NY	
Harmonaires	1955	NYC (Manhattan)	NY	Harlem
Harmonizing Four	1927	Richmond	VA	So. Richmond/Dunbar Elementary School
Harptones	1953	NYC (Manhattan)	NY	Harlem (115th St.) & lower Manhattan
Harris, Thurston (with the Sharps)	1957	Los Angeles	CA	
Hawks	1954	St. Louis	MO	
Heartbeats	1956	NYC (Queens)	NY	Jamaica
Heartbreakers (RCA)	1951	Washington	DC	
Heartbreakers (Vik)	1957	NYC (Bronx)	NY	
Hearts (Billy Austin & the)	1952	NYC	NY	
Hearts (female)	1955	NYC (Manhattan)	NY	Harlem (122nd St. & Eighth Ave.)
Hearts (Lee Andrews & the)	1954	Philadelphia	PA	Southwest Philadelphia/49th & Woodland/ Bertram H.S.
Heartspinners (Dino & the)	1954	NYC (Manhattan)	NY	Harlem/J.H.S. 139
Hemlocks (Little Bobby Rivera & the)	1957	NYC (Bronx)	NY	Melrose Projects
Hi Lites	1962	Danbury	CT	
Hi Tensions	1960	Santa Cruz	CA	
Hi-Fives	1958	Garfield	NJ	
Hi-Lites (Ronnie & the)	1962	Jersey City	NJ	
Hide-A-Ways	1954	Philadelphia	PA	West Philadelphia
Highlands	1961	?	?	
Hits (Tiny Tim & the)	1958	NYC (Manhattan)	NY	
Hollywood Flames	1953	Los Angeles	CA	Jefferson H.S.
Hollywood Saxons	1961	Los Angeles	CA	
Hornets (Flash)	1957	San Diego	CA	
Hurricanes	1955	NYC (Brooklyn)	NY	Bedford-Stuyvesant
Hy-Tones (aka Shytones)	1958	NYC (Brooklyn)	NY	Bensonhurst
Imaginations	1961	Bellmore	NY	Long Island
Impalas	1958	NYC (Brooklyn)	NY	Canarsie & Brownsville (Jefferson H.S.)
Imperials (Great Lakes)	1953	Detroit	MI	
Imperials (Little Anthony & the)	1958	NYC (Brooklyn)	NY	Greenpoint
Imperials (Savoy)	1952	Newark	NJ	Central Ward
Impressions (Jerry Butler & the)	1958	Chicago	IL	Near North
Initials (Angelo & the)	1959	Pittsburgh	PA	
Ink Spots	1935	Indianapolis	IN	
Innocents (Indigo)	1959	Los Angeles	CA	
Intentions (Jamie)	1963	Philadelphia	PA	South Philadelphia
Intervals	1958	St. Louis	MO	
Isley Brothers	1957	Cincinnati	OH	
Ivy-Tones	1958	Philadelphia	PA	North Philadelphia
Jaguars	1955	Los Angeles	CA	Fremont H.S./S. Central L.A.
Jamies	1958	Dorchester	MA	
Jarmels	1961	Richmond	VA	
Jayhawks/Vibrations	1956	Los Angeles	CA	Jefferson H.S.
Jaynells	1963	NYC (Bronx)	NY	
Jaytones (Timely)	1958	NYC	NY	

Group	Year	City or Area	State	Comments
Jelly Beans	1964	Jersey City	NJ	
Jesters	1957	NYC (Manhattan)	NY	Harlem/Cooper J.H.S./119th St. & Park Ave.
Jets (Gee)	1956	NYC	NY	
Jets (Rainbow)	1953	Washington	DC	
Jewels (male)	1954	San Bernadino	CA	
Jive Bombers	1952	NYC	NY	Partially from Palmer Brothers from Pawtucket, RI
Jive Five	1961	NYC (Brooklyn)	NY	Bedford-Stuyvesant (Hart St. & Myrtle Ave.) P.S. 54
Joytones	1956	NYC (Manhattan)	NY	Harlem (Cita's house on 119th St.)
Jubilaires	1932	Jacksonville	FL	
Juniors (Danny & the)	1957	Philadelphia	PA	John Bartram H.S.
Juniors (Jimmy Castor & the)	1956	NYC (Manhattan)	NY	Sugar Hill
Kac-Ties	1962	NYC (Brooklyn)	NY	
Keynotes	1954	NYC (Manhattan)	NY	Harlem (115th St.)
Keystoners	1956	Philadelphia	PA	South Philadelphia
Keytones	1957	Newark	NJ	
King Krooners	1959	Jacksonville	FL	
Kings (featuring Bobby Hall)	1953	Baltimore	MD	
Knight, Bob (The Bob Knight Four)	1961	NYC (Brooklyn)	NY	East New York
Knockouts	1959	North Bergen	NJ	
Kodaks (aka Kodoks)	1957	Newark	NJ	
Kool Gents	1956	Chicago	IL	West Side/Marshall H.S.
Kuf-Linx	1958	Los Angeles	CA	
Ladders	1957	NYC (Manhattan)	NY	Harlem (115th St. & Lenox Ave.)
Laddins	1957	NYC (Manhattan)	NY	Harlem (118th St.)
Lamplighters	1953	Los Angeles	CA	Southeast/Jordan and Jefferson H.S.
Lanes (Gee)	1956	NYC (Manhattan)	NY	
Larks	1951	Durham	NC	
Larks (on Sheryl)	1961	Philadelphia	PA	West Philadelphia
Laurels (Flair)	1955	Los Angeles	CA	
Leaders	1955	Newport News	VA	
Lee, Curtis (with the Halos)	1960	NYC	NY	
Legends (Melba/Hull)	1957	NYC (Brooklyn)	NY	
Lexingtons (Joey & the)	1962	Paterson	NJ	Lexington Ave.
Limelighters	1956	NYC (Bronx)	NY	Morris H.S.
Limelites (Shep & the)	1960	NYC	NY	
Lollypops	1958	NYC (Brooklyn)	NY	
Loungers (Herald)	1958	NYC (Staten Island)	NY	
Love Notes (Holiday)	1957	NYC (Brooklyn)	NY	Williamsburg
Love Notes (Imperial)	1953	Roxbury	MA	
Ly-dells	1961	Philadelphia	PA	Southwest Philadelphia
Lyrics	1958	San Antonia	TX	
Lyrics (Fernwood)	1961	Memphis	TN	
Magnificent Four	1961	NYC (Brooklyn)	NY	Ft. Greene
Magnificents	1956	Chicago	IL	South Side/Hyde Park H.S.
Majestics (Chex)	1962	Detroit	MI	
Majestics (Nitey Nite)	1956	Miami	FL	
Majors (Derby)	1951	NYC (Brooklyn)	NY	
Majors (Imperial)	1960	Philadelphia	PA	
Marcels	1961	Pittsburgh	PA	Woodstrun Ave. on North Side/Oliver Allegheny H.S.
Marigolds	1955	Nashville	TN	
Marquis (Onyx)	1962	NYC (Manhattan)	NY	Broadway & 130th St.
Marvelettes	1962	Inkster	MI	Inkster H.S.
Marvelows (ABC)	1965	Chicago	IL	
Marylanders	1952	Stevensville	MD	
Master-Tones	1954	NYC	NY	
Masters (Rick & the)	1962	Philadelphia	PA	South Philadelphia/24th & McKean
Matadors	1958	NYC (Manhattan)	NY	Harlem

Group	Year	City or Area	State	Comments
Meadowlarks (Don Julian & the)	1955	Los Angeles	CA	Fremont H.S.
Medallions (Vernon Green & the)	1954	Los Angeles	CA	Jordan H.S.
Mel-O-Dots	1952	NYC	NY	
Mello-Harps	1955	NYC (Brooklyn)	NY	
Mello-Kings	1957	Mt. Vernon	NY	Washington H.S.
Mello-Moods	1952	NYC (Manhattan)	NY	Resurrection Grammar School/West 151st St.
Mellows (Lillian Leach & the)	1954	NYC (Bronx)	NY	Morrisania/Morris H.S.
Meloaires	1958	Nashville	TN	
Metronomes	1957	NYC (Manhattan)	NY	Harlem (134th St. between 7th and 8th Aves.)
Midnighters (aka Royals)	1953	Detroit	MI	Dunbar H.S.
Mills Brothers	1931	Piqua	OH	
Minors	1957	NYC (Manhattan)	NY	
Mint Juleps	1956	Springfield	MA	
Monarchs (Neil)	1956	NYC	NY	
Moniques	1962	Philadelphia	PA	
Monotones	1957	Newark	NJ	
Montclairs	1956	NYC (Brooklyn)	NY	
Montereys (Onyx)	1957	NYC	NY	
Moonglows	1952	Louisville	KY	
Moroccos	1955	Chicago	IL	Englewood H.S.
Mystery Quartet	1950	Philadelphia	PA	
Mystery Quartette	1950	Philadelphia	PA	
Mystics	1959	NYC (Brooklyn)	NY	Bensonhurst
Native Boys	1954	Los Angeles	CA	Watts/Cathedral H.S.
Neons	1956	NYC	NY	
New Yorkers 5	1955	NYC (Manhattan)	NY	Harlem
Nitecaps	1955	Detroit	MI	
No Names	1963	Philadelphia	PA	
Nobles (Nicky & the)	1957	New haven	CT	
Nomads (Josie)	1958	NYC	NY	
Note-Torials	1959	Philadelphia	PA	
Nutmegs	1955	New Haven	CT	
Ocapellos	1965	Newark	NJ	
Olympics	1958	Compton	CA	Centennial H.S.
Opals	1954	NYC (Manhattan)	NY	Harlem (St. Nicholas & Amsterdam Aves. in the 140s)
Orchids (Parrot)	1955	Chicago	IL	South Side/Wentworth Ave. Projects
Orients	1964	Long Island	NY	
Orioles	1948	Baltimore	MD	
Orlons	1961	Philadelphia	PA	
Oxfords (Darryl & the)	1959	NYC (Brooklyn)	NY	Brighton Beach
Packards	1956	NYC	NY	
Palmer Brothers	1937	Pawtucket	RI	
Paradons	1960	Bakersfield	CA	
Paragons	1957	NYC (Brooklyn)	NY	Bedford-Stuyvesant (Greene Ave.)
Parakeets	1956	Newark & Elizabeth	NJ	
Passions	1958	NYC (Brooklyn)	NY	Bensonhurst
Pastels	1957	Greenland	N/A	
Pearls (Onyx)	1956	Detroit	MI	
Pelicans	1953	Detroit	MI	
Penguins	1954	Los Angeles	CA	Jefferson H.S. & Fremont H.S.
Pentagons	1958	San Bernadino	CA	
Perfections	1959	Philadelphia	PA	
Personalities	1957	NYC	NY	Morrisania
Phillips, Phil (with the Twilights)	1959	Lake Charles	LA	
Pipes	1956	Oakland	CA	McClymonds H.S.
Pips	1961	Atlanta	GA	
Pixies Three (Mercury)	1963	?	?	
Platters	1953	Los Angeles	CA	Jefferson H.S.
Plurals (Wanger)	1958	Newark	NJ	

Group	Year	City or Area	State	Comments
Poets	1958	Los Angeles	CA	Jefferson H.S.
Ponitails	1957	Lyndhurst	OH	Near Cleveland
Precisions (Highland)	1960	Los Angeles	CA	
Premiers (Dig)	1956	Los Angeles	CA	
Premiers (Palm) (with Herb Johnson)	1960	Baltimore	MD	
Premiers (with Roger Koob)	1959	New Haven	CT	
Pretenders	1955	NYC (Manhattan)	NY	Sugar Hill
Prisonaires	1953	Nashville	TN	Tennessee State Penitentiary
Prophets (Atco)	1956	Philadelphia	PA	
Pyramids (Federal)	1955	Los Angeles	CA	
Pyramids (Shell)	1958	NYC (Brooklyn)	NY	
Quails (Bill Robinson & the)	1954	Miami	FL	
Queens (Shirley Gunter & the)	1954	Los Angeles	CA	
Quin-Tones	1958	York	PA	William Pen Sr. H.S.
Quinns	1958	NYC (Brooklyn)	NY	
Quotations	1961	NYC (Brooklyn)	NY	Kings Highway/James Madison H.S.
Rainbows	1955	Washington	DC	Northwest
Rainbows (Randy & the)	1963	NYC (Queens)	NY	Maspeth
Raindrops	1963	NYC	NY	
Raindrops (Spin-It)	1956	Los Angeles	CA	
Ramblers (Jax)	1953	Baltimore	MD	
Ramblers (Trumpet)	1963	Atlanta	GA	
Ravels (Sheriff & the)	1959	?	IL	
Ravens	1946	NYC (Manhattan)	NY	Harlem
Rays	1955	NYC (Brooklyn)	NY	
Re-Vels	1956	Philadelphia	PA	
Reflections	1964	Detroit	MI	
Regents	1961	NYC (Bronx)	NY	
Revalons	1958	NYC (Brooklyn)	NY	
Rhythm Aces	1954	Chicago	IL	
Rialtos (CB)	1962	?	?	
Riffs	1964	NYC (Brooklyn)	NY	
Rivals (Apollo)	1950	Camden	NJ	
Rivera, Lucy (& group) (End)	1959	NYC (Manhattan)	NY	
Rivieras	1958	Englewood	NJ	
Rivileers	1954	NYC (Queens)	NY	Jamaica/Jamaica H.S.
Rivingtons	1962	Los Angeles	CA	Jefferson H.S.
Rob Roys (Norman Fox & the)	1957	NYC (Bronx)	NY	Near Henry Hudson Parkway/DeWitt Clinton H.S.
Robins	1949	San Francisco	CA	Not fully formed until L.A.
Rocketeers	1958	Los Angeles	CA	
Rocketones	1957	NYC (Brooklyn)	NY	Saratoga Ave. & Dean St./J.H.S. 178
Rockin' Chairs (Lenny Dean & the)	1959	NYC (Queens)	NY	
Romancers	1956	San Francisco	CA	
Romans (Little Caesar & the)	1961	Los Angeles	CA	
Roommates	1960	NYC (Queens)	NY	Kew Gardens/Forest Hills H.S.
Rosebuds (Gee)	1957	NYC	NY	
Roulettes	1957	NYC	NY	
Royal Notes (Kelit)	1958	NYC (Bronx)	NY	
Royal Teens	1957	Fort Lee	NJ	
Royals (Richie & the)	1961	Philadelphia	PA	South Philadelphia
Royals/Midnighters	1952	Detroit	MI	Dunbar H.S.
Royaltones	1956	NYC (Brooklyn)	NY	
Safaris	1960	Los Angeles	CA	
Salutations (Vito & the)	1962	NYC (Brooklyn)	NY	Brownsville & Canarsie (Jefferson H.S.)
Scarlets	1954	New Haven	CT	Hillhouse H.S.
Schoolboys	1956	NYC (Manhattan)	NY	Harlem (Cooper J.H.S./Madison Ave. between 119th and 120th Sts.)
Scott Brothers (Skyline)	1959	NYC (Queens)	NY	Jamaica
Selections	1958	NYC (Bronx)	NY	

Group	Year	City or Area	State	Comments
Senors	1962	Atlanta	GA	
Sensations	1956	Philadelphia	PA	South Philadelphia
Sequins (Red Robin)	1956	NYC	NY	Harlem
Serenaders (aka Royal Jokers/Muskateers)	1952	Detroit	MI	
Serenaders (on MGM)	1957	Newark	NJ	Miller St. & Sherman Ave.
Shadows	1950	New Haven	CT	
Sharmeers	1958	Philadelphia	PA	
Sharps	1957	Los Angeles	CA	
Shells	1957	NYC (Brooklyn)	NY	Saratoga & Civic St., Esther's Candy Store
Shepherd Sisters	1954	?	?	
Sheppards	1959	Chicago	IL	South Side H.S.
Shields	1958	Los Angeles	CA	
Shirelles	1958	Passaic	NJ	Passaic H.S.
Showmen	1961	Norfolk	VA	
Shy-Tones (aka Hy-Tones)	1960	NYC (Brooklyn)	NY	
Silhouettes	1957	Philadelphia	PA	S. Phila./10th & Bainbridge
Silva-Tones (Monarch/Argo)	1957	Boston	MA	
Sinceres (Richie)	1960	NYC	NY	
Six Teens	1956	Los Angeles	CA	
Skarlettones	1959	Akron	OK	
Skyliners	1959	Pittsburgh	PA	South Hills area
Solitaires	1954	NYC (Manhattan)	NY	Harlem (142nd St. between Lenox & 7th Aves.)
Sophomores (Anthony & the)	1963	Philadelphia	PA	South Philadelphia
Souvenirs (Dooto)	1957	Los Angeles	CA	
Spaniels	1953	Gary	IN	Roosevelt H.S.
Sparrows	1953	NYC	NY	
Spectors Three	1960	Los Angeles	CA	
Spiders	1954	New Orleans	LA	
Spinners (Claudine Clark & the)	1958	Philadelphia	PA	
Squires	1954	Pasadena	CA	Suburb of Los Angeles/John Muir H.S.
Starlarks (Ember)	1957	New Haven	CT	
Starlites (Eddie & the)	1959	NYC (Brooklyn)	NY	
Starlites (Peak)	1957	NYC (Brooklyn)	NY	Bedford-Stuyvesant
Stereos	1959	Steubenville	OH	
Storytellers	1959	Los Angeles	CA	East L.A.
Strangers	1954	NYC (Brooklyn)	NY	Putnam & Tompkins Aves.
Students (New York)	1958	NYC	NY	
Students (Philadelphia)	1957	Philadelphia	PA	South Philadelphia
Sultans	1954	Omaha	NE	Omaha Technical H.S.
Summits	1961	NYC (Bronx)	NY	
Sunbeams	1955	Long Island	NY	
Superiors	1957	Philadelphia	PA	Southeast Philadelphia/Bartram H.S.
Supremes (Ace)	1956	Columbus	OH	East H.S.
Supremes (Kitten)	1956	Lawrence	MA	Park St. areas
Supremes (Ruth McFadden & the)	1956	NYC (Manhattan)	NY	Harlem
Swallows	1951	Baltimore	MD	
Swans	1954	Philadelphia	PA	
Swinging Hearts (620)	1960	Chicago	IL	
Teardrops (Josie)	1954	NYC	NY	
Techniques (Stars/Roulette)	1957	Atlanta	GA	
Teddy Bears	1958	Los Angeles	CA	Fairfax H.S.
Teenagers (Frankie Lymon & the)	1956	NYC (Manhattan)	NY	Sugar Hill (Stitt J.H.S.)
Teenchords (Lewis Lymon & the)	1957	NYC (Manhattan)	NY	Sugar Hill
Tempo-Tones	1957	Long Island	NY	Copiague
Temptations (Goldisc)	1960	NYC (Queens)	NY	Flushing
Temptations (King)	1958	NYC	NY	
Three Chuckles (with Teddy Randazzo)	1954	NYC	NY	Three Chuckles from Brooklyn, T. Randazzo from 115th St. Manhattan
Three Friends	1956	NYC (Brooklyn)	NY	

Group	Year	City or Area	State	Comments
Thrillers (Little Joe & the)	1956	Philadelphia	PA	North Philadelphia
Tigers (Julian Herrera & the)	1956	Los Angeles	CA	East L.A.
Timetones (aka Time-Tones)	1961	NYC	NY	
Tokens	1961	NYC (Brooklyn)	NY	Brighton Beach/Lincoln H.S.
Tokens (Gary)	1957	NYC (Brooklyn)	NY	Brownsville
Tonettes	1956	NYC (Bronx)	NY	South Bronx (Claremont Pkwy. & Bathgate Ave.)/Grace Vocational
Toppers (Billy Mitchell & the)	1953	New Orleans	LA	
Tops (Little Jimmy (Rivers & the)	1961	Philadelphia	PA	North Philadelphia
Travelers (Roger & the)	1961	New Haven	CT	
Treble Chords	1959	NYC (Bronx)	NY	
Tremaines	1958	(NYC (Bronx)	NY	Coney Island
Tremonts	1961	NYC (Bronx)	NY	
Tru-Tones (chart)	1957	Miami	FL	
Tuneweavers	1957	Boston	MA	
Turbans	1955	Philadelphia	PA	S. Philadelphia/10th & Bainbridge
Turks	1955	Los Angeles	CA	Jefferson H.S.
Tuxedos	1960	Los Angeles	CA	
Twilighters (Marshall)	1953	Washington	DC	Dunbar H.S.
Twilighters (Tony & the)	1960	Philadelphia	PA	South Philadelphia
Tyce, Napoleon (& group) (Norwood)	1960	Washington	DC	
Tymes	1963	Philadelphia	PA	N. Philadelphia/Gratz H.S.
Uniques (Flippin')	1959	NYC	NY	
Uniques (Gone)	1958	NYC (Brooklyn)	NY	South Brooklyn
Universals (27th St. & Girard Ave.)	1957	Philadelphia	PA	N. Philadelphia
Upfronts	1961	Los Angeles	CA	South L.A.
V-Eights	1959	Asbury Park	NJ	
Vacels (Ricky & the)	1962	Valley Stream (L.I.)	NY	
Val-Chords	1957	NYC	NY	
Valentines	1954	NYC (Manhattan)	NY	Harlem (Colonial Projectson 8th Ave. near PoloGrounds)
Valiants	1957	Los Angeles	CA	
Valrays (Parkway)	1963	Long Island	NY	
Van Dykes (Decca)	1958	Paterson	NJ	
Vanguards	1958	NYC	NY	
Vel-Tones (Zara)	1960	NYC	NY	
Velours	1956	NYC (Brooklyn)	NY	Bedford-Stuyvesant/Boys H.S.
Velvatones (Nu Kat)	1959	Richmond	VA	
Velvets	1959	Odessa	TX	
Velvets (Red Robin)	1953	NYC (Manhattan)	NY	Sugar Hill
Vibranaires	1954	Asbury park	NJ	Springwood Ave.
Videls	1960	Providence	RI	
Videos	1958	NYC (Queens)	NY	Jamaica/Jamaica H.S.
Viscaynes (Tropo)	1961	Vallejo	CA	
Vocalaires (aka Blue Sonnets)	1962	NYC (Brooklyn)	NY	Bensonhurst
Vocaleers	1951	NYC (Manhattan)	NY	Harlem (142nd St. between Amsterdam Ave. & Broadway)
Vocaltones	1956	NYC (Manhattan)	NY	Harlem
Voices	1955	Los Angeles	CA	
Volumes	1962	Detroit	MI	
Voxpoppers (Amp-3)	1958	?	?	
Wanderers	1953	NYC (Manhattan)	NY	Harlem (116th St. & Lenox Ave.)
Wanderers (Tony Allen & the)	1961	Los Angeles	CA	
Wheels	1956	NYC	NY	
Whirlers (aka Empires)	1957	NYC (Manhattan)	NY	Harlem
Whirlwinds (Philips)	1963	Jersey City	NJ	
Whispers	1954	Baltimore	MD	
Willows	1953	NYC (Manhattan)	NY	Harlem (115th St. & Lenox Ave.)
Wrens	1955	NYC (Bronx)	NY	
Youngsters (Empire)	1956	Los Angeles	CA	
Youngtones	1958	NYC (Brooklyn)	NY	Coney Island
Zodiacs (Maurice	1959	Lancaster	SC	Barr Street H.S/Williams & the)/Gladiolas

Introduction to Songography

One of the most difficult tasks in assembling a songography of doo-wop music, as we have defined it, lay in deciding which groups to include and which to leave out. These decisions were especially troublesome for groups singing at the beginning of the doo-wop era and for those singing at its end.

Since we conceptualize the "doo-wop-ishness" of a song as a continuum, we had to make some hard choices that are, in truth, arbitrary and open to question. For the purposes of this songography, we have done the following: For groups that sang almost exclusively in doo-wop style, we have listed all of their works. For those that only recorded a few songs in doo-wop style before making their name in another genre (e.g. Miracles and Supremes), we have included only doo-wop-styled versions. For groups that made significant contributions to both doo-wop and other genres (e.g., Dells and Little Anthony & the Imperials) we have listed only their doo-wop works.

The songography that follows is quite extensive, primarily because we had so many excellent sources to rely on. Our most important sources are listed below, with the works by Robert Ferlingere, Fernando Gonzales and Jeff Kreiter being of greatest help. Aside from its completeness, ours differs from its predecessors primarily on being exclusively a doo-wop songography, while others have focused on the broader field of rhythm and blues. Further, many other lists, especially those published by Jerry Osborne, focus on record prices, while ours does not. Our primary sources were:

Clee, Ken. The Directory of American 45 R.P.M. Records (4 Vols). Philadelphia: Stak-O-Wax, 1989.

Ferlingere, Robert. A Discography of Rhythm & Blues and Rock 'N' Roll Vocal Groups, 1945 to 1965.

Hayward, CA: California Trade School, 1976.

Gart, Galen. American Record Label Directory and Dating Guide (4th ed.). Milford, N.H.: Big Nickel

Publications, 1990.

Gonzales, Fernando L. Disco-File (2nd ed.). Flushing, N.Y.: Fernando L. Gonzales, 1977.

Hill, Randall C. The Official Price Guide to Collectible Rock Records, 2nd ed. House of Collectibles, 1980.

Kreiter, Jeff. 45 R.P.M. Group Collector's Record Guide, 7th ed. Bridgeport, OH: Boyd Press, 1999.

Mawhinney, Paul C. The Music Master: The 45 RPM Record Directory By Artist (V.I) Pittsburgh, PA:

Record-Rama Sound Archives, 1983.

Mawhinney, Paul C. The Music Master: The 45 RPM Record Directory By Title (V. II) Pittsburgh, PA:

Record-Rama Sound Archives, 1983.

Nite, Norm N. Rock On, Vol. I New York: Thomas Y. Crowell Co., 1974.

Osborne, Jerry. Record Collector's Price Guide, 1st ed. O'Sullivan, Warside, 1976.

Osborne, Jerry. Blues, R&B and Soul Price Guide, 1st ed. O'Sullivan, Warside, 1980.

Osborne, Jerry. The Complete Library of American Phonograph Recordings, 1959. Tempe, AR: Osborne Enterprises, 1987.

Osborne, Jerry. The Complete Library of American Phonograph Recordings, 1960. Tempe, AR: Osborne Enterprises, 1987.

Osborne, Jerry. The Complete Library of American Phonograph Recordings, 1961. Tempe, AR: Osborne Enterprises, 1987.

Osborne, Jerry. Rockin' Records: Buyers and Sellers Reference Book and Price Guide. Port Townsend, WA: Osborne Enterprises, 1989.

Propes, Steve. Those Oldies But Goodies: A Guide to 50s Record Collecting. New York: MacMillan, 1973.

Propes, Steve. Golden Oldies: A Guide to 60s Record Collecting. New York: Chilton, 1974.

Whitburn, Joel. The Billboard Book of Top 41 Hits: 1955-1987. New York: Billboard Books, 1989.

Unfortunately, two sources occasionally presented conflicting information about the titles, flip sides, year and even record number and label. Many of the sources we relied on often had incomplete information about a record; for example, the year was missing, and we often could not fill in the blank. Especially troublesome was the confusion surrounding groups singing under the same name. For example, one source may have presented a (hypothetical) group called the Ostriches recording on the A, B and C labels and a second group of Ostriches singing on D and E. A second source may have reported the first Ostrich group as being on labels A, D and E. A third source may have recommended that three separate Ostrich groups recorded for labels A through E. We have done our best to sort out these puzzles.

Our goal was to give the reader as many song titles as we could find. We have concentrated our efforts in the years that define the doo-wop era, approximately 1950 to the early 1960s. While recordings outside of these years are listed, the information is less complete. The overwhelming majority of titles have complete information (i.e., flip side, year, record label and record number), and were recorded as singles. In some cases, however, songs appear that are missing a flip side, a year and/or a record label. Most often, when this occurs, the song was recorded for an LP or

EP. A single may exist somewhere, but we could not unearth it. We would welcome help from our readers in filling in the blanks.

Group name: Most entries in this column are the names of groups, listed in alphabetical order. A group with the moniker "Tiny Tony & the Tots" is listed as "Tots (Tiny Tony & the)." Occasionally, individual names are listed, e.g., "Mouse, Matthew (& group)." The presence of a group is certain, but the name of this group is unknown.

If other information is known, it is given in parenthesis. "Tots (with Tiny Tony)" or "Tots (featuring Tiny Tony)" means that Tiny Tony's name appeared on the recording. Other information is supplied (because it may be of interest to the reader) using the following abbreviations in parenthesis: "fb" is fronted by, "bb" is backed by, and "gm" is group member. Where these three abbreviations are used, the information that follows them is not on the recording itself.

Often, groups with identical (or nearly so) members sang under more than one group name. In these cases, one name is referenced by another using the phrase, "also known as" or "aka." For example, "Tots (aka Toddlers/aka Kid-Tones)" means that the three groups had identical (or nearly so) membership. If the groups are not identical, but are related to one another, "ref" (standing for "refer to") is used; e.g., Oldsters (ref Seniors).

Numbers in parenthesis following the name of a group (e.g., "Tots (1)" or "Tots (2)" are used to differentiate between different groups of singers that sang under the same group name. Decisions about whether groups were identical or separate, as mentioned ear-lier, were not always easy to make. Often, these decisions were made on little but the labels recorded on and the years of release. Again, any help from our readers is welcome.

Song titles: In most cases, "A" sides are listed first and "B" sides second, when this distinction could be made. Flip sides are separated by the slash symbol ("/"). In some instances, the flip side is unknown, but some information is included such as "flip is instrumental" or "Flip has no group." If the flip side was recorded by a different group, its name appears in parenthesis after the title of the flip side.

Year: The year refers to the first known release date for the record. If a date is given for an unreleased song, it refers to the recording date for the song.

Label: Label and label numbers are given for each song when known. If a label name is followed by a number, a "/" and another number, e.g., "Superlabel 1001/1002," the two numbers refer to the two sides of the record. If the same record was released by two different labels (or the same label at two different points in time), both names appear, with the first release coming first, and they are separated by a "/" (e.g., "Goodlabel 104/Betterlabel 5003"). If release dates are known for the second, third, etc. labels, they are included in parenthesis.

Label listings imply that the second was released as a single, most often a "45," occasionally a "78." In the interest of completeness, songs released only on albums are included in the songography. Information about the album (LP) or extended play (EP) are given, if known, as for example: "Goodlabel LP only" or "Goodlabel LP 1011."

Artist	Song	Year	Label
4 MOST (AKA FOUR MOST (1)) (LINCOLN CHASE & THE)			
	Watch My Smoke/If I Were A Countryside	1956	Dawn 217
A MOMENT'S PLEASURE			
	I Need Your Kisses/Sweet One	1986	Starlight 39
	Lost Love/What Cha Gonna Do	1986	Starlight 42
A-TONES (ROGER & THE) (ROGER BAILON)			
	Why/Look A Who	1961	Nike 002
ACADEMICS			
	At My Front Door/Darla, My Darling	1956	Ancho 100/Relic 509 (64)
	Heavenly Love/Too Good To Be True	1957	Ancho 101/Relic 510 (64)
	Girl That I Love/I Often Wonder	1958	Ancho 104 (unreleased)
	Drive-In Movie/Something Cool	1958	Elmont 1001/1002
ACCENTS (1)			
	Baby Blue/Don't Expect A Miracle	1955	Blue Mill 111
	Where Will You Be/Voice Of The Bayous	1956	Accent 1036
	Name Song/This Ole Body	1956	Accent 1037
	22 Del Rio Avenue/Red Light	1959	Jubilee 5353
	Till You Bring Your Love Back/Cassius Clay	1962	Joker 200
ACCENTS (1) (FEATURING ROBERT DRAPER JR.)			
	Wiggle Wiggle/Dreamin' And Schemin'	1958	Brunswick 55100
	I Give My Heart To You/Ching A Ling	1959	Brunswick 55123
	Anything You Want Me To Be/ Autumn Leaves (Les Ferrilles Mortes)	1959	Brunswick 55151/ Coral 62151 (59)
ACCENTS (1) (JACKIE ALLEN & THE)			
	Don't Go/Cool-A-Roo	1955	Accent 1025
	Bop Me Baby/Mood To Be Wooed	1955	Accent 1027
	Forever Yours/Yes, Yes	1955	Accent 1031
ACCENTS (2) (GARY TREXLER & THE)			
	Teen Baby/Cloud Full Of Tears	1957	Rev 3507
ACCENTS (2) (JIM MURPHY & THE)			
	I'm Gone Mama/Plumb Crazy	1957	Rev 3508
ACCENTS (2) (TED NEWMAN & THE)			
	I Double Dare You/None Of Your Tears	1957	Rev 3511
ACCENTS (3)			
	Our Wonderful Love/A Hundred Wailin' Cats	1962	Jive 888/Vee Jay 484 (62)
	Little Boy Blue/Movin' Along	1962	Matt 0001
	Here Comes The Pain/All I Want Is You	1963	Spokane 4007
	Where Can I Go/Rags To Riches	1963	Sultan 5500
ACCENTS (3) (SCOTT ENGLISH & THE)			
	High On A Hill/When (by the Dedications)	1963	Sultan 4003/ Spokane 4003 (63)
ACCENTS (4)			
	Enchanted Garden/Tell Me Now	19	Mercury 72154
ACCENTS (5) (FEATURING SANDI)			
	I've Got Better Things To Do/Then He Starts To Cry	1964	Charter 1017
	Better Watch Out Boy/ Tell Me (What's On Your Mind)	1964	Commerce 5012/ Challenge 59254 (64)
	He's The One/On The Run	1964	Karate 529
	Tell Me/Sweet Talk	1965	Challenge 9294
	Friendly Stranger/People Are Funny	N/A	Gazzari 90391
ACCENTS (6) (DANNY & THE)			
	Her Diary/She Can't Be Real	1965	Valli 307
ACCENTS (7) (RON PETERSON & THE)			
	Sticky/Linda Lou	1965	Jerden 728
ACCIDENTALS			
	No Reason/Twangin' Marie	1962	Beau Monde 1633
	Loser's Advice	N/A	Harbor 7593
ACEY, JOHNNY (& GROUP)			
	Why/Please Don't Go (Back To Baltimore)	1960	Fire 1015
ACORNS			
	Angel/I'm Going To Stick To You	1958	Unart 2006
	Please Come Back/Your Name And Mine	1959	Unart 2015
ACQUINETS (CARL GREEN'S) (FEMALE)			
	Apple Of My Heart/Give In	1961	Lilly 5008
ACTORS (AKA JARMELS)			
	Cool Water/Peanut Brittle	1962	Laurie 3135
ACTUALS			
	We Build A Nest/Dream Ship (by the Vocalaires)	1976	Ronnie 200
AD LIBS			
	The Boy From New York City/Kicked Around	1965	Blue Cat 102
	He Ain't No Angel/Ask Anybody	1965	Blue Cat 114
	On The Corner/Oo-Wee Oh Me Oh My	1965	Blue Cat 119
	Just A Down Home Girl/Johnny My Boy	1965	Blue Cat 123
ADAMS, LINK (& GROUP)			
	Angel Or Not/Lonely Teen	1961	A Okay 111
ADAMS, RICHIE (& GROUP)			
	No Mistakin' It/The Right Way	1961	Beltone 1001
	Are You Changing/The King	1964	Congress 226
ADAPTERS			
	Believe Me (flip has no group)	N/A	Richie 65
ADDICTION			
	Daddy's Home (a capella)/When We Get Married (a capella)	1972	Kelway 102
ADELPHIS			
	Darling It's You/Kathleen	1958	Rim 2020
	Kiss-A-Kiss/(The Sun Will) Shine Again	1958	Rim 2022
	Canadian Sunset	1973	Merry-Go-Round 103
ADLIBS			
	I Stayed Home/Santa's On This Way	1988	Johnnie Boy 1
ADMIRAL TONES			
	Hey Hey Pretty Baby/Rocksville, Pa. (instrumental)	1959	Felsted 8563
ADMIRALS			
	Oh Yes/Left With A Broken Heart	1955	King 4772
	Close Your Eyes/Give Me Your Love	1955	King 4782
	It's A Sad, Sad Feeling/Ow (with Cathy Ryan)	1955	King 4792
ADMIRATIONS (1) (FEATURING JOSEPH LORELLO)			
	The Bells Of Rosa Rita/Little Bo Peep	1958	Mercury 71521
	To The Aisle/Hey Senorita	1962	Mercury 71883/Jason Scott
	Over The Rainbow/In My Younger Days	1974	Kelway 108
	It All Happened So Fast	N/A	Mercury (unreleased)
	Remember The Day	N/A	Mercury (unreleased)
	Bells Of Rosa Rita/Please Be My Love (by the Charades)	N/A	Popular Request 107
ADMIRATIONS (2)			
	Just Like A Baby/My Baby	1961	Apollo 753
ADMIRATIONS (3) (AKA BEL MARS)			
	Coo Coo Cuddle Coo/Down To Earth (by the Nutmegs)	1963	Times Square 19
	Mixture Of Love/I've Searched (by the Heartspinners)	1963	Times Square 20/Relic 537 (65)
ADMIRATIONS (3) (NORVEEN BASKERVILLE & THE) (AKA BEL MARS)			
	Gonna Find My Pretty Baby/ Li'l Li'l Lulu (by the Bel Mars) (61)	1960	X-Tra 100/Candlelite 414
ADMIRATIONS (4)			
	Moonlight/Ain't It Funny	1964	Hull 1202
	Memories Are Here To Stay/Dear Lady	N/A	Atomic 12871
ADMIRATIONS (5) (KEITH & THE)			
	Dream/Caravan Of Lonely Men (no group)	1965	Columbia 43268
ADOLESCENTS (LITTLE WILLIE & THE)			
	Get Out Of My Life	N/A	Tener 1009
ADORABLES			
	School's All Over/Be	1964	Golden World 10
	Deep Freeze/Daddy Please	1964	Golden World 4
	Oh Boy/Devil In His Eyes	1965	Golden World 25
ADORABLES (GINGER & THE)			
	He's Gone (acapella)	1975	Relic LP 104

Artist	Song	Year	Label
ADORATIONS			
	Linda/That Lucky Old Sun	1971	Dreamtone 200
	Canadian Sunset/		
	Not Too Young (by the Four		
	Starlings)	1972	Dreamtone 202
ADRIAN, LEE (BB THE CHAPERONES)			
	Barbara, Let's Go Steady/I'm		
	So Lonely	1959	Richcraft 5006/SMC 1385 (62)
	School Is Over/A In Love	1962	SMC 1386
ADVENTURERS			
	Rip Van Winkle/Trail Blazer	1959	Capitol 4292
	Little Genie/Excelsior	1959	Jerden 105
	Shaggin'/Two O'Clock Express	1959	Mecca 11
	Peppermint Stick	1961	Columbia
	Rock And Roll Uprising/My		
	Mama Done Tole Me	1961	Columbia 42227
	It's Alright/I Don't Mind	1962	Ran-Dee 106
	Baby, Baby, My Heart/Lover		
	Doll	1966	Reading 602
	Wallflower	N/A	Columbia LP 8547
	Bill's Place	N/A	Columbia LP 8547
	Another Bachelor	N/A	Columbia LP 8547
AFFECTIONS (JUDY & THE)			
	Dum Dum De Dip/Marie,		
	Give Him Back	N/A	Dode
AFTERBEATS (GLORIA WOOD & THE)			
	Ching Ching/Doo Dee Doo		
	Doop	1960	Buena Vista 361
AGEE, RAY (& FEMALE GROUP)			
	I Need You/Without A Friend	1955	R&B 1311
AGEE, RAY (& GROUP)			
	These Things Are True/Love		
	Bug	1962	Marjan 001
AGENTS			
	The Love I Hold/Trouble	N/A	Liberty Bell 3260
	Gotta Help Me	N/A	Rally 504
AIRDALES (WESS & THE)			
	I Miei Giorni Felici/I'll Never		
	Turn My Back On You	1967	Durium 9259
AIRE-DALES (ROCKY ROBERTS & THE)			
	Buzz Buzz Buzz/Too Much	1965	Brunswick 55357
AKTONES (WILL WENDEL & THE)			
	Lonely Blue Boy/Lover	1962	Trans America 10000
ALADDIN, JOHNNY (BB THE PASSIONS)			
	Why Did You Go/Happy		
	Together	1960	Chip 1001
ALADDINS (1)			
	Cry, Cry Baby/Remember	1955	Aladdin 3275
	Get Off My Feet/I Had A Dream		
	Last Nite	1955	Aladdin 3298
	All Of My Life/So Long,		
	Farewell, Bye-Bye	1956	Aladdin 3314
	Help Me/Lord Show Me	1957	Aladdin 3358
ALADDINS (2)			
	Dot, My Love/My Charlene	1958	Frankie 6
ALADDINS (3)			
	I'll Be There/I'll Kiss Your		
	Teardrops Away	1959	Angie
ALADDINS (4)			
	Gee/Then	1962	Prism 6001
	Please Love Me/Munch	1962	Witch 109
	Our Love Will Be/Simple Simon	1963	Witch 111
ALADDINS (5)			
	Magic Carpet/A Thousand		
	Times Every Day	N/A	Duplex 9012
ALAIMO, CHUCK (CHUCK ALAIMO QUARTET)			
	That's My Desire/Leap Frog		
	(instrumental)	1957	MGM 12449
	How I Love You/Local 66		
	(instrumental)	1957	MGM 12508
ALAM-KEYS			
	Please Come Back To		
	Me/Jumpin' Twist	1962	Kiski 2056
ALAMOS			
	Donkey Walk/Pork Chops	1957	Hi-Q 5030
ALAMOS (SAMMY HOUSTON & THE)			
	Summer Souvenir/Hey		
	Swamper	1960	Cleveland 104
ALAMOS (TONY VALLA & THE)			
	Jane Why Did You Do It/La		
	Bamba	1961	Fortune 858
	Love, Boy (Made A Fool Out Of		
	You)/Maria Christina	1961	Fortune 859
ALCONS			
	Black Jack/One Note Samba	1959	Brunswick 55128
ALCOVES			
	Heaven/The Ballad Of Cassius		
	Clay	1964	Carlton 602
ALDENAIRES (PAUL ALDEN & THE)			
	Crazy Memories/How Do		
	You Break An Angel's Heart	N/A	Glolite 106
ALEXANDER, JEFF (THE JEFF ALEXANDER QUARTET)			
	I'll Pay As I Go/Dr. Geek	1955	Aardell 0001
ALGERS (SKIP & FRUIT & THE)			
	Heavenly Father/Oh Baby	1960	Northern 3730
ALIENS			
	Wild Love	N/A	Stilt 66801
ALL AMERICANS (JOEY ROGERS & THE)			
	Jeannine/They Didn't Believe		
	Me	1958	Nu-Clear (no number)
ALL NIGHTERS			
	You Talk Too Much/Summertime		
	Blues	1964	GMA 1
ALLAN, JOHNNY (BB THE KRAZY KATS)			
	Unfaithful One/Rubber Dolly	1962	Viking 1016
ALLEN TRIO			
	That's What I Like/Teach Me		
	Tonight (by the Five Dips)	1955	Original 1005
ALLEN, ANISTEEN (BB THE CUES)			
	Fuji Yama Mama/Wheels Of		
	Love	1955	Capitol 3048
ALLEN, BOB (& GROUP)			
	I'm Alone Again/Everybody's		
	Got A Little Something	1966	Diamond 197
ALLEN, CHARLIE (& GROUP)			
	Sweetie Pie/Wheelin' And		
	Dealin'	1961	Portrait 107
ALLEN, GEORGE (& GROUP)			
	I Must Be Crazy/Times Won't		
	Always Be Hard (no group)	1961	Sotoplay 0031
ALLEN, MIMI (& GROUP)			
	Do You Miss Me/Whoopee		
	(Love's A Wonderful Thing)	1961	Three Speed 711
ALLEN, RICH (BB THE EBONISTICS)			
	Echoes Of November/Fanarri	1968	Groovey Grooves 160
ALLEN, SUE (& GROUP)			
	I Dedicate My Heart/Don't		
	Leave Me Here To Cry	1954	Groove 0037
ALLEN, TONY (& GROUP)			
	The Back Door/No One	1988	Classic Artists 102
ALLEN, TONY (BB THE WONDERS)			
	Train Of Love/God Gave Me		
	You	1959	Jamie 1143
	Dreamin'/Be My Love, Be		
	My Love	1961	Kent 364
ALLEY CATS (1)			
	This Thing Called		
	Love/Spang-A-Lang	1956	Whippet 202
	Last Night/Snap, Crackle		
	And Pop	1957	Whippet 209
ALLEY CATS (2)			
	Puddin' 'N Tain' (Ask Me Again,		
	I'll Tell You The Same)/Feel		
	So Good	1962	Philles 108
	I Should Have Stayed At Home		
	Tonight/Lily Of The West	1965	Epic 9778
ALLEYCATS (JOE ALLEN & THE)			
	I Cried Enough/Baby, Baby,		
	Baby	1958	Jalo 201
	I Want To Thrill You/Mike's Riff	1958	Jalo 202
ALLIE OOP'S GROUP (FB GERRY GRANAHAN)			
	Bloop, Bloop/Dinosaur	1960	Caprice 102
ALLISON, GENE (& GROUP)			
	You're My Baby/Somebody		
	Somewhere	1956	Calvert 106/Decca 30185 (56)
	Hey, Hey, I Love You/You Can		
	Make It If You Try	1957	Vee Jay 256
	Let's Sit And Talk/I Don't Know		
	Why	1958	Vee Jay 286
ALLISONS			
	Lessons In Love/Oh, My Love	1962	Smash 1749
	Money/Surfer Street	1963	Tip 1011

Artist	Song	Year	Label
ALLUMNS			
	Tell Me Why/Winner Take All	1978	Crystal Ball 118
ALLURES			
	King Love	1963	Melron 5009
	It Wasn't A Lie/You Came To Me	1985	Starlight 26
	Lorraine/Here Goes A Fool	1986	Starlight 32
	Our Songs Of Love/The Stars	1986	Starlight 48
	Your Very First Love/Happy Happy Birthday	1987	Starlight 50
	Lovers Never Say Goodbye/Magic Moon	1989	Starlight 71
ALMA-KEYS			
	Please Come Back To Me/Jumpin' Twist	1980	Kiski 2056
ALSTON, HENRY (& GROUP)			
	Once In A Beautiful Lifetime/I Dare You Baby	1959	Skyline 500
	Once In A Beautiful Lifetime/ What Is There Left For Me	1959	Skyline 551
ALSTON, JO ANN (& GROUP)			
	He Left Me Crying/Looking Like A Fool	1963	Vest 8001
ALSTON, WALTER (& GROUP)			
	Gypsy Lady/Hey Baby	1961	Gamut 101
ALTAIRS (GM GEORGE BENSON)			
	If You Love Me/Groovie Time	1960	Amy 803
ALTECS			
	Easy/Recess	1961	Felsted 8618
	Yok Yok Yok/Tweeda	N/A	Cloister 6201
ALTEERS			
	Words Can't Explain/Keep Laughin'	1961	Laurie 3097
	This Lovely Night/No End	1964	G-Clef 705
ALTONES			
	Summer Love/Love Me, Love Me	1961	Archer 104
	Love Me Love Me/Eileen	1961	Gardena 121
ALVANS			
	Love Is A Game/What Can It Be	1961	May 102
AMAKER, DONALD (& GROUP)			
	Don't Let Me Shed Any More Tears/Pleasing	1959	Raines 418
AMATO, JERRY (& GROUP)			
	Dream On Little Fool/When I Met You	N/A	Tacit 109
AMBASSADORS (1) (AKA FOUR ARCS/AKA GAYLORDS/AKA IMPERIALS (1))			
	Darling I'm Sorry (I Made You Cry)/Willa-Bea	1954	Timely 1001
	Keep On Trying/The Switch	1956	Air 5065
	Lorraine/Come On And Dance	1963	Playbox 202
	Moanin'	1987	Relic LP 5071
	Calling For Love	1987	Relic LP 5071
AMBASSADORS (2) (VERN YOUNG & THE)			
	Cindy Lou/One Last Look At My Darling	1960	Chords 101
AMBASSADORS (3) (FEMALE)			
	I Wonder Why/The Power Of Love	1962	Bon 001/Reel 117 (62)
AMBASSADORS (4)			
	Oh Nancy/Ambassador Blues	1963	Bay 210
AMBERS (1) (GM RALPH MATHIS)			
	Never Let You Go/I'll Make A Bet	1958	Ebb 142
	Listen To Your Heart (Caroline)/Loving Tree	1959	Greezie 501
	All Of My Darling/So Glad	1960	Todd 1042
AMBERS (2) (JOEY & THE)			
	Treasure In My Heart/Sweet, Sweet Memory	1960	Big Top 3052
AMBERTONES			
	Charlena/Bandido	1964	GNP Crescendo 329
	One Summer Night/Chocolate Covered Ants	1965	Dottie 1129
	I Need Some/If I Do	1965	Dottie 1130
	I Only Have Eyes For You	N/A	Rayjack 1002
AMBITIONS			
	Traveling Stranger/Come Back To Me	1962	Cross 1005
AMBROSE, KENNY (& GROUP)			
	Don't Be A Fool For Love/Come On And Marry Me	1958	Hamilton 50019
	Your Love Is My Love/Won't You	1959	Willett 109
AMERICAN BEETLES			
	She's Mine/Them Of American Beetles	1964	BYP 1001
AMORETTES (ARMOND ADAMS & THE)			
	The Storm/Diamond Pins And Broken Beads	1964	Fortune 572
ANASTASIA (& GROUP)			
	Time Bomb/That's My Kind Of Love	1960	Laurie 3066
	Seven Days A Week/Nothing Beats My Girl	1961	Stasi 1001
	Every Road (I Walk Along)/Bicycle Hop	1962	Stasi 1002
ANDERS, BERNIE (& GROUP)			
	My Heart Believes/Too Late I Learned	1955	King 4833
ANDERS, TERRI (& GROUP)			
	Come Back My Love/All In My Mind	1960	Chief 7027
ANDERSON, BUBBA (& GROUP)			
	Where Has My Lover Gone/Please Don't Leave Me	1962	Ace 662
ANDREWS, GENE (& GROUP)			
	Linda Linda/Lonely Room	1963	Rust 5054
ANDREWS, LEE (BB THE HEARTS) (REF HEARTS (3))			
	I've Got A Right To Cry/I Miss You So	1960	Swan 4065
ANGEL, GARY (BB THE HALOS)			
	Oh Judy/Memories Of A Summer Day	1961	Kama 501
ANGEL, JOHNNY (& GROUP)			
	Doubt/Falling Teardrops	1960	Imperial 5673
ANGEL, JOHNNY (BB THE TRICKLES)			
	Starlight/The Story Of Love	1958	Power 250
ANGELENOS			
	As Long As I Have You/Don't Cry Baby	1961	Peepers 2824
	As Long As I Have You/On An Island	1961	Peepers 2824
	Come On Baby/Hully Gully Fever	1961	Peepers 2827
ANGELENOS (CAMILLE BROWN & THE)			
	Angels In Heaven/You're Gonna Be Sorry	1961	Peepers 2825
ANGELETTES			
	You And Only You/Mine And Mine Alone	1957	Josie 813
ANGELONES			
	Praying For A Miracle	N/A	Relic LP 5044
ANGELS (1) (WITH SONNY GORDON) (MALE)			
	Wedding Bells (Are Ringing In My Ears)/Times Have Changed	1954	Grand 115
	A Lovely Way To Spend An Evening/You're Still My Baby	1955	Grand 121
ANGELS (10) (LONNY & THE)			
	Before I Saw You Smile/Bargain Love	1961	Pledge 102
ANGELS (11) (LITTLE BETTY & THE)			
	Why Did You Do It/I May Be Wrong	1961	Savoy 1603
ANGELS (12) (FB JOEL KATZ)			
	Dearest Little Angel	1964	N/A
ANGELS (2)			
	Glory Of Love/It's You I Love Best	1956	Gee 1024
ANGELS (3)			
	Leaving You Baby/Sha-Wa-Wa	1956	Irma 105
ANGELS (4) (LITTLE BOBBY BELL & THE)			
	Came, Saw, Conquered/Whole Wide World	1957	Demon 1501
ANGELS (5) (REF SAFARIS)			
	A Lover's Poem (To Her)/A Lover's Poem (To Him)	1959	Tawny 101
ANGELS (6) (GABRIEL & THE)			
	That's Life (That's Tough)/ Don't Wanna Twist No More	1959	Casino 107/Swan 4118 (62)/Itzy 7 (62)
ANGELS (6) (GABRIEL & THE)			
	Hey/Chumba	1960	Amy 802
	Zing Went The Strings Of My Heart/The Rooster	1961	Amy 823
	I'm Gabriel/Ginza	1961	Norman 506

Artist Song	Year	Label	Artist Song	Year	Label
All Work, No Play/Peanut Butter Song	1963	Swan 4133	**APOLLO BROTHERS**		
ANGELS (7) (FEMALE) (AKA STARLETS (1))			My Beloved One/Riot Locket 108 (60)	1960	Cleveland 108/
P. S. I Love You/Where Is My Love Tonight	1960	Astro AS202-1	**APOLLOES**		
Til/A Moment Ago (with Linda Jansen)	1961	Caprice 107	Summertime Blues	1964	Look 001
Cry Baby Cry/That's All I Ask Of You (with Linda Jansen)	1962	Caprice 112	**APOLLOS (1)**		
Everybody Loves A Lover/Blow, Joe	1962	Caprice 116	I Love You Darling/Bandstand Baby	1959	Harvard 803
I'd Be Good For You/You Should Have Told Me	1962	Caprice 118	I Can't Believe It/Sometimes I Feel	1961	Galaxy 707
A Moment Ago/Cotton Fields	1962	Caprice 121	Lord, Lord, Lord/Say A Prayer	1961	Galaxy 708
Cotton Fields/Irresistible	1963	Ascot 2139	**APOLLOS (2)**		
My Boyfriend's Back/(Love Me) Now	1963	Smash 1834	Just Dreaming/Rockin' Horses	1960	Mercury 71614
I Adore Him/Thank You And Goodnight	1963	Smash 1854	**APOLLOS (3) (PAUL STEFEN & THE)**		
Wow Wow Wee (He's The Boy For Me)/Snowflakes And Teardrops	1964	Smash 1870	Good For A Laugh/For Pete's Sake	1962	Cite 5006
Little Beatle Boy/Java	1964	Smash 1885	You/Cry Angel Cry	1962	Cite 5008
Dream Boy/Jamaica Joe	1964	Smash 1915	Hey Lonely One	1963	Citation 5007
The Boy From 'Cross Town/A World Without Love	1964	Smash 1931	**APOLLOS (4) (BOBBY CHARLES & THE)**		
What To Do/I Had A Dream I Lost You	1967	RCA 9129	No Money/Forget	1962	Tide 1084/1085
You'll Never Get To Heaven/Go Out And Play	1967	RCA 9246	**APOSTLES**		
With Love/You're The Cause Of It	1967	RCA 9404	Stranded In The Jungle/Tired Of Waiting	1966	A-Square 401
The Modley/If I Didn't Love You	1968	RCA 9541	**APPARITIONS**		
The Boy With The Green Eyes/But For Love	1968	RCA 9612	Part Of Our Love (acapella)	1975	Relic LP 103
Merry Go Round/So Nice	1968	RCA 9681	Autumn Leaves (acapella)	1975	Relic LP 105
Papa's Side Of The Bed/You're All I Need To Get By	1974	Polydor 14222	Don't Leave Me Baby (acapella)	1975	Relic LP 105
ANGELS (8) (AKA HI TENSIONS)			Forgotten Spring (acapella)	1975	Relic LP 105
I'm Saying Goodbye/A Real Sensation	1960	Audio 203/Milestone	Image Of A Girl (acapella)	1975	Relic LP 108
ANGELS (9) (HANNIBAL & THE)			Since I Fell For You (acapella)	1975	Relic LP 108
Please Take A Chance On Me/Love Is Funny	1960	Pan World 517	Valerie (acapella)	1975	Relic LP 109
ANGLETONES			**AQUA-NITES**		
Darling	1985	Relic LP 5051	Carioca/Lover Don't You Weep	1965	Astra 1000/Astra 2003 (65)
ANGLOES (JULIE GIBSON & THE)			Christy/Lover Don't You Weep	1965	Astra 2001
I Got News For You/You've Been Cheatin' On Me	1962	Herald 575	**AQUALADS (ANTHONY & THE)**		
ANGLOS (LINDA MARTELL & THE)			The Heart That's True/I Remember	N/A	Gold Bee 1650
A Little Tear/The Things I Do For You	1962	Fire 512	**AQUATONES**		
ANGORIANS			You/She's The One For Me	1958	Fargo 1001
Lullaby/Raindrops	1964	Tishman 9078	Say You'll Be Mine/So Fine	1958	Fargo 1002
ANNUALS			Our First Kiss/The Drive-In	1958	Fargo 1003
Hungry, I'm Hungry/Once In A Lifetime	1962	Marconn CR1	My One Desire/My Treasure	1959	Fargo 1005
ANSWERS			Every Time/There's A Long Long Trail	1959	Fargo 1015
Have No Fear/Keeps Me Worried All The Time	1957	United 212	Crazy For You/Wanted (A Solid Gold Cadillac)	1960	Fargo 1016
ANTEATERS (CHUCK HARROD & THE)			My Darling/For You, For You	1960	Fargo 1111
Sandy/They Wanna Fight	1959	Champion 1013	My Treasure/Say You'll Be Mine	1962	Fargo 1022
ANTELL, PETE (& GROUP)			Light Up The Sky	N/A	Fargo LP 5033X
Keep It Up/You In Disguise	1963	Cameo 264	**ARABIAN KNIGHTS (HAJI BABA & THE)**		
ANTENNAS			Early One Morning/Don't Put Me Down Baby	1956	Gotham 313
Thirty Minutes To Go	1962	United (unreleased)	**ARABIAN KNIGHTS (RAY GANT & THE)**		
Ubangi Baby	1962	United (unreleased)	I Need A True Love/Don't Leave Me, Baby	1971	Jay Walking 014
Fuji-Yama Mama/Be Yourself	N/A	Clay 201	**ARABIANS (1)**		
ANTHONY, MIKE (& GROUP)			Heaven Sent You/The Shack	1960	Jam 3738/Twin Star 1018 (60)
Little Linda/My Secret Heartache	1961	Imperial 5813	My Heart Beats Over And Over Again/Crazy Little Fever	1960	Magnificent 102/ Magnificent 102 (60)
ANTHONY, PAUL (& GROUP)			Teardrops In The Night/Take Me	1960	Magnificent 114
My Promise To You/Bop Bop Bop	1958	Roulette 4099	**ARABIANS (2)**		
Step Up/Look At Me Now	N/A	Metro International 1003	I Love You So/Now You Have To Cry Alone	1960	Lanrod 1605
ANTLERS			Tell Me/School Is Cool	N/A	Mary Jane 1006
Just In Case You	1952	Artists 1260	**ARABIANS (2) (EDWARD HAMILTON & THE)**		
ANTONES			Thank You Mother/Thank You Mother (instrumental)	N/A	Mary Jane 1007/1008
Jeanette/You Are The One	1956	Black Crest 106	**ARABIANS (3)**		
ANTONES (JOEY PFARR & THE)			My One Possession/Somebody Tell Me	1961	Carrie 1516
All My Life/Time For Love	1957	Black Crest 107	**ARABIANS (4)**		
ANTWINETTS (FEMALE)			You Upset Me Baby/Please Take A Chance On Me	1964	Le Mans 001
Johnny/Kill It	1958	RCA 7398	**ARABIANS (5)**		
			Condition Your Heart/Bouncing Ball	1964	Teek 4824-1/4824-2
			ARABIANS (6) (LAWRENCE & THE)		
			I'll Try Harder	N/A	Hem
			ARC-ANGELS		
			Little Wheel/Goddess	1961	Lan-Cet 142

Artist Song	Year	Label
ARCADES		
Blackmail/June Was The End Of August	1959	Guyden 2015
Fine Little Girl (w. King Curtis)/ My Love	1959	Johnson 116/ Johnson 320 (62)
Our Love/The Pal	1960	Julia 1100
ARCADOS		
When You Walked Out/Sugar Sweet	1963	Fam 502
ARCHIADS		
I Told You So	N/A	Ro-Cal
ARCS (J. LAMBERT & THE)		
Alone/Rockin' Strings	1958	K&C 100
ARDEES (PHIL ALAN & THE)		
Tell Me Why/Four Leaf Clover	N/A	Ko Co Bo 1010
ARDELLS (FB JOHNNY MAESTRO)		
Every Day Of The Week/Roll On	1961	Marco 102
Eefenanny/Lonely Valley	1963	Epic 9621
Seven Lonely Nights/You Can Fall In Love	1963	Selma 4001
ARGYLES (1)		
Everytime You Smile/Moonbeam	1957	Bally 1030
ARGYLES (2) (AKA HOLLYWOOD ARGYLES)		
Vacation Days Are Over/It Takes Time	1959	Brent 7004
ARIST-O-KATS		
I Don't See Me In Your Eyes Anymore/Chasin' The Blues	1957	Vita 168
ARISTOCATS		
So In Love With You/Lawdy When She Kissed Me	1958	Sue 714
ARISTOCATS (BOBBY BLUE & THE)		
You're Mine	1958	N/A
ARISTOCRATS (1)		
Believe Me/I'm Waiting For Ships	1954	Essex 366/Sound 101
ARISTOCRATS (1) (MURRAY SCHAFF & THE)		
Ooh How I Love Ya/The Unfinished Rock	1955	Josie 788
ARISTOCRATS (2)		
Don't Go/Squeeze Me	1962	Home Of The Blues 237
ARISTOCRATS (2) (JACKIE LEONARD & THE)		
Another Love	1963	Lesley 1926
ARISTOCRATS (3) (TONY SMITH & HIS)		
Rippling Waters/By Nellie's	N/A	Mad 1006
ARK ANGELS (LITTLE CAESAR & THE)		
The Ghost Of Mary Meade	1960	Jack Bee 1008
ARKETTS (ARGIE & THE)		
You're The Guy/Hey Baby	1961	Ronnie (no number)
ARLIN, BOB (& GROUP)		
East L.A./Pearl Of My Heart	1960	Olympia 823/824
ARLINGTON, BRUCE (& GROUP)		
You Made Me Cry/How Could You Know	1964	King 5918
ARMEN, MICKEY (& GROUP)		
Cheating On Me/Tell My Why	1958	Peek-A-Boo 1001
ARMPITS (SNAKE & THE)		
Can't We Be Sweethearts/My Son	N/A	Explo 013
ARNELLS		
Take A Look/Heart Repair Shop	1963	Roulette 4519
ARONDIES		
All My Love/Sixty-Nine (69)	N/A	Sherry 69
ARPEGGIOS		
Mary/I'll Be Singing	1963	Aries 001
ARRIBINS (DUKE SAVAGE & THE)		
Your Love/Hey Baby!	1959	Argo 5346
ARROGANTS (FB RAY MORROW)		
Tom Boy/Make Up Your Mind	1960	Big A 12184/12185
Take Life Easy/Stone Broke	1962	Vanessa 200
Mirror Mirror/Canadian Sunset	1963	Lute 6226/Candlelite 425 (63)
ARROWS		
What's New With You/We Ain't Gonna Ride No More	1973	Baron 102
ARROWS (1) (JOE LYONS & THE)		
Honey Chile/What's New With You	1956	Hollywood 1065
No End To True Love/One Too Many Times	1956	Hollywood 1071
Shim Sham Shufflin' Jive/Bop-A-Loop	1959	Hit Maker 600

Artist Song	Year	Label
ARROWS (2)		
Annie Mae/Indian Bop Hop	1958	Flash 132
I'm Checking On You Baby/No Other Arms	1964	Hugo 1174
ARROWS (3)		
Run Like The Wind/When You Were Sweet 16	1960	Cupid 105
ARROWS (4) (BIG BO & THE)		
It Keeps Raining	1962	Duchess 1016
A Thousand Miles Away/I Done Got Over It	1964	Checker 1068
ARTELLS (AKA CRESTS)		
You Can Fall In Love/7 Lonely Nights		Selma 4001
ARTIS, RAY (& GROUP)		
Art Of Love/That's All I Want From You	1961	A 111
ARTISTICS		
Life Begins At Sixteen/One Way	1962	S&G 302
ARVETTES (FEMALE)		
At A School Dance/Lovely Emotions	1961	Hac 104
Pledge Of Love/I Want To Dance With You	1966	Ideal 100A
Pledge Of Love/Stolen Hours	1966	Ideal 3776
ASCOTS (1)		
What Love Can Do/Everything Will Be All Right	1956	J&S 1628/1629
ASCOTS (2)		
It It Really You/Easier Said Than Done	1959	Arrow 736
ASCOTS (3)		
Perfect Love/I'm Touched	1962	Ace 650
She Did/Hip Talk	1962	Bethlehem 3046
(Darling I'll See You) Tonight/I Don't Care One Bit	1962	King 5679
ASCOTS (4)		
Acapulco Run/The Gladiator	1963	Dual-Tone 1120
Miss Heartbreaker/This Old Heartache	1965	M.B.S. 106
ASCOTS (5)		
Sometimes I Wonder/Anytime	1965	Mir-A-Don 1001
Mother Said/Yes It's All Right	1965	Mir-A-Don 1002
Another Day/Love	1965	Mir-A-Don 1004
ASHLEY, JOHN (& GROUP)		
Seriously In Love/I Want To Hear It From You	1960	Silver 1002
ASTORS		
What Can It Be/Just Enough To Hurt Me	1963	Stax 139
I Found Out/Candy	1965	Stax 170
ASTRA-LITES		
Space Hop/Lonely	1962	Tribute 101
ASTRO JETS		
Boom-A-Lay/Hide And Seek	1961	Imperial 5760
ASTRONAUTS (1)		
Come Along Baby/Tryin' To Get To You	1961	Palladium 610
ASTRONAUTS (2)		
Farewell/Chili Charlie	1960	Trial 3521
ASTROS (PEPE & THE)		
Judy My Love (Judy Mi Amor)/ Now Ain't That A Shame	1961	Swami 553/554
ATLANTICS (BARRY WHITE & THE)		
Flame Of Love/Tracy (All I Have Is Yours)	1963	Faro 613
ATLANTICS (GM BARRY WHITE)		
Boo-Hoo-Hoo/Everything Is Gonna Be All Right	1961	Linda 103
Remember The Night/Flame Of Love	1962	Linda 107
Let Me Call You/Home On The Range	1965	Rampart 614
Fine, Fine, Fine/Beaver Shot	1965	Rampart 643
ATOMICS (DENNIS BROWN & THE)		
Hiding My Tears With A Smile/Show Me The Rose	1957	Atomic 57-101
ATTITUDES (GM RANDY SILVERMAN)		
That Old Black Magic/Mama's Doin' The Jerk	1967	Times Square 110
ATTRACTIONS (J.R. & THE) (AKA JOHNNY RAND & GROUP)		
I'm Yours/Bristol Stomp	1965	Hunch 928

Artist	Song	Year	Label	Artist	Song	Year	Label
ATTRIBUTES1				**AVONS (4) (FEMALE)**			
	Valerie/Another Night With The Boys	1979	U.G.H.A. 12		Talk To Me/Got To Get Used To You	1967	A-Bet 9419
AUDIOS (CELL FOSTER & THE)				**AZALEAS (FEMALE)**			
	Honest I Do/I Prayed For You	1956	Ultra 105		Hands Off/Our Drummer Can't	1963	Romulus 3001
AUSTIN, LITTLE AUGIE (BB THE CHROMATICS)				**AZTECS (1) (JOSE & THE)**			
	My Love For You/I Thank My Lucky Star	1960	Pontiac 101		Does She Know	1955	Roadhouse LP
AUTOMATIONS					My Aching Heart	1955	Roadhouse LP
	Miracle Of The Bells/Here's That Rainy Day	1974	Clifton 6		Why Did She Leave Me	1955	Roadhouse LP
AUTUMNS					Baby Baby/Zoop (by the Hi-Lites)	1976	Monogram 122
	Maureen/Dearest Little Angel	1962	Medieval 208/Clifton 34 (79)		My Aching Heart/Why Did She Leave	1976	Monogram 123
	Never/Exodus (acapella)	1966	Amber 856/Power	**AZTECS (2)**			
	Seven-Up Jingles/Lovely Way To Spend An Evening	1980	Clifton 52		The Answer To My Prayer/It's You That I Love	1962	Zin-A-Spin 002
	Thank You Pretty Lady/Dancer	1981	BAB 128	**AZTECS (3)**			
AUTUMNS (JOEL & THE)					Teenage Hall Of Fame/Traffic Jam	1964	Card 901
	A 1950s Love Song/The Second Time Around	1979	J & M 646		Da Doo Ron Ron/Hi-Heel Sneakers	1964	World Artists 1029
AVALONS (1)				**AZTECS (4) (BILLY THORPE & THE)**			
	Chains Around My Heart/Ooh! She Flew	1956	Groove 0141		Over The Rainbow/That I Love	1965	GNP Crescendo 340
	It's Funny But It's True/Sugar Sugar	1956	Groove 0174		Summertime Blues/What'Cha Gonna Do About It	1965	GNP Crescendo 346
	My Heart's Desire/Ebb Tide	1958	Unart 2007		Twilight Time/My Girl Josephine	1965	GNP Crescendo 359
	You Do Something To Me/ You Can Count On Me	1959	Casino 108	**BABY DOLLS (1)**			
	Begin The Beguine/Malanese	1963	Olimpic 240/NPC 302 (64)		Cause I'm In Love/Tutti Frutti (Pop-Pi)	1958	RCA 7296
	You Do Something To Me/You Can Count On Me	1972	Bim Bam Boom 106		Hey Baby/Quiet	1959	Warner Bros. 5086
	What's Wrong	N/A	Collectables LP 5037		Go Away Baby/I'm Lonely	1961	Maske 103
	I Follow The Stars	N/A	Groove (unreleased)		Thanks, Mr. Dee-Jay/What A Wonderful Love	1961	Maske 701
	Little Cutie	N/A	Groove (unreleased)		I Will Do It (Cause He Wants Me To)/Now That I've Lost You	1966	Boom 60002
AVALONS (2)					There's A Small Hotel/Bleeding Hearts	N/A	Parnaso 227
	I Miss You/Love Me	1956	Aladdin (unreleased)	**BABY DOLLS (1) (BILL BAKER & THE)**			
	Louella/You Broke Our Hearts	1958	Dice 90/91		Another Sleepless Night/It Shouldn't Happen In A Dream	1965	Parnaso 110
AVALONS (3)					Is This The End?/Boy Friend	1959	Elgin 021
	Is It The End/Many Things From Your Window	1964	Roulette 4568	**BABY DOLLS (2)**			
AVALONS (4)					Why Can't I Make Him Like You/Got To Get You In My Life	1961	Hollywood 1111
	Suddenly	1987	Relic LP 5072	**BABY DOLLS (3) (ROSIE'S)**			
	A Star	1987	Relic LP 5072		In Between (Wishing I Was Sweet Sixteen)/Should Have Known	1961	Fargo 1017
	I Don't Know	1987	Relic LP 5072	**BACHELOR THREE**			
	Baby Looka Here	1988	Relic LP 5075		Lover Man/Enchanted Summer	1961	Vi-Way 288
	Love Me Or Let Me Go	1988	Relic LP 5075		Mary Mary/Head Bo Thread Bo	1961	Vi-Way 289
	Do Something For Me	1988	Relic LP 5075	**BACHELORS (1) (DEAN BARLOW & THE)**			
AVANTIS					Is This Goodbye/Weekend Blues	1951	International 777
	Keep On Dancing/I Wanna Dance	1963	Argo 5436		Baby/Tell Me Now	1955	Earl 102
AVERONES (BOB & THE)					In A Little Inn In Italy/Bachelor Mambo	1955	Excel 105
	Please Say You Want Me/Patti	1964	Brent 7054		I'm Lost/Texas	1955	Excel 106
AVONS (1)					Delores/I Want To Know About Love	1955	Earl 101
	Our Love Will Never End/I'm Sending S.O.S.	1956	Hull 717	**BACHELORS (2) (AKA JETS)**			
	Baby/Bonnie	1957	Hull 722		Can't Help Loving You/Pretty Baby	1953	Aladdin 3210
	You Are So Close To Me/Gonna Catch You Nappin'	1958	Hull 726		You've Lied/I Found Love	1956	Royal Roost 620
	What Will I Do (If You Go Away)/ Please Come Back To Me	1958	Hull 728		After/You Know! You Know! (I Love You)	1957	Poplar 101
	What Love Can Do/On The Island	1959	Hull 731		Raining In My Heart	N/A	Royal Roost (unreleased)
	Someone For Everybody	1960	Hull LP 1000		Baby	N/A	Royal Roost (unreleased)
	Fairy Tales/Once Upon A Time	1960	Hull LP 1000/	**BACHELORS (3)**			
	Monogram 129 (77)				Selfish	1955	Palace 140
	Baby/Whisper (Softly)	1963	Astra 1023		From Your Heart/A Million Teardrops	1957	National 104
	A Girl To Call My Own/ The Grass Is Greener On The Other Side	1963	Hull 754		Sometimes/Teenage Memory	1958	MGM 12668
AVONS (1) (WITH THE MILLER SISTERS)					I Want A Girl/Today, Tomorrow, Forever	1958	National 115
	Whisper (Softly)/If I Just (Had My Way) (with the Miller Sisters)	1961	Hull 744		Bachelor's Club/Do The Madison	1960	Epic 9369
AVONS (2) (FEMALE)					The Day I Met You/Hey Little Girl	1961	Smash 1723
	We Fell In Love/Pickin' Petals	1960	Mercury 71618	**BACHELORS (4) (T. LA MAR & THE)**			
	Push A Little Harder/Oh, Gee Baby	1963	Groove 0022		Don't Leave Me/You Do Something To Me	1963	Five-Four 5440
AVONS (3) (FEMALE)							
	Rolling Stone/Words Written On Water	1963	Groove 0033				
	Tonight Kiss Your Baby Goodbye/Whatever Happened To Our Love	1963	Groove 0039				

Artist Song	Year	Label
BACKUS, GUS (& GROUP)		
You Can't Go It Alone/My Chick Is Fine	1958	Carlton
BAD BOYS		
What Do You Want With Me/It's More Like Voodoo	1964	Herald 592
BAD BOYS (JESSIE PERKINS & THE)		
One More Kiss/Madly In Love	1960	Savoy 1584
BAILEY, DON (& GROUP)		
Be My Own/Wedding	1962	USA 723
BAILEY, HERB (& GROUP)		
Precious Lilly/Someway Somehow	1964	Movin' 126
BAILEY, JIMMY (& GROUP)		
Constantly/Let Your Conscience Be Your Guide	1958	Wynne 103
BAKER'S SATINS		
Crying In The Chapel/In The Still Of The Night	1984	Clifton 74
BAKER, BILL (& GROUP)		
Just To Be Near You/To The Aisle	1962	Audicon 118/Musictone 1108 (62)
Teenage Triangle/Why Did Summer Have To End	1962	Musicnote 119
BAKER, BILL (BB THE DEL SATINS)		
Is It A Dream/I Wanna Know	1961	Audicon 115
BAKER, CHARLIE (& GROUP)		
Star Of Wonder/You Crack Me Up	1959	Mun Rab 106/Liberty 55226
BAKER, JOAN		
Satisfy Me/Everybody's Talking	1964	Diamond 164
BAKER, ROY BOY (& GROUP)		
Bridge Of Love/I Thought I Heard You Call My Name	1963	Dess 7011
BALLADEERS		
Goodbye Little Girl/I Wish I Was Single Again	1952	RCA 4612
Red Sails In The Sunset/Give Me You	1992	Clifton 96
On Sunday Afternoon/11th Hour Melody	1990	Clifton 89
BALLADIERS		
What Will I Tell My Heart?/Forget Me Not	1952	Aladdin 3123
BALLADIERS (BILLY MATTHEWS & THE)		
Dance The Rhythm And Blues/ My Love For You (by the Rockets (2))	1956	Wrimus 701
BALLADS (1)		
Before You Fall In Love/Broke	1956	Franwil 5028
Somehow/Knee Bop	1960	Ron-Cris 1003
BALLADS (2)		
A Fool/That's My Baby	1972	Klik 1021
BALLADS (3)		
We Know/This Is Magic	1964	Tina 102
BALLARDS		
I Hope I Never Fall In Love/Do It Now	N/A	Veltone 1738
BALLARDS (BILLY BROWN & THE)		
I See A Girl/Why, Baby, Why	1963	El Tone 439
BALLIN, ROGER (& GROUP)		
Why/Look A Who	1960	Nike 002
BALTINEERS		
Moments Like This/New Love	1956	Teenage 1000
Tears In My Eyes/Joe's Calypso	1956	Teenage 1002
BAN LONS		
I Like It/Hey Good Lookin'	1959	Fidelity 4056
BANDITS		
Nothing Can Change My Love For You/This Love Of Ours (by the Dynamics)	1963	Emjay 1935
Tell Me/Little Sally Walker	N/A	Jerden 773
BANDMASTERS (LOU RALL & THE)		
Never Let Me Go/Party At Lesters	1964	Way Out (no number)
BANKS, OTIS (& GROUP)		
She's My Baby/Sazarac (instrumental)	1957	Bow 304
BANLONS		
Hey Baby/Highest Mountain	1959	Fidelity 4051/Baron 108 (73)
I Like It/Hey Good Lookin'	1962	Fidelity 4056

Artist Song	Year	Label
Fortune Tellers/Sales Talk	1960	MGM 12862
BARBARIANS (BB VITO PICCONE & THE ELEGANTS)		
Are You A Boy Or Are You A Girl/Take It Or Leave It	1965	Laurie 3308
I'll Keep On Seeing You/Moulty	1965	Laurie 3326
BARDS		
Easy Going Baby/I'm A Wine Drinker	1954	Dawn 208
Avalon/Gravy	1955	Dawn 209
BARIN, PETE (BB THE BELMONTS)		
So Wrong/Broken Heart	1962	Sabina 504
The Loneliest Guy In The World/Look For Cindy	1963	Sabina 512
BARITONES		
After School Rock/Sentimental Baby	1958	Dore 501
BARLOW, DEAN (& GROUP)		
Baby Doll/Third Window From The Right	1961	Lescay 3004
Love, Is That You?/Little Sister	1961	Seven Arts 704
It's All In Your Mind/Friendly People	1961	Warwick 618
BARNES, BIG SYL (& GROUP)		
Cherry/Come On Back	1960	Corvair 900
BARNES, JIMMY (& GROUP)		
Keep Your Love Handy/No Regrets	1959	Gibraltar 101
BARNES, JOHNNY (& GROUP)		
(There Is) No Love For Me/ Tell Me Why (That's What I Want To Know)	1961	Flippin' 105
BARNES, OTHEA (& GROUP)		
Your Picture On The Wall/Same As Before	1963	ABC 10434
BARNETTE, BILLY (& GROUP)		
Marlene/Two Brothers	1961	Parkway 826
BARON, NANCY (& GROUP)		
Oh Yeah	1962	Chelsea 102
BARONAIRES		
I Have A Father Who Cares	1960	Carrie
BARONS (1) (AKA MEL WILLIAMS & THE MONTCLAIRS/AKA BUDDIES (2))		
Exactly Like You/Forget About Me	1954	Decca 29293
A Year And A Day/My Baby's Gone	1954	Decca 48323
BARONS (2)		
Cryin' For You Baby/So Long, My Darling	1954	Imperial 5283
Eternally Yours/Boom Boom	1955	Imperial 5343
My Dream, My Love/I Know I Was Wrong	1955	Imperial 5359
Searching For Love/Cold Kisses	1955	Imperial 5370
Don't Walk Out/Once In A Lifetime	1956	Imperial 5397
My Secret/Darling Please (by the Bees)	1974	Owl 325
My Secret/I Love You Baby	N/A	Imperial (unreleased)
Hold Me Baby/Shake The Dice	N/A	Imperial (unreleased)
BARONS (3) (WALTER MILLER & THE)		
My Last Mile/Standing On The Highway	1956	Meteor 5037
BARONS (4) (FORMERLY THE PEPPERMINTS)		
Gravel Gert/The Fight	1959	Demon 1520
If You Want A Lovin'/Jay Walk	1959	Key 1001
Dog Eat Dog/Money Don't Grow On Trees	1961	Soul 837
Willow Weep For Me/I've Been Hurt	1961	Spartan 400
I Miss You So/Money Don't Grow On Trees	1961	Spartan 402
BARONS (5)		
Song Of Songs/Bridgitte	1959	Whitehall 30008
BARONS (6)		
Drawbridge	1958	Tender 511
BARONS (6)		
Lula Mae/Lovely Loretta	1960	Dart 126
The Bandit/Wanderin'	1963	Bellaire 103
Perfect Love/Until The 13th Chime	1963	Dart 134
Pledge Of A Fool/Don't Go Away (Pretty Little Girl)	1963	Epic 9586/Epic 10093 (66)

Artist / Song	Year	Label
Remember Rita/Lucky Star	1964	Epic 9747
(I Just Go) Wild Inside/Silence	1964	Imperial 66057
BARONS (7)		
When You Dance (acapella)	1975	Relic LP 101
BARONS (8)		
Come To Me	N/A	Blue Jay 154
BARRETT, RICHARD (& GROUP)		
Remember Me/Smoke Gets In Your Eyes	1958	MGM 12616
Summer's Love/Let Me Down Easy (no group)	1963	Crackerjack 4012
BARRETT, RICHARD (BB THE CHANTELS)		
Come Softly To Me/Walking Through Dreamland	1959	Gone 5056
BARRIES		
Why Don't You Write Me/Mary-Ann	1962	Vernon 102
Tonight Tonight/Mary-Ann	1963	Ember 1101
When You're out Of School/Loneliest Man In Town	1964	Di-Nan 101
BARRONS (AKA CRESCENDOS (2))		
Oh Julie	N/A	Guest Star LP 1481
Katie Doll	N/A	Guest Star LP 1481
I'm So Ashamed	N/A	Guest Star LP 1481
Janie	N/A	Guest Star LP 1481
Julie Anna	N/A	Guest Star LP 1481
Without Love	N/A	Guest Star LP 1481
Angel Face	N/A	Guest Star LP 1481
Let's Take A Walk	N/A	Guest Star LP 1481
BARTLEY, CHRIS (& GROUP)		
Love Me Baby/The Sweetest Thing This Side Of Heaven	1967	Vando 101
BASICS		
Basic Surf/Jailer Bring Me Water	N/A	Lavender 1851
Oh Lonely Me/Time	N/A	Lavender 2002
BASIN ST. BOYS		
I Sold My Heart To The Junkman/Lost In The Night (by Charles Brown)	1948	Exclusive 39/Cash 1052 (56)
BATCHELORS		
Mountain Dew/The Ballad Of Betsy Ross	1955	Rama 176
BATTERY PARK		
I Believe/Something	1973	Vintage 1001
BAUM, ALLEN (BB THE LARKS)		
My Kinda Woman/Too Much Competition	1953	Red Robin 124
BAXTER, RONNIE (BB THE CHANTELS)		
Is It Because/I Finally Found You	1959	Gone 5050
BAY BOPS		
Joanie/Follow The Rock	1958	Coral 61975
To The Party/My Darling My Sweet	1958	Coral 62004
BAY CITY 5 (LUIGI MARTINI & THE)		
Please Don't Talk About Me/Basin Street Blues	1954	Jaguar 3001
Oh Marie/I'm Sorry I Made You Cry	1954	Jaguar 3002
BAY-TONES		
Completely Lost My Mind/Oh My Darling	1976	Monogram 116
BAYSIDERS		
Over The Rainbow/My Bonnie	1960	Everest 19366
Look For The Silver Lining/Trees	1960	Everest 19386
The Bell's Of St. Mary's/Comin' Through The Rye	1960	Everest 19393
BEACHAM, RUFUS (& GROUP)		
I Can't Believe/All Right (no group)	1956	Chart 627
BEACHCOMBERS		
This Is My Love/Surfin' The Summer Away	1964	Diamond 168
BEAR CATS		
Rama Lama Ding Dong	N/A	Bravo EP 70-2
BEARD, DEAN (& GROUP)		
Little Lover/Holding On To A Memory	1959	Challenge 59048
BEASLEY, BILLY (& GROUP)		
A Million Teardrops/Too Long	N/A	Dee Cal 500
BEASLEY, JIMMY (& GROUP)		
My Happiness/Jambalaya	1956	Modern 1009

Artist / Song	Year	Label
BEATNICKS		
Blue Angel/Shakey Mae	1960	Key-Lock 913
BEATNIKS (CHARLES WALKER & THE)		
Just Me And You/My Eyes On The World	1958	Rhythm 116
BEAU BELLES (FEMALE)		
Wonderful You/Honky Tonk Hop	1958	Arrow 729
BEAU BRUMMELS		
In Self Defense/I Haven't The Heart	1956	Vik 0208
BEAU JIVES		
Dip Dip/Don't Put All Your Onions In One Basket	1961	Vision 111/Lord Bingo 111
I'll Never Be The Same/What Would You Do	1962	Shepherd 2202
Brightest Star In The Sky/But I Love You	N/A	Lord Bingo 102
Brightest Star In The Sky/Mr. Sandman	N/A	Lord Bingo 107
BEAU-MARKS		
Clap Your Hands/Daddy Said	1960	Shad 5017/
Mainstream 688 (68)		
'Cause We're In Love/Jimmy Went Walkin'	1960	Shad 5021
Classmate/School Is Out	1961	Rust 5035
Rockin' Blues/Oh Joan	1961	Time 1032
Lovely Little Lady/Little Miss Twist	1962	Quality 1370/Port 70029 (62)
Tender Years/I'll Never Be The Same	1962	Rust 5050
BEAUMONT, JIMMY (& GROUP)		
Everybody's Cryin'/Camera	1961	May 112
BEAUS (BOBBIE & THE)		
Losing Game/Melvin	1959	Unart 2009
BEAVERS		
Rockin' At The Drive In/Sack Dress	1958	Capitol 3956
Low As I Can Be/Road To Happiness	1958	Capitol 4015
BECK, CARLTON (& GROUP)		
The Girl I Left Behind/You'll Be Coming Home Soon	1963	Troy 100
BEE HIVES		
Beatnik Baby/I Just Can't	1961	Fleetwood 215
BEE JAY (& GROUP)		
I'll Go On/There's No One For Me	1961	Clock 1743
BEE JAYS (BUDDY JOHNSON & THE) (ELLA JOHNSON WITH)		
Bring It On Home To Me/Rock On (no group)	1956	Mercury 70912
BEE, RICHIE (RICHARD BARRETT BB THE CHANTELS)		
Summer's Love/All Is Forgiven	1961	Gone 5060
BEECHWOODS		
I'm Not A Kid Anymore/Place	1963	Smash 1843
BEES (1) (GM BOBBY BLAND)		
Baby Blues	1954	Imperial (unreleased)
Sunny Side Of The Street	1954	Imperial (unreleased)
Why Don't You Do Right	1954	Imperial (unreleased)
Toy Bell/Snatchin' Back	1954	Imperial 5314
I Want To Be Loved/Get Away Baby	1954	Imperial 5420
Dreaming In The Meadow/Eyes For You Only	1974	Firefly 325
Darling Please (recorded in 1954)/My Secret (by the Barons)	1974	Owl 325
BEES (2) (HONEY & THE)		
Almost Eighteen/Please Go Away	1959	Pentagon 500
Sunday Kind Of Love/Baby Do That Thing	1968	Arctic 158
You Better Go Now/Why Do You Hurt The One Who Loves You	N/A	Arctic 141
That's What Boys Are Made For/Has Somebody Taken My Place	N/A	Bell 217
Let's Get Back Together Now	N/A	Garrison 3005
BEES (3)		
So Jealous/Tough Enough	N/A	Finch 506

Artist Song	Year	Label
BEGINNERS		
I'm So Lonely Over You/		
Someday You'll Be My Girl	1964	Dot 16629
BEL MARS (AKA ADMIRATIONS (2))		
Lil' Lil' Lulu/Gonna Find My Pretty		
Baby (by the Admirations)	1962	Candlelite 414
BEL RAVES (LOU BERRY & THE)		
Hot Rod/What A Dolly	1959	Dreem 1001
BEL-AIRES (1)		
Tick-Tock/Cherry Pie	1954	Crown 126
BEL-AIRES (2)		
My Yearbook/Rockin' And		
Strollin'	1958	Decca 30631
BEL-AIRES (3) (DONALD WOODS & THE) (AKA DONALD WOODS & THE VEL-AIRES)		
This Paradise/Let's Party Awhile	1955	Flip 303 (first pressing, second is by Vel-Aires)
White Port Lemon Juice/This Is Goodbye	1955	Flip 304
BEL-AIRES (4) (FB LARRY LEE)		
Hope And Pray/Space Walk	1959	Arc 4451
BEL-AIRES (5) (EDDY BELL & THE)		
Anytime/The Masked Man (Hi-Yo Silver)	1960	Mercury 71677
The Great, Great Pumpkin/I'm Still In Love With You	1961	Lucky Four 1012
Knock, Knock, Knock (Knocking On My Door)/		
Wear My Class Ring On A Ribbon	1961	Mercury 71763
BEL-AIRES (6) (LITTLE D & THE)		
Are You My Girl/Scratch	1962	Raft 604
BEL-AIRS FIVE		
Bring Back My Baby/The Time Has Come	1964	USA 764
BEL-LARKS		
Getting Married In June/A Million And One Dreams	1963	Hammer 6313
A Million And One Dreams/Satisfied	1963	Ransom 5001
BELAIRS (1)		
You'll Never Be Mine Again/Hoppin' & Boppin'	1955	GG 521
BELAIRS (2) (LEE BANTELL & THE)		
Sweet Sixteen/Louisiana Rug Roll	1956	Coral 61605
By You By You/Sonya's Place	N/A	Coral 61735
BELAIRS (3) (AKA DECOYS (1)/AKA FOUR BEL-AIRES)		
Tell Me Why/Where Are You?	1958	X-Tra 113/Times Square 23 (63)/Relic 536 (65)
It's Going To Be Allright/Oh Baby (Decoys)	1963	Times Square 8
Rosa	N/A	Relic LP 5029
Bells	N/A	Relic LP 5029
BELAIRS (4) (BARRY PETRICOIN & THE)		
Pretty Little Angel/Come Back To Sorrento	1958	Al-Stan 103
BELAIRS (5) (MIKE & THE)		
She's Mine/Buscando (Searchin')	1963	Cobra 6666
BELGIANETTES (FEMALE)		
My Blue Heaven/The Train	1963	Okeh 7172
You're Far From Home/Do The Crank	1963	USA 731
BELGIANS		
Pray Tell Me/Changed	1964	Teek 4824-3/4824-4
BELL BOYS		
Are You For Me/I Love Thee	1960	Era 3026
BELL HOPS (1)		
Please Don't Say No To Me/Merchant St. Blues	1956	Tin Pan Alley 153
BELL HOPS (2)		
Angela/Ring Dang Doo Ting A Ling	1958	Barb 100
Teenage Years/Carmella	1958	Barb 101/102
BELL HOPS (3) (BUDDY WHITE & THE)		
For Your Love/Who But A Fool	N/A	The Wheeler Dealers 501
BELL NOTES		
I've Had It/Be Mine	1959	Time 1004
Old Spanish Town/She Went That-A-Way	1959	Time 1010
That's Right/Betty Dear	1959	Time 1013

Artist Song	Year	Label
You're A Big Girl Now/Don't Ask Me Why	1959	Time 1015
White Buckskin Sneakers And Checkerboard Socks/No Dice	1959	Time 1017
A Sad Guitar	1959	Time EP 100
Dream Street	1959	Time EP 100
Little Girl In Blue/Too Young Or Too Old	1960	Autograph 204
Shortnin' Bread/To Each His Own	1960	Madison 136
Friendly Star/Wild Child	1960	Madison 141
BELL TONES (1)		
Heart To Heart/The Wedding	1955	Rama 170
BELL TONES (2) (AKA FIVE BELLS)		
My Pledge To You/There She Goes	1959	Clock 71889/Mercury 71889 (61)
BELL, JOHNNY (& GROUP)		
Ev'ry Day/I'm So Glad	1959	Fleetwood 1001
BELL-AIRES (GM BILLY FORD)		
I'd Never Forgive Myself/I'm Looking For A Lover	1955	Ruby 103
BELLA TONES (EULIS MASON & THE)		
Carol Lee/Rockin' Santa Claus	1959	Bella 20
BELLATONES		
Forgotten Spring/Va Va Voom	1959	Bella 21
BELLES (1) (TERRY & THE)		
I'm Alone Because I Love You/Keep That Beat	1958	Hanover 4505
I'll Always Be Nearby/I'd Want You	1959	Ducky 711
BELLES (2)		
Hear The Word/Trouble In My Soul	1961	Choice 18
Everyday, Everyday/Wonderful Is His Name	1962	Choice 29
BELLES (2) (GLORIUS WILSON & THE)		
Try Me And You'll See/I Hear Bells Ding Dong	1956	Fairbanks 2002
BELLES (3)		
Melvin/Come Back	N/A	Tiara 100
BELLS (GM JOE VAN LOAN)		
What Can I Tell Her Now/Let Me Love You, Love You	1955	Rama 166
BELLTONES (1)		
Carol	1953	Grand 100
Estelle/Promise Love	1954	Grand 102
BELLTONES (10)		
(Please Try) To Understand Me/Swinging Little Chickie	1962	Olimpic 1068/Itzy 1 (62)
BELLTONES (2) (AKA RONNIE BAKER & THE DELTONES)		
The Merengue/I Love You, Darling	1956	Scatt 1609/1610/J&S 1609/1610 (58)
I Want To Be Loved/You've Got What It Takes	1962	Jell 188
Glory Be/This Big Wide World	1963	Jell 200
BELLTONES (3) (LACILLE WATKINS & THE)		
His Hand In Mine/Maybe You'll Be There	1956	Kapp 145
BELLTONES (4) (JOHNNY & THE)		
Ev'ry Day/My Little Baby	1957	Cecil 5050
BELLTONES (5) (J. BROTHERS WITH THE)		
The Girl I Used To Know	1958	Mermaid 3360
BELLTONES (6) (KIRK TAYLOR & THE)		
Been So Long/My Rosemarie	1958	Tek 2634
BELLTONES (7) (TONY MORRA & THE)		
Claire/My Baby Scares Me	1959	Arcade 152
BELLTONES (8)		
My Pledge To You/There She Goes	1961	Mercury 71889
BELLTONES (9) (RONNIE DOVE & THE) (AKA BELTONES)		
No Greater Love/Saddest Hour	1962	Jalo 1406
BELMONTS		
I Need Someone/That American Dance	1961	Sabina 502
Don't Get Around Much Anymore/Searching for A New Love	1961	Sabrina 501
Tell Me Why/Smoke From Your Cigarette	1961	Surprise 1000/Sabrina 500 (61)

Artist / Song	Year	Label
I Confess/Hombre	1962	Sabina 503
Come On Little Angel/How About Me?	1962	Sabina 505
Diddle-De-Dum/Farewell	1962	Sabina 507
Ann-Marie/Accentuate The Positive	1963	Sabina 509
Walk On By/Let's Call It A Day	1963	Sabina 513
More Important Things To Do/Let's Call It A Day	1964	Sabina 517
C'Mon Everybody/Why	1964	Sabina 519
Nothing In Return/Summertime	1964	Sabina 521
I Don't Know Why/Summertime	1965	United Artists 809
(Then) I Walked Away/Today My Love Has Gone Away	1965	United Artists 904
I Got A Feeling/To Be With You	1965	United Artists 966
Come With Me/You're Like a Mystery	1966	United Artists 5007
She Only Wants To Do Her Own Thing/Reminiscences	1968	Dot 17173
Have You Heard/Answer Me, My Love	1969	Dot 17257
The Worst That Could Happen/Answer Me, My Love	1969	Dot 17257
Cheek To Cheek/The Voyager	1976	Strawberry 106
BELMONTS (BOB THOMAS & THE)		
My Day/Believe Me My Darling	1959	Abel 232
BELMONTS (DION & THE)		
Teenage Clementine/Santa Margarita	1957	Mohawk 106
We Went Away/Tag Along	1957	Mohawk 107
I Wonder Why/Teen Angel	1958	Laurie 3013
No One Knows/I Can't Go On (Rosalie)	1958	Laurie 3015
Don't Pity Me/Just You	1958	Laurie 3021
A Teenager In Love/I've Cried Before	1959	Laurie 3027
Every Little Thing I Do/A Lover's Prayer	1959	Laurie 3035
I Got The Blues	1959	Laurie LP 1002/Laurie LP 2002 (60)/Collectables LP 5025
You Better Not Do That	1959	Laurie LP 1002/Laurie LP 2002 (60)/Collectables LP 5025
Where Or When/That's My Desire	1960	Laurie 3044
When You Wish Upon A Star/Wonderful Girl	1960	Laurie 3052
In The Still Of The Night/A Funny Feeling	1960	Laurie 3059
It's Only A Paper Moon	1960	Laurie LP 2006
My Day	1960	Laurie LP 2006
September Song	1960	Laurie LP 2006
My Private Joy	1960	Laurie LP 2006
Swinging On A Star	1960	Laurie LP 2006
When The Red, Red Robin Comes Bob, Bob, Bobbin' Along	1960	Laurie LP 2006
I'm Through With Love	1960	Laurie LP 2006
All The Things You Are	1960	Laurie LP 2006
In Other Words	1960	Laurie LP 2006
We Belong Together/Such A Long Way	1961	Laurie 3080
Come Take A Walk With Me	1962	Laurie LP 2016/Ace LP 155
That's How I Need You	1962	Laurie LP 2016/Ace LP 155
Will You Love Me Still	1962	Laurie LP 2016/Ace LP 155
My Girl, The Month Of May/Berimbau	1966	ABC 10868
Movin' Man/For Bobby	1967	ABC 10896
BELMONTS (FRANK LYNDON WITH THE)		
Earth Angel/Don't Look At Me	1964	Sabina 520
BELMONTS (FREDDY CANNON & THE)		
Mama Ain't Always Right	1981	Mia Sound 1002
BELTONES		
I Talk To My Echo/Oof Goof	1957	Hull 721
Yes Darling I'll Be Around/Party Doll	1961	Decca 31288
BELTONES (L. FARR & THE)		
Mary Lisa/Too Much Ain't Enough	1964	N-Joy 1001
BELVADERES		
Don't Leave Me To Cry/I Love You	1956	Hudson 4
Come To Me Baby/Dear Angels Above (by Jimmy Morris)	1955	Baton 214
We Too/Pepper-Hot Baby	1955	Baton 217
Suzanne/Hey Honey	1958	Dot 15852
Let's Get Married/Wow Wow Mary Mary	1958	Trend 30-009
Walkin' In The Garden/Buena Sera	1959	Jopz 1771
He's A Square	1961	Lucky Four 1003
Why Do You Treat Me This Way/Lost Love	1962	Poplar 114
From Out Of Nowhere/Tormented	N/A	Count
The McCoy/Tired Out	N/A	Rhapsody 5163
BELVIN, ANDY (& GROUP)		
With All My Heart/You Were Meant To Be	N/A	Cal State 3200
BELVIN, JESSE (& GROUP)		
All That Wine Is Gone/Don't Cry Baby	1951	Imperial 5115
Dream Girl/Hang Your Tears Out To Dry	1951	Recorded In Hollywood 120
Confusin' Blues/Baby Don't Go	1952	Specialty 435
Love Comes Tumbling Down (aka Love Song)	1953	Recorded In Hollywood 412
I'm Only A Fool/Trouble And Misery	1955	Money 208
Beware/Dry Your Eyes	1956	Cash 1056
Goodnight My Love/Let Me Love You Tonight	1956	Modern 1005
Goodnight My Love/I Want You With Me Christmas	1956	Modern 1005
Dear Heart/Betty My Darling	1956	Recorded In Hollywood 1059
Senorita/I Need You So	1957	Modern 1013
Don't Close The Door/By My Side	1957	Modern 1015
Sad And Lonesome/I'm Not Free	1957	Modern 1020
You Send Me/Summertime	1957	Modern 1025
Just To Say Hello/My Satellite	1957	Modern 1027
Sentimental Reasons/Senorita	1958	Kent 326
Little Darling/Deacon Dan Tucker	1958	Knight 2012
Ever Since We Met/Volare	1958	RCA 7310
Funny/Pledging My Love	1958	RCA 7387
Deep In My Heart/I'm Confessin'	1959	Class 267
Goodnight My Love/My Desire	1959	Jamie 1145
Guess Who/My Girl Is Just Enough Woman For Me	1959	RCA 7469
It Could've Been Worse/Here's A Heart	1959	RCA 7543
Give Me Love/I'll Never Be Lonely Again	1959	RCA 7596
Something Happens To Me/The Door Is Always Open	1960	RCA 7675
Let's Make Up	N/A	Crown LP 5187
BELVIN, JESSE (BB THE FEATHERS)		
Gone/One Little Blessing	1955	Specialty 550
Where's My Girl/The Love Of My Life	1955	Specialty 559
Sugar Doll/Let Me Dream	1958	Aladdin 3431
BENGALS (BOBBY & THE)		
No Parking/Double Rock	1960	B&W 601
BENNET, RON (& GROUP)		
Dingle Dangle Doll/My Only Girl	1961	Ta-Rah 1
BENNETT, BUDDY (BB THE MARGILATORS)		
Our Love Can Never Be/Baby Don't Go	1959	Blue Moon 412
BENNETT, CHUCK (& GROUP)		
Seven Days/I Went To Your House	1962	Bonnie 101
BENNETTS		
One Love/All My Loving	1964	Amcan 401
BENTLEYS (AKA VAMPIRES)		
Why Didn't I Listen To Mother/Did Anybody Lose A Tear	1965	Smash 1988
BERETS		
Sonny Boy/The Bells	1973	Night Train 904
BERMUDAS (FB RICKIE PAGE)		
Donnie/Chu Sen Ling	1964	Era 3125
Blue Dreamer/Seeing Is Believing	1964	Era 3133

Artist	Song	Year	Label
BERNARD, ROD (& GROUP)			
	These Were Our Songs/Just		
	Another Lie	1966	Arbee 105
BERRY CUPS (TERRY CLINTON & THE)			
	Dolores Darlin'/Hurt By A Letter	1959	Khoury's 710
BERRY KIDS			
	Love Me, Love/Go, Go, Go		
	Right Into Town	1956	MGM 12379
	You're My Teenage		
	Baby/Rootie Tootie	1957	MGM 12496
	Suzie	N/A	Soo 12
BERRY, RICHARD (& GROUP)			
	Walk Right In/It's All Right	1960	Warner Bros. 5164
	I'm Your Fool/In A Real Big Way	1961	K&G 1004
BERRY, RICHARD (BB THE DREAMERS)			
	Wait For Me/Good Love	1956	RPM 477
	Besame Mucho/Do I Do I	1958	Flip 339
BERRY, RICHARD (BB THE FLAIRS)			
	I'm Still In Love With You/One		
	Little Prayer	1953	Flair 1016
	What You Do To Me/The Big		
	Break	1955	Flair 1055
	Oh! Oh! Get Out Of The		
	Car/Please Tell Me	1955	Flair 1064
	God Gave Me You/Don'tcha Go	1955	Flair 1068
	Together/Jelly Roll	1956	Flair 1075
BETTY JEAN (& GROUP)			
	I Want To Be Your Girl/Joey		
	Or Jim	1963	JR 5001
BEY SISTERS (FEMALE)			
	Patience/Wake Up	1956	Jaguar 3016
	Sentimental Journey/Sugar		
	Cookie	1956	Jaguar 3018/Flip 328 (57)
BI-LANGOS (DONNY & THE)			
	I'm Not A Know-It-All/I	N/A	Colton 101
BI-TONES			
	Beatnik Girl/Oh How I Love		
	You So	1960	Bluejay 1000
BIFIELD, LENORE (& GROUP)			
	Lies	1964	Sketch 217
BIG 5			
	Baby I Miss		
	You/Wob-Ding-A-Ling	1958	Junior 5000
	Blue Eyes/Stardust In Her Eyes	1960	Shad 5019
BIG BOYS			
	If I Had My Chance/Rock Rock		
	Rock A Bye Baby	1964	Melmar 113
BIG DOG (& GROUP)			
	Doris/Just Wait For Me	1962	Joey 501
BIG EDSEL BAND			
	Desire/Whispering Bells	1978	Clifton 27
	Once In Awhile/		
	Why Do Lovers Break Each		
	Other's Hearts	1980	Clifton 48
BIG FIVE			
	Blue Eyes/Stardust In Her Eyes	1960	Shad 5019
BIG TOPS			
	I'm In Love/The Dance They Did	1958	Warner 1017
BIG TOWN GIRLS (SHIRLEY MATTHEWS & THE) (FEMALE)			
	(You Can) Count On That/Big		
	Town Boy	1963	Atlantic 2210
BILLBOARDS			
	With All My Heart/Around The		
	World	1961	Vistone 2023
BILLIE & LILLIE (BB THE THUNDERBIRDS)			
	Love Me Sincerely/Whip It To		
	Me Baby	1963	ABC 10421
BINDERS (GM CORNELIUS HARP)			
	When We Were Young/Mojo		
	Hannah	N/A	Sara 7771
	You Don't Have To Cry Any		
	More/Save The Last Dance		
	For Me	N/A	Sara 7772/Ankh 7772
BING BONGS (DICKY DELL & THE)			
	Ding-A-Ling-A-Ling Ding		
	Dong/The Cling	1958	Dragon 10205
BIRDIES (ROBERT BYRD & HIS)			
	Bippin' & Boppin' (Over		
	You)/Strawberry Stomp	1956	Spark 501/Jamie 1039 (57)
BIRDS (1) (BOBBY BYRD & THE)			
	The Truth Hurts/Let's Live		
	Together As One	1956	Cash 1031
BIRDS (2) (DON MIKKELSEN & THE)			
	Chapel Of Love/Where I Came		
	In (no group)	1961	Deck 600
BIRDSONG, LARRY (& GROUP)			
	Tell Me The Truth/Three Times		
	Seven (no group)	1956	Calvert 104
BISCAYNES (AKA VISCAYNES)			
	Uncle Sam Needs You/Yellow		
	Moon	1961	VPM 1006
BISHOPS			
	Masquerade Ball/Open Up		
	Your Heart	1961	Lute 6010
BISHOPS (WITH THE MELLOW-TONES)			
	The Wedding/Pretty	1961	Bridges 1105
BITTER SWEETS			
	Another Chance/In The Night	1967	Original Sound 70
BLACKHAWKS			
	Love Me When I'm Old/Beatrice		
	My Darling	1972	Roadhouse 1000
BLACKWELLS			
	Here's The Question/Please		
	Don't Come Crying	1959	G&G 126
	Oh My Love/Holy Sombrero	1959	G&G 131/Guyden 2020 (59)
	You Are Free, I'm Alone/Depot	1959	Jamie 1141
	Always It's You/Honey, Honey	1960	Jamie 1150
	Mansion On The Hill/Unchained		
	Melody	1960	Jamie 1157
	Christmas Holiday/Little Match		
	Girl	1960	Jamie 1173
	Love Or Money/Big Daddy And		
	The Cat	1961	Jamie 1179
	You Took Advantage Of Me/I	1961	Jamie 1199
BLADES, CAROL (WITH THE HARPTONES)			
	When Will I Know/What Did		
	She Do Wrong	1957	Gee 1029
BLAIR, RONNIE (& GROUP)			
	A Tear In My Eye/Twenty One	1961	Crest 1084
BLAIR, SANDY (& GROUP)			
	The Clock Says/When The		
	Bells Stop Ringing	1963	Bobby 111
	When The Bells Stop		
	Ringing/The Clock Says	N/A	Bobby 111
BLAKE, CICERO (& GROUP)			
	Don't Do This To Me/See What		
	Tomorrow Brings	1963	Success 107
BLAKELY, CORNEL (& GROUP)			
	Don't Touch The Moon/Promise		
	To Be True	1957	Fulton 2543
BLANDERS			
	Desert Sands/Jitterbug	1965	Smash 2005
BLASERS (1) (AKA FOUR BLAZERS)			
	She Needs To Be Loved/Done		
	Got Over	1956	United 191
BLASERS (2) (EDDIE FOSTER & THE)			
	You Are The Only One/I Need		
	Love	1961	Lyons 108
BLASTERS			
	Day Train/I Do (by the		
	Youngtones)	1964	Times Square 31
BLAZE, JOHNNY (& GROUP)			
	Oh Lovin' Baby/Lolita Cha Cha	1959	Apon 2142
BLAZERS (1) (JOHNNY MOORE'S)			
	Why Johnny Why/Johnny Ace's		
	Last Letter	1955	Hollywood 1031
	Christmas Eve Baby/Christmas		
	Every Day	1955	Hollywood 1045
	I Send My Love/Next Time We		
	Meet	1956	Hollywood 1056
BLAZERS (2) (RODNEY & THE)			
	Teenage Cinderella/Rolling		
	Stone	1960	Dore 572
	Teenage Cinderella/		
	Summertime	1960	Kampus 100
	Snow White/Tell Me Baby	1961	Dore 588
	All Over But The Crying/Little		
	Orphan Annie	1956	Chan 110
BLAZERS (3) (WITH DAVE "BABY" CORTEZ)			
	So Nice/Wobble Party	1961	Winley 1001
BLAZERS (4) (JIMMY FEAGANS & THE)			
	No Matter/Saturday Night	1961	Howard 501

Artist Song	Year	Label
BLAZERS (5) (LITTLE BERNIE & THE)		
My Love, I Have You/By The Light Of The Silvery Moon	1962	Josie 884
BLAZERS (6)		
I Don't Need You	1963	Brass 306
BLAZONS		
Magic Lamp/Little Girl	N/A	Fanfare 5001/Bravura 5001
BLEATERS		
I'm Gonna Be A Wheel Some Day/Come And Get Your Baby	1963	Guyden 2100
BLEN-DELLS		
Say You're Mine/Forever	1962	Bella 608
BLEND TONES		
She's Gone/Lights Please	1961	Chic-Car 100/Don-El 106 (61)/Imperial 5758 (61)
BLEND-AIRES		
Call On Me/Sweet Sue	1977	Arcade 104
He's Gone/Lucky Guy	1978	Story Untold 500
Shouldn't I/Gee Whiz	1978	Story Untold 501
I Beg For Your Love/Don't Leave Me	1982	Story Untold 503
Guaranteed/I Got It Bad And That Ain't Good	1959	Decca 30938
My Love Is Just For You/Repitition	1958	Tin Pan Alley 252
BLEND-TONES		
Lights, Please/She's Gone	1979	Clifton 36
BLENDAIRES (BOBBY CARLE & THE)		
Walk With Me/Anytime, Any Place, Anywhere	1958	Decca 30605
I Couldn't Stand It/ A Time To Love And A Time To Lie	1958	Decca 30699
BLENDELLS (1)		
La La La La/Huggie's Bunnies	1964	Rampart 641/Reprise 0291 (64)
BLENDELLS (2)		
Night After Night/The Love That I Needed	1968	Cotillion 44020
BLENDERS (1) (AKA MILLIONAIRES (1)/AKA SPARROWS (1))		
Gone/Honeysuckle Rose	1950	Decca 48156
I'd Be A Fool Again/Just A Little Walk With Me	1952	Decca 28092
Don't Play Around With Love/ You'll Never Be Mine Again	1953	Jay-Dee 780
I Don't Miss You Anymore/ If That's The Way You Want It, Baby	1953	MGM 11488
Please Take Me Back/Isn't It A Shame?	1953	MGM 11531
Don't Fuck Around With Love (alternate take of Jay Dee 780)/I'm Gonna Do That Woman In (by the Sparrows)	1971	Kelway 101
BLENDERS (2)		
Darline	1987	Relic LP 5069
BLENDERS (2) (EARL CURRY & THE)		
Late Rising Moon/I Want To Be With You	1954	R&B 1304
Dream Dream/Try And Get Me	1956	R&B 1313
BLENDERS (2) (RAY FRAZIER & THE)		
Darling/King Of Lovers	1960	Combo 161/Relic LP 5069 (87)
BLENDERS (3)		
My Heart's Desire/Little Rose	1958	Class 236
I Won't Tell The World/But I Know	1959	Paradise 111
BLENDERS (4)		
Soda Shop/Two Loves	1959	Aladdin 3449
Angel/Old MacDonald	1959	Wanger 189
Craving Your Love/Find Yourself Another Job	N/A	Wonder 722
BLENDERS (5) (AKA CANDLES (2))		
I Asked For Your Hand/Dance In The Night	1957	Vision 1000
Everybody's Got A Right/What Have You Got	1962	Cortland 103
Daughter/Everybody's Got A Right	1963	Witch 114
Boys Think (Every Girl's The Same)/Squat And Squirm	1963	Witch 117

Artist Song	Year	Label
One Time/One Time	1963	Witch 122
Love Is A Good Thing Going/ Your Love Has Got Me Down	1966	Mar-V-Lous 6010
BLENDERS (5) (BABY JANE & THE) (AKA CANDLES (2))		
You Trimmed My Christmas Tree	1963	Witch 112
BLENDERS (5) (GOLDIE COATES & THE) (AKA CANDLES (2))		
Love Is A Treasure/Fisherman	1962	Cortland 102
BLENDERS (6)		
It Takes Time/Graveyard	1962	Afo 305
BLENDORS		
Tell Me What's On Your Mind/ When I'm Walkin' With My Baby	1961	Decca 31284
BLENDS		
A Thousand Miles Away/Music, Maestro, Please	1960	Casa Grande 5000
Hey! Little Fool/Baby You're Wrong, Dead Wrong	1960	Casa Grande 5001
Someone To Care/Now It's Your Turn	1960	Casa Grande 5037
Tell Me/The Way I Want You	1960	Talent 110/Skylark 108 (61)
BLENDS (GLENN WELLS & THE)		
Write Me A Letter/Lesson	1960	Jin 122
Written In The Stars/You're Mine Tonight	1960	Jin 133/
United Artists 244 (60)		
As My Tears Fall/In Memory Of Our Love	1960	Jin 139
BLENDTONES		
Lovers/Dear Diary	1963	Success 101
The Slide/Come On Home	1963	Success 105
Lilly/Military Kick	1959	MGM 12782
BLEU LIGHTS		
A Lonely Man's Prayer/Bony Maronie	1968	Bay Sound 67007
BLISTERS		
Shortnin' Bread/Cookie Rockin' In Her Stockings	1963	Liberty 55577
BLOSSOMS		
Lonely Friday Night/The Last Letter	1989	Classic Artists 110
BLOSSOMS (FEMALE)		
Move On/He Promised Me	1957	Capitol 3822
Little Louie/Have Faith In Me	1958	Capitol 3878
No Other Love/Baby Daddy-O	1958	Capitol 4072
I'll Wait/Son-In-Law	1961	Challenge 9109
Write Me A Letter/Hard To Get	1961	Challenge 9122
Big Talkin' Jim/The Search Is Over	1962	Challenge 9138
I'm In Love/What Makes Love	1963	Okeh 7162
Things Are Changing/Things Are Changing (instrumental with Brian Wilson on piano)	1965	EEOC-8472
BLUE ANGELS		
In The Sun/Sobbin'	1959	Palette 5038
Desirie/Like Heaven	1961	Edsel 781
My May/Cottage In The Country	1961	Palette 5077
BLUE BEARDS		
Romance/Crawlin'	1958	Guide 1002
BLUE BELLES (1) (FEMALE)		
Cancel The Call/The Story Of A Fool	1953	Atlantic 987
BLUE BELLES (2) (FEMALE)		
I Sold My Heart To The Junkman/Itty Bitty Twist	1962	Newtown 5000
I Sold My Heart To The Junkman/I've Got To Let Him Know	1962	Newtown 5000
I Found A New Love/Pitter Patter	1962	Newtown 5006 (1st printing)
I Found A New Love/Go On	1962	Newtown 5006 (2nd printing)
When Johnny Comes Marching Home/Cool Water	1962	Newtown 5009
Where Are You/You'll Never Walk Alone	1963	Nicetown 5020
BLUE BELLES (2) (PATTI LABELLE & THE) (FEMALE)		
Go On (This Is Goodbye)/Tear After Tear	1962	Newtown 5007
Decatur Street/Academy Award	1962	Newtown 5019
Down The Aisle/C'Est La Vie	1963	Newtown 5777/ King 5777 (63)
You'll Never Walk Alone/Decatur Street	1963	Nicetown 5020/ Parkway 896 (63)

Artist Song	Year	Label
One Phone Call/You Will Fill		
My Eyes No More	1964	Parkway 913
Danny Boy/I Believe	1964	Parkway 935
You Better Move On/You're		
Just Fooling Yourself	1964	Rainbow 1900
All Or Nothing/You Forgot How		
To Love	1965	Atlantic 2311
Over The Rainbow/Groovy		
Kind Of Love	1965	Atlantic 2318
Ebb Tide/Patti's Prayer	1966	Atlantic 2333
I'm Still Waiting/Family Man	1966	Atlantic 2347
Take Me For A Little While/		
I Don't Want To Go On		
Without You	1966	Atlantic 2373
Tender Words/There's		
Always Something There		
To Remind Me	1966	Atlantic 2390
Unchained Melody/Dreamer	1966	Atlantic 2408
Oh My Love/I Need Your Love	1967	Atlantic 2446
He's My Man/Wonderful	1968	Atlantic 2548
Dance To The Rhythm Of		
Love/He's Gone	1969	Atlantic 2610
Pride's No Match For		
Love/Loving Rules	1969	Atlantic 2629
Suffer/Trustin' In You	1970	Atlantic 2712
BLUE BELLES (3) (FEMALE)		
A Place Called Happiness/Snow		
White And The Three Stooges	1961	20th Fox 249
BLUE BOYS (MR. BO & THE)		
Lost Love Affair	N/A	Diamond 852
BLUE CHIPS (1) (CARLRON LANKFORD & THE)		
Appointment With Love/Come		
Back	1956	DeLuxe 6100
BLUE CHIPS (2)		
I'm So In Love With You/Try		
My Arms	1959	Wren 302
The New Year's In/Double		
Dutch Twist	1961	Laurel 1026
Puddles Of Tears/The Contest	1961	RCA 7923
Let It Ride/Adios, Adios	1961	RCA 7935
Promise/One Hen	1962	Groove 0006
Wishing Well/Deep Freeze	1962	Sparta 001
BLUE CHORDS		
So Far Away/The Mini Movement	N/A	Reverb 6745
BLUE COUNTS (MIKE LANZO & THE)		
At The Fair/Ghost Town	1964	Debra 2006
BLUE CRYSTALS		
Broke Up/Queen Of All The Girls	1959	Mercury 71455
BLUE DENIMS (WILD BILL & THE)		
Mona My Love/The Chase	1960	Gone 5082
BLUE DIAMONDS (1) (FB ERNIE "K-DOE" KADOR)		
Honey Baby/No Money	1954	Savoy 1134
BLUE DIAMONDS (2)		
Ramona/All Of Me	1960	London 1954
Little Ship/Carmen My Love	1962	London 10006
BLUE DIAMONDS (3) (DON & THE)		
Too Late To Love/How About		
That	1961	Skylark 113
BLUE DOTS (1)		
Don't Do That, Baby/You've		
Got To Live For Yourself	1954	DeLuxe 6052
Don't Hold It/Street Of Sorrow	1954	DeLuxe 6055
God Loves You, Child/Save All		
Your Love For Me	1954	DeLuxe 6061
Hold Me Tight/Let Me Know		
Tonight	1954	DeLuxe 6067
Please Don't Tell 'Em/Saturday		
Night Fish Fry	1957	Ace 526
BLUE DOTS (2)		
I Wanna Know/Looking For My		
Baby	1958	Zynn 511
BLUE DOTS (3) (EWARD HARRIS & THE)		
You're Closer To My Heart Than		
My Shadow/All You Gotta Do	1958	NRC 504
BLUE DOTS (4)		
My Confession/Oh Baby		
(by the Nobles)	1976	Robin Hood 136
BLUE ECHOES		
It's Witchcraft	N/A	Bon 2112
BLUE EMOTIONS		
Sincerely/The Best I Feel Is Sad	1982	Ambient Sound 03409

Artist Song	Year	Label
BLUE FLAMERS		
Driving Down The		
Highway/Watch On	1954	Excello 2026
BLUE FLAMES (1)		
Skylark	1954	Grand 113
BLUE FLAMES (1) (FB CHRIS POWELL)		
Uh Uh Baby/Sweet Sue Mambo	1954	Grand 108
BLUE FLAMES (2) (BUDDY LOVE & THE)		
I Love You/I'm Leaving	1958	Thunder 1A
BLUE FLAMES (3)		
That Crazy Little House On		
The Hill/You Don't Love		
Me Anymore	1961	Spry 113
Close To Me/Moon Eyes	1962	Spry 115
BLUE FLAMES (4)		
Just A Stranger	N/A	Flame 1102
BLUE JAYS (1)		
White Cliffs Of Dover/Hey,		
Pappa	1953	Checker 782
BLUE JAYS (2)		
Sweet Georgia Brown/J. J.'s		
Blues	1959	Laurie 3037
Barbara/Practical Joker	1959	Roulette 4169
Cave Man Love/Kum Ba Yah	1960	Roulette 4264
BLUE JAYS (3)		
Lover's Island/You're Gonna		
Cry	1961	Milestone 2008
Tears Are Falling/Tree Top Len	1961	Milestone 2009
Let's Make Love/Rock Rock		
Rock	1961	Milestone 2010
The Right To Love/Rock Rock		
Rock	1962	Milestone 2012
Venus My Love/Tall Len	1962	Milestone 2014
Rock Rock Rock/The Right To		
Love	1963	Milestone 2021
Could I Adore You/Sweet		
Pauline	1972	Roadhouse 1004
A Magic Island	1987	Relic LP 5064
Darlene	1987	Relic LP 5064
The Heart You Break May Be		
Your Own	1987	Relic LP 5064
So Long, Lover's Island	1987	Relic LP 5064
Woe Is Me	1987	Relic LP 5064
That's All It Took	1987	Relic LP 5064
A Casual Kiss	1987	Relic LP 5064
Cottonhead Joe	1987	Relic LP 5064
BLUE JAYS (4) (AKA SQUIRES (3))		
Earth Angel	1956	Dig EP 777
Sincerely	1956	Dig EP 777
Hearts Of Stone	1956	Dig EP 777
Pledge Of Love	1956	Dig EP 777
Ling Ting Tong	1956	Dig EP 778
Don't Drop It	1956	Dig EP 780
Shoo Do Be Do	1956	Dig EP 780
Write A Letter/I Really Love You	1961	Blujay 1002
BLUE JEANS (BOB B. SOXX & THE)		
Zip-A-Dee Doo Dah/Flip &		
Nitty (instrumental)	1962	Philles 107
Why Do Lovers Break Each		
Others Hearts/		
Dr. Kaplan's Office		
(instrumental)	1963	Philles 110
Not Too Young To Get		
Married/Annette	1963	Philles 113
The Bells Of St. Mary's	1963	Philles EP X-EP/
Philles LP 4005 (63)		
My Heart Beats A Little Faster	1963	Philles LP 4002
Everything's Gonna Be All Right	1963	Philles LP 4002
I Shook The World	1963	Philles LP 4002
White Cliffs Of Dover	1963	Philles LP 4002
This Land Is Your Land	1963	Philles LP 4002
Baby (I Love You)	1963	Philles LP 4002
Jimmy Baby	1963	Philles LP 4002
Dear (Here Comes My Baby)	1963	Philles LP 4002
Let The Good Times Roll	1963	Philles LP 4002
Here Comes Santa Claus	1963	Philles LP 4005
BLUE KINGS (ANDY CHARLES & THE)		
Love Come Back/Baby Don't Go	1959	D 1061
BLUE KNIGHTS (STEVE COLT & THE)		
Gloria/Train Of No Return	1962	Fleetwood 4550
BLUE MOONS		
A Sunday Kind Of Love/Peace		
Of Mind	N/A	Jaguar 1001

Artist Song	Year	Label
BLUE NIGHTHAWKS (IRVIN RUCKER & THE)		
Two People In Love	N/A	Duplex
BLUE NOTES (1)		
Darling Of Mine/I Love Her So	1958	TNT 150/Dot 15720 (58)
Rufus/Your Tender Lips	1961	Accent 1069
My Heart Cries For You/Shrimp		
Boats Are Coming	1961	Gamut 100
Blue Star/Is There A Doctot In		
The House	1975	Red Top 132
BLUE NOTES (1) (HAROLD MELVIN & THE)		
She Is Mine/Letter	1960	Lost 105
My Hero/A Good Woman	1960	Val-Ue 213/Red Top 135 (63)
Oh Holy Night/Winter		
Wonderland	1960	Val-Ue 215
Blue Star/Pucker Your Lips	1961	20th Century 1213
Get Out/You May Not Love Me	1962	Landa 703
BLUE NOTES (1) (TODD RANDALL & THE)		
Charlotte Amalie/Make A Box	1955	Tico 1083
If You Love Me/There's Some-		
thing In Your Eyes, Eloise	1956	Josie 800/Port 70021 (61)
With This Pen/Letters	1957	Josie 814
The Retribution Blues/Wagon		
Wheels	1957	Josie 823
W-P-L-J/While I'm Away	1962	3 Sons 103
BLUE NOTES (1) (WITH JOE LOCO & QUINTETTE)		
If You'll Be Mine/Too Hot To		
Handle	1953	Rama 25
BLUE NOTES (2) (JOE WEAVER & HIS)		
Soft Pillow/15-40 Special	1953	DeLuxe 6006
J.B. Boogie/Baby I'm In Love		
With You	1953	DeLuxe 6021
I'm On My Merry Way/Loose		
Caboose	1955	Fortune 820
All I Do Is Cry/Too Hot To Trot		
(instrumental)	1960	Fortune 852
BLUE NOTES (2) (JOE WEAVER & THE)		
Do You Wanna Work Now/The		
Lazy Susan	1955	Jaguar 3011
BLUE NOTES (3) (LITTLE BILL & THE)		
Bye Bye Baby/I Love An Angel	1959	Dolton 4
Sweet Cucumber/Why Was I		
Ever Born	1960	Topaz 1302
Little Angel/The Next Time You		
See Me	1961	Bolo 725
Louie, Louie/Boy Next Door	1961	Topaz 1305
BLUE NOTES (4)		
Never Never Land/I Waited	1958	Colonial 9999
I Don't Know What It Is/Summer		
Love	1959	Brooke 111 (first pressing)
I Don't Know What It Is/You		
Can't Get Away From Love	1959	Brooke 111
		(second pressing)
I'm Gonna Find Out/Forever		
On My Mind	1960	Brooke 116
Summer Love/It Had To Be You	1960	Brooke 119
BLUE NOTES (5) (BERNARD WILLIAMS & THE)		
It's Needless To Say/Focused		
On You	1964	Harthon 136
BLUE NOTES (6) (TRACY PENDARVIS & THE)		
It Don't Pay/(flip has no group)	1961	Scott 1202
BLUE RAYS (1) (JOE HAMMOND & THE)		
Kiss Me My Love	1958	Bee 1102
BLUE RAYS (2)		
Come On Baby/Who		
(Will It Be Today)	1964	Philips 40186
BLUE ROCKERS		
Calling All Cows/Johnny Mae	1955	Excello 2062
BLUE SKY BOYS		
You Came To Me/Call On Me	1971	Blue Sky 100
Cherie/I'm Just Another One		
In Love With You	1972	Blue Sky 101
Wedding Bells Are Ringing In		
My Ears/The Story Of		
Daddy Cool	1973	Blue Sky 107
This Silver Ring/Darling		
(by Mel Dark & the Giants)	1974	Blue Sky 108
Darlene/My Vow To You	1974	Blue Sky 109
BLUE SONNETS (AKA VOCALAIRES)		
Thank You Mr. Moon/It's Never		
Too Late	1963	Columbia 42793
BLUE STARS		
Erlene/My Love Will Never Die	1977	Arcade 101

Artist Song	Year	Label
I Only Have Eyes For You/Hey		
Pretty Baby	1977	Arcade 102
Can't We Be Sweethearts/Your		
Way	1977	Arcade 103
Love Is The Thing/False Alarm	1991	Clifton 95
BLUE TONES		
Shake, Shake/Oh Yeah!	1957	King 5088
BLUEBIRDS		
Can't Help But Sing The		
Blues/Feel Like Riding On	1952	Rainbow 199
BLUEDOTS		
My Very Own/Mary Had A		
Rock N' Roll Lamb	1959	Hurricane 104
BLUEJAYS (LEON PEELS & THE)		
Once Upon A Love/Alice From		
Above	1989	Classic Artists 111
BLUENOTES (1) (IVAN GREGORY & THE)		
Kathy/Elvis Presley Blues	1956	G&G 110
BLUENOTES (2) (AKA BLUE NOTES (1))		
Page One/Mighty Low	1957	Colonial 434
BLUENOTES (2) (AKA BLUE NOTES (1))		
Let Her Know/Christmas Chimes	1958	Colonial 7779
BLUENOTES (2) (HAROLD MELVIN & THE) (AKA BLUE NOTES (1))		
What A Man Can Do/Go Away	1966	Arctic 135
BLUENOTES (3) (HENRY WILSON & THE)		
My Steady Girl/Mighty Lou	1958	Dot 15692
BLUENOTES (4)		
Winter Wonderland/Oh Holy Night	1960	Valve 115
BLUENOTES (5) (DONNIE WILLIAMS & THE)		
Cry Your Heart Out/Is Your Love	1959	Viking 1005
BLUENOTES (5) (JAMES EASTERLING & THE)		
Angel Of Mine/You Think		
You're Smart	N/A	Reno 133
BLUENOTES (5) (PHIL CAY & THE)		
Meet Me In The Barnyard/If		
They Ask Me	1959	Hart 1001
BLUENOTES (5) (VINCE ANTHONY & THE)		
Clarabel/All Over Again	1963	Viking 1018
BLUENOTES (6) (GM JOEY VILLA)		
I'll Love You (Till The End Of		
TIme) Pt. 1/I'll Love You		
(Till The End Of TIme) Pt. 2	1965	Bluejay 101
BLUES BUSTERS		
Tell Me Why/Behold	1962	Capitol 4895
BOARDWALKERS (RONNIE & THE)		
She Won't Go Steady/What'll		
I Do	1961	Rex 103
BOB-O-LINKS		
I Promise/Mr. Frog	1962	Hi-Ho 101
BOB-WHEELS		
She's Gone/Love Me	1963	Tarx 1008
BOBBETTES (FEMALE)		
Mr. Lee/Look At The Stars	1957	Atlantic 1144
Come-A Come-A/Speedy	1957	Atlantic 1159
Zoomy/Rock And Ree-Ah-Zole	1958	Atlantic 1181
The Dream/Um Bow Wow	1958	Atlantic 1194
You Are My Sweetheart/Don't		
Say Goodnight	1959	Atlantic 2027
I Shot Mr. Lee/Untrue Love	1960	Atlantic 2069
I Cried/Oh My Papa	1960	Galliant 1006
I Shot Mr. Lee/Billy	1960	Triple-X 104
Have Mercy Baby/Dance With		
Me Georgie	1960	Triple-X 106
Teach Me Tonight/Mr. Johnny Q	1961	End 1093
I Don't Like It Like That Pt. 1/		
I Don't Like It Like That Pt. 2	1961	End 1095
I Don't Like It Like That/		
Mr. Johnny Q	1961	Gone 5112
Oh Mein Papa/Dance With Me		
Georgie	1961	King 5490
Looking For A Lover/Are You		
Satisfied (With Your Love)?	1961	King 5551
Over There (Stands My		
Baby)/Loneliness	1962	Jubilee 5427
The Broken Heart/Mama Papa	1962	Jubilee 5442
My Dearest/I'm Stepping Out		
Tonight	1962	King 5623
Teddy/Row, Row, Row	1963	Diamond 133
Close Your Eyes/Somebody		
Bad Stole De Wedding Bell	1963	Diamond 142
My Mama Said/Sandman	1964	Diamond 156

Artist Song	Year	Label
In Paradise/I Am Climbing A Mountain	1964	Diamond 166
You Ain't Seen Nothing Yet/ I'm Climbing A Mountain	1965	Diamond 181
Love Is Blind/Teddy	1965	Diamond 189
I've Gotta Face The World/Having Fun	1966	RCA 8832
It's All Over/Happy-Go-Lucky Me	1966	RCA 8983
That's A Bad Thing To Know/All In Your Mind	1971	Mayhew 712297/712298
Tighten Up Your Own Thing/ Looking For A New Love (Bad Thing To Know)	1972	Mayhew 712237
It Won't Work Out/Good Man	1974	Mayhew 712861
BOBBETTES 1981 (FEMALE)		
Love Rhythm/I'll Keep Coming Back	1981	QIT
BOBBIES		
Lonely And Blue/Want Your Lovin'	1964	Crusader 115
BOBBINAIRES		
Just Another Way To Break A Heart	N/A	Jen-D
BOBBY & JIMMY (& GROUP)		
Day And Night/Down The Road And Over The Hill	1963	King 5757
BOBBY-PINS		
Darling Don't Leave Me Now/I Want You	1959	Okeh 7110
Why Did You Go/I Wanna Love	1963	Mercury 72193
BOBOLINKS		
Elvis Presley's Sergeant/Your Cotton Pickin' Heart	1958	Key 573
Chocolate Ice Cream/Mechanical Man	1958	Key 575
Lonesome Wind/Message From Me	1961	Tune 226
BOHEMIANS		
Some Happy Day/Say Sweet Things	1962	Chex 1007
BOLEROS (CARMEN TAYLOR & THE)		
Freddie/Ooh I	1954	Atlantic 1041
Teen-Age Ball/Oh Please	1956	Apollo 489
BOMBERS		
Malena/I'll Never Tire Of You	1955	Orpheus 1101
Two-Time Heart/Sentence Of Love	1956	Orpheus 1105
BON BONS		
Three Teens/A Girl Without A Fella	1956	Columbia 40800
The Kiss In Your Eyes/Love Me Or I'll Die	1957	Columbia 40887
BON-AIRES		
Broken Heart (live)/Share (live) (by the Brooklyn Connection)	1982	50th U.G.H.A. Show Commemoration 45
BON-AIRES (1)		
Bermuda/Stop The World	1956	King 4975
BON-AIRES (2)		
Blue Beat/Driving Along	1962	Rust TR3
Bye Bye/My Love My Love	1964	Rust 5077
The Shrine Of St. Cecilia/Jeanie Baby	1964	Rust 5097
My Heart's Desire/New Me	1976	Catamount 130
Cherry/At Night (acapella)	1976	Flamingo 1000
Out Of Sight, Out Of Mind/I Love You (acapella)	1976	Flamingo 1001
The Angels Sang/What Did She Use	1977	Flamingo 1002
BON-BONS (1) (FEMALE)		
Pass It Along/Momma Llama, Poppa Llama	1955	London 1585
Listen My Heart/Lovin' Up A Storm Tonight	1964	Sampson 1003
BON-BONS (2) (FEMALE)		
Come On Baby/What's Wrong With Ringo	1964	Coral 62402
Each Time/Everybody Wants My Boyfriend	1964	Coral 62435
BONAIRES		
Lolita/Evergreen	1960	Shasta 126

Artist Song	Year	Label
BONAIRS		
It's Christmas Time/I'm Alone Tonight (by the Ernie Tavares Trio)	1953	Dootone 325
BOND, DAVE (& GROUP)		
Tell Me/Rocking Good Feeling	1961	Khoury's 723
BONNETS		
Ya Gotta Take A Chance/Ya Gotta Take A Chance (instrumental)	1963	Unical 3010
BONNEVILLES		
Give Me Your Love/Until You Say We're Through	1959	Capri 102
My Love	1959	Ka-Hi 121
I Do/Make Believe Lovin'	1959	Whitehall 30002
Lorraine/Zu Zu	1960	Munich 103/Barry 104 (62)
BONNIE SISTERS		
Cry Baby/Broken	1956	Rainbow 328
BONNIE SISTERS (FEMALE)		
Cry Baby/I Saw Mommy Cha Cha Cha With You Know Who	1956	Rainbow 328
Track That Cat/Wandering Heart	1956	Rainbow 333
Do You Know/Little Bo Peep	1956	Rainbow 336
BOOGIE RAMBLERS		
Cindy Lou/Such Is Love	1957	Goldband 1030
BOP CHORDS		
My Darling To You/Castle In The Sky	1957	Holiday 2601
When I Woke Up This Morning/ I Really Love Her So	1957	Holiday 2603
So Why/Baby	1957	Holiday 2608
BOP SHOP		
Don't Say Goodnight/Seven Wonders Of The World (by the Del Statens)	1972	Kelway 105
The Stars/That's How I Feel	N/A	Horizon Ent. Ltd.
Nuts 'N' Sprinkles/Cry Baby Cry	N/A	Larric 7301
BOPPERS (ALONZO & THE)		
I'm On My Way/Juicy Melon	1963	Rojac 8127
BOPTONES		
Be My Pussy Cat/I Had A Love	1958	Ember 1043
BOSS MEN		
Self Pity/I'm Ready	1964	Score 1003
BOSSMEN		
Fever Of Love/Good Lookin' Woman	1964	Busy Bee 1001
You And I/Baby Boy	1966	Lucky Eleven 231
BOSSTONES (AKA BOSS-TONES)		
Mope-itty Mope/Wings Of An Angel	1959	Boss 401/V-Tone 208 (60)
BOSTICK, CALVIN (& GROUP)		
Christmas Won't Be Christmas Without You/Four Eleven Boogie (no group)	1953	Chess 1530
BOULEVARDS		
Delores/Chop Chop Hole In The Wall	1959	Everest 19316
BOUQUETS		
Welcome To My Heart/Ain't That Love	1965	Blue Cat 115
BOUQUETS (TOOTIE & THE)		
You Done Me Wrong/The Conqueror	1963	Parkway 887
BOWERY BOYS		
Sometimes	1985	N/A
BOWMAN, JANE (& GROUP)		
Dearest Little Angel/Comin Down With The Blues	1961	Sapien 1002
BOWMAN, PRISCILLA (& GROUP)		
Why Must I Cry/Like A Baby	1959	Abner 1033
BOWMAN, PRISCILLA (BB THE SPANIELS)		
I Ain't Givin' Up Nothin'/A Rockin' Good Way	1958	Abner 1018
BOWTIES (CIRINO & THE)		
My Rosemarie/My Baby's In Love With Me	1955	Royal Roost 614
This Must Be The Place/Again	1956	Royal Roost 619
Snap Jack/After Love	1956	Royal Roost 622
Ever Since I Can Remember/ Rock, Pretty Baby (with Ivy Schulman)	1956	Royal Roost 624
Road Man	N/A	Royal Roost (unreleased)

Artist	Song	Year	Label
	Blind In Love	N/A	Royal Roost (unreleased)
BOY FRIENDS (1) (JEANIE & THE)			
	It's Me Knocking/Baby	1959	Warwick 508
BOY FRIENDS (2) (TERRY CORIN & THE)			
	Dream Date/Sick Sick Sick	1960	Colony 110
BOY FRIENDS (3)			
	Shy Boy/Snake In The Grass	1961	Glasser 1000
BOYCE, TOMMY (& GROUP)			
	I'll Remember Carol/Too Late			
	For Tears	1962	RCA 8074
BOYD, EDDIE (WITH HIS CHESS MEN)			
	I Love You/Save Her Doctor	1957	J.O.B. 1114
	Come On Home/Reap What			
	You Sow (no group)	1959	Keyhole 107
	All The Way/Where You Belong	1959	Keyhole 114
BOYFRIENDS (1) (WINI BROWN & THE)			
	Here In My Heart/Your			
	happiness In Mine	1952	Mercury 5870
	Heaven Knows Why/Be			
	Anything, Be Mine	1952	Mercury 8270
BOYFRIENDS (2) (JANIS & HER)			
	Please Be My Love/Bang Bang	1958	RCA 7318
BOYFRIENDS (3) (AKA FIVE DISCS)			
	Let's Fall In Love/Oh Lana	1964	Kapp 569
BOYS (1) (BARBARA & THE)			
	Hooty Sapperticker/Cobra	1958	Dot 15798
BOYS (2)			
	Angel Of Mine/I Wanna Know	1964	SVR 1001
	It's Hopeless/How Do You Do			
	With Me	1964	SVR 1002
BOYS NEXT DOOR			
	We Got Together/Now You're			
	Talking Baby	1956	Rainbow 349
	Sweet Love Of Mine/You Talk			
	Too Much	1956	Vik 0207
BQE			
	Tonight Tonight/Zing Went The			
	Strings Of My Heart	1988	Starlight 58
	The Lion Sleeps Tonight/Stand			
	By Me	1988	Starlight 60
	I Love You/Tonight Could Be			
	The Night	1988	Starlight 61
BRACELETS			
	I'll Play Along/Waddle, Waddle	1962	Congress 104
	You're Just Fooling Yourself/You			
	Better Move On	1964	20th Century Fox 539
BRADFORD BOYS			
	That Feeling/Little Boy Blue	1955	Rainbow 307
BRADFORD, CHUCK (& GROUP)			
	You're Going To Miss Me			
	(When I'm Gone)/Say It Was			
	A Dream	1961	Fire 505
	You Can't Hurt Me			
	Anymore/Wherever You Are	1962	Fire 511
BRADFORD, SYLVESTER (& GROUP)			
	I Like Girls/Live Just To Love			
	You	1958	Atco 6130
BRADLEY, MAMIE (& GROUP)			
	I Feel Like A Million/The Patty			
	Cake	1958	Sue 702
BRAVADOES (LITTLE MAC & THE)			
	Cinderella/Dance Baby			
	(With Me)	1961	Little Mac 101
BREAKAWAYS			
	He Doesn't Love Me/That's			
	How It Goes	1964	Cameo 323
BREAKERS			
	Balboa Memories/Long Way			
	Home	1963	Marsh 206
BREEDLOVE, JIMMY (& GROUP)			
	Jealous Fool/Li'l Ol' Me	1963	Diamond 144
BRENTWOODS			
	Midnight Star/As I Live From			
	Day To Day	1960	Dore 559
	Gee, But I Miss Him/Oh, Dear,			
	What Can The Matter Be	1963	Talent 1003
BREWER, MIKE (& GROUP)			
	The Most Important Thing/I'm			
	Counting On You	1963	Lesley 1929
BRIAN, EDDIE (THE EDDIE BRIAN GROUP)			
	Back To '55/Christmas Shopping	1988	BAB 130

Artist	Song	Year	Label
BRIDGES, CURLEY (& GROUP)			
	A Prayer Of Love/(no group)	1960	DC 0436
BRIGHTONES			
	Rumors/Swim Swim Swim	1964	Warner Bros. 5472
BROADWAYS			
	Are You Telling Me			
	Goodbye/Goin', Goin', Gone	1966	MGM 13486
	Sweet And Heavenly			
	Melody/You Just Don't Know	1967	MGM 13592
BROCHURES			
	They Lied/My In-Laws Are			
	Outlaws	1961	Apollo 757
BROKEN HEARTS			
	Shining Star/Ten Lonely Guys	1962	Diamond 123
	Crying Over You/Thrill Upon			
	A Hill	N/A	Rosina 147
BROOKLYN ALLSTARS			
	Ten Commandments/			
	Storehouse Of His Love	1974	Jewell 236
BROOKLYN BOYS			
	If She Should Call/Every Night	1956	Ferris 902
BROOKLYN CONNECTION			
	Share (live)/Broken Heart (live)			
	(by the Bon-Aires	1982	50th U.G.H.A. Show
			Commemoration 45
BROOKTONES			
	There Must Be A Reason/Cute			
	Collegiate	1958	Coed 502
	Never Again/School Girl's Crush	1958	Coed 507
BROTHERS			
	My True Love/One Lonely Heart	1961	Checker 995
BROTHERS (LITTLE TONI & THE)			
	Princess/I Love You	1960	Top Rank 2090
BROWN, BILLY (& GROUP)			
	Lost Weekend/Just Out Of Reach	1960	Republic 2007
BROWN, BOBBY (& GROUP)			
	Falling From Paradise/Dreamer	1962	Pak 1313
BROWN, CHARLES (& GROUP)			
	Angel Baby/Baby Oh Baby	1961	King 5439
BROWN, RUTH (BB THE RHYTHMAKERS)			
	Oh What A Dream I Had Last			
	Night/Please Don't Freeze	1955	Atlantic 1036
BROWN, SAMMY (& GROUP)			
	I'm In Love/Let's Leave It Like			
	It Is	1964	Bee Bee 701
BROWNE, DORIS (BB THE CAPRIS)			
	Oh Baby/Please Believe Me	1953	Gotham 290
	Until The End Of Time/Why			
	Don't You Love Me Now,			
	Now, Now	1953	Gotham 296
	My Cherie/The Game Of Love	1953	Gotham 298
BROWNS (BARBARA & THE)			
	Big Party/You Belong To Her	1964	Stax 150
	In My Heart/Please Be Honest			
	With Me	1964	Stax 158
BRUNO, BRUCE (& GROUP)			
	Dear Joanne/Venus In Blue			
	Jeans	1962	Roulette 4427
BRYANT, HELEN (& GROUP)			
	That's A Promise/I've Learned			
	My Lesson	1961	Fury 1042
BUA, GENE (& GROUP)			
	Well Honey/Golly Gee	1958	Safari 1007/ABC 9928 (58)
BUCCANEERS (1)			
	The Stars Will Remember/Come			
	Back My Love	1953	Rama 21
	In The Mission Of St.			
	Augustine/You Did Me Wrong	1953	Rama 24
	Dear Ruth/Fine Brown Frame	1953	Southern 101/Rainbow 211 (53)
BUCCANEERS (2)			
	Over And Over Again/Let's			
	Drink To Happiness	1954	Tiffany 1308
BUCCANEERS (3)			
	Who Are You Foolin' Now/Blonde			
	Hair, Blue Eyes And Ruby Lips	1958	Crystalette 718
BUCKEYES			
	Since I Fell For You/Be Only			
	You	1957	DeLuxe 6110
	Dottie Baby/Begging You,			
	Please	1957	DeLuxe 6126

Artist Song	Year	Label
BUDDIES (1) (BILLY BUNN & THE)		
I'm Afraid/I Need A Shoulder		
To Cry On	1951	RCA 4483
That's When Your Heartaches		
Began/Until The Real Thing		
Comes Along	1952	RCA 4657
BUDDIES (2) (AKA BARONS (1)/AKA MEL WILLIAMS & THE MONTCLAIRS)		
I Stole Your Heart/I Waited	1955	Glory 230
BUDDIES (3) (LITTLE BUTCHIE SAUNDERS & HIS)		
Lindy Lou/Rock And Roll Indian		
Dance	1956	Herald 485
Great Big Heart/I Wanna Holler	1956	Herald 491
Over The Rainbow/Sometimes		
Little Girl (by Little Butchie &		
the Vells)	1959	Angle Tone 535
BUDDIES (4)		
Two Skeletons On A Roof/Most		
Happy Fella	1956	Decca 29840
Every Time The Phone		
Rings/Bag Of Bones	1957	Decca 29953
A Prom And A Promise/Lottery	1957	Decca 30355
BUDDIES (5) (CARL ELL (AKA CARL WHITE) & THE)		
Bobby, My Love/Sunshine	1959	Combo 154
BUDDIES (6)		
Castle Of Love/Give Me Your		
Love	1959	Okeh 7123
Heartless/She's A Loser	1959	Tiara 6121
BUDDIES (7)		
Must Be True Love/Hully		
Gully Mama	1961	Comet 2143
Lebone Delada/Spooky Spider	1961	Swan 4073
The Beatle/Pulsebeat	1964	Swan 4170
BUDDIES (8) (AKA TOKENS (2))		
On The Go/My Only Friend	1964	Swing 102
BUMBLE BEES		
A Girl Called Love/Echo Boogie	1963	Joey 6220
Please Let It Be/Please Don't Go	N/A	Relic LP 5043
BURGESS, DEWAYNE (& GROUP)		
Moments To Recall/Roller	N/A	Branley 103
BURNETT, CARL (& GROUP)		
Sweet Memories/Jerk Baby Jerk	1965	Carmax 102
BURRAGE, HAROLD (& GROUP)		
Crying For My Baby/What You		
Don't Know	1959	Vee Jay 318
BURT, WANDA (BB THE CRESCENDOS)		
Your True Love Is Standing		
Here/Scheming	1961	Music City 840
BUSSY, TERRY (& GROUP)		
How Could You/Calypso		
Peacock	1956	Jazzmar 103
BUTANES		
That's My Desire/Don't Forget I		
Love You	1961	Enrica 1007
BUTLER, B. B. (& GROUP)		
I Hope I Don't Cry/As Long As		
You Love Me	1964	Barry 111
BUTLER, CLIFF (& GROUP)		
That's How I Go For		
You/Devoted To You	1958	Nasco 6010
BUTLERS (1)		
Lovable Girl/When I Grow Older	1963	Guyden 2081
She Tried To Kiss Me/The		
Sun's Message	1964	Liberty Bell 1024
BUTLERS (2) (FRANKIE BEVERLY & THE)		
She Kissed Me/Don't Cry Little		
Boy Sad	1967	Fairmount 1012
BUTTERBALLS		
Butterball/Give Me A Chance		
(by the Chanells)	1963	Times Square 24
BUTTERFLYS (FEMALE)		
Goodnight Baby/The Swim	1964	Red Bird 10-009
Gee Baby Gee/I Wonder	1964	Red Bird 10-016
BUZZ-OFF BOYS QUINTET		
Frannie, Come Back To		
Me/Please Mister Moon	1978	Clifton 28
BUZZARDS (BIG JOHN & THE)		
Mean Woman/Hey, Little Girl	1954	Columbia 40345
Oop Shoop/Your Cash Ain't		
Nothin' But Trash	1954	Okeh 7045
BYE BYES		
Do You/Blond Hair, Blue Eyes,		
Ruby Lips	1959	Mercury 71530
BYRD, BOBBY (& GROUP)		
Please Don't Hurt Me/Delicious		
Are Your Kisses	1955	Sage & Sand 203
If We Should Meet Again/Looby		
Loo	1957	Zephyr 70-018
BYSTANDERS		
Power Of A Prayer/		
Yellow Mellow Hardtop	1957	Demon 1502
BYSTANDERS (FB RAY JOHNSON)		
Love A La Mode/No Stone		
Unturned	1956	Dot 15512
C & C BOYS		
Hey Marvin/You Stole My Heart	1962	Duke 358
It's All Over Now/My Life	1964	Duke 379
C-LARKS		
Time/Please Write Me A Letter	1956	Nova 106
C-NOTES (1) (AKA C-TONES)		
On Your Mark/From Now On	1957	Everlast 5005
We Were Meant For Each		
Other/Last Saturday Night	1959	Arc 4447
C-NOTES (1) (FRANKIE & THE)		
Forever And Ever/Union Hall		
(by the Montels)	1961	Richie 2/Times Square 10 (63)
C-NOTES (2) (RON JONES & THE)		
Goodbye Linda/Why	1962	Mobie 3419
C-QUENTS		
Merry Christmas Baby/All I		
Want For Christmas Is You	1968	Captown 4027
Dearest One/It's You And Me	1968	Essica 004
C-QUINS		
My Only Love/You've Been		
Crying	1962	Ditto 501/Chess 1815 (62)
C-TONES (AKA C-NOTES)		
On Your Mark/From Now On	1957	Everlast 5005
CABARETTES		
There Must Be A Way/Times Is		
Tough	1963	Saxony 1002
CABOT, JOHNNY (& GROUP)		
On My Own Again/Night And		
Day	1962	Columbia 42283
CADDELL, SHIRLEY (& GROUP)		
The Big Bounce/Don't Hurt A		
Good Thing	1963	Lesley 1927
CADDY'S (JESSE POWELL & THE)		
Ain't You Gonna/Turnpike		
(instrumental)	1958	Josie 834
CADETS (1) (AARON COLLINS & THE) (AKA JACKS)		
Pretty Evey (Evelyn)/Rum		
Jamaica Rum	1957	Modern 1019
CADETS (1) (AKA JACKS)		
Don't Be Angry/I Cry	1955	Modern 956
Rollin' Stone/Fine Lookin' Baby	1955	Modern 960
Fine Lookin' Baby/I Cry	1955	Modern 963
Ay La Ba/My Man (Dolly Cooper)	1955	Modern 965
I Got Loaded/Dancin' Dan		
(Sixty Minute Man)	1956	Modern 1000
Fools Rush In/I'll Be Spinning	1956	Modern 1006
Annie Met Henry/So Will I	1956	Modern 969
Do You Wanna Rock		
(Hey Little Girl)/If It Is Wrong	1956	Modern 971
Church Bells May		
Ring/Heartbreak Hotel	1956	Modern 985
Stranded In The Jungle/I Want		
You	1956	Modern 994
Love Bandit/Heaven Help Me	1957	Modern 1012
You Belong To Me/Wiggie		
Waggie Woo	1957	Modern 1017
You Belong To Me/Heaven		
Help Me	1957	Modern 1017
Ring Chimes/Baby Ya Know	1957	Modern 1026
Car Crash/Don't	1960	Jan-Lar 102/Firefly 328 (74)
The Riddle	1963	Crown LP 5370
I Had Fifty Cents	1963	Crown LP 5370
Marie My Love	1963	Crown LP 5370
John Henry	1963	Crown LP 5370
Stranded In The Jungle/Rollin'		
Stone	1975	Relic 1032
Smack Dab In The Middle	N/A	Modern LP 1215
Let's Rock And Roll	N/A	Relic LP 5025
Memories Of You	N/A	Relic LP 5025

Artist	Song	Year	Label
CADETS (1) (BENNIE BUNN & THE) (AKA JACKS)			
	One More Chance/I'm Looking For A Job	1960	Sherwood 211
CADETS (1) (WILL JONES & THE) (AKA JACKS)			
	Hands Across The Table/ Love Can Do Most Anything	1957	Modern 1024
CADETS (2) (KENNY & THE)			
	Barbie/What Is A Young Girl Made Of	1960	Randy 422
CADILLACS			
	Gloria/I Wonder Why	1954	Josie 765
	Wishing Well/I Want To Know About Love	1954	Josie 769
	Party For Two	1954	unreleased
	Corn Whiskey	1954	unreleased
	No Chance/Sympathy	1955	Josie 773
	Down The Road/Window Lady	1955	Josie 778
	Speedoo/Let Me Explain	1955	Josie 785
	Zoom/You Are	1956	Josie 792
	Betty My Love/Woe Is Me	1956	Josie 798
	(That's) All I Need/The Girl I Love	1956	Josie 805
	Shock-A-Doo/Rudolph The Red-Nosed Reindeer	1956	Josie 807
	Oh! Whatcha Do	1956	unreleased
	Don't Take Your Love From Me	1956	unreleased
	Sugar, Sugar/About That Girl Named Lou	1957	Josie 812
	My Girl Friend/Broken Heart	1957	Josie 820
	If You Want To Be A Woman Of Mine	1957	unreleased
	Peek-A-Boo/Oh, Oh, Lolita	1958	Jo-Z 846 (first pressing)/ Josie 846 (58) (second pressing)
	Speedo Is Back/A Looka Here	1958	Josie 836
	Holy Smoke Baby/I Want To Know	1958	Josie 842
	Jelly Bean	1958	unreleased
	It's Spring	1958	unreleased
	Great Googly Moo	1958	unreleased
	Jay Walker/Copy Cat	1959	Josie 857
	Please, Mr. Johnson/Cool It Fool	1959	Josie 861
	Romeo/Always My Darling	1959	Josie 866
	Bad Dan McGoon/Dumbell	1959	Josie 870
	Carelessly	1959	Jubilee LP 1089
	Don't Be Mad With My Heart	1959	Jubilee LP 1089
	Baby's Coming Home To Me	1959	Jubilee LP 1089
	Why, Why	1959	Jubilee LP 1089
	Zoom Boom Zing	1959	Jubilee LP 1089
	You're Not in Love With Me	1959	unreleased
	The Vow	1959	unreleased
	Frankenstein	1959	unreleased
	Your Heart Is So Blind	1959	unreleased
	I Want To Be Loved	1959	unreleased
	That's Why/The Boogie Man	1960	Josie 883
	Louise	1960	unreleased
	I'm In Love	1960	unreleased
	Rock 'n' Roll Is Here To Stay	1960	unreleased
	Lucy	1961	Jubilee LP 1117
	Let Me Down Easy	1961	Jubilee LP 1117
	Hurry Home	1961	Jubilee LP 1117
	C'mon Home Baby	1961	Jubilee LP 1117
	It's Love	1961	Jubilee LP 1117/ Jubilee LP 5009 (62)
	Buzz Buzz Buzz	1961	Jubilee LP 1117/ Jubilee LP 5009 (62)
	Dum De Dum Dum	1962	Jubilee LP 5009
	Still You Left Me Baby	1962	Jubilee LP 5009
	Speedo/Baby It's All Right	1964	Lana 118
	Gloria/Hay Bob E Re Bob	1964	Lana 119
	Let's Get Together/She's My Connection	1966	Roulette 4654
	I'll Never Let You Go	N/A	Josie (unreleased)
CADILLACS (BOBBY RAY & THE)			
	I'm Willing/Thrill Me So	1961	Mercury 71738
	I Saw You/La Bomba	1963	Capitol 4935
CADILLACS (RAY BREWSTER & THE) (AKA SOLITAIRES)			
	Fool/The Right Kind Of Lovin'	1963	Arctic 101
CADILLACS (SPEEDO & THE)			
	Tell Me Today/It's Love	1960	Josie 876
CADILLACS (THE ORIGINAL CADILLACS)			
	Hurry Home/Lucy	1957	Josie 821
	What You Bet/You Are To Blame	1961	Smash 1712
	White Gardenia/Groovy Groovy Love	1962	Capitol 4825
	Deep In The Heart Of The Ghetto Pt. 1/Pt. 2	1972	Polydor 14031
CAESARS			
	Get Yourself Together/(La La) I Love You	N/A	Lanie 2001
CHAPERONES (AKA CHAPERONES (1)			
	Cruise To The Moon/Dance With Me	1960	Josie 880 (first pressing, second is by the Chaperones)
CAINE, GLADYS (& GROUP)			
	Please, Mr. D.J. Play A Song/ I Got My Mind Make Up	1963	Togo 602
CAITON, RICHARD (& GROUP)			
	You Look Like A Flower/Listen To The Drums	1964	GNP Crescendo 327
CAL-CONS			
	Daddy Cool/Mash Potato Party	1962	Allrite 621
CALDWELL, JOE (& GROUP)			
	Rollin' Tears/Rowdy Mae	1959	Esta 100
	Guess I'm Still The Lonely One/Rowdy Mae Is Back In Town Again	N/A	M-C-I
CALENDARS (1)			
	I'm Gonna Laugh At You/You're Too Fast	1961	Coed 564
	One Week Romance/Roasted Peanuts (by the Milestones)	1961	Swingin' 649
	If I Could Hold Your Hand	1974	Relic LP 5019
	What Are You Gonna Be	1974	Relic LP 5019
CALENDARS (1) (SHELL DUPONT & THE)			
	Share My Love/Stop Driving Me Crazy	1965	Tribune 1001
CALENDARS (2) (FREDDY MEADE & THE)			
	Just Give Her My Love/Mepri Stomp	1961	20th Fox 287
CALENDARS (3) (ROBERTA WATSON & THE)			
	Dear Donnie/You Insulted Me	1963	Corsican 111
CALHOUN, LENA (BB THE EMOTIONS (2))			
	I Can Tell/Been Lookin' Your Way	1962	Flip 358
CALHOUN, MILLIE (& GROUP)			
	This Love Will Last Forever/I Go For You	1965	Lo Lace 708
CALIFORNIANS			
	My Angel/Heavenly Ruby	1955	Federal 12231
CALIPHS			
	Darling If I Had You/Mother Dear	1958	Scatt 111
	I Need You/Party Time	1973	Vintage 1008
CALLENDER, BOB (& GROUP)			
	Baby I'm Ready/All With You	1964	Gold 102
CALLENDERS			
	If I Could Hold Your Hand/What Are You Gonna Be	1959	Cyclone 5012
CALTONES			
	Get Offa The Telephone	1960	Verve 10205
CALVAES			
	Fine Girl/Mambo Fiesta	1956	Cobra 5003
	Born With Rhythm/Lonely, Lonely Village	1957	Cobra 5014
CALVAES (OSCAR BOYD & THE)			
	Anna Macora/So Bad	1959	Checker 928
CALVANES			
	They Call Me Fool	1955	Dooto EP 205
	Crazy Over You/Don't Take Your Love From Me	1955	Dootone 371
	Florabelle/One More Kiss	1956	Dootone 380
	Dreamworld/5, 7 Or 9	1958	Deck 579
	My Love Song/Horror Pictures	1958	Deck 580
	Have You No Heart/Take Me Back	1991	Classic Artists 127
	Fleeoowee	N/A	Dootone LP 855/ Collectables LP 5048
CALVERT, DUANE (& GROUP)			
	Somewhere Somehow/My Love For You	1964	D.M.D. 102
CALVEYS			
	The Wind/I Need Love	1961	Comma 84349/Comma 445

Artist	Song	Year	Label	Artist	Song	Year	Label
CAMELOTS					As Time Goes By/Never, Never,		
	Music To My Ears/Daddy's				Never	1963	Philips 40111
	Going Away/Pocahontas/Don't			**CANDIES (2)**			
	Leave Me Baby	N/A	Clifton EP 507		I'm Only Making It Easier For		
CAMELOTS (1)					You/Yes I Love You	1962	Ember 1092
	Never Been In Love Before/Lulu	1961	Nix 101		If You Wanna Do A Smart		
CAMELOTS (2) (AKA CUPIDS (6)/AKA HARPS (2))					Thing/Stop	1963	Fleetwood 7003
	Don't Leave Me Baby			**CANDLES (1) (ROCHELL & THE)**			
	(acapella)/The Letter	1961	Crimson 1001		Once Upon A Time/When My		
	Your Way/Don't Leave Me Baby	1963	AAnko 1001		Baby Is Gone	1960	Swingin' 623
	Sunday Kind Of Love/My				Goodnight	1961	Swingin'
	Imagination	1963	AAnko 1004		Hey, Pretty Baby/So Far Away	1961	Swingin' 634
	Pocahontas/Searching For				Peg Of My Heart/Squat With		
	My Baby	1963	Ember 1108		Me Baby	1961	Swingin' 640
	Don't Leave Me Baby				Big Boy Pete/A Long Time Ago	1961	Swingin' 652
	(acapella)/Love Call				Each Night/Turn Her Down	1962	Challenge 9158
	(by the Ebonaires)	1964	Cameo 334		Let's Run Away And Get		
	Dance Girl/That's My Baby				Married/Annie's Not An		
	(by the Suns)	1964	Times Square 32/		Orphan Anymore	1962	Challenge 9191
			Relic 541 (65)		One Night With You	1985	Relic LP 5060
	Chain Of Broken Hearts/Rat			**CANDLES (2) (AKA BLENDERS (5))**			
	Race	1965	Relic 530		Junior/Down On My Knees		
	Your Way/I Wonder	1973	Dream 1001		(by the Starr Brothers)	1964	Nike 1016
CAMELOTS (3)				**CANDLETTES**			
	Scratch/Charge	1962	Comet 930		Wrapped Up In A Dream/		
CAMEOS (1) (FB VERNON GREEN)					Moments To Remember	1963	Rhonda 1001
	Craving/Only For You	1955	Dootone 365		Angel Love/Everybody Loves		
CAMEOS (2)					To Rock And Roll	1958	Vita 179
	Merry Christmas/New Year's				My Only Love/It's Misery	1959	Vita 182
	Eve	1957	Cameo 123	**CANDY CANES (JIMMY JAMES & THE)**			
	Best Of The Can Can Pt. 1/				Teen-Age Beauty/Marjolaine	1958	Columbia 41192
	Best Of The Can Can Pt. 2	1959	Cameo 176	**CANDY GIRLS**			
CAMEOS (3)					Tomorrow My Love/Run	1964	Rotate 5001
	Please Love Me/Shanga Langa				Runaround/Run	1964	Rotate 5005
	Ding Dong	1959	Flagship 115	**CANDY MAKERS**			
CAMEOS (4)					And So Tomorrow/Chop Chop		
	We'll Still Be Together/I				Chop	N/A	Urban 124
	Remember When	1960	Matador 1808/Astra 5002		Comin' Through The		
			(85)		Rye/Chapel In My Memory	N/A	Urban 125
	Canadian Sunset/Never Before	1960	Matador 1813	**CAP-TANS (AKA L'CAPTANS/AKA L'CAP-TANS)**			
	He/Can You Remember?	1963	Gigi 100		Yes/Satchelmouth Baby	1950	DC 8048
CAMEOS (5)					You'll Always Be My		
	Wait Up/Lost Lover	1960	Dean 504/Johnson 108 (60)		Sweetheart/Coo-Coo Jug-Jug	1950	DC 8054
CAMEOS (5) (TY TAYLOR & THE)					I'm So Crazy For Love/Crazy		
	The Beginning Of Love/Big Pearl	1959	Design 834		'Bout My Honey Dip	1950	Dot 1009
CAMEOS (6) (LITTLE WILLIE BROWN & THE)					With All My Love/Chief Turn		
	Gonna Make It On Back/Cut It Out	1961	Do-Ra-Mi 1404		The Hose On Me	1950	Dot 1018
CAMEOS (7) (LONDIE & THE)					Asking/Who Can I Turn To	1951	Coral 65071
	Foolin' Me/Straight From The				Never Be Lonely/My, My, Ain't		
	Grapevine	1963	ABC 10508		She Pretty	1951	Gotham 233
CAMEOS (8)					Yes/Waiting At The Station	1951	Gotham 268
	Comin' On Down	N/A	Relic LP 5028		I'm So Crazy For Love/With All		
CAMERON, KEN (& GROUP)					My Love	1953	Dot 15114
	Don't Forget/The Prisoner's				Let's Put Our Cards On The		
	Song	1961	Zynn 500		Table/Goodnight Mother	1959	DC 8064
CAMERONS					Tight Skirts And Crazy		
	Laura/Red Red Robin	1977	Crystal Ball 112		Sweaters/I'm Afraid	1960	Anna 1122
CAMERONS (1)					Looking Ahead	1962	Design LP DLP705
	Cheryl/Boom Chic-A-Boom				I Love You So/I Thought I		
	(by the Jiveleers)	1960	Cousins 1/2		Could Forget You	1974	Roadhouse 1016
	Lonely Teenager/Cheryl	1960	Cousins (unreleased)		Feel Like Balling Some		
	Baby Don't You Know/She's				More/I'm Seeking Revenge	1974	Roadhouse 1023
	Got It	1960	Cousins (unreleased)		Grateful/Don't Believe What		
CAMERONS (2) (AKA DEMILLES)					They Say	1975	Gotham 261
	Guardian Angel/A Girl I Marry	1961	Cousins 1003/		Nobody's Here	N/A	International Award
			Felsted 8638 (61)				LP AK222
CAMPANIONS (AKA DEL SATINS)				**CAP-TANS (BETHEA & THE)**			
	I Want A Yul Brenner				Whenever I Look At You/Round		
	Haircut/Dorothy, My Monster	N/A	Dee-Dee 1047		the Rocket	1963	Sabu 103
CAMPBELL, CHARLOTTE (& GROUP)					You Better Mind/I Wanna Make		
	True Lover/Where Did My				Love	1963	Sabu 501
	Dreamboat Go	1959	Wanger 194	**CAP-TANS (BETHEA & THE) (AKA L'CAPTANS/AKA L'CAP-TANS)**			
CAMPBELL, JO ANN (BB THE DUBS)					Crazy About A Woman/Revenue		
	Jim Dandy/Five Minutes More	1962	Rori 711		Man	1962	Loop 100/International
CANADIAN METEORS (BUDDY BURKE & THE)							Award LP AK222
	Street Of Sorrow/That Big Old				Rockin' In The Jungle/Annie		
	Moon	1957	Bullseye 1002		Penguin	1962	Hawkeye 0430
CANARIES				**CAPERS (FEMALE)**			
	I'm Sorry Baby/Runaround				Miss You, My Dear/Early One		
	Ronnie	1964	Dimension 1047		Morning	1958	Vee Jay 297
CANDIES (1) (ACE KENNED & THE)					High School Diploma/Candy		
	Arms Around You/You Promise	1960	XYZ 609		Store Blues	1959	Vee Jay 315

Artist	Song	Year	Label
CAPES			
	The Vow	N/A	Chat 5005
CAPISTRANOS (JOHN LITTLETON & THE) (WITH JAMES BROWN)			
	Now Darling/Po' Mary	1958	Duke 179
CAPITOLS (1)			
	Angel Of Love/Cause I Love You	1958	Pet 807
CAPITOLS (1) (MICKEY TOLIVER & THE)			
	Rose-Marie/Millie	1957	Cindy 3002
CAPITOLS (1) (MICKEY TOLIVER & THE)			
	Day By Day/Little Things	1958	Gateway 721
CAPITOLS (2) (JOHNNY HOUSTON & THE)			
	But It's Too Late/Hula Hands	1957	East West 100
CAPITOLS (3)			
	I Let Her Go/I've Got A Girl	1958	Carlton 461
CAPITOLS (4)			
	Write Me A Love Letter/Three O'Clock Rock	1959	Triumph 601
CAPITOLS (5)			
	I'll Drink A Toast/Fine Momma's Daughter	1962	Portrait 109
CAPITOLS (6)			
	Honey, Honey/ Alone In The Night (by the Jones Boys)	1973	Baron 103
CAPREEZ			
	Rosanna/Over You	1956	Sound 126/Sound 149 (65)
CAPRI SISTERS (FEMALE)			
	After School Rock 'N' Roll/The Occarina Roll	1956	Jubilee 5244
	Run-A-Round/Hawaiian Sway	1958	Dot 15851
	In Between/It's All Over	1959	Hanover 4531
	I'm Gonna Wish For You/There But For Her Go I	1960	ABC 10158
	Poco Loco/The Blues Came Tumbling Down	1961	Warwick 673
	I Want You To Be My Boy/Fairy Tales	1962	Newtown 5002
CAPRI, BOBBY (& GROUP)			
	One-Sided Love/Charm Bracelet	1961	Artiste 101
	You And I/Cleopatra	1963	Johnson 124
	The Night/I'm Gonna Be Another Man	1963	Johnson 126
CAPRI, JOHN (BB THE FABULOUS FOUR)			
	When I'm Lonely/Love For Me	1959	Bomarc 306
CAPRI, JOHNNY (& GROUP)			
	Don't Say Goodbye/Mine Alone	1961	Master 13
CAPRI, MIKE (& GROUP)			
	She's My Baby/Dontcha Keep Me Wanting	N/A	Cecil 4450
CAPRI, TONY (& GROUP)			
	Sandy/Why Do You Do Me	1961	Liban 1001
	Counting Wishes/That's The Way	1961	Liban 1005
CAPRIS (1)			
	God Only Knows/That's What You're Doing To Me	1954	Gotham 7304/20th Century 7304 (57)
	It Was Moonglow/Too Poor To Love	1955	Gotham 7306
	My Weakness/Yes, My Baby Please	1956	20th Century 1201
	It's A Miracle/Let's Linger Awhile	1956	Gotham 7308
	Oh, My Darling/Rock Pretty Baby	1958	Lifetime 610/Candlelite 422 (63)
	Please Believe Me	N/A	Collectables LP 5000
	He Still Loves Me	N/A	Collectables LP 5000
	She Still Loves Me	N/A	Collectables LP 5000
	Just A Fool	N/A	Collectables LP 5000
	Bless You	N/A	Collectables LP 5000
	I Miss Your Love	N/A	Collectables LP 5000
	You're Mine Again	N/A	Collectables LP 5000
	Yes My Baby Please	N/A	Collectables LP 5000
	How Long	N/A	Collectables LP 5000
CAPRIS (2) (AKA JESSE BELVIN & STUDIO GROUP)			
	Endless Love (slow version)/ Endless Love (fast version)	1959	Impact 34
	Endless Love/Beware	1959	Tender 518
CAPRIS (3)			
	Can't Get Over You/This Is Goodbye	1959	Fable 665
	My Promise To You/Bop! Bop! Bop!	1959	Sabre 201/202
CAPRIS (4)			
	There's A Moon Out Tonight/Indian Girl	1958	Planet 1010/1011/Old Town 1094 (60)/Lost Nite 101 (60)/Trommers 101 (60)
	Where I Fell In Love/Some People Think	1961	Old Town 1099
	Tears In My Eyes/Why Do I Cry	1961	Old Town 1103
	Girl In My Dreams/My Island In The Sun	1961	Old Town 1107
	Limbo/From The Vine Came The Grape	1962	Mr. Peacock 118/ Mr. Peeke 118 (63)
	Morse Code Of Love/There's A Moon Out Again	1982	Ambient Sound 02697
	A Hum Diddily Dee Do	N/A	Collectables LP 5016
	Stars In The Sky	N/A	Collectables LP 5016
	Little Girl/When	N/A	Lost Nite 148
CAPRIS (5) (AKA MEL WILLIAMS & THE MONTCLAIRS)			
	Ooh Wah/Fools Fall In Love	1955	Rage 101
CAPRISIANS			
	A Lovely Way To Spend An Evening/Yibby-Yah	1960	Indigo 109
	Oh What A Night/Why Do You Have To Go	1961	Lavender 004
CAPTANS (JERRY HOLLAND & THE)			
	A Big Bite Of The Blues/Ain't No Big Thing (instrumental)	1959	DC 0433
CARALLONS (LONNIE & THE)			
	Chapel Of Tears/My Heart	1959	Mohawk 108/ Streetcorner 101 (73)
	Trudy/Hold Me Close	1959	Mohawk 111
	You Say/Backyard Rock	1960	Mohawk 112
	The Gang All Knows/Ike Hammer	1960	Mohawk 113
	Chapel Of Tears/Wild Weekend (by the Barons)	1963	Mohawk 902
CARAMAN, ART "TURK" (& GROUP)			
	Falling For You/Eternity Of Love	1962	Dasa 101
CARAVELLES			
	Angry Angel/Pink Lips	1961	Star Maker 1925
	Falling For You/Shake Baby	1962	Joey 301
	One Little Kiss/Twistin' Marie	1962	Joey 6208
CARBO, CHUCK (BB THE SPIDERS)			
	Times/I Miss You	1957	Imperial 5479
CARBO, LEONARD (& GROUP)			
	So Tired/Pigtails And Blue Jeans	1958	Vee Jay 291
CARDELL, NICK (& GROUP)			
	How Can I Help It/Arlene	1963	Liberty 55556
	I Stand Alone/Everybody Jump	1964	Amcan 405
CARDELLS			
	Helen/Lovely Girl	1956	Middle-Tone 011
CARDIGANS (1)			
	Your Graduation Means Goodbye/Boll Weevil On The Mountain Top	1958	Mercury 71251
	It's Better That You Love/Wacky Wacky	1959	Mercury 71349
	Make Up Your Mind/Half Breed	1959	Spann 431
CARDIGANS (2) (DAVE & THE)			
	My Falling Star/Cha Cha Baby	1963	Bay 216
CARDINALS			
	Train	1974	Atlantic EP/Bim Bam Boom EP 1000 (74)
CARDINALS (1)			
	(Give Me) A Little Something	1951	Atlantic (unreleased)
	Give Me Another Chance	1951	Atlantic (unreleased)
	Shouldn't I Know/Please Don't Leave Me	1951	Atlantic 938
	Pretty Baby Blues/I'll Always Love	1951	Atlantic 952
	This Can't Be The End	1952	Atlantic (unreleased)
	If You See My Baby	1952	Atlantic (unreleased)
	Wheel Of Fortune/Kiss Me Baby	1952	Atlantic 958
	She Rocks/The Bump	1952	Atlantic 972
	For A While	1953	Atlantic (unreleased)
	Lovie Darling/You Are My Only Love	1953	Atlantic 995
	Please Baby/Under A Blanket Of Blue	1954	Atlantic 1025
	Love Came Tumbling Down	1955	Atlantic (unreleased)

Artist Song	Year	Label
You Won't Be True To Your		
Heart	1955	Atlantic (unreleased)
Today, Tomorrow, Forevermore	1955	Atlantic (unreleased)
Bang A Lang	1955	Atlantic (unreleased)
The Door Is Still Open/Misirlou	1955	Atlantic 1054
Come Back My Love/Two		
Things I Love	1955	Atlantic 1067
Lovely Girl/There Goes My		
Heart To You	1955	Atlantic 1079
The Show Is All Over	1956	Atlantic (unreleased)
Let The Sunshine Shine On You	1956	Atlantic (unreleased)
Nek I Hok I	1956	Atlantic (unreleased)
Off Shore/Choo-Choo	1956	Atlantic 1090
I Won't Make You Cry Anymore/		
The End Of The Story	1956	Atlantic 1103
One Love/Near You	1957	Atlantic 1126
Go Go Baby	1962	Cha Cha 741
Why Don't You Write		
Me/Sh-Boom	1963	Rose 835
My Love	1974	Atlantic EP/Bim Bam Boom EP 1000 (74)
Have I Been Gone Too Long	1974	Atlantic EP/Bim Bam Boom EP 1000 (74)
Sure Enough	1974	Atlantic EP/Bim Bam Boom EP 1000 (74)
Would I Love You/I'll Always		
Love You	1977	Robin Hood 154
Bim Bam Boom	N/A	Atlantic EP only
I Want You	N/A	Cha Cha 740
I'm Gonna Tell On You	N/A	Cha Cha 748
CARDINALS (2) (BOBBY GREGORY & THE)		
Just Waiting/Precious One	1959	Kip 403
CARDINALS (3) (CLAUDIA & THE)		
Much Too Much Too Soon	N/A	Teltone
CARELESS FIVE		
I'm Lonely/The Question		
Mark Twist	1962	Careful 1010
Summertime/Tell Me Right Now	N/A	Vitose 101
CARI, EDDIE (& GROUP)		
Wishing Time/This Love Of Mine	1963	Mermaid 104
CARIANS		
She's Gone/Snooty Friends	1961	Indigo 136
Only A Dream/Girls	1961	Magenta 04
CARIBBEANS		
Keep Her By My Side/I Knew	1958	20th Fox 112
CARIBBEANS (GEORGE TORRENCE & THE)		
Too Soon/Sweet Little Thing		
(Called Love)	1958	Galliant 1003
CARLO (AKA CARLO MASTRANGELO) (BB THE TREMONTS)		
Write Me A Letter/Baby Doll	1963	Laurie 3151
Little Orphan Doll/Mairzy Doats	1963	Laurie 3157
Story Of My Love/Five Minutes		
More	1963	Laurie 3175
Ring-A-Ling/Stranger In My		
Arms	1964	Laurie 3227
Claudine/Fever	1970	Raftis 110
Let There Be Love	1970	Raftis 112
CARLOS BROTHERS		
Under Stars Of Love	1959	Cascade-Drop LP 1008
Tonight/Come On, Let's Dance	1959	Del-Fi 4112
It's Time To Go/Little Cupid	1959	Del-Fi 4118
La Bamba/It's Time To Go	1960	Del-Fi 4145
CARLTON, CHICK (& GROUP)		
Tomorrow Never Comes/Give		
Me Courage	1962	Imperial 5873
Beyond Belief/Two Left Feet	1962	Imperial 5925
CARMACKS		
With All My Heart/I've Got		
To Know	1960	Autograph 205
CARMELETTES (FEMALE)		
My Foolish Heart/Promise Me		
A Rose	1959	Alpine 53
Aching For You/Something		
Tells Me I'm In Love	1960	Alpine 61
CARMEN, JERRY (& GROUP)		
Cherry Pie/Could This Be Love	1962	Barrish 500
Soldier Baby (Of Mine)	1965	Cameo 355
CARNATIONS (1)		
Tree In The Meadow/Clown Of		
The Masquerade	1952	Derby 789
The Angels Sent You To Me/		
Night Time Is The Right Time	1955	Savoy 1172

Artist Song	Year	Label
CARNATIONS (2)		
You Gave Me Peace Of Mind	1954	Music City 736
CARNATIONS (3)		
Gimme, Gimme, Gimme/Love,		
Open Up My Heart	1959	Enrica 1001
Casual/Red Wing	1960	Fraternity 863
Sleepy Hollow/Barbary Coast	1960	Terry Tone 199
CARNATIONS (4) (RAY ALLEN & THE)		
A Fool In Love/Betty Jo	1959	Ace 130
CARNATIONS (5)		
I'm Sorry/Oh Yeah	1959	Checker 914
A Wing And A Prayer/Leap Year	1960	University 606
CARNATIONS (6) (AKA STARTONES)		
Long Tall Girl/Is There Such		
A World	1961	Lescay 3002
CARNATIONS (7) (COSMO & THE)		
Scorpion/Fireball Mail	1961	Tilt 780
I'm A Little Mixed Up/You Can't		
Get Kissed	1961	Tilt 787
Funny Time/Punctuation	1963	Laurie 3163
CARNEGIES (ALPHONSO JONES & THE)		
Goodbye/Tell Her You Love Her	1963	Brunswick 55230
CAROLE, NANCY (& GROUP)		
The Memories We Share/My		
Joey	1964	Luxor 1029
CAROLONS		
Let It Please Be You/Let's		
Make Love Tonight	1964	Mellomood 1003
CARONATORS		
Senorita/Long Hot Summer	1960	Clock 1045/Clock 227
Lonely Street/Fairy Tales	1960	Clock 1047
This Is The Time/Casanova	1960	Clock 1049
CAROUSELS (1)		
Rendezvous/Drive-In Movie	1959	Jaguar 3029/Spry 121 (59)
I've Cried Enough/Lotsa Lotsa		
Lovin'	1959	Spry 116
Fading Away/Solitude	1960	G&C 201
CAROUSELS (2) (FEMALE)		
Symptoms Of Love/Hush Of Love	1961	ABC 10233
You Can Come/Pretty Little		
Thing	1961	Gone 5118 (first pressing)
If You Want To/Pretty Little Thing	1961	Gone 5118 (second pressing)
Never Let Him Go/Dirty Tricks	1962	Gone 5131
I Wanna Fly/Something Else	1964	Guyden 2102
Beneath The Willow/Sail Away	1965	Autumn 13
Just For Your Love/Goodbye	1973	Vintage 1012
CARPENTER, FREDDIE (& GROUP)		
Money Money Money/Take		
Me Back Lover	1958	East West 112
CARPETS		
Why Do I?/Let Her Go	1956	Federal 12257
Lonely Me/Chicken Backs	1956	Federal 12269
CARR, WYNONIE (& GROUP)		
What Do You Know About		
Love/Heartbreak Melody	1957	Specialty 600
CARRIBEANS		
Wonderful Girl/Oh My Love	1963	Amy 871
CARRIBIANS		
Baby/Wonderland	1961	Brooks 2000/2001 /Johnson/Clifton 7 (74)
CARROL, EDDIE (& GROUP)		
Rules Of Love/Gone From Me	1961	Guyden 2046
CARROLL BROTHERS		
Dearly Beloved/(My Gal Is)		
Red Hot	1958	Cameo 145
CARROLL, CATHY (BB THE EARLS)		
Jimmy Love/Deep In A Young		
Boy's Heart	1961	Triodex 11
Poor Little Puppet/Love And		
Learn	1962	Warner Bros. 5284
CARROLL, EDDIE (& GROUP)		
Wait Eternally/I'm Sorry	1962	Santo 504
CARROLL, YVONNE (& GROUP)		
Gee What A Guy/Stuck On You	1963	Domain 1018
My Sad Love/Earth Angel	1963	Domain 1020
CARTER QUARTET, EDDIE		
Don't Turn Your Back On		
Me/Eat 'Em Up	1953	MGM 11405
Take Everything But		
You/Cool Wailin' Papa	1954	Grand 107 (first pressing)

Artist Song	Year	Label
CARTER RAYS (AKA CARTERAYS)		
My Secret Love/Ding Dong Daddy	1957	Lyric 2001/Gone 5006 (57)
Bless You/Keep Listening To Your Heart	1961	Mala 433
CARTER RAYS (AKA CARTERAYS) (EDDIE CARTER & THE)		
Take Everything But You/Cool Wailin' Papa	1954	Grand 107 (second pressing)
CARTER RAYS (AKA CARTERAYS) (GLORIA MANN & THE)		
Goodnight, Sweetheart, Goodnight/Love-Me-Boy	1954	SLS 102/Jubilee 5142 (54)
CARTER, EDDIE (THE EDDIE CARTER QUINTET)		
Little Joe/Ooh Lovin' Baby	1975	Monogram 107
CARTER, MARTHA (& GROUP)		
Nobody Knows/I'm Through Crying	1961	Ron 336
CARTER, SONNY (& GROUP)		
Crying Over You/My Lonely Life	1959	Dot 15921
CARTERAYS (EDDIE CARTER & THE) (AKA CARTER RAYS)		
Ooh Baby/These Are The Things That Matter	1954	Sound 105
CARTERAYS (GLORIA MANN & THE)		
I'm Living My Life For You/The Waltz	1954	Sound 102
CARTHAYS		
Betty-Jo/So Bad	1961	Tag 446
CARUSO, DICK (& GROUP)		
Blue Denim/I'll Tell You In This Song	1959	MGM 12811
Teenage Blues/Playing The Field	1959	MGM 12827
If I/Dee Dee Dum	1960	MGM 12852
CARUSOS		
Confessions Of Love/Haunting Memories	1974	Roadhouse 1020
CARVELLS		
When We Get Married/Please Say You Want Me	1978	Clifton 30
CARVELS		
It's You, It's You I Love/I Love You So	1985	Relic LP 5050
CARVER, BOBBY (& GROUP)		
Never Leave Me/Roller Coaster	1962	Coral 62337
CARVETTES		
A Lover's Prayer/Never Gonna Leave Me	1959	Copa 200-1/200-2
CARYL, NAOMI (& GROUP)		
Before You Say Goodbye/ If You Want To Be My Baby	1956	Ember 1006
CASALS		
Eight O'Clock Scene/Teacher Crush	1961	Seville 105
CASANOVAS (1)		
That's All/Are You For Real?	1955	Apollo 471
It's Been A Long Time/Hush-A-Meca	1955	Apollo 474
I Don't Want You To Go/Please Be My Love	1955	Apollo 477
My Baby's Love/Sleepy Head Mama	1955	Apollo 483
Please Be Mine/For You And You Alone	1957	Apollo 519
You Are My Queen/(I Got A) Good Lookin' Baby	1958	Apollo 523
Pleading From My Heart To You	1989	Relic LP 5081
My Love For You	N/A	Apollo LP 1004/Relic LP 5073 (87)
Listen To The Bells	N/A	Apollo LP 1004/Relic LP 5073 (87)
Love Me Baby	N/A	Apollo LP 1004/Relic LP 5073 (87)
Night Rider	N/A	Apollo LP 1004/Relic LP 5073 (87)/Relic LP 5075 (88)
CASANOVAS (2)		
In My Land Of Dreams/Deep In The Heart Of The Jungle	1962	Planet 1027
CASANOVAS (LITTLE ROMEO & THE)		
Remember Lori/That's How Little Girls Get Boys	1965	Ascot 2192
CASCADES		
She Was Never Mine (To Lose)/My Best Girl	1964	Charter 1018
CASHER, BILLY (& GROUP)		
Give Her Back/No Matter What I Do	1961	Epic 9478
CASHIERS (EDDIE CASH & THE)		
Doing All Right/Land Of Promises	1958	Peak 1001
CASHMAN, TERRY (& GROUP)		
Pretty Face	1966	Boom 60005
CASHMERES (1)		
Yes Yes Yes/My Sentimental Heart	1954	Mercury 70501
Don't Let It Happen Again/ Boom Mag-Azeno Vip Vay	1955	Mercury 70617
There's A Rumor/Second Hand Heart	1955	Mercury 70679
Little Dream Girl/Do I Upset You?	1956	Herald 474
CASHMERES (2)		
Stairsteps To Heaven/Nag-Nag (Pack Your Bag)	1959	ACA 1216/1217
Everything's Gonna Be Alright/Four Lonely Nights	1960	Lake 703
Satisfied (Pt. 1)/Satisfied (Pt. 2)	1960	Lake 705/Relic 1005 (65)
Life-Line/Where Have You Been	1961	Josie 894
A Very Special Birthday/I Believe In St. Nick	1961	Laurie 3078
I Gotta Go/Singing Waters	1961	Laurie 3088
Baby Come On Home/Life Line	1961	Laurie 3105
CASHMERES (3) (DALE & THE)		
Last Night/Pete The Mongoose	1961	Matt 161
CASHMERES (4)		
This Moment/Darling You Send Me	N/A	Rubbertown 103
CASINOS (1)		
I'm Falling/Speedy	1959	Maske 803
CASINOS (2)		
My Love For You/Why Am I A Fool	1960	Casino 111
CASINOS (3)		
I Like It Like That/Baby Don't Do It	1961	Alto 2002
CASINOS (4)		
Please Let Her/When Love Was Born	1962	S&G 301
Please Let Her/When Love Is Born	1962	S&G 301
CASINOS (5)		
Do You Recall/Swim	1963	Itzy 404/Olimpic 251 (65)
CASINOS (6)		
Gee Whiz/Lovely One	1964	Terry 115
Too Good To Be True/That's The Way	1964	Terry 116/Airtown 886
CASLONS		
Anniversary Of Love/The Quiet One	1961	Seeco 6078
For All We Know/Settle Me Down	1962	Amy 836
CASTALEERS		
Come Back/Hi Fi Baby	1958	Felsted 8504
Lonely Boy/My Bull Fightin' Baby	1958	Felsted 8512
You're My Dream/I'll Be Around	1959	Felsted 8585
That's Why I Cry/My Baby's All Right	1960	Planet 44/Donna 1349 (61)
CASTANETS (FEMALE)		
I Love Him/Funky Wunky Piano	1963	TCF 1
CASTANETS (YOLANDA & THE)		
Meet Me After School/What About Me	1961	Tandem 7002
CASTAWAYS (1)		
Teasin'/I Wish	1954	Excello 2038
CASTAWAYS (2) (AKA IRIDESCENTS)		
I Found You/Hey There	1962	Assault 1869
CASTAWAYS (3) (TONY RIVERS & THE)		
I Love You/I Love The Way You Walk	1964	Constellation 128
CASTELLES		
My Girl Awaits Me/Sweetness	1953	Grand 101
This Silver Ring/Wonder Why	1954	Grand 103
Do You Remember/If You Were The Only Girl	1954	Grand 105
Over A Cup Of Coffee/Baby Can't You See	1954	Grand 109

Artist Song	Year	Label
Marcella/I'm A Fool To Care	1954	Grand 114
It's Christmas Time/Over The Rainbow	1954	Grand 118
Heavenly Father/My Wedding Day	1955	Grand 122
Happy And Gay/Hey, Baby, Baby	1956	Atco 6069
The Joke's On Me	N/A	Atco (unreleased)
Cheree	N/A	Atco (unreleased)
CASTELLES (GEORGE GRANT & THE)		
One Little Teardrop/At Christmas Time	1989	Classic Artists 114
Surrender To Love/Baby Please Don't Stop	1991	Classic Artists 126
CASTELLS		
Little Sad Eyes/Romeo	1961	Era 3038
Sacred/I Get Dreamy	1961	Era 3048
Make Believe Wedding/My Miracle	1961	Era 3057
The Vision Of You/Stiki De Boom Boom	1961	Era 3064
So This Is Love/On The Street Of Tears	1962	Era 3073
Oh What It Seemed To Be/Stand There Mountain	1962	Era 3083
Echoes In The Night/Only One	1962	Era 3089
Eternal Love, Eternal Spring/Clown Prince	1962	Era 3098
Initials/Little Sad Eyes	1963	Era 3102
What Do Little Girls Dream Of?/Some Enchanted Evening	1963	Era 3107
I Do (with Brian Wilson)/Teardrops	1964	Warner Bros. 5421
Could This Be You/Shinny Up Your Own Side	1964	Warner Bros. 5445
Love Finds A Way/Tell Her If I Could	1964	Warner Bros. 5486
An Angel Cried/Just Walk Away	1965	Decca 31834
Life Goes On/I Thought You'd Like That	1966	Decca 31967
In A Letter To Me/We Better Slow Down	1967	Solomon 1351
Rock Ridges/I'd Like To Know	1968	Laurie 3444
Two Lovers/Jerusalem	1968	United Artists 50324
Some Enchanted Evening/Jerusalem	1968	United Artists 50324
Save A Chance	N/A	Black Gold 306
CASTLE KINGS		
Loch Lomond/You Can Get Him-Frankenstein	1961	Atlantic 2107
Jeanette/The Caissons Go Rolling Along	1962	Atlantic 2158
CASTLE SISTERS		
Will You Love Me Tomorrow/Thirteen	1960	Roulette 4220
Goodbye Dad/Wishing Star	1962	Terrace 7506
CASTLE-TONES		
Goodnight/No Pork In The Beans	1959	Rift 502
We Met At A Dance/At The Hot Dog Stand	1960	Rift 504/Firefly 321 (74)
CASTON, BOBBY (& GROUP)		
Call Me Darling/Why Wasn't I Told	1957	Atlas 1103
CASTRO, VINCE (BB THE TONETTES)		
'Cause I Love You/Too Proud To Cry	1958	Apt 25025
Bong Bong (I Love You Madly)/You're My Girl	1958	Doe 102/Apt 25007 (58)
You're My Girl/Bongo Twist	1960	Apt 25047
CASTROES		
Dearest Darling/Dance With Me	1959	Grand 2002
CASTROS		
Lucky Me/Darling, I Fell For You	1959	Lasso 501
In My Dreams/Is It Right?	1959	Lasso 502
CASUAL CRESCENDOS		
Wish That You Were Here/Uncle Ben's Concentrated Blueberry Jam	1963	MRC 12001
CASUAL TEENS		
Need You So/She's Swinging	1958	Felsted 8529

Artist Song	Year	Label
CASUAL THREE (AKA CASUAL 3)		
Some Other Fellow/The Invisible Thing	1956	Luniverse 109
Candy Store Blues/Be-Bop Way Marie	1957	Mark-X 7009
CASUAL-AIRES		
Candy/Thunderbird	1958	Brunswick 55064
CASUALAIRS		
Satisfied/At The Dance	1959	Mona Lee 136
Cruising/Bossa Nova Twist	1961	Craig 5001
CASUALS (1) (AKA ORIGINAL CASUALS)		
Till You Come Back To Me/Hello Love	1957	Dot 15671
My Love Song For You/Somebody Help Me	1957	Nu-Sound 801/Dot 15557 (57)
So Tough/I Love My Darling	1958	Back Beat 503 (first pressing,second is by Original Casuals)
Someday/Siboney (instrumental)	1963	Moonbeam 71613
We Go Together/Pardners	N/A	Black Hawk 500
My Usual Self/Beautiful Friendship	N/A	Kern 2755
CASUALS (2) (GARY & THE)		
My One Desire/Someone Like You	1962	Vandan 609
CASUALS (3) (FB SUE KENNY)		
Look/Fool In Love	1963	Tribute 118
CASUALS (4) (HAROLD & THE)		
Darling Do You Love Me/You Can Shake A Tail Feather	1959	Scotty 628
CASUALS (5) (SKIP MAHONEY & THE)		
Wherever You Go	1976	Abet
CASUALTONES		
Summer School/The Very End	1963	Success 102
CATALINA 6		
Would You Believe It/Moon 2000	1962	Flagship 126
It Had To Rain/Baby Please Come Home	1962	Flagship 127/Candlelite 413 (62)
CATALINAS (1)		
Castle Of Love/Give Me Your Love	1958	Little 811/812/Jayne 502
CATALINAS (2)		
Long Walk/Destruction	1959	Fortune 535
CATALINAS (3) (AKA INVENTIONS)		
Marlene/With Your Girl	1958	Glory 285
Peanuts/Row Boat	1960	Up
CATALINAS (4)		
Speechless/Flying Formation With You	1958	Back Beat 513
Ring Of Stars/Wooly Wooly Willie	1960	Rita 107/Rita 1006 (60)
CATALINAS (5)		
Unchained Melody/Sweetheart	1961	20th Fox 286
Hey Little Girl/Hey Senorita	1961	Zebra 101
Safari/Pretty Little Nashville Girl	1963	20th Fox 299
Bail Out/Bulletin	1963	Dee Jay 1010/Sims 134 (63)
Stormy Weather/Whole Lot Of Lovin' To Do	1963	Million 77
Banzai Washout/Beach Walkin'	1963	Ric 113
Your Tender Lips/Gonna Tell	1964	Original Sound 48
Surfer Boy/Boss Barracuda	1966	Ric 164
You Haven't The Right/Tick Tock	1967	Scepter 12188
Why Do Fools Fall In Love/I'm So Tired	1973	Jayne 500
Castle Of Love/The Stars Tonight	1973	Jayne 501
I Love You/Give Me Your Love	1973	Jayne 502
Until Next Year/Litterbug	1973	Jayne 503
Back In My Arms/Blue Velvet	1973	Jayne 504
Hey Little Girl/Dancin' And Romancin'	1980	Catalinas 16560
Why Oh Why	N/A	Wonder 14
CATALINAS (6) (BILLY HUHN & THE)		
Baltimore/Freshman Queen	1962	Lesley 1923
CATALINAS (7) (PHIL & THE)		
Our Love Is So True/Clementine	1960	Olimpic (no number)
Bobby Layne/June 30th	1960	Olimpic (no number)/Triodex 106 (60)

Artist	Song	Year	Label
CATALINAS (8)			
	How I Love You/Jingles	1979	Crystal Ball 132
	That Lucky Old Sun/Who's		
	That Knocking	1979	Crystal Ball 135
CATAMOUNTS (CALVIN & THE)			
	Creation Of Love/I Know By		
	Baby Cares	1976	Catamount 131
CATES, RONNIE (BB THE TRAVELERS)			
	For My Very Own/Long Time	1962	Terrace 7508
CAVALIERS (1)			
	Honor Bright/Somewhere,		
	Sometime, Someday	1955	Decca 29556
	Nobodys Business If I Do	1958	Gilt-Edge 3935
	I Wanna Dance/Messed Up	1959	Tel 1006
	The Magic Age Of Sixteen/So		
	Young, So Warm, So Beautiful	1963	Music World 101
	Merry Christmas My Love	N/A	Herald (unreleased)
CAVALIERS (1) (FB SCOTT STEVENS)			
	Dance, Dance, Dance/Play By		
	The Rules Of Love	1958	Apt 25004
	Sunday In May/Why Why Why	1959	Apt 25031/ABC
CAVALIERS (1) (TOMMY ROCCO & THE)			
	Let There Be Love/Midnight		
	Train	1960	F-M 3264
CAVALIERS (2) (JERRY COX & THE)			
	Sherry/Debbie Jean	1959	Frantic 751
CAVALIERS (3) (LITTLE BERNIE & THE)			
	Lonely Soldier/The Waddle	1962	Jove 100
	Poor Town	N/A	Ascot 2183
CAVALIERS (4)			
	I Wanna Know/Put Your Trust		
	In Me	1962	Gum 1002
	The Right Time/The Quiver	1962	Gum 1004
CAVERLIERS QUARTET (FB ART SHELTON)			
(AKA FI-TONES/AKA CHANCES (2))			
	You Thrill Me So/Dynaflow	1954	Atlas 1031
CELEBRITIES (1)			
	Goodnight/You Didn't Tell		
	The Truth	1959	Boss 502
CELEBRITIES (2)			
	I Want You/Mambo Daddy	1961	Music Makers 101
CELEBRITYS			
	Juanita/This Is My Plea	1956	Caroline 2301
	We Made Romance/Absent		
	Minded	1956	Caroline 2302
CELESTIALS (BOBBY GEE & THE)			
	Blue Jean/Julie Is Mine	1959	Stacy 922
	Little Miss Fantasy/Sealed		
	With A Kiss	1960	XYZ 611
CELESTRALS			
	Alone/Alone	1963	Don-El 125
	Alone/Checkerboard Love	1963	Don-El 125
CELLOS			
	Rang Tang Ding Dong (I Am		
	The Japanese Sandman)/		
	You Took My Love	1957	Apollo 510
	Juicy Crocodile/Under Your		
	Spell	1957	Apollo 515
	The Be-Bop Mouse/Girlie		
	That I Love	1957	Apollo 516
	I Beg For Your Love/What's		
	The Matter For You?	1958	Apollo 524
	Doo Doo Wah	1988	Relic LP 5074 (88)
	Buffalo Bill	1988	Relic LP 5074 (88)
	Love That Girl	1988	Relic LP 5074 (88)
CELTICS (1)			
	Can You Remember/Send Me		
	Someone To Love	1957	Al Jacks 2
	I Can Remember	1957	Al-Jack's 1
	Darlene Darling/Only The		
	Lonely	1960	War Conn 2216
CELTICS (1) (BOBBY LANZ & THE)			
	Let Them Talk/If This World		
	Were Mine	1973	Bridges 5003
	Sinner Man	N/A	Bridges 2204
CELTICS (2)			
	Wondering Why	N/A	Coronado 133
CELTICS (3)			
	And She'll Cry	N/A	Linjo 106
CENTENNIALS			
	My Dear One/The Wayward		
	Wind	1961	Dot 16180
CENTURIANS			
	We Mean More To Each Other/		
	Since You Left My World	1959	Tiger 1001
CENTURIES (1)			
	In This Whole World/Mine,		
	All Mine	1961	Life 501
CENTURIES (2) (RONNIE & THE)			
	I Don't Care/Mister Mirror	1962	Luna 3076
CENTURIES (3) (AKA JAYTONES/AKA REVLONS (3))			
	Crying For You/Oh Darling		
	(by the Jaytones)	1963	Times Square 5
	Betty/Ride Away (by the		
	Revlons (3))	1963	Times Square 15
	Crying For You/Betty	N/A	Klik
CENTURIES (4)			
	I'd Cry For You	N/A	Rich 102
	Just Today/Don't Let It Fade		
	Away	N/A	Rich 112
CENTURIES (5)			
	Please Don't Go	1985	Relic LP 5053
	When I'm With You	1985	Relic LP 5053
	Time After Time	1985	Relic LP 5053
	Willette	1985	Relic LP 5053
CENTURYS			
	Take My Hand/Oh Joe, Joe	1959	Fortune 533
	Strollin' Time/Paradiddle	1960	Veltone 104
CEZANNES (FEATURING CERRESSA)			
	Pardon Me/All At Once	1963	Markay 108
CHADONS			
	Let's Start All Over Again/It's A		
	Crying Shame	1964	Chattahoochie 664
CHAINS			
	I Can Learn/It Happens This		
	Way	1963	Peacock 1922
CHALETS			
	Fat-Fat-Fat! Mom-Mi-O/Who's		
	Laughing Who's Crying	1961	Tru-Lite 1001/Dart 1026 (61)/Musicnote 1115 (61)
	My Foolish Heart/Walking My		
	Baby Back Home	1982	L.I.R.R.A. 1000
	Fat Fat Mommio/Lily Maebelle	1984	Starlight 20
CHALLENGERS (1) (WALTER WARD & THE) (AKA OLYMPICS)			
	I Can Tell/The Mambo Beat	1957	Melatone 1002
CHALLENGERS (2) (AKA EXECUTIVES (2))			
	Honey, Honey, Honey/Stay	1962	Tri-Phi 1012
	The Butterfly/Who Shot The		
	Hole In My Sombrero	1962	Tri-Phi 1015/Challenge 1105 (62)
	Why/Come On Baby	1963	Explosive 3621-10
	Before You	N/A	GNP Crescendo 400
CHALLENGERS III (AKA CHALLENGERS (2))			
	Every Day/I Hear An Echo	1962	Tri-Phi 1020
CHALONS			
	Oh You/Leave Me Baby	1958	Dice 89
CHAMP, BILLY (& GROUP)			
	Hush-A-Bye/Believe Me	1964	ABC 10518
CHAMPAGNES			
	Crazy/Cash	1963	Skymac 1002/Laurie 3189 (63)
CHAMPIONS			
	Annie Met Henry/		
	Keep-A-Rockin'	1954	Scott/Chart 602
	The Same Old Story/Pay Me		
	Some Attention	1956	Chart 620
	Come On/Big Bad Beulah	1956	Chart 631
	It's Love, It's Love/Mexico		
	Bound	1956	Scott 1201/Chart 611
	I'm So Blue/Cute Little Baby	1958	Ace 541 (duplicate # IS correct!)
	I Do/My Heart	1958	Ace 541 (duplicate # IS correct)
CHAMPLAINS (FB FRED PARRIS)			
	Ding Dong/Have You		
	Changed Your Mind?	1961	United Artists 346
CHAMPS (1) (TONY ALLEN & THE)			
	Nite Owl/I	1955	Specialty 560
CHAMPS (2) (AKA MYSTICS (2))			
	Teenage Sweetheart/Rockin'		
	Yodel	N/A	Chatam 350
CHANACLAIRS			
	Yuletide Love/See See Rider	1955	Coleman 1056

Artist	Song	Year	Label
CHANCE, WAYNE (& GROUP)			
	Send Her To Me/Just A Little Bit O' Lovin'	1964	Whirlybird 2006
CHANCELLORS (1) (AKA FIVE CHANCELLORS)			
	Too Many Memories/Everything Has Its Place	1956	Unique 341
	There Goes My Girl/Tell Me You Love Me	1957	Port 5000
	I'm Coming Home/Gotta Little Baby	1957	XYZ 104/XYZ 601 (59)
	Seaport At Sunset/Chalypso Train	1958	XYZ 105
	I Really Really Do/My Thoughts To You	1959	Storm 503
CHANCELLORS (2)			
	Sad Avenue/All The Way From Heaven	1959	Capacity 61023
	Upside Down/Straightaway	1962	Brent 7031
	Yo Yo/Little Latin Lupe Lu	1965	Soma 1421
	So Fine	1965	Soma 1435
	My Girl/Jenny Jenny	1965	USA 783
	Once In A Million/Journey	1966	Fenton 2066
	Dear John/5 Minus 3	1966	Fenton 2072
CHANCERS			
	Shirley Ann/My One	1958	Dot 15870
CHANCES (1) (FEMALE)			
	One More Chance/It Takes More Than A Loan	1961	Bea & Baby 130
CHANCES (2) (AKA CAVERLIERS QUARTET/AKA FI-TONES)			
	Through A Long And Sleepless Night/What Would You Say?	1964	Roulette 4549
CHANCES (3) (CHUCK CORBY & THE)			
	Happy Go Lucky	N/A	Sound 717
CHANDELIERS (1) (AKA CHANDELIERS QUINTET)			
	Wild Cherry	1958	Angle Tone (unreleased)
	Blueberry Sweet/One More Step	1958	Angle Tone 521
	Dolly/Dancin' In The Congo	1958	Angle Tone 529
	Tender Love	1973	Relic LP 5012
CHANDELIERS (2)			
	Give Me Your Love/She's A Heartbreaker	1962	Sue 761
CHANDELIERS (3)			
	Once More/Bicycle Hop	1962	Du-Well 102
CHANDELIERS (4)			
	It's A Good Thought/Double Love	1964	Loadstone 1601
CHANDLER, GENE (BB THE DUKAYS)			
	Duke Of Earl/Kissin' In The Kitchen	1961	Vee Jay 416/Nat 4003 (62)
	Walk On With The Duke/London Town	1962	Vee Jay 440
CHANDLER, LENNY (& GROUP)			
	Wait For Me/Heart	1963	Laurie 3158
CHANELLS			
	Give Me A Chance/Butterball (by the Butterballs)	1963	Times Square 24
CHANELS (AKA FIVE CHANELS) (FEMALE)			
	The Reason/Skidilly Doo	1958	Deb 500
CHANNELLS (AKA CHANNELS (2))			
	In My Arms To Stay/You Hurt Me	1963	Hit Record 700
CHANNELS (1) (EARL LEWIS & THE)			
	The Closer You Are/Now You Know (I Love You So)	1956	Whirlin' Disc 100/Port 70014 (59)
	The Gleam In Your Eyes/Stars In The Sky	1956	Whirlin' Disc 102/Port 70017 (60)
	I Really Love You/What Do You Do?	1956	Whirlin' Disc 107/Port 70023 (60)
	My Love Will Never Die/Bye Bye Baby	1957	Fury 1021/Fury 1071 (58)
	That's My Desire/Stay As You Are	1957	Gone 5012
	Flames In My Heart/My Loving Baby	1957	Whirlin' Disc 109/Port 70022 (61)
	Altar Of Love/All Alone	1958	Gone 5019
	My Heart Is Sad/The Girl Next Door	1959	Fire 1001
	Gloria (recorded in 1956)/You Said You Loved Me (recorded in 1956)	1971	Channel 1000
	She Blew My Mind/Breaking Up Is Hard To Do	1971	Rare Bird 5017
	We Belong Together/Hey Girl, I'm In Love With You	1972	Channel 1001
	You Got What It Takes/Crazy Mixed Up World	1972	Channel 1002
	Close Your Eyes/Work With Me Annie	1973	Channel 1003
	Over Again/In My Arms To Stay	1973	Channel 1004
	A Thousand Miles Away/Don't Let The Green Grass Fool You	1974	Channel 1006
	You Came To Me/Tell Me Baby	1978	King Tut 173
	I'm Sorry You're Gone/Dear Lord	1978	King Tut 174
	Yo Te Quiro (I Love You)/22 Years Of Love	1978	King Tut 175
	The Closer You Are/Donna	1987	Soul Jam 712
	Do What Lovers Do/You Promised Me Love	1990	Classic Artists 124
	What Do You Do (Fast Ver.)	N/A	Collectables LP 5012
CHANNELS (2) (AKA CHANNELLS)			
	My Love/Sad Song	1963	Enjoy 2001
	Anything You Do/I've Got My Eyes On You	1964	Groove 0046
	You Can Count On Me/Old Chinatown	1965	Groove 0061
CHANNELS (2) (EDIE & THE)			
	Did I Hear You Right/Love's Burning Fire	1963	Ember 584/Herald 584 (63)
CHANNELS (3)			
	Lonely	1959	Mercury
	Earthquake/Jungle Lights	1959	Mercury 71501
CHANSONAIRES			
	If You Were Here Tonight/Love Always Finds The Way	1958	Hamilton 50012
CHANTECLAIRS			
	Baby Please/Someday My Love Will Come My Way	1954	Dot 1227
	Believe Me My Beloved/I've Never Been There	1955	Dot 15404
CHANTEERS			
	She's Coming Home/Mr. Zebra	1962	Mercury 71979
	I Waited/Just A Little Boy	1962	Mercury 72037
CHANTELS (FEMALE)			
	He's Gone/The Plea	1957	End 1001
	Tasty Kisses	1957	unreleased
	Maybe/Come, My Little Baby	1958	End 1005
	Every Night (I Pray)/Whoever You Are	1958	End 1015
	I Love You So/How Could You Call It Off	1958	End 1020
	Prayee/Sure Of Love	1958	End 1026
	Congratulations/If You Try	1958	End 1030
	I Can't Take It (There's Our Song Again)/Never Let Me Go	1958	End 1037
	Memories Of You	1958	End EP 202/End LP 312 (61)
	C'est Si Bon	1958	End EP 202/End LP 312 (61)
	I'll Walk Alone	1958	End EP 202/End LP 312 (61)
	I've Cried	1958	unreleased
	I'm Confessin'/Goodbye To Love	1959	End 1048
	Two Loving Hearts	1959	unreleased
	Miracle Of Love	1959	unreleased
	Chantel Rock	1959	unreleased
	Whoever You Are/How Could You Call It Off	1960	End 1069
	Love, Love, Love/He Knows I Love Him Too Much	1961	Big Top 3073
	Look In My Eyes/Glad To Be Back	1961	Carlton 555
	Well I Told You/I Still	1961	Carlton 564
	Here It Comes Again/Summertime	1961	Carlton 569
	There's Our Song Again/I'm The Girl	1961	End 1105
	My Darlin'	1961	End LP 312
	Ific	1961	End LP 312/Murray Hill LP 000385 (87)
	Cotton Fields	1961	unreleased
	You'll Never Know	1962	Carlton LP 144
	Eternally/Swamp Water	1963	Ludix 101
	Some Tears Fall Dry/That's Why You're Happy	1963	Ludix 106

Artist Song	Year	Label
Everything/Good Girls	1963	Spectorious 150
Take Me As I Am/There's No Forgetting You	1965	TCF-Arrawak 123
From This Moment On	1966	unreleased
Lonely Am I	1966	unreleased
Lover's Chant	1966	unreleased
Soul Of A Soldier/You're Welcome To My Heart	1966	Verve 10387
It's Just Me/Indian Giver	1966	Verve 10435
Maybe/He's Gone	1969	Roulette 7064
I'm Gonna Win Him Back/Love Makes All The Difference In The World	1970	RCA 0347
So Real	1987	Murray Hill LP 000385
Peruvian Wedding Song	1987	Murray Hill LP 000385
CHANTELS (FEMALE) (ACTUALLY THE VENEERS)		
Believe Me (My Angel)/I	1960	Princeton 102/End 1103 (61)
CHANTERS (1)		
Tell Me, Thrill Me/She Wants To Mambo	1954	RPM 415
Lonesome Me/Golden Apple	1955	Kem 2740
Do You Remember	1988	Relic LP 5076
CHANTERS (1) (BROTHER WOODMAN & THE)		
Why?/Watts	1955	Combo 78
CHANTERS (1) (GENE FORD & THE)		
I Love You/Hot Mamma	1955	Combo 92
CHANTERS (2)		
My My Darling/I Need Your Tenderness (I Love You Darling)	1958	DeLuxe 6162
Row Your Boat/Stars In The Skies	1958	DeLuxe 6166
Five Little Kisses/Angel Darling	1958	DeLuxe 6172
I Make This Pledge (To You)/No, No, No	1961	DeLuxe 6191
At My Door/My My Darling	1961	DeLuxe 6194
Row Your Boat/No, No, No	1963	DeLuxe 6200
Free As A Bird/Bongo Bongo	1967	MGM 13750
Heavenly You/What Are You Doing	N/A	SSP
CHANTERS (2) (BUD JOHNSON & THE)		
No, No, No/Over The Rainbow	1958	DeLuxe 6177
CHANTEURS (1)		
New Rockin' Baby/Wishin' Well	1961	La Salle 501
You've Got A Great Love/The Grizzly Bear	1963	Vee Jay 519 (63)
CHANTEURS (2)		
No Doubt About It/Mr. Jones	1963	Bolo 745
CHANTICLEERS		
To Keep Your Love/Daddy Must Be	1958	Lyric 103
Necklace Of Roses/Green Satin	1963	Old Town 1137
CHANTIERS		
Peppermint/Dear Mr. Clock	1964	DJB 112
CHANTIERS (RODNEY BAKER & THE)		
Teenage Wedding Song/Graduation	1961	Jan Ell 8
CHANTONES		
It's Just A Summer Love/Five Little Numbers	1958	Carlton 485
Dear Diary/Cocoanuts And Palm Trees	1959	TNT 167
Tangerock/Don't Open That Door	1960	Top Rank 2066
Stormy Weather/Sweet Georgia Brown	1961	Capitol 4661
CHANTS		
Come Go With Me/I Don't Care	1963	Cameo 268/Pye 15557
CHANTS (1)		
Close Friends/Lost And Found	1958	Capitol 3949
Respectable/Kiss Me Goodbye	1961	Tru Eko 3567/UWR 4243 (61)MGM 13008 (61)
Dick Tracy/Choo-Choo	1961	Verve 10244
Surfside/Chicken 'N Gravy	1968	Checker 1209
CHANTS (2) (LITTLE JERRY & THE)		
Ooh Wee Baby/The Shape You Left Me In	1960	Ace 606
CHANTS (3)		
Heaven And Paradise/When I'm With You	1960	Nite Owl 40
Come Go With Me/I Don't Care	1963	Cameo 277

Artist Song	Year	Label
A Thousand Stars/I Could Write A Book	1964	Cameo 297/Pye 15591
She's Mine/Then I'll Be Home	1964	Interphon 7703
CHANTS (4) (JIMMY SOUL & THE)		
Respectable/I Wish I Could Dance (no group)	1963	20th Fox 413
CHANTS (5) (CASANOVA & THE)		
Geraldine/I Know You	N/A	Sapphire 2254
CHAPARRALS (FEATURING TOOTER BOATMAN)		
Sweet Lies/Pool Gal	1958	Rebel 108
CHAPELAIRES		
I'm Still In Love With You/Not Good Enough	1961	Hac 101
Gloria/Under Hawaiian Skies	1961	Hac 102
CHAPELAIRES (JONI KAY & THE)		
Lonely Star/Happy Memories	1964	Gateway 744
It's Impossible, Why Try/Vacation Time	1965	Gateway 746
CHAPERONES (1)		
Cruise To The Moon/Dance With Me	1960	Josie 880 (second pressing, first is by the Cahperones)/Port
Shining Star/My Shadow And Me	1962	Josie 885
The Man From The Moon/Blueberry Sweet	1963	Josie 891
CHAPERONES (2) (MARIA MAE & THE)		
Teenage Love/Till The End Of Our Days	1961	Phantom 986
CHAPMAN, GRADY (BB THE SUEDES)		
I Need You So/Don't Blooper	1955	Money 204
Say You Will Be Mine/Starlight Starbright	1958	Knight 2003
Let's Talk About Us/Come Away	1959	Imperial 5611
CHAPPIES		
Suddenly There Were Tears/Big Beach Bully	N/A	Chelton 750
CHAPS		
They'll Never Be/Heaven Must Have Run Out Of Angels	1959	Matador 1814
One Lovely Yesterday/Perfect Night For Love	1960	Brent 7016
CHAPTERS (1)		
Goodbye My Love/Love You, Love You	1953	Republic 7038
CHAPTERS (1) (HELEN FOSTER & THE)		
They Tell Me/Somebody, Somewhere	1953	Republic 7037
CHAPTERS (2) (REUBEN & THE)		
Cara Mia/Zing Went The Strings Of My Heart	1979	Surfside 3
CHARADES		
Make Me Happy Baby/Shang Lang A Ding Dong	1958	United Artists 132
Let Me Love You/Bright Red Skinny Pants	1959	United Artists 183
For You/Sophia	1962	Northridge 1002
Please Be My Love Tonight/Turn Him Down	1963	Ava 154
Christina/Surf 'N' Stomp	1964	Impact 2
Close To Me/Take A Chance	1964	Original Sound 47
Flamingo/Someone's In The Kitchen With Dinah	1964	Skylark 502
Hey, Operator/He's Not Your Boyfriend	1964	Warner Bros. 5415
Please Be My Love/Bells Of Rosa Rita (by the Admirations)	N/A	Popular Request 107
CHARGERS (1)		
Large Charge	1959	B.E.A.T. 1006
CHARGERS (2) (FB JESSE BELVIN)		
Old MacDonald/Dandelion	1958	RCA 7301
Here In My Heart/The Counterfeiter	1958	RCA 7417
CHARIOTS		
Gloria/A Sunday Morning Love	1959	Time 1006/Brent
Open House/A Tiger In Your Tank	1964	RSVP 1105
CHARLES, JIMMY (WITH THE REVELETTS)		
A Million To One/Hop Scotch Hop	1960	Promo 1002
The Age For Love/Follow The Swallow	1960	Promo 1003

Artist Song	Year	Label
CHARLES, NICK (& GROUP)		
For You/I Wonder	1961	Guyden 2049
CHARLETTES		
The Fight's Not Over/Whatever		
Happened To Our Love	1963	Angie 1002
CHARLETTES (LARRY & THE)		
Love Notes/Judy	1963	Sapien 1004
CHARLIE & DON (& GROUP)		
Young Man's Fancy/Hush		
Little Baby	1962	Duel 513
CHARM		
It's So Hard To Say Goodbye		
To Yesterday (rec. 1983)/		
Morse Code Of Love	1992	Clifton 98
CHARMAINES		
If You Were Mine/Rockin'		
Old Man	1961	Fraternity 873
What Kind Of Girl (Do You		
hink I Am)/All You Gotta Do	1961	Fraternity 880
Where Is The Boy Tonight/On		
The Wagon	1962	Dot 16351
Where Is The Boy Tonight/		
Walking Down Main Street	1996	Saxony 2005
CHARMANES (YOLANDA & THE)		
There Oughta Be A Law	1962	Smash 1777
CHARMERS (1)		
The Beating Of My Heart/Why		
Does It Have To Be Me	1954	Central 1002
Tony, My Darling/In The Rain	1954	Central 1006
I Was Wrong/The Mambo	1954	Timely 1009
The Church On The Hill/Battle		
Axe	1954	Timely 1011
For Sentimental Reasons	N/A	Relic LP 5051 (85)
CHARMERS (2)		
All Alone/Johnny My Dear	1956	Aladdin 3337
He's Gone/Oh! Yes	1956	Aladdin 3341
CHARMERS (3)		
Letters Don't Have Arms/Rock		
Rhythm And Blues	1957	Silhouette 522
CHARMERS (3) (JIM BEASLEY & THE)		
Caught Raped And Tied	1957	Silhouette 519
CHARMERS (4)		
Little Fool/Hard To Get	1961	Jaf 2021
The Letter/Watch What You Do	1963	Co-Rec 101
CHARMERS (5) (PRINCE CHARLES & THE)		
Good Luck Charm/Twistin' At		
The Pool	1962	Class 301
CHARMERS (6)		
Visiting Day/Whatever		
Happened To Baby Jane?	1962	Terrace 7512
CHARMERS (6) (MARK STEVENS & THE)		
Magic Rose/Come Back To		
My Heart	1962	Allison 921
CHARMERS (7)		
Johnny/My Kind Of Love	1962	Laurie 3142
I Cried/Shy Guy	1963	Laurie 3173
Sweet Talk/Work It Out	1963	Laurie 3203
Looking For Trouble/After You		
Walk Me Home	1964	Pip 8000
It's A Funny Way We Met/		
Where's The Boy	1965	Louis 6806
CHARMERS (8)		
Lesson From The Stars/My Love	1963	Sure Play 104
CHARMERS (9) (JANICE CHRISTIAN & JOHNNY & THE)		
Promises/Just A Bad Thing	1964	Swan 4174
CHARMETTES (FEMALE)		
Skating In The Blue Light/My		
Love	1958	Hi 2003
School Letter/Johnny, Johnny	1959	Federal 12345
I Love You To The Nth Degree/		
Deeds To My Heart	1960	Mona 553
Donnie/Too Much True Lovin'	1962	Markay 101
One More Time/Surrender My		
Love	1962	Marlin 16001
On A Night Like Tonight/Why		
Oh Why	1962	Tri Disc 103
Please Don't Kiss Me Again/		
What Is A Tear	1963	Kapp 547
0021-0021-Ooh/He's A		
Wise Guy	1964	Kapp 570
My Lover Is A Boy Scout/Mailbox	1964	Mala 491
Sugar Boy/Stop The Wedding	1965	World Artists 1053

Artist Song	Year	Label
CHARMS (1) (OTIS WILLIAMS & HIS) (REF O.W. & HIS NEW GROUP)		
Rollin' Home/Do Be You	1956	DeLuxe 6092
Ivory Tower/In Paradise	1956	DeLuxe 6093
It's All Over/One Night Only	1956	DeLuxe 6095
Whirlwind/I'd Like To Thank		
You Mr. D.J.	1956	DeLuxe 6097
Gypsy Lady/I'll Remember You	1956	DeLuxe 6098
Pardon Me/Blues Stay Away		
From Me	1957	DeLuxe 6105
Walkin' After Midnight/I'm		
Waiting Just For You	1957	DeLuxe 6115
Nowhere On Earth/No Got De		
Woman	1957	DeLuxe 6130
One Kind Word From You/		
Talking To Myself	1957	DeLuxe 6137
United/Don't Deny Me	1957	DeLuxe 6138
Well Oh Well/Dynamite Darling	1957	DeLuxe 6149
Could This Be Magic/Oh Julie	1958	DeLuxe 6158
Let Some Love In Your Heart/		
Baby-O	1958	DeLuxe 6160
Burnin' Lips/Red Hot Love		
(Oo This Love)	1958	DeLuxe 6165
You'll Remain Forever/Don't		
Wake Up The Kids	1958	DeLuxe 6174
My Prayer Tonight/Watch Dog	1959	DeLuxe 6183
I Knew It All The Time/Tears		
Of Happiness	1959	DeLuxe 6185
Creation Of Love/Away (by the		
Jacks)	1974	Owl 329
Happy Are We/What Do You		
Know About That	1953	DeLuxe 6014
Heaven Only Knows/Loving		
Baby	1953	Rockin' 516/DeLuxe 6000 (53)
Please Believe In Me/Bye		
Bye Baby	1954	DeLuxe 6034
Quiet Please/Fifty-Five Seconds	1954	DeLuxe 6050
My Baby Dearest Darling/		
Come To Me Baby	1954	DeLuxe 6056
Hearts Of Stone/Who Knows?	1954	DeLuxe 6062
Two Hearts/The First Time		
We Met	1954	DeLuxe 6065
Crazy, Crazy Love/Mambo		
Sh-Mambo	1954	DeLuxe 6072
Ling, Ting, Tong/Bazoom		
(I Need Your Lovin')	1955	DeLuxe 6076
Ko Ko Mo (I Love You So)/		
Whadaya Want	1955	DeLuxe 6080
Crazy, Crazy Love/Whadaya		
Want	1955	DeLuxe 6082
When We Get Together/Let		
The Happening Happen	1955	DeLuxe 6087
One Fine Day/It's You, Yes You	1955	DeLuxe 6089
That's Your Mistake/Too Late I		
Learned (by O.W. & His		
New Group)	1956	DeLuxe 6091
My Friends/Secret	1958	DeLuxe 6178
Welcome Home/Pretty Little		
Things Called Girls	1959	DeLuxe 6181
In Paradise/Who Knows	1959	DeLuxe 6186
Blues Stay Away From Me/Funny		
What True Love Can Do	1959	DeLuxe 6187
It's A Treat/Chief Um	1960	King 5323
Silver Star/Rickety Rickshaw		
Man	1960	King 5332
Image Of A Girl/Wait A Minute		
Baby	1960	King 5372
So Be It/First Sign Of Love	1960	King 5389
Wait/And Take My Love	1960	King 5421
Little Turtle Dove/So Can I	1961	King 5455
You Know I Care/Just Forget		
About Me	1961	King 5497
Panic/Pardon Me	1961	King 5527
The Secret/Two Hearts	1961	King 5558
When We Get Together/Only		
Young Once	1961	King 5682
Baby, You Turn Me On/Love		
Don't Grow On Trees	1965	Okeh 7225
I Fall To Pieces/Gotta Get		
Myself Together	1966	Okeh 7235
Welcome Home/I Got Loving	1966	Okeh 7248
Your Sweet Love/Ain't Gonna		
Walk Your Dog No More	1966	Okeh 7261

Artist Song	Year	Label
CHARMS (1) (REF O.W. & HIS NEW GROUP)		
Love's Our Inspiration/Love		
Love Stick Stov	1955	Chart 608
Heart Of A Rose/I Offer You	1956	Chart 613
I'll Be True/Boom Diddy Boom		
Boom	1956	Chart 623
CHARMS (1) (TINY TOPSY & THE)		
Come On, Come On, Come On/		
Ring Around My Finger	1957	Federal 12309
CHARMS (2) (TOMMY G & THE)		
I Want You So Bad/I Know		
What I Want	1961	Hollywood 1109
CHARTBUSTERS		
She's The One/Slippin'		
Through Your Fingers	1964	Mutual 502
CHARTERS (1)		
My Rose/El Merengue	1962	Tarx 1003
CHARTERS (2)		
I Lost You/My Little Girl	1963	Alva 1001
Lost In A Dream/This Makes		
Me Mad	1963	Merry-Go-Round 103
CHARTS		
Deserie/Zoop	1957	Everlast 5001/Everlast 5026 (63)/Lost Nite 173 (81)
Dance Girl/Why Do You Cry	1957	Everlast 5002/Lost Nite 180 (81)
You're The Reason/I've Been		
Wondering	1957	Everlast 5006/Lost Nite 186 (81)
All Because Of Love/I Told		
You So	1957	Everlast 5008
My Diane/Baby Be Mine	1957	Everlast 5010
Ooba-Gooba/For The Birds	1959	Guyden 2021
Desiree/Fell In Love With You		
Baby	1966	Wand 1112
Livin' The Night Life/Nobody		
Made You Love Me	1966	Wand 1124
CHASE, BOBBY (& GROUP)		
Missing Someone/Knowing It		
Was Heartbreak	1965	Ascot 2195
CHASE, EDDIE (& GROUP)		
If You Only Knew/Ginger	1959	Viscount 529
CHATEAUS (1)		
Let Me Tell You, Baby/Darling		
Je Vous Aime Beaucoup	1956	Epic 9163
Brown Eyes/Satisfied	1958	Warner Bros. 5023
The Masquerade Is Over/If I		
Didn't Care	1959	Warner Bros. 5043
Ladder Of Love/You'll Reap		
What You Sow	1959	Warner Bros. 5071
CHATEAUS (2)		
Honest I Will/Summer's Here	1963	Coral 62364
CHATTERS		
My Darling One/Teenage		
Love Affair	1959	Viking 1001
CHAUNTES		
Bohemian Love	N/A	Tonix 15
CHAVELLES (AKA UNTOUCHABLES/AKA SABERS)		
Valley Of Love/Red Tape	1956	Vita 127
CHAVIS BROTHERS (AKA FIVE CHAVIS BROTHERS)		
Baby Don't Leave Me/Old		
Time Rock And Roll	1961	Coral 62270
So Tired/I Love You	1962	Clock 1025
CHEATERS		
You're Mine/Barefootin'	1964	Raynard 1056
Suzanne	1965	Wax 213
Please Come Home	N/A	JBJ
CHECK MATES		
Hey Mrs. Jones, Pt. 1/Hey		
Mrs. Jones, Pt. 2	1961	Arvee 5030
Swingin' Summer	N/A	Arvee 5037
CHECKER DOTS		
Alpha Omega/All I Hear	1959	Peacock 1688
CHECKER, CHUBBY (BB THE DREAMLOVERS)		
The Twist/Toot (no group)	1960	Parkway 811
CHECKERS		
Flame In My Heart/Oh Oh		
Oh Baby	1952	King 4558
Night Curtains/Let Me Come		
Back	1952	King 4581
My Prayer Tonite/Love Wasn't		
There	1953	King 4596

Artist Song	Year	Label
Ghost Of My Baby/I Wanna		
Know	1953	King 4626
You Never Had It So Good/		
I Promise You	1954	King 4673
White Cliffs Of Dover/Without		
A Song	1954	King 4675
House With No Windows/		
Don't Stop Dan	1954	King 4710
Over The Rainbow/You've		
Been Fooling Around	1954	King 4719
I Wasn't Thinkin', I Was		
Drinkin'/Mama's Daughter	1954	King 4751
Can't Find My Sadie/Tryin' To		
Hold My Gal	1955	King 4764
Heaven Only Knows/Nine		
More Miles	1958	King 5156
So Fine/Sentimental Heart	1959	Federal 12355
Teardrops Are Falling/Rocka		
Locka (by the Five Wings)	1959	King 5199/King 4781 (55) (as the Five Wings)
White Cliffs Of Dover/Let Me		
Come Back	1960	Federal 12375
CHECKMATES (1) (EMIL FORD & THE)		
What Do You Want To Make		
Those Eyes At Me For?/		
Don't Tell Me Your Troubles	1959	Andie 5018/Cub 9063 (60)
CHECKMATES (2)		
What Do You Do/Shoo-be		
Shoo-be do	1962	Regency 26
CHEERETTES (FEMALE)		
Lullabye My Love/Told The		
Sunshine	1956	Vita 143/Vita 145 (56)
CHEERIOS (1)		
Ding Dong Honeymoon/Where		
Are You Tonight	1961	Infinity 11/Golden Oldies 1 (61)
CHEERIOS (2) (BOBBY LONG & THE)		
Flip Flop/Station Hurt	1963	Cub 9120
CHEERTONES		
Rose Anna/I'll Come To You	1961	ABC 10277
CHELL-MARS (AKA CHELMARS)		
Roamin' Heart/Feel All Right	1963	Jamie 1266
CHELLOS		
Have You Heard/Fatso	1961	Columbia 42044
CHELLOWS		
I Want To Be A Part Of You/Be		
My Baby	1961	Poncello 713
Candy Girl/Hello Muddah,		
Hello Faddah (by Dick Martin)	1964	Hit 77
Rag Doll/A Hard Day's Night		
(by the Jalopy Five)	1966	Hit 134
Barbara Ann/No Matter What		
Shape (by the Upsetters)	N/A	Hit 237
CHELMARS (AKA CHELL-MARS)		
Confess/Jigsaw Puzzle	1962	Select 712
CHEQUES		
A Thousand Miles Away/		
Go On, Girl	1969	Sur-Speed 214
CHERLOS		
Tell It Like It Is/99 1/2 Won't Do	1956	Ultra D'Or 8
Little Little	N/A	Relic LP 5022
Cry Fool	N/A	Relic LP 5022
CHEROKEES (1)		
Rainbow Of Love/I Had A Thrill	1954	Grand 106
Please Tell Me So/Remember		
When?	1954	Grand 110
Is She Real?/Drip, Drip,		
The Coffee Grinder	1955	Peacock 1656
Brenda/By The Candleglow	N/A	Lost Nite 379/Grand 111 (78)
CHEROKEES (2)		
My Heavenly Angel/Bed Bug	1961	United Artists 367
CHEROKEES (3)		
It's Gonna Work Out Fine	N/A	Gary
CHERUBS		
Julie, Julie (16 & 23)/They		
Go Ape	1960	Dore 545
CHERYL ANN (& GROUP)		
Goodbye Baby/I Can't Let Him	N/A	Patty 52
CHESSMEN (1)		
Du-Whop/I Live For You	1958	Mirasonic 1002/Mirasonic 1868 (58)
Keeper Of My Love/Why	1959	Safari 1011

Artist Song	Year	Label
Mr. Cupid/What's To Become Of Me	1962	AMC 101/Don-Dee 101 (62)/Mercury 72559 (65)
Stormy Dreams/Pick It Up	1962	Amy 841
Voyage/Sorry	1964	G-Clef 707
I Apologize (acapella)/Dance (acapella)	1965	Relic 1015
Ways Of Romance (acapella)/ Heavenly Father (acapella)	1965	Relic 1016
Stars Fell (acapella)/That's My Desire	1965	Relic 1017
Don't Have To Shop Around (acapella)/Love Is What The World Is Made Of (acapella)	1965	Relic 1020
Two Kinds Of People (acapella)	1975	Relic LP 101
For All We Know (acapella)	1975	Relic LP 101/Relic LP 106 (75)
All Nite Long (acapella)	1975	Relic LP 101/Relic LP 106 (75)
A Teardrop (acapella)	1975	Relic LP 102
Sentimental Reasons (acapella)	1975	Relic LP 102
Let Me Come Back (acapella)	1975	Relic LP 102
Is Everybody Happy (acapella)	1975	Relic LP 102/Relic LP 106 (75)
I Want To Dance (acapella)	1975	Relic LP 102/Relic LP 106 (75)
Ooh Baby Baby (acapella)	1975	Relic LP 105
Danny Boy (acapella)	1975	Relic LP 105
Dance Gypsy (acapella)	1975	Relic LP 106
When We Were So In Love (acapella)	1975	Relic LP 106
I've Been Good To You (acapella)	1975	Relic LP 106
Flowers On The Wall (acapella)	1975	Relic LP 106
You Know My Heart Is Yours (acapella)	1975	Relic LP 106
The One Love Forgot (acapella)	1975	Relic LP 106
There Goes My Baby (acapella)	1975	Relic LP 106
A Teardrop Fell From My Eyes (acapella)	1975	Relic LP 106
CHESSMEN (2)		
Mustang/Mr. Meadowlands	1964	Jerden 743
CHESSMEN (3)		
It'll Be Me	1959	Salem 001
CHESSMEN (4)		
I Believe/Lola	1961	Pac 100
CHESSMEN (5) (BARBARA MCBRIDE & THE)		
The Only Reason (flip by Woody Carr)	N/A	Mari 451
CHESSMEN (6)		
Bells Bells/Prayer Of Love	1959	Golden Crest 2661
CHESTERFIELDS (1)		
I'm In Heaven/All Messed Up	1953	Chess 1559
CHESTERFIELDS (2) (FB AL RENO)		
I Got Fired/Meet Me At The Candy Store	1958	Cub 9008
CHESTERFIELDS (3)		
A Dream Is But A Dream/You Walked Away	1962	Philips 40060/Philips 40083 (63)
CHESTERS (REF LITTLE ANTHONY & THE IMPERIALS)		
The Fires Burn No More/ Lift Up Your Head	1958	Apollo 521
Tears On My Pillow/Two People In The World	1958	End 1027
CHESTNUTS (1)		
Don't Go/I Wanna Come Home	1954	Mercury 70489
CHESTNUTS (2)		
Love Is True/It's You I Love	1956	Davis 447
Forever I Vow/Brother Ben	1956	Davis 452
Who Knows Better Than I?/ I Feel So Blue	1957	Eldorado 511
Who Knows Better Than I?/ Mary, Hear Those Love Bells	1957	Standord 100
This Is My Love/Wiggle Wiggle	1958	Aladdin 3444
CHESTNUTS (2) (BILL BAKER & THE)		
Won't You Tell Me, My Heart?/ Tell Me Little Darling	1959	Elgin 007/008
Wonderful Girl/Chit Chat	1959	Elgin 013/014
CHESTNUTS (3)		
Endless Love/Wobble Shank	1960	Coral 62176

Artist Song	Year	Label
CHESTNUTS (4)		
Rock 'N Roll Tragedy/I'm So Blue	1973	Night Train 906
CHEV-RONS		
The Defense Rests/It's Saturday Night	1962	Gait 100
CHEVELLES (1)		
I'm Sorry	1964	Infinity 029
CHEVELLES (2) (FEMALE)		
It's Goodbye/Another Tear Must Fall	1963	Butane 777
CHEVELLES (3) (MARVIN NASH & THE)		
Dina/Happiness	1963	Courier 111
CHEVELLES (4) (G.W. & THE)		
Walking With My New Love	1968	Flaming Arrow 37
CHEVELLES (5) (ART BARRON & THE)		
One Kiss/My Lucy Lou	1964	Golden 101
CHEVELLES (6)		
Red Tape	1973	Relic LP 5007
Valley Of Love (Fast & Slow Versions)	1973	Relic LP 5007
CHEVELLS		
Pretty Little Girl	N/A	Justice 1004
CHEVELLS (DON & THE)		
The Only Girl	1964	Speedway 1000
CHEVIERES		
Last Nite I Dreamed (acapella)	1975	Relic LP 109
Uncle Sam (acapella)	1975	Relic LP 109
CHEVIES (WAYNE JOHNSON & THE)		
I Love That Girl So/Come On And Love Me	1959	Dove 1033
CHEVRONS		
That Comes With Love/Don't Be Heartless	1959	Brent 7000
Lullabye/Day After Forever	1959	Brent 7007
Little Darlin'/Little Star	1960	Brent 7015
Come Go With Me/I'm In Love Again-All Shook Up	1960	Time 1
For Your Love/Good Good Lovin'	1961	Cuca 6381
Please Don't Make Me Cry/ Still In Love With You	1962	Sara 6462
Who Does He Cry To/The Jones Girl	1964	Kiski 2065
Mine Forever More/In The Depths Of My Soul	1968	Indpendence 94
CHEX (TEX & THE) (AKA LYRICS)		
I Do Love You/My Love	1961	Atlantic 2116
Love Me Now/Beach Party	1963	20th Fox 411
Be On The Lookout For My Love/Watching Willie Wobble	1963	Newtown 5010
CHIC-CHOCS		
Them There Eyes/Sugar	1961	Broadway 103
CHIC-LETS (FEMALE)		
I Want You To Be My Boyfriend/Don't Goof On Me	1964	Josie 919
CHICKLETTES (ANGIE & THE) (FEMALE)		
Tommy/Treat Him Tender, Maureen (Now That Ringo Belongs To You)	1965	Apt 25080
CHICKS (KELL OSBORNE & THE)		
Little Chick-A-Dee/Do You Mind	1962	Class 302
CHIEF-TONES		
Do Lord	N/A	Cuca 1287
CHIFFONS (1) (FEMALE) (AKA FIVE PENNIES)		
Tonight's The Night/Do You Know?	1960	Big Deal 6003/Zircon 1012
No More Tomorrows/Never Never	1961	Wildcat 601
After Last Night/Doctor Of Hearts	1962	Reprise 20103
He's So Fine/Oh My Lover	1963	Laurie 3152
A Love So Fine/Only My Friend	1963	Laurie 3159
Why Am I So Shy?/Lucky Me	1963	Laurie 3166
One Fine Day/Why Am I So Shy?	1963	Laurie 3179
A Love So Fine/Only My Friend	1963	Laurie 3195
I Have A Boyfriend/I'm Gonna Dry My Eyes	1963	Laurie 3212
Tonight I Met An Angel/Easy To Love	1963	Laurie 3224
My Boyfriend's Back/I Go Plenty O Nuttin'	1963	Laurie 3364

Artist Song	Year	Label	Artist Song	Year	Label
Sailor Boy/When Summer Is Through	1964	Laurie 3262	**CHIMES (8) (DAVE BURGESS & THE)**		
What Am I Gonna Do With You, Baby/Strange Strange Feeling	1965	Laurie 3275	Lulu/I Don't Want To Know	1959	Challenge 59037
Nobody Knows What's Going On/The Real Thing	1965	Laurie 3301	Just For Me/Everlovin'	1959	Challenge 59045
			CHIMES (9)		
Nobody Knows What's Goin' On/Did You Ever Go Steady?	1965	Laurie 3301	Tears From An Angels Eyes	1959	House Of Beauty 3
			CHIPETTES (CHIP ALLAN & THE)		
Tonight I'm Gonna Dream/ Heavenly Place	1965	Laurie 3318	Tell Me Today/Summertime	1963	Corsican 100
Sweet Talkin' Guy/Did You			**CHIPPENDALES**		
Ever Go Steady	1966	Laurie 3340	What A Night/Drip Drop	1959	Andie 5013
Out Of This World/Just A Boy	1966	Laurie 3350	Voodoo/Day Will Come	1960	Rust 5023
Stop Look And Listen/March	1966	Laurie 3357	**CHIPS (1)**		
Keep The Boy Happy/If I Knew Then	1967	Laurie 3377	Rubber Biscuit/Oh, My Darlin'	1956	Josie 803/Jozie 803 (56)
Just For Tonight/Teach Me How	1967	Laurie 3423	**CHIPS (2) (BILLY BOBBS & THE)**		
My Secret Love/Strange Strange Feeling	1968	B.T. Puppy 558	Shim Sham/Tweedle De Dum Dum	1958	Edison International 400/ Edison International 416 (59)
Up On The Bridge/March	1968	Laurie 3460	**CHIPS (3)**		
Love Me Like You're Gonna Lose Me/Three Dips Of Ice Cream	1969	Laurie 3497	As You Can See/You Make Me Feel So Good	1960	Satellite 105
So Much In Love/Strange Strange Feeling	1970	Buddah 171	**CHIPS (4) (FB JOE SOUTH)**		
			Bye Bye My Love/What A Lie	1961	Ember 1077
My Sweet Lord/Main Nerve	1975	Laurie 3630	Darling I Need Your Love/ You're On My Mind (61)	1961	Venice 101/Strand 25027
Dream Dream Dream/Oh My Lover	1976	Laurie 3648	Party People/Long Lonely Winter	1965	Tollie 9042
Will You Still Love Me Tomorrow?	N/A	Collectables LP 5042	**CHIPS (5)**		
When I Go To Sleep At Night	N/A	Collectables LP 5042	When I'm With You/Everyone's Laughing	1980	Clifton 54
The Locomotion	N/A	Collectables LP 5042	**CHIRPS (MARVIN & THE)**		
It's My Party	N/A	Collectables LP 5042	I'll Miss You This Christmas/ Sixteen Tons	1958	Tip Top 202
Da Doo Ron Ron	N/A	Collectables LP 5042	**CHOCOLATEERS**		
CHIFFONS (2) (GINGER & THE) (FEMALE)			For Sentimental Reasons/ Don't (by the Spiders)	1974	Owl 334
Where Were You Last Night/She	1962	Groove 0003	**CHOICE**		
CHIMES (1) (AKA FLAIRS (1))			Mr. Rock & Roll/Kiss And Say Goodbye	1988	Clifton 80
Love Me, Love Me, Love Me/ My Heart's Crying For You	1954	Flair 1051	**CHORALETTERS**		
CHIMES (10) (LEIGH BELL & THE)			Hear My Prayer/I've Got To Run On	1957	Duke 214
Terry/Eternity	1961	Rust 5031	**CHORALETTES**		
CHIMES (11)			I Destroyed Your Letters/ Won't You Call Me	1964	Fargo 1063
Losing You Baby/Swanee River Rock	N/A	Jay-Tee 1000	**CHORALS**		
CHIMES (2)			In My Dream/Rock And Roll Baby	1956	Decca 29914
Dearest Darling/A Fool Was I	1954	Royal Roost 577	**CHORD SPINNERS**		
CHIMES (3)			Call Me/Love Is A Many Splendored Thing	1961	Liberty 55368
The Chimes Ring Out/I'm Leaving Baby	1955	Specialty 549 (unreleased)	**CHORD'R NOTES**		
Tears On My Pillow/Zindy Lou	1955	Specialty 555	Livin' The Life/How Still The Night	1964	Fargo 1061
Pretty Little Girl/Chop Chop	1956	Specialty 574	**CHORD-A-ROYS (BOBBY ROY & THE)**		
Jonelle/I Found An Angel	1957	Dig 148 (unreleased)	Little Girl Lost/Girls Were Made For Boys	1960	Roys 5001/JDS 5001 (60)
CHIMES (3) (GENE MOORE & THE)			**CHORDCATS (AKA CHORDS)**		
Only A Dream/Reap What You Sow	1955	Combo 63	Zippety Zum (I'm In Love)/Bless You (For Being An Angel)	1954	Cat 109
CHIMES (3) (TONY ALLEN & THE)			A Girl To Love/Hold Me, Baby	1954	Cat 112
Check Yourself, Baby/Especially	1956	Specialty 570	**CHORDELLS (1)**		
CHIMES (4) (FB FREDDIE SCOTT)			Here's A Heart For You/ I Started Out	1956	Onyx 504/Relic 523 (64)
Please Call/The Letter Came This Morning	1957	Arrow 724	**CHORDELLS (2)**		
Lovin' Baby/A Faded Memory	1957	Arrow 726	At Last/September Song	1959	Jaro 77005
CHIMES (5) (FB LENNY COCCO)			**CHORDELLS (2) (LITTLE CHIPS & THE)**		
Once In A While/Oh How I Love You (by the Bi-Tones)	1960	Tag 444	A Little More Love/Amazon Girl	1961	Hull 746
Once In A While/Summer Night	1960	Tag 444/Music Note 1101 (61)	**CHORDELLS (3) (WILLIE HOWARD & THE)**		
			Letters Of Love/Louise	1961	Mascot 127
I'm In The Mood For Love/ Only Love	1961	Tag 445	**CHORDELLS (4)**		
Let's Fall In Love/Dream Girl	1961	Tag 447	Yea-Yea (I Was Blind)/Quit While You're Ahead	1963	Tiger 601
Whose Heart Are You Breakin' Now/Baby's Coming Home	1963	Metro 1/Laurie 3211 (63)	**CHORDIALS**		
New York City Lady/Why Is Love So Bad	1986	Freedom 223	I Wish It Were Summer/Tug Of War	1964	Big Top 513
CHIMES (5) (LENNY & THE)			**CHORDLINERS**		
Paradise/My Love	1962	Tag 450	Kathleen/Never Let Me Go	1988	Blue Sky 110
Two Times Two/Only Forever	1964	Vee Jay 605	Dance Between The Stars/ Dream Girl	1989	Blue Sky 111
CHIMES (6)			**CHORDLINERS (MIKE & THE)**		
Angel Child/Cry Cry Baby	1957	Limelight 3000	She's Gone/Don't Know What To Do	1989	Crystal Ball 154
Du Wap/Stop Look And Listen	1957	Limelight 3002			
Nervous Heart/When School Starts Again	1957	Reserve 120			
CHIMES (7)					
Coming Back To You	1959	Storm 501			

Artist	Song	Year	Label
CHORDONES (LEON D. TARVER & THE)			
	Oo-Ee What's Wrong With Me/		
	I'm A Young Rooster	1954	Checker 791
CHORDS (1)			
	Daddy Loves Mommy/In The		
	Woods	1953	Gem 211
CHORDS (2)			
	Sh-Boom/Cross Over The Bridge	1954	Cat 104 (first pressing)
	Sh-Boom/Little Maiden	1954	Cat 104 (second pressing)
	Zippety Zum/Bless You	1954	Cat 109
CHORDS (3)			
	Tears In Your Eyes/Don't Be		
	A Jumpin' Jack	1958	Casino 451
CHORDS (4)			
	Pretty Face/Elephant Walk	1959	Metro 20015
CHORDS (5) (PHIL MOORE & THE)			
	Little Angel/My Baby And Me	1959	Time 101
CHORDS (6)			
	Cool, Cool Daddy/I'll Never		
	Fool My Heart (by the Arrows)	1973	Baron 107
CHRIS-TONES (TOMMY CHRISTY & THE)			
	Teen-Age Jive/Choo-Choo-		
	Choo-Choo-Cha-Cha-Cha	1958	Scot 19999
CHRISTAIN, DIANE (& GROUP)			
	There's So Much About My		
	Baby (That I Love)/Has		
	Anybody Seen My Boyfriend	1963	Smash 1862
CHRISTIE, CHARLES (BB THE CRYSTALS)			
	In The Arms Of A Girl/Young		
	And Beautiful	1966	HBR 473
CHRISTIE, DEAN (& GROUP)			
	I'm A Loser/Heart Breaker	1962	Select 715
CHRISTIE, LOU (& GROUP) (AKA LUGEE & THE LIONS)			
	The Jury/Little Did I Know	1963	American Music Makers 006
CHRISTMAS, CONNIE (& GROUP)			
	What A Night (What A		
	Morning)/Big Chief	1962	Checker 1015
CHRISTOPHER, ROD (& GROUP)			
	Daybreak/Tattle Tale Blues	1962	Tru-Lite 111
CHROMATICS			
	Wild, Man, Wild/Devil Blues	1956	Crest 1011
	Don't Know Why I Cry/Here		
	In The Darkness	1956	Million 2014
	My Conscience/Got To Keep		
	Her Down On The Farm	1960	Ducky 716
CHROMATICS (AUGIE AUSTIN & THE)			
	Too Late/My Heart Let Me Be		
	Free	1958	Brunswick 55080
CHROMATICS (BOB WILLIAMS & THE)			
	Believe Me/Who's Fooling Who		
	(with the Tornados)	1955	Blend 1005
	I'll Never Change/Rockin' Beat	1955	Blend 1006
CHROMATICS (EDDIE SINGLETON & THE)			
	Too Late/Kiss-A-Kiss,		
	Hug-A-Hug	1958	Amasco 3701
CHROMATICS (SHERRY WASHINGTON & THE)			
	Here In The Darkness/La De		
	Do De Do	1955	Million 2010
	Honey Bug/Wabble Loo	1956	Million 2016
CHRYSLERS (LITTLE NATE & THE)			
	Cry Baby Cry/Someone Up		
	There	1959	Johnson 318
CHRYSTALIGHTS			
	Oh Baby/The Bells	1953	Sunset 1141
CHUCK-A-LUCKS			
	Heaven Knows/Chuck-A-Luck	1957	Bow 305/Candlelite 424 (63)
	Who Am I/The Devil's Train	1958	Lin 5010
	Disc Jockey Fever/The Magic		
	Of First Love	1958	Lin 5014
	Unconditional Surrender/		
	Tarzan's Date	1961	Jubilee 5415
	Pick Up And Deliver/Long John	1961	Warner Bros. 5198
	Cotton Pickin' Love/I'm		
	Hospitalized Over You	1961	Warner Bros. 5234
CHUCKLES (1) (CHUCK & THE)			
	Bury The Hatchet/One Hundred		
	Baby	1959	Shad 5015
CHUCKLES (2) (AKA THREE CHUCKLES)			
	Runaround/Lonely Traveler	1961	ABC 10276
CHUCKLES (3) (AKA CONSORTS (2)/AKA FOUR CLEFS)			
	On The Street Where You Live/		
	I'll Wait	1964	West Side 1019
CHUMS (MARY EUSTACE & THE)			
	That's It/Never A Moment	N/A	Apt 25009
CHURCHILL, SAVANNAH (& GROUP)			
	My Memories Of You/I Cried	1954	Decca 29194
CHYMES			
	If I Give My Heart To You/On		
	The Street Where You Live	1964	Musictone 6125
CINCINNATIANS			
	Magic Genie/Do What You		
	Want To Do	1962	Roosevelt Lee 16115/
			Emerald 16116 (63)
CINCOS (BEN HARPER & THE)			
	Here Goes My Girl/Drive		
	Away Blues	1960	Talent 106
CINDERELLAS			
	Yum Yum Yum/Mister Dee-Jay	1959	Decca 30830
	I Was Only Fifteen/You Never		
	Shoulda Gone Away	1959	Decca 30925
	Baby, Baby (I Still Love You)/		
	Please Don't Wake Me	1964	Dimension 1026
	More Than Yesterday/It's A		
	Wonderful Night	1964	Tamara 763
	Fairy Tale/Mr. Happy Love Joy	1965	Mercury 72394
CINDERS			
	Cinnamon Cinder/C'mon		
	Wobble	1963	Warner Bros. 5326
	I'll Follow You/The Story	1964	Original Sound 43
	Poison Ivy/Good Lovin's Hard		
	To Find	1965	Ric 156
CINEEMAS			
	Never Gonna Cry/A Crush		
	On You	1963	Dave 911
CINERAMAS			
	Life Can Be Beautiful/It Must		
	Be Love	1959	Champ 103
	Crying For You/I'm Sorry, Baby	1960	Rhapsody 71963/
			71964/Candlelite 433
	Playing For Keeps	1960	Rhapsody 71984
	Is This All Mine/Crying For You	1973	Clifton 4
CITADELS			
	Let's Fall In Love/When You		
	Said Goodbye	1962	Monogram 501
	When I Woke Up This Morning		
	(acapella)	1975	Relic LP 102
	When I Fall In Love (acapella)	1975	Relic LP 102
	New Love Tomorrow (acapella)	1975	Relic LP 102
	Tonite I Fell In Love (acapella)	1975	Relic LP 103
	Pennies From Heaven		
	(acapella)	1975	Relic LP 103
	Dream World (acapella)	1975	Relic LP 103
	I'll Never Let You Go (acapella)	1975	Relic LP 104
	Castle In The Sky (acapella)	1975	Relic LP 105
	Earth Angel (acapella)	1975	Relic LP 109
CITATIONS (1)			
	It Hurts Me/Kiss In The Night	1961	Don-El 113/Clifton 23 (77)
CITATIONS (2) (FB NICKI NORTH)			
	Magic Eyes/Mystery Of Love	1962	Canadian American 136/
			Jason Scott 23 (82)
CITATIONS (3)			
	Just For You	1962	Sara 101
	Slippin' And Slidin'/Moon Race		
	(instrumental)	1962	Sara 3301/Epic 9603 (63)
	The Stomp/Chicago	1964	Mercury 72286
	Down Went The Curtain/That		
	Girl Of Mine	1965	MGM 13373
	I Will Stand By You/To Win The		
	Race	1967	Ballad 101
CITATIONS (4)			
	The Girl Next Door/Ten Miles		
	From Nowhere	1963	Vangee 301/Fraternity 910
			(63)/Fraternity 992 (67)
CITATIONS (5) (BUDDY & THE)			
	Juvenile Delinquent/Don't Let		
	Her Have Her Way	1964	IRC 6918
CITATIONS (6)			
	Take Me	1959	University 101
CITATIONS (7) (ANGIE & THE)			
	Dance Her By Me/Headache	N/A	Angela 102
CITIZENS			
	Tammy/The Ballad Of Seymour	1961	Laurie 3107
CITRONES (FREDDY POWELL & THE)			
	Faded Pictures/Flip To The		
	Twist	1962	Sheraton 105

Artist Song	Year	Label
CIUFO, JERRY (& GROUP)		
Fools Fall In Love/Don't Cry	1965	Jeree 65
CLAIR-TONES		
Lost In A Dream/Checking On You Baby	N/A	Announcing 1000
CLAIRMONTS (AKA CLAREMONTS/AKA TONETTES)		
Angel Of Romance/Why Keep Me Dreaming	1957	Apollo 517
CLANTONES		
May I Never Love Again/If You Were Mine	1959	Emony 1021
CLAREMONTS (AKA CLAIRMONTS/AKA TONETTES))		
Angel Of Romance/Why Keep Me Dreaming	1963	Apollo 751
CLARENDONS (LEE & THE)		
Night Owl	N/A	H.S.
CLARK, DEE (BB THE KOOL GENTS)		
Gloria/Kangaroo Hop	1957	Falcon 1002
Gloria/You're Lookin' Good (Dee Clark)	1957 355 (60)	Falcon 1002/Vee Jay
When I Call On You/Nobody But You	1958	Abner 1019
All Alone In My Lonely Room/ As Long As You're In Love With Me	1963	Atco 6266
I Just Can't Help Myself	N/A	Vee Jay LP 1019/Charly LP 1113
Just Like A Fool	N/A	Vee Jay LP 1019/Charly LP 1113/Solid Smoke LP 8026
CLARK, JIMMY (& GROUP)		
Shirley/Everything's Fine	1964	Diamond 157
CLARK, LEE (& GROUP)		
As Long As You're In Love With Me/All Alone In My Lonely Room	1963	Atco 6266
CLARK, LUCKY (& GROUP)		
Two Kinds Of People/So Sick	1961	Chess 1732
CLASS CUTTERS (HERBIE & THE)		
Just A Summer Kick/Like Those Ivy Walls	1959	RCA 7649
CLASS-AIRES		
My Tears Start To Fall/Too Old To Cry	N/A	Honey Bee 1/Jason Scott 16 (82)
CLASS-NOTES		
You Inspire Me/Goodness Gracious	1958	Dot 15786
Take It Back/Bessie's House	1958	Hamilton 50011
CLASSIC IV (FOUR)		
Early Christmas/Limbo Under The Christmas Tree	1962	Algonquin 1650
What Will I Do/True Story	1962	Algonquin 1651
Island Of Paradise/What Will I Do (Without You)	1962	Twist 1001
Please Be Mine/Heavenly Bliss	1962	Twist 1003/1004
CLASSICALS		
One More River/Camel Caravan	1962	Kent 379
CLASSICS (1)		
If Only The Sky Was A Mirror/ Gosh But This Is Love	1957	Class 219
CLASSICS (2)		
You're The Prettiest One/Let Me Dream	1959	Crest 1063
CLASSICS (3)		
You're Everything/Burning Love	1960	Top Rank 2061
CLASSICS (3) (FB EMIL STUCCIO)		
Cinderella/So In Love (63)	1959	Dart 1015/Musictone 1114
Angel Angela/Eenie, Meenie, Minie And Mo	1960	Dart 1032
Life Is But A Dream Sweetheart/ That's The Way	1961	Dart 1038/Mercury 71829 (61)
Life's But A Dream/Nuttin' In The Noggin'	1961	Streamline 1028
Till Then/Eenie, Meenie, Minie And Mo	1963	Musicnote 1116
P.S. I Love You/Wrap Your Troubles In Dreams(And Dream Your Troubles Away)	1963	Musictone 118
Too Young/Who's Laughing, Who's Crying	1964	Musictone 6131
You'll Never Know/Dancing With You	1965	Stork 2
Over The Weekend/Dancing With You	1966	Josie 939
I Apologize/Love For Today	1967	Piccollo 500
Wind/Vagabond	1971	Sire 353
Again/The Way You Look Tonight	N/A	Bed-Stuy 222
CLASSICS (3) (JIMMY RINGO & THE)		
Full Race Cam	1959	Dart
CLASSICS (4) (FB LOU CHRISTIE)		
Close Your Eyes/Funny Thing	1961	Starr 508/Alcar 207 (63)
CLASSICS (4) (LOU CHRISTIE & THE)		
Tomorrow Will Come/You're With It	1963	Alcar 208
CLASSICS (5) (HERB LANCE & THE)		
Blue Moon/Little Boy Lost (no group)	1961	Promo 1010
CLASSICS (6)		
The Wheel Of Love/Noah's Ark	N/A	Karen 316
CLASSICS (7)		
Christmas Is Here	1960	MV 1000
CLASSICS (8) (MIKE SABEH & THE)		
So Fine	N/A	Empress 1001
CLASSICS FOUR (BOB GERARDI & THE)		
Nobody Wants You Anymore/ You're Everything To Me	1960	Recorte 441
CLASSINETTES (FEMALE)		
To The Church/Little Boy	1962	Markay 107
CLASSMATES (1) (AKA FOUR CLASSMATES)		
What Am I Gonna Do/A Kiss Is Not A Kiss	1955	King 1487
Return My Heart/Who's Gonna Take You To The Prom	1956	Dot 15460
Break Down And Love Me/ Two Straws In The Wind	1956	Dot 15464
Friends/I Want My Love Close By	1956	Dot 15504
You Do Something To Me/You Aren't The Only One	1957	Dot 15589
High School/Don't Make Me Cry	1960	Marquee 101
Until Then/Pretty Little Pet	1960	Marquee 102
Homework/Here Comes Suzy	1961	Seg-Way 104
All I Want Is To Love You/Some Of These Days	1962	Radar 3962
Did You Ever/Will You Love Me Tomorrow	1962	Stacy 935
Graduation/Teenage Twister	1963	Radar 2624
CLASSMATES (2)		
Gotta Go And See My Baby/ Washed My Heart Of Love	1956	Silhouette 509/510
CLASSMATES (3) (RONNIE JONES & THE)		
Little Girl Next Door/Teenage Rock	1957	End 1002
Lonely Boy/My Baby Cries	1958	End 1014
Lonely Boy/Teenage Rock	1963	End 1125
CLASSMATES (4) (MARC CAVELL & THE)		
I Didn't Lie/I See It	1961	Candix 329
CLASSMATES (5)		
A Summer Place	1963	Felsted 8673
CLASSMATES (6) (DWAIN LOUIS & THE)		
That's All Right	N/A	Carole 611
CLASSMEN (1)		
True Love/Silver Medal	1963	Gateway 712
Love Is Gone/My Special Angel	1963	Limelight 3012
All Time Fool/Do You Wanna Dance	1964	Limelight 3016
CLASSMEN (2)		
I'm Warning You/I Won't Cry	1963	CM 8464
CLASSMEN (3)		
Why Did You Put Me On/Why Does Everybody	1964	JR 5006
CLEAN CUT CLAN (DAN & THE)		
The Perfect Example/Broken Hip Party	1962	Accent 1116
CLEARWATER, EDDIE (& GROUP)		
Twist Like This/I Was Gone	1962	Federal 12446
CLEESHAYS (DANNY TYRELL & THE)		
You're Only Seventeen/Let's Walk	1958	Eastman 784

Artist	Song	Year	Label
CLEESHAYS (SONNY KNIGHT & THE)			
	Lipstick Kisses/Eat Your Mush And Hush	1958	Eastman 787
CLEF DWELLERS			
	Redheaded Woman With Green Velvet Eyes/The Way You Gotta Swing Today	1958	Singular 713
CLEFFTONES (AKA WHIRLPOOLS)			
	My Dearest Darling/The Masquerade Is Over	1955	Old Town 1011
	Little Girl	1955	Old Town/Murray Hill LP 000083
	Gloria	1955	Old Town/Murray Hill LP 000083
	Guess Who	1955	Old Town/Murray Hill LP 000083
CLEFS (1) (FB SCOTTY MANN)			
	We Three/Ride On	1952	Chess 1521
	What Did I Do	1954	Peacock (unreleased)
	I'm Wondering	1954	Peacock (unreleased)
	I'll Be Waiting/Please Don't Leave Me	1954	Peacock 1643
CLEFS (2)			
	Sorry/I Really Had A Ball (by the Ontarios)	1973	Baron 104
CLEFTONES			
	You Baby You/I Was Dreaming	1956	Gee 1000
	Little Girl Of Mine/You're Driving Me Mad	1956	Gee 1011
	Can't We Be Sweethearts/Neki-Hokey	1956	Gee 1016
	String Around My Heart/Happy Memories	1956	Gee 1025
	Why Do You Do Me Like You Do/I Like Your Style Of Making Love	1957	Gee 1031
	See You Next Year/Ten Pairs Of Shoes	1957	Gee 1038
	Hey Baby/What Did I Do That Was Wrong	1957	Gee 1041
	Since We Fell In Love	1957	Roulette LP 25021
	Honey Bun	1957	unreleased
	Lover Boy/Beginners At Love	1958	Gee 1048
	After The Dance	1959	Roulette LP 25059
	Cool It, Fool	1959	unreleased
	Heart And Soul/How Do You Feel	1961	Gee 1064
	I Love You For Sentimental Reasons/Deed I Do	1961	Gee 1067
	Earth Angel/Blues In The Night	1961	Gee 1074
	Do You/Again	1961	Gee 1077
	Lover Come Back To Me/There She Goes	1961	Gee 1079
	How Deep Is The Ocean/Some Kind Of Blue	1961	Gee 1080
	One Hundred Pounds Of Clay	1961	Gee LP 705
	Time Is Running Out On Our Love	1961	Gee LP 705
	The Glory Of Love	1961	Gee LP 705
	You And I Can Climb	1961	Gee LP 705
	Red Sails In The Sunset	1962	Gee LP 707
	My Babe	1962	Gee LP 707
	Sweet And Lovely	1963	unreleased
	Blue Skies	1963	unreleased
	Slippin' And Slidin'	1963	unreleased
	Since We Fell In Love/Heavenlyn Father	1976	Robin Hood 132
	Please Say You Want Me/So You And I Can Climb	1976	Robin Hood 133
	My Angel Lover/You Lost The Game Of Love	1990	Classic Artists 121
	She's So Fine/Trudy	1958	Roulette 4094
	Cuzin' Casanova/Mish Mash Baby	1959	Roulette 4161
	She's Gone/Shadows On The Very Last Row	1960	Roulette 4302
	She's Forgotten You/Right From The Git Go	1964	Ware 6001
CLEFTONES (FEATURING PAT SPANN)			
	Heavenly Father	1961	Gee LP 705
	Please Say You Want Me	1961	Gee LP 705
CLEFTS			
	Dreaming/Come On	1960	V-Tone 212
CLEOPATRA (& GROUP)			
	Heaven Only Knows/My Darling	1961	Sheryl 335
CLICHES			
	What's Your Name/Little Egypt	1959	Maar C 1530
	Save It For Me	N/A	Wes Mar 1020
CLICK-CLACKS			
	Is It Wrong/A Kiss Goodbye	1958	Algonquin 714
	Rocket Roll/A Kiss Goodbye	1958	Algonquin 715/Apt 25032 (59)
	Pretty Little Pearly/Roma Rocka-Rolla	1958	Apt 25010
CLICK-ETTES (AKA CLICKETTES (1)) (FEMALE)			
	A Teenager's First Love/Jive Time Turkey	1958	Dice 83/84
	But Not For Me/I Love You I Swear	1960	Dice 100
	To Be A Part Of You/Because Of My Best Friend	1960	Dice 92/93
	Warm, Soft And Lovely/Why Oh Why	1960	Dice 96/97
	Lover's Prayer/Grateful	1960	Dice 98/99
	I Just Can't Help It/I Just Can't Help It (instrumental)	1963	Checker 1060
	I Understand Him/I Understand Him (instrumental)	1963	Tuff 373
CLICKETTES (1) (AKA CLICK-ETTES) (FEMALE)			
	Where Is He/Lone Lover	1960	Guyden 2043
CLICKETTES (2) (ANGIE & THE)			
	Tommy	1959	Apt 25080
CLICKS			
	Come Back To Me/Peace And Contentment	1955	Josie 780
	You Ran Away From My Heart/Twisting Saturday Night	1963	Rush 2004
CLIENTELLS			
	Church Bells May Ring/My Love	1961	M.B.S. 7
CLIF-TONES			
	School Is Over/Nunca (by the Latin Lads)	1976	Clifton 15
CLIFFORD, BUZZ (BB THE TEENAGERS)			
	Three Little Fishes/Simply Because	1962	Columbia 41979
CLIMATES			
	Breaking Up Again/No You For Me	1967	Sun 404
CLIMATICS			
	All Alone/Help, There Is A Burglar	1959	Request 3007/3008
	My Gift From Heaven/Light Finger Willie	1962	Re-No 1000
CLIMBERS			
	My Darlin' Dear/Angels In Heaven Know I Love You	1957	J&S 1652
	I Love You/Trains, Cars, Boats	1957	J&S 1658
CLINTON, BUDDY (& GROUP)			
	How My Prayers Have Changed/Across The Street From Your House	1959	Time 1016
CLINTONIAN CUBS (FB JIMMY CASTOR)			
	Confusion/She's Just My Size	1960	My Brother's 508
	She's Just My Style/Confusion	1960	My Brother's 7
CLIPPERS (1) (BIG MIKE GORDON & THE)			
	Careless Lover/The Clipper	1956	Baton 233
CLIPPERS (2) (JOHNNY BLAKE & THE)			
	Bella-Marie/I'm Yours	1957	Gee 1027
CLIPPERS (3)			
	Rain/You Can't Trust A Woman	1957	Fox 961
CLIPPERS (4)			
	Goodnight, Irene/Beanie	1960	Beacon 210
	Now And Always/Forgotten Love	1961	Tri 211
CLIPS			
	Wish I Didn't Love You So/Your Lovin' Moves Me	1954	Republic 7102
	Kiss Away/Let Me Get Close To You Baby	1956	Calvert 105
CLIQUES (AKA JESSE BELVIN)			
	Why Oh Why/Don't Stop Loving Me	1956	Modern 967 (unreleased)
	Girl In My Dreams/I Wanna Know Why	1956	Modern 987

Artist / Song	Year	Label
My Desire/I'm In Love With A Gal	1956	Modern 995
CLOCKS & CLASSMEN		
It's Written/Think You're Smart	1958	Mail Call 1011
CLOUDS (1)		
I Do/Rock And Roll Boogie	1956	Cobra 5001
CLOUDS (2)		
Darling I Love You/T.V. Mix Up	1959	Round 1008
CLOUDS (3) (LITTLE SUNNY DAYE & THE)		
Lou Ann/Baby Doll	1961	Tandem 7001
CLOUDS (4) (DONNA DEE & THE)		
Can't You See (Oo-Wee)/The More I See Him	1961	Ramada 501
CLOUDS (5)		
All I Do Is Worry/Baby It's Me	1961	Skylark 116
CLOUDS (6) (FB BILL MEDLEY)		
My Tears Will Go Away/ Night Owl	1964	Medley 1001
CLOUDS (7)		
A Lovely Way To Spend An Evening/Say Hey Hey	N/A	Vons 1000
CLOUDS (8)		
Say You Love Me	1990	Relic LP 5088
CLOVERMEN (TIPPIE & THE) (AKA TIPPIE & THE CLOVERS)		
Please Mr. Sun/I Like It Like That	1962	Stenton 7001
CLOVERS		
Yes Sir, That's My Baby/When You Come Back To Me	1950	Rainbow 11-122
Skylark/Don't You Know I Love You	1951	Atlantic 934
Fool, Fool, Fool/Needless	1951	Atlantic 944
One Mint Julep/Middle Of The Night	1952	Atlantic 963
Ting-A-Ling/Wonder Where My Baby's Gone	1952	Atlantic 969
I Played The Fool/Hey, Miss Fannie	1952	Atlantic 977
Good Lovin'/Here Goes A Fool	1953	Atlantic 1000
Comin' On/The Feeling Is So Good	1953	Atlantic 1010
Crawlin'/Yes, It's You	1953	Atlantic 989
Lovey Dovey/Little Mama	1954	Atlantic 1022
I've Got My Eyes On You/Your Cash Ain't Nothin' But Trash	1954	Atlantic 1035
I Confess/Alrighty, Oh Sweetie	1954	Atlantic 1046
Blue Velvet/If You Love Me	1955	Atlantic 1052
In The Morning Time/Lovebug	1955	Atlantic 1060
Nip Sip/If I Could Be Loved By You	1955	Atlantic 1073
Devil Or Angel/Hey, Doll Baby	1956	Atlantic 1083
Your Tender Lips/Love, Love, Love	1956	Atlantic 1094
From The Bottom Of My Heart/ Bring Me Love	1956	Atlantic 1107
Baby Baby, Oh My Darling/ A Lonely Fool	1956	Atlantic 1118
You Good-Looking Woman/ Here Comes Romance	1957	Atlantic 1129
So Young/I-I-I Love You	1957	Atlantic 1139
Down In The Valley/There's No Tomorrow	1957	Atlantic 1152
Wishing For Your Love/All About You	1958	Atlantic 1175
Please Come On To Me/The Gossip Wheel	1958	Poplar 110/Poplar 139 (59)
The Good Old Summertime/ Idaho	1958	Poplar 111
Old Black Magic/Rock And Roll Tango	1959	United Artists 174
Love Potion No. 9/Stay Awhile	1959	United Artists 180
To Each His Own	1959	United Artists LP 3033
Kentucky Babe	1959	United Artists LP 3033
Pennies From Heaven	1959	United Artists LP 3033
What Is This Thing Called Love	1959	United Artists LP 3033
Jamaica Farewell	1959	United Artists LP 3033
Vaya Con Dios	1959	United Artists LP 3033
My Mother's Eyes	1959	United Artists LP 3033/ Broadcast 1124 (75)
One Mint Julep/Lovey	1960	United Artists 209
Easy Lovin'/I'm Confessin' That I Love You	1960	United Artists 227
Yes It's You/Burning Fire	1960	United Artists 263
The Bootie Green/Drive It Home	1961	Atlantic 2129
The Honeydripper/Have Gun	1961	United Artists 307
Wrapped Up In A Dream/Let Me Hold You	1961	Winley 255
I Need You Now/Gotta Quit You	1961	Winley 265
Love Love Love/The Kickapoo	1963	Brunswick 55249
He Sure Could Hypnotize/ Poor Baby	1965	Port 3004
Too Long Without Some Loving/For Days	1968	Josie 992
Try My Lovin' On You/Sweet Side Of A Soulful Woman	1968	Josie 997
CLOVERS (BUDDY BAILEY & THE)		
Stop Pretending/One More Time	1963	Porwin 1001
It's All In The Game/That's What I Will Be	1963	Porwin 1004
CLOVERS (TIPPIE & THE)		
Bossa Nova Baby/Bossa Nova (My Heart Said)	1963	Tiger 201
Cocksucker's Ball/Darbytown	1975	Jett 3019
Cocksucker's Ball/It's Too Soon To Know	1975	Jett 3019
CLUSTERS		
Darling Can't You Tell/Pardon My Heart	1958	Tee Gee 102/End 1115 (62)
Long Legged Maggie/Forecast Of Our Love	1959	Epic 9330
CLUSTERS (GUS COLETTI & THE)		
Hold My Hand/Without Your Love	1957	Tin Pan Alley 206
Sample Kiss/My Darling Wait For Me	1957	Tin Pan Alley 207
CO-EDS (1) (FB GWEN EDWARDS)		
Love You Baby All The Time/ I Beg Your Forgiveness	1956	Old Town 1027
I Love An Angel/I'm In Love	1957	Old Town 1033
CO-EDS (2)		
Juke Box/Big Chief	1958	Cameo 129
La La La (Lessons Of The Cha Cha)/Juke Box	1958	Cameo 134
With All My Heart/A Man	1959	Dwain 802
When It's Over/Annabelle Lee	1961	Cha Cha 715/ Checker 996 (61)
Time After Time/To Be Or Not To Be	1961	Sheryl 337
The Magic Of Your Love/ Heartthrob	1962	USA 724
CO-EDS (3) (AKA BLOSSOMS)		
Son-In-Law/I'll Wait	1961	Challenge 9109
CO-HEARTS		
My Love/Cry Baby	1958	Vee Jay 289
CO-OPS		
Your Love/Shame, Shame, Shame	1959	Versailles 100
COACHMEN (1)		
Caring/Fame And Fortune	1954	X 0044
COACHMEN (2)		
Teen Bride/Marianne	1960	Iona 1004
COACHMEN FIVE		
Oh Joan/This I Know	N/A	Janson 100
COANJOS		
Dance The Boomerang/ Speaking Of Love	1961	Dapt 208
COASTERS		
Down In Mexico/Turtle Dovin'	1956	Atco 6064
One Kiss Led To Another/Brazil	1956	Atco 6073
Searchin'/Young Blood	1957	Atco 6087
Idol With The Golden Head/ (When She Wants Good Lovin') My Baby Comes To Me	1957	Atco 6098
What's The Secret Of Your Success/Sweet Georgia Brown	1957	Atco 6104
Dance/Gee Golly	1958	Atco 6111
Yakety Yak/ Zing Went The Strings Of My Heart	1958	Atco 6116
The Shadow Knows/Sorry But I'm Gonna Have To Pass	1958	Atco 6126
Riot In Cell Block #9	1958	Atco LP 101
Charlie Brown/Three Cool Cats	1959	Atco 6132
Along Came Jones/That Is Rock 'n' Roll	1959	Atco 6141
Poison Ivy/I'm A Hog For You	1959	Atco 6146
Run Red Run/What About Us	1959	Atco 6153

Artist	Song	Year	Label
	Besame Mucho Pt. 1/Besame Mucho Pt. 11	1960	Atco 6163
	Wake Me, Shake Me/Stewball	1960	Atco 6168
	Shoppin' For Clothes/Snake And The Bookworm	1960	Atco 6178
	Wait A Minute/Thumbin' A Ride	1961	Atco 6186
	Little Egypt/Keep On Rolling	1961	Atco 6192
	Girls, Girls, Girls Pt. 1/Girls, Girls, Girls Pt. 2	1961	Atco 6204
	Just Like Me (Ain't That)/Bad Blood	1961	Atco 6210
	Ridin' Hood/Teach Me How To Shimmy	1962	Atco 6219
	The Climb/The Climb	1962	Atco 6234
	My Babe	1962	Atco LP 135
	The P.T.A./Bull Tick Waltz	1963	Atco 6251
	T'ain't Nothin' To Me/Speedoo's Back In Town	1964	Atco 6287
	Bad Detective/Lovey Dovey	1964	Atco 6300
	Wild One/I Must Be Dreaming	1964	Atco 6321
	Hongry/Lady Like	1965	Atco 6341
	Let's Go Get Stoned/Money Honey	1965	Atco 6356
	Bell Bottom Slacks/Crazy Baby	1966	Atco 6379
	She's A Yum Yum/Saturday Night Fish Fry	1966	Atco 6407
	Soul Pad/Down Home Girl	1967	Date 1552
	She Can/Everybody's Woman	1968	Date 1607
	Everybody's Woman/ D.W. Washburn	1968	Date 1617
	Love Potion No. 9/ D.W. Washburn	1971	King 6385
COASTERS TWO PLUS TWO (AKA COASTERS)			
	Searchin' 75/Young Blood	1975	Chelan 2000
	If I Had A Hammer/If I Had A Hammer	1976	American International 1122
COASTIERS			
	The Angels Listened In/Teen Beat (instrumental)	N/A	Coast 1287
COASTLINERS			
	Wonderful You/Alright	1960	Back Beat 554
	She's My Girl/I'll Be Home	1960	Back Beat 566
	I See Me/California On My Mind	1967	Dear 1300
COBANAS (ROY HINES & THE)			
	We Have Love/I Can Live	N/A	Solitaire 1001
COBRAS (1)			
	Cindy (or Sindy)/I Will Return	1955	Modern 964
COBRAS (2)			
	La La (Hey Baby)/Goodbye Molly	1964	Casino 1309/Swan 4176 (64)
	Thumpin'/Don't Even Know Your Name	1964	Monogram 519
COCOAS			
	Flip Your Daddy/Ooooo! Ooooo!	1955	Chesterfield 364
CODAS (CHARLES GULLY & THE)			
	Hey Little Baby/Strange Lady	1963	C.J. 641
COEDS (JOHNNY MAESTRO WITH THE)			
	Mr. Happiness/Test Of Love	1961	Coed 552
COEDS (WITH THE TOKENS)			
	Mark My Words/You're My First Love	1964	Swing 101
COGNACS			
	Charlena/Heaven Only Knows	1961	Roulette 4340
COINS (1) (AKA COLONIALS (1))			
	Blue, Can't Get No Place With You/Cheatin' Baby	1954	Gee 10
	Look At Me Girl/S.R. Blues	1954	Gee 11
	Look At Me Girl/Two Loves Have I (by the Colonials)	1956	Gee 1007
COINS (2)			
	Loretta/Please	1955	Model 2001
COLBERT, BERTHA (& FEMALE GROUP)			
	Teardrops On A Letter/Poor Bonnie	1962	Roulette 4435
COLE, ANN (BB THE SUBURBANS (1))			
	Are You Satisfied/Darling Don't Hurt Me	1955	Baton 218
	New Love/Easy Easy Baby	1956	Baton 224
COLE, CLAY (BB THE CAPRIS)			
	Twist Around The Clock/Don't Twist	1961	Imperial 5804
COLE, FREDDY (& GROUP)			
	Don't Be Mad/Little Boy	1963	Titantic 100

Artist	Song	Year	Label
COLEMAN, LENNY (BB NINO & THE EBBTIDES)			
	Four Seasons/Shake It Easy	1965	Laurie 3290
COLLEAGUES			
	A Tear Fell/I Want You I Need You	1961	Glodus 1651
COLLEGIANS (1) (JACKIE ROY & THE)			
	The Leaf/You Made A Fool Of Me	1953	Okeh 6970
	Devil Eyes/My Heart Knows	1953	Okeh 6987
COLLEGIANS (2)			
	Rickety Tickety Melody/The Sackbut, The Psaltery And The Dulcimer	1954	Cat 110
	Blue Solitude/Please Let Me Be The One	1956	Groove 0163
COLLEGIANS (3)			
	Zoom Zoom Zoom/On Your Merry Way	1957	Winley 224
	Let's Go For A Ride/Heavenly Night	1958	X-Tra 108/Times Square 11 (63)
	Tonite Oh Tonite/Oh I Need Your Love	1961	Winley 261
	Right Around The Corner/ Teenie Weenie Little Bit	1961	Winley 263
COLLEGIANS (4)			
	Happy Parakeet/Cookin'	1961	Hilltop 1868
	I'm Ready/Grandma Told Me So	1962	Post 10002
COLLEGIANS (5) (PROFESSOR MARCELL & THE)			
	My College Girl, Pt. 1/ My College Girl, Pt. 2	1967	Mayhams 212
COLLEGIATES (1) (DICKY LEE & THE)			
	Good Lovin'/Memories Never Grow Old	1957	Sun 280
COLLEGIATES (1) (DICKY LEE & THE)			
	Dream Boy/Stay True Baby (no group)	1957	Tampa 131
COLLEGIATES (1) (DICKY LEE & THE)			
	Fool, Fool, Fool/Dreamy Nights	1958	Sun 297
COLLEGIATES (2)			
	Restless Lover/Brief Romance	1959	Capo 001
	Say Hello To An Angel/What Is A Dream	1960	Campus 10
	Heartaches Don't Care/The Effigy	1961	Campus 123
	I Had A Dream/Growing Up	1961	Heritage 105
COLLEGIATES (3) (HAROLD TEEN & THE)			
	The Genevieve Jump/Moon Over Miami	1960	Goldisc 3014
COLLEGIATES (4)			
	Teenage Plea/A Kid In His Teens	1960	RD Globe 009
COLOGNES			
	A River Flows/A Bird And A Bee	1959	Lummtone 102
COLONAIRS			
	Sandy/Can't Stand To Lose You	1957	Ember 1017
	Do-Pop-Si/Little Miss Muffet	1963	Tru-Lite 127
COLONIALS (1) (AKA COINS (1))			
	Two Loves Have I/Look At Me Girl (by the Coins)	1956	Gee 1007
COLONIALS (1) (BILL "BASS" GORDON & THE) (AKA COINS (1))			
	Two Loves Have I/Bring My Baby Back	1954	Gee 12
COLONIALS (2)			
	Where Is My Love/Why Didn't You Tell Me Girl	N/A	Senate 1003
COLOS (DAVID DAYTON & THE)			
	The Search Is Over/I Gotta Have Love	1955	Lomar 704
COLTS			
	Adorable/Lips Red As Wine	1955	Vita 112/Mambo 112 (55)
	Sweet Sixteen/Honey Bun	1956	Vita 121
	Never No More/Hey You, Shoobeoohbee	1956	Vita 130
	Never No More/Sheik Of Araby	1959	Antler 4003
	Guiding Angel/Sheik Of Araby	1959	Antler 4007
	I Never Knew/Oh, When You Touch Me (by the Red Coats)	1959	Del-Co 4002
	Sweet Sixteen/Hey, Hey, Pretty Baby	1962	Plaza 505
COLTS (JACKIE KELSO & THE)			
	Kwela, Kwela/Rat-A-Tat	1955	Vita 114

Artist Song	Year	Label
COLUMBO, JOE (& GROUP)		
I Need You/I Wonder If I Care As Much	1963	Taurus 359
COLUMBUS PHARAOHS (AKA FOUR PHARAOHS/AKA KING PHARAOH & THE EGYPTIANS)		
Give Me Your Love/China Girl	1957	Esta 290/Ransom 101 (58)/ Paradise 109 (59)/Nanc 1120 (59)
COMBINATIONS		
Back Home Again/Rockin' Chair Rock	1959	Combo 167
Just One More Chance/Voodoo	1970	Carrie 010
Mother Was Right	N/A	Fortune LP 8017
COMBINATIONS (ARTIE MORRIS & THE)		
Back Home Again/I'm A Travelin' Man	1959	Coco 163
COMBO KINGS		
All I Could Do Was Cry/Mish Mash	N/A	Flo-Jo 4095
COMBO-NETTES (CLEMONS PENIX & THE)		
I've Been Searching/No Evil	1956	Combo 117
COMBO-NETTES (JANE PORTER & THE) (FEMALE)		
If I Had My Wish/Hi-Diddle-Diddle	1955	Combo 74
I Ain't Got Time/What Kind Of Man Is This?	1956	Combo 118
Got To Have You Baby	1988	Relic LP 5076
COMETS (1) (HERB KENNY & THE)		
Only You/When The Lights Go On Again	1952	Federal 12083
COMETS (2) (LYNN TIATT & THE)		
Dad Is Home/Vilma's Jump-Up	N/A	Pussycat 1
COMIC BOOKS		
Manuel/Black Magic And Witchcraft	1961	New Phoenix 6199/ Citations 5001 (62)
COMMANDS		
No Time For You/Hey It's Love	1964	Dynamic 104
No Time For Love	N/A	Back Beat 570
COMMODORES (1)		
Riding On A Train/Uranium	1955	Dot 15372
Close To My Heart/Cream Puff	1955	Dot 15425
Speedoo/Whole Lotta Shakin' Goin' On	1956	Dot 15439
Two Loves Have I/Who Said I Said That	1956	Dot 15461
Not A Day Goes By/Sweet Angel	1957	Challenge 1004
I'll Be There/Faith	1957	Challenge 1007
Laughing With Tears In My Eyes/Who Dat	1959	Brunswick 55126
Home	N/A	4-S
COMMODORES (2) (DARRELL GLENN & THE)		
Hello Baby/Zinga Zingo	1957	RPM 488
COMO, NICKY (BB THE DEL SATINS)		
Your Guardian Angel/Just A Little While	N/A	Tang 1231
COMPANIONS (1)		
Falling/Oh, What A Feeling!	1958	Dove 240
Why Oh Baby Why/I Didn't Know	1959	Brook's 100/Federal 12397 (60)
No Fool Am I/How Could You	1962	Amy 852
It's Too Late/These Foolish Things	1963	Arlen 722/Gina 722 (63)
COMPANIONS (2)		
I'll Always Love You/A Little Bit Of Blue	1962	Columbia 42279
COMPANIONS (3)		
Be Yourself/Help A Lonely Guy	1962	General American 711
COMPLIMENTS (1) (MICHAEL ZARA & THE)		
Angels Of Mercy/Nobody Knows	1963	Shell 313
COMPLIMENTS (2)		
Borrow Til Morning/Beware Beware	1965	Midas 304
COMPOSERS		
Woe Is Me/Elephant Drag	1963	Ampen 221
I Had A Dream/You And Yours	1963	Era 3118
COMPUTONES		
Flip Flip Zu-Wah/Summer Night	1978	U.G.H.A. 1
Dancing With You/So Lonely	1978	U.G.H.A. 3
This Is My Wedding Day/I Had A Dream	1979	Clifton 32
Joyce/Dottie	1981	Clifton 61

Artist Song	Year	Label
I'll Stay Home/Rudolph The Red Nosed Reindeer (by Patty & the Street-Tones)	1981	Clifton 66
CON CHORDS (BOB BRADY & THE)		
Goodbye Baby/Tell Me Why	1966	Chariot 100
I Love You Baby/Illusion	1966	Chariot 525
CON-DONS		
Dear Abby/Centennial March	1962	Carlton 587
CONCEPTS (1)		
Jungle/Whisper	1961	Apache 1515/Musictone 1109 (61)
CONCEPTS (2)		
Sad Little Boy/Blue Sea	1964	ABC 10526
CONCEPTS (3)		
Yo Me Pregunto/The Vow (acapella)	1966	Catamount 112
CONCEPTS (4) (WITH THE EMANONS)		
Cry (Only You Cry Alone)/ The Sway	N/A	J&J 3000
CONCERTONES		
Just One More Time/All Is Well And Fine	1961	Legrand 1011
CONCORDS (1)		
Candlelight/Monticello	1954	Harlem 2328
I'm Satisfied With Rock 'N' Roll/I'll Always Say Please	1956	Ember 1007
CONCORDS (1) (PEARL REAVES & THE)		
You Can't Stay Here (Step It Up And Go)/I'm Not Ashamed (Ugly Woman)	1955	Harlem 2332
CONCORDS (2) (AKA SNOWMEN/AKA SHERWOODS (3))		
Cross My Heart/Our Last Goodbye	1961	Gramercy 304
Again/The Boy Most Likely	1961	RCA 7911
My Dreams/Scarlet Ribbons	1962	Gramercy 305
Marlene/Our Love Wasn't Meant To Be	1962	Herald 576
Cold And Frosty Morning/ Don't Go Now	1962	Herald 578 (first pressing, second is by the Snowmen)
One Step From Heaven/Away	1962	Rust 5048
Should I Cry/It's Our Wedding Day	1964	Epic 9697
Down The Aisle Of Love/I Feel A Love Comin' On	1966	Boom 60021/Polydor 14036 (70)
CONCORDS (2) (FB NEAL SCOTT)		
Bobby/I Haven't Found It With Another	1961	Portrait 102
Run To Me/Tomboy	1962	Comet 2151
One Piece Bathing Suit/Little Girl	1963	Herald 581
I Don't Stand A Ghost Of A Chance/Let Me Think It Over	1967	Cameo 476
CONCORDS (3) (TONY COLTON & THE)		
Goodbye Cindy Goodbye/Tell The World	1963	Roulette 4475
CONCORDS (4) (SUE KENNY & THE)		
Look/A Fool In Love	1963	Tribute 118
CONDORS		
Sweetest Angel/Little Curly Top	1962	Hunter 2503/2504
CONES (CONNIE & THE)		
Let Us Pretend/I See The Image Of You	1959	NRC 5006
Lonely Girl's Prayer/I Love My Teddy Bear	1960	Roulette 4223
Take All The Kisses/No Time For Tears	1960	Roulette 4313
CONFESSIONS		
Be-Bop Baby/Before You Change Your Mind	1961	Epic 9474
CONFIDENTIALS (BILLY JOE & THE)		
Feeling Blue/Got You On My Mind	1965	BJ 64
CONNER, HAROLD (& GROUP)		
I'll Be There/Please Don't Tell Me (no group)	N/A	Recona 3504
CONNOTATIONS		
Two Hearts Fall In Love/Before I Go	1962	Technichord 1000/1001/ Clifton 25 (78)
When You Wish Upon A Star/ When I Fall In Love	1980	Clifton 51

Artist	Song	Year	Label
CONNOTATIONS (JOEL & THE)			
	Stormy Weather/Zoom	1979	Clifton 33
CONQUERORS (FEMALE)			
	Billy Is My Boyfriend/Duchess			
	Conquers Duke	1962	Lu Pine 108
CONSERVATIVES			
	That's All/Chunchin' Song	1968	Ebonic Sound 6569
CONSOLES (BOBBY & THE)			
	My Jelly Bean/Nita, I Need			
	You So	1963	Diamond 141
	Karine//Maybe	1966	Verve 10402
CONSORTS			
	Star Above/Carrie	1977	Crystal Ball 111
	BarbaraAnn/A Fool In Love/			
	Runaround/A Mother's Love	N/A	Clifton EP 501
CONSORTS (1) (LES LEVO & THE)			
	Nina/Got Me A Sweetheart	1959	Nina 1601
CONSORTS (2) (AKA CHUCKLES (3)/AKA FOUR CLEFS)			
	Please Be Mine/Time After Time	1961	Cousins 1004/Apt 25066 (62)
CONSTELLATIONS (1)			
	Come Sit By Me/God Loves			
	You Child	1956	Groove 0140
CONSTELLATIONS (2)			
	My Dear/Oh Mary	1963	Violet 1053
CONSULS (1)			
	Runaway/I'm Happy	1959	Abel 222
CONSULS (2) (LITTLE CAESAR & THE) (AKA LITTLE CAESAR & THE ROMANS)			
	My Girl Sloopy/Poison Ivy	1965	Mala 512
CONTELS			
	Hey You/Lover's Dream	1959	Warwick 103
CONTENDERS (AKA FIVE SCRIPTS/AKA KAPTIONS/AKA LYTATIONS/AKA ZIPPERS)			
	Mr. Dee Jay/Yes I Do	1959	Blue Sky 105
	The Clock/Peace Of Mind	1963	Long Fiber 201
	Whenever I Get Lonely/That's			
	The Way	1963	Saxony 1001/Saxony 1001 (93)
	The Dune Buggy/Go Ahead	1964	Chattahoochie 644
	Johnny B. Goode/Rise And			
	Shine	1964	Chattahoochie 656
	The Clock/Look At Me	1966	Java 101
	Lovely Lover/Surprise	1966	Java 102
	Lonely Lover/I Like It Like That	1966	Java 103
	Hetta Hetta/I Know Somewhere	1966	Java 104
	Gunga Din/Wake Up In The			
	Morning	1967	Whitney Sound 1929
CONTESSAS (FEMALE)			
	Boy Of My Heart/Hard Guy To			
	Please	1963	Witch 113
CONTINENTAL FIVE			
	Moe & Joe/Perdelia	1959	Nu Kat 10132
	My Lonely Friend/King Of Rock			
	And Roll	1959	Nu Kat 104/105
CONTINENTAL GEMS			
	My Love Will Follow You/			
	Everywhere	1963	Guyden 2091
CONTINENTALS (1)			
	Dear Lord/Fine Fine Frame	1956	Whirlin' Disc 101/Port 70018 (59)
	Picture Of Love/Soft And Sweet	1956	Whirlin' Disc 105/ Port 70024 (59)
	Peace Of Mind	N/A	Relic LP 5036
CONTINENTALS (10) (MICHAEL & THE)			
	Little School Girl/Rain In My			
	Eyes	1965	Audio Fidelity 139
CONTINENTALS (11)			
	My Lonely Friend/Impossible			
	(by the Velvatones)	1961	Candlelite 412
CONTINENTALS (12)			
	It Doesn't Matter/Whisper It	1962	Hunter 3503
CONTINENTALS (13)			
	No Money No Luck Blues	N/A	Vandan 8067
	Pink Champagne	N/A	Vandan 8453
CONTINENTALS (14)			
	Man With A Broken Heart	N/A	M
CONTINENTALS (15) (MORRIS ROGERS & THE)			
	Wonders Of Love/The Leg	N/A	Delta 601
CONTINENTALS (16)			
	Goodbye/This Is Why	1974	Owl 331
CONTINENTALS (2)			
	Don't Do It Baby/Tongue Twister	1959	Davis 466
CONTINENTALS (3)			
	Take A Gamble On Me/			
	Meanwhile Back At The Ranch	1956	Key 517
	You're An Angel/Giddy-Up And			
	Ding-Dong	1956	Rama 190
CONTINENTALS (4) (BILL HARRIS & THE)			
	Danny Boy/I'm So Glad	1958	Eagle 1002
CONTINENTALS (5)			
	Sad Love Affair/White Buck			
	Shoes	1959	Red Top 121
CONTINENTALS (6) (TEDDY & THE)			
	Tick Tick Tock/Everybody Pony	1961	Richie 1001/Pik 235 (61)
	Do You/Tighten Up	1961	Richie 445
	Crying Over You/Crossfire With			
	Me Baby	1961	Richie 453
	Tick Tick Tock/Wild Christening			
	Party (by the Teen Kings)	1962	Rago 201
CONTINENTALS (7) (BILLY JOHN & THE)			
	Ooh Pooh Pah Doo/Does			
	Someone Care (For Me)	1962	N-Joy 1012
	Lover Boy Blue/Put The Hurt			
	On You	1962	N-Joy 1014
CONTINENTALS (8) (LENNY & THE)			
	Little Joe And Linda Lee/The			
	Shack (instrumental)	1963	Tribute 119
	Dance The Last Dance/Rosebud	1963	Tribute 125
CONTINENTALS (9) (JOEY & THE)			
	She Rides With Me/Rudy Vadoo	1965	Claridge 304
	Linda/Will Love Ever Come			
	My Way	1965	Komet 1001
	Sad Girl/Baby	1965	Laurie 3294
CONTINETTES			
	Boys Who Don't Understand/			
	Billy The Kidder	1963	Richie 452
CONTOURS			
	Funny/The Stretch	1961	Motown 1012
CONTOURS (MIKE HANKS & THE)			
	Christen/Can I Be Your Lover			
	Boy	1960	Brax 221/222
CONTOURS (TEXAS RED & THE)			
	Comin' Home/Turn Around	1957	Bullseye 1009
CONTRAILS			
	Someone/Mummy Walk	1965	Reuben 711/Diamond 213 (66)
	Make Me Love You/Feel So Fine	1967	Millage 104
CONTRASTS (BILLY VERA & THE)			
	My Heart Cries/All My Love	1962	Rust 5051
CONVINCERS			
	Rejected Love/Go Back Baby	1962	Movin' 100
COOK, GENE (& GROUP)			
	Ann Marie/Silly Girl	N/A	Jarrell 101
COOK, JOHNNY (& GROUP)			
	My Dear My Darling/It's All In			
	Your Mind	1957	Lamp 2006
COOKE, DALE (AKA SAM COOKE) (& GROUP)			
	Loveable/Forever	1957	Specialty 596
COOKE, L.C. (& GROUP)			
	Please Think Of Me/I'm Falling	1959	Checker 925
COOKE, SAM (& GROUP)			
	Forever/I'll Come Running			
	Back To You	1957	Specialty 619
	That's All I Need To Know/			
	I Don't Want To Cry	1958	Specialty 627
	Just For You/Made For Me	1961	Sar 122
COOKIES (1) (FEMALE)			
	Don't Let Go/All Night Mambo	1954	Lamp 8008
	Precious Love/Later, Later	1955	Atlantic 1061
	In Paradise/Passing Time	1956	Atlantic 1084/Atlantic 2079 (60)
	My Lover/Down By The River	1956	Atlantic 1110
	Hippy-Dippy-Daddy/King Of			
	Hearts	1957	Josie 822
COOKIES (2) (FB EARL-JEAN MCCREE) (FEMALE)			
	Chains/Stranger In My Arms	1962	Dimension 1002
	Don't Say Nothin' Bad (About			
	My Baby)/Softly In The Night	1963	Dimension 1008
	Will Power/I Want A Boy For			
	My Birthday	1963	Dimension 1012
	Girls Grow Up Faster Than			
	Boys/Only To Other People	1963	Dimension 1020

Artist Song	Year	Label
I Never Dreamed/The Old Crowd	1964	Dimension 1032
COOL CATS (ROBIN & THE)		
Give Me Your Love/(no flip)	N/A	Pussy Cat 501
COOL GENTS (DEROY GREEN & THE)		
Beggar To A Queen/At The Teen Center	1961	Cee Jay 584
Phoebe	N/A	unreleased
COOL TONES		
Hello Mama/Cry All Night	N/A	Dice 750
Ginchy/Movin' Out	1959	Warwick 505
The Dixie Blues/Daylight In Dixie	1962	Radiant 1510
COOLBREEZERS		
You Know I Go For You/My Brother	1957	ABC 9865
The Greatest Love Of All/Eda Weda Bug	1958	Bale 100/101
Let Christmas Ring/Hello, Mr. New Year	1958	Bale 102/103
Just Room For Two/You Know I Go For You	1974	Roadhouse 1019
COOPER, BABS (& GROUP)		
Just Couldn't Please You/ Honest I Do	1962	Indigo 144
COOPER, DOLLY (& GROUP)		
My Man/Ay La Bah	1955	Modern 965
I'm Looking Through Your Window/Big Rock Inn	1956	Dot 15495
COOPER, WADE (& GROUP)		
Oh Me Oh My/I'm Gonna Love You So	1960	Ember 1059
COPAS		
When I'm With You	1967	Catamount 118
Swanee/When You Dance	1979	U.G.H.A. 10
Traveling Stranger/Island Of Love	1979	U.G.H.A. 11
COPASETICS		
Collegian/Believe In Me	1956	Premium 409
COPYCATS (SUZY & THE)		
No Other Love (Like Yours)/ Come Back To Me	1961	Brent 7020
COQUETTES (MIKE BURNETTE & THE)		
Ricky/Parking Meter	1959	Imperial 5610
CORALAIRS (T. RENALDI & THE)		
Baby Blue Eyes/A Lover Is A Fool	1958	Bee 1543
CORALITES		
True Love/Unchained Melody	N/A	Carib 1008
CORALS (FEMALE)		
Tell Me Yes/The Puppet	1962	Cheer 1001
My Best Friend/Dancin' And Cryin'	1962	Kram 1001/Rayna 5010 (62)
CORALTONES (DAVE BRYAN & THE)		
Please Forgive Me, Don't Forget Me/Let's Make It Real	1956	Speck 103
CORBY, DOUG (& GROUP)		
Let's Get Together Again/The Wonderful World Of Children	1963	Vault 922
CORDELL, RICHIE (& GROUP)		
Tick Tock/Please Don't Tell Her	1962	Rori 707
CORDELLS		
Believe In Me/Please Don't Go	1958	Bullseye 1017
The Beat Of My Heart/Laid Off	1961	Bargain 5004
Happy Time	1964	Ador 6402
CORDIALS (1)		
I'm Ashamed/Sentimental Journey	1960	Cordial 1001
CORDIALS (2)		
Dawn Is Almost Here/Keep An Eye	1961	7 Arts 707
CORDIALS (3) (GM BOBBY PICKETT)		
A Fool In Love/Eek	1961	Stan 111
Once In A Lifetime/What Kind Of Fool Am I?	1962	Felsted 8653
Eternal Love/The International Twist	1962	Reveille 106
CORDIALS (4)		
Listen To My Heart/My Heart's Desire	1962	Whip 276
CORDIALS (5) (FEMALE)		
I'm Not Crying Anymore/What's The Matter With Me	1962	Bethlehem 3019
CORDIALS (6)		
Oh How I Love Her/You Can't Believe In Love	1965	Liberty 55784
CORDOVANS		
Come On Baby/My Heart	1960	Johnson 731
CORDUROYS		
Forever Yours/Ain't Gonna Let You Go	1961	Hale 100
COREY, JOHN (WITH THE FOUR SEASONS)		
Pollyanna/I'll Forget	1961	Vee Jay 466
CORLETTES		
I Love You/Crazy Baby	1962	Kansoma 02
Tears On My Pillow/How Do You Feel	N/A	Pace/Nita 711
CORONA, LARRY (& GROUP)		
Revenge/Jane	1956	Fortune 523
CORONADOS (1)		
Let's Get Acquainted/I Came Back To Say I'm Sorry	1956	Vik 0217
My Beautiful Dream/No No Blues	1957	Vik 0265
Good Night Kiss/World Of Confusion	1958	United Artists 135
CORONADOS (2)		
The Nature Of My Love/I Believe	1960	Columbia 41550
CORONADOS (3)		
Saturday Hop/Why	1961	Peerless 5134
My Elise/Lying	1961	Ric 979
CORONAS		
I Need Your Lovin' Again/All Out Vota (instrumental)	1965	Corona 520
CORONDOLAYS (CHICO & THE)		
My Wishes/Little Green Man	1965	Style 1927
CORONETS		
Nadine/I'm All Alone	1953	Chess 1549
It Would Be Heavenly/Baby's Coming Home	1953	Chess 1553
I Love You More/Crime Doesn't Pay	1955	Groove 0114
Hush/The Bible Tells Me So	1955	Groove 0116
Don't Deprive Me/Little Boy	1955	Sterling 903
CORONETS (SAMMY GRIGGS & THE)		
Footsteps/Long John Silver	1960	J.O.B. 100
CORRENTE, SAL (& GROUP)		
Run Run Run/Love Me	1966	Roulette 4673
CORRIDORS		
Dear One/I Want To Marry You	1963	Zone 4323/Wildcat 0057 (63)
CORSAIRS (1)		
Goodbye Darling/Rock Lilly Rock	1957	Hy-Tone 110
CORSAIRS (2)		
Time Waits/It Won't Be A Sin	1961	Smash 1715
Smoky Places/Thinkin' (Maybe She's Changed Her Ways)	1961	Tuff 1808/Chess 1808 (61)
I'll Take You Home/Sittin' On Your Doorstep	1962	Tuff 1818/Chess 1818 (62)
Dancing Shadows/While At The Stroke Of Midnight/Listen To My Little Heart	1962	Tuff 1830/Chess 1830 (62)
	1962	Tuff 1840/Chess 1840 (62)
Stormy//(It's Almost) Sunday Morning	1963	Tuff 1847/Chess 1847 (63)
Save A Little Monkey/ (flip is instrumental)	1963	Tuff 375
CORSAIRS (2) (LANDY MCNEIL & THE)		
The Change In You/On The Spanish Side	1964	Tuff 402
CORSELLS		
Nobody Heard About Me/Party Time	1964	Hudson 8104
CORVAIRS (1)		
Sing A Song Of Sixpence/Yeah Yeah	1960	Cub 9065
CORVAIRS (2)		
Whatcha Gonna Do/Love Her So	1961	Clock 1037
Something Wild/Darlin'	1961	Crown 004
True True Love/Hey Sally Mae	1962	Comet 2145
CORVAIRS (3)		
Gee Whiz/It's Aw'rite	1962	Twin 1001
I'm Gonna Marry You/I Need You So	1962	Twin 19671

Artist Song	Year	Label
CORVAIRS (4)		
The Girl With The Wind In		
Her Hair/I Don't Wanna Be		
Without You Baby	1963	Leopard 5005
Because I Love You	N/A	Relic LP 5028
CORVAIRS (5)		
Get A Job/Ain't No Soles In		
These Old Shoes	1966	Columbia 43861
CORVAIRS (6)		
A Victim Of Her Charms/Love		
Is Such A Good Thing	N/A	Sylvia 5003
CORVAIRS (7) (BILLY MARTIN & THE)		
I Found My Baby/Sweeney's		
Twist	N/A	Monitor 1402
CORVANS		
Sleepless Nights/Love Angel	1959	Cabot 131
CORVELLS		
We Made A Vow/Miss Jones	1957	Lido 509/Tip Top 509 (57)
The Bells/Don't Forget	1961	Blast 203
Daisy/Take My Love	1962	ABC 10324
He's So Fine/Baby Sitting	1962	Lu Pine 104/Lu Pine 1004 (62)
One (Is Such A Lonely Number)/		
The Joke's On Me	1963	Cub 9122
CORVETS (1)		
Lenora/My Darling	1958	Way-Out 101
Only Last Night (In A Garden)/		
Shark In The Park	1960	20th Fox 223
So Long/Alligator In The		
Elevator	1960	Laurel 1012
I'm Pleadin'/Let's Do The Pony	1961	Sure 1003
CORVETS (2) (ARTHUR & THE)		
I'm Going To Cry/You're Blue	1959	Moon 100
Darling I Love You/Poor Girl	1964	Na-R-Co 203
I Believe/Miracles	1964	NRC 2781
Aritha/Flossie Mae	1964	NRC 2871
CORVETS (3)		
You Don't Want Me/Want To		
Be Happy	1965	Soma 1425
CORVETTES (1)		
String Band Hop/Don't Restrain		
Me Joe	1958	ABC 9891
CORVETTES (2)		
Rockin' Around The Mountain/		
Shasta	1959	Arco 104
CORVETTES (3) (IRVING FULLER & THE)		
And Mine/I Can't Stop	1960	Emery 121
CORVETTES (4)		
In The Chapel/The Swinging		
Smitty	1961	Sheraton 201
CORVETTES (5) (LITTLE SONNY & THE)		
She's Mine	1986	Relic LP 8008
CORVETTES (6)		
Janice	N/A	Duncan 401
CORVETTES (7)		
Little Heart Attacks/Sweet Thing	N/A	Oak 4429/4430
CORWINS		
Little Star/When	N/A	Gilmar 222
COSMIC RAYS		
Bye Bye/Somebody's In Love	1960	Saturn 222
Daddy's Gonna Tell You No		
Lies/Dreaming	1960	Saturn 401
COSMO (BB THE CARNATIONS)		
Sweetheart Please Don't Go/		
Just Words	1962	Tilt 789
COSMOS		
(I Feel) You're Torturing My		
Heart/Angel, Angel	1962	Big L 502
COSYTONES (AKA COZYTONES)		
Speak To Me Of Love/Ride		
Along	1956	Melba
I'm Alone/Little Flirt	1957	Willow 1001
COTILLIONS		
Surf Twist/Sahara	1962	Alley 1003
What Kind Of Day Has It Been/		
This Road	1962	Ascot 2105
Sometimes I Get Lonely/One		
Of These Days	1963	ABC 10413
COUNT DOWNS (CHUCK HIX & THE)		
Sandy/Sixteen	1959	Verve 10169
Ballad Of A Badman/Is You Is	1959	Verve 10190
Loretta/Cookie Duster	1961	Flair 101

Artist Song	Year	Label
COUNT FIVE		
There Was A Time (acapella)	1975	Relic LP 103
Bells Of Love (acapella)	1975	Relic LP 103
I Do Believe (acapella)	1975	Relic LP 103
Sound Of Heartbreak (acapella)	1975	Relic LP 105
COUNT VICTORS		
Bye Bye Love/The Story Of		
Bonnie	1961	Rust 5034
Lorie	1962	Coral 62356
COUNTDOWNS		
Watermelon	1961	Image 5002
Satellite Dan/The Answer In		
Your Heart	1962	Rori 706
Lost Horizon	1963	Summit 0004
COUNTS (1) (AKA FIVE DOTS)		
Darling Dear/I Need You Always	1954	Dot 1188/Dot 16105 (61)
Hot Tamales/Baby Don't You		
Know?	1954	Dot 1199
My Dear, My Darling/She		
Won't Say Yes	1954	Dot 1210
Baby I Want You/Waitin' Around		
For You	1954	Dot 1226
Let Me Go Lover/Wailin' Little		
Mama	1955	Dot 1235
From This Day On/Love And		
Understanding	1955	Dot 1243
Sally Walker/I Need You Tonight	1955	Dot 1265
Heartbreaker/To Our Love	1955	Dot 1275
Sweet Names/I Guess I Brought		
It All On Myself	1956	Note 20000
COUNTS (2) (FRANKIE BRENT & THE)		
Cold As Ice/Playing The Field	1958	Vik 0322
No Rock And Rollin' Here/		
Lover's Lane//	1960	Strand 25014
COUNTS (3)		
Teen-Age Guy And Gal/Shake		
The Town	1958	Mercury 71318
COUNTS (4) (BOBBY & THE)		
Three Signs Of Love/Cellar Stomp	N/A	Count 6985
COUNTS (4) (BOBBY COMSTOCK & THE)		
Sweet Talk/Tennessee Waltz	1959	Blaze 349
Jealous Fool/Zig Zag	1959	Triumph 602
Let's Talk It Over/Jambalaya	1960	Atlantic 2051
Bony Maronie/Do That Little		
Thing	1960	Jubilee 5392
Everyday Blues/Wayward Wind	1960	Mohawk 124
The Garden Of Eden/Just A		
Piece Of Paper	1961	Festival 25000
I Want To Do It/Let's Stomp	1962	Lawn 202
Jezebel/Your Big Brown Eyes	1963	Jubilee 5396
Susie Baby/Take A Walk	1963	Lawn 210
Sunny/Chicken Back	1963	Lawn 217
This Little Love Of Mine/Your		
Boyfriend's Back	1963	Lawn 219
I Can't Help Myself/Run My		
Heart	1963	Lawn 224
Since You Been Gone/The		
Beatle Bounce	1964	Lawn 229
Ain't That Just Like Me/Can't It		
Be True	1964	Lawn 232
COUNTS (4) (FREDDY DAVIS & THE)		
I Hope You're Happy/Faith Can		
Move Mountains	1958	Count 405
COUNTS (5)		
Touch Me/Twistin' All Night	1961	Sunset 502
COUNTS (6)		
Don't Hafta Shop Around/Just		
A Little Bit	1964	Rich Rose 711
COUNTS (6) (TOMMY BURK & THE)		
You'll Feel It Too/Counted Out	1962	Nat 100
Stormy Weather/True Love Gone	1962	Nat 101/Smash 1821 (63)
You Better Move On	1964	Atco 6340
Rainy Day Lovin'	1964	H.I.P. 101
Cute/Ding-A-Ling	1964	Rich Rose 1001
You Took My Heart/She Told		
A Lie	1964	Rich Rose 1003
Without Me	1965	Southern Artists 2026
COUNTS (7) (COSMO & THE)		
Things I'd Like To Do/Small		
Town Gossip	1963	Sound Stage 7 2504
Soft And Pretty/You Gotta Dance	1963	Sound Stage 7 2520

Artist Song	Year	Label	Artist Song	Year	Label
COUNTS (8) (DANNY & THE)			**CREATIONS (4)**		
You Need Love	N/A	Coronado 136	Seventeen/You'll Always		
COUPLINGS			Be Mine	1962	Patti-Jo 1703
Young Dove's Calling/I Can See	1958	Josie 831	**CREATIONS (5)**		
COURT JESTERS			Through Eternity (acapella)	1975	Relic LP 109
The Trial Of My Love/Roaches	1961	Blast 201/Blast 208 (63)	My Best Friend's Girl (acapella)	1975	Relic LP 109
Drive Me Crazy	N/A	Jester 2034	**CREATIONS (6)**		
COURTIERS			Sweet Lovin'/Day Dreaming	N/A	Tan
I've Been Mistreated/Mean			Darling/I Don't Want To See		
Poor Girl	1959	Case 107	Tomorrow	N/A	Tan
COUSINS (1)			**CREATORS**		
Mademoiselle	1957	Nar 224	I've Had You/Drafted,		
COUSINS (2)			Volunteered And Enlisted	1961	Dooto 463
Be Nice To Me/I'm In Love			Do You Remember?/There's		
With You	1958	Decca 30609	Going To Be An Angel	1961	Time 1038
What'd I Say/Boston Hop			Too Far To Turn Around/Hello		
(by the Playboys)	1961	Chancellor 1074	There Mister Grave Digger	1962	Dore 635/Lummtone
COUSINS (3)			I'll Never, Never Do It		
Little Girl/Molly Bee	1960	Swirl 102	Again/Boy, He's Got It!	1962	T-Kay 110
Down That Lonely Road/			Cross Fire/Crazy Love	1963	Epic 9605
Everlovin' (Baby Mine)	1960	Versatile 105	Boy, He's Got It!/Yeah, He's		
COVACS			Got It	1963	Philips 40058
Say You'll Be Mine/Shouldn't I	N/A	Herald (unreleased)	I Stayed Home (New Year's		
COVAY, DON (& GROUP)			Eve)/Shoom Ba Boom	1963	Philips 40060
Please Don't Let Me Know/			I'll Stay Home/I'll Stay Home		
Take This Hurt Off Me	1964	Rosemart 802	(by the Jaynells)	1982	Jason Scott 24
COVINAS			Jungle Fever	N/A	Fortune LP 8017
Thanks For The Memories/			**CREATORS (WITH THE ALAMOS)**		
Five Minutes More	N/A	Hilton 3751	Wear My Ring/Booga Bear	1957	Hi-Q 5021
COX, HERBIE (BB THE CLEFTONES)			**CREELS**		
Vacation In The Mountains/			See Me Once Again/Do You		
Leave My Woman Alone	1958	Rama 233	Wanna Jump	1959	Judd 1005
COYNE, RICKY (& GROUP)			**CRENSHAWS (REF EBBTIDES (3)/REF FOUR AFTER FIVES/REF LAMPLIGHT-**		
Angel From Heaven/I Want			**ERS/REF RIVINGTONS/REF SHARPS/REF TENDERFOOTS)**		
You To Know	1959	Event 4294	Moonlight In Vermont/He's Got		
CRACKERJACKS (O. JAY OLIVER & THE)			The Whole World In His Hands	1961	Warner Bros. 5254
Real Love And Affection/			(Come On Baby) Let The Good		
Good Gravy	1958	Coed 500	Times Roll	1961	Warner Bros. EP 5505
CRAFTSMEN			Wishing Star/Off Shore	1961	Warner Bros. EP 5505
What's The Matter With			Off Shore	1961	Warner Bros. EP 5505
Grownups//(flip is instrumental)	1962	Warwick 678	Manana	1961	Warner Bros. EP 5505
CRAFTYS (AKA HALOS)			**CREOLES (LIL MILLET & HIS)**		
L-O-V-E/Heart Breaking World	1961	Lois 5000/Seven Arts 5708 (61)	Hopeless Love/Rich Woman	1956	Specialty 565
			CRESCENDOS (1)		
Zoom Zoom Zoom/I Went			Sweet Dreams/Finders Keepers	1956	Atlantic 1109
To A Party	1962	Elmor 310	I'll Be Seeing You/Sweet		
CRANE, LOR (& GROUP)			Dreams	1959	Atlantic 2014
When I Lay Me Down To			**CRESCENDOS (2) (AKA BARRONS/AKA CRESCHENDOS)**		
Sleep/Hey Cleopatra	1961	Radiant 1512	My Heart's Desire/Take My		
CRAVERS			Heart	1957	Music City 831/Gone 5100 (61)
Windstorm/Flavor Craver	1958	Chock Full Of Hits 109			
CRAYONS			**CRESCENDOS (3)**		
Crazy Dream/Teach Me Mama	1963	Counsel 121	Oh Julie/My Little Girl	1957	Tap 7027/Nasco 6005 (57)
Love At First Sight/I Saw You	1963	Counsel 122	School Girl/Crazy Hop	1958	Nasco 6009
CREATIONS (1)			Young And In Love/Rainy		
There Goes The Girl I Love/			Sunday	1958	Nasco 6021
You Are My Darling	1956	Lido 501/Tip Top 501 (56)	Let's Take A Walk/Strange Love	1960	Scarlet 4007
Every Night I Pray/Mommy			Angel Face/I'm So Ashamed	1961	Scarlet 4009
And Daddy	1956	Tip Top 400	**CRESCENDOS (4) (JOHNNY WOODSON & THE)**		
The Bells/Shang Shang	1961	Jamie 1197	All That's Good/Dreamer From		
Woke Up In The Morning/			My Heart	1958	Spry 108
Strolling Through The Park	1961	Pine Crest 101	**CRESCENDOS (5)**		
This Is Our Night/You Are My			A Fellow Needs A Girl/Black Cat	1963	Domain 1025
Inspiration	1962	Mel-o-Dy 101	**CRESCENDOS (6)**		
I've Got A Feeling/The Wedding	1962	Meridian 7550	Ding A Ling/Baby Doll	1976	Robin Hood 144
Don't Listen To What Others			**CRESCENTS (1)**		
Say, Pt. 1/Don't Listen To			Everybody Knew But Me/		
What Others Say, Pt. 2	1964	Radiant 103	You Have No Heart	1957	Joyce 102
CREATIONS (1) (JOHNNY ANGEL & THE)			Roseann/You Have No Secrets	1957	N/A
We're Old Enough/Where's My			**CRESCENTS (1) (PAT CORDEL & THE)**		
Love	1959	Jamie 1134	Darling Come Back/My Tears	1956	Club 1011/Michele M 503 (59)/Victory 1001 (63)
CREATIONS (2)					
Lady Luck/We're In Love	1962	Penny 9022/Take Ten 1501 (63)	**CRESCENTS (2) (BILLY WELLS & THE)**		
			Julie/I Love Only You	1956	Reserve 105
Oh Baby/Plenty Of Love	1967	Globe 1000	**CRESCENTS (3) (DICK WATSON & THE)**		
Just Remember Me/Times			Be On The Lookout For The		
Are Changing	1967	Globe 102	Woman/Groover	1962	Gone 5144
I've Got To Find Her/Times			**CRESCENTS (4)**		
Are Changing	1967	Globe 103	Smoke Gets In Your Eyes/		
CREATIONS (3) (BOBBY RICHARDSON & THE)			Johnny Won't Run Around	1963	Arlen 743
This Is My Love/Nobody			When You Wish Upon A Star/		
Loves Me	1961	Ember 1076	Hey There	1963	Hamilton 50033

Artist Song	Year	Label
CRESCENTS (5) (CHIYO & THE)		
Pink Dominoes	1963	Break Out 4/Era 3116 (63)
CRESCENTS (6)		
Here You Come Again/That's		
All She Left Me	1965	Watch 1902
CRESCENTS (7)		
I'll Make A Vow/Come Back Baby	1965	Seven B 7013
CRESCENTS (8)		
You Are	1985	Relic LP 5053
Sympathy	1985	Relic LP 5053
Be Mine	1985	Relic LP 5053
Bewitched	1985	Relic LP 5053
Please Don't Tease	1985	Relic LP 5053
You're A Sweetheart	1985	Relic LP 5053
Zoom	1985	Relic LP 5053
CRESCENTS (9) (CLARA HARDY & THE)		
Call My Name	N/A	Astra 3010
CRESCHENDALS		
Oh My Love/Oh My Love		
(instrumental)	1963	Fortune 566
CRESCHENDOS (AKA CRESCENDOS (2))		
My Heart's Desire/Take My		
Heart	1960	Music City 831/Gone 5100 (61)
Teenage Prayer/I Don't Mind	1960	Music City 839
CRESLYNS		
Boom Chip-A-Boom/You've		
Been Going Steady Too Long	1963	Beltone 2036
CRESTONES		
She's A Bad Motorcycle/The		
Grasshopper Dance	1964	Markie 117
Hey, Little Girl Of Mine/I've Had It	1964	Markie 123
The Chopper	1964	Markie 127
CRESTONES (JIMMY & THE)		
Angel Maureen/New Girl On		
My Block	1964	Maria 101/Avenue D 11 (85)
CRESTS		
My Juanita/Sweetest One	1957	Joyce 103/Musictone 1106 (62)
Let Me Be The One	1958	Coed (unreleased)
Strange Love	1958	Coed (unreleased)
Pretty Little Angel/I Thank		
The Moon	1958	Coed 501
Sixteen Candles/Beside You	1958	Coed 506
Young Love	1959	Coed (unreleased)
Journey Of Love	1959	Coed (unreleased)
Six Nights A Week/I Do	1959	Coed 509
Flower Of Love/Molly Mae	1959	Coed 511
The Angels Listened In/		
I Thank The Moon	1959	Coed 515
A Year Ago Tonight/Paper		
Crown	1959	Coed 521
Keep Away From Carol	1960	Coed (unreleased)
Let True Love Begin	1960	Coed (unreleased)
Learning About Love	1960	Coed (unreleased)
You Took The Joy Out Of Spring	1960	Coed (unreleased)
Step By Step/Gee (But I'd		
Give The World)	1960	Coed 525
Trouble In Paradise/Always You	1960	Coed 531
Journey Of Love/If My Heart		
Could Write A Letter	1960	Coed 535
Isn't It Amazing/Molly Mae	1960	Coed 537
Party Doll	1960	Coed LP 901
A Rose And A Baby Ruth	1960	Coed LP 901
My Special Angel	1960	Coed LP 901
Party Doll	1960	Coed LP 901
Butterfly	1960	Coed LP 901
Silhouettes	1960	Coed LP 901
Dream Maker	1961	Coed (unreleased)
Out In The Cold Again	1961	Coed (unreleased)
I Remember (In The Still Of		
The Night)/Good Golly		
Miss Molly	1961	Coed 543
Little Miracles/Baby I Gotta Know	1961	Coed 561
Guilty/Number One With Me	1962	Selma 311
The Actor/Three Tears In A		
Bucket	1962	Trans Atlas 696
Fifty Million Heartbeats/Before		
I Loved her	1962	United Artists 474
I'll Be True/Over The Weekend		
(The "Crests" were		
actually the Tymes)	1963	Cameo 256
Tears Will Fall/Did I Remember	1963	Selma 4000
Baby/I Love You So (acapella)	1963	Times Square 6/Times Square 97 (64)
Lean On Me/Make Up My Mind	1964	Cameo 305
You Blew Out The Candles/		
A Love To Last A Lifetime	1964	Coral 62403
Phone Booth On The Highway/		
She's All Mine Alone	1965	Apt 25075
I'm Stepping Out Of The		
Picture/Afraid Of Love	1965	Scepter 12112
Try Me/Heartburn	1966	Parkway 987
I Care About You/Come See Me	1966	Parkway 999
My Time/Is It You?	1967	Parkway 118
Earth Angel/Tweedle Dee	1978	King Tut 172
You Blew Out The Candles/		
Tonight We Love (by the		
Four Directions)	N/A	Popular Request 108
CRESTS (WITH JOHNNY MAESTRO)		
Noone To Love/Wish She		
Was Mine	1957	Joyce 105/Times Square 2 (62)
CRESTWOODS		
Angel Of Love/Lucky Star	1961	Impact 6
CREW (RON & JOE & THE)		
Riot In Cell Block #9/Ain't Love		
Grand	1959	Strand 25001
CREWE, BOB (& GROUP)		
Oh How I Miss You Tonight/		
Ev'ry Time	1960	Warwick 601
CREWNECKS		
I'll Never Forget You/Crewnecks		
And Khakis	1959	Rhapsody 71960
Rockin' Zombie/When I First		
Fall In Love	1959	Rhapsody 71961
CRICKETS (DEAN BARLOW & THE)		
Be Faithful/Sleepy Little Cowboy		
(by the Deep River Boys)	1953	Beacon 104
When I Met You/Dreams And		
Wishes	1953	Jay-Dee 777
I'm Not The Same One You		
Love/Fine As Wine	1953	Jay-Dee 781
You're Mine/Milk And Gin	1953	MGM 11428
I'll Cry No More/For You I		
Have Eyes	1953	MGM 11507
Changing Partners/Your Love	1954	Jay-Dee 785
Just You/My Little Baby's Shoes	1954	Jay-Dee 786
Never Give Up Hope/Are You		
Looking For A Sweetheart	1954	Jay-Dee 789
I'm Going To Live My Life Alone/		
The Man From The Moon	1954	Jay-Dee 795/Davis 459 (58)
Be Faithful/I'm Not The Same		
One You Love	1963	Beacon 555
CRISIS (LONNIE & THE)		
Bells In The Chapel/Santa		
Town, U.S.A.	1961	Universal 103/Times Square 25 (63)/Relic 532 (65)
CRITERIONS (1)		
Don't Say Goodbye/Crying		
The Blues Over You	1959	Cecelia 1010
I Remain Truly Yours/You		
Just You	1959	Cecelia 1208/Laurie 3305 (65)
CRITERIONS (2) (TYGH & THE)		
To Be Mine/Do What You		
Wanna	1963	Flite 101
CRONIES (HERB & THE)		
In The Middle Of Love/		
The Phantom	1960	Personality 700
CROOM BROTHERS (FB DILLARD CROOM JR.)		
It's You I Love/Rock And		
Roll Boogie	1958	Vee Jay 283
CROSSTONES (1) (BB THE CHRISS CHROSS ORCHESTRA)		
Congratulations/Lies	1955	Jaguar 3014
CROSSTONES (2)		
Crush On You/Dream Girl/		
Joanne/Since Love's		
Been Knockin'	N/A	Clifton EP 510
Johnny/Rockin' Around The		
Christmas Tree/Merry		
Christmas Darling/All I		
Want This Christmas	N/A	Clifton EP 511

Artist Song	Year	Label
CROWNS (1) (ARTHUR LEE MAYE & THE)		
Set My Heart Free/I Wanna Love	1954	Modern 944
Please Say You Love Me/		
Cool Lovin'	1955	RPM 420 (unreleased)
Truly/Oochie Pachie	1955	RPM 424
Love Me Always/Loop De		
Loop De Loop	1955	RPM 429
Please Don't Leave Me/Do		
The Bop	1955	RPM 438
Earth Angel/Honey Love	1956	Dig 100 (unreleased)
This Is The Nite For Love/		
Honey, Honey	1956	Dig 124
Gloria/Oh-Rooba-Lee	1956	Specialty 573
A Fool's Prayer/Whispering		
Winds	1957	Dig 133
Gee/Only You	1957	Dig 146 (unreleased)
Sh-Boom/Sincerely	1957	Dig 149 (unreleased)
Honey Love/At My Front Door	1957	Dig 151
Cause You're Mine Alone/		
Hey Pretty Girl	1957	Flip 330
Honey, Honey/Will You Be Mine	1958	Cash 1063/Imperial 5790 (61)
All I Want Is Someone To Love/		
Pounding	1958	Cash 1065
Breaks Of Life/Only A Dream	1964	Jamie 1284
That's What I'm Gonna Do	1985	Relic LP 5052
Don't You Know (I Love You So)	1985	Relic LP 5054
At My Front Door/One Mint Julep	N/A	Dig (unreleased)
CROWNS (10) (TERRY & THE)		
Shelly My Love/Teenage		
Romance	1977	Harvey 103
CROWNS (2) (AKA FIVE CROWNS/REF DRIFTERS)		
Kiss And Make Up/I'll Forget		
About You	1958	R&B 6901
CROWNS (3) (HENRY STROGIN & THE)		
Why Did You Go Away/My		
Aching Feet	1960	Dynamic 1002
I'll Tag Along/I Love L.A.	1962	Amazon 1001
I Wanna Love/Old Folks		
Boogie While The Young		
Ones Twist	1963	Ball 1012
Why Did You Go Away/I'll Tag		
Along	1963	Ball 1015
CROWNS (4)		
Heart Breaking Train/Lonely		
For You	1959	Wheel 1001
CROWNS (5) (STARK WHITEMAN & THE)		
Graduation Day/Noise	1960	Sho-Biz 1004
CROWNS (6)		
Party Time/Amazon Basin Pop	1962	Chordette 1001
Possibility/Watch Out		
(with Larry Chance)	1963	Old Town 1171
CROWNS (7) (FB PHILIP HARRIS)		
I Wonder Why (You Make Me		
Blue)/Better Luck Next Time	1963	Vee Jay 546
CROWNS (8) (DANNY & THE)		
Night Moon/The Story Of Jack		
And Jill	1963	Mercury 72096
CROWNS (9)		
Gonna Get Right Tonight/It's		
Still Love	1964	Limelight 3031
CROWS (AKA JEWELS (1))		
Seven Lonely Days/No Help		
Wanted	1953	Rama 3
Gee/I Love You So	1953	Rama 5
Heartbreaker/Call A Doctor		
(by the Jewels)	1954	Rama 10
Untrue/Baby	1954	Rama 29
Miss You/I Really Really		
Love You	1954	Rama 30
Baby Doll/Sweet Sue (It's You)	1955	Rama 50 Mambo Shevitz/ Mambo #5
(by Melino & Orchestra)		
(instrumental)	1955	Tico 1082
CRUISERS (1)		
Baby, What A Fool I've Been/		
The Moon Is Yours	1957	Finch 353
Foolish Me/There's A Girl	1958	Zebra 119/Jason Scott 15 (81)
I Want Your Love/I Said Hear	1959	Arch 1611
Betty Ann/You Made A Fool		
Out Of Me	1959	Coda 3005
My Mary Lou/Cruisin'	1959	Winston 1033
Another Lonely Night/Please		
Let Me Be	1961	Pharaoh 128
CRUISERS (2)		
A Ring Around A Chain/Buoys		
And Gulls	1958	Era 1052
CRUISERS (3)		
Miss Fine/If I Knew	1960	V-Tone 207
Don't Tease Me/Crying Over		
You	1960	V-Tone 213/Guyden 2069 (62)
CRUSADERS (1)		
Seminole	1962	D.K.R.
CRUSADERS (2)		
I Found Someone/Swinging		
Week-End	1963	Dooto 472
CRYSTAL TONES		
Debra-Lee/A Girl I Love	1959	MZ 007/008/Zebra
CRYSTAL TONES (BILLY JAMES & THE)		
Never For Me/It's The Twist	1959	M-Z 111
CRYSTAL, LOU (& GROUP)		
Dreaming Of An Angel/Sheila		
Baby	1962	SFAZ 1001
CRYSTALAIRES		
Nobody Knows/Henry Said		
Goodbye	1963	Sound Souvenir 1/2
First Time Romance/For Lovers		
Only	1990	Crystal Ball 156
Back To School/School Is Over	1990	Crystal Ball 158
Mona/Ding Dong Teenage Bells	1990	Crystal Ball 159
Picture Of An Angel/		
Mr. Moon/Telephone/		
Man From The Moon	1990	Magic Carpet EP 512
Elevator Of Love/Tokyo Girl	1995	Crystal Ball 163
Little Miss Pinocchio/		
Cinderella Baby	1998	Sweet Beat 101
Pinocchio/Very First Tear	N/A	Mickey B Juke Box Review 101
CRYSTALETTES (FEMALE) (FB CHAKA KHAN)		
Shy Guy/Please Stay Away	1962	Crystalette 752
Just Think Of Me/Billy, My Billy	1963	Crystalette 753
I've Got Everything/We're In		
Love	1963	Crystalette 755
CRYSTALIERS (CLEO & THE)		
Please Be My Guy/Don't Cry	1957	Johnson 103/Cindy 3003 (57)
Please Be My Guy/Don't Cry	1976	Arcade 1001
CRYSTALS (1) (AKA OPALS (1))		
Four Women/My Dear	1953	DeLuxe 6013
My Girl/Don't You Go	1953	Rockin' 518
Have Faith In Me/My Love	1954	DeLuxe 6037
Come To Me, Darling/Squeeze		
Me, Baby	1954	Luna 100/101/Luna 5001 (54)
God Only Knows/My Girl	1955	DeLuxe 6077
CRYSTALS (10) (JESSE & THE)		
Tell Me	N/A	Geno 12348
CRYSTALS (11)		
Laughing On The Outside	N/A	Iona 1009
CRYSTALS (2) (FEMALE)		
I Love My Baby/I Do Believe	1957	Aladdin 3355
CRYSTALS (3) (SAM HAWKINS & THE)		
King Of Fools/The		
Whatchamacallit	1959	Gone 5042
CRYSTALS (4)		
Blind Date/Mary Ellen	1959	Felsted 8566
CRYSTALS (5)		
Love You So/In The Deep	1959	Specialty 657
CRYSTALS (6)		
That's Where I Belong/Better		
Come Back To Me	1959	Metro 20026
Gypsy Ribbon/Malaguena		
(instrumental)	1960	Brent 7011
CRYSTALS (6) (AKA METROS (2))		
Watching You/Oh My, You	1959	Cub 9064
CRYSTALS (7) (FEMALE)		
Dreams And Wishes/Mr. Brush	1961	Indigo 114
There's No Other (Like My		
Baby)/Oh Yeah Maybe Baby	1961	Philles 100
Pony In Dixie/Espresso	1961	Regalia 17
Uptown/What A Nice Way To		
Turn Seventeen	1962	Philles 102

Artist Song	Year	Label
He's A Rebel/I Love You Eddie	1962	Philles 106
He's Sure The Boy I Love/ Walkin' Along (instrumental)	1962	Philles 109
Let's Dance The Screw Pt. 1/ Let's Dance The Screw Pt. 11	1963	Philles 111
Da Doo Ron Ron (When He Walked Me Home)/Git It (instrumental)	1963	Philles 112
Then He Kissed Me/Brother Julius (instrumental)	1963	Philles 115
Little Boy/Harry (from W. Va.) And Milt (instrumental)	1964	Philles 119/Philles 119X (63)
All Grown Up/Irving (Jaggered Sixteenths) (instrumental)	1964	Philles 122
My Place/You Can't Tie A Good Girl Down	1965	United Artists 927
I Got A Man/Are You Trying To Get Rid Of Me Baby	1966	United Artists 994
Ring-A-Ting-A-Ling/Should I Keep On Waiting	1967	Michelle 4113

CRYSTALS (8) (CLAUDIA & THE)
| This Is Your Life/Little Love Of Mine | 1961 | Dore 601 |

CRYSTALS (9) (HOWIE & THE)
| Golly Gee | N/A | Fleetwood 4521 |

CUBANS (1) (JOE ALEXANDER & THE)
| Oh Maria | 1955 | Ballad 1008 |

CUBANS (2)
| Don't Go Baby/Oh Miss Dolly | 1958 | Flash |

CUBANS (2) (FB DAVIE "LITTLE CAESAR" JOHNSON)
| Tell Me (Will You Ever Be Mine)/ You've Been Gone So Long | 1958 | Flash 133 |

CUBS
| I Hear Wedding Bells/Why Do You Make Me Cry | 1956 | Savoy 1502 |

CUES
Forty 'Leven Dozen Ways/ Scoochie Scoochie	1954	Lamp 8007
Oh My Darlin'/Burn That Candle	1955	Capitol 3245
Only You/I Fell For Your Loving	1955	Jubilee 5201
Charlie Brown/You're On My Mind	1956	Capitol 3310
Don't Make Believe/Destination Twenty-One Hundred And Sixty-Five	1956	Capitol 3400
The Girl I Love/Crackerjack	1956	Capitol 3483
Why/Prince Or Pauper	1956	Capitol 3582
Crazy Crazy Party/I Pretend	1957	Prep 104
Old Man River/Always Remember (Not To Forget)	1960	Festival

CUFF LINKS (REF CUFF LINX)
Guided Missles/My Heart	1957	Dootone 409
How You Lied/The Winner	1957	Dootone 413
Off-Day Blues/Twinkle	1957	Dootone 414
It's Too Late Now/Saxophone Rag	1957	Dootone 422
Changing My Love/I Don't Want Nobody	1963	Dooto 474
So Tough/My Love Is With You	1958	Dooto 433
A Fool's Fortune/Trick Knees	1958	Dooto 434

CUFF LINX (REF CUFF LINKS)
| Lawful Wedding/Zoom | 1958 | Dooto 438 |

CUFFLINKS
| Only One Love/Next To You | 1962 | Gait 543 |

CULMER, LITTLE IRIS (BB THE MAJESTICS)
| Frankie, My Eyes Are On You/ Show Me The Way To Your Heart | 1956 | Marlin 803 |

CUNNINGHAM, DALE (& FEMALE GROUP)
| Trust Me/Too Young | 1958 | Cash 1067 |

CUPCAKES (1) (COOKIE & THE) (AKA TWILIGHTS) (FB TERRY "COOKIE" CLINTON)
Matilda/Married Life	1958	Khoury's 703/Judd 1002 (59)
Until Then/Close Up The Back Door	1959	Judd 1015/Lyric 1012 (63)
Part Of Everything/Matilda Has Finally Come Back	1961	Mercury 71748
I've Been So Lonely/Got You On My Mind	1963	Chess 1848
Matilda/I'm Twisted	1963	Lyric 1003/Paula 221 (65)
Until Then/Close Up The Back Door	1963	Lyric 1004

Artist Song	Year	Label
I Heard That Story Before/ All My Lovin' Baby	1963	Lyric 1008
Breaking Up Is Hard To Do/ I Cried	1963	Lyric 1009/Paula 312 (68)
Hey, Little Schoolgirl/Charged With Cheating	1964	Lyric 1015
Even Though/Walking Down The Aisle (by Little Alfred)	1964	Lyric 1016/Jewel 744 (65)
Long Time Ago/Kissin' Someone Else (no group)	1964	Lyric 1017
Belinda/Trouble In My Life	1964	Lyric 1020/Paula 230 (65)

CUPCAKES (1) (L. ALFRED WITH THE)
| Even Though/Walking Down The Aisle | 1965 | Jewel 744 |

CUPCAKES (1) (SHELTON DUNAWAY & THE)
| I Had The Blues/Who Would Have Thought | 1959 | Khoury's 715 |
| Since Your Love Has Grown Cold/Frankochinese Cha Cha Cha | 1961 | Khoury's 727 |

CUPCAKES (2)
| It's Willy/Deutsche Rock And Roll | 1959 | Time 1011 |
| Winter Blue/Pied Piper | 1965 | Diamond 177 |

CUPIDS (1)
| I Don't Know/Troubles Not At End | 1956 | Chan 107 |

CUPIDS (2) (FEMALE)
| My Dog Likes Your Dog/The Answer To Your Prayer | 1957 | Decca 30279 |

CUPIDS (3)
| Now You Tell Me/Lillie Mae | 1958 | Aladdin 3404 |

CUPIDS (4) (CARLO & THE)
| Teenage Blues/Crazy Rock | 1959 | Parker 501/Judd 1007 (59) |

CUPIDS (5) (DARWIN & THE)
| How Long/Chloe (instrumental) | 1960 | Jerden 1 |
| Goodnight My Love/Won't You Give Me A Chance | 1960 | Jerden 9 |

CUPIDS (6) (AKA CAMELOTS (2)/AKA HARPS (2))
Brenda/For You	1962	KC 115/AAnko 1002 (63)
True Love, True Love/Let's Twist	1962	UWR 4241/4242
Pretty Baby/Let's Rock	1964	Times Square 1
Heavenly Angel	N/A	unreleased

CUPIDS (7) (SANDY & THE)
| Rebel/I Didn't Know Him | 1963 | Charter 2 |

CUPIDS (8)
| Lorraine/Little Girl Of Mine | 1963 | Musicnote 119 |

CUPONS (MATERLYN & THE)
| I'll Be Your Love Tonight/ Turn Her Down | 1964 | Impact 28 |

CURIOS (1) (BUCKY BROWN & THE)
| Dream Date/Everybody Had A Dream | 1960 | XYZ 610 |

CURIOS (2) (BOBBY BROWN & THE)
| I Got The Blues/Down At Mary's House | 1959 | Vaden 100 |
| Please, Please Baby | 1959 | Vaden 109 |

CURLS
| Imaginez Vous/Why Didn't I Go | 1959 | Everest 19319 |
| Like A Waterfall/He's My Hero | 1960 | Everest 19350 |

CURRY, EARL (BB THE BLENDERS)
| Love Somebody/Hobo | 5 | Post 2011 |

CURRY, JAMES (BB THE JAYHAWKS)
| Please Baby/My Promise | 1956 | Flash 110 |

CURTAINS (MR. LEE &)
| It's Fair To Me/The Lonesome Walk | 1970 | Boardwalk 18 |

CURTIN, LEE (& GROUP)
| Hot Dog/Gee I'm Sorry | 1961 | Gizmo 003 |

CURTIS, EDDIE "TEX" (& GROUP)
| Don't Cry/You're Just Too Pretty For Me | 1956 | Dot 15505 |

CURTIS, TEX (& GROUP)
| Prayer To The Moon/Shake, Pretty Baby, Shake | 1954 | Gee 9 |

CURTIS, JIMMY (& GROUP)
| Without You/Simple Things | 1960 | United Artists 215 |

CURTISS, JIMMY (BB THE REGENTS)
| Let's Dance Close/Girl From The Land Of 1000 Dances | 1965 | Laurie 3315 |

CUSTOMS (1)
| Because Of Love/Earthquake | 1963 | Arlen 511 |

Artist Song	Year	Label
CUSTOMS (2) (DAVE &)		
Shortnin' Bread	1965	Dac 500
You Should Be Glad	1965	Dac 501
Bonie Maronie	65	Dac 502
CUTE-TEENS		
When My Teen-Age Days Are Over/From This Day Forward	1959	Aladdin 3458
CUTOUTS (BRIAN BRENT & THE)		
For Eternity/Vacation Time	1963	Penny 2201
CUTUPS		
She Has Gone/Double Date	1962	Jim 852
Cutups/Romeo	1962	Music Makers 301
CYCLONES (1)		
My Dear/Do You Love Me	1957	Flip 324
Good Goodnight/Big Mary	1959	Forward 313
Give Me Love/Say What	1961	Festival 25003
CYCLONES (2) (BILL TAYLOR & THE)		
Nelda Jane/(flip is instrumental)	1958	Trophy 500
CYCLONES (2) (BOB WILLIAMS & THE)		
You Can't Make Me Cry/Aftermath	1958	Trophy 503
CYCLONES (3) (WAYNE BROOKS & THE)		
Secret Love/Runaways	1961	Warwick 629
CYCLONES (4)		
Angel/I Need Love	N/A	Cyclone 500
CYMBALS (1)		
The Voice Of A Fool/Way In The Night	1963	Dot 16472
CYMBALS (1) (AKA FRED HUGHES & GROUP)		
One Step Too Far/Shout Mama Linda	1962	Amazon 709
CYMBALS (2) (LEE WILLIAMS & THE)		
Peepin' Through The Window/Lost Love	1965	Carnival 527
What Am I Guilty Of	N/A	Rapda
CYMBOLS (LITTLE SONNY KNIGHT & THE)		
My Darling/Tears On My Pillow	N/A	New Teenage 5001
CYPRESS, BUDDY (& GROUP)		
Don't Forsake Me/I'm In Love With You (no group)	1957	Flash 118
CYTATIONS (CHRIS & THE)		
The Glory Of Love/Unbelievable	1963	Catamount 100
CYTONES (JOHNNY DURAINE & THE)		
My Last Love/Shang-Dang-Do	1961	Dore 624
CZARS OF RHYTHM		
You Show Me The Way/Please Don't Leave Me	1965	De-Voice 2501
D'ACCORDS		
Runnin' Around/Who's Been Loving You?	1961	Don-El 110
DA-PREES		
Sometimes (When I'm All Alone)/Pay Day	1963	Twist 70913
DAARTS		
Beloved Stranger/Cut Me Up	1961	Dyna 109
DABETTES (KAREN CAPLE & THE) (FEMALE)		
One Dab Man/Why Do You Care	1962	Advance 3933
DADDY COOL (& GROUP)		
I'll Never Smile Again/Daddy Rocks Off	1972	Reprise 1090
I'll Never Smile Again/I'll Never Smile Again	1972	Reprise 1090
DADDY-O'S		
Freddie	N/A	Shell
DADDY-O'S (JOEY CASTLE & THE)		
Rock And Roll Daddy/Wild Love	1959	Headline 1008
DAFFODILS		
Wine/These Kissable Lips	1955	CJ 100
Walk	1955	CJ 101
Slave To Love/Be No Fool No More	1959	Champion 1014
DAHILLS		
Michelle/Why Do We Have To Say Goodnight	1964	Musicor 1041
Do You Want To Go Steady/Please Be My Girlfriend	1976	Clifton 13
She's An Angel/I Who Love You	1978	Crystal Ball 107
DAHLIAS		
Storm Tossed Sea Of Love/Go 'Way And Leave Me	1957	Big H 612

Artist Song	Year	Label
DAIDEMS		
What More Is There To Say?/Ala Vevo	1961	Lavere 187
DAISIES		
I Wanna Swim With Him/You Just Said You Love Me	1964	Roulette 4571
DALE, ALAN (& GROUP)		
Monday To Sunday/That's A Teenage Girl	1961	Sinclair 1003
DALE, BOBBY (& GROUP)		
You Love Me Only In Your Dreams/Love Me More	1961	De Rose 8469
DALES (1)		
If You Are Meant To Be/Lonely Women, Lonely Men	1957	Onyx 509
DALES (2)		
Rockin' Nellie/Sweet Annie	1960	Crest 1069
DALTON, DANNY (& GROUP)		
Who's Gonna Hold Your Hand/Walkin'	1959	Teen 505
DAME, FREDDY (& GROUP)		
Love Is A Game/(Right) After School	1962	Nic Nac 331
DAMONS (CARL LAWRENCE & THE)		
High School Dreams	1958	Jean 0001
DANDERLIERS (AKA DANDOLIERS)		
Chop Chop Boom/My Autumn Love	1955	States 147/B&F 1344 (61)
The New Way (Shu-Wop)/My Loving Partner	1955	States 150/B&F 150 (61)
May God Be With You/Little Man	1955	States 152
All The Way/Walk On With Your Nose Up	1967	Midas 9004
DANDEVILLES		
Heavenly Angel/Psychology	1959	Forte 314
Nasty Breaks/There's A Reason	1959	Guyden 2014
DANDIES		
Have I Lost Your Love/Red Light	1959	Peach 726
DANDLEERS (AKA DANLEERS)		
One Summer Night/Wheelin' And Dealin'	1958	Amp-3 2115 (first pressing, second is by the Danleers)
DANDOLIERS (AKA DANDERLIERS)		
My Love/She's Mine	1956	States 160/B&F 160
DANES		
Most Of All/Come On Baby	1961	Le Cam 718
DANIELS (AKA ELGINS (1))		
Big City/Finally	1963	Lantam 01
DANIELS, DOTTY (& GROUP)		
Play A Sad Song/I Wrote You A Letter	1963	Amy 885
DANLEERS		
One Summer Night/Wheelin' And Dealin'	1958	Amp-3 2115 (second pressing, first is by the Dandleers)/Mercury 71322(58)/Amp 3 1005 (58)
I Really Love You/My Flaming Heart	1958	Mercury 71356
A Picture Of You/Prelude To Love	1959	Mercury 71401
I Can't Sleep/Your Love	1959	Mercury 71441
If You Don't Care/(I Live) Half A Block From An Angel	1960	Epic 9367
I'll Always Be In Love With You/Little Lover	1960	Epic 9421
Foolish/I'm Lookin' Around	1961	Everest 19412
The Truth Hurts/Baby You've Got It	1964	Lemans 004
I'm Sorry/This Thing Called Love	1964	Lemans 008
If/Were You There?	1964	Smash 1872
Where Is Love?/The Angels Sent You	1964	Smash 1895
DANTE'S INFERNOS		
My First True Love (There She Goes)/Teenage Blues	1957	Lido 507
DANTES (1)		
Zebra Shoot/Dragon Walk	1964	Courtney 713
Top Down Time/How Many Times	1964	Rotate 850
DANTES (2)		
Can't Get Enough Of Your Love/80-96	1966	Jamie 1314

Artist Song	Year	Label	Artist Song	Year	Label
DAPPER DANS			**DARLINGS (1)**		
Bird Brain/Lonely One	1960	Ember 1065	In The Evening/Let's Go Fishing	1959	Penguin 0698
DAPPERS (1)			**DARLINGS (2)**		
Come Back To Me/Mambo			To Know Him Is To Love Him/		
Oongh	1955	Peacock 1651	Train Of Of Memphis	1963	Dore 663
Bop Bop Bu/How I Need You,			He Played 1, 2, 3, 4/My Pillow	1963	Dore 677
Baby!	1956	Rainbow 373	Please Let Me Know/Two Time		
My Love Is Real/Baby You			Loser	1963	Mercury 72185
Know You're Wrong	1960	Epic 9423	**DARNELL, LARRY (& GROUP)**		
DAPPERS (2)			That's All I Want From You/		
Unwanted Love/That's All,			Who Showed My Baby		
That's All, That's All	1956	Groove 0156	How To Love	1955	Savoy 1151
DAPPERS (3)			If You Go/Fing Fang Foy	1957	DeLuxe 6136
We're In Love/Spellbound	1958	Star-X 505	**DARNELLS (1)**		
DAPPERS (4)			She, She, Little Sheila	1962	Sara 1055
Chicken Twist/Lonely Street	1961	Foxie 7005	**DARNELLS (2) (AKA MARVELETTES)**		
DAPPERS QUINTET			Come On Home/Too Hurt To		
Look What I've Found/It's			Cry, Too Much In Love To		
Almost Christmas	1955	Flayr 500	Say Goodbye	1963	Gordy 7024
DAPPS (JOHNNIE MAE MATTHEWS & THE)			**DARNELS (1) (GUS GORDON & THE)**		
Dreamer/Indian Joe	1960	Northern 3727	In The Valley Of The Roses/		
Some Day/Mr. Fine	1960	Northern 3729	My Little Homin' Pigeon	1957	Bana 525
DAPS			**DARNELS (2) (DEBBIE & THE) (FEMALE) (AKA TEEN DREAMS)**		
When You're Alone/Down			The Time/Why, Why	1961	Vernon 100
And Out	1956	Marterry 5249	Daddy/Mr. Johnny Jones	1962	Columbia 42530
DAR-LETTS (FEMALE)			The Time/Santa, Teach Me To		
He's Gonna Get It/Til I Fell In			Dance	1962	Vernon 101
Love	1964	Shell 101	**DARRELLS**		
DARCHAES			So Tenderly/Without Warning	1961	Lyco 1003
Y-O-U/Life Is But A Dream	1980	Clifton 56	**DARROW, JAY (& GROUP)**		
Pain In My Heart/Danny Boy	1983	Nobell 7001	Girl Of My Dreams/I Love		
DARCHAES (BEN WHITE & THE)			That Girl	1961	Keen 82124
Jocko Sent Me/Nationwide Stamps	1962	Aljon 1247/1248/Coney	**DARTS (1) (SHERMAN & THE)**		
Island		Island	Remember/Rockin' At Midnight	1957	Fury 1014
DARCHAES (NICKY ADDEO & THE) (REF RAY & THE DARCHAES/REF			**DARTS (2)**		
UNIQUES)			On My Mind/Well Baby	1958	Apt 25023
Gloria/Bring Back Your Heart	1963	Savoy 200/Earls 1533	Sweet Little Baby/Gee-Ver-		
Where There Is Love/You Can			Men-Nee-Vers	1958	Dot 15752
Depend On Me	1964	Melody 1417	**DARTS (3) (HERB PRICE & THE)**		
Over The Rainbow/Fool #2	1964	Selsom 104	Gone Too Long/Shimmy		
DARCHAES (RAY & THE) (REF NICKY ADDEO & THE DARCHAES/REF			Shimmy (Cha Cha Cha)	1959	Tempus 1506
UNIQUES)			**DARTS (4)**		
Carol/Little Girl So Fine	1962	Aljon 1249/1250	Come Back My Love	1978	Magnet-United Artists LP
Darling Forever/There Will					850G
Always Be	1962	Buzzy 202	Sometime Lately	1978	Magnet-United Artists LP
DARDENELLES					850G
Now You're Gone/Feel Allright	1953	Entre 102	False Alarm	1981	Kat Family LP JW37356
A Thing Worth Remembering/			**DARVELL, BARRY (& GROUP)**		
Star Dream (instrumental)	1960	Pennington 108	All I Need Is You	1959	Colt 45 301
My Baby/Soft Is The Breeze	N/A	Playgirl 501	Lost Love/Silver Dollar	1961	Atlantic 2128
DARES (JOEY DAYE & THE)			Fountain Of Love/Little Angel		
True True Love/Talking About			Lost	1961	Cub 9088
My Love	1961	Fortune 868	Adam And Eve/A King For		
DARIENS			Tonight	1962	Atlantic 2138
Tell Me Love/Kid Me Not Baby	N/A	Carlson International 0027	**DARVELS (1)**		
DARIN, BOBBY (& GROUP)			I Lost My Baby/Gone	1963	Eddies 69
Judy, Don't Be Moody/Splish			**DARVELS (FRANKIE & THE)**		
Splash (no group)	1958	Atco 6117	Mr. Fortune Teller/Last Goodbye	1977	Crystal Ball 109
Lost Love/Queen Of The Hop			**DARWIN, RICKY (& GROUP)**		
(no group)	1958	Atco 6127	The Great Thinker/Deep In Love	1959	Buzz 103
Dream Lover (with Neil			**DATES (LINCOLN FIG & THE)**		
Sedaka on piano)/Bullmoose			Kiss Me Tenderly/Way Up	1958	Worthy 1006
(no group)	1959	Atco 6140	**DAVE & LARRY (& GROUP)**		
Somebody To Love/Artificial			Only A Dream/My Confession		
Flowers (no group)	1960	Atco 6179	To You	1965	B'n Kc 102
DARLENES			**DAVI (BB THE SPIDELS)**		
(I'm Afraid) You Hurt Me/I Still			Reason For Love/Go, Charley,		
Like Rock And Roll	1963	Stacy 965	Go	1962	Stark 110
DARLETTES (DIANE & THE) (FEMALE)			**DAVIES (JOHNNY GRECO & THE)**		
Just You/The Wobble	1962	Dunes 2016	High School Dance/Hogwalk	1959	Sonic 813
Just You/Here She Comes	1962	Dunes 2026	Rocket Ride/Why Don't You		
DARLETTES (FEMALE)			Love Me	1963	Pageant 602
Lost/Sweet Kind Of Loneliness	1965	Mira 203	**DAVIS BROTHERS**		
Love Will Make You Cry/To			Why Can't They Understand/		
Reconcile	N/A	Taffi 100	The Best You Can	1965	Guyden 2120
DARLIN, CHRIS (& GROUP) (FEMALE)			**DAVIS, BILLY (& GROUP)**		
A Casual Look/Please Write			Anne Marie/Small Fry	1960	R-Dell 118
Me A Letter	1961	Dore 578	**DAVIS, EUNICE (& GROUP)**		
DARLING, JOHNNY (& GROUP)			24 Hours A Day/Get Your Enjoys	1954	DeLuxe 6068
Baseball Baby/I Don't Want To			**DAVIS, GEORGE (& GROUP)**		
Wind Up In Love	1958	DeLuxe 6167	Out Of A Million Girls/Soft Touch	1962	Philips 40082

Artist Song	Year	Label
DAVIS, HAL "SONNY" (& FEMALE GROUP)		
The Way You Look Tonight/Way To My Heart	1959	Kelley 105
DAVIS, HAL "SONNY" (& GROUP)		
Sweet And Lovely/My Young Heart	1959	Alden 1301
King Of Lovers/Sweet And Lovely	1959	Alden 1303
You're Playing With Me/Read The Book Of Love	1960	Del-Fi 4146
You'll Find Love/I'll Tell It	1960	M.J.C. 104
What Do You Mean To Me/ Merchant Of Love	1961	Wizard 101/Vee Jay 387 (61)
One More Chance/Show Me	1962	Gardena 125
I Don't Know/Lover's Plan	1963	G.S.P. 2
DAVIS, JAN (& GROUP)		
You're Not Welcome (Anymore)/ Don't Walk Away	1963	Rendezvous 214
DAWN (AKA FIVE DISCS)		
I'm Afraid They're All Talking About Me/Lovers' Melody	1967	Laurie 3388
Sandy/For The Love Of Money	1967	Laurie 3417
Bring It On Home/Baby I Love You	1968	Rust 5128
DAWN QUARTET (BILLY DAWN QUARTET) (AKA DUKES (1)/AKA FOUR DUKES/AKA DONNY MILES & THE DUKES/AKA HERALDS)		
This Is The Real Thing Now/ Crying For My Baby	1952	Decatur 3001
Tonight Must Live On/Crying For My Baby	1974	Firefly 330
This Is The Real Thing/You Will Always Find Me True	1974	Firefly 332
DAWN QUARTET (BILLY DAWN QUARTET) (AKA FOUR DUKES/AKA DONNY MILES & THE DUKES)		
Miracle Of Love/Proud Of You	1973	Vintage 1010
DAWNS		
Love You So Tonight/Travelin'	1959	Catalina 1000
How Deep Is The Ocean/Why Did You Let Me Love You	1959	Climax 104
It Seems Like Yesterday/From You, Only You	1964	Atco 6296
DAWNS (BILLY HARTON [AKA HORTON] & THE)		
Like To See You In That Mood/Shadow	1964	Lawn 241
I Wanna Know/No One Can Take Your Place	1970	KayDen 403
DAWSON, RONNIE (& GROUP)		
Decided By The Angels/ Summer's Comin'	1960	Swan 4054
DAY BROTHERS		
A Thousand Miles Away/ Somebody Else	1960	Chancellor 1059
Cleopatra Brown/Wait For Me	1962	Firebird 103
DAY DREAMS (TONY & THE)		
I'll Never Tell/Why Don't You Be Nice	1958	Planet 1008/1009
Christmas Lullabye/Hand In Hand	1958	Planet 1054
Hand In Hand/I'll Never Tell	1961	Planet 1055
DAY, BOBBY (BB THE BLOSSOMS)		
My Blue Heaven/Don't Want To	1959	Class 263
DAY, DARLENE (BB THE IMAGINATIONS)		
Will/I Love You So	1961	Music Makers 106
DAY, DAWN & DUSK		
Let The Tears Fall/Miss Petunia	1955	Apollo 476
Let The Tears Fall/A Cheat's A Cheat	1955	Kent 519
Anytime, Anyplace, Anywhere/ Who Are You Kissing	1956	Josie 794
DAY, TRACEY (& GROUP)		
Jerry (I'm Your Sherry)/Once In A Blue Moon	1961	Vee Jay 467
DAYBREAKERS		
I Wonder Why?/Up, Up And Away (58)	1958	Lamp 2016/Aladdin 3434
DAYCHORDS (ROXY & THE)		
I'm So In Love/Mary Lou	1962	Don-El 116/Candlelite 430/ Clifton 24 (77)
Too Bad/One More Time	1962	Don-El 120
DAYE, BILLIE (WITH MALE GROUP)		
When A Girl Gives Her Heart To A Boy/Twenty Four Hours	1961	Bliss 1002
DAYLIGHTERS		
Mad House Jump/You're Breaking My Heart	1959	Bea & Baby 103
I'll Never Let You Go/ Something Is Wrong	1959	Domino 904
Come On Home/Reap What You Sow	1959	Key Hole 107
Tough Love/Sweet Rocking Mama	1960	C.J. 614
Oh What A Way To Be Loved/ Why Do You Do Me Wrong	1961	Nike 10011/Dot 16326 (62) Tip Top 2001 (62)
This Heart Of Mine/Bear Mash Stomp	1961	Nike 1011/Astra 1001 (65)
Cool Breeze/Baby I Love You	1962	Tip Top 2002
No One's Gonna Help You/ War Hoss Mash	1963	Checker 1051
Whisper Of The Wind/I Can't Stop Crying	1963	Tip Top 2007
Hard Headed Girl/Oh Mom	1964	Tip Top 2008
I Can't Stop Crying/Magic Touch	1964	Tip Top 2009
For My Baby/Sweeter	1964	Tip Top 2010
Whisper Of The Wind/Here Alone	1964	Tollie 9028
Tell Me/What About Me	1966	Smash 2040
DAYLIGHTERS (BETTY EVERETT & THE)		
Please Come Back/Why Did You Have To Go	1960	C.J. 611
DAYLIGHTERS (CHUCK & THE)		
I Can't Stop Crying/Bottomless Pit	1963	Tip Top 2006
DAYLIGHTS		
Billy Is The Boy/A Tear Fell From My Eyes	1963	Propulsion 601
DAYTONES		
Bless My Love/Krambuli	1963	Jubilee 5452
DAYTONS		
King Of Broken Hearts/Friday Better Come	1959	Norgolde 101
DAYTRIPPERS		
You Cheated	N/A	AMM 005
DAZZLERS		
Gee Whiz/Somethin' Baby	1958	Lee 100
DAZZLERS (TEDDY RANDAZZO & THE)		
Dance To The Locomotion/ Cotton Fields	1962	ABC 10350
DE BONAIRS		
Lanky Linda/Mother's Son	1956	Ping 1000
Say A Prayer For Me/Cracker-Jack Daddy	1956	Ping 1001
DE HAVILONS (EDDIE & THE)		
Baby Dumplin'/Xmas Party	1962	Peacock 1920
DE MARCO, LOU (& GROUP)		
Careless Love/My Lady Fair	1956	Ferris 903
DE VAURS (FEMALE)		
Baby Doll/Teenager	1956	D-Tone A-3
Where Are You/Boy In Mexico	1959	Moon 105/Red Fox 104
DE VELLES		
Misery/Let's Do The Hunch	N/A	Emanuel 107
DE VILLE SISTERS (RUEBEN GRUNDY & THE)		
Every Word/Sail Away	1958	Spry 110
DE VILLES		
Do Wop/Kiss Me Again And Again	1958	Aladdin 3423
Without Warning/Troubled Heart	1960	Dixie 1108
DE-ICERS		
Callin' My Love/After Five	1957	De-Icer 100
DE-LIGHTS		
I'm Comin' Home/One, Two, Button My Shoe	1962	Ad Lib 0207/Pop Line
DEALERS (FLOYD WHITE & THE)		
Cinderella/Cha Cha Rock (instrumental)	1960	Criterion 1
DEAN & JEAN (BB THE DEL SATINS)		
Please Don't Tell Me Now/ Hey Jean, Hey Dean	1964	Rust 5075
DEAN, TERRY (& GROUP)		
Dream Boy (Oh, Oh, Oh)/ It's Just Your Kiss	1957	Poplar 102
DEANE, JANET (BB THE SKYLINERS)		
Another Night Alone/I'm Glad I Waited	1958	Gateway 719

Artist Song	Year	Label
DEANS (1) (BARRY & THE)		
Rock With Me Baby/I'll Love You	1960	Zirkon 1001
DEANS (2)		
My Heart Is Low/I'll Love You Forever	1960	Mohawk 114
Humpty Dumpty/Le Chaim (Good Luck)	1960	Mohawk 119
Little White Gardenia/I Don't Want To Wait	1961	Laurie 3114
It's You/I Don't Want To Wait	1961	Mohawk 126
Oh Little Star/You Got Me Baby	1963	Dean 1928/Star Maker 1928 (63)
Chills, Chills, Chills/(Lady Of The) Caravan	1963	Star Maker 1931
I'm Gonna Love You/Don't Let Her Cry Tonight	N/A	Tin Pan Alley 316
Pretty Nola	N/A	Tin Pan Alley 319
DEANS (3) (DOLLY & THE)		
The Happiest Years/What For	N/A	Thornett 1008
DEB-TEENS (FEMALE)		
Darling/Drip Drop	1959	Boss 403
DEB-TONES (FEMALE)		
Miss Lonely Hearts/Cuddly Baby	1958	RCA 7242
Give It Up/Rock-A-Bye	1958	RCA 7384
Knock, Knock, Who's There/ I'm In Love Again	1959	RCA 7539
DEBELAIRES (FEMALE)		
The Wa-Wabble/So Long, My Sailor	1962	Lectra 502
DEBERONS		
It Only Takes One/He's Lazy	1960	Bond 1480
DEBONAIRES (1)		
Won't You Tell Me/I'm Gone	1956	Gee 1008
Darling/Whispering Blues	1957	Herald 509
Every Once In A While/Mama Don't Care	1959	Dore 526
Every Other Day/Jivin' Guy	1959	Maske 804
We'll Wait/Make Believe Lover	1960	Gee 1054
Every Once In A While/Gert's Skirts	1961	Dore 592/Dore 702 (63)
Hold Back The Dawn/Mama Don't Care	1962	Dore 654
Everybody's Movin'/Mama Don't Care	1964	Dore 712
I Want To Talk About It (World) Pt. 1/I Want To Talk About It (World) Pt. 2	1967	Galaxy 787
Cause Of A Bad Romance	1987	Relic LP 5069
Best Love/I'd Climb The Highest Mountain	N/A	Gee (unreleased)
DEBONAIRES (2)		
This Must Be Paradise/I Need You Darling	1958	Elmont 1004
DEBONAIRES (3) (BOB & THE)		
So Blue/Guess I'm Through With Love	1961	Debonair 2251
DEBONAIRES (4) (DICKIE & THE)		
Please Mr. Disc Jockey/Yo Yo Girl	1965	Valli 302/Jason Scott 19 (82)
DEBONAIRES (5)		
Please Don't Say We're Through/A Little Too Long	1964	Golden World 17
Please Don't Say We're Through/ Eenie Meenie Gypsaleenie	N/A	Golden World 26
How's Your New Love Treating You	N/A	Golden World 38
DEBONAIRES (6)		
In The Rain	N/A	Tobin 340
DEBONAIRS (1)		
As Other Lovers Do/ The Bill Collector	1957	Combo 129
Cause Of A Bad Romance/For The Woman I Love	1958	Combo 149
DEBONAIRS (2)		
Crazy Kind Of Love/To Be Without You	1960	Winter 502
DEBONAIRS (3)		
Fools Love/Ah-La-La	1961	B&F 1353
DEBS (1) (FEMALE)		
Shoo Doo De Doo/Whadaya Want?	1955	Bruce 129
If You Were Here Tonight/Look What You're Doin' To Me	1955	Crown 153
DEBS (2) (FEMALE)		
Johnnie, Darling/Doom-A-Rocka	1957	Keen 34003
DEBS (3) (FEMALE) (WITH THE ESCORTS)		
(We Like) Crew Cuts/Swingin' Sam (by the Pastels)	1958	Josie 833
DEBS (4) (FEMALE)		
If Wishes Were Kisses/Mucha Cha	1961	Echo 1008
Just Another Fool/Danger Ahead	1963	Double L 727
DEBS (5) (FEMALE)		
Dream Boat/The Mask	1962	Infinity 035
DEBS (6) (TY ROBIN & THE) (FEMALE)		
Please Be Good To Me/I'm Not Sure	1960	Rex 1010
DEBUTANTES (1)		
Just Leave It To Me/It It Too Soon?	1956	Savoy 1191
DEBUTANTES (2)		
Going Steady/Memories	1958	Kayo 928
DEBUTS		
Gettin' Mellow	N/A	Scudder 101
DECADES (3)		
Please Say It Isn't So/Buzz Buzz Buzz	1980	Avenue D 1
Stand By Me/Teenage Rose	1980	Avenue D 2
To Make A Long Story Short/ Everybody's Somebody's Fool	1980	Avenue D 3
DECADES (1) (BROTHER ZEE & THE)		
Sha-Boom Bang/Smokey The Bear	1962	Ramco 3725
DECADES (2)		
Dance Forever	1963	Daytone 1306
Lonely Drummer	1964	Daytone 6403
DECALS		
Londonderry Air/There In The Moonlight	1975	Monogram 103
Decaro Brothers		
My Heart Stood Still/Candy Coated Lies	1964	Liberty 55700
DECCORS (MARIE & THE)		
Queen Of Fools/I'm The One	1962	Cub 9115
DECKERS (1)		
Sincerely With All My Heart/ Come Back Baby	1958	Yeadon 101
Sincerely With All My Heart/ The Thing	1958	Yeadon 1041
DECKERS (1) (LYNN CHRISTIE & THE)		
Oh Where Did You Go/What Did I Do	1957	Nar 225
DECKERS (2) (JIGGER & THE)		
Falling Teardrops	N/A	GWS 3105
DECOYS (1) (AKA BELAIRS (3))		
I Only Want You/For You	1963	Aanko 1005
Memories/Happy Honeymoon (by the Four Fellows (2))	1963	Aljon 1261
It's Gonna Be Allright/Oh Baby (by the Bel-Airs)	1963	Times Square 8
Tomorrow/I Only Want You	1964	Times Square 9/Times Square 96 (64)
DECOYS (2)		
Listen To Me/Always Be Good	1964	Velvet 1001
DEDICATIONS (1)		
Why Don't You Write Me/ Boppin' Around	1962	Card 335/336/Card 2001 (62)
Shining Star/Mary Lou	1963	C&A 506/Jason Scott 10 (81)
Someone To Love/ Mr. Taxicab Driver	1964	Ramarca 602
Teardrops/Teardrops	1970	White Whale
Why Don't You Write Me/Juanita	1983	Avenue D 8
Crazy For You/Never	1983	Avenue D 9
Angel/Flower Of Love	1989	Clifton 86
For Your Love/Come Back My Love	1990	Clifton 92
DEDICATIONS (2) (DENNY & THE)		
Lost Love/I'll Show You How To Love	1965	Susan 1111
DEE CALS		
Stars In The Blue What Should I Do/A Wonderful Day	1959	Co-Ed 1960/Mayhams 1960 (61)

Artist Song	Year	Label
DEE JAYS (1)		
I'm Really In Love	1954	After Hours 102
DEE JAYS (1) (CHICO SHEPHERD & THE)		
You Actin' Funny Honey	1954	After Hours 101
DEE JAYS (2)		
You Took Your Love From Me/		
Canadian Sunset	1962	Sonata 1100
DEE, FERN (& GROUP)		
Dream Man/You'll Never Know	1958	Ember 1035
DEE, JOEY (& GROUP)		
Lorraine/The Girl I Walk To		
School	1958	Little 813/814/Bonus 7009
The Face Of An Angel/		
Shimmy Baby	1960	Scepter 1210
DEE, LARRY (& GROUP)		
Am I Just Your Clown/Turtle		
Dove	1961	Lagree 703
DEE, RICKY (BB THE EMBERS)		
Save Your Love For Me	1960	Palette 5068
DEE, RONNIE (& GROUP)		
Little Boy Blue/Never Leave		
The One You Love	1961	Wye 1008
DEE, SONNY (& GROUP)		
Here I Stand/I'm Not The One		
For You	1961	Kapp 421
DEE-VINES		
I Believe/World's Greatest Lover	1960	Lano 2001/Relic 514 (64)
DEE-VINES (FB NEIL STEVENS)		
More And More/What Could		
Be Better	1958	Brunswick 55095
DEEJAYS		
Love Me Baby/Don't Leave		
Me Here To Cry	N/A	SRC 101
DEEP RIVER BOYS		
Truthfully/Doesn't Make Sense		
To Me	1951	Beacon 9143
DEEPS		
Calypso Rock 'N' Roll/The		
Night Is Young	1957	Que 1000
DEEPTONES		
My Prayer	1954	Music City 736/Musicon 736
DEFENDERS		
Island Of Love/I Laughed So		
Hard	1964	Parkway 926
DEJA-VU		
Maybe/Over The Rainbow	1984	Starlight 22
DEL AIRS		
It Took A Long Time/Ma Ma		
Marie	1965	Delsey 302
DEL AMOS		
She's So Wonderful/I'm So		
Weak	1959	Nikko 703
DEL CADES		
World's Fair U.S.A./(It Takes)		
Two To Fall In Love	1964	United Sound Associates 175
DEL CAPRIS		
Speak To Me Of Love/Theresa	1963	Almont 304
Forever My Love/Hey Little Girl	1967	Ronjerdon 39/Kama Sutra 235 (67)
DEL CHORDS		
September Song/In Togetherness	1962	Midas 09
DEL COUNTS (RONALD BOBO & THE)		
Mother Nature/Lone Stranger	1960	Rose 23/Arcade 1002 (76)
DEL KNIGHTS		
Wrapped Too Tight/Wherever		
You Are	1961	Chancellor 1075
DEL MATES (JOHN STEELE & THE)		
You're Gonna Miss Me/Fat Man	1965	Wand 194
DEL PRIS		
Womp/The Time	1961	Varbee 2003
I Don't Want To Cry/It Must		
Have Been Love	N/A	Varbee (unreleased)
DEL RAYS (1)		
My Darling/The One I Adore	1958	Warner Bros. 5022
Around The Corner/Have A		
Heart	1959	Moon 110
DEL RAYS (2)		
Lily Maebelle/When We're		
Alone	1958	Future 2203

Artist Song	Year	Label
DEL RAYS (3)		
Our Love Is True/One Kiss,		
One Smile And A Dream	1958	Cord 101
DEL RAYS (4)		
Fortune Teller/Dimples	N/A	R&H 1005
DEL REYS		
Let's Stay Together/Young		
And Innocent	1960	Columbia 41784
DEL RIOS (1)		
Alone On A Rainy Nite/Lizzie	1956	Meteor 5038
There's A Love/Just Across		
The Street	1962	Stax 125
DEL RIOS (2)		
The Vines Of Love/The Session	1958	Big 613
Valerie/Mystery	1963	Rust 5066
DEL RIOS (3) (JIMMY HURT & THE)		
You Know Darling/Oh, What		
A Feeling	1959	Do-Re-Mi 1401
DEL RIOS (4) (FEMALE)		
I'm Crying/Wait, Wait, Wait	1959	Neptune 108
DEL RIOS (5) (LINDA & THE)		
Come On, Let Me Try/I Don't		
Want To Be Loved	1962	Crackerjack 4005
DEL RIOS (6)		
Heavenly Angel/Dangerous		
Lover	1962	Bet-T 7001
DEL ROYALS		
You Can't Run Away/Trust		
In Love	1960	Destiny 101
Who Will Be The One?/She's		
Gone	1960	Minit 610
Barbara/I'd Wait Forever	1960	Warwick 111
Got You On My Mind/Close		
To You	1961	Minit 620
I Fell In Love With You/Always		
Naggin'	1961	Minit 637
DEL ROYS		
Love Me Tenderly/Pleasing You	1961	Carol 4113
DEL ROYS (AKA DELROYS)		
Strange Land/Wise Old Owl	1959	Sparkell 102
Love Me Tenderly/Pleasing You	1961	Carol 4113
Alimony	1964	Moon LP AB1
Happy Life	N/A	Carol unreleased
Mexico	N/A	Carol unreleased
DEL SATINS		
I'll Never Know/I Don't Care	1995	Park Ave. 11
DEL SATINS (AKA CAMPANIONS)		
I'll Pray For You/I Remember		
The Night	1961	End 1096
Counting My Teardrops/		
Remember	1961	Win 702
Teardrops Follow Me/Best		
Wishes, Good Luck, Goodbye	1962	Laurie 3132
Ballad Of A D. J./Does My		
Heart Stand A Chance	1962	Laurie 3149
Feelin' No Pain/Who Cares	1963	Columbia 42802
Two Broken Hearts/Believe In		
Me	1964	Mala 475
Hang Around/My Candy Apple		
Vet	1965	B.T. Puppy 506
Sweets For My Sweet/A Girl		
Named Arlene	1965	B.T. Puppy 509
Relief/Throwaway Song	1965	B.T. Puppy 514
A Little Rain Must Fall (with		
Carl Parker)/Love, Hate		
And Revenge	1967	Diamond 216
DEL SATINS (DION & THE)		
Come Go With Me/King		
Without A Queen	1963	Laurie 3171
DEL SATINS (LINDA LAURIE WITH THE)		
Stay At Home Sue/Lazy Love		
(instrumental)	1962	Rust 5042
DEL STATENS		
Seven Wonders Of The World/		
Don't Say Goodnight (by the		
Bop Shop)	1973	Kelway 105
DEL TONES		
Please Talk To Me/And The		
Angels Sang	1961	USA 711
DEL VICTORS		
Baby Sitter I Love You/Oh Lover	1963	Hi-Q 5028

Artist	Song	Year	Label
DEL-AIRS (1) (AKA DEL-AIRES/AKA RONNIE & THE DELAIRES)			
	While Walking/Lost My Job	1960	MBS 001
	It Took A Long Time/Ma Ma Marie	1961	Delsey 302
	Elaine/Just Wigglin' 'N Wobblin'	1963	Coral 62370
	My Funny Valentine/Drag (Ronnie & the Delaires)	1964	Coral 62404
	Arlene/I'm Your Baby	1964	Coral 62419
DEL-AIRS (2) (FEMALE)			
	Why Did He Leave/I'm Lonely	1962	Arrawak 1003
DEL-BROOKS			
	Darling Barbara/Thunderbird	1958	Kid 101
DEL-CAPRIS			
	Up On The Roof/If I Should Lose You (acapella)	1966	Amber 854
	Teardrops Follow Me/Man In The Moon	1966	Catamount 115
DEL-CAPRIS (BEVERLY & THE)			
	Mildred/Mama I Think I'm In Love	1964	Columbia 43107
DEL-CHORDS (1)			
	Help Me/Say That You Love Me	1960	Jin 126
DEL-CHORDS (2) (DONNIE & THE)			
	When You're Alone/So Lonely	1961	Taurus 352/Epic 9495 (62)
	I Don't Care/I'll Be With You In Apple Blossom Time	1963	Taurus 357
	That Old Feeling/Transylvania Mist	1963	Taurus 361
	I Found Heaven/Be With You	1963	Taurus 363
	I'm In The Mood For Love/I've Got A Woman	1963	Taurus 364
	Guardian Angel	1963	Taurus LP 1000
	Please Say You Want Me	1963	Taurus LP 1000
	Out Of Sight, Out Of Mind	1963	Taurus LP 1000
DEL-CHORDS (3)			
	Marsha-Mellow/At The Hop	1960	Cool 5816
DEL-CORDS			
	Everybody's Gotta Lose Someday/Your Mommy Lied To Your Daddy	1960	Impala 215/Genius 401 (63)
DEL-FIS (JERRY & THE)			
	Little Suzanne	N/A	Hound 102
DEL-HEARTS (DALE & THE)			
	I've Waited So Long/Always And Ever	1961	Herald 564
	High Blood Pressure/Please	1961	Herald 565
DEL-KNIGHTS			
	Everything/Compensation	1959	Unart 2008
	I'm Comin' Home/One Two Button My Shoe	1961	Sheryl
DEL-LARKS			
	Remember The Night/Lady Love	1958	East West 116
	Remember The Night/Bubble Gum	1992	Park Ave. 8
DEL-LARKS (SAMMY & THE)			
	I Never Will Forget/Baby Come On	1961	Ea-Jay 100/Clifton 29 (78)
	Little Darling/Sleep Walk	1961	Stop 101
DEL-LOURDS			
	Alone/All Alone (Acapella)	1963	Solar 1001
	Gloria/All Alone (Acapella)	1963	Solar 1003
DEL-MARS			
	That's My Desire/You Know	1963	ABC 10426
	Snacky Poo, Part. 1/Snacky Poo, Pt. 2	1964	Mercury 72244
DEL-MINGOS			
	Young Queen Chunka Bo Bo/ Goodnight My Love	1963	Lomar 702
DEL-PHIS (FEMALE) (AKA MARTHA & THE VANDELLAS)			
	It Takes Two/I'll Let You Know	1961	Checkmate 1005
DEL-PRADOS			
	Oh, Baby/The Skip	1962	Lucky Four 1021
DEL-RAYS (1) (DETROIT JR. & THE)			
	Zig Zag/I'm Gonna Find Me Another Girl	1964	C.J. 636
	Can't Take It/Mother-In-Law	1964	C.J. 637
DEL-RAYS (2)			
	I Want To Do It/Don't Let Her Be Your Baby	1968	Stax 162
DEL-RAYS (3)			
	Lorraine/Girl In My Heart	1981	Jason Scott 8
DEL-RAYS (3) (DAVE T. & THE)			
	Girl In My Heart/Scooter Town	1959	Carousel 213
DEL-RAYS (3) (FB DAVE T.)			
	Lorraine/The Bounce	1961	Planet 52
DEL-RAYS (4)			
	Runaround Lou/Mary Is Her Name	1963	Tammy 1020
DEL-REYS			
	Should I Ever Love Again/ Fannie Mae	1960	Delreco 500
DEL-RHYTHMETTS			
	I Need Your Love/Chic-A-Boomer	1958	J-V-B 5000
DEL-RIOS			
	Just For Tonite	N/A	Fortune LP 8017
DEL-SHARPS (SONNY ACE & THE)			
	If My Teardrops Could Talk/ Swingin' Stroll	1958	TNT 153
DEL-TINOS			
	Pa Pa Ooh Mau Mau/Nightlite	1964	Sonic 1451
DEL-TONES			
	Best Wishes/Walking Out The Back Door	1959	Ro-Ann 1001
DEL-VONS (AKA CHANTERS (2))			
	All I Did Was Cry/Gone Forever	1963	Wells 1001
DELACARDOS			
	A Letter To A School Girl/I'll Never Let You Down	1959	Elgey 1001/Candlelite (63)
	I Got It/Thing-A-Ma-Jig	1960	United Artists 276
	Dream Girl/I Just Want To Know	1961	Shell 308
	Hold Back The Tears/Mr. Dillon	1961	United Artists 310
	Love Is The Greatest Thing/ Girl Girl	1962	Shell 311
DELAIRS (FB RAY ADAMS)			
	I'm Gone/Rattle My Bones	1956	Rainbow 348
DELATONES			
	Ik-Heb-Je-Lief/Teenager's Love	1960	TNT 9028
DELCHORDS (DAVID CAMPANELLA & THE)			
	Somewhere Over The Rainbow/ Everybody's That Way	1959	Kane 25593/Candlelite 415 (62)
DELCONTE, DAVID (& GROUP)			
	Face In The Crowd/I Lie	N/A	Delcon 1
DELCOS			
	Those Three Little Words/Arabia	1962	Ebony 01/02/Showcase 2501 (63)/Sound Stage 7 2501 (63)
	Still Miss You So/Just Ask	1963	Sound Stage 7 2515
	Just Ask/I Miss You So	N/A	Monument
	When You Dance/Why Do You Have To Go	N/A	Monument
DELEGATES (1) (AKA KOOL GENTS)			
	The Convention/Jay's Rock (Big Jay McNeely)	1956	Vee Jay 212
	Mother's Son/I'm Gonna Be Glad	1957	Vee Jay 243
DELEGATES (2)			
	The Peeper/Pygmy	1965	Aura 88120
DELFIS 117			
	My Darling/Hope, Prayer And A Dream	1978	Crystal Ball 117
DELFONICS (1) (GM CARLTON LEE)			
	There They Go/You Can Tell	1962	Fling 727
DELFONICS (2)			
	You've Been Untrue	1963	Cameo 272
DELI-CADOS			
	Now I've Confessed/Granny Baby	1960	PMP (no number)
DELICATES			
	Black And White Thunderbird/ Ronnie Is My Lover	1959	Unart 2017
	Meusurry/Ringa Ding	1959	Unart 2024
	Flip, Flip/Your Happiest Years	1960	United Artists 210
	Too Young To Date/The Kiss	1960	United Artists 228
	My Pillow/I Played 1, 2, 3, 4	1961	Celeste 676/Dee Dee 677 (61)
	Not Tomorrow/Little Ship	1961	Roulette 4321
	Little Boy Of Mine/Dickie Went And Did It	1961	Roulette 4360
	Strange Love/I Don't Know Why	1961	Roulette 4387
	C'Mon Everybody/I've Been Hurt	1964	Challenge 59232
	I Want To Get Married/I've Been Hurt	1965	Challenge 59267

Artist Song	Year	Label
Comin' Down With Love/Stop Shovin' Me Around	1965	Challenge 59304
DELIGHTERS (2) (LITTLE "D" & THE)		
Oh My Darling/A Love So Fine	1958	Little "D" Records 1010
DELIGHTERS (1) (DONALD & THE) (AKA FORTUNES)		
Adios My Secret Love/ Somebody Help Me	1963	Cortland 112
(Native Girl) Elephant Walk/ Wang Dang Dula	1963	Cortland 109
I've Settled Down	1963	Cortland 116
DELIGHTS		
My One Desire/Please Take My Love	1961	Nite 1034
That Lucky Old Sun/Don't You Cry	1962	Golden Crest 574
I Cry/Breaking Hearts To Him Is Just A Game	1964	Arlen 753
DELL MATES		
Angela/Cross My Heart And Hope To Die	1964	Fontana 1934/Smash 1934 (64)
DELL TONES		
Yours Alone/My Heart's On Fire	1953	Brunswick 84015
DELL VIKINGS (AKA DEL VIKINGS/AKA DEL-VIKINGS)		
Come Go With Me/How Can I Find True Love	1956	Fee Bee 205/Dot 15538 (57)/Dot 16092 (60)
Down In Bermuda/Maggie	1956	Fee Bee 206
True Love/Uh Uh Baby	1956	Fee Bee 210
What Made Maggie Run?/ Uh, Uh, Baby	1956	Fee Bee 210
What Made Maggie Run?/ Down By The Stream	1956	Fee Bee 210/Dot 15571 (56)
True Love/Baby, Let Me Be	1956	Fee Bee 902
What Made Maggie Run?/ Little Billy Boy	1957	Dot 15571
I'm Spinning/When I Come Home	1957	Dot 15636/Mercury 71198 (57)
Whispering Bells/Don't Be A Fool	1957	Fee Bee 214/Dot 15592 (57)
I'm Spinning/You Say You Love Me	1957	Fee Bee 218/Dot 15636 (57)
Willette/I Want To Marry You	1957	Fee Bee 221
Willette/Woke Up This Morning	1957	Fee Bee 221/Dot 15673 (58)
Tell Me I'm The One For You/ Finger Poppin' Woman	1957	Fee Bee 227
Somewhere Over The Rainbow/Hey, Senorita	1957	Luniverse 106
A Sunday Kind Of Love/Come Along With Me	1957	Mercury 30112
Cool Shake/Jitterbug Mary	1957	Mercury 71132
Come Along With Me/ What'Cha Gotta Lose	1957	Mercury 71180
Your Book Of Love/Snowbound	1957	Mercury 71241
Heart And Soul	1957	Mercury EP 3362
I'm Sittin' On Top Of The World	1957	Mercury EP 3362
My Foolish Heart	1957	Mercury EP 3362
Is It Any Wonder	1957	Mercury LP 20314/ Mercury EP 3363 (57)
Yours	1957	Mercury LP 20314/ Mercury EP 3363 (57)
Summertime	1957	Mercury LP 20314/ Mercury EP 3363 (57)
The Voodoo Man/Can't Wait	1958	Mercury 71266
You Cheated/Pretty Little Things Called Girls	1958	Mercury 71345
Flat Tire/How Could You	1958	Mercury 71390
Pistol Packin' Mama/The Sun	1960	Alpine 66
I'll Never Stop Crying/Bring Back Your Heart	1961	ABC 10208
I Hear Bells (Wedding Bells)/ Don't Get Slick On Me	1961	ABC 10248
Kiss Me/Face The Music	1961	ABC 10278
One More River To Cross/ The Big Silence	1962	ABC 10304
Confession Of Love/Kilimanjaro	1962	ABC 10341
An Angel Up In Heaven/ The Fishing Chant	1963	ABC 10385
Too Many Miles/Sorcerer's Apprentice	1963	ABC 10425
Be Mine	1963	Crown LP 5368

Artist Song	Year	Label
This Heart Of Mine	1963	Crown LP 5368
We Three/I've Got To Know	1964	Gateway 743
Cold Feet/I Want To Marry You	1972	Bim Bam Boom 111
Come Go With Me/When You're Asleep	1972	Scepter 12367
Watching The Moon/You Say You Love Me	1973	Bim Bam Boom 113
Girl Girl/I'm Spinning	1973	Bim Bam Boom 115
Hey Senorita/Over The Rainbow	1973	Blue Sky 104
Yours/Heaven And Paradise	1973	Luniverse 110
In The Still Of The Night/The White Cliffs Of Dover	1973	Luniverse 113
There I Go/Girl Girl	1973	Luniverse 114
Milk Shake Mama (acapella)	1975	Relic LP 109
How Do You Like It (acapella)	1975	Relic LP 109
Hollywood And Vine/Welfare Blues	1977	Fee Bee 173
Come Go With Me/How Can I Find True Love	1980	Collectables 1251
Whispering Bells/Don't Be A Fool	1980	Collectables 1252 BVM
My Heart/Rock 'n' Roll Remembered	1991	BVM 001
Can't You See?/Oh I	N/A	D.R.C. 101
Come Go With Me/Whispering Bells	N/A	Lightning 9013
DELL VIKINGS (BUDDY CARLE & THE) (AKA DEL VIKINGS/AKA DEL-VIKINGS)		
Understand/It's Too Late	N/A	Eedee 3501/Star 223
DELL VIKINGS (WITH CHARLES JACKSON)		
Cold Feet/Watching The Moon	1959	Petite 503
DELL WOODS		
Don't Put Onions On Your Hamburger/Her Moustache	1963	Big Top 3137
DELL, JOEY (& GROUP)		
Let's Find Out Tonight/Only Last Night	1962	Roulette 4422
DELL, TONY (& GROUP)		
My Girl/Magic Wand	1963	King 5766
DELL-COEDS		
Love In Return/Hey Mr. Banjo	1962	Enith 712/Dot 16314 (62)
DELL-FI'S (LEON PETERSON & THE)		
Together Just We Two/My Love Came Tumbling Down	1960	Kable 437
DELL-OS (JOHN SHAW & THE) (AKA SENSATIONAL DELL-OS)		
Why Did You Leave Me/Why Does It Have To Be Her (no group)	1958	U-C 5002/U-C 1031
DELL-RAYS		
Darling I Pray/Pauline	1958	Boptown 102
DELLRAYS		
The Way You Look Tonight/ Hum Gully Gully	N/A	Lavette 1007
DELLS (AKA EL RAYS)		
Tell The World/Blues At Three (by Count Morris)	1955	Vee Jay 134
Dreams Of Contentment/ Zing Zing Zing	1955	Vee Jay 166
Oh What A Night/Jo Jo	1956	Vee Jay 204
Movin' On/I Wanna Go Home	1956	Vee Jay 230
Why Do You Have To Go?/ Dance, Dance, Dance	1957	Vee Jay 236
A Distant Love/O-Bop, She-Bop	1957	Vee Jay 251
Time Makes You Change/ Pain In My Heart	1957	Vee Jay 258
What You Say Baby/ The Springer	1957	Vee Jay 274
Jeepers Creepers/I'm Calling	1958	Vee Jay 292
Wedding Day/My Best Girl	1958	Vee Jay 300
Dry Your Eyes/Baby Open Up Your Heart	1959	Vee Jay 324
Oh What A Night/I Wanna Go Home	1959	Vee Jay 338
Swingin' Teens/Hold On To What You've Got	1961	Vee Jay 376
God Bless The Child/I'm Going Home	1962	Argo 5415
The (Bossa Nova) Bird/Eternally	1962	Argo 5428
If It Ain't One Thing It's Another/ Hi Diddley Dee Dum Dum	1963	Argo 5442
After You/Goodbye Mary Ann	1963	Argo 5456
Shy Girl/What Do We Prove?	1964	Vee Jay 595

Artist Song	Year	Label
Oh What A Good Night/Wait 'Til Tomorrow	1964	Vee Jay 615
Stay In My Corner/It's Not Unusual	1965	Vee Jay 674
Hey Sugar (Don't Get Serious)/ Poor Little Boy	1965	Vee Jay 712

She's Just An Angel/I Can't
   Help Myself
	1979	Skylark 558/Solid Smoke
		   LP 8029 (84)

Now I Pray/Someone To Call
   Me Darling
	1979	Skylark 581/Solid Smoke
		   LP 8029 (84)/Charly LP
		   1055 (85)

Restless Days, Sleepless Nights	1983	Charly LP 1056
Cherry Bee	1983	Charly LP 1056
I Can't Dream	1983	Charly LP 1056
Baby Do	1983	Charly LP 1056
At The Bandstand (The Springer)	1983	Charly LP 1056
Come On Baby	1983	Charly LP 1056
Rain	1984	Solid Smoke LP 8029/ Charly LP 1055 (85)
You're Still In My Heart	1984	Solid Smoke LP 8029/ Charly LP 1055 (85)
Don't Tell Nobody	1984	Solid Smoke LP 8029/ Charly LP 1055 (85)
Let's Do It Over	1984	Solid Smoke LP 8029/ Charly LP 1055 (85)
It Looks Like It's Over	1985	Charly LP 1055
DELLTONES (1)		
Baby Say You Love Me/ Don't Be Long	1955	Baton 212
DELLTONES (1)		
My Special Love/Believe It	1956	Baton 223
DELLTONES (1) (& THE KELLY OWENS ORCHESTRA)		
I'm Not In Love With You/ Little Short Daddy	1954	Rainbow 244
DELLTONES (2)		
No Darlin' No/Lookin' For A Gal	N/A	Maestro 1919
DELLTONES (3) (DINO & THE)		
Daydream	1965	Cobra 1117
DELLTONES (3) (J. JAY & THE)		
Too Late To Forgive/Just A Matter Of Time	1963	Cobra 5555
DELMAR, EDDIE (BB THE BOB KNIGHT FOUR)		
Garden In The Rain/My Heart Beckons You	1965	Vegas 628
DELMAR, EDDIE (WITH THE BOB KNIGHT FOUR)		
Blanche/Love Bells	1961	Madison 168
DELMARS (WITH THE MORDERN TRENAIRE BAND)		
Drive-In	N/A	RST 135
DELMIROS		
Dry Your Eyes/The Big Sound	1961	Dade 1821
DELMONICOS		
There They Go/You Can Call	1963	Aku 6318
Until You/World's Biggest Fool	1964	Musictone 6122
Heaven On Earth/Close Your Eyes	1990	Clifton 88
DELMONICOS (DENISE G. & THE)		
Teenage Idol/I'm Fed Up	1961	Aku 6139
DELMONICOS (FB DENISE GERMAINE)		
Teenage Idol/I'm Fed Up	1963	Aku 6139
DELONGS		
I Want Your Love/You're Never Too Young	N/A	Art Flow 3906
DELPHIS (TONY & THE)		
(Please) Don't Say Goodbye/ Going To Miami	N/A	New Group 6001
DELRONS (1) (REPERATA & THE) (FEMALE)		
Your Big Mistake/Leave Us Alone	1964	Laurie 3252
Whenever A Teenager Cries/ He's My Guy	1964	World Artists 1036
I Can Tell/Take A Look Around You	1965	RCA 8721
I'm Nobody's Baby Now/ Loneliest Girl In Town	1965	RCA 8820
Tommy/Mama Don't Allow	1965	World Artists 1051
The Boy I Love/I Found My Place	1965	World Artists 1062
He's The Greatest/Summer Thoughts	1965	World Artists 1075
Mama's Little Girl/He Don't Want You	1966	RCA 8921

Artist Song	Year	Label
I Believe/It's Waiting There For You	1967	Mala 573
The Kind Of Trouble I Love/ Boys And Girls	1967	RCA 9123
I Can Hear The Rain/Always Waitin'	1967	RCA 9185
Weather Forecast/You Can't Change A Boy's Mind	1968	Mala 12016
Captain Of Your Ship/Toom Toom (Is A Little Boy)	1968	Mala 589
We're Gonna Hold The Night/ San Juan	1969	Kapp 2010

(That's What Sends Men
   To The) Bowery/I've Got An
   Awful Lot Of Losing To Do
	1969	Kapp 989

Walking In The Rain/I've Got An Awful Lot Of Losing To Do	1970	Kapp 2050
Octopus' Garden/Your Life Is Gone	1971	Laurie 3589
DELRONS (2)		
This Love Of Ours/Over The Rainbow	1961	Forum 700
DELROYS (AKA DEL ROYS)		
Bermuda Shorts/Time (Milton Sparks bb Delroys)	1957	Apollo 514
DELSHAYS		
I'll Love You Forever/Fake It	1964	Charger 102
DELSTARS		
Zoop Bop (acapella)/For Your Love (acapella)	1964	Mellomood 1001

Why Do You Have To Go
   (acapella)/Who Said You
   Wasn't Mine (acapella)
	1964	Mellomood 1004/Relic
		   1014 (65)

Your Way (acapella)	1975	Relic LP 102
DELTAIRS (FEMALE)		
Lullaby Of The Bells/ It's Only You Dear	1957	Ivy 101
You Won't Be Satisfied/ Who Would Have Thought It	1958	Felsted 8525
I Might Like It/Standing At The Altar	1958	Ivy 105
Whoever You Are/There He Goes	1973	Vintage 1005
DELTARS (PEARL & THE) (FB PEARL MCKINNON)		
Teenager's Dream/Dance, Dance, Dance	1961	Fury 1048
Where Are You?/Back To School Again	N/A	unreleased
DELTAS (1)		
Lamplight/Let Me Share Your Dreams	1957	Gone 5010/Sold 504 (73)
DELTAS (2) (JIM WALLER & THE)		
I've Been Blue/What I Want	1961	Trac 502
Surfin' Wild/Church Key	1962	Arvee 5072
Goodnight My Love/Give My Love A Chance	1964	Cambridge 124/125
DELTAS (3)		
My Own True Love/The Work Song	1962	Philips 40023
My Own True Love/Hold Me, Thrill Me, Kiss Me	1962	Philips 40023
DELTAS (4) (JAY & THE)		
Bells Are Ringing/Super Hawk	1964	Warner Bros. 5404
DELTEARS (FEMALE)		
There He Goes/Whoever You Are	N/A	Ray-Born 132/133
DELTEENS		
A Lover's Prayer/First Man To The Moon	1958	Vee Jay 303
DELTEENS (WITH THE ORBITS)		
Listen To The Rain/ (Why Don't You) Love Me	1961	Fortune 541
DELTONES (1)		
I'm Coming Home/Early Morning Rock	1958	Vee Jay 288
DELTONES (2)		
Bow Legged Annie/La La La	1959	Jubilee 5374
I Never Knew/Framed	1960	20th Century Fox 175
Since I Met You/Hey, Little Girl	1961	Dayhill 1002
DELTONES (3) (RONNIE BAKER & THE) (AKA BELTONES)		
My Story/I Want To Be Loved	1962	Laurie 3128

Artist / Song	Year	Label
DELTONES (4)		
Jerry/Rock'n Cha Cha	1958	Roulette 4081
DELTONES (5)		
Dateless Night	N/A	Moon 302
DELUSIONS (W. KELLEY & THE)		
Do What You Did/I Do	1975	Kelway 115
DELVERTS		
Listen To The Raindrops	N/A	Salem 1302
DELVETS		
I Want A Boy For Christmas/		
Repeat After Me	1961	End 1106
Will You Love Me In Heaven/		
Repeat After Me	1961	End 1107
DELVONS		
Stay Clear Of Love/Please Stay	1967	J.D.F. 760
DEMARCO, RALPH (WITH THE PARAMOUNTS)		
More Than Riches/Old Shep	1959	Guaranteed 202
DEMATRONS		
The Boy Who's Sixteen/		
East Is East	1963	Southern Sound 202
DEMENS (1) (AKA EMERSONS)		
Take Me As I Am/You Broke		
My Heart	1957	Teenage 1006
I'm Not In Love With You/		
Short Daddy	1957	Teenage 1007
The Greatest Of Them All/		
Hey, Young Girl	1957	Teenage 1008
DEMENS (2) (RAY SCOTT & THE)		
You Drive Me Crazy	N/A	Satellite 104
DEMENSIONS		
Over The Rainbow/Nursery		
Rhyme Rock	1960	Mohawk 116
Don't Take Your Love From		
Me/Zing! Went The Strings		
Of My Heart	1960	Mohawk 120
Ave Maria (Schubert)/God's		
Christmas	1960	Mohawk 121
A Tear Fell/Theresa	1960	Mohawk 123
Count Your Blessings Instead		
Of Sheep/Again	1961	Coral 62277
As Time Goes By/Seven Days		
A Week	1961	Coral 62293/Coral 65611
(67)		
Young At Heart/Your Cheatin'		
Heart	1962	Coral 62323
My Foolish Heart/Just One		
More Chance	1963	Coral 62344
Fly Me To The Moon/You'll		
Never Know	1963	Coral 62359
Just A Shoulder To Cry On/		
Don't Worry About Bobby	1963	Coral 62382
Don't Cry Pretty Baby/A Little		
White Gardenia	1963	Coral 62392
This Time Next Year/My Old		
Girl Friend	1964	Coral 62432
Over The Rainbow/Zing Went		
The Strings Of My Heart	1966	Coral 65559
As Time Goes By/My Foolish		
Heart	1966	Coral 65611
Take My Love	N/A	Coral LP 57430
DEMENSIONS (LENNY DELL & THE)		
Ting Aling Ting Toy/Once A Day	1964	Coral 62444
DEMILLES (AKA CAMERONS (2)) (GM CARLO MASTRANGELO)		
Donna Lee/Um-Ba-Pa	1964	Laurie 3230
Cry And Be On Your Way/Lazy		
Love	1964	Laurie 3247
DEMIRES		
Wheels Of Love/The Spiders	1959	Lunar 519
DEMOLYRS		
Rain/Hey Little Rosie	1964	U.W.R. 900/Jason Scott 7
		(80)
DEMONS (1)		
Doo Doo Dah	1958	Unart 2002
DEMONS (2) (BOBBY & THE)		
Oh, Dale/The Woo	1960	MCI 1028
DEMONS (3) (EDDIE JONES & THE)		
The Greatest Of Them All/Long		
Tall Texan (with Jim Mann)	N/A	Kairay 1003
DEMURES		
Raining Teardrops/He's Got		
Your Number	1963	Brunswick 55284
DENELS		
Here Come The Ho-Dads	1962	Union 502/Bamboo 517
DENHAMS		
I'm So Lonely/Cry Baby Cry	1957	Note 10009
DENIMS		
Sad Girl/Everybody Let's Dance	1965	Columbia 43367
DENNIS, BRADFORD (& GROUP)		
The Wings Of An Angel/Hey Girl	1960	Canadian 1600
DENNY & LENNY (BB THE HOLLYWOOD GHOULS)		
Monster's Love/Ghoul Love	1963	Chance (N.Y.) 569
DENOIA, PAUL (& GROUP)		
Dear Abby/Maureen	1962	Kenco 5020
DENOTATIONS		
Nena/Lone Stranger	1965	Lawn 253
DENTON, MICKEY (& GROUP)		
Mi Amore/Ain't Love Grand	1965	Impact 1002
DEPIPPO SISTERS		
This Time Last Year/He Said	1964	Magnifico 104
DEPUTEES (PETER MARSHALL & THE)		
My Lovely One/Nice And Cozy	1956	Melba 103
DERBYS		
I Ain't Gonna Love You	1953	Central 1001
Night After Night/Just Leave		
Me Alone	1959	Mercury 71437
Lead Me On/Traveling Man	1962	Savoy 1609
Any Old Way/The Huckster Man	1963	KC 111
DERRINGERS		
True Love, True Love		
(If You Cry)/Sheree	1961	Capitol 4532
Maybe Baby/Don't Deceive Me	1961	Capitol 4572
DESIDEROS		
I Pledge My Love/Flat Foot		
Charlie	1963	Renee 1040
DESIRES (1) (AKA JIVETONES)		
Bobby You/Cold Lonely Heart	1958	Herald 532
Let It Please Be You/Hey, Lena	1959	Hull 730
I Wanna Rendezvous With You/		
Set Me Free (My Darling)	1960	Hull 733
Me And You	N/A	Hull (unreleased)
Coast Of Red	N/A	Hull (unreleased)
A Talk To Mother	N/A	Hull (unreleased)
I Love Paris	N/A	Hull (unreleased)
Sidewalks Of New York	N/A	Hull (unreleased)
So Close To An Angel	N/A	Hull (unreleased)
DESIRES (2)		
I Don't Know Why/Longing	1960	20th Fox 195
Need Someone/Ha-Ha-		
Ha-Ha, Ha	1962	Dee Impulse/Moneytown
		602 (62)
There I Go Again/I Never		
Loved Like This	1962	Smash 1763
DESIRES (3) (AKA REGENTS (3))		
Story Of Love/I Ask You	1962	Seville 118
Barbara Ann/Teenage Love	N/A	unreleased
DESIRES (4)		
Phyllis Beloved/The Girl For Me	1962	Dasa 102
DESIRES (5) (ROSKO & THE)		
Pledging My Love/The EMT	1963	Domain 1021
DESIRES (6) (JULIE & THE)		
Kiss And Tell/Sand Dune	1964	Laurie 3266
DESTINAIRES		
Traveling Stranger/(I Hear)		
Silver Bells	1964	Old Timer 64
Rag Doll/Teardrops (Acapella)	1965	Old Timer 609
Chapel Bells/It's Better This		
Way (Acapella)	1965	Old Timer 610
Diamonds And Pearls/More	1965	Old Timer 613
You're Cheating On Me/		
The Sky (by the Lancers)	1965	Old Timer 614
DESTINATIONS		
Valley Of Tears/Come On And		
Let Me Love You	1961	Fortune 864
Tell Her/I'd Rather Be Hurt All		
At Once	1966	Cameo 422
I Can't Leave You/Ando's		
Theme (no group)	1968	Ando 114
DESTINEERS		
So Young/Take A Look	1962	RCA 8049
DETERMINATIONS		
Only Love, Sweet Love/		
Memories Can't Be Broken	1959	Space 304

Artist / Song	Year	Label
DETROIT HARMONETTES		
I Gave Up Everything/I Need Thee	1954	DeLuxe 6039
DETROIT JR. (& GROUP)		
This Time For Christmas/ Christmas Day	1961	Foxy 002
DEUCES WILD		
Meaning Of Love/I'm In A Whirl	1958	Specialty 654
By Golly Gee/Just The Boy Next Door	1960	Sheen 108
DEVILLES (1)		
Kiss Me Again And Again/ Do Wop	1958	Aladdin 3423
Without Warning/Troubled Heart	1960	Dixie 1108
DEVILLES (2)		
Joan Of Love/Tell Me So	1959	Orbit 540
Mary Lou/Searching For Love	1960	Jerden 107
Just Keep Me In Mind/Goddess Of Angels	1960	Talent 103
Give Your Love To Me/Down On The Farm	1961	Acclaim 1002
I Do Believe/No Money	1962	Arrawak 1001
DEVLIN, JOHNNY (& GROUP)		
Angel Of Love/Stayin' Up Late	1962	Coral 62335
DEVONS		
Wise Up And Be Smart/Groovin' With My Thing	1969	Mr. G 825
DEVOTIONS (1)		
Silly Milly/Worried About You Baby	1958	Cub 9020
DEVOTIONS (2)		
Rip Van Winkle/I Love You For Sentimental Reasons	1961	Delta 1001/Roulette 4406 (61)/Roulette 4541 (64)
A Sunday Kind Of Love/ Tears From A Broken Heart	1964	Roulette 4556
Zindy Lou/Snow White	1964	Roulette 4580
How Do You Speak To An Angel?/Teardrops Follow Me	1972	Kape 701
Who Can She Be/My Foolish Heart (by the Five Discs)	1976	Robin Hood 137
Erlene/Portrait Of Love	1994	Avenue D 22
DEVOTIONS (3) (LITTLE MARCUS & THE)		
The Lone Stranger Went Mad/ I'll Always Remember	1964	Gordie 1001
DEW DROPS (1) (HENRY CLEMENT & THE)		
I'm So In Love With You/ Please, Please Darling	1961	Zynn 503
DEW DROPS (1) (LITTLE CLEM & THE) (AKA GAY NOTES (3))		
Plea Of Love/Waiting In The Chapel	1958	Zynn 504
DEW DROPS (2) (FEMALE)		
No Other Guy/Johnny Run Run	1963	Jeff 1963
DEWDROPS (HONEY & THE) (FEMALE)		
Come My Little Baby/ Confucius Say	1959	MMC 005
DEWTONES		
When My Baby Was Born	1954	States (unreleased)
Rockalick Baby	1954	States (unreleased)
DEY, TRACEY (& GROUP)		
Jerry (I'm Your Sherry)/ Once In A Blue Moon	1962	Vee Jay 467
DI SENTRI, TURNER (BOB GAUDIO BB THE FOUR SEASONS)		
Spanish Lace/Ten Million Tears	1961	Topix 6001
DIABLOS (AKA VELVET ANGELS)		
Harriet/Come Home, Little Girl	1958	Fortune 841
Playboy (Don't You Play In School)/I Won't Be Your Fool	1963	Fortune 551
Fools Rush In	1984	Fortune LP 8016
Old McDonald	1984	Fortune LP 8016
Tender Passion	1984	Fortune LP 8016
That's What You're Doing To Me	1984	Fortune LP 8016
Wild Side Of My Baby	1984	Fortune LP 8016
(So Long) Gee, I Hate To See You Go	1984	Fortune LP 8020
My Kind Of Lovin'	1984	Fortune LP 8020
I Want To Know	1984	Fortune LP 8020
Come Home With Me	1984	Fortune LP 8020
Daddy Nolan Strong	1984	Fortune LP 8020
Since I Fell For You & Rockin' Robin	1984	Fortune LP 8020
Remember Me (I'm The One Who Loves You)	1984	Fortune LP 8020

Artist / Song	Year	Label
White Christmas	N/A	Fortune LP 8010
Someday You'll Want Me To Want You	N/A	Fortune LP 8010
DIABLOS (ANDRE WILLIAMS & GINO PARKS WITH THE)		
(Georgia May Is) Movin' (Andre Williams & Gino Parks)/(H-mmm, Andre Williams Is) Movin'	1960	Fortune 851
DIABLOS (FEATURING NOLAN STRONG) (AKA VELVET ANGELS)		
Adios My Desert Love/(I Want) An Old Fashioned Girl (as the Diablos)	1954	Fortune 509/510
The Wind/Baby Be Mine	1954	Fortune 511
Hold Me Until Eternity/Route 16	1955	Fortune 514
Daddy Rockin' Strong/Do You Remember What You Did?	1955	Fortune 516
The Way You Dog Me Around/ Jump, Shake And Move	1955	Fortune 518
DIABLOS (NOLAN STRONG & THE) (AKA VELVET ANGELS)		
You Are/You're The Only Girl, Dolores	1955	Fortune 519
A Teardrop From Heaven/ Try Me One More Time	1956	Fortune 522
Can't We Talk This Over?/ The Mambo Of Love	1957	Fortune 525
For Old Time's Sake/My Heart Will Always Belong To You	1959	Fortune 529
I Am With You/Goodbye Matilda	1959	Fortune 531
If I Could Be With You Tonight/ I Wanna Know	1959	Fortune 532
Since You're Gone/Are You Gonna Do	1960	Fortune 536
Blue Moon/I Don't Care	1962	Fortune 544
Mind Over Matter (I'm Gonna Make You Mine)/Beside You	1962	Fortune 546
If I, Oh I/I Wanna Know	1963	Fortune 532
I Really Love You/You're My Love	1963	Fortune 553
You're Every Beat Of My Heart/ (Yeah, Baby) It's Because Of You	1963	Fortune 556
Are You Making A Fool Out Of Me/I Want To Be Your Happiness (N. S. with the Diablos & Tony Valla & the Alamos)	1963	Fortune 564
(What Did That Genie Mean When He Said) Ali Coochie/ (You're Not Good Looking- But) You're Presentable	1963	Fortune 569
Village Of Love/(I'm In Love) Real True Love	1964	Fortune 563
The Way You Dog Me Around/ Jump With Me (N.S. with the Diablos/acapella)	1980	Fortune 574
DIADEMS		
What More Is There To Say/ Ala Vevo	1961	Lavere 187
Why Don't You Believe Me/ Yes I Love You Baby	1963	Star 514
Dancing On Moonbeams/ My Little Darling	1964	Goldie 207
Goodnight Irene/I'll Do Anything	1964	Goldie 715
DIALS (1)		
Wondering About Your Love/ Sorrento	1960	Hilltop 2009
School Bells Are Ringing/ Ring Ting-A-Ling	1960	Hilltop 2010
Ring Ting-A-Ling/All Kinds Of Twistin'	1960	Norgolde 105
No Hard Feelings/Win Yourself A Lover	1961	Hilltop 219
DIALS (2) (FB SAL CORRENTE/AKA SAL ANTHONY)		
These Foolish Things/At The Start Of A New Romance	1962	Philips 40040
DIALTONES (1)		
Cherry Pie/Again	1959	Dandy Dan 1
So Young/Chicago Bird	1963	Lawn 203
DIALTONES (2) (JOHNNY & THE)		
I Ran Around/My Dream Love	1960	Jin 134
DIALTONES (2) (JOHNNY BERSIN & THE)		
The Only Girl/Don't Feel That Way	1959	Jin 117

Artist	Song	Year	Label
DIALTONES (3) (AKA RANDY & THE RAINBOWS)			
	Till I Heard It From You/Johnny	1960	Goldisc 3005/Goldisc 3020 (61)
DIAMOND, RONNIE (& GROUP)			
	Close To My Heart/Zig Zag	1958	Imperial 5554
DIAMONDS (1) (FB HAROLD "SONNY" WRIGHT)			
	A Beggar For Your Kisses/ Call Baby Call	1952	Atlantic 981
	Two Loves Have I/I'll Live Again	1953	Atlantic 1003
	Romance In The Dark/Cherry	1953	Atlantic 1017
DIAMONDS (2)			
	Black Denim Trousers And Motorcycle Boots/Nip Sip	1955	Coral 61502
	Be My Lovin' Baby/Smooch Me	1955	Coral 61577
	Why Do Fools Fall In Love/ You Baby You	1956	Mercury 70790
	Church Bells May Ring/Little Girl Of Mine	1956	Mercury 70835
	Love, Love, Love/Ev'ry Night About This Time	1956	Mercury 70889
	Ka-Ding-Dong/Soft Summer Breeze	1956	Mercury 70934
	My Judge And Jury/Put Your House In Order	1956	Mercury 70983
	A Thousand Miles Away/ Ev'ry Minute Of The Day	1956	Mercury 71021
	Little Darlin'/Faithful And True	1957	Mercury 71060
	Words Of Love/Don't Say Goodbye	1957	Mercury 71128
	Zip Zip/Oh, How I Wish	1957	Mercury 71165
	Silhouettes/Daddy Cool	1957	Mercury 71197
	The Stroll/Land Of Beauty	1957	Mercury 71242
	High Sign/Chick-Lets (Don't Let Me Down)	1958	Mercury 71291
	Kathy-O/Happy Years	1958	Mercury 71330
	Walking Along/Eternal Lovers	1958	Mercury 71366
	Young In Years/Twenty Second Day	1959	Mercury 10017/ Mercury 71505 (59)
	She Say (Oom Dooby Doom)/ From The Bottom Of My Heart	1959	Mercury 71404
	Mother's Love/Gretchen	1959	Mercury 71449
	Holding Your Hand/Sneaky Alligator	1959	Mercury 71468
	Walkin' The Stroll/Batman, Wolfman, Frankenstein Or Dracula	1959	Mercury 71534
	Tell The Truth/Real True Love	1960	Mercury 71586
	Slave Girl/Pencil Song	1960	Mercury 71633
	You'd Be Mine/The Crumble	1960	Mercury 71734
	I Sho Lawd Will/You Short Changed Me	1961	Mercury 71782
	Munch/Woomai	1961	Mercury 71818
	One Summer Night/It's A Doggone Shame	1961	Mercury 71831
	The Horizontal Lieutenant/ Vanishing American	1962	Mercury 71956
DIANTE, DENNY (& GROUP)			
	Little Lover/Faraway Places	1964	Holiday 1210
	What Makes Little Girls Cry/ Traveled	1964	Holiday 1211
DIATONES			
	Oh, Baby, Come Dance With Me/Ruby Has Gone	1960	Bandera 2509
DIAZ, VICKIE (& GROUP)			
	For Eternity/Your Mama Said No	1960	Del-Fi 4149
DICKSON, RICHIE (& GROUP)			
	You Broke My Heart/Moonlight And Roses	1962	Class 308
DIKES			
	Light Me Up/Don't Leave Me Poor	1955	Federal 12249
DILLARD, VARETTA (BB THE FOUR STUDENTS)			
	Got You On My Mind/Skinny Jimmy	1956	Groove 0159
DIMENSIONALS (DONNIE BAKER WITH THE)			
	Sleepy Time Girl/Drinkin' Pop Sodee Odee	1953	Rainbow 219
DIMENSIONS			
	She's Boss/Penny	1966	Panorama 25/HBR 1477 (66)/Hanna Barbera 477 (66)
	Baby What Do You Say/ Knock You Flat	1967	Panorama 41
DIMPLES (1) (EDDIE COOLEY & THE)			
	Priscilla/Got A Little Woman	1956	Royal Roost 621
	A Spark Met A Flame/Driftwood	1957	Royal Roost 626
	Hey You/Pull, Mon, Pull	1957	Royal Roost 628
	Leona/Be My Steady	1959	Triumph 609
	Priscilla/A Spark Met A Flame	1960	Roulette 4272
DIMPLES (2)			
	Toy Telephone/Gimme Jimmy	1958	Era 1079/Era 3079 (62)
	Invitation To A Party/My Sister's Beau	1959	Dore 517
	Dreaming Of You/Please Don't Be Angry With Me	1964	Cameo 325
DIMUCCI, DION			
	I'm Your Hoochie Coochie Man/Gloria	1969	Warner Bros.
DIMUCCI, DION (BB THE DEL SATINS)			
	Lonely Teenager/Little Miss Blue	1960	Laurie 3070
	Havin' Fun/Northeast End Of The Corner	1961	Laurie 3081
	Kissin' Game/Heaven Help Me	1961	Laurie 3090
	Somebody Nobody Wants/ Could Somebody Take My Place Tonight?	1961	Laurie 3101
	Runaround Sue/Runaway Girl	1961	Laurie 3110
	The Wanderer/The Majestic	1961	Laurie 3115
	Runaround Sue/Ya Ya Twist (by Joey Dee & the Starliters)	1961	Monument (No #)
	Lovers Who Wander/(I Was) Born To Cry	1962	Laurie 3123
	Little Diane/Lost For Sure	1962	Laurie 3134
	Love Came To Me/Little Girl	1962	Laurie 3145
	Ruby Baby/He'll Only Hurt You	1963	Columbia 42662
	This Little Girl/The Loneliest Man In The World	1963	Columbia 42776
	Be Careful Of Stones That You Throw/I Can't Believe (That You Don't Love Me Anymore)	1963	Columbia 42810
	Donna The Prima Donna/ You're Mine	1963	Columbia 42852
	Drip Drop/No One's Waiting For Me	1963	Columbia 42917
	Sandy/Faith	1963	Laurie 3153
	Come Go With Me/King Without A Queen	1963	Laurie 3171
	Lonely World/Tag Along	1963	Laurie 3187
	Then I'll Be Tired Of You/After The Dance	1963	Laurie 3225
	I'm Your Hoochie Coochie Man/The Road I'm On	1964	Columbia 42977
	Johnny B. Goode/Chicago Blues	1964	Columbia 43096
	Shout/Little Girl	1964	Laurie 3240
	Unloved, Unwanted Me/ Sweet Sweet Baby	1965	Columbia 43213
	Spoonful/Kickin' Child	1965	Columbia 43293
	I Got The Blues/(I Was) Born To Cry	1965	Laurie 3303
	Southern Train/I Can't Help But Wonder Where I'm Bound	1969	Columbia 44719
DIMUCCI, DION (BB THE WANDERERS)			
	Tomorrow Won't Bring The Rain/You Move Me, Babe	1965	Columbia 43423
DING DONGS (1) (AKA RINKY-DINKS) (FEATURING BOBBY DARIN)			
	Early In The Morning/Now We're One	1958	Brunswick 55073
DING DONGS (2)			
	Ding Dong/Sweet Thing	1960	Eldo 109
	Late Last Night/Lassie Come Home	1960	Todd 1043
DING-A-LINGS			
	Oink Jones/C. Percy Mercy (Of Scotland)	1960	Capitol 4467
DINGOES			
	What Would You Do/Dallas	1957	Dallas 2001
DINKS			
	Ugly Girl/Rocka-Mow-Mow	1966	Sully 925
DINNING SISTERS			
	Truly/Drifting And Dreaming	1955	Essex 392
DINOS			
	Darling Oh Darling/Twistin' Irene	1962	Fox 101
	Lover's Holiday/Happy Fool	1962	Fox 105
	This Is My Story	N/A	Van 03265

Artist	Song	Year	Label
DIPLOMATS (1) (DEBBIE & THE)			
	Burnin' The Torch/Unchangeable Heart	1958	Stepheny 1826
DIPLOMATS (2) (DINO & THE)			
	My Dream/I Can't Believe	1961	Laurie 3103
	Hushabye My Love/Homework	1961	Vida 0100/0101
	Soft Wind/Such A Fool For You	1961	Vida 0102/0103
DIPLOMATS (3)			
	Janie Girl/Let's Be In Love	1961	May 105
	Unchained Melody/Cards On The Table	1964	Arock 1000
DIPPERS (GEORGIE TORRENCE & THE)			
	So Good To Me (You've Been)/Go Away (Far Away)	1960	King 5376
	Such A Fool Was I/Way Over Yonder	1961	Epic 9453
	Together At Last/Fine Foxy Frame	1965	Duo-Disc 117
	Juanita/For Sentimental Reasons (by the Clovers)	1978	King Tut 170
DISCHORDS			
	Wipe Out/Mary's Little Lamb	1963	Bonneville
DISCIPLES			
	I Found Out/Disciples	1964	Fortune 573
DISCORDERS			
	Nothing Else Matters/My Hula Hula Lulu	1957	Stepheny 1806
DISCORDS (EDDIE CORNER & THE)			
	The World Of Make Believe/Bad Habit	1960	Smoke 101
DISCOUNTS (BOBBY & THE)			
	Doreen	N/A	Generation 100
DISSONAIRES (MIKE L. & THE)			
	One Love/Blitzkrieg (instrumental)	1959	Altair 101
DISTANTS			
	Always/Come On	1960	Northern 3732/Warwick 546 (60)
	Open Your Heart/Always	1960	Warwick 577
DISTANTS (RICHARD STREET & THE) (GM EDDIE KENDRICKS)			
	Answer Me/Save Me From This Misery	1961	Thelma/Harmon 1002 (62)
DITALIANS			
	I Gotta Go/Forever And Always (by the Traditions)	1996	Saxony 2004
DITTOS			
	Come On Strong/Mustard	1961	Warner Bros. 5247
DIVOTS			
	Diddy-Wah-Diddy/Missing You	1961	Savoy 1596
	Dry Cereal	N/A	Mark 3516
DIXON, WILLIE (& GROUP)			
	Twenty-Nine Ways/The Pain In My Heart (no group)	1956	Checker 851
DO-REYS			
	I Live For Your Love/A New World	1956	Joy 2401
DO-WELLS (TONY MORRA & THE)			
	Looking For My Baby/I Can't Believe	1960	Du-Well 1005
DOCKETT, JIMMY (& GROUP)			
	How Hurt I Am	N/A	Camille 3002
DODD, CALLY (& GROUP)			
	Too Young/Empty Halls	1959	Calico 110
DODDS, BILLY (& GROUP)			
	Praying For You/Waiting	1962	Prime 2601
DODGERS (1)			
	Let's Make A Whole Lot Of Love/You Make Me Happy	1955	Aladdin 3259
	Drip Drop/Cat Hop	1955	Aladdin 3271
DODGERS (2)			
	Pretty Baby/Boogie Man	1957	Skyway 117
	Oh Little One/Where Did The Bums Go	1958	Skyway 118
	Poor Little Fool/Big Mo	1958	Skyway 119
DOLLARS (LITTLE EDDIE & THE)			
	Yellow Moon/My Momma Said	1959	Fortune 845
DOLLETTES (JIMMY CARTER & THE)			
	I'll Never Let You Go	N/A	Cayce 2002
DOLLS (1) (FEMALE)			
	Tell Me Now/Suspicious Of You, Baby	1958	Kangaroo 101
	Just Before You Leave/I Love	1958	Teenage 1010
	In Love/Please Come Home	1959	Okeh 7122
	This Is Our Day/What's Next	1965	Maltese 100
DOLLS (2) (SPONGY & THE) (FEMALE)			
	It Looks Like Love/Really, Really, Really, Really, Really Love	1966	Bridgeview 7001
DOLPHINS (1) (DOUGIE & THE)			
	Yesterday's Dreams/Double Date	1959	Angle Tone 542
DOLPHINS (2)			
	Tell-Tale Kisses/I Found True Love	1960	Shad 5020
	Rainbow's End/One More For The Road	1961	Empress 102
	Hang On/Swingin' Soiree	1963	Laurie 3202
	Hey-Da-Da-Dow/I Don't Want To Go On Without You	1964	Fraternity 937
	Little Donna/Beautiful Woman	1965	Fraternity 940
	Surfin' East Coast/I Should Have Stayed	1966	Yorkshire 125
DOLPHINS (3) (DAVEY JONES & THE)			
	Love Is Strange/Velvet Waters	1961	Audicon 116
	Bull Fight/Strictly Polynesian	1961	Audicon 117
	Dance Dance, Little Girl Dance/Annabelle-Lee	1961	Sinclair 1005
	Hell Cats/The Only Way To Fly	1968	Tower 4527
DOLPHINS (4)			
	Dance/Pony Race (62)	1962	Tip Top 2003/Gemini 501
	It Might Break Your Heart/Why Will You Break My Heart	1962	Tip Top 2005
DOLPHINS (5) (DOC & THE)			
	Something About You Darling/Topless Bathing Suit	N/A	Dino 2
DOMAINS (JERRY WRIGHT & THE)			
	Do You Remember/At The Party	1960	Lanjo 2394
DOMINEERS			
	Nothing Can Go Wrong/Richie, Come On Down	1960	Roulette 4245
DOMINIONS			
	Spanish Harlem/I Need Her	N/A	Graves 1091
DOMINO, BOBBY (& GROUP)			
	Marilyn/Your Love For Me	1961	Donna 1339
DOMINOES (1)			
	Chicken Blues/Do Something For Me	1950	Federal 12001
	Harbor Lights/No! Says My Heart	1951	Federal 12010
	Sixty Minute Man/I Can't Escape From You	1951	Federal 12022
	I Am With You/Weeping Willow Blues	1951	Federal 12039
	That's What You're Doing To Me/When The Swallows Come Back To Capistrano	51	Federal 12059
	Have Mercy Baby/Deep Sea Blues	1952	Federal 12068
	That's What You're Doing To Me/Love, Love, Love	1952	Federal 12072
	These Foolish Things Remind Me Of You/Don't Leave Me This Way	1953	Federal 12129
	Have Mercy Baby/Love, Love, Love	1957	Federal 12308
DOMINOES (1) (BILLY WARD & THE)			
	I'll Be Satisfied/No Room	1952	Federal 12105
	Yours Forever/I'm Lonely	1952	Federal 12106
	The Bells/Pedal Pushin' Papa	1952	Federal 12114
	Where Now, Little Heart/You Can't Keep A Good Man Down	1953	Federal 12139
	Rags To Riches/Don't Thank Me	1953	King 1280
	Ringing In A Brand New Year/Christmas In Heaven	1953	King 1281
	My Baby's 3-D/Until The Real Thing Comes Along	1954	Federal 12162
	I'm Gonna Move To The Outskirts Of Town/Tootsie Roll	1954	Federal 12178
	One Moment With You/Handwriting On The Wall	1954	Federal 12184
	Above Jacob's Ladder/Little Black Train	1954	Federal 12193

Artist Song	Year	Label
Gimme Gimme Gimme/Come To Me Baby	1954	Jubilee 5163
Tenderly/A Little Lie	1954	King 1342
Three Coins In The Fountain/ Lonesome Road	1954	King 1364
Little Things Mean A Lot/I Really Don't Want To Know	1954	King 1368
Can't Do Sixty No More/If I Never Get To Heaven	1955	Federal 12209
Cave Man/Love Me Now Or Let Me Go	1955	Federal 12218
Sweethearts On Parade/Take Me Back To Heaven	1955	Jubilee 5213
Learnin' The Blues/May I Never Love Again	1955	King 1492
Over The Rainbow/Give Me You	1955	King 1502
St. Therese Of The Roses/ Home Is Where You Hang Your Heart	1956	Decca 29933
Will You Remember (When You Are Far A-Way/ Come On, Snake, Let's Crawl	1956	Decca 30043
Half A Love (Is Better Than None)/Evermore	1956	Decca 30149
St. Louis Blues	1956	Decca EP 2549/Decca LP 7885 (57)/Decca LP 8621 (57)
Bobby Sox Baby/How Long, How Long Blues	1956	Federal 12263
'Til Kingdom Come/Rock, Plymouth Rock	1957	Decca 30199
I Don't Stand A Ghost Of A Chance With You/To Each His Own	1957	Decca 30420
When The Saints Go Marching In/September Song	1957	Decca 30514
Oh, Lady Be Good	1957	Decca LP 7885/Decca LP 8621 (57)
Am I Blue	1957	Decca LP 8621
When Irish Eyes Are Smiling	1957	Decca LP 8621
One Moment With You/St. Louis Blues	1957	Federal 12301
Stardust/Lucinda	1957	Liberty 55071
Deep Purple/Do It Again	1957	Liberty 55099
My Proudest Possession/ Someone Greater Than I	1957	Liberty 55111
Solitude/(You Grow) Sweeter As The Years Go By	1958	Liberty 55126
Music, Maestro, Please/ Jennie Lee	1958	Liberty 55136
Eatin' And Sleepin'	1958	Liberty LP 3083
I'll Never Ask For More Than This	1958	Liberty LP 3083
Please Don't Say No/Behave, Hula Girl	1959	Liberty 55181
Sea Of Glass	1959	Liberty LP 3056
Deep River	1959	Liberty LP 3056
Joshua	1959	Liberty LP 3056
Bye And Bye	1959	Liberty LP 3056
Were You There	1959	Liberty LP 3056
You're Mine/The World Is Waiting For The Sunrise	1960	ABC 10128
The Gypsy/You	1960	ABC 10156
Have Mercy Baby/Sixty Minute Man	1960	King 5322
Lay It On The Line/ That's When You Know You're Growing Old	1961	King 5463
Man In The Stained Glass Window/My Fair Weather Friend	1961	Ro-Zan 10001
I'm Walking Behind You/ This Love Of Mine	1965	King 6002
O Holy Night/What Are You Doing New Year's Eve?	1965	King 6016

DOMINOES (1) (LIL GREENWOOD & THE)

Artist Song	Year	Label
Mercy Me/All Is Forgiven	1954	Federal 12165

DOMINOES (1) (LITTLE ESTHER & THE)

Artist Song	Year	Label
The Deacon Moves In/Other Lips Other Arms	1951	Federal 12016
Heart To Heart/Lookin' For A Man (no group)	1951	Federal 12036

DOMINOES (2) (JOE TAYLOR & THE)

Artist Song	Year	Label
Never Let Me Go/You Don't Love Me	N/A	HMF 2002

DOMINOS (DON & THE)

Artist Song	Year	Label
Weary Blues/Whole Lotta Love	1962	Cuca 1109

DON CLAIRS (HAROLD PERKINS & THE)

Artist Song	Year	Label
I Lost My Job/Santa Fe	1958	Amp-3 1001/1002

DON JUANS (1)

Artist Song	Year	Label
I'm On My Merry Way	1956	Fortune 831
Baby I Don't Care/Yum Yum	1956	Jaguar 3020

DON JUANS (1) (ANDRE WILLIAMS & THE)

Artist Song	Year	Label
Going Down To Tia Juana/ Pulling Time	1956	Fortune 824
It's All Over/Bobby Jean	1956	Fortune 828
Just Because Of A Kiss/Bacon Fat	1956	Fortune 831/Epic 9196 (56)
You Are My Sunshine (with Gino Purifoy)/Mean Jean (no group)	1956	Fortune 834
My Tears (with Gino Purifoy) /Jail Bait (no group)	1956	Fortune 837
Come On Baby/The Greasy Chicken (no group)	1956	Fortune 839
My Last Dance With You/Hey! Country Girl	1958	Fortune 842
Ooh, Ooh, Those Eyes/Cha Cha Of Love	1956	Fortune 520

DON JUANS (1) (JOE WEAVER & THE)

Artist Song	Year	Label
Baby I Love You So/It Must Be Love (no group)	1956	Fortune 825
Baby Child/Looka Here, Pretty Baby	1956	Fortune 832

DON JUANS (1) (LITTLE EDDIE & THE)

Artist Song	Year	Label
This Is A Miracle/Calypso Beat	1955	Fortune 836

DON JUANS (1) (MARSHA RENAY & THE)

Artist Song	Year	Label
It's Nice/Our Cha-Lypso Of Love	1960	Hi-Q 5017

DON JUANS (2)

Artist Song	Year	Label
The Girl Of My Dreams/Dolores	1959	Onezy 101

DON-TELS

Artist Song	Year	Label
I Found A Love/People Gonna Talk	1963	Witch 119
Lonely Boy/The Old Man	1963	Witch 121

DONATO, MIKE (& GROUP)

Artist Song	Year	Label
Dora/Summertime Love	N/A	PM 0101

DONAYS (FEMALE)

Artist Song	Year	Label
Bad Boy/The Devil In His Heart	1962	Brent 7033

DONETTES (DON EDDY & THE)

Artist Song	Year	Label
Carrot Top/Sugar Coated Candy Kisses	1960	Rona 1002

DONNA LOU (& GROUP)

Artist Song	Year	Label
Only Heaven Knows/White Cadillac	1963	Lomar 703

DONNELLS (JO BABY & THE)

Artist Song	Year	Label
I'm Gonna Move To The Outskirts/Little Sally Walker	1965	Ty-Tex 114

DONNELS (FEMALE)

Artist Song	Year	Label
Johnny Oh/Here Comes The Bride	1963	Alpha 001

DONNYBROOKS

Artist Song	Year	Label
Every Time We Kiss/Break The Glass	1959	Calico 108
Coming Home From School/ Mandolins Of Love	1959	Calico 112

DONS (1) (GENE KENNEDY & THE)

Artist Song	Year	Label
If You Give Me A Chance/ I'll Still Be Loving You	1959	Paradise 112

DONS (2)

Artist Song	Year	Label
Dream Girl/Marcheta	N/A	Heartbeat 1

DONTELLS

Artist Song	Year	Label
Lover's Reunion/Make A Chance	1963	Beltone 2040
In Your Heart/Nothing But Nothing	1965	Vee Jay 666
I Can't Wait/Gimmie Some	N/A	Ambassador 3346

DOO DROPS (MISTY & THE)

Artist Song	Year	Label
Answer Me My Love/Come Shake Hands With A Fool	1963	Imperial 5975

DOO RAYS (DAVEY & THE)

Artist Song	Year	Label
It's The Beat/Do Dee Do Dee Do Wah	1958	Guyden 2002

Artist Song	Year	Label
DOODLERS		
Two Hearts/Don't Shake The Tree	1955	RCA 6074
DOOTONES		
Teller Of Fortune/Ay, Si, Si	1955	Dootone 366
Strange Love Affair/The Day You Said Goodbye	1962	Dooto 470
Sailor Boy/Down The Road	1962	Dooto 471
DORELLS		
Maybe Baby/The Beating Of My Heart	1963	Gei 4401/Atlantic 2244 (64)
DORIES		
I Loved Him So/Tragedy Of Love	1959	Dore 528
Don't Jump/They Go Ape	1960	Dore 556
Stompin' Sh-Boom/Breakup	1962	Dore 629
DORN, JERRY (BB THE HURRICANES)		
Wishing Well/Sentimental Heaven	1956	King 4932
The Key/Quicksand	1957	King 5029
DORSETS		
Pork Chops/Cool It	1961	Asnes 101
DOTS (1) (FB JEANETTE BAKER) (FEMALE)		
I Confess/I Wish I Could Meet You	1956	Caddy 101
I Lost You/Johnny	1957	Caddy 107
Good Luck To You/Heartsick And Lonely	1957	Caddy 111
DOTS (2) (LENNY CAPELLO & THE)		
Cotton Candy/Tootles	1960	Ric 960
Genevieve/90 Pound Weakling	1962	Ric 991
DOTS (3) (TINY DEE & THE)		
My Honey/Telegraph	1963	Success 104
DOUBLE DATERS		
Blondie Baby/Senior Stroll	1958	Carlton 457
Beach Umbrella/Summer In The Mountains	1958	Dot 15780
DOUBLE DATES		
I Love You Girl/Tatoo	1959	Luck 103
DOUG & FREDDY (BB THE PYRAMIDS)		
Need Your Love/Campus Girl	1961	K&G 100
DOUG & FREDDY (WITH THE PYRAMIDS)		
A Lover's Plea/I Believe In Love	1959	Rendezvous 111
DOUGLAS, RONNIE (& GROUP)		
You Say/Run, Run, Run	1961	Everest 19413
Candy And Gum/You'll Come Back	1961	Everest 19425
Say Didd-I-Lee Hey (Gonna See My Baby)/Worth Waiting For	1965	Epic 9843
DOVE, DIANE (& GROUP)		
Why/To Prove My Love	1959	NRC 018
DOVELLS (FB LEN BARRY)		
No No No/Letters Of Love	1961	Parkway 819
Bristol Stomp/Out In The Cold Again	1961	Parkway 827 (first pressing)
Bristol Stomp/Letters Of Love	1961	Parkway 827 (second pressing)
Do The New Continental/Mope-itty Mope Stomp	1962	Parkway 833
Bristol Twistin' Annie/The Actor	1962	Parkway 838
Hully Gully Baby/Your Last Chance	1962	Parkway 845
The Jitterbug/Kissin' In The Kitchen	1962	Parkway 855
Foot Stompin'	1962	Parkway LP 7006
Little Girl Of Mine	1962	Parkway LP 7006
I Really Love You	1962	Parkway LP 7006
Deserie	1962	Parkway LP 7006
You Can't Run Away From Yourself/Help Me Baby	1963	Parkway 861
You Can't Sit Down/Wildwood Days	1963	Parkway 867
You Can't Sit Down/Stompin' Everywhere	1963	Parkway 867
Betty In Bermudas/Dance The Froog	1963	Parkway 882
Stop Monkeyin' Aroun'/No No No	1963	Parkway 889
Be My Girl/Dragster On The Prowl	1963	Parkway 901
Happy Birthday Just The Same/One Potato, Two Potato	1964	Parkway 911
Watusi With Lucy/What In The World's Come Over You?	1964	Parkway 925
(Hey Hey Hey) Alright/Happy	1965	Swan 4231
Happy Summer Days/Long After	1966	Diamond 198
There's A Girl/Love Is Everywhere	1966	MGM 13628
Here Comes The Judge/Girl (by the Magistrates)	1968	MGM 13946
One Winter Love/Blue	1969	Jamie 1369
Kiss The Hurt Away/He Cries Like A Baby	1970	Decca 32919
Roll Over Beethoven/Something About You Boy	1970	Event 3310
Mary's Magic Show/Don't Vote For Luke McCabe	1972	MGM 14568
Sometimes/Far Away	1972	Verve 10701
Dancing In The Street/Back On The Road Again	1974	Event 216
Baby Work Out/Hully Gully Baby	1983	Abkco 4029
L-O-V-E, Love/We're All In This Together	N/A	Paramount 0134
DOVERS (1) (FB MIRIAM GRATE)		
Sweet As A Flower/Boy In My Life	1959	Davis 465
The Sentence/Devil You May Be	1961	New Horizon 501
Your Love (acapella)	1988	Relic LP 5075
Only Heaven Knows (acapella)	1988	Relic LP 5075
DOVERS (1) (MIRIAM GRATE & THE)		
My Angel/Please Squeeze	1955	Apollo 472
My Love	1988	Relic LP 5075/Relic LP 5078 (89)
DOVERS (2)		
Alice My Love/A Lonely Heart	1962	Valentine 1000
DOVES		
When You Love/People Will Talk	1954	States 123
Don't Turn Away From Me/Let's Make Up	1960	Big Top 3046
DOWN BEATS		
Hard Rockin' Daddy/Down Beat (instrumental)	1958	Dee-Cee 714
Amor/Drifting Easy (instrumental)	1960	Conn 201
Again/I'm Gonna Put You Down	1961	Entente 001
Soul Fool/I Can't Hear You No More	1965	Down Beat
Dedicated To The One I Love/Over My Room	1965	Down Beat 1029
You're No Good/Bony Maronie	1965	Down Beat 1030
Why Do You Love Another/You're The One	N/A	Dawn 1031
Say The Word/Together	N/A	Dawn 4531
Come On Over/Lady Of The Sea	1956	Sarg 162
DOWNBEATS (1)		
Come On Over (Baby)/Darling Of Mine	1956	Sarg 168
Run To Me, Baby/I Need Your Love	1956	Sarg 173
I Couldn't See/Oh, Please	1956	Sarg 186
Playing Possum/One At A Time	1960	Wilco 16
DOWNBEATS (1) (BETH MURPHY WITH GENE TERRY & THE)		
Where Were You/Walking On Air	1959	Goldband 1083
DOWNBEATS (1) (GENE TERRY & THE)		
Cindy Lou	1958	Goldband 1066
No Mail Today/Never Let Her Go	1959	Goldband 1081
Cinderella, Cinderella/Guy With A Million Dollars	1959	Goldband 1088
Fine, Fine (with Ronnie Dee)/This Should Go On Forever	1959	Savoy 1559
DOWNBEATS (1) (O. S. GRANT & THE)		
Falling Stars/I Just Can't Understand	1956	Sarg 197
You Did Me Wrong/Tanya	1956	Sarg 200
DOWNBEATS (2)		
My Girl/China Doll	1956	Gee 1019
Let's Go Steady/So Many Tears	1958	Peacock 1679
Someday She'll Come Along/You're So Fine	1959	Peacock 1689
You Gotta Tell Me/It Won't Be Easy	1962	Dynamite 243/Diamond 243
DOWNBEATS (3)		
Here/Big-N-Heavy (instrumental)	1958	Safari 1010

Artist / Song	Year	Label
DOWNBEATS (4)		
Request Of A Fool/Your		
Baby's Back	1962	Tamla 54056
DOWNBEATS (5)		
Growing Love/Sweet Little Jane	N/A	Hampshire 1002
DOWNBEATS (6)		
1-2-3	N/A	Kanwic 137
DOWNES, VINNIE (& GROUP)		
Foolish Pride/An Angel Never		
Cries	1959	Transcontinental 1011
DOWNS, BOBBIE (& GROUP)		
Darling/It Won't Be Long	1960	Correc-Tone 3807
DOYLE, DICKY (& GROUP)		
Dreamland Last Night/		
My Little Darlin'	1961	Wye 1009
DRAGONAIRES (BYRON LEE & THE)		
Behold/You're No Good	N/A	Bra 503
DRAGONS (ST. GEORGE & THE)		
Donna Alone	N/A	Dragon
DRAKE SISTERS		
Smoke From Your Cigarette	1964	Chattahoochee 649
DRAKES (1)		
Let Them Talk	1955	States (unreleased)
Take A Giant Step	1955	States (unreleased)
DRAKES (2)		
Oo Wee So Good/Kitty	1958	Conquest 1001
DRAKES (3)		
I Made A Wish/Ole King Cole	1965	Olimpic 252
DRAPERS (1)		
Merry Go Round/The Love		
I Wish I Had	1960	Unical 3001
Best Love/One More Time	1960	Vest 831
DRAPERS (2) (REF DRIFTERS)		
You Got To Look Up/		
Your Love Has Gone Away	1962	Gee 1081
DREAM GIRLS (BOBBIE SMITH & THE) (FEMALE)		
Don't Break My Heart/Oh,		
This Is Why	1959	Cameo 165
Crying In The Night/I'm In		
Love With You	1959	Metro 20029
I Could Write A Book/Don't		
Break My Heart	1960	Big Top 3059
Love Him/Heartaches	1960	Metro 20034
Mr. Fine/Wanted	1961	Big Top 3085
Dutchess Of Earl/Mine All Mine	1962	Big Top 3100
Here Comes Baby/I Get A		
Feeling, My Love	1962	Big Top 3111
Your Lovey Dovey Ways/Now		
He's Gone	1962	Big Top 3129
DREAM KINGS		
More Than Yesterday, Less		
Than Tomorrow/Oh, What		
A Baby	1957	Checker 858
DREAM-TIMERS (BB THE FLIPPIN' TEENS ORCHESTRA)		
An Invitation/The Dancin' Lady	1961	Flippin' 107
DREAMAIRES (L. FLAYTUS & THE)		
Buy A Van/Forever In Love	1985	Antrell 101
DREAMERS (1)		
Please Don't Leave Me/Walkin'		
My Blues Away	1952	Mercury 70019
DREAMERS (10)		
I Sing This Song (That's Why)/		
Mary's Little Lamb	1960	Apt 25053
Natalie/Teenage Vows Of Love	1960	Goldisc 3015
Mary Mary/Canadian Sunset	1960	Guaranteed 219
Because Of You/Little Girl	1961	Cousins 1005/May 133 (61)
DREAMERS (11)		
I Really Love You/You Made		
Me Darling	1960	Blue Star 8001
DREAMERS (12) (DONNIE & THE) (AKA KENNY & THE WHALERS)		
Carole/Ruby My Love	1961	Decca 31312
Count Every Star/Dorothy	1961	Whale 500
My Memories Of You/		
Teenage Love	1961	Whale 505
DREAMERS (13) (LEON & THE)		
If It Hadn't Been For You/Haircut	1962	Parkway 843
DREAMERS (14) (HAL HEDGES & THE)		
On My Knees/Pennies From		
Heaven	1963	ABC 10406
DREAMERS (15)		
Daydreamin' Of You/		
The Promise	1963	Fairmount 612
DREAMERS (16) (FEMALE)		
Love, Love, Love/Henry,		
Henry, Henry	1965	United Artists 841
DREAMERS (17)		
Dear I/Only Time	N/A	Tri-Dec 8757
DREAMERS (2)		
No Man Is An Island/Melba	1954	Rollin' 5/Rollin' 1001 (55)
Tears In My Eyes/535	1955	Grand 131
DREAMERS (3)		
Do Not Forget/Since You've		
Been Gone	1956	Flip 319/Flip 354 (61)
DREAMERS (3) (ELOISE BROOKS & THE)		
My Plea/Charles My Darling	1955	Aladdin 3303
DREAMERS (3) (RICHARD BERRY & THE)		
At Last/Bye, Bye	1954	Flair 1052
Daddy, Daddy/Baby Darling	1955	Flair 1058
Jelly Roll/Together	1955	Flair 1075
Baby Baby	1963	Crown LP 5371
Pretty Brown Eyes	1963	Crown LP 5371
I Am Bewildered	1963	Crown LP 5371
The Big Break	1963	Crown LP 5371
Good Love	1963	Crown LP 5371
Next time	1963	Crown LP 5371
Wait For Me	1963	Crown LP 5371
Please Tell Me	1963	Crown LP 5371
DREAMERS (3) (SIDNEY ESTER & THE)		
After You've Gone/Let Me		
Walk With You	1958	Dangold 2001/Goldband 1087 (59)
DREAMERS (4)		
Right Time For Love/Girl Down		
The Street	1956	ABC 9746
DREAMERS (5) (FEMALE)		
No Obligation/Lips Were Meant		
For Kissing	1956	Manhattan 503
DREAMERS (6)		
Oh Yeah/Only Your Love	1958	Bullseye 1013
DREAMERS (7) (JOY ANTHONY & THE)		
Earth Angel/Eternally Yours	1958	Sinclair 1001
DREAMERS (8)		
Seconds/Mama Lucie	1958	Dream 101
Little Girl/This I Swear	N/A	Dream 1223
DREAMERS (8) (DANNY & THE)		
Forgive Me/Venus	1960	Dream 7
DREAMERS (9)		
Don't Cry/It's Gonna Be Alright	1959	Nugget 1000
DREAMETTES		
Run Steven Run/Gonna Make		
That Little Boy Mine	1965	United Artists 921
DREAMLINERS		
Just Me And You/Daiquiri		
(instrumental)	1963	Cobra 013
DREAMLOVERS		
Take It From A Fool/For The		
First Time	1960	Len 1006
Annabelle Lee/Home Is		
Where The Heart Is	1960	V-Tone 211
When We Get Married/		
Just Because	1961	Heritage 102
Welcome Home/Let Them Love	1961	Heritage 104
Zoom Zoom Zoom/While We		
Were Dancing	1961	Heritage 107
Time/May I Kiss The Bride	1961	V-Tone 229
If I Should Lose You/I Miss You	1962	Down/End 1114 (62)
Sad Sad Boy/If I Were A		
Magician	1963	Columbia 42698
Sad Sad Boy/Black Bottom	1963	Columbia 42752
Pretty Little Girl/I'm Thru		
With You	1963	Columbia 42842
Together/Amazons And Coyotes	1963	Swan 4167/Casino 1308 (63)/Swan 5619
These Will Be The Good Old		
Days/Oh Baby Mine	1964	Cameo 326
You Gave Me Somebody		
To Love/Doin' Things		
Together With You	1965	Warner Bros. 5619
Bad Times Make The Good		
Times/Bless Your Soul	1966	Mercury 72595
Callin' Joann/You Gave Me		
Somebody To Love	1966	Mercury 72630
Mother	1982	Collectables LP 5004
Let Them Talk	1982	Collectables LP 5004

Artist / Song	Year	Label
Let's Twist Again	1982	Collectables LP 5004
For The First Time	1982	Collectables LP 5005/ Relic LP 5066
DREAMS (1)		
I'm Losing My Mind/Under The Willow	1954	Savoy 1140
I'll Be Faithful/My Little Honeybun	1955	Savoy 1157
DREAMS (1) (REF KENNY ESQUIRE & THE STARLITES) (GM GEORGE TINDLEY)		
Darlene/A Letter To My Girl	1954	Savoy 1130
DREAMS (2) (FRANK ROSSI & THE)		
Dream Boy/Around The Corner	1957	Mark 7001
DREAMS (3) (JOHNNY & THE)		
You're Too Young For Me/ Are You With That	1961	Richie 457
DREAMS (4)		
Too Late/Inexperience	1962	Smash 1748
I Love You/Popeye	1963	Talent 1004
DREAMS (5) (DARNELL & THE)		
The Day Before Yesterday /I Had A Love	1964	West Side 1020/Cousins
DREAMTONES (FB MAJOR LANCE)		
Was I Dreaming/Say Hey Baby	1957	Mercury 71222
Stand Behind Me/Love Me In The Afternoon	1958	Klik 8505/Sold 501 (75)/ Early Bird 005 (96)
A Lover's Answer/Mean Man	1959	Astra 551
Praying For A Miracle/Jelly Bean	1959	Express 501
DREW-VELS (PATTI DREW & THE)		
Tell Him/Just Because	1963	Capitol 5055
It's My Time/Everybody Knows	1964	Capitol 5145
I've Known/Creepin'	1965	Capitol 5244
DRIFTERS		
Money Honey/The Way I Feel	1953	Atlantic 1006
Summertime/Besame Mucho	1953	Rama 22
Such A Night/Lucille	1954	Atlantic 1019
Honey Love/Warm Your Heart	1954	Atlantic 1029
Bip Bam/Someday You'll Want Me To Want You	1954	Atlantic 1043
White Christmas/The Bells Of St. Mary's	1954	Atlantic 1048
The World Is Changing/ Sacroiliac Swing	1954	Crown 108
Gone/What'cha Gonna Do	1955	Atlantic 1055
Everyone's Laughing/ Hot Ziggety	1955	Atlantic 1070
Adorable/Steamboat	1955	Atlantic 1078
Ruby Baby/Your Promise To Be Mine	1956	Atlantic 1089
Soldier Of Fortune/I Gotta Get Myself A Woman	1956	Atlantic 1101
Fools Fall In Love/It Was A Tear	1957	Atlantic 1123
Hypnotized/Driftin' Away From You	1957	Atlantic 1141
I Know/Yodee Yakee	1957	Atlantic 1161
Drip Drop/Moonlight Bay	1958	Atlantic 1187
There Goes My Baby/Oh My Love	1959	Atlantic 2025
Dance With Me/(If You Cry) True Love, True Love	1959	Atlantic 2040
This Magic Moment/Baltimore	1960	Atlantic 2050
Let The Boogie Woogie Roll (recorded in 1953)/ Deep Sea Ball	1960	Atlantic 2060
Lonely Winds/Hey Senorita	1960	Atlantic 2062
Save The Last Dance For Me/ Nobody But Me	1960	Atlantic 2071
I Count The Tears/Suddenly There's A Valley	1960	Atlantic 2087
Souvenirs	1960	Atlantic LP 8041
Sadie My Lady	1960	Atlantic LP 8041
Honky Tonk	1960	Atlantic LP 8041
Some Kind Of Wonderful/ Honey Bee	1961	Atlantic 2096
Please Stay/No Sweet Lovin'	1961	Atlantic 2105
Sweets For My Sweet/ Loneliness Or Happiness	1961	Atlantic 2117
Room Full Of Tears/Somebody New Dancin' With You	1961	Atlantic 2127
When My Little Girl Is Smiling/ Mexican Divorce	1962	Atlantic 2134
Stranger On The Shore/What To Do	1962	Atlantic 2143
Sometimes I Wonder/Jackpot	1962	Atlantic 2151
Up On The Roof/Another Night With The boys	1962	Atlantic 2162
On Broadway/Let The Music Play	1963	Atlantic 2182
Rat Race/If You Don't Come Back	1963	Atlantic 2191
I'll Take You Home/I Feel Good All Over	1963	Atlantic 2201
Vaya Con Dios/In The Land Of Make Believe	1964	Atlantic 2216
One Way Love/Didn't It	1964	Atlantic 2225
Under The Boardwalk/I Don't Want To Go On Without You	1964	Atlantic 2237
I've Got Sand In My Shoes/ He's Just A Playboy	1964	Atlantic 2253
Saturday Night At The Movies/ Spanish Lace	1964	Atlantic 2260
The Christmas Song/ I Remember Christmas	1964	Atlantic 2261
At The Club/Answer the Phone	1965	Atlantic 2268
Chains Of Love/Come On Over To My Place	1965	Atlantic 2285
Follow Me/The Outside World	1965	Atlantic 2292
I'll Take You Where The Music's Playing/Far From The Maddening Crowd	1965	Atlantic 2298
We Gotta Sing/Nylon Stockings	1965	Atlantic 2310
Tonight	1965	Atlantic LP 8113
As Long As She Needs Me	1965	Atlantic LP 8113
The Good Life	1965	Atlantic LP 8113
Temptation	1965	Atlantic LP 8113
What Kind Of Fool	1965	Atlantic LP 8113
I Wish Your Love	1965	Atlantic LP 8113
Desifinado	1965	Atlantic LP 8113
On The Street Where You Live	1965	Atlantic LP 8113
Who Can I Turn To	1965	Atlantic LP 8113
More	1965	Atlantic LP 8113
Quando, Quando, Quando	1965	Atlantic LP 8113
Memories Are Made Of This/ My Islands In The Sun	1966	Atlantic 2325
Up In The Streets Of Harlem/ You Can't Love Them All	1966	Atlantic 2336
Baby What I Mean/Aretha	1966	Atlantic 2366
Aint The Truth/Up Jumped The Devil	1967	Atlantic 2426
Still Burning In My Heart/I Need You Now	1968	Atlantic 2471
Steal Away/Your Best Friend	1969	Atlantic 2624
Black Silk/You Got To Pay Your Dues	1970	Atlantic 2746
Three Thirty Three	1971	Atco LP 375
I Should Have Done Right	1971	Atco LP 375
Be My Lady/A Rose By Any Other Name	1971	Atlantic 2786
Kissin' In The Back Row Of The Movies/I'm Feelin' Sad	1974	Bell 45,600
DRIFTERS (CHARLIE THOMAS GROUP)		
Peace Of Mind/The Struggler	1973	Steeltown 671
DRIFTERS (JOHNNY MOORE GROUP)		
Every Night/Something Tells Me	1972	Bell 1269
You've Got Your Troubles/ I'm Feeling Sad (And Oh So Lonely)	1973	Bell 45,320
Like Sister And Brother/ The Songs We Used To Sing	1973	Bell 45,387
Say Goodbye To Angelina/I'm Free (For The Rest Of Your Life)	1974	Bell 1339
DRIVERS (1)		
Smooth, Slow And Easy/Women	1956	DeLuxe 6094
My Lonely Prayer/Midnight Hours	1957	DeLuxe 6104
Oh, Miss Nellie/Dangerous Lips	1957	DeLuxe 6117
Blue Moon/I Get Weak	1957	RCA 7023
DRIVERS (2) (& THE SPACEMEN)		
Doe Doe/Ho Ho	1959	Alton 252
DRIVERS (3)		
A Man's Glory/Teeter Totter	1960	Lin 1002
DRIVERS (4)		
Mr. Astronaut/Dry Bones Twist	1962	King 5645

Artist	Song	Year	Label
DU DROPPERS			
	Can't Do Sixty No More/Chain Me, Baby (Blues Of Desire)	1952	Red Robin 108
	Balabam	1953	RCA (unreleased)
	I Wanna Know/Laughing Blues	1953	RCA 5229
	I Found Out (What You Do When You Go Around There)/Little Girl, Little Girl (You'd Better Stop Talkin' In Your Sleep)	1953	RCA 5321
	Whatever You're Doin'/Somebody Work On My Baby's Mind (The Seven Sisters)	1953	RCA 5425
	Don't Pass Me By/Get Lost	1953	RCA 5504
	Come On And Love Me Baby/Go Back	1953	Red Robin 116
	My Thrill Girl	1953	unreleased
	Ten Past Midnight	1953	unreleased
	Baby Don't Leave Me In This Mood	1953	unreleased
	Train Keep Rolling On	1953	unreleased
	You're Wrong	1954	Groove (unreleased)
	Dead Broke/Speed King	1954	Groove 0001
	Just Whisper/How Much Longer?	1954	Groove 0013
	Let Nature Take It's Course/Boot 'Em Up	1954	Groove 0036
	Had To Play My Number	1954	unreleased
	Drink Up	1954	unreleased
	If You Just Don't Leave	1954	unreleased
	You've Been Good To Everybody	1954	unreleased
	Talk That Talk/Give Me Some Consideration	1955	Groove 0104
	You're Mine Already/I Wanna Love You	1955	Groove 0120
	Honeybunch	1955	Groove EP EGA-2
	I Only Had A Little	1955	Groove EP EGA-2
	Smack Dab In The Middle	1955	Groove EP EGA-5
	That's All I Need	1955	Groove EP EGA-5
	Rollin' Stone	1955	Groove EP EGA-5
	Story Untold	1955	Groove EP EGA-5
DU DROPPERS (SUNNY GALE & THE)			
	Mama's Gone, Good Bye/The Note In The Bottle	1953	RCA 5543
	Goodnight, Sweetheart, Goodnight/Call Off The Wedding	1954	RCA 5746
DU MAURIERS			
	All Night Long/Baby, I Love You	1957	Fury 1011
DU WOPPERS			
	Oh Stop It/Peace Of Mind (by the Young Lords)	1970	Kelway 100
DU-KANES			
	Our Star	1964	HSH 501
DUAL TONES			
	Bubble Gum Bop/I'll Belong To You	1960	Sabre 204
DUALS (1)			
	Wait Up Baby/For Ever And Ever	1957	Fury 1013
DUALS (2)			
	Nearest To My Heart/Bye Bye	1959	Arc 4446
DUBS (AKA MARVELS (1))			
	This To Me Is Love/The Letter (by the Larktones)	N/A	Popular Request 109
	Angel Mine	1955	unreleased
	Hurry Up Honey	1955	unreleased
	Workin' For My Baby	1956	unreleased
	Could This Be Magic/Such Lovin'	1957	Gone 5011/Musictone 1141 (61)
	Don't Ask Me (To Be Lonely)/Darling	1957	Johnson 102/Gone 5002 (57)/Musictone 1142 (61)
	Beside My Love/Gonna Make A Change	1958	Gone 5020
	Be Sure My Love/Song In My Heart	1958	Gone 5034/Mark-X 8008 (60)
	Chapel Of Dreams/Is There A Love for Me	1958	Gone 5046/Gone 5069 (59)
	Early In The Morning/No One	1959	ABC 10056
	Don't Laugh At Me/You'll Never Belong To Me	1960	ABC 10100
	For The First Time/Ain't That So	1960	ABC 10150
	If I Only Had Magic/Joogie Boogie	1961	ABC 10198
	Down, Down, Down I Go/Lullaby	1961	ABC 10269
	Now That We Broke Up/This To Me Is Love	1961	End 1108
	You've Discovered Love	1961	unreleased
	Two Hearts Are Better Than One	1961	unreleased
	You're Free To Go/Is There A Love For Me	1962	Gone 5138
	Blue Velvet	1962	Josie LP 4001
	This I Swear/Wisdom Of A Fool	1963	Josie 911
	Your Very First Love/Just You	1963	Wilshire 201
	Could This Be Magic (version 2)/Blue Velvet	1964	Lana 115
	Your Very First Love/Don't Ask Me To Be Lonely (version 2)	1964	Lana 116
	Where Do We Go From Here/I Only Have Eyes For You	1972	Clifton 2
	We Three/We Build A Nest (by the Actuals)	1973	Candlelite 438
	Connie/Home Under My Hat	1973	Johnson 097 (recorded in 1957)
	I Won't Have You Breaking My Heart/Somebody Goofed	1973	Johnson 098 (recorded in 1957)
	You're Welcome/This To Me Is Love	1975	Clifton 5
DUBS (RICHARD BLANDON & THE)			
	I'm Downtown/Lost In The Wilderness	1971	Vicki 229
	Don't Ask Me/Peace Of Mind	1987	Starlight 51
	Beside My Love/Heartache To Me	1987	Starlight 53
	Wherever You Are/Please The Crowd	1990	Classic Artists 120
DUBS (THE CLEVELAND STILL)			
	Beside My Love (live)/If I Didn't Care (by Lillian Leach & the Mellows)	1986	100th U.G.H.A. Show Commemoration 45
	Could This Be Magic/Teddy Bear	1986	Clifton 77
DUCANES			
	I'm So Happy (Tra La La)/Little Did I Know	1961	Goldisc 3024
DUCHESSES (FEMALE) (AKA FOUR DUCHESSES)			
	Why/You Told Everyone But Me	1960	Chief 7019
	Every Boy In Town/Will I Ever Make It	1960	Chief 7023
DUDADS			
	I Heard You Call Me Dear/My Baby Misses Me Too	1955	DeLuxe 6083
DUDES (GM FREDDY DOUGLAS)			
	Who Would Have Thought/You Ought To Be Ashamed	1961	Keith 6501
DUDS (DOUGIE & THE)			
	Lifetime/Cowboy Joe	1963	Amy 869
DUETS (LEO & THE)			
	Down The Aisle/Goodnight Sweetheart	1967	Co-Op 514
DUKAYS			
	The Girl's A Devil/The Big Lie	1961	Nat 4001
	Nite Owl/Festival Of Love	1962	Nat 4002/Vee Jay 430 (62)
	Please Help/I'm Gonna Love You So	1962	Vee Jay 442
	I Feel Good All Over/I Never Knew	1962	Vee Jay 460
	Combination/Every Step	1963	Vee Jay 491
	The Jerk/Mo' Jerk	1964	Jerry-O 105
	Mellow-Feznecky/Sho Nuf M.F.	1964	Jerry-O 106
	Night Owl/The Big Lie	1975	Monogram 102
DUKE OF EARL (& GROUP) (AKA GENE CHANDLER BB THE DUKAYS)			
	Daddy's Home/The Big Lie	1962	Vee Jay 450
DUKES (1) (AKA FOUR DUKES/AKA BILLY DAWN QUARTETTE/AKA HERALDS)			
	I'll Find Her/So Long Love	1954	Specialty
	Ooh Bop She Bop/Oh-Kay	1954	Specialty 543
	I Found A Love/Come On And Rock	1955	Imperial 5344 (unreleased)
	Bad Luck Blues	1956	Imperial (unreleased)
	The Last Ride	1956	Imperial (unreleased)
	Lost Dreams	1956	Imperial (unreleased)

Artist	Song	Year	Label	Artist	Song	Year	Label
	Someday Somewhere/				I'm Yours/Wishing Ring	1964	Coed 596
	Tell Me Why	1956	Imperial 5385 (unreleased)		Around The Corner/They		
	My Love Is Blue/I Was A Fool	1956	Imperial 5399 (unreleased)		Said It Couldn't Be Done	1965	Columbia 43336
	Teardrop Eyes/Shimmies				She Waits For Him/Norma Jean	1965	Columbia 43464
	And The Shakes	1956	Imperial 5401		Let Them Talk/Exodus Song	1966	Columbia 43577
	Lovin' You/Three Time Loser	1956	Imperial 5408		It's Not Time Now/Don't Want		
	Wini Brown/Cotton Pickin' Hands	1956	Imperial 5415		To Have To Do It	1966	Columbia 43802
	Looking For You/Groceries, Sir	1959	Flip 343		Be My Love/I Understand	1967	Columbia 44078
	I Love You/Leap Year Cha Cha	1959	Flip 345		My Special Angel/Ring Of Love	1968	Heritage 804
	Baby Please	N/A	Imperial (unreleased)		Goodnight My Love/Ring Of Love	1968	Heritage 805
DUKES (1) (LLOYD PRICE & THE)					My Love, My Love/The Sky's		
	Oo-Ee-Baby/Chee Koo Baby	1954	Specialty 535		The Limit	1969	Heritage 808
DUKES (2) (BILLY DUKE & THE)					Two Different Worlds/Hope	1969	Heritage 811
	I Cried/The High And The Mighty	1954	Coral 61203		The Sky's The Limit/Delicious	1975	RCA 10407
	Flip, Flop And Fly/Fun			**DUPRIES**			
	Lovin' Mama	1955	Casino 138		Baby Doll/Kissy Face	1960	Thunderbird 106
	This Is What I Ask/By Now	1956	Sound 130	**DURHAMS**			
	I Know I Was Wrong/				Sincerely/Seconds Of Soul	1965	Relic 1018
	Paradise Princess	1956	Teen 110		This Is My Love (acapella)	1975	Relic LP 103
	Daddy Rock And Roll/				Maureen (acapella)	1975	Relic LP 103
	Rocky Piano	1956	Teen 112		Don't Say We're Through		
	Chalypso	1957	Peak		(acapella)	1975	Relic LP 103
DUKES (3) (DON BARBER & THE)					I Remember (acapella)	1975	Relic LP 104
	What's Your Name/The Waddle	1960	Thunderbird 105	**DUSTERS**			
DUKES (4) (KEITH ALEXANDER & THE)					Give Me Time/Sallie Mae	1956	Arc 3000
	Poor Orphan Boy/Cheater Sam	1962	Gemini 901		Don't Leave Me Today/		
DUKES (5) (SKIP ARNE & THE)					Why Do I Love You	1956	Hudson 4
	Sunshine And Rain/Angel	1964	Little Fort 8688/Dot 16627 (64)		Pretty Girl/Coolation	1957	ABC 9886
					Rock At The Hop	1958	Cupid 5003
DUMONTS					Darling Love/Teenage		
	But Only With You/Hoopla	1961	King 5552		Jamboree	1958	Glory 287
DUNDEES (CARLYLE DUNDEE & THE)					The Great Pretender	N/A	4 Hits EP only
	Evil One/Never	1954	Space 201	**DUVALS (1)**			
DUNES					Guide Me/Happiness	1956	Gee 1003
	Lonely Sands/Sloppy Jalopy	1961	Madison 156	**DUVALS (2) (REF FIVE CROWNS (1)/REF DRIFTERS)**			
DUNGAREE DARLINGS (FEMALE)					You Came To Me/Ooh Wee		
	Little Wallflower/Boy Of My				Baby	1956	Rainbow 335/Riviera 990 (56)
	Dreams	1956	Rego 1003/Karen 1005 (59)				
DUNHAM, JACKIE (& GROUP)				**DUVALS (3) (PHIL JOHNSON & THE) (AKA ROYAL NOTES)**			
	Slow Down Your Life/I Think				Kisses Left Unkissed/		
	Of You	1961	Imperial 5768		Three Speed Girl		
DUNHILLS					(by the Royal Notes)	1958	Kelit 7032
	Sound Of The Wind/Ricochet	1961	Royal 110		I Lied To My Heart/Money	1958	Kelit 7033
DUNN, LEONA (& GROUP)					Wee Small Hours/You Are My		
	Our Songs Of Love/				Love (by the Royal Notes)	1958	Kelit 7034
	Baby Don't Play Around	1965	Hallmark 500	**DUVALS (4)**			
DUOTONES					I Wanna Be Free/Yes I Do	1961	La Salle 502
	I Just Got Kissed/Tumblin' Down	N/A	Harlequin 611026	**DUVALS (5)**			
DUPONTS (1) (FB LITTLE ANTHONY GOURDINE)					What Am I/Cotton	1963	Boss 2117/Red Rocket 471 (63)
	You/Must Be Falling In Love	1955	Winley 212/Savoy 1552 (58)				
	Prove It Tonight/Somebody	1957	Royal Roost 627	**DUVALS (6)**			
DUPONTS (2)					The Last Supper/Ferny Roast	1963	Prelude 110
	Screamin' At Dracula's Ball/			**DUVELLS**			
	Half Past Nothing	1958	Roulette 4060		Danny Boy/How Come	1962	Rust 5045
DUPREE, LEBRON (& GROUP)				**DWELLERS**			
	Wanda/Yea, Yea, Yea	1959	Spann 411		Lonely Guy/Come Home		
DUPREE, NELSON (& GROUP)					Right Away	1958	Conrose 101
	Lost/Red Ruby	1960	Palm 201		Oh, Sweetie/What's That		
DUPREES (1) (WILLIS SANDERS & THE)					Thing Called Love	1959	Oasis 101
	Summertime/I'm Movin' On	1961	Regatta 2000		Tell Me Why/Annie	1963	Howard 503
DUPREES (2)				**DYMENSIONS (JOEL & THE)**			
	You Belong To Me/Take				A Thousand Miles Away/		
	Me As I Am	1962	Coed 569		My Juanita	1991	Classic Artists 130
	My Own True Love/Ginny	1962	Coed 571	**DYMNESTICS (EVONNE ROBINSON & THE)**			
	I'd Rather Be Here In Your Arms/				Darling Hear My Plea	N/A	Spacey
	I Wish I Could Believe You	1963	Coed 574	**DYNA-SORES**			
	Gone With The Wind/Let's				Alley-Oop/Jungle Walk	1960	Rendezvous 120
	Make Love Again	1963	Coed 576	**DYNAMICS (1)**			
	I Gotta Tell Her Now/Take Me				When The Saints Come		
	As I Am	1963	Coed 580		Marching In/Gone Is My Love	1957	Cindy 3005
	Why Don't You Believe Me/			**DYNAMICS (10)**			
	My Dearest One	1963	Coed 584		That's Bad/Nothing Can Change		
	Why Don't You Believe Me/				My Love For You		
	The Things I Love	1963	Coed 584		(by the Bandits)	1963	Emjay 1928
	Have You Heard?/Love Eyes	1963	Coed 585/Heritage 826 (69)		This Love Of Ours/Nothing Can		
	It's No Sin/The Sand And				Change My Love For You		
	The Sea	1964	Coed 587		(by the Bandits)	1963	Emjay 1935
	Where Are You/Please Let			**DYNAMICS (11)**			
	Her Know	1964	Coed 591		Yes I Love You Baby/		
	So Many Have Told You/				Soul Sloopy	N/A	Top Ten 100
	Unbelievable	1964	Coed 593		Whenever I'm Without You/		
	It Isn't Fair/So Little Time	1964	Coed 595		Love To A Guy	N/A	Top Ten 927

Artist	Song	Year	Label
DYNAMICS (12) (RAY MURRAY & THE)			
	Warm/I Never Knew	1963	Fleetwood 7005
DYNAMICS (2)			
	A Hundred Million Lies/Ka Joom	1957	Warner 1016
	Someone/Moonlight	1958	Impala 501/Seeco 6008 (59)
	Enchanted Love/Happiness And Love	1959	Arc 4450
	No One But You/Always, I Have Loved You	1959	Capri 104
	Blue Moon/Pigeon	1959	Delta 1002
	Don't Leave Me/Wasted	1959	Dynamic 1001
	The Girl I Met Last Night/ Nobody's Going Out With Me	1959	Dynamic Sound 504
	Aces Up/Baby	1959	Guaranteed 201
	Seems Like Only Yesterday/ How Should I Feel	1960	Decca 31046/Decca 31450 (62)
	At The End Of Each Day/ The Girl By The Gate	1960	Decca 31129
	If She Should Call/Dream Girl	1961	Dynamic 1008
	Wrap Your Troubles In Dreams/ I Can't Give You Anything But Love	1961	Lavere 186
	Christmas Plea/Dream Girl	1962	Dynamic Sound 578/9
	If I Give My Heart To You/ Blind Date	1962	Liban 1006
	Misery/I'm The Man	1963	Big Top 3161
	Delsinia/So Fine	1963	Dynamic 1002/Reprise 20183 (63)
	Chapel On A Hill/Conquistador	1963	Liberty 55628
	I Wanna Know/And That's A Natural Fact	1964	Big Top 516
	Take The Freeway	N/A	Corsican 651
DYNAMICS (2) (FB SKIP MILO)			
	Jo Baby/What's Wrong With Me	1959	Arc 4453
DYNAMICS (3) (JOHNNY CHRISTMAS & THE)			
	Soft Lips/Dum Dum	1959	P.D.Q. 5002
DYNAMICS (4) (RAY MURRAY & THE)			
	Baby What You Want Me To Do/With All My Love	1960	Arbo 222
DYNAMICS (5) (TONY MARESCO & THE) (AKA ANTHONY & THE SOPHOMORES)			
	Betty My Own/Forever Love	1961	Herald 569
DYNAMICS (6)			
	I Love To Be Loved/You Don't Seem To Realize	1961	Douglas 200
DYNAMICS (7) (MICKEY FARRELL & THE)			
	Baby Mine/I'm Calling On You	1963	Bethlehem 3080
DYNAMICS (8) (SUSAN & THE)			
	Letter To An Angel/Happy Birthday To Julie	1963	Dot 16476
DYNAMICS (9)			
	I Guess You Don't Love Me (No More)/Oh Night Of Nights	1963	Do-Kay-Lo 101
DYNAMO, SKINNY (& GROUP)			
	So Long So Long/Jingle Bell	1956	Excello 2097
DYNAMOS (1)			
	Woh Woh Yea Yea/Manhunt	1961	Cub 9096
	Teen Blues/Harem	1961	Press 101
DYNAMOS (2)			
	Darling/No One But You	1964	Azuza 1002
DYNATONES			
	The Girl I'm Searching For/ Pushin' And A-Slidin' (instrumental)	1959	Bomarc 303
DYNELS			
	Boy Friend/Let's Do It Again	1962	Dot 16382
	C'Mon Little Darlin'/Just A Face In The Crowd	1964	Natural 7001
EAGER, JOHNNY (& GROUP)			
	So Glad/Stay By Me	1959	End 1054
	I Understand/Blessing Of Love	1959	End 1061
EAGLEAIRES			
	Cloudy Weather/Number One Baby (no group)	1954	J.O.B. 1104
	I Love You/Save Her Doctor	1954	J.O.B. 1114
EAGLES			
	Please, Please/Tryin' To Get To You	1954	Mercury 70391
	(Will You, Won't You, Can't You) Don't You Wanna Be Mine?/ Such A Fool	1954	Mercury 70464
	What A Crazy Feeling/I Told Myself	1955	Mercury 70524
	Kiss Them For Me/Ladies In The Sky	1957	Prep 118
EARLINGTON, LYN (& GROUP)			
	Love Drops/My Last Phone Call	N/A	Lemonade 1501
EARLS (2)			
	Remember When/Sister Sookey/ Remember When/Give Me Time	1978	Crystal Ball 131
	My Heart's Desire/Lost Love	1980	Clifton 43
EARLS (1) (AKA FIVE THRILLS/REF ORCHIDS)			
	Believe Me, My Love/Spinnin'	1954	Gem 221/Crystal 100
	Love Tears/Don't Leave My Broken Heart	1974	Roadhouse 1009
	I'm All Alone/Good Lovin' Man	1974	Roadhouse 1021
	My Marie/Out Of This World (recorded in 1954)	1975	Gem 227
	Darlene	1990	Relic LP 5087
	Laverne	1990	Relic LP 5087
EARLS (1) (PAUL CRAWFORD & THE) (AKA FIVE THRILLS/REF ORCHIDS)			
	Let Me Back In There Again	1956	DC 0400
EARLS (2)			
	Life Is But A Dream/Without You	1961	Rome 101
	Life Is But A Dream/It's You	1961	Rome 101
	Lookin' For My Baby/Cross My Heart	1961	Rome 102/Clifton 39 (79)
	My Hearts Desire/I'll Never Cry	1961	Rome 5117
	Remember Then/Let's Waddle	1962	Old Town 1130
	Never/Keep A-Tellin' You	1963	Old Town 1133
	Eyes/Lookin' My Way	1963	Old Town 1141
	Cry Cry Cry/Kissin'	1963	Old Town 1145
	I Believe/Don't Forget	1964	Old Town 1149/Barry 1021
	Ask Anybody/Oh What A Time	1964	Old Town 1169
	Remember Me Baby/Amor	1965	Old Town 1181/1182
	If I Could Do It Over Again/Papa	1966	Mr. G. 801
	My Lonely Lonely Room/It's Been A Long Time Coming	1969	ABC 11109
	I Believe/Remember Then	1971	Cotillion 44114
	Dreams Come True/ My Heart's Desire	1973	Clifton 47
	A Sunday Kind Of Love/ Dream Come True	1975	Harvey 100
	Goin' Uptown/Mrs. Women	1976	Columbia 10225
	Stormy Weather/Could This Be Magic (by the Pretenders)	1976	Rome 111/Power-Martin 1005 (76)
	Little Boy And Girl/Lost Love	1976	Rome 112
	Whoever You Are/Lost Love	1976	Rome 113
	All Through Our Teens/ Whoever You Are	1976	Rome 114
	Get On Up And Dance The Continental/Love Epidemic	1976	Woodbury 1000
	Tonight (Could Be The Night)/ Meditation	1977	Woodbury 101
	Our Day Will Come	N/A	Woodbury LP 104
	Out In The Cold Again	N/A	Woodbury LP 104
	Old Man River	N/A	Woodbury LP 104
EARTHBOYS			
	Barbara Ann/Space Girl	1958	Capitol 4067
EARTHMEN			
	She's Mine	N/A	Tropical 123
EARTHQUAKES			
	Darling, Be Mine/Bashful Guy	1959	Fortune 534
EARTHQUAKES & RHYTHM KINGS			
	This Is Really Real/Crazy Bop	1960	Fortune 538
EARTHQUAKES (ARMANDO KING WITH THE)			
	Look What You've Done/ Baby, Only You	1962	Fortune 549
EARTHQUAKES (TINO CAIRO WITH THE)			
	Love In Portofino/ Wow Baby Sitter	1957	Hi-Q 5020
EAST-MEN (HAL JAXON & WATSIE LUMBARD & THE) (AKA EASTMEN)			
	Hum-Dibby-Do-Wah/Passion	N/A	Glow 100
EASTMEN (REF DELL VIKINGS)			
	Lover, Come Home/Bye, Bye, My Baby	1959	Mercury 71434
EBB TIDES			
	Franny Franny/Darling I'll Love Only You	1957	Acme 720
	Only Be Mine/What's Your Name Dear	1957	Teen 121

Artist Song	Year	Label
EBB TIDES (NINO & THE)		
Puppy Love/You Make Me		
Want To Rock And Roll	1958	Recorte 405
Purple Shadows/The Real		
Meaning Of Christmas	1958	Recorte 408
I'm Confessin'/Tell The World		
I Do	1959	Recorte 409
I Love Girls/Don't Look Around	1959	Recorte 413
Tonight/Nursery Rhymes	1961	Madison 151
Those Oldies But Goodies		
(Remind Me Of You)/Don't		
Run Away	1961	Madison 162
Juke Box Saturday Night/		
Someday (I'll Fall In Love)	1961	Madison 166
Little Miss Blue/Someday		
(I'll Fall In Love)	1961	Marco 105
A Happy Guy/Wished I		
Was Home	1961	Mr. Peacock 102
Stamps Baby Stamps/		
Lovin' Time	1962	Mr. Peacock 117
Low Tide/A Ballad Of Jed		
Clampett	1962	R&R 303
A Week From Sunday/Say No		
More (by Miss Frankie Nolan		
with the Ebbtides)	1963	Mr. Peeke 123
Automatic Reaction/Linda		
Lou Garrett (Likes 24 Karat)	1964	Mala 480
Mr. Moto/Surfin' '69	1969	R&R
EBB TONES		
Boogie Woogie/Rebel Beat	1961	Bee 301
EBB TONES (DON GRISSOM & THE)		
Recess In Heaven/Just Fall		
In Love	1956	Million $ 2011
Baby Stop	1956	Million $ 2012
EBB-TONES		
I Want You Only/That's All	1956	Crest 1016
Baby/What Makes A Man		
Fool Around?	1956	Crest 1024
Dust Off The Bible/Hum	1957	Crest 1032
EBBONAIRES (JACKSON TRIO & THE) (AKA EBONAIRES)		
Let's Kiss Hello Again/		
Jivarama Hop	1956	Hollywood 1062
EBBS (AKA EBB TIDES)		
Cartoons/Vickie Sue	1959	Dore 521
EBBTIDES (1) (DAVID FORD & THE)		
My Confession/The Sound		
Of Your Voice	1956	Specialty 588
EBBTIDES (2)		
Come On And Cry/Straightaway	1962	Monument 520
EBBTIDES (3) (REF CRENSHAWS/REF FOUR AFTER FIVES/REF LAMPLIGHT-ERS/REF RIVINGTONS/REF SHARPS/REF TENDERFOOTS)		
Lonesome/Love Doctor	1959	Jan-Lar 101/Firefly 329 (74)
EBBTIDES (4)		
Star Of Love/First Love	1964	Duane 1022
EBBTONES		
I've Got A Feeling/Danny's		
Blues	1957	Ebb 100
EBON-KNIGHTS		
Poor Butterfly/The Way The		
Ball Bounces	1958	Stepheny 1817
First Date/Only Only You	1958	Stepheny 1822
EBONAIRES (1)		
Love For Christmas/Jingle		
Bell Hop	1955	Hollywood 1046
The Very Best Luck In The		
World/Hey, Baby, Stop	1956	Money 220
We're In Love/Thinkin' And		
Thinkin'	1959	Colonial 117
EBONAIRES (2)		
Love Call/Somewhere In		
My Heart	1959	Lena 1001
Love Call/Don't Leave Me Baby		
(a capella) (by the Camelots)	1964	Cameo 334
EBONAIRES (3)		
Sposin'	1988	Relic LP 5076
Bring Me A Bluebird	1988	Relic LP 5076
You	1988	Relic LP 5076
Sioux City Sioux	1988	Relic LP 5076
Rosetta	1988	Relic LP 5076
Doodle Doo Doo	1988	Relic LP 5076
EBONAIRES (1) (BB THE MAXWELL DAVIS ORCH.)		
Three O'Clock In The Morning/		
Baby, You're The One	1953	Aladdin 3211

Artist Song	Year	Label
You're Nobody Till Somebody		
Loves You/Lawd, Lawd, Lawd	1953	Aladdin 3212
EBONETTES (FEMALE)		
All Alone/Wild Man Walk	1958	Ebb 147
EBONIERS		
Hand In Hand/Shut Your Mouth	1959	Port 70013
EBONY MOODS		
I've Got News For You/Grand,		
Nice, Swell	1955	Theron 108
ECCENTRICS		
Share Me/Stars	1964	Applause 1008
ECHELONS		
A Christmas Long Ago/Mystery	1987	BAB 129
A Christmas Long Ago/Snowtime	1991	BAB 132
It's So Hard To Say Goodbye		
To Yesterday/Under The		
Boardwalk	1992	Clifton 102
Streetlite Serenade/Pledging		
My Love	1992	Clifton 97
ECHOES (1)		
All That Wine Is Gone/Please		
Say You're Mine	1953	Rockin' 523
My Little Honey/Aye Senorita	1956	Combo 128
Have A Heart	1987	Relic LP 5069
Take My Hand	1988	Relic LP 5076
Please Come Back	N/A	Rockin' (unreleased)
ECHOES (10)		
Bluebirds Over The Mountain/		
A Chicken Ain't Nothin'		
But A Bird	1962	Smash 1766
Keep An Eye On Her/A Million		
Miles From Nowhere	1963	Smash 1807
Annabelle Lee/If Love Is	1963	Smash 1850
ECHOES (11) (BILLY & THE)		
Come Softly/Bodacious Twist	1962	Gala 121
ECHOES (12) (MITCH & THE)		
One Chance/I Could Try	1963	Bethlehem 3077
ECHOES (13) (TOMMY VANN & THE)		
Too Young/Give A Little Bit	1966	Academy 118
Is This Love/What Can You		
Do With A Broken Heart	1966	Academy 123
I'm Hopin' You'll Be Mine/		
Baby That's No	1966	Hollywood 101
ECHOES (14) (ALLAN ROBERTS & THE)		
School Days/Walk In With Love	N/A	Spotlight 101
ECHOES (2) (BENNY BARNES & THE)		
Lonely Street/Moon Over My		
Shoulder	1958	Mercury 71284
ECHOES (3) (FRANKIE & THE)		
Come Back Baby/Until We		
Meet Again	1958	Savoy 1544
ECHOES (4)		
Ding Dong/My Heart Beats		
For You	1957	Gee 1028
Over The Rainbow/Someone	1957	Specialty 601
Bye-Bye My Baby/Do I Love You	1960	Columbia 41549
Loving And Losing/Ecstasy	1960	Columbia 41709
Angel Of Love/Twistin' Town	1961	Hi-Tide 106/Felsted 8614
(61)		
I Love Candy/Paper Roses	1965	Ascot 2188
I Love Candy/Cinderella		
(by Gary Kay & the Passions)	1982	Jason Scott 20
Soldier Boy	N/A	4 Hits EP 11
ECHOES (4) (SONNY ROBERTS & THE)		
Honey Chile/I'll Never Let		
You Go	1958	Impala 1001
Scratch My Back/The Little		
Green Man	1958	Swan 4013
ECHOES (5)		
Time/Dee-Dee-Di-Oh	1959	Andex 22102
ECHOES (6) (JERRY STARR & THE)		
Teenage Tangle/Do Be True	1959	Ron 321
ECHOES (7)		
Born To Be With You/		
My Guiding Light	1960	Dolton 18
ECHOES (8)		
Without You/Heartbeat	1960	Edco 100
ECHOES (9)		
Angel Of My Heart/Gee Oh Gee	1961	Seg-Way 1002
Sad Eyes/It's Rainin'	1961	Seg-Way 106
Baby Blue/Boomerang	1961	SRG 101/Seg-Way 103 (61)

Artist	Song	Year	Label
ECHOLETTES			
	My Beau Joe/My Baby Loves Me	1963	Imperial 5934
ECHOMORES			
	Cute Chick/Little Chick	N/A	Rocket 1042
	How Does It Feel To Be Lonely	N/A	Rocket 1048
ECHOS			
	Land Of Rock And Roll	1982	Crystal Ball 150
ECHOTONES			
	So In Love/My Baby Doll	1959	Dart 1009
ECHOTONES (SKIP & THE)			
	Born To Love/Ooh-La-La	1959	DR 1001/Warwick 634 (60)
ECSTASIES			
	That Lucky Old Sun/A Time For Love	1962	Amy 853
	Dream Of A Lifetime/Chapel In The Moonlight	1979	Clifton 31
	White Christmas/Silent Night	1979	Clifton 40
	I'll Never Tell/Sixty Minute Man	1979	U.G.H.A. 4
	That's The Way It Goes/I Don't Know Why	1979	U.G.H.A. 5
	Adorable/Cry Like I Cried	1986	Clifton 78
	Out Of Sight, Out Of Mind/You Foolish Thing	1990	Clifton 87
	Until The Real Thing Comes Along/The Pleasure's All Mine	1991	Ronnie 207
	A G.I. Wish/It's Too Soon To Know/Gee/You Do Something To Me	N/A	Clifton EP 508
ECUADORS			
	I'll Be The One	1958	RCA EP 4286
	Stay A Little Longer	1958	RCA EP 4286
	Sputnik Dance	1958	RCA EP 4286
	A Vision	1958	RCA EP 4286
	Say You'll Be Mine/Let Me Sleep Woman	1959	Argo 5353
	You're My Desire/Someone To Call My Own	1961	Miracle 7
EDGEWOODS			
	Those Golden Oldies/So Fine	1968	Epic 10275
EDSELS			
	Lama Rama Ding Dong/Bells	1958	Dub 2843
	Do You Love Me?/Rink-A-Din-Ki-Do	1959	Roulette 4151
	What Brought Us Together?/Don't Know What To Do	1960	Tammy 1010
	Rama Lama Ding Dong/Bells	1961	Dub 2843/Twin 600 (61)/Winley 700/Musictone 1144 (64)
	Three Precious Words/Let's Go	1961	Tammy 1014/Ember 1078 (61)
	The Girl I Love/Got To Find Out About Love	1961	Tammy 1023
	Count The Tears/Twenty Four Hours	1961	Tammy 1027
	My Jealous One/Bone Shaker Joe	1962	Capitol 4588
	Shake Shake Sherry/If Your Pillow Could Talk	1962	Capitol 4675
	Shaddy Daddy Dip Dip/Don't You Feel	1962	Capitol 4836
	Could It Be/My Whispering Heart	1962	Dot 16311
EDWARDS, JACK (& GROUP)			
	All Night Long/When We Get The Word	1963	Michelle 508
EDWARDS, JOEY (& GROUP)			
	This Little Girl/Shirley Shirley	1960	Lilly 501
EDWARDS, SONNY (& GROUP)			
	This Time I'm Gonna Cry	1963	Cavetone 508
	I Love You Tenderly	1963	Cavetone 516
EFICS (WITH HARVEY CONNELL)			
	Autumn Heart/Sentimental Journey	1961	Fraternity 891
EGYPTIAN KINGS (AKA COLUMBUS PHARAOHS/FOUR PHARAOHS)			
	Give Me Your Love/I Need Your Love	1961	Nanc 1120
	School Days/The Move Around	N/A	Nanc (unreleased)
EGYPTIANS			
	That's Alright/Flippin' Their Top	N/A	Danae 1002
EGYPTIANS (KING PHARAOH & THE) (AKA COLUMBUS PHARAOHS/FOUR PHARAOHS)			
	By The Candlelite/Shimmy Sham	1961	Federal 12413
EKHOES (CON PIERSON & THE)			
	I Heard Those Bells/Six Pretty Girls	1964	LeMans 007
EKO'S (PENNY & THE)			
	Share Your Love/Gimme What You Got	1958	Argo 5295
EL CAMINOS (1) (MR. LEE & THE)			
	My Woman/I'm A Hog For You Baby	1964	Camelot 107/Nolta
EL CAMINOS (2)			
	Black Magic (a capella)/Darling Can't We Talk (a capella)	1965	Fellatio 101
EL CAPRIS			
	(Shimmy, Shimmy) Ko Ko Wop/Oh, But She Did	1956	Bullseye 102/Argyle 1010 (61)
	Your Star/To Live Again	1957	Fee Bee 216
	They're Always Laughing At Me/Ivy League Clean	1958	Paris 525
	Safari/Quit Pulling My Woman	1960	Ring-O 308
EL CAPRIS (FB SAM CRUNBY)			
	Girl Of Mine/These Lonely Nights	1958	Hi-Q 5006
EL DOMINGOES			
	Evening Bells/I'm Not Kidding You	1958	Kappa Rex 206
	Lucky Me, I'm In Love/Made In Heaven	1962	Chelsea 1009/Candlelite 418 (63)
	Are You Ready To Say I Do/I Want To Know	1964	Karmin 1001
EL DORADOS (1)			
	It's No Wonder/A Fallen Tear	N/A	Oldies 45 171
	Baby I Need You/My Lovin' Baby	1954	Vee Jay 115
	One More Chance/Little Miss Love	1955	Vee Jay 127
	At My Front Door/What's Buggin' You, Baby?	1955	Vee Jay 147
	I'll Be Forever Loving You/I Began To Realize	1955	Vee Jay 165
	Now That You've Gone/Rock 'n' Roll's for Me	1956	Vee Jay 180
	A Fallen Tear/Chop Ling Soon	1956	Vee Jay 197
	Bim Bam Boom/There In The Night	1956	Vee Jay 211
	Tears On My Pillow/A Rose For My Darling	1957	Vee Jay 250
	Three Reasons Why/Boom Diddle Boom	1957	Vee Jay 263
	Lights Are Low/Oh What A Girl	1958	Vee Jay 302
	In Over My Head/You Make My Heart Sing	1970	Torrid 100
	She Don't Run Around	1981	Charly LP 1022
	Trouble Trouble	1981	Charly LP 1022
	Love Of My Own	1984	Solid Smoke LP 8005
	It's No Wonder/A Fallen Tear	N/A	Oldies 45 171
EL DORADOS (1) (WITH HAZEL MCCOLLUM)			
	Annie's Answer/Living With Vivian (Al Smith's Combo)	1954	Vee Jay 118
EL DORADOS (2) (AKA KOOL GENTS)			
	Since You Came Into My Life/Looking In From The Outside	1971	Paula 347
	Loose Bootie/Loose Bootie (instrumental)	1972	Paula 369
EL JAYS (LEO WRIGHT & THE)			
	It Is I/I Wonder	1964	CB 5008/Red Fox 103 (65)
EL POLLOS			
	School Girl/Why Treat Me This Way?	1957	Neptune 1001
	High School Dance/These Four Letters	1958	Studio 999
	Three Little Letters	N/A	Neptune
EL RAYS (1) (AKA DELLS)			
	Darling I Know/Christine	1954	Checker 794
EL RAYS (2) (FEMALE)			
	Till The End Of Time/My Baby From Me	1963	M.M. 104/Wolf 104
EL REYES (AKA EL REYS)			
	Mr. Moonglow/Need Your Love	1958	Jade 501
EL REYS (AKA EL REYES)			
	Diamonds And Pearls/Rocket Of Love	1965	Ideal 94706

Artist Song	Year	Label
Beverly/Angalie	1965	Ideal 95388
EL SIERROS (AKA TOMMY & THE TEARS/AKA TEAR STAINS)		
Sunday Kind Of Love/Daddy's Comin' Home	1963	Yussels 7702
Life Is But A Dream/Pretty Little Girl	1964	Times Square 101
Love You So/Valerie	1964	Times Square 29/Relic 534 (65)
Picture Of Love/Sweeter Than (by the Young Ones)	1964	Times Square 36/Relic 527 (65)
EL TEMPOS		
My Love Grows Deep/My Dream Island	1963	Vee Jay 561 (first pressing)
My Dream Island/My Love Goes Deep Within	1963	Vee Jay 580 (second pressing)
EL TEMPOS (BIG MIKE GORDON & THE)		
Rain Or Shine/Down In New Orleans	1955	Savoy 1152
EL TEMPOS (MIKE GORDON & THE)		
You Got To Give/Why Don't You Do Right?	1954	Cat 101
EL TONES (1)		
Like Mattie/Lovin' With A Beat	1958	Cub 9011
EL TONES (2) (JO ANN BOSWELL & THE)		
You Were Meant For Me/I Won't Be Your Fool	1955	Chief 800
EL TORROS (1)		
Dance With Me/Yellow Hand	1957	Duke 175
You Look Good To Me/Barbara Jean	1958	Duke 194
What's The Matter/Dance With Me	1960	Duke 321
You May Say Yes/Two Lips	1961	Duke 333
Mama's Cookin'/Doop Doop A Walla Walla	1962	Duke 353
EL TORROS (2)		
All The Tears Is Gone/Love Is Love	1958	Fraternity 811
EL VENOS (AKA EL VINOS)		
Are You An Angel/You're Gonna Be My Girl	1990	Park Ave. 1
Now We're Together/Geraldine	1956	Groove 0170
My Heart Beats Faster/You Must Be True	1957	Vik 0305
Lonely Girl/Lover's Prayer (by Anne Keith and the Altairs)	1959	Memo 96
Little Things/Stereophonic	1960	Calico (unreleased)
My Heart Beats Faster/You WON'T Be True	1964	RCA 8303
Pretty Knees/I Am Just A Lonely Girl	N/A	Amp 3 (unreleased)
EL VIREOS		
First Kiss/Silly Willy	1959	Revello 1002
EL-DEENS		
Why Can't I Find You/My Love For You	1959	Federal 12347
Where Are You/Club For Broken Hearts	1959	Federal 12356
EL-DEROCKS		
Back Room/Hound Dog Blues	1958	Sapphire 1004
EL-RICH TRIO		
This I Swear/House Of Blue Lights	1966	Elco SK-1
ELADS (AKA LITTLE JOEY & THE FLIPS)		
African Twist/Ring Dong	N/A	unreleased
ELBERT, DONNIE (& GROUP)		
Believe It Or Not/Tell Me So	1957	DeLuxe 6143
Leona/I Have Sinned	1957	DeLuxe 6148
My Confession Of Love/Peek-A-Boo	1958	DeLuxe 6161
ELCHORDS (BUTCHIE SAUNDERS & THE)		
Peppermint Stick/Gee, I'm In Love	1957	Good 544/Musictone 1107 (59)
ELDAROS		
Rock-A-Bock/Please Surrender	1958	Vesta 101/102
ELDEES		
Don't Be Afraid To Love/You Broke My Happy Heart	N/A	Dynamics 1013
ELDER, NELVIN (& GROUP)		
I Dream/Find Me A Dream	1961	Brent 7027
ELDORAYS		
Nights Of Ecstacy/Everything's Gonna Be Alright	1961	Bud 114
ELECTRAS (1)		
You Lied/Ten Steps To Love	1961	Infinity 012/Constellation
Boo Babe/The Stomp	1962	Infinity 016
You Know/Boo Baby	1962	Lola 100
You Know/Don't Tell Me (by the Surgeons)	1963	Cee Jam 100
Boo Baby/Can't You See It In My Eyes	1963	Challenge 59245
Little Girl Of Mine/Mary, Mary	1966	Ruby-Doo 2
ELECTRAS (2)		
Get Lost Baby	N/A	Dauphin
ELECTRONAIRES (CHUCK RANADO & THE)		
Why Do I Cry/My Baby's Gone	1959	Count 508
One Lonely Night/Oh My	1959	Count 505
My Baby's Gone/Why Did I Cry	1959	Count 507
ELECTRONS		
For Sale/They Talk Too Much	1964	Laguna 103
ELEGANT IV		
Time To Say Goodbye/I'm Tired	1961	Cousins 1005/Mercury 72516 (65)
ELEGANTS		
Little Star/Getting Dizzy	1958	Apt 25005
Please Believe Me/Goodnight	1958	Apt 25017
Rain Rain Go Away	1958	Hull (unreleased)
Still Waiting	1958	Hull LP 1002
True Love Affair/Payday	1959	Apt 25029
Little Boy Blue (Is Blue No More)/Get Well Soon	1959	Hull 732
Green Eyes	1960	United Artists (unreleased)
Bluffin'	1960	United Artists (unreleased)
Let My Prayers Be With You/Speak Low	1960	United Artists 230
I've Seen Everything/Tiny Cloud	1961	ABC 10219
Happiness/Spiral	1961	United Artists 295
Promises/The Young Years	1963	Limelight 3013
A Dream Can Come True/Dressin' Up	1963	Photo 2662
Barbara, Beware/A Letter From Vietnam	1965	Laurie 3283
Bring Back Wendy/Wake Up	1965	Laurie 3298
Lonesome Weekend/It's Just A Matter Of Time	1974	Bim Bam Boom 121
Woo Woo Train/Maybe	1980	Crystal Ball 139
I Tried/Love Me And Don't Fool Around	N/A	Elegants 101
ELEGANTS (VITO & THE)		
Belinda/Lazy Love (instrumental)	1965	Laurie 3324
ELEGANTS (VITO PICCONE WITH THE)		
Path In The Wilderness/Get On The Right Track	1963	IPG 1016
ELEKTRAS		
Poor Amigos Rock/Little Lamb	1960	End 1082
All I Want To Do Is Run/It Ain't As Easy As That	1963	United Artists 594
ELEMENTS		
Lonely Hearts Club/Bad Man	1960	Titan 1708
ELEMENTS OF LIFE		
In A Fairy Tale/Disco Mama, Disco Man	1981	Starlight 14
ELGINS (1) (AKA DANIELS)		
Mademoiselle/A Picture Of You	1958	MGM 12670
Uncle Sam's Man/Casey Cop	1961	Flip 353
Extra, Extra/My Illness	1961	Titan 1724 (first pressing)
Heartache Heartbreak/My Illness	1961	Titan 1724 (second pressing)
Once Upon A Time/The Huddle	1962	Joed 716
Cheryl/Tell Gina	1963	Dot 16563
Johnny I'm Sorry/A Winner Never Quits	1963	Lummtone 109
Johnny I'm Sorry/You Got Your Magnet On Me Baby	1963	Lummtone 110
Finally/I Lost My Love In The Big City	1963	Lummtone 112
Your Lovely Ways/Finding A Sweetheart	1964	Lummtone 113
ELGINS (2) (LITTLE TOMMY & THE)		
Never Love Again/I Walk On	1962	Elmar 1084/ABC 10358 (62)

Artist Song	Year	Label
ELGINS (3)		
The Times We've Wasted/		
Ritha Mae	1964	Congress 214
Here In Your Arms/We're		
Gonna Have A Good Time	1964	Congress 225
Street Scene/You Found		
Yourself Another Fool	1965	Valiant 712
ELGINS (4) (DE JAN & THE)		
That's My Girl/Reality	1960	Lessie 99
That's My Girl/Heartbeat		
(by the Whirlwinds (1))	1967	Times Square 112
ELGINS (5)		
Pretending/Lonesome	1961	A-B-S 113
Darling Baby/Put Yourself In		
My Place	1965	V.I.P. 25029
ELITES (1)		
You Mean So Much To Me/		
Tell Him Again	1960	Hi-Lite 106
Tree Of Love/You'll Break		
Two Hearts	1963	ABC 10460
ELITES (2)		
In The Little Chapel/Northern		
Star	1959	Abel 225
ELITES (3) (FEMALE)		
Dapper Dan/Darling What		
About You	1960	Chief 7028
Jack The Ripper/Mama Look		
At Me	1960	Chief 7032
Come On And Dance/The Blues	1961	Chief 7040
ELJAYS (LEO WRIGHT & THE)		
It Is I/I Wonder	1962	CB 5008/Red Fox 103
		(65)/Pam
ELLINGTONS		
Hurry Home	1964	G-Clef 708
ELLIOTS (ANDRE & THE)		
Willie Jones Got Married/		
Willie Jones	1962	Barry 106
ELLIS BROTHERS		
Wow Baby/Sneaky Alligator	1958	ABC 9954
ELLIS, LORRAINE (BB THE CROWS)		
Piano Player Play A Tune/		
Perfidia	1954	Gee 1/Bullseye 100 (55)
ELOISE TRIO		
(Sorry I Just Had To) Li'l Darlin'	N/A	Carib 1032
ELRODS (RONNIE SPEEKS & THE)		
What Is Your Technique/		
Please Wait For Me	1961	King 5548
EMANON FOUR		
Oh! That Girl/Blues For Monday	1956	Flash 106
EMANONS		
Ol' Man River/Emanons Rock	1960	Delbert 5290
EMANONS (1)		
Change Of Time/Hindu Baby	1956	Gee 1005
Blue Moon/Wish I Had My Baby	1956	Josie 801
EMANONS (2)		
We Teenagers (Know What		
We Want)/Dear One	1958	Winley 226/ABC 9913 (58)
Connie/Buzz Buzz	N/A	Connie (unreleased)
You Know I Miss You/Cow		
Cow Dulywah	N/A	GGS 443
EMANONS (2) (WITH THE CONCEPTS (4))		
Cry (Only You Cry Alone)/		
The Sway	N/A	J&J 3000
EMBERGLOWS		
Sack And Chemise Gang		
Fight/Have You Found		
Someone New	1961	Dore 591
Sentimental Reasons/Make		
Up Your Mind	1962	Amazon 1005
EMBERS (1)		
Paradise Hill/Sound Of Love	1953	Ember 101/Herald 410 (53)
EMBERS (10) (RAY ALLEN & THE)		
Ham The Space Monkey/		
The Wibble	1961	Sinclair 1002
EMBERS (11) (PETE BENNETT & THE)		
Fever/Soft	1961	Sunset 1002
EMBERS (12) (RICKY DEE & THE)		
Tunnel Of Love/Workout	1962	Newtown 5001
EMBERS (13)		
In My Lonely Room/Good		
Good Lovin'	1964	JCP 1008

Artist Song	Year	Label
EMBERS (14)		
I Wonder Why/Little Girl Next		
Door	1965	Ara 210
EMBERS (15) (GENE PITNEY & THE)		
So Tired	1990	Relic LP 5085
Runaway Lover	1990	Relic LP 5085
Darkness	1990	Relic LP 5085
Victory	1990	Relic LP 5085
EMBERS (15) (LARRY LEE & THE)		
That Little Girl Was Mine	1990	Relic LP 5085
Tremble	1990	Relic LP 5085
Winter's Romance	1990	Relic LP 5085
EMBERS (2)		
Sweet Lips/There'll Be No		
One Else But You	1954	Columbia 40287
EMBERS (3)		
Wait For Me/Couldn't Wait		
Any Longer	1960	Dot 16101
My Dearest Darling/Please,		
Mr. Sun	1960	Dot 16162
EMBERS (3) (WILLIS SANDERS & THE)		
Your Souvenirs/Taking A		
Chance On You	1957	Juno 213/Jvpiter 213 (57)
Honey-Bun/Lovable	1958	Millionaire 775/Unart 2004 (58)
Time Out For Tears/Hungry		
For Your Love	1959	Coral 62146
EMBERS (4) (FRANKIE JOE & THE)		
Down Be The Stream/Margaritte	1957	Fee Bee 224
EMBERS (5) (JEFF MILNER & THE)		
No Greater Love/Let Me Know,		
Let Me Know, Let Me Know	1959	Dale 113
My Vow To You/Then		
(I'll Stop Loving You)	1959	Dale 114
EMBERS (6) (BILLY SCANDLIN & THE)		
You'll Always Have Someone/		
I Keep On Walking	1959	Viking 1002
EMBERS (7) (JERRY BRIGHT & THE)		
Be Mine/I'll Always Be	1959	Yucca 143
EMBERS (8) (JOE D'AMBRA & THE)		
Please Come Home/		
Don't Forget To Write	1960	Mercury 71725
EMBERS (9) (AKA TWILIGHTS (2))		
Solitaire/I'm Feeling Alright		
Again	1961	Empress 101
I Won't Cry Any More/I Was		
Too Careful	1961	Empress 104
Abigail/I Was Too Careful	1961	Empress 107
What A Surprise/I Was Too		
Careful	1961	Empress 108
I Wish I Didn't Love You So	N/A	Valmor
EMBERTONES		
I Remember/Falling For You	1962	Bay 203
EMBLEMS (1)		
Please Forgive Me	1959	Topic 8570
Poor Humpty Dumpty/		
Would You Still Be Mine	1962	Bay Front 107
Too Young/Bang Bang,		
Shoot 'Em Up Daddy	1962	Bay Front 108
EMBLEMS (2) (EDDIE CARL & THE)		
Little Willie Wampum/Every		
Little Dream Comes True	1962	Oh My 1000
The Thrust, Pt. 1/The Thrust,		
Pt. 2	1962	Oh My 1001
EMBLEMS (3) (PATTY & THE)		
Mixed Up, Shook Up Girl/		
Ordinary Guy	1964	Herald 590
The Sound Of Music Makes		
Me Want To Dance/You Took		
Advantage Of A Good Thing	1964	Herald 593
You Can't Get Away From Me/		
And We Danced	1964	Herald 595
Easy Come, Easy Go/It's		
The Little Things	1966	Congress 263
Let Him Go Little Heart/Try It,		
You Won't Forget It	1966	Kapp 791
All My Troubles Are Gone/		
Please Don't Ever Leave		
Me Baby	1967	Kapp 850
I'll Cry Later/One Man Woman	1967	Kapp 870
I'm Gonna Love You A Long		
Long Time/My Heart Is So		
Full Of You	1967	Kapp 897

Artist Song	Year	Label
EMBRACEABLES		
From Somebody Who Loves You/Gotta Pretty Little Baby	1959	Sandy 1025
Don't Call For Me/My Foolish Pride	1962	Cy 1004
(There's A) Wall Between Us/Sam (The 8th Of May)	1962	Dover 4100
Come Back/Destiny	1962	Dover 4101
EMERALDS (1) (LUTHER BOND & THE)		
What If You/See What You Done?	1954	Savoy 1124
You Were My Love/Starlight, Starbright	1954	Savoy 1131
I Won't Believe You Anymore/It's Written In The Stars	1955	Savoy 1159
He Loves You, Baby/I Cry	1956	Federal 12279
Old Mother Nature/Six Foot Hole	1959	Federal 12368
Gold Will Never Do/Jitterbug Jamboree	1959	Showboat 1501/Briar 114
Someone To Love Me/Should I Love You So Much?	1960	Showboat 1505
EMERALDS (2)		
Sally Lou/Why Must I Wonder?	1954	Kicks 3/Allied 10002/10003 (58)
That's The Way It's Got To Be/Maria's Cha Cha	1959	Bobbin 107
All The Time/Gotta Be On Time	1959	Rex 1004
Lover's Cry/Rumblin' Tumblin' Baby	1960	Bobbin 121
I Kneel At Your Throne/Custer's Last Stand	1960	Rex 1013
The Web/Trapped	1960	Yale 232
Silver/Roadrunner	1961	Toy 7734
EMERALDS (2) (WITH LITTLE MILTON)		
Cross My Heart/I'm In Love	1960	Bobbin 128
EMERALDS (3)		
The One I Adore/You Belong To My Heart	1957	ABC 9889
Confess/I'm Dreaming	1958	ABC 9948
EMERALDS (4)		
Mademoiselle/The Lover	1959	Venus 1002
Marsha/You're Driving Me Crazy	1959	Venus 1003
EMERALDS (5) (BOBBY WOODS & THE)		
Falling Rain/Friendly Mr. Hendley	1960	Dot 16053
I Need Your Love/Please Come Back	1961	Rumble 348
EMERALDS (6) (PAUL CHAPLAIN & HIS)		
Shortnin' Bread/Nicotine	1960	Harper 100
EMERALDS (7)		
You're A Fallen Angel/You Hold The Strings To My Heart	1962	Pel 3836
EMERALDS (8) (FEMALE)		
Dancing Alone/Wanna Make Him Mine	1964	Jubilee 5474
Did You Ever Love A Guy/I'm Gonna Ask That Boy To Dance	1964	Jubilee 5489
EMERALS		
Please Don't Crush My Dreams/(Soda Pop) Jukebox Rock	1960	Triple X 100/101/Times Square 111
EMERSON, BILLY "THE KID" (& FEMALE GROUP)		
Somebody Show Me/The Pleasure Is All Mine	1957	Vee Jay 247
EMERSONS (AKA DEMENS)		
Joannie Joannie/Hungry	1958	Newport 7004
Hokey Pokey/Dr. Jekyll And Mr. Hyde	1959	Cub 9027
Down In The Valley/Loneliness	1961	United Artists 379
EMERY'S		
Sincerely/Sweeter Than Sunday Kind Of Love/Then	1977	Clifton 18
You Can Tell Me Goodbye	1977	Clifton 19
Good Old Acappella/That's My Desire	1977	Clifton 17
EMJAYS (FB JIMMY CURTIS)		
This Is My Love/Waitin' (The Pitty Pat Song)	1959	Greenwich 411
Cross My Heart/All My Love, All My Life	1959	Greenwich 412
Over The Rainbow/Cookie Jar	1959	Paris 538
EMMETS (FB CHIP FISHER)		
No One/Poor Me	1959	Addison 15002
EMMY LOU (& GROUP)		
Love Ya, Need Ya/I Wanna Know	1961	Lute 6018
EMOTIONS (1)		
Echo '90/You Were There	1990	Crystal Ball 155
Mr. Night/Make Me A Love	1961	Laurie 3112
The Nearest Thing To Heaven/Lover's Lane	1961	Pio 107
Echo/Come Dance Baby	1962	Kapp 490
A Story Untold/One Life, One Love, One You	1963	20th Fox 430
Rainbow/Little Miss Blue	1963	20th Fox 452
L-O-V-E/A Million Reasons	1963	Kapp 513
Starlit Night/Fool's Paradise	1963	Laurie 3167
Boomerang/I Love You Madly	1964	20th Fox 478
I Wonder/Hey Baby	1964	Karate 506
She's My Baby/Baby I Need Your Loving	1965	Calla 122
Heart Strings/Every Time	1966	20th Fox 623
You're A Better Man Than I/Are You Real?	N/A	Johnson 746
Color My World/You're A Better Man Than I	N/A	South Park 1000
When You Dance	N/A	unreleased
EMOTIONS (2)		
It's Love/Candlelight	1958	Fury 1010
I Ran To You/Been Lookin' Your Way	1961	Flip 356
Been Lookin' Your Way/I Can Tell	1961	Flip 358
(By The Light Of The) Silvery Moon/Do You Love Me	1962	Card 600/Jason Scott 12 (81)
Love Of A Girl/Do This For Me	1965	Vardan 201
EMOTIONS (2) (LENA CALHOUN & THE)		
I Ran To You/First Love Baby	1961	Flip 357
EMPALAS		
It's Been A Long Time/Smoochin' In The Sewer	1958	Mark V 501
EMPERORS (1)		
I May Be Wrong/Come Back, Come Back	1954	Haven 511
EMPERORS (2)		
No Regrets/Nursery Rhyme	1958	3-J 121
EMPERORS (3)		
Darlin' In The Moonlight/Steve Allen	1964	Olimpic 245
EMPERORS (4) (ERNIE & THE)		
Meet Me At The Corner/Got A Lot I Want To Say	1965	Reprise 0414
EMPERORS (5)		
If You Don't Want Me	N/A	Graham
EMPERORS (6)		
I Want My Woman	N/A	Sabra 5555
EMPIRES (1)		
Corn Whiskey/My Baby, My Baby	1954	Harlem 2325
Make Me Or Break Me (vocal by Johnny Ace Jr.)/Magic Mirror	1955	Harlem 2333
I Want To Know/Shirley	1955	Wing 90023
Tell Me, Pretty Baby/By The Riverside	1955	Wing 90050
Linda/Whispering Heart	1956	Whirlin' Disc 104
My First Discovery/Don't Touch My Gal	1956	Wing 90080
If I'm A Fool/Zippety Zip	1957	Amp-3 132
EMPIRES (1) (LIGHTNING JUNIOR & THE)		
Ragged And Hungry/Somebody Changed The Lock	1955	Harlem 2334
EMPIRES (2)		
Only In My Dreams/Definition Of Love	1961	Calico 121
Love You So Bad/Come Home Girl	1962	Chavis 1026/Candi 1026 (62)
Everybody Knew But Me/Three Little Fishes	1962	Colpix 680
You're On Top, Girl/Slide On By	1963	Candi 1033
Love Is Strange/Have Mercy	1964	DCP 1116
EMPIRES (2) (EDDIE FRIEND & THE)		
Tears In My Eyes/Single And Free	1959	Colpix 112

Artist Song	Year	Label	Artist Song	Year	Label
EMPIRES (3)			I Still Remember/Picture Of Love	1975	Barrier 102
Over The Summer Vacation/			Trickle Trickle/Five Hundred		
You're So Popular	1961	Lake 711	Miles	1976	Barrier 104
EMPIRES (4) (FB JAY BLACK)			Sure As The Flowers/Baby		
A Time And A Place/			I Love You	1980	Clifton 41
Punch Your Nose	1962	Epic 9527	**ENDORSERS**		
EN-SOLIDS (DRAKE & THE)			Crying/Hold My Hand	1959	Moon 109
Please Leave Me/I'll Always			**ENDS**		
Be There	N/A	Alteen 8652	It Ain't No Use/Row Row		
ENCENADAS			Your Boat	1960	Vin 1029
Love I Beg Of You	1964	N/A	**ENGLISH, ANNA (& GROUP)**		
ENCHANTED FIVE			Baby Come Home/		
Try A Little Love/Have You Ever	1961	CVS 1002	My Favorite Record	1958	Felsted 8524
ENCHANTERS (1) (AKA SUGAR TONES (1)) (FEMALE)			**ENGLISH, SCOTT (BB THE ACCENTS (4))**		
Today Is Your Birthday/How			White Cliffs Of Dover/		
Could You (Break My Heart)	1952	Jubilee 5072	4000 Miles Away	1960	Dot 16099
I've Lost/Housewife Blues	1952	Jubilee 5080	When/Ugly Pills (You're Takin')	1962	Joker 777
ENCHANTERS (2)			High On A Hill/When		
True Love Gone (Come On			(by the Dedications)	1963	Sultan 4003/Spokane
Home)/Wait A Minute, Baby	1956	Mercer 992/Coral 61756 (57)			4003 (63)
There Goes (A Pretty Girl)/			Rags To Riches/Where Can I Go	1963	Sultan 5500
Fan Me, Baby	1957	Coral 61832	Here Comes The Pain/All I		
Bottle Up And Go/Mambo			Want Is You	1964	Spokane 4007
Santa Mambo	1957	Coral 61916	Brandy/Lead Me Back	1971	Janus 171
True Love Gone/The Day	1963	Coral 62373	Woman In My Life/Ballad Of		
True Love Gone/There Goes			The Unloved	1972	Janus 192
A Pretty Girl	1963	Coral 65610	**ENSENADAS**		
One Hand, One Heart	N/A	Coral	On And On/Love I Beg Of You	1963	Tarx 1005/Tarx 1005 (97)
ENCHANTERS (3) (AKA ENCHANTMENTS)			**ENSENATORS**		
Spellbound By The Moon/			Just Like Before/I Had A Little		
Know It All	1956	Stardust 102	Too Much	1962	Tarx 1001/Tarx 1001 (97)
Come On Baby, Let's Do			**ENTERTAINERS (1)**		
The Stroll/Rock Around	1958	Bald Eagle 3001	Danny Boy/How Much Do		
Touch Of Love/Cafe Bohemian	1959	Orbit 532/Bamboo 513 (61)	You Love Me	1963	Demand 2932
We Make Mistakes/The Decision	1960	Sharp 105	**ENTERTAINERS (2) (CORTEZ & THE)**		
I Lied To My Heart/Talk While			Life	N/A	Your Town
You Walk	1961	Musitron 1072	**ENTREES (CHUCK CORLEY & THE)**		
I Need Your Love/Goddess			Honey Let Me Stay/I Need		
Of Love	1962	Epsom 103	Your Love	1957	Fee Bee 219
Oh Rosemarie/Bewildered	1962	JJ&M 1562/Candlelite 432	City Of Strangers/Bring My		
On A Little Island	1963	Tee Pee 65	Daddy Home	1966	Sonic 118
I Should Be Loving You	N/A	Delta Ltd. 156	**ENTROS (GLORIA FOWLER & THE)**		
ENCHANTERS (4)			Will You Be My Guy/Train		
You Worry Me/So Much	1964	Vargo 10	Of Love	1965	Cee Jay 654
ENCHANTMENTS (AKA ENCHANTERS (3))			**ENVOYS (2)**		
(I Love You) Sherry/Come			Declaration Of Love/Springtime	1977	Crystal Ball 110
On Home	1962	Gone 5130	**ENVOYS (1) (BILL TALLY & THE)**		
Popeye/Lonely Heart	1962	Romac 1001	Summer Sun/Stop On Red,		
Oh Rosemarie/Bewildered	1963	J.J.&M. 1562	Go On Green	1959	Canadian American 104
I Love My Baby/Pains In			I've Waited/Goodbye, Goodbye	1959	Canadian American 105
My Heart	1963	Ritz 17003	**EPICS (1)**		
I'm In Love With Your			Let's Dance/Lonely	1958	Lifetime 1004
Daughter, Pt. 1/			So Many Times/I Want To		
I'm In Love With Your			Be Your Girl	1960	Dante 3004
Daughter, Pt. 2	1964	Faro 620	Rowdy Mae/Summer's		
Oh Rosemarie/Juke Box			Coming In	1961	Bandera 2512
Saturday Night	1972	Clifton 3	Ho-Hum-Deedle-Dum/		
Down On My Knees (acapella)	1975	Relic LP 103	Girl By The Wayside	1961	Lynn 510
Rock 'N' Roll Cha Cha			Magic Kiss/Last Night I Dreamed	1961	Lynn 516/Sabra 516
(acapella)	1975	Relic LP 103	**EPICS (2) (LINDA & THE)**		
Good Old Acappella/I Could			Memories Of Love/Gonna		
Never Love Another	N/A	Rogue (no #)	Be Loved	1959	Blue Moon 415
ENCHANTONES			**EPICS (3)**		
My Picture Of You/We Fell			Wishing You Were Mine/		
In Love	1962	Poplar 116	Grounded	1962	Eric 7001
ENCHORDS			**EPICS (4)**		
Zoom Zoom Zoom/I Need			Wild One	1962	Kim 101
You, Baby	1961	Laurie 3089	**EPICS (5)**		
ENCORES			The Bells Are Ringing/		
When I Look At You/			White Cliffs Of Dover	1964	Mercury 72283
Young Girls, Young Girls	1953	Checker 760	**EPIKS**		
Ha-Chi-Bi-Ri-Bi-Ri/Time			When We're Apart/Give Me		
Is Moving On	1954	Look 105/Ronnex 1003	A Chance	1965	Process 146
		(54)/Hollywood 1034 (55)	**EPISODES**		
Barbara/Thank You	1957	Bow 302	Where Is My Love/		
ENCOUNTERS			The Christmas Tree	1965	Four Seasons 1014
Don't Stop/A Place In Your Heart	1965	Swan 4205/Lost Nite 235	**EPITOMES (BUFORD BUSBEE & THE)**		
ENDELLS			Nobody But Me/This Is All I Ask	1959	Dee Dee 101
The Monkey Dance/Vicky	1963	Heigh Ho 604/605	**EPPS, ARTHUR (& GROUP)**		
ENDINGS			Mona/There Was A Party	1961	Spark 900
Can't Help Loving That Girl Of			**EPSILONS**		
Mine/You Never Loved Me	1974	Barrier 101	The Echo/Really Rockin'	1969	Stax 0021

Artist	Song	Year	Label
	I'm So Devoted/Mad At The World	N/A	Shrine 106
EQUADORS	I'll Be The One/A Vision/S putnik Dance/Stay A Little Longer	1958	RCA EP 4286
EQUALLOS	Beneath The Sun/In Between Tears	1955	M&M/Romantic Rhythm (55)
EQUALOS	Yodelin' Mad/Patty Patty	1959	Mad 1296
ERHARDT, DIAN (& GROUP)	I'll Wait/Mama Worries	1957	RCA 7137
ERLENE AND HER FRIENDS	Because Of You/Casanova	1963	Old Town 1052
ERMINES (GM CORNEL GUNTER) (AKA FLAIRS)	True Love/Peek, Peek-A-Boo	1955	Loma 701
ERMINES (GM CORNEL GUNTER) (AKA FLAIRS)	You Broke My Heart/I'm So Used To You Now	1956	Loma 703
	Keep Me Alive/Muchacha, Muchacha	1956	Loma 704
	I'm Sad/One Thing For Me	1956	Loma 705
ERRICO, RAY (BB THE HONEYTONES)	Humpty Dumpty Rock/My Sweetheart	1956	Masquerade 56003
ERVIN, FRANKIE (& FEMALE GROUP)	Believe Me/Why Don't You Go	1959	Guyden 2010
ERVIN, FRANKIE (& GROUP)	Annie Laurie/Wilhemina	1959	Contender 1316
	The Story/Blessing In Disguise	1959	Rendezvous 112
	You Hurt Me/If We Should Meet Again	1960	Rendezvous 126
	Such A Fool/Detour	1962	Indigo 138
ERVIN, FRANKIE (BB THE SHIELDS)	Some Other Guy/Be My Girl	1960	Hart 1691-52
ERVIN, FRANKIE (BB THE SPEARS)	Why Did It End/Try To Care	1961	Don 202
ESCAPADES (1) (GEORGIE SALO & THE)	End Of Time/I'll Love You Forever	1960	Hi-Q 5014
ESCAPADES (2)	Nobody Knows/Peaches	N/A	Glow 87896
ESCORTS (1)	Oh Honey/You Won't Be Satisfied	1954	Essex 372
	Paradise Hill/Bluebird Of Happiness	1954	Essex 383
	I've Been Thinking	1955	Essex 389
	Bad Boy/Tore Up Over You	1957	RCA 6834
	Lonely Man/So Hard To Laugh, So Easy To Cry	1957	RCA 6963
	You Can't Even Be My Friend	1963	RCA 8228
ESCORTS (10)	Gloria/Seven Wonders Of The World	1962	Coral 62302
	As I Love You/Gaudamaus	1962	Coral 62317
	Back Home Again/Something Has Changed Him	1963	Coral 62372
	My Heart Cries For You/Give Me Tomorrow	1963	Coral 62385
ESCORTS (10) (GOLDIE & THE)	Somewhere/Submarine Race Watching	1962	Coral 62336
	One Hand, One Heart/I Can't Be Free	1963	Coral 62349
ESCORTS (11) (CHARLIE MCCOY & THE)	Will You Still Love Me Tomorrow/My Babe	N/A	Monument 842
ESCORTS (2)	Sorry/It's Love To Me	1956	Premium 407
ESCORTS (3)	Misty Eyes/Arrow Two Hearts	1957	O.J. 1010
ESCORTS (3) (BOBBY CHANDLER & THE)	Winter Time/Junior Prom	1958	O.J. 1012
ESCORTS (4) (DEBS & THE)	Crew Cuts (We Like)/Swingin' Sam (instrumental by the Pastels)	1958	Josie 833
ESCORTS (5) (DON CRAWFORD & THE)	Why Why Why/Ugly Duckling	1959	Scepter 1201
ESCORTS (6)	One More Kiss Goodnight/Do-Ba-Ba-Do	1959	Wells 102
ESCORTS (7)	My First Year/Clap Happy	1959	Judd 1014
	I Will Be Home Again/Leaky Heart And His Red Go-Kart	1960	Scarlet 4005
	Judy Or Jo Ann/Main Drag	1961	Soma 1144
ESCORTS (8) (DEL & THE)	You Don't Love Me/Skokian (by Dell & the Escorts)	1960	Symbol 913
	Baby Doll/Someone To Watch Over Me	1961	Rome 103
	Happy/You're For Me (And I'm For You)	1961	Taurus 350
ESCORTS (9) (FELIX & THE) (GM FELIX CAVALIERE)	The Syracuse/Save	1962	Jag 685
ESCOS	Chick-A-Dee/I'm Lonesome For You	1959	Esta 100
	Diamonds And Pearls/We Dance	1960	Federal 12380
	Golden Rule Of Love/Watcha Bet	1961	Federal 12430
	Yes I Need Someone/Thank You Mister Ballard (For Creating The Twist)	1961	Federal 12445
	Shame Shame Shame/That's Life	1963	Federal 12493
ESKRIDGE, MURRIE (& GROUP)	So In Need For Love/Never Felt Like This Before	1961	Apex 7764
ESQUIRES (1) (AKA FIVE TINOS)	If You Only Knew What A Three Cent Stamp Could Do/Now, Now, Now	1954	Epic 9024
	Only The Angels Know/One Word For This	1955	Hi-Po 1003
	Yackety Yak/A Girl Named Joe	1956	Meteor 5022
ESQUIRES (2) (LORD LUTHER & THE)	Tremble/Tell Ya What (by the Five Hearts)	1960	Music City 833
ESQUIRES (3)	Mission Bells/When I Fall In Love	1962	Meridian 6283
ESQUIRES (4)	Boat Of Love/With A Feeling	1963	Argo 5435
ESSENTIALS (1) (BILLY & THE)	Maybe You'll Be There/Over The Weekend	1962	Jamie 1239
	Lonely Weekend/Young At Heart	1963	Mercury 72127
	Last Dance/Yes Sir, That's My Baby	1963	Mercury 72210
	Remember Me, Baby/The Actor	1965	Cameo 344
	Babalu's Wedding Day/My Way Of Saying	1966	Smash 2045
	Don't Cry (Sing Along With The Music)/Baby, Go Away	1966	Smash 2071
	I Wrote A Song/Oh What A Feeling	1967	SSS International 706
ESSENTIALS (1) (LITTLE BILLY & THE)	Steady Girl/The Dance Is Over	1962	Landa 691/Jamie 1229 (62)
ESSENTIALS (2) (JOHNNY LLOYD & THE)	On Our Wedding Day/Desire	1965	Reading 16000
ESSENTIALS (1) (BILLY & THE)	Resolutions/You're So Fine	1981	Crystal Ball 145
ESSENTS	Barbara/I Just Can't Understand	1966	Laurie 3335
ESSEX (1)	Easier Said Than Done/Are You Going My Way	1963	Roulette 4494
	A Walkin' Miracle/What I Don't Know Won't Hurt Me	1963	Roulette 4515
	She's Got Everything/Out Of Sight, Out Of Mind	1963	Roulette 4530
	I Hate To Cry	1963	Roulette LP 25234
	Every Night	1963	Roulette LP 25234
	We Belong Together	1963	Roulette LP 25234
	I Want You To Be My Boy/Tonight Tonight	1964	Roulette 4591
	Young And Lively	1964	Roulette LP 24246

Artist	Song	Year	Label
	The Eagle/Moonlight, Music And You	1966	Bang 537
ESSEX (1) (ANITA HUMES & THE)			
	Curfew Lover/What Did I Do?	1964	Roulette 4542
	Are You Going My Way/ Everybody's Got You	1967	Roulette 4750
ETERNALS			
	Rockin' In The Jungle/ Rock 'n' Roll Cha Cha	1959	Hollywood 68/Musictone 1111 (61)
	Babalu's Wedding Day/My Girl	1959	Hollywood 70/71/ Musictone 1110 (59)
	Blind Date/Today	1961	Warwick 611
	Come Go With Me/Love Me With All Your Heart	1968	Quality 1884
ETIQUETTES (LITTLE NAT & THE)			
	You're So Close/Blah Blah Blah	1961	Clock 2001
EUNIQUES			
	Pretty Baby/Cry Cry Cry	1961	620 1003
	Cry Cry Cry/Chicken (Yeah)	1961	620 1006
	Silvery Moon/Cry Cry Cry	1980	Jason Scott 6
EVANS SISTER (WITH MALE GROUP)			
	I Need Somebody flip is instrumental by Rusty Bryant)	1956	Dot 15449
EVANS, DONNA (& GROUP)			
	Sorry/Foolish Me	1962	Cheer 1003
EVANS, JERRY (BB THE OFF KEYS)			
	Out Of My Mind/Knock On Wood	1962	Bubble 1333
EVANS, KAY (& GROUP)			
	Lover (How Much Longer)/ Prove It	1961	Whip 274
EVELS (FEMALE)			
	The Magic Of Love/ Wonderful Guy	N/A	Tra-X 14-152
EVENTUALS			
	Just The Things That You Do/Charlie Chan	1961	Okeh 7142
EVERETT, BRACEY (& GROUP)			
	I Want Your Love/The Lover's Curse	1959	Atlantic 2013
EVERGLADES (1)			
	While Waiting In The Chapel/ Do You Miss Me	1963	BPV 112577
EVERGLADES (1) (JERRY HAYWARD & THE)			
	You Stole My Heart Away/ Shimmy, Shimmy, Shimmy, Shimmy	1963	Symbol 916
EVERGLADES (2)			
	I Went To The S&S/Tell Me Pretty Baby	N/A	Brenne 502
EVERGREENS (1)			
	Very Truly Yours/Guitar Player	1955	Chart 605
EVERGREENS (2) (DANTE & THE)			
	Alley-Oop/The Right Time	1960	Madison 130
	Time Machine/Dream Land	1960	Madison 135
	What Are You Doing New Year's Eve/Yeah Baby	1960	Madison 143
	Think Sweet Thoughts/Da Doo	1961	Madison 154
EVERGREENS (3) (EDDIE & THE) (REF SHA NA NA)			
	In The Still Of The Night/ In The Still Of The Night	1973	Kama Sutra 578
EX-CELS FIVE			
	Talk Is Cheap/Dancing Girl	1964	Enith 722
EX-TONES (MR. X & THE)			
	Yours Is My Heart Alone/ I'm In Love	N/A	H.O.B. 1000
EXCELLENTS (1) (AKA EXCELLONS)			
	White Cliffs Of Dover	1961	unreleased
	She's Not Coming Home	1961	unreleased
	Coney Island Baby/You Baby You	1962	Blast 205
	Love No One But You/When The Red Red Robin Comes Bob, Bob Bobbin' Along	1963	Mermaid 106
EXCELLENTS (2)			
	I Hear A Rhapsody/Why Did You Laugh	1963	Blast 207
EXCELLONS (AKA EXCELLENTS (1))			
	Sunday Kind Of Love/Helene (Your Wish Came True)	1964	Bobby 601/Old Timer 601 (64)
EXCELS (1)			
	You're Mine Forever/Baby Doll	1957	Central 2601
	Baby Doll/My Greatest Thrill	1965	Relic 1007
EXCELS (2)			
	On Bended Knee/I Miss You So	1955	X 0108
	My Foolish Heart/Just You And I Together	1960	Gone 5094
	Til You Were Gone/Can't Help Lovin' That Girl Of Mine	1961	R.S.V.P. 111
EXCELS (2) (BILL DANIELS & THE)			
	Rock And Roll Baby	1955	X
EXCELS (2) (SANDY STEWART & THE)			
	Johnny Darling	1955	X 0126
EXCEPTIONS			
	Down By The Ocean/Pancho's Villa	1963	Pro 1/Cameo 378 (65)
EXCITEMENTS (ELROY & THE)			
	My Love Will Never Die/ No One Knows	1961	Alanna 188/Alanna 565 (63)
EXCITING INVICTAS			
	I Don't Care/Not Again	1960	Kingston 427
EXCLUSIVES			
	My Girl Friend/It's Over	1958	K&C 102
EXECS			
	Walkin' In The Rain/Palladium	1958	Fargo 1055
EXECUTIVE FOUR			
	You Are/I Got A Good Thing Going	N/A	Lumar 202
EXECUTIVES (1) (MARGIE MILLS & THE)			
	Knock On Any Door/All Of Me	1963	Vee Jay 549
EXECUTIVES (2) (AKA CHALLENGERS)			
	River Of Tears/Come On Now	1963	Explosive 3821/Mink 5004
	Why/Come On Baby	1963	Revenge 5003/Explosive 3621 (63)
EXODUS (AKA FOUR EPICS)			
	M And M/Silhouettes-You Cheated You Lied	1972	Wand 11248
EXOTICS (1)			
	That's My Desire/Darling I Want To Get Married	1961	Coral 62268
	The Gang That Sang "Heart Of My Heart"/Hotcha Mighty Knows	1961	Coral 62289
	Manpower/Fortune Hunter	1962	Coral 62310
	My Life's Desire, Pt. 1/My Life's Desire, Pt. 2	1962	Coral 62343
	Sad Sad Song/Let's Get Together	1964	Coral 62399
	Like You Hurt Me/Big Time Charlie	1964	Coral 62439
EXOTICS (2)			
	Lorraine/Gee	1963	Springboard 101
EXPLOITS (BOBBY MAXWELL & THE)			
	You're Laughing At Me/ Stay With Me	1959	Fargo 1009
EXPLORERS			
	Vision Of Love/On A Clear Night	1960	Coral 62147
	In The Wee Small Hours Of The Morning/Don't Be A Fool	1960	Coral 62175/Coral 65575 (63)
	Don't Be A Fool/Vision Of Love	N/A	Popular Request 101
EXPLORERS (DENNIS & THE)			
	Remember/Every Road	1961	Coral 62295
EXPRESSIONS (1)			
	Now That You're Gone/Crazy	1956	Teen 101
EXPRESSIONS (2)			
	My Love, My Love/The Sign Of Happiness	1961	Arliss 1012
	Come Back Karen/Thrill	1963	Smash 1848
	You Better Know It/Out Of My Life	1964	Federal 12533
	Be Bop A Lula/Skinny Minnie	1965	Guyden 2122
	One Plus One/Playboy	1965	Reprise 0360
EXPRESSIONS (3) (AKA IMAGINATIONS)			
	To Cry/On The Corner	1963	Parkway 892
EXPRESSIONS (3) (BILLY HARNER & THE)			
	Anymore/Watcha Gonna Do	1964	Lawn 239
EXPRESSIONS (4) (JOHNNY & THE)			
	Where Is The Party/Something I Want To Tell You	1965	Josie 946
	Shy Girl/Now That You're Mine	1966	Josie 955
	Give Me One More Chance/ Boys And Girls Together	1966	Josie 959

Artist	Song	Year	Label
EXQUISITES			
	Dedicated To The One I Love/		
	Hey Senorita	1985	Avenue D 12
	Chapel Of Dreams/At My		
	Front Door	1985	Avenue D 13
EXTENSIONS (FEMALE)			
	I Want To Know/My Need	1963	Success 109
EXTREMES (AKA BOBBY & THE VELVETS)			
	Come Next Spring/Let's Elope	1958	Everlast 5013
	The Bells/That's All I Want		
	(with Bobby Sanders)	1962	Paro 733
EXZELS			
	Canadian Sunset/Hip Talk	N/A	Crossfire 228
F. J. BABIES			
	And The Moon Came Down/		
	She Has	1961	Apt 25068
FABIANS (FEMALE)			
	Confidential/Would You Believe	N/A	Blue Rocket 315
FABLES			
	Angel/Cleopatra 30 B.C.	1962	Elgo 3001
FABULAIRES			
	While Walking/No, No	1957	East West 103/Main Line 103 (58)
	Wedding Song/Lonely Days, Lonely Nights	1963	Chelsea 103
FABULEERS			
	If I Had Another Chance/I Had A Feeling This Morning	1960	Kenco 5002
FABULONS (1)			
	Smoke From Your Cigarette/ Give Me Back My Ring	1960	Ember 1069
	Connie/This Is The End	1963	Benson Ritco 100/ Benson 100 (63)
FABULONS (2) (WITH THE TIKIS)			
	Since You've Been Gone/ Don't Ask Me	1966	Tower 259
FABULONS (3) (FEMALE)			
	Lonely Boy/Trying	1963	Jo-Dee 1001
FABULONS (4) (BOBBY WINSLOW & THE)			
	House Of Tears	N/A	Fabulous 1001
FABULOUS BLENDS			
	A Thousand Miles Away/ Music Maestro Please	1964	Casa Grande 5000
	Someone To Care/It's Your Turn	N/A	Casa Grande 3037
FABULOUS BLENDS (BIG JOHN & THE)			
	Hey Little Fool/Baby You're Wrong	1964	Casa Grande 5001
FABULOUS CHIMES (FB ARLENE SMITH)			
	Faithful To Me/Faithful To Me (instrumental)	1964	Invincible Arts 1177
FABULOUS CLOVERS (AKA CLOVERS)			
	They're Rockin' Down The Street/Be My Baby	1961	Winley 265
FABULOUS DENOS			
	Bad Girl/Once I Had A Love	1964	King 5908
	Hard To Hold Back Tears/I've Enjoyed Being Loved By You	1965	King 5971
FABULOUS DESIRES			
	Dance With Me (flip has no group)	1964	Era 3138
FABULOUS DIALS			
	Forget Me Not/Bossa Nova Stomp	1963	Joy 276/DnB 1000
FABULOUS DINOS			
	That Same Old Song/ Where Have You Been	1962	Musicor 1025
	Instant Love/Retreat	1964	Saber 1009
FABULOUS DUDES			
	Davilee/Go On	1989	Presence 4502
	Betty Blue Moon/Ding Dong Darling	1994	Presence 4503
FABULOUS EARTHQUAKES			
	Please Be My Girl/In The Chapel In The Moonlight	1960	Meridian 1518
FABULOUS ECHOES			
	I Never Knew/Keep Your Love Strong	1964	Liberty 55769
	Sunshine	1965	Diamond 187
	Candy/Cry I Do	1965	Liberty 55801
FABULOUS EGYPTIANS			
	End Of Time/The Cowboy	1965	Cindy 96750
FABULOUS EL DORADOS			
	Ease The Pain/Remember Sherrie	1987	Delano 1099
FABULOUS EMBERS (WILLIS SANDERS & THE) (AKA EMBERS)			
	Lovable You/Honey Bun	1958	Millionaire 775
FABULOUS ENCHANTERS			
	Why Are You Crying/ Something Blue	1961	Finer Arts 1007
FABULOUS FABULIERS			
	She Is The Girl For Me/I Found My Baby	1959	Angle Tone 539
FABULOUS FALCONS			
	Dolly/I Wanna Be With You	1966	White Cliffs 249
FABULOUS FANATICS			
	Givin' Up On Love/Sweeter Than Wine	1961	T-Bird 201
FABULOUS FIDELS			
	Westside Boy, Eastside Girl/ Soul St.	N/A	Jaa Dee 106
FABULOUS FIVE			
	Gettin' Old/Janie Made A Monster	1959	King 5220
FABULOUS FIVE FLAMES			
	Lonely Lover/No More Tears	1960	Time 1023
FABULOUS FLAMES			
	My Joan/Josephine	1958	Rex 3000
	Do You Remember?/Get To Stepping	1961	Bay-Tone 102
	Lover/I'm So All Alone	1961	Bay-Tone 105
FABULOUS FORTUNES (NORM N. NITE & THE)			
	Let's Try It Again/Good Old Rock & Roll Music	1971	Globe 107
FABULOUS FOUR (AKA FOUR JS)			
	In The Chapel In The Moonlight/Mr. Twist	1960	Chancellor 1062
	Let's Try Again/Precious Moments	1961	Chancellor 1068
	Why Fools Fall In Love/ The Sound Of Summer	1961	Chancellor 1078
	Betty Ann/Prisoner Of Love	1961	Chancellor 1085
	I'm Comin' Home/Everybody Knows	1961	Chancellor 1090
	Mr. Twist/Everybody Knows	1961	Chancellor 1098
	Forever/It's No Sin	1962	Chancellor 1102
	Oop-Shoobie-Doop Bam-A-Lam/ Welcome Me Home	1962	Melic 4114
	Got To Get Her Back/Now You Cry	1964	Brass 311/Coral 62479 (64)
	Happy/Who Could It Be	1964	Brass 314
	Yound Blood/I'm Always Doing Something Wrong	1964	Brass 316
	Rita	N/A	Fortune LP 8017
FABULOUS FOUR (WITH FABIAN)			
	The Love That I'm Giving To You/You're Only Young Once	1961	Chancellor 1079
FABULOUS FUTURAS			
	La Do Da Da/When You Ask About Love	N/A	Okon (no #)
FABULOUS GARDENIAS (AKA GARDENIAS (2))			
	What's The Matter With Me?/ It's You, You, You	1962	Liz 1004
FABULOUS IDOLS			
	Baby/Nellie	1961	Kenco 5011
FABULOUS KOOLCATS (RUBEN SIGGERS & THE)			
	Those Love Me Blues/ Please Pretty Baby	1957	Spinks 600
FABULOUS MARCELS (AKA MARCELS)			
	That Lucky Old Sun/ Peace Of Mind	1975	St. Clair 13711/ Rocky 13711
FABULOUS PEARL DEVINES			
	So Lonely/You've Been Gone	1959	Alco 101
FABULOUS PEARLS			
	My Heart's Desire/Jungle Bunny	1959	Dooto 448
FABULOUS PERSIANS			
	Save The Last Dance For Me/ Ling Ting Tong	N/A	Bobby-O 3123
FABULOUS PHARAOHS			
	Church Key	N/A	Three Star 2668
FABULOUS PLAYBOYS (AKA FALCONS (5))			
	I Fooled You/Sweet Peas And Bronc Busters	1959	Contour 004
	Honkey Tonk Woman/Tears, Tears, Tears	1960	Apollo 760

Artist	Song	Year	Label
	Nervous/Forget The Past	1960	Daco 1001/Apollo 758 (60)
FABULOUS ROYALS			
	I Only Have Eyes For You/		
	Land Of 1000 Dances	N/A	Aegis 1006
FABULOUS SILVER TONES			
	Dimples	N/A	West Coast 452
FABULOUS SPLENDORS			
	Canadian Sunset/Your		
	Change Of Heart	1960	O-Gee 105
FABULOUS TEARS (LITTLE DOOLEY & THE)			
	I Love You/She's So Fine	1965	Baylor 101
FABULOUS THREE (GORGEOUS GEORGE & THE)			
	Cross Every Mountain/		
	Teach Me	1962	Hale 501
FABULOUS TWILIGHTS (NATHANIEL MAYER & THE)			
	My Last Dance With You/		
	My Little Darling	1961	Fortune 542
	Village Of Love/I Want A Woman	1962	Fortune 545/United Artists 449 (62)/Fortune 563 (63)
	Hurtin' Love/Leave Me Alone	1962	Fortune 547
	Well, I've Got News/Work It Out	1962	Fortune 550
	Well, I've Got News/		
	Mr. Santa Claus	1962	Fortune 550X
	I Had A Dream/I'm Not		
	Gonna Cry	1963	Fortune 554
	Going Back To The Village		
	Of Love/My Last Dance		
	With You	1963	Fortune 557
	Place I Know/Don't Come Back	1963	Fortune 562
	From Now On/I Want Love		
	And Affection	1963	Fortune 567
FABULOUS UPTONES			
	New Love I Have Found/Turtle	1962	Tulip 100
FABULOUS VALIENTS			
	Your Golden Teardrops/		
	Carmelita	1962	Holiday 61005
FABULOUS WINDS (JOE BOOT & THE)			
	That's Tough/Rock And		
	Roll Radio (no group)	1958	Celestial 111
FABUTONES			
	I Found A Love/Baby	1972	Bim Bam Boom 100
FACES			
	Christmas/New Year's		
	Resolution	1965	Iguana 601
	What Is This Dream (I Have)/		
	Skier Jones	1965	Regina 1326
	I'll Walk Alone/I Didn't Want Her	1965	Regina 1328
FADS (BUDDY & THE)			
	Won't You Love Me/Is It Just		
	A Game	1958	Morocco 1001
FAIRFIELD FOUR			
	Memories (Of My Mother)/		
	Don't Let Nobody	1960	Old Town 1081
FAIRLANES (1)			
	Seventeen Steps/Johnny		
	Rhythm	1959	Lucky Seven 102
	If The World Don't End		
	Tomorrow	1960	Argo
	Little Girl, Little Girl/Comin'		
	After You	1960	Argo 5357
	I'm Not The Kind Of Guy/		
	The Dagwood	1962	Minaret 103
	Surf Train/Lonely Weekends	1963	Reprise 20213
	Baby Baby/Tell Me	1964	Radiant 101
	The New York Sound, Pt. 1/		
	The New York Sound, Pt. 2	1964	Radiant 104
	Memories Of The Past	1989	Relic LP 5079
FAIRLANES (2)			
	Just For Me/Bullseye	1959	Dart 109
FAIRLANES (3)			
	Writing This Letter/Playboy	1961	Continental 1001
FAIRLANES (4) (CHARLES PERRYWELL & THE)			
	Come Along With Me/		
	You're Lonesome Now	N/A	Tic Toc 104
FAIRMOUNTS			
	Times And Places/Lucky Guy	1962	Planet 53
FAITHFULS (PHILIP & THE)			
	Love Me/Rhythm Marie	1964	Goldwax 109
FALCONS (1)			
	I Can't Tell You Now/How Blind		
	Can You Be	1952	Regent 1041
	You're The Beating Of My		
	Heart/It's You I Miss	1953	Savoy 893

Artist	Song	Year	Label
	Stepping Stone/Jigsaw Puzzle	1957	RCA 7076
FALCONS (2)			
	Stay Mine/Du-Bi-A-Do	1954	Flip 301
	Tell Me Why/I Miss You, Darling	1955	Cash 1002
FALCONS (2) (CANDY RIVERS & THE)			
	Baby Tonight/You Are The		
	Only One	1954	Flip 302
FALCONS (3) (AKA LYRICS)			
	My Only Love/Now That It's Over	1957	Quality 1721/Falcon 1006 (57)/Abner 1006 (57)
FALCONS (4) (GM WILSON PICKETT & EDDIE FLOYD)			
	Baby That's It/This Day	1956	Mercury 70940
	Can This Be Christmas?/		
	Sent Up	1957	Silhouette 521
	This Heart Of Mine/Romanita	1958	Kudo 661
	Just For Your Love/This Heart		
	Of Mine	1959	Chess 1743/Anna 1110 (60)
	You're So Fine/Goddess		
	Of Angels	1959	Flick 001/Unart 2013 (59)/United Artists 2013X (59)/United Artists 420 (62)
	You're Mine/Country Shack	1959	Unart 2022
	That's What I Aim To Do/You		
	Must Know I Love You	1960	Flick 008
	Waiting For You/The Teacher	1960	United Artists 229
	I + Love + You/Wonderful Love	1960	United Artists 255
	Workin' Man's Song/Pow!		
	You're In Love	1961	United Artists 289
	Lah-Tee-Lah-Tah/Darling	1962	Atlantic 2153
	I Found A Love/Swim	1962	Lu Pine 103/Lu Pine 1003
	Take This Love I've Got/		
	Let's Kiss And Make Up	1963	Atlantic 2179
	Oh Baby/Fine Fine Girl	1963	Atlantic 2207
	Lonely Nights/Has It Happened		
	To You	1964	Lu Pine 124/Lu Pine 1020 (64)
	You're On My Mind/Anna	1965	Lu Pine 003
	Please Don't Leave Me Dear	1985	Relic LP 8005
	Whose Little Girl Are You	1985	Relic LP 8005
	Girl Of My Dreams	1985	Relic LP 8005
	Anytime, Anyplace, Anywhere	1985	Relic LP 8005
	Juke Hop	1985	Relic LP 8005
	I Wonder	1985	Relic LP 8005
	No Time For Fun	1985	Relic LP 8005
	Let It Be Me	1985	Relic LP 8005
	I'll Never Find Another Girl		
	Like You	1985	Relic LP 8005
	She's My Heart's Desire	1986	Relic LP 8006
	Billy The Kid	1986	Relic LP 8006
	What To Do	1986	Relic LP 8006
	Part Time Love	1986	Relic LP 8006
	Feels Good	1986	Relic LP 8006
FALCONS (5) (AKA FABULOUS PLAYBOYS)			
	I Can't Help It/Standing On		
	Guard	1966	Big Wheel 1967
	(I'm A Fool) I Must Love You/		
	Love, Love, Love	1966	Big Wheel 321/322
	Love Look In Her Eyes/		
	In Time For The Blues	1967	Big Wheel 1971
	Good Good Feeling/Love You		
	Like You've Never Been Loved	1967	Big Wheel 1972
FALCONS (6) (JACK RICHARDS & THE)			
	Pretty Baby/We Dream	1958	Dawn 233
FALLEN ANGELS			
	So Young, So Fine/Up On		
	The Mountain	1965	Tollie 9049
	A Little Love From You Will		
	Do/Everytime I Fall In Love	1966	Laurie 3343
	Bad Woman/Pimples And		
	Braces	N/A	Eceip 1004
FAMOUS FLAMES (1) (WITH JOHNNY SPAIN)			
	I'm In Love/Family Rules	1958	Back Beat 516
FAMOUS FLAMES (2)			
	So Long My Darling/I'm Going		
	To Live My Life Alone	1960	Harlem 114
FAMOUS HEARTS (AKA LEE ANDREWS & THE HEARTS)			
	Aisle Of Love/Momma	1962	Guyden 2073
FANADOS			
	The One I Love/She Must Be		
	From A Different Planet	1957	Carter 2050
FANATICS			
	Is There Still A Chance/		
	Oogly Googly Eyes	1961	Skyway 127

Artist	Song	Year	Label
FANTASTIC FIVE KEYS (AKA FIVE KEYS)			
	From The Bottom Of My Heart/ Out Of Sight, Out Of Mind	1962	Capitol 4828
FANTASTIC VONTASTICS			
	Oh Happy Day (Tra-La-La)/ Gee What A Boy	1965	Tuff 406
FANTASTICS (1)			
	There Goes My Love/I Wanna Be A Millionaire Hobo	1959	RCA 7572
	This Is My Wedding Day/ I Got A Zero	1960	RCA 7664/Popular Request 102
	Dancing Doll/I Told You Once	1961	United Artists 309/ Park Ave. 4 (91)
	Believe In Me/My Girls	1990	Park Ave. 3
	Angie Lee/Drum Beat	1990	Park Ave. 2
	There Goes My Love/ Oh Rosemarie (by the Fascinators)	N/A	Popular Request 106
FANTASTICS (2)			
	Goodbye To Love/I Don't Know	1964	DMD 103
FANTASTICS (3)			
	In Times Like These/Where There's A Will	1961	Impresario 124
FANTASYS			
	No One But You/Why, Oh Why	1960	Guyden 2029
FARRER, TONY (& GROUP)			
	A Blast From The Past/ Following You	1961	Trans Atlas 001
FASCINATIONS (5)			
	Goodnight/1-2-3	1978	Crystal Ball 123
FASCINATIONS (1)			
	Midnight (or It's Midnight)/ Boom Bada Boom	1960	Sure 106
FASCINATIONS (1)			
	If I Had Your Love/Why	1961	Paxley 750/Dore 593 (61)
FASCINATIONS (2) (JORDAN & THE)			
	Give Me Your Love/ Once Upon A Time	1961	Carol 4116
	My Imagination/I'll Be Forever Loving You	1961	Dapt 203
	Love Will Make Your Mind Go Wild/My Baby Doesn't Smile Anymore	1961	Dapt 207
	I'm Goin' Home/If You Love Me Really Love Me	1962	Josie 895
	If You Love Me/Once Upon A Time/Delores/Love Will Make Your Mind Go Wild	1990	Magic Carpet EP 509
FASCINATIONS (3) (FEMALE)			
	Mama Didn't Lie/Someone Like You	1963	ABC 10387
	Tears In My Eyes/You're Gonna Be Sorry	1963	ABC 10443
FASCINATIONS (4)			
	I'm Gonna Cry/Since You Went Away (recorded in 1962)	1972	A&G 101
FASCINATORS (1)			
	Can't Stop/Don't Give My Love Away	1955	Blue Lake 112
FASCINATORS (2)			
	Teardrop Eyes/Shivers And Shakes	1958	Dooto 441
	Cuddle Up With Carolyn/ Tee Vee	1958	King 5119
	Oh Rosemarie/There Goes My Love (by the Fantastics)	N/A	Popular Request 106
	Dear Lord	N/A	Relic LP
FASCINATORS (3)			
	Chapel Bells/I Wonder Who (61)	1958	Capitol 4053/Capitol 4544
	Who Do You Think You Are/ Come To Paradise	1959	Capitol 4137
	Oh Rose Marie/Fried Chicken And Macaroni	1959	Capitol 4247
	Oh Rose Marie/Forgive Me My Darling	1972	Bim Bam Boom 110
	Teenage Wedding/Recess (recorded in 1959)	1995	Park Ave. 10
	Dear Lord	N/A	Capitol LP 1008
FASCINATORS (4)			
	The Bells Of My Heart/ Sweet Baby	1959	Your Copy 1135
	My Beauty, My Own/ Don't Give It Away	1959	Your Copy 1136
FASCINATORS (5)			
	You're To Blame	1962	Trans Atlas 688
FASCINATORS (6)			
	I'll Be Gone/Can't You See I'm Lonely	1965	Burn 845
FASCINATORS (7) (GLIN LITTLETON & THE)			
	Sherry My Love/Tipsy (instrumental)	N/A	Lake 1003
FASHIONETTES (FEMALE)			
	Daydreamin' Of You/Only Love	1964	GNP Crescendo 322
FASHIONS (1) (FEMALE)			
	I'm Dreaming Of You/I Love You So	1959	V-Tone 202
	I'm Dreaming Of You/ Lonesome Road	1959	V-Tone 202
	I Just Got A Letter/Try My Love	1961	Ember 1084
	Dearest One/All I Want	1961	Warwick 646
FASHIONS (2)			
	Fairy Tales/Please Let It Be Me	1962	Elmor 301
	When Love Slips Away	1968	20th Fox
FASHIONS (3)			
	Why Don't You Stay A Little Longer/I Set A Trap For You	1963	Amy 884
	Surfer's Memories/Surfin' Back To School	1963	Felsted 8689
FASHIONS (4) (DOLLY & THE)			
	Just Another Fool	1965	Ivanhoe 5019
FASHIONS (5) (FRANKIE & THE)			
	My Love For You/Linda	1993	Avenue D 19
	Blame It On Another Rainy Day/Say What You Mean	1994	Avenue D 21
	Guardian Angel/United In Harmony	1994	Crystal Ball 162
FAT BOYS (FREDDIE & THE)			
	Why Do Fools Fall In Love/ Ballad Of Freddie And Rich	N/A	Fat Man 101
FAULKNER, FREDDY (& GROUP)			
	Cigarettes And Matches/ Little Drifter Amy	1963	Swan 4134
FAWNS			
	Until I Die/Come On	1958	Apt 15035/Apt 25015 (58)
	Girl In Trouble/Bless You	1965	Tec 3015
	Wish You Were Here With Me/Nothing But Love Can Save Me	1967	Capacity 105
FAY, FLO (& GROUP)			
	I'm The Richest One Of All/ I Promise	1963	Lawn 206
FAYETTES (HATTIE LITTLES & THE)			
	Here You Come/Your Love Is Wonderful	1962	Gordy 7007
FEATHERS			
	Johnny, Darling/Shake 'Em Up	1954	Aladdin 3267
	Nona/Johnny, Darling	1954	Show Time 1104
	Why Don't You Write Me?/ Busy As A Bumble Bee (by Johnny & Louis Stanton)	1954	Show Time 1105/ Candlelite 427 (63)
	Love Only You/Crashing The Party	1954	Show Time 1106
	I Need A Girl/Standin' Right There	1955	Aladdin 3277
	Dear One/Lonesome Tonight	1955	Hollywood 1051
	Walkin' And Talkin'	1955	Show Time
	Why Don't You Write Me/ Love Song (by Jesse Belvin & the Five Keys)	1963	Candlelight 427
FEATHERS (JOHNNY STATON & THE)			
	Charlene/Irene My Darling	1989	Classic Artists 109
	More Than Enough For Me/ Happy Holiday (by the Jaguars)	1989	Classic Artists 117
	At The Altar/A Girl Like You	1991	Classic Artists 125
FEATHERS (JUNE MOY & THE)			
	Desert Winds/Castle Of Dreams	1955	Show Time 1103
FEDERALS			
	Come Go With Me/Cold Cash	1957	DeLuxe 6112
	While Our Hearts Are Young/ You're The One I Love	1957	Fury 1005
	Dear Lorraine/She's My Girl	1957	Fury 1009

Artist Song	Year	Label
FELLOWS (EUGENE CHURCH & THE)		
Pretty Girls Everywhere/		
For The Rest Of My Life	1958	Class 235
FENDER, FREDDY (& GROUP)		
Holy One/Mean Woman	1958	Duncan 1000/Imperial 5659 (60)
In The Still Of The Nite/		
You Don't Have To Go	1964	Norco 108
Since I Met You Baby	N/A	Duncan 1004
FENTONES (SHANE FENTON & THE)		
Don't Do That/I'll Know	1963	Laurie 3287/20th Fox 439 (63)
FENWAYS		
Humpty Dumpty/Nothing		
To Offer You	1964	Bevmar 401
Number One Song In The		
Country/Nothing To Offer You	1964	Ricky L 106
FERNS (BABY RAY & THE) (GM FRANK ZAPPA)		
How's Your Bird/World's		
Greatest Sinner	1963	Donna 1378
FERROS		
Come Home My Love/		
Tough Cat	1958	Hi-Q 5008
FESTIVALS		
Music/I'll Always Love You	1966	Smash 2056
FI DELLS		
Time And Time Again	1961	India 5822
FI DELS		
You Never Do Right (My Baby)/		
Try A Little Harder	N/A	Keymen 106
FI-DELLS (1) (FEMALE)		
No Other Love/Come Back		
To Me	1957	Warner 1014
FI-DELLS (2)		
What Is Love/Don't Let Me		
Love You	1961	Imperial 5780
FI-DELLS (3) (DEAN PURKISS & THE)		
Alone Without Love	1964	United Southern Artists 5-110
FI-TONES (AKA FI-TONES QUINTETTE/AKA CAVERLIERS QUARTET)		
Foolish Dreams/Let's Fall		
In Love	1955	Atlas 1050
My Faith/My Heart	1957	Old Town 1042
You'll Be The Last/Wake Up	1958	Angle Tone 525
What Am I Goin' To Do?/		
It Wasn't A Lie	1958	Angle Tone 530
I Found My Baby/She Is The		
Girl For Me	1959	Angle Tone 539
Deep In My Heart/Minnie	1959	Angle Tone 536
Peddler Of Dreams	1973	Relic LP 5010
Delores	1973	Relic LP 5010
FI-TONES (CARL THOMAS & THE)		
I Love You Judy/Sweet Lovin'		
Maryann	1959	Stroll 101/O Gee 1004 (59)
FI-TONES QUINTETTE (AKA FI-TONES/AKA CAVERLIERS QUARTET)		
It Wasn't A Lie/Lots And Lots		
Of Love	1955	Atlas 1051
I Call To You/(Don't You Know)		
Love You, Baby	1956	Atlas 1052
I Belong To You/Silly And		
Sappy	1956	Atlas 1055
Waiting For Your Call/		
My Tired Feet	1956	Atlas 1056
FIATS		
Speak Words Of Love/		
Before I Walk Out The Door	1964	Universal 5003
FIDELITONES		
Pretty Girl/Game Of Love	1958	Aladdin 3442
Say Hey Pretty Baby/Playboy	1961	Marlo 1518
It It Too Late	N/A	Aladdin (unreleased)
FIDELITYS		
The Things I Love/Hold On To		
What Cha Got (And Get		
One More)	1958	Baton 252
Can't You Come Out/		
Memories Of You	1958	Baton 256
Captain Of My Ship/		
My Greatest Thrill	1959	Baton 261
Marie/The Invitation	1959	Sir 271
Walk With The Wind/Only To		
You	1959	Sir 274
Where In The World/This Girl		
Of Mine	1960	Sir 276

Artist Song	Year	Label
Wishing Star/Broken Love	1960	Sir 277
FIDELS		
Love Me Tender/After The		
Lights Go Down	1957	Music City 806
FIDELTONES		
Whispering Words Of Love/		
For Your Love	1960	Poop Deck 101
FIESTAS		
So Fine/Last Night I Dreamed	1958	Old Town 1062
I'm Your Slave/Grandma Gave		
A Party	1959	Old Town 1067
Our Anniversary/I'm Your Slave	1959	Old Town 1069
That Was Me/Good News	1959	Old Town 1074
It Don't Make Sense/Dollar Bill	1960	Old Town 1080
You Could Be My Girl Friend/		
So Nice	1960	Old Town 1090
Look At That Girl/Mr. Dillon,		
Mr. Dillon	1961	Old Town 1104
She's Mine/The Hobo's Prayer	1961	Old Town 1111
Julie/Come On Everybody	1961	Strand 25046
Broken Heart/The Railroad		
Song	1962	Old Town 1122
I Feel Good All Over/Look At		
That Girl	1962	Old Town 1127
The Gypsy Said/Mama Put		
The Law Down	1963	Old Town 1134
The Party's Over/Try It One		
More Time	1963	Old Town 1140
Rock-A-Bye Baby/Foolish		
Dreamer	1963	Old Town 1148
Rock-A-Bye Baby/All That's		
Good	1964	Old Town 1166
Anna/Think Smart	1964	Old Town 1178
Love Is Strange/Love Is Good		
To Me	1965	Old Town 118
Ain't She Sweet/I Gotta Have		
Your Lovin'	1965	Old Town 1189
Broken Heart/So Fine	1971	Cotillion 44117
So Fine/Darling You've		
Changed	1974	Vigor 712
The Lawman	N/A	Ace LP CH173
Mexico	N/A	Ace LP CH173
FIFES (EDWARD HAMILTON & THE)		
Call Me	N/A	Jameco 1630
FILETS OF SOLE		
Come On Let's Dance/		
Since I Fell For You	1968	Savoy 1630
FINGERPOPPERS (RONNY WILLIAMS & THE)		
Strange Are The Ways Of Love/		
Feeling Is Real	1960	Ultra Sonic 111
FIRE BALLS (BILLY ELDRIDGE & HIS)		
Let's Go Baby/My Blue Tears	1959	Vulco 1501/Unart 2011 (59)
FIREBALLS (CHUCK THARP & THE)		
Let There Be Love/Long,		
Long Ponytail	1960	Jaro 77029/Lucky 0012
FIREFLIES (AKA FIREFLYS) (FB RICHIE ADAMS)		
You Were Mine/Stella's Got		
A Fella	1959	Ribbon 6901
I Can't Say Goodbye/What		
Did I Do Wrong	1959	Ribbon 6904
Marianne/Give All Your Love		
To Me	1960	Canadian American 117
My Girl/Because Of My Pride	1960	Ribbon 6906
You Were Mine (For Awhile)/		
One O'Clock Twist	1962	Taurus 355
Love Me Do	1962	Taurus LP 1002
Our Day Will Come	1962	Taurus LP 1002
Twist And Shout	1962	Taurus LP 1002
Hully Gully Baby	1962	Taurus LP 1002
Moon River	1962	Taurus LP 1002
For Sentimental Reasons	1962	Taurus LP 1002
Irresistible You	1962	Taurus LP 1002
Walk Don't Run	1962	Taurus LP 1002
Please Please Me	1962	Taurus LP 1002
Bye Bye Love	1962	Taurus LP 1002
Traveling Man	1962	Taurus LP 1002
Blacksmith Blues/Tuff-A-Nuff	1963	Hamilton 50036
My Prayer For You/Good Friends	1964	Taurus 366
Runaround/Could You Mean		
More	1966	Taurus 376
Tonight/A Time For Us	1967	Taurus 380
Old Man River/Love You	N/A	G.M. 1001

Artist Song	Year	Label
The Crawl/Where The		
Candlelight Glows	1958	Roulette 4098
FIRESIDE SINGERS		
Pretty Girl/Darlin' Come Home	1963	Herald 582
FIRESIDERS		
(I'll Remember) One And All/		
No One Cares For Me	1961	Swan 4074
FIRESTONE, JOHNNY (& GROUP)		
Is It Love/It Happens Every Night	1958	Elmont 1003/D&M 001 (85)
FIRST PLATOON		
Ten Ways/Physical Fitness	1963	SPQR 3303
FIRST WARD DUKES		
Welcome Home/		
Call Somebody Please	1977	Clifton 20
FIVE ("5") ROYALES		
Too Much Of A Little Bit/Give		
Me One More Chance	1951	Apollo 434
You Know I Know/Courage		
To Love	1952	Apollo 441
Baby Don't Do It/Take All Of Me	1952	Apollo 443
Help Me Somebody/Crazy		
Crazy Crazy	1953	Apollo 446
Laundromat Blues/Too Much		
Lovin'	1953	Apollo 448
I Want To Thank You/All Righty!	1953	Apollo 449
Good Things/I Do	1954	Apollo 452
Cry Some More/I Like It Like That	1954	Apollo 454
Let Me Come Back Home/		
What's That	1954	Apollo 458
Behave Yourself/I'm Gonna		
Run It Down	1954	King 4740
Monkey Hips And Rice/Devel		
With The Rest	1954	King 4744
One Mistake/School Girl	1954	King 4762
Six O'Clock In The Morning/		
With All Your Heart	1955	Apollo 467
You Didn't Learn It Home/		
Every Dog Has His Day	1955	King 4770
How I Wonder/Mohawk Squaw	1955	King 4785
When I Get Like This/I Need		
Your Lovin' Baby	1955	King 4806
Women About To Make Me		
Go Crazy/Do Unto You	1955	King 4819
Someone Made You For Me/		
I Ain't Gettin' Caught	1955	King 4830
Right Around The Corner/When		
You Walked Through The Door	1956	King 4869
My Wants For Love/I Could		
Love You	1956	King 4901
Come On And Save Me/		
Get Something Out Of It	1956	King 4952
Just As I Am/Mine Forever More	1956	King 4973
Tears Of Joy/Thirty Second Lover	1957	King 5032
Think/I'd Better Make A Move	1957	King 5053
Say It/Messin' Up	1957	King 5082
Dedicated To The One I Love/		
Don't Be Ashamed	1957	King 5098
The Feeling Is Real/Do The		
Cha Cha Cherry	1958	King 5131
Double Or Nothing/Tell The		
Truth	1958	King 5141
Don't Let It Be In Vain/		
The Slummer The Slum	1958	King 5153
The Real Thing/Your Only Love	1959	King 5162
Miracle Of Love/I Know		
It's Hard But It's Fair	1959	King 5191
Wonder Where Your Love		
Has Gone/Tell Me You Care	1959	King 5237
My Sugar Sugar/It Hurts Inside	1959	King 5266
Please, Please, Please/I Got		
To Know	1960	Home Of The Blues 112
Don't Give No More Than		
You Can Take/I'm With You	1960	King 5329
Why/Within My Heart	1960	King 5357
If You Don't Need Me/I'm		
Gonna Tell Them	1961	Home Of The Blues 218
Not Going To Cry/Take Me		
With You Baby	1961	Home Of The Blues 232
They Don't Know/Much In Need	1961	Home Of The Blues 234/
		Vee Jay 412 (61)
Dedicated To The One You		
Love/Miracle Of Love	1961	King 5453

Artist Song	Year	Label
What's In The Heart/I Want It		
Like That	1962	ABC 10368
Goof Ball/Catch That Teardrop	1962	Home Of The Blues 257/
		ABC 10348
Help Me Somebody/Talk		
About My Woman	1962	Vee Jay 431
Tears Of Joy/Dedicated To		
The One I Love	1963	King 5756
I'm Standing In The Shadows/		
doin' Everything	1963	Todd 1086
Baby Don't Do It/There's		
Somebody Over There	1963	Todd 1088
I Need Your Lovin' Baby/Wonder		
Where Your Love Has Gone	1964	King 5892
FIVE (5) BELL AIRES (HENRY HALL & THE)		
My Friends	1990	Relic LP 5085
Come On To My Love House	1990	Relic LP 5085
House Of Love	1990	Relic LP 5085
I'm So Happy	1990	Relic LP 5085
FIVE (5) BELL AIRES (JOHN HALL & THE)		
Wedding Bells	1990	Relic LP 5085
Come On Home	1990	Relic LP 5085
FIVE (5) GENTS		
I Never Told You/Rock With		
Me Marie	1958	Crest 516
Sandy/Baby Doll	N/A	Viking 101
FIVE (5) KIDS		
Carolyn/Oh Baby	1955	Maxwell 101
FIVE ARCADES		
Ruby Lee/Malcolm's Boogie		
(instrumental)	1973	Sacto 101
Hoping You'll Fall In Love/		
Heaven's One Desire	1973	Sacto 103
FIVE ARCADES (S. J. & THE)		
Heaven's Own Desire/You		
Took Advantage Of Love	1985	Antrell 103
FIVE ARROWS (GLORIA VALDEZ, THE PAUL BASCOMB ORCH. & THE)		
Pretty Little Thing/You've Got		
Me Losing My Mind	1955	Parrot 816
FIVE BARONS		
Fine As Wine/(no flip)	1952	Beacon 9144/Krazy Kat
		LP 797
FIVE BARS		
Somebody Else's Fool/		
Stormy Weather	1957	Money 224
I'm All Dressed Up With A		
Broken Heart/To Make A		
Long Story Shorter	1963	Bullet 1009
Deep In My Heart/Bars' Boogie	1963	Bullet 1010
FIVE BELLS		
My Cutie Pie/Please		
Remember My Heart	N/A	Stolper 100
FIVE BELLS (AKA BELL TONES (2))		
My Pledge To You/It's You	1960	Clock 1017
FIVE BILLS		
Can't Wait For Tomorrow/		
Till I Waltz Again With You	1953	Brunswick 84002
Till Dawn And Tomorrow/		
Waiting, Wanting	1953	Brunswick 84004
FIVE BIRDS (WILLIE HEADEN & THE)		
Back Home Again/I Wanna Know	1956	Authentic 703/Dooto 703
Let Me Cry/The Skinny		
Woman Story	1957	Authentic 410/Dootone 410
FIVE BLACKS		
Forever In Love/Come One	1961	B&C 100
FIVE BLIND BOYS		
Brother Bill/Well Done Baby		
(by the Spartones)	1972	Vintage 1000
FIVE BLUE FLAMES (CHRIS POWELL & THE)		
My Love Has Gone/In The		
Cool Of The Evening	1951	Columbia 39407
FIVE BLUE NOTES		
My Gal Is Gone/Ooh Baby	1954	Sabre 103
You Gotta Go Baby/The Beat		
Of Our Hearts	1954	Sabre 108
Thunderbird/My Special		
Prayer (by the Jammers)	1959	Onda 108
My Special Prayer/Something		
Awful	1964	Onda 888
FIVE BOB-O-LINKS		
Trying/Mailman Blues	1952	Okeh

Artist	Song	Year	Label
FIVE BOPS			
	Unforgotten Love/Jitterbuggin'	1959	Hamilton 50023
FIVE BOROUGHS			
	Sunday Kind Of Love/For Your Precious Love	1988	Avenue D 15
	One Too Many Lies/Apart	1990	Classic Artists 119
	Heaven And Cindy/A Kiss From Your Lips	1990	Classic Artists 122
	Recess In Heaven/Over The Rainbow	1991	Mona 31866
	Only At Christmas/Like A Kid At Christmas	N/A	Classic Artists 135
FIVE BUDDS			
	I Was Such A Fool (To Fall In Love With You)/Midnight	1953	Rama 1
	I Want Her Back/I Guess It's All Over Now	1953	Rama 2
FIVE C'S			
	Tell Me/Whoo-Wee, Baby	1954	United 172
	My Heart's Got The Blues/Goody, Goody	1955	United 180
	There's No Tomorrow	1981	P-Vine Special LP 9036
	I Long For You	1981	P-Vine Special LP 9036
	Going My Way	1981	P-Vine Special LP 9036
	Only By You (I Want To Be Loved)	1981	P-Vine Special LP 9036
FIVE CAMPBELLS			
	Hey, Baby/Morrine	1956	Music City 794
FIVE CANDLELIGHTS			
	Romance In The Spring/(Baby) Please Tell Me	N/A	Candlelite 431
FIVE CASHMERES			
	Walkin' Through The Jungle/The Hitchhiker	1962	Golden Leaf 108
FIVE CATS			
	He Follows She/Santa Lucie	1954	RCA 5885
	Rockin' Chair/Mine Mine Mine	1955	RCA 6012
	I Was So Wrong/Someone's Gonna Cry	1955	RCA 6181
FIVE CHANCELLORS (AKA CHANCELLORS (1))			
	There Goes My Girl/Tell Me You Love Me	1957	Port 5000
FIVE CHANCELLS			
	Love No One But You/Please Let Me Love You (acapella)	1965	Fellatio 103/Dawn 302
FIVE CHANCES			
	I May Be Small/Nagasaki	1954	Chance 1157
	All I Want/Shake-A-Link	1955	Blue Lake 115
	Bashful Boy	1956	States (unreleased)
	Gloria/Sugar Lips	1956	States 156
	My Days Are Blue/Tell Me Why	1957	Federal 12303
	Need Your Love/Land Of Love (despite label, not by Five Chances)	1960	Corina 2002
	Need Your Love/Is This Love	1960	P.S. 1510
	Make Love To Me/California	1977	Atomic 2494
FIVE CHANELS (AKA CHANELS) (FEMALE)			
	The Reason/Skiddily Doo	1958	Deb 500
FIVE CHESTNUTS			
	My Kind Of Baby/Chi Chi	1959	Elgin 003
FIVE CHESTNUTS (HAYES BASKERVILLE & THE)			
	My One And Only Love/My Billy	1958	Drum 003/004
FIVE CHESTNUTS (MARVIN BASKERVILLE & THE)			
	Chapel In The Moonlight/Chi Chi	1958	Drum 001
FIVE CHIMES			
	A Fool Was I/Dearest Darling	1954	Royal Roost 577/Betta 2017 (55)
	Rosemarie/Never Love Another	1955	Betta 2011
FIVE CHORDS			
	Jeannie/Red Wine	1961	Cuca 1031
FIVE CHORDS (JOHNNY JONES & THE)			
	Love Is Like Music/Don't Just Stand There	1958	Jamie 1110
FIVE CHUMS			
	High School Affair/Give Me The Power	1958	Excello 2123
FIVE CLASSICS			
	My Imagination/Come On Baby	1960	Arc 4454/A 317 (61)
	Love Me/Mississippi Mud	1961	Pova 6142
	Old Cape Cod/Magic Star	1962	Medieval 204/Rode 101
FIVE COOKIES			
	Cook, Cook, Cookie/Keep Twisting	1962	Everest 19429
FIVE COUNTS			
	Spanish Nights/Watermelon Man	1962	Brent 7034
FIVE CROWNS (1) (AKA CROWNS (2)/REF DRIFTERS)			
	Good Luck Darlin'/Again	1952	Old Town 777 (unreleased)/Relic LP 5030
	The End Of The Fair/The Man From The Moon	1952	Old Town 778 (unreleased)/Relic LP 5030
	You Could Be My Love/Good Luck Darling	1952	Old Town 790
	Lullaby Of The Bells/Later Later Baby	1952	Old Town 792
	A Star/You're My Inspiration	1952	Rainbow 179
	Who Can Be True/$19.50 Bus	1952	Rainbow 184
	Keep It A Secret/Why Don't You Believe Me	1953	Rainbow 202
	Alone Again/Don't Have To Hunt No More	1953	Rainbow 206
	I Was Wrong/Hug Me Baby	1954	Rainbow 251
	You Ran Away With My Heart	1954	Rainbow 281
	I Can't Pretend/Popcorn Willie	1955	Caravan 15609/Trans-World 717 (56)
	You Came To Me/Ooh Wee Baby	1955	Riviera 990/Rainbow 335 (56)
	God Bless You/Do You Remember	1956	Gee 1011
	Kiss And Make Up/I'll Forget About You	1958	R&B 6901
	Memories Of Yesterday/A Surprise From Outer Space	1959	De'Besth 1122
	I Want You/Hillum Boy	1959	De'Besth 1123
	Just A Part Of Life/Just A Part Of Life	N/A	Five-O 503
FIVE CROWNS (2) (WITH JAN ANDRE)			
	It's Funny To Everyone But Me/Speak With Your Eyes	1955	Emerald 2007
FIVE CROWNS (3) (CHUCK EDWARDS & THE)			
	If I Were King/Lucy And Jimmy Got Married	1959	Alanna 557/558
FIVE CROWS			
	When I See Elephants Fly/Darling Here's My Heart (by the Paramours)	1986	Ronnie 205
FIVE CRYSTALS			
	Path Of Broken Hearts/Heaven's Own Choir	1958	Music City 821/Delcro 827
	Hey, Landlord/Good Looking Out	1959	Kane 25592/Relic 1003 (65)
FIVE DAPS			
	Do Whop-A-Do/You're So Unfaithful	1958	Brax 207/208
FIVE DEBONAIRES			
	Darlin'/Whispering Blues	1957	Herald 509
FIVE DELIGHTS			
	There'll Be No Goodbye/Okey Dokey, Mama	1958	Newport 7002/Unart 2003 (58)
	The Thought Of Losing You/That Love Affair	1959	Abel 228
FIVE DIAMONDS			
	Ten Commandments Of Love /I Cried And Cried	1955	Treat 501
	The Night/My Love	1977	Treat 9/10
FIVE DIPS			
	Teach Me Tonight/That's What I Like (by the Allen Trio)	1956	Original 1005
FIVE DISCS (AKA BOYFRIENDS/AKA DAWN/AKA IMPALAS (4))			
	I Remember/The World Is A Beautiful Place	1958	Emge 1004/Vik 0327 (58)/Rust 5027 (63)
	My Chinese Girl/Roses	1959	Dwain 6072/Dwain 803 (59)/Mello Mood 1002 (64)/Downstairs 1001
	Adios/My Baby Loves Me	1961	Calo 202
	When Love Comes Knocking/Go-Go	1961	Yale 240
	Come On Baby/I Don't Know What I'll Do	1961	Yale 243/244/Candlelite 429

Artist Song	Year	Label
Never Let You Go/That Was The Time	1962	Cheer 1000
Rock 'N' Roll Revival/Gypsy Woman	1972	Laurie 3601
My Foolish Heart/Who Can She Be (by the Devotions)	1976	Robin Hood 137
Mirror Mirror/Most Of All/I Wonder	1978	Crystal Ball 114
Unchained Melody/ The Shrine Of St. Cecilia	1978	Crystal Ball 120
Playing A Game Of Love/Bells	1979	Crystal Ball 136
This Love Of Ours/To Be Fair	1980	Crystal Ball 141
Zu-Zu/Your Way	1991	0-0-1
Let's Fall In Love/That Was The Time	N/A	Pyramid 166
FIVE DOLLARS		
Doctor Baby/Harmony Of Love	1955	Fortune 821/Fraternity 821 (58)
So Strange/You Know I Can't Refuse	1956	Fortune 826
Hard-Working Mama/I Will Wait	1956	Fortune 830
You Fool/How To Do The Bacon Fat	1957	Fortune 833
You Fool/I'm Wanderin' (by the Five Jets)	1957	Fortune 833
That's The Way It Goes/ My Baby-O	1960	Fortune 854
The Bells/Weekend Man	1979	Skylark 561/Fortune LP 8016 (84)
FIVE DOLLARS (ANDRE WILLIAMS & THE)		
(H-mmm, Andre Williams Is) Movin'/(Georgia May Is) Movin' (Andre Williams & Gino Parks)	1960	Fortune 851
FIVE DOLLARS (JIM SANDS WITH THE)		
We're Gonna Rock/You Don't Know My Mind	1958	Hi-Q 5010
FIVE DOTS (AKA COUNTS (1))		
The Other Night/Each Night	1954	Dot 1204
I Just Love The Things She Do/ Well, Little Baby	1955	Note 10003
FIVE DREAMERS (1) (EDDIE BANKS & THE)		
Sugar Diabetes/Rock A Bye Blues	1956	Josie 804
FIVE DREAMERS (2) (AKA 5 DREAMERS)		
You Don't Know/Beverly	1957	Port 5001
FIVE DREAMS		
You Are My Only/Up All Night	1957	Mercury 71150
FIVE DUKES (BENNIE WOODS & THE) (AKA ROCKIN' TOWNIES)		
Wheel Baby Wheel/ I Cross My Fingers	1955	Atlas 1040
FIVE DUKES OF RHYTHM		
Soft, Sweet And Really Fine/ Everybody's Singing The Blues	1954	Rendezvous 812/Fortune 812 (54)
FIVE ECHOES (AKA FIVE ECHOS)		
Baby, Come Back To Me/ Lonely Mood	1953	Sabre 102
So Lonesome/Broke	1954	Sabre 105
Soldier Boy/Down The Road I Go	1956	Vee Jay 190
If You Don't Love Me/The Hunt	1971	Sabre 106
That's My Baby/Why Oh Why	1971	Sabre 111
Lonely Mood	N/A	Oldies 45 419
Tell Me, Baby/I Really Do	1955	Vee Jay 129
Fool's Prayer/Tastee Freeze	1955	Vee Jay 156
FIVE ELGINS		
The Wind/Blast Off (instrumental by the Satellites)	1977	Ronnie 204
FIVE EMBERS		
Please Come Home/Love Birds	1954	Gem 224
Love Tears/All Alone	1955	Gem 227 (unreleased)
I'm Free/My Fragile Heart	1960	Royce 0006/X-Bat 1006 (95)
FIVE EMERALDS		
I'll Beg/Let Me Take You Out Tonight	1954	S-R-C 106
Darling/Pleasure Me	1954	S-R-C 107
FIVE EMPREES (AKA FIVE EMPRESSIONS)		
Little Miss Sad/Hey Lover	1965	Freeport 1001 (second pressing)
Why/Hey Baby	1965	Freeport 1002

Artist Song	Year	Label
FIVE EMPRESSIONS (AKA FIVE EMPREES)		
Little Miss Sad/Hey Lover	1965	Freeport 1001 (first pressing)
FIVE ENCORES		
Double Date/Whistlin' Willie	1955	Rama 180
Readin' Ritin' Rithmetic' & Rock 'n' Roll/Ben Ben Quaker Ben	1955	Rama 185
Dance With The Rock/One Scotch, One Bourbon, One Beer	1955	Rama 187
FIVE FABULOUS DEMONS		
You'd Better Come Home/ Yeah Since You Went Away	1963	King 5761
FIVE FASHIONS		
Pennies From Heaven/ Ten Commandments Of Love	1964	Catamount 102
Over The Rainbow/Solitaire	1965	Catamount 103
My Girl/Kiss, Kiss, Kiss	1965	Catamount 107
I'll Be Home For Christmas	1966	Catamount 116
FIVE FLAMES		
I Want You So Bad/ There Must Be A Reason	1959	Federal 12348
FIVE FLEETS		
I Been Crying/Oh, What A Feeling	1958	Felsted 8513
Slight Case Of Love/ Yo' Good Lovin'	1958	Felsted 8522
Cheer Up/Pitter Patter	1961	Seville 112
FIVE FORTUNES		
You Are My Only Love/ Time Out For Love	1958	Ransom 103
FIVE G'S		
Forget Her/I Think I Know	1959	Washingtonian (no number)
FIVE GENTS		
I Never Told You/Rock With Me Marie	1958	Crest 516
FIVE GLOW TONES		
At A Dance/Quiet Village	1959	Jax 101
FIVE GRANDS		
Kiss Me/Two For The Blues	1958	Brunswick 55059
FIVE HARMONAIRES (ELAINE GAY & THE) (AKA HARMONAIRES)		
Rock Love/Ebony Eyes	1955	DeLuxe 2029
FIVE HEARTS (1) (AKA FLAIRS/AKA FIVE HOLLYWOOD BLUE JAYS)		
Please, Please, Baby/ The Fine One	1954	Flair 1026
FIVE HEARTS (2)		
Tell Ya What/Tremble (by Lord Luther & the Esquires)	1960	Music City 833
FIVE HEARTS (3) (REF LEE ANDREWS & THE HEARTS)		
Unbelievable/Aunt Jenny	1959	Arcade 107
FIVE HEARTS (4)		
My Prayer Tonight	N/A	Ransom
FIVE HI LIGHTERS (AKA HIGHLIGHTERS (2))		
Sweet Little Baby Of Mine/ Mi Amor	1959	Cannon 580488
FIVE HOLLYWOOD BLUE JAYS (AKA FLAIRS/AKA FIVE HEARTS (1))		
Cloudy And Raining/So Worried	1951	Recorded In Hollywood 185
Put A Nickel In The Jukebox/ Safronia Ida B. Brown	1952	Recorded In Hollywood 162
I Had A Love/Tell Me You're Mine	1952	Recorded In Hollywood 396
FIVE HUNGRY MEN		
We Belong Together	1964	Melmar 122
FIVE IVORIES (AKA IVORYS)		
Why Don't You Write Me/ Deep Freeze	1962	Sparta 001
FIVE J'S (AKA FIVE JOHNSON BROTHERS/AKA JOHNSON BROTHERS)		
My Darling/Calypso Jump	1958	Fulton 2454
FIVE JADES (1)		
Without Your Love/Rock And Roll Molly	1958	Duke 188
FIVE JADES (2) (AKA FIVE SHADOWS)		
Rosemarie (acapella)/ My Reverie (acapella)	1965	Your Choice 1011
My Girl Friend (acapella)/How Much I Love You (a capella)	1965	Your Choice 1012
Out Of Sight Out Of Mind/ Hold Me	1972	Kelway 103
That's My Desire (acapella)	1975	Relic LP 107
Begin The Beguine (acapella)	1975	Relic LP 107
I Was Such A Fool (acapella)	1975	Relic LP 107
If Someone Would Care (acapella)	1975	Relic LP 107

Artist / Song	Year	Label
Unchained Melody (acapella)	1975	Relic LP 107
That's The Way It Goes (acapella)	1975	Relic LP 107
Ebb Tide (acapella)	1975	Relic LP 107
In The Still Of The Nite (acapella)	1975	Relic LP 107
When I Fall In Love (acapella)	1975	Relic LP 107
I Wish You Love (acapella)	1975	Relic LP 107
Tell Her That I Love Her (acapella)	1975	Relic LP 107
If I Were To Lose You (acapella)	1975	Relic LP 107
Are You Sorry (acapella)	1975	Relic LP 107
Endless Night (acapella)	1975	Relic LP 107
Shout (acapella)	1975	Relic LP 108
When You Dance (acapella)	1975	Relic LP 109
Falling In Love/That's The Way It Goes	1984	Clifton 73

FIVE JETS (1)

Song	Year	Label
Not A Hand To Shake/I Am In Love	1953	DeLuxe 6018
I'm Stuck/I Want A Woman	1954	DeLuxe 6053
Tell Me You're Mine/Give In	1954	DeLuxe 6058
Crazy Chicken/Everybody Do The Chicken	1954	DeLuxe 6064
Please Love Me Baby/Down Slow	1954	DeLuxe 6071
I'm Wanderin'/You Fool (by the Five Dollars)	1957	Fortune 833

FIVE JETS (2)

Song	Year	Label
Sugaree/The Shake	1964	Jewel 739

FIVE JETS (3)

Song	Year	Label
I'm Going To Live My Life Alone/Why Oh Why	N/A	Broadcast 999

FIVE JOHNSON BROTHERS (AKA FIVE J'S/AKA JOHNSON BROTHERS)

Song	Year	Label
Sleep With A Dream/Happy Rock & Roll	1958	Fulton 2455

FIVE JOYS (JUANITA ROGERS & LYNN HOLLINGS & MR. J'S)

Song	Year	Label
Teenager's Letter Of Promises/I'm So Glad You Love Me	1961	Pink Clouds 333

FIVE KEYS

Song	Year	Label
Ling Ting Tong/I'm Alone	1954	Capitol 2945
I Took Your Love For A Toy/Ziggus	1959	King 5251
Dream On/Dancing Senorita	1959	King 5273
How Can I Forget You?/I Burned Your Letter	1960	King 5302
Gonna Be Too Late/Rosetta	1960	King 5330
I Didn't Know/No Says My Heart	1960	King 5358
Valley Of Love/Bimbo	1960	King 5398
Girl You Better Stop It	1960	King LP 692
Will You	1960	King LP 692
Now I Know I Love You	1960	King LP 692
Wrapped Up In A Dream	1960	King LP 692
You Broke The Only Heart/That's What You're Doing To Me	1961	King 5446
Stop Your Crying/Do Something For Me	1961	King 5496
I'll Never Stop Loving You/I Can't Escape From You	1964	King 5877
Hey Girl/No Matter	1965	Inferno 4500
Glory Of Love/Red Sails In The Sunset	1971	Aladdin 3125
Goddess Of Love/Stop What You're Doing	1973	Landmark 101
A Dreamer/Your Teeth And Tongue Will Get You Hung	1973	Owl 321
When Will My Troubles End	N/A	Detour LP 33-010
Teeth & Tongue Will Get You Hung	N/A	Detour LP 33-010
Wisdom Of A Fool	N/A	Popular Request 110
Ling Ting Tong	N/A	Popular Request 112
I Dreamt I Dwelt In heaven/Wisdom Of A Fool	N/A	Popular Request 1999
Out Of Sight, Out Of Mind/Tell Me You Love Me	N/A	Popular Request 2001
Sweetheart/Sittin' Here Wondering	1972	Roadhouse 1003

FIVE KEYS (FEATURING RUDY WEST)

Song	Year	Label
Just Like Two Drops Of Water	1951	Aladdin (unreleased)
Your Teardrops	1951	Aladdin (unreleased)
Happy Am I	1951	Aladdin (unreleased)
With A Broken Heart/Too Late	1951	Aladdin 3085
The Glory Of Love/Hucklebuck With Jimmy	1951	Aladdin 3099
It's Christmas Time/Old McDonald (Had A Farm)	1951	Aladdin 3113
I'll Follow You/Lawdy Miss Mary	1951	Groove 0031
Yes Sir, That's My Baby/Old McDonald Had A Farm	1952	Aladdin 3118
Red Sails In The Sunset/Be Anything But Be Mine	1952	Aladdin 3127
Mistakes/How Long	1952	Aladdin 3131
I Hadn't Anyone Till You/Hold Me	1952	Aladdin 3136
Serve Another Round/I Cried For You	1952	Aladdin 3158
Can't Keep From Crying/Come Go My Bail, Louise	1953	Aladdin 3167
There Ought To Be A Law (Against Breaking A Heart)/Mama (Your Daughter Told A Lie On Me)	1953	Aladdin 3175
These Foolish Things/Lonesome Old Story	1953	Aladdin 3190
Teardrops In My Eyes/I'm So High	1953	Aladdin 3204
My Saddest Hour/Oh! Babe!	1953	Aladdin 3214
How Could You Do This To Me	1953	Audio-Video (unreleased)
Someday Sweetheart/Love My Loving	1954	Aladdin 3228
Deep In My Heart/How Do You Expect Me To Get It	1954	Aladdin 3245
My Love/Why Oh Why	1954	Aladdin 3263
Trapped, Lost, Gone	1954	Capitol (unreleased)
I'm Just A Fool	1954	Capitol (unreleased)

FIVE KEYS (FEATURING RUDY WEST)

Song	Year	Label
So Glad	1954	Capitol (unreleased)
Story Of Love/Serve Another Round	1955	Aladdin 3312
Shook My Head	1955	Capitol (unreleased)
Close Your Eyes/Doggone It, You Did It	1955	Capitol 3032
The Verdict/Me Make Um Pow Wow	1955	Capitol 3127
Don't You Know I Love You/I Wish I'd Never Learned To Read	1955	Capitol 3185
Gee Whittakers/Cause You're My Lover	1955	Capitol 3267
Just Sittin'	1956	Capitol (unreleased)
What Goes On/You Broke The Rules Of Love	1956	Capitol 3318
She's The Most/I Dreamed I Dwelt In Heaven	1956	Capitol 3392
Peace And Love/My Pigeon's Gone	1956	Capitol 3455
Out Of Sight, Out Of Mind/That's Right	1956	Capitol 3502
Wisdom Of A Fool/Now Don't That Prove I Love You	1956	Capitol 3597
From The Bottom Of My Heart	1956	Capitol LP 828/Capitol EP 1-828 (57)
Dog Gone Baby	1957	Capitol (unreleased)
Open Sesame	1957	Capitol (unreleased)
Let There Be You/Tiger Lily	1957	Capitol 3660
Four Walls/It's A Groove	1957	Capitol 3710
This I Promise/The Blues Don't Care	1957	Capitol 3738
The Face Of An Angel/Boom Boom	1957	Capitol 3786
Do Anything/It's A Crying Shame	1957	Capitol 3830
From Me To You/Whippety Whirl	1957	Capitol 3861
Who Do You Know In Heaven	1957	Capitol LP 828/Capitol EP 1-828 (57)
To Each His Own	1957	Capitol LP 828/Capitol EP 1-828 (57)
All I Need Is You	1957	Capitol LP 828/Capitol EP 2-828 (57)
C'Est La Vie	1957	Capitol LP 828/Capitol EP 2-828 (57)
Maybe You'll Be There	1957	Capitol LP 828/Capitol EP 2-828 (57)
Dream	1957	Capitol LP 828/Capitol EP 2-828 (57)
The Gypsy/Just For A Thrill	1957	Capitol T-828 (D.J. copy)
With All My Love/You're For Me	1958	Capitol 3948

Artist Song	Year	Label
Emily Please/Handy Andy	1958	Capitol 4009
One Great Love/Really-O Truly-O	1958	Capitol 4092
Just To Be With You/You Were Mine	1959	King 5276
My Mother's Prayers/As Sure As I Live	1959	King 5285
The Measure Of My Love/This Is Something Else	1959	King 5305
I've Always Been A Dreamer	1960	King LP 688
Your Teeth And Your Tongue	1960	King LP 688
When Paw Was Courtin' Maw	1960	King LP 688
Hucklebuck With Jimmy/ Ghost Of A Chance (recorded in 1951)	1971	Aladdin 3099A
Do I Need You/Can't Keep From Crying (recorded in 1951)	1971	Aladdin 3113A
Darling/Goin' Downtown (recorded in 1952)	1971	Aladdin 3119
Serve Another Round/If You Only Knew (recorded in 1953)	1971	Aladdin 3167A
When You're Gone/White Cliffs Of Dover (recorded in 1953)	1971	Aladdin 3175A
I'll Always Be In Love With You/ Rocking And Crying Blues (recorded in 1953)	1971	Aladdin 3182
Will My Heart Stand A Chance/ Yearning (recorded in 1953)	1971	Aladdin 3182A
Out Of Sight, Out Of Mind (a capella)/Close Your Eyes (a capella)	1973	Bim Bam Boom 116
Lawdy Miss Mary	1989	Detour LP 33-010
Every Heart Is Home At Christmas	1990	Capitol CDP 7-94701-2
If You Only Knew	1991	EMI CDP7-92709
FIVE KEYS (JESSE BELVIN & THE)		
Love Song/Why Don't You Write Me (by the Feathers)	N/A	Candlelight 427
FIVE KEYS (RUDY WEST & THE)		
Out Of Sight, Out Of Mind/ You're The One	1961	Seg-Way 1008
FIVE KIDS		
Carolyn/Oh Baby	1955	Maxwell 101
FIVE KINGS		
Light Bulb/Don't Send Me Away	1964	Columbia 43060
Here Comes My Baby/Tina	1966	Yvette 101
FIVE KNIGHTS		
Miracle/Yo Te Amo	1959	Specialty 675
She's Allright/Take Me In Your Arms	1959	Tau 104
Let Me In/Times Are Getting Harder	1961	Minit 626
Dark Was The Night/She's My Baby	1963	Bumps 1504
FIVE KNIGHTS (TOMMY TAYLOR & THE)		
I Want Somebody/Polly Want A Cracker	1961	Minit 636
FIVE LARKS (AKA LARKS (1))		
Coffee, Cigarettes And Tears/ My Heart Cries For You	1951	Apollo 1177
FIVE LETTERS		
Hold My Baby/Your First Love	1958	Ivy 102
FIVE LORDS		
Oo-La-La/Falling Tears	1960	D.S. 2078
FIVE LYRICS		
I'm Traveling Light/My Honey, Sweet Pea	1956	Music City 799
FIVE MASKS		
Polly Molly/Forever And A Day	1958	Jan 101
FIVE MASQUERADERS (SEAPHUS SCOTT & THE) (REF MASQUERADES)		
Nature's Beauty/Summer Sunrise	1958	Joyce 303
FIVE MASTERS		
We Are Like One/Cheap Skate	1959	Bumble Bee 502
Cheap Skate	1986	Relic LP 8008
FIVE MONEYS		
Believe	N/A	Charlie
FIVE NOTES (1) (HENRY PIERCE & THE)		
Thrill Me Baby/Hey Fine Mama	1952	Specialty 461
FIVE NOTES (2) (AKA NOTES)		
You Are So Beautiful/Broken Hearted Baby	1955	Jen D 4185/Josie 784 (55)

Artist Song	Year	Label
Park Your Love/Show Me The Way	1956	Chess 1614
FIVE NOTES (3) (SAMMY & THE)		
North By Northeast/African Cha Cha	1960	Lucky Four 1010
The Lion Is Awake (answer song)/Doodle Bug Twist	1962	Lucky Four 1019
FIVE ORLEANS (AKA ROULETTES)		
The Way You Carry On/ You Don't Care Anymore	1957	Ebb 124
FIVE OWLS		
Pleading To You/I Like Moonshine	1955	Vulcan 1025
The Thrill Is Gone/Lima Beans	1974	Owl 327
FIVE PALMS (AKA PALMS)		
Little Girl Of Mine/Tear Drops	1957	States 163
FIVE PASTELS		
You're Just An Angel/Listen Baby	1962	Dome 249
FIVE PEAKS		
Sittin' On The Porch/Hair-Net	1987	Jay-R 100
FIVE PEARLS (REF PEARLS (1)/REF SHEIKS (1))		
Please Let Me Know/ Real Humdinger	1954	Aladdin 3265
FIVE PENNIES		
Mr. Moon/Let It Rain	1955	Savoy 1182
My Heart Trembles/Money	1956	Savoy 1190
The Wedding Bells/For A Lifetime	1978	King Tut 176
Wedding Bells/Put This Ring On Your Finger	N/A	Herald (unreleased)
FIVE PENNIES (BIG MILLER & THE)		
All Is Well/Try To Understand	1955	Savoy 1181
FIVE PLAYBOYS		
Pages Of My Scrapbook/Love Me Right	1957	Fee Bee 213
Pages Of My Scrapbook/ When We Were Young	1957	Fee Bee 213/Dot 15605 (57)
Angel Mine/She's My Baby	1958	Fee Bee 232
Why Be A Fool/Time Will Allow	1958	Mercury 71269
She's My Baby/Mr. Echo	1959	Petite 504
FIVE PYRAMIDS		
It's Wonderful/Sugar Doll	1975	Nile 101
FIVE QUAILS (1)		
Jungle Baby/Hop Scotch Rock	1957	Mercury 71154
FIVE QUAILS (2) (FB HARVEY FUQUA)		
Been A Long Time/Get To School On Time	1962	Harvey 114/Harvey 4818
My Love/Never Felt Like This Before	1962	Harvey 116
FIVE RAMBLERS		
I Want You To Know/Slide, Slide, Slide	1963	Lummtone 111
FIVE REASONS		
Go To School/Three O'Clock Rock	1958	Cub 9006
FIVE ROSES		
Romance In The Spring/ Don't Cry, Della (75)	1959	Nu Kat 100/101/Clifton 11
FIVE ROVERS		
Down To The Sea/Change Your Mind	1956	Music City 798
FIVE ROYALS ((AKA FIVE ("5") ROYALES))		
Baby Don't Do It/I Like It Like That	1964	Smash 1936
Never Turn Your Back/Faith	1965	Smash 1963
FIVE SATINS (REF SCARLETS)		
When The Swallows Come Back To Capistrano/Dance Girl Dance (by Gerry Granahan & group)	1995	X-Bat 1000
FIVE SATINS (FRED PARRIS & THE)		
Memories Of Days Gone By/ Loving You	1982	Elektra 47411
FIVE SATINS (REF SCARLETS)		
Wonderful Girl/Weeping Willow	1956	Ember 1008
All Mine/Rose Mary	1956	Standord 100/Times Square 4 (63)
I Remember (In The Still Of The Nite)/The Jones Girl	1956	Standord 200/Ember 1005 (56)

Artist	Song	Year	Label
	Oh Happy Day/Our Love Is Forever	1957	Ember 1014
	To The Aisle/Wish I Had My Baby	1957	Ember 1019
	Our Anniversary/Pretty Baby	1957	Ember 1025
	A Million To One/Love With No Love In Return	1957	Ember 1028
	Again	1957	Ember LP 100
	Sugar	1957	Ember LP 100/Ember EP 101
	Moonlight and I	1957	Ember LP 100/Ember EP 102
	I'll Get Along	1957	Ember LP 100/Ember EP 102
	Pretty Baby	1957	Ember LP 100/Ember EP 104
	A Night To Remember/Senorita Lolita	1958	Ember 1038
	Shadows/Toni My Love	1959	Ember 1056
	When Your Love Comes Along/Skippity Doo	1959	First 104
	Your Memory/I Didn't Know	1960	Cub 9071
	These Foolish Things/A Beggar With A Dream	1960	Cub 9077
	I'll Be Seeing You/A Night Like This	1960	Ember 1061
	Candlelight/The Time	1960	Ember 1066
	Wishing Ring/Tell Me Dear	1960	Ember 1070
	I've Got Time	1960	Ember LP 401
	You Must Be An Angel	1960	Ember LP 401
	I've Lost	1960	Ember LP 401
	She's Gone (With The Wind)/(Somewhere) A Voice Is Calling	1961	Candlelite 411
	Can I Come Over Tonight?/Golden Earrings	1961	Cub 9090
	To The Aisle/Just To Be Near You	1961	Musictone 1108
	On A Lover's Island/Till The End	1961	United Artists 368
	The Masquerade Is Over/Raining In My Heart	1962	Chancellor 1110
	Downtown/Do You Remember	1962	Chancellor 1121
	Paradise On Earth/Monkey Business (by the Pharotones)	1963	Times Square 21/Times Square 94 (64)
	Remember Me/Kangaroo	1963	Warner Bros. 5367
	You Can Count On Me/Ain't Gonna Cry	1964	Roulette 4563
	In The Still Of The Night "67"/Heck No (instrumental)	1967	Mama Sadie 1001
	Summer In New York/Dark At The Top Of My Heart	1971	RCA 74-0478
	Very Precious Oldies/You Are Love	1973	Kirshner 4251
	I Love You So/Story To You (by the Rajahs)	1973	Klik 1020
	All Mine/The Voice	1973	Night Train 901
	Two Different Worlds/Love Is Such A Beautiful Thing	1974	Kirshner 4252
	Silver Waters	N/A	Relic LP 5024
	My Present Love	N/A	Relic LP 5024
	Annie's Back	N/A	Relic LP 5024
	Lover's Hill	N/A	Relic LP 5024
	Lonely Hearts	N/A	Relic LP 5024
	Wonder Why	N/A	Relic LP 5024
	Church Bells Played The Blues	N/A	Relic LP 5024
	Noone Knows/Musical Chairs	N/A	Sammy 103
FIVE SCALDERS			
	If Only You Were Mine/There Will Come A Time	1956	Drummond 3000/Sugarhill 3000 (56)
	Girlfriend/Willow Blues	1956	Drummond 3001
FIVE SCAMPS			
	With All My Heart/Red Hot	1954	Okeh 7049
FIVE SCRIPTS (AKA CONTENDERS/AKA KAPTIONS/AKA LYTATIONS/AKA ZIPPERS)			
	Peace Of Mind/The Clock	1963	Long Fiber 201
	My Friends Call Me/You Left My Heart	1965	Script 103
FIVE SECRETS (AKA SECRETS (1)/AKA LOUNGERS)			
	Queen Bee/See You Next Year	1957	Decca 30350 (first pressing, second is by the Secrets)
FIVE SEQUINS (GARY HAINES & THE)			
	Another Girl Like You/Tsetse Fly	1961	Kapp 383
FIVE SHADES			
	Mary Had A Little Lamb/Lonely Boy	1961	Ember 1074
	One Hot Dog/Sherlock Jones	1961	MGM 13035
	Vickie/I'll Give You Love	1965	Veep 1208
FIVE SHADOWS (AKA FIVE JADES (2))			
	Blue Moon/My Love Bug	1960	Frosty 1
	Sunday Kind Of Love (acapella)/Don't Say Goodnight (acapella)	1965	Mellomood 011/012
FIVE SHARKS (AKA SHARKS)			
	Let's Not Break Up/Up On The Roof	1986	Starlight 34
	Gloria (acapella)/Flames (acapella)	1964	Old Timer 604/Siamese 404 (64)/Old Timer 611 (65)
	Stand By Me (acapella)/I'll Never Let You G	1964	Old Timer 605
	Stormy Weather (Short & Long Versions)/If You Love Me	1964	Times Square 35/Relic 525 (65)
	The Lion Sleeps Tonight (acapella)/Land Of A 1000 Dances (acapella)	1966	Amber 852
FIVE SHARPS			
	Stormy Weather/Sleepy Cowboy	1952	Jubilee 5104
	Stormy Weather/Mammy Jammy	1964	Jubilee 5478
	Stormy Weather/Sleepy Cowboy	1972	Bim Bam Boom 103
FIVE SHILLINGS			
	Letter To An Angel/The Snake	1958	Decca 30722
FIVE SHITS			
	Stormy Weather/My Pretty Little Girl	1970	Chance 1163
	Let Me Tell You/Dreaming Of You	1973	Lost Cause 100
FIVE SOUNDS			
	The Greatest Gift Of All/Chalypso Baby	1958	Deb 1006
	Good Time Baby/That's When I Fell In Love	1960	Baritone 940/941
FIVE SOUNDS (RUSS RILEY & THE)			
	Tonight Must Live On/Crazy Feeling	1957	Aljon 115
	Tonight Must Live On/Crazy Feeling	1977	Arcade 1005
FIVE SPARKS			
	Little Bo Peep/A Million Tears	1959	Jimbo 1
FIVE SPEEDS			
	Tell Me/Goodbye	1959	Wiggie 131
FIVE SPENDERS (AKA REGENTS (2))			
	No Hard Feelings/That's What I Call A Good Time	1960	Versatile 113
FIVE SPLENDORS			
	Your Dog Hates Me/The Elephant Walk	1960	Stroll 106
FIVE STARS (1)			
	Where Did Caledonia Go?/Walkin' An' Talkin'	1954	Show Time 1102
	Let's Fall In Love/We Danced In The Moonlight	1955	Treat 505
FIVE STARS (2)			
	Take Five/Humpty Dumpty	1956	Atco 6065
	So Lonely, Baby/Hey, Juanita	1957	Blue Boys Kingdom 106
	Atom Bomb Baby/You Sweet Little Thing	1957	Kernel 319574/Dot 15579 (57)
	Ooh, Shucks/Dead Wrong	1957	Mark-X 7006
	Baby, Baby/Blabber Mouth	1958	End 1028/Columbia 42056 (61)
	Dreaming/Pickin' On The Wrong Chicken	1958	Note 10011/Hunt 318 (58)/ABC 9911 (58)
	Friction/My Paradise	1958	Note 10016
	Am I Wasting My Time/Gamblin' Man	1959	Note 10031
FIVE STARS (2) (DOTTIE FERGUSON & THE)			
	You And Me Baby/Slow Burn	1957	Kernel 003/Mercury 71129
FIVE STARS (3) (GARY ROBERTS & THE)			
	You Made Me A Prisoner Of Love	N/A	Sterling 681

Artist Song	Year	Label
FIVE SUPERIORS		
Big Shot/There's A Fool Born		
Every Day	1962	Garpax 44170
FIVE SWANS		
Li'l Girl Of My Dreams/Li'l		
Tipa-Tina	1956	Music City 795
A Mother's Love	N/A	Music City (unreleased)
FIVE TECHNIQUES		
Heaven Above/Don't Tell Me	1961	Imperial 5742
FIVE TEENBEATS		
Autumn Mood/Time To Rock	1960	Big Top 3062
FIVE THRILLS (AKA EARLS (1))		
Wee, Wee Baby/Gloria	1954	Parrot 800
Girl Of My Dreams/Laverne	1981	Parrot 803
All I Want	1990	Relic LP 5087
Ride Jimmy Ride	1990	Relic LP 5087
So Long Young Girl	1990	Relic LP 5087
Rockin' At Midnight	1990	Relic LP 8020
FIVE THRILLS (AKA EARLS (2))		
My Baby's Gone/Feel So Good	1953	Parrot 796
FIVE TINOS		
Sitting By My Window/Don't		
Do That!	1955	Sun 222
Gonna Let You Go/Mambo Baby	1976	Sun 514
FIVE TROJANS		
Alone In This World/Don't Ask		
Me To Be Lonely	1958	Tender 516
Little Doll/Lola Lee	1959	Edison International 412
FIVE TROJANS (NICKY ST. CLAIR & THE)		
I Hear Those Bells/Creator Of		
Love	1959	Edison International 410
FIVE VETS		
You're In Love/Right Now	1956	Allstar 713/Bruce
FIVE VULTURES		
Lonesome/Soldier In Korea		
(recorded in 1952)	1973	Roadhouse 1006
FIVE WHISPERS		
Moon In The Afternoon/		
Midnight Sun	1962	Dolton 61
Especially For You/Awake		
Or Asleep	1962	Dolton 69
FIVE WILLOWS (AKA WILLOWS (1))		
My Dear, Dearest Darling/		
Rock, Little Francis	1953	Allen 1000
Dolores/All Night Long	1953	Allen 1002
White Cliffs Of Dover/		
With These Hands	1953	Allen 1003
Love Bells/Please, Baby	1953	Pee Dee 290
Baby, Come A Little Closer/		
Lay Your Head On My		
Shoulder	1954	Herald 433
Look Me In The Eyes/		
So Help Me	1954	Herald 442
FIVE WINGS (1)		
Johnny Has Gone/Johnny's		
Still Singing	1955	King 4778
Teardrops Are Falling/		
Rock-A-Locka	1955	King 4781/King 5199
FIVE WINGS (2) (BILLY NELSON & THE)		
Walk Along/Shack, Pack And		
Stack Your Blues Away	1956	Savoy 1183
My Gal/Hurry Up Honey	N/A	Savoy 999 (unreleased)
FLAIRS (1)		
I Had A Love/She Wants To		
Rock	1953	Flair 1012
You Should Care For Me/		
Tell Me You Love Me	1953	Flair 1019
Gettin' High/Love Me Girl	1954	Flair 1028
Baby Wants/You Were Untrue	1954	Flair 1041
This Is The Night For Love/		
Let's Make With Some Love	1954	Flair 1044
Hold Me, Thrill Me, Chill Me/		
I'll Never Let You Go	1955	Flair 1056
My Darling, My Sweet/		
She Loves To Dance	1955	Flair 1067
I'd Climb The Hills And		
Mountains/Swing Pretty Mama	1959	Antler 4005
I Want You To Be Mine	1963	Crown LP 5356
Tell Me You're Mine	1963	Crown LP 5356
My Heart's Crying For You	1963	Crown LP 5356
Lonesome Desert	1963	Crown LP 5356
Rock Bottom	1963	Crown LP 5356

Artist Song	Year	Label
I Love You	1963	Crown LP 5356
Cool, Baby, Cool	1984	Cadet
FLAIRS (1) (CORNEL GUNTER & THE)		
In Self Defense/She Loves		
To Rock	1956	ABC 9698
Aladdin's Lamp/Steppin' Out	1956	ABC 9740
Where You Live/You Got To		
Steal	N/A	Rap 007
FLAIRS (1) (ETTA JAMES & THE)		
Sunshine Of Our Love/		
Baby Baby Every Night	1959	Kent 304
FLAIRS (1) (FATSO THEUS & THE)		
Be Cool, My Heart/		
Rock 'N' Roll Drive-In	1956	Aladdin 3324
FLAIRS (1) (JAMES STALLCUP & THE)		
Baby Let's Make Love/		
Sad Feeling	1961	Le Cam 724
FLAIRS (1) (RICHARD BERRY & THE)		
The Big Break/What Would		
You Do To Me	1955	Flair 1055
(Oh Oh) Get Out Of The Car/		
Please Tell Me	1955	Flair 1064
God Gave Me You/Don't Cha Go	1955	Flair 1068
FLAIRS (1) (SHIRLEY GUNTER & THE)		
How Can I Tell You?/Ipsy		
Opsie Ooh	1955	Flair 1076
Fortune In Love/I Just Got Rid		
Of A Heartache	1956	Modern 1001
Headin' Home/I Want You	1956	Modern 989
FLAIRS (2) (AKA REDWOODS) (GM JEFF BARRY)		
The Memory Lingers On/Shake		
Shake Sherry	1961	Epic 9447
FLAME TONES (RICHARD WILLANS & THE)		
Oldies But Goodies/Little		
Sister Nell	1972	Bell 192
FLAMES (1) (AKA HOLLYWOOD FLAMES)		
Young Girl/Please Tell Me Now	1950	Selective 113
Strange Land Blues/Cryin' For		
My Baby	1952	Spin 101
Keep On Smiling/Baby, Baby,		
Baby	1953	7-11 2106
Baby, Pretty Baby/Together	1953	7-11 2107
Let's Talk It Over/Tears Keep		
Tumbling Down	1953	7-11 2108 (unreleased)
Volcano/Sorrowful Heart		
(lead by Patti Anne Mesner)	1953	7-11 2109 (unreleased)
I'll Hide My Tears/Got A Little		
Shadow	1953	7-11 2110 (unreleased)
So All Alone/Flame Mambo	1956	Aladdin 3349
So Long My Darling/I'm Gonna		
Try To Live My Life All Over	1960	Harlem 114
FLAMES (1) (PATTI ANNE MESNER & THE)		
Midnight/My Heart Is Free Again	1952	Aladdin 3162
Sorrowful Heart/Beginning To		
Miss You (no group)	1953	Aladdin 3198
FLAMES (2) (TOMMY "MARY JO" BRADEN & HIS)		
Do The Do/Did You Ever See		
A Monkey	1955	United 177
FLAMES (3)		
I'll Never Let You Go/Crazy	1959	Bertram 203
FLAMES (4) (ALLAN & THE)		
Till The End Of Time/Winter		
Wonderland (instrumental)	1960	Colonial 7006/Campbell 225-1
FLAMES (5) (FARRELL & THE)		
Dreams And Memories/		
You'll Be Sorry	1961	Fransil 14
FLAMES (6) (CAROL PEGUES & THE)		
Darling Jane/Blues Around		
My Door	N/A	GM 101
FLAMES (7) (ALTON & THE)		
Nothing Sweeter	N/A	Duchess
FLAMES (8) (JOHNNY SPAIN & THE)		
I'm In Love	N/A	Back Beat 516
FLAMETTES		
You You You/Hee Hee Ha Ha	1961	Laurie 3109
FLAMING EMBERS		
Gone Gone Gone/You Can		
Count On Me	1961	Fortune 869
FLAMING HEARTS		
I Don't Mind/Baby	1958	Vulco V1

Artist Song	Year	Label
FLAMINGO, JOHNNY (& FEMALE GROUP)		
Will She Think Of Me/Paradise Hill	1958	Specialty 640
FLAMINGO, JOHNNY (& GROUP)		
I/It Were You	1957	Canton 1785
United/I Just Cry	1959	Malynn 101
FLAMINGOS		
If I Can't Have You/Someday Someway	1953	Chance 1133
That's My Desire/Hurry Home Baby	1953	Chance 1140
Golden Teardrops/Carried Away (61)	1953	Chance 1145/Vee Jay 384
Plan For Love/You Ain't Ready	1953	Chance 1149
Cross Over The Bridge/ Listen To My Plea	1954	Chance 1154
Blues In A Letter/Jump Children	1954	Chance 1162
Dream Of A Lifetime/On My Merry Way	1954	Parrot 808
When/(Chica Boom)That's My Baby	1955	Checker 815
Please Come Back Home/ I Want To Love You	1955	Checker 821
I Really Don't Want To Know/ Get With It	1955	Parrot 811
I'm Yours/Ko Ko Mo	1955	Parrot 812
Cry	1956	Checker (unreleased)
I'll Be Home/Need Your Love	1956	Checker 830
A Kiss From Your Lips/ Get With It	1956	Checker 837
The Vow/Shilly Dilly	1956	Checker 846
Would I Be Crying/Just For Kicks	1956	Checker 853
That Love Is You	1957	Decca (unreleased)
The Ladder Of Love/ Let's Make Up	1957	Decca 30335
My Faith In You/Helpless	1957	Decca 30454
Where Mary Go/Rock And Roll March	1958	Decca 30687
Without A Song	1958	End (unreleased)
Lovers Never Say Goodbye/ That Love Is You	1958	End 1035
Dream Of A Lifetime/ Whispering Stars	1959	Checker 915
Stolen Love	1959	Checker LP 3005/Chess LP 1433 (59)
Chickie Um Bah	1959	Checker LP 3005/Chess LP 1433 (59)
Nobody's Love	1959	Checker LP 3005/Chess LP 1433 (59)
Kiss-A-Me/Ever Since I Met Lucy	1959	Decca 30880
Jerri Lee/Hey Now	1959	Decca 30948
We Were Made For Each Other	1959	End (unreleased)
River Of Tears	1959	End (unreleased)
But Not For Me/I Shed A Tear At Your Wedding	1959	End 1040
Love Walked In/At The Prom	1959	End 1044
I Only Have Eyes For You/ At The Prom	1959	End 1046
I Only Have Eyes For You/ Goodnight Sweetheart	1959	End 1046
Love Walked In/Yours	1959	End 1055
I Was Such A Fool/Heavenly Angel	1959	End 1062
Where Or When	1959	End LP 304
The Breeze And I	1959	End LP 304
Begin The Beguine	1959	End LP 304
As Time Goes By	1959	End LP 304
Music Maestro Please	1959	End LP 304/End EP 205 (59)
I'm In The Mood For Love	1959	End LP 304/End EP 205 (59)
Mio Amore/You, Me And The Sea	1960	End 1065
Nobody Loves Me Like You/ Besame Mucho	1960	End 1068
Besame Mucho/You, Me And The Sea	1960	End 1070
Mio Amore/At Night	1960	End 1073
When I Fall In Love/Beside You	1960	End 1079
Your Other Love/Lovers Gotta Cry	1960	End 1081
Kokomo/That's Why I Love You	1960	End 1085
Maria Elena	1960	End LP 307
Crazy, Crazy, Crazy	1960	End LP 307

Artist Song	Year	Label
My Foolish Heart	1960	End LP 307
You Belong To My Heart	1960	End LP 307
Sweet And Lovely	1960	End LP 307
Never In This World	1960	End LP 307
Bridge Of Tears	1960	End LP 307
Tell Me How Long	1960	End LP 307
You'll Never Walk Alone	1960	End LP 308
Every Time I Think Of You	1960	End LP 308
Happy Birthday Elise	1960	End LP 308
In The Still Of The Night	1960	End LP 308
Tenderly	1960	End LP 308
Everybody's Got A Home	1960	End LP 308
Lover Come Back	1961	End (unreleased)
Dream Girl/Time Was	1961	End 1092
My Memories Of You/I Want To Love You	1961	End 1099
I'm No Fool Anymore/It Must Be Love	1962	End 1111
For All We Know/Near You	1962	End 1116
I Know Better/Flame Of Love	1962	End 1121
(Talk About) True Love/Come On To My Party	1962	End 1124
(When You're Young And) Only Seventeen	1962	End LP 316
The Sinner	1962	End LP 316
Danny Boy	1962	End LP 316
Ol' Man River	1962	End LP 316
You're Mine	1962	End LP 316
Too Soon To Know	1962	End LP 316
Moonlight In Vermont	1962	End LP 316
Shout It Out	1963	End (unreleased)
My Lovely One	1963	End LP 316
Without His Love	1963	End LP 316
I'm Coming Home	1963	End LP 316
Ol' Man River Pt. 1/Ol' Man River Pt. 2	1963	Roulette 4524
Lover Come Back To Me/ Your Little Guy	1964	Checker 1084
Goodnight Sweetheart Good- night/Does It Really Matter	1964	Checker 1091
September Song	1964	Constellation LP 3
If I Could Love You/I Found A New Baby	1964	Constellation LP 3/Chess LP 702 (76)/Skylark 541 (78)
Lovely Way To Spend An Evening/Walking My Baby Back Home	1964	Times Square 102
If I Can't Have You/I'll Be Home	1973	Owl 322
Stolen Love/Honey (by the Honey Boys)	1974	Owl 333
Welcome Home/Gotta Have All Your Lovin'	1974	Ronze 111
Someone To Watch Over Me/ Heavy Hips	1975	Ronze 115
Love Keeps The Doctor Away/ Love Keeps The Doctor Away	1976	Ronze 116
If I Could Love You	1990	Relic LP 5088
I Found A New Baby	1990	Relic LP 5088
FLANNELS		
Hey Rube/So Shy	1956	Tampa 121
FLARES (AKA CADETS (1)/AKA JACKS)		
Loving You/Hotcha Cha-Cha Brown	1960	Felsted 8604
Jump And Bump/What Do You Want If You Don't Want Love?	1960	Felsted 8607
Foot Stomping Pt. 1/Foot Stomping Pt. 2 (instrumental)	1961	Felsted 8624
Rock And Roll Heaven Pt. 1/ Rock And Roll Heaven Pt. 2	1961	Press 2800
Doing The Hully Gully/Truck And Trailer	1961	Press 2802
Mad House/Make It Be Me	1961	Press 2803
Do It With Me/Yon We Go	1961	Press 2807
Hand Clappin'/Shimmy And Stomp	1961	Press 2808
The Monkey Walk/Do It If You Wanna	1961	Press 2810
Fish And Twist	N/A	London (England) LP 8034
Huckle-Buck	N/A	London (England) LP 8034
The Stroll	N/A	London (England) LP 8034
The Twist	N/A	London (England) LP 8034
Doing The Watusi	N/A	London (England) LP 8034

Artist Song	Year	Label
Shake, Shimmy And Stroll	N/A	London (England) LP 8034
Sock Hop	N/A	London (England) LP 8034
The Pony	N/A	London (England) LP 8034
Write A Song About Me/		
I Didn't Lose A Doggone Thing	N/A	Press 2814
FLARES (COOKIE JACKSON & THE) (REF CADETS (1)/REF JACKS)		
I Didn't Lose A Doggone Thing/		
Write A Song About Me	1961	Press 2814
FLARES (PAUL BALLENGER & THE) (REF CADETS (1)/REF JACKS)		
I Still Love You/Seven Times		
Heaven	1958	Reed 711
FLASHER BROTHERS		
Love Gave Me To You/To Live		
The Life Of A Lie	1952	Aladdin 3156
Lowdown Dirty/It's The Last		
Thing I Do	1953	Aladdin 3186
FLASHES (JESS DAVIS & THE)		
With All My Heart And Soul/		
Come What May	1959	Bob-O-Link 100/101
FLEAS		
Tears/Scratchin'	1961	Challenge 9115
FLEETONES		
Your Lover Man/Please Tell me	1961	Bandera 2511
FLEETWOODS		
Come Softly To Me/I Care So		
Much	1959	Dolton 1/Liberty 55188 (59)/Liberty 77188 (59)
Graduation's Here/Oh Lord,		
Let It Be	1959	Dolton 3/Dolton S-3 (59)
Mr. Blue/You Mean Everything		
To Me	1959	Dolton 5
Outside My Window/Magic Star	1960	Dolton 15
Runaround/Truly Do	1960	Dolton 22
The Last One To Know/		
Dormilona	1960	Dolton 27
Confidential/I Love You So	1960	Dolton 30
Tragedy/Little Miss Sad One	1961	Dolton 40
(He's The) Great Impostor/		
Poor Little Girl	1961	Dolton 45
Billy Old Buddy/Trouble	1961	Dolton 49
Lovers By Night, Strangers		
By Day/They Tell Me It's		
Summer	1962	Dolton 62
You Should've Been There/		
Sure Is Lonesome Downtown	1963	Dolton 74
Goodnight My Love/Jimmy		
Beware	1963	Dolton 75
What'll I Do/Baby Bye-O	1963	Dolton 86
Before And After (Losing You)/		
Lonely Is As Lonely Does	1964	Dolton 302
I'm Not Jimmy/Come Softly To		
Me	1964	Dolton 307
Rainbow/Just As I Needed You	1964	Dolton 310
For Lovin' Me/This Is Where I		
See Her	1964	Dolton 315
Lonesome Town/Ruby Red,		
Baby Blue	1964	Dolton 93
Ten Times Blue/Ska Light,		
Ska Bright	1964	Dolton 97
Mr. Sandman/This Is My Prayer	1964	Dolton 98
FLINTS		
Over The Ocean/Chickie		
Chop Chop	1958	Petite 101
People Say/Skippin' And		
Jumpin'	1959	Okeh 7126
Why Do You Go/When Summer		
Gets Back	1962	Hart 100
FLIPPERS		
You Yakity Yak Too Much/		
My Aching Heart	1955	Flip 305
FLIPS (1)		
Why Should I/Yes Ma'am		
(no group)	1955	Sapphire 1052
Gone Away/It Will Never Be		
The Same	1959	Mercury 71426
FLIPS (2) (KIP TYLER & THE)		
Jungle Hop/Ooh Yeah Baby	1958	Challenge 59008
FLIPS (3) (MARIO & THE)		
Once In A While/Nobody's		
Sweetheart	1959	Cross Country 100
Twistin' Train/You Made Me		
Love You	1961	Decca 31252

Artist Song	Year	Label
FLIPS (4) (JOEY & THE)		
The Beachcomber/Fool, Fool,		
Fool	1964	Cameo 327
FLIPS (4) (LITTLE JOEY & THE)		
Our Own Little World/My First		
Love Letter	1960	Joy 243
Bongo Stomp/Lost Love	1962	Joy 262
Bongo Gully/It Was Like Heaven	1962	Joy 268
The Mystery Of The Night/		
Hot Rod	1976	Monogram 111 (bootleg)
FLIPS (5)		
Rockin' With Rosie	N/A	Arctic 102
FLIPS (4) (LITTLE JOEY & THE)		
The Mystery Of The Night/		
Hot Rod	1975	Monogram 111
FLORES, TEDDY (& GROUP)		
Karen My Darling	N/A	Deflor 65729
FLORESCENTS		
What Are You Doing Tonight?/		
Being In Love	1963	Bethlehem 3079
FLORIDIANS		
That Lucky Old Sun/I Love Marie	1961	ABC 10185
FLUORESCENTS		
The Facts Of Love/Shoopy		
Pop-A-Doo	1959	Hanover 4520/Candlelite 420 (63)
FLYERS		
On Bended Knee/My Only		
Desire	1957	Atco 6088
Island Love	N/A	Fabbi
FOOTE, CHUCK (& GROUP)		
Come On Back/You're Running		
Out Of Kisses	1961	Soncraft 401
FORD, ANN (& GROUP)		
The Fool/Can't Tell You	1959	Apollo 532
FORD, JERRY (& GROUP)		
Love Will Make Your Mind Go		
Wild	N/A	Double B 101
FOREIGN INTRIGUE (AKA ERNIE MARESCA & THE DEL SATINS)		
The Wanderer/Blind Date	N/A	E.M. 1001
FORETELLS		
Exodus (acapella)/Return To		
Me (acapella)	1965	Catamount 109
Somewhere, Somewhere	1966	Catamount 113
FOREVERS		
Isn't That A Lovely Way To		
Say Goodnight	1958	Apt
Baby/Slow Down	1958	Apt 25022
FORTES		
Waiting For My Baby/		
Why Won't You Change		
Your Ways For Me	1964	Current 103
FORTUNE BRAVOS (SPIDER TURNER & THE)		
Ride In My 225/One Stop	1963	Fortune 570
FORTUNE TELLERS		
Song Of The Nairobi Trio/		
Camel Train	1961	Music Makers 105
School Prom/Just A Little Bit		
Of Your Love	1961	Sheryl 340
Marry Her Joe/I Love You		
(Inka Doo)	1963	Atlantic 2197
FORTUNE, BILLY (& GROUP) (AKA BILLY JONES & THE SQUIRES)		
Listen To Your Heart/Every		
Word Of The Song	1958	Dice 478
FORTUNE, JIMMY (& GROUP)		
Moonlight Shadows/I Feel A		
Heartache Comin' On	1961	Chancellor 1097
FORTUNE, JOHNNY (BB THE PARAMOURS)		
I'm Talking About You/		
My Wandering Love	1963	Park Ave. 4905
FORTUNEERS		
Look A' There/Oh, Woh, Baby	1963	Skytone 1000
FORTUNES (1) (AKA DONALD & THE DELIGHTERS)		
Believe In Me/My Baby Is Fine	1955	Checker 818
Love/Bread	1981	Parrot 804/Relic LP 5088 (90)
Break	1990	Relic LP 5088
FORTUNES (2)		
Who Cares?/Tarnished Angel	1958	Decca 30541
How Clever Of You/Trees	1958	Decca 30688
FORTUNES (3)		
Steady Vows/In The Night	1959	Top Rank 2019

Artist	Song	Year	Label
	Nothing Matters Anymore/		
	Ugly Duckling	1961	Queen 24010
	The Laugh Of The Town/		
	This Is Love	1964	Yucca 168/170
FORTUNES (3) (LARRY DARNELL & THE)			
	Congratulations/Look At Me,		
	Look At You	1960	Argo 5364
FORTUNES (4)			
	Running Away From Love/		
	Tell Me	1962	DRA 320
FORTUNES (5)			
	The Ghoul In School/You Don't		
	Know (What I've Been Through)	1963	Cub 9123
FORTUNES (6)			
	Lonely Teardrops/This Is Love	N/A	Bishop 1005
FOSTER BROTHERS			
	Tell Me Who/I Said She		
	Wouldn't Do	1957	El-Bee 161
	Never Again/I Could Cry	1958	Hi Mi 3005
	Show Me/If You Want My Heart	1958	Mercury 71360
	Trust In Me/Why-Yi-Yi	1959	Profile 4004
	Revenge/Pretty, Fickle Woman	1960	B&F 1333
FOSTER BROTHERS (LEFTY "GUITAR" BATES & THE)			
	Land Of Love/Let's Jam	1960	Dilly 101
FOUNTAIN, MORRIS (& GROUP)			
	Cryin' My Heart Out/Juicin'		
	And Goofin'	1954	Savoy 1139
FOUR (4) GENTS			
	I Refuse To Pay/My Bernadette	1963	Vida 0123
FOUR (4) UNIQUES			
	Endlessly/Maybe Next Summer	1964	USA 753
FOUR AFTER FIVES (REF CRENSHAWS/REF EBBTIDES (3)/REF LAMPLIGHT-ERS/REF RIVINGTONS/REF SHARPS/REF TENDERFOOTS)			
	Hello, Schoolteacher!/I Gotta		
	Have Somebody (Lonely Boy)	1961	All Time 9076
FOUR ARCS (AKA AMBASSADORS (1)/AKA GAYLORDS/AKA IMPERIALS (1))			
	Life Of Ease/It Won't Be Very		
	Long	1954	Boulevard 102
FOUR B'S			
	Love Eternal/I Played The Fool	1958	D 1013
FOUR BARONS (1) (AKA LARKS)			
	Got To Go Back Again/		
	Lemon Squeezer	1950	Regent 1026
FOUR BARONS (2)			
	Old Enough To Know/Bambinella	1957	Roman 400
FOUR BARS (1)			
	Hey Baby/Grief By Day,		
	Grief By Night	1954	Josie 762
	If I Give My Heart To You/		
	Stop It! Quit It!	1954	Josie 768
	Memories Of You/When		
	Did You Leave Heaven?	1954	Republic 7101
	Why Do You Treat Me This		
	his Way/Let Me Live	1955	Josie 783
	Love Me Forever More/		
	What's On Your Mind?	1960	Cadillac 2006
	Phony Baloney/Why Did You		
	Do It	1960	Time 4
FOUR BARS (2)			
	Just Bid Me Farewell/The		
	Game Of Romance	1961	Len 1014
	Try Me One More Time/		
	Comin' On Home	1962	Dayco 101/Shelley 180
	Poor Little Me/Stay On My J.O.B.	1962	Dayco 2500
	Try Me One More Time/		
	What's On Your Mind	1963	Shelley 180
	I've Got To Move/Waitin'		
	On The Right Guy	1964	Falew 108
	What Am I Going To Do/		
	Guess Who Loves You	N/A	Shrine
FOUR BARS (2) (BETTY WILSON & THE)			
	Anything To Please My Man/		
	If I Had It To Do All Over Again	1962	DAyco
	I'm Yours/All Over Again	1962	Dayco 1631
	Lean On Me When Heartaches		
	Get Rough/Why I've Got		
	To Know	1962	Dayco 4564
FOUR BARS (2) (SHANE HUNTER & THE)			
	I'm So Helpless/Follow Me	1959	IPS 101
FOUR BARS (3)			
	We Are Together/Speak Now	1964	Flying Hawk 1501

Artist	Song	Year	Label
FOUR BEATS (DONN BRUCE & THE)			
	Love Leads A Fool/Let's Start		
	All Over Again	1956	Tuxedo 914
FOUR BEAUS			
	Tight Shoes/Partners Paradise	1959	Todd 1028
FOUR BEL-AIRES			
	Tell Me Why/Where Are You	1958	X-Tra 113
	Where Are You/Blue Moon	1976	King Tut 169
FOUR BEL-AIRES (LARRY LEE & THE)			
	Can I Be In Love/Stolen Love	1959	M-Z 006
FOUR BELLS			
	Please Tell It To Me/Long Way		
	To Go	1953	Gem 207/Crystal 102
	Here/Dream, Dream, Dream	1954	Bell 1039
	Hey Nita/When I Needed You		
	Most	1954	Bell 5047
	Only A Miracle/My Tree	1954	Gem 220/Crystal 101
FOUR BITS			
	Hey Dreamboat/Glad Glad Glad	1958	Coin 1501
FOUR BLADES			
	I Want You To Be My Girl/		
	Can You Find It In Your Heart	1956	Gateway 1170
	Church Bells May Ring/Stardust	1956	Gateway 1174
	You Didn't Sign Your Letter		
	With Love/Bake That		
	Chicken Pie	1963	Alert 422
	The Green Door	N/A	Big 4 Hits EP 203
	It Isn't Right	N/A	Big 4 Hits EP 203
FOUR BLUEBIRDS (GM BOBBY NUNN)			
	My Baby Done Told Me/Court		
	Room Blues (Johnny Otis		
	& Orchestra)	1949	Excelsior 540
FOUR BLUES			
	Re Bop-De-Boom/		
	The Vegetable Song	1950	Apollo 1145
	Missing You/As Long As I Live	1950	Apollo 1160
FOUR BROTHERS AND A COUSIN			
	Trust In Me/Whistle Stop Blues	1954	Jaguar 3003
	Whispering Winds/Can It Be	1954	Jaguar 3005
FOUR BUDDIES (1)			
	I Will Wait/Just To See You		
	Smile Again	1951	Savoy 769
	Don't Leave Me Now/		
	Sweet Slumber	1951	Savoy 779
	My Summer's Gone/Why At A		
	Time Like This	1951	Savoy 789
	I'm Yours/Moonlight In Your		
	Eyes	1951	Savoy 809 (unreleased)
	Heart And Soul/Sin	1951	Savoy 817
	Simply Say Goodbye/		
	Window's Eyes	1951	Savoy 823
	You're Part Of Me/Story Blues	1952	Savoy 845
	What's The Matter With Me/		
	Sweet Tooth For My Baby	1952	Savoy 866
	My Mother's Eyes/Ooh-Ow	1953	Savoy 888
	I Love You Yes I Do/It Could		
	Have Been Me	N/A	Savoy 951 (unreleased)
	You Left Me Blue/Got		
	Everything But You	N/A	Savoy 955 (unreleased)
	Close To You/Stop Your Hittin'		
	On Me	N/A	Savoy 959 (unreleased)
FOUR BUDDIES (1) (DOLLY COOPER & THE)			
	I'd Climb The Highest Mountain/		
	I Wanna Know (no group)	1953	Savoy 891
FOUR BUDDIES (2)			
	Delores/Look Out	1956	Club 51 105
FOUR BUDDIES (2) (BOBBIE JAMES & THE)			
	I Need You So/Baby, I'm Tired		
	(Bobbie James)	1956	Club 51 104
FOUR BUDDIES (2) (RUDY GREENE & THE)			
	You Mean Everything To Me/		
	Highway No. 1 (no group)	1956	Club 51 103
FOUR BUDDIES (3)			
	Hurt/Moonglow	1961	Coral 62217
	The Light/Cin Cin (Che Bell)	1962	Coral 62325
	I Want To Be The Boy You Love/		
	Just Enough Of Your Love	1964	Imperial 66018
	Slow Locomotion/Lonely		
	Summer	1965	Philips 40122
FOUR BUDDIES (4)			
	Allright Already/Don't Know		
	Why I Love You	1959	Willett 100

Artist	Song	Year	Label
FOUR BUDS (AKA FOUR BUDDIES (1)/AKA BUDDIES (2)/AKA BARONS (1))			
	Just To See You Smile Again/		
	I Will Wait	1950	Savoy 769
FOUR CAL-QUETTES (AKA FOUR COUQUETTES)			
	Starbright/Billy, My Billy	1961	Capitol 4574
	Most Of All/I'm Gonna Love		
	Him Anyway	1961	Capitol 4657
	I'll Never Come Back Silly Boy/		
	Again	1962	Capitol 4725
	I Cried/Movie Magazines	1963	Liberty 55549
FOUR CASTS			
	Stormy Weather/Working		
	At The Factory	1964	Atlantic 2228
FOUR CHANELS (VIRGIL & THE) (AKA 5 CHANELS)			
	Waiting/Don't Keep It To		
	Yourself	1959	Deb 508
FOUR CHAPS			
	Completely Yours/Foolish		
	Little Butterfly	1956	Rama 195
	Roll Over Beethoven/Wrong		
	Number	1956	Rama 199
	True Lovers/Will You Or Won't		
	You	1962	Co & Ce 231 (65)
FOUR CHECKERS			
	Broken Heart/Sheila	1959	Ace 129
FOUR CHECKS			
	I'll Be Around/Big Feet Mary	1961	Tri Disc 101
FOUR CHEERS			
	Fatal Charms Of Love/		
	Perriwinkle Blue	1958	End 1034
FOUR CHEVELLES			
	This Is Our Wedding Day/		
	Darling, Forever	1957	Band Box 357/Delft 357 (64)
	I Can't Believe/I Know	1957	Band Box 358
FOUR CHICKADEES (FEMALE)			
	Ding Dong/Teenage Blues	1956	Checker 849
FOUR CHIMES (AKA MOROCCOS)			
	Before I Met You	1954	States (unreleased)
	My Easy Baby	1954	States (unreleased)
	When My Baby Was Born	1954	United (unreleased)
FOUR CHYMES			
	The Gypsy/Now Look At		
	Who's Crying	1963	Musicnote 121
FOUR CLASSMATES (AKA CLASSMATES (2))			
	A Kiss Is Not A Kiss/What Am I		
	Gonna Do	1955	King 1487
FOUR CLEFS (AKA CHUCKLES (3)/AKA CONSORTS (2))			
	Time After Time (acapella)/		
	Please Be Mine (a capella)	1966	B-J 1000
FOUR CLIPPERS			
	You Can't Trust A Woman/Rain	1957	Fox 960/961
FOUR CLOSURES			
	Maybe/Rock-A-My Soul	1958	Specialty 643
FOUR COACHMEN			
	If You Believe/Nothing But		
	Love, Love, Love	1959	Castle 507
	Shalom/Swamp Legend	1960	Adonis 106/Stellar 712 (60)/Dot 16297 (61)
	Wintertime/That Thing Called		
	A Girl	1960	Adonis A-102
FOUR COUNTS (1)			
	Young Hearts/I'm Gonna Love		
	You	1958	Dart 1014
FOUR COUNTS (2)			
	Yum-mee, Yum-mee/Cuckoo	1958	Josie 840/Go 103
FOUR COUNTS (3)			
	I Love You With All My Heart/		
	Rock & Roll's Good for the Soul	1958	Cham 003
FOUR COUNTS (4)			
	Heavenly/Blue Eyes	1960	Ace 597
FOUR COUNTS (5)			
	Graduation/Fanny Mae	1962	Fine 2562
FOUR COUQUETTES (AKA FOUR CAL-QUETTES) (FEMALE)			
	Sparkle And Shine/In This World	1961	Capitol 4534
	Again/I'll Never Come Back	1962	Capitol 4725
FOUR COUSINS (BILL MURRAY & THE)			
	Time And Time Again/		
	Guaranteed	1955	20th Century 75020
FOUR CRICKETS			
	A Thousand Miles Away	N/A	Tops 702
FOUR CRUISERS (JOSEPH DOBBIN & THE)			
	On Account Of You/Beale		
	St. Shuffle	1953	Chess 1547
FOUR DATES (FABIAN & THE)			
	Gingerbread/Blue Betty		
	(no group)	1958	Chancellor 1021
	Lilly Lou/Be My Steady Date	1958	Chancellor 1024
FOUR DATES (FB FABIAN FORTE)			
	I'm Happy/Eloise	1957	Chancellor 1014
FOUR DATES (FB JOHNNY OCTOBER)			
	I Say Babe/Hey Roly Poly	1958	Chancellor 1019
	Teenage Neighbor/I Feel Good	1958	Chancellor 1027
FOUR DEALS			
	It's Too Late Now/There Ain't		
	No Bears In The Forest	1950	Capitol 1313
FOUR DEANS			
	So Very Much/Mr. Echo		
	(recorded in 1958)	1992	Park Ave. 7
FOUR DEL-AIRES (LUCY ANN GRASSI & THE)			
	Boy Crazy/Scuba Duba	1964	Volcanic 1002
FOUR DEUCES			
	W-P-L-J/Here Lies My Love		
	(by Mr. Undertaker)	1955	Music City 790
	Down It Went/Goose Is Gone	1956	Music City 796
	Polly/Yella Shoes	1959	Everest 19311
FOUR DIRECTIONS			
	Tonight We Love/(Doin' The)		
	Arthur	1965	Coral 68456
	Tonight We Love/You Blew		
	Out The Candles		
	(by the Crests)	N/A	Popular Request 108
FOUR DOLLS			
	Proud Of You/Three On A Date	1957	Capitol 3766
	Whoop-A-Lala/I'm Following		
	You	1958	Capitol 3895
FOUR DOTS (1) (AKA HEARTBREAKERS)			
	You Won't Let Me Go/My Dear	1951	Dot 1043
	Rita/He Man Looking For A		
	She Girl	1956	Bullseye 103
	Peace Of Mind/My Dear	1956	Bullseye 104
	Peace Of Mind/Kiss Me,		
	Sugar Plum	1956	Bullseye 104
FOUR DOTS (2) (JERRY STONE & THE) (WITH EDDIE COCHRAN & JEWEL AKENS)			
	It's Heaven/My Baby		
	(She Loves Me)	1958	Freedom 44002
FOUR DOTS (3) (JERRY STONE & THE) (WITH EDDIE COCHRAN & JEWEL AKENS)			
	Pleading For Your Love/		
	Don't Wake Up The Kids	1959	Freedom 44005
FOUR DOTS (4) (DEKE WATSON & THE)			
	Strange As It Seems/		
	Saturday Night Function	1952	Castle 2006
FOUR DUCHESSES (FEMALE) (AKA DUCHESSES)			
	Cry For My Baby/Queen		
	Without A King	1957	Chief 7014
	Why/You Told Everyone But Me	1957	Chief 7019
FOUR DUKES (1)			
	Crying In The Chapel/I Done		
	Done It	1953	Duke 116
	Angel Dear/Baby Doll	1976	Sun 515
	Walking Alone/Annie	1976	Sun 518
FOUR DUKES (2)			
	Baby Won't You Please Come		
	Home/John Henry	1960	Imperial 5653
FOUR EKKOS			
	My Love I Give/Toodaloo		
	Kangaroo	1958	RIP 12558
	Hand In Hand/Think Twice	1959	Label 2022
FOUR EKKOS (BERNIE CAMPBELL & THE)			
	Baby You Belong To Me/		
	Will I Ever Find My Baby	1961	Fine 26574
FOUR EKKOS (JERRY ENGLER & THE)			
	Unfaithful One/Sputnik		
	(Satellite Girl)	1957	Brunswick 55037
FOUR ELDORADOS (AKA EL DORADOS (1))			
	A Lonely Boy/Go! Little Susie	1958	Academy 8138
FOUR EMBERS			
	But Beautiful/You've Been		
	Away Too Long	1963	Smash 1846

Artist	Song	Year	Label
FOUR EPICS (AKA EXODUS/AKA VESPERS)			
	I'm On My Way To Love/When		
	The Music Ends	1962	Heritage 109
	Again/I Love You Diane	1963	Laurie 3155
	How I Wish I Was Single		
	Again/Dance Joanne	1963	Laurie 3183
	Mr. Cupid/When I Walk With		
	My Angel (by the Vespers)	1963	Swan 4156
FOUR ESCORTS (1)			
	Love Me/Loop De Loop Mambo	1954	RCA 5886
FOUR ESCORTS (2)			
	My Special Girl/Don't You		
	Remember	1961	Skyla 1113
FOUR ESCORTS (3) (DAVE PASSECALLO & THE)			
	By The Fire/Baby, Where Are		
	You?	1961	Bi-Mi 102
FOUR ESQUIRES			
	Follow Me/Summer Vacation	1956	Pilgrim 717
	Follow Me/Land Of You And Me	1958	Paris 526
	Can't Help Falling In Love/		
	Merry-Go-Round Of Home	1962	Terrace 7502
FOUR EVERS			
	Dream Land/I'm Gonna Tell		
	Your Mother	1978	Crystal Ball 121
FOUR EXCEPTIONS			
	A Sad Goodbye	1966	Parkway
FOUR FEATHERS (GENE FORREST & THE)			
	Wiggle/Dubio	1954	Aladdin 3224
FOUR FELLOWS			
	Soldier Boy (rec. live, 1956)/		
	Skylark (rec. 1980)	1980	U.G.H.A. 15
FOUR FELLOWS (1)			
	I Tried/Bend Of The River	1954	Derby 862
	I Wish I Didn't Know You/		
	I Know Love	1955	Glory 231
	Soldier Boy/Take Me Back, Baby	1955	Glory 234
	Angels Say/In The Rain	1955	Glory 236
	Fallen Angel/Hold 'Em, Joe	1956	Glory 238
	Petticoat Baby/I'm Past Sixteen		
	(with Bette McLaurin)	1956	Glory 241
	Darling You/Please Don't		
	Deprive Me Of Love	1956	Glory 242
	I Sit In My Window/Please		
	Play My Song	1956	Glory 244
	You Don't Know Me/You		
	Sweet Girl	1956	Glory 248
	Give Me Back My Broken		
	Heart/Loving You, Darling	1957	Glory 250
FOUR FELLOWS (1) (BETTE MCLAURIN & THE)			
	Grow Old Along With Me/		
	So Will I	1955	Glory 233
	Just Come A Little Bit Closer/		
	A Love That's True	1955	Glory 237
FOUR FELLOWS (1) (CATHY RYAN & THE)			
	24 Hours A Day/With You	1955	King 1495
FOUR FELLOWS (1) (MISS TONI BANKS & THE)			
	Johnny The Dreamer/		
	You're Still In My Heart	1957	Glory 263
FOUR FELLOWS (1) (SCATMAN CRUTHERS & THE)			
	I Want You To Be My Girl	N/A	Tops EP 285
FOUR FELLOWS (2)			
	Break My Bones/Stop Crying	1953	Tri-Boro 101
	Remember/That Kiss You		
	Gave Me	1955	Nestor 27
	That's Why I Pray/The City	1962	Ad Lib 0208
	Happy Honeymoon/Memories		
	(by the Decoys (2))	1963	Aljon 1261
FOUR FIFTHS			
	Come On Girl (Be Mine)/		
	After Graduation	1963	Hudson 8101
	If You Still Want Me/Have You		
	Ever Loved A Girl	1966	Columbia 43913
FOUR FLAMES (AKA HOLLYWOOD FLAMES)			
	Tabarin/W-I-N-E	1951	Fidelity 3001
	The Bounce Pt. 2/		
	The Bounce Pt. 1 (instrumental		
	by Sherman Williams)	1951	Fidelity 3002
FOUR FLAMES (AKA HOLLYWOOD FLAMES) (BOBBY DAY & THE)			
	Wheel Of Fortune/Later	1952	Specialty 423
FOUR FLARES			
	Jump Back Honey Ride/		
	Riders In The Sky	1958	Edison International 402

Artist	Song	Year	Label
FOUR FLICKERS			
	Is There A Way/Yo Yo	1959	Lee 1002
	Long Tall Texan/Aimez-Moi	1959	Lee 1003
FOUR FRIENDS			
	My Young And Foolish Heart/		
	Save This Fallen Heart	1957	Fee Bee 225
FOUR GABRIELS			
	Gloria/Recess In Heaven	1948	World 2505
FOUR GEMS			
	Outside Of Paradise/Darling		
	You Know	1971	Broadcast 4/Broadcast 1001
FOUR GENTS			
	On Bended Knee/Linda	1957	Park 113
	You're Just A Little Too Young/		
	Please Don't Ask Me	1961	Nite Owl 50
FOUR GRADUATES (AKA HAPPENINGS)			
	May I Have This Dance/Caught		
	In A Lie	1978	Crystal Ball 116
	Your Initials/Every Year About		
	This Time	1978	Crystal Ball 119
	Lovely Way To Spend An		
	Evening/Picture Of An Angel	1963	Rust 5062
	Candy Queen/A Boy In Love	1964	Rust 5084
FOUR GUYS (1)			
	This May Be Your Life/By Bye		
	For Just A While	1955	Wing 90036
	Drive-In Rock/Do Unto Others	1956	Mercury 70908
FOUR GUYS (2)			
	You Took My Heart By Surprise/		
	You Didn't Have To Tell Me	1959	Kent 311
FOUR GUYS (3)			
	Teardrops From My Eyes/		
	Hey Junior	1963	Stride 5001
FOUR HAVEN KNIGHTS (AKA HAVEN KNIGHTS)			
	In My Lonely Room/I'm Just		
	A Dreamer	1956	Atlas 1066/Josie 824 (57)/
			Angletone 1066 (58)
	Why Go On Pretending?/		
	Just To Be In Love	1957	Atlas 1092/Angletone
			1092 (58)
FOUR HAVENS			
	What Time Is It?/Let's Have		
	A Good Time Baby	1965	Veep 1214
FOUR HITS & A MISS			
	She Wobbles (All Night Long)	1962	Flamingo
	Do It	1962	Flamingo 540
FOUR HOLIDAYS			
	Nobody Loves You Like-A Me/		
	Who Can Say	1959	United Artists 163
			(unreleased)
	I Don't Wanna Go To School/		
	Love Ya	1960	Verve 10204/Verve 740
FOUR HOLLIDAYS			
	Step By Step/Grandma Bird	1963	Markie 109
	I Won't Need You	1963	Markie 115
FOUR HORSEMEN			
	A Dear John Letter/No Story		
	Unturned	1953	MGM 11566
	My Heartbeat/A Long Long Time	1958	United Artists 134
FOUR HUES			
	Rock-A-Bye/Take Me Out Of		
	Your Heart	1956	Crown 159
FOUR IMPERIALS			
	My Girl/Teen Age Fool	1958	Chant 101
	Look Up And Live/Give Me		
	One More Chance	1958	Fox 102
	Lazy Bonnie/Let's Make A Scene	1958	Lorelei 4444/Dot 15737 (58)
	Valley Of Tears/Time Out	1959	Dial 101
	Santa's Got A Coupe De Ville/		
	Seven Lonely Days	1959	Twirl 2005
FOUR INTERNS			
	I'm Troubled/It's All Right Now	1955	Federal 12239
FOUR INTRUDERS (AKA INTRUDERS)			
	Come Home Soon/I'm Sold	1961	Gowen 1401
	My Baby/This Is My Song	1961	Gowen 1404
	Goodnight/Sweet Girl	1979	King Tut 179
FOUR J'S (1) (I.E. JAMES, JOSEPH, JIMMY & JOE) (AKA FABULOUS FOUR)			
	Dreams Are A Dime A Dozen/		
	Kissin' At The Drive-In	1958	Herald 528
	Rock And Roll Age/Be Nice,		
	Don't Fight	1958	United Artists 125

Artist / Song	Year	Label
Here I Am Broken Hearted/		
She Said That She Loved Me	1964	Jamie 1267
By Love Possessed/My Love,		
My Love	1964	Jamie 1274
Dreamin'/Love My Love	1969	Congress 6003
FOUR J'S (2)		
The Nursery/Will You Be My		
Love	1963	4-J 506
FOUR JACKS		
You Met A Fool/Goodbye Baby	1952	Federal 12075
I'll Be Home Again/The Last Of		
The Good Rockin' Men	1952	Federal 12087
Darling I'm Lonesome For		
You/You're In Love With		
Someone Else	1952	MGM 11179-A
Don't Be Angry	1956	Gateway 1121
R-O-C-K/Gum Drop	1956	Gateway 1136
Only You	1956	Gateway 1147
The Great Pretender/Woman		
In Love	1956	Gateway 1151
My Prayer	1956	Gateway 1183-B
Too Much	1956	Gateway 1204
Little Darlin'	1956	Gateway 1211-A/Big 4 Hits EP 213
Come Go With Me/Rockabilly	1956	Gateway 1213
I Can't Forget/Becky Ann	1958	Rebel 1313
Whispering Bells	N/A	Big 4 Hits EP 213
FOUR JACKS (BEN JOE ZEPPA & THE)		
Why Do Fools Fall In Love/		
No Not Much	1956	Gilmar 278
FOUR JACKS (BILL ERWIN & THE)		
Too Young To Be Blue/		
Too Young To Be Blue	1960	Pel 501/Fairlane 21020 (62)
I've Waited Long Enough/		
Like Man It's Spring	1960	Pel 601
FOUR JACKS (JANET SHAY & THE)		
Busy Bee/If And When	1960	Alcar 1502
FOUR JACKS (LIL GREENWOOD & THE)		
My Last Hour/Monday		
Morning Blues	1952	Federal 12082
Never Again/Grandpa Can		
Boogie Too	1952	Federal 12093
FOUR JACKS (MAC BURNEY & THE)		
Tired Of Your Sexy Ways/		
This Is My Last Affair	1955	Aladdin 3274
Let Me Get Next To You/		
Walking And Crying	1956	Hollywood 1058
FOUR JACKS (SHIRLEY HAVEN & THE)		
Troubles Of My Own/Stop		
Foolin' Around	1952	Federal 12092
FOUR JACKS (with CORA WILLIAMS & SHIRLEY HAVEN)		
I Ain't Comin' Back Anymore/		
Sure Clue For The Blues	1952	Federal 12079
FOUR JAYS		
Class Ring/Weird	1958	MGM 12687
FOUR JEWELS (AKA IMPALAS (3)/AKA RUBIES (1)) (FEMALE)		
Dapper Dan/Loaded With		
Goodies	1963	Checker 1039
Loaded With Goodies/Fire	1963	Start 638 (same # used twice)
Johnny Jealousy/Someone		
Special	1963	Start 638 (same # used twice)
Time For Love/That's What They		
Put Erasers On Pencils For	1964	Checker 1069
Opportunity/Gotta Find A Way	1964	Dimension 1034
But I Do/Smokey Joe	1964	Dimension 1048
All That's Good/I Love Me		
And You	1964	Start 641
Baby It's You/She's Wrong		
For You Baby	1964	Tec 3007
FOUR JOES		
Lifetime Of Happiness/Uh-Huh	1957	Darl 1005
FOUR JOKERS (1)		
Caring/Tell Me Now	1954	MGM 11815
FOUR JOKERS (2)		
You Did/Transfusion	1956	Diamond 3004
FOUR JOKERS (3)		
Written In The Stars/The Run		
Around	1958	Sue 703

Artist / Song	Year	Label
FOUR JOKERS (4)		
Your Decision/We Met In		
Catalina	1959	Crystalette 730
FOUR JOKERS (5)		
Uggaboo/She's A Flirt	1962	Amy 832
FOUR KAYS (LEROY TAYLOR & THE)		
I'll Understand/Takin' My Time	N/A	Shrine 101
FOUR KINGS (1)		
Hurry Back Home/She Don't		
Want Your Rocking (no group)	1952	Fortune 807
My Head Goes Acting Up/		
You Don't Mean Me, Right?	1954	Fortune 811
Doo-Li-Op/Rose Of Tangier	1955	Fortune 517
Willingly/It's Not The End Of		
The World	1956	Fraternity 752
Walking Along/Rag Mop	1958	Stomper Time 1163
Early In The Morning/I Want		
To Be There	1963	M.O.C. 655
Hallelujah/The Graveyard Is		
Waiting	N/A	Gotham 763
FOUR KINGS (1) (BEN & THE)		
Forever Mine/Imprison Me Baby	1961	Revival 635
FOUR KINGS (1) (WILLIE MITCHELL & THE)		
Walking At Your Will/Tell It To		
Me Baby	1958	Stomper Time 1160
FOUR KINGS (2)		
You Never Knew/Do You		
Want To Rock?	1954	Jax 323
FOUR KINGS (3)		
I Don't Want Nobody But You/		
Guess Who	1960	Cee Jay 580
FOUR KINGS (4) (RAY AGEE & THE)		
Pray For Me/Swingin' Partner	1960	Check 102/Plaid 105
FOUR KINGS (5) (SUE TORNAY & THE)		
You Went Away/Tell Me	1961	Dore 594
FOUR KINGS (6)		
One Night/Lonely Lover	1964	Canadian American 173
FOUR KINGS AND A QUEEN		
Just A Fool	1952	United (unreleased)
Lean Pretty Baby	1952	United (unreleased)
Wheelin' And Dealin'	1952	United (unreleased)
Grass In Your Own Backyard	1952	United (unreleased)
FOUR KITTENS ("FAT MAN" MATTHEWS & THE)		
When Boy Meets Girl/Later Baby	1952	Imperial 5211
FOUR KNIGHTS		
La La/Tic-Toc	1962	Triode 104
FOUR LABELS		
Susie/Lookin'	1958	Gralow 5524
FOUR LARKS		
Go, Baby, Go/Night And Day	1954	Guyden 707
It's Unbelievable/Keep		
Climbing Brothers	1967	Uptown 761
FOUR LOCKS		
A Little Bit Of Soap	N/A	Uptown 761
FOUR LORDS		
Pancakes/Angel From Nowhere	1978	Crystal Ball 124
FOUR LOVERS (REF FOUR SEASONS)		
The Girl In My Dreams/You're		
The Apple Of My Eye	1956	RCA 6518
Honey Love/Please Don't		
Leave Me	1956	RCA 6519
Be Lovey Dovey/Jambalaya	1956	RCA 6646
Happy Am I/Never Never	1956	RCA 6768
Pucker Up/My Life For Your		
Love	1957	Epic 9255
Shake A Hand/The Stranger	1957	RCA 6812
The Stranger/Night Train		
(instrumental)	1957	RCA 6819
I Want A Girl Just Like The		
Girl That Married Dear Old Dad	1957	RCA LP 1317
Such A Night	1957	RCA LP 1317
For Sentimental Reasons	1957	RCA LP 1317
Lawdy Miss Clawdy	1957	RCA LP 1317
It's Too Soon To Know	1957	RCA LP 1317
Memories Of You	1957	RCA LP 1317
Cimarron	1957	RCA LP 1317
White Christmas	1957	RCA LP 1317
San Antonio Rose	1957	RCA LP 1317
This Is My Story	1957	RCA LP 1317
It May Be Wrong/Please Take		
A Chance	1959	Decca 30994

Artist / Song	Year	Label
FOUR LYRICS		
It's Not For Me To Say	1964	Phillips 40218
FOUR MARKSMEN		
The Birth Of Love/One Love	1958	Radio 107
FOUR MINTS		
What'Cha Gonna Do/Night Air	1956	Choctaw 8002/Imperial 5432 (57)
Gold/Ruby Baby	1957	Decca 30465
Hey, Little Neil/Teenage Wonderland	1958	NRC 003
You Belong To My Heart/Wolf	1958	NRC 011
Tomorrow Night/Pina Colada	1959	NRC 037
FOUR MOST (1) (AKA 4 MOST)		
Ooh! Baby It Scares Me/Let A Smile Be Your Umbrella	1956	Dawn 220
FOUR MOST (2)		
The Breeze And I/I Love You	1959	Milo 107/Relic 501 (63)
FOUR NATURALS (AKA NATURALS (1))		
How Strange/Blue Moon	1958	Red Top 113
I Hear A Rhapsody/When I'm In Your Arms	1959	Red Top 119
The Thought Of You Darling/Long Long Ago	1959	Red Top 125/Arcade 1004 (77)
FOUR NUGGETS		
No Time For Lovin'/Shortcut To A Heartache	1963	Songbird 204
FOUR OF A KIND		
Dedicated To You/Rock My Heart	1956	Melba 110
Fools Fall In Love/Dreamy Eyes	1957	Melba 117
You Were Made To Love/Love Every Moment	1958	Cameo 154
It's Better That Way/I Care For You	1958	Chancellor 1012/Bomarc 302 (59)
Next Fall/U-Turn Baby	1961	Rex 104
FOUR OF US		
Loving A Girl Like You/I'm Some Kind Of Wonderful	1961	Adore 902/Bruce
I Don't Need No One/Iga Diga Doo	1963	Brunswick 55288
Be Mine	N/A	Modern 222
FOUR PAGES		
Autograph Book/Much As I Do	1962	Plateau 101
FOUR PALMS		
Consideration/Jeanie, Joanie, Shirley, Toni	1957	Aladdin 3411
FOUR PALS (1)		
If I Can't Have The One I Love/I Flipped	1955	Royal Roost 610
No One Ever Loved Me/Can't Stand It Any Longer	1956	Royal Roost 616
FOUR PALS (2) (DEAN BEARD & THE)		
On My Mind Again/Rakin' And Scrapin'	1957	Atlantic 1137
FOUR PALS (3)		
Long Black Stockings/Yours To Possess	1959	Roulette 4127
FOUR PEARLS		
Look At Me/It's Almost Tomorrow	1960	Dolton 26
FOUR PENNIES (1) (AKA CHIFFONS) (FEMALE)		
When The Boy's Happy/Hockaday Pt. 1	1963	Rust 5070
My Block/Dry Your Eyes	1963	Rust 5071/Collectables LP 5042
FOUR PENNIES (2) (MALE)		
You Have No Time To Lose/You're A Gas	1964	Brunswick 55304
FOUR PERSUASIONS		
Echo/Fool No More	1972	Pay-4-Play 100
FOUR PHARAOHS (AKA COLUMBUS PHARAOHS/AKA KING PHARAOH & THE EGYPTIANS)		
Pray For Me/The Move Around	1957	Ransom 100
Give Me Your Love/China Girl	1958	Ransom 101/Paradise 109 (58)
Is It Too Late/It Was A Night Like This	1958	Ransom 102
FOUR PIPS (POP & THE)		
For You/Teenage Rock	1959	Mercedes 5001
FOUR PLAID THROATS		
My Inspiration/The Message	1953	Mercury 70143
FOUR RIFFS (JULIE LANG & THE)		
Exactly Like You/I Be Good To You	1955	Campus 104
FOUR RIVERS (LITTLE LYNN & THE)		
Send My Records C.O.D./I Walk In Circles	1962	Music City 845
FOUR SAINTS		
Window Of Dreams/When I'm With You Again	1970	Era 701
FOUR SEASONS (GIGI PARKER & THE)		
Lonely Girl Blue/Someday, Someday	1962	Coral 62314
FOUR SENSATIONS		
Heaven Knows/Believing In You	1951	Rainbow 157
FOUR SEVILLES		
Heart 'n' Soul/What Are You Doing New Year's Eve	1985	Starlight 30
Heartbeat	N/A	Rainbow 157
Little Maiden/Oh Baby Don't	N/A	Starlight 10
In Between Tears/Darling	N/A	Starlight 12
If I/What's Your Name	N/A	Starlight 3
If You Didn't Mean It/Melba	N/A	Starlight 5
Heartbeat/You're Mine	N/A	Starlight 6
I'm Not A Know It All/Heartbreaker	N/A	Starlight 8
FOUR SHADES OF RHYTHM		
My Blue Walk/Baby I'm Gone	1949	Old Swingmaster 13
I Can Dream/Master Of Me	1949	Old Swingmaster 23
Yesterdays/So There	1952	Chance 1126
I Don't Stand A Ghost Of A Chance/Come Here	1958	Mad 1206
FOUR SHOTS		
Love Hit Me And I Hollered/Get Off The Fence Hortence	1955	Cadillac 154
FOUR SIERRAS (AKA SIERRAS (1))		
Chance/Stormy Weather	1963	Mail Call 2333/2334
FOUR SKINS (EDDIE GEE & THE)		
Chapel Of Cream Cheese/Havertown Doo Doo Hoe Down	1974	Lost Cause 200
FOUR SOUNDS		
Afraid/Tall Lanky Papa	1957	Celeste 3010
You Stole My Heart/Noisy Clock	1957	Celeste 3013
When I Find My Love/Someone To Show Me The Way	1961	Federal 12421
It Won't Be A Sin/The Change In You	1961	Tuff
The Ring/Peter's Gun	1961	Tuff 1
Nobody Wants Me/Mama Ubangi Bangi	1962	Ran-Dee 104
FOUR SOUNDS (LOIS BLAINE & THE)		
I Need You So/Here Am I	1963	Open-G 00
FOUR SPARKS		
My Sweet Juanita/Out Of This World	1958	ABC 9906
The Same Way/The Key To My Heart	1958	Cleff-Tone 152
FOUR SPEEDS		
I Need You, Baby/The Girls Back Home	1954	DeLuxe 6070
FOUR SPORTSMEN		
Surrender/Franklin Delano Brown	1960	Sunnybrook 1
Lucille/Mother In Law	1961	Sunnybrook 2
Pitter Patter/Git Up Paint	1961	Sunnybrook 4
Sixty Minute Man/Jelly Roll Brown	1962	Sunnybrook 5
If Your Heart Can Take It/Records, Records, Records	1962	Sunnybrook 6
FOUR STARLINGS		
Not Too Young/Canadian Sunset (by the Adorations)	1972	Dreamtone 202
FOUR STARS		
Win Or Lose/Honey, I Could Fall In Love	1954	King 1382
My Sentimental Heart/The Chapel By The Sea	1958	Kay-Y 66781
Play It Again	1961	Bamboo 512
FOUR STEPS OF RHYTHM (BILL JOHNSON & THE)		
Right To Love/You Better Dig It	1959	Talos 402
FOUR STUDENTS		
So Near And Yet So Far/		

Artist Song	Year	Label
Hot Rotten Soda Pop (Oh, My Toe)	1955	Groove 0110
FOUR STUDENTS (BIG JOHN GREER & THE)		
A Man And A Woman/Blam (instrumental)	1955	Groove 0131
I'll Never Stop Loving You	1955	RCA (unreleased)
FOUR STUDENTS (CHARLES CALHOUN & THE)		
Jamboree/My Pigeon's Gone	1956	Groove 0149
FOUR STUDENTS (LIL MCKENZIE & THE)		
Run Along/The Others Like I	1955	Groove 0113
FOUR STUDENTS (OSCAR BLACK & SUE ALLEN WITH THE)		
Think Of Tomorrow/Set A Wedding Day	1955	Groove 0130
FOUR STUDENTS (PIANO RED WITH THE)		
Goodbye/Six O'Clock Bounce (no group)	1955	Groove 0118
FOUR STUDENTS (TOMMY BROWN & THE)		
The Thrill Is Gone/Gambler's Prayer	1956	Groove 0143
FOUR STUDENTS (VARETTA DILLARD & THE)		
Darling, Listen To The Words Of This Song/Mama Don't Want (What Poppa Don't Want) (no group)	1956	Groove 0139
FOUR STUDENTS (VARETTA DILLARD & THE)		
Cherry Blossom/I'm Gonna Tell My Daddy	1956	Groove 0152
FOUR STUDENTS (ZILLA MAYS & THE)		
Come Back To Me/Right Now	1955	Groove 0127
FOUR TEENS		
Spark Plug/Go Little Go Cart	1958	Challenge 59021
FOUR TEES		
I Said, She Said/Like My Baby	1964	Vee Jay 627
FOUR TEMPS (PEE WEE CRAYTON WITH ESTHER & THE)		
Give Me One More Chance/Look Up And Live	1958	Fox 102
FOUR TEMPTATIONS (AKA TEMPTATIONS (2))		
Cathy/Rock And Roll Baby	1958	ABC 9920
FOUR THOUGHTS		
When I'm With You/Kisses And Roses	N/A	Womar 103
FOUR TIERS (JIMMY KEMPER & THE)		
Lonely For Kathy/I'm Free To Choose	1964	Le Mans 2
FOUR TONES (DUSTY BROOKS & THE)		
Heaven On Fire/Tears And Wine (by Juanita Brown)	1953	Sun 182
FOUR TOPS (1)		
Could It Be You?/Kiss Me Baby	1956	Chess 1623
Lonely Summer/Ain't That Love	1960	Columbia 41755/ Columbia 43356 (65)
Pennies From Heaven/Where You Are	1962	Riverside 4534
FOUR TOPS (2) (CAROLYN HAYES & THE)		
Baby Say You Love Me/Really	1956	Chateau 2001
FOUR TOPS (2) (DELORES CARROLL & THE)		
Everybody Knows/I Just Can't Keep The Tears From Tumblin' Down	1956	Chateau 2002
FOUR TOWNS		
I'll Follow You/Do Do Baby	N/A	A1 1001
FOUR TOWNSMEN		
It Wasn't So Long Before/Sometimes	1960	Artflow 145
It Wasn't So Long Before (Graduation Is Here)/Sometimes	1963	Artflow 145
FOUR TRIUMPHS		
I've Waited All My Life For You/Rivers In The Sky	1958	Mira 2050
FOUR TROYS		
In The Moonlight/Suddenly You Want To Dance	1959	Freedom 44013
FOUR TRUMPETS (SUSIE & THE)		
Starry Eyes/Blue Little Girl	1962	United Artists 471
FOUR UNIQUES		
Looking For A Love/Too Young	1961	Adam 9002
Island Of Love/Good Luck Charm	1961	Deer 3002
She's The Only Girl/Twistin' Around	1962	Adam 9004

Artist Song	Year	Label
FOUR VAGABONDS		
P.S. I Love You/Lazy Country Side	1953	Lloyds 102
FOUR VANNS		
So Young And So Pretty/Sha-Bee-Dah-Ah Ding	1956	Vik 0246
FOUR VIBES		
You're All I Live For/You Got Soul	1962	Swa-Ray 1001
FOUR WHEELS		
Uh Huh/Come On Baby (recorded in 1961)	1992	Park Ave. 6
FOUR WHEELS (FB TERRI DEAN)		
I Blew Out The Flame/I'm Confessin' That I Love You	1959	Laurel 1003
FOUR WHEELS (NICK THERRY & THE)		
Grateful/Adios, My Pretty Baby	1956	Spin-It 108
FOUR WINDS (1) (SONNY WOODS & THE)		
I Promise/Do You Love Me?	1956	Middle-Tone 008
Living In A Dream/Do You Mean It	1956	Middle-Tone 013
FOUR WINDS (2)		
Find Someone New/Colorado Moon	1956	Vik 0221
Short Shorts/Five Minutes More	1957	Decor 175
Daddy's Home/Bull Moose Stomp	1961	Warwick 633
Playgirl/Jennifer	1964	Derby 10022/Felsted 8703 (64)
Come Softly To Me/Dear Judy	1978	Crystal Ball 102
Arlene/Goodbye, Maureen	1978	Crystal Ball 105
Doin' The Stroll	N/A	Explorer 713
Old Man River/Popcorn Party	N/A	Sherluck 1027
FOUR WINDS (3) (AKA TOKENS (2))		
Remember Last Summer/Strange Feelings	1964	Swing 100
Let It Ride/One Face In The Crowd	1968	B.T. Puppy 555
FOUR WINDS (4)		
To Love Or Not To Love/Down And Out	1964	Chattahoochie 655
FOUR WINDS (5)		
Mission By The Sea/These Hearts Were Mine	1958	Hide-A-Way 101
FOUR XS (AKA FOUR ZS)		
I'll Remember/Why Can't You Love Me	1960	Lost 103
FOUR YOUNG MEN		
You Been Torturing Me/See Them Laugh	1961	Crest 1076
Sweetheart Of Senior High/Just For Tonight	1961	Crest 1083
Garden In The Rain/That Man Paul	1961	Dore 621
FOUR YOUNG MEN (BOBBY EDWARDS & THE)		
You're The Reason	1961	Crest 1075
FOUR ZS (AKA FOUR XS)		
I'll Remember/Why Can't You Love Me	1960	Lost 20
FOUR-EVERS (AKA FOUR EVERS)		
I Confess/Sooner Or Later	1961	Josie 901
You Belong To Me/Such A Good Night For Dreaming	1962	Columbia 42303/ Jason Scott 4 (80)
One More Time/Everybody South Street	1963	Jamie 1247
Lover Come Back To Me/It's Love	1963	Smash 1853
Come Up In The World/Colors	1964	Chattahoochie 630
Please Be Mine/If I Were A Magician	1964	Smash 1887 (first pressing)
Be My Girl/If I Were A Magician	1964	Smash 1887 (second pressing)
Doo Be Dum/Everlasting	1964	Smash 1921
Stormy/I'm Walkin' (Into The Crowd)	1965	Constellation 151
A Lovely Way To Spend An Evening/The Girl I Wanna Bring Home	1966	Columbia 43886
What A Scene/You Never Had It So Good	1966	Red Bird 10-078

Artist Song	Year	Label	Artist Song	Year	Label
Dreamland/Marianne/You're So Fine/I'm Gonna Tell Your Mother	N/A	Magic Carpet LP 1004	**FRIDAY KNIGHTS** Don't Open That Door/ Poor Mans Roses	1960	Strand 25019
FOURMOST			**FRIENDS (1) (JUNIOR & HIS)**		
Why Can't I Have You/ Twist-A-Taste	1962	Lu Pine 105	ABC's Of Love/Whos's Our Pet, Annette	1960	ABC 10089
Hello Little Girl/Just In Case	1963	Atco 6280	**FRIENDS (2) (GARY CANE & HIS)**		
Respectable/I'm In Love	1963	Atco 6285	C'Mere Baby Doll/The Fight	1960	Shell 717
If You Cry/Little Bit Of Loving	1964	Atco 6307	The Yen Yet Song/I'll Walk The Earth	1960	Shell 719
How Can I Tell Her/You Got That Way	1964	Atco 6317	**FRIENDS (3) (DANTE & HIS) (AKA DANTE & THE EVERGREENS)**		
Why Do Fools Fall In Love/ Girls, Girls, Girls	1966	Capitol 5591	Something Happens/Are You Just My Friend	1961	Imperial 5798
Here There And Everywhere/ You've Changed	1966	Capitol 5738	Miss America/Now I've Got You	1962	Imperial 5827
It Was A Lie/Girl You Do Something	1966	Red Bird 10-071/D.W. 105	**FRIENDS (4) (MORNINGSIDE DRIVE &)** Na-Na-Na/Lazy Love (instrumental)	1973	Laurie 3615
FOURMOSTS (BOBBY MOORE & THE)			**FRONTERA, TOMMY (& GROUP)**		
Dance Of The Land/You Got To Live For Yourself	1964	Fantasy 585	After Tonight/How To Love Him	1960	Rem 103
It Was A Lie/Girl, You Do Something To Me	N/A	D.S. 105	**FRONTIERS (1)** Ding Dong Doo/Why Pretend	1961	King 5481
FOURTEEN KARAT SOUL			Nearest Thing To Heaven/ Oh Nurse	1961	King 5534
The Sun/Boogie Woogie Bugle Boy	1979	Catamount 120	Each Night I Pray/You Shake Me Up	1962	King 5609
Doo-Wopp Disco/(flip is instrumental)	1979	Catamount 737	**FRONTIERS (2) (FB ROGER KOOB)** I Only Have Eyes For You/ Don't Come Crying	1963	Philips 40113
Please Say You Want Me/ The Trouble With Love	1980	Catamount 738	I Just Want You/I'm Still Loving You	1963	Philips 40148
FOXES			You/When I See You	1967	MGM 13722
I Just Might Fall In Love/Tip Toe Through The Tulips With Me	1963	ABC 10446	**FUGITIVES (FB DELNA LEE)** One Year Today/Big Man	1957	Fabor 141
FOXES (JOHNNY FOX & THE)			**FULLER, JERRY (& GROUP)**		
You Laff Too Much/Mountain Dew	1962	Newtime 507	Betty My Angel/Memories Of You	1959	Challenge 59052
FOXETTES (LADY FOX & THE) (FEMALE)			**FULLER, WALTER (& GROUP)**		
I Think Of You/Our Love	1962	Don-El 114	Closer To My Heart/Pecan Mambo	1954	Kicks 4
It Must Be Love/How Are You	1962	Don-El 118	**FULLYLOVE, LEROY (& GROUP)**		
FRANCETTES			I'm So Lonely/Jumpin' Over The Moon	1961	Tandem 7002
Cradle Love/Late In The Evening	1963	Besche 100	**FULTON, SONNY (& GROUP)**		
He's So Sweet/I'm Leaving You	1963	Wolfie 104	A Lovely Relationship/ Here She Comes Now	1959	Lash 1127
FRANCISCANS			**FULTON, SONNY (& HIS GROUP)**		
Mother Please Answer Me/Walk To The Bottom Of The Sea	N/A	JimBo 4001	Honest I Do/Fire	1959	Chelsea 533
FRANK, CAROL (& GROUP)			**FUN-ATICS**		
Emmitt Lee/One Look At You	1957	Excello 2118	Wise Guy/I Wanna Know How To Twist	1962	Versailles 100
Hold Me/One More Chance	1959	Excello 2175	Just In The Nick Of Time/ I Don't Wanna Make You Cry	1967	Select 571
FRATERNITY BROTHERS			**FUNKYTONES (VINCENT MacREE & THE)**		
Big Town/Sad Little Boy	1960	Date 1528	Oh Baby You/My Love For You Will Never Change	1957	Gametime 110
Dearest Darling/Moonlight And Roses	1960	Verve 10195	**FUNNY BUNNIES**		
FRATERNITY MEN			Midnight Sun/Sick Song	1960	Dore 542
Little Star/Lynne	1964	Courier 114	**FURNESS BROTHERS**		
FRAZIER, RAY (& GROUP)			Paul Revere/I'm In The Mood For Love	1952	MGM 11356
Days/Turn Me On	1955	Excel 111	Please Don't Call Me Fool/ King Of The Blues	1957	Prep 107
Walking With My Love	1956	Excel 111	You Name It/I Want A Date	1960	Future 1002
FRAZIER, RAY (BB THE MOONRAYS)			One Little Moment With You/ Duke's Place	1960	Rae-Cox 104
All My Love/Fat Mouth	1956	Excel 112	Only Fate/Lookin' Out The Window	1964	Melmar 114
FRECKLES			Say It Isn't So/King Of The Blues	1964	Melmar 116
Little Star/Freckle Face	1961	Madison 158	**FURNESS BROTHERS (AL BERRY & THE)**		
FREDERICK, TOMMY (& GROUP)			Please Don't Call Me A Fool/ King Of The Blues	1964	Melmar 115
Sundown/Where'd Ja Go	1960	Coral 62170	**FURYS (1) (RAY & THE)**		
FREEDOMS			Kiss And Run Driver	1961	Coed 558
Ten Steps To Love/You Lied	1964	Constellation 105	**FURYS (2)**		
FREELANCERS (DAN WILLIAMS & THE)			Zing! Went The Strings Of My Heart/Never More	1963	Mach IV 112
High School Flame/Why	N/A	Beth 20/Freelance 20	If There's A Next Time/ Another Fella	1963	Mach IV 114
FREELOADERS (1) (BOBBY SUE & THE)			I Really Feel Good	1963	Mach IV 115
It Takes A Lot Of Love/ Relief Check	1955	Harlem 2335	I Lost My Baby	1963	Mach IV 118
FREELOADERS (2) (LITTLE PRINCE & THE)			Lost Caravan	1963	Manor 51621
Nursery Love/Sat It	1973	M&M 1263	Anything For You/Cat 'N' Mouse	1963	World Pacific 386
FREESE, HARRISON (& GROUP)					
Earth Angel/Mary Lou	N/A	Freshman 302			
FREEWAYS					
My Baby Loves Me/I've Been A Fool	1965	Hugo 11723			
FRESANDOS					
Your Last Goodbye/I Mean Really (by Eddie Bartell)	1958	Star-X 501			
FRETTS					
Full Moon Above/Rock'n Baby	1959	Blue Moon 414			

Artist Song	Year	Label
Gone In The Night	N/A	Fleetwood 4569
FUTURES (1)		
Breaking Up/Our Thing	N/A	Amjo 3033
FUTURES (2) (VIC FONTAINE & THE)		
Rosina	N/A	Adam & Eve LP 504
FUTURETONES		
Roll On/I Know	1959	Tress 1/2
FUTURETONES (JIM HOLIDAY & THE)		
All I Want Is You/Voice Of		
The Drums	1958	4 Star 1720
FYDELLS		
That Certain One/Pandora	1959	Camelia 100
G-CLEFS		
Ka-Ding-Dong/Darla My Darlin'	1956	Pilgrim 715
'Cause You're Mine/		
Please Write While I'm Away	1956	Pilgrim 720
Symbol Of Love/		
Love Her In The Mornin' And		
Love Her In The Night Time	1957	Paris 502
Is This The Way/Zing Zang Zoo	1957	Paris 506
I Understand (Just How You		
Feel)/Little Girl, I Love You	1961	Terrace 7500
I'll Remember All You Kisses/		
Ka-Ding-Dong	1962	Ditto 503
A Girl Has To Know/Lad	1962	Terrace 7503
Make Up Your Mind/They'll		
Call Me Away	1962	Terrace 7507
Lover's Prayer (All Through		
The Night)/Sitting In The		
Moonlight	1962	Terrace 7510
All My Trials/The Big Rain	1963	Terrace 7514
I Believe In All I Feel (Je Croix		
En Tout A Que Je Resent)/To		
The Winner Goes The Prize	1964	Regina 1314
Angel, Listen To Me/Nobody		
But Betty	1964	Regina 1319
On The Other Side Of Town/		
I Have	1965	Veep 1218
Little Lonely Boy/Party '66	1966	Loma 2034
I Can't Stand It/The Whirlwind	1966	Loma 2048
This Time/On The Other Side		
Of Town	1966	Veep 1226
The Whirlwind/I Can't Stand It	1966	Veep 2048
G-NOTES (FEMALE)		
I Would/Ronnie	1958	Tender 510/Jackpot 48000 (59)
If They Only Knew/Say You're		
Mine	1959	Form 102
Johnny, Johnny, Johnny/Broken		
Down Merry-Go-Round	1959	Guyden 2012
GADABOUTS		
By The Waters Of Minnetonka/		
Giuseppe Mandolino	1954	Mercury 70495
Go Boom Boom/Oochi Pachi	1955	Mercury 70581
Two Things I Love/Glass Heart	1955	Wing 90008
Teen Age Rock/If You Only		
Had A Heart	1955	Wing 90043
Busy Body Rock/All My Love		
Belongs To You	1956	Mercury 70823/Wing 90062 (56)
Stranded In The Jungle/		
Blues Train	1956	Mercury 70898
GAILTONES (FEMALE)		
Lover Boy/Please Don't Go	1958	Decca 30726
GAINORS		
The Secret/Gonna Rock Tonite	1958	Cameo 151
You Must Be An Angel/Follow		
Me	1958	Red Top 110/Cameo 156 (59)
Message With Flowers/		
She's My Lollipop	1959	Mercury 71466
She's Gone/Please Consider	1960	Mercury 71569
I'm In Love With You/Nothing		
Means More To Me	1960	Mercury 71630/Mercury 71632
This Is A Perfect Moment/		
Where I Want To Be	1961	Tally-Ho 102
Tell Him/Darlin'	1961	Tally-Ho 105
GALABOOCHIES		
She Doesn't Care	N/A	Staff 108
GALAXIES (3)		
Just Another Date/Little Man	1976	Ronnie 201

Artist Song	Year	Label
GALAXIES (1) (BB EDDIE COCHRAN ON GUITAR)		
My Tattle Tale/Love Has Its		
Ways	1960	Guaranteed 216
GALAXIES (2)		
The Big Triangle/Until The		
Next Time	1960	Capitol 4427
Tremble/My Blue Heaven	1961	Dot 16212
Dear Someone/The Leopard	1961	Richie 458
GALAXYS		
A Lover's Prayer/Jelly Bean	1959	Carthay 103
GALE, SUNNY (& GROUP)		
Church Bells May Ring/		
My Foolish Heart	1960	Warwick 540
GALENS		
Baby I Do Love You/Love Bells	1963	Challenge 59212
Stranger In Paradise/Chinese		
Lanterns	1964	Challenge 59253
Young Dreams/I Love You		
More Than You Know	1966	Challenge 59402
GALES (1)		
Don't Let The Sun Catch You		
Crying/My Eyes Keep Me		
In Trouble	1955	J.V.B. 34
Darling Patricia/All Is Well,		
All Is Well	1955	J.V.B. 35/J.O.B. 3001
GALES (2) (AKA MARVELS (2)/AKA SENATORS)		
Guiding Angel/If I Could Forget	1958	Mel-O 111/113
Josephine/If I Could Forget	1958	Mel-O 113
I Love You/Squeeze Me	1960	Winn 916
Tommy/Around The Clock With		
You	1963	Debra 1002
GALLAHADS		
Ooh Ah/Careless	1955	Capitol 3060
Do You Believe Me/If It Wasn't		
For You	1955	Capitol 3175
The Fool/The Morning Mail	1956	Jubilee 5252
If I Give You My Word/Take		
My Love	1956	Jubilee 5259
One Love Alone/Take Back		
My Ring	1957	Vik 0291
Best Wishes/Steady Man	1958	Vik 0316
Silently/Barracuda	1958	Vik 0332
Keeper Of Dreams/Sad Girl	1960	Beechwood 3000/Starla 15
Be Fair/I'm Without A Girl Friend	1960	Del-Fi 4148
Lonely Guy/Jo Jo The Big Wheel	1960	Donna 1322/Del-Fi 4137 (60)
Gone/So Long	1961	Nite Owl 20
Why Do Fools Fall In Love/Gone	1961	Rendezvous 153
Have Love, Will Travel/		
My Offering	1964	Sea Crest 6005
GALLAHADS (JIMMY PIPKIN & THE)		
This Letter To You/The Answer		
To Love	1962	Donna 1361
GALLAHADS (WITH THE COUNTS)		
Have Love Will Travel/		
My Offering	1964	Sea Crest 6005
GALLANT MEN		
Foreign Girl/Lost Romance		
(by the Ultimates (2))	1962	Ford 117
GALLANT, BILLY (BB THE ROULETTES)		
Scribbling On The Wall/		
Thinking, Hoping And Wishing	1961	Dee Dee 501
Thinking, Hoping And Wishing/		
If You'd Only Be My Love	1962	Goldisc G6
GALLAWAY, BILL (& GROUP)		
It's For Real	N/A	Clarke 1605
GALLEONS		
I Played The Fool/Pick Up	1959	Vita 184
GANG (TEDDY FIELD & THE)		
When We Get Married	N/A	Vita 184
GANTS		
My Unfaithful Love/		
Happening After School	1957	Aladdin 3387
GARDENIAS (1)		
Flaming Love/My Baby's Tops	1956	Federal 12284
I'm Laughing At You/Houdini	1958	Hi-Q 5005
GARDENIAS (2)		
What's The Matter With Me/		
Darling It's You, You, You	1962	Fairlane 21019
GARDNER, DON (& GROUP)		
A Dagger In My Chest/This		
Nearly Was Mine	1957	DeLuxe 6133

Artist	Song	Year	Label
	I Don't Want To Go Home/		
	There! I've Said It Again	1957	DeLuxe 6155
GARI, FRANK (& GROUP)			
	There's Lots More Where		
	This Came From/		
	You Better Keep Runnin'	1961	Crusade 1024
	Do-Be-Do	N/A	Ritco 555
GARNETS (1) (BUEL MOORE & THE)			
	Really Really Baby/Sputnik 3	1957	Vita 174
GARNETS (2) (LORD LUTHER & THE)			
	Turn The Key/Teenage Creature		
	(by the Kingsmen)	1958	Frantic 107
GARRETT, SCOTT (BB THE MYSTICS (1))			
	Love Story/Graduation		
	Souvenirs	1959	Laurie 3029
GASSERS			
	Tell Me/Hum De Dum	1956	Cash 1035
	Dody Mighty/Doggonit	1957	Encino 1011
GATES			
	Letter To Dick Clark/Wrapped		
	In Green Made For A Teen	1959	Peach 628
	Summer Night Love/Wedding		
	Bells Gonna Ring	1959	Peach 716
GATES, DAVID (& GROUP)			
	What's This I Hear/		
	You'll Be My Baby	1960	Mala 413
GATORVETTES			
	If It's Tonight/Midnight	1958	Thunder 1001/Bocaldun 1001 (59)
GAY CHARMERS (FEMALE)			
	Groovey Shoes/Dance		
	D-D-Dance	1958	Savoy 1549
	What Can I Do/Get In And		
	Shut The Door	1959	Grand 2001/Swan 4032 (59)
	Walk Beside Him/Why Do You		
	Hurt Me Darling	1959	Savoy 1561
GAY KNIGHTS			
	The Loudness Of My Heart/		
	Angel	1958	Pet 801
GAY NOTES (1) (FEMALE) (AKA HONEY BEES)			
	Hear My Plea/Crossroads	1955	Post 2006
GAY NOTES (2)			
	For Only A Moment/Pu Pu		
	Pa Doo	1955	Drexel 905
GAY NOTES (3)			
	Something Special/Cherie	1959	Vim 501
GAY NOTES (3) (AKA LITTLE CLEM & THE DEW DROPS)			
	Waiting In The Chapel/		
	Plea Of Love	1958	Zynn 504
GAY POPPERS			
	You Better Believe/I Need		
	Your Love	1959	Savoy 1573
	I've Got It/I Want To Know	1960	Fire 1026
	You Got Me Uptight/Please		
	Mr. Cupid	1961	Fire 1039
GAY TUNES (AKA GAYTUNES)			
	Wh-y-y Leave Me This		
	Way-ay-ay/Thrill Of Romance	1953	Timely 1002
	Got You On My Mind/Don't Go	1958	Dome 502
	I'll Always Love You	1987	Relic LP 5071
	I Want You To Love Me Too	1987	Relic LP 5071
GAY-TUNES			
	There Goes A Fool/Get A Mule	1974	Broadcast 1100
GAYLADS			
	Popeye The Sailor Man/Ah So	1961	Audan 120
GAYLARKS			
	Tell Me, Darling/Whole Lot		
	Of Love (by the Rovers (2))	1955	Music City 792
	Romantic Memories/		
	Lil' Dream Girl	1955	Music City 793
	My Greatest Sin/Teenage		
	Mambo	1956	Music City 805
	Mr. Rock 'n' Roll/Church On		
	The Hill	1957	Music City 809
	Somewhere In This World/Just		
	One More Chance (no group)	1957	Music City 812
	Ivy League Clothes/		
	The Doodle-Doo	1958	Music City 819
GAYLES			
	My Boy Flat Top/I Get So Happy	1955	King 4846
	I Had To Lose You/Too Late		
	I Learned	1955	King 4860

Artist	Song	Year	Label
	Yes Sir, That's My Baby/		
	All I Want Is You	1956	Media 1021
GAYLORDS (AKA AMBASSADORS (1)/AKA FOUR ARCS/IMPERIALS (1))			
	Get Mad Baby/Go On Baby	1952	Savoy 852
GAYNELS			
	Chubby/Uh-Huh	1959	Okeh 7114
GAYNOTES (FEMALE)			
	Once He Loved Me/Strange		
	As It May Seem	1958	Aladdin 3424
GAYS			
	Alone At The Harbor/Command		
	My Heart	1959	Decca 30988
GAYTEN, PAUL (& GROUP)			
	Be My Baby/The Music Goes		
	Round And Round	1956	Argo 5257
GAYTUNES (AKA GAY TUNES)			
	I Love You/You Left Me	1957	Joyce 101
	Plea In The Moonlight/Pen Pal	1958	Joyce 106
GAZELLES			
	Honest/Pretty Baby, Baby	1956	Gotham 315
GEE, BILLY (& GROUP)			
	King Of Hearts/If You Have Faith	1959	Coronet 1303
GEE, FRANKIE (& GROUP)			
	Date With The Rain/Ya Ya	1975	Claridge 410
GEE-CHORDS			
	Dreams Come True/		
	Mello-Jello Pt. 2	1974	Romantic Rhythm 101
GEE-CHORDS (DINO & THE)			
	Darling/Baby Can I Take		
	You Home	1977	Robin Hood 152
GEE-TONES (AKA GREGORY HOWARD WITH THE CADILLACS)			
	When In Love (Do As		
	Lovers Do)/Sweet Pea	1956	Gee 1013 (unreleased)
GEES (1) (DICKIE & THE)			
	Foolish Tears/Baby Bye Bye	1958	Argo 5288
GEES (2)			
	It's All Over/Love Is A		
	Beautiful Thing	1966	Port 3011
GEMS (1)			
	'Deed I Do/Talk About The		
	Weather	1954	Drexel 901
	I Thought You'd Care/		
	Kitty From New York City	1954	Drexel 903
	You're Tired Of Love/Ol' Man		
	River	1954	Drexel 904
	One Woman Man/The Darkest		
	Night	1956	Drexel 909
	Till The Day I Die/Monkey		
	Face Baby	1957	Drexel 915
	Ow' You're So Fine/Please		
	Tell Me When	1973	Broadcast 995 (unreleased)
	I Can't Believe/Ow' You're So		
	Fine	1975	Drexel 900 (unreleased)
GEMS (2)			
	I Never Dreamed	1955	20th Century 5037
GEMS (3)			
	Waiting/Please Change Your		
	Mind	1958	Recorte 407
	Nursery Rhymes/The Night Is		
	Over	1958	Win 701
	Crazy Chicken/Hippy Dippy	1961	Mercury 71819
	School Rock/There's No One		
	Like My Love	1961	Pat 101
	Runch Happy	1961	Vergelle 711
GEMS (4) (PEARL WOODS & THE)			
	Think Of Poor Me/I'll Be A		
	Cry Baby	1962	Wall 551
	One More Time/Sloppin'	1962	Wall 552
GEMTONES (EDDIE WOODS & THE)			
	Heaven Was Mine/Prima Vera	1953	Gem 204
GENELLS			
	Linda Please Wait/Rainy Night	1963	Dewey 101
GENERALS (MICKEY FARRELL & THE)			
	Never Too Late/I'm Searchin'	1960	Tammy 1009
GENIES (1) (GM EUGENE PITT)			
	No More Knockin'/On The		
	Edge Of Town	1959	Hollywood 69
	Who's That Knockin'/First Time	1959	Shad 5002
	There Goes That Train/		
	Crazy Love	1960	Warwick 573
	Just Like The Bluebird/		
	Twistin' Pneumonia	1960	Warwick 607

Artist	Song	Year	Label
	Come Here My Darling/		
	Love Love Love	1961	King 5568
	Crazy Feeling/Little Young Girl	1961	Warwick 643
GENIES (2) (GENE WILSON & THE)			
	Come Here My Darling/Love,		
	Love, Love D-R-E-A-M	1961	King 5568
GENIES (3) (FEMALE)			
	I'm Going Home/Shoo Fly Pie	1963	Lennox 5562
GENOS			
	Wishful Dreaming/Slim Little		
	Annie	1959	Sundance 202
GENOTONES			
	City Lights (Thank Her For Me)/		
	Counting Stars	1961	Casino 52261
	Rita My Teenage Bride/		
	Midnight Walk	N/A	WGW 3003
GENTLEMEN			
	Something To Remember		
	You By/Tired Of You	1954	Apollo 464
	Don't Leave Me Baby/Baby		
	Don't Go	1954	Apollo 470
	Story Of A Love Gone Cold/		
	You're Driving Me Crazy	1955	Apollo
GENTRYS			
	There's A Love/You Make		
	Me Feel So Good	1967	MGM 13690
GENTS (1)			
	Why Do I Love Her/Jump In		
	The Line	1961	Liberty 55332
GENTS (10) (GIN & THE)			
	Boy And Girl	N/A	Eldorado 102
GENTS (2)			
	Golly Golly/It's Too Late To Cry	1961	All Boy 8501
GENTS (3)			
	I'll Never Let You Go/Darling I		
	Love You (by the Teen 5)		
	(Acapella)	1964	Times Square 2/Times Square 99 (64)
	Island Of Love/Till The End		
	Of Time (by the Teen 5)		
	(Acapella)	1964	Times Square 4/Times Square 98 (64)
GENTS (4) (LARRY & THE)			
	Little Queenie/Can't You Tell	1964	Delaware 1700
	You Mean Everything To Me/		
	I'm Just A Loser In Love	1965	Delaware 1711
GENTS (5) (VIC & THE)			
	Lydia (acapella)/The Sign From		
	Above (acapella)	1964	Dorana 1170
GENTS (6) (LITTLE FREDDIE & THE)			
	Betty/Push, Kick And Shout	1965	Showcase 402
GENTS (7)			
	If You Don't Come Back	1966	Duane
GENTS (8)			
	I Wonder Why	1967	Normandy 91067
GENTS (9)			
	Facing This World Without You/		
	Down In The Alley	N/A	Midnight 102
GEOLES (LIL MILLET & THE)			
	Rich Woman/Hopeless Love	1955	Specialty 565
GEORGE, OTHEA (& GROUP)			
	Now That You're Gone	1962	Chex 1008
	Come To Me/Keep On Writin'	N/A	Volume 1100
GEORGE, SUNNY (& GROUP)			
	Lip Lockin'/Tell Me Tell Me	1958	MGM 12697
GEORGE, TERRY (& GROUP) (AKA GEORGE TERRY & GROUP)			
	My Love Dreamy Eyes/Write Me	1961	Comet 2144
GEORGETTES (FEMALE)			
	Oh Tonight/Love Like A Fool	1957	Ebb 125
	Dizzy Over You/Oh, Oh Yes	1959	Jackpot 48001
	Down By The River/Pair Of Eyes	1960	Fleet 1111/United Artists 237 (60)
	Forget Me Not/How Do I Know	1960	Goldisc 3006
	The Story/Little Boy	1963	Troy 1001
GIANT, JIMMY (& GROUP)			
	Everything's Gonna Be Alright/		
	Suddenly	1960	Vee Jay 345
GIANTS (1) (LITTLE GUY & THE)			
	So Young/It's You	1961	Lawn 103
GIANTS (2) (MEL DARK & THE) (AKA SPARROWS QUARTETTE)			
	Darling/This Silver Ring		
	(by the Blue Sky Boys)	1974	Blue Sky 108

Artist	Song	Year	Label
GIBRALTERS (JIMMY BARNES & THE)			
	No Regrets/Keep Your Love		
	Handy	1958	Gibraltar 101
	Be Careful With My Love/		
	I Need You So Much	1959	Gibraltar 102
	Love Made Me A Fool/Don't Let		
	Nothing Stand In Your Way	1959	Gibraltar 106
	Our Wedding Day/Crying Cause		
	I Lost	1960	Savoy 1581
GIBRALTERS (NAPPY BROWN & THE)			
	My Baby Knows/Down In The		
	Alley	1960	Savoy 1582
GIBSON, CINDY (& GROUP)			
	(A Lovely) Summer Night/I'll		
	Always Love You	N/A	General 700
GIBSON, DOLORES (& GROUP)			
	Call Me, Call Me, Call Me/		
	Hey Little Boy	1954	Aladdin 3255
GIFTS (LITTLE NATALIE & HENRY & THE)			
	Teardrops Are Falling/		
	It's Uncle Willie	1963	Roulette 4540
GIFTS (YOUNG HENRY FORD & THE)			
	Treat Her Nice/Two Hearts		
	Make A Romance	1964	Roulette 4552
GIGI (& GROUP)			
	This Time Next Summer/		
	Little Bit Of Lovin'	1961	Seg-Way 1010
GIGOLOS			
	Black And Blue	N/A	Broadway 1000
GIGOLOS (JAMIE COE & THE)			
	Cleopatra/But Yesterday	1962	Big Top 3107
GILLETTES			
	24 Hours A Day/The Same		
	Identical Thing	1964	J&S 1391
GILMAN, TONY (& GROUP)			
	Who Put The Bomp	N/A	J&S 1391
GINGER (& GROUP)			
	Dry Tears/Spare Time	1962	Titan 1717
GINGER (BB THE SAFARIS)			
	Spare Time/Dry Tears	1961	Titan 1717
GINGERSNAPS (FEMALE)			
	Gingerbread/Lenny Lenny	1958	Kapp 226
GINO (& GROUP)			
	Gotta Travel On	1963	Golden Crest 588
GINO (BB THE DELLS)			
	Altar Of Dreams/Baby Don't		
	Go Now	1961	Golden Crest 567
GINOS (JEFF & THE)			
	One Summer In A Million/		
	Let Me Out	1963	Mercury 72138
GIRLFRIENDS (1) (FEMALE)			
	Four Shy Girls (In Their Itsy		
	Bitsy Teenie Weenie		
	Yellow Polka-Dot Bikinis)		
	(answer song)/Jackie	1960	Pioneer 71833
	My One And Only, Jimmy Boy/		
	For My Sake	1963	Colpix 712
	No More Tears/I Want To Be		
	Happy	1963	Melic 4125
	Baby Don't Cry/I Don't Believe		
	In You	1964	Colpix 744
GIRLFRIENDS (2) (ERLENE & THE) (FEMALE)			
	A Guy Is A Guy/My Dada Say	1963	Old Town 1150
	Because Of You/Casanova	1963	Old Town 1152
GLAD RAGS			
	My China Doll/Just One Love	1957	Excello 2121
GLADIATORS (1)			
	Girl Of My Heart/My Baby Doll	1957	Dig 135
GLADIATORS (2)			
	I Need You/Turning To Stone	1958	Donnie 701
GLADIATORS (3) (BRUNO & THE)			
	Istambul/Warm Is The Sun	1962	Vault 901
GLADIOLAS			
	Running Around/We're Lovers	1974	Owl 326
GLADIOLAS (FB MAURICE WILLIAMS)			
	Little Darlin'/Sweetheart		
	Please Don't Go	1957	Excello 2101
	Run, Run, Little Joe/Comin'		
	Home To You	1957	Excello 2110
	Hey! Little Girl/I Wanna Know	1957	Excello 2120
	Say You'll Be Mine/		
	Shoop Shoop	1958	Excello 2136

Artist Song	Year	Label
GLASERS (TOMPALL & THE)		
Yakety Yak/Sweet Lies	1958	Robbins 1006
GLEAMS (1)		
Give Me A Chance/Bad Boy	1960	J-V 101
You Broke My Heart/I Don't		
Know Why You Sent For Me	1962	Kip 236/237
Mr. Magic Moon/Pile Driver	1963	Kapp 565
GLEAMS (2) (BERLIN PERRY & THE)		
Tennessee Waltz/Put That		
Tear Back	1959	Ribbon 6902
GLEEMS		
Sandra Baby/Are You The One	1963	Parkway 893
GLEEPERS (COKE WILLIS & THE)		
Ooh, But You're Nice To Hold/		
The Gleep	N/A	Daco 101
GLENNS		
In The Chapel In The Moonlight/		
More And More	1960	Rendezvous 118
GLENS (1) (BILLY & THE)		
I Believe In You/Oh Boy	1959	Jaro 77006
GLENS (2)		
A Little Less Talk/Cherish		
My Love	1960	Laitini 6666
Cherish My Love/A Little		
Less Talk	1961	Sudden 104
Image Of Love/I Feel So Blue	N/A	Ro-Nan 1002
GLENWOODS (AKA CHATEAUS)		
Elaine/That's The Way It'll Be	1960	Jubilee 5402
GLIDERS		
School Days/Baby Come On	1962	Southern Sound 103
No Time	N/A	Alva 112
GLIDERS (GLEN PACE & THE)		
Tell Me/Next Year	1960	ABC 10091
GLITTERS		
Sherry (flip by Alan Freed)	1962	You 6
Little Star	N/A	Promenade A552
You Don't Know/Lighten-Up		
Slim	N/A	Rubaiyat 413
GLOBELITERS		
Gotta Find Me A Love/		
Turn It On	1964	Guyden 2119
GLOBETROTTERS		
Rainy Day Bells	N/A	Collectables LP 7000
GLORY TONES		
You Only Came Back To Hurt		
Me/Was That The Right		
Thing To Do	1957	Epic 9243
GLOWTONES		
The Girl I Love/Ping Pong	1957	East West 101/Atlantic 1156 (57)
GO BOYS		
Sombody's Got My Baby	N/A	Robbins
GO BOYS (DUDLEY CALLICUTT & THE)		
Get Ready Baby/Heart Trouble	1959	DC 0412
GO-TOGETHERS		
Train/Time After Time	N/A	Coast 100
GODS		
Beneath The Sun/In Between		
Tears	1975	Romantic Rhythm 102
GOLD BUGS		
Stop That Wedding/It's So Nice	1965	Coral 62453
GOLD COASTERS		
Let's Make A New Start	1964	Blue River 206
GOLD TONES (BILL BRYAN & THE)		
Wasted Words/Rocking Chair	1962	Pike 5913
GOLDEN ARROW QUARTET		
That's My Desire/I Want To Be		
Loved	N/A	Continental 6048
GOLDEN BELLS		
Pretty Girl/Bells Are Ringing	1959	Sure 1002
GOLDEN NUGGETS		
I Was A Fool/Teenage		
Josephine	1959	Futura 2-1691
GOLDEN TONES		
I'm Wrong/Crying The Blues	1955	Samson 107/108
GOLDEN TONES (FB JOE SIMON AND BB JOHNNY GUITAR'S BAND)		
Little Island Girl/Doreetha	1959	Hush 101
GOLDEN TONES (FB JOE SIMON)		
You Left Me Here To Cry Alone/		
Ocean Of Tears	1960	Hush 102
Blackboard Of My Heart/		
Mister Moon	1961	Lodestar 22
GOLDEN TONES (MARIE REYNAUD & THE)		
My Man/This Little Man Of Mine	1958	Goldband 1049
GOLDEN TONES (STICKS HERMAN & THE)		
The Natural Thing To Do/Wipe		
The Tears From Your Eyes	1958	Goldband 1056
GOLDENAIRES		
My Only Girl/All About You	1959	Ron 325
Love Letters/Dingbats	1960	Ron 332
GOLDENKEYS		
Let's Vote For Tom Berkeley	1956	Irma 100
GOLDENRODS		
Wish I Was Back In School/		
Color Cartoons	1959	Vee Jay 307
GOLDENTONES		
The Meaning Of Love/Run,		
Pretty Baby	1955	Jay-Dee 806/Beacon 560 (55)
She's Funny That Way/		
Our Love Is Our Affair	1956	Rainbow 351
GOLDTONES		
Wings Of An Angel/I'm So		
Lonely	1961	YRS 1001
Without You/Journey Bells	1962	YRS 1002
GOLDTONES (BILL BRYAN & THE)		
Wasted Words/Rockin' Chair	1962	Pike 5913
Three Hearts/I Know Better	1962	Pike 5915
GOMEZ, YVONNE (& GROUP)		
Ease The Pain/My Man A-Go-Go	1967	Hawaii 128
GONDOLIERS (JOHNNY ADAMS & THE)		
Knocked Out/You Call		
Everybody Darling	1959	Ric 957
Nowhere To Go/Come Home	1960	Ric 963
GOOD GUYS (1)		
Dom-De-Dom/I Love My Baby	1964	San-Dee 1007
GOOD GUYS (2) (DOUG ROBERTSON & THE)		
Love You So/Desirie	1964	Jerden 703/Uptown 703 (64)
Quiet Riot/Sweets For My Sweet	1964	Jerden 729
Greenfields/Sweets For My		
Sweet	1964	Jerden 729
Desirie/Driving Home	1964	Jerden 739
Runaround Sue/Gloria	1965	Jerden 767
GOODE, RAY (& GROUP)		
Stupid Heart/Fool's Paradise	1959	Vel-Tone 25
GOODFELLOWS		
Another Chance/Pretty Little Girl	1958	Sun-Nel 0535
GOODIES		
In Bermuda/The Deep Blue Sea	1959	Chess 1731
GOODTIMERS (DON COVAY & THE)		
(Where Are You) Now That I		
Need You/Teen Life Swag	1962	Columbia 42197
GOOFERS		
Hearts Of Stone/You're The One	1954	Coral 61305
Flip Flop And Fly/My Babe	1955	Coral 61383
Goofy Dry Bone/Nare	1955	Coral 61431
Dee-Do Dee-Do/What Does		
That Dream Mean	1955	Coral 61480
Sick Sick Sick/Twenty-One	1955	Coral 61545
Crave Me/Oh How I Miss		
You Tonight	1956	Coral 61593
Teardrop Motel/Tennessee		
Rock And Roll	1956	Coral 61650
I'm Gonna Rock And Roll 'Til		
I Die/Our Miss Brooks	1956	Coral 61664
'S O.K., 'S Alright/Little Bit		
Square, But Nice	1959	Tiara 6123
Nameless/Perfidia	1959	Tiara 6127
GOOGLES (BARNEY & THE)		
Fall Is Here/Doin' The Shimmy	1960	Shimmy 1055
GORDAN, JONI (& GROUP)		
I'm Watching A Wedding/		
I Guess I'll Miss The Prom	1964	Musicnote 125
GORDON, BIG MIKE (& GROUP)		
Rain Or Shine/Down In		
New Orleans	1955	Savoy 1152
GORDON, GARY (& GROUP)		
No One/Let's Have A Ball	1959	Fleetwood 1002
GORDON, PHIL (& GROUP)		
Get A Load Of Crazy/		
Good Morning Judge	1953	Hub Of Hollywood 1105
GORDON, ROSCOE (& GROUP)		
You'll Never Know/Dillyn Bop	1960	Duke 320
What I Wouldn't Do/Let 'Em Try	1961	Vee Jay 385

Artist	Song	Year	Label
GORDON, SONNY (& GROUP)			
	(I'm Gonna) Tell On You/		
	Don't Leave Me	1962	Bethlehem 3017
GOTHICS			
	Marilyn/Sunday Kind Of Love	1959	Dynamic 101
	My Dream/Love You Too Much	1961	Carol 4115
GOTHICS (STEPHANIE & THE)			
	Oh Happy Day/I'll String Along		
	With You (no group)	1961	Shelley 126
GRADUATES			
	What Good Is Graduation/		
	Lonely	1959	Corsican 0058
	Wendy, Wendy, Went Away	1960	Malvern 500
GRADUATES (AKA JOHNNY HOLLIDAY & THE GRADUATES)			
	Ballad Of A Girl And Boy/Care	1959	Shan-Todd 0055
	Ballad Of A Boy And Girl/		
	Goodbye My Love	1963	Lawn 208
GRADY, PAUL (& GROUP)			
	Darling I Understand/Baby		
	Boy And Girl From Home	1963	Glaze 109
GRANAHAN, GERRY (& GROUP)			
	Love's Young Dream/Oh		
	Well-A-Watcha Gonna Do	1958	Mark 121
	Girl Of My Dreams/No Chemise		
	Please	1958	Sunbeam 102
	Dance Girl Dance/When		
	The Swallows		
	Come Back To Capistrano		
	(by the Five Satins)	1995	X-Bat 1000
GRANAHAN, GERRY (BB THE WILDWOODS (REF FIVE SATINS))			
	Dance Girl, Dance/Too Big		
	For Her Bikini	1961	Caprice 108
GRAND CENTRAL ECHOES			
	Jeannie/Fine, Fine Frame	1985	Clifton 76
GRAND PREES			
	Alone/I'm Gone	1962	Haral 780
	Sit And Cry/Jungle Fever	1963	Candi 1020
	Heartbreak Hotel	N/A	Go Go 101
	No Time To Lose	N/A	Scotty 825
GRAND PRIXS			
	Linda	1962	Sara 6354
	Last Summer Love	1963	Pancho
GRANDISONS			
	True Romance/All Right	1962	RCA 8159
GRANT, JASON (& GROUP)			
	It Doesn't Matter/House Of		
	Cards	1959	20th Fox 151
GRASSHOPPERS			
	Hushabye	N/A	20th Fox 151
GRAY, CAROL (& GROUP)			
	Cha-Cha Bop/Cha Cha Baby		
	(no group)	1958	Rhythm 126
GRAY, MAUREEN (& GROUP)			
	Crazy Over You/Today's		
	The Day	1961	Chancellor 1082
	I Don't Want To Cry/Come		
	On And Dance	1961	Chancellor 1091
	I'm So Young/There Is A Boy	1961	Chancellor 1100
	Dancin' The Strand/Oh My	1962	Landa 689
	People Are Talking/On My	1962	Landa 692
GRAY, RUDY (& GROUP)			
	Please Big Mama	1955	Capitol 3149
GRAY, WILHEMINA (& GROUP)			
	Don't Wake Me Up/When The		
	One You Love Loves You	1957	MGM 12500
GRAYDON, JOE (& GROUP)			
	Again/It Happened To Me	1959	Hamilton 50027
GRECO, JOHNNY (& GROUP)			
	Why Don't You Love Me/		
	Rocket Ride	1963	Pageant 602
GREEN, BARBARA (& GROUP)			
	Long Tall Sally/Slippin' And		
	Slidin'	1963	Atco 6250
	Young Boy/I Should Have		
	Treated You Right	1964	Vivid 105/Hamilton 50027
GREEN, BIRDIE (& GROUP)			
	How Come/Tremblin'	1962	End 1117
GREEN, JANICE (& GROUP)			
	With All My Heart/Jackie	1958	Nasco 6013
GREENWOOD, LIL (BB THE DOMINOES)			
	I'll Go/I'm Crying	1954	Federal 12158
GREENWOOD, PAUL (BB THE FOUR BEL-AIRES)			
	You Won My Heart		Arc
GRIER QUARTET (THE FRANKIE GRIER QUARTET) (ACTUALLY THE SIGNATURES)			
	Oh Gloria/Lonesome For You	1958	Swan 4019
GRIFFIN BROTHERS			
	My Baby's Done Me Wrong/		
	Black Bread	1954	Dot 1145
GRIFFIN, HERMAN (& GROUP)			
	I Need You/I'm So Glad I Learned		
	To Do The Cha Cha Cha	1959	House Of Beauty 112
GRIFFIN, JIMMY (& FEMALE GROUP)			
	A Love Like You/You Took My		
	Loving	1954	Dot 15223
GRIFFINS (1) (AKA WARBLERS)			
	I Swear By All The Stars Above/		
	Sing To Me	1955	Mercury 70558
	Bad Little Girl/Scheming	1955	Mercury 70650
	My Baby's Gone/Why Must		
	You Go?	1956	Mercury 70913
	Forever More/Leave It To Me	1956	Wing 90067
GRIFFINS (2) (JEAN SIMMS & THE)			
	Groovy/Goin' Steady	N/A	Dot
GROGAN, TOBY (& GROUP)			
	Angel/Just A Friend	1963	Vee Jay 560
GROOVERS (1) (JOE DODO & THE)			
	Goin' Steady/Groovy	1958	RCA 7207
GROOVERS (2)			
	Just Go For Me/I'm A Bashful		
	Guy	N/A	Minit 32010
GROSS SISTERS			
	Oom Baby!/My Baby Ain't		
	Nothing But Bad	1959	Checker 932
GROVES			
	Out Of The Blue	N/A	Riff 104
GUARDIANS (KEMPY & THE)			
	Never	N/A	Romunda 1/Lucky Sound 1006
GUERILLAS			
	Lonely	1965	Donna 1406
GUIDES (AKA SWALLOWS (2))			
	You Must Try/How Long Must		
	A Fool Go On	1959	Guyden 2023 (second pressing, first is by the Swallows)
GUM DROPS			
	Gum Drop/Don't Take It So		
	Heard	1955	King 1496
	Don't Take It So Hard/I'll Wait		
	For One More Train	1955	King 8853/King 1499 (55)
	I'll Follow You/I Wonder		
	And Wonder	1956	King 4913
	Chapel Of Hearts/Natural		
	Born Lover	1956	King 4963
	Pigeon/Ba-Bee Da Boat Is		
	Leaving	1957	King 5051
	My Own True Love/On The		
	Wings Of The Wind	1958	Coral 62003
	You're The One/Gum Drop		
	Shoes And Bells In Her Hair	1958	Decca 30584
	I Spoke Too Soon/Sie Tu		
	(It's You, It's You)	1959	Coral 62102
	It Happens Every Day/They		
	Wake Me	1959	Coral 62138
GUNGA DINS			
	Stick With Her/No One Cares	N/A	Busy-B 2
GUNTER, CORNEL (& GROUP)			
	Wishful Thinking/Key To		
	Your Heart	1964	Challenge
GUNTER, CORNEL (BB THE ERMINES)			
	Call Me A Fool/You Send Me	1957	Dot 15654
	Baby Come Home/I Want		
	You Madly	1957	Eagle 301
GUNTER, CORNELL (& GROUP)			
	Lift Me Up Angel/Rope Of Sand	1962	Warner Bros. 5266
GUNTER, GLORIA (& GROUP)			
	Move On Out/Your Love		
	Reminds Me	1959	Arch 1610
GUNTER, SHIRLEY (& GROUP)			
	Believe Me/Crazy Little Baby	1957	Tender 503
GUYS (1)			
	Walkin' By The School/Funny		
	Feelin'	1965	Original Sound 56

Artist	Song	Year	Label
GUYS (2) (LITTLE SAMMY ROZZI & THE)			
(AKA LITTLE SAMMY & THE TONES)			
	Over The Rainbow/Christine	1963	Pelham 722
GUYTONES			
	You Won't Let Me Go/Ooh		
	Bop Sha Boo (Give All Your		
	Love To Me)	1957	DeLuxe 6144
	She's Mine/Not Wanted	1957	DeLuxe 6152
	This Is Love/Hunky Dory	1958	DeLuxe 6159
	Baby I Don't Care/Young		
	Dreamer	1958	DeLuxe 6163
	Tell Me (How Was I To Know)/		
	Your Heart's Bigger Than Mine	1958	DeLuxe 6169
GYPSIES (1)			
	One, Two, Three, Go/I'm Good		
	To You Baby	1955	Groove 0117
	You've Been Away Too Long/		
	Rock Around The Christmas		
	Tree	1955	Groove 0129
	You've Been Away Too Long/		
	Rockin' Pretty Baby	1956	Groove 0137
GYPSIES (2) (FEMALE)			
	Why?/Young Girl To Calypso	1957	Atlas 1073/Angletone 1073 (57)
HAFF-TONES			
	I Need You/Turnaround	1961	Twilight 001
HALL BROTHERS			
	My White Convertible/Now You		
	Say We Are Through	1958	Arc 4444
HALL BROTHERS			
	I'm Still Lonely/Toy Boy	1962	Four Star 1760
HALL, BETTY (& GROUP)			
	Paradise For Two/I'm On		
	A Holiday	1962	Ember 1096
HALL, BETTY (& GROUP)			
	Paradise For Two/I'm On		
	A Holiday	1963	Ember 1096
HALLIQUINS			
	Haunting Memories/		
	Confession Of Love	1996	Early Bird 004
HALLMARKS (1)			
	Congratulations/		
	My Little Sailor Boy	1962	Dot 16418
HALLMARKS (2) (RICKIE & THE) (FB RICKI LISI)			
	Wherever You Are/Joanie		
	Don't You Cry	1963	Amy 877
HALO, JOHNNY (WITH THE FOUR SEASONS)			
	Betty Jean/More Lovin'		
	Less Talkin'	1962	Topix 6004
HALOS (1) (AKA CRAFTYS)			
	Nag/Copy Cat	1961	7 Arts 709
	Come On/What'd I Say	1961	7 Arts 720
	Village Of Love/Mean Old World	1962	Trans Atlas 690
	Bird Dog	1962	Warwick LP 2046
	Crazy Bells	1962	Warwick LP 2046
	I Want To Party	1962	Warwick LP 2046
	Oh What A Night	1962	Warwick LP 2046
	Your Precious Love	1962	Warwick LP 2046
	If I Had Known	1962	Warwick LP 2046
HALOS (1) (CAMMY CAROL & THE)			
	Until The Day I Die/Out Of Sight	1961	Elmor 302
HALOS (1) (CARL SPENCER & THE)			
	Prayer/Tired Of Work	1959	Southside 1002
HALOS (1) (ERNIE & THE) (FB ERNIE K-DOE)			
	Girl From Across The Sea		
	(Angel Marie)/Darling		
	Don't Make Me Cry	1963	Guyden 2085
HALOS (1) (JOHNNY ANGEL & THE)			
	Lady Of Spain/Without Her Heart	1961	Felsted 8633
	One More Tomorrow/		
	Mashed Potato Stomp	1962	Felsted 8646
	Roller Motion/Looking For A Fool	1962	Felsted 8659
HALOS (2) (FEMALE)			
	Do I/Just Keep On Loving Me	1965	Congress 244
	Since I Fell For You/You're		
	Never Gonna Find	1965	Congress 249
	Baby What You Want Me To		
	Do/Hey Hey Love Me	1965	Congress 253
HAMBER, KENNY (& GROUP)			
	Tears In My Eyes/Do The		
	Hully Gully	1963	Spar 101
HAMILTON SISTERS			
	Oop Shoop/Do You Wanna		
	Ride	1954	Columbia 40319
	My Blue Heaven/Garden Of		
	Eden	1954	Columbia 40368
	You Are The One/Lonely Cabin	1956	King 4892
HAMILTON, BOB (& GROUP)			
	Geraldine	N/A	Lu Pine
HAMILTON, GIL (& GROUP)			
	When Are You Coming Home/		
	Move And Groove	1962	Vee Jay 479
HAMILTON, JUDD (& GROUP)			
	Dream/Your Only Boy	1963	Dolton 80
HAMILTON, ROY (BB THE CUES)			
	Don't Let Go/The Right To Love	1957	Epic 9257
HAMILTON, WILLIE (& GROUP)			
	I'm So Glad You're Mine/		
	Hangin' Around	1960	Contour 500
HAMILTONS (ALEXANDER & THE)			
	Over The Rainbow/I Don't		
	Need You	1966	Warner Bros. 5844
HAMMEL JR., KARL (& GROUP)			
	Summer Souvenirs/The Magic		
	Of Summer	1961	Arliss 1007
	Sittin' Alphabetically/		
	A Smile On My Face, A Tear		
	In Your Eye	1961	Arliss 1011
HAMPTONS (GM BROTHER KENNEDY)			
	I Know Why Dreamers Cry/		
	Once In A Lifetime	1961	Legrand 1007
HANKS, MIKE (& GROUP)			
	I've Got A Feeling	1962	Al-Jacks 000.1
HANNIBAL (BB THE ANGELS)			
	Please Take A Chance On		
	Me/Love Is Funny	1960	Pan World 517
HANSEN BROTHERS			
	Mary Anna/Best Girl Of Summer	1979	Crystal Ball 137
	Doo Wop Jingle Bells/		
	Christmas Peace	1981	Crystal Ball 146
HAPPY JESTERS			
	Just Because/Heart Of My Heart	1957	Dot 15566
HAPPY TEENS			
	One More Kiss/Cha Cha Boots	1960	Paradise 114
HAPPYTONES			
	Summertime Nights/Papa Shame	1963	Colpix 693
HARBOR LIGHTS (AKA HARBOR LITES) (WITH JAY BLACK)			
	Angel Of Love/		
	Tick-A-Tick-A-Tock	1960	Mala 422
HARBOR LITES (AKA HARBOR LIGHTS) (WITH JAY BLACK)			
	What Would I Do Without You/		
	Is That Too Much To Ask	1960	Jaro 77020
HARBORSIDE			
	Solitaire/Lost In Your Eyes	1991	Clifton 93
HARDIN-AIRES			
	Teenage Love	1956	Ebony 1015
HARGRO, CHARLES (& GROUP)			
	Baby Oh Baby/Over And Over	1959	DAB 101
HARLEMS (LITTLE "D" & THE)			
	Who's Gonna Pick Up The		
	Pieces/Deep In The Heart Of		
	A Woman	1963	Josie 914
HARLEQUINS			
	Confession Of Love/		
	Haunting Memories	1958	Juanita 102
HARMONAIRES			
	Lorraine/Come Back	1957	Holiday 2602
HARMONAIRES (BILLY FORD & THE)			
	Put Yourself In My Place	1961	Slate 3065
HARMONAIRES (BONNIE LOU & THE)			
	Drop Me A Line/Old, Faithful		
	And True Love	1955	King 1476
	Miss The Love/Barnyard Hop	1955	King 1506
	Miss The Love/Daddy-O	1955	King 4864
HARMONAIRES (EDDIE ELDERS & THE)			
	With A Tear In My Heart/Gee!		
	I Love You Baby	1957	Vita 176
HARMONAIRES (ELAINE GAY & THE) (AKA FIVE HARMONAIRES)			
	Rock Love/Ebony Eyes	1955	DeLuxe 2029
HARMONAIRES (LULA REED & THE)			
	Heavenly Road/My Mother's		
	Prayers	1953	King 4590

Artist	Song	Year	Label
HARMONIZERS (PREMO & THE)			
	So Good	N/A	Doctor Bird
HARMONY			
	Sweet Was The Wine/Guilty	N/A	Starlight 7
HARMONY GRITS (REF ORIGINAL DRIFTERS)			
	Am I To Be The One/I Could		
	Have Told You	1959	End 1051
	Gee/Santa Claus Is Coming		
	To Town	1959	End 1063
HARMONY KINGS (CLYDE TILLIS & THE)			
	Swinging Affair/It Makes		
	No Difference	1958	Cash 1064
HARPER, CHUCK (& GROUP)			
	Summer Is Through/Call On Me	1962	Felsted 8658
HARPER, THELMA (& GROUP)			
	At Last/Unchain My Heart	1962	Jell 191
HARPS (1) (LITTLE DAVID (BAUGHAN) & THE)			
	I Won't Cry/You'll Pay	1955	Savoy 1178
HARPS (2) (AKA CAMELOTS (2)/AKA CUPIDS (6))			
	Marie/Daddy's Going Away		
	Again	1964	Laurie 3239
HARPTONES			
	A Sunday Kind Of Love/		
	I'll Never Tell	1953	Bruce 101/Relic 1022 (73)
	My Memories Of You/It Was		
	Just For Laughs	1954	Bruce 102/Relic 1023 (73)
	I Depended On You/		
	Mambo Boogie	1954	Bruce 104
	Why Should I Love You/		
	Forever Mine	1954	Bruce 109
	Since I Fell For You/		
	Oobidee-Oobidee-Oo	1954	Bruce 113
	Loving A Girl Like You/		
	High Flyin' Baby	1954	Bruce 123
	Life Is But A Dream/You Know		
	You're Doing Me Wrong	1954	Paradise 101
	I Almost Lost My Mind/		
	Oo-Wee, Baby	1955	Bruce 128
	My Success (It All Depends		
	On You)/I've Got A Notion	1955	Paradise 103
	It All Depends On You/		
	Guitar Shuffle	1955	Paradise 105
	What Is Your Decision/		
	Gimme Some	1956	Andrea 100
	I Got A Fine Little Girl	1956	Rama (unfinished)
	Three Wishes/That's The		
	Way It Goes	1956	Rama 203
	On Sunday Afternoon/		
	The Masquerade Is Over	1956	Rama 214
	My Memories Of You/		
	High Flyin' Baby	1956	Tip Top 401
	Cry Like I Cried/So Good,		
	So Fine, You're Mine		
	(with Harriet "Toni" Williams)	1957	Gee 1045
	The Shrine Of St. Cecilia/		
	Oo-Wee, Baby	1957	Rama 221
	Laughing On The Outside/		
	I Remember	1959	Warwick 500
	Love Me Completely/		
	Hep Teenager	1959	Warwick 512
	Rain Down Kisses/Answer Me,		
	My Love	1960	Coed 540
	No Greater Miracle/What Kind		
	Of Fool (Do You Think I Am)	1960	Warwick 551
	All In Your Mind/The Last Dance	1961	Companion 102
	What Will I Tell My Heart/		
	Foolish Me	1961	Companion 103
	Devil In Velvet/Your Love Is		
	A Good Love	1961	Cub 9097
	A Sunday Kind Of Love/		
	Mambo Boogie	1962	Raven 8001
	Sunset/I Gotta Have Your Love	1963	KT 201
	Until The Real Thing		
	Comes Along	1972	Roulette LP 114/Murray Hill LP 001098 (88)
	That's The Way It Goes/Marie	1974	Rama 197/Broadcast 1135 (76)
	Until The Real Thing Comes		
	Along/Love You As You Love		
	Me (by the Metronomes)	1976	Robin Hood 131
	Love Needs A Heart/It's You	1982	Ambient Sound 02807
	You're Gonna Need My		
	Help Someday	1985	Murray Hill LP 000083
	School Girl	1985	Murray Hill LP 000083
	What Is Your Secret	1988	Murray Hill LP 001098
	The Wobble	N/A	Diplomat LP 2311
HARPTONES (WITH BUNNY PAUL)			
	I'll Never Tell/Honey Love	1954	Essex 364
HARRIS, BILL (& GROUP)			
	I'm So Glad	N/A	Essex 364
HARRIS, BILLY (& GROUP)			
	The Wedding	1959	Plaid 101
HARRIS, DIMPLES (& GROUP)			
	This I Do Believe/If You'll		
	Be True	1956	Crest 1013
HARRIS, KURT (& GROUP)			
	Emperor Of My Baby's Heart/		
	Goon	1963	Diamond 158
HARRIS, STERLING (& GROUP)			
	The Church Bells Ring	N/A	VVVV
HARRIS, THURSTON (BB THE SHARPS)			
	Little Bitty Pretty One/I Hope You		
	Won't Hold It Against Me	1957	Aladdin 3398
	Do What You Did/I'm Asking		
	Forgiveness	1957	Aladdin 3399
	Be Baba Leba/I'm Out To		
	Getcha	1958	Aladdin 3415
	Only One Love Is Blessed/		
	Smokey Joes	1958	Aladdin 3428
	Over And Over/You're Gonna		
	Need Me	1958	Aladdin 3430
	Tears From My Heart/Over		
	Someone Else's Shoulder	1958	Aladdin 3435
	From The Bottom Of My Heart/		
	You Don't Know How Much		
	I Love You (no group)	1959	Aladdin 3448
	My Love Will Last/Hey Little Girl	1959	Aladdin 3450
	Bless Your Heart/Runk Bunk	1959	Aladdin 3452
	Paradise Hill/Slip-Slop	1959	Aladdin 3456
HARRISON, LEE (& GROUP)			
	Mine Alone/So Unimportant	1958	Judd 1003
HARRISON, OSCAR (& GROUP)			
	I Need Love/I Don't Want To Cry	N/A	Tap 1003
HART, ROCKY (BB THE MYSTICS)			
	Every Day/Come With Me	1959	Cub 9052
HART, ROCKY (BB THE PASSIONS)			
	Crying/Baby You've Got It Made	1961	Big Top 3069
	I Play The Part Of A Fool/		
	Someone Stole My Baby		
	While Doing The Twist	1961	Glo 216
HARVEY (HARVEY FUQUA WITH THE MOONGLOWS)			
	Ten Commandments Of Love/		
	Mean Old Blues	1958	Chess 1705
	I Want Somebody/Da Da		
	Goo Goo	1958	Chess 1713
	Don't Be Afraid To Love/		
	Twelve Months Of The Year	1959	Chess 1725
	Unemployment/Mama Loocie	1959	Chess 1738
	Oooh Ouch Stop! (Teacher,		
	You're Hurting Me)/Blue Skies	1959	Chess 1749
HARVEY BOYS			
	Nothing Is Too Good For You/		
	Marina Girl	1956	Cadence 1306
HARVEY SISTERS			
	Kiss Of Fire/This Is The Same	1962	Newtime 512
HATFIELD, BOBBY (& GROUP)			
	I Need A Girl/Hot Tamale	1963	Moonglow 220
HAVEN KNIGHTS (AKA FOUR HAVEN KNIGHTS)			
	Just To Be In Love/Why Go		
	On Pretending	1973	Sold 503
HAVENS			
	Want You/Only You	1963	Poplar 123
HAWKETTS			
	Mardi Gras Mambo/Your		
	Time's Up	1955	Chess 1591
HAWKINS, SAM (& GROUP)			
	King Of Fools/The		
	Whatchamacallit	1959	Gone 5042
	When Nobody Loves You/		
	She Didn't Notice Me	1959	Gone 5054
HAWKS (1)			
	Joe The Grinder/Candy Girl	1954	Imperial 5266
	Good News/She's All Right	1954	Imperial 5281
	It Ain't That Way/I-Yi	1954	Imperial 5292
	Give It Up/Nobody But You	1954	Imperial 5306

Artist	Song	Year	Label
All Women Are The Same/	That' What You Are	1954	Imperial 5317
It's Too Late Now/Can't See	For Lookin'	1955	Imperial 5332
These Blues/Why Oh Why?		1955	Post 2004
It's All Over/Ever Since You	Been Gone	1956	Modern 990
A Little More Wine, My Dear/	Fussy	1958	Del-Fi 4108
Schoolgirl		N/A	Imperial (unreleased)
He's The Fatman		N/A	Imperial (unreleased)
I Want My Loving Now		N/A	Imperial (unreleased)

HAWKS (2) (RONNIE HAWKINS & THE)

Artist	Song	Year	Label
Need Your Lovin'/Mary Lou		1959	Roulette 4177

HAWKS (2) (RONNIE HAWKINS & THE)

Artist	Song	Year	Label
Southern Love/Love Me Like	You Can	1959	Roulette 4209

HAWKS (3) (LITTLE TONY & THE)

Artist	Song	Year	Label
Cry Cry Cry/Do What You Did		1966	Original Sound 63

HAYDEN SISTERS

Artist	Song	Year	Label
Silent Tears/Mr. Blues		1961	Tilt 784

HAYDEN, GIL (& GROUP)

Artist	Song	Year	Label
So Left Alone/Think Before	You Say Goodbye	1961	V-Tone 219

HAYES, LINDA (& GROUP)

Artist	Song	Year	Label
Our Love's Forever Blessed/	You're The Only One For Me	1955	Recorded In Hollywood 1032/Decca 29644 (55)

HAYES, LINDA (BB THE FLAIRS)

Artist	Song	Year	Label
I Had A Dream/You Ain't	Movin' Me	1956	Antler 4000

HAYES, LINDA (BB THE PLATTERS)

Artist	Song	Year	Label
Let's Babalu/My Name Ain't	Annie	1955	King 4752

HEADHUNTERS (CANNIBAL & THE)

Artist	Song	Year	Label
Show You How To Make	Love To Me/Land Of 1,000 Dances (not doo-wop)	1965	Rampart 642

HEADLINERS (1)

Artist	Song	Year	Label
Comin' On Down With Love/	B.I. Moore	1962	Beltone 2020

HEADLINERS (2) (GEORGE GOODMAN & THE)

Artist	Song	Year	Label
Let Me Love You/Let Me Love	You (instrumental)	1964	Val 1
Let Me Love You/I'm So Tired		1965	Val 1000/Warner Bros. 5632(65)/A&M 1011 (68)
I'll Cherish You Love/Secret	Love	1965	Val 5
Starlight And Moonbeams/	I'm So Tired	1965	Val 6

HEADLINERS (3)

Artist	Song	Year	Label
Back To School Again/	Traveler Traveler	N/A	Keno 1002

HEALEYS (TOM AUSTIN & HIS)

Artist	Song	Year	Label
Summer's Over/Maybe You'll	Be There	1963	Old Town 1147

HEARD, LONNIE (BB THE HALOS)

Artist	Song	Year	Label
A Sunday Kind Of Love/	Romance In The Park	1961	Arliss 1008

HEART BEATS QUINTET (AKA HEARTBEATS (2))

Artist	Song	Year	Label
Tormented/After Everybody's	Gone	1955	Network 71200/Candlelite 437(72)/Candlelite 1135 (76)

HEART-ATTACKS

Artist	Song	Year	Label
Babba Diddy Baby/I'm Angry	Baby	N/A	Remus 5000

HEART-THROBS

Artist	Song	Year	Label
So Glad/All The Way Home		1957	Aladdin 3394/Lamp 2010 (57)

HEARTACHES (JO ANN & THE)

Artist	Song	Year	Label
I'm So Young (acapella)/	A Lovers Call (acapella)	1966	Catamount 114

HEARTBEATS (1) (AKA THREE FRIENDS)

Artist	Song	Year	Label
Finally/Boil And Bubble		1955	Jubilee 5202

HEARTBEATS (2)

Artist	Song	Year	Label
Crazy For You/Rock 'n'	Rollin' 'n' Rhythm 'n' Blues-n'	1956	Hull 711
Darling How Long/	Hurry Home Baby	1956	Hull 713/Gee 1062 (61)
People Are Talking	(Slow Version)/Your Way	1956	Hull 716/Gee 1061 (61)
A Thousand Miles Away/	Oh Baby Don't	1956	Hull 720/Rama 216 (57)

Artist	Song	Year	Label
Stars In The Sky		1956	Rama (unreleased)
Tell Me		1956	Rama (unreleased)
When I Found You/Hands	Off Baby	1957	Gee 1043
After New Year's Eve/	Five Hundred Miles To Go	1957	Gee 1047
Lovin' Sickness		1957	Rama (unreleased)
Be Mine		1957	Rama (unreleased)
Wedding Bells/I Won't Be The	Fool Anymore	1957	Rama 222
Everybody's Somebody's Fool/	I Want To Know	1957	Rama 231
Down On My Knees/I Found	A Job	1958	Roulette 4054
One Day Next Year/Sometimes	I Wonder	1958	Roulette 4091
One Million Years/Darling,	I Want To Get Married	1959	Guyden 2011
Down On My Knees/	Crazy For You	1959	Roulette 4194
Have Rock, Will Roll		1960	Roulette LP 25107/Broadcast 1125 (75)
It's Alright With Me		1960	Roulette LP 25107/Broadcast 1125 (75)
Lonely Lover		1960	Roulette LP 25107/Broadcast 1125 (75)
Easy To Remember		1981	Collectables 1021

HEARTBEATS (3) (RICHIE HART & THE)

Artist	Song	Year	Label
I Want You		1960	MCI 1025

HEARTBREAKERS (1) (FB ROBERT EVANS)

Artist	Song	Year	Label
Heartbreaker/Wanda		1951	RCA 4327
I'm Only Fooling My Heart/	You're So Necessary To Me	1951	RCA 4508
Why Don't I/Rockin' Daddy-O		1952	RCA 4662
There Is Time/It's O.K. With Me		1952	RCA 4849
Cry Wind Cry/I Swear By All	The Stars Above	1973	Roadhouse 1007 (unreleased bootleg)
Hey Baby/I Only Want To Be	Your Guy	1973	Roadhouse 1008 (unreleased bootleg)
Heartbreaker/Embraceable		1974	Roadhouse 1010 (unreleased bootleg)
Is It Real/Ain't Nothin' Shakin'		1974	Roadhouse 1011 (unreleased bootleg)
Goodbye Baby/We're Gonna	Have Some Fun	1974	Roadhouse 1012 (unreleased bootleg)

HEARTBREAKERS (2) (FB PAUL HIMMELSTEIN)

Artist	Song	Year	Label
1, 2, I Love You/Without A Cause		1957	Vik 0261
Love You Till/My Love		1957	Vik 0299
Come Back My Love/	Jenny Lee (by the Students (2))	1959	Fordham 109/Vanguard 9093
Corrida Mash/I'm Leaving It	All Up To You	1962	Brent 7037
Since You've Been Gone/	John Law	1962	Markay 106
The Willow Wept/You Had Time		1963	Atco 6258
Please Answer/She Is My Baby		1964	Linda 114
Come Back My Love/Who Does	She Think She Is (by the Keynoters)	1975	Vanguard 9093
She's Gone/I Don't Want	Nobody	N/A	Broadcast 99

HEARTBREAKERS (3) (TV SLIM & HIS)

Artist	Song	Year	Label
Darling Remember/	Flatfoot Sam (no group)	1957	Cliff 103/Checker 870 (57)

HEARTBREAKERS (4) (FB FRANK ZAPPA)

Artist	Song	Year	Label
Everytime I See You/Cradle	Rock	1963	Donna 1381

HEARTBREAKERS (5) (FEMALE)

Artist	Song	Year	Label
It's Hard Being A Girl/Special	Occasions	1963	MGM 13129

HEARTIES (KIP HALE & THE)

Artist	Song	Year	Label
Don't You Care/Don't Say	You Love Me	1954	Jubilee 5166

HEARTS (1) (BILLY AUSTIN & THE)

Artist	Song	Year	Label
Angel Baby/Night Has Come		1953	Apollo 444

HEARTS (2)

Artist	Song	Year	Label
Lonely Nights/Oo Wee		1955	Baton 208/Main Line 102 (57)
All My Love Belongs To You/	Talk About Him, Girlie	1955	Baton 211

Artist Song	Year	Label
Until The Real Thing Comes Along/Gone, Gone, Gone	1955	Baton 215
Like, Later Baby/I Want Your Love Tonite	1955	J&S 1626/1627
Goin' Home To Stay/Disappointed Bride	1956	Baton 222
She Drives Me Crazy/I Had A Guy	1956	Baton 228
If I Had Known/There Are So Many Ways	1956	J&S 1002/1003
You Weren't Home/I Couldn't Let You See Me Crying	1956	J&S 1180/1181
My Love Has Gone/You Or Me Have Got To Go	1956	J&S 425/426
A Thousand Years From Today/I Feel So Good	1956	J&S 995/Zells 3377 (63)
Dancing In A Dream World/You Wouldn't Tell	1957	J&S 1657
So Long Baby/You Say You Love Me	1957	J&S 1660
There Is No Love At All/Goodbye Baby	1957	J&S 4571/4572
Dear Abby/Dear Abby (instrumental)	1963	Tuff 370
Do You Remember	1963	Zells 3378

HEARTS (2) (WITH CLARENCE ASHE)
Dancing In A Dreamworld/Trouble I've Had	1964	J&S 1466

HEARTS (3) (AKA LEE ANDREWS & THE HEARTS)
On My Honor/It's Unbelievable	1960	Chancellor 1057

HEARTS (3) (LEE ANDREWS & THE)
Maybe You'll Be There/Baby, Come Back	1954	Rainbow 252/Riviera 965 (54)
The White Cliffs Of Dover/Much Too Much	1954	Rainbow 256
The Bells Of St. Mary's/The Fairest	1954	Rainbow 259
Bluebird Of Happiness/Show Me The Merengue	1956	Gotham 318
Lonely Room/Leona	1956	Gotham 320
Just Suppose/It's Me	1956	Gotham 321
Teardrops/The Girl Around The Corner	1957	Grand 156/Main Line 105 (57)/Argo 1000 (57)/Chess 1675 (57)
Long, Lonely Nights/The Clock	1957	Grand 157/Main Line 102 (57)/Chess 1665 (57)
Try The Impossible/Nobody's Home	1958	Casino 452/United Artists 123 (58)
Why Do I/Glad To Be Here	1958	United Artists 136
All I Ask Is Love/Maybe You'll Be There	1958	United Artists 151
Lonely Room/Together Again	1962	Gowen 1403
Much Too Much/The Fairest	1965	Lost Nite 104
Quiet As It's Kept/You're Taking A Long Time Coming Back	1966	RCA 8929
Island Of Love/Nevertheless	1967	Crimson 1009
I've Had It/Little Bird	1968	Crimson 1015
Cold Grey Dawn/All You Can Do	1968	Lost Nite 1001
Oh My Love/Can't Do Without You	1968	Lost Nite 1004
Quiet As It's Kept/Island Of Love	1968	Lost Nite 1005
Sipping A Cup Of Coffee/Just Suppose	1981	Gotham 323
Window Eyes/Long Lonely Nights (alternate)	1981	Gotham 324
I Miss My Baby/Boom (alternate)	1981	Gotham 325
Abide (By The Golden Rule)	N/A	Collectables LP 5003
Strollin' Baby	N/A	Collectables LP 5003

HEARTS (3) (LEE ANDREWS & THE) (AS LEE ANDREWS)
I Wonder/Baby Come Back	1959	Casino 110
Just Suppose/Boom	1959	United Artists 162
A Wise Man Said/If You Only Cared	1960	Jordan 121
I've Got A Right To Cry/I Miss You So	1961	Swan 4065
A Night Like Tonight/You Gave To Me	1961	Swan 4076
P.S. I Love You/I Cried	1961	Swan 4087
I'm Sorry Pillow/Gee But I'm Lonesome	1962	Parkway 860/Parkway 5213/5214 (63)
Looking Back/Operator	1963	Parkway 866
You You You/Hug-A-Bee	1965	V.I.P. 1601

HEARTS (4) (FEMALE) (EUGENE BALL WITH THE)
California Baby/Why Oh Why	1957	Melatone 1001

HEARTS (5) (BUDDY & THE)
Thirty Days/Let It Rock	1964	Landa 701

HEARTSPINNERS (1)
Fire Of Romance/Boy Meets Girl	1953	Universal

HEARTSPINNERS (2)
I've Searched/Oh So Much	1958	X-Tra 109
I've Searched/Mixture Of Love (by the Admirations)	1963	Times Square 20

HEARTSPINNERS (3) (DINO & THE)
Cry Like I Cried/That's My Girl	1972	Bim Bam Boom 108
I Love You So/Two Kinds Of People In The World	1972	Bim Bam Boom 112
Hey Senorita/I'm Not A Know It All	1973	Bim Bam Boom 119
Cry Like I Cried/That's My Girl	1976	Barrier 103
Zoom!/Let's Go Back To Yesterday	1976	Robin Hood 141
Who Do You Think You Are?/A Thousand Miles Away	1976	Robin Hood 142
The Bells Of Love/The Wind	1981	Starlight 13
Flames/Shirley	N/A	Pyramid 164
The Lover's Plea/Mexico	N/A	Starlight 11
I Believe In You/Gee	N/A	Starlight 9

HEARTSTRINGS (JOHNNY JASON & THE)
Last Years Christmas Tree/Be There (by the Shadettes)	N/A	Romantic 101/102

HEATHENS
The Other Way Around	N/A	Vibra 104

HEATWAVES (FB BILLY CARLUCCI) (REF BILLY & THE ESSENTIALS)
I'll Do My Crying Tomorrow/Nowhere To Go	65	Josie 941

HEMLOCKS (LITTLE BOBBY RIVERA & THE)
Coralee/The Joys Of Love	57	Fury 1004

HENDERSON, FLOYD (& GROUP)
Nosy Rosy/Tenderly	59	Triangle 51315

HENDRICKS, BOBBY (BB THE COASTERS)
Itchy Twitchy Feeling/A Thousand Dreams	58	Sue 706
Dreamy Eyes/Molly Be Good	58	Sue 708
It's Misery/Cast Your Vote	59	Sue 710

HENRY, EARL (& GROUP)
My Suzanne/Believe A Traveler	1958	Dot 15875

HENRY, STACY (BB THE DREAM-TIMERS)
Sweetest Darlin'/I'm Not Ashamed	1961	Flippin' 108

HEP CATS
What In The World Can I Do/The Dilly Up	1961	Del-Fi 4159

HEPCATS (DAISY MAE & THE)
Woman Trouble/Lonesome Playgirl	1956	Gotham 317

HEPSTERS
I Had To Let You Go/Rockin' 'n' Rollin' With Santa Claus	1955	Ronel 107
I Gotta Sing The Blues/This-A-Way	1956	Ronel 110

HEPTONES
I'm So In Love With You/Anna Bell	1956	Abbco 105

HERALDS (AKA FOUR DUKES/AKA BILLY DAWN QUARTETTE/AKA DONNIE MILES & THE DUKES/AKA DUKES)
Eternal Love/Gonna Love You Every Day	1954	Herald 435
Peggy/Wonder Boy	1968	Tamborine 2
Freeze	N/A	Herald (unreleased)
Why Can't I Have You	N/A	Herald (unreleased)

HESITATIONS (DON SWEET & THE)
Remember/Wild Little Willie	1964	D-Town 383

HI FI'S
Why Can't I Stop Loving You/I Keep Forgettin'	1965	Cameo 349

HI LARKS
Mine/Take A Hike	1959	Beat 0050

HI LIGHTERS
Feeling Alright	N/A	Charly LP 1115

Artist Song	Year	Label
HI LITERS (BUDDY ROBERTS & THE)		
Ding Dong/Black And Blue	1960	Bonanza 689/690
HI LITES		
I'm So Jealous	1965	Daran 222
HI TENSIONS (AKA ANGELS (8))		
Got A Good Feeling/		
Ebbing Of The Tide	1963	Milestone 2018
Wedding Song (If You Say I Do)	N/A	Milestone
Old Times	N/A	Milestone
Traveling Lady	N/A	Milestone
Come What May	N/A	Milestone
HI TENSIONS (LEON PEELS & THE) (REF ANGELS (8))		
So Far Away/The Clock	1960	Audio 201/K&G 101
She'll Break Your Heart/		
Mary Had A Little Man	1964	Whirlybird 2005
A Magic Island/Darlene	1964	Whirlybird 2008
HI TIMERS		
You're Everything/Why Should		
We Keep On Pretending	1959	Sonic 1502
HI TONES (CHARLES ANDREA & THE)		
Didn't We Have A Nice Time/		
Open Up Your Heart	1961	Tori Ltd. T-2X
HI TOPPERS (V. JAMES & THE)		
My Heart Is Not A Toy/		
By And By My Love	1961	Kent 354
HI-BOYS		
Billy Boy/Draw	1959	Mala 400
HI-FASHIONS		
Yes, Oh Yes/Ooh, What A Guy	1958	Paris 524
HI-FI FOUR		
Band Of Gold/Davy You		
Upset My Life	1955	King 4856
HI-FI-DELS		
Did I Cry/Tricky Tricky	1961	Atlantic 2121
HI-FIDELITIES		
Street Of Loneliness/Help!		
Murder! Police!	1957	Hi-Q 5000
HI-FIDELITIES (GINO PARKS & THE)		
Last Night I Cried/Just Go		
(by Gino Parks)	1958	Fortune 528
HI-FIS		
I'm So Lonely/My Dear	1959	Montel 1005
Each Passing Day/Sally	1960	Mark 148/Devere 006
HI-FIVES (1)		
Hong Kong/Throwing Pebbles		
In The Pond	1956	Flair-X 3000
HI-FIVES (2)		
My Friend/How Can I Win	1958	Decca 30576
Dorothy/Just A Shoulder To		
Cry On	1958	Decca 30657
What's New, What's New/		
Lonely	1958	Decca 30744
Felicia/Windy City Special	1960	Bingo 1006
HI-FIVES (3)		
Julie/Son Of Raunchy	1964	Bell 634
HI-JACKS		
Wonderful One/The Letter		
I Wrote Today	1956	ABC 9742
HI-LIGHTERS		
Ain't Giving Up Nothing/		
Undecided Now	1956	Celeste 3005
You Must Come In/		
Dance Everyone, Dance	1958	Hanover 4506
Cha Cha Rock/Dance Me		
To Death	1958	Mercury 71342
HI-LIGHTS		
Oh Lover Of Mine/Man On		
The Shelf	1963	JR 5003
HI-LITERS (1)		
Route 66/Baby Don't Treat		
Me This Way	1955	Wen-Dee 1927
HI-LITERS (2)		
Over The Rainbow/Baby		
Please Be True	1958	Hico 2433/Zircon 1006
HI-LITERS (2) (WITH KING BASSIE & THE THREE ACES)		
In The Night/Let Me Be True		
To You	1958	Hico 2432
HI-LITES (1)		
I Found A Love/Zanzee	1954	Okeh 7046
HI-LITES (2)		
The Next Four Years/The Girl		
With The Bells	1956	Mercury 70987

Artist Song	Year	Label
Friday Night Go Go/Chicka-		
Rocka-Chee-Che-Cho	1958	Brunswick 55102
Beach Baby/One Love For Me	1958	Wonder 102
HI-LITES (3)		
The Pony Pt. 1/The Pony Pt. 2	1961	Jet 501
4000 Miles Away/Woke Up		
This Morning	1961	Jet 502
HI-LITES (4)		
Walking My Baby Back Home/		
I'm Falling In Love	1961	Record Fair 500/Dandee LP 206
Zoop	1962	Dandee LP 206
Everybody's Somebody's Fool/		
Moonlight	1962	Dandee LP 206/ Monogram 119 (76)
Zoom Zoom Zoom/To The Aisle	1962	Dandee LP 206/ Monogram 120 (76)
Pretty Face/Maybe You'll		
Be There	1962	Dandee LP 206/ Monogram 121 (76)
Gloria (My Darling)/For Your		
Precious Love	1962	Julia 1105/Dandee LP 206
For Sentimental Reasons/		
For Your Precious Love	1962	Record Fair 501/Dandee LP 206
Zoop/Baby Baby (by Jose &		
the Aztecs)	1976	Monogram 122
HI-LITES (5)		
Twistin' Time/Twistin' Pony	1962	Twist Time 12
Death Of An Angel		
Our Winter Love	1963	King 5730
Groovy/Hey Baby	1965	Wassel 701
HI-LITES (6) (RANDY HARD & THE)		
Honey Doll/May It Be My Fortune	1958	NRC 013
HI-LITES (7) (RONNIE & THE)		
I Wish That We Were Married/		
Twistin' And Kissin'	1962	Joy 260
Send My Love/Be Kind	1962	Joy 265
Valerie/The Fact Of The Matter	1962	Raven 8000
A Slow Dance/What The		
Next Day May Bring	1963	Win 250/Reo
The Fact Of The Matter/		
You Keep Me Guessin'	1963	Win 251
High School Romance/		
Uptown-Downtown	1963	Win 252
Too Young/High School		
Romance	1965	ABC 10685
For Lovers/What A Pretty		
Bride You'll Be	1982	U.G.H.A. 16
HI-LITES (8) (SKIPPY & THE)		
Waiting To Take (You Home)/		
Old Man River	N/A	Stream-Lite 1027/Elmor
HI-LITES (9) (ROY SMITH & THE)		
Love You So Much/She's Fine	1959	Nu-Tone 1182/Key 1182
HI-NOTES (TOMMY FREDERICK & THE)		
The Prince Of Players/		
I'm Not Pretending	1958	Carlton 450
HI-TIDES (MIKE HARRIS & THE)		
I'm So Proud	1963	Krimmie 24
HI-TOMBS		
Sweet Rockin' Mama	N/A	Cannon 832
HI-TONES (AKA HITONES)		
That's All I Want To Do/You		
Didn't Have To Laugh	1958	Skyline 701
The Special Day/I've Never		
Seen A Straight Banana	1960	Candix 307
Fool, Fool, Fool/Let's Have A		
Good Time	1960	King 5414
What Was The Cause Of It All/		
Don't Leave Me No Choice	1961	Eon 101
Lover's Quarrel/Just For You	1961	Fonsca 201
No More Pain/I Don't Know Why	1961	Fonsca 202
Girls/Sure As The Flowers	1961	Seg-Way 105
HI-TONES (BOB JAXON & THE) (AKA HITONES)		
Why Does A Woman Cry/		
Ali Baba	1955	Cadence 1264
HI-TONES (CHARLES ANDREA & THE)		
Didn't We Have A Nice Time/		
Open Up Your Heart	1961	Tori Ltd. 2
HI-TONES (JOHNNY WYATT & THE)		
Wondering Why/We Met At		
A Dance	1959	Big Time 1927

Artist	Song	Year	Label
HI-TONES (WILLIE MAE THORNTON & THE) (AKA HITONES)			
	Don't Talk Back	N/A	Irma 13
HIDE-A-WAYS			
	Cherie/Me Makem Powwow	1955	MGM 55004
HIDEAWAYS			
	Can't Help Loving That Girl Of Mine/I'm Coming Home	1954	Ronni 1000
	Lovin' Time/You're So Hard To Say Goodnight To	1963	Duel 521
HIGGINS, BEN (BB THE FIVE SATINS)			
	Really Paradise/A Whole Lot Of Lovin'	1962	Jamie 1217
HIGGINS, CHUCK (& GROUP)			
	Shot Gun Wedding/Groove	1954	Kicks 6
	I'll Be There/Broke	1954	Specialty 532
HIGGS & WILSON (& GROUP)			
	When You Tell Me Baby/Mannyon	1960	Time 1028
HIGH LITERS			
	Hello, Dear/Bobby Sox Baby	1956	Vee Jay 184
HIGH SEAS			
	Sunday Kind Of Love/We Go Together	1960	D-M-G 1001/D-M-G 4000
HIGH TENSIONS			
	Looking For A Summertime Girl	1964	Hitt 6601
HIGH TYPE FIVE (BILLY CARR & THE)			
	Champagne	1959	C&P 105
HIGH TYPE FIVE (CLARENCE GREEN WITH THE)			
	Mary My Darling/Old Grandpa	1959	Chess 1732
HIGHBROWS (SHADOE & THE)			
	Tomboy/Pony Express Riders	1961	Gem 102
HIGHLANDERS (1)			
	Sunday Kind Of Love/Beg And Steal	1957	Ray's 36
HIGHLANDERS (2) (SANDRA & THE)			
	Written In The Stars	1961	Highland 1015
HIGHLANDS			
	I Laughed	1961	unreleased
HIGHLIGHTERS (1)			
	Christmas Is Coming At Last/White Christmas	1950	Apollo 1141
	Flang Dang Do/The Bull	1958	New Song 116
	Well/Las Vegas Drive (instrumental)	1959	New Song 133
HIGHLIGHTERS (2)			
	Sweet Little Baby Of Mine/Mi Amor	1959	Cannon 80488
HIGHLIGHTERS (2) (JIMMY HALL & THE)			
	Jeannie/At The Hippety Hop	1959	Cannon 369/370
HIGHLIGHTERS (3) (WALTER WEBB & THE)			
	Your Time Is Gonna Come/Lulu	1970	Chess 2091
HIGHLIGHTS (1) (FB FRANK PIZANI)			
	City Of Angels/Listen My Love	1956	Bally 1016
	To Be With You/Will I Ever Know	1957	Bally 1027
	Indiana Style/Turn Around Shoes	1958	Bally 1044
HIGHLIGHTS (2) (BARRY & THE)			
	Christmas Bell Rock/Chil-E Baby	1960	Baye 511/Airmaster 700 (60)
HIGHLIGHTS (3)			
	Ah So	N/A	Play
HIGHLITES			
	No One To Tell Her	1965	Pit 403
HIGHLITES (LITTLE ANGIE & THE)			
	Baby Doll	N/A	Essay
HIGHSCHOOL CHANTERS			
	Hoodoo The Voodoo/Teenage Chant	1959	Fashion 001
HIGHTONES (CLAUDE & THE)			
	Bucket Head/Doodle Bug	1959	Baytone 113
	Monkey Stuff/High Sailing	N/A	Pammar 614
HIGHTOWER, DONNA (BB THE JACKS)			
	Dog Gone It/Love Me Again	1955	RPM 432
	Since You/Bob-O-Link (by the Jacks)	1955	RPM 439
	I Ain't Gonna Tell/He's My Baby	1956	RPM 481
HILITES (ROY SMITH & THE)			
	She's Fine/Love You So Much	1961	Nu Tone 1182
HILL, GRANT (& GROUP)			
	She's Going Away/Looking For A Girl	1959	Topaz 1300
HILLSIDERS (BOBBY ANGEL & THE)			
	Baby-O/That's The Way I Want To Go	1961	Rhum 101
	Heartbreak Hotel/Submarine Races	1962	Astra 300
HINES, WILLIAM A. (& GROUP)			
	Bring Back Your Heart/The Old Master Painter	1960	Ball 508
HINTON, JOE (& GROUP)			
	I Know/Ladder Of Prayer	1958	Back Beat 519
	Pretty Little Mama/Will You	1959	Back Beat 526
HIPPIES (AKA STEREOS (1)/AKA TAMS (1))			
	Memory Lane/Teenage Kids	1963	Parkway 863
HISTORIANS (BARBAROSO & THE) (FB NICKY ADDEO)			
	Zoom (a capella)/When I Fall In Love (a capella)	1957	Jade 110
HIT-MAKERS			
	Pretty Little Mama/Will You	1959	Beat 526
HITCHHIKERS (CHUCK THOMAS & THE)			
	Let Our Hearts Be Our Guide/Why Baby	1957	Band Box 360
HITMAKERS (1)			
	Chapel Of Love/Cool School	1958	Original Sound 1
	I Can't Take It Anymore/Too Cool	1959	Angletone 1104
	How To Make A Hit Record/Buttermilk	1965	Dore 738
HITMAKERS (2) (LINDA LOU & THE)			
	The Torch Is Out/The Difference In Our Ages	1965	Lama 7786
HITONES (LEONARD WAYNE & THE) (AKA HI-TONES)			
	That's All I Want To Do/You Don't Have To Laugh	1964	Andre 701
HITS (TINY TIM & THE)			
	Wedding Bells/Doll Baby	1958	Roulette 4123
HOBBS, LOUIS (& GROUP)			
	All That Heaven Sent/Mama, Mama, Mama	N/A	Buddy Buddy 460
HOBSON, EMMETT (& GROUP)			
	Looka Here, Mattie Bee/Oo-Wee Mr. Jeff	1953	Central 1001
HODGES, CHARLES (BB THE FI-TONES)			
	There Is Love/Can I Run To You	1965	Alto 2016
HODGES, EDDIE (WITH SUE WRIGHT & GROUP)			
	Bandit Of My Dreams/Mugmates	1961	Cadence 1410
HOLDEN, RON (& GROUP)			
	Lover's Never Say Goodbye	N/A	VMC 748
HOLIDAY, BOBBY (& GROUP)			
	My Letter/Come Home	1961	Port 70027
HOLIDAY, JIMMY (& GROUP)			
	Janet/How Can I Forget	1963	Everest 2022
HOLIDAYS (1)			
	Ima-Lika-You (Pizza Pie)/Rolling River	1953	King 1217
	(Shine 'Em! Shake 'Em! Roll 'Em!) Let The Dice Decide/Just Out Of Reach	1954	King 1246
	You'll Never Get Away/List'nin' To The Green Grass Grow	1956	King 1520
HOLIDAYS (10)			
	Cathy Darling/Down By The Shore	N/A	Mark IV 725
HOLIDAYS (11)			
	Love That's True/To Me	N/A	Willjer 6002
HOLIDAYS (12) (GM EDWIN STARR)			
	I'll Love You Forever/(flip is instrumental)	N/A	Golden World 36
	No Greater Love/Watch Out Girl	N/A	Golden World 47
HOLIDAYS (2)			
	Irene/Aw-Aw Baby	1954	Specialty 533
HOLIDAYS (3)			
	Desperately/The Robin	1957	Melba 112
	Sands Of Gold/French Riviera	1958	Brunswick 55084
	Never Go To Mexico/(flip has no group)	1958	Music City 818
	Refreshing/Crazy Discharge	1959	Pam 111
	Very Merry Christmas/Merry Christmas Song	1960	Monument 431
	One Little Kiss/My Girl	1961	Nix 537
	Pretend/Miss You	1961	Robbee 103
	Then I'll Be Tired Of You/Lonely Summer	1961	Robbee 107

Artist Song	Year	Label
I Got News For You	N/A	Dixie 1145
HOLIDAYS (4) (TONY & THE)		
There Goes My Heart Again/		
My Love Is Real	1959	ABC 10029/ABC 10295 (62)
HOLIDAYS (5)		
Who Knows/My Heart Never		
Knows	1959	Wonder 115
Stars Will Remember/		
Who Knows, Who Cares	1960	Andie 5019
Come Back To Me/No Other		
Love	1961	Brent 7018
Got Your Letter/The New		
Trucking	1961	Lyons 107
Patty Ann/Big Brown Eyes	1962	Track 101
Send Back My Love/		
Deacon Brown	1963	Galaxy 714
HOLIDAYS (6) (DICK HOLLER & THE)		
King Kong/The Girl Next Door	1961	Herald 566
Hey Little Fool/Mooba-Grooba	1962	Comet 2146
Double Shot Of My Baby's		
Love/Yea-Boo	1962	Comet 2152
HOLIDAYS (7) (BUDDY SHEPPARD & THE) (AKA BELMONTS)		
Brahm's Lullabye/(Time To		
Dream) My Love Is Real	1962	Sabina 506
Now It's All Over/		
That Background Sound	1963	Sabina 510
HOLIDAYS (8)		
I Want You To Love Me/		
Love And Learn	1964	Coral 62430
HOLIDAYS (9)		
This I Swear/Summertime	1966	Relic 542
Chant Of The Isles (acapella)	1975	Relic LP 102
Adios (acapella)	1975	Relic LP 102
It Happened Today (acapella)	1975	Relic LP 102
My Baby Loves Me (acapella)	1975	Relic LP 102
Time After Time (acapella)	1975	Relic LP 102
HOLLAND, BRYANT (& GROUP)		
Where's The Joy In Nature Boy/		
Shock	1958	Kudo 667
HOLLAND, EDDIE (& GROUP)		
Merry-Go-Round/It Moves Me	1959	Tamla 102/United Artists 172 (59)
HOLLIDAYS		
The Wonder Of Love/I'm Not		
Ashamed	1958	Prep 136
HOLLOWAY, BRENDA (BB THE CARROLLS)		
Echo/Hey Fool	1962	Donna 1358
HOLLYHAWKS		
I Cry All The Time/When Came		
The Fall	1963	Jubilee 5441
HOLLYHOCKS		
Don't Say Tomorrow/You for Me	1957	Nasco 6001
HOLLYWOOD ALLSTARS		
Justine/Dance The Slossin	1963	Admiral 501
HOLLYWOOD ARGYLES		
Alley Oop/Sho' Know A Lot		
About Love	1960	Lute 5905
Gun Totin' Critter Named		
Jack/Bug Eye	1960	Lute 5908
Hully Gully/So Fine	1960	Lute 6002
See You In The Morning/		
Morning After	1961	Finer Arts 1002
You've Been Torturing Me/		
The Grubble	1961	Paxley 752
Bossy Nover/Find Another Way	1963	Felsted 8674
Long Haired Unsquare Dude		
Named Jack/Ole	1965	Chattahoochie 691
HOLLYWOOD ARIST-O-KATS		
Amazon Beauty/I'll Be Home		
Again	1953	Recorded In Hollywood 406
HOLLYWOOD BLUEJAYS		
I Had A Love/Tell Me You		
Love Me	1953	Recorded In Hollywood 396
HOLLYWOOD FLAMES (AKA SATELLITES) (FB BOBBY DAY)		
Let's Talk It Over/I Know	1953	Swing Time 345/Lucky 009 (55)/Decca 48331 (55)
One Night With A Fool/Ride,		
Helen, Ride	1954	Lucky 001
I Shall Return	1954	Lucky 002
Peggy/Ooh-La-La	1954	Lucky 006/Decca 29284 (55)/Hollywood 104
Fare Thee Well/Clickety Clack,		
I'm Leaving	1954	Money 202

Artist Song	Year	Label
Go And Get Some More/		
Another Soldier Gone		
(by the Question Marks (1))	1954	Swing Time 346
Buzz-Buzz-Buzz/Crazy	1957	Ebb 119/Mona Lee 135
Give Me Back My Heart/		
A Little Bird	1958	Ebb 131
Strollin' On The Beach/		
Frankenstein's Den	1958	Ebb 144
Chains Of Love/Let's Talk It		
Over	1958	Ebb 146
I'll Get By/A Star Fell	1958	Ebb 149
If I Thought You Needed Me/		
Every Day, Every Way	1959	Atco 6155
I'll Be Seeing You/Just For You	1959	Ebb 153
So Good/There Is Something		
On Your Mind	1959	Ebb 158
Now That You're Gone/		
Hawaiian Dream	1959	Ebb 162
In The Dark/Much Too Much	1959	Ebb 163
Ball And Chain/I Found A Boy	1960	Atco 6164
Devil Or Angel/Do You Ever		
Think Of Me	1960	Atco 6171
Money Honey/My Heart's On		
Fire	1960	Atco 6180
Yes They Do/Gee	1961	Chess 1787
Believe In Me/I Can't Get A		
Hit Record	1962	Coronet 7025
Drop Me A Line/Letter To My		
Love	1963	Vee Jay 515
Dance Senorita/Annie Don't		
Love Me Anymore	1965	Symbol 211
I'm Comin' Home/I'm Gonna		
Stand By You	1965	Symbol 215
Two Little Bees	1988	Specialty LP 2166
So Good	1988	Specialty LP 2166
Ooh Baby Ooh	1988	Specialty LP 2166
This Heart Of Mine	1988	Specialty LP 2166
HOLLYWOOD FLAMES (DAVE FORD & THE) (AKA SATELLITES)		
Elizabeth/Believe In Me	1962	Goldie 1101
HOLLYWOOD FOUR FLAMES		
Dividend Blues/W-I-N-E	1951	Unique 003
Tabarin/Cry For My Baby	1951	Unique 009
Please Say I'm Wrong/		
The Masquerade Is Over	1951	Unique 015
I'll Always Be A Fool/She's		
Got Something	1952	Recorded In Hollywood 164
Young Girl/Baby Please	1952	Recorded In Hollywood 165 (first pressing)
Young Girl/Glory Of Love	1952	Recorded In Hollywood 165 (second pressing)
HOLLYWOOD PLAYBOYS (1) (FB NICK MASSI)		
Talk To Audrey/Ding Dong,		
School Is Out	1960	Sure 105
HOLLYWOOD PLAYBOYS (2)		
I'm Lonely/You Can't Fool Me		
Baby	1961	Rita 118
HOLLYWOOD PRODUCERS		
You're Not Welcome/		
White Silk Gloves	1966	Parkway 993
HOLLYWOOD SAXONS (AKA SAXONS (1))		
Everyday's A Holiday/		
L. A. Lover	1961	Hareco 102/Swingin' 631 (61)/Elf 101 (61)/20th Century 312 (63)
I'm Your Man/It's You	1961	Swingin' 651/Elf 103 (61)
Loving You/Laughing Blues	1962	Action-Pac 111
Is It True?/Rock & Roll Show	1965	Relic 1011
Merry Go Round/Laughing Girl	1968	Swingin' 654
HOLLYWOOD SAXONS (STAN BEVERLY & THE)		
Spinning/Diamonds	1958	Entra 711
The Tears Came Rolling Down/		
Diamonds	1963	Entra 1214
HOLLYWOOD TEENERS (JIMMY NORMAN & THE)		
A Boy And A Girl/Bride	1960	Fun 101
My Thanks/Para Siempre	1960	Fun 102
HOLMAN, EDDIE (& GROUP)		
This Can't Be True/A Free		
Country (no group)	1965	Parkway 960
Never Let Me Go/Why Do		
Fools Fall In Love	1966	Parkway 157
HOLMES, EDDIE (& GROUP)		
Together Again/At Night	1958	Eagle 1000

Artist	Song	Year	Label
HOMESTEADERS			
	Lonely Day/Riff Rock	1958	End 1017
HOMETOWNERS			
	Ding Dong/I Wanna Go Home	1959	Fraternity 842
HONDAS			
	Send It/Twelve Feet High	1962	Eden 4
HONEY BEARS (MALE)			
	One Bad Stud/It's A Miracle	1954	Spark 104
	I Love Brooklyn/Cuca Monga	1955	Cash 1004
	I Shall Not Fail/Whoa!	1955	Spark 111
HONEY BEES (1)			
	Let's See What's Happening/		
	Endless	1956	Imperial 5400
	What's To Become Of Me/		
	Just To Live Again	1956	Imperial 5416
HONEY BEES (2)			
	Kiss Me My Love/Give Your		
	Love To Me	1964	Bee 1101
	One Wonderful Night/		
	She Don't Deserve You	1964	Smash 1939
	One Girl, One Girl/No Guy	1964	Vee Jay 611
	Some Of Your Lovin'/You		
	Turn Me On Boy	1965	Fontana 1505
	Let's Get Back Together/Never		
	In A Million Years	1966	Wand 1141
HONEY BOYS			
	Never Lose Faith In Me/		
	Vippity Vop	1956	Modern 980
	Unchained Melody/Honey Lov	1974	Boogie Music 1
	Honey/Stolen Love		
	(by the Flamingos)	1974	Owl 333
HONEY DREAMERS			
	Time Was/Copper Kettle	1959	Dot 15925
HONEY-DO'S (MALE)			
	Honey-Dew/Someone	1961	Sue 746
HONEYBIRDS			
	Ain't That Just Like A Boy/		
	Who You Gonna Run To	1964	Coral 62414
HONEYCONES			
	Op/Vision Of You	1958	Ember 1036
	Gee Whiz/Rockin' In The Knees	1958	Ember 1042
	Tell Me Baby/Your Face	1959	Ember 1049
HONEYCONES (ERNIE CAST & THE)			
	Betty Morretti/Cool It Baby	1958	Ember 1033
HONEYDREAMERS (KIRK STUART & THE)			
	Gladly/The Swingin' Shepherd		
	Blues	1958	Josie 832
HONEYMOONS (DENNY DALE & THE)			
	Why Did You Leave Me/		
	Mr. Moon	1966	Soma 1447
HONEYTONES (1)			
	Somewhere, Sometime,		
	Someday/Too Bad	1955	Mercury 70557
	False Alarm/Honeybun Cha Cha	1955	Wing 90013
HONEYTONES (1) (GENE WORTH & THE)			
	When You Are Mine/I'll Never		
	Leave You Alone	N/A	Ace 118
HONEYTONES (2)			
	Don't Look Now, But/I Know		
	I Know	1958	Big Top 3002
HONG KONG WHITE SOX			
	Cholley-Oop (parody)/		
	He'd Better Go	1960	Trans-World 6906
HONKERS			
	Do You Promise/Honk	1959	Okeh 7124
HONORABLES			
	Castle In The Sky/How About		
	A Date	1961	Honor Records 100
HOOD, DARLA (BB THE ROCKETEERS)			
	No Secret Now/Witches Brew	1957	Encino 1007/Acama 122 (60)
HOOTENAIRES			
	Baby Baby (I Love You)/		
	Bill Bailey	1963	Enjoy 2003
HOPE, LYNN (THE LYNN HOPE QUINTET)			
	Don't Worry 'Bout Me/Move It		
	(instrumental)	1952	Aladdin 3155
HOPPERS			
	Linda Loves Me/Linda Loves Me	1959	Valley's Meadow 104
HORIZONS (1)			
	Hey Now Baby/Strange Oh		
	Strange	1964	Regina 1321
HORIZONS (1) (SUNNY & THE)			
	Nature's Creation/Because		
	They Tell Me	1962	Luxor 1015
HORIZONS (2)			
	Why Did You Make Me Cry		
	(acapella)	1975	Relic LP 103
	A Story Of Love (acapella)	1975	Relic LP 104
HORNETS (1) (AKA CLEVELAND QUARTET)			
	I Can't Believe That You're In		
	Love With Me/Lonesome Baby	1953	States 127
	Ridin' And Rockin'	1981	P-Vine Special LP 9036
	You Played The Game	1981	P-Vine Special LP 9036
	Big City Bounce	1981	P-Vine Special LP 9036
HORNETS (2)			
	Crying Over You/Tango Moon	1957	Flash 125
	Strollin'/Slow Dance	1958	Rev 3515
HORNETS (3)			
	She's My Baby/Give Me A Kiss	1964	V.I.P. 25004
HORNETS (4) (DON RAY & THE)			
	I Dreamed Of You/Silly Dilly	1959	Hornet 501
HOSEA, DON (& GROUP)			
	Since I Met You/Uh Huh Huh	1961	Sun 368
HOT RODS (1) (LITTLE SHY GUY & THE)			
	My Little Baby	1956	Calvert 107
HOT RODS (2) (DOUG CONNELL & THE)			
	On Our Way From School/		
	You're My Girl	1959	Alton 600
HOT SHOTS			
	Blue Hours/Horse's Neck	1954	Savoy 1128
	Blue Nights/Blue Dreams	1954	Savoy 1136
HOT TAMALES			
	Mr. Starlight/Loves Intentions	1964	Detroit 101
HOUND DOGS			
	I'm Beginning To Understand		
	Them/The Girl	1964	Dee Dee 773
HOUSE, HERMAN (& GROUP)			
	Evie My Darling	N/A	Call 106
HOUSTON, DAVID (& GROUP)			
	Waited So Long/All I Do Is		
	Dream Of You	1958	NRC 005
HOUSTON, JOE (& GROUP)			
	Shtiggy Boom/Joe's Gone		
	(instrumental)	1955	RPM 426
HOWARD, GREGORY (BB THE CADILLACS) (AKA GEE-TONES)			
	When In Love (Do As Lovers		
	Do)/Sweet Pea	1963	Kapp 536
HOWARD, VINCE (& GROUP)			
	If You Believe, If You Believe/		
	Moonlight Mountain	1961	Era 3056
HOWARDS			
	Lola/Mi Mi Girl	1958	ABC 9897
HUBBCAPS (FRANK HUBBELL & THE)			
	Broken Date, Pt. 1/		
	Broken Date, Pt. 2	1963	Topix 6005
HUBCAPS (HOLT DAVEY & THE)			
	Pittery Pat/You Move Me	1958	United Artists 110X
HUDSON, EDDIE (& GROUP)			
	She's Sugar Sweet/That Long		
	Lost Baby	1958	Excello 2135
HUDSON, GLINDA (& GROUP)			
	I'll Wait	N/A	Smalltown 300
HUDSON, POOKIE (BB THE IMPERIALS)			
	I Know I Know/Jealous Heart	1963	Double L 711
HUEYS			
	Coo Coo Over You/You Ain't		
	No Hippie	1968	Instant 3289
HUFF, CHAUNCEY (& GROUP)			
	Does She Love Me/Swimmin'		
	U.S.A.	1964	Fantasy 587
HUGHES, FRED (& GROUP) (AKA CYMBALS (1)			
	One Step Too Far/Shout Mama	1965	Minasa 709
HULL, TERRY (BB THE STARFIRES)			
	Those Pretty Brown Eyes/		
	Meant To Be	N/A	Staff 103
HUMDINGERS			
	Necklace Of Tear Drops/		
	The Clock In Lovers Lane	1957	Dale 106
HUME, DON (& GROUP)			
	Perfect Night/Go Right Ahead	1963	Felsted 8679
HUMMINGBIRDS			
	You And Me/My Ship	1962	Cannon 4600

Artist	Song	Year	Label
HUMPHRIES, FATMAN (BB THE FOUR NOTES (AKA CROWS))			
	I Can't Get Started With You/		
	Lulubell Blues	1952	Jubilee 5085
HUMPHRIES, TEDDY (& GROUP)			
	This Love Is True Love/		
	Without A Song	1958	King 5151
HUNTER, HERBERT (& GROUP)			
	I'm So Satisfied/Don't Pity Me	1961	Poncello 711
HUNTERS (1) (AKA FLAIRS)			
	Rabbit On A Log/Down At		
	Hayden's	1953	Flair 1017
HUNTERS (2) (LITTLE MOOSE & THE)			
	Lovely One/Granny Rock	1959	SMC 1373
HURLEY, JOHN (& GROUP)			
	Lonely Boy/Cry Baby	1958	AKA 103
HURRICANES (1) (BOB GAYE & THE)			
	I Keep Crying/Teardrops	1954	Audivox 109
HURRICANES (2)			
	Poor Little Dancing Girl/Pistol		
	Packin' Mama	1955	King 4817
	Maybe It's All For The Best/		
	Yours	1956	King 4867
	Raining In My Heart/Tell Me,		
	Baby	1956	King 4898
	Little Girl Of Mine/Your Promise		
	To Me	1956	King 4926
	Sentimental Heaven/		
	Wishing Well	1956	King 4932
	Dear Mother/You May Not Know	1956	King 4947
	Fallen Angel/I'll Always Be In		
	Love With You	1957	King 5018
	Priceless/Now That I Need You	1957	King 5042
	I'll Be Glad	N/A	UGHA LP 001
HUSHABYES (HALE & THE)			
	Yes Sir, That's My Baby/		
	900 Quetzals	1964	Apogee 104/Reprise 0299
HUSKIES			
	Go Out And Buy Yourself A		
	Hat/Alaska, U.S.A.	1958	Imperial 5544
HUSKIES (KENNY KOLE & THE)			
	Sorry/Who	1958	Klik 8205
HUSTLERS (1) (RICHARD WARD & THE)			
	The Well Of Loneliness/The		
	Long Drink Of Water In A		
	Topless Bathing Suit	1964	Downey 121
HUSTLERS (2)			
	Goodbye/That's What Makes		
	Her Boss	1965	Fascination 6570
	Linda	1965	Rich 113
HUSTLERS (3) (CARL BURNETT & THE) (REF LITTLE CAESAR & THE ROMANS)			
	Sweet Memories/Jerk Baby Jerk	1965	Carmax 102
HY-TONES			
	I'm A Fool/Chinese Boogie	1958	Hy-Tone 120
	I've Got My Baby/Bigger And		
	Better	1966	A-Bet 9415
HY-TONES (GEORGIA HARRIS & THE)			
	It's Time To Rock/Let's Exchange		
	Hearts For Christmas(by		
	Georgia Harris & the Lyrics)	1958	Hy-Tone 117
	Let Me Hold Your Hand/		
	I Want To Kiss You	1958	Hy-Tone 121
HYPNOTICS			
	Eloise/Your'er The Best For Me	1959	Warkee 905
I. V. LEAGUERS			
	Ring Chimes/The Story	1957	Porter 1003/1004/Dot 15677 (58)
	Told By The Stars/Jim Jam	1959	Nau-Voo 803
IDEALS (1)			
	Do I Have The Right/You		
	Won't Like It	1958	Cool 108
IDEALS (2)			
	My Girl/Annie Was A Stroller	1958	Decca 30720
	Ivy League Lover/Don't Be A		
	Baby, Baby	1959	Decca 30800
	Please Jan/Always Yours	1959	Stars Of Hollywood 1001
	Together/What's The Matter		
	With You, Sam	1961	Paso 6401/Dusty Disc
	Teens/Magic	1961	Paso 6402/Dusty Disc
	Trans Zistor/The Duchess	1962	Fargo 1024
IDEALS (2) (JOHNNY BRANTLEY & THE)			
	Mary's Lamb/Knee Socks	1959	Checker 920/Checker 979 (61)
IDENTICALS			
	Jamie/Dreaming Of You	1963	Firebird 101
IDENTITIES			
	When You Find Love Slipping		
	Away	N/A	Together 1410
IDETS			
	Look My Way/Doggie In The		
	Window	N/A	Shiptown 007
IDOLS (1)			
	Just A Little Bit More/Why Must		
	I Cry (by the Swans)	1961	Reveille 1002/Dot 16210 (61)
IDOLS (2)			
	The Prowler/Thirty Days	1958	RCA 7339
	Jeannine/Can't Tag Along	1961	E-Z 1214
IDOLS (3)			
	The Stars Will Remember/Tell Me	1961	Galaxie 77
IDOLS (4)			
	You're Good For Me/		
	That's The Game To Play	1958	Redd-E 1017
IDOLS (5)			
	I Love You	N/A	Collectables LP 5039
IDOLS (6) (LITTLE JOE BONNER & THE)			
	Tell Me Baby/Do You Love Me	1955	B&S 1570
IDYLLS			
	Annette/Love Me Again	1960	Spinning 6012
ILLUSIONS (1)			
	The Letter/Henry And Henrietta	1960	Coral 62173
	Can't We Fall In Love/How High		
	Is The Mountain	1961	Ember 1071
	The Closer You Are/For		
	Sentimental Reasons	1962	Kape 1001/Kape 100 (74)
	Hey Boy/Lonely Soldier	1962	Mali 104/Sheraton 104 (62)/ Northeast 801 (62)/Relic 512 (64)
	I Know/Take My Heart	1966	Columbia 43700
ILLUSIONS (2)			
	Jezebel	1963	Round 1018
ILLUSIONS (3)			
	In The Beginning (I May Be		
	Wrong)/Maybe	1964	Laurie 3245
	Story Of My Life/Walking Boy	1964	Little Debbie 105
ILLUSIONS (4) (JIMMY & THE)			
	Karen	1963	Jolynn 36
ILLUSIONS (5)			
	City Of People	N/A	Michelle 1
IMAGE			
	All Mine/Over The Rainbow	1982	Clifton 68
IMAGINATIONS (1)			
	I Want A Girl/I Love You More		
	(Than Anyone)	1961	Bacon Fat 101
IMAGINATIONS (2) (AKA EXPRESSIONS (3))			
	I Hate To See A Little Girl Crying	1961	Music Makers (unreleased)
	Goodnight Baby/The Search		
	Is Over	1961	Music Makers 103
	Hey You/Guardian Angel	1961	Music Makers 108/Duel 507 (61)/Bo Marc 301 (61)
	Mama's Little Baby/Wait A		
	Little Longer Son	1962	Ballad 500
	I'll Never Let You Go/The		
	Mystery Of You	1976	Harvey 101
	Autumn Leaves	1985	Relic LP 5058
	Never Let You Go	1985	Relic LP 5058
	The Mystery Of You	1985	Relic LP 5058
	Harry Goody	1985	Relic LP 5058
	Fannie Mae	1985	Relic LP 5058
	My Little Girl	1985	Relic LP 5058
	Chapel Bells	1985	Relic LP 5058
IMAGINATIONS (2) (DARLENE DAY & THE)			
	I Love You So/Will	1961	Music Makers 106
IMMORTALS			
	Theme For A Broken Heart/		
	Moonshine	1961	Laurie 3099
IMPACS			
	Forever And A Day/Hold-Out	1963	Arlen 741
	I'm Gonna Make You Cry/		
	Tears In My Heart	1963	Parkway 865
	Jo-Ann/Two Strangers	1964	King 5851
	Shimmy, Shimmy/Zot		
	(instrumental)	1964	King 5863
	Kool It/She Didn't Even Say		
	Hello	1964	King 5891

Artist	Song	Year	Label	Artist	Song	Year	Label
	Ain't That The Way Life Is/				I'm Still Dancing/Bermuda		
	Don't Cry Baby	1964	King 5910		Wonderful	1963	Capitol 4924
IMPACTS (1)				**IMPERIALS (2) (LITTLE ANTHONY & THE)**			
	Croc-O-Doll/Bobby Sox Squaw	1959	RCA 7583		Little Girl	1958	End (unreleased)
	Now Is The Time/Soup	1959	Watts 5599		I Cover The Waterfront	1958	End (unreleased)
	Canadian Sunset/They Say	1959	Watts 5600/RCA 7609 (59)		Tears On My Pillow/Two		
	Summer/Linda	1964	Anderson 104		People In The World	1958	End 1027(second pressing,
IMPACTS (2)							first is by the Imperials)
	Help Me Somebody/Darling,				So Much/Oh Yeah	1958	End 1036
	Now You're Mine	1961	Carlton 548		The Diary/Cha Cha Henry	1958	End 1038
IMPACTS (3)					Must Be Falling In Love/You	1958	Savoy 1552
	Where Are You/I'm So Glad	1966	Brunswick 55393		Dry Your Eyes	1959	End (unreleased)
IMPAKS					When You Wish Upon A Star/		
	Make Up Your Mind/Climb				Wishful Thinking	1959	End 1039
	Upon Your Rockin' Chair	1962	Express 716		A Prayer And A Juke Box/		
IMPALAS (1)					River Path	1959	End 1047
	All But The Memory	1958	Cub EP CX5000		So Near And Yet So Far/		
	Chum	1958	Cub EP CX5000		I'm Alright	1959	End 1053
	Sorry (I Ran All The Way				Shimmy, Shimmy, Ko-Ko-Bop/		
	Home)/Fool Fool Fool	1959	Cub 9022		I'm Still In Love With You	1959	End 1060
	Oh What A Fool/Sandy Went				Love Is A Many Splendored		
	Away	1959	Cub 9033		Thing	1959	End LP 303/End EP 204 (59)
	Peggy Darling/Bye Everybody	1959	Cub 9053		Over The Rainbow	1959	End LP 303/End EP 204 (59)
	First Date/I Was A Fool	1959	Hamilton 50026		What Did I Do	1959	End LP 303/End EP 204 (59)
	My Hero/There Is Nothing				My Empty Room/Bayou Bayou		
	Like A Dame	1982	U.G.H.A. 17		Baby	1960	End 1067
	My Hero/There Is Nothing				I'm Taking A Vacation From		
	Like A Dame	1982	UGHA 17		Love/Only Sympathy	1960	End 1074
IMPALAS (1) (SPEEDO & THE)					Limbo Pt. 1/Limbo Pt. 2	1960	End 1080
	When My Heart Does All The				Formula Of Love /Dream		
	Talking/All Alone	1960	Cub 9066		(or Two People In The World)	1960	End 1083
IMPALAS (2)					Please Say You Want Me/		
	The Lonely One/Lost Boogie	1959	Sundown 115		So Near And Yet So Far	1960	End 1086
	Last Night I Saw A Girl/There				The Fires Burn No More/I Know		
	Is Nothin' Like A Dame	1963	20th Fox 428		(Lift Up Your Head)	1961	Apollo 755
	I Still Love You/Whip It On Me	1969	Bunky 7762		Traveling Stranger/Say Yeah	1961	End 1091
IMPALAS (2) (BOBBY BYRD & THE)					A Lovely Way To Spend An		
	Why?/Gotta Girl	1958	Corvet 1017		Evening/Dream	1961	End 1104
IMPALAS (3) (FEMALE) (AKA FOUR JEWELS/AKA RUBIES (1))					I've Got A Crush On You	1961	End LP 311
	I Need You So Much/For The				I Couldn't Sleep A Wink Last		
	Love Of Mike	1961	Checker 999		Night	1961	End LP 311
IMPALAS (4) (AKA FIVE DISCS)					I'll Never Smile Again	1961	End LP 311
	When You Dance/I Can't See				All Or Nothing At All	1961	End LP 311
	Me Without You	1966	Red Boy 113/Steady 044		If You Are But A Dream	1961	End LP 311
	I Can't See Me Without You/				Ooh Looka There, Ain't She		
	Old Man Mose	N/A	Rite-On 101		Pretty	1961	End LP 311
IMPALOS					Don't Get Around Much		
	You're To Blame/Wrong About				Anymore	1961	End LP 311
	You	1961	United Artists 327		Undecided	1961	End LP 311
IMPAX					They Say It's Wonderful	1961	End LP 311
	Baby, You're My Love/				This Love Of Mine	1961	End LP 311
	Cool Breeze	1960	Warner Bros. 5153		That Lil' Ole Lovemaker Me/		
IMPERIAL GENTS					It Just Ain't Fair	1963	Roulette 4379
	Little Darlin'/The Imperial				Lonesome Romeo/I've Got A		
	Gents Stomp	1970	Laurie 3540		Lot To Offer Darling	1963	Roulette 4477
IMPERIAL WONDERS					I'm On The Outside (Looking In)/		
	When I Fall In Love/Trying To				Please Go	1964	DCP 1104/Veep 1240 (66)
	Get To You	1969	Black Prince 317		Goin' Out Of My Head/Make It		
IMPERIALITES					Easy On Yourself	1964	DCP 1119/Veep 1241 (66)
	Have Love Will Travel/Let's				Hurt So Bad/Reputation	1965	DCP 1128/Veep 1242 (66)
	Get One	1964	Imperial 66015		Take Me Back/Our Song	1965	DCP 1136/Veep 1243 (66)
IMPERIALS (1) (AKA AMBASSADORS (1)/AKA FOUR ARCS/					I Miss You So/Get Out Of My Life	1965	DCP 1149/Veep 1244 (66)
AKA GAYLORDS)					Hurt/Never Again	1966	DCP 1154/Veep 1245 (66)
	My Darling/You Should Have				It's Not For Me	N/A	Rhino LP 70919
	Told Me	1952	Savoy 1104/Buzzy 1 (62)	**IMPERIALS (3)**			
	Why Did You Leave Me?/				The Glory Of Love/Come On		
	Hard Workin' Woman	1953	Derby 858		Tiger	1958	Liberty 55119
	You'll Never Walk Alone/			**IMPERIALS (4) (STACY HENRY & THE)**			
	Ain't Gonna Tell It Right	1953	Gem 212/Great Lakes		Sweetest Darlin'/I'm Not		
			1212 (54)		Ashamed	1961	Flippin' 108
	Life Of Ease/It Won't Be			**IMPLACEABLES**			
	Very Long	1954	Great Lakes 1201		My Foolish Pride/Don't Call		
IMPERIALS (2)					For Me	1960	Kain 1004
	Tears On My Pillow/Two People			**IMPOLLOS (FB BOBBY RUSSELL)**			
	In The World	1958	End 1027 (first pressing,		The Raven/She's Gonna Be		
			second is by Little		Right	1958	Felsted 8520
			Anthony & the Imperials)	**IMPOLLOS (JOHNNY INMAN & THE)**			
	Faithfully Yours/Vut Vut	1961	Carlton 566		You Never Realized/I'm So		
	A Short Prayer/Where Will				Sorry	1958	Aladdin 3426
	You Be	1962	Newtime 503	**IMPOSSIBLES (1)**			
	The Letter/Go And Get Your				Mr. Maestro/Well It's Alright	1959	RMP 1030
	Broken Heart	1962	Newtime 505		Well It's Alright/Everywhere I Go	1960	RMP 501

Artist Song	Year	Label	Artist Song	Year	Label
I Can't Dance/The Tenants' Blues	1961	RMP 508	He's Coming Home/What Good Am I Without You	1965	Cor 6581/Verve Folkways 5002
IMPOSSIBLES (2) (LINDA CARR & THE)			Woo Woo Pretty Girl/Servant Of Love	1977	Arcade 1006
Shy One/(I'm In Love With The) Garbage Man	1961	Ray Starr 779	**INDIVIDUALS (1)**		
I'll Never Get Married/ Happy Teenager	1961	Skyla 1111	Met Her At A Dance/ Jungle Superman	1959	Show Time 595
IMPOSSIBLES (3)			Dear One/Jungle Superman	1959	Show Time 598/Red Fox 105 5002
Chapel Bells/Little By Little	1963	Blanche 029			
Lonely Bluebird/Paint Me A Pretty Picture	1964	Reprise 0305	Woo Woo Pretty Girl/Servant Without Success/I've Been Hurt	1959	Sparrow 101
IMPRESSIONS (1)			**INDIVIDUALS (2) (JOE BLACKWELL & THE)**		
The Gift Of Love/At The Country Fair	1958	Abner 1023	Beverly My Darling/April Love (by Andy Taylor)	1961	Music City 838
Listen/Shorty's Got To Go	1958	Bandera 2504/Port 70031 (60)	**INDIVIDUALS (3) (CHUCK RIO & THE)**		
Lonely One/Senorita I Love You	1959	Abner 1025	Cell Block #9/If You Were The Only Girl In The World	1961	Tequila 103
Meanwhile, Back In My Heart/ All Through The Night	1960	20th Fox 172	**INDIVIDUALS (4) (WITH THE MERCEEDEES)**		
That You Love Me/New Love	1960	Abner 1034	Please Baby Be Mine/Not Me	1962	Gold Seal 1000
I Need Your Love/Don't Leave Me	1962	Swirl 107	**INDIVIDUALS (5)**		
Say That You Love Me/Senorita I Love You	1962	Vee Jay 424/Vee Jay 621 (64)	Wedding Bells/Pillow Wet With Tears	1964	Chase 1300
IMPRESSIONS (1) (JERRY BUTLER & THE)			**INDIVIDUALS (6)**		
Come Back My Love/Love Me	1958	Abner 1017	Here I Am	1959	Delwood
For Your Precious Love/ Sweet Was The Wine	1958	Vee Jay 280/Falcon 1013 (58)/Abner 1013 (58)/Vee Jay 396 (61)	**INELIGIBLES**		
			Just The Things That You Do/ Do The Groove	1960	Capella 501
The Gift Of Love/At The Country Fair	1963	Vee Jay 574	**INFASCINATIONS**		
A Long Time Ago/Believe In Me	1976	Robin Hood 139/Vee Jay LP 1075	One Chance/I'm So In Love	1961	Clauwell 003/004
			INFATUATORS		
Don't Drive Me Away/ Young Lover	1976	Robin Hood 140/Vee Jay LP 1075	I Found My Love/Where Are You?	1961	Destiny 504/Vee Jay 395 (61)
			INFATUATORS (LARRY LEE & THE)		
Let Me Know/Lover's Lane	1976	Robin Hood 147/Vee Jay LP 1075	Desire/Kentucky	1961	Destiny 503
			INFERNOS (1)		
IMPRESSIONS (2) (JOEY & THE)			Goin' Cruisin'	1963	Hawk 101
The Week Is Over/Lonesome Teenager	N/A	Cagg 101	In My Diary/False Alarm	1981	Clifton 59
IMPRESSORS			Ronnie I Jingle/Shrine Of St. Cecilia/Chapel Of Dreams/I'll Be True	N/A	Clifton EP 502
Is It Too Late/No No No	1957	Onyx 514	**INFERNOS (2)**		
Do You Love Her/Loneliness	1958	Cub 9010	That Lady Of Mine/Looking	1980	BAB 126
IMPS			The Angel On 4th Avenue/ Rainy Days In New York	1980	BAB 127
Uh-Oh/That'll Get It	1961	Do-Ra-Mi 1414	**INFORMERS (1)**		
INADEQUATES			Don't Cry, Sure It Hurts/Dora, He Told Me To Tell You It Hurts	1960	Dore 562
Pretty Face/Audie	1959	Capitol 4232			
INCAS			**INFORMERS (2)**		
Cottage By The Sea/Your Love Is Just Plain	1976	Monogram 125	If You Love Me/Hard Way To Go	1965	J-Rude 1400
The Time For Love/A Wink And A Grin	1977	Monogram 126	**INITIALS (ANGELO & THE)**		
			Bells Of Joy/You	1959	Dee 1001/Sherry 667
You're Gone/Sweet Lucy	1977	Monogram 127	School Day/This Song Is Number One	1964	Congress 207
INCIDENTALS			Seventeen Guys On A Blanket At The Beach/Dancing On The Sand	1964	Congress 219
Barbara/Where's My True Love	1961	Gar-Lo 1000			
All Night/Driving Guitars	1964	Ford 134	Someday She'll Love Me/ I Should Have Listened	1964	Congress 229
Lucille/Fireside	1964	Ford 138	You Didn't Answer My Letter/ Someday Someway	1973	Vintage 1006
It's In Your Mind	N/A	Paris Tower 126	**INNOCENTS**		
INCOGNITOS			Time/Dee Dee Di Oh	1959	Andex 22012/Indigo 141 (62)
Dee Jay's Dilemma/Forget It	1961	Zee 001	Honest I Do/My Baby Hully Gully's	1960	Indigo 105
INCONQUERABLES			Tick Tock/The Rat (instrumental)	1960	Trans World 7001
Wait For Me/For Your Love	1964	Flodavieur 803	Gee Whiz/Please Mr. Sun	1961	Indigo 111
INCREDABLES			Kathy/In The Beginning	1961	Indigo 116
If You Give A Party/Little Bitty Bandit	N/A	Kelrich 850/851	Beware/Because I Love You	1961	Indigo 124
INCREDIBLE UPSETTERS			Donna/You Got Me Goin'	1961	Indigo 128
My Life, My Loved One	1959	Audio Lab EP 2	Pains In My Heart/When I Become A Man	1961	Indigo 132
INDELGENTS			I Believe In You	1961	Indigo LP 503
Give Up	N/A	Jenges	Walking Along	1961	Indigo LP 503
INDEXES (JOHN GOLDEN & THE)			Girl Of My Dreams	1961	Indigo LP 503
Take A Chance/You Changed My Mind (with Blanton McFarlin)	1961	Douglas 101	It Was A Tear	1961	Indigo LP 503
			Chiquita	1961	Indigo LP 503
INDIGOS			Come On Lover/Don't Cry	1963	Decca 31519
Woo Woo Pretty Girl/Servant Of Love	1958	Cornel 3001	My Heart Stood Still/Don't Call Me Lonely Any More	1964	Warner Bros. 5450
Everything Plus/High School Social	1958	Cornel 515	**INNOCENTS (KATHY YOUNG & THE)**		
Girl By The Wayside/Ho-Hum Deedle-Dum	1961	Image 5001	A Thousand Stars/Eddie My Darling	1960	Indigo 108/Port 3025 (60)
My Dream Girl/Beyond Your Wildest Dreams	1963	Cadette 8003			

Artist Song	Year	Label
Happy Birthday Blues/Someone To Love	1961	Indigo 115
Our Parents Talked It Over/Just As Though You Were Here	1961	Indigo 121
Magic Is The Night/Du Du'nt Du	1961	Indigo 125
Baby Oh Baby/The Great Pretender	1961	Indigo 137
Lonely Blue Nights/I'll Hang My Letters Out To Dry	1962	Indigo 146
Dream Awhile/Send Her Away	1962	Indigo 147
Dream Boy/I'll Love That Man	1962	Monogram 506
All You Had To Do (Was Tell Me)/Love Me (with Chris Montez)	1962	Monogram 517
Oh How I Miss My Baby/Be Mine	1962	Reprise 20112
Oh How I Miss My Baby/You're Never Satisfied	1963	Reprise 20125
Sparkle And Shine	N/A	Indigo EP 1001
INNOCENTS (RAL DONNER & THE)		
Beyond The Heartbreak/Run Little Linda	1963	Reprise 20192
INQUISITORS (LITTLE ISADORE & THE)		
Woo Woo Train/I Pray For You	1995	Early Bird 5000
Why Do You Cry/Bongo Stomp	1995	Early Bird 5001
INSPIRATIONS (1)		
Raindrops/Maggie	1956	Apollo 494
Don't Cry/Indian Jane	1958	Lamp 2019
Pretty Mama	1989	Relic LP 5080
INSPIRATIONS (2)		
Dry Your Eyes/Goodbye	1956	Jamie 1034/Jamie 1212 (62)
The Genie/Feeling Of Her Kiss	1959	Sultan 1
Angel In Disguise/Stool Pigeon	1960	Al-Brite 1650/1651/Sparkle 102 (60)/Gone 5097 (60)
The Girl By My Side/Neckin'	1963	Beltone 2037
INSPIRATIONS (3) (RONNIE VARE & THE)		
Let's Rock Little Girl/Love Is Just For Two	1959	Dell 5202/5203
INSPIRATIONS (4) (BENNY BUNN & THE)		
If I Were King/In Desperation	1959	Eastmen 790
INSPIRATIONS (5) (ANDRE "BACON FAT" WILLIAMS & THE)		
I Still Love You/Jailhouse Blues	1960	Fortune 856
INSPIRATIONS (6)		
Ay Yai Yai/My Inspiration	1972	Bim Bam Boom 109
INSPIRATIONS (7) (MAURICE WILLIAMS & THE)		
The Day Has Come/Never Leave You Again	1963	Candi 1031
INSPIRATIONS (8)		
Ring Those Bells/The Cumberland And The Merrimac	1961	Rondak 9787
INSPIRATORS		
If Loving You Is Wrong/Three Sixty	1955	Treat 502
Starlight Tonight/Oh, What A Feeling!	1958	Old Town 1053
INSTANTS		
Always Be True/Gravy Train	1962	Rendezvous 193
INTENSIONS		
I Don't Care Anymore	N/A	Bluelight 1214
INTENTIONS		
Summertime Angel/Mr. Misery	1963	Jamie 1253/Jason Scott 2 (80)
I'm In Love With A Go-Go Girl/Wonderful Girl	1964	Melron 5014
Time/Cool Summer Night	1965	Uptown 710
My Love She's Gone/Dancing Fast, Dancing Slow	1967	Kent 455
Don't Forget That I Love You/Night Rider	1967	Philips 40428
What Am I Gonna Do With You/Hey Baby	N/A	Black Pearl 100
INTERIORS (GM JAYOTIS WASHINGTON)		
Darling Little Angel/Voodoo Doll	1961	Worthy 1008
Echoes/Love You Some More	1961	Worthy 1009
INTERLUDES (1)		
I Shed A Million Tears/Oo-Wee	1958	RCA 7281
INTERLUDES (2)		
I Want You To Know/Split A Kiss	1959	Star-Hi 103
Heartbreaker/Scandalous	1959	Valley 1005
No One For Me/Fort Lauderdale	1960	Valley 106
White Sailor Hat/Evil	1960	Valley 107

Artist Song	Year	Label
INTERLUDES (3)		
Number One In The Nation/Beautiful, Wonderful, Heavenly You	1961	ABC 10213
Darling I'll Be True/Wilted Rose Bud	1962	King 5633
INTERNATIONALS		
Goin' To A Party/I Love You So	1958	ABC 9964
INTERPRETERS		
Pretty Little Thing/Be Kind To Love	1967	A-Bet 9425
INTERVALS		
Side Street/I Still Love That Man	1958	Ad 104/Apt 25019 (58)
Love So Sweet/Try To Realize	1958	Irma 820
Please Come Back To Me/Don't Leave Me	1959	Ad 103
You Are My Only Love/Funny How Time Goes By	1962	Class
Here's That Rainy Day/Wish I Could Change My Mind	1962	Class 304
INTIMATES		
Got You Where I Want/Only Girl For Me	1964	Amcan 402
Smart Too Late/I've Got A Tiger In My Tank	1964	Epic 9743
INVADERS		
Paradise/Sloop It Out	1963	El Toro 503
I Won't Be Lonely	1964	Calendar 223-66
INVENTIONS (AKA CATALINAS (3))		
Hey, Peanuts/Row Boat	1960	Up 111
INVICTAS		
Lest You Forget/Over The Wall	1958	Pix 1101
Gone So Long/Nellie	1959	Jack Bee 1003
I Met Him At A Dance/Oh Mama	1963	Mavis 221
INVICTAS (SONNY PATTERSON & THE)		
Gone So Long/Troubles (by the Pastel Six)	1963	Vault 903
INVICTORS		
I'll Always Care For You/I Don't Wanna Go	1959	Bee 1117
This Thing Called Love/The Wiggle	1962	TPE 8217
Don't Take My Love/Babalonian	1963	TPE 8219
Where All Lovers Meet/That's All Right	1963	TPE 8221
I Took A Chance/Put Her Down	1963	TPE 8223
INVINCIBLES		
Mr. Moonglow/Swayback	1959	Chess 1727
IRIDESCENTS (FEMALE)		
Three Coins In The Fountain/Strong Love	1963	Hudson 8102
I Found You/Hey There	1963	Hudson 8107
IRRIDESCENTS		
The Angels Sang/I Know	1960	Ultrasonic 104/Ultrasonic 109
IRWIN, BIG DEE (BB THE PASTELS)		
I Can't Help It	N/A	Astra 1024
ISLANDERS (1)		
Hey, Hey Baby (acapella)	1975	Relic LP 103
My True Story (acapella)	1975	Relic LP 103
Walking In The Rain (acapella)	1975	Relic LP 104
You Never Loved Me (acapella)	1975	Relic LP 105
When We Get Married (acapella)	1975	Relic LP 108
ISLANDERS (2) (RICK & THE)		
Just For You (Dance Dance)/Everybody	N/A	H&G 185
ISLEY BROTHERS		
Angels Cried/The Cow Jumped Over The Moon	1956	Teenage 1004
This Is The End/Don't Be Jealous	1958	Cindy 3009
I Wanna Know/Everybody's Gonna Rock & Roll	1958	Gone 5022
My Love/The Drag	1959	Gone 5048
The Drag/Rockin' MacDonald	1959	Mark-X 8000
Turn To Me/I'm Gonna Knock On Your Door	1959	RCA 7537
ITALIAN ASPHALT AND PAVEMENT COMPANY (AKA DUPREES)		
Check Yourself/The Sky's The Limit	1970	Colossus 110
ITELS		
Star Of Paradise/Chubby Isn't Chubby Anymore	1961	Magnifico 101

Artist	Song	Year	Label
ITHACAS			
	If You Want My Love/Gonna Fix You Good	1957	Fee Bee 220
IVES, JIMMY (& GROUP)			
	My Fumbling Heart/Settle Down	1961	Comet 2141
IVIES			
	Sunshine/Come On	1958	Ivy 110/Brunswick 55112 (58)
	I Really Want To Know/Voodoo	1959	Roulette 4183
IVIES (EZRA & THE)			
	Comic Book Crazy/Rockin' Shoes	1959	United Artists 165
IVOLEERS			
	Lover's Quarrel/Come With Me	1959	Buzz 101
IVORIES (1)			
	Alone/Baby, Send A Letter	1956	Jaguar 3019/Jaguar 3023 (57)
IVORIES (2) (FEMALE)			
	Me And You/I'm In Love	1957	Mercury 71239
IVORYS (AKA FIVE IVORIES)			
	Wishing Well/Deep Freeze	1962	Darla (no number)
	Why Don't You Write Me/Deep Freeze	1962	Sparta 001
IVORYTONES			
	Little Fool/The Things We Did Last Summer	1960	Norwood 101
	Wo! Wo! Wo!/Move It Over	1960	Unidap 448
IVY JIVES			
	Million Dollar Girl/Knockout	1960	Jaro 77036
IVY LEAGUE			
	What More Do You Want/Wait A Minute	1965	Cameo 343
	Lonely Room/Funny How Love Can Be	1965	Cameo 356
	That's Why I'm Crying/A Girl Like You	1965	Cameo 365
	Graduation Day/Tossing And Turning	1965	Cameo 377
IVY LEAGUERS			
	Beware Of Love/Deposit Your Love In The Bank Of My Heart	1957	Flip 325
IVY THREE			
	Yogi/Was Judy There	1960	Shell 720
	Hush Little Baby/Alone In The Chapel	1960	Shell 723
	Nine Out Of Ten/I've Cried Enough For Two	1961	Shell 302
	Bagoo/Suicide	1961	Shell 306
IVY, SHERON (& GROUP)			
	I Need You/Believe Me	1961	Heritage 106/Coed 572 (62)
IVY-TONES			
	Oo-Wee Baby/Each Time	1958	Red Top 105
IVYLIERS			
	Echo From The Blue/When The Reign Of Love Begins	1957	Donna A-3
IVYS			
	All I Want/Lost Without You	1959	Coed 518
J'S (1) (JIMMY J. & THE)			
	Girlfriend (Please Be My)/I've Lost	1961	Salco 647
J'S (2) (WITH JAMIE)			
	Little Me/Come On Strong	1962	Columbia 42635
JAC-O-LACS (FB CORNEL GUNTER)			
	Cindy Lou/Sha-Ba-Da-Ba-Doo	1955	Tampa 103
JACK, JOHNNY (& GROUP)			
	The Beggar That Became King/Touch Me	1962	Gone 5132
	Let's Have A Party/True Love At First Sight	1964	Lawn 226
	Forever (And A Day)/Love Must Be	64	Lawn 230
JACKAELS (J. J. JACKSON & THE) (AKA JACKALS (2))			
	A Lifetime From Today/That Look In Your Eye	1959	Storm 501
	Oo-Ma-Liddi/Let The Show Begin	1959	Storm 502/Prelude 502 (59)
JACKALS (1) (FRANK SANDY & THE)			
	Let's Go Rock 'N Roll/Midnight Stomp	1958	MGM 12678
JACKALS (2) (J. J. JACKSON & THE) (AKA JACKAELS)			
	Ring Telephone/False Face	1963	Everest 2012
JACKS			
	Away/Creation Of Love (by the Charms	1974	Owl 329
JACKS & JILLS			
	I Hear A Melody/Roses Never Fade	1956	Empire 101
	I Can't Forget/Red Dog	1958	MGM 12671
JACKS (AKA CADETS (1))			
	Why Don't You Write Me/Smack Dab In The Middle	1955	RPM 428 (first pressing)
	Why Don't You Write Me/My Darling	1955	RPM 428 (second pressing)
	I'm Confessin'/Ever Since My Baby's Been Gone	1955	RPM 433
	Bob-O-Link/Since You (Donna Hightower)	1955	RPM 439
	This Empty Heart (My Love Has Gone)/My Clumsy Heart	1955	RPM 444
	So Wrong/How Soon?	1956	RPM 454
	Why Did I Fall In Love/Sugar Baby	1956	RPM 458
	Dream A Little Longer/Let's Make Up	1956	RPM 467
	I Confess/Blau-Wile Devest Fontaine (P. Anka)	1956	RPM 472
	Oo Wee Baby	1957	RPM LP 3006
	You Belong To Me	1957	RPM LP 3006/Crown LP 5021 (57)
	Wiggie Waggie Woo	1957	RPM LP 3006/Crown LP 5021 (57)
	Do You Wanna Rock (aka Hey Little Girl)	1957	RPM LP 3006/Crown LP 5372 (58)
	Why Don't You Write Me/This Empty Heart	1960	Kent 344
	You Are The First One	1963	Crown LP 5372
	Lovey Dovey	1963	Crown LP 5372
	Why Don't You Write Me/So Wrong	1975	Relic 1031
	Away	N/A	Relic LP 5023
	Why Don't You Write Me/Sugar Baby	N/A	Victory
JACKS (JULIE JORDAN & THE)			
	Sincerely	N/A	Rush 1003
JACKSON BROTHERS			
	The Wrong Door/Love Was Here With You	1952	Arrow 1003
	Love Me/Tell Him No	1954	Atlantic 1034/Atco 6139 (59)
	Troubles/Baby Baby	1959	Candy 002
JACKSON TRIO (BB THE EBONAIRES)			
	Love For Christmas/Jingle Bell Hop	1955	Hollywood 1046
JACKSON, CHUCK (& GROUP)			
	Baby I Want To Marry You/Never Let Me Go	1961	Atco 6197
JACKSON, DIMPLES (& GROUP)			
	Where Are You/Love Came Tumbling Down	1960	Gardena 114
JACKSON, GEORGE (BB THE JIVE FIVE)			
	When I Stop Loving You/Lonely Night	N/A	Double R 248
JACKSON, LEE (& GROUP)			
	The Christmas Song	1957	Bea & Baby 121
JADES (1)			
	Beverly/Leave Her To Me	1958	Dot 15822
	Leave Her For Me/So Blue	1958	Time 1002
	Big Beach Party/Oh Why	1959	Christy 110
	Applesauce/Tell Me Pretty Baby	1959	Christy 111
	Don't Be A Fool/Friday Night With My Baby	1959	Christy 113
	Blue Memories/Look For A Lie	1959	Christy 114
	Hey Little Girl/Walking All Alone	1959	Nau-Voo 807
	Hold Back The Dawn/When They Ask About You	1963	Dore 687
JADES (1) (BOBBY KLINT & THE)			
	Moana/Rock Me The Blues	1959	Christy 109
	Lovely Lady Please Be Mine/Pretend	1959	Christy 117
JADES (1) (CHRIS NEWTON & THE)			
	Impala/Hello And Good-Bye	1961	Mikesell 134
JADES (1) (JERRY COULSTON & THE)			
	Bon Bon Baby/Cave Man Hop	1959	Christy 112
	Go Ask Your Mama/What's A Personality	1959	Christy 119

Artist	Song	Year	Label
	Bon Bon Baby/Go Ask Your Mama	1960	Christy 131
JADES (1) (JOE BEILIN & THE)			
	Just You And I And Love/ With Hope In My Heart	1960	Christy 122
JADES (1) (MCMILLIN BROTHERS & THE)			
	Let It Be Me/Satisfied	1959	Christy 120
JADES (2) (EMMETT & THE)			
	No One/Blowin' The Rock	1961	Rustone 1405
JADES (3) (FREDDY KOENIG & THE)			
	One Last Teardrop/Hey, Clarice	1963	Lori 9548/Valerie 225 (63)
JADES (4)			
	He's My Guy/There Will Come A Day	1964	Port 70042
JADES (5)			
	Hey Senorita	1962	Adona 1445
	Walking Along	N/A	Prism 1924
JADES (6)			
	My Loss, Your Gain/I Know The Feelin'	N/A	Poncello 7703
JADES (7)			
	I'm All Right	1964	Ector 101
JAGS (STEVE CARL WITH THE)			
	Curfew/Eighteen Year Old Blues	1958	Meteor 5046
JAGUARS (1)			
	Rock It, Davy, Rock It/The Big Bear (with Patti Ross)	1955	Aardell 107
	I Wanted You/Rock It, Davy, Rock It	1956	Aardell 0003
	Be My Sweetie/Why Don't You Believe Me?	1956	Aardell 0006
	The Way You Look Tonight/ Moonlight And You	1956	Aardell 0011
	The Way You Look Tonight/ Baby Baby Baby	1956	R-Dell 11/Baronet 1 (62)
	I Love You Baby/(City Zoo) Baby Baby Baby	1957	R-Dell 16
	Hold Me Tight/Picadilly	1958	Ebb 129
	I Wanted You/Rock It, Davy, Rock It	1958	R-Dell 45
	Roundabout/Jaguar	1959	Epic 9308
	Exit 6/Drive In	1959	Epic 9325
	Big Noise/I Could If I Would	1959	Janet 201
	Thinking Of You/Look Into My Eyes	1959	Original Sound 06/ Original Sound 20 (62)
	Girl Of My Dreams/Don't Go Home	1960	R-Dell 117
	Fine, Fine, Fine/It Finally Happened	1961	Rendezvous 159/ Rendezvous 216 (63)
	The Way You Look Tonight/ Baby, Baby, Baby, Baby	1965	Original Sound 59
	You Have Come Back/ Be My Sweetie	1976	Monogram 124
	Mellow Sunday/Our Summer Song	1988	Classic Artists 106
	Play A Love Song/All On Me	1989	Classic Artists 113
	Happy Holiday/More Than Enough For Me (by Johnny Staton & the Feathers)	1989	Classic Artists 117
JAGUARS (2) (NICK & THE)			
	Cool And Crazy/Ichi Bon, Volume I	1960	Tamla 5501
JAGUARS (3)			
	Where Lovers Go/Discover A Lover	1964	Faro 618
JAI, LORI (& GROUP)			
	Thrills And Heartaches/ Hold Me Close	1956	Rim 2016
JAMECOS (DIANA TYLER & NAT BROWN WITH THE)			
	Most Of All/Second Hand Love	1965	Jameco 2004
JAMES BOYS			
	Ah Ha Crazy	1960	Edsel 780
JAMES, ARTAMER (& GROUP) (AKA TAMMY JAMES & GROUP)			
	Congratulations/Ditty Bop Walk	1958	Code 711
JAMES, BOBBY (& GROUP)			
	True Blue/Let's Go	N/A	Lant 66009
JAMES, JESSE (BB THE ROYAL ACES)			
	Somebody Really Mine/ Dreams Never Hurt Nobody	1961	Musicor 1008

Artist	Song	Year	Label
JAMES, JIMMY (& GROUP)			
	She Don't Know/Time's Running Out	1963	Coed 583
JAMES, TAMMY (& GROUP) (AKA ARTAMER JAMES & GROUP)			
	Congratulations/Caesar Haircut	1963	Janlene 776
JAMIES			
	Summertime, Summertime/ Searching For You	1958	Epic 9281
	Snow Train/When The Sun Goes Down	1958	Epic 9299/Epic 9565 (63)
	Don't Darken My Door/ The Evening Star	1959	United Artists 193
JAMMERS			
	My Special Prayer/Thunderbird (by the Five Blue Notes)	1959	Onda 108
JAMMERS (JOHNNY & THE) (FB JOHNNY WINTER)			
	School Day Blues/You Know I Love You	1960	Dart 131
JANETTES			
	He's Crying Inside/We Belong To Each Other	1962	Goldie 1102
JANSSEN, DANNY (& GROUP)			
	Mirror On The Wall/Blue Moon	1960	Stepheny 1841
JANUARYS (LITTLE JUNE & HIS) (FB JUNE COLEMAN)			
	Hello/Burgers, Fries And Shakes	1957	Salem 188
JANUARYS (LITTLE JUNE & HIS) (FB JUNE COLEMAN)			
	Oh, What A Feeling/Oh, My Love	1959	Profile 4009
JARMELS			
	Little Lonely One/She Loves To Dance	1961	Laurie 3085
	A Little Bit Of Soap/The Way You Look Tonight	1961	Laurie 3098
	I'll Follow You/Gee Oh Gosh	1961	Laurie 3116
	Red Sails In The Sunset/ Loneliness	1962	Laurie 3124
	One By One/Little Bug	1962	Laurie 3141
	Come On Girl/Keep Your Mind On Me	1963	Laurie 3174
	Why Am I A Fool For You	N/A	Collectables LP 5044
	You Don't Believe A Word I Say	N/A	Collectables LP 5044
JAVALONS			
	Took A Chance (I Took A Chance)/That Is Why (I Love You)	1961	Tru-Eko 6901/Pip 6902
JAXON PLAYBOYS (EDDIE BUSH & THE)			
	Little Darling	1953	Jaxon 503
JAXON SISTERS			
	For A Lifetime	1957	Big 605
JAY BIRDS (1) (VINNIE MONTE & THE)			
	Your Cute Little Ways/Without Your Love	1956	Josie 793
	Always/A Love Of My Own	1958	Decanter 101
JAY BIRDS (2) (LENNY YOUNG & THE)			
	Joyce/Lovable	1958	Jay Scott 1001/Jackpot 48006 (58)
JAY CEES			
	Just Say The Word/The Waddle	1962	Enjoy 1004
JAYBIRDS (BOBBY DARIN & THE)			
	Silly Willie/Blue-Eyed Mermaid	1956	Decca 29922
JAYCEES (CHUCK JACKSON & THE)			
	Forever Is A Long Long Time/ Goodnight Irene	1964	Gateway 738
JAYE SISTERS			
	Going To The River/Pitter Patter Boom Boom	1958	Atlantic 1171
	Real Love/School's Out	1958	Atlantic 1190
	Little Daddy/Stop, You're Knocking Me Out	1958	Atlantic 2000
JAYE, JERRY (& GROUP)			
	I'm Goin' Home/Let's Make Love	1963	Carlton 598
JAYES			
	You're Gonna Grieve When I Leave/Panic Stricken	1958	Arc 4443
JAYHAWKS (AKA VIBRATIONS/AKA MARATHONS)			
	Counting My Teardrops/ The Devil's Cousin	1956	Flash 105
	Stranded In The Jungle/ My Only Darling	1956	Flash 109
	Love Train/Don't Mind Dyin'	1956	Flash 111
	The Creature/Everyone Should Know	1957	Aladdin 3393

Artist Song	Year	Label
Start The Fire/I Wish The World Owed Me A Living	1957	Eastman 792
New Love/Betty Brown	1958	Eastman 798/Firefly 327 (74)
Lonely Highway/La Macerena	1961	Argyle 1005
JAYHAWKS (EARL PALMER & THE)		
Johnny's House Party, Pt. 1 (instru.)/Johnny's House Party, Pt. 2 (instru.)	1957	Aladdin 3379
JAYNELLS		
I'll Stay Home New Year's Eve/ Down Home	1963	Cameo 286/Diamond 153
Out Of A Million Girls/At The End Of A Sunset	1984	Angela 101
Portrait Of Love/Hollywood Actor	1984	Angela 102
JAYNES (LONNIE JAY & THE)		
Somewhere/Around And Around We Go	1963	Arlen 724
JAYOS (JOHNNY OTIS & THE)		
Tough Enough/The Blooper (no group)	1957	Dig 131
Earth Angel	1957	Dig LP 104
At My Front Door	1957	Dig LP 104
Sh-Boom	1957	Dig LP 104
Sincerely	1957	Dig LP 104
Only You	1957	Dig LP 104
One Mint Julep	1957	Dig LP 104
Honey Love	1957	Dig LP 104
Gee	1957	Dig LP 104
JAYOS (MEL WILLIAMS & THE)		
Don't Cry Baby/My Love	1956	Dig 123
JAYS (1) (ARMONDA & THE)		
Present Of Love/Pony Tails	1959	Apollo 540
JAYS (2) (MIKE & THE)		
Dingle Dangle Doll/My Only Girl	1960	Doyl 1001
JAYS (3)		
Turn To Me/Stanwyck Theme	1961	Barry 103
JAYS (4) (JOHNNY & THE)		
Lugene/Baby Do	1961	Fairbanks 2001
JAYS (KELLY TROY & THE)		
Lucky In Love/In The Still Of The Night	N/A	Harvey
JAYTONES (AKA REVLONS (3)/AKA CENTURIES (3))		
The Clock/Gasoline	1958	Brunswick 55087
Oh Darling/The Bells	1958	Timely 1003/1004
My Only Love/Absolutely Right	1960	Cub 9057
Oh Darling/Crying For You (by the Centuries)	1963	Times Square 5
JAYWALKERS		
Oh Babe/My Bonnie (Lies Over The Ocean)	1962	Pam 210
JEANETTES (GENE & THE)		
You're A Star/A Lover	1963	Fortune 565
JEETERS (RON WILLIS & THE)		
Don't Come Too Late/Someday You'll Want Me To Want You	1960	Ace 588
JEFFRIES, BOB (BB THE MONDELLOS)		
Never Let Me Go/Irina Special (instrumental)	1957	Rhythm 110
JELLY BEANS		
I Wanna Love Him So Bad/ Long	1964	Red Bird 10-003
The Kind Of Boy You Can't Forget/Baby Be Mine	1964	Red Bird 10-011
I'm Hip To You/You Don't Mean No Good To Me	1965	Eskee 001
JEROME, PATTI (& GROUP)		
Johnny Has Gone/After The Lights Go Down Low	1955	Josie 774
JEROMES		
Rockin' Chair Song/Getting Even	1961	Dar 300
JESTERS		
The Beating Of My Heart/ What Now My Love	1986	Starlight 41
JESTERS (1)		
So Strange/Love No One But You	1957	Winley 218
Please Let Me Love You/ I'm Falling In Love	1957	Winley 221
I Laughed/Now That You're Gone	1958	Cyclone 5011
The Plea/Oh Baby	1958	Winley 225
The Wind/Sally Green	1960	Winley 242

Artist Song	Year	Label
That's How It Goes/Tutti Fruitti	1961	Winley 248
Come Let Me Show You/ Uncle Henry's Basement	1961	Winley 252
The Buffalo/Alexander Graham Bull	1962	Amy 859
JESTERS (1) (LENDON SMITH WITH THE)		
Women/Lost Love	1956	Meteor 5030
JESTERS (2)		
Since You're Gone/Messy Bessy	1960	Shimmy 1054
JESTERS (3) (RICHIE THOMPSON & THE)		
Ring A Ling A Ding/Too Late To Worry	1961	Diamond 103
JESTERS (4)		
My Babe/Cadillac Man	1966	Sun 400
JESTERS (5)		
To Be Or Not To Be	1959	Spry 118
JESTERS (6) (JUNIOR CHARD & THE)		
Be Bop A Lula/Locked Out	1959	Madison 127
JET STREAMS		
Who Me/Hey Phoebe, Get Off The Phone	1958	Decca 30743
JETS (1)		
The Lovers/Drag It Home, Baby	1953	Rainbow 201
JETS (2)		
Volcano/Gomen Nasai	1953	7-11 2101/2102
Got A Little Shadow/I'll Hide My Tears	1954	Aladdin 3247
JETS (2) (RONNIE GRETT & THE)		
Sweet Baby/Run Manny Run	1955	Capitol 3174
JETS (3)		
Heaven Above Me/Millie Brown	1956	Gee 1020
JETS (4) (ROY JORDAN & THE)		
Keep Cool/Jeebla Jabla Jingo	1956	Orpheus 1102
JETS (5) (BUCK ROGERS & THE)		
Rose Marie/Crazy Baby	1959	Montel 2002
JETS (6) (REF MARCELS)		
You Still Got Time To Change Your Mind/Soul Dinner	1963	Arrow 100
JEWELS (1) (AKA CROWS)		
Call A Doctor/Heartbreaker (by the Crows)	1953	Rama 10
JEWELS (2) (AKA MARBLES)		
Hearts Of Stone/Runnin'	1954	R&B 1301
A Fool In Paradise/Oh Yes I Know	1954	R&B 1303
Try And Get Me/Dream	1954	R&B 1313/Ram 1102
Hearts Can Be Broken/Angel In My Life	1955	Imperial 5351
Please Return/Natural, Natural Ditty	1955	Imperial 5362
How/Rickety Rock	1956	Imperial 5377
My Baby/Goin', Goin', Gone	1956	Imperial 5387
She's A Flirt/B-Bomb Baby	1956	RPM 474
The Wind/Pearlie Mae	1959	Antler 1102
I Worry 'Bout You/Are You Comin' To The Party	1959	Shasta 115
Hearts Of Stone/Oh Yes I Know	1964	Original Sound 38
No Shoulder To Cry On/Keep Your Feet On The Floor	1974	Imperial 5374
One Night	N/A	Imperial (unreleased)
Skid Row	N/A	Imperial (unreleased)
Keep Your Feet On The Floor	N/A	Imperial LP only
JEWELS (2) (JOHNNY TORRANCE WITH THE)		
Rosalie/Living From Day To Day	1954	R&B 1306
JEWELS (3)		
My Song/This Is My Story	1963	Federal 12541
JEWELS (4) (BILLY ABBOTT & THE)		
Groovy Baby/Come On And Dance With Me	1963	Parkway 874
JEWELS (5) (FEMALE) (AKA FOUR JEWELS)		
Opportunity/Gotta Find A Way	1964	Dimension 1034
Smokey Joe/But I Do	1964	Dimension 1048
Jimmy Lee/The Hash	1964	Olimpic 244
Smokie Joe's/Lookie Cookie	1966	King 6068
JEWELS (6)		
I Had A Dream/Strawberry Peak	1976	Monogram 117
JILLETTES (FEMALE)		
Daddy Do/Please Say You'll Love Me	1962	Amazon 711
Why Did I Cry/Can't Play A Playgirl	1963	Philips 40140

Artist	Song	Year	Label
JILLS (JACQUELINE & THE)			
	He Loves Me He Loves Me Not/Gee But It's Great To Be In Love	1961	Goldisc 3023
JIV-A-TONES			
	Flirty Gertie/Fire Engine Baby	1957	Fox 1/Felsted 8506 (58)
	And Then It Happened/Wild Bird	N/A	Fraternity 823
JIVE BOMBERS			
	It's Spring Again/Pork Chop Boogie	1952	Citation 1160
	Brown Boy/Peewee's Boogie	1952	Citation 1161
	Bad Boy/When Your Hair Has Turned To Silver	1957	Savoy 1508
	The Blues Don't Mean A Thing/If I Had A Talking Picture	1957	Savoy 1513
	Cherry/You Took My Love	1957	Savoy 1515
	Is This The End/Just Around The Corner	1958	Savoy 1535
	You Give Your Love To Me/Stardust	1959	Savoy 1560
	Anytime/The Days Of Wine And Roses	1964	Middle-Tone 020
JIVE FIVE			
	My True Story/When I Was Single	1961	Beltone 1006/Relic 1026 (75)
	Never, Never/People From Another World	1961	Beltone 1014/Relic 1030 (78)
	No Not Again/Hully Gully Callin' Time	1962	Beltone 2019/Relic 1027 (75)
	What Time Is It/Beggin' You Please	1962	Beltone 2024/Relic 1028 (76)
	These Golden Rings/Do You Hear Wedding Bells	1962	Beltone 2029/Relic 1029 (77)
	You Know What I Would Do/Hurry Back	1962	Beltone 3001
	The Girl With The Wind In Her Hair/I Don't Want To Be Without You Baby	1962	Beltone 3002
	Johnny Never Knew/Lili Marlane	1963	Beltone 2030
	Rain/She's My Girl	1963	Beltone 2034
	Prove Every Word You Say/United	1964	Sketch 219/United Artists 807 (64)
	Kiss, Kiss, Kiss/I'm A Happy Man	1965	United Artists 853
	Oh Baby/Magic Make, Music Maker	1982	Ambient Sound 02742
	Don't Believe Him Donna/Hey Sam	1982	Ambient Sound 03053
	Where Do We Go From Here	1982	Ambient Sound LP 801
	I Don't Want To Be Without You	N/A	Beltone (unreleased)
	Hurry Back	N/A	Relic LP 5020
	You/You Promised Me Great Things	N/A	United Artists 50107
	A Bench In The Park/Please Baby Please (Come On Back To Me)	N/A	United Artists 936
JIVELEERS			
	Boom Chic-A-Boom/Cheryl (by the Camerons (1))	1960	Cousins 1/2
JIVERS (1)			
	Cherie/Little Mama	1956	Aladdin 3329
	Ray Pearl/Dear Little One	1956	Aladdin 3347
JIVERS (2)			
	I Wonder If You Know/What Do You Know About Heartaches	1959	RCA 7478
JIVES (BOBBY TAYLOR WITH CHARLIE & THE)			
	Seven Steps To An Angel/Ubangi Stomp	1962	Hour 102
JIVES (CHARLIE & THE)			
	Coffee Grind, Pt. 1/Coffee Grind, Pt. 2	1962	Hour 104
JIVETONES			
	Ding Ding Dong/Geraldine	1958	Rhythm 5001/Apt 25020 (58)
	Zip Zip	N/A	Apt (unreleased)
	When	N/A	Apt (unreleased)
JIVING JUNIORS			
	Moonlight Lover/Sweet As An Angel	1961	Asnes 103
	I Wanna Love/Duke's Cookies	1961	Blue Beat 24
	Dearest Darling/Lollipop Girl	1961	Blue Beat 4
JO-VALS			
	Ballerina/I Want You To Be My Girl	1964	Alwil 101/102
	Well It's Alright/Well It's Alright (instrumental)	1964	Grove 105
	Sometimes I'm Happy/You You My Love	1964	Laurie 3229
JOEY (& GROUP)			
	I Got Feelings/A Place In Your Heart	1962	Taurus 353
JOEY, GUY (& GROUP)			
	Philly Stomp/Anna	1961	Coed 563
JOGETTES			
	Your Love/Johnnie's Coming Home	1962	Mar 102
JOHNNY (WITH THE KIDS)			
	There Is Love/The Bounce	1962	Luck 101
JOHNSON 3 PLUS 1			
	High School Queen/Treatment For The Cure	1969	Tangerine 1013
JOHNSON BROTHERS (AKA FIVE J'S/AKA FIVE JOHNSON BROTHERS)			
	Sleep With A Dream/Happy Rock 'n' Rollers	1958	Carrie 012
	Zombie Lou/Casting My Spell	1959	Valor 2006
JOHNSON QUARTET, BILL (THE BILL JOHNSON QUARTET)			
	Maria Mia/We're Gonna Love	1955	Jubilee 5211
JOHNSON, ARTHUR (& GROUP)			
	Honey Please Believe Me/Something About My Baby	1959	Wanger 190
JOHNSON, BILL (THE BILL JOHNSON QUINTET)			
	So Sweet Of You/Traveling Stranger	1957	Baton 239
JOHNSON, BUBBER (BB THE WHEELS)			
	Drop Me A Line/Ding Dang Doo	1955	King 4793
JOHNSON, DAVE (& GROUP)			
	Angel Of Mine/Teenage Jamboree	1960	Apt 25054
JOHNSON, DELORES (& FEMALE GROUP)			
	Give Me Your Love/Gotta Find My Baby (no group)	1960	Bobbin 132
JOHNSON, ERNIE (& GROUP)			
	Tell Her For Me/You Need Love	1961	Asnes 104
JOHNSON, HERB (BB THE CRUISERS)			
	Guilty/Have You Heard	1960	Len 1007
JOHNSON, JESSE (& GROUP)			
	So Loved Am I/Cute Little Girl	1958	Symbol 901
JOHNSON, KRIPP (& GROUP)			
	A Door That Is Open/Still I Forgive You	1959	Mercury 71486
JOHNSON, MARV (& GROUP)			
	Once Upon A Time/Baby You (Baby-O)	1958	Kudo 663
JOHNSON, STELLA (& MALE GROUP)			
	The Ways Of Love/What Do They Know	1960	Vin 1022
JOKERS (1) (JIVIN' GENE & THE)			
	Up, Up And Away/Going Out With The Tide	1959	Jin 109/Jin 7331
	My Need For Love/Breaking Up Is Hard To Do	1959	Jin 116
	Breakin' Up Is Hard To Do/My Need For Love	1959	Mercury 71485
	You're Jealous/Go On, Go On	1960	Mercury 71561
	Poor Me/That's What It's Like	1961	Mercury 71751
JOKERS (2) (JOHNNY & THE)			
	Do-Re-Mi Rock/Why Must It Be	1959	Harvard 804
	I Know/Where Did My Baby Go	1962	Beltone 2028
JOKERS (3)			
	I Do/Pretty Little Hula Girl	1960	Danco 117
JOKERS (3) (DARLENE & THE)			
	Love Me, Love Me/Frankie	1960	Danco 115
JOKERS (3) (TY STEWART & THE)			
	Young Girl/Here Am I	1961	Amy 828
JOKERS (4)			
	Little Mama/Say You're Mine	1961	Grace 510
JOKERS (5) (FB KENNY TIBBS)			
	I'm Still Alone/The Worm	1962	Viking 1009
JOKERS (5) (WILLIE & THE)			
	She Won't Hang Up/I Promise	1962	Viking 1007
JOKERS (6) (JOHNNY WILLIAMS & THE)			
	Only A Tear/Sidewalk Rock & Roll	1959	Simpson 1130
	Dearest Darling/Long Black Veil	1961	Pic 1 105
JOKERS (7)			
	Don't Want No Woman	N/A	Teen 1006

Artist	Song	Year	Label
JOKERS (8) (JOHNNY & THE)			
	The Seven Teens/The Seven		
	Teens (by the Pretenders)	1980	Clifton 46
JOLLY JACKS			
	There's Something On Your		
	Mind/Rock The House	1963	Landa 707
JONES BOYS (1)			
	The Song Is Ended/You Make		
	Me Feel Like A Penny Waitin'		
	For Change	1954	S&G 5007
JONES BOYS (2) (JIMMY JONES & THE)			
	Heaven In Your Eyes/		
	The Whistlin' Man	1957	Arrow 717
JONES BOYS (3)			
	Alone In The Night/Honey,		
	Honey (by the Capitols)	1973	Baron 103
JONES, BILLY (BB THE SQUIRES)			
	Listen To Your Heart/Every		
	Word Of The Song	1958	Deck 478
JONES, DAVEY (& GROUP)			
	Love Your Way/Come On And		
	Love Me	1958	Apt 25013
	No More Tears/Tootsie Wootsie	1959	Glades 601
	Our Love/Change Your Mind	1959	Marlin 6062
	I'm In Pain/Let's Do It	1961	Apt 25064
JONES, DEE (& GROUP)			
	Hideaway Heaven/Dreamland	1961	Brent 7023
JONES, HILLARD (& GROUP)			
	Prison Of Love/What Have		
	You Got	1962	Cortland 101
JONES, JIMMY (& GROUP)			
	You For Me To Love/Whenever		
	You Need Me	1959	Epic 9339
JONES, JIMMY (BB THE CUES)			
	Handy Man/The Search Is Over		
	no group)	1959	Cub 9049
JONES, JIMMY (BB THE PRETENDERS)			
	Lover/Plain Old Love	1960	Roulette 4232
	Close Your Eyes/Part Time		
	Sweetheart	1961	Port 70040
JONES, TONI (& GROUP)			
	Dear (Here Comes My Baby)/		
	Love Is Strange	1963	Smash 1814
JONES, VIVIAN (& GROUP) (FEMALE)			
	Open Arms/I Wanna Know	1962	Twirl 1017
JORDAN, LOU (BB THE CHAPERONES (1))			
	Paradise For Two/Close Your		
	Eyes	1962	Josie 888
JOSEPH, DAVE (& GROUP)			
	Another Mile To Go/Oo La La	1958	Vanguard 35004
JOSEPH, MIKE (& GROUP)			
	Sandy/King Of Wealth	1962	Lucky Four 1017
JOSIE, LOU (& GROUP)			
	Lonely Years/I'm Gonna Getcha	1959	Baton 269
	Talk To The Angels/Jeannie	1961	Rendezvous 143
JOVATIONS			
	Take You Back Agian/		
	My Dreams	1963	Taurus 362
JOY BOYS (CHUCK HIGGINS & THE)			
	Broke/I'll Be There	1954	Specialty 532
JOY, ARLENE (& GROUP)			
	Too Young/Twistin' Susie Q	1962	Rendezvous 185
JOY-TONES			
	This Love/I Wanna Party		
	Some More	1964	Coed 600
JOYETTES (FEMALE)			
	Story Of Love/Boy Next Door	1956	Onyx 502
JOYJUMPERS (FB JIMMY ANDERSON)			
	Angel Please/I Wanna Boogie	1962	Zynn 1014
JOYLARKS			
	In The Rain/Betty, My Love	1959	Snag 107/Candlelite 426 (63)
JOYLETS (FEMALE)			
	Say Yeah/Stewed Tomatoes	1963	ABC 10403
JOYS			
	I Still Love Him/(Sing Along)		
	I Still Love Him	1964	Valiant 6042
JOYTONES (FEMALE)			
	All My Love Belongs To You/You		
	Just Won't Treat Me Right	1956	Rama 191
	Gee! What A Boy/Is This Really		
	The End?	1956	Rama 202
	My Foolish Heart/Jimbo Jango	1956	Rama 215

Artist	Song	Year	Label
JULIANA (& GROUP)			
	You Can Have Any Boy/		
	You're Saying Goodnight	1961	RCA 7906
JULIETTES			
	Bye, Bay Baby/Carol's Theme	1980	Catamount 779
JUMPERS (JAY NELSON & THE)			
	Sleepytime Rock/A Fool That		
	Was Blind	1959	Excello 2149
	Wild Love/To You, My Darling	1959	Excello 2165
JUMPIN' JACKS (1)			
	Do Let That Dream Come True/		
	Why, Oh, Why?	1953	Lloyds 101
	Long Head Leggy Rascal	1989	Relic LP 5077
	Julocka Jolly	1989	Relic LP 5077
JUMPIN' JACKS (1) (DANNY LAMEGO & THE)			
	Embraceable You/Pa-Pa-Ya,		
	Baby	1954	Bruce 115
	Hickory Dickory Rock/		
	Chicken Feed	1956	Andrea 101
JUMPIN' JACKS (1) (DANNY PEPPERMINT & THE)			
	The Peppermint Twist/		
	Somebody Else Is Taking My		
	Place	1961	Carlton 565
JUMPIN' JACKS (2)			
	Mop-Top/Let There Be Rockin'	1956	One-O-One 100
JUMPIN' JAGUARS			
	Shut The Door, Baby/		
	Knock-Kneed Nellie From		
	Knox	1956	Decca 29938
	You'll Wonder Where/Frantic		
	Antic	1956	Decca 29973
JUMPIN' JAY (& GROUP)			
	Come On Home/Bad Buc	1961	Turban 101
JUMPIN' TONES			
	I Had A Dream/I Wonder	1964	Raven 8004
	Grandma's Hearing Aid/		
	That Angel Is You	1964	Raven 8005
	Jingle Bell Stomp/Even Now	1989	Avenue D 16
	Japanese Sandman	N/A	unreleased
	Come On Home	N/A	unreleased
	I See A Star	N/A	unreleased
	You're My Love	N/A	unreleased
JUMPING JACKS (1)			
	About A Quarter To Nine/Lady,		
	Play Your Mandolin	1956	Capitol 3415
	Valencia/Toki-Roll, Toki-Rock	1956	Capitol 3496
JUMPING JACKS (2)			
	Tried And Tasted/My Girl,		
	My Girl	1957	ABC 9859
JUNE VOICES (JIMMY VON CARL & THE)			
	This Doesn't Seem Real/		
	Lonely Night	1959	Flick 002
JUNIOR FIVE			
	On My Birthday/I Can't Wait		
	Till Tomorrow	1963	Laurie 3213
JUNIORS (1) (JIMMY CASTOR & THE)			
	I Promise/I Know The Meaning		
	Of Love	1956	Wing 90078
	This Girl Of Mine/Somebody		
	Mentioned Your Name	1957	Atomic 100
JUNIORS (2) (DANNY & THE)			
	Rock And Roll Is Here To Stay/		
	School Boy Romance	1957	ABC 9888
	At The Hop/ Sometimes		
	When I'm All Alone	1957	Singular 711 (57)/ABC
			9871 (57)
	Dottie/In The Meantime	1958	ABC 9926
	A Thief/Crazy Cave	1958	ABC 9953
	Sassy Fran/I Feel So Lonely	1958	ABC 9978
	Do You Love Me/Somehow I		
	Can't Forget	1959	ABC 10004
	Playing Hard To Get/Of Love	1959	ABC 10052
	Twistin' U.S.A./A Thousand		
	Miles Away	1960	Swan 4060
	O Holy Night/Candy Cane		
	Sugary Plum	1960	Swan 4064
	Pony Express/Daydreamer	1961	Swan 4068
	Cha Cha Go Go (Chicago		
	Cha Cha)/Mr. Whisper	1961	Swan 4072
	Back To The Hop/Charleston		
	Fish	1961	Swan 4082

Artist	Song	Year	Label	Artist	Song	Year	Label
	Just Because/Your Hair's Too Long/Some Kind Of Nut (3 songs on record)	1961	Swan 4084	**KELLOGGS (FB VITO BALSAMO)**	Snap, Crackle, Pop/Like A Mad Fool	1969	Laurie 3476
	Oo-La-La-Limbo/Now And Then	1962	Guyden 2076	**KELLUM, MURRY (& GROUP)**	Long Tall Texan/I Gotta Leave This Town	1964	MOC 653
	Twistin' All Night Long (with Freddy Cannon)/Some Kind Of Nut	1962	Swan 4092	**KELLY, KAROL (& GROUP)**	Slow Dance/I Wanna Talk To You	1962	Joy 272
	Doin' The Continental Walk/ (Do The) Mashed Potato	1962	Swan 4100	**KELWAY QUINTET**	Working On A Groovy Thing/He Ain't Heavy, He's My Brother	1972	Kelway 104
	We Got Soul/Funny	1962	Swan 4113	**KENDALL SISTERS**	Three Wishes/Make It Soon	1957	Checker 884
	Twistin' All Night Long/ Twistin' England	1962	Top Rank 604	**KENJOLAIRS**	Little White Lies/Story Of An Evergreen Tree	1962	A&M 704
	Let's Go Skiing/Sad Girl	1964	Mercury 72240	**KENNEDY, ACE (& GROUP)**	I Made A Mistake/Buck Dancin'	1961	Swan 4080
	Rock And Roll Is Here To Stay/ Sometimes	1968	Lub 252	**KENNEDY, TOM (& GROUP)**	Careless Love	N/A	Golden Crest 103
	I Can't See Nobody/Mo'Reen	1968	Ronn 24	**KENT, AL (& GROUP)**	Hold Me/You Know Me	1959	Wizzard 100
	Let The Good Times Roll/ At The Hop	1973	Crunch 18001	**KENTONES**	Marie/Please Make Up Your Mind	1958	Siroc 202
	Tallahassee Lassie	N/A	Singular LP 569	**KENTS (1)**	I Found My Girl/With All My Heart And Soul	1958	Argo 5299
	When The Saints Go Twistin' In	N/A	Singular LP 569		I Love You So/Happy Beat	1958	Dome 501
JUPITORS	I Want/It Takes Two	1958	Planet X 9621	**KENTS (2)**	Don't Say Goodbye/My Juanita	1965	Relic 1013
JUSTIFIERS	Lonely Boy/My Love Has Gone	1958	Kim 101	**KESTRELS**	In The Chapel In The Moonlight/ There Comes A Time	1960	Laurie 3053
JUVENILES	The Beat In My Heart/I've Lied	1958	Mode 1	**KEY BROTHERS**	My Baby Doll/Lulu's Party	1960	Gardena 102
K'S (LITTLE ROBERT & THE)	Fabulous 50's/Gwendolyn (by the Super Heroes)	N/A	Dice	**KEY, TROYCE (& GROUP)**	Drown In My Tears/Baby Please Don't go	1958	Warner Bros. 5007
K-DOE, ERNIE (& GROUP)	Hello My Lover/Taint It The Truth	1960	Minit 614		Ain't I Cried Enough/Watch Your Mouth	1959	Warner Bros. 5035
	My Love For You/Shirley's Tuff	1961	Ember 1075		Most Of All/She's Sumpin' Else	1959	Warner Bros. 5070
KA-RILLONS	Love Boat/Open Up Your Heart	1964	Laurie 3244	**KEY-NOTERS**	The Vision/Starlight And You (instrumental)	1959	Swan 4048
KAC-TIES (AKA KACT-TIES)	Walking In The Rain/Smile	1962	Trans Atlas 695/Kape 502 (63)	**KEYAVAS (HARRY & THE)**	If This Is Goodbye/Tears	1963	IPG 1011
	Happy Birthday/Girl In My Heart	1963	Kape 501/Kape 51563 (63)	**KEYMASTERS**	Been So Long	N/A	Quality Sound 001
	Over The Rainbow/Donald Duck	1963	Kape 702	**KEYNOTERS**	Who Does She Think She Is/ Come Back My Love (by the Heartbreakers)	1975	Vanguard 9093
	The Rest Of My Life (acapella)	1975	Relic LP 108	**KEYNOTERS (FB NORMA BROCK)**	I'm Gonna Build A Mountain/ Evergood	1959	Pepper 896
	What Did I Do Wrong (acapella)	1975	Relic LP 108	**KEYNOTES (1)**	Who/They Say	1954	Dot 15225
	Let Your Love Light Shine/ Were-Wolf	1963	Shelley 163/Kape 503 (63)		Suddenly/Zenda	1955	Apollo 478
	Oh What A Night/Let Me In Your Life	1963	Shelley 165/Atco 6299 (64)		I Don't Know (Why I Love You Like I Do)/A Star	1955	Apollo 484
KAPERS (PAUL LONDON & THE)	Sugar Baby/Never Like This	1962	Check Mate 1006		Oh Yeah Hm-m-m/A Star	1956	Apollo 485
KAPPALIERS (GM NOEL SOOKEY)	Down In Mexico/Goodbye Baby	N/A	Shadow 1229		Really Wish You Were Here/ Bye, Bye, Baby	1956	Apollo 493
KAPPAS	Sweet Juanita/Your Love	1959	Wonder 112		Zup Zup (Ooh You Dance So Nice)/Now I Know	1956	Apollo 498
KAPTIONS (AKA CONTENDERS/AKA FIVE SCRIPTS/AKA LYTATIONSAKA ZIPPERS)	Dreaming Of You/I Know Somewhere	N/A	Ham-Mil 1520		In The Evening/Oh, Yeah, Hm-m-m	1956	Apollo 503
KARTELS (WILBERT LOMBARD & THE)	That's How We'll Be/Lovely, Wonderful, Beautiful	1957	Deb 1002		One Little Kiss/Now I Know	1957	Apollo 513
KARTUNES (FB TEDDY RANDAZZO)	Raindrops/Will You Marry Me	1958	MGM 12598		Early One Morning	1989	Relic LP 5080
	Dedicated To Love/Willie The Weeper	1958	MGM 12680		Chapel Bells Are Ringing	1989	Relic LP 5080
KASHMIRS	Heaven Only Knows/ Tippi-Tippi-Wang-Wang	1958	Wonder 104		Tell Me You Love Me	1989	Relic LP 5080
KATZ, RONNIE (& GROUP)	Long Time	1961	N/A		Surely	N/A	Apollo LP 1000/Relic LP 5072 (1000)
KAYS	To Be With You/Cool It	N/A	Choice 3757		Zoop Zoop (Darling I Love You)	N/A	Apollo LP 1000/Relic LP 5072 (1000)
KEENS (RICK & THE)	Peanuts/I'll Be Home	1961	Austin 313/Le Cam 721 (61)/Smash 1705 (61)		Girl In The Chapel	N/A	Apollo LP 1000/Relic LP 5072 (1000)
	Maybe/Popcorn	1961	Smash 1722	**KEYNOTES (2) (BILL ALLEN & THE)**	Butterfly/Oo-Wee-Baby	1957	Eldorado 505
	Your Turn To Cry/Tender Years	1962	Le Cam 958/Jamie 1219 (62)				
	Darla/Someone New	1964	Le Cam 113/Tollie 9016 (64)				
KEITH, ANN (& GROUP)	Lover's Prayer/Lonely Girl (by the El Venos)	1959	Memo 96				
KELLER, JERRY (& GROUP)	Never Wake Up/Be Careful How You Drive Young Joey	1961	Capitol 4630				
KELLEY, CHARLES (BB THE 3 OF US TRIO)	Telegram/Sugar Jump (instrumental)	1958	York 3332				

Artist Song	Year	Label
KEYNOTES (3)		
A Sunday School Romance/		
Only In A Dream	1959	Bell-O-Tonic 001
With These Rings/We're Not		
Getting Along		
(Like We Used To)	1959	Top Rank 2005
KEYNOTES (4)		
Dum Doodee Dum Dum/		
Open The Door	N/A	Index
KEYNOTES (5)		
Congratulations Baby/		
Carelessly	1957	Pop 111
KEYNOTES (6) (GENE ANDERSON & THE)		
Susie/I've Got It Bad	N/A	Top Ten 252
KEYS (1)		
Am I In Love/Barefoot Days	1952	MGM 11168
KEYS (2) (RICKY & THE)		
Can't You See/Come On Liza	1958	Savoy 1529
KEYS (3)		
When You Wish Upon A Star/		
Barbara	1965	Jam 501
KEYS (4)		
My Love Has Gone	N/A	Lee 0759
KEYS (5) (RUDY WEST & THE)		
Miracle Moment Of Love/		
When Was The Last Time	1989	Classic Artists 112
I Want You For Christmas/		
Express Yourself Back Home	1989	Classic Artists 115
KEYSTONERS		
The Magic Kiss/After I Propose	1956	Epic 9187/Okeh 7210 (64)
Magic Kiss/I'd Write About The		
Blues	1956	G&M 102
Sleep And Dream/T. V. Gal	1961	Riff 202
I'll Always Remember/I Don't		
Know Why	1984	Starbound 501
That's Why I Dream/Say Always	1984	Starbound 502
It's Too Soon To Know	1988	Starbound 509
It's Never Too Soon/Little Darlin'	1991	Starbound 512
My Heart Beats Again/You're		
All I Want For Christmas	1991	Starbound 514
Them There Eyes/Sweet		
Was The Wine	1992	Starbound 516
Gossip/Call My Name	1992	Starbound 515
KEYTONES (1)		
Wonder Of The World/A Fool		
In Love	1957	Old Town 1041 (first pressing)
Seven Wonders Of The World/		
A Fool In Love	1957	Old Town 1041(second pressing)
KEYTONES (2)		
Don't Tell William/Parking		
Field 4	1961	Chelsea 1002
I Don't Care/La-Do-Da-Da	1962	Chelsea 101
One, Two, Three/Sweet Chariot	1963	Chelsea 1013
KEYTONES (3)		
Time After Time/Lover Of Mine	1962	Chess 1821
KID, THE (& GROUP)		
Sleep Tight/True Love		
(Is Hard To Find)	N/A	Rumble 1347
KIDDIEOS (JAY BRYANT & THE)		
Don't Stop Now/Want You To		
Know	N/A	Alfa 201
KIDDS		
Drunk, Drunk, Drunk/Are You		
Forgetting Me	1955	Imperial 5335
You Broke My Heart/I Won't		
Be Back	1955	Post 2003
Down In Mexico/Miss Lucy	N/A	Post 2010
KIDDS (MORRY WILLIAMS & THE)		
Are You My Girlfriend/Oh Louise	1958	Tee Vee 301/Carlton 477 (58)
Time Runs Out/Grasshopper		
(instrumental)	1960	Luck 102
Time Runs Out/Long Foor Jean	1974	Firefly 319
KIDS (1) (HERMAN & THE)		
Daddy Daddy/March On	1959	Columbia 41411
KIDS (2) (BILLY & THE)		
Take A Chance On Love/		
The Way It Used To Be	1961	Lute 6016/Lute 312
Say You Love Me	N/A	Julian 104
KIDS (3)		
Good Loving	N/A	Gaylord 2203

Artist Song	Year	Label
KIDS (4)		
Dear Mom And Dad	N/A	Hurd 80
KIDS FROM CLEVELAND		
Someone In Love/NightTrain	1957	Whippet 204
KIDS FROM TEXAS		
Long Legged Linda/I'm So		
Lonely	1958	Hanover 4500
KILLERS (HANK BLACKMAN & THE)		
Everyone Has Someone/		
Itchy Koo	1962	Brent 7030
KILTS (1) (HERMAN JONES & THE) (GM TONY LeMAR)		
I'll Be True/Mashed Potatoes	1958	Gaynote 105
KILTS (2) (CHARLIE JESTER & THE)		
Sylvia/If Only I Had Known	1961	Le Cam 722
KING BEES		
Puppy Love/Give Me Your		
Number	1957	Flip 323
Can't You Understand?/		
Lovely Love	1957	KRC 302
Buzzin'/Good Rockin' Tonight	1958	Checker 909
What Could Have Been Can't		
Be/Tender Love	1959	Noble 715
Look My Way/Good Rockin'		
Daddy	1974	Outhouse 101
KING COBRAS		
To Hold Your Love/		
Blue Diamond	1959	Irvanne 117
KING CROONERS (AKA KING KROONERS)		
Now That She's Gone/Won't		
You Let Me Know	1959	Excello 2168
Lonely Nights/She's Mine All		
Mine	1959	Hart 1002
KING KROONERS (FB LITTLE RICO) (AKA KING CROONERS)		
Memoirs/School Daze		
(no group)	1960	Excello 2187
KING TOPPERS		
You Were Waiting For Me/		
Walkin' And Talkin' Blues	1956	Josie 811
Walkin' And Talkin' The Blues/		
You Were Waiting For Me	1957	Josie 811
KING TROTTERS (GENE MORRIS & HIS)		
Bongo Washie Wado	N/A	Cal-West 108
KING, BUZZY (& GROUP)		
Your Picture/School Boy Blues	1959	Top Rank 2027
KING, CLYDIE (& GROUP)		
Our Romance/Written On		
The Wall	1957	Specialty 605
KING, FREDDY (& GROUP)		
Fortune Teller/Lonesome		
Old World	N/A	Roulette 7003
KING, MABEL (BB THE HARPTONES)		
Love/When We Get The Word	1963	Amy 874
KING, SLEEPY (& GROUP)		
Begging/My Time Ain't Long	1959	Symbol 904
KING, SONNY (& GROUP)		
Do You Love Me	N/A	Marida 101
KING-PINS		
Lucky Guy/Dance Romeo		
Dance	1963	Vee Jay 494
KINGLETS (FEMALE)		
You Gotta Go/Six Days A Week	1956	Calvert 101
My Baby Don't Need Chargin'/		
Pretty Please	1959	Bobbin 104
KINGPINS		
Ungaua	1958	United Artists 111
KINGS & QUEENS		
Voices Of Love/I'm So Lonely	1957	Everlast 5003
KINGS (1) (BOBBY HALL & THE) (REF RAMBLERS (1))		
Why? Oh, Why?/I Love You,		
Baby	1953	Jax 314/Blue Sky 106 (73)
Baby, Be There/You Made		
Me Cry	1953	Jax 316
Sunday Kind Of Love/Love		
No One	1953	Jax 320/Blue Sky 105 (73)
Count Your Blessings/How To		
Start A Romance	1963	Century 1300/Little Rick 909 (63)/Chess 1867 (63)
KINGS (1) (REF RAMBLERS (1)		
Fire In My Heart/You Never		
Knew	1954	Harlem 2322
What Can I Do?/Til I Say		
Well Done	1954	Specialty 497

Artist Song	Year	Label
God Made You Mine/The Good Book	1956	Gotham 316
Don't Go/Love Is Something From Within	1957	Gone 5013
Angel/Come On, Little Baby	1958	Jalo 203
Till You/Elephant Walk	1958	RCA 7419
Surrender/Hold Me	1959	Jay-Wing 5805
Your Sweet Love/Troubles Don't Last	1959	RCA 7544
I Want To Know/Bump-I-Dy Bump	1960	Lookie 18/Epic 9370 (60)
Creation	N/A	Collectables LP 5037/ Collectables LP 7003
KINGS (2) (FB JOE VAN LOAN)		
Long Lonely Nights/Let Me Know	1957	Baton 245
KINGS (3) (VICKI FRANCE & THE)		
Cry On My Shoulder/My France	1959	Sparkette 1002
KINGS (4) (JOHNNY & THE) (AKA JOHNNY & THE TOKENS)		
The Taste Of A Tear/Never Till Now	1961	Warwick 658
KINGS (5) (ALBERT WASHINGTON & THE)		
Your Gonna Miss Me	1964	Vim 10990
Woman Is A Funny Thing	N/A	Fraternity 982
KINGS (6) (CHET RENI & THE)		
A Love Of My Own/What's Wrong With Me?	N/A	Georgie 101
KINGS FIVE		
The Voodoo Man/I Hear The Rain	1959	Trophy 9
KINGS MEN		
Don't Say You're Sorry/ Kicking With My Stallion	1957	Club 51 108
KINGSMEN (1)		
One Foolish Mistake/ Stranded Love	1956	Neil 102
Guardian Angel/I'm Your Lover Man	1957	Allstar 500/East West 115 (58)/East West 120 (58)
KINGSMEN (2)		
Teenage Creature/Turn The Key (by Lord Luther & the Garnets (2))	1959	Frantic 107
KINGSMEN (3)		
Ladies Choice	1961	Jalynne 108
KINGSMEN (4) (JOHNNY KNIGHT & THE)		
Secret Heart/Push A Little Button	1963	Chance (N.Y.) 568
KINGSMEN (5)		
Wish For An Angel	1961	Musictone 102
Pygmy	1962	Shelly 164
Goodnight Sweetheart/ Humpty Dumpty	N/A	Arnold 2106
KINGTONES		
To Have A Little Girl/A Love I Had	1962	Kitoco/Drummond 105 (65)
Twins/Have Good Faith	1964	Derry 101
It Doesn't Matter Anymore	N/A	Eucalyptus 002/Cotillion 44069
KINNEY, MARY (& GROUP)		
Bobby My Love/I'm Anxious	1959	Andex 4031
KIT KATS		
You're An Angel/Cold Walls	1965	Lawn 249
KITTENS (FEMALE)		
Letter To Donna/It's All Over Now	1959	Unart 2010
Something Tells Me I'm In Love/Aching For You	1960	Alpine 61
Itsy Bitsy, Teenie Weenie, Yellow Polka Dot Bikini/ Dark, Dark Sunglasses	1960	Alpine 64
Letter On His Sweater/ Broken Dreams	1960	Alpine 67
Count Every Star/I'm Worried	1963	Chestnut 203
Walter/Lite Bulb	1963	Don-El 122
I Need Your Love Tonight/ Johnny's Place	1963	Don-El 205
I Love You So	1985	Relic LP 8004
He's My Guy	1985	Relic LP 8004
KITTENS (TERRI & THE) (FEMALE)		
Wedding Bells (Just For You And Me)/You Cheated	1961	Imperial 5728
KITTENS FIVE (FEMALE)		
Don't Let It Happen Again/ Nothin'	1964	Herald 588

Artist Song	Year	Label
KLEIN, ROBERT (& GROUP)		
Fabulous 50's/Fabulous 50's (stereo)	1973	Brut 802
KLIXS		
It's All Over/This Is The End Of Love	1958	Music City 817
Elaine/This Is The End Of Love	1958	Music City 823
KNICK-KNACKS		
Baby Sittin' With You/Loneliness	1959	Cub 9030
Tracks Of My Tears (acapella)	1975	Relic LP 108
KNICKERBOCKERS (1)		
You Must Know/Somewhere, Somehow, Sweetheart	1953	It's A Natural 3000
KNICKERBOCKERS (2)		
Please Don't Love Him/Can You Help Me	1966	Challenge 59348
KNICKERBOCKERS (2) (BUDDY RANDELL & THE)		
All I Need Is You/Bite Bite Barracuda	1965	Challenge 59268
Lies/The Coming Generation	1965	Challenge 59321
KNIGHT LITES (GARY & THE)		
Will You Go Steady/I Can't Love You Anymore	1959	Prima 1016
Lonely Soldier's Pledge/ So Far Away From Home	1965	Bell 643
KNIGHT RIDERS (GM BILLY VERA)		
Annie's Place	1961	United Artists 366
KNIGHT, ALAN (& GROUP)		
Until I Know/Chills	1960	Tide 007
Here With Me	1960	Tide 016
KNIGHT, BOB (THE BOB KNIGHT FOUR)		
Good Goodbye/How Old Must I Be	1961	Laurel 1020
For Sale/You Gotta Know	1961	Laurel 1023
Well, I'm Glad/(no flip)	1961	Laurel 1025
So So Long (Good Goodbye)/ You Tease Me	1961	Taurus 100
Memories/Somewhere	1962	Josie 899
I'm Selling My Heart/The Lazy Piano (instrumental by the Lazy Four)	1962	Taurus 356
Two Friends/Crazy Love	1963	Jubilee 5451
Tomorrow We'll Be Married/ Willingly	1964	Goal 4/Jubilee
KNIGHT, GLORIA (& GROUP)		
Lonely Girl/Come Home	1964	Emerson 2101
KNIGHT, MARIE (& GROUP)		
Look At Me/Grasshopper Baby	1956	Mercury 70969
Tell Me Why/As Long As I Love	1956	Wing 90069
Am I Reaching For The Moon/ I'm The Little Fooler	1957	Mercury 71055
KNIGHT, SONNY (& GROUP)		
Keep A Walkin'/Baby Don't Want me	1955	Specialty 547/Specialty 594 (57)
End Of A Dream/Worthless And Lowdown	1957	Dot 15542
Insha Allah/Lovesick Blues (female group)	1957	Dot 15597
Barbara/I'm Lost Without You	1959	Eastman 791
Those Oldies But Goodies Are Dedicated To You/She Had Me Reelin'	1962	Original Sound 18
KNIGHTBEATS		
Hey Girl	1962	Planet 55
KNIGHTCAPS		
Honey Bee	1958	Punch 6000
KNIGHTS (1) (FRANKIE DAYE & THE)		
Dance Party Rock/Drag It	1959	Studio 9904
KNIGHTS (2)		
Forgive Me/I've Got The Feeling	1965	USA 800
KNIGHTS (3) (MARY WHEELER & THE)		
A Falling Tear/I Feel In My Heart	N/A	Atom 701
KNIGHTS (4) (EDDIE SHAW & THE)		
Lucky Star/Give Me Love	N/A	Rand 2
KNIGHTSMEN		
Darlin' Why/Pistol Packin' Mama	1961	Bocaldun 1006
KNOCKOUT MAYS		
You Are Laughing/Sweet Talk	1960	Cos-De 1003

Artist	Song	Year	Label
KNOCKOUTS			
	Darling Lorraine/Riot In Room 3C	1959	Shad 5013
	Rich Boy Poor Boy/Please Be Mine	1960	Shad 5018
	You Can Take My Girl/Fever	1961	MGM 13010
	Mo Jo, Pt. 1/Mo Jo, Pt. 2	1964	Tribute 199
	What's On Your Mind/Tweet-Tweet	1964	Tribute 201
	Don't Say Goodbye/Ecuador	1965	Tribute 1039
KO KOS (FEMALE)			
	The First Day Of School/You've Been Cheating	1957	Combo 141
	Teardrops	N/A	Gilt-Edge
KODAKS (AKA KODOKS)			
	Little Boy and Girl/Teenager's Dream	1957	Fury 1007
	Oh Gee Oh Gosh/Make Believe World	1957	Fury 1015
	My Baby And Me/Kingless Castle	1958	Fury 1019
	Runaround Baby/Guardian Angel	1960	Fury 1020
	Don't Want No Teasing!/Look Up To The Sky	1960	J&S 1683/1684
	Dance Dance Dance	1990	Relic LP 5083
	Let's Rock/Twista Twistin'	1961	Wink 1004
	Love Wouldn't Mean A Thing/Mister Magoo	1961	Wink 1006
KOKOMOS (WITH THE FOUR SEASONS)			
	Yours Truly/Mamma's Boy	1962	Gone 5134
	Open House Party/No Lies	1962	Josie 906
KOKONUTS (FB MEL CAVIN)			
	I Love You/My Mummy	1962	Bertram International 215
KOOKIE BEAVERS			
	Doggie In The Window/Three Little Fishes	1960	Gone 5086
KOOL GENTS (AKA DELEGATES) (GM DEE CLARK)			
	This Is The Night/Do Ya Do?	1956	Vee Jay 173
	You Know/I Just Can't Help Myself	1956	Vee Jay 207
	Picture On The Wall/Come To Me	1963	Bethlehem 3061
	Just Like A Fool/When I Call On You	1974	Broadcast 1102
	Crazy Over You	N/A	Charly LP 1115/Solid Smoke LP 8026
	Just Like A Fool	N/A	Vee Jay LP 1019/Charly LP 1113/Solid Smoke LP 8026
KOOLTONES			
	Traveling Stranger (acapella)	1975	Relic LP 101
KOOLTOPPERS			
	Is That Exactly What You Wanna Do/Cause I Love You So	1955	Beverly 702
KORMAN, JERRY (& GROUP)			
	Blind Date Fate/Hurry Back	1959	Meadow 1001/ABC 10024 (59)
KOUNTS (LEE HARRISON & THE)			
	Mine Alone/So Unimportant	1958	Pearl 717
KRAFTONES			
	Memories/Everybody's Got A Home But Me	1962	Medieval 206
KRANTZTONES			
	Zoop/Two Radio Jingles for WHBI	1980	Crystal Ball 140
KRUISERS			
	Karen/C'Mon Sweet Baby	1965	Kiski 2068
KUF-LINX			
	So Tough/What'Cha Gonna Do	1958	Challenge 1013/Challenge 59002 (58)
	Eyeballin'/Service With A Smile	1958	Challenge 59004
	Climb Love's Mountain/All That Good	1958	Challenge 59015
L'CAP-TANS (AKA CAP-TANS/AKA L'CAPTANS)			
	The Bells Ring Out/Call The Doctor	1958	Hollywood 1092
	Say Yes/Home Work	1959	Savoy 1567/D.C. 0416 (59)
LA CHORDS			
	To Be/Flame Out	1962	Gay 629
LA DOLLS			
	I'll Be Back	1985	Relic LP 8004
	Sick Spell	1985	Relic LP 8004
LA DONNA, MARIE (& GROUP)			
	How Can I Let You Know/Georgie Porgie	1960	Gateway 730
LA FETS & KITTY (AKA LA FITS & KITTY)			
	Christmas Letters/Can Can Rock & Roll	1957	Apollo 520
LA MAR, TONY (& GROUP)			
	Come Out Tonight/Promises	1960	Duco 5001
LA RAYS			
	A Woman Like You/Yesterday And You	1963	Arlen 517
LA RELLS			
	Everybody Knew/Please Be Fair	1961	Robbee 109
	Public Transportation/I Just Can't Understand	1961	Robbee 114
	I Guess I'll Never Stop Loving You/Sneaky Alligator	1962	Liberty 55430
LA ROC, DAL (& GROUP)			
	Stop What You're Doing/What A Fool	1961	Arteen 1010
LA SALLES			
	Chopsticks/Yum Yum	1958	Back Beat 515
LABRADORS			
	Queen Of Swing/When Someone Loves You	1958	Chief 7009
LADDERS			
	Counting The Stars/I Want To Know	1957	Holiday 2611
	My Love Is Gone/Hey, Pretty Baby	1959	Vest 826
LADDINS			
	Did It/Now You're Gone	1957	Central 2602/Times Square 3 (61)
	My Baby's Left Me	1958	Central (unreleased)
	I'm Falling In Love	1958	Central (unreleased)/Isle (unreleased) (60)
	Eternally	1959	Grey Cliff (unreleased)
	So Long Darling	1959	Grey Cliff (unreleased)
	Yes, Oh Baby Yes/Light A Candle	1959	Grey Cliff 721
	A Certain Kind Of Love	1960	Isle (unreleased)
	She's The One/Come On	1960	Isle 801
	Oh How I Hate To Go Home/There Once Was A Time	1961	Theatre 111
	I'll Kiss Your Teardrops Away/If You Need Me, I'll Be There	1962	Angie 1790
	Try, Try Again/That's What You Do To Me	1962	Groove 4-5
	Push, Shake, Kick And Shout/Push, Shake, Kick And Shout (instrumental)	1963	Angie 1003/Bardell 776 (63)
	Dream Baby/Dizzy Jones Birdland	1963	Butane 779
	Every Beat Of My Heart	1974	Relic LP 5018
	You Talk Too Much	1974	Relic LP 5018
	Diamonds And Pearls	1974	Relic LP 5018
	A Hundred Pounds Of Clay	1974	Relic LP 5018
	Tossin' And Turnin'	1974	Relic LP 5018
	That's What You Do To Me	1974	Relic LP 5018
	Mother-In-Law	1974	Relic LP 5018
LADDS (GEORGE DEE & THE)			
	I Can't Go On Like This/More	N/A	Kon-Ti-Ki 230
LADELLES (FEMALE)			
	Borrowed Time/No	N/A	Debonair 1218
LADY BUGS (FEMALE)			
	Who Sent This Love Note/Fraternity, U.S.A.	1962	Legrand 1033
LADYBIRDS			
	Yes I Know/Yes I Know	1964	Lawn 231
LAFAYETTES			
	Nobody But You/Life's Too Short	1962	RCA 8044
	I Still Do/Caravan Of Lonely Men	1962	RCA 8082
LAINE, LINDA (& GROUP)			
	After Today/Low Grades And High Fever	1964	Tower 108
LAKE, ARTHUR (BB THE WHEELS)			
	The Good Earth/May I Count On You	1956	Premium 406
LAKE, TONY (& GROUP)			
	I Declared My Love/Glamor Girl	1959	Herald 543

Artist Song	Year	Label	Artist Song	Year	Label
LAKETTES (FEMALE)			**LAPELS**		
Here Comes The Fool/Do You			Sneakin' Around/Sneaky Blues	1960	Melker 103/Dot 16129 (60)
Know	1960	Thunderbird 102	Big Bad Mollie/I Want A		
LALARETTES (LA LA & THE)			True Friend	1960	Melker 104
This Day Is Ours/Gettin' Ready			Bad Luck/Dusty Roads	1961	Fortune 862
For Freddy	1963	Elpeco 2922	**LARADOS**		
LAM, TOMMY (& GROUP)			Now The Parting Begins/		
Teenagers Dream/Weeping			Bad Bad Guitar Man	1957	Fox 963
Willow	1962	R 303	Rock N' Roll Mama	1957	unreleased
LAMAR, CHRIS (& GROUP)			Angels In Heaven	1957	unreleased
Love So True/Treat Me So Good	1963	Don-El 121	Will You Love Me Tomorrow?/		
LAMARR, GENE (BB THE BLUE FLAMES (3))			You Didn't Care	N/A	Madog 801
That Crazy Little House/			**LARADOS (DANNY ZELLA & THE)**		
You Don't Love Me Anymore	1958	Spry 113	You Made Me Blue/Sapphire	1957	Dial 100
Close To Me/Moon Eyes	1958	Spry 115	Wicked Ruby/Black Sax	1959	Fox 10056
LAMBERT, RUDY (BB THE LYRICS)			**LARAND, JOHNNY (& GROUP)**		
That Old Feeling/Sunday Kind			Heaven To Me/Don't Get Mad	1965	Octavia 0005
Of Love	1958	Rhythm 128	**LARGOS**		
LAMP LIGHTERS			Just A Picture/Saddle Up	1961	Starmaker 1002
Big Joke/After All	1955	Decca 29669	I Wonder Why?/Saddle Up	1961	Starmaker/Dot 16292 (62)
LAMPKIN, TOMMY (BB THE KIDDS)			**LARKS (1)**		
Lover's Plea/Eternal Love	1955	Imperial 5361	My Heart Cries For You/Coffee,		
LAMPLIGHTERS (JIMMY WITHERSPOON & THE)			Cigarettes And Tears	1951	Apollo 1177
Sad Life/Move Me Baby	1953	Federal 12156	Hopefully Yours/When I Leave		
LAMPLIGHTERS (REF CRENSHAWS/REF EBBTIDES (3)/REF FOUR AFTER			These Prison Walls	1951	Apollo 1180
FIVES/REF RIVINGTONS/REF SHARPS/REF TENDERFOOTS)			My Reverie/Let's Say A Prayer	1951	Apollo 1184
Turn Me Loose/Part Of Me	1953	Federal 12149	Eyesight To The Blind/I Ain't		
Be Bop Wino/Give Me	1953	Federal 12152	Fattenin' Frogs For Snakes	1951	Apollo 427
Smootchie/I Can't Stand It	1953	Federal 12166	Little Side Car/Hey! Little Girl	1951	Apollo 429
I Used To Cry Mercy, Mercy/			Oh It Feels So Good/I Don't		
Tell Me You Care	1953	Federal 12176	Believe In Tomorrow	1951	Apollo 430
Salty Dog/Ride, Jockey, Ride	1954	Federal 12182	Shadrack/Honey In The Rock	1952	Apollo 1189
Five Minutes Longer/You Hear	1954	Federal 12192	In My Lonely Room/Stolen Love	1952	Apollo 1190
Yum Yum/Goody Good Things	1954	Federal 12197	Hold Me/I Live True To You	1952	Apollo 1194
I Wanna Know/Believe In Me	1954	Federal 12206	My Lost Love/How Long Must I		
Roll On/Love, Rock And Thrill	1955	Federal 12212	Wait For You?	1952	Apollo 435
Hug A Little, Kiss A Little/			Darlin'/Lucy Brown	1952	Apollo 437
Don't Make It So Good	1955	Federal 12242	Margie/Rockin' In The Rocket		
You Were Sent Down From			Room	1954	Lloyds 108
Heaven/Bo Peep	1956	Federal 12255	If It's A Crime/Tippin' In	1954	Lloyds 110
It Ain't Right/Everything's			When You're Near/Who Walks		
All Right	1956	Federal 12261	In When I Walk Out	1954	Lloyds 111
LANCE, HERB (BB THE CLASSICS)			No Other Girl/The World Is		
You Can't Be Sure Of Anything/			Waiting For The Sunrise	1954	Lloyds 112
By The Candle Glow	1957	DeLuxe 6150	Forget It/Os-Ca-Lu-Ski-O	1954	Lloyds 114
LANCERS (1)			Johnny Darlin'/You're Gonna		
Were You Ever Mine To Lose	1953	Trend 63	Lose Your Gal	1954	Lloyds 115
It's You I Love	1954	Trend 73	Honey From The Bee/		
Live And Let Live	1954	Trend 82	No, Mama, No	1955	Apollo 475
LANCERS (2)			Danny Boy/Without A Song	1971	Dreamtone 201 (unreleased)
Oh Little Girl/You're The			She's A Good One/Baby Wants		
Right One	1963	Lawn 205	To Rock (by the Clouds)	1974	Broadcast 1002
The Warmth Of The Sun/			Christmas To New Year's	1988	Relic LP 8013
Hushabye	1965	Vee Jay 654	It's Breaking My Heart	1988	Relic LP 8013
LANCERS (3) (WITH LARRY SMITH)			Jam Session	1988	Relic LP 8013
Don't Make Me A Lonely Boy/			If You Were The Only Girl In		
The Moocher	N/A	Central 6001	The World	1988	Relic LP 8013
LANDERS, BOB (& GROUP)			For The Love Of You	1988	Relic LP 8014
Cherokee Dance/Guitar Rock			All I Want For Christmas	1988	Relic LP 8014
(by Willie Joe)	1956	Specialty 576	What's The Matter	1988	Relic LP 8014
LANDI, TONY (& GROUP)			**LARKS (2) (DON JULIAN & THE)**		
Angels Cried/Bubbily Bubbily	1957	Safari 1001	Shorty The Pimp, Pt. 1/Shorty		
LANDIS, JERRY (& GROUP) (AKA PAUL SIMON & GROUP)			The Pimp, Pt. 2	1965	Jerk 202
I Wish I Weren't In Love/			**LARKS (2) (GM DON JULIAN)**		
I'm Lonely	1961	Canadian American 130	Fabulous Cars And Diamond		
Lone Teen Ranger/Lisa	1962	Amy 875/Jason Scott 22 (82)	Rings/Life Is Sweeter Now	1961	Cross Fire 74-49/74-50/
LANDS, LIZ (BB THE TEMPTATIONS)					Guyden 2103 (61)
Keep Me/Midnight Journey	1963	Gordy 7030	I Want Her To Love Me/I Want		
LANE, RUSTY (BB THE MYSTICS)			Her To Love Me (instrumental)	1961	Guyden 2098/Violet 1051
Karen/Comes The Day	1959	Laurie 3031			(63)
LANES			It's Unbelievable/I Can't		
Open Up Your Heart/You Alone	1956	Gee 1023	Believe It	1961	Sheryl 334/Uptown (65)
LANHAM, RICHARD (BB THE TEMPO-TONES)			There Is A Girl/Let's Drink		
On Your Radio/Dance Of Love	1955	Acme 712	A Toast	1961	Sheryl 338
Wishing All The Time/The Day			I Want Her To Love Me/		
I Met You	1956	Acme 722	Muddy Road	1963	Violet 1050
Don't Believe Him/Have A			For The Love Of Money/		
Little Faith	1965	Josie 985	Another Sleepless Night	1964	Arock 1010
LANTERNS			The Jerk/Forget Me	1964	Money 106
Gloria (acapella)/I Miss You			Mickey's East Coast Jerk/		
So Much	1973	Baron 110	Soul Jerk	1964	Money 110
			Heavenly Father/The Roman	1964	Money 112

Artist Song	Year	Label
Love You So/Love Me True	1965	Jett 3001
Sad Sad Boy/Can You Do		
The Duck	1965	Money 115
The Answer Came Too Late/		
Lost My Love Yesterday	1965	Money 119
Philly Dog/Heaven Only Knows	1965	Money 122
Come Back Baby/The Skate	1965	Money 127
I Want You Back/I Love You	1971	Money 601
LARKS (3) (IRMA & THE)		
Don't Cry/Without You Baby	N/A	Priority 322
LARKTONES		
The Letter/Rockin', Swingin'		
Man	1958	ABC 9909
Nosy Neighbor/Why Are You		
Tearing Us Apart	1960	Riki 140
The Letter/This To Me Is Love		
(by the Dubs)	N/A	Popular Request 109
LARSON, KEY (& GROUP)		
Web Of Lies/A Little Lovin'	1961	Lawn 106
LASABERS (LAFAYETTE & THE)		
Cure For Love/Free Way		
(instrumental)	1960	Port 70036
LASSITER, ART (& GROUP)		
Just Another Day In The Life		
Of A Fool/Bermuda	1956	Ballad 1020
Too Late For Tears/Just		
Another Day In The Life		
Of A Fool	1956	Ballad 1024
LATARS		
Rita/Another Miracle Of Love	1975	Monogram 100
LATIN LADS		
The Way You Look Tonight/		
When I Fall In Love	1987	Ronnie 206
LATIN LADS (JULITO & THE)		
Nunca (Never)/Poesia En		
Movim lento	1963	Rico-Vox 27
LATINAIRES (LITTLE JOE & THE)		
Why Don't You Write Me/		
Crazy Baby	1970	White Whale 304
LATONS		
So In Love/Love Me	1962	Port 70030
LAURELS (1)		
Truly, Truly/'Tis Night	1955	X 0143
LAURELS (1) (BOBBY RELF & THE)		
Yours Alone/Farewell	1955	Flair 1063
LAURELS (2) (JAKE PORTER & THE)		
Fine Fine Baby/		
T. J. (instrumental)	1955	Combo 66
LAURELS (3) (KENNY LORAN & THE)		
Lonely Boy/Change Of Love	1958	Challenge 59010
LAURELS (4)		
Picture Of Love/Hand In Hand	1959	ABC 10048
Baby Talk/You Left Me	1960	Spring 1112
LAURELS (5) (JOHN GAUDET & THE)		
Your Name Shall Be		
Remembered/XMas Will		
Soon Be Here	1961	Mary Glen 1001
LAURELS (6)		
A Little Romance/Summer's		
Gonna Be A Ball	1982	Alexis 6873
I Wonder/Every Minute		
Of The Day	1982	Bishop 1016
Don't Just Stand There/Rhythm	1985	Nobletown 821
Honey, I Love You/So		
Much In Love	1985	R.A.M. 501012
When I'm With You/Truthfully	1986	R.A.M. 706005
Hydrogen Bomb/Crying In		
The Chapel/Lonely Summer/		
Barbara	1986	R.A.M. EP 509049
Don't Go/Darling How Long	1989	World 102
Our Anniversary/Walking		
The Dog	1995	Swing Club 028
LAURIE, LINDA (& GROUP)		
Prince Charming/Soupin' Up		
Your Motor	1960	Rust 5022
Stay At Home Sue/Lazy Love	1962	Rust 5042
LAVENDERS (1) (ROBIN LEE & THE)		
Pretty Patti	1960	Circle Dot 103
LAVENDERS (2)		
Angel/The Slide	1961	C.R. 103
The Bells/I Said Look	1961	Lake 706
One More Time/One More Once	1963	Mercury 72126

Artist Song	Year	Label
This I Feel/Daddy, Daddy	1964	Dot 16584
LAVENDERS (3) (ERNIE MORALES & THE)		
I'm So Lonely/A Little Bit Of		
Everything	1977	Crystal Ball 100
LAVETTE, BETTY (& GROUP)		
You Killed The Love/		
Witchcraft In The Air	1964	LuPine 123
LAWRENCE BROTHERS (BILL LAWRENCE & THE)		
Hey Baby	1959	Bertram International 207
Please Don't Leave Me	1960	Bertram International 227
LAWRENCE, BERNIE (& GROUP)		
Collecting Girls/That Was		
Yesterday	1961	United Artists 388
LAWRENCE, BOB (& GROUP)		
Come My Little Baby/		
Honey Dew	1957	Mark-X 7005
LAWSON BOYS (TEDDY LAWSON & THE)		
There's No Return From Love/		
I Knew It Was You All The Time	1957	Mansfield 611/612
LEADERS		
Stormy Weather/A Lover		
Of The Time	1955	Glory 235
Dearest, Beloved Darling/		
Nobody Loves Me	1956	Glory 239
Can't Help Lovin' That Girl Of		
Mine/Lovers	1956	Glory 243
LEAPING FLAMES		
It's Been So Long/Hurts Me		
To Work	1963	MRC 1201
LEDO, LES (& GROUP)		
Scarlet Angel/Don't Fight	1960	Shell 721
LEE (BB THE REGENTS)		
Goddess Of Love/Lonely		
Summer	1961	Scepter 1222
LEE, ADDIE (& GROUP)		
C'Mon Home/Please Buy My		
Record	1958	End 1018
LEE, CURTIS (BB THE HALOS)		
Special Love/D-In Love	1960	Dunes 2001
California GL-903/Then I'll		
Know	1960	Dunes 801
I Never Knew What Love		
Could Do/Gotta Have You	1960	Hot 7
I'm Asking Forgiveness/		
Let's Take A Ride	1960	Sabra 517
With All My Heart/Pure Love	1960	Warrior 1555
Pledge Of Love/Then I'll Know	1961	Dunes 2003
Pretty Little Angel Eyes/		
Gee How I Wish	1961	Dunes 2007
Under The Moon Of Love/		
Beverly Jean	1961	Dunes 2008
Just Another Fool/A Night At		
Daddy Gee's	1962	Dunes 2012
The Wobble/Does He Mean		
That Much To You	1962	Dunes 2015
LEE, JAMES WASHINGTON (& GROUP)		
I Need Somebody/Don't Ask Me	1962	L&M 1003
LEE, JERRY (& GROUP)		
Unwritten Law/Count Ten	1961	Rendezvous 147
LEE, JIMMY (& GROUP)		
It Must Be Love/Intermission	1958	Apollo 525
My Dear Little Doll/I Wonder		
(Can It Be True)	1961	Canadian American 122
LEE, JIMMY (& WAYNE WALKER & GROUP)		
Love Me	1955	Chess 4863
LEE, JIMMY (BB THE EARLS)		
Daddy's Home/If I Could Do It		
Once Again	1978	Bo-P-C 100
LEE, MABEL (& GROUP)		
Dearest Dream/He's My Guy	1956	Hull 712
LEE, SHIRLEY (& GROUP)		
Behind The Make Up/Keep		
The Magic Working	1961	Seven Arts 711
LEE, WARREN (& GROUP)		
Geraldine/London Bridge	1963	Jin 173
LEEDS		
Heaven Only Knows/Mr. Cool	1959	Wand 102
LEEDS, RANDY (& GROUP)		
My Oh My/Insurance	1959	Roulette 4153
LEEN TEENS		
So Shy/Dream Around You	1959	Imperial 5593

Artist Song	Year	Label
LEERICS		
Island Of Love/Hey Patty	N/A	Un-Released Gold 799
LEFEMMES (COLE & THE)		
Love Is No Stranger/		
Aut-a-mation	N/A	Varbee 5001
LEGACY (AKA BEL-AIRES)		
Loretta/Dreams Of Heaven	1987	Crystal Ball 151
Down The Road/A Little Bit		
Of Soap	1988	Crystal Ball 153
LEGENDS (1)		
I'll Never Fall In Love Again/		
The Eyes Of An Angel	1957	Melba 109
The Legend Of Love/		
Now I'm Telling You	1958	Hull 727
LEGENDS (2) (BILLY DAVIS & THE)		
Goodbye Jesse/Spunky Onions	1960	Peacock 1694
LEGENDS (3)		
Get Out Of The House/		
You Little Nothin'	1961	Magenta 02
Jungle Lullabye/Go Away		
With Me	1962	Caldwell 410
My Love For You/Say Mama	1962	Ermine 39
Bop-A-Lena/I Wish I Knew	1962	Ermine 43
Temptation/Marionette	1962	Ermine 45
Tell The Truth/You'll Never		
See The Forest	1962	Jamie 1228
Run To The Movies/		
Summertime Blues	1963	Capitol 5014
Well Darling/Over Yonder	1963	Falco 305
LEGENDS (4) (RICK & THE)		
I Wonder Why/Love Me Like I		
Know You Can	1963	JD 162/United Artists 50093 (66)
LEGENDS (5) (LARRY & THE) (WITH THE FOUR SEASONS)		
Don't Pick On Me Baby/		
The Creep	1964	Atlantic 2220
LEGENDS (6)		
Here Comes The Pain/		
Don't Be Ashamed	1964	Warner Bros. 5457
LEGENDS (7) (LONNIE & THE)		
I Cried/Baby Without You	1966	Impression 109
LEGENDS (8)		
Gail/Lariat	N/A	Key 1002
LEGGERIORS		
Flame Of Love/Justine	1963	Goliath 1351
LEGS, STICK (& GROUP)		
The Wedding/Flying Twist	1962	Hard Times 3002
LEIGH, LINDA (& GROUP)		
Move Out/It's Real	1959	Rendezvous 103
LEISURE LADS		
Baby, I'm All Alone/A Teenage		
Memory	1959	Delco 801
LEMON DROPS		
Cute Little Wiggle/Lo-o-ve	1959	Coral 62145
Marcheta/Mexicali Moon	1960	Aladdin 3465
LEN-DELLS (AKA LYDELLS)		
(Don't Be A) Litterbug/Maryann	1964	Reach 2
LEOPARDS (1) (LEE & THE)		
Come Into My Palace/Trying To		
Make It	1962	Gordy 7002/Laurie 3197 (63)
What About Me/Don't Press		
Your Luck	1964	Fortune 867
LEOPARDS (2)		
Mah Mah (Chicken Pot Pie)/		
Valerie	1963	Leopard 5006
LESTER, BOBBY (ACTUALLY THE MOONGLOWS)		
Lonely Hearts/Am I The Man?	1959	Checker 921
LEVEE SONGSTERS (AKA MELLO-HARPS/AKA TEENTONES)		
Out Love Is A Vow/Walkie		
Talkie Baby	1959	Karen 1004/Relic 515 (64)
LEVERETT, CHICO (BB THE SATINTONES)		
Work Work/Baby Don't Leave	1963	Bethlehem 3062
LEVONS (FEMALE)		
Come To Me/Everytime	1962	Columbia 42506
We're Just Friends Now/		
Love Is Better Than Ever	1963	Columbia 42798
LEWIS, BILLY (& GROUP)		
Stool Pigeon Baby/I Won't Tell		
A Soul	1956	Flo-Lou 101
LEWIS, BOBBY (& FEMALE GROUP)		
Tossin' And Turnin'/Oh Yes,		
I Love You	1961	Beltone 1002

Artist Song	Year	Label
LEWIS, JAMES (& GROUP)		
I Cried Last Night/Tell Me		
That You Love Me	1958	Arrow 730
LEWIS, LITTLE JUNIOR (& GROUP)		
And That's All I Need/Come		
On Back Where You Belong	1960	Fury 1039
LEXING, BOBBY (& GROUP)		
Flame In My Heart	1961	Good Sound 107
LEXINGTONS (1)		
When My Baby Went Away/		
I Found My Baby	1960	Everest 19369
LEXINGTONS (2) (JOEY & THE)		
Heaven/The Girl I Love	1962	Comet 2154
Bobbie/Tears From My Eyes	1963	Dunes 2029
LEXINGTONS (3)		
My Honey Loves Another Girl/		
Ba Ba Doo	1963	International 500
LEXONS		
Angels Like You/		
Rock 'N Roll 'N Rock 'N Roll	1958	Lexington 100
LIDOS		
Trudy/Since I Last Saw You	1957	Band Box 359
LIFESAVERS (LUCIEN FARRAR & THE)		
Didn't You Know/Help	1957	Jupiter 1
Tomorrow Night/Bohemia Night	1957	Jupiter 2
LIGHTERS (MARY HYLOR & BILLY ROLLE & THE)		
We Walk Down The Aisle/		
Runnin'	1963	El-Lor 1058
LILE, BOBBY (& GROUP)		
Story-Book Love	1963	Marsh 204
LIMELIGHTERS		
Cabin Hideaway/My Sweet		
Norma Lee	1956	Josie 795
This Lonely Boy/Sister Sookey		
Comes Home	1957	Gilco 213
LIMELITES (SHEP & THE)		
Freckle Face	1959	Apt (unreleased)
Little Star	1959	Apt (unreleased)
Too Young To Wed/Two Loving		
Hearts (Shane Sheppard)	1960	Apt 25039
I'm So Lonely (What Can I Do?)/		
One Week From Today	1960	Apt 25046
Daddy's Home/This I Know	1961	Hull 740
Ready For Your Love/You'll		
Be Sorry	1961	Hull 742/Hull 1009
Three Steps From The Altar/		
Oh What A Feeling	1961	Hull 747
Three Steps From The Altar/		
Ready For Your Love	1961	Roulette 102
Our Anniversary/Who Told The		
Sandman	1962	Hull 748
What Did Daddy Do/Teach Me		
How To Twist	1962	Hull 751
Everything Is Gonna Be Alright/		
Gee Baby What About You	1963	Hull 753
Remember Baby/The Monkey	1963	Hull 756
Stick By Me (And I'll Stick By		
You)/It's All Over Now	1963	Hull 757
Steal Away (With Your Baby)/		
For You My Love	1963	Hull 759
Why, Why Won't You Believe		
Me/Easy To Remember		
(When You Want To Forget)	1963	Hull 761
Why Did You Fall For Me/		
I'm All Alone	1964	Hull 767
Party For Two/You Better Believe	1965	Hull 770
I'm A Hurtin' Inside/In Case		
I Forget	1965	Hull 772
LINCOLN'S QUINTETT		
Dream Of Romance/Tell Me		
What Is Wrong	1958	Angle Tone 522
LINCOLNS (1)		
I Cried/Madly In Love	1957	Aljon 113/114/Bim Bam Boom 105 (72)
Don't Let Me Shed Any		
More Tears/Pleasin' You		
Pleases Me	1957	Atlas 1100
Baby, Please Let Me Love		
You/Can't You Go For Me?	1959	Mercury 71553
LINCOLNS (2)		
Sometime, Somewhere/		
Sukiyaki Rocki	1961	Bud 113

Artist / Song	Year	Label
LINKS		
Scrunchy/Pyramid	1958	Brunswick 55081
Baby/She's The One	1958	Teenage 1009
LINNETTES		
Someday/Big Eyed Baby	1960	Palette 5112
LIONS (1)		
No One (No One But You)/Giggles	1960	Everest 19388/Mark IV 1
Hickory Dickory/The Yokel (He Went To Town)	1960	Imperial 5678
Two Timing Love/Feast Of The Beast	1960	Rendezvous 116
'Til The 13th Month	1961	Mark IV 104
LIONS (2) (LUGEE & THE) (FB LOU CHRISTIE)		
The Jury/Little Did I Know	1961	Robbee 112
LISI, RICKY (BB THE CONCORDS)		
The River/Don't Go Now	1963	Roulette 4511
LITATIONS		
Let Me Tell You	1963	N/A
LITTERBUGS		
Valerie/Calypso	1963	Okeh 7164
LITTLE ALFRED (& GROUP)		
Walking Down The Aisle	1962	Lyric 1016
LITTLE ANGEL		
Come On And Rock/Help Me Baby	1959	Award 126
LITTLE ANGELS		
I'll Be A Little Angel/Santa Claus Parade	1961	Warwick 672
LITTLE BEATS		
Someone For Me/Love Is True	1957	Mercury 71155
LITTLE BEAVERS (JOHNNY BRISCOE & THE)		
Why Do Fools Fall In Love/Sugar Love	1971	Atlantic 2822
LITTLE BOYS BLUE (BONNIE & THE)		
You'd Better Run/Bells	1960	Nikko 611
LITTLE BUCK (& GROUP)		
I'll Follow You/Let It Be Now	1960	Duke 324
LITTLE CAESAR (& GROUP)		
I'm Reachin'/Who Slammed The Door	1958	RCA 7270
LITTLE CHERYL (& GROUP)		
Heaven Only Knows/Can't We Just Be Friends	1963	Cameo 270
Come On Home/I Love You Conrad	1964	Cameo 292
LITTLE COOLBREEZERS		
Won't You Come In/Pack Your Bags And Go	1956	Ebony 1015
LITTLE DAVID (& GROUP)		
So Long/Home Is Where You Come From	1963	Savoy 1617
Love Me	N/A	521 1001
LITTLE DIPPERS		
Forever/Two By Four	1959	University 210
Be Sincere/Tonight	1960	University 6053/6054
Lonely/I Wonder, I Wonder, I Wonder	1960	University 608
Sails/For Just A Little While Tonight	1964	Dot 16602
LITTLE DIXIE (& GROUP)		
Be Fair/I'm Growing Up	1959	Las Vegas 101/Strip 101
LITTLE ELLEN (& GROUP)		
Answer Me My Love/That Other Guy	1961	Smash 1724
LITTLE ERNIE (& GROUP)		
You Lied And I Cried/Queen Of The Hop	1963	Summit 0008
LITTLE ESTHER (BB THE DOMINOES)		
Heart To Heart/Lookin' For A Man	1951	Federal 12036
LITTLE ESTHER (BB THE ROBINS)		
Saturday Night Daddy/Mainliner (by Bobby Nunn with the Robins)	1952	Federal 12100
LITTLE EVA (& GROUP)		
The Locomotion/He Is The Boy	1962	Dimension 1000
LITTLE FOUR QUARTET		
Tee-U-Eee/Don't Forget To Be True	N/A	Southern 122
LITTLE HERMAN (& GROUP)		
Gotta Keep On Walking/I'm Gonna Put The Hurt On You	1964	Arlen 751
LITTLE JERRY (& GROUP) (JERRY WILLIAMS)		
(I'll Always Remember) The Chapel On The Hill/I'm So Mad	1960	Aldo 502
LITTLE KINGS (PHIL ORSI & THE)		
Oh My Darling/Come On Everybody	1963	Lucky 1009
LITTLE LINDA (& GROUP)		
After I Told You/You Know	1961	Coral 62286
LITTLE MISS PEGGY (& GROUP)		
Tears Of Love/Freddie, Freddie	1960	Goldband 1109
LITTLE MISS WANDA (& GROUP)		
My Johnny/You Go To My Head (no group)	1961	Aries 1020
LITTLE NAT (BB THE SHELLS)		
Tally Wally/Do This Do That	1961	Pik 242
LITTLE PEOPLE (MIKE LYNAM & THE)		
Message To Pretty/I Need You	N/A	Emanon 101
LITTLE RICHARD (& GROUP)		
True, Fine Mama/Ooh My Soul (no group)	1958	Specialty 633
LITTLE SAMMY (& GROUP)		
Can You Love Me/Papa Did The Chicken	1956	Shade 1002
LITTLE STEVIE (& GROUP)		
I See A Star/The Letter	1961	Guyden 2060
LITTLE, HORACE (& GROUP)		
Five Hundred Years/Texas Stomp	1962	Ascot 2102
LITTLE, LEE ROY (& GROUP)		
Hurry Back, Please Come Home/Let Me Go Home Whiskey	1960	Cee Jay 579
LITTLEFIELD, LITTLE WILLIE (& FEMALE GROUP)		
Theresa/The Day The Rains Came	1958	Rhythm 124
LITTLEFIELD, LITTLE WILLIE (BB THE MONDELLOS)		
Ruby, Ruby/Easy Go (instrumental)	1957	Rhythm 108/Bullseye 1005 (57)/Argyle
LIVE WIRES (ANDY & THE)		
Maggie/You've Done It Again	1960	Applause 1249
LLOYD, JACKIE (BB THE HARBOR LIGHTS)		
Come And Get Me/Warm Love	1960	Heros 342
LOCKETS		
Don't Cha Know/Little Boy	1963	Argo 5455
LOCKETTES (FEMALE)		
Puddin' Pie/You Don't Want Me	1958	Flip 334
LOCKETTES (RICHARD BERRY & THE)		
Heaven On Wheels/The Mess Around	1958	Flip 336
LOCOMOTIONS		
Little Eva/Adios My Love	1962	Gone 5142
LOCOS		
Professor Loco/Oh Yes, Indeed I Do	1958	20th Fox 102
LOGAN, DOROTHY (BB THE GEMS)		
Since I Fell For You/Small Town Man (no group)	1954	Drexel 902
LOGICS		
One Love/Everybody's Doing The Pony	1960	Everlast 5015
LOLLIPOPS (1) (LITTLE BOB & THE)		
Twisting Home/You Don't Have To Cry	1962	Decca 31412
LOLLIPOPS (2) (BECKY & THE)		
I Don't Care/Come On Home	1964	Troy 6493/Epic 9736 (64)
LOLLYPOPPERS		
A Bottle Of Pop And A Lollypop/Miss Selma's Boogie	1955	Aladdin 3291
Miss Selma's Boogie/A Bottle Of Pop And A Lollypop	1955	Harlem 104/Aladdin 3291 (55)
LOLLYPOPS		
Believe In Me/My Love Is Real	1958	Universal International 7420/Holland 7420 (58)
Dream Street/Norman	1960	Kandee 6001
LONDON, LLOYD (BB THE YACHTSMEN)		
Will There Ever Be A Girl/Cry Baby	1959	Destiny 530

Artist Song	Year	Label
LONDON, PAUL (& GROUP)		
Hey Boy/Keep Your Heartaches		
To Yourself	1963	Limelight 3015
LONDON, RALPH (& GROUP) (AKA ADAM WADE & GROUP)		
Someday You'll Be My Girl/		
Lovely Lovely Girl	1964	Coed 588
LONELY BOYS		
A Spoken Letter/My Girl	1959	NuWay 555
LONELY GUYS		
The Way You Look Tonight/		
Moon Flight	1957	Caddy 117
LONELY ONES		
I Want My Girl/My Wish	1959	Baton 270/Sir 270 (59)
Debbie/Swanee River Fling	1960	Rendezvous 125
LONG, BOBBY (& HIS CHERRIOS)		
Patty/By My Side	1958	Arrow 727
I Slipped-Tripped/Don't You		
Run	1959	Glow-Hill 503
Hold Me/Ooh La La	1959	Glow-Hill 504
Calling/Did You Ever Dream		
Lucky	1959	Unart 2023
LOPEZ, TRINI (& GROUP)		
Since I Don't Have You/		
Rock On	1959	King 5187
Love Me Tonight/Here		
Comes Sally	1959	King 5198
LORAN, KENNY (& GROUP)		
Magic Star/Mama's Little Baby	1959	Capitol 4276
LORD, EMMETT (& GROUP)		
Turn Him Down/Women	1962	Liberty 55491
Been So Long/Beggar Of Love	N/A	Antel 520
LORDS (1) (YVETTE & THE)		
We Must Carry On/How Can		
I Tell Him	1964	Yvette 103
LORDS (2)		
When She Was My Girl/Elvira	1987	Starlight 52
Just My Imagination/Don't		
Look Back	1988	Starlight 62
LORELEIS		
Have Fun Baby/Now I'm		
Broken Hearted	1955	Dot 15268
You're So Nice To Be Near/		
Wildsville	1955	Spotlight 390
LORNETTES		
His Way With The Girls/Down		
The Block And Up To Heaven	1965	Gallico 110
LOUISIANA JEMMS (SUGAR PIE DESANTOS & THE)		
Crazy Lovin'/Love Me Tonight	1963	Checker 1056
LOUNGERS (AKA FIVE SECRETS/AKA SECRETS (1))		
Remember The Nite/Dizzy Spell	1958	Herald 534
Teenage Bells/Wedding Bells	1991	Park Ave. 5
LOURDES		
My Favorite Dream/Yours	1960	Mercury 71655
LOVE BUGS (FB PRESTON LOVE)		
Boom Diddy Wawa Baby/		
A Man Goin' Crazy	1955	Federal 12216
LOVE BUGS (PRESTON LOVE & THE)		
If You Ever Get Lonesome/		
Groove Juice	1955	Ultra 101
LOVE LETTERS		
Walking The Streets Alone/		
Owee-Nellie	1957	Acme 714
LOVE NOTES (1)		
Crawling	1953	Family Library of Music EP 1040
You're Mine	1953	Family Library of Music EP 1040
LOVE NOTES (2)		
Surrender Your Heart/Get		
On My Train	1953	Imperial 5254
I'm Sorry/Sweet Lulu	1954	Riviera 970/Rainbow 266 (54)
Since I Fell For You/Don't Be		
No Fool	1954	Riviera 975
LOVE NOTES (3)		
United/Tonight	1957	Holiday 2605
If I Could Make You Mine/		
Don't Go	1957	Holiday 2607
LOVE NOTES (4)		
Our Songs Of Love/Nancy	1963	Wilshire 200
Gloria/Mathematics Of Love	1964	Wilshire 203
LOVE NOTES (5) (HONEY LOVE & THE)		
We Belong Together/Mary Ann	1965	Cameo 380
LOVE NOTES (6) SYBIL LOVE & THE)		
I Love You Darling/No More		
Tears	N/A	Valex 505
LOVE, DARLENE (& GROUP)		
(Today I Met) The Boy I'm		
Gonna Marry/My Heart		
Beat A Little Faster	1963	Philles 111
(Today I Met) The Boy I'm		
Gonna Marry/Playing For		
Keeps	1963	Philles 111
Wait 'Til My Bobby Gets Home/		
Take It From Me (instrumental)	1963	Philles 114
A Fine Fine Boy/Nino And		
Sonny (instrumental)	1963	Philles 117
Christmas (Baby, Please		
Come Home)/Harry And Milt		
Meet Hal B. (instrumental)	1963	Philles 119
(He's A) Quiet Guy/Stumble		
And Fall	1964	Philles 123
Christmas (Baby, Please Come		
Home)/Winter Wonderland	1964	Philles 125
White Christmas	1964	Philles EP X-EP
Christmas/Winter Blues	1965	Philles 125X
Too Late To Say You're Sorry/If	1966	Reprise 534
Christmas (Baby, Please Come		
Home)/Wait Till My Bobby		
Gets Home	1974	Warner-Spector 0401
Lord, If You're A Woman/		
tumble And Fall	1976	Warner-Spector 0410
LOVE, FRANKIE		
First Star/Save Her For Me	1962	La Rosa 101
LOVE, JIMMY (& GROUP)		
Let Me Down Easy/Way Down		
Yonder In New Orleans	1963	Violet 1052
LOVE, RONNIE (& GROUP)		
Judy/Detroit, Michigan	1965	D-Town 1047
LOVE-LORDS		
Burning Love/Simmerfast		
(instrumental)	1962	Al-King 11021
LOVE-TONES (GINO PARKS & THE)		
Fire/For This I Thank You	1962	Tamla 54066
LOVE-TONES (MARY WELLS & THE)		
You Beat Me To The Punch/		
Old Love	1962	Motown 1032
Laughing Boy/Two Wrongs		
Don't Make A Right (no group)	1963	Motown 1039
LOVEJOY, LOVEY (& GROUP)		
Crazy Crazy 'Bout You/		
(flip is instrumental)	N/A	Award 116
LOVEJOYS (FEMALE)		
It's Mighty Nice/Payin'		
(For The Wrong I've Done)	1964	Tiger 105/Red Bird 003 (64)
LOVEJOYS (LEOLA & THE) (FEMALE)		
He Ain't No Angel/Wait 'Round		
The Corner	1964	Tiger 101
LOVELARKS (1)		
More And More/Diddle-Le-Bom	1961	Masons 3-070/Fellatio 301
LOVELARKS (2) (STEVE KASS & THE)		
Darling My Love/You Made A		
Boo Boo	1957	Class 10
LOVELITES		
I Found Me A Lover/You Better		
Stop It	1961	Bandera 2515
(When) I Get Scared	N/A	Phi-Dan 5008
LOVELLS		
Here Comes The Heartaches/		
My Time To Cry	1967	Brent 7073
LOVENOTES (1) (AKA TRUE LOVES)		
A Love Like Ours/Never Look		
Behind	1957	Premium 411
LOVENOTES (2) (SYBIL LOVE & THE)		
I Love You Darling/No More		
Tears	1959	Valex 505
LOVER BOY (& GROUP)		
Incidentally/Dance A Little		
Closer	1963	Crystalette 758
LOVERS (1)		
Don't Touch Me/Let Me Be		
The First To Know	1956	Decca 29862
Darling It's Wonderful/Gotta		
Whole Lot Of Lovin' To Do	1957	Lamp 2005
I Wanna Be Loved/Let's Elope	1957	Lamp 2013

Artist / Song	Year	Label
Tell Me/Love Bug Bit Me	1958	Aladdin 3419/Lamp 2018 (58)
Strange As It Seems/Party Line	1961	Keller 101
Darling It's Wonderful/I Want To Be Loved	1962	Imperial 5845/Post 10007 (63)
You Are Welcome To My Heart/ With All My Heart	1962	MC B-003
Let's Elope/Tell Me	1963	Imperial 5960
Someone/Do This For Me	1966	Gate 501/Philips 40353 (66)
LOVERS (2)		
Let's/Big Axe	1958	Casino 103
LOVERS (3) (RAY FRAZIER & THE)		
King Of Lovers/Darling	1959	Combo 161
LOVERS (4) (PETE PETER & THE)		
A Lonely Island/Pistol Packing Mama	1960	Derby 1030
LOVERS (5) (VALENTINO & THE)		
I'm Gonna Love/One Teardrop Too Late	1960	Donna 1345
LOVERS (6) (LITTLE LOUIE & THE) (GM LOU CHRISTIE)		
Someday You'll Pay/Nothing But The Two-Step	1962	Viscount 102
LOVERS (7) (BILLY LOVE & THE)		
Legend Of Love/Hold Me Close	1964	Dragon 4403
LOVERS (8)		
Caravan Of Lonely Men/In My Tenement	1965	Agon 1011
LOVERS (9) (CLIFF BUTLER & THE)		
I Can't Believe/Everybody Needs Somebody	N/A	Frantic 801
LOVETONES (1)		
Talk To An Angel/Take It Easy, Baby	1956	Plus 108
When I Asked My Love/You Can Tell That This Is Christmas	1962	Love-Tone 101
LOVETONES (2)		
It's Mighty Easy/I Want You Now	1961	Marlo 1515
LOVETONES (3) (RAYMOND POPE & THE)		
I Love Nadine/Star	1962	Squalor 1313
LOVETONES (4)		
For Your Love/So Strange	1974	Barrier 100
LOVETTES		
Written In The Stars/Puzzling Love	1959	Knight 2010
Puzzling Love/Lost Weekend	1959	Knight 2010
LOYE JR., BOBBY (& GROUP)		
Loving Tree/Another Mr. Blue	1963	Wilshire 202
LP's (DENNY & THE)		
Why Not Give Me Your Heart?/ Slide-Cha-Lypso	1958	Rock-It 001
LULLABIES (LISA & THE) (REF CONCORDS)		
Why Do I Cry/He's So Good	1964	Coed 589
LULLABYES (1)		
My Heart Cries For You/ You Touch Me	1964	Dimension 1039
LULLABYES (2)		
You Belong To Me/Do What You Did	1961	Embassy 204
LULLABYES (3) (TOMMY TUCKER & THE)		
That Lucky Old Sun/Oh Baby (Don't Keep Chasing Me)	1975	Kelway 111
LUMPKIN, HENRY (& GROUP)		
We Really Love Each Other/ I've Got A Notion	1961	Motown 1005
LUVS		
We Kiss In The Shadows/ You Used To Be	1963	Stallion 1002
LY-DELLS (AKA LENDELLS)		
Genie Of The Lamp/Teenage Tears	1961	Master 111
Wizard Of Love/Let This Night Last	1961	Master 251
Book Of Songs/Hear That Train	1962	SCA 18001
Karen/Doing The Wiggle Wobble	1963	Roulette 4493
Three Little Monkeys/Playing Hide And Seek	1964	Southern Sound 122
Sherry/Little Lover	1978	King Tut 177
Book Of Songs/Let This Night Last	1981	Clifton 67
Stormy Weather	N/A	Clifton LP 2002
Don't Be A Litter Bug	N/A	Clifton LP 2002
Maryann	N/A	Clifton LP 2002

Artist / Song	Year	Label
LYDELLS		
There Goes The Boy/Talking To Myself	1959	Pam 103/Parkway 897 (64)
LYNDON, FRANK (BB THE REGENTS)		
Tonight We Wail/Cry Cry Cry	N/A	Jab 1004
LYNN, BILL (& GROUP)		
Only One For Me/Little Pony Tail	1961	Amy 820
LYNN, BOBBY (& GROUP)		
Tonight My Love/Charleston	1961	CR 1002
LYNN, GLORIA (BB THE WHEELS)		
Run For Your Love/I Can't Waste My Tears	1957	Premium 412
LYNN, SANDY (BB THE CORVETS)		
Hurry, Hurry Home/Little Johnny	1961	Laurel 1024
LYRES (AKA NUTMEGS)		
Ship Of Love/Play Boy	1953	J&G 101
LYRICS (1)		
I'm In Love/You	1958	Hy-Tone 111
Let's Exchange Hearts For Christmas/It's Time To Rock (by Georgia Harris & the Hy-Tones)	1958	Hy-Tone 117
LYRICS (2)		
Did She Leave You/Lovely Charms	1958	Marvels 1005
Every Night/Come Back Baby	1958	Rhythm 126/127
Come On Home/Why Don't You Stop?	1958	Vee Jay 285
Oh, Please Love Me/The Girl I Love	1959	Harlem 101/Wildcat 0028 (59)/Coral 62322 (62)
I Want To Know/The Beating Of My Heart	1959	Harlem 104
Crying Over You/Down In The Alley	1959	Mid South 1500
Let's Be Sweethearts Again/ You And Your Fellow	1961	Fernwood 129/Fleetwood 233 (61)
LYRICS (2) (LEO VALENTINE & THE)		
Please Don't Leave Me This Way/Baby Doll	1962	Skylight 201
Got To Get Along/Come Back	1962	Skylight 202
LYRICS (2) (WILLIAM WIGFALL & THE)		
Darling/How A Woman Does Her Man	1963	(Russel's) Gold Wax 101/ Goldwax 910 (63)
So Hard To Get Along/The Side Wind	1963	Goldwax 105/ABC 10560 (64)
LYRICS (3) (KENNETH CHURCHILL & THE)		
Fate Of Rock And Roll/Would You Rather	1958	Joyce 304
LYRICS (4) (IKE PERRY & THE)		
Stairsteps To Heaven/ The Love Bug's Got Me	1958	Bridge 110
I've Got You Covered/You Can Be My Honey	1960	Cowtown 801
In My Letter To You/My Honey Sweet Pea	1963	Mama 1/2/Mama 1074 (63)
At The Party/Don't Let It Get You Down	1963	Mama 3614/Courier 828 (63)/Naurline 100 (65)
Lovin' Papa/She's Got His Nose Wide Open	1965	Bee 95/Bee 1875
You Belong To Me/It's Too Soon To Know	1979	King Tut 180
God Must Have Sent You To Me/Please Don't	1979	King Tut 181
LYRICS (5)		
Broken Love/I Can't Get Along Without You	1962	Dan-Tone 1002
LYTATIONS (AKA CONTENDERS/AKA FIVE SCRIPTS/AKA KAPTIONS/AKA ZIPPERS)		
Over The Rainbow/Look Into The Sky	1964	Times Square 107
MAC, BOBBY (& GROUP)		
How Was Your Weekend/ Shy Guy	1962	Vended 104
MAC, LOU (BB THE PALMS)		
Slow Down/Baby (no group)	1955	Blue Lake 114
MACK, DELL (BB THE GOLDEN GATE QUARTET)		
The Way Love Goes/You Can't Judge A Book By The Cover	1958	Goldband 1064

Artist	Song	Year	Label
MACK, LONNIE (& FEMALE GROUP)			
	Say Something Nice To Me (flip has no group)	1964	Fraternity 920
MACKINTEERS (TEDDY MACK & THE)			
	Is There Any Doubt/Hey Hey Gypsy Woman	N/A	Monroe 1
MACREE, VINCENT (& GROUP)			
	Teenage Talk/Candy Doll	1957	Gametime 103
MACS (TERRY & THE)			
	Baby-O-Mine/Love Is A Beautiful Thing	1956	ABC 9668
	You Don't Have To Explain/ Spinning, Spinning, Spinning	1956	ABC 9721
MAD LADS			
	Why/Hey, Man	1962	Mark Fi 1934
MAD LADS (FRANK DEATON & THE)			
	My Love For You/Just A Little Bit More	1957	Bally 1042
MAD LADS (LITTLE BECKY COOK & THE)			
	Let's Dance/Saving My Love For You	1961	CBM 504
MADARA, JOHNNY (& GROUP)			
	Lovesick/Be My Girl	1957	Prep 110
	A Story Untold/Vacation Time	1961	Bamboo 511
	Heavenly/Save It	1962	Landa 687
MADDOX, WALT (AND THE MARCELS)			
	A Letter Full Of Tears/How Do You Speak To An Angel	1982	Super M 203073
	Blue Moon/Clap Your Hands (When I Clap My Hands)	1983	Super M 304027
MADHATTANS			
	Wowie/A Basketful Of Blueberries	1957	Atlantic 1142
MADISON BROTHERS			
	Trusting In You/What's The Matter, Baby	1960	Cedargrove 314/Apt 25050 (60)
	Give Me Your Heart/Baby Don't	1961	Sure 1002
MADISON BROTHERS (FARRIS HILL & THE)			
	Did We Go Steady Too Soon/ The Twirl	1962	V-Tone 231
MADISON, GLEN (& GROUP)			
	Why Do You Have To Go/ When You Dance	1962	Ebony 105/Monument
MADISONS (1) (FB LARRY SANTOS)			
	Can You Imagine/The Wind And The Rain	1964	Lawn 240
	Bad Baboon/Because I Got You	1964	Limelight 3018
	Only A Fool/Stagger	1965	Jomada 601/Jumaca 601
	Cheryl Anne/Looking For True Love	1965	MGM 13312
	Valarie/I'll Be Around (by the Monterays)	1965	Twin Hit 2865
MADISONS (2) (BILLY KIDD & THE)			
	First Time/If Only You Cared	1961	Madison 153
MAESTRO, JOHNNY (& GROUP)			
	Model Girl/Got To Tell Them	1961	Coed 545
	What A Surprise/The Warning Voice	1961	Coed 549
	Test Of Love/Mr. Happiness	1961	Coed 552
	I.O.U./The Way You Look Tonight	1961	Coed 557
	Besame Baby/It Must Be Love	1961	Coed 562
	Fifty Million Heartaches/Before I Loved Her	1962	United Artists 474
	I'll Be True/Over The Weekend (bb the Tymes)	1963	Cameo 256
	Lean On Me/Make Up My Mind	1964	Cameo 305
	She's All Mine Alone/Phone Booth On The Highway	1965	Apt 25075
	I'll Be True/Over The Weekend	N/A	Popular Request 103
MAGIC CHORDS			
	Be Sure/I've Got The Right To Be Blue	1950	Domino 311
	It's Over Because We're Through/Doubt In Your Mind	N/A	Domino 360
MAGIC MOMENTS			
	Good Goodbye/Lost Love	1990	Clifton 90
	Magic Moments With You/ Please Say	1999	Magic Moments 100
MAGIC NOTES			
	Never Again/The Wrong Door	1957	Era 1035
MAGIC TONES			
	When I Kneel Down To Pray/ Good Googa Mooga	1953	King 4665
	How Can You Treat Me This Way?/Cool, Cool Baby	1954	King 4681
	Tears In My Eyes/Spanish Love Song	1957	Howfum 101
	Great Day/Look Away	N/A	Ram-Brock 2001
MAGIC TOUCH (1) (AKA VITO & THE SALUTATIONS)			
	Baby, You Belong To Me/ Lost And Lonely Boy	1973	Roulette 7143
MAGIC TOUCH (2)			
	I'll Be Forever Loving You/ That's Why I Love You	1990	Starlight 73
MAGIC-TONES			
	Does She Know/Wait A Minute Baby	1974	Broadcast 1101
MAGICHORDS			
	I Beeped When I Shoulda Bopped/Darling	1950	Regal 3238
	See Here Pretty Baby/Why Feel This Way About You	N/A	Tri-Tone 1002
MAGICIANS (1)			
	Rain Don't Fall/An Invitation To Cry	1965	Columbia 43435
MAGICIANS (2) (FEMALE)			
	Why Do I Do These Foolish Things/Is It All Gone?	1966	Villa 704
	Why Must You Cry/Keep Your Hands Off	1966	Villa 706
MAGICS			
	Chapel Bells/She Can't Stop Dancing	1963	Debra 1003
	If I Didn't Have You/Let's Boogaloo	N/A	RFA 100
MAGNATONES			
	I Need You/McDonald's Rock (60)	1960	Cedargrove 313/Time 108
	Adios My Desert Love/I Love You With Tender Passion	1963	Fortune 555
MAGNETICS (1)			
	Where Are You/The Train	1962	Allrite 620
MAGNETICS (2)			
	Oh Love/Wasting Time	N/A	JV 2501
MAGNETS			
	You Just Say The Word/ Surprise	1955	Groove 0058
	When The School Bells Ring/ Don't Tarry Little Mary	1958	RCA 7391
MAGNIFICENT 6			
	Forever More/Hold On Baby	N/A	L-Brown 01659
MAGNIFICENT FOUR			
	The Closer You Are/Uncle Sam	1961	Whale 506/Blast 210 (63)
MAGNIFICENTS			
	Up On The Mountain/Why Did She Go?	1956	Vee Jay 183
	Caddy Bo/Hiccup	1956	Vee Jay 208
	Off The Mountain/Lost Lover	1957	Vee Jay 235
	Don't Leave Me/Ozeta	1958	Vee Jay 281
	Let's Do The Cha Cha/Up On The Mountain	1960	Vee Jay 367
	Do You Mind?/The Dribble Twist	1962	Kansoma 03/Checker 1016 (62)
	Yes, She's My Baby	1984	Solid Smoke LP 8030
	This Ole Love Of Mine	1984	Solid Smoke LP 8030
MAGNIFICENTS (RELEASED AS BY THE EL DORADOS)			
	My Heart Is Calling/On Main Street	1966	Dee Gee 3008
MAHARAJAHS			
	I Do Believe/Why Don't You Answer?	1958	Flip 332
	Sweet Loretta/Oh, Shirley	1958	Flip 335
MAIDENS (SIR JOE & THE)			
	Jivin' Jean/Pen Pal	1962	Lenox 5563
MAJESTICS (1)			
	Divided Heart/Please Don't Say No	1958	NRC 502
	TV Cowboys/So You Want To Rock	1959	Faro 592
	Sweet One (with the Nightwinds)/The Lone Stranger	1959	Sioux 91459/20th Century 171(59)/Foxie 7004 (59)

Artist Song	Year	Label	Artist Song	Year	Label
Teen Age Gossip/Hard Times	1960	Contour 501	**MAJORS (6)**		
Searching For A New Love/			Say You'll Be Mine/Lost In A City	N/A	Big Three 403
Angel Of Love	1961	Pixie 6901/Jordan 123 (61)/Nu-Tone 123 (61)	**MALDONEERS (WITH THE DELTAIRS)**		
			Maria My Love/What A Pity	1973	Vintage 1015
Strange World/Everything Is			**MALIBUS**		
Gonna Be All Right	1963	Linda 111	Cry/Leave Me Alone	1963	Planet 58
Girl Of My Dreams/It Hurts Me	1965	Linda 121	**MANDELLS**		
Girl Of My Dreams/Baby Let			Darling, I'm Home/Who, Me?	1961	Smart 323/Chess 1794 (61)
Me Bang Your Box	1991	Boardwalk 121	I Don't Have You/Because I		
MAJESTICS (2)			Love You	1961	Smart 325
Nitey Nite/Cave Man Rock	1956	Marlin 802	It's No Good/Don't Know		
The Love Stranger/Sweet One	1959	20th Fox 171	What You've Got	1963	York 202
Pennies For A Beggar/Boom			True Love Is Hard To Find/		
Da Da Boom	1960	Knight 105	Doin' The Look	1966	Jubilee 5519
Oasis/Oasis, Pt. 2	1962	Chess 1802	Now I Know	N/A	Trans World 695
Shoppin' And Hoppin'/Give			How To Love A Woman/I Can't		
Me A Cigarette	1962	Chex 1000	Get Enough Of Your Stuff	N/A	Trans World 711
So I Can Forget/Give Me A			Think Back/I Miss You Baby	N/A	Trans World 821
Cigarette	1962	Chex 1000	**MANDELS**		
Treat Me Like You Want To Be			The Scotch/My Kissin' Cousin	1961	Lilly 502
Treated/Unhappy And Blue	1962	Chex 1004	**MANDERINS**		
Lonely Heart/Gwendolyn	1962	Chex 1006	Going Away/Let The Bells Ring	1960	Band Box 236
Teach Me How To Limbo/Baby	1962	Chex 1009	**MANHATTAN TRANSFER**		
MAJESTICS (2) (KIRK TAYLOR & THE)			Trickle Trickle/Foreign Affair	1980	Atlantic 3772
From Out Of This World/You			That's The Way It Goes/		
Didn't Learn That In School	1959	Bandera 2507	Baby Come Back To Me	1984	Atlantic 89594
MAJESTICS (3)			**MANHATTANS (1)**		
Smile Through My Tears/Love			How Do I Say I'm Sorry/Love Is		
Has Forgotten Me	1966	MGM 13488	Where You Find It	1958	Warner 1015
MAJESTICS (4)			**MANHATTANS (2) (ELI PRICE & THE)**		
Symbol Of Love/Two Purple			My Big Dream/That'll Make It Nice	1959	Dooto 445
Shadows	1973	Vintage 1002	**MANHATTANS (3)**		
Ave Maria (acapella)	1975	Relic LP 104	La-La-La/Sing All The Day	1962	Capitol 4730
Twilight (acapella)	1975	Relic LP 105	**MANHATTANS (4) (RONNIE & THE)**		
MAJESTICS (4) (LITTLE JOE & THE)			Come On Back/Long Time No		
I'm So Young (acapella)	1975	Relic LP 104	See	1963	Enjoy 2008
Every Day Of The Week			**MANHATTANS (5)**		
(acapella)	1975	Relic LP 104	Call Somebody Please	1972	Rim LP 101
This Magic Moment (acapella)	1975	Relic LP 105	**MANHATTANS (6)**		
MAJORETTES (FEMALE)			Why Should I Cry/The Feeling		
White Levis/Please Come Back	1963	Troy 1000	Is Mutual	1963	Big Mack 3911
Let's Do The Kangaroo/Dance			**MANIS, GEORGIE (& GROUP)**		
With Me	1963	Troy 1004	Teen Angel/Hep, 2, 3, 4	1958	Eclaire 105
MAJORS (1)			**MANN, BARRY (BB THE EDSELS)**		
Laughing On The Outside,			Who Put The Bomp (In The		
Crying On The Inside/Come			Bomp, Bomp, Bomp)/		
On To My Room	1951	Derby 763	Love, True Love	1961	ABC 10237
You Ran Away With My Heart/			**MANN, BILLY (& GROUP)**		
At Last	1951	Derby 779	Lost Angel/Find Yourself		
MAJORS (2)			Another Guy	1956	Dig 111
Big Eyes/Go Way	1954	Original 1003	**MANN, BILLY (& GROUP)**		
MAJORS (2) (JESSE POWELL & THE)			A Million Heartaches Ago/		
Oh Baby/String-A-Long	1958	Josie 845	Just Like Before	1956	Dig 120
MAJORS (3) (OTIS BLACKWELL & THE)			**MANN, GLORIA (& GROUP)**		
It's Love And It's Real/			I Played The Fool/Pretty Eyes	1955	Sound 114
Don't Take My Word	1957	Gale 102	**MANNISH BOYS (EDDIE HOPE & THE)**		
MAJORS (4)			A Fool No More	1956	Marlin 804
Rockin' The Boogie/Blue Sunset	1957	Felsted 8501	**MANSELLES**		
Come Go With Me/Les Qua	1959	Felsted 8576	Love Him/Paradise Is Where		
Go With Me/I Found My Love	1965	Felsted 8707	He Is	1965	Diamond 172
MAJORS (5) (AKA VERSATILES/AKA PERFORMERS)			**MAPLES**		
Lundee Dundee/I'll Whisper			I Must Forget You/99 Guys	1954	Blue Lake 111
In Your Ear (as the Versatiles)	1960	Rocal 1002	**MAR, JERRY (& GROUP)**		
A Wonderful Dream/Time			Sittin' On Top Of The World/		
Will Tell	1962	Imperial 5855	Brokenest Heart In Town	1957	Amp-3 131
A Little Bit Now/She's A			**MAR-VELLS (AKA MAR-VELS)**		
Troublemaker	1962	Imperial 5879	Go On And Have Yourself A		
Anything You Can Do/What In			Ball/How Do I Keep The		
The World	1963	Imperial 5914	Girls Away	1963	Butane 778
Tra-La-La/What Have You			Tonight	N/A	Harlem 1002
Been Doin'?	1963	Imperial 5936	**MAR-VELS (AKA MAR-VELLS)**		
Get Up Now/One Happy Ending	1963	Imperial 5968	Cherry Lips/Could Be You	1958	Love 5011/5012
Your Life Begins (At Sweet			Somewhere In Life/Voo Doo		
Sixteen)/Which Way Did			Hurt	1961	Tammy 1016
She Go	1963	Imperial 5991	My Guardian Angel/Marvel		
I'll Be There/Ooh Wee Baby	1963	Imperial 66009	Stomp	1961	Tammy 1019
Twist And Shout	1964	Imperial LP 9222	Endless Nights/Surfing At		
Don't Lose Your Cool	1964	Imperial LP 9222	Makaha	1964	IN 102
I Wonder Who's Dancing With			**MAR-VILLES**		
Her Now	1964	Imperial LP 9222	The Drag/Nights Are So Lonely	1962	Infinity 027
Come On Come On	1964	Imperial LP 9222	**MARATHONS (1)**		
			Don't Know Why/The Stranger	1959	Sabrina 334/JC 101 (59)

Artist Song	Year	Label	Artist Song	Year	Label
MARATHONS (2) (AKA JAYHAWKS/AKA VIBRATIONS)			**MARCELS (BOB JEFFRIES & THE)**		
Peanut Butter/Talkin' Trash	1961	Arvee 5027	Take Me Back/Betty Lou	1958	Jody 123
C. Percy Mercy Of Scotland			**MARCELS (WALT MADDOX & THE)**		
Yard/Tight Sweater	1961	Arvee 5038	A Letter Full Of Tears/How Do		
Peanut Butter/Down In New			You Speak To An Angel	1982	Super M 3073
Orleans	1961	Chess 1790/Argo 5389 (61)	Blue Moon/Clap Your Hands	1983	Super M 4027
Chicken Spaceman/You Bug			**MARCHAN, BOBBY (BB THE CLOWNS)**		
Me Baby	1962	Arvee 5048	Quit My Job/Hush Your Mouth	1960	Ace 595
Little Pancho/Mashed Potatoes			**MARCHAND, DONNY (& GROUP)**		
One More Time	1962	Plaza 507	Round In Circles/Along Came		
Oink Jones	N/A	Collectables LP 5081	Susie	1960	Craft 3000
Gee	N/A	Collectables LP 5081	**MARCO (& GROUP)**		
High Blood Pressure	N/A	Collectables LP 5081	Let's Leave It That Way/I'm So		
MARAUDERS (HAYWARD LEE & THE)			Alone	1963	Mohawk 135
Mother Dear	N/A	Jet	**MARENO, LEE (BB THE REGENTS)**		
MARBLES (AKA JEWELS (2))			Goddess Of Love/He's Gone	1961	New Art 103/Scepter
Golden Girl/Big Wig Walk	1954	Lucky 002			1222 (61)
MARCEL, VIC (& GROUP)			**MARESCA, ERNIE (BB THE DEL SATINS)**		
Come Back To These Arms/			Shout! Shout! (Knock Yourself		
That's My Girl	1963	Don-But 17349	Out)/Crying Like A Baby		
MARCELS			Over You	1962	Seville 117
Blue Moon/ Goodbye To Love	1961	Colpix 186/Eric 113	Mary Jane/Down On The Beach	1962	Seville 119
Summertime/Teeter Totter Love	1961	Colpix 196	Lorelei/The Love Express	1963	Seville 125
You Are My Sunshine/Find			Please Be Fair/Rovin' Kind	1963	Seville 129
Another Fool	1961	Colpix 606	**MARGILATORS**		
Heartaches/My Love For You	1961	Colpix 612	Wait For Me/Arlinda	1959	Blue Moon 409
Merry Twist-Mas/Don't Cry For			**MARGILATORS (BUDDY BENNETT & THE)**		
Me This Christmas	1961	Colpix 617	Our Love Can Never Be/		
My Melancholy Baby/Really			Baby Don't Go	1959	Blue Moon 412
Need Your Love	1961	Colpix 624	**MARGILATORS (TOBY & RAY & THE)**		
Sunday Kind Of Love	1961	Colpix LP 416	Bom Do Wa/Just Waiting For You	1959	Blue Moon 411
Tell Them About It	1962	Colpix (unreleased)	**MARGLOWS (ANDY & THE)**		
Baby Where Y'Been	1962	Colpix (unreleased)	Just One Look/Symphony	1963	Liberty 55570
Footprints In The Sand/			I'll Get By/Superman Lover	1963	Liberty 55627
Twistin' Fever	1962	Colpix 629	**MARIA (& GROUP)**		
Hold On/Flowerpot	1962	Colpix 640	Departed/Goodbye Angel Baby	1980	BAB 125
Friendly Loans/Loved Her The			**MARIE ANN (& GROUP)**		
Whole Week Through	1962	Colpix 651	Dream Boy/High Heel Shoes	1960	Warwick 605
All-Right-OK You Win/Lollipop			**MARIE, ELENA (& GROUP)**		
Baby	1962	Colpix 665	Soldier Boy/Blue Mood	1962	Gee Bee 01
Lonely Boy/How Deep Is The			**MARIGOLDS**		
Ocean	1963	888 101	Rollin' Stone/Why Don't You?	1955	Excello 2057
Tell Me/Letter Full Of Tears	1963	Chartbound 009	Two Strangers/Love You,		
That Old Black Magic/Don't			Love You, Love You	1955	Excello 2061
Turn Your Back On Me	1963	Colpix 683	**MARIGOLDS (JOHNNY BRAGG & THE)**		
I Wanna Be The Leader/Give			Foolish Me/Beyond The Clouds	1956	Excello 2078
Me Back Your Love	1963	Colpix 687	It's You, Darling, It's You/		
One Last Kiss/You Got To Be			Juke Box Rock 'n' Roll	1956	Excello 2091
Sincere	1963	Colpix 694	**MARINERS**		
One Last Kiss/Teeter Totter Love	1963	Colpix 694	Zindy Lou/Everybody's Doin'		
Honestly Sincere	1963	Colpix LP 454	It Now	1955	Cadence 1278
One Last Kiss	1963	Colpix LP 454	**MARIONETTES (CHRIS ALLEN & THE)**		
Comes Love/Your Red Wagon			Thank You Mister Moon/		
(You Can Push It Or Pull It)	1964	Kyra	Saxophone Pete	1959	Hollywood 1908
Betty Lou/Take Me Back	1973	Baron 109	**MARK III**		
In The Still Of The Night/High			Valerie/The Man	1961	ABC 10280/BRB 100
On a Hill	1973	Queen Bee 47001	**MARK IV**		
Peace Of Mind/Crazy Bells	1974	Owl 324	(Make With) The Shake/		
I'll Be Forever Loving You/			45 R.P.M.	1958	Cosmic 704
A Fallen Tear	1975	Monogram 112	I Got A Wife/Ah-OOO-Ga	1959	Mercury 71403
Over The Rainbow/Sweet Was			Dante's Inferno/Move Over		
The Wine	1975	Monogram 113	Rover	1959	Mercury 71445
Two People In The World/Most			**MARK IVS**		
Of All	1975	Monogram 115	The Tide Has Turned/Whoa		
Tell Me	1977	Extra Play LP 10101	Baby, That's All	1962	Barry 105
Tell Them All About It	1977	Pop N' Rock LP	**MARK V**		
Hard To Please/You'll Never			Cry Baby/Bull Fight Cha Cha		
Know (by the Mondellos)	1984	Rhythm 118	Cha	1960	Milo 110
Blue Heartaches	1986	Murray Hill LP 000229	**MARK, RONALD (& GROUP)**		
Bells/One Last Kiss	1988	Want List 1	Moonlight Sky/And Now		
You Might As Well Tell The			You're Gone	1964	Gateway Custom 102
Truth	N/A	Colpix (unreleased)	**MARKAYS (DOUG SAHM & THE)**		
Mr. Bassman	N/A	Colpix (unreleased)	If You Ever Need Me/Why, Why,		
Crazy Bells In My Heart/			Why	1961	Harlem 107/Swingin' 625 (61)
Sunday Kind Of Love	N/A	Cycle 2001/Colpix LP 416	**MARKEETS**		
Heartaches/Summertime	N/A	Eric 114	Teardrops/Baby Please	1957	Melatone 1005
Blue Moon/I Love You 1000			**MARKELLS**		
Times (by the Platters)	N/A	Ripete 185	The Letter Of Love/Darling I		
My Melancholy Baby/Over The			Really Love You	1958	R&M 407/408
Mountain (by Johnnie & Joe)	1988	Royale 1003B	**MARKEYS**		
MARCELS (AS THE FABULOUS MARCELS			Eternal Love/You've Got Me		
Peace Of Mind/That Lucky Old Sun	1975	St. Clair 13711/Rocky 13711	On A String	1956	20th Century 1210

Artist Song	Year	Label
Along Came Love/Special Delivery	1958	Gone 5028
Yakity Yak/Hot Rod	1958	RCA 7256
A Time To Love/Make A Record Man	1958	RCA 7412
MARKSMEN		
Don't Gamble With My Heart/ You Hurt Me So	1957	Starday 320/Mercury 71139
MARKTONES		
Hold Me Close/Talk It Over	1957	Ember 1022
Yes, Siree/Hey, Girlee	1958	Ember 1030
MARLAND, CLETUS (& GROUP)		
I'll Take Care Of You/Like I Never Felt Before	1961	Roulette 4388
MAROONS		
Don't Leave Me Baby, Don't/ Someday I'll Be The One	1962	Queen 24012
MARQUEES (1)		
The Bells/The Rain	1956	Grand 141
MARQUEES (2) (BILLY STEWART & THE)		
Baby, You're My Only Love/ Billy's Heartache	1957	Okeh 7095
MARQUEES (2) (GM MARVIN GAYE)		
Hey Little School Girl/Wyatt Earp	1957	Okeh 7096
MARQUEES (3)		
Say Hey/I'm In Misery	1958	Len 100
MARQUEES (4)		
Love Machine/Who Will Be The First One	1959	Warner Bros. 5072
Christmas In The Congo/ Santa Done Got Hip	1959	Warner Bros. 5127
Don't Be Mean, Geraldine/ Until The Day I Die	1960	Warner Bros. 5139
MARQUEES (4) (TERRY BROWN & THE)		
That's The Way I Feel/Stay With Me	1960	Jo-Ann 128
I Need A Helping Hand/Don't You Do Me Like That	1961	Jo-Ann 130
MARQUEES (5)		
Ecstasy/Close To Me	1958	Day-Sel 1001
MARQUEES (6)		
In The Halo Of Your Love/ Can It Be Wrong	1960	Do-Ra-Mi 1407
MARQUIS (1)		
I Don't Want Your Love/ Popcorn Willie	1956	Rainbow 358
MARQUIS (2)		
Bohemian Daddy/Hope He's True	1956	Onyx 505/Relic 505 (64)
MARQUIS (3)		
Strange Is Love/Six Gun	1959	Class 251
MARSH, BILLY (& GROUP)		
Run And Tell/Don't Tell Me	1956	Arrow 716
MARSHALL BROTHERS		
Who'll Be The Fool From Now On/Mr. Santas Boogie	1951	Savoy 825
Why Make A Fool Out Of Me/ Just A Poor Boy In Love	1952	Savoy 833
My Life Is My Life	N/A	Savoy (unreleased)
It All Comes (Back To Me Now)	N/A	Savoy (unreleased)
I Didn't Know	N/A	Savoy (unreleased)
MARSHALLS (BILL COOK & THE)		
A Soldier's Prayer/Just Because (by Bill Cook)	1951	Savoy 828
MARSHANS		
I Remember/It's Almost Tomorrow	1964	Etiquette
My Letter To Santa/Main Man	1965	Johnson 736
MARSMEN (MARVIN & JOHNNY & THE)		
Jo Jo/How Long Has She Been Gone	1954	Specialty 488
MARTELLS (1) (AKA MARTELS)		
Forgotten Spring/Va Va Voom	1961	Cessna 477/Bella 45 (61)/ Relic 517 (64)
MARTELLS (2)		
Since I've Been Away/ What Can I Do	1965	Atco 6336
MARTELS (AKA MARTELLS (1))		
Where Did My Woman Go/ Teacher Don't Keep Me In	1959	Nasco 6026
MARTELS (EULIS MASON & THE) (AKA MARTELLS (1))		
Rockin' Santa Claus/Carol Lee	1959	Bella 20

Artist Song	Year	Label
MARTIN, BENNY (& GROUP)		
Darling Goodbye/This Is Why I Love You	1960	Astro 109
MARTIN, JERRY (& GROUP)		
Lovers Promise/Young Boy's Love	1962	R 507
MARTIN, KENNY (& GROUP)		
I'm The Jivin' Mr. Lee/Come Back For Me (no group)	1958	Federal 12310
I'm Sorry/Yum Yum	1958	Federal 12330
Now I Know/Tell Me Not To Go	1959	Federal 12350
Ask Me/It's All Over	1959	Federal 12354
MARTIN, SONNY (& GROUP)		
When True Love Is Gone/ How To Win Your Love	1959	Rocko 518
MARTIN, STEVE (& GROUP)		
Lonely Little Girl/My Little Angel	1963	Magnasound 700
MARTIN, TRADE (& GROUP)		
Joanne/Liverpool Baby	1964	Coed 594
MARTINELS		
Baby, Think It Over/I Don't Care	1963	Success 110
MARTINEQUES		
Tonight Is Another Night/ Unknown Love	1962	Danceland 777/Roulette 4423 (62)
Broken Hearted Me/Everything Will Be Alright	1962	Danceland 779
If You Want To Call Me	1965	Me O 1002
MARTINO, LOU (& GROUP)		
Someone To Watch Over Me/ Please (Give Me A Little Love)	1964	Columbia 43126
MARVEL, TINA (& MALE GROUP)		
I Can't Love No One But You/ Beautiful Love	1963	Lu Pine 121
MARVELEERS		
For The Longest Time/ One-Sided Love Affair	1953	Derby 829
All My Heart/I've Only Myself To Blame	1953	Derby 842
Love Me, Want Me/I Miss You Most Of All	1953	Derby 844
These Are The Things We'll Share/Marlina, Marlina	1955	Dot 15320
MARVELETTES		
Forever/Locking Up My Heart	1963	Tamla 54077
MARVELIERS		
When We Dance/Down	1960	Cougar 1868
Little Girl/The Spider	N/A	Joanie 4439
MARVELLOS (1)		
You're The Dream/Calypso Mama	1955	Theron 117
Red Hot Momma/I Need A Girl	1958	Marvello 5005
Come Back My Love/Boyee Yoing	1958	Stepheny 1818/Cha Cha 756
MARVELLOS (2)		
She Told Me Lies/Salty Sam	1962	Exodus 6214/Reprise 20008 (62)
I Ask Of You/Hip Enough	1962	Exodus 6216
MARVELLS (AKA GALES (2)/AKA MARVELS (2)/AKA SENATORS)		
Did She Leave You/Lovely Charms	1959	Magnet 1005
Miracle Of Life/What About The Mountain	1961	Finer Arts 2019
For Sentimental Reasons/ Come Back	1961	Winn 1916
How Could You Hurt Me So/ 'Cause I'm Loving You	1962	Finer Arts 2024
Tomorrow/I'm A Fool For Losing You	1962	Finer Arts 2026
This Can't Go On	N/A	Yorsey
MARVELOWS		
I Do/Me Heart	1965	ABC 10629
MARVELS (1) (AKA DUBS)		
I Won't Have You Breaking My Heart/Jump, Rock And Roll	1956	ABC 9771
MARVELS (1) (HARRY M & THE)		
What's The Use/The "U-T"	1961	ABC 10243
MARVELS (2) (AKA GALES (2)/AKA MARVELLS/AKA SENATORS)		
So Young, So Sweet/I Shed So Many Tears	1958	Laurie 3016

Artist	Song	Year	Label
MARVELS (3)			
	Just Another Fool/You Crack Me Up	1959	Mun Rab 1008
MARVELS (4)			
	Somewhere In Love (You'll Find Your Love)	1960	Bishop 1002
MARVELS (5)			
	Guiding Angel/Hallelulu-la	1962	Pyramid 6211
	Guiding Angel/I'll Never Forget (by Buzz Clifford)	1982	Jason Scott 21
MARVELS (5) (NEIL SEDAKA & THE)			
	Oh Delilah/Neil's Twist	1962	Pyramid 623
MARVELTONES			
	So (It's Over)/My Heart Is Yours	1952	Regent 194
	Three Sundays/Care	1952	Regent 196
MARX (AKA THE MARX)			
	One Minute More/You Are My Love	1959	Chante 1002/Dahlia 1002 (59)
MARYLANDERS			
	Make Me Thrill Again/Please Love Me	1952	Jubilee 5091
	Fried Chicken/Good Old 99	1953	Jubilee 5114
	Sittin' Here Wondering/ Sweetheart (by the Five Keys)	1972	Roadhouse 1003
	I Really Don't Care/Last Night (recorded in 1954)	1974	Roadhouse 1015
	I'm A Sentimental Fool/Sittin' By The River	1952	Jubilee 5079
MASCOTS (1)			
	The Story Of My Heart/ Do The Wiggle	1960	King 5377
	Lonely Rain/That's The Way I Feel	1960	King 5435
MASCOTS (2)			
	Once Upon A Love/Hey Little Angel	1962	Blast 206
	Bluebirds Over The Mountain/ Timberlands	1962	Mermaid 107
MASCOTS (3)			
	Waited So Long/I Want Love	1974	Rumble 4197
MASKED MARAUDERS			
	I Am The Japanese Sandman	N/A	Deity LP 6378
MASON, BARBARA (BB THE LARKS)			
	Dedicated To You/Trouble Child	1964	Crusader 114/Arctic (65)
MASON, LITTLE BILLY (BB THE RHYTHM JESTERS)			
	Make Me Your Own/I Love My Baby	1956	Rama 212
	School Kid/Young, Broke And In Love	1957	Gee 1042
	Thinking Of You/You Are My Sunshine	1957	Rama 223
MASON, PETER (& GROUP)			
	Lonely Drummer Boy/Thank Heaven For Little Girls	1960	Lawn 105
MASQUERADES (REF SEAPHUS SCOTT & THE FIVE MASQUERADERS)			
	These Red Roses/Mister Man The Guitar Man	1960	Formal 1011/1012
	Fanessa/The Whip	1961	Boyd 1027
	Portia	N/A	unreleased
	These Foolish Things	N/A	unreleased
	Good Golly Miss Molly	N/A	unreleased
	That's When Your Heartaches Begin	N/A	unreleased
MASQUINS (TONY & THE)			
	My Angel Eyes/Fugi Womma	1961	Ruthie 1000
MASSEY, BARBARA (& GROUP)			
	You Call Me Angel/I'll Tell You In The Morning	1961	Imperial 5786
MASSI, NICK (& GROUP)			
	Little Pony	N/A	One Way 244
MASTER FOUR			
	It's Not The End/Love From The Far East	N/A	Tay-Ster 6012
MASTER, RONNIE (& GROUP)			
	I Don't Know (If You Really Love Me)/I Love You So	1961	Landa 669
MASTER-TONES			
	Tell Me/What'll You Do?	1954	Bruce 111/Tip Top
MASTERETTES (FEMALE)			
	Never Never/Follow The Leader	1958	Le Sage 716
MASTERS (1) (SCOTTY MANN & THE)			
	Just A Little Bit Of Loving/ The Mystery Man	1956	Peacock 1665
MASTERS (2) (THURSTON HARRIS & THE)			
	I Hear A Rhapsody/Purple Stew	1958	Aladdin 3440
MASTERS (3)			
	Johnny Clean-Up/'Til I Return	1958	Len 103
MASTERS (4)			
	I'm Searching/Crying My Heart Out	1958	Le Sage 713/714
	A Lovely Way To Spend An Evening/Dore's Blues	1960	Bingo 1008
	A Man Is Not Supposed To Cry/Look Out	1961	End 1100
MASTERS (5) (RICK & THE)			
	Bewitched Bothered And Bewildered/A Kissin' Friend	1962	Haral 778
	Flame Of Love/Here Comes Nancy	1962	Taba 101/Cameo 226 (62)
	Let It Please Be You/I Don't Want Your Love	1963	Cameo 247
	Nutmegs Medley/Sit And Hold My Hand	1992	Clifton 104
MASTERS, JOHNNY (AKA JOHNNY MAESTRO) (BB THE CRESTS)			
	Say It Isn't So/The Great Physician	1960	Coed 527
MASTERS, RICK & THE			
	Flame Of Love/Here Comes Nancy	1962	Cameo 226
MASTERTONES (1)			
	Are You Lonely/I Made A Boo Boo	1957	Future 1001
MASTERTONES (2)			
	Fannie Mae	1959	Band Box 226
MASTERTONES (2) (ELAINE TAYLOR & THE)			
	Yes Sir, That's My Baby/Baby Won't You Please Come Home	1960	Band Box 233
MASTERTONES (2) (SCOTTY & BOBO & THE)			
	For The Rest Of My Life/ Mamacita Mia	1960	Band Box 238
MASTERTONES (3) (FB RAY WILLIAMS)			
	Baby (You Got To Change) /I Want To Know	1961	Le Cam 717
MATADORS (1)			
	Vengeance (Will Be Mine)/ Pennies From Heaven	1958	Sue 700
	Be Good To Me/Have Mercy Baby	1958	Sue 701
MATADORS (10) (FRANKIE & THE)			
	With A Girl Like You	N/A	Peerless 9012
MATADORS (2) (HANK AYALA & THE)			
	Betty Jo/Handsome	1959	Back Beat 530
MATADORS (3)			
	If I Had Another Chance/ Nonsense	1961	Duchess 1005
MATADORS (4)			
	Listen/So Near	1962	Jamie 1226
	If You Left Me Today/It Ain't Nothin' But Rock 'N' Roll	1963	Keith 6502
	You'd Be Crying Too/My Foolish Heart	1963	Keith 6504
MATADORS (5)			
	Ace Of Hearts/Perfidia	1963	Colpix 698
	La Corrida/I've Gotta Drive (by Jan & Dean)	1964	Colpix 718
	C'mon, Let Yourself Go/C'mon, Let Yourself Go, Pt. 2	1964	Colpix 741
MATADORS (6) (TOMMY LISS & THE)			
	Just In Make Believe/Time Is Tough	1963	Saxony 1005/Savoy 2007 (97)
	That's The Way/Whenever I Get Lonely	1993	Saxony 1001
MATADORS (7)			
	Please Say You Want Me/ Should I Ever Love Again	1963	Lee 5466
MATADORS (8)			
	Let Me Dream/Wobble Wobble	1966	Chartmaker 404/Forbes 230 (67)
MATADORS (9)			
	Carmen, I Wish You Were Here/Say Yes Baby	1962	Chavis 103

Artist Song	Year	Label
MATCHES		
She Laughed At Me/Gonna Build Myself A Castle	N/A	Jaguar 712
MATES (MARCI & THE)		
Shall I Tell Him You're Not Here/ Let Us Part For A Year	1962	Big Top 3116
Suddenly We're Strangers/Oops, There Goes Another Year	1963	Big Top 3136
MATHEWS BROTHERS		
Stupid/Mora Dora	1963	ABC 10473
MATTHEWS, DINO (& GROUP)		
The Girl That I Love/Lenore	1962	Dot 16365
MAYE, ARTHUR LEE (& GROUP)		
Moonlight/I'm Happy In Love	1985	Antrell 102
MAYE, HARTSY (& GROUP)		
As The Years Go By/Hi Ho Merry O	N/A	Zell 4397
MAYE, JEAN (& GROUP)		
He Makes Me Feel So Crazy/ Dew Drop Inn	1964	Diamond 170
MAYFIELD, PERCY (& GROUP)		
Please Believe Me/Diggin' The Moonglow	1957	Specialty 607
One Love/My Reward (no group)	59	Imperial 5577
MAYTONES (PERCY MAYFIELD & THE)		
The Voice Within/Baby, You're Rich	1954	Specialty 544
MCCAIN, JERRY (& GROUP)		
Love Me Right/Ting Tang Tagalu	1965	Continental 777
MCCALL, LITTLE J. (& GROUP)		
My Love I Can't Hide/Half Ton Tillie	1961	Wow 1000/Donna 1334 (61)
MCCALLISTER, LON (& GROUP)		
One Desire/Empty Heart	1961	Apt 25061
MCCLEESE, JAMES (& GROUP)		
I Love You So/A Million Tears	1961	Marco 106
MCCLINE, CHARLES (& GROUP)		
You Conquered Me/Say That You Care	1964	Larry-O 101
MCCOY, VAN (& GROUP)		
Mr. D.J./Never Trust A Friend	1961	Rock'N 101
MCCRACKLIN, JIMMY (& GROUP)		
I Need Your Loving/ The Swinging Thing	1958	Peacock 1683
MCDONALD, KEN (& GROUP)		
Candy From A Baby/What Have I Got To Lose	1957	DeLuxe 6121
One Love Alone/The Picture	1958	Prep 128
MCDOWALL, CHESTER (& GROUP)		
I Wonder Why/Baby Don't Leave me	1959	Duke 302
MCELROY, SOLLIE (& FEMALE GROUP)		
Angel Girl/Party Time	N/A	Ja-Wes 101
MCFADDEN, RUTH (BB THE HARPTONES)		
School Boy/United We Stand (no group)	1956	Old Town 1030
MCGEE, AL (& GROUP)		
Lucky Joe/You Can Count On Me	1961	Aries 7-10-2
Tender Beloved/Oldies But Goodies Show	1961	Donna 1348
MCHUGH, JIMMY (& GROUP)		
I Don't Want Everything/ Do The Kangaroo	1963	Success 106
MCHUGH, RICHIE (& GROUP)		
Jo Ann/You'll Need Me Some Day	1963	Raewood 587
MCKAY, JOHNNY (& GROUP)		
After You/I Whisper Your Name	1960	United Artists 21
MCKINNON, PRESTON (& GROUP)		
I Have Problems/Till I Met Sweet You	1960	Sharp 104
MCKNIGHT, JUNE (& GROUP)		
Why Don't You Come Home/ Twist Me Henry	1962	Jeannie 1225
MCLAIN, TOMMY (& GROUP)		
I Need You So/Sweet Dreams	N/A	MSL 197
MCNEIL, ANGELE (& GROUP)		
Can You Tell Me Why/Please Daddy	1957	Felsted 8503

Artist Song	Year	Label
MCPHATTER, CLYDE (& FEMALE GROUP)		
I'm Lonely Tonight/Thirty Days	1956	Atlantic 1106
I'm Not Worthy Of You/Seven Days	1955	Atlantic 1081
MCPHATTER, CLYDE (& GROUP)		
Let The Boogie Woogie Roll (with the Drifters)/Deep Sea Ball (with the Cookies & the Cues)	1960	Atlantic 2060
I Just Want To Love You/ You're For Me	1960	Mercury 71692
MCPHATTER, CLYDE (BB THE COOKIES & THE CUES)		
Just To Hold My Hand (Cues only)/No Matter What	1957	Atlantic 1133
Heartaches/Long Lonely Nights (Cues only)	1957	Atlantic 1149
You'll Be There/Rock And Cry	1957	Atlantic 1158
No Love Like Her Love/ That's Enough For Me	1958	Atlantic 1170
A Lover's Question (Cues only)/I Can't Stand Up Alone	1958	Atlantic 1199
Since You've Been Gone/ Try Try Baby	1959	Atlantic 2028
You Went Back On Your Word/ There You Go (with the Drifters)	1959	Atlantic 2038
Go! Yes Go!/If I Didn't Love You Like I Do (with the Drifters)	1960	Atlantic 2082
MCPHATTER, CLYDE (BB THE CUES)		
I Make Believe/Without Love (There Is Nothing)	1956	Atlantic 1117
MCPHATTER, CLYDE (BB THE DRIFTERS)		
Don't Dog Me/Just Give Me A Ring (with the Cookies & the Cues)	1960	Atlantic 2049
MCQUINN, KEVIN (& GROUP)		
Every Step Of The Way/ Keep Me On Your Mind	1961	Diamond 101
Same Time Same Place/ Adventure	1962	Diamond 109
MEADOWBROOKS		
Seems Like Only Yesterday/ Time After Time	1965	Catamount 106
Lovers Quarrel (acapella)/Is Everybody Happy (acapella)	1965	Catamount 108
MEADOWLARKS		
Brother Bill/Raisin' A Ruckus	1951	Imperial 5146
LSMFT Blues/Pass The Gin	1954	RPM 406
Lie/The Booglay	1964	Magnum 716
MEADOWLARKS (DON JULIAN & THE)		
Love Only You/Real Pretty Mama	1954	RPM 399
Heaven And Paradise/ Embarrassing Moments	1955	Dootone 359
Always And Always/I Got Tore Up	1955	Dootone 367
This Must Be Paradise/Mine All Mine	1955	Dootone 372
Thrill Me Night And Day	1955	Dootone EP 103/Dootone EP 203
Please Love A Fool/Oop Boopy Oop	1956	Dootone 394/ Original Sound 004 (58)
I Am A Believer/Boogie Woogie Teenage	1956	Dootone 405
Blue Moon/Big Momma Wants To Rock	1957	Dooto 424
Untrue	1957	Dooto LP 224
Please (Say You Love Me)/ Doin' The Cha Cha Cha	1958	Original Sound 03
Blue Mood/There's A Girl	1960	Original Sound 12
Popeye/Heaven Only Knows	1962	Dynamite 1112
Slauson Shuffle, Pt. 1/ Slauson Shuffle, Pt. 2	1962	Dynamite 1114
Philly Jerk/How Can You Be So Foul	1965	Jerk 100
Quickie Wedding/Our Love	1988	Classic Artists 101
White Christmas/Merry Christmas Baby	1988	Classic Artists 105
Everytime	N/A	Chance
MEADOWS, LARRY (& GROUP)		
Phyllis/We're Through	1959	Strato-Lite 969
MED-TONES (JOHNNY DARIL & THE)		
Come Back/Weak In My Knees	1959	Vita 188
Come Back/Weak In My Knees	1959	Vita 188

Artist Song	Year	Label
MEDALIONS (AKA MEDALLIONS (3))		
Love Letters/Since You've Gone Away	1960	Card 1
MEDALLIONAIRES		
Magic Moonlight/Teen-Age Caravan	1958	Mercury 71309
MEDALLIONS (1)		
The Letter/Buick '59	1954	Dootone 347
The Telegram/Coupe De Ville Baby	1955	Dootone 357
Edna/Speedin'	1955	Dootone 364
Dear Darling/Don't Shoot Baby	1955	Dootone 379
Mary Lou	1955	Dootone EP 202
I Want A Love/Dance And Swing	1956	Dootone 393
Give Me The Right/She's The One	1960	Dooto 456 EP
How/Meet Me Tonight	1972	Dootone 344 (unreleased)
MEDALLIONS (1) (JOHNNY TWOVOICE & THE)		
My Pretty Baby/I'll Never Love Again	1955	Dootone 373
MEDALLIONS (1) (VERNON GREEN & THE)		
Shedding Tears For You/Pushbutton Automobile	1956	Dootone 400
Did You Have Fun?/My Mary Lou	1956	Dootone 407
For Better Or For Worse/I Wonder, I Wonder, I Wonder	1957	Dooto 419
A Lover's Prayer/Unseen	1957	Dooto 425
Magic Mountain/'59 Volvo	1959	Dooto 446
Behind The Door/Rocket Ship	1959	Dooto 454
Deep, So Deep/Dear Ann	1962	Pan World 10000
Dear Ann/Shimmy Shimmy Shake	1962	Pan World 71
Look At Me, Look At Me/Am I Ever Gonna See My Baby Again	1964	Minit 30234
Can You Talk/You Don't Know	1973	Dootone 479
So Bad/Accept Me For What I Am	1988	Classic Artists 103
For Your Precious Love/Drinkin' Wine	1991	Classic Artists 129
MEDALLIONS (2)		
I Know/Laki-Lani	1955	Essex 901
MEDALLIONS (3) (AKA MEDALIONS)		
A Broken Heart/Lolo Baby	1957	Singular 1002
Love That Girl/Carachi	1959	Sultan 1004
MEDALLIONS (4)		
I Love You True/My Baby's Gone	1961	Sarg 191
Lovin' Time/Home Town	1961	Sarg 194
You Are Irresistible/Why Do You Look At Me	1962	Reo 8693/Lenox 5556 (62)
MEDLIN, JOE (& GROUP)		
No One But You/I'll Be All Right (no group)	1957	King 5054
Searchin' In Vain/Johnny Brown	1959	Duke 311
MEL-O-AIRES (RUDY JACKSON & THE)		
I'm Crying/Enfold Me	1955	R&B 1310
Teasing Me/Give Me Your Hand	1957	Imperial 5425
MEL-O-DOTS		
One More Time/Just How Long	1952	Apollo 1192
Baby Won't You Please Come Home	1989	Relic LP 5077
Rock My Baby	1989	Relic LP 5077
MELLARDS		
That's Life/Love Me Crazy	1956	Ballad 1016
MELLARDS (FRED GREEN & THE)		
My Sweetheart/You Can't Keep Love	1955	Ballad 1012
MELLO KINGS		
The Kiss/Shirley	1950	Imperial 5105
MELLO-CHORDS		
Golden Vanity/Desperado	1961	Lyco 1001
I'm So All Alone/A Teardrop Falls	N/A	Palm 5000
MELLO-DEES (HERMAN GRIFFIN & THE)		
Hurry Up And Marry Me/Do You Want To See My Baby	1960	Anna 1115/Stepp 237
MELLO-FELLOWS		
Iddy Biddy Baby/My Friend Charlie	1954	Lamp 8006
MELLO-HARPS (AKA LEVEE SONGSTERS/AKA TEENTONES)		
Love Is A Vow/Valerie	1955	Do-Re-Mi 203
I Love Only You/Ain't Got The Money	1955	Tin Pan Alley 145/146
What Good Are My Dreams?/Gone	1956	Tin Pan Alley 157/158
I Couldn't Believe/My Bleeding Heart	1956	Tin Pan Alley 159
Gumma Gumma/No Good	1959	Casino 104
MELLO-KINGS (AKA MELLOKINGS/AKA MELLOTONES (1))		
Tonight, Tonight/Do Baby Do	1957	Herald 502 (second pressing,first is by Mellotones)
Chapel On The Hill/Sassafras	1957	Herald 507
Baby Tell Me (Why, Why, Why)/The Only Girl (I'll Ever Love)	1958	Herald 511
Valerie/She's Real Cool	1958	Herald 518
Running To You/Chip Chip	1959	Herald 536
Our Love Is Beautiful/Dear Mr. Jock	1960	Herald 548
Kid Stuff/I Promise	1960	Herald 554
Til There Were None/Penny	1961	Herald 561
Love At First Sight/She's Real Cool	1961	Herald 567
Walk Softly/But You Lied	62	Lescay 3009
Thrill Me	N/A	Relic LP 5035
MELLO-LARKS (VINCE MASSEY & THE)		
Smile/Did I Remember	1953	Herald 414
MELLO-MAIDS (FEMALE)		
Oh-h-h/Will You Ever Say You're Mine	1956	Baton 231
I Remember, Dear/A Million Years Ago	1957	Baton 238
MELLO-MEN		
My Love, The Blues, And Me/I'd Give A Million Yesterdays	1953	MGM 11607
MELLO-MOODS		
Where Are You? (Now That I Need You)/How Could You	1951	Robin 105
I Couldn't Sleep A Wink Last Night/And You Just Can't Go Through Life Alone	1952	Red Robin 104
I'm Lost/When I Woke Up This Morning	1953	Prestige 856
How Could You (different version from Red Robin 105)	1964	Oldies 45 167
Christmas Song/Love Me (by the Rainbows)	1977	Ronnie 202
I'm Lost/They Say (by the Rainbows)	N/A	Hamilton 143
MELLO-MOODS (BB TEACHO WILTSHIRE BAND)		
Call On Me/I Tried And Tried And Tried	1952	Prestige 799
MELLO-QUEENS (JOHN LESTER & THE)		
Getting Nearer/At Last	1959	C&M 500
MELLO-TONE 3 (LITTLE E & THE)		
Bye Bye Pretty Baby/Candy Apple Red Impala	1961	Falco 302
MELLO-TONES (1)		
I'm Just Another One In Love With You/I'm Gonna Get	1954	Decca 48319
Little Bit More/When Love Is Young	1958	Key 5804
MELLO-TONES (1) (MARGA BENITEZ & THE)		
Man Love Woman/Winos On Parade	1954	Decca 48318
Darling I Will	N/A	Sampson 102
MELLO-TONES (2)		
Rosie Lee/I'll Never Fall In Love Again	1957	Fascination 1001/Gee 1037 (57)
Ca-Sandra/Rattlesnake Roll	1957	Gee 1040
MELLO-TONES (2) (NAT WILLIAMS & THE)		
You Excite Me/A Friend	1959	Aries 1014
MELLOMEN (KITTY WHITE & THE)		
If You Only Take The Time/Someone Like Joe	1955	Century 711
MELLOMEN (SCATMAN CROTHERS & THE)		
Dearest One/Keep That Coffee Hot	1955	Century 710
MELLOMOODS		
Song Of Love/That Dubonnet Wine	1954	Recorded In Hollywood 399

Artist Song	Year	Label
MELLOMOODS (CHUCK HIGGINS & THE)		
Beautiful Love/Rock & Roll (instrumental)	1956	Money 214
MELLOS (TERRI CORIN & THE)		
Truly, I Love You Truly/Why Did You Do It	N/A	Rider 108
MELLOS (TERRY & THE)		
Love Express/The Bell's Of St. Mary's	1960	Amy 812
MELLOTONES (1) (AKA MELLO KINGS)		
Tonight, Tonight/Do Baby Do	1957	Herald 502 (first pressing, second is by Mello-Kings)
MELLOTONES (2) (DOUG WILLIAMS & THE)		
How Many Souls/Sorrow Valley	1958	Hy-Tone 103
Sorrow Valley/The Battle Of Jericho	1959	Hy-Tone 122
Send Me/Trust In God	1959	Hy-Tone 125
MELLOW DROPS		
When I Grow Too Old To Dream/The Crazy Song	1954	Imperial 5324
I Want Your Love	N/A	Imperial (unreleased)
She'll Stand Up For You	N/A	Imperial (unreleased)
MELLOW JACKS		
Gina Baby/Mellow You Down	1962	Marquee/Ascot 2115 (62)
MELLOW KEYS		
Listen, Baby/I'm Not A Deceiver	1956	Gee 1014
MELLOW LARKS		
Farewell To You My Love/ Sing A Silly Sing Song	1957	Argo 5285
MELLOWS (CARL SPENCER & THE)		
Farewell, Farewell/No More Loneliness	1956	Candlelight 1012
MELLOWS (LILLIAN LEACH & THE)		
How Sentimental Can I Be?/ Nothin' To Do	1954	Jay-Dee 793
Smoke From Your Cigarette/ Pretty Baby, What's Your Name?	1955	Jay-Dee 797
I Was A Fool To Let You Go/ I Still Care	1955	Jay-Dee 801
Yesterday's Memories/ Lovable Lily	1955	Jay-Dee 807
My Darling/Lucky Guy	1956	Celeste 3002/Celeste 3012 (74)
Sweet Lorraine/I'm Yours	1956	Celeste 3004/Celeste 3014 (74)
Ain't She Got Nerve (acappella)/ You're Gone	1974	Celeste 3008
When The Lights Go On Again/ I'm Gonna Pick Your Teeth With An Ice Pick (a capela)	1974	Celeste 3009
I Call To You/Noisy Clock	1974	Celeste 3011
Be Mine	1989	Relic LP 5080
So Strange	1989	Relic LP 5080
If I Didn't Care/Beside My Love (live, by Cleveland Still's Dubs)	N/A	100th UGHA Show Commemoration 45
Moon Of Silver/You've Gone	1956	Candlelight 1011
MELLOWS (MACK STARR & THE)		
Drifting Apart/Oh, My Love	1962	Cub 9117
MELO GENTS		
Baby Be Mine/Get Off My Back	1959	Warner Bros. 5056
MELO-AIRES		
You Know Baby/Indebted To You	1958	Nasco 6019
MELODEARS		
Summer Romance/Charock	1958	Gone 5033
It's Love Because/They Don't Say	1959	Gone 5040
MELODEERS		
Rudolph The Red-Nosed Reindeer/Wishing Is For Fools	1960	Studio 9908
The Letter/Naima Naima	1961	Shelley 127
Happy Teen-Age Times/ Goo Goo (Sounds)	1961	Studio 9909
Born To Be Mine/Three Deuces And Twin Pipes	1962	Shelley 161
MELODEERS (TONY THOMAS & THE)		
Say You Care/Sometimes I'm Happy	1955	Capri 777
MELODEES		
Daddy Daddy	1960	Nu Kat 124

Artist Song	Year	Label
MELODETTES (NORMAN DUNLAP WITH THE)		
A Dream And A Prayer/It's Easy To Remember	1953	Aladdin 3213
MELODY MASTERS		
I'll Never Be The Same/ Problem Child	1957	Renown 107
MELODY MASTERS & THE SPORTSMEN (WAYNE HARDY WITH THE)		
Betcha Didn't Know/Don't Be Unfair	1957	Renown 104
MELODY MATES		
Promenade/Enchantment	1961	Nix 100
MELODYMACKS (GEORGE MACK & THE)		
I Want To Be With You Baby	N/A	Mac
MELODYMAKERS		
Let's Make Love Worthwhile/ Carolina Moon	1957	Hollis 1001
MELOTONES		
Father Time/Prayer Of Love	1962	Lee Tone 700
MELSON, JOE (& GROUP)		
Love Is A Dangerous Thing/ Dance	1962	Hickory 1175
MELVETTES		
Take One Step/Quiet Now	N/A	Tela-Star 110
MELVETTS (JOYCE SPIVEY & THE)		
Dreaming/Angel	1965	Olimpic 254
MEMBERS (WAYNE MARSHALL & THE)		
Tell Me Who/Her Final Letter	1965	Josie 930
MEMORIES (1)		
Love Bells/I Promise	1962	Way-Lin 101
MEMORIES (2) (DANNY & THE) (GM NEIL YOUNG)		
Don't Go/Can't Help Lovin' That Girl Of Mine	1964	Valiant 705
MEMORIES (3)		
Darling You're My Angel (a capella)/Will I (a capella)	1964	Times Square 11/Times Square 95 (64)
Love Me Once Again	N/A	Klik
MEMORIES (4)		
U.G.H.A./Canadian Sunset (by the Ribitones)	1980	U.G.H.A. 14
MEMORY		
Street Corner Serenade/ He'll Be Back	1981	Avenue D 5
Daddy's Home/Under The Boardwalk	1981	Avenue D 6
MEMORY LANE		
The Night/Little Star	1982	Crystal Ball 149
MEMOS		
My Type Of Girl/The Biddy Leg	1959	Memo 34891
I'm Going Home/My Most Precious Possession	1959	Memo 5000/5001
MEN FROM MARS (MARVIN PHILLIPS & THE)		
Wine Woogie/Old Man's Blues	N/A	Specialty 445
MENDELL, JOHNNY (& GROUP)		
Pretty Little Rita/Please Be My Love	1962	Jamie 1214
MERCEEDEES (WITH THE INDIVIDUALS (4))		
Please Baby, Be Mine/Not Me	1962	Gold Seal 1000
MERCURYS		
Someone Touched Me/ The B. B. Bug	1959	Madison 119
MERIDIANS		
Blue Victory/Have You Forgotten	N/A	Parnaso 107
Blame My Heart/He Can't Dance	N/A	Parnaso 120
MERRI MEN (ROBIN HOOD & HIS) (AKA ROBIN HOOD & HIS MERRI MEN)		
Maryann/We Had A Quarrel	1961	Delsey 303
MERRI MEN (1) (ROBIN HOOD & HIS) (AKA ROBIN HOOD & HIS MERRI MEN)		
Mister Santa, Bring Me A Doll/ Ellen	1962	Mohawk 130
MERRY MEN (2) (STEVE DOUGLAS & HIS)		
Yes Sir, That's My Baby/ Lt. Colonel Bogey's Parade	1962	Philles 104
METALLICS		
Drop By/Get Lost	1962	Baronet 14
It Hurts Me/I'll Conquer The World	1962	Baronet 18
Need Your Love/Itchy Twitchy Too	1962	Baronet 2
METALLICS (J. D. WRIGHT & THE)		
Let Me Love You/In The Middle Of The Night	1962	Baronet 16

Artist Song	Year	Label
METAPHORS		
You Have Everything/Come On Back	N/A	Rad (no #)
METEORS (1) (JUNIOR THOMPSON WITH THE)		
Mama's Little Baby/Raw Deal	1956	Meteor 5029
METEORS (2)		
Let's Start Anew/Trying To Get Back Home	1963	Beltone 2041
METEORS (3) (JIMMY DEE & THE)		
Don't Hurt Me No More/Wanda	1961	Pixie 7411
METER-TONES		
Believe In Me/Talk To Me	1959	Jax 1002
METRICS		
I Found You/Wishes	1964	Chadwick 101
METRO-CHORDS		
It's A Shame/Slide My Baby Slide	1961	Admiral 300
METRO-LINERS		
I Don't Stand A Ghost Of A Chance/Your Troubles Will Be My Troubles	1976	Catamount 132
METRONOMES (1)		
Ride/I Want You	1953	Specialty 462 (unreleased)
METRONOMES (1) (GENE MOORE & THE)		
She's Gone/That's Bad	1953	Specialty 472
METRONOMES (2) (FB HAROLD "SONNY" WRIGHT)		
I Love My Girl/I'm Gonna Get Me A Girl Somehow	1957	Cadence 1310
Dear Don/How Much I Love You	1957	Cadence 1339
Embraceable You (60)	1960	Wynne EP/Wynne LP 706
Pennies From Heaven (60)	1960	Wynne EP/Wynne LP 706
Fools Rush In	1960	Wynne LP 706
Don't Blame Me	1960	Wynne LP 706
Heaven Help Me	N/A	Cadence (unreleased)
Lonely Woman	N/A	Cadence (unreleased)
METRONOMES (3)		
Tears Tears Tears/Hot Time	1962	Challenge 9157
My Dearest Darling/The Chickie-Goo	1962	Maureen 1000
Back Door Blues/This Could Be The Start Of Something Big	1962	Riverside 4523
METRONOMES (4) (LEON & THE)		
Buy This Record For Me/I'll Catch You On The Rebound	1965	Carnival 515
METRONOMES (5)		
If You Care/Fountain Of Love	N/A	Milestone
METRONOMES (6)		
Love Is The Thing/Blue	1975	Broadcast 1131
METRONOMES (7)		
Love You As You Love Me/Until The Real Thing Comes Along (by the Harptones)	1976	Robin Hood 131
METROPOLITANS		
So Much In Love/My Heart Is True	1958	Junior 395
METROS (1) (EDDIE JOY & THE)		
Young Love Is An Old Story	1959	Dart 1008
METROS (2) (AKA CRYSTALS (6))		
Lookin'/All My Life	1959	Just 1502
METROS (3)		
Someone	N/A	Ra-Sel
METROS (4)		
Egyptian Lover	N/A	RCA LP 3776
METROTONES (1)		
A-Ting-A-Ling/Tonight	1955	Columbia 40420
Write Me Baby/Even Then	1955	Columbia 40486
METROTONES (2)		
More And More	1957	Reserve 114
METROTONES (2) (BB THE LITTLE WALKIN' WILLIE QUARTET)		
Please Come Back/Skitter, Skatter	1957	Reserve 116
MIAMIANS		
Call Me A Coward/When My Teenage Days Are Through	1958	Amp-3 1006
MICHELS, GINNY (& GROUP)		
True Confession/Everyone Was There	1962	Mala 446
MICROGROOVES		
Hey You/Why Do You Make Me Cry	1990	Crystal Ball 160
MID-KNIGHTERS		
Charlena/Flower Of Love	N/A	Paragon 814

Artist Song	Year	Label
Flower Of Love/Charlena	N/A	Paragon 814
MIDDLETON, TONY (& GROUP)		
Count Your Blessings/I Just Want Somebody	1959	Triumph 600
MIDDLETONES		
Ain't Gonna Waste No Tears On You	1955	Cadillac 156
MIDNIGHT LIGHTERS (HANK BALLARD & THE) (AKA MIDNIGHTERS)		
Finger Poppin' Time/From The Love Side	1972	Polydor 14128
MIDNIGHT RIDERS (KASANDREA & THE)		
Turtle Dovin'/I Couldn't Let You Down	1959	Imperial 5638
MIDNIGHTERS (AKA ROYALS (1))		
Work With Me Annie/Sinner's Prayer	1953	Federal 12169
Work With Me Annie/Until I Die	1953	Federal 12169
Give It Up/That Woman	1953	Federal 12177
Sexy Ways/Don't Say Your Last Goodbye	1954	Federal 12185
Annie Had A Baby/She's The One	1954	Federal 12195
Annie's Aunt Fanny/Crazy Loving (Stay With Me)	1954	Federal 12200
Stingy Little Thing/Tell Them	1954	Federal 12202
Moonrise/She's The One	1954	Federal 12205
Ring-A-Ling-A-Ling/Ashamed Of Myself	1955	Federal 12210
Switchie Witchie Titchie/Why Are We Apart	1955	Federal 12220
Henry's Got Flat Feet (Can't Dance No More)/ Whatsoever We Do	1955	Federal 12224
It's Love Baby/Looka Here	1955	Federal 12227
Give It Up/That Woman	1955	Federal 12230
That House On The Hill/Rock And Roll Wedding	1955	Federal 12240
Don't Change Your Pretty Ways/ We'll Never Meet Again	1955	Federal 12243
Sweet Mama Do Right/ Partners For Life	1956	Federal 12251
Open Up The Back Door/ Rock Granny Roll	1956	Federal 12260
Tore Up Over You/Early One Morning	1956	Federal 12270
I'll Be Home Some Day/ Come On A Get It	1956	Federal 12285
Let Me Hold Your Hand/ Ooh Bah Baby	1957	Federal 12288
In The Doorway Crying/ E Basta Cosi	1957	Federal 12293
Oh So Happy/Is Your Love For Real	1957	Federal 12299
Let 'Em Roll/What Made You Change Your Mind	1957	Federal 12305
Daddy's Little Baby/Stay By My Side	1958	Federal 12317
Baby Please/Ow Wow Oo Wee	1958	Federal 12339
Don't Go I Love You	1960	King LP 700
Young Lady	1960	King LP 700
MIDNIGHTERS (FB HENRY MOORE)		
Doin' Everything/Big Frog	1961	King 5513
MIDNIGHTERS (HANK BALLARD & THE) (AKA ROYALS (1))		
The Twist/Teardrops On Your Letter	1959	King 5171/Federal 12345 (59)
Kansas City/I'll Keep You Happy	1959	King 5195
Sugaree/Rain Down Tears	1959	King 5215
House With No Windows/ Cute Little Ways	1959	King 5245
Never Knew/I Could Love You	1959	King 5275
Look At Little Sister/I Said I Wouldn't Beg You	1959	King 5289
The Coffee Grind/Waiting	1960	King 5312
Finger Poppin' Time/I Love You, I Love You So-o-o	1960	King 5341
Let's Go, Let's Go, Let's Go/ If You'd Forgive Me	1960	King 5400
The Hoochi Coochi Coo/ I'm Thinking Of You	1960	King 5430
Rock Junction/Spongie	1961	King 5449
Let's Go Again/Deep Blue Sea	1961	King 5459

Artist	Song	Year	Label
	The Continental Walk/What's This I See?	1961	King 5491
	The Switch-A-Roo/The Float	1961	King 5510
	Nothing But Good/Keep On Dancing	1961	King 5535
	Can't You See, I Need A Friend/Big Red Sunset	1961	King 5550
	I'm Gonna Miss You/Do You Remember?	1961	King 5578
	Do You Know How To Twist/Broadway	1962	King 5593
	It's Twistin' Time/Autumn Breeze	1962	King 5601
	Good Twistin' Tonight/I'm Young	1962	King 5635
	I Want To Thank You/Excuse Me	1962	King 5655
	When I Need You/Dreamworld	1962	King 5677
	I Love And Care For You/Shakey Mae	1962	King 5693
	She's The One/Bring Me Your Love	1962	King 5703
	The Rising Tide/All The Things I Love	1962	King 5713
	That Low Down Move/House On The Hill	1963	King 5719
	Christmas Time For Everyone But Me/Santa Claus Is Coming	1963	King 5729
	Walkin' And Talkin'/How Could You Leave	1963	King 5746
	Those Lonely, Lonely Feelings/It's Love	1963	King 5798
	Buttin' In/I'm Learning	1963	King 5821
	Don't Let Temptation/Have Mercy	1964	King 5835
	Don't Fall In Love With Me/I'm So Mad	1964	King 5860
	These Young Girls/I Don't Know But One	1964	King 5884
	Stay Away From My Baby/She's Got Soul	1964	King 5901
	What's Your Name/Daddy Rolling Stone	1964	King 5931
	A Winner Never Quits/Let's Get Show	1964	King 5954
	One Monkey Don't Stop The Show/Watch What...	1964	King 5963
	Poppin' The Whip/You Just You	1965	King 5996
	Sloop And Slide/My Sun Is Going Down	1965	King 6018
	I'm Ready/Togetherness	1965	King 6031
	He Came Along/Annie Had A Baby	1966	King 6055
	You're In Real Good Hands/Unwind Yourself	1967	King 6119
	Funky Soul Train/Which Way Should I Turn	1967	King 6131
	You Can't Keep A Good Man Down	1969	King LP 1052
	Hey There Sexy Lady/Hey There Sexy Lady (instrumental)	1974	Stang 5058
MIDNIGHTERS (HENRY BOOTH & THE)			
	Every Beat Of My Heart/Starting From Tonight	1960	DeLuxe 6190
MIDNIGHTERS (LIL' RAY & THE)			
	Loretta/My Girl	1964	Impact 30
MIDNIGHTS			
	Annie Pulled A Hum-Bug/Hear My Plea	1954	Music City 746
	She Left Me/Cheating On Me	1954	Music City 762
MIDNITE RAIDERS (MILLS ALLEN & THE)			
	Dorothy Jane	N/A	Black Gold 304
MIDNITERS (AL CHASE & THE)			
	Oh Yes My Darling/Lubby Lou	1960	Jin 118
MIFLIN TRIPLETS			
	I Do/Someone Should Have Told Me	1958	Ember 1045
MIGHTY DUKES			
	Not Other Love/Why Can't I Have You	1952	Duke 104
MIGHTY JUPITERS			
	Your Love/Hy Wocky Toomba	1958	Warner 1020
MIGHTY MELLOTONES			
	Beams Of Heaven	N/A	Honey-B 1017
MILESTONES			
	Roasted Peanuts/One Week Romance (by the Calendars)	1961	Swingin' 649
MILKY WAYS			
	Teenage Island/My Love	1960	Liberty 55255
MILLER BROTHERS			
	Try/If I Had A Car	1958	Mercury 71293
	Let Me Know/Lawrence Was His Name	1963	Coed 577
MILLER SISTERS (FEMALE)			
	Until You're Mine/Hippity Ha	1955	Herald 455/Herald 527 (58)
	There Is No Right Way To Do Me Wrong/You Can Tell Me	1955	Sun 230
	Guess Who/How Am I To Know	1956	Ember 1004
	Someday You Will Pay/You Didn't Think I Would	1956	Flip 504
	Please Don't Leave/Do You Wanna Go	1956	Hull 718
	Finders Keepers/Ten Cats Down	1956	Sun 255
	The Flip Skip/Let's Start Anew	1957	Acme 111/Acme 721 (58)
	You Made A Promise/Crazy Billboard Song	1957	Acme 717
	My Own/Sugar Candy	1957	Onyx 507
	Just Wait And See/Black Pepper (instrumental by Leo Price)	1960	Hull 736
	Oh Lover/Remember That	1960	Miller 1140
	Pony Dance/Give Me Some Old Fashioned Love	1960	Miller 1141
	Please Mr. D.J.	1960	Miller 1143
	Pop Your Finger/You Got To Reap What You Sow	1961	Glodis 1003
	Roll Back The Rug And Twist/Don't You Forget	1962	Hull 750
	I Cried All Night/Holly Golly Reel	1962	Hull 752
	I Miss You So/Dance Little Sister	1962	Rayna 5001
	Oh Why/Walk On	1962	Rayna 5004
	Tell Him/Dance Close	1963	Riverside 4535
	Baby Your Baby/Silly Girl	1963	Roulette 4491
	Cooncha/Feel Good	1964	Stardust 3001
	Looking Over My Life/Si Senor	1965	Yorktown 75
	I'm Telling It Like It Is/Until You Come Home I'll Walk Alone	1967	GMC 10006
	Hey You	N/A	Capri
MILLER SISTERS (JEANNIE & THE) (FEMALE)			
	Don't You Forget/Roll Back The Rug (And Twist)	1962	Hull 750
MILLIONAIRES (1) (AKA BLENDERS (1)/AKA SPARROWS (1))			
	Somebody's Lyin'/Kansas Kapers	1955	Davis 441
MILLIONAIRES (2)			
	Cherry Baby/I Thought About You	1965	Bunny 506
MILLIONAIRES (3) (ROCKY & THE)			
	Remember Me/Frisco Sands	1963	Orchestra 102
MILLIONAIRES (4) (BENNY CURTIS & THE)			
	I Wonder/Troubles	1961	Bridges 1102
MILLIONAIRES (5) (FB BEN E. KING) (REF DRIFTERS)			
	Once A Heart/Tasty Kisses (by the Tunemasters)	1990	Mark-X 7010
MILNER, JIMMY (& GROUP)			
	A Place In My Heart/Is It Fair	1959	Ember 1052
MINOR BOPS (DAVE ATKINS & THE)			
	Ballad Of Robert E. Lee	N/A	Contour 503
MINOR CHORDS			
	Many A Day/Let Her Go Man	1962	Lu Pine 112
	So What	1986	Relic LP 8008
MINOR CHORDS (CHARLES HENDERSON & THE)			
	Bad Bulldog/Fire	1959	Flick 005
MINOR CHORDS (SUNNIE ELMO & THE)			
	Don't Let Me Down/I'm Falling In Love With You	1960	Flick 006
	Indian Love Call/Let Me	1960	Flick 009
MINOR TONES (ROBBIE MELDANO & THE)			
	Forever Darling/I Need You Baby	1958	Music City 816
MINORBOPS			
	Need You Tonight/I Want You For My Own	1957	Lamp 2012

Artist	Song	Year	Label
MINORS			
	Jerry/Where Are You?	1957	Celeste 3007/Mello 554
MINT JULEPS			
	Bells Of Love/Vip-A-Dip	1956	Herald 481
	Queen Of Love	N/A	Herald (unreleased)
MINT, LITTLE EDDIE (& GROUP)			
	Bring Yourself Back Here/		
	Two More Days	1959	Memo 17921
MINTS			
	Busy Body Rock/Don't Leave		
	Me Alone	1956	Lin 5001
	Night Air/Pledge Of Love		
	(by Ken Copeland)	1956	Lin 5007/Imperial 5432 (57)
	Magic Of Love/Swimming		
	Around The World	1958	Airport 103
MINUTE MEN			
	My Love Is Gone/Please Keep		
	The Beatles In England	1964	Argo 5469
MIRACLES (1)			
	A Lovers' Chant/Come Home		
	With Me	1955	Baton 210
MIRACLES (2)			
	You're An Angel/A Gal Named Jo	1955	Cash 1008
MIRACLES (3) (CARL HOGAN & THE)			
	I Love You So/Your Love		
	(Is All I Need)	1957	Fury 1001
MIRACLES (4) (FB SMOKEY ROBINSON)			
	Got A Job/My Mama Done		
	Told Me	1958	End 1016
	Money/I Cry	1958	End 1029/End 1084 (60)
	Bad Girl/I Love You Baby	1959	Motown G1/G2/Chess 1734 (59)
	All I Want Is You/I Need A		
	Change	1960	Chess 1768
MIRACLETONES			
	Tell Me My Darling/Mambo Train	1958	Jam 5803
MIRANDA, BILLY (& GROUP)			
	Go Ahead/Run Rose	1960	Checker 957
MISFITS			
	Midnight Star/I Don't Know	1961	Aries 7-10-3
	Give Me Your Heart/My		
	Mother-In-Law	1961	Hush 105
MISHEL, BILLY (& GROUP)			
	Paradise Found/The Agency	1961	Time 1036
MISSILES			
	We Belong Together/Space		
	Ship	1960	Novel 200
MISSION BELLS			
	Sincerely/When A Girl Really		
	Loves You	1965	London 9760
MISTAKES			
	Chapel Bells/I Got Fired	1959	Lo-Fi 2311/2312/Tip Top
MISTERS (1)			
	Too Many Girls/Why Don't We		
	Do This More Often	1959	Chante 1002/Decca 31026 (59)
MISTERS (2) (MIKE MALONE & THE)			
	It Must Be Raining/Daddy's		
	Gone Away	1964	Token 1002
MISTICS			
	Memories/Without Love	1963	Capri 631
	You'll Be There/What		
	Happened To Saturday	1964	Kirk 636
MITCHELL, BILLY (& GROUP)			
	Bottomless Pit/The Rock And		
	Roll Tango	1957	Poplar 105
MITCHELL, TONY (& GROUP)			
	Candle In The Wind/Million		
	Drums	1963	Canadian American 157
MITCHUM, JIM (& GROUP)			
	Lonely Birthday/Oh, What A		
	Wonderful Feeling	1960	20th Century 277
MITLO SISTERS (WITH THE DREAMTONES)			
	Let Me Tell You/Lonely Sea	1958	Klik 8405
MIXERS			
	You Said You're Leaving Me/		
	Johnny's Got A Girl Friend	1958	Bold 101
	Love And Kisses/Casanova	1959	Bold 102
MIXMASTERS (SONNY FULTON & THE)			
	Fingerprints/No Not Now	1959	Sunbeam 125
MOBLEY, JOHN (& GROUP)			
	Tunnel Of Love (Pt. 1)/Tunnel		
	Of Love (Pt. 2)	1962	Town & Country 6601

Artist	Song	Year	Label
MODERN RED CAPS			
	They Can Dream/Don't You		
	Hear Them Laughing	1963	Rowax 801
	Our Love Will Never Be The		
	Same/Empty World	1965	Lawn 254
	Lovers Never Say Goodbye/		
	We Walked In The Moonlight	1965	Penntown
	Golden Teardrops/Never Too		
	Young	1966	Swan 4243
MODERN RED CAPS (GEORGE TINDLEY & THE)			
	Done Being Lonely/I Couldn't		
	Care Less	1962	Smash 1768
	Free/Never Kiss A Good Man		
	Goodbye	1965	Penntowne 101
MODERNISTICS			
	Who Can I Turn To/Down At		
	The Go Go	1965	Pioneer 7315
MODERNISTICS (AL LEWIS & THE)			
	What Will The Outcome Be/		
	Just One More Chance	1959	Music City 829
MODERNISTICS (LITTLE E & AL & THE)			
	Hurts My Soul/I'm Knockin' Love	1961	Falco 304
MODIFIERS (MIKE & THE)			
	I Found Myself A Brand New		
	Baby/It's Too Bad	1962	Gordy 7006
MOHAWKS (1)			
	Bewitched (Bothered And		
	Bewildered)/I Got A Gal	1960	Val-Ue 211
MOHAWKS (2) (FB RICHARD "POPCORN" WYLIE)			
	I'll Be Around/Money	1961	Motown 1009
MOHAWKS (2) (POPCORN & HIS)			
	Pretty Girl/You're The One	1960	Northern 3732
	Shimmy Gully/Custer's Last Man	1960	Motown 1002
	Money/I'll Still Be Around	1961	Motown 1009
	Have I The Right/Real Good Lovin'	1962	Motown 1019
MOHAWKS (3)			
	Shoplifting Molly	1964	Mutual 504
MON-CLAIRS			
	Please Come Back/Baby Sue	1962	Joey 6101
MON-VALES			
	Carol Ann/White Bucks	1958	Pen Joy 501
	Carol Ann/White Bucks	1958	Pen Joy 501
MONARCHS (1)			
	Angels In The Sky/Wanna Go		
	Home	1955	Wing 90040
MONARCHS (2)			
	Pretty Little Girl/In My Younger		
	Days	1956	Neil 101/Melba 101 (56)
	Always Be Faithful/How Are		
	You?	1956	Neil 103/Melba 103 (56)
	Love You That's Why/Coming		
	Home	1961	Liban 1002
MONARCHS (3) (CHUCK MILLS & THE)			
	She's Mine/Who Was The Fool	1959	Band Box 221
	Who Was The Fool/Ding Dong	1959	Band Box 227
MONARCHS (4)			
	This Old Heart/'Til I Hear From		
	You	1962	Jam 104
MONARCHS (5) (PORGY & THE)			
	Stay/Somebody Said (I'd Cry		
	Someday)	1963	Mala 462
MONARCHS (6)			
	Look Homeward Angel/What		
	Made You Change Your Mind	1964	Sound Stage 7 2516
MONARCHS (7)			
	Over The Rainbow/Guess Who	1962	Reegal 512
MONCLAIRS			
	Call The Police	N/A	Fortune LP 8017
MONDAY, JULIE (& GROUP)			
	Baby, Let Me Be Your Girl/Come		
	Share The Good Times With Me	1966	Rainbow 500/501
MONDELLOS			
	That's What I Call Love/		
	Daylight Saving Time	1957	Rhythm 106
	Hard To Please/Happiness		
	Street	1957	Rhythm 109
	You'll Never Know/Hard To		
	Please (by the Marcels)	1984	Rhythm 118
MONDELLOS (ALICE JEAN & THE)			
	100 Years From Today/		
	Come Back Home	1957	Rhythm 102

Artist Song	Year	Label	Artist Song	Year	Label
MONDELLOS (RUDY LAMBERT & THE)			**MONTAGUES**		
My Heart/That's What I Call Love	1958	Rhythm 114	School Rock/Teenagers Are Really Hep	1995	Early Bird 002
MONDELLOS (YUL MCCLAY & THE)			**MONTALVO, LENNY (BB THE CRYSTAL CHORDS)**		
Never Leave Me Alone/ Over The Rainbow	1957	Rhythm 105	Be Mine Again/When In The World	1958	3-D 373
MONDELLS (JOHNNY C & THE)			**MONTCLAIRS (1)**		
No Love/Lonely One	1972	Saluda 106	Give Me A Chance/My Every Dream	1956	Premium 404
MONDO, JOE (& GROUP)			All I Want Is Love/I've Heard About You	1956	Sonic 104
Last Summer Love/ Doin' The Thing	1963	EPI 1003	Golden Angel/Don Juan	1957	Hi-Q 5001
MONELS			**MONTCLAIRS (1) (FLOYD SMITH WITH THE)**		
Everyday Of The Week/Please Say You Want Me	1989	Starlight 66	Grandpa's Gully Rock/This Is A Miracle	1961	Fortune 540
MONIQUES			**MONTCLAIRS (1) (MEL WILLIAMS & THE) (AKA CAPRIS (5))**		
Hey Girl/Goin' Down To Birdland	1962	Benn-X 55	O-O-Wah/Lessons In Love	1954	Decca 29370
Love So Wonderful/Teach Me How To Dance	1962	Benn-X 58	Ooh Wah/Fools Fall In Love	1955	Rage 101
Halo/Don't Throw Stones	1963	Centaur 104	**MONTCLAIRS (2)**		
I'm With You All The Way/ Rock Pretty Baby	1963	Centaur 105	Goodnight, Well It's Time To Go/A Broken Promise	1960	Audicon 111
MONITORS (1)			I Believe (In Your Love)/No Baby	1963	ABC 10463
Candy Coated Kisses/ Tonight's The Night	1955	Aladdin 3309	**MONTCLAIRS (3)**		
Our School Days/I've Got A Dream	1957	Specialty 595	Wait For Me/Happy Feet Time	1965	Sunburst 106
Closer To Heaven/ Rock 'N' Roll Forever	1957	Specialty 622	Sore Feet/Poopsie	1965	Sunburst 115
Hop Scotch/Mamma Linda	1958	Specialty 636	**MONTCLAIRS (4)**		
MONITORS (2)			Lisa/Tap Tap Daisy	1967	United International 1007
A Boyfriend's Prayer/Nita	1958	Circus 219	**MONTCLAIRS (5) (EDDIE CAROL & THE)**		
MONOGRAMS			Where Are You/Wow-Wow Baby	1958	Rulu 6098
My Baby Dearest Darling/ Please Baby Please	1957	Saga 1000	**MONTE, VINCE (& GROUP)**		
Tears And Dreams/That's What He Said	1960	Safire 102	Mashed Potato Girl/You Can't Compare With My Baby	1962	Jubilee 5428
Baby Blue Eyes/Little Suzie	1961	Rust 5036	I Wrote A Poem/Naughty Naughty Baby	1958	Fargo 1000
Come Back My Love/Dunkin' Boy (by the Hi-Liters)	1975	Monogram 101	**MONTELLS**		
Baby/This Letter To You	1975	Monogram 105	Ranga Lang Lang/Soldier Boy, I'm Sorry	1963	Golden Crest 582
Tears In My Eyes/Dear One	1975	Monogram 106	Gee Baby/My Prince Will Come	1963	Golden Crest 585
MONORAILS			**MONTELS (1)**		
Come To Me Darling/Will Ya William	1961	Lute 6017	Union Hall/That's Alright With Me	1956	Universal 101
Come To Me Darling/Untrue (by the Meadowlarks)	1973	Sold 506	Union Hall/Forever And Ever (by Frankie & the C-Notes)	1963	Times Square 10
Juanita/Sad And Blue	1976	Broadcast 1136	**MONTELS (2)**		
MONORAYS (AKA MONTEREYS (2))			Rondevous/The Way I Feel	1961	Kink 9365
It's Love Baby/What's Your Name	1958	Nasco 6020	**MONTERAYS (1)**		
Face In The Crowd/Step Right Up	1963	Astra 1018	Deep Within My Heart/ Push-Em Up	1964	Dominion 1019/Ultima 704
You're No Good/Love	1965	20th Fox 594	**MONTERAYS (2)**		
MONORAYS (WITH TONY MARCH)			I'll Be Around/Valerie (by the Madisons)	1965	Twin Hit 2865
My Guardian Angel/Five Minutes To Love You	1959	Tammy Records 1005 (first pressing)/Tammy 1005 (59) (second press ing)/Red Rocket 476 (60)	**MONTERAYS (3)**		
			You Never Cared/Blast Off	1957	Planet 57
			MONTEREYS (1)		
MONOTONES (1) (REF TERRACETONES)			Someone Like You/Train Whistle Blues	1956	Nestor 15/Teenage 1001 (56)
Book Of Love/You Never Loved Me	1957	Mascot 124/Argo 5290 (58)	**MONTEREYS (1) (DEAN BARLOW & THE)**		
Tom Foolery/Zombi	1958	Argo 5301	Dearest One/Through The Years	1957	Onyx 513/Relic 511 (64)
The Legend Of Sleepy Hollow/ Soft Shadows	1959	Argo 5321	Angel/Tell Me Why	1957	Onyx 517
Fools Will Be Fools/Tell It To The Judge	1959	Argo 5339	**MONTEREYS (2) (AKA MONORAYS)**		
Reading The Book Of Love/ Dream	1960	Hull 735	My Girl/With You	1956	Saturn 1002
Daddy's Home But Mama's Gone/Tattletale	1961	Hull 743	Goodbye My Love/Slipping Away	1956	Saturn 1005
Toast To Lovers	1962	Hull LP 1002	I'll Love You Again/The American Teens	1958	East West 124
Book Of Dance	1962	Hull LP 1002	You're The Girl For Me/ Ape Shape	1958	Rose 109
Book Of Dance/Toast To Lovers	1974	Owl 323	Goodbye My Love/It Hurts Me So	1959	Arwin 130
What Would You Do If There Wasn't Any Rock 'N' Roll	1986	Murray Hill LP 000180	Without A Girl/So Deep	1959	Impala 213
Forever Yours	1986	Murray Hill LP 000180	Rita/Billy Budd	1960	Prince 5060
MONOTONES (2)			Face In The Crowd/Step Right Up	1963	Blast 219 (63)
What Would I Do/Is It Right	1964	Hickory 1250	First Kiss/Just One More Kiss	1964	Dominion 1019
When Will I Be Loved/If You Can't Give Me All	1965	Hickory 1306	I Still Love You/For Sentimental Reasons	1964	GNP Crescendo 314
			One More Fool Than I	N/A	Saturn
			MONTEREYS (2) (SANDRA PATRICK & THE)		
			I Want Your Love/Broken Heart Prayer	1964	Dominion 1008
			MONTEREYS (3)		
			A Crowded Room/You Said That You Loved Me	1959	Major 1009

Artist Song	Year	Label
MONTEREYS (4)		
Darlin' Send Me A Letter/Darlin' (Love You So)	N/A	Trans American 1000/1001
MONTEREYS QUARTET		
Ballad Of Take Me Back To Baltimore (Pt. 1)/Ballad Of Take Me Back To Baltimore (Pt. 2)	1964	JC Records 9317
MONTGOMERYS		
Promise Of Love/Gotta Make A Hit Record	1963	Amy 883
MOOD MAKERS		
Dolores/Dream A Dream	1961	Bambi 800
MOODS		
Little Alice/Lady Of The Sea	1959	Sarg 162
Let Me Have Your Love/Broke Up	1959	Sarg 179
Teenagers Past/Rockin' Santa Claus	1959	Sarg 184
Easy Going/Duck Walk	1960	Sarg 176
Teenager's Past/On The Move	1960	Sarg 185
MOON BEAMS		
Don't Go Away/A Lover's Plea	1959	Grate 100
MOON MISTS		
Didn't You Get The Letter	N/A	Modern 201
MOONBEAMS (AKA MOONBEEMS)		
Crying The Blues//Mardi Gras Mambo (by the Hawketts)	1958	Sapphire 2250
MOONBEAMS (JEANNE STERLING & THE)		
It's Too Soon To Know/Star Of Love (with Johnny Otis)	1957	Capitol 3802
MOONBEEMS (AKA MOONBEAMS)		
Teen Age Baby/Cryin' The Blues	1955	Sapphire 1052/Sapphire 100/(58)/Checker 912 (59)
Maria	N/A	Sapphire (unreleased)
The Way You'll Always Be	N/A	Sapphire (unreleased)
MOONGLOWS		
I Just Can't Tell No Lie/I've Been Your Dog (Ever Since I've Been Your Man)	1952	Champagne 7500
Whistle, My Love/Baby, Please	1953	Chance 1147
Just A Lonely Christmas/ Hey! Santa Claus	1953	Chance 1150
Secret Love/Real Gone Mama (62)	1954	Chance 1152/Vee Jay 423
I Was Wrong/Ooh Rocking Daddy	1954	Chance 1156
219 Train/My Gal	1954	Chance 1161
Fine Fine Girl/My Love	1954	Chance 1166 (unreleased)
So All Alone/Shoo Doo Be Doo (My Lovin' Baby)	1954	Checker 806
Sincerely/Tempting	1954	Chess 1581
Most Of All/She's Gone	1955	Chess 1589
Foolish Me/Slow Down	1955	Chess 1598
Starlight/In Love	1955	Chess 1605
In My Diary/Lover, Love Me	1955	Chess 1611
We Go Together/Chickie Um Bah	1956	Chess 1619
See Saw/When I'm With You	1956	Chess 1629
Over And Over Again (fast version)/I Knew From The Start	1956	Chess 1646
Over And Over Again (slow version)/I Knew From The Start	1956	Chess 1646
I'm Afraid The Masquerade Is Over/Don't Say Goodbye	1956	Chess 1651
Please Send Me Someone To Love/Mr. Engineer (Bring Her Back To Me)	1957	Chess 1661
The Beating Of My Heart/ Confess It To Your Heart	1957	Chess 1669
Too Late/Here I Am	1957	Chess 1681
In The Middle Of The Night/ Soda Pop	1958	Chess 1689
This Love/Sweeter Than Words	1958	Chess 1701
Rock Rock Rock	1958	Chess LP 1425
I'll Never Stop Wanting You/ Love Is A River	1959	Chess 1717
Cold Feet	1959	Chess LP 1430
Kiss Me Baby	1959	Chess LP 1430/Chess LP 701 (76)
Junior/Beatnik	1960	Chess 1770
The First Time/Mama	1961	Chess 1781
My Inspiration/Gee	1961	Crimson 1003
Sincerely/Time After Time	1964	Lana 130
What A Difference A Day Makes/Most Of All	1964	Lana 131
Blue Velvet/In My Diary	1964	Lana 132
See Saw/Love Is A River	1964	Lana 133
We Go Together/Shoo Doo Be Doo	1964	Lana 134
Half A Heart/Ten Commandments Of Love	1964	Lana 135
I've Got The Right/Baby Please	1964	Times Square 30
Sincerely "72"/You've Chosen Me	1971	Big P 101
We Go Together/Please Send Me Someone	1972	All Platinum 109
Sincerely '72/I Was Wrong	1972	RCA 74-0759
When I'm With You/You've Chosen Me	1972	RCA 74-0839
In The Still Of The Night/I Pray For Love	1973	Relic 1024
Thrill Me/Let's Go	1976	Chess LP 701/Skylark 552 (79)
I'm Only Trying/Ten Commandments Of Love	1976	Robin Hood 143
She's All Right With Me/ Someone For Everyone	1977	Monogram 128
MOONGLOWS (BOBBY LESTER & THE)		
Blue Velvet/Penny Arcade	1962	Chess 1811
MOONGLOWS (HARVEY & THE)		
The Ten Commandments Of Love/Mean Old Blues	1958	Chess 1705
Mama Loocie/Unemployment	1959	Chess 1738
MOONLIGHTERS (1) (BOBBY LESTER & THE) (AKA MOONGLOWS)		
So All Alone/Shoo Doo Be Doo (My Lovin' Baby)	1954	Checker 806
New Gal/A Hug and A Kiss	1955	Checker 813
MOONLIGHTERS (2)		
Broken Heart/Glow Of Love	1958	Tara 100/Josie 843 (58)
Never, Never, Never/ Rock-A-Bayou-Baby	1958	Tara 102
MOONLIGHTERS (3) (BILLY & THE)		
You Made Me Cry/Little Indian Girl	1978	Crystal Ball 101
MOONRAYS (1) (RAY FRAZIER & THE)		
Days/Turn On Me	1956	Excel 111
My Dream Love/Heaven's Not So Far	1962	Dynamite 1009
MOONRAYS (2) (LEE WILLIAMS & THE)		
I'm So In Love/(No) I Won't Cry Any More	1960	King 5409
MOONTARS (DON DEAL & THE)		
Sweet Love/The First Teenager	1958	Era 1070
MOONTUNES (SMILEY MOON & THE)		
You Don't Understand/Whip It On	1967	Star 601
MOORE, RUDY MAY (BB THE RAYTONES)		
Easy Easy Baby/Miss Wonderful	1960	World Pacific 821
MOORE, SONNY (& GROUP)		
My True Love And I/Prisoner To You	1958	Old Town 1063
MOOVERS		
I Love You Baby/One Little Dance	1967	Brent 7065
MORELAND, PRENTICE (& GROUP)		
Oh Pretty Baby/Please, Please, Please	1959	Edsel 778
You Are My Sunshine/Chubby Ain't Chubby No More	1962	Challenge 9154
MORNING ECHOES		
Dear Mother	1951	Premium 877
MOROCCANS (AKA MOROCCOS)		
Believe In Tomorrow/You Fascinate Me (by the Phillipairs)	1957	Salem 1014
MOROCCANS (SAMMY FITZHUGH & THE)		
Sadie Mae/Linda Baby	1958	Poplar 115
MOROCCOS		
Morocco Chant	1955	United (unreleased)
Pardon My Tears/Chicken	1955	United 188
Somewhere Over The Rainbow/Red Hots And Chili Mac	1955	United 193/B&F 193 (60)
My Love	1956	United (unreleased)

Artist	Song	Year	Label
	What Is A Teen-Ager's Prayer?/		
	Bang Goes My Heart!	1956	United 204/B&F 1347
	Sad, Sad Hours/The Hex	1957	United 207
MOROCCOS (LILLIAN BROOKS & THE)			
	For Only You/She Boodle Dee,		
	Boodle Dee	1956	King 4934
	Sweet Sweet William/No Parking	1956	King 4956
MORRA, TONY (& GROUP)			
	Claire/My Baby Scares Me	1958	Arcade 152
MORRIS, PETE (& GROUP)			
	When You're Hurt/Walkin'		
	Together	1957	End 1006
MORRIS, ROSE (BB THE DELIGHTERS)			
	It's No Secret/I Love The Life		
	I Live	1962	Puff 1002
MORROCOS (LITTLE JOE & THE)			
	Trouble In The Candy Shop/		
	Bubble Gum	1959	Bumble Bee 500
MORSE, ELLA MAE (& GROUP)			
	Goodnight Sweetheart		
	Goodnight/Happy Habit	1954	Capitol 2800
	Lovey Dovey/Bring Back My		
	Baby To Me	1954	Capitol 2992
MOSQUITOS			
	Wait A Minute/Blind Date	1964	Herald 587
MOTIFS			
	She's My Girl/My Babe	N/A	Baton 23112
MOTIONS (AKA EMOTIONS (1))			
	Mr. Night/Make Me A Love	1961	Laurie 3112
MOTIONS (RON & THE)			
	Last Nights Dream/When My		
	Little Girl Is Smiling	N/A	Red Bug 0006
MOTIVATIONS			
	I'm Loving You, You're Leaving		
	Me/I Love You	1973	Eastbound 604
MOTOR SCOOTER (BEVERLY & THE)			
	I Had To Walk Home Myself/		
	He's My Boy	1964	Epic 9654
MOY, JUNE (BB THE FEATHERS)			
	Desert Winds/Castle Of Dreams	1954	Show Time 1103
MR. BASSMAN (AKA DEVOTIONS)			
	Rip Van Winkle/You're The One		
	(by Marty & the Symbols)	1963	Graphic Arts 1000
MR. LEE (1) (BB THE CHEROKEES)			
	The Decision/What's Your		
	Name	1960	Winter 501
	Dear One/Mr. Lee's Plea	N/A	Terry 220
MR. LEE (2) (BB THE FRANK ANDRADE 5)			
	Let The Four Winds Blow/		
	Hey Mrs. Jones	1964	Skylark 503
MUDLARKS			
	Love Game/My Grandfather's		
	Clock	1959	Roulette 4143
MUFFINS			
	Walk Alone/Just One More Time	1963	Planet 59
MULRAYS			
	Lily Marlane/I Got The Blues	1957	Trans World 719
MURALS			
	See You In September/Ambush	1959	Climax 110
MURPHY, BOB (& GROUP)			
	Hey You/Hootin' In The Kitchen		
	(by Billy Boyle)	1963	Lawn 221
MURRAYMEN			
	Oasis/It Won't Always Be		
	Raining	1955	Arcade 131
MUSICAL NOTES (BILL JOHNSON & THE)			
	When Your Hair Has Turned		
	To Silver	1954	Tru-Blue 414
MUSKATEERS (AKA ROYAL JOKERS/AKA ROYALS (2)/AKA SCOOTERS/AKA SERENADERS (1))			
	Goodbye My Love/Love You		
	'Til My Dying Day	1953	Roxy 801
	Deep In My Heart/Love You		
	'Til My Dying Day	1953	Swingtime 331
MUSKETEERS (DEBBIE ANDREWS & THE)			
	Don't Make My Cry/Love Me,		
	Please Love Me	1952	United 144
MUSTANGS			
	Over The Rainbow/Look	1965	Vest 8005
MYRON, MITCH (& GROUP)			
	Runnin' Around Town/		
	True Love Is Hard To Find	1960	Bay-Tone 109

Artist	Song	Year	Label
MYSTERY MEN			
	Feel Like A Million/On A		
	Saturday Night	1963	Pow 1001
MYSTICS (1)			
	Hushabye/Adam And Eve	1959	Laurie 3028
	Don't Take The Stars/So		
	Tenderly	1959	Laurie 3038
	Red Red Robin	1959	unreleased
	Wim O Weh	1959	unreleased
	All Through The Night/(I Begin)		
	To Think Again Of You	1960	Laurie 3047
	White Cliffs Of Dover/Blue Star	1960	Laurie 3058
	Star Crossed Lovers/Goodbye		
	Mr. Blues	1961	Laurie 3086
	A Sunday Kind Of Love/		
	Darling I Know Now	1961	Laurie 3104
	In My Faithful Heart	1965	unreleased
	Now That Summer Is Here/		
	Prayer To An Angel	1982	Ambient Sound 02871
	Again	N/A	Collectables LP 5043
	It's Only A Paper Moon	N/A	Collectables LP 5043
	Let Me Steal Your Heart Away	N/A	Collectables LP 5043
	Over The Rainbow	N/A	Collectables LP 5043
MYSTICS (2)			
	Life To Go/Ballad Of Barbara		
	Allen	1959	Lee 1004
	Mash Potatoes With Me/The		
	Hoppy Hop	1962	King 5678
	Just For Your Love (I Would Do		
	Anything)/The Jumpin' Bean	1963	King 5735
	Fox/Dan	1963	Nolta 353
	Just A Loser/She Got Everything	1964	Constellation 138/Safice 333
	Didn't We Have A Good Time/		
	Now And For Always	1965	Dot 16862
	Ooh Poo Pah Doo	1966	Black Cat 501
	Teenage Sweetheart/		
	Rockin' Yodel	N/A	Chatam 350/351
	Get A Job/That's All	N/A	Jenny Lynn 101
	Steppin' Stones	N/A	Olympia 2131
	Ride My Pony/This Is What I		
	Was Made For	N/A	Ren-Vell 320
MYSTICS (2) (GENE FISHER & THE)			
	Remember (You're My Girl)/		
	Listen To Me	1962	Plateau 101
MYSTICS (3) (ED GATES & THE)			
	In The Jungle/Chewing Gum	1962	Robins Nest 2
MYSTICS (4)			
	That's The Kind Of Love/		
	I Really Love You	1964	Teako 370
NACKS (NICKY & THE)			
	The Night/That Old Black Magic	1962	Barry 108
	Love Is A Many Splendored		
	Thing (acapella)	1975	Relic LP 103
	A Lovely Way To Spend An		
	Evening (acapella)	1975	Relic LP 103
	White Cliffs Of Dover (acapella)	1975	Relic LP 104
	Good Good-Bye (acapella)	1975	Relic LP 105
	Linda/The ABC's Of Love	1977	Crystal Ball 103
NASH, MARVIN (& GROUP)			
	Say A Prayer For Me	N/A	Pharoah 1001
NASH, MARVIN (WITH THE CHEVELLES)			
	Darling/Dina	1961	Pharoah 115
NATIVE BOYS			
	Native Girl/It Won't Take Long	1954	Modern 939
	Strange Love/Cherrlyn	1956	Combo 113
	Tears/When I Met You	1956	Combo 115
	Laughing Love/Valley Of Lovers	1956	Combo 119
	Oh, Let Me Dream/I've Got A		
	Feeling	1956	Combo 120
NATURAL FACTS			
	What Time Is It/Girl Don't Cry	N/A	Lucky Lou 813
NATURALS (1)			
	You Give Me So Much/What A		
	Shape I'm In	1958	Beacon 462
	Don't Send Me Away/		
	The Mummy	1959	Era 1089
NATURALS (1) (AKA FOUR NATURALS)			
	Blue Moon/How Strange	1958	Red Top 113/Hunt 325 (58)
NATURALS (2) (JACK BAILEY & THE)			
	Oh What Love Is	1959	Ford 105
	Your Magic Touch/Tiger Lil	1959	Ford 113

Artist	Song	Year	Label
NATURALS (3) (YOLANDA & THE)			
	My Memories Of You/Jawbone	1962	Kimley 923
NATURALS (4)			
	Why Don't They Understand/		
	Just In Case You Change		
	Your Mind	1964	Chattahoochie 633
NEANDERTHALS (DAVE MEADOWS & THE)			
	Angel/I Don't See Stars In Your		
	Eyes	1960	Magnum 41160
NEEVETS			
	The Hum/You're Gonna Pay	1964	Reon 1303
NELSON, CHIP (& GROUP)			
	Honey For Sale	1960	Edsel 783
NELSON, VIKKI (BB THE WHEELS)			
	By My Side/Bright And Early	1956	Premium 402
NEONS (1)			
	Angel Face/Kiss Me Quickly	1956	Tetra 4444
	Road Of Romance/		
	My Chickadee	1957	Tetra 4449
	Golden Dreams/Angel Face	1960	Gone 5090
	Honey Bun/Golden Dreams	1974	Vintage 1016
NEONS (2)			
	My Lover/Tucson	1961	Waldon 1001
	Fat Girls/Magic Moment	1962	Challenge 9147
NEPTUNES			
	Fraidy Cat/As Long As	1957	Glory 269
	If You Care/She Went		
	That-A-Way	1958	Payson 101/102
	So Little Time/She'll Understand	1960	Checker 967
	This My Love/Curiosity Killed		
	The Cat	1961	RCA 7931
	Turn Around Girl/Girl, That's An		
	Awful Thing To Say	1963	Gem 100
	Make A Memory/House Of		
	Heartache	1963	Instant 3255
	A King Without A Crown/		
	I Met You	1964	Marlo 1534
	I'm Coming Home/I Don't Cry		
	Anymore	1964	Victoria 102
NEVILLE, AARON (& GROUP)			
	Show Me The Way/Get Out Of		
	My Life (no group)	1960	Minit 618
	I've Done It Again/For		
	Everybody There's A Girl	1967	Instant 3282
NEVILLE, ART (& GROUP)			
	My Dear Dearest Darling/		
	My Baby	1965	Cinderella 1400
	Little Liza Jane/My Dear		
	Dearest Darling	1965	Cinderella 1401
NEW EMAGE			
	Falling In Love/It's Summer	1985	Starlight 29
	All In The Game/Frankie And		
	Johnny	1987	Starlight 55
	It's Summer/Ain't No Sunshine	1987	Starlight 57
NEW GROUP (OTIS WILLIAMS & HIS) (REF CHARMS)			
	Miss The Love (I've Been		
	Dreaming Of)/Tell Me Now	1955	DeLuxe 6088
	Gumdrop/Save Me, Save Me	1956	DeLuxe 6090
	Too Late I Learned/That's		
	Your Mistake (by O.W. &		
	the Charms)	1956	DeLuxe 6091
NEW HOLLYWOOD ARGYLES (AKA HOLLYWOOD ARGYLES)			
	Alley Oop '66/Do The Funky		
	Foot	1966	Kammy 105
NEW INVICTAS			
	Deeply In Love With You/		
	She Wouldn't Quit	1962	Hale 500
NEW SILHOUETTES (AKA SILHOUETTES)			
	Climb Every Mountain/		
	We Belong Together	1967	Jamie 1333
	Not Me Baby/Gaucho Serenade	1968	Goodway 101
NEW YORKERS (1) (FB FRED PARRIS)			
	Miss Fine/Dream A Little Dream	1961	Wall 547
	Tears In My Eyes/A Little Bit	1961	Wall 548
NEW YORKERS (2)			
	You Should Have Told Me/		
	Don't Want To Be Your Fool	1964	Tac-Ful 101
NEW YORKERS (3)			
	I Know Why/Little Girl 5'3"	1963	Park Ave 100
NEW YORKERS 5			
	Gloria, My Darling/Cha Cha		
	Baby	1955	Danice 801

Artist	Song	Year	Label
NEWCOMERS (WADE FLEMONS & THE)			
	Here I Stand/My Baby Likes		
	To Rock	1958	Vee Jay 295
NEWLYWEDS			
	Love Walked Out/The Quarrel	1961	Homogenized Soul 601
NEWMARKS			
	Why/Goody Goody Gum Drop	1963	Chattahoochie 627
NEWPORTS (1) (AKA FALCONS (4))			
	Chicky Chop Chop/Hurry, Arthur		
	Murray (lead by Eddie Floyd)	1959	Contour 301
NEWPORTS (2) (CAL LINLEY & THE)			
	Mess Around/Can't Find A Girl	1960	DC 0431
NEWPORTS (3)			
	If I Could Tonight/A Fellow		
	Needs A Girl	1961	Kane 007/Guyden 2067 (62)
	Dixie Women/The Wonder		
	Of Love	1961	Kent 380
	Tears/Disillusioned Love	1964	Guyden 2116
NEWPORTS (4) (TYRONE & THE) (AKA NU PORTS)			
	I Feel Like A Million/On A		
	Saturday Night	1963	Darrow 5-20
NEWPORTS (5)			
	I Want You/The Trouble Is You	1965	Laurie 3327
NEWPORTS (6)			
	Hands/Wishing Star	1978	Image 501
NEWPORTS (7)			
	Dooly Bump/go To Sleep My		
	Little Girl	1977	Crystal Ball 108
	Looking For Love/The Night		
	We First Met	1978	Crystal Ball 113
	Jingle Bells/My Juanita	1978	Crystal Ball 129
	Denise/Your Way	1979	Crystal Ball 134
	Crazy For You/Gloria	1981	Crystal Ball 143
NEWPORTS (8)			
	I Dreamt I Dwelt In Heaven/		
	Look Into The Future	1993	Avenue D 18
	My Movie Queen/The Great		
	Pretender	1994	Avenue D 20
NEWTONES (1)			
	Going Steady/Remember The		
	Night	1959	Baton 260
NEWTONES (2) (AKA NUTONES (2))			
	Can't You See/I Remember		
	The Night	1965	Relic 1009
	Come On/We're Going Steady	1965	Relic 1010
NIC NACKS			
	Jolene/Since You Came	1963	Ovation 6201
NICHOL, JOEY (& GROUP)			
	Ashamed/Steady Love	1958	ABC 9951
NICHOLLS, DAVE (BB THE COINS)			
	Bells Will Ring/Time For Dreams	1961	Sparton 1062
NICKELS & THE THREE PENNIES (ED HENRY WITH THE)			
	I Love Only You/I Only Love		
	You (instrumental)	N/A	Nu Sound 180
NIGHT OWLS			
	Loop The Hoop/You Shouldn't		
	Oughta Don It	1957	NRC 015
	Bells Ring/Let's Go Again	1964	Bethlehem 3087
NIGHT OWLS (TONY ALLEN & THE)			
	I Found An Angel/I'm Dreamin'	1956	Dig 109
	Why In The World	1960	Crown LP 5231
	Dreamin'	1960	Crown LP 5231
	Home Wrecker	1960	Crown LP 5231
	Have Faith In Me	1960	Crown LP 5231
	Cute Thing	1960	Crown LP 5231
	Give Me A Chance	1960	Crown LP 5231
	Be My Love	1960	Crown LP 5231
	If I Had Aladdin's Lamp	1960	Crown LP 5231
	If Love Was Money	1960	Crown LP 5231
	Lover's Mountain	1960	Crown LP 5231
NIGHT RIDERS			
	Lookin' For My Baby/St. Lou	1959	Sue 719
	Talk To Me Baby/Night Ridin'	1960	Sue 731
NIGHT RIDERS (DOC STARKES & THE)			
	Women & Cadillacs/Say Hey	1954	Apollo 460
	Rags/Doctor Velvet	1954	Apollo 466
NIGHT RIDERS (JOHNNY FAIRCHILD & THE)			
	I Was A Fool/Please, Please,		
	Please	1959	Ace 565
NIGHT RIDERS (MEL SMITH & THE)			
	Pretty Plaid Skirt/I'll Never		
	Change	1959	Sue 713

Artist	Song	Year	Label	Artist	Song	Year	Label
NIGHT ROCKERS (FREDDIE HALL & THE)					I Sure Do Love You Baby/		
	Love And Affection/She Was				Honky Tonk Hardwood Floor	1958	Bullseye 1008
	My First Love	1959	CJ 610	**NITELITES (NICKIE & THE) (FB NICK MASSI)**			
NIGHT-RIDERS (AKA NIGHT RIDERS)					I'm Lonely/Tell Me You Care	1959	Brunswick 55155
	Big Game Hunter/Doin' The			**NO NAMES**			
	Cha Cha In Havana	1961	Dore 613		Love/Jam (instrumental)	1964	Guyden 2114
NIGHTBEATS				**NOBELLS (AKA ROBINS (4))**			
	Lonesome Road Rock/Cryin'				Searchin' For My Love/Crying		
	All Night	1958	Zoom 002		Over You	1962	Mar 101
NIGHTBEATS (ELRAY & THE)				**NOBLE, BEVERLY (& GROUP)**			
	My Secret	N/A	Revive 103		You Cheated/Why Must I Cry	1959	Sparrow 100
NIGHTCAPS				**NOBLEMEN (1)**			
	Darlin'/Mystery Train	1961	Vandan 7066		Sleep Beauty Sleep/		
NIGHTHAWKS (1)					He Won't Tell	1963	USA 1215
	All'A Your Love/When Sin Stops	1958	Hamilton 50006	**NOBLEMEN (2)**			
NIGHTHAWKS (2) (B. GUITAR & THE)					On The Other Side Of The		
	Here Comes Night/You				World/I Just Want To Know	N/A	Clarity 106
	Should Have Loved Her More	1958	Decca 30634	**NOBLEMEN (2) (AKA NOBLEMEN 4)**			
NIGHTHAWKS (3) (JOHNNY GOSEY & THE)					Everytime/All The Love I Got	N/A	Clarity 103
	Fools Will Take Chances/			**NOBLEMEN 4 (AKA NOBLEMEN (2))**			
	I Lost My Baby	N/A	MOA 1001		What's Your Name/Get Out Of		
NIGHTINGALES					My Life Woman	N/A	Recap 291
	Love In Return/Private Party	1961	Ray Star 784		I Can Hear Raindrops/Hang It		
NIGHTRIDERS (AKA NITE RIDERS)					In Your Ear	N/A	Recap 292
	Never/Tell The Truth	1956	Sound 128	**NOBLES (1)**			
NIGHTWINDS (FRANK & JACK & THE)					Do You Love Me/Who's Been		
	Oh My Darling/Pretty Betty Jean	1958	Felsted 8539		Riding My Mule	1958	Sapphire 1051
NIPTONES (NIPPY HAWKINS & THE)				**NOBLES (1) (NICKY & THE)**			
	Angie/It's Gonna Be Too Late	1965	Lorraine 100		Poor Rock 'N' Roll/Ting-A-Ling	1957	Klik 305/Times Square 1
NITE LITERS							(62)/Lost Nite 153
	Jealous Heart/Nervous	1962	Verve 10256		Schoolhouse Rock/A Way To		
NITE RIDERS					Tell Her	1958	End 1021
	When A Man Cries/Waiting				School Bells/School Day Crush	1958	Gone 5039/End 1098
	In The Schoolroom	1958	Teen 120				(61)/Times Square 37
NITE RIDERS (AKA NIGHTRIDERS)							(64)/Relic 544 (66)
	Starlight And You/I Know				Crime Don't Pay/Darkness	1962	Times Square 12
	You're In There	1958	Teen 116		Why Be A Fool/The Search	1963	Times Square 33
	Got Me A Six Button Benny/				Oh Baby/My Confession		
	Don't Hang Up The Phone	1958	Teen 118		(by the Blue Dots)	1976	Robin Hood 136
NITE RIDERS (DOC STARKES & THE)				**NOBLES (2) (AKA TIMBERS (2))**			
	Apple Cider/Six Button Benny	1958	Swan 4003		Till The End Of Time/Standing		
	Apple Cider/Way In The				Alone	1958	ABC 9984
	Middle Of A Dream	1958	Teen 114		Oops Oh Lawdy/Stop Crying	1958	Tee Gee 101
	Keep It A Secret	1989	Relic LP 5078		Just For Me/To Me	1959	ABC 10012
NITE RIDERS (MELVIN SMITH & THE)				**NOBLES (3) (FB SOLLIE MCELROY)**			
	Ugly George/Nobodys Fault	1962	Chime 101		Serenade/You Ain't Right	1962	Stacy 926
NITE SOUNDS				**NOBLES (4) (AKI ALEONG & THE)**			
	Cheese Cake/I Love You				Without Your Love/Tradewinds		
	With Tender Passion	1962	Fortune 548		Tradewinds	1961	Reprise 20021
	Harem Girl/The Roll	1962	Fortune 552		Body Surf/Mary Ann	1963	Vee Jay 520
	Get Clean/On Broadway	1962	Seafair 112	**NOBLETONES**			
NITE SOUNDS (MELVIN DAVIS WITH THE DIABLOS & THE)					Who Cares About Love/		
	Playboy (Don't You Play In				Cha-Lyp-So Baby	1958	C&M 182/Times Square
	School) (with the Diablos)/						18 (63)
	I Won't Be Your Fool	1962	Fortune 551		I'm Really Too Young/I Love		
NITE-LITERS					You	1958	C&M 183/Times Square 17
	Fat Sally/Parents Keep-A						(63)/Relic 529 (65)
	Preachin'	1960	Sudden 101		I'm Really Crying/Mambo		
NITE-LITES					Boogie	1958	C&M 188/C&M 438
	I Get Blue/Lover's Twist	1962	Sequoia 502		Who Cares About Love/		
NITEBEATERS					Cha-Lypso	1973	Bim Bam Boom 118
	Dream Lover	N/A	Carib 1010		I Still Love You/Rock And Roll		
NITEBEATS					Nursery Rhymes	1973	Vintage 1014
	Teen-Age Lover	1959	Peach 718	**NOCTURNES**			
NITECAPS					I Fell For You	N/A	Sensation 22
	A Kiss And A Vow/Be My Girl	1955	Groove 0134	**NOLAN, MISS FRANKIE (BB NINO & THE EBBTIDES)**			
	Tough Mama/Sweet Thing	1956	Groove 0147		A Week From Sunday/		
	Bamboo Rock & Roll/You May				Say No More	1961	Madison 151
	Not Know	1956	Groove 0158	**NOLAN, MISS FRANKIE (BB THE FOUR SEASONS)**			
	In Each Corner Of My Heart/				I Still Care/(I Wish It Were)		
	Let Me Know Tonight	1956	Groove 0176		Summer All Year Round	1961	ABC 10231
	Wine Wine Wine/Nightcap Rock	1960	Vandan 7491	**NOMADS (1)**			
	24 Hours/No Parking	1961	Vandan 3587		The Perfect Crime/Paris After		
	Next Time You See Me	1966	Vandan 4280		Dark	1958	Balboa 006/Josie 851 (58)
	Wine Wine Wine/Walking The				Desert Tramp/Bounty Hunter	1961	Rust 5028
	Dog	1966	Vandan 4733		Tell It Like It Is/Rainbow's End	1963	Josie 905
	You're Gonna Be Sorry	N/A	Detour LP 33-010	**NOMADS (2)**			
	Oh, You Sweet Girl	N/A	Detour LP 33-010		You're The Only One/Heart		
	Snap Crackle & Pop	N/A	Detour LP 33-010		Attack	1959	Northern 503
NITECAPS (CLYDE STACY & THE)				**NOMADS (3) (BEN ATKINS & THE)**			
	Hoy Hoy/So Young	1957	Candlelight 1015		Love Is A Beautiful Thing	N/A	Goldwax 336

Artist / Song	Year	Label
NORMAN, ZACK (& GROUP)		
Hey Doll/Givin' Up Love	1957	Poplar 111
NORMANAIRES		
My Greatest Sin/Wrap It Up	1953	MGM 11622
NORNETTS		
Happy Boy/Pappa Knew	1964	Wand 153
NORTHERN LIGHTS		
All Alone	1959	Patt 058
Please Love Me Now	1960	Patt 059
NORTONES		
Susie Jones/That's The Way		
The Cookie Crumbles	1959	Warner Bros. 5065
Smile, Just Smile/Boy	1959	Warner Bros. 5115
Cookie Man/I'm Gonna Find You	1960	Stack 502
NORVELLS		
Greasy Kid Stuff/As I Walk Alone	1963	Checker 1037
Without You	N/A	Janis 6366
NOTABLES		
Moonlight And Roses/Under		
The Bridges Of Paris	1958	Big Top 3001
Surfside/Lisa Maree	1963	Big Top 3141
NOTATIONS		
Chapel Doors/What A Night		
For Love	1980	Jason Scott 9
NOTATIONS (1)		
What A Night For Love/		
Chapel Doors	1958	Wonder 100
NOTATIONS (2) (AUGIE RIOS & THE)		
I've Got A Girl/There's A Girl		
Down The Way	1963	Shelley 181
NOTATIONS (3)		
Danny Boy/You Can Run	1965	Relic 1019
Kentucky Babe (a capella)	1975	Relic LP 104
For Your Precious Love		
(a capella)	1975	Relic LP 104
Lost Love (a capella)	1975	Relic LP 104
Hang On Sloopy (a capella)	1975	Relic LP 105
When I Fell In Love (a capella)	1975	Relic LP 105
My Foolish Heart (a capella)	1975	Relic LP 108
Peace Of Mind (a capella)	1975	Relic LP 109
NOTE MAKERS		
It Hurts To Wonder/Do I Have		
A Chance	1958	Sotoplay 007
NOTE-TORIALS		
My Valerie/Loved And Lost	1959	Sunbeam 119
NOTEMAKERS		
Take Me As I Am/Sally,		
The Cosmetic Queen	1976	Monogram 118
NOTES (1) (AKA FIVE NOTES (2))		
Don't Leave Me Now/		
Cha Jezebel	1956	Capitol 3332
Trust In Me/Round And Round	1956	MGM 12338
One More Time	1956	MGM 12421
NOTES (2) (REED HARPER & THE)		
I Miss You So/Sweetheart Of		
The Prom	1958	Vik 0328/Smart 1001 (58)
Three Charms/It's Worth		
Remembering	1960	Luck 105
NOTES (3)		
Little Girl/G.I. Blues	1959	Sarg 177
NOTES (4) (BEBO SINGLETON & THE)		
The Shrine Of The Echo/		
Feeny Jones	1960	Stentor 101
NOVAIRS (CARL BELL & THE)		
Birth Of The Beat/Open House		
In Your Heart	1958	Laurie 3014
NOVAS (LITTLE TED & THE)		
All Your Lovin'/Baby Baby Baby	N/A	Kay-Gee 440/Kay-Gee 1068
NOW & THEN		
He's Gone/Since I've Lost You	1981	Clifton 65
NU LUVS		
Baby You Belong To Me/		
Hello Lover	1965	Clock 2003
NU PORTS (TYRONE & THE) (AKA NEWPORTS)		
Feel Like A Million/On A		
Saturday Night	1963	Darrow 5-20
The Combination/Look At		
Her Eyes	1963	Darrow 71/72
NU-TONES (1)		
Sharon Lee/Feel In Love For		
The Very First Time	1961	Cha Cha 716

Artist / Song	Year	Label
NU-TONES (2)		
Teen-Age Heart/Guitar Shuffle	1959	Spin Time 1001
NU-TONES (3)		
I Never Dreamed	1958	20th Century 75030
NU-TRONS		
Searchin'	N/A	Eldee 85
NUGGETS		
Curl Up In My Arms/So Help		
Me I Love You	1954	Capitol 2989
Shtiggy Boom/Anxious Love	1955	Capitol 3052
Before We Say Goodnight/		
Angel On The Dance Floor	1961	RCA 7930
Just A Friend/Cat Snapper	1962	RCA 8031
Whisper/Wish She Were Mine	1973	Vintage 1003
NUMBERS		
Big Red/My Pillow	1962	Bonneville 101/Dore 641 (62)
NUNN, BOBBY (BB THE ROBINS)		
Mainliner/Saturday Night Daddy		
(by Little Esther)	1952	Federal 12100
NUNN, BOBBY (WITH THE ROBINS & LITTLE ESTHER)		
You Took My Love Too Fast/		
Street Lights	1953	Federal 12122
NUNN, DOLLY (& GROUP)		
Why Do Fools Fall In Love	N/A	Worthmore EP 183
NUTMEGS (AKA RAJAHS/AKA LYRES)		
Story Untold/Make Me Lose		
My Mind	1955	Herald 452
Ship Of Love/Rock Me,		
Squeeze Me	1955	Herald 459
Whispering Sorrows/Betty Lou	1955	Herald 466
The Joker	1956	Herald (unreleased)
Key To The Kingdom		
(Of Your Heart)/Gift O'		
Gabbin' Women	1956	Herald 475
A Love So True/Comin' Home	1956	Herald 492
My Story/My Sweetest Dream	1959	Herald 538
A Dream Of Love/Someone,		
Somewhere (Help Me)	1960	Tel 1014
Crazy 'Bout You/Rip Van Winkle	1962	Herald 574
The Way Love Should Be/		
Wide Hoop Skirts	1963	Times Square 14/Relic 533 (65)
Down To Earth/Coo Coo		
Cuddle Coo (Admirations)	1963	Times Square 19/ Candlelite 434
Why Must We Go To School?/		
Ink Dries Quicker Than		
Tears (by the Volumes)	1963	Times Square 22/Relic 535 (65)
Down In Mexico/My Sweet		
Dreams	1963	Times Square 27/Relic 528 (65)
Let Me Tell You/Hello	1963	Times Square 6/Relic 531 (65)
You're Crying/Wa-Do-Wa	1964	Times Square 103
Shifting Sands/Out Of My Heart	1965	Relic 1006
Help Me	1971	Relic LP 5002
I Like To Cha Cha	1971	Relic LP 5002
Story Untold '72/Tell Me	1972	Baby Grand 800
Shifting Sands/Take Me And		
Make Me Yours	1973	Night Train 905
Come Down To Earth (same		
as "Down To Earth")	N/A	Herald (unreleased)
NUTONES (1)		
Goddess Of Love/Niki Niki		
Mambo	1955	Hollywood Star 797
Believe/Annie Kicked The		
Bucket	1955	Hollywood Star 798
Believe/You're No Barking Dog	1955	Hollywood Star 798
At Midnight/Beans 'N' Greens	1956	Combo 127
NUTONES (2) (AKA NEWTONES (2))		
I Remember The Nite/		
Can't You See	1965	Relic 1009
We're Going Steady/Come On	1965	Relic 1010
NUTONES (3)		
Love Me All The Time/Time		
And Again	1963	Dart 135
NUTONES (4) (TERRY DALY & THE)		
Why Did This Happen/You		
Don't Bug Me	1958	Mark 122
NUTRENDS		
Together/Spooksville	1963	Lawn 216

Artist Song	Year	Label
O'HENRY, LENNY (BB THE FOUR SEASONS)		
The Touch Of You/Goin' To A Party	1961	ABC 10272
OASIS		
When I Woke Up This Morning/ My Imagination	1978	Arcade 105
There Goes My Love/Never	1979	Story Untold 502
OBERLE, SCOTT (& GROUP)		
Cupid's Poison Dart/You're My Dream Girl	1964	Lawn 216
OBJECTIVES		
Oh My Love/Love Went Away	1965	Jewel 751
OBSESSIONS		
Love Always/A Fool	1964	Accent 1182
OCAPELLOS		
The Stars/Anytime	1965	General 107/Checker 1144 (66)
OCTAVES		
Mambo Carolyn/You're Too Young	1958	Val 1001
OCTOBERS		
Stop It Little Girl/I Should'A Listened To Mama	1963	Chairman 4402
OFF BEATS		
Doodlum/Have Love Will Travel	1964	Guyden 2101
OFF KEYS		
Our Wedding Day/Singing Bells	1962	Rowe 003/Technicord 1001 (62)
OFF KEYS (JERRY EVANS & THE)		
Oh Little Girl/You Are	1962	Rowe 002
OFFBEATS (HAROLD L & THE)		
Connie/Three Years	1961	Happy Hearts 124
OFFBEATS (JIMMY DEE & THE)		
You're Late Miss Kate/Here I Come	1958	Dot 15721
I Feel Like Rockin'/Rock Tick Tock	1959	TNT 161
You Say You Beat Me To The Punch (answer record)/I've Got A Secret	1963	Cutie 1400
OFFBEATS WITH THE MONTCLAIRS (JIMMY DEE & THE)		
Don't Cry No More/Henrietta (no group)	1957	TNT 148/Dot 15664 (57)
OFFITT, LILLIAN (& GROUP)		
Can't Go On/Darling Please Don't Change	1958	Excello 2139
OHIO UNTOUCHABLES (AKA FALCONS (4))		
She's My Heart's Desire/ What To Do	1962	Lu Pine 1009/Lu Pine 109 (62)
I'm Tired/Up Town (instrumental)	1962	Lu Pine 1011/Lu Pine 116/ 117 (64)
Love Is Amazing/Forgive Me Darling	1962	Lu Pine 110/Lu Pine 1010 (62)
OLENN, JOHNNY (BB THE BLOCKBUSTERS)		
Teenie/Devil Darling	1959	Personality 1002
OLIVER, BIG DANNY (& GROUP)		
Sapphire/I Wanna Go Steady	1958	Trend 012X/Kapp 941
OLIVER, JOHNNY (& GROUP)		
I Must Have Love/Lemonade Baby	1954	MGM 55001
Darling, Is It True?/My Love Lady	1955	MGM 55012
I Need You So/The Things I Might Have Been	1956	MGM 12319
OLYMPICS		
Western Movies/Well	1958	Demon 1508
Dance With The Teacher/ Ev'rybody Needs Love	1958	Demon 1512
(Baby) Hully Gully/Private Eye	1959	Arvee 562
Chicken/Your Love	1959	Demon 1514
I Wish I Could Shimmy Like My Sister Kate/Workin' Hard	1960	Arvee 5006
Dance By The Light Of The Moon/Dodge City	1960	Arvee 5020
Big Boy Pete/The Slop	1960	Arvee 595
Stay Away From Joe	1960	Arvee LP A-423
Boo-Dee Green	1960	Arvee LP A-423
Little Pedro/Bull Fight (instrumental)	1961	Arvee 5023
Dooley/Stay Where You Are	1961	Arvee 5031
The Stomp/Mash Them 'Taters	1961	Arvee 5044
Big Boy Pete '65/Stay Where You Are	1961	Arvee 6501/Everest

Artist Song	Year	Label
Just Like That	1961	Arvee LP A-424
Chicken/Cool Short	1961	Titan 1718
Twist/Everybody Likes To Cha Cha Cha	1962	Arvee 5051
The Scotch/Baby It's Hot	1962	Arvee 5056
What'd I Say Pt. 1/What'd I Say Pt. 2	1962	Arvee 5073
The Boogler Pt. 1/ The Boogler Pt. 2	1962	Duo Disc 104
Return Of Big Boy Pete/Return Of The Watusi	1962	Duo Disc 105
The Bounce/Fireworks	1963	Tri Disc 106
Dancin' Holiday/Do The Slauson Shuffle	1963	Tri Disc 107
Bounce Again/A New Dancin' Partner	1963	Tri Disc 110
The Broken Hip/So Goodbye	1963	Tri Disc 112
I'm Comin' Home/Rainin' In My Heart	1964	Loma 2010
Good Lovin'/Olympic Shuffle (instrumental)	1965	Loma 2013
Baby I'm Yours/No More Will I Cry	1965	Loma 2017
We Go Together (Pretty Baby)/ Secret Agents	1965	Mirwood 5504
Mine Exclusively/Secret Agents	1966	Mirwood 5513
Baby Do The Philly Dog/ Western Movies	1966	Mirwood 5523
The Duck/The Bounce	1966	Mirwood 5525
We Go Together	1966	Mirwood LP 7003
Pretty Baby	1966	Mirwood LP 7003
Mine Exclusively	1966	Mirwood LP 7003
I'll Do A Little Bit More/ The Same Old Thing	1967	Mirwood 5529
Hully Gully/Big Boy Pete	1967	Mirwood 5533
Lookin' For A Love/Good Things	1968	Parkway 6003
The Cartoon Song/Things That Made Me Laugh	1969	Jubilee 5674
Please Please Please/Girl, You're My Kind Of People	1969	Warner Bros. 7369
I'll Never Fall In Love/Time After Time (by the Vibrations)	1977	Robin Hood 151
OMEGAS		
Crazy Bones/Razzamatazz	1959	Chord 1305
When You Touch Me/Froze	1959	Decca 31008
Study Hall/(So How Come) No One Loves You	1960	Decca 31094
No One Will Ever Know/ Falling In Love	1960	Decca 31138
Midnight Run/I Wanna Go Home	1961	Groove G-4
ONE, BOBBY (& GROUP)		
Undecided/Hummingbird	1959	NRC 021
ONE-O-TWO'S (102'S) (SKIP & THE)		
Gotta Pay The Price	1963	KayBee 106
ONTARIOS		
Memories Of You/Lovers' Mambo	1965	Big Town 121/Firefly 324 (74)
It's Wrong/Is This The Real Thing (by the Warblers)	1973	Baron 101
I Really Had A Ball/Sorry (by the Clefs)	1973	Baron 104
Love Me Baby/Scheming (by the Warblers)	1973	Baron 106
I'll Drink A Toast/I'm Gonna Move	1974	Firefly 323
OPALS (1) (AKA CRYSTALS (1))		
My Heart's Desire/Oh, But She Did	1954	Apollo 462
Come To Me, Darling/ Squeeze Me, Baby	1954	Luna 100/101
OPALS (2) (FEMALE)		
Love/Hop, Skip And Jump	1962	Beltone 2025
OPALS (3)		
No, No, Never Again/Just Like A Little Bitty Baby	1965	Laurie 3288
OPPOSITES		
Karen/Ding Dong	1962	Columbia 42641
ORBITS (1)		
Message Of Love/I Really Do	1956	Flair-X 5000
Who Are You?/Mr. Hard Luck	1957	Argo 5286
Knock Her Down/My Love	1959	Nu Kat 116/117
Tell Me Baby/Two Crazy Scientists	N/A	Dooto 601

Artist	Song	Year	Label
ORBITS (2) (BOBBY & THE)			
	Felicia/Bandstand Dance	1959	Seeco 6005/Seeco 6067 (61)
	Teenage Love/What Do I Say (When I'm Close To You)	1959	Seeco 6030
	Your Cheatin' Heart/I Don't Stand A Chance	1962	Gone 5126
ORBITS (2) (BOBBY GRAYSON & HIS)			
	I'll Follow You/Look Over Here Girl	1963	Jamco 105
ORBITS (2) (FB LANI ZEE)			
	Funny, Funny, Funny/Sea Tides	1961	Seeco 6074
ORBITS (3) (J. LYNDON & THE)			
	My One Desire/Bill Bailey	N/A	Whiteley 4282
ORBITS (4)			
	I Need You/I'm Home	N/A	Don-J 48798
ORBITS (5)			
	My Rosa-Lee	N/A	Friddell 102
ORBITS (6)			
	Queen Bee	N/A	Space 1116
ORCHIDS (1)			
	Oh Why?/All Night Long	1953	King 4661
	I've Been A Fool From The Start/Beginning To Miss You	1953	King 4663
ORCHIDS (2) (AKA EARLS (1)/REF FIVE THRILLS)			
	You're Everything To Me/ Newly Wed	1955	Parrot 815
	I Can't Refuse/You Said You Loved Me	1955	Parrot 819
ORCHIDS (3)			
	My Story/Is It True	N/A	Savoy 964 (unreleased)
ORCHIDS (4)			
	Soft Shadows/Good Gully	1961	Wall 549
ORCHIDS (5) (FEMALE)			
	I Don't Think You Missed Me/ We're In Love	1962	Harlow 101
	That Boy Is Messin' Up My Mind/The Harlem Tango	1964	Columbia 42913
ORCHIDS (6) (DICK BARDI & THE)			
	Stormy Weather/The Hard Way	N/A	Maestro 409/410
ORDELLS			
	Sippin' A Cup Of Coffee/ Big Dom	N/A	Dionn 505
ORIENTALS			
	Get Yourself To School/ Please Come Back Home	1958	Kayo 927
	Misty Summer Night/Soul Ain't You Thrilled	N/A	New Dawn 413
ORIENTS			
	Queen Of Angels/Shouldn't I?	1964	Laurie 3232
ORIGINAL CADILLACS (AKA CADILLACS)			
	Lucy/Hurry Home	1957	Josie 821
	I'll Never Let You Go/The Wayward Wanderer	1964	Josie 915
ORIGINAL CADILLACS (EARL CARROLL & THE) (AKA CADILLACS)			
	Buzz-Buzz-Buzz/Yea, Yea, Baby	1958	Josie 829
ORIGINAL CASUALS (AKA CASUALS (1))			
	So Tough/I Love My Darling	1958	Back Beat 503 (second pressing, first is by Casuals)
	Ju-Judy/Don't Pass Me By	1958	Back Beat 510
	Three Kisses Past Midnight/ It's Been A Long Time	1958	Back Beat 514
ORIGINAL CHARMERS			
	For Sentimental Reasons/ Bashful Boy	1960	Angle Tone 550
	Fools Rush In/Someday You'll Want Me	1972	Blue Sky 102
ORIGINAL CHECKERS			
	Love Wasn't There/Over The Rainbow	1962	King 5592
ORIGINAL DRIFTERS (BILL PINKNEY & THE) (REF DRIFTERS)			
	Don't Call Me/Do The Jerk	1964	Fontana 1956
ORIGINAL DRIFTERS (REF DRIFTERS)			
	The Masquerade Is Over/ I Found Some Lovin'	1967	Veep 1264
	Old Man River/Millionaire	1971	Game 394
ORIGINAL EMOTIONS (AKA EMOTIONS (1))			
	You're A Better Man Than I/ Are You Real	N/A	Johnson 746
ORIGINAL FOUR ACES (AKA FOUR ACES)			
	I Can See An Angel/You Were My First Affair	1954	Big Town 112/ Big Town 118 (55)
ORIGINAL JAGUARS			
	Our Young Love/Making Love Girl	N/A	Val-Vo 110
ORIGINAL MUSTANGS (DOLORES CURRY & THE)			
	Oh Baby/Jump Lula	1959	Hi-Q 5040
ORIGINAL PYRAMIDS (AKA PYRAMIDS (3))			
	Ankle Bracelet/Hot Dog Dooly Wah	1961	Shell 304
ORIGINAL RHYTHM ROCKERS			
	Madness/Oh! Oh! Honey	1959	Gone 5073
ORIGINAL THREE FRIENDS (JOEY & THE)			
	Blanche/The Oriental	1963	Chevron 500
ORIGINALS (1)			
	Anna/Sleepless Nights	1959	Jackpot 48012
ORIGINALS (10)			
	Dreams Can Come True/ Dressin' Up	1988	Starlight 64
	I Was Such A Fool/You'll Never Walk Alone	1990	Starlight 72
ORIGINALS (2) (TONY ALLEN & THE)			
	Let Me Hear You Say Yeah/ Wishing Star	1960	Original Sound 10
	Little Lonely Girl/I Still Love You	1960	Original Sound 13
ORIGINALS (3) (ROSIE & THE)			
	A Kiss From Your Lips/Let Me Be Your Girl	1960	Brunswick 55171
	Angel Baby/Give Me Love	1960	Highland 1011
	Lonely Blue Nights/We'll Have A Chance	1961	Brunswick 55205/ Highland 1031 (61)
	My Darlin' Forever/The Time Is Near (Rosie)	1961	Brunswick 55213
	Angel From Above/Why Did You Leave Me?	1961	Highland 1025
ORIGINALS (4)			
	Lend Me Your Ear/Bandstand Sound	1960	Poor Boy 110
ORIGINALS (5) (FB LONNIE NYE)			
	Careless With Love/I Gotta Know	1960	Lo-Lon 101
ORIGINALS (6)			
	At Times Like This/Gimme A Little Kiss, Will Ya Huh	1961	Diamond 102
	You And I/Summer School	1962	Diamond 116
ORIGINALS (7) (BILL PINKNEY & THE)			
	The Masquerade Is Over/ I Found Some Lovin'	1967	Veep 1264
ORIGINALS (8)			
	Old Enough To Break A Heart	N/A	Van 04166
ORIGINALS (9) (RACHAEL & THE)			
	I'll Always Remember/ The Sound	1962	Night Star 010
ORIGINELLS 4			
	I Can Make You Mine/ Four Nights	1965	Apt 25074
ORIOLES (FEATURING BOBBY THOMAS			
	Don't Make It A Sad Holiday/ Danny Boy	1992	Clifton 105
ORIOLES (SONNY TIL & THE)			
	It's Too Soon To Know/ Barbra Lee	1948	It's A Natural 5000/ Jubilee 5000 (48)
	Exactly Like You	1948	Jubilee (unreleased)
	Two Party Line	1948	Jubilee (unreleased)
	Lazy River Rolls By	1948	Jubilee (unreleased)
	I'm Losing Something I N ever had	1948	Jubilee (unreleased)
	To Be With You/Dare To Dream	1948	Jubilee 5001
	(It's Gonna Be A) Lonely Christmas/To Be With You	1948	Jubilee 5001
	Please Give My Heart A Break/It Seems So Long Ago	1949	Jubilee 5002
	Tell Me So/Deacon Jones	1949	Jubilee 5005
	I Challenge Your Kiss/ Donkey Serenade	1949	Jubilee 5008
	A Kiss And A Rose/It's A Cold Summer	1949	Jubilee 5009
	Forgive And Forget/So Much	1949	Jubilee 5016
	What Are You Doing New Year's Eve/(It's Gonna Be A) Lonely Christmas	1949	Jubilee 5017
	If It's To Be	1950	Jubilee (unreleased)

Artist Song	Year	Label
Would You Still Be The One In My Heart/Is My Heart Wasting Time	1950	Jubilee 5018
At Night/Every Dog-Gone Time	1950	Jubilee 5025
Moonlight/I Wonder When?	1950	Jubilee 5026
You're Gone/Everything They Said Came True	1950	Jubilee 5028
I'd Rather Have You Under The Moon/We're Supposed To Be Through	1950	Jubilee 5031
I Need You So/Goodnight Irene	1950	Jubilee 5037
I Crossed My Fingers/Can't Seem To Laugh Anymore	1950	Jubilee 5040
Oh Holy Night/The Lord's Prayer	1950	Jubilee 5045
This I'll Do My Darling	1951	Jubilee (unreleased)
I Miss You So/You Are My First Love	1951	Jubilee 5051
Pal Of Mine/Happy Go Lucky Local Blues	1951	Jubilee 5055
When You're A Long Long Way Away From Home/ Would I Love You (Love You, Love You)	1951	Jubilee 5057
My Prayer/I Never Knew	1951	Jubilee 5060
I'm Just A Fool In Love/Hold Me, Squeeze Me (Hold Me Tight)	1951	Jubilee 5061
Baby, Please Don't Go/Don't Tell Her What's Happened To Me	1951	Jubilee 5065
Yes Indeed	1952	Jubilee (unreleased)
Baby, I Love You So	1952	Jubilee (unreleased)
It Ain't Gonna Be Like That	1952	Jubilee (unreleased)
A Scandal	1952	Jubilee (unreleased)
How Blind Can You Be/ When You're Not Around	1952	Jubilee 5071
Trust In Me/Shrimp Boats	1952	Jubilee 5074
Proud Of You/You Never Cared For Me	1952	Jubilee 5076
Waiting/It's All Over Because We're Through	1952	Jubilee 5082
Barfly/Getting Tired, Tired, Tired	1952	Jubilee 5084
See See Rider/Don't Cry, Baby	1952	Jubilee 5092
You Belong To Me/I Don't Want To Take A Chance	1952	Jubilee 5102
Till Then/I Miss You So	1953	Jubilee 5107
Teardrops On My Pillow/ Hold Me, Thrill Me, Kiss Me	1953	Jubilee 5108
Dem Days (Are Gone Forever)/ Bad Little Girl	1953	Jubilee 5115
I Cover The Waterfront/One More Time	1953	Jubilee 5120
Crying In The Chapel/Don't You Think I Ought To Know	1953	Jubilee 5122/Lana 109 (64)
Write And Tell Me Why/In The Mission Of St. Augustine	1953	Jubilee 5127
Robe Of Calvary/There's No One But You	1953	Jubilee 5134
Don't Go To Strangers/Secret Love	1954	Jubilee 5137
Maybe You'll Be There/ Drowning Every Hope I Ever Had	1954	Jubilee 5143
In The Chapel In The Moonlight/ Thank The Lord, Thank The Lord	1954	Jubilee 5154
Longing/If You Believe	1954	Jubilee 5161
Count Your Blessings (Instead Of Sheep)/Runaround	1954	Jubilee 5172
Sure Fire	1955	Jubilee (unreleased)
Don't Cry	1955	Jubilee (unreleased)
I Love You Mostly/Fair Exchange	1955	Jubilee 5177
I Need You Baby/That's When the Good Lord Will Smile	1955	Jubilee 5189
Please Sing My Blues Tonight/ Moody Over You	1955	Jubilee 5221
Don't Go To Strangers/Angel	1956	Jubilee 5231
Happy Till The Letter/I Just Got Lucky	1956	Vee Jay 196
For All We Know/Never Leave Me Baby	1956	Vee Jay 228

Artist Song	Year	Label
Sugar Baby/Didn't I Say	1957	Abner 1016/Vee Jay 244 (57)
Tell Me So/At Night (with chorus)	1959	Jubilee 5363
The First Of Summer/Come On Home (with the Helen Way Singers)	1959	Jubilee 5384
Crying In The Chapel/Forgive And Forget (with chorus)	1959	Jubilee 6001
Live It Up	1960	Vee Jay LP 1021
Secret Love/Wobble	1962	Charlie Parker 211
In The Chapel In The Moonlight/Hey! Little Woman	1962	Charlie Parker 212
Back To The Chapel Again/ Lonely Christmas	1962	Charlie Parker 213
What Are You Doing New Year's Eve/Don't Mess Around With My Love	1962	Charlie Parker 214
It's Too Soon To Know/ I Miss You So	1962	Charlie Parker 215
I Miss You So/Hey! Little Woman	1962	Charlie Parker 219
Write And Tell Me Why/Don't Tell Her What Happened To Me	1963	Charlie Parker 216
What Are You Doing New Year's Eve/Crying In The Chapel	1964	Lana 109
Walking By The River	1983	Murray Hill LP M61277
Feeling Low	1983	Murray Hill LP M61277
I Promise You	1983	Murray Hill LP M61277
Wanted	1983	Murray Hill LP M61277
I'm Beginning To Think You Care For Me	1983	Murray Hill LP M61277
Why Did You Go	1983	Murray Hill LP M61277
Pretty, Pretty Rain	1983	Murray Hill LP M61277
Once Upon A Time	1983	Murray Hill LP M61277
Don't Keep It To Yourself	1983	Murray Hill LP M61277
Don't Stop	1983	Murray Hill LP M61277
Good Looking Baby	1983	Murray Hill LP M61277
My Baby's Gonna Get It	1983	Murray Hill LP M61277
Along About Sundown	1983	Murray Hill LP M61277
Blame It On Yourself	1983	Murray Hill LP M61277
I May Be Wrong	1983	Murray Hill LP M61277
My Loved One	1983	Murray Hill LP M61277
Bring The Money Home	1983	Murray Hill LP M61277
I Had To Leave Town	1983	Murray Hill LP M61277
Cigareetos	1983	Murray Hill LP M61277
What Happened To You	N/A	Collectables LP 5014

ORIOLES (SONNY TIL & THE) (BB THE SID BASS ORCHESTRA)
If You Believe/Laughing	1954	Jubilee 5161

ORLANDO, TONY (& GROUP)
Ding Dong/You And Only You	1959	Milo 101

ORLANDOS
Old MacDonald/Cloudburst	1957	Cindy 3006

ORLONS
I'll Be True/Heart Darling Angel	1961	Cameo 198
Mr. Twenty One/Please Let It Be Me	1962	Cameo 211

ORO, EMMY (& GROUP)
Is It A Sin/Some Of These Days	1962	Chelsea 1005

OSBURN, BOBBY (& GROUP)
My Heart's Been Broken/ Susie-Q	1964	Arlen 747

OSPREYS
Do You Wanna Jump Children/ It's Good To Me (You Don't Know And I Don't Know)	1957	East West 110

OUR GANG
What Kind Of Fool Am I/ The Lady Is A Tramp	N/A	Starlight 4

OUTCASTS (MAC BOSWELL & THE)
Rang Dang Do Lally/ I Thought You Knew	1960	Wonder 117

OVATIONS (1)
Whole Wide World/My Lullabye	1960	Andie 5017
The Day We Fell In Love/ My Lullabye	1961	Barry 101
Oh What A Day (same song as Day We Fell In Love)/ Real True Love	1961	Epic 9470

OVATIONS (2)
I Don't Wanna Cry/Loneliness Never Entered My Mind	1963	Capitol 5082

OVATIONS (3)
Remembering/Who Needs Love	1964	Josie 916

Artist Song	Year	Label
OVATIONS (4)		
Runaround/I Still Love You	1964	Hawk 153
OVATIONS (5)		
She's My Angel/Laura	1986	Starlight 43
Let's Make Love Tonight/ Pledging My Love	1986	Starlight 45
The Bells Of Rosa Rita/If You Want To	1988	Starlight 59
OVERONS (REF MYSTICS (1))		
The Bells Are Ringing	1958	unreleased
Prayer To An Angel	1958	unreleased
Why Do You Pretend	1958	unreleased
Big Brown Eyes	1958	unreleased
OVERTONES		
I Can't Fall In Love/This Old Love Of Mine	1961	Slate 3072
From My Heart/ Sally Put Your Red Dress On	1966	Ajax 174
Home Type Girl/There's A Girl Down The Way	1967	Ajax 175
You're The Only Girl/I've Been There Before You	1967	Ajax 176
OVERTONES (PENNY & THE)		
What Made You Forget/ Walkin' My Baby Back Home	1958	Rim 2021
OVERTONES (TONY RICE & THE)		
My Darling Y-O-U/I Thank You, Baby	1961	Action 100
Little School Girl/Bluebird Of Happiness	1961	Rae-Cox 106
OWENS, BUDDY (& GROUP)		
Bon Voyage/Sugar Lump	1964	Tec 3003
OWENS, FREDDY (& GROUP)		
Heavenly One/Chapel	1961	Wall 550
OWENS, GARLAND (& GROUP)		
Dancing With Tears In My Eyes	N/A	Lemonade 1502
OWLS		
So Lost/Kasanutu	N/A	Arden 1000
OX-TONES		
Fatty Patty	1958	Phonograph 1024
OXFORDS (DARRELL & THE) (AKA TOKENS (2))		
Picture In My Wallet/Roses Are Red	1959	Roulette 4174
Can't You Tell?/But Your Mother She Said No	1960	Roulette 4230
OZELLS		
The Gossip/Please Don't Go	1963	Cub 9126
PACERS (1)		
I Wanna Dance With You/ I Found A Dream	1958	Calico 101
PACERS (2)		
How Sweet/No Wonder	1961	Guyden 2064/Jason Scott 1 (80)
PACERS (3)		
You Got Me Bugged/Sassy Sue	1963	Coral 62398
PACESETTERS		
That's All/Ronnie's Beat (instrumental)	1962	Wink 1008
PACETTES		
Don't Read The Letter/You Don't Know Baby	1963	Regina 1306
PACKARDS		
That Night	1956	Decca (unreleased)
You Are	1956	Decca (unreleased)
S.O.S.	1956	Decca (unreleased)
Love Is Wonderful	1956	Decca (unreleased)
Pretty Eyes	1956	Decca (unreleased)
Dream Of Love/Ding Dong	1956	Paradise 105
Ladise/My Doctor Of Love	1956	Pla-Bac 106
PAGANS		
Lover's Plea/Bad Man Brown	1960	Music City 832
PAGANS (LYNN DEE & THE)		
Fool That I Am/I've Got What You Want	1960	Music City 835
PAGE BOYS		
Waiting/This I Give To You	1957	Prep 117
Hey Now Baby/Out To Lunch	1959	Tel 1007
If Tears Could Speak/ Old Buttermilk Sky	1963	Decca 3105
Our Love/Things Are Going To Break Up	N/A	Camelot 114
PAGE, JOEY (& GROUP)		
Blue Velvet/Party Season	1961	Roulette 4373
PAGE, PRISCILLA (& GROUP)		
Dreaming/My Letter	1961	Rose 500
PAGE, RICKY (& FEMALE GROUP)		
I Understand/Everytime (You're Mine)	1961	Coin 711/Dot 16261
PAGEANTS (1)		
Show Them You Can Dance/ It's Been So Long	1955	Beacon 559
We Belong Together/Theme From "Sleeping Moondog"	1961	Paxley 753
PAGEANTS (1) (FB TONY DEE)		
Happy Together/Why Did You Go	1960	Goldisc 3013
Saturday Romance/Make You My Queen	1962	Du-Well 101/Arlen 731 (62)
PAGEANTS (2)		
She Is Your Girl/Make It Last	1965	Groove 0056
I'm A Victim/Are You Ever Coming Home	1965	RCA 8601
PAGEANTS (3)		
Tender Love	N/A	Club
PAGEANTS (4)		
Long Ago	N/A	Vira
PAGEBOYS		
When I Meet A Girl Like You/ I Have Love	1963	Seville 135
PAGENTS		
Glenda	1964	Era 3124
Sad And Lonely/Pa-Cha	1964	Era 3134
PAGES (1) (GENE MORRIS & THE)		
I've Gotta Love/Lovin' Honey	1957	Vik 0287
PAGES (2)		
Donna Marie/Wind	1958	Eagle 1005/Don Tan 0001
PAL, RICKI (& GROUP)		
Just Outside Of Love/No Need For Crying	1958	Arwin 115
PALISADES (1)		
Oh My Love/Hometown Girl	1961	Dore 609
This Is The Nite/Relic Rock (instrumental)	1962	Medieval 205
Make The Night A Little Longer/ It's Heaven Being With You	1963	Chairman 4401
PALISADES (1) (GM CAROLE KING)		
Close Your Eyes/I Can't Quit	1960	Calico 113
Dear Joan/The Shrine	1960	Leader 806
PALISADES (2) (FRANK GONZALES & THE)		
Let's Make Up/Sweet Little Surfing Girl	1961	FG 1001
PALISADES (3)		
Chapel Bells/She Can't Stop Dancing	1963	Debra 1003
PALMS		
Dianne	1956	States (unreleased)
Knew I Had A Chance	1956	States (unreleased)
One More Time	1957	States (unreleased)
Love Is No Thing To Play With	1957	States (unreleased)
Edna/Teardrops	1957	United 208
PALMS (ARTIE WILKINS & THE)		
Darling Patricia/Please Come Back (no group)	1956	States 157
PALS (1)		
My Baby Likes To Rock/ Summer Is Here	1958	Turf 1000/1001/Guyden 2019 (59)
PALS (2) (GERRY PATT & HIS)		
It's So Strange/Dancing By Myself	1965	Ascot 2129
PANICS		
Heartaches/You're Driving Me Crazy	1959	ABC 10072
PANTHERS (CHARLES GRAY WATSON & THE)		
I Found My Love/Don't Do It	N/A	Village 103
PARADONS (AKA TREND-TONES)		
Diamonds And Pearls/I Want Love	1960	Milestone 2003
Bells Ring/Please Tell Me	1960	Milestone 2005
Never Again/This Is Love	1960	Tuffest 102
Take All Of Me/So Fine, So Fine, So Fine	1960	Warner Bros. 5186
I Had A Dream/Never, Never	1962	Milestone 2015

Artist / Song	Year	Label
PARAGONS		
Florence/Hey, Little School Girl	1957	Winley 215
Let's Start All Over Again/ Stick With Me Baby	1957	Winley 220
Two Hearts Are Better Than One/Give Me Love	1957	Winley 223
Twilight/The Vows Of Love	1958	Winley 227
So You Will Know/Don't Cry, Baby	1958	Winley 228/Times Square 9 (63)
Blue Velvet/Wedding Bells	1960	Musicraft 1102/Musictone 1102 (62)
So You Will Know/Doll Baby	1960	Winley 240
If/Hey Baby	1961	Tap 500
In The Midst Of The Night/ Begin The Beguine	1961	Tap 503
These Are The Things I Love/ If You Love Me	1961	Tap 504
Time After Time/Baby, Take My Hand	1963	Music Clef 3001/3002
Florence Don't Leave Me/ Danny Boy	1977	Robin Hood 145
Blue Velvet/Florence	1984	Starlight 23
Danny Boy/Hey Little School Girl	1986	Starlight 46
Don't Ever Leave Me	N/A	Winley LP 6003
PARAGONS (MACK STARR & THE)		
Just A Memory/Kneel And Pray	1961	Winley 250
PARAGONS (TOMMY COLLINS & THE)		
Darling, I Love You/Doll Baby	1959	Winley 236
PARAKEETS (1) (FB FRANK MOTLEY)		
Give Me Time/I'm Losing My Mind Over You (by Frank Motley)	1954	Gem 218
My Love Is True/ Can't You See I Love You (by the Rainbows)	1973	Baron 105
Candy Bar Boogie/Give Me Time	1973	Roadhouse 1005
PARAKEETS (2) (VIC DONNA & THE)		
Teenage Rose/Silly And Sappy	1957	Atlas 1071
Love Was A Stranger To Me/ Count The Tears	1957	Atlas 1075/Angletone 1075
PARAKEETS (2) QUINTET		
I Have A Love/The Rain Starts To Fall	1956	Atlas 1068/Angletone 1068
PARAKEETS (2) QUINTET (LEROY WILLIAMS & THE)		
My Heart Tells Me/Yvonne	1956	Atlas 1069
PARAKEETS (3)		
Shangri-La/Come Back	1961	Jubilee 5407
I Want You Right Now/I Love You Like I Do	1962	Big Top 3130
PARAMOUNTS (1)		
Take My Heart/Thunderbird Baby	1959	Combo 156
Christopher Columbus/I Know You'll Be My Love	1960	Fleetwood 1014
Where's Carolyn Tonight/ When I Dream	1963	Centaur 103
Shedding Teardrops/In A Dream	1963	Ember 1099
Time Will Bring A Change/ Under Your Spell	1964	Magnum 722
Rumba	1987	Relic LP 5069
PARAMOUNTS (2)		
Trying/Girl Friend	1960	Carlton 524
Congratulations/Why Do You Have To Go?	1961	Dot 16175
When You Dance/You're Seventeen	1961	Dot 16201
Just to Be With You/One More For The Road	1963	Laurie 3201
PARAMOUNTS (3) (EDDIE SAXON &)		
Blues No More/If It's Meant To Be	1962	Empress 106
PARAMOUNTS (4)		
Gosh Golly Gee/King Of Love	1976	Broadcast 1138
PARAMOUNTS (5)		
Tell Me Why/Stand By Me	1982	Avenue D 7
We Belong Together/ The Lions Sleeps Tonight/ Pledging My Love/It Happened Today	1985	Avenue D 10
PARAMOURS (1) (BILL MEDLEY & BOBBY HATFIELD)		
That's The Way We Love/ Prison Break	1961	Smash 1701
Cutie Cutie/Miss Social Climber	1961	Smash 1718

Artist / Song	Year	Label
That's All I Want Tonight/There She Goes (She's Walking)	1962	Moonglow 214
PARAMOURS (2)		
Darling Here's My Heart/When I See An Elephant Fly (by the Five Crows)	1986	Ronnie 205
PARAMOURS (3) (JOHNNY FORTUNE & THE)		
I'm Talking About You/ My Wandering Love	1964	Park Ave 4905
PARIS, BOBBY (& GROUP)		
Little Miss Dreamer/ Who Needs You	1963	Chattahoochie 631
Night Owl/Tears On My Pillow	1966	Cameo 396
PARISIANS		
Silhouettes/Planters Cafe	1959	Bullseye 1028
Silhouettes/Esther	1961	Argyle 1006
Fifi's Place/Ambush	1961	Felsted 8627
Why (I Want To Know)/On The Sunny Side Of The Street	1962	Pova 1003/1004
PARKAYS		
Late Date/Get It	1961	ABC 10242
PARKER, BOBBY (& GROUP)		
Foolish Love/Stop By My House	1960	Amanda 1001
PARKER, LITTLE JUNIOR (& GROUP)		
Belinda Marie/Dangerous Woman (no group)	1959	Duke 315
PARKTOWNS		
Stop, Look And Listen/ You Hurt Me Inside	1960	Impala 214/Thor 3258
That Day Will Never Come/ You Hurt Me Inside	1961	Crimson 1006
PARKWAY		
Maybe Next Christmas/ Take Time	1990	BAB 131
Where Can I Go Without You/ Lonesome For You	1992	Clifton 99
PARLAY BROTHERS		
My Girl/Do You Really Wanna Dance	1965	Valjay 2725
PARLETTES		
Tonight I Met An Angel/ Because We're Very Young	1963	Jubilee 5467
PARLIAMENTS (1)		
Don't Need You Anymore/ Honey, Take Me Home With You	1958	Len 101
PARLIAMENTS (2)		
Party Boys/Poor Willie	1959	Apt 25036
Lonely Island/You Make Me Wanna Cry	1960	Flipp 100/101
To Be Alone/My Only Love	1961	U.S.A. 719
You're Cute/I'll Get You Yet	1963	Symbol 917
PARLIAMENTS (3) (FREDDIE & THE)		
Darlene/That Girl	1959	Twirl 1003
PARLIAMENTS (4) (SAMMY & THE)		
No Hard Feelings/Win Yourself A Lover	1960	Arnold 1001
PARRISH, TROY (BB THE METALLICS)		
Gloria/Laugh	1962	Baronet 10
PARROTS		
Please Don't Leave Me/Weep, Weep, Weep	1953	Parrot 758/Checker 772 (54)
PARTYLIGHTS (SHONA & THE)		
Nice Guy/Miracle Maker	1963	Chicory 1601
PASSIONETTES		
My Plea/My Fault	N/A	Path 101
PASSIONS (1)		
Tango Of Love/Nervous About Love	1958	Dore 505
Just To Be With You/ Oh Melancholy Me	1959	Audicon 102
I Only Want You/This Is My Love	1960	Audicon 105
Gloria/Jungle Drums	1960	Audicon 106
Beautiful Dreamer/One Look At You Is All It Took	1960	Audicon 108
Made For Lovers/You Don't Love Me Anymore	1960	Audicon 112
I Gotta Know/Aphrodite	1961	Octavia 8005
Lonely Road/One Look Is All It Took	1962	Jubilee 5406
The Bully/Empty Seat	1963	ABC 10436
Sixteen Candles/The Third Floor (instrumental)	1963	Diamond 146

Artist Song	Year	Label
Aphrodite/I've Gotta Know	1981	Jason Scott 9
Waiting For You/Brooklyn	1990	Crystal Ball 157
PASSIONS (1) (GARY KAY & THE)		
Cinderella/I Love Candy		
(by the Echoes)	1981	Jason Scott 20
PASSIONS (2)		
Jackie Brown/My Aching Heart	1958	Era 1063/Capitol 3963 (58)
PASSIONS (3)		
Too Many Memories/		
The Reason (Why I Love You)	1961	Unique 79X/79XX/
		Fantastic 79
PASSIONS (4)		
Baby I Do/Man About Town	1966	Back Beat 573
PASSIONS (5)		
It Ain't Fair/I'm So Afraid	N/A	Topaz 1317
PASTEL KEYS (RONNIE GILL & THE)		
Standing On The Mountain/		
Geraldine	1958	Rip 108/Rio 129/Expiditus 500
PASTEL KEYS (RONNIE KING & THE)		
Girl, Break Away	N/A	Gateway 786
PASTELS (1)		
Bye Bye	1955	States (unreleased)
Goodbye	1955	States (unreleased)
Put Your Arms Around Me/		
Boom De De Boom	1956	United 196
PASTELS (2) (FB BIG DEE IRWIN)		
Been So Long/My One And		
Only Dream	1957	Mascot 123/Argo 5287 (57)
Let's Go To The Rock & Roll		
Ball/You Don't Love Me		
Anymore	1958	Argo 5297
So Far Away/Don't Knock	1958	Argo 5314
PASTELS (3)		
Swingin' Sam/(We Like) Crew		
Cuts (by the Debs & Escorts)	1958	Josie 833
PASTELS (4)		
King Of Fools/Mary	1963	Limelight 3007
PASTELS (5)		
Do You Ever Think Of Me/		
Sleep Tight	1964	Pastel 506
PASTELS (6)		
Oh Me Oh My	1974	Owl 332
PASTIMES		
Can't Find The Time To Tell		
You/Too Late	1986	Starlight 36
PATIOS (BILLY & THE)		
Love Is A Story/You Name It	1961	Lite 9002
PATTERNS		
Here's Why I Love You/		
Give Me Your Love	1980	Clifton 55
PATTI ANNE (PATTI ANNE MESNER WITH THE FLAMES)		
Shtiggy Boom/Baby, Baby I'm		
In Love With You (no group)	1955	Aladdin 3280
PAUL, BUNNY (BB THE HARPTONES)		
Such A Night/I'm Gonna		
Have Some Fun	1954	Essex 352
Answer The Call/Lovey Dovey	1954	Essex 359
PAUL, CLARENCE (& GROUP)		
I'll Be By Your Side/I Need		
Your Lovin'	1959	Hanover 4519
Falling In Love Again/May		
Heaven Bless You	1959	Roulette 4196
PAWNS		
Summer	N/A	Bay-State 1267
PAYMENTS		
Cantina/Brand New Automobile	N/A	Kit 101
PAYNE, CHUCK (& GROUP)		
Baby/La De Da	1957	Atlas 1072
PAYNE, LITTLE LEON (& GROUP)		
History Of Love	N/A	Daco 701
PEACHEROOS		
Be Bop Baby/Every Day My		
Love Is True	1954	Excello 2044
PEACHETTES (LYNN TAYLOR & THE) (FEMALE)		
Sweet Little Girl/The Bells Of		
St. Mary's	1960	Clock 1033/Hawk 2001
PEACOCKS		
My New Hi-Fi/Teen Hoppers		
Ball	1958	4 Star 1718
I Want You To Know/		
Tender Love	1958	Noble 711
PEACOCKS (JOHNNY OTIS & THE)		
Young Girl/(flip has no group)	1955	Peacock 1625
PEACOCKS (JUNIOR RYDER & THE)		
Sad Story/Better Stop (no group)	1954	Duke 119
PEACOCKS (NUNNIE MOORE & THE)		
Fontella/Bouquet Of Roses	1957	L&M 1002/Firefly 322 (74)
PEANUTS (M&M & THE)		
Open Up Your Eyes/Lil Valley	1964	Money 101
I Found My Love/The Phillie	1964	Money 107
My Belief/Without A Word	1965	Money 111
PEARLETTES (FEMALE)		
He's Gone/Just In Case	1961	Craig 501/502
Just In Case/Just In Case	1961	Craig 562/Seg-Way 1003 (61)
Can I Get Him/Never Be		
Another Boy Like You	1961	Vee Jay 422/Go 712
Can This Be Love/Cheated	1962	Vault 100
Duchess Of Earl/Everybody	1962	Vee Jay 435
PEARLS (1) (REF FIVE PEARLS/REF SHEIKS (1))		
Shadows Of Love/Yum Yummy	1956	Atco 6057
The Bells Of Love/Come On		
Home	1956	Atco 6066
Let's You And I Go Steady/		
Zippety Zippety Zoom	1956	Onyx 503/Relic 513 (64)
Tree In The Meadow/My, Oh My	1956	Onyx 506/Relic 519 (64)
I Sure Need You/Your		
Cheatin' Heart	1957	Onyx 510/Relic 520 (64)
Ice Cream Baby/Yuz-A-Ma-Tuz	1957	Onyx 511/Relic 521 (64)
The Wheel Of Love/It's Love,		
Love, Love	1957	Onyx 516/Relic 522 (64)
Band Of Angels/Ugly Face	1959	On The Square 320
It Must Be Love/I Cried	1961	Amber 2003
There's No Forgetting You/		
I Just Can't Stand It	N/A	Astor 1005
PEARLS (2) (SPEEDO & THE) (REF CADILLACS)		
Who Ya Gonna Kiss/Naggity		
Nag	1959	Josie 865
PEARLS (3)		
Jungle Bunny/My Heart's Desire		
(as the Fabulous Pearls)	1959	Dooto 448
Look At Me/It's Almost Tomorrow	1960	Dolton 26
PEARLS (4) (FEMALE)		
If I Had A Choice/Happy Over		
You	1962	Warner Bros. 5300
PEBBLES		
Ooo Wee/Let Me Hear It Again	1955	Middle-Tone 2002
Oh What A Beautiful Dream/		
That Was My Girl	1965	Eiffel 2085
PEDAL PUSHERS (B. DALE & THE)		
Love You Lovely Stranger/		
Foolish Little Fool	N/A	Ko Ko 8803
PEDESTRIANS (JAYWALKER & THE) (FEATURING PETE ANTELL)		
Hey Now/Never Happen	1962	Amy 848
PEDRICK, BOBBY (& GROUP)		
Maybe/Karine	1966	Verve 10402
PEE WEES		
Tootsie Roll/Blue Jean		
Cinderella	1958	Josie 838
PEEBLES, ROBERT (& GROUP)		
This Little Light Of Mine/		
Gift From Heaven	1959	Jax 1001
PEEK, PAUL (& GROUP)		
I'm Not You Fool Anymore/		
Oldsmo William	1958	NRC 008
PEELS		
Juanita Banana/Fun	1966	Karate 522
PEELS, LEON (BB THE BLUE JAYS)		
A Casual Kiss/Cottonhead Joe	1964	Whirlybird 2002
PELICANS (1)		
Chimes/Ain't Gonna Do It	1954	Imperial 5307
Aurelia/White Cliffs Of Dover	1954	Parrot 793
Miss Lucy	N/A	Imperial (unreleased)
Down In Mexico	N/A	Imperial (unreleased)
PELICANS (2) (EARL NELSON & THE)		
I Bow To You/Oh Gee, Oh Golly	1957	Class 209
PEMBERTON, JIMMY (BB THE CHANTELS)		
From Rags To Riches/That's		
What You Think	1959	End 1059/Mark-X 8002 (59)
PENDULUMS		
Time Marches On/Masquerader	1962	May 109
PENGUINS		
No There Ain't No News Today/		
When I'm Gone (by Willie		
Headen & D. Williams Orch.)	1954	Dootone 345

Artist Song	Year	Label
Earth Angel/Hey Senorita	1954	Dootone 348/Power 7023 (54)
I Ain't Gonna Cry No More	1955	Dooto EP 101 (55)/Dooto LP 224 (57)/Authentic LP 224 (57)
Love Will Make Your Mind Go Wild/Ookey-Ook	1955	Dootone 353
Kiss A Fool Goodbye/Baby, Let's Make Some Love	1955	Dootone 362
Be Mine Or Be A Fool/Don't Do It	1955	Mercury 70610
Walkin' Down Broadway/ It Only Happens To You	1955	Mercury 70654
Devil That I See/Promises, Promises, Promises	1955	Mercury 70703
A Christmas Prayer/Jingle Jangle	1955	Mercury 70762
My Troubles Are Not At An End/ She's Gone, Gone	1956	Mercury 70799
Earth Angel/Ice	1956	Mercury 70943
Dealer Of Dreams/Peace Of Mind	1956	Wing 90076
Pledge Of Love/I Knew I'd Fall In Love	1957	Atlantic 1132
That's How Much I Need You/ Be My Lovin' Baby	1957	Dooto 428
Will You Be Mine/Cool Cool Baby	1957	Mercury 71033
Sweet Love/Let Me Make Up Your Mind	1958	Dooto 432
Do Not Pretend/If You're Mine	1958	Dooto 435
Heart Of A Fool	1959	Dooto LP 242/Dooto EP 241
Lover Or Fool	1959	Dooto LP 242/Dooto EP 241
Money Talks	1959	Dooto LP 242/Dooto EP 241
Cold Heart	1959	Dooto LP 242/Dooto EP 241
Butterball	1959	Dooto LP 242/Dooto EP 241
Want Me	1959	Dooto LP 242/Dooto EP 241
Mr. Junkman	1960	Dooto EP 456
You're An Angel	1960	Dooto EP 456
Believe Me/The Pony Rock	1962	Sun State 101
Memories Of El Monte/Be Mine	1963	Original Sound 27
Heavenly Angel/Big Bobo's Party	1965	Original Sound 54
PENGUINS (CLEVE DUNCAN & THE)		
To Keep Our Love/Universal Twist	1961	Eldo 119
PENN BOYS		
Have A Party/Baby Baby	1959	Bobby 502
PENN MEN (BILLY LEHMAN & THE)		
Audrey/First Sign Of Love	1959	ARP 014
PENN, DAN (& GROUP)		
Let Them Talk/Close To Me	1964	Fame 6402
PENN, TONY (& GROUP)		
King Or A Fool/I Don't Like It	1959	P.R.I. 101
PENNANTS		
Don't Go/Workin' Man	1961	World 102
PENTAGONS		
Silly Dilly/It's Spring Again	1958	Specialty 644
To Be Loved (Forever)/Down At The Beach	1960	Fleet Int'l 100/Donna 1337 (61)
For A Love That Is Mine/ Like The Way You Look At Me	1961	Donna 1344
I Wonder (If Your Love Will Ever Belong To Me)/She's Mine	1961	Jamie 1201
Forever Yours/Gonna Wait For You	1961	Sutter 100
Until Then/I'm In Love	1962	Jamie 1210/Caldwell 411 (62)
PEPPERMINTS (1)		
Teen Age Idol/Believe Me	1959	House Of Beauty 1
Peppermint Jerk/We All Warned You	1965	RSVP 1112
PEPPERMINTS (2)		
Cheryl Ann/Now I Cry	1965	Peppermint 1001
PEPPERS (1)		
Rocking Chair Baby/Hold On	1954	Chess 1577
Yoko Hoko Homa/Blossoms	1958	Jane 105
PEPPERS (2)		
One More Chance/A Place In My Heart	1961	Ensign 1076
Little Piece Of Paper/ It Wouldn't Be The Same	1961	Press 2809

Artist Song	Year	Label
PERCELLS		
Cheek To Cheek/What Are Boys Made Of	1963	ABC 10401
Look At That Guy/Boy Friends	1963	ABC 10449
My Guy/Hully Gully Guitar	1963	ABC 10476
I Stand Alone/The Greatest	1963	ABC 10516
PERENIALS		
I Need Your Lovin'/Please Please (by the Scholars)	N/A	Ruby-Ray 2
PERENNIALS		
I'm Yours 'Til The End/ My Big Mistake	1963	Ball 1016
PERFECTIONS		
Hey Girl/My Baby	1962	Lost Nite 111
Am I Gonna Lose You/I Love You, My Love	1964	S.V.R. 1005
No More Love For You/ My Perfection	N/A	Pam-O 101
PERFORMERS (1)		
Give Me Your Heart/I'll Make You Understand	1956	All Star 714/Tip Top 402 (57)
PERFORMERS (2) (BOBBY SANDERS & THE)		
Cleopatra/Dead Pigeon	1963	Sound-O-Rama 117
PERFORMERS (3) (AKA MAJORS/AKA VERSATILES)		
Just Dance/Love Is The Answer (by the Majors)	1966	ABC 10777
PERIDOTS		
Hully Gully All Nite Long/ It's The Bomp	1961	Deauville 100
PERKINS, AL (& GROUP)		
So Long/Love Me Baby	1966	Jive 1003
PERKINS, ROY (& GROUP)		
You're Gone/Here Am I	1955	Meladee 112
PERKS (BILL PINKY & THE) (GM BILL PINCKNEY)		
After The Hop/Sally's Got A Sister	1958	Phillips International 3524
PERMANENTS		
Oh Dear, What Can The Matter Be/Let Me Be Baby	1963	Chairman 4405
PERRI'S (FEMALE)		
Jerrilee/Ballad Of A Happy Heart	1958	Madison 105
PERRY, CHARLES (& GROUP)		
Walk Through The Darkness/ If There Wasn't Any You	1962	Melic 4119
PERRY, TONY (& GROUP)		
Trust In Our Love/I'm Yours Forever	1957	Ember 1015
PERRYMAN, PAUL (& GROUP)		
Teen-Age Romeo/Paul Loves Betty	1959	Duke 305
PERSIANETTES (TIMMY & THE)		
Timmy Boy/There Comes A Time	1963	Olympia 100
Summertime Is Near/ Summertime Is Near	1963	Olympia 101
PERSIANETTES (TIMMY CARR & THE)		
Only Now And Then/I Could Never Stop Crying	1964	Guyden 2104
PERSIANS (1)		
Your Love/Keep On Moving	1955	Capitol 3230
PERSIANS (2)		
Teardrops Are Falling/Vault Of Memories	1961	Goldisc G1/Goldisc 1004 (63)
Gee What A Girl/Love Me Tonight	1962	Gold Eagle 1813
Tears Of Love/Dance Now	1962	RSVP 114
Sunday Kind Of Love/When We Get Married	1962	RTO 100
(When You Said) Let's Get Married/(Let's Monkey) At The Party	1963	Goldisc G17/Music World 102 (63)
Get A Hold Of Yourself/The Steady Kind	1963	Pageant 601
That Girl Of Mine/Don't Let Me Down	1963	Sir Rah 501
PERSIANS (3) (PARIS & THE)		
Credit Man	1961	AKU 921
PERSONALITIES		
Woe Woe Baby/Yours To Command	1957	Safari 1002

Artist Song	Year	Label
PERSUADERS		
What Could It Be/Tears	1959	Winley 235/Relic 1002 (65)
PERSUASIONS		
Stardust/I Could Never Love		
Another	1970	Catamount 1957
Without A Song/Since I Fell		
For You	1971	Reprise 0977
Good Old Acappella/You		
Must Believe	1973	MCA 40080
Love You/Most Of All	1973	MCA 40118
The Sun/The ABC's Of Love	1978	King Tut 171
PERSUASIONS (DONNA & THE)		
For Your Love/In The Still Of		
The Night	1973	Blue Sky 103
PERY MATES		
It Was You/Great Red Rat	1961	CaJo 210
PETITE TEENS		
My Singing Idol And Poor Little		
Fool/We're In Our Teens	1959	Brunswick 55119
PETITES		
Marguerite/Blessed Are They	1958	Spinning 6003
Sweetie Pie/Who Kicked The		
Light Plug Out Of The Socket	1958	Spinning 6005
Get You Daddy's Car Tonight/		
Sun Showers	1960	Columbia 41662
Making Miracle/Little Love	1961	Columbia 42053
The Beating Of My Heart/		
Nobody But You	1961	Elmor 304
I'm Gonna Love Him/Is		
Thirteen Too Young To		
Fall In Love	1964	Ascot 2166
PETS		
Cha-Hua-Hua/Cha-Kow-Ski	1958	Arwin 109
PETS (JERRY WARREN & THE)		
Street Of Love/Monkey Walk	1959	Arwin 118
PETTY, DARYL (& GROUP)		
Flaming Love/The Day I Die	1959	Hornet 502
PETTY, EDDIE "PRINCE" (& GROUP)		
That's You, That's Me/I Simply		
Crack Up	1957	Guest 1003
PHAETONS (1)		
I Love My Baby/As You Know	1959	Vin 1015
Fling/Homemade	1959	Hi-Q 5012
PHAETONS (2) (GM DEAN TORRENCE)		
I'm So Lonely/Road Of Blues	1963	Sahara 102
PHANTOMS		
Lost And Found/Channel Fever	1957	Baton 244
PHANTOMS (LYNN ROBERTS & THE)		
Miss You Tonite/I'll Be Around	1956	Oriole 101
PHANTOMS (VERNON GREEN & THE)		
Sweet Breeze/The Old Willow		
Tree	1956	Specialty 581
Tell Me Why/How	1956	Specialty unreleased
PHANTONES		
This Is Love/Get Ready,		
Get Right	1958	Code 707
Is This The End/Waiting For		
Your Love	1959	Bale 105
PHARAOHS (1)		
Somewhere There's A Rainbow/		
I'll Never Ever Love Again	1960	Flip 352
My Little Girl	N/A	Specialty
PHARAOHS (1) (RICHARD BERRY & THE)		
Take The Key (And Open Up		
My Heart)/No Kissin' And		
A Huggin'	1956	Flip 318
Louie, Louie/You Are My		
Sunshine	1957	Flip 321
Rock, Rock, Rock (This Dance		
Is Crazy)/Sweet Sugar You	1957	Flip 327
You're The Girl/You Look So		
Good	1958	Flip 331
Do I Do I/Besame Mucho	1958	Flip 339
Have Love Will Travel/No Room	1959	Flip 349
You Are My Sunshine/		
You Look So Good	1962	Flip 360
PHARAOHS (2) (RICKY & THE)		
Teenager's Love Song/Watusi	1956	Class 202
PHARAOHS (3)		
Walking Sad/Come On Baby	1957	Fascination 101/Skylor 101
PHARAOHS (4) (AL EPP & THE)		
My Dream Girl/Breaking My		
Heart	1959	Wildcat 0018

Artist Song	Year	Label
PHARAOHS (5)		
Come To Me/If I Had The Power	1961	Pharaoh 1
PHARAOHS (6) (ARTIE & THE)		
I'll Take Care Of You/Foxy Devil	1964	Cuca 1162
PHARAOS		
Tender Touch/Heads Up,		
High Hopes Over You	1960	Donna 1327
PHAROADS		
My Little Girl/All Alone	1952	RPM 355 (unreleased)
PHAROTONES		
Monkey Business/Paradise		
On Earth (by the Five Satins)	1963	Times Square 21/Times
Square 94 (64)		
PHEASANTS		
Out Of The Mist/Hot Biscuits	1963	Throne 802
PHILADELPHIANS		
Church Bells/Coming Home		
To You	1961	Campus 103
Dear/The Love That I Lost	1961	Chesapeake/Campus 101 (61)
The Vow/I Missed Her	1962	Cameo 216
PHILADELPHIANS (BIG JOHN & THE)		
My Love, My Love/Cleo's		
Theme (Vince Mon Tanta)	1963	Guyden 2093
PHILETTES		
Again Again And Again/Riddle		
Riddle Mar Randy O	1964	Hudson 8105
PHILHARMONICS		
Why Don't You Write Me?/		
Teen Town Hop	1958	Future 2200
PHILLIPAIRS		
You Fascinate Me/Believe In		
Tomorrow (by the Moroccans)	1957	Salem 1014
PHILLIPS, PHIL (BB THE TWILIGHTS (AKA COOKIE & THE CUPCAKES))		
Sea Of Love/Juella (with the		
Twilights)	1959	Khoury's 711/Mercury 71465 (59)
Take This Heart/Verdie Mae	1959	Mercury 71531
PICADILLY PIPERS		
Where's My Baby/I Loved		
Only You	1956	Chart 615
Lonely Lover's Prayer/		
Mr. Butterball	1956	Chart 619
PICTURES (C.L. & THE)		
Let's Take A Ride/I'm Asking		
Forgiveness	1961	Dunes 2010/Sabra 517 (60)
Afraid/Mary Go Round	1962	Dunes 2017
Love Will Find A Way/Then		
I'll Know	1963	Cadette 8005
Lonely Weekends/Better Him		
Than Me	1963	Dunes 2020
Pickin' Up The Pieces Of My		
Heart/Mr. Mistaker	1963	Dunes 2021
I'm Sorry/That's What's		
Happening	1963	Dunes 2023
I'm Not A Know It All	1964	Kirk 635
He'll Only Hurt You/Talking		
About My Baby	1964	Kirk 639/Monument 854 (64)
Could This Be Magic/Yolanda	1965	Monument 888
Baby Not Now/Jigsaw Puzzle	1966	Monument 958
PIECES OF EIGHT		
It Will Stand/Party Time	1967	A&M 907
PILGRIMS		
Careless Love/Walkin' Down		
The Track	1956	Baton 235
PILLOWS (PENNY BAKER & THE)		
Since I've Been Going With Him	1964	Witch 123
PIN-UPS (FEMALE)		
Lookin' For Boys/Kenny	1964	Stork 1
PING PONGS (1)		
In The Chapel In The		
Moonlight/Big Ben		
(Hoffman-Siegel Orch.)	1960	Cub 9062
Zyzzle/Summer Reverie	1960	United Artists 236
PING PONGS (2)		
You Belong To Me/Falabalon	1962	Marco 107
PING PONGS (3)		
You And Only You/I Don't		
Want To Wait	1964	G-Note
PIONEERS		
For You/48 Hours	1961	Golden Crest 565
PIPES (1)		
Be Fair/Let Me Give You Money	1956	Dootone 388

Artist Song	Year	Label
I Love The Life I Live/You Are		
An Angel	1956	Dootone 401
So Long/Baby Please Don't Go	1958	Jacy 001
Teamwork/Soon I Will Be Done	1962	Carlton 575
PIPES (2) (RUDY HARVEY & THE)		
I Need You So/Popcorn	1959	Capri 103
PIPS (FB GLADYS KNIGHT)		
Ching Chong/Whistle, My Love	1958	Brunswick 55048
Every Beat Of My Heart/Room		
In Your Heart	1961	Huntom 2510/Vee Jay
		386 (61)/Fury 1050 (61)
Linda/Darling	1962	Fury 1067
Happiness/I Had A Dream		
Last Night	1963	Everlast 5025
PIRATES (1) (TERRY & THE)		
What Did He Say/Talk About		
The Girl	1958	Valli 100/Chess 1695 (58)
PIRATES (2) (BLACK BEARD & THE)		
Lovers Never Say Goodbye/Show		
Me The Way To Go Home	1958	Ad 101
PIRATES (3) (JOHNNY KIDD & THE)		
Yes Sir, That's My Baby/Shakin'		
All Over	1960	Apt 25040
I'll Never Get Over You/Then I		
Got Everything	1963	Capitol 5065
PIRATES (4) (AKA TEMPTATIONS (4))		
Mind Over Matter (I'm Gonna		
Make You Mine)/I'll Love You		
'Til The Day I Die	1962	Mel-O-Dy 105
PIROUETTES		
If You See My Baby/The		
Wrangler Stretch	1964	Diamond 165
PITCH PIKES		
Zing Zong/Never Never Land	1957	Mercury 71099
How Will I Know/Come Back		
To Me	1957	Mercury 71147
PITNEY, GENE (& GROUP)		
Every Breath I Take/Mr. Moon,		
Mr. Cupid And I	1961	Musicor 1011
PITT, EUGENE (& GROUP)		
Why Why Why/Another Rainy		
Day	1966	Veep 1229
PITTER PATS		
Baby You Hurt Me/Whatcha Bet	1967	Instant 3284
PIXIES		
Cry Like A Baby/Just Like A Tear	1962	AMC 102/Don-Dee 102 (63)
Geisha Girl/He's Got You	1965	Autumn 12
PIXIES 3 (FEMALE)		
Birthday Party/Our Love	1963	Mercury 72130
442 Glenwood Avenue/Cold,		
Cold Winter	1963	Mercury 72208
Love Walked In/Orphan Boy	1964	Mercury 72231
Gee/After The Party	1964	Mercury 72250
The Hootch/It's Summer Time	1964	Mercury 72288
Love Me, Love Me/Your Way	1964	Mercury 72357
PIZANI, FRANK (BB THE HIGHLIGHTS)		
Every Time/Angry	1957	Bally 1040
It's No Fun/Wanna Dance	1959	Afton 616
The Stars Will Remember/		
Steady Cha Cha	1959	Afton 617
PLAIDS (1)		
Keeper Of My Heart/I Sing		
For You	1956	Darl 1001
Al-Lee-O! Al-Lee-Ay!/Halfway		
To Heaven	1956	Darl 1003
PLAIDS (2)		
Hungry For Your Love/Chit-Chat	1958	Liberty 55167
My Pretty Baby/Till The End Of		
The Dance	1958	Nasco 6011
Around The Corner (From		
My House)/He Stole Flo	1959	Era 3002
PLAIDS (3) (WILLIE LOGAN & THE)		
You Conquered Me/Say That		
You Care	1964	Jerry-O 103
Never Again/Stand There		
Mountain	1957	Era 1038
Be Sure/Wild Leaves	1957	Era 1049
Sharin' Lockers/I Need You So	1959	Nu-Clear 7422
Be Sure/Once In A Lifetime	1962	Aljon 1244
PLANETS (2)		
Mr. Moon/You Are My Sunshine	1964	Roulette 4551

Artist Song	Year	Label
PLANETTS		
The Magic Age Of Sixteen/So		
Young, So Warm, So Wonderful	1963	Goldisc G7
PLANTS		
Dear I Swear/It's You	1957	J&S 1602
From Me/My Girl	1958	J&S 1617/1618
I Searched The Seven Seas/		
I Took A Trip Way Over The		
Sea	1958	J&S 248/249/J&S 1604 (58)
PLATINUMS		
Life Is But A Dream/My True		
Story	1979	J & M 647
One Summer Night/Teardrops		
Follow Me	1979	J&M 122648
Blanche/Walking In The Rain	1980	J & M 649
PLATTERS		
Give Thanks/Hey Now	1953	Federal 12153
I Need You All The Time/		
I'll Cry When You're Gone	1953	Federal 12164
Roses Of Picardy/Beer Barrel		
Boogie	1954	Federal 12181
Tell The World/Love All Night	1954	Federal 12188
Voo-Vee-Ah-Bee/Shake It Up		
Mambo	1954	Federal 12198
Maggie Doesn't Work Here		
Anymore/Take Me Back,		
Take Me Back	1954	Federal 12204
Only You (And You Alone)/		
You Made Me Cry	1955	Federal 12244
I Need You All The Time/		
Tell The World	1955	Federal 12250
Glory Of Love	1955	Federal LP 395-549/King LP
		549 (56)/Mercury LP 20146 (56)
Only You (And You Alone)/		
Bark, Battle And Ball	1955	Mercury 70633
The Great Pretender/I'm Just		
A Dancing Partner	1955	Mercury 70753
Only You (And You Alone)/		
Voo-Vee-Ah-Bee	1955	Power 7012
Give Thanks/I Need You		
All The Time	1956	Federal 12271
(You've Got) The Magic		
Touch/Winner Take All	1956	Mercury 70819
My Prayer/Heaven On Earth	1956	Mercury 70893
You'll Never Never Know/		
It Isn't Right	1956	Mercury 70948
One In A Million/On My Word		
Of Honor	1956	Mercury 71011
Heart Of Stone	1956	Mercury LP 20216/
		Mercury EP 3343
I'm Sorry/He's Mine	1957	Mercury 71032
My Dream/I Wanna	1957	Mercury 71093
Only Because/The Mystery		
Of You	1957	Mercury 71184
For The First Time/Twilight		
Time	1958	Mercury 30075
Helpless/Indiff'rent	1958	Mercury 71246
Twilight Time/Out Of My Mind	1958	Mercury 71289
My Old Flame/You're Making		
A Mistake	1958	Mercury 71320
I Wish/It's Raining Outside	1958	Mercury 71353
Smoke Gets In Your Eyes/		
No Matter What You Are	1958	Mercury 71383/Mercury
		10001 (58)
Enchanted/The Sound And		
The Fury	1959	Mercury 71427
Remember When/Love Of a		
Lifetime	1959	Mercury 71467
Wish It Were Me/Where	1959	Mercury 71502/Mercury
		10018 (59)
My Secret/What Does It Matter	1959	Mercury 71538
Harbor Lights/Sleepy Lagoon	1960	Mercury 71563
Ebb Tide/(I'll Be With You In)		
Apple Blossom Time	1960	Mercury 71624
Red Sails In The Sunset/		
Sad River	1960	Mercury 71656/Mercury
		10038 (60)
To Each His Own/Down The		
River Of Dreams	1960	Mercury 71697
By The River Sainte Marie	1960	Mercury LP 20481/
		Mercury 60160 (60)

Artist Song	Year	Label
Lazy River	1960	Mercury LP 20481/ Mercury LP 60160 (60)
Rainbow On The River	1960	Mercury LP 20481/ Mercury LP 60160 (60)
Moonlight On The Colorado	1960	Mercury LP 20481/ Mercury LP 60160 (60)
Reflections In The Water	1960	Mercury LP 20481/ Mercury LP 60160 (60)
On A Slow Boat To China	1960	Mercury LP 20481/ Mercury LP 60160 (60)
Whispering Grass	1960	Mercury LP 20589/ Mercury LP 60254 (60)
When You Wore A Tulip	1960	Mercury LP 20589/ Mercury LP 60254 (60)
Jeanine	1960	Mercury LP 20589/ Mercury LP 60254 (60)
Honeysuckle Rose	1960	Mercury LP 20589/ Mercury LP 60254 (60)
If I Didn't Care/True Lover	1961	Mercury 71749
Trees/Immortal Love	1961	Mercury 71791
I'll Never Smile Again/You Don't Say	1961	Mercury 71847
You'll Never Know/Song For The Lonely	1962	Mercury 71904
It's Magic/Reaching For A Star	1962	Mercury 71921
More Than You Know/Every Little Movement	1962	Mercury 71986
Memories/Heartbreak	1963	Mercury 72060
Once In A While/I'll See You In My Dreams	1963	Mercury 72107
Here Comes Heaven Again/ Strangers	1963	Mercury 72129
Cuando Caliente El Sol/ Viva Ju Juy	1963	Mercury 72194
Full Moon And Empty Arms	1963	Mercury LP 20759/Mercury LP 60759 (63)
In A Little Spanish Town	1963	Mercury LP 20759/Mercury LP 60759 (63)
Moonlight Memories	1963	Mercury LP 20759/Mercury LP 60759 (63)
Sentimental Journey	1963	Mercury LP 20759/Mercury LP 60759 (63)
Moon Over Miami	1963	Mercury LP 20759/Mercury LP 60759 (63)
Shine On Harvest Moon	1963	Mercury LP 20759/Mercury LP 60759 (63)
My Reverie	1963	Mercury LP 20759/Mercury LP 60759 (63)
Moonlight And Roses	1963	Mercury LP 20759/Mercury LP 60759 (63)
Oh How I Miss You Tonight	1963	Mercury LP 20759/Mercury LP 60759 (63)
Row The Boat Ashore/Java Jive	1964	Mercury 72242
Sincerely/P. S., I Love You	1964	Mercury 72305
Love Me Tender/Little Things Mean A Lot	1964	Mercury 72359
Are You Sincere/Sixteen Tons	1973	Owl 320
Don't Blame Me	N/A	Mercury EP
I'd Climb The Highest Mountain	N/A	Mercury EP 3343
You've Changed	N/A	Mercury EP 3343
I'll Get By	N/A	Mercury EP 3344
You Can Depend On Me	N/A	Mercury EP 3345
I Don't Know Why	N/A	Mercury EP 3345
Take Me In Your Arms	N/A	Mercury EP 3345
Temptation	N/A	Mercury EP 3345
You Are Too Beautiful	N/A	Mercury EP 3353
No Power On Earth	N/A	Mercury EP 3353
Sweet Sixteen	N/A	Mercury EP 3353
Darktown Strutter's Ball	N/A	Mercury EP 3353
Don't Forget	N/A	Mercury EP 3355
Time And Tide	N/A	Mercury EP 3355
Oh Promise Me	N/A	Mercury EP 3355
Mean To Me	N/A	Mercury EP 3355
I Love You 1000 Times/ Blue Moon (by the Marcels)	N/A	Ripete 185
PLATTERS '65 (FEATURING LINDA HAYES)		
Won't You Be My Friend/ Run While It's Dark	1965	Entree 107
PLATTERS (LINDA HAYES & THE)		
Please Have Mercy/Oochi Pachi	1955	King 4773
PLAYBOY BAND (JOHN FRED & HIS)		
Mirror Mirror (On The Wall)/ To Have And To Hold	1962	Montel 2001

Artist Song	Year	Label
PLAYBOYS (1)		
Tell Me (Are You Really Mine)/ Rock, Moan And Cry	1954	Cat 108
PLAYBOYS (1) (CHARLES WHITE & THE)		
Good Golly, Miss Molly/ Honey Bun	1955	Cat 115
PLAYBOYS (2)		
One Question/So Good	1956	Tetra 4447
PLAYBOYS (3)		
Don't Do Me Wrong/Why Do I Love You, Why Do I Care	1957	Mercury 71228
Over The Weekend/Double Talk	1958	Martinique 101/Cameo 142 (58)
Golly Gosh Oh Gee/Sugar Lump	1958	United Artists 124
Memories/You're All I See	1959	ABC 10070
Icy Fingers/Party Ice	1959	Dolton 8
Crazy Daisy/Sweet Talk	1959	Imperial 5586
Please Forgive Me/Sing Along	1959	Martinique 400
Jungle Fever/Shotgun	1959	Rik 572
Believe It Or Not/Hawaiian War Chant	1959	Souvenir 1001
Boston Hop/What'd I Say? (by the Cousins)	1961	Chancellor 1074
Duck Walk/If I Had My Way	1962	Chancellor 1106
Careful With My Heart/Girl Of My Dreams	1962	Cotton 1008
Mope De Mope/The Night Before Christmas	1963	Legato 101
Shortnin' Bread/Cheater Stomp	N/A	Catalina 1069
PLAYBOYS (4)		
Cross My Heart	1961	Nite Owl 30
PLAYBOYS (5)		
When I Meet A Girl Like You/ I Have Love	1963	Seville 135
PLAYBOYS (6) (GENE VITO & THE)		
Playboy/I Want You Back Again	1964	Blast 214
PLAYBOYS (7) (CALEB & THE)		
I'm Yours/See About Me	1963	Olimpic 4575
PLAYBOYS (8) (GARY GILLESPIE & THE)		
Honest I Do/Dancing Girl	1962	Delta 520
PLAYBOYS (9) (JOHN FRED & THE)		
Shirley/High Heel Sneakers	1962	Montel 998
PLAYERS (1) (LEROY LOVETT & THE)		
Unchained Melody/Midnight Sun	1955	Atlantic 1058
PLAYERS (2)		
You Need A Love/What About Me	1963	Tarx 1007
PLAYGIRLS (1) (AKA BLOSSOMS)		
Hey Sport/Young Love Swings The World	1959	RCA 7546
Gee, But I'm Lonesome/ Sugar Beat	1960	RCA 7719
PLAYGIRLS (2)		
Bells/Donnie	1962	Galaxy 713
PLAYGROUND		
Four Seasons 1960s Medley/ Ronnie	1983	Clifton 72
PLAYMATES (AKA THREE PLAYMATES)		
It Must Be Love/Giddy-Up-A-Ding-Dong	1957	Savoy 1523
PLAYTHINGS		
Lipstick/Sittin'	1958	Liberty 55147
PLAZAS (1) (ERIC & THE)		
I Wish/It's The Last Kiss	1963	Production 612
PLAZAS (2) (NICKY ADDEO & THE)		
Danny Boy/Lovely Way To Spend An Evening	1962	Revelation 7-101
PLEASERS (1) (LITTLE WILBUR & THE)		
Heart To Heart/Alone In The Night	1957	Aladdin 3402
PLEASERS (1) (WILBUR WHITFIELD & THE)		
P.B. Baby/The One I Love	1957	Aladdin 3381
Plaything/I Don't Care	1957	Aladdin 3396
Heart To Heart/Alone In The Night	1957	Aladdin 3402
PLEASERS (2) (BOBBIE PLEASE & THE)		
The Monster/The Switch	1959	Jamie 1118
Your Drivers License, Please/ Heartache Street	1961	Era 3044
PLEASURES		
Music City	1963	Catch 100
Don't You Know (I Love You)/ Plaything	1964	RSVP 1102

Artist	Song	Year	Label
PLEDGES (1) (AKA SKIP & FLIP)			
	Betty Jean/Her Bermuda Shorts	1957	Revere 3517
PLEDGES (2)			
	I'm Sorry/Won't You Give Your Love To Me	1959	Hamilton 50028
PLURALS			
	Donna My Dear/Miss Annie	1958	Wanger 186/187/Bergen 186/187 (59)
	Goodnight/I'm Sold	1959	Wanger 188
PLUSH PUPS (TERRIE PARKER & THE)			
	A Dream In The Night/'Cause I'm Your Friend	1961	Queen 24011
PLUSHTONES			
	Raindrops/Penny Loafers	1960	Plush 601
PO BOYS (EDGAR ALLEN & THE)			
	Lenore/Panic Button	1962	Rust 5053
POE RATS (AL DOWNING & THE)			
	Oh Babe/Down On The Farm	1958	Challenge 59006
POET, THE (AKA POETS (2))			
	Vowels Of Love/Dead	1958	Pull 305
POETS (1)			
	Never Let Me Go/I'm Falling In Love	1960	Shade 1001
POETS (2) (AKA THE POET)			
	Vowels Of Love/Dead	1958	Flash 129 (58)
POETS (3)			
	I'm In Love/Honey Chile	1960	Spot 107/Imperial 5664 (60)
POETS (4)			
	Merry Christmas Baby/I'm Stuck On You	1964	Red Bird 046
POETS (5)			
	She Blew A Good Thing	N/A	Symbol 214
	So Young/A Sure Thing	N/A	Symbol 216
POKA-DOTTS (FEMALE)			
	Ting-A-Ling/Stairway To Love	1954	Modern 945
PONI-TAILS			
	It's Just My Luck To Be Fifteen/Wild Eyes And Tender Lips	1957	ABC 9846
	Can I Be Sure/Still In Your Teens	1957	Marc 1001
	Your Wild Heart/Que La Bozena	1957	Point 8
	Born Too Late/Come On, Joey, Dance With Me	1958	ABC 9934
	Seven Minutes In Heaven/Close Friends	1958	ABC 9969
	Moody/Oom-Pah Polka	1959	ABC 10027
	I'll Be Seeing You/I'll Keep Tryin'	1959	ABC 10047
	Before We Say Goodnight/Come Be My Love	1959	ABC 10077
	Father Time/Early To Bed	1959	ABC 9995
	Who, When And Why/Oh, My, You	1960	ABC 10114
POOR BOYS (KING RICHARD & THE)			
	Didn't We Fool Them?/I'm Not Ashamed	1961	Apollo 1201
	Washboard/I'm Going To Spend My Money	1961	Apollo 1203
POORE, BOBBY (& GROUP)			
	One And Two/Heartbreak Of Love	1958	Beta 1003
POP OVERS			
	Time's Run Out	N/A	Toppette 1020
POPCORNS			
	I Loved You/Pluto	1963	Vee Jay 537
POPPIES (FEMALE)			
	Lullaby Of Love/I Wonder Why	N/A	Epic 9893
POPSICLES			
	Thumb Print/This Is The End	1958	Knight 2002
	Baby I Miss You/I Don't Want To Be Your Baby Anymore	1965	GNP Crescendo 336
POPULAIRES			
	Island Of Paradise/I Lost My Heart	1957	Marvello 5001
POPULAR FIVE			
	Sh-Boom/Tomorrow Night	1967	Rae-Cox 1001
	I'm A Love Maker/Litlle Bitty Pretty One	1968	Minit 32050
	Baby I've Got It/Best Friend Worst Enemy	1970	Mister Chand 8001
PORK CHOPS			
	I Wanna See My Lovin' Baby/Everything's Cool	1956	Herald 493
PORTEE, ROBIN (& GROUP)			
	Casanova/I Am So Proud	1963	Diamond 151
PORTER, JAKE (WITH THE BUZZARDS)			
	Wine, Women And Gold/The Bop (no group)	1955	Combo 91
PORTO, BILLY (& GROUP)			
	Ruby Ruby/Foolish Dreams	1957	Mercury 71205
PORTRAITS			
	Close To You/Easy Cash	1959	Capitol 4181
	Yo-Yo Girl/My Big Brother's Friend	1961	RCA 7900
	Three Blind Mice/We're Gonna Party	1963	Tri-Disc 109
	A Million To One/Let's Tell The World	1967	Sidewalk 928
	Over The Rainbow/Runaround Girl	1968	Sidewalk 935
POSSE (MARSHALL LAWS & THE)			
	Mama's House/Little Baby	1961	Forum 702
POSSESSIONS			
	Hey There	1964	Britton
	No More Love/You And Your Lies	1964	Britton 1003/Parkway 930 (64)
POWELL QUINTET (THE AUSTIN POWELL QUINTET)			
	Some Other Spring/All This Can't Be True	1951	Decca 48206
POWELL, AUSTIN (BB THE JAMES QUINTET)			
	Wrong Again/What More Can I Ask	1952	Atlantic 968
POWELL, SANDY (& GROUP)			
	Bon Bon/Pistol Packin' Mama	1960	Herald 557/Impala 211
POWELL, TINY (& GROUP)			
	Take Me With You/My Time (no group)	1964	Wax 101
POWERS, RONI (& GROUP)			
	An Angel Up In Heaven/I Wish	1961	LT Productions 1022
POWERS, WAYNE (& GROUP)			
	My Love Song/Point Of View	1958	Phillips International 3523
PRANCERS			
	Rudolph The Red-Nosed Reindeer/Short Short'nin'	1959	Guaranteed 204
PRE-HISTORICS			
	Alley Oop Cha-Cha-Cha	1960	Edsel 779
PRECISIONS (1)			
	You Can't Play Games/Dream On	1960	Strand 25038
	Cleopatra/Someone To Watch Over Me	1962	Golden Crest 571
	Eight Reasons Why (I Love You)/Mama Told Me	1962	Highland 300
PRECISIONS (2) (TOMMY GENOVA & THE)			
	What Has Happened To You/The Lover	1962	Bella 606
PRECISIONS (3)			
	Sweet Dreams/Stop Leading Me On	1963	Debra 1001
PRECISIONS (4)			
	Brenda/White Christmas	N/A	Rayna 1001
PRECISIONS (5)			
	The Love (I Found In You)/What Would You Do	N/A	Wild 903
PREETEENS			
	What Makes Me Love You/Pass It On	1959	J&S 1756
PRELLS			
	It's A Wig/Cash	1964	Skyline 1004
PRELUDES (1)			
	Don't Fall In Love Too Soon/I Want Your Arms Around Me (All The Time)	1956	Empire 103
PRELUDES (2)			
	Vanishing Angel/Kingdom Of Love	1958	Acme 730/Cub 9005 (58)
PRELUDES (3)			
	Lorraine/Oh, Please, Genie	1961	Arliss 1004
	A Place For You (In My Heart)/That Would Be So Good	1962	Octavia 8008
PRELUDES (4)			
	Flip Flop	N/A	Imperial
PRELUDES FIVE			
	Don't You Know Love/Starlight	1961	Pik 231

Artist Song	Year	Label
PREMEERS		
Diary Of Our Love/Gee Oh Gee	1962	Herald 577
PREMIERES & THE INVICTAS		
Do It/Magic Of Love	1959	F-M 677
PREMIERS (1)		
Baby/New Moon	1956	Dig 106
Have A Heart/My Darling	1956	Dig 113
Red Sails In The Sunset/Your		
Kiss	1957	Dig 141 (unreleased)/Relic LP 5052 (85)
When You Are In Love/The		
Trap Of Love	1957	Fortune 527
Is It A Dream?/Valerie	1957	Gone 5009
Hey Miss Fancy/Run Along		
Baby	1957	RCA 6958
China Doll/Life Is Grand	1958	Cindy 3008
Red Light Bandit (Caryl		
Chessman)/True Deep Love	1960	Dore 547
Reverie/Double Date	1961	Clock 1042
She Goes Oonka Chicka/		
What Makes Little Girls Cry	1961	Dore 614
Frantic/The Beatle Walk		
(by the Phaetons)	1964	Sahara 103
Lonely Weatherman	N/A	Mohican
Speaking Of You/Funky Monkey	N/A	Odex 1711
PREMIERS (1) (ARTIE & LINDA & THE)		
Laughing On The Outside/		
Blueberry Hill	1964	Chancellor 1147
PREMIERS (1) (JULIE STEVENS & THE)		
Blue Mood/Crazy Bells	1956	Dig 115/Eldo 107 (60)/Dice 115
Take My Heart/I Don't Want		
To Know	1957	Dig 129
Evening Star/Last Of The Real		
Smart Guys	1961	Dore 603
Angel Love/False Love	1962	Best 1004
PREMIERS (2) (JOHN MCKINNEY & THE)		
Angels In The Sky/Gee (How		
I Love You)	1958	Mad 1009
PREMIERS (3)		
Hop And Skip/Uh-Huh	1958	Bond 5803/5804
Firewater/Younger Than You	1959	Nu-Phi 429/Nu-Phi 701
PREMIERS (4)		
I Think I Love You/Tonight	1959	Mink 021/Parkway 807 (60)
PREMIERS (5) (FB ROGER KOOB) (AKA ROGER & THE TRAVELERS)		
Jolene/Oh Theresa	1959	Alert 706
Pigtails Eyes Are Blue/I Pray	1960	Fury 1029
Falling Star/She Gives Me Fever	1961	Rust 5032
Run Along Baby	N/A	Coast 102
PREMIERS (6) (RONNIE & THE)		
Sharon/Cha Cha Rock	1961	Highland 1014
PREMIERS (7) (HERB JOHNSON & THE)		
Help/Crying Blues	1959	Palm 301
PREMONITIONS		
My Girl Pearl	1967	Jade
My Girl Pearl/Once In Love	1979	Crystal Ball 133
PRESIDENTS		
The Toast/Pots And Pans	1962	Mercury 72016
PRESS, DON (BB THE MYSTICS (1))		
More Than Ever/Ask The Robin	1959	Laurie 3036
PRESTOS		
Lookin' For Love/Till We Meet		
Again	1955	Mercury 70747
PRETENDERS (1) (FEATURING JIMMY JONES) (AKA SAVOYS (3))		
Close Your Eyes/Part Time		
Sweetheart	1955	Whirlin' Disc 106/ Port 70040 (61)
Posessive Love/I've Got To		
Have You, Baby	1956	Rama 198
Tonight/I Love You So	1957	Holiday 2610
Blue And Lonely/Daddy		
Needs Baby	1958	Central 2605/Apt 25026 (59)/ABC 10094 (60)
Pennies From Heaven		
(acapella)	1975	Relic LP 101
PRETENDERS (1) (JIMMY JONES & THE) (AKA SAVOYS (3))		
Lover/Plain Old Love	1956	Rama 210/Roulette 4322 (60)
PRETENDERS (2)		
I'm So Happy/Smile	1961	Power-Martin 1001/Relic 1004 (65)
Could This Be Magic/Stormy		
Weather (by the Earls on		
Rome 111)	1976	Power-Martin 1005

Artist Song	Year	Label
Could This Be Magic/		
A Very Precious Love	1976	Power-Martin 1006/1007
PRETENDERS (3)		
The Day You Are Mine/		
Ding Dong Bells	1962	Bethlehem 3050
PRETENDERS (4) (LINDA & THE)		
It's Not My Will/Believe Me	1963	Assault 1879/1880
PRETENDERS (5) (JAMES MOORE & THE)		
To Be Loved/A Man Should		
Never Cry	1964	Tishman 905
PRETENDERS (6)		
The Seven Teens/The Seven		
Teens (by Johnny & the Jokers)	1980	Clifton 46
PRICE, DEL (& GROUP)		
Stand By Me/Pretty Statue	1975	Kelway 113
PRIME		
Walk On The Wild Side/Ooh Baby		
Baby/Don't Have To Shop		
Around/We Belong Together	N/A	Clifton EP 506
PRIMETTES (AKA SUPREMES (4))		
Tears Of Sorrow/Pretty Baby	1961	Lu Pine 120
PRIMETTES (AKA SUPREMES (4)) (AL GARNER & THE)		
All I Need Is You	1986	Relic LP 8008
PRINCE, ROD (& GROUP)		
Rainbow Of Love/My Star All		
Alone	1961	Comet 2140
PRINDER, SHAD		
Here Goes A Fool/Willow Tree	1962	Infinity 009
PRISONAIRES		
Just Walking In The Rain/		
Baby Please	1953	Sun 186
My God Is Real/Softly And		
Tenderly	1953	Sun 189
A Prisoner's Prayer/I Know	1953	Sun 191
There Is Love In You/What'll		
You Do Next	1954	Sun 207
I Wish/All Alone And Lonely	1976	Sun 511
No More Tears/Don't Say		
Tomorrow	1976	Sun 512
If I Were King/The Chick's Too		
Young To Fry	1976	Sun 513
What A Fool/Rockin' Horse	1976	Sun 516
Two Strangers/Lucille, I Want		
You	1976	Sun 517
Dreaming Of You/Surleen	1976	Sun 519
PRIVATEERS (JOYCE & THE) (FB JOYCE HEATH)		
Honor Role Of Love/The Bunny		
Tale	1962	Agon 1003
PRIZES		
I Found Someone New/		
Summer's Here At Last	1964	Parkway 917
PRODIGALS (1)		
Judy/Marsha	1958	Falcon 1011/Abner 1011 (58) /Tollie 9019 (64)/Lost Nite 276 /Collectables 1458
Won't You Believe/Vangie	1958	Falcon 1015/Abner 1015 (58)
PRODIGALS (2)		
I Need You/You Better Move On	N/A	Acadian 1000
PROFESSIONALS (TOMMY VANN & THE)		
I'm So Alone/Does Your		
Mama Know About Me	1969	Congress 6001
PROFILES (1)		
Take A Giant Step/Watusi		
Wobble	1962	Goldie 1103
PROFILES (2)		
Right By Her Side/Never	1965	Gait 1444
PROFILES (3)		
I Still Love You	N/A	Bamboo 108
PROFITS (AKA CLASSICS WITH EMIL STUCCHIO)		
Wind/Vagabond	1971	Sire 353
PROMINENTS		
Just A Little/You're Gonna		
Lose Her	1965	Lummtone 116
PROPHETS (1)		
Sugar Lump/Come Back,		
Baby, Come Back	1955	Go-Lish 101
Stormy/Baby Come Back	1956	Atco 6078
Little Miss Dreamer/Sha-La-La	1963	Jairick 201
The Wind/Vagabond	1971	Sire 353
I Still Love You	N/A	Shell
PROPHETS (2) (RONNIE DIO & THE)		
Love Pains/Ooh-Poo-Pah-Do	1962	Atlantic 2145

Artist / Song	Year	Label
Gonna Make It Alone/Swingin' Street	1963	Lawn 218
10 Days With Brenda/Walking In Different Circles	1967	Parkway 143
PROSPECTS		
Would You Be Mine/Way Beyond Tomorrow	1989	Starlight 69
PUFFS		
I Only Cry Once A Day Now/Moon Out There	1966	Dore 757
PUSSYCATS		
Anniversary Of Love/Mickey Mouse March	1963	Keyman 600
PUZZLES		
I Need You/My Sweet Baby	1968	Fatback 216
PYRAMIDERS		
Don't Ever Leave Me/How It Feels	1958	Scott 1505
PYRAMIDS (1)		
Deep In My Heart For You/And I Need You	1955	Federal 12233
Someday/Bow-Wow	1955	Hollywood 1047/"C" Note 1206 (56)
PYRAMIDS (2)		
At Any Cost/Okay, Baby!	1956	Davis 453
Why Did You Go?/Before It's Too Late	1957	Davis 457
PYRAMIDS (2) (RUBY WHITAKER & THE)		
I Don't Want To Set The World On Fire/I Get The Feeling	1957	Mark-X 7007
PYRAMIDS (3)		
Ankle Bracelet/Hot Dog Dooly Wah	1958	Shell 711
Cryin'/I'm The Playboy	1962	Cub 9112
Shakin' Fit/What Is Love	1963	Vee Jay 489
PYRAMIDS (4)		
Oh No You Won't/Long Long Time	1959	RCA 7556
Here Comes Marsha/Penetration	1963	Best 102/Best 13002 (64)
PYRAMIDS (5) (DAVE WHITE & THE)		
24 Hours/Write My Name	1960	Pink 705
PYRAMIDS (6) (DOUG & FREDDY & THE) (AKA DOUG & FREDDY WITH THE PYRAMIDS)		
Take A Chance On Love/I Know Your Lyin' (But Say It Again)	1961	Finer Arts 1001
PYRAMIDS (7) (LITTLE RICHARD MORELAND & THE)		
Bells In My Heart/Mailman Blues	N/A	Picture 7722
Q TONES (DON Q & THE)		
Private Property/Baby I Don't Need You Now	N/A	Bullet 330
Q'S (BRUCE CLARK & THE)		
A Penny For Your Thoughts/Went To Chinatown	1964	Hull 762
QUADRELLS		
Come To Me/What Can The Matter Be?	1956	Whirlin' Disc 103
QUADRELLS (ALAN & THE)		
The Woody Surfer/Loafin'	1961	Goldisc G14
QUAILS (1)		
The Things She Used To Do/Pretty Huggin' Baby	1955	DeLuxe 6085
The Cow/Take Me Back, Baby	1963	American 1023
You're Mine	1963	American 1024
QUAILS (1) (BILL ROBINSON & THE)		
Lonely Star/Quit Pushin'	1954	DeLuxe 6030
I Know She's Gone/Baby Don't Want Me No More	1954	DeLuxe 6047
A Little Bit Of Love/Somewhere, Somebody Cares	1954	DeLuxe 6057
Why Do I Wait?/Heaven Is The Place	1954	DeLuxe 6059
Love Of My Life/Oh, Sugar	1955	DeLuxe 6074
QUAILS (2) (FB HARVEY FUQUA)		
It's Been A Long Time/Get To School On Time	1961	Harvey 114
My Love/Never Felt Like This Before	1962	Harvey 116
Over The Hump/I Thought	1962	Harvey 120
QUAILTONES (SAX KARI & THE)		
Tears Of Love/Roxanna	1955	Josie 779
QUANTRILS (FREDDIE & THE)		
If I Give My Heart To You/Thunderbird	1964	Karem 1004
QUARDELLS (BILLY KOPE & THE)		
It's All My Fault/Lulu	1958	Kudo 662
QUARTER NOTES (1)		
Come De Nite/Loneliness	1957	DeLuxe 6116
My Fantasy/Ten Minutes To Midnight	1957	DeLuxe 6129
QUARTER NOTES (2)		
Like You Bug Me/Please Come Home	1957	Dot 15685
Punkanilla/The Interview	1958	RCA 7327
Record Hop Blues/Suki-Yaki-Rocki	1959	Whizz 715
Frantic Flip/Canadian Sunset	1960	Imperial 5647
Pretty Pretty Eyes/I Don't Want To Go Home	1963	Guyden 2083
I've Been Loved/Hey Little Girl	1966	Boom 60018
QUARTER NOTES (2) (NEIL DARROW & THE)		
Charlene/She's A Fine Chick	1959	Whizz 717
QUARTER TONES (CHIP & THE)		
Simple Simon/You Were My Baby	1964	Carlton 604
QUARTERNOTES		
Baby/Hold Me Darling	1962	Little Star 112
QUEEN CITY RAMBLERS (LAURA GUNTER & THE)		
He's My Man	1958	Excellent 807
QUEENS (SHIRLEY GUNTER & THE)		
Oop Shoop/It's You	1954	Flair 1050
You're Mine/Why?	1955	Flair 1060
Baby, I Love You So/What Difference Does It Make?	1955	Flair 1065
That's The Way I Like It/Gimme, Gimme, Gimme	1955	Flair 1070
QUENTINS		
Mi Amore/You'll Never Know	1960	Andie 5014
QUESTION MARKS (1)		
Another Soldier Gone/Go And Get Some More (by the Hollywood Flames)	1954	Swing Time 346
QUESTION MARKS (2)		
Ballad Of A Boy And A Girl/Concerto Rock	1959	First 102
QUILLS		
Going To The Moon/Whose Love But Yours	1959	Casino 106
QUIN-TEENS (FEMALE)		
I Hurt So/Dickie	1963	Pike 5922
QUIN-TONES (FEMALE)		
Ding Dong/I Try So Hard	1958	Chess 1685
What Am I To Do? (The Letter)/There'll Be No Sorrow	1958	Hunt 322 (58)
Oh My Love	1958	Red Top
Down The Aisle Of Love/Please Dear	1958	Red Top 108/Hunt 321 (58)
Oh, Heavenly Father/I Watch The Stars	1958	Red Top 116
My Aloha Sand/Ay! Ay!	N/A	Courtney 134
Choo Choo Boogie/Boogie Woogie Pony	N/A	Courtney 135
Fool That I Am/When My Sugar	N/A	Vo 5172
QUINNS		
Oh Starlite/Hong Kong	1958	Cyclone 111
Unfaithful/Who Stole The Cookies	1965	Relic 1012
QUINTONES (1)		
I'm Willing/Strange As It Seems	1956	Gee 1009
QUINTONES (2)		
The Lonely Telephone/Just A Little Loving	1954	Jordan 1601
South Sea Island/More Than A Notion	1957	Park 57-111/57-112
Power Of Love/Liverlips	1961	Lee 1113
Times Sho' Gettin' Rough/Softie	1962	Phillips International 3586
QUINTONES (2) (JIMMY WITHERSPOON & THE)		
Still In Love/My Girl Ivy	1956	Atco 6084
QUINTONES (2) (PAT FOSTER & THE)		
In The Doorway Crying/That's What They Say	1960	Lee 1114
QUOTATIONS		
Imagination/Ala-Men-Sa-Aye	1961	Verve 10245/Relic 1025 (73)

Artist	Song	Year	Label
This Love Of Mine/We'll Reach Heaven Together		1962	Verve 10252
See You In September/ Summertime Goodbyes		1962	Verve 10261
Listen My Children And You Shall Hear/Speak Softly And Carry A Big Horn		1963	Liberty 55527
In The Night/Oh No, I Still Love Her		1964	Admiral 753
It Can Happen To You/I Don't Have To Worry		1968	DeVenus 107
Can I Have Someone/Havin' A Good Time (With My Baby)		1968	Imperial 66368
Imagination (acapella)/ Ala-Men-Sa-Aye (acapella)		1973	Relic 1025
Night/Why Do You Do Me Like You Do		1974	Downstairs 1003
I've Seen Everything (acapella)		1975	Relic LP 103
I Wonder Why (acapella)		1975	Relic LP 103
Maybe You'll Be There (acapella)		1975	Relic LP 103
Why Do You Do Me Like You Do (acapella)		1975	Relic LP 104
I'll Be Home (acapella)		1975	Relic LP 104
To The Aisle (acapella)		1975	Relic LP 105
I Don't Want To Cry (acapella)		1975	Relic LP 105
My Blue Heaven (acapella)		1975	Relic LP 108
Ala-Men-Sa-Aye (acapella)		1975	Relic LP 109
Imagination/Ala-Men-Saye		N/A	Popular Request 104

R-DELLS

Artist	Song	Year	Label
You Know Baby/You Say		1960	Dade 1806
Candy Stick Twist/That's What I Want		1962	Gone 5128

RADIANTS (1) (REF VALENTINOS)

Artist	Song	Year	Label
I'll Never Be Mean/Ra Cha Cha		1958	Wizz 713

RADIANTS (2) (CLEVE DUNCAN & THE)

Artist	Song	Year	Label
I'm Betting My Heart/To Keep Our Love (by the Penguins)		1959	Dooto 451

RADIANTS (3) (LITTLE JAN & THE)

Artist	Song	Year	Label
Now Is The Hour/Is It True?		1960	Clock 180
Heart And Soul/If You Love Me		1960	Vim 507
If You Love Me/Now Is The Hour		1961	Goldisc G15
If You Love Me/Is It True		1961	Queen 24007

RAGAMUFFINS

Artist	Song	Year	Label
Don't Be Gone Long/The Fun We Had		1964	Tollie 9027

RAGING STORMS

Artist	Song	Year	Label
Down At The Corner/So Hard To Take		1962	Trans Atlas 691
Hound Dog/Dribble Twist		1962	Warwick 677

RAGMOPS (LITTLE B. COOK & THE)

Artist	Song	Year	Label
God Bless This Moment/ Dancing The Scratch		1961	CBM 314

RAIDERS (1) (HAL GOODSON & THE)

Artist	Song	Year	Label
Later Baby		1957	Solo 108

RAIDERS (2)

Artist	Song	Year	Label
The Castle Of Love/Raiders From Outer Space		1958	Atco 6125
My Steady Girl/Walking Through The Jungle		1958	Brunswick 55090

RAIDERS (3)

Artist	Song	Year	Label
You Said/Blue Day		1958	Mercury 71395

RAIDERS (4) (TONY CASTLE & THE)

Artist	Song	Year	Label
Salty/Hi Lily, Hi Lo		1961	Gone 5099
Sincerely/Tara's Theme		1961	Gone 5105

RAIDERS (5) (JOEY VEL & THE)

Artist	Song	Year	Label
Acts Of Love/Goodbye		1962	Promo Rel 102

RAINBEAUS

Artist	Song	Year	Label
Maybe It's Wrong/That's All I'm Asking Of You		1960	World Pacific 810

RAINBEAUS (VINNIE ROME & THE)

Artist	Song	Year	Label
Come Home/Crazy Maisie		1959	Apt 25035

RAINBOWS (1)

Artist	Song	Year	Label
My Heart Is Yours/Can't You See I Love You		1954	Gem 214

RAINBOWS (2)

Artist	Song	Year	Label
Mary Lee/Evening		1855	Red Robin 134/Pilgrim 703 (56)/Fire 1012 (60)
Shirley/Stay		1956	Pilgrim 711/Argyle 1012 (62)
They Say/Minnie		1957	Rama 209
Love Me/Christmas Song (by the Mello-Moods)		1977	Ronnie 202

Artist	Song	Year	Label
They Say/I'm Lost (by the Mello-Moods)		N/A	Hamilton 143
Honey Hush		N/A	Red Robin (unreleased)
Jelly Bean		N/A	Red Robin (unreleased)
The Bug		N/A	Red Robin (unreleased)
Baraboo		N/A	Red Robin (unreleased)

RAINBOWS (3) (RANDY & THE) (AKA DIALTONES)

Artist	Song	Year	Label
Denise/Come Back		1963	Rust 5059
Why Do Kids Grow Up?/She's My Angel		1963	Rust 5073
Dry Your Eyes/Happy Teenager		1964	Rust 5080
Little Star/Sharin'		1964	Rust 5091
Joyride/Little Hot Rod Susie		1964	Rust 5101
Lovely Lies/I'll Forget Her Tomorrow		1966	Mike 4001
Quarter To Three/He's A Fugitive		1966	Mike 4004
Bonnie's Part Of Town/Can It Be?		1966	Mike 4008
I'll Be Seeing You/Oh, To Get Away		1967	B.T. Puppy 535
Angel Face/I Wonder Why		1977	Crystal Ball 106
Try The Impossible/Debbie		1982	Ambient Sound 02872
Remember (Walking In The Sand)/Happy Teenager		1982	Ambient Sound 451

RAINBOWS (4)

Artist	Song	Year	Label
Till Tomorrow/Mama, Take Your Daughter Back		1962	Gramo 5508
I Know/Only A Picture		1963	Dave 908
It Wouldn't Be Right/Family Monkey		1963	Dave 909
Key To My Heart/Good Thing Goin'		1968	Instant 3291

RAINBOWS (5)

Artist	Song	Year	Label
It's Terrific/Undertaker (by Sonny Walker)		1973	Baron 100
Can't You See I Love You/My Love Is True (by the Parakeets)		1973	Baron 105

RAINBOWS (6)

Artist	Song	Year	Label
Gonna Go Down		N/A	Mercury

RAINDROPS (1)

Artist	Song	Year	Label
(I Found) Heaven In Love/ I Prayed For Gold		1956	Spin-It 104
Little One/Rockin' On The Farm		1958	Spin-It 106
Rock-A-Baby Rock/Rain		1959	Capitol 4136
Without Love, Love, Love/Oh My		1959	Hamilton 50021

RAINDROPS (2)

Artist	Song	Year	Label
Dim Those Lights/Oh, Oh, Baby		1958	Vega 105

RAINDROPS (3)

Artist	Song	Year	Label
Love Is Like A Mountain/Maybe		1960	Corsair 104/Dore 561 (60)

RAINDROPS (4)

Artist	Song	Year	Label
I Remember In The Still Of The Night/The Sweetheart Song		1961	Imperial 5785

RAINDROPS (5) (TONY & THE)

Artist	Song	Year	Label
While Walking/Our Love Is Over		1962	Chesapeake 609
Tina/My Heart Cried		1962	Crosley 340

RAINDROPS (6)

Artist	Song	Year	Label
What A Guy/It's So Wonderful		1963	Jubilee 5444
The Kind Of Boy You Can't Forget/Even Though You Can't Dance		1963	Jubilee 5455
That Boy John/Hanky Panky		1963	Jubilee 5466
Book Of Love/I Won't Cry		1964	Jubilee 5469
Let's Get Together/You Got What I Like		1964	Jubilee 5475
One More Tear/Another Boy Like Mine		1964	Jubilee 5487
Don't Let Go/My Mama Don't Like Him		1964	Jubilee 5497

RAINDROPS (7)

Artist	Song	Year	Label
I Still Love You		1964	Sotoplay 0028
If You See Mary Lee/Ooh My Soul		1974	Firefly 313

RAINDROPS (8) (JACKIE & THE)

Artist	Song	Year	Label
My Heart Is Your Heart/Down Our Street		1964	Colpix 738

RAINSFORD, BILLY (& GROUP)

Artist	Song	Year	Label
Starry Eyes/Magnolia		N/A	Hermitage 803

RAJAHS (AKA NUTMEGS/AKA LYRES)

Artist	Song	Year	Label
Shifting Sands/I Fell In Love		1957	Klik 7805
Rose Ann (a capella)/You're Crying (a capella)		1973	Klik 1019

Artist Song	Year	Label
Story To You (a capella)/I Love You So (by the Five Satins)	1973	Klik 1020
RAMADAS		
Teenage Dream/My Angel Eyes	1963	Philips 40097
Summer Steady/Lonely Tears	1963	Philips 40117
I'm Going To Be Blue/Walking Down The Hall	1964	New World 2000
RAMBLERS (1) (REF KINGS (1))		
Search My Heart/50-50 Love	1953	Jax 319
Vadunt-Un-Va-Da Song/Please Bring Yourself Back Home	1954	MGM 11850
Bad Girl/Rickey-Do, Rickey-Do	1955	MGM 55006
RAMBLERS (2)		
The Heaven And Earth/Don't You Know?	1956	Federal 12286
RAMBLERS (3)		
Hurry Hurry Baby/Everything Is Wrong	1956	Flash 101
RAMBLERS (4)		
Rambling/Devil Train	1960	Addit 1257
RAMBLERS (5)		
Yaba Dab Ah Doo/Funny Papers	1961	Impact 10
RAMBLERS (6)		
I Need You So/She's A Heartbreaker	1963	Larkwood 1104
RAMBLERS (7)		
Father Sebastian/Barbara (I Love You)	1964	Almont 311
Birdland Baby/School Girl	1964	Almont 313
Surfin' Santa/Silly Little Boy	1964	Almont 315
RAMBLERS (8)		
Come On Back/So Sad	1963	Trumpet 102
RAMBLERS (9)		
Bye Bye Bye/Lost Symphony	1964	Cora 101
RAMS		
Sweet Thing/Rock Bottom	1955	Flair 1066
RAMSEY, GLORIA (& GROUP)		
My Love/Good Poppin' Daddy	1960	Hap 1894
RAN-DELLS		
Sound Of The Sun/Come On And Love Me Too	1963	Chairman 4407
The Martian Hop/Forgive Me Darling	1964	Chairman 4403
Beyond The Stars/Wintertime	1964	RSVP 1104
RAND, JOHNNY (& GROUP) (AKA J.R. & THE ATTRACTIONS)		
I'm Yours/Exodus	1965	Keno 928
RAND, ROSE MARIE (& GROUP)		
Lies, Lies, Lies/Gimmie	1956	Vik 0206
RANDELL, DENNY (& GROUP)		
Hey! Chickie Baby	1963	Cameo 255
RANDELL, RICK (& GROUP)		
Take My Name And Number/Stars	1962	United Artists 448
RANDELLS (RICK & THE)		
Let It Be You/Honey Doll	1959	ABC 10055
RANDLE, JOHNNY (& FEMALE GROUP)		
My One And Only One/Pulling String	1961	Jayree 2205
RANDOLPH, DEAN (& GROUP)		
False Love/Girl In The White Convertible	1963	Chancellor 1138
RANDOLPH, LEROY (& GROUP)		
(I've Fallen Into) The Tender Trap/Good to The Last Drop	1971	Spring 121
RANDOLPH, LIL (& GROUP)		
Satellite Love/Give Me A Girl	1958	Chock Full Of Hits 103
RANGOONS		
My Heart Is A Ball Of String/Moon Guitar	1961	Laurie 3096
RANNELS		
Blue Island/Boom, Baby	1963	Boss 2122
RAPHAEL, JOHNNY (& GROUP)		
We're Only Young Once/Lonely Road To Nowhere	1958	Aladdin 3409
RAPID TRANSIT		
Living Just For You/My Own True Love	1978	Clifton 26
RAPID-TONES (WILLIE WINFIELD & THE) (REF HARPTONES)		
Sunday Kind Of Love/Memories Of You	1962	Rapid 101
RAVELS (SHERIFF & THE)		
Shombalor/Lonely One	1959	Vee Jay 306

Artist Song	Year	Label
RAVENAIRES (AKA RIVIERAS (2))		
Together Forever/A Night To Remember	1958	Algonquin 718 (second pressing, first is by the Rivieras)
RAVENETTS		
Too Young To Know/Misery	1959	Moon 103
RAVENS (1)		
Out Of A Dream/My Sugar Is So Refined	1946	Hub 3032
Bye Bye Baby Blues/Once And For All	1946	Hub 3033
Honey/Lullabye	1946	Hub 3030
Mahzel/For You	1947	National 9034
Ol' Man River/Would You Believe Me?	1947	National 9035
Write Me A Letter/Summetime	1947	National 9038
Searching For Love/For You	1947	National 9039
Fool That I Am/Be I Bumble Bee Or Not	1947	National 9040
Bye Bye Baby Blues/Once And For All	1948	King 4234
Out Of A Dream/Blues In The Clouds (by the Three Clouds)	1948	King 4260
Together/There's No You	1948	National 9042
Until The Real Thing Comes Along/Send For Me If You Need Me	1948	National 9045
September Song/Once In A While	1948	National 9053
It's Too Soon To Know/Be On Your Merry Way	1948	National 9056
How Could I Know/I Don't Know Why I Love You Like I Do	1948	National 9059
Silent Night/White Christmas	1948	National 9062/Mercury 70505 (54)/Savoy 1540 (54)
Always/Rooster	1948	National 9064
Out Of A Dream/My Baby Is So Refined	1949	King
Honey/Bye Bye Baby Blues	1949	King 310
Honey/Matinee Hour In New Orleans(by the Three Clouds, instrumental)	1949	King 4272
My Sugar Is So Refined/Playing Around (by the Three Clouds, instrumental)	1949	King 4293
Deep Purple/Leave My Gal Alone	1949	National 9065
Ricky's Blues/The House I Live In	1949	National 9073
There's Nothing Like A Woman In Love/Careless Love	1949	National 9085
If You Didn't Mean It/Someday	1949	National 9089
I'm Afraid Of You/Get Wise Baby	1949	National 9098
I've Been A Fool/I Don't Have To Ride No More	1949	National 9101
Time Takes Care Of Everything/Don't Look Now	1950	Columbia 39050
My Baby's Gone/I'm So Crazy For Love	1950	Columbia 39070
Midnight Blues/You Don't Have To Drop A Heart To Break It	1950	Columbia 39112
Count Every Star/I'm Gonna Paper All My Walls With Your Love Letters	1950	National 9111
Phantom Stage Couch/I'm Gonna Take To The Road	1950	National 9131
You're Always In My Dreams/Gotta Find My Baby	1951	Columbia 39194
You Fooling Thing/Honey I Don't Want You	1951	Columbia 39408
Out In The Cold Again (with Dinah Washington)/Hey Good Lookin' (with Dinah Washington)	1951	Mercury 8257
Lilacs In The Rain/Time Is Marching On	1951	National 9148
The Whiffenpoof Song/I Get All My Lovin' On A Saturday Night	1951	Okeh 6825
That Old Gang Of Mine/Everything But You	1951	Okeh 6843
Write Me A Letter/Marie	1951	Rendition 5001

Artist	Song	Year	Label
	There's No Use Pretending/		
	Wagon Wheels	1951	Mercury 5764
	Begin The Beguine/Looking		
	For My Baby	1952	Mercury 5800
	Chloe-e/Why Did You Leave Me	1952	Mercury 5853
	Don't Mention My Name/		
	I'll Be Back	1952	Mercury 70060
	Write Me One Sweet Letter/		
	Rock Me All Night Long	1952	Mercury 8291
	Mam'Selle/Calypso Song	1952	Okeh 6888
	Come A Little Bit Closer/		
	She's Got To Go	1953	Mercury 70119
	Who'll Be The Fool/		
	Rough Ridin'	1953	Mercury 70213
	Without A Song/Walkin' My		
	Blues Away	1953	Mercury 70240
	September Song/Escortin' or		
	Courtin'	1954	Mercury 70307
	Going Home/The Lonesome		
	Road	1954	Mercury 70330
	Love Is No Dream/I've Got		
	You Under My Skin	1954	Mercury 70413
	Bye Bye Baby Blues/Happy		
	Go Lucky Baby	1955	Jubilee 5184
	Green Eyes/The Bells Of San		
	Raquel	1955	Jubilee 5203
	On Chapel Hill/We'll Raise A		
	Ruckus Tonight	1955	Jubilee 5217
	Old Man River/Write Me A Letter	1955	Mercury 70554
	Kneel And Pray/I Can't Believe	1956	Argo 5255
	Water Boy/A Simple Prayer	1956	Argo 5261
	Boots And Saddles/I'll Always		
	Be In Love With You	1956	Jubilee 5237
	Dear One/That'll Be The Day	1957	Argo 5276/Checker 871 (57)
	Here Is My Heart/Lazy Mule	1957	Argo 5284
	Into The Shadows/The Rising		
	Sun	1959	Top Rank 2003
	Solitude/Hole In The Middle		
	Of The Room	1959	Top Rank 2014
	It's The Talk Of The Town/		
	Count Every Star	1972	National 9158
	It's The Talk Of The Town/		
	Count Every Star	1972	National 9158
RAVENS (2) (MIKE & THE)			
	I've Taken All I Can/		
	Mr. Heartbreak	1962	Empire 1
RAVENS (3) (RICO & THE)			
	In My Heart/Don't You Know	1965	Rally 1601/Autumn 6 (65)
RAVENS (4) (BILLY & THE)			
	Someone To Love	N/A	Sahara 108
RAVES (1)			
	Don't Bug Me Baby/If I Knew		
	The Way	1956	Liberty 55013
	Tell Me One More Time/		
	Billy The Kid	1959	Swade 104
RAVES (2) (JIMMY RICKS & THE)			
	Homesick/Daddy Rollin' Stone	1962	Atco 6220
	Daddy Rollin' Stone/Umgowa	1962	Festival 25004
RAVONS (1)			
	Teenage Hop/Wrapped,		
	Tangled And Tied	1958	Arrow 734
	Teen-Age Idol/I'm A Fugitive	1959	Davis 464
RAVONS (2)			
	Why Did You Leave Me?/		
	Everybody's Laughing At Me	1962	Yucca 142
RAVONS (3) (BOBBY ROBERTS & THE)			
	I'm In Love Again/How Can I		
	Make Her Mine	1964	Cameo 339
	Big Sandy	N/A	Syy 101
RAY, LITTLE JIMMY (& GROUP)			
	Make Her Mine/You Need To		
	Fall In Love	1959	Galliant 1001
RAY-DOTS			
	I Need Someone/Lu La	1960	Vibro 1651
RAY-O-VACS			
	What Can I Say/Start Lovin' Me	1952	Jubilee 5098
	Darling (with Herb Milliner)/		
	Riding High	1954	Josie 763
	Crying All Alone/Party Time	1956	Kaiser 384
	Wino O/Hong Kong	1956	Kaiser 389
	Party Time/Crying Alone	1957	Atco 6085
	Little Boy/I'll Always Be In		
	Love With You	1960	Sharp 103
RAY-O-VACS ("FLAP" McQUEEN & THE)			
	Daddy (vocal by Babe Hutton)/		
	I Still Love You So (vocal		
	by Herb Milliner)	1955	Josie 781
RAY-VONS			
	Judy/Regina	1964	Laurie 3248
RAYBER VOICES (HERMAN GRIFFIN & THE)			
	I Need You/I'm So Glad	N/A	H.O.B. 112
RAYBER VOICES (MARV JOHNSON & THE)			
	Come To Me/Whisper	1959	United Artists 160/Tamla 101 (59)
RAYE, CAL (& GROUP)			
	We Belong Together/Lovely		
	Lies	1965	Providence 412
	My Tears Start To Fall/You're		
	My Lovin' Baby	1966	Super 101
RAYE, JAN (THE JAN RAYE QUARTET)			
	Sweet Sue/Whatever Happened		
	To You (by W.L. Carroll)	1955	Baton 213
RAYE, JAN (THE JAN RAYE QUARTET) (LILY ANN & THE)			
	Soda Pop/You Fool	1956	Baton 221
RAYE, JEAN (& GROUP)			
	Open Your Eyes/The Very		
	Young	1961	Whip 275
RAYS (1)			
	Tippity Top/Moo Goo Gai Pan	1955	Chess 1613
	How Long Must I Wait?/Second		
	Fiddle	1957	Argo 1074/Chess 1678 (57)
	My Steady Girl/Nobody Loves		
	You Like I Do	1957	XYZ 100
	Silhouettes/Daddy Cool	1957	XYZ 102/Cameo 117 (57)
	Crazy Girl/Dressin' Up	1958	Cameo 127
	Triangle/Rendezvous	1958	Cameo 128
	Elevator Operator/Souvenirs		
	Of Summertime	1958	XYZ 2001
	Why Do You Look The Other		
	Way/Zimba Lulu	1959	XYZ 600
	Mediterranean Moon/It's A		
	Cryin' Shame	1959	XYZ 605
	Silver Starlight/Old Devil Moon	1960	XYZ 608
	Magic Moon (Claire De Lune)/		
	Louie Hoo Hoo	1961	XYZ 607
	Sad Saturday/Love Another Girl	1964	Amy 900
RAYS (1) (BOB CREWE & THE)			
	Charm Bracelet/Do Be Do Be Do	1957	Vik 0307
RAYS (1) (DOUG WARREN & THE)			
	If The World Doesn't End		
	Tomorrow(I'm Comin'		
	After You)/Around Midnight	1960	Image 1011
RAYS (1) (FB FRANKIE VALLI)			
	Are You Happy Now/Bright		
	Brown Eyes	1962	Perri 1004
RAYS (1) (FEATURING HAL MILLER)			
	Rags To Riches/The Man Above	1958	Cameo 133
RAYS (1) (HAL MILLER & THE)			
	An Angel Cried/Hope, Faith		
	And Dreams	1961	Topix 6003
	I Still Care/On My Own Two		
	Feet	1964	Amy 909
RAYS (2) (RICH & THE)			
	My Heart/The Way You Look		
	Tonight	1956	Richloy 101
RAYTONES (1) (LAVERNE RAY & THE)			
	I've Got That Feeling/I'm In		
	Love Again	1957	Okeh 7091
RAYTONES (2)			
	My Baby Pt. 1/My Baby Pt. 2	1958	Ball 0503
	Until You're In My Arms/		
	Ready, Willing And Able	1958	Cash 1059
RAYTONES (2) (RUDY RAE MOORE & THE)			
	Dear Ruth/Skitter Skatter Pitter		
	Patter	1957	Ball 0500
	Your Tender Touch/My		
	Country Gal	1958	Ball 0504
	I'm Ready/So Good To Me	1958	Cash 1060
RE'VELLS			
	Let It Please Be You/Love		
	Walked In	1962	Roman Press 201
RE-VELS (AKA RE-VELS QUARTETTE)			
	You Lied To Me/Later, Later,		
	Baby	1956	Sound 129
	Dream, My Darling, Dream/		
	Cha-Cha-Toni	1956	Sound 135

Artist Song	Year	Label
So In Love/It Happened To Me	1956	Teen 122
False Alarm/When You Come Back To Me	1958	Chess 1708
RE-VELS QUARTETTE (AKA RE-VELS)		
My Lost Love/Love Me, Baby	1954	Atlas 1035
REACTIONS		
Just A Little Love/Let Me Hang Around You	1964	Cool Sound 701/Cloud 10498 (64)
Our Wonderful Love/That Girl	1965	Mutual 509
REAL McCOYS		
Gonna Take A Chance/ I Must Forget About You	N/A	Pico 523
REALISTICS		
Please Baby Please/Too Shy	1970	De-Lite 528
REALITY		
Dry Your Eyes/Trickle Trickle	1978	U.G.H.A. 02
Endlessly/ABC's Of Love	1979	U.G.H.A. 13
At Night/Who' Lovin' You	1980	Bey 130
REALTONES		
Dumb Dora	N/A	Famous LP 501
REARDON, EDDIE (BB THE THREE FRIENDS)		
Who Is Eddie	1958	Brunswick 55062
REASONS (RIA & THE)		
Memories Linger On/Sorry I Lied	1964	Amy 888
REBELAIRES		
Once We Loved/Keep Singing And Look Ahead	1957	B&K 103
REBELS (1) (GENE SUMMERS & THE)		
School Of Rock And Roll	1958	Jan 101
REBELS (2) (JIMMY & THE)		
Shiek Of Araby/You Are My Sunshine	1959	Roulette 4201
REBELS (3)		
In The Park/In My Heart	1959	Kings-X 3362
REBELS (4)		
Just Give Me Your Heart/ The Donkey Step	1961	Peacock 1909
RED CAPS (STEVE GIBSON & THE)		
Cheryl Lee/Bless You	1959	Hunt 326
RED COATS		
Oh, When You Touch Me/I Never Knew (by the Colts)	1959	Del-Co 4002
Love Unreturned/Dum Dum Song	1965	Laurie 3319
Teenage Broken Heart	N/A	Kikko 610
RED HOTS (JOHNNY HANSLEY & THE)		
Please Try To Love Me/Shaggin'	1959	Kip 402
RED TOPS		
Hello Is The You?/Swanee River Rock	N/A	Sky 703/RCA 7144
REDCOATS (STEVE ALAIMO & THE)		
Home By Eleven	1959	Dade 1800
Love Letters/You Can Fall In Love	1959	Dade 1805
I Want You To Love Me/Blue Fire	1959	Marlin 6064/Imperial 5699 (60)
She's My Baby/Should I Call	1959	Marlin 6067
Blue Fire/My Heart Never Said Goodbye	1960	Dickson 6445
REDJACKS		
Big Brown Eyes/To Make You Mine	1958	Apt 25006/Oklahoma 5005 (58)
REDTOPPERS (LEE OVERBY)		
I Never Had A Girl Like You/ All Night Jump	N/A	Dan 3214
REDTOPS (EDDIE DUGOSH & THE)		
Release My Heart/One Mile	1958	Award 116
REDWOODS (AKA FLAIRS (2)) (GM JEFF BARRY)		
Shake Shake Sherry/The Memory Lingers On	1961	Epic 9447
Never Take It Away/ Unemployment Insurance	1961	Epic 9473
Where You Used To Be/ Please Mr. Scientist	1962	Epic 9505
REED, A. C. (& GROUP)		
Talkin' 'Bout My Friends/ Boogaloo Tramp (no group)	N/A	Nike 2002
REED, JOHN (& GROUP)		
Darling Please/Yeah Little Girl	N/A	Fore 611
REED, JOHNNY (& GROUP)		
A Thousand Miles Away/ Promises	1958	Major 100
REED, LULA (BB THE TEENERS)		
Just Whisper/If The Sun Isn't Shining	1954	King 4714
Why Don't You Come On Home/ I'm Giving All My Love	1955	King 4811
Give Me The Right/Anything To Say You're Mine	1958	Argo 5298
Idle Gossip/Lovin'	1959	Argo 5355
REED, URSULA (BB THE SOLITAIRES)		
You're Laughing Cause I'm Crying/Ursula's Blues	1954	Old Town 1001
REEVES, HARRIET (& GROUP)		
Come To Me/Just Friends	1961	Eon 103
REFLECTIONS (1) (HOWIE BUTLER & THE)		
Treasure Of Love/Have A Good Time	1960	Gaity 6017
REFLECTIONS (2)		
I Really Must Know/Maybe Tomorrow	1961	Crossroads 401
Rocket To The Moon/Because Of You	1962	Crossroads 402
Tic Toc/In The Still Of The Night	1962	Tigre 602
I Need Your Love/You Don't Love Me	N/A	Went 001
REFLECTIONS (3)		
Like Columbus Did/Lonely Girl	1964	Golden World 12
Talkin' 'Bout My Girl/Oowee Wow	1964	Golden World 15
Don't Do That To Me/A Henpecked Guy	1964	Golden World 16
(Just Like) Romeo & Juliet/ Can't You Tell By The Look In My Eyes	1964	Golden World 8/9
You're My Baby/Shabby Little Hut	1965	Golden World 19
Poor Man's Son/Comin' At You	1965	Golden World 20
Deborah Ann/Wheelin' And Dealin'	1965	Golden World 22
Out Of The Picture/June Bride	1965	Golden World 24
Girl In The Candy Store/Your Kind Of Love	1965	Golden World 29
Like Adam And Eve/Vito's House	1966	ABC 10794
Long Cigarette/You're Gonna Find Out	1966	ABC 10822
You Said Goodbye/Helpless	1981	Adam & Eve 1
REGAL DEWEY		
Love Music/Where Would I Be Without You	1977	Milennium 603
REGAL, MIKE (& GROUP)		
Too Young/Is It True What They Say About Barbara	1963	Kapp 506
REGALS (1)		
May God Bless And Keep You/ Run Pretty Baby	1954	Aladdin 3266
When You're Home/There'll Always Be A Christmas	1954	MGM 11869
I'm So Lonely/Got The Water Boiling	1955	Atlantic 1062
REGALS (2)		
Yes My Love/See You In The Morning	1960	Lavender 1452
REGAN, TOMMY (& FEMALE GROUP)		
I Adore You/Nine To Five	1965	World Artists 1049
REGAN, TOMMY (BB THE MARCELS)		
I'll Never Stop Loving You/ This Time I'm Losing You	1964	Colpix 725
REGENTS (1)		
Bamboo Tree/Isle Of Trinidad	1957	Argo 5268
REGENTS (2) (AKA FIVE SPENDERS)		
That's What I Call A Good Time/ No Hard Feelings	1960	Kayo 101
Summertime Blues	N/A	Peoria 0008
REGENTS (3) (AKA DESIRES (3)/AKA RUNAROUNDS (2))		
Barbara-Ann/I'm So Lonely	1961	Cousins 1002/Gee 1065 (61)
Runaround/Laura My Darling	1961	Gee 1071
Liar/Don't Be A Fool	1961	Gee 1073
Lonesome Boy/Oh Baby	1961	Gee 1075
Your Love Captured Me	1961	Gee LP 706

Artist Song	Year	Label
Just Cry	1961	Gee LP 706
Summertime	1961	Gee LP 706
Autumn Leaves	1961	Gee LP 706
A Fool In Love	1961	Gee LP 706
Jeanette, Jeanette	1961	Gee LP 706
Sunday Kind Of Love	1961	Gee LP 706/Forum Circle LP
Let Them Talk	1962	K-C
Unbelievable/Hooray For Love (by the Run-A-Rounds)	1962	KC 116
Over The Rainbow	N/A	unreleased
REGENTS (4)		
Me And You/Playmates	1965	Blue Cat 110
Words/Worryin' Kind	1966	Penthouse 502
REID, MATTHEW (BB THE FOUR SEASONS)		
Jane/Why Start	1961	ABC 10259
Through My Tears/Me Tarzan Twist	1962	ABC 10305
RELATIONS		
Smile (Baby)/Until We Two Are One	1963	Kape 504
Too Proud To Let You Know/ What Did I Do Wrong?	1963	Kape 703
All Night Long/When We Get The Word	1963	Michelle 506
Crowd With The Phony Tattoo/ Say You Love Me	1963	Zells 712
Don't Let Me Down This Weekend/Puddin' And Tain	1971	Lebby 7966
When We Get The Word	N/A	Club
Yes I Do	N/A	Club
Burying Ground	N/A	Club
Back To The Beach/Too Proud To Let You Know	N/A	Demand 501/Davy Jones 664
RELATIONS (GLORIA & THE)		
Date With My Man/ Hook, Line And Sinker	N/A	Bonnie 101/102
RELATIVES (1) (RONNIE & THE) (AKA RONETTES)		
Sweet Sixteen/I Want A Boy	1961	Colpix 481/Colpix 601 (61)
My Guiding Angel/I'm Gonna Quit While I'm Ahead	1961	May 111
RELATIVES (2)		
Never Will I Love You Again/ I'm Just Looking For Love	1963	Almont 306
RELF, BOBBY (BB THE LAURELS)		
Our Love/The Shuck (by Ernie Freeman)	1956	Cash 1019
Little Fool/I'm Not Afraid	1956	Dot 15510
REMAINDERS		
Pen In Hand/Over The Rainbow	N/A	Vico 1
REMAINING FEW		
What Are You Gonna Be/ Who Do You Think You Are?	1991	Clifton 94
REMARKABLES (1) (REGGIE & THE)		
The Year That Gave Me You/ Come On Baby	1962	Musicor 1030
REMARKABLES (2)		
Write Me/Whirl-A-Round	1964	Chase 1600
REMINISCENTS		
Cards Of Love/Flames	1962	Marcel 1000
For Your Love/Please Lie To Me	1963	Cleopatra 104
Zoom Zoom Zoom/Oh Let Me Dream	1963	Day 1000
Hey You (acapella)	1975	Relic LP 109
Oh Let Me Dream (acapella)	1975	Relic LP 109
RENAULTS		
Stella/Melancholy	1959	Warner Bros. 5094
Just Like Mine/Another Train Pulled Out	1962	Wand 114
Only You/Hully Gully Lamb	1962	Wand 120
Two Face/Ten Questions	1963	Chicory 160
RENAULTS (BOBBY COLQUITT & THE)		
Searching/Tell Daddy Baby	1961	Colt 621/CJ 621
I'm Not A Know It All	N/A	Colt 101
RENDEZVOUS		
It Breaks My Heart/Take A Break	1961	Rust 5041
Congratulations Baby/Faithfully	1962	Reprise 20089
Ruby Baby/Ram-Bunk-Shus	N/A	Paradise 1017
RENDITIONS (BILLY DE MARCO & THE)		
Out Of My Mind/Goodbye Mister Blues	1960	Up 113
RENEGADES		
Stolen Angel/Keep Laughin'	1961	Dorset 5007

Artist Song	Year	Label
RENEGADES (PATTI MCCOY & THE)		
I Love Him So/Double Trouble	1962	Counsel 119
Goodbye/Stranger	1962	Counsel 116
RENO, AL (& GROUP)		
Cheryl/Congratulations	1961	Kapp 432
RENO, FRANK (& GROUP)		
I Love You So/I Want My Love	1962	Diamond 118
RENO, NICKY (& GROUP)		
I Had A Dream/My Darling	1959	Ges 100
RENOWNS (1)		
My Mind's Made Up/Wild One	1961	Everest 19396
RENOWNS (2) (RICHIE & THE)		
Please Say You Want Me/That's What You're Doing To Me	1963	Streke 247
REPTILES (JOHNNY COLE & THE)		
Wrap My Heart In Velvet/ Lizard Grizzard	1961	Radiant 1503
RESOLUTIONS		
January 1st, 1962/Traveling Salesman	1962	Valentine 1001
RESONICS		
Split Personality/Pepe La Phew	1963	Unity 101
I'm Really In Love/Think Right	1964	Lucky Token 108
With Your Love To Guide Me/ It Won't Be Long	N/A	Lil-Larry 1005
RESTLESS HEARTS (FRED PARRIS & THE) (REF FIVE SATINS)		
Walk A Little Faster/No Use In Crying	1965	Checker 1108
Land Of Broken Hearts/Bring It On Home To Daddy	1966	Atco 6439
Blushing Bride/Giving My Love To You	1966	Green Sea 106
I'll Be Hanging On/I Can Really Satisfy	1966	Green Sea 107
In The Still Of The Night "67"/ Heck No (instrumental)	1967	Mama Sadie 1001
RETROSPECT		
The Girl I Love/My Love Will Never Die	1980	Clifton 42
Lorraine/Row Your Boat	N/A	Collage
REUNION		
Wonderful Tonight/Cool Change	1987	Clifton 79
You Were Always On My Mind/ Where Are You Tonight	1990	Clifton 91
Drift Away/Lean On Me	N/A	Starlight 17
Slipping Into Darkness/Heart Of Saturday Night	N/A	Starlight 18
REUNITED		
Unbelievable/Heavenly Father	1980	Clifton 50
REV-LONS (FEMALE)		
Give Me One More Chance/ Boy Trouble	1962	Garpax 44168
Love Can't Be A One Way Deal/ I Can't Forget About You	1963	Reprise 20200/Starburst 123
REVALONS		
Dreams Are For Fools/This Is The Moment	1958	Pet 802
REVELAIRES		
Only The Angels Know/Down By The Well	1954	Burgundy 1001
It's A Miracle/Crazy Doctor	1954	Burgundy 105
Rockin' The Tease/New Kind Of Gold	1960	Crystalette 737
You Must Be Blind/She Wears My Ring	1965	Decca 31830
REVELATIONS		
Higher And Higher/Spanish Harlem	N/A	Starlight 15
Love Potion No. 9/Don't Look Back	N/A	Starlight 16
REVELERS		
Give Me A Second Chance/ The Ghaly Ghaly Man	N/A	Masquerade 22458
REVELIERS		
I Still Love Her	1962	Soma 1180
REVELLETTS (JIMMY CHARLES & THE)		
A Million To One/Hop Scotch Hop	1960	Promo 1002
The Age For Love/Follow The Swallow	1960	Promo 1003
REVELLONS (RIA & THE)		
She Fell In Love/He's Not There	1964	RSVP 1110

Artist Song	Year	Label
REVELS		
Dead Man's Stroll/Talking To My Heart	1959	Norgolde 103 (first pressing)
Midnight Stroll/Talking To My Heart	1959	Norgolde 103 (second pressing)
Foo Man Choo/Tweedley Dee	1959	Norgolde 104
Good Grief/Six Pack	1959	Swingin' 620
Please/Two Little Monkeys	1960	Andie 5077
Oh How I Love You/I Met My Lost Love	1961	Palette 5074
Lots Of Luck/Gotta Have Some Fun	1963	Diamond 143
REVERES (1)		
Leonore/Honeystrollin' (instrumental by the Honeystrollers)	1958	Glory 272
REVERES (2) (FEMALE)		
Beyond The Sea/The Show Must Go On	1963	Jubilee 5463
REVIERAS		
Walk Away/I'll Wait	1964	Victoria 103
REVIVALS		
My Prayer To Heaven/Oh Please	1984	Memory Lane 100
Too Young/I'm Not A Juvenile Delinquent	1987	Avenue D 14
Under The Boardwalk/I Believe	1987	DCA 100/Clifton 84 (89)
Quarter To Three/Sea Cruise	1989	Sultra 101
No No No/Slow Dance	1991	Avenue D 17
REVLONS (1)		
This Restless Heart/I Promise Love	1961	Rae-Cox 105
Dry Your Eyes/She'll Come To Me	1962	Capitol 4739
It Could Happen To You/Ya Ya	1964	Parkway 107
REVLONS (2) (TINO & THE)		
Story Of Our Love/Black Bermudas And Knee Socks	1960	Mark 154
Wedding Bells Will Ring/Heidi	1963	Pip 4000
Little Girl, Little Girl/Rave On	1965	Dearborn 525
Lazy Mary Memphis/I'm Coming Home	1966	Dearborn 530
REVLONS (3) (AKA CENTURIES (3)/AKA JAYTONES)		
Ride Away/Betty (by the Centuries (3))	1963	Times Square 15
My Love	N/A	Klik
REVLONS (4)		
What A Love This Is/Did I Make A Mistake	1962	Toy 101
REVLONS (5)		
Love's Burning Fire/Bye, Bye Baby	N/A	VRC 112
REVLONS (6)		
Moonlight Angel/You Don't Love Me	1980	Crystal Ball 138
REVOLVERS		
The Pounding Of My Heart/ Walkin' My Baby Back Home	1994	JL 101
REXETTES (LARRY & THE)		
Mercy/That Ain't All	N/A	Zorro 420
REY, TONY (& GROUP)		
Something On Your Mind/ Play It Cool	1959	King Bee 101
RHOADES, DARRYL (& GROUP)		
Burgers From Heaven/Surfin' Shark	1976	Wonder 1976-1
RHYTHM ACES (1)		
Crazy Jealous/Boppin' Sloppin' Baby	1960	Mark-X 8004
RHYTHM ACES (2) (PRESTON JACKSON & THE)		
Be Mine/Joni	1961	Vee Jay 417
RHYTHM BOYS (HANK FARELL & THE)		
Bad Boy	1960	Solar 1013
RHYTHM CADETS		
Dearest Doryce/Rocking Jimmy	1957	Vesta 501/502
RHYTHM CADETS (LITTLE WILLIE & THE)		
Eleanor/I Need Your Love	1988	Crystal Ball 152
RHYTHM CASTERS		
Love, Love, Baby/Oh, My Darling	1957	Excello 2115
RHYTHM FIVE		
Baby Please Don't Go/I Tried	1962	Tifco 829
RHYTHM FOUR (JOE THERRIEN & THE)		
Tell Me/Siam	1961	Sentinel 8906
RHYTHM GENTS		
Linda	1964	Merri 6008
RHYTHM HEIRS		
Strange World/Cradle Rock	1959	Yucca 105
RHYTHM JESTERS		
Hole In The Bucket/Rock To The Music	1956	Rama 213
Please Be Mine/Ooh Sha-La	1962	Lectra 501
RHYTHM JESTERS (BOB DAVIS & THE)		
Never Anymore/She'll Never Know	1957	Rama 224
RHYTHM KINGS		
Night After Night/I Shouldn't Have Passed Your House	1949	Ivory 751
Merry Christmas One And All/ Christmas Is Coming At Last	1951	Apollo 1171
Why My Darling Why/I Gotta Go Now	1951	Apollo 1181
RHYTHM MASTERS (AKA VEL-AIRES)		
Patricia/Baby We Two	1956	Flip 314
RHYTHM ROCKERS (1) (JIMMY REAGAN & THE)		
Lonely Lonely Heart/Can't You See It In My Eyes	1959	G&G 128/129/Mona-Lee
RHYTHM ROCKERS (2)		
Oh Oh Henry/Madness	1960	Square 505
RHYTHM ROCKERS (2) (FB MIKE PATTERSON)		
We Belong Together/Oh Boy	1960	Satin 921
RHYTHM ROCKERS (3)		
We Three	N/A	Emperor 112
RHYTHM STARS		
Oh Moon/Lynn	1959	Clock 1007
My Girl Babe/Bandstand March	1959	Corsican 0057
RHYTHM STEPPERS		
Hey Little Lola/My First Broken Heart	1959	Spinning 6010
RHYTHM TONES		
Please Come Back To Me/ Something Wrong	1959	Vest 828
RHYTHMAIRES (CURT JENSEN & THE)		
Just For You/If I Only Knew	1958	Pet 806
RHYTHMAIRES (JESSIE LEE WITH THE)		
Lonely Broken Heart/Won't Have To Cry Anymore	1958	Mida 110
RHYTHMAIRES (WITH GAYLE LARK)		
Melody Of Love	N/A	Tops EP 250
Sincerely	N/A	Tops EP 252
Earth Angel	N/A	Tops EP 252
RHYTHMASTERS		
Until Now/I Was The Third On A Match	N/A	Bennett 401
RHYTHMERES		
Elaine/Bow Legged Baby	1958	Brunswick 55083
RHYTHMETTES		
Mister Love/Mind Reader	1957	Brunswick 55012
Till My Baby Comes Home/ That's A Plenty	1958	Brunswick 55050
Page From The Future	1958	Brunswick 55097
High School Lovers/Snow Queen	1960	Coral 62186
RIALTOS (1) (CHANO & THE)		
Guardian Angel/Don't Forget To Write	1960	Jin 154
RIALTOS (2) (BOBBY HOLLISTER & THE)		
Love's Gamble/Ring Around Your Neck	1961	Pike 5910
RIALTOS (3)		
Let Me In/It Hurts	1962	CB 5009
RIBBONS		
Ain't Gonna Kiss Ya/My Baby Said	1962	Marsh 202
RIBITONES		
Most Of All/Crazy Little Mama	1979	Clifton 38
Crazy Little Mama/Crazy Little Mama (acapella)	1979	Off The Wall 69
Canadian Sunset/U.G.H.A.	1980	U.G.H.A. 14
RICARDO, RICKY (& GROUP)		
I Wish For Someone/Peek A Boo Mary Loo	1961	Wye 1011
Precious One	N/A	Taylor 801

Artist	Song	Year	Label
RICARDOS			
	Mary's Little Lamb/I Mean Really	1958	Star-X 512
RICH, DAVE (& GROUP)			
	I've Thought It Over/School Blues	1959	RCA 7141
RICHARDS, DONALD (BB THE VOLUMES (3))			
	I Cried For Your Love/Hello Operator	1962	Chex 1003
RICHARDS, JAY (& GROUP)			
	Echoes On My Mind/Little Sheryl	1959	Hollywood 1100
RICHARDS, LEE (& GROUP)			
	I'm Waitin'	1959	Wanger 193
RICHARDS, NORM (& GROUP)			
	Tease Me/Datin' With You	1959	Imperial 5567
RICHARDS, RICKY (& GROUP)			
	I Wish For Someone/Peek-A-Boo Mary Lou	1961	Wye 1011
RICHARDSON, RUDI (& GROUP)			
	Why Should I Cry/Fools Hall Of Fame	1957	Sun 271
RICHETTES			
	Love And Happiness/This Is Our First Date	1962	Apt 25069
RICHIE (& GROUP)			
	Cherie/Dream Lover	1961	Kip 240
RICKATEERS (JIMMY RICKS & THE)			
	She's Fine-She's Mine/The Unbeliever	1956	Josie 796
RICKS, JIMMY (& FEMALE GROUP)			
	Romance In The Dark/Trouble In Mind	1964	Atlantic 2246
RICKS, JIMMY (& GROUP)			
	Do You Promise/The Sugar Man Song	1957	Paris 504
	Goodnight My Love/At Sunrise	1959	Signature 12013
RICKY (& GROUP) (FB RICHARD BERRY)			
	Baby Please Come Home (flip has no group)	1956	Empire 106
RICQUETTES (DANNY SKEENE & THE)			
	Over The Rainbow/Seven Days	N/A	Valex 105/106
RIDGLEY, TOMMY (& GROUP)			
	Double Eye Whammie/Should I Ever Love Again	1961	Ric 978
RIFF-TONES (RIFF RUFFIN & THE)			
	I'm Confessin'/Solitude	1957	Ball 0501
RIFFS (AKA CHIMES (5))			
	Tell Her/I Been Thinkin'	1964	Jamie 1296
	Little Girl/Why Are The Nights So Cold	1964	Sunny 22
	Tell Tale Friends/Why Are The Nights So Cold	1965	Old Town 1179
	Storm/Where There's A Will	1978	Crystal Ball 130
RILEY, PAT (& GROUP)			
	Without You To Love/Get With It	1957	Tin Pan Alley 175
RING-A-DINGS			
	Snaky Poo, Pt. 1/Snaky Poo, Pt. 2	1962	Infinity 014
RINGO, EDDIE (& GROUP)			
	Teardrops On My Letter/Full Racing Cam	1960	Twin Star 1016
RINKY-DINKS (AKA DING DONGS (1)) (FEATURING BOBBY DARIN)			
	Early In The Morning/Now We're One	1958	Atco 6121
	Mighty Mighty Man/You're Mine	1958	Atco 6128
	Catch A Little Moonbeam/Choo Choo Cha Cha	1959	Capitol 4146
RIOS, AUGIE (& GROUP)			
	When You Dance/No One	1964	Shelley 186
RIP CHORDS (1)			
	I Laughed So Hard/You And I	1958	MMI 1236
RIP CHORDS (2) (FB BRUCE JOHNSTON)			
	Ding Dong/Karen	1962	Columbia 42641
	Karen/Here I Stand	1963	Columbia 42687
	She Thinks I Still Care/Gone	1963	Columbia 42812
	Hey Little Cobra/The Queen	1963	Columbia 42921
	Three Window Coupe/Hot Rod USA	1964	Columbia 43035
	One Piece Topless Bathing Suit/Wah-Wahini	1964	Columbia 43093
	Don't Be Scared/Bunny Hill	1965	Columbia 43221
RIP TIDES (JOHNNY HUDSON & THE)			
	Let's Run Away/Hanky Panky	1959	Challenge 59062
RIP-CHORDS			
	I Love You The Most/Let's Do The Razzle Dazzle	1956	Abco 105
RIPPLES			
	Battle Of Love/Please Let Me Love You	1960	Bond 1479
RIPTIDES			
	April/Sally Ann	1966	Sidewalk 904
RITUALS			
	This Is Paradise/Gone	1959	Arwin 127
RITUALS (FB ARNIE GINSBURG)			
	Girl In Zanzibar/Guitarro	1959	Arwin 120
RIVALS (1)			
	Rival Blues/Don't Say You're Sorry	1950	Apollo 1166
RIVALS (2) (FB LETHA JONES)			
	I Need You/I Got That Feeling	1960	Anna 1113
RIVALS (3)			
	I'll Never Walk Alone/Sally, Sally	1963	Treyco 401
RIVALS (4)			
	Make Up Your Mind/She's Mine	1962	Puff 3912
	It's Gonna Work Out/Love Me	1964	Puff 1001/Lu Pine 118 (64)
RIVALS (5)			
	Rigetty Tick/I Must See You Again	1957	Darryl 722
	Come To Me/I Must See You Again	1963	Junior 990
RIVER ROVERS (LYDIA LARSEN & THE)			
	Delta Drag/Bald Headed Daddy	1951	Apollo 432
	Just Love You So	1989	Relic LP 5077
RIVERA, LUCY (& GROUP)			
	Make Me Queen Again/I F I C	1959	End 1041
RIVIERAS (1)			
	Count Every Star/True Love Is Hard To Find	1958	Coed 503
	Moonlight Serenade/Neither Rain Nor Snow	1958	Coed 508
	Our Love/True Love Is Hard To Find	1959	Coed 513
	Our Love/Midnight Flyer	1959	Coed 513
	Since I Made You Cary/Eleventh Hour Melody	1959	Coed 522
	Moonlight Cocktails/Blessings Of Love	1960	Coed 529
	My Friend/Great Big Eyes	1960	Coed 538
	Stay In My Heart/Easy To Remember	1960	Coed 542
	El Dorado/Refrigerator	1961	Coed 551
	Moonlight Cocktails/Midnight Flyer	1964	Coed 592
	My Silent Love	N/A	Coed LP only
	Scarlet Hour	N/A	Coed LP only
	Serenade In Blue	N/A	Post LP 2000
RIVIERAS (2) (AKA RAVENAIRES)			
	Together Forever/A Night To Remember	1958	Algonquin 718 (first pressing, second is by the Ravenaires)
RIVIERAS (3) (BOBBY MEYER & THE)			
	You Got To Tell Me/Behold	1964	Lawn 238/Casino 103
RIVILEERS			
	Forever/Darling, Farewell	1954	Baton 201
	Eternal Love/Carolyn	1954	Baton 205
	For Sentimental Reasons/I Want To See My Baby	1955	Baton 207
	Don't Ever Leave Me/Little Girl	1955	Baton 209
RIVILEERS (GENE PEARSON & THE)			
	A Thousand Stars/Hey, Chiquita	1954	Baton 200
	A Thousand Stars/Who Is The Girl	1957	Baton 241/Dark 241
RIVINGTONS (REF CRENSHAWS/REF EBBTIDES (3)/REF FOUR AFTER FIVES/REF LAMPLIGHTERS/REF SHARPS/REF TENDERFOOTS)			
	Papa-Oom-Mow-Mow/Deep Water	1962	Liberty 55427/Wand 11253 (63)
	My Reward/Kickapoo Joy Juice	1962	Liberty 55513
	Mama-Oom-Mow-Mow/Waiting	1963	Liberty 55528
	The Bird's The Word/I'm Losing My Grip	1963	Liberty 55553
	The Shaky Bird Pt. 1/The Shaky Bird Pt. 2	1963	Liberty 55585
	Little Sally Walker/Cherry	1963	Liberty 55610

Artist	Song	Year	Label
	Doin' The Bird	1963	Liberty LP 3282/Liberty LP 7282 (63)
	Weejee Walk/Fairy Tales	1964	Liberty 55671
	I Tried/One Monkey	1964	Reprise 0293
	All That Glitters/You Move Me Baby	1964	Vee Jay 634/A.R.E. American 100 (64)
	Years Of Tears/I Love You Always	1964	Vee Jay 649
	The Willy/Just Got To Be Mine	1964	Vee Jay 677
	Tend To Business/A Rose Growing In The Ruins	1966	Columbia 43581
	Yadi-Yadi-Yum-Dum/Yadi Yadi Revisited	1966	Columbia 43772
	Teach Me Tonight/Reach Our Goal	1967	Baton Master 202
	I Don't Want A New Baby/You're Gonna Pay	1967	Quan 1379
	I Lost The Love/Mind Your Man	1968	AGC 5
	Pop Your Corn Pt. 1/Pop Your Corn Pt. 2	1969	RCA 74-0301
	Papa-Oom-Mow-Mow/I Don't Want A New Baby	1973	Wand 11253
ROACHES			
	Angel Of Angels/Beatlemania Blues	1964	Crossway 447
ROAMERS			
	I'll Never Get Over You/Deep Freeze	1954	Savoy 1147
	Never Let Me Go/Chop, Chop, Ching-A-Ling	1955	Savoy 1156
ROAMERS (VARETTA DILLARD & THE)			
	You're The Answer To My Prayer/Promise, Mr. Thomas (no group)	1955	Savoy 1160
ROAMERS (WILBERT HARRISON & THE)			
	Da Dee Ya Da/Women And Whiskey	1954	Savoy 1149
ROB ROYS			
	Conversation/Now, Only Me	1960	Columbia 41650
ROB-ROYS (NORMAN FOX & THE)			
	Tell Me Why/Audrey	1957	Back Beat 501
	Dance, Girl, Dance/My Dearest One	1958	Back Beat 508
	Dream Girl/Pizza Pie	1958	Hammer 544/Capitol 4128 (59)
	Lover Doll/Little Star	1988	Back Beat 499
	Rainy Day Bells/That's Love	1988	Back Beat 500
	Lover Doll/Do-Re-Mi	1990	Back Beat 501
	Tell Me Why/Dance Girl Dance	N/A	Popular Request 105
ROBBINS (AKA ROBINS)			
	Rockin'/That's What The Good Book Says	1951	Modern 807
	I Made A Vow/Double Crossin' Baby	1954	Crown 106
	Key To My Heart/All I Do Is Rock	1954	Crown 120
ROBBINS, BILLY (& GROUP)			
	Bring Her Back To Me/Baby Please Come Back Home	1957	Dig 127
ROBBINS, EDDIE (& GROUP)			
	A Girl Like You/Dear Parents	1958	Power 214/Dot 15702 (58)
	Janice/It Was Fun	N/A	David 1001
ROBERTS, ALLEN (& GROUP)			
	Give Me Your Hand/Angel In My Life	1959	Knight 2009
ROBERTS, DAVE (& GROUP)			
	Wondrous/Fancy Talk	1958	PL 14
ROBERTS, LOU (& GROUP)			
	My Promise To You/Rattle Snake Shake	1966	Genie 102
ROBERTS, PENNY (BB THE PARAMOURS)			
	I'll Be Yours/The Only Way	1962	Moonglow 201
ROBIN, RICHIE			
	Strange Dreams/Branded	1960	Gone 5083
ROBIN, RUTH (& GROUP)			
	Lonely Eyes/Footsteps To The Sea	1962	Titan 1725
ROBINS (1)			
	If It's So Baby/If I Didn't Love You So	1949	Savoy 726
	Around About Midnight/You Sure Look Good To Me	1949	Score 4010
	Don't Like The Way You're Doin'/Come Back Baby	1950	Aladdin 3031
	School Girl Blues/Early Morning Blues	1950	Recorded In Hollywood 150
	I'm Not Falling In Love With You/Cry Baby (by Mel Walker & the Bluenotes)	1950	Regent 1016
	I Found Out	1950	Savoy (unreleased)
	Have A Merry Christmas	1950	Savoy (unreleased)
	The Turkey Hop Pt. 1 (with Johnny Otis)/The Turkey Hop Pt. 2 (instrumental)	1950	Savoy 732
	Our Romance Is Gone/There Ain't No Use Beggin'	1950	Savoy 738
	I'm Living OK/There's Rain In My Eyes	1950	Savoy 752
	I'm Through/You're Fine But Not My Kind	1950	Savoy 762
	A Fool Such As I/My Heart's The Biggest Fool	1952	RCA 5175
	All Night Baby/Oh Why?	1953	RCA 5271
	How Would You Know/Let's Go To The Dance	1953	RCA 5434
	My Baby Done Told Me/I'll Do It	1953	RCA 5486
	Ten Days In Jail/Empty Bottles	1953	RCA 5489
	Don't Stop Now/Get It Off Your Mind	1954	RCA 5564
	Framed/Loop De Loop Mambo	1955	Spark 107
	If Teardrops Were Kisses/Whadaya Want	1955	Spark 110
	One Kiss/I Love Paris	1955	Spark 113
	I Must Be Dreamin'/The Hatchet Man	1955	Spark 116
	Smokey Joe's Cafe/Just Like A Fool	1955	Spark 122/Atco 6059 (56)
	Cherry Lips/Out Of The Picture	1955	Whippet 200
	Merry Go Rock/Hurt Me	1956	Whippet 201X
	Since I First Met You/That Old Black Magic	1957	Whippet 203
	A Fool In Love/All Of A Sudden My Heart Sings	1957	Whippet 206
	Every Night/Where's The Fire?	1957	Whippet 208
	Pretty Little Dolly/Quarter To Twelve	1958	Knight 2001
	A Little Bird Told Me/It's Never Too Late	1958	Knight 2008
	In My Dreams/Keep Your Mind On Me	1958	Whippet 211
	Snowball/You Wanted Fun	1958	Whippet 212
	Just Like That/Whole Lot Imagination	1960	Arvee 5001
	Live Wire Suzie/Oh No	1960	Arvee 5013
	Baby Love/We Loved	1961	Gone 5101
	White Cliffs Of Dover/How Many More Times?	1961	Lavender 001
	Magic Of A Dream/Mary Lou Loves To Hootchy Kootchy Koo	1961	Lavender 002
	I Found Out My Troubles	1987	Savoy Jazz LP 1188
	Trouble/Moving Out	N/A	Push 764
ROBINS (1) (FB RICHARD BERRY)			
	Riot In Cell Block #9/Wrap It Up	1954	Spark 103
ROBINS (1) (LITTLE ESTHER & THE)			
	Double Crossin' Blues/Back Alley Blues (by the Beale Street Gang)	1950	Savoy 731
	Double Crossin' Blues/Ain't Nothin' Shakin (with Little Esther & Johnny Otis)	1950	Savoy 731
	Mistrustin' Blues/Misery	1950	Savoy 735
	Deceivin' Blues/Lost Dream Blues	1950	Savoy 759
ROBINS (1) (MAGGIE HATHAWAY & THE)			
	Race Of A Man/Bayou Baby Blues	1950	Recorded In Hollywood 112
	A Falling Star/When Gabriel Blows His Horn (vocals by Maggie Hathaway)	1951	Recorded In Hollywood 121
ROBINS (2) (FEMALE)			
	Johnny/Doing The Popeye	1962	Sweet Taffy 400/New Hit 3010
ROBINS (3) (AKA NOBELLS)			
	Lucy Watusi/Cry Over You	1964	Musicor 1050

Artist	Song	Year	Label
ROBINS (4) (MIKE ROBIN & THE)			
	So Glad I'm Crying/Now That I've Found You	N/A	Clarity 105
ROBINSON, FAITH (& GROUP)			
	My Birthday Wish/Randy The Snow Shoe Rabbit	1960	Dolphin
ROBINSON, MIKE (& GROUP)			
	Lula/Red Light	1961	Vibro 4000
ROCCO, LENNY (& GROUP)			
	Rochelle/Sugar Girl	1961	Delsey 301
ROCHELLS			
	Teardrops/Please Hear My Plea	N/A	Spacey 202
ROCK AND ROLLERS (DEACON & THE)			
	Rockin' On The Moon	1959	Nau-Voo 804
ROCK-A-BOPS (JEANNIE DELL, JOHNNIE B & THE)			
	Kiss You A Thousand Times/ Rock-A-Bye Boogie	1960	Josie 878
ROCK-A-BOUTS			
	She's A Fat Girl/Beatnik	1959	Chancellor 1030
ROCK-A-BYES (BABY JANE & THE)			
	Hickory Dickory Dock/Half Deserted Street	1962	Spokane 4001
	My Boy John/How Much Is That Doggie In The Window	1962	United Artists 560
	Get Me To The Church On Time/Half Deserted Street	1963	Spokane 4004
ROCK-A-FELLAS			
	Red Lips/Don't Torment Me	1958	ABC 9923
ROCK-A-FELLAS (EDDIE BELL & THE)			
	High School Girl/Shindig	1958	Coed 505
	Countin' The Days/Night Party	1959	Coed 512
	Super Chick/To The School House	1959	Coed 517
ROCK-A-TONES			
	Young Lady/Please Don't Talk About Me	N/A	Judytone 369
ROCK-A-WAYS (RICKY VAC & THE)			
	How Do You Think I Feel/ Colleen	1961	Hilltop 1871
ROCK-FELLERS			
	Ours/Orange Peel	1959	Valor 2004
ROCK-ITS			
	It's Love/If You've Never Been In Love	1958	Spangle 2010
ROCK-ITS (DALE WRIGHT & THE)			
	She's Neat/Say That You Care	1957	Fraternity 792
ROCKABEATS (JIMMY KELLY & THE)			
	Little Chickie/Bonnie	1958	Cobra 5028/Astra 101 (58)
ROCKAFELLAS (AKA ROCKAFELLERS)			
	Strike It Rich/My Baby, She's The Talk Of The Town	1963	SCA 18003
ROCKAFELLERS (AKA ROCKA-FELLAS)			
	Dear Someone/Strike It Rich	1963	Southern Sound 112
ROCKAWAYS (1) (ALICIA & THE)			
	Why Can't I Be Loved?/Never Coming Back	1956	Epic 9191
ROCKAWAYS (1) (KEN DARRELL & THE)			
	I'm Not Going Steady/Faleroo	1957	Epic 9226
ROCKAWAYS (2) (AKA TOKENS (2))			
	Top Down Time/Don't Cry (Tomorrow's Tears Tonight)	1964	Red Bird 10-005
ROCKBUSTERS			
	Tough Chick/Chico	1959	Cadence 1371
ROCKENETTES (DONALD SIMPSON & THE)			
	Woe-Oh Baby	1958	Major 1002
ROCKERS (1) (PAUL WINLEY & THE)			
	My Confession/Angel Child	1955	Premium 401
ROCKERS (2)			
	Tell Me Why/Count Every Star	1956	Carter 3029
	What Am I To Do?/I'll Die In Love With You	1956	Federal 12267
	Down In The Bottom/Why Don't You Believe?	1956	Federal 12273
ROCKERS (3) (RICK RANDLE & THE)			
	I'm Hurt/That Day	1958	Arc 4445
ROCKERS (4) (ROCKIN' BRADLEY & THE)			
	She's Mine Not Yours/Loomy	1958	Hull 729
ROCKET-TONES			
	Too Many Loves	1963	3-Sons Records 928
ROCKETEERS (1)			
	Foolish One/Gonna Feed My Baby Poison	1953	Herald 415
ROCKETEERS (2) (AKA RHYTHM ACES)			
	Hey Rube/Talk It Over	1956	Modern 999
	My Reckless Heart/They Turned The Party Out Down At Bessie's House	1958	M.J.C. 501/Firefly 326 (74)
ROCKETONES			
	Mexico/Dee I	1957	Melba 113
ROCKETS (1) (HERB KENNY & THE)			
	My Song/You Never Heard A Word I Said	1952	MGM 11332
	I Don't Care/Calling You	1952	MGM 11360
	Take A Little/I Miss You So	1953	MGM 11397
	But Always Your Friend/(I Dreamed Of A) Star Spangled Banner	1953	MGM 11487
	Don't Take My Word (Take My Heart)/Do I Have To Tell You I'm Sorry	1953	MGM 11648
ROCKETS (2)			
	Open The Door/Big Leg Mama	1953	Atlantic 988
	My Love For You/Dance The Rhythm And Blues (by Billy Matthews & the Balladiers)	1956	Wrimus
	Boogie Woogie Mama	N/A	Atlantic (unreleased)
	Ride In My Oldsmobile	N/A	Atlantic (unreleased)
	Where'd She Go	N/A	Atlantic (unreleased)
ROCKETS (3) (AKA RHYTHM ACES)			
	You Are The First One/Be Lovey Dovey	1956	Modern 992
	Johnny's House Party, Pt. 1/ Johnny's House Party, Pt. 2	1957	Modern 1021
ROCKETS (3) (LITTLE FREDDY & THE)			
	All My Love/Too Fat	1957	Chief 33
ROCKETS (4) (BILL BODAFORD & THE)			
	Little Girl/Teardrops	1958	Back Beat 507
ROCKETS (5) (DICK HOLLER & HIS)			
	Uh-Uh-Baby/Livin' By The Gun	1958	Ace 540
ROCKETS (6) (RANDY & THE)			
	Genevieve/If You Really Care	1959	Viking 1000
	Let's Do The Cajun Twist	1962	Jin 161
ROCKETS (7) (LOIS LEE & THE)			
	Always Alone	N/A	Cool 712
ROCKETS (8) (BILL MARINE & THE)			
	At My Front Door	N/A	Prom 1132
ROCKETS (9) (JOE THERRIEN JR. & HIS)			
	"Hey Babe" Let's Go Downtown/ Come Back To Me Darling	1957	Lido 505/Brunswick 55005
ROCKETTES			
	Love Nobody/I Can't Forget	1954	Parrot 789
ROCKIN R'S			
	Walking You To School/Bewitched (Bothered And Bewildered)	1960	Stepheny 1842
ROCKIN' BRADLEY (& GROUP)			
	I Have News For You/Look Out	1959	Fire 1007
ROCKIN' CHAIRS			
	A Kiss Is A Kiss/Rockin' Chair Boogie	1959	Recorte 402
	Come On Baby/Please Mary Lou	1959	Recorte 404
ROCKIN' CHAIRS (LENNY DEAN & THE)			
	Memories of Love/Girl Of Mine	1959	Recorte 412
ROCKIN' DUKES (1)			
	Angel And A Rose/My Baby Left Me	1957	O.J. 1007
ROCKIN' DUKES (2) (WITH JOE HUDSON)			
	Baby, Give Me A Chance/ Ooh-Wee, Pretty Baby	1957	Excello 2112
ROCKIN' KIDS			
	Yea Yea/Black Stockings	1958	Dot 15749
ROCKIN' KINGS (RONNIE & THE)			
	You Know/Rock 'N Roll Sal	1958	RCA 7248
ROCKIN' R'S (RON VOLZ & THE)			
	I'm Still In Love With You/ Mustang (instrumental)	1959	Tempus 1515/Vee Jay 334 (59)
ROCKIN' TOWNIES (BENNIE WOODS & THE) (AKA FIVE DUKES)			
	I Cross My Fingers/Wheel Baby Wheel	1955	Atlas 1040
ROCKING REBELS (RAY FOURNIA & THE)			
	You Done Me Wrong/Settle Down	N/A	Diamond Disk 101
ROCKMASTERS			
	My Lonely One/A Wonderful Thing	1963	One-Derful 4820

Artist	Song	Year	Label
ROCKY FELLERS (1) (LEROY & THE)			
	Unfinished Fifth/River Wide	1961	Cameo 194
ROCKY FELLERS (2)			
	Long Tall Sally/South Pacific Twist	1962	Parkway 836
	Santa Santa/Great Big World	1962	Scepter 1245
	Killer Joe/Lonely Teardrops	1963	Scepter 1246
	Like The Big Guys Do/Great Big World	1963	Scepter 1254
	Ching-A-Ling Baby/Hey Little Donkey	1963	Scepter 1258
	She Makes Me Wanna Dance/ Bye Bye Baby	1963	Scepter 1263
	My Prayer/Two Guys From Trinidad	1963	Scepter 1271
	The Beachcomber Song/Don't Sit Down	1964	Donna 1383
	Tiger (Everybody Wants To Be A)/Jeannie Memsah	1964	Warner Bros. 5440
	Nina/Better Let Her Go	1964	Warner Bros. 5469
	Don't Throw My Toys Away/The Man With The Blue Guitar	1965	Warner Bros. 5497
	Rented Tuxedo/Two Steps Downstairs In The Basement	1965	Warner Bros. 5613
RODANS			
	Time Is Passing/Queenie Bee	1959	Vest 825
ROECKER, SHERRILL (& GROUP)			
	Don't Say Nothin'/It's All Over	1964	Swan 4173
ROGERS, DAN (& GROUP)			
	I'd Be Lost Without You/ No Girl For Me	1964	Era 3131
ROGERS, FRANTIC JOHNNY (& GROUP)			
	Sassy/Ramrod (instrumental)	1958	Cindy 3010
ROGERS, JUANITA (BB THE FIVE JOYS)			
	Teenager's Love Letter/I'm So Glad You Love Me	1961	Pink Clouds 333
ROGERS, KENNETH (AKA KENNY ROGERS) (& GROUP)			
	That Crazy Feeling/We'll Always Have Each Other	1958	Carlton 454
ROGERS, LEE (& GROUP)			
	Troubles/Walk On By	1962	Mah's 000.9
ROGERS, MENARD (& GROUP)			
	I Found Someone	N/A	Drum Boy 45104
ROGERS, PAULINE (& GROUP)			
	Up Till Now/You're Everything To Me	1955	Atco 6050
	Round And Round/Come Into My Parlor	1956	Atco 6071
	I've Been Pretending/ Everything's All Right	1956	Flair-X 5001
ROGUES			
	If You Love Me/World Of Love	1956	Old Town 300
	It's True/Puppy Love	1956	Old Town 304
	Dream/I've Been Dreaming	1958	Old Town 1056
	Bitter Tears	N/A	Beckingham 1083
ROLEAKS (FEMALE)			
	As Long As You Love Me/ Keep On Loving You	N/A	Hope 557
ROLLERS			
	Bonneville/Got My Eye On You	1961	Liberty 55303
	The Continental Walk/I Want You So	1961	Liberty 55320
	Bounce/Teenager's Waltz	1961	Liberty 55357
ROLLETTES (FEMALE)			
	More Than You Realize/ Kiss Me, Benny	1956	Class 203
	An Understanding/I'm Trying (To Make You Love Me)	1960	Melker 103
ROLLETTES (GOOGIE RENE & THE) (FEMALE)			
	Sad Fool/Wham Bam (instrumental)	1956	Class 201
ROLLINS, BIRD (& GROUP)			
	You Are My Angel/Hurry Up Honey	1958	Vanguard 35003
	I'll Love You Forever/Bumble Bee	1960	Harvard 805
ROLLINS, DEBBIE (& GROUP)			
	Meet Me Tonight/Don't Let It Get Your Girl	1964	Ascot 2159
ROMA, TEENA (& GROUP)			
	Just For You/Love Is Like A Mountain	1961	Arteen 1002

Artist	Song	Year	Label
ROMAINES			
	Long Time Dead	1954	Groove (unreleased)
	Weight Broke The Wagon Down	1954	Groove (unreleased)
	Your Kind Of Love/Till The Wee, Wee Morning	1954	Groove 0035
ROMAINES (ROMAINE BROWN & HIS)			
	Autumn Leaves/Soft Summer Breeze	1956	Decca 30054
	Hole 'Em Joe	1956	Decca 30122
	When Your Lover Has Gone/ Satin Doll	1957	Decca 30399
ROMAN, NAT (& GROUP)			
	Tears In My Eyes/This Is The Night	1964	Sahara 103
ROMAN, NIP (& GROUP)			
	Darling I Need You/With These Words	1957	Flash 121
ROMANAIRES			
	Is It Too Late/Lollypops And Shotguns	N/A	D&J 100
ROMANCERS (1)			
	I Still Remember/House Cat	1956	Dootone 381
	This Is Goodbye/Jump And Hop	1956	Dootone 404
	You Don't Understand/Baby, I Love You So	1958	Bay-Tone 101
ROMANCERS (2)			
	Take Me To Paradise/We Met At The Altar	1959	Marquee 701
ROMANCERS (3)			
	Moody/Jumpin' Jungle	1960	Palette 5067
	Addio Maria/It Only Happens To You	1961	Medieval 202/Palette 5075 (61)
	That Lucky Old Sun/Hard Head	1961	Palette 5085
	What About Love/Marie That's You	1962	Palette 5095
	Don't Let Her Go/I Did The Wrong Thing	1964	Linda 117
	My Heart Cries/Tell Her I Love Her	1965	Linda 119
	Do You Cry/Love's The Thing	1965	Linda 120
	She Gives Me Love/Take My Heart	1966	Linda 123
	She Took My Oldsmobile/ That's Why I Love You	1966	Linda 124
ROMANCERS (4)			
	No Greater Love/You'll Never Know	1961	Celebrity 701/Beacon 701
ROMANCERS (5) (ROCKY HOMAN & THE)			
	My Precious Love/Love Me All The Way	1961	Flip 355
ROMANCERS (6)			
	Eternal Love/You Win Again	1973	Vintage 1013
ROMANS (1)			
	Honey Love/Why Can't This Be So	1956	Haven 111
	Why Can't This Be So/Honey Love	1956	Haven 111
	Wild Ideas/Uh Uh	1958	MMI 1238
ROMANS (2) (FRANKIE VALLE & THE) (REF FOUR SEASONS)			
	Real (This Is Real)/Come Si Bella	1959	Cindy 3012
ROMANS (3) (CAESAR & THE)			
	Baby Let's Wait	N/A	GJM 9000
	Your True Love/Let The Four Winds Blow	N/A	Hi-Note 602
ROMANS (3) (LITTLE CAESAR & THE)			
	Those Oldies But Goodies (Remind Me Of You)/She Don't Wanna (Dance No More)	1961	Del-Fi 4158
	Those Oldies But Goodies (Remind Me Of You)/Fever	1961	Del-Fi 4158
	Hully Gully Again/Frankie And Johnny	1961	Del-Fi 4164
	Memories Of Those Oldies But Goodies/Fever	1961	Del-Fi 4166
	The Ten Commandments Of Love/C. C. Rider	1961	Del-Fi 4170
	Popeye Once More/Yoyo Yo Yoyo	1961	Del-Fi 4177
	Annie Had A Baby	1961	Del-Fi LP 1218
	Little Star	1961	Del-Fi LP 1218

Artist Song	Year	Label
Work With Me Annie	1961	Del-Fi LP 1218
Searchin'	1961	Del-Fi LP 1218
I Need You So	1961	Del-Fi LP 1218
We Belong Together/Disco Hully Gully	1977	Essar 7803
ROMANS (4)		
The Cat's Meow/You Are My Only Love	1958	Juno 013/014
ROME, BILLY (& GROUP)		
Donna/You Runaround	1961	Sultan 5501
ROMEO, AL (& GROUP)		
Moonlight Becomes You/Hot Fudge Sundae	1963	Laurie 3177
ROMEOS (1) (AKA JUMPING JACKS (1))		
Love Me/I Beg You Please	1954	Apollo 461
Rags/Doctor Velvet	1954	Apollo 466
Oh Baby Oh	1989	Relic LP 5078
Somebody's Been Plowing My Mule	1989	Relic LP 5078
ROMEOS (2)		
Gone, Gone, Get Away/Let's Be Partners	1957	Fox 748/749
Fine, Fine Baby/Moments To Remember You By	1957	Fox 845/846/Atco 6107 (57)
ROMEOS (3)		
Two Innocent Loves/Love Mobile	1958	Felsted 8528
Julie/I'm Gonna Rebuild This World	1963	Felsted 8672
ROMEOS (4)		
The Tiger's Wide Awake/Hitch Hiken	1962	Amy 840
ROMEOS (5)		
Precious Memories/Juicy Lucy	N/A	Mark II 101
Searching/A Tear And A Smile	N/A	Mark II 103
ROMEOS (6) (KENNY GAMBLE & THE)		
Ain't It Baby, Pt. 1/Ain't It Baby, Pt. 2 (instrumental)	N/A	Arctic 114
ROMEOS (7) (JIMMY & THE)		
Kathy/Lunale	1960	Southside 1003
ROMMELS		
Those Wedding Bells/Mister Sam	1960	Trend 4104
RON-DELLS (AKA RONDELS)		
I'll Be Gone/Slow Down	1963	Arlen 723
RON-DELS (FB DELBERT MCCLINTON)		
If You Really Want Me To, I'll Go/Walk About	1965	Brownfield 18/Smash 1986 (65)
RONDELLS (1)		
Dreamy/Good Good	1958	Carlton 467
RONDELLS (2)		
My Prayer (acapella)	1975	Relic LP 104
RONDELS		
Oh Baby/Be Mine	1981	Clifton 58
RONDELS (AKA RON-DELLS)		
Matilda/Tina	1963	Shalimar 104/Dot 17323 (70)
ROOKIES (1) (JOE PERKINS & THE)		
Time Alone Will Tell/Ain't You Glad Nature Did It	1957	King 5005
A New Feeling/How Much Love Can One Heart Hold	1957	King 5030
ROOKIES (2)		
Blabbermouth/The Penalty	1959	Donna 1313
ROOMATES (AKA ROOMMATES)		
I Want A Little Girl/Making Believe	1960	Promo 2211
Glory Of Love/Never Knew	1961	Valmor 008
Band Of Gold/Oh Baby Love	1961	Valmor 010
My Foolish Heart/My Kisses For Your Thoughts	1961	Valmor 013
Come Go With Me	1961	Valmor LP 78/Valmor LP 789(62)/Relic LP 5041
One Summer Night	1961	Valmor LP 78/Valmor LP 789 (62)/Relic LP 5041
To The Aisle	1961	Valmor LP 78/Valmor LP 789 (62)/Relic LP 5041
There Goes My Heart	1961	Valmor LP 78/Valmor LP 789 (62)/Relic LP 5041
Answer Me, My Love/Gee	1963	Philips 40105
The Nearness Of You/Please Don't Cheat On Me	1963	Philips 40153/Philips 40161 (63)

Artist Song	Year	Label
A Place Called Love/Knowing You	N/A	Ban 691
Song Of The Dreamer	N/A	Relic LP 5041
The Only Girl For Me	N/A	Relic LP 5041
Yes My Love	N/A	Relic LP 5041
ROOMATES (CATHY JEAN & THE)		
Please Love Me Forever/ Canadian Sunset (no group)	1960	Valmor 007
Make Me Smile Again/Sugar Cake	1961	Valmor 009
I Only Want You/One Love	1961	Valmor 011
Turn Me Loose	1961	Valmor LP 78/Valmor LP 789 (62)
Believe Me/Double Trouble	1962	Philips 40143
Please Tell Me/Sugar Cake	1962	Valmor 016
You Don't Have To Say You Love Me/It's So Hard	1991	Cure 91-02801
ROOMATES (FB CATHY JEAN) (AKA ROOMMATES)		
My Heart Belongs To Only You/I Only Want You	1963	Philips 40106
ROOMMATES (AKA ROOMATES)		
Sunday Kind Of Love/A Lovely Way To Spend An Evening	1962	Cameo 233
My Heart/Just For Tonight	1964	Canadian American 166
Someone To Watch Over Me	N/A	Canadian American (unreleased)
ROOMMATES (DICK DIXON & THE)		
Be Good, Be Good, Be Good/ Caterpillar Crawl	1959	Kapp 292
ROOSTERS		
Fun House/Chicken Hop	1959	Shar-Dee 704
Pretty Girl/Let's Try Again	1962	Epic 9487/Felsted 8642 (62)
ROSE, ANDY (WITH THE THORNS)		
Love-A Love-A Love/Just Young	1958	Aamco 100
Crazy For You/This Is The Nite	1961	Coral 62271
Don't Ask Me To Be Lonely/ You Weren't There	1961	Coral 62284
ROSEBUDS (1) (FEMALE)		
Dearest Darling/Unconditional Surrender	1957	Gee 1033
ROSEBUDS (2) (FEMALE)		
Joey/Kiss Me Goodnight	1959	Lancer 102
ROSEBUDS (3) (ROSEMARY & THE) (FEMALE)		
Dreamtime/What Do I Mean To You	1963	Larkwood 1101
ROSEBUDS (4) (RICHIE DIXON & THE)		
Moonlight And Roses/You Broke My Heart	1963	Class 308
ROSES		
Almost Paradise/I Kissed An Angel	1958	Dot 15816
ROSES (DON & HIS)		
Since You Went Away To School/Right Now	1958	Dot 15755
Leave Those Cats Alone	1958	Dot 15784
ROSETTES		
You Broke My Heart/It Must Be Love	1961	Herald 562
ROSS, TED (& GROUP)		
The Brain/All Cried Out	1959	Arwin 121
ROULETTES (1)		
The Way You Carry On/You Don't Care Anymore	1957	Ebb 124
I See A Star/Come On, Baby	1958	Champ 102
Hasten Jason/Wouldn't Be Going Steady	1959	Scepter 1204
ROULETTES (2)		
Can You Go/Soon You'll Be Leaving Me	1964	United Artists 718
ROULETTES (2) (ADAM FAITH & THE)		
I Just Don't Know/It's Alright (no group)	1964	Amy 913
ROUND ROBINS		
Since I Don't Have You/Peter Gunn (instrumental by Joe Cenna)	1953	Bell 108
ROUNDERS (JIMMY TIG & THE)		
Small Town Girl/Foolish Lover	1963	Spar 779
ROUZAN, WANDA (& GROUP) (FEMALE)		
Here's A Letter From Home/ Long Time No See	1963	Frisco 115

Artist Song	Year	Label	Artist Song	Year	Label
ROVERS (1) (HELEN FOSTER & THE)			Sam's Back/Grabitis	1960	Metro 20032
You Belong To Me/Oop Dee			Red Hot/Hard Times	1961	Big Top 3064
Doo	1952	Republic 7013	You Tickle Me Baby/You		
ROVERS (2)			Came Along	1963	Fortune 560
Why, Oh-H?/Ichi-Bon Tami			**ROYAL KINGS (1)**		
Dachi	1954	Music City 750/Capitol 3078 (55)	Teachin' And Preachin'/		
			Bouncin' The Boogie	1952	Specialty 444
Salute To Johnny Ace/Jadda	1955	Music City 780	**ROYAL KINGS (2)**		
Whole Lot Of Love/Tell Me,			Peter Peter/Keep It To Yourself	1961	Forlin 502/Candlelite 410 (61)
Darling (by the Gaylarks)	1955	Music City 792	**ROYAL KINGS (3)**		
ROVERS (3)			My Last Song	1957	Lance 1035
Most Of All/Sweet Slumber	1974	Vintage 1018	**ROYAL KNIGHTS**		
ROYAL ACES (JESSE JAMES & THE)			You Should Have Told Me/		
I Will Go/Cha Cha Minnie	1962	Shirley 103	There's Going To Be A Way	N/A	Radio City 1001
ROYAL BOYS			Have You Heard	N/A	Rendezvous 01
Darling Angel/Lover's Bells	1960	Tropelco 1007	**ROYAL LANCERS (1) (RONNIE PREMIERE & THE)**		
Is It Me/Marry Young	1961	United Artists 228	So Loved Am I/You May Not		
ROYAL COUNTS			Be An Angel	1961	Sara 1020
That's How I Feel (acapella)/			**ROYAL LANCERS (2) (PAUL STEFAN & THE)**		
Way Over There	1970	Catamount 1958	Say Mama	1963	Citation 5003
ROYAL DEBS			Baby I Don't Care/Angel In		
Jerry/I Do	1962	Tifco 826	My Eyes	1963	Citation 5004
ROYAL DEMONS			Good, Good Lovin'/This Time	1963	Hi Mar HM-501
Baby Don't/What's A Matter			**ROYAL LANCERS (3)**		
Baby	1958	Rhythm 5004	Hey Little One/Hey Everybody	1963	Lawn 215
Kiss Kiss/Trembling Hand	1961	Pek 8101	Together/Spooksville	1963	Lawn 216
ROYAL DRIFTERS			**ROYAL MASTERS**		
Little Linda/S' Why Hard	1959	Teen 506	You're The One/Don't Leave		
To Each His Own/Da Kind	1959	Teen 508	Me This Way	1962	Guyden 2078
ROYAL DUKES (DON ELLIS & THE)			**ROYAL MONARCHS**		
Blue Diamonds	1958	Bee 1110	My Baby	N/A	Star
Come In World	1959	Bee 1111	**ROYAL NOTES (AKA PHIL JOHNSON & THE DUVALS)**		
Half Of Me/You Won't			Three-Speed Girl/Kisses Left		
Remember Me	1959	Bee 1114	Unkissed (by Phil Johnson		
Party Doll/A Woman's Love	1960	Bee 201	& the Duvals)	1958	Kelit 7032
ROYAL FIVE			You Are My Love/Wee Small		
Ain't No Big Thing/Peace Of			Hours (by Phil Johnson &		
Mind	1968	Arctic 160	the Duvals)	1958	Kelit 7034
ROYAL FLAIRS			**ROYAL PLAYBOYS**		
Dream Angel	N/A	Sam 119	Walking On/Don't Be No Square	1961	Imperial 5782
ROYAL HALOS			**ROYAL PREMIERS**		
Nobody But Me And My Girl/			Who Am I Without Your Love/		
My Love Is True	1959	Aladdin 3460	I Wanna Love Love Love	1962	Toy 103
ROYAL HOLIDAYS			Make Love To Me/I Can Make		
I'm Sorry (I Did You Wrong)/			It If I Try	1965	M.B.S. 105
Margaret	1958	Penthouse 9357/ Carlton 472 (58)	**ROYAL RAVENS**		
			Grand Spanish Lady/All Over		
Down In Cuba/Rockin' At The			You	1963	Mah's 0015
Bandstand	1959	Herald 536	**ROYAL REVEROS**		
ROYAL JACKS			Such A Fool/If I Had My Life		
I'm In Love Again/The Big Ring	1958	20th Fox 100	To Live Over	N/A	Jump Up 114
Night After Night/Who, What,			**ROYAL ROBINS (1)**		
When, Where And Why?	1959	Studio 9903	The Country Fool/Turn Me		
Tam-O-Shanter/Anticipation	1962	Amy 865	Loose	1963	ABC 10504
ROYAL JESTERS			How High The Moon/		
Those Dreamy Eyes/My Angel			Something You've Got Baby	1964	ABC 10542
Of Love	1960	Harlem 105	**ROYAL ROBINS (2) (PATRICIA CONLEY & THE)**		
Love Me/Let's Kiss And Make Up	1961	Cobra 2222	We're Gonna Get Married/		
Ask Me To Move A Mountain/			Mama What'll I Do	1962	Aldo 504
Is That Good Enough For You	1961	Cobra 611025	**ROYAL SONS QUINTET (AKA FIVE ROYALES)**		
I Want To Be Loved/I Never			Bedside Of A Neighbor/		
Will Forget	1962	Cobra 7777	Journey's End	1952	Apollo 253
Wisdom Of A Fool/What Love			Come Over Here/Let Nothing		
Has Joined Together	1962	Jester 102	Separate Me	1952	Apollo 266
We Go Together/I Want You			**ROYAL TEENS (GM BOB GAUDIO & JOE VILLA)**		
Round	1962	Jester 104	Sittin' With My Baby/Mad Gas	1957	Astra 1012/Power 113 (59)
Let There Be You/I Really			Short Shorts/Planet Rock	1957	Power 215/ABC 9882 (58)
Don't Want To Know	1962	Jester 106	Big Name Button/Sham Rock	1958	ABC 9918
Please Say You Want Me Too/			Harvey's Got A Girl Friend/		
What'Cha Gonna Do 'Bout It	1965	Jox 029	Hangin' Around	1958	ABC 9945
ROYAL JOKERS (AKA MUSKATEERS/AKA ROYALS (2)/AKA SCOOTERS/AKA SERENADERS (1))			My Kind Of Dream/Open The		
			Door (I Forgot My Key)	1958	ABC 9955
You Tickle Me, Baby/Stay Here	1955	Atco 6052	Believe Me/Little Cricket	1959	Capitol 4261
Don't Leave Me, Fanny/			I'll Not Be The One (To Say		
Rocks In My Pillow	1956	Atco 6062	Goodbye)/Royal Blue		
Ride On, Little Girl/She's Mine,			(instrumental)	1959	Mighty 111
All Mine	1956	Atco 6077	Leotards/Royal Blue		
September In The Rain/Spring	1957	Hi-Q 5004	(instrumental)	1959	Mighty 111
Sweet Little Angel/I Don't Like			Cave Man/Wounded Heart	1959	Mighty 112
You That Much	1958	Fortune 840	The Moon's Not Meant For		
Lovey Dovey/Nickel, Three			Lovers (Anymore)/Was It		
Dimes and Five Quarters	1960	Keldon 322	a Dream?	1960	Capitol 4335

Artist	Song	Year	Label
It's The Talk Of The Town/			
With You	1960	Capitol 4402	
My Memories Of You/			
Little Trixie	1961	Mighty 200	
Short Short Twist/Royal Twist	1962	Allnew 1415/Jubilee 5418 (62)	
I'll Love You Till The End Of			
Time Pt. 1/I'll Love You Till			
The End Of Time Pt. 2 (by the			
Blue Tones/instrumental)	1965	Swan 4200/Blue Jay 101	
Bad Girl/Do The Montoona	1965	TCF 117	
Smile A Little Smile For Me/			
Hey Jude	1969	Musicor 139	
Lazy Walker	N/A	Empire 1001	
ROYAL TEENTONES (BOBBY SANDS & THE)			
Secret Lover/Teenage Joy	1959	Nugget 1003	
ROYAL TONES			
Seesaw/Little Bo	1959	Jubilee 5362	
ROYAL, BILL JOE (& GROUP)			
We Haven't A Moment To Lose/			
Never In A Hundred Years	1961	Fairlane 21009	
We Haven't A Moment To Lose/			
Never In A Hundred Years	1961	Fairlane 21009	
ROYAL-AIRES			
Friendship Ring/Baby Baby	1957	Gallo 108	
Please Don't Leave Me Now/			
You're In Love	1957	Gallo 110	
ROYALE CITA CHORUS			
I Understand/Chang			
Chang A-Lang	1956	Gee 1021	
ROYALE CITA CHORUS (FB MABEL KING)			
Second Hand Love/Symbol			
Of Love	1956	Rama 204	
ROYALLS (AKA FIVE ROYALES)			
Too Much Of A Little Bit/Give			
Me One More Chance	1952	Apollo 434	
ROYALS (1) (AKA MIDNIGHTERS)			
Every Beat Of My Heart/All Night			
Long (with Wynonie Harris)	1952	Federal 12064/	
		Federal 12064AA (52)	
Starting From Tonight/I Know			
I Love You So	1952	Federal 12077	
Moonrise (with Alonzo Tucker)/			
Fifth St. Blues	1952	Federal 12088	
I'll Never Let Her Go/A Love			
In My Heart	1952	Federal 12098	
Are You Forgetting/What Did I Do	1952	Federal 12113	
The Shrine of St. Cecilia/I Feel			
So Blue	1953	Federal 12121	
Get It (with Alonzo Tucker)/			
No It Ain't	1953	Federal 12133	
I Feel That-A-Way/Hello Miss			
Fine	1953	Federal 12150	
Someone Like You/That's It	1953	Federal 12160	
Give It Up/That Woman	1953	Federal 12177	
Work With Me Annie/Until I Die	1954	Federal 12169	
ROYALS (1) (CHUCK WILLIS & THE)			
I've Been Treated Wrong Too			
Long/Don't Deceive Me			
(no group)	1953	Okeh 6985	
ROYALS (1) (FB CHUCK WILLIS)			
If You Love Me/Dreams Of You	1951	Okeh 6832	
ROYALS (2) (AKA MUSKATEERS/AKA ROYAL JOKERS/AKA SCOOTERS/AKA SERENADERS (1))			
Someday We'll Meet Again/			
I Want You To Be My Mambo			
Baby	1954	Venus 103	
ROYALS (3) (FAY SIMMONS & THE)			
Shake It Up/Forgive This Fool	1960	Jordan 122	
ROYALS (4) (RONNIE BENNETT & THE)			
True Love, True Love/Have You			
Ever Watched A Teardrop	1960	Jin 143	
ROYALS (5) (RICHIE & THE)			
And When I'm Near You/Goody			
Goody	1961	Rello 1	
Be My Girl/We're Strollin'	1962	Rello 3/Golden Crest 573 (63)	
ROYALS (6)			
I Lost My Love	N/A	Liban	
ROYALS FIVE			
Say It To My Face/Gonna Keep			
Lovin' You	N/A	Tyler 200	
ROYALTONES (1)			
Crazy Love/Never Let Me Go	1956	Old Town 1018	
Latin Love/Hey, Norman!	1956	Old Town 1028	
Hong Kong Jelly Wong	N/A	Murray Hill LP 000083	
I Give You My Word	N/A	Old Town (unreleased)	
A Castle In The Sky	N/A	Old Town (unreleased)	
Do You Remember	N/A	Old Town (unreleased)	
ROYALTONES (1) (RUTH MCFADDEN & THE)			
Two In Love (With Only One			
Heart)/You For Me (no group)	1956	Old Town 1020	
Short Line/Big Wheel	1960	Goldisc 3004	
The Flip/Secret Love	1960	Goldisc 3011	
Butterscotch/Dixie Cup	1960	Goldisc 3016	
Dixie Rock/Royal Whirl	1960	Goldisc 3017	
Do The Early Bird/Scotch 'N'			
Soda	1961	Goldisc 3028	
ROYALTONES (2) (EL PAULING & THE)			
I'm A Cool Teenager/Solid Rock	1960	Federal 12383	
Now Baby Don't Do It/			
Everybody Knows	1960	Federal 12396	
You're Ruinin' My Gladness/			
The Way I See It	1960	Lute 5801	
RPMs			
Love Me/Street Scene	1963	Port 70032	
RU-BEE-ELS			
Evil/I'll Try	1962	Flip 359	
RU-TEENS (AKA RUE-TEENS)			
Happy Teenager (a capella)/Come			
A Little Bit Closer (a capella)	1965	Old Timer 612	
RUBBER BISCUITS			
A Hundred Pounds Of Clay/			
Rags To Riches	1986	Starlight 35	
Gloria/Boni Maroni	1986	Starlight 37	
RUBIES (1) (AKA FOUR JEWELS/AKA IMPALAS (3)) (FEMALE)			
Zing! Went The Strings Of My			
Heart/Wobble With Me Baby	1953	TNT 101/KT	
Loaded With Goodies/Take It			
Easy Casanova	1961	District 301	
He Was An Angel/He Was Mine	1961	Empress 103	
Spanish Boy/Deeper	1964	Vee Jay 596	
RUBIES (2)			
Someday/Just You And I	1955	Verne 103	
RUBIES (3) (JEWELL & THE)			
A Thrill/Kidnapper	1963	La Louisianne 8041/ABC 10485 (63)	
Days Go By	1963	La Louisianne 8055	
RUBIES (4) (FEMALE)			
Is A Man Really Worth It/			
Sugar Cane	1964	Enith International 720	
RUE-TEENS (AKA RU-TEENS)			
Lucky Boy/I Don't Cry Over Girls	1964	Louis 6805	
RUMBLERS			
Boss/I Don't Need You Anymore	1963	Downey 103/Dot 16421 (63)	
Riot In Cell Block #9/The			
Hustler	1964	Downey 119	
RUN-A-ROUNDS (AKA RUNAROUNDS (2)/AKA REGENTS (3)/AKA DESIRES (3))			
Unbelievable/Hooray For Love			
(by the Run-A-Rounds)	1963	KC 116	
Let Them Talk/Are You Looking			
For A Sweetheart			
(by the Run-A-Rounds)	1963	Tarheel 065	
A Lovely Way To Spend An			
Evening	N/A	unreleased	
Crazy Love	N/A	unreleased	
Tonight (Could Be The Night)	N/A	unreleased	
RUNAROUNDS (1) (AKA EMOTIONS (1))			
The Nearest Thing To Heaven/			
Lover's Lane	1961	Pio 107/Jason Scott 13 (81)	
RUNAROUNDS (2) (AKA RUN-A-ROUNDS/AKA REGENTS (3)/AKA DESIRES (3))			
Mashed Potato Mary/I'm All			
Alone	1961	Cousins 1004	
Carrie (You're An Angel)/			
Send Her Back	1964	Felsted 8704	
Perfect Woman/You're a Drag	1966	Capitol 5644	
You Lied/My Little Girl(with			
Tommy Cosgrove & the			
Elegant Four)	1967	MGM 13763	
RUNAROUNDS (3) (RITCHIE & THE) (GM LOU CHRISTIE/GM KRIPP JOHNSON)			
Lost In The Crowd/Don'tcha			
Back Track	1963	Ascot 2136	
RUNAWAYS			
Pardon Me/It's Love Baby	1961	Lavender 003	
Pachuko Hop/The Stinger	1962	Moonglow 202	
Laughing With Tears In My			
Heart/Shake	1978	Crystal Ball 125	

Artist Song	Year	Label
18th Floor Girl/Your Foolish Ways	N/A	Alamo 105
What's Happening, Baby?	N/A	Hitt 2001
Kangaroo Hop/Teenage Style	N/A	Teensound 1924
RUNNERS		
Charlie Brown/She Say (by the Treetoppers)	1953	Bell 107
RUSS, LONNIE (& GROUP)		
Something Old Something New/ My Wife Can't Cook	1962	4-J 501
RUSSELL, BOBBY (& GROUP)		
You Were Mine/Once A Day	1965	Monument 899
RUSSELL, RICK (& GROUP)		
My Angel/It's Time To Cry	1963	Poplar 120
RYAN, ALLEN (& GROUP)		
My Reverie	1957	Sonic 1600
RYAN, CATHY (BB THE ADMIRALS)		
Come Home/The Cricket	1955	King 4848
Only A Dream/High Falutin' Honey	1956	King 4890
RYDELL, BOBBY (& GROUP)		
Please Don't Be Mad/Makin' Time (no group)	1959	Cameo 160
RYDER, JUNIOR (BB THE PEACOCKS)		
Better Stop	1954	Duke
SA-SHAYS (FEMALE)		
Boo Hoo Hoo/You Got Love	1961	Alfi 1/Zen 101
This Is My Story/On That Beautiful Day	1961	Zen 110
SABER, JOHNNY (& GROUP)		
The Note That I Wrote/Baby It's Gotta Be Love	1962	Hitsville 1137
SABER, JOHNNY (BB THE PASSIONS)		
Wish It Could Be Me/Dolly In A Toy Shop	1960	Adonis 103
SABERS (1) (FB BILLY STORM)		
Cool, Cool Christmas/Always Forever	1955	Cal-West 847
SABERS (2) (J. & THE)		
Twist Mary Sue/Little One	1962	Vavrey 1003
SABERS (3)		
It's Not Like You	N/A	Prism 1893
SABIANS		
Crazy Dream	1961	Yale 241
SABRES		
You Can Depend On Me/ Calypso Baby	1955	Bullseye 101
Your Face/Lulu	1958	Liberty 55128
Most Of All/Sweet Slumber	1965	Jameco 2004
SAD SACKS		
Sack Dresses/Guard Your Heart	1958	Imperial 5517
SAFARIS (FB JIMMY STEPHENS) (AKA SUDDENS)		
Image Of A Girl/Four Steps To Love	1960	Eldo 101
Girl With The Story In Her Eyes/Summer Nights	1960	Eldo 105
In the Still Of The Night/Shadows	1960	Eldo 110
Soldier Of Fortune/Garden Of Love	1961	Eldo 113
Legion Of The Lost	N/A	Image LP
SAIGONS		
You're Heavenly/Honey Gee	1955	Dootone 375
SAINTS (1)		
With You/I Rocked When I Should Have Rolled	1957	Cue 7934
SAINTS (2) (DANNY & THE)		
Peggy's Party/No One Has Eyes For Me	1959	Warner Bros. 5134
Big Lulu/Long Long Ago	N/A	Fanelle 101
SAINTS (3) (DAVE & THE)		
Fever/Leavin' Surf City	1963	Band Box 341
SAINTS (3) (ORLIE & THE)		
King Kong/Pittsburgh Twist And Freeze	1961	Band Box 253
SAINTS (3) (TOM ALLEN & THE)		
Lone Lonely One/Never	1961	Band Box 249
SAINTS (4) (RICKY & THE)		
When The Saints Twist/My Special Angel	1962	7 Teen 101
SAINTS (5)		
Snap Dragon/Doin' The Stroll	1958	Prescott 1570

Artist Song	Year	Label
SAINTS (6) (LOLA & THE)		
Crazy For You	1984	N/A
Wishful Thinking	1984	N/A
SAINTS (7)		
The Sun Don't Shine (Everyday)	N/A	Kent 480
SAINTS (8)		
White Christmas/Please Come Home For Christmas	1984	Angela 103
Wishful Thinking/ABC's Of Love	1984	Angela 104
I'm So Young/I'm On The Outside	1988	Clifton 81
SALEMS		
My Precious Love/I'll Still Go On Loving You	1961	Mercury 71754
SALLYCATS (SALLY & THE)		
Bread Fred/Depending On You	1959	Rendezvous 105
SALUTATIONS (VITO & THE)		
Your Way/Hey, Hey Baby	1962	Kram 1202/Kram 5002
Gloria/Let's Untwist The Twist	1962	Rayna 5009/Red Boy 5009 (66)
Unchained Melody/Hey, Hey Baby	1963	Herald 583
Eenie Meenie/Extraordinary Girl	1963	Herald 586
Girls I Know/Get a Job	1964	Regina 1320
Can I Depend On You/ Liverpool Bound	1964	Wells 1008
Don't Count On Me/Day-O (Banana Boat Song)	1964	Wells 1010
Walkin'/High Noon	1965	Apt 25079
Bring Back Yesterday/I Want You To Be My Baby	1966	Boom 60020
So Wonderful (My Love)/I'd Best Be Going	1966	Red Boy 1001/Sandbag 103
Can I Depend On You/Hello Dolly	1966	Rust 5106
Keep A Light In The Window	N/A	unreleased
SAMS		
My Guardian Angel	N/A	Ebony 008
SAMUELS, CLARENCE (& GROUP)		
Without You/We're Goin' To The Hop	1959	Apt 25028
SANDELLES		
Hit 'N' Run Lover/All That I Need	1964	Debonair 309
SANDERS, BOBBY (BB THE PERFORMERS)		
It Was You/I'm On My Way	1961	Kaybo 618
SANDERS, WILL (& GROUP)		
The Living Truth/Stay Put	1961	Regatta 2003
SANDETTS		
Cutting Silhouettes/Without You	1960	Smokey 109
SANDETTS (FEMALE)		
Without You/Cutting Silhouettes	1960	Smokey 109
SANDMEN (1)		
Somebody To Love/When I Grow Too Old To Dream	1955	Okeh 7052
SANDMEN (1) (BROOK BENTON & THE)		
Ooh/The Kentuckian Song (Brook Benton)	1955	Okeh 7058
SANDMEN (1) (CHUCK WILLIS & THE)		
I Can Tell/One More Break (Chuck Willis)	1955	Okeh 7055
SANDMEN (1) (FB BROOK BENTON)		
Come On Be Nice/I Wanna Do Everything For You	1957	Vik 0285
SANDMEN (1) (LINCOLN CHASE & THE)		
The Message/That's All I Need	1955	Columbia 40475
SANDMEN (2)		
Searching For A New Love/ If You Want Me	1965	Blue Jay 5002
SANDPIPERS		
Ali Baba/Young Generation	1966	Kismet 394
SANDS OF TIME (AKA TOKENS (2))		
Benji's Cincinnati/A Tribute To The Beach Boys '76	1976	Kirshner 4263
SANDS, JERI LYNN (& GROUP)		
As Long As I (Can Dream)/ Steady Freddy	1959	Arcade 153
SANTELLS		
Why Are We Apart/There's A Time And Place For Everything	1964	Courier 103
So Fine/These Are Love	1964	Courier 115
SANTOS, LARRY (BB THE FOUR SEASONS)		
Someday (When I'm Gone)/True	1964	Atlantic 2250

Artist	Song	Year	Label
SANTOS, LARRY (BB THE TONES (1))			
	Three Little Lovers/We Belong Together	1959	Baton 265
SAPPHIRES (1)			
	So Glad/Everyone Knows	1958	RCA 7357
SAPPHIRES (2) (HOWIE & THE) (AKA PEARLS)			
	More Than The Day Before/ Rockin' Horse	1959	Okeh 7112
SAPPHIRES (3)			
	Goodnight Kiss	1964	Swan LP 513
SARATOGAS			
	I'll Be Loving You/Get It In A Minute	1961	Imperial 5738
SATELITES (BABY BOY JENNINGS & THE)			
	Little Girl/Goin' Home	1960	Savoy 1589
SATELITES (RONNY & THE)			
	Blue Moon/Bunny Lee	1960	Dolly 22254
SATELLITES (1) (SONNY KING & THE)			
	You Shouldn't/So Doggone Lonely	1955	Nocturne 1003/1004
SATELLITES (10) (JOE NETTLES & THE)			
	Oh Baby	N/A	Circle 1174
SATELLITES (2) (JOE POTITO & THE)			
	Say A Prayer/Can't Let Your Lovin' Go	1957	Safari 1003
SATELLITES (3)			
	Heavenly Angel/You Ain't Sayin' Nothin'	1958	Class 234/Malynn 234 (58)
	My Piggie's Gotta Dance/ I Found A Girl	1958	United Artists 141
	Blast Off/Man In Orbit	1961	Chess 1789
	One More Time/Red And Yellow Polka Dots	N/A	Arc 149
SATELLITES (3) (BOBBY DAY & THE)			
	So Long Baby/Come Seven	1957	Class 207
	Little Bitty Pretty One/Heavenly Angel	1957	Class 211
	Little Bitty Pretty One/When The Swallows Come Back To Capistrano	1957	Class 211
	Beep Beep Beep/Darling If I Had You (no group)	1957	Class 215
	Sweet Little Thing/Honeysuckle Baby	1958	Class 220
	Little Turtle Dove/Saving My Love For You (no group)	1958	Class 225
	Rockin' Robin/Over And Over	1958	Class 229/Trip 29
	The Bluebird, The Buzzard And The Oriole/Alone Too Long	1958	Class 241
	That's All I Want/Say Yes	1959	Class 245
	Mr. & Mrs. Rock 'n' Roll/Gotta New Girl	1959	Class 252
	Love Is A One Time Affair/ Ain't Gonna Cry No More	1959	Class 255
	Unchained Melody/Three Young Rebs From Georgia	1959	Class 257
	My Blue Heaven/I Don't Want To	1959	Class 263
	Undecided/Slow Pokey Joe	1962	Rendezvous 175
SATELLITES (4)			
	Linda Jean/Rockateen	1959	Cupid 5004/ABC 10038 (59)
	Each Night/Darktown S trutters Ball	1960	D-M-G 4001
	Buzz Buzz/We Like Birdland	1960	Palace 102
SATELLITES (5) (PAT & THE)			
	Jupiter-C/Oh! Oh! Darlin'	1959	Atco 6131
SATELLITES (6) (DICK & SLIM & THE)			
	Chalypso Rock/My Truest Love	1959	Cool 113
SATELLITES (7) (RONNY & THE)			
	Dream Of You/Last Night I Dreamed	1959	Rose 1001
SATELLITES (8) (COLLAY & THE)			
	Last Chance/Little Girl Next Door	1960	Sho-Biz 1002
SATELLITES (9) (BOBBY LONG & THE)			
	Red Roses Will Never Fade	1964	Vegas 555-2
	You've Got What It Takes	1964	Vegas 700
SATIN ANGELS (FEMALE)			
	Town Sensation/Pity Me	1985	Relic 8004
SATINS (SUNNY & THE)			
	In My Memories/This Night Is Our Night	1978	Crystal Ball 122
SATINS (TOMMY ROE & THE)			
	I Got A Girl/Caveman	1960	Judd 1018
SATINS FOUR (WITH THE CINAMMON ANGELS)			
	Oh Cathy/I Can't Find The Girl On My Mind	1965	B.T. Puppy 515
SATINTONES			
	My Beloved (versions with and without strings)/Sugar Daddy	1960	Motown 1000
	I'll Never Love Again/Solid Sender	1960	Tamla 54024
	Motor City/Going To The Hop	1960	Tamla 54026
	Tomorrow And Always/A Love That Can Never Be (versions with and without strings)	1961	Motown 1006 (first pressing)
	Angel/A Love That Can Never Be	1961	Motown 1006 (second pressing)
	I Know How It Feels/My Kind Of Love	1961	Motown 1010
	Zing! Went The Strings Of My Heart/Faded Letter	1961	Motown 1020
SATISFACTIONS			
	Oh Why/We Will Walk Together	1962	Chesapeake 610
	Give Me Your Love/Take It Or Leave It	1964	Smash
SATISFIERS			
	Lies/All Over Nothing	1955	Jubilee 5205
	Come Away, Love/Where'll I Be Tomorrow Night	1956	Coral 61727
	Solitude/Over The Rainbow	1957	Coral 61788
	Will-O-The-Wisp/Remember That Crazy Rock	1958	Coral 61945
	Ghost Of A Chance/Fair Exchange	1960	Vegas 626
SAUCERS			
	Why Do I Dream?/Oh Wailey Routa	1959	Felco 104
	Flossie Mae/Hi-Oom	1964	Kick 100
	Hello, Darling/Giggle Goo	1964	Lynne 101
SAUNDERS, JAY (& GROUP)			
	I'm Still In Love With You/ Heaven Have Mercy	1956	Club 1012
SAVAGE, AL (& GROUP)			
	Trouble On My Mind/A Fool Was I	1957	Herald 505
SAVOYS (1)			
	Let's Ride, Ride, Ride/Oh, That'll Be Joyful (by Jack McVea)	1954	Combo 55
	Darling Stay With Me/Yacka Hoom Boom	1955	Combo 75
	Evil Ways/Loving Man	1955	Combo 81
	Chop Chop Boom/Nobody In Mind (by Jack McVea)	1955	Combo 90
SAVOYS (2) (SONNY BROOKS & THE)			
	Here I Am/Rocka Rolla Rock	1956	Tip Top 1007
	Sweetheart Darling/I'm So Down Hearted	1956	Tip Top 1008
SAVOYS (3) (AKA PRETENDERS (1))			
	You/Say You're Mine	1956	Savoy 1188
SAVOYS (3) (JIMMY JONES & THE) (AKA PRETENDERS (1))			
	With All My Heart/Please Say You're Mine	1955	Savoy 1186
SAVOYS (4)			
	I Love My Baby/You And I	1959	Bella 18
SAVOYS (5) (MARVA & THE)			
	Don't Let Him Go/Just In Your Imagination	1963	Coed 582
SAVOYS (6)			
	Oh What A Dream (acapella)/ If You Were Gone From Me (a capella)	1963	Catamount 101
	When I Fall In Love/Crazy	1965	Catamount 104
	Gloria (acapella)/The Closer You Are (acapella)	1965	Catamount 105
	Oh Gee Oh Gosh/Vision Of Love	1980	Catamount 778
SAVOYS (7)			
	Hopin' For Your Return/Darling Please (by the Bees)	1973	Sold 505
SAVOYS (8)			
	Charlena/Pretty One	N/A	Raynard RS 10019
SAXON, EDDIE (& GROUP)			
	Blues No More/(No Flip)	1962	Empress 106

Artist	Song	Year	Label
SAXONS (1) (AKA HOLLYWOOD SAXONS)			
	Please Be My Love Tonight/		
	Home On The Range	1957	Our
	Is It True?/Rock And Roll Show	1958	Contender 1313
	My Love Is True/Trying	1958	Tampa 139
	Everyday Holiday/L.A. Lover	1961	Hareco 102
SAXONS (1) (MARY EDWARDS & THE)			
	Oh Oh Mama/Chilly Willy	1956	Meteor 5031
SAXONS (2)			
	Camel Walk	1960	Sho-Biz 1003
SAXONS (3)			
	The Power Of Love	N/A	Jim Dandy 1002
SCALE-TONES			
	Everlasting Love/Dreamin' And		
	Dreamin'	1956	Jay-Dee 810
SCAMPS			
	Yes My Baby/Waterproof	1955	Peacock 1655
SCARFS			
	Give A Little Try	N/A	Arc 7452
SCARLETS			
	Teardrops Fell/Yes You're Mine		
	(by the Vocaleers)	1976	Robin Hood 134
SCARLETS (FRED PARRIS & THE) (REF FIVE SATINS)			
	She's Gone (With The Wind)/		
	The Voice	1958	Klik 7905/Candlelite 411 (61)
SCARLETS (REF FIVE SATINS)			
	Dear One/I've Lost	1954	Red Robin 128/Event " 4287 (55)
	Love Doll/Darling I'm Yours	1955	Red Robin 133
	True Love/Cry Baby	1955	Red Robin 135
	Kiss Me/Indian Fever	1955	Red Robin 138
	Truly Yours/East Of The Sun	1960	Fury 1036
SCAVENGERS			
	The Angels Listened In/My		
	over Waits For Me	1963	Mobile Fidelity 1005
SCHAEFER, FREDDY (& GROUP)			
	Zoom Zoom Zoom/Why Is It	1962	King 5621
SCHARMEERS			
	I've Waited So Long/Traveling		
	Stranger (by the Jive Chords)	1974	Vintage 1017
SCHOLARS			
	What Did I Do Wrong/Poor		
	Little Doggie	1956	Cue 7927
	Rocky Road/Spin The Wheel	1956	Dot 15498
	If You Listen With Your Heart/		
	Poor Little Doggie	1956	Dot 15519
	Beloved/I Didn't Want To Do It	1957	Imperial 5449
	Kan-Cu-Wa/I Didn't Want To		
	Do It	1957	Imperial 5459
	Please Please/I Need Your		
	Lovin' (by the Perenials)	N/A	Ruby-Ray 2
SCHOOL BELLES			
	Waitin' For My Date/Billy Boy,		
	Billy Boy	1958	Dot 15746
	Turtle Dovin'/Cool It Baby	1958	Dot 15801
	Swing Swang/Count Down	1959	Hanover 4526
	Whistling Bells/Whistling At		
	The Boys	1961	Buena Vista 378
	Don't Believe Him/Valley High	1962	Crest 1104
SCHOOL BOYS			
	Dream Lover	1960	Studio 1
SCHOOL GIRLS			
	The Reason Why I Love Him/		
	Guess We're Not In Love	1962	Express 712
SCHOOLBOYS (1)			
	Shirley/Please Say You Want		
	Me	1956	Okeh 7076
	Mary/I Am Old Enough	1957	Okeh 7085
	Carol/Pearl (Leslie Martin bb		
	the Cadillacs)	1957	Okeh 7090
	Angel Of Love/The Slide	1958	Juanita 103/Bim Bam Boom 107 (72)
	Mary/Ding A Ling Coo Coo		
	Mop/I Am Old Enough	1990	Magic Carpet EP 511
SCHOOLBOYS (2) (BOB HAMILTON & THE)			
	School's Beginning	1986	Relic LP 8008
SCHOOLBOYS (2) (PROFESSOR HAMILTON & THE)			
	Back To School/Juanita Of		
	Mexico	1961	Contour 0001
SCHOOLGIRLS (WENDY & THE) (FEMALE)			
	My Guy/Merry Go Round	1958	Golden Crest 502
SCHOOLMATES (1) (COLLEEN & THE)			
	Mairzy Doats/My Heart Is On A		
	Merry-Go-Round	1958	Coral 62024
SCHOOLMATES (2) (RONNIE & THE)			
	Don't Don't Don't (Drop Out)/		
	Just Born (To Be Your Baby)	1964	Coed 605
SCHOONERS (1)			
	Viddley Biddley Baby/Schooner		
	Blues	1958	Ember 1041
SCHOONERS (2) (SMOKEY ARMEN & THE)			
	Baby What Am I Gonna Do/		
	Say You Love Me	1958	Peek-A-Boo 102
SCOOTERS (AKA MUSKATEERS/AKA ROYAL JOKERS/AKA ROYALS (2)/AKA SERENADERS (1))			
	Someday We'll Meet Again/		
	Really	1957	Dawn 224
	Everybody's Got A Girl/A Ring		
	Around A Chain	1958	Era 1065
	Everybody's Got A Girl/Big Lies	1958	Era 1072
SCOTCHTONES			
	Do You Have The Right/		
	Sake Wa Duke	1960	Rustone 1402
SCOTT BROTHERS			
	Do You Want My Love/		
	Celebrity Party	1959	Skyline 501
	Part Of You/Kingdom Of Love	1959	Skyline 502
	Stolen Angel/Keep Laughing	1960	Ribbon 6905
	Lost Love/Only Then	1960	Ribbon 6911
	Lonely Bluebird/Kingdom Of		
	Love	1961	FTP 415
	Memories/Beggin' For Your Love	1962	Parkway 841
	Letter From My Baby/Love Me		
	Tenderly	1963	Comet 2153
	Love Me Tenderly/Welcome Me	1963	Comet 2161
SCOTT, CHYVONNE (& GROUP)			
	I Won't Stand In The Way		
	(with Chick Willis)/Everybody		
	Needs A Friend	1963	Alto 2010
SCOTT, JIMMY (& GROUP)			
	What Sin/When Day Is Done	1957	King 5086
	Somewhere Down The Line/		
	Home	1958	King 5104
SCOTT, NEIL (BB THE CONCORDS (2))			
	Oh Genie/Go Bohemian	1960	Clown 3011
	Run To Me/Tomboy	1962	Comet 2151
	One Piece Bathing Suit/		
	Little Girl	1963	Herald 581
SCOTT, RICKY (& GROUP)			
	Darling Darlin'/I Didn't Mean It	1960	X-Clusive/Cub 9079 (60)
SCOTTIES			
	Let Me Love You Tonight/		
	Patiently	1959	Scottie 1305
SCRUBS (DAVE COLLINS & THE)			
	Bluesy Me/Don't Break-A My		
	Heart	1954	Imperial 5294
SEARCHERS			
	Wow Wow Baby/Ooo-Wee	1958	Class 223
	Yvonne/Little Wanda	1961	Mac 351
SEBASTIAN (& GROUP)			
	Too Young/Darlin' I Do	1959	Mr. Maestro 801/Take 2 2002 (59)
SECRETS (1) (AKA FIVE SECRETS/AKA LOUNGERS)			
	See You Next Year/Queen Bee	1957	Decca 30350 (second pressing, first is by the Five Secrets)
SECRETS (1) (AKA LOUNGERS/AKA FIVE SECRETS)			
	Wedding Bells/Teenage Bells	1991	Park Ave. 5
SECRETS (2)			
	Quien Sabe (Who Knows, Who		
	Knows)/Now Is The Hour	1960	Columbia 41861
SECRETS (3) (CARLO & THE)			
	Pony Party/100 Pounds Of		
	Potatoes	1962	Throne 801
SECRETS (4) (COLLEEN KAYE & THE)			
	Joey's Diamond Ring/The One		
	I Love	1963	Big Top 3151
SECRETS (5)			
	Everyday/A Smile Upside Down	1966	Red Bird 10-076
SEDATES			
	Please Love Me Forever/		
	I Found	1958	MRB 171/20th Century 1011 (59)/Port 70004 (59)/20th Century 1212 (61)

Artist / Song	Year	Label
Girl Of Mine/Bei Mir Bist Du Schon	1962	Trans Atlas 692
SEEGRAMS (BASIL SWIFT & THE)		
Farmer's Daughter	1965	Mercury 72386
SELECTIONS		
Guardian Angel/Soft And Sweet	1958	Antone 101/Mona Lee 129
SELECTONES (JAY JAY & THE)		
Humpty Dumpty/When I Look Around	1962	Guest 6201/6202
SEMESTERS		
Summer Nights (a capella)	1975	Relic LP 104
Spiral (a capella)	1975	Relic LP 104
Laura My Darling (a capella)	1975	Relic LP 104
SEMINOLES		
Meant To Be/Cheating Heart	1960	Hi-Lite 109
True Love/Open Your Eyes	1961	Go-Gee 287
I Can't Stand It/It Takes A Lot	1962	Check Mate 1012
Forever/You Can Lump It	1962	Mid Town 101
Trouble In Mind	N/A	Hi-Lite 87568
SEMITONES (RON RICKY & THE)		
There's A Girl In My Heart/My Babe	N/A	Semitone 1
SENATORS (AKA GALES (2)/AKA MARVELS (2))		
Loretta/Poor Little Puppet	1958	Golden Crest 514
Julie/It Doesn't Matter	1959	Abner 1031
Scheming/Tafu	1959	Bristol 1916
Wedding Bells/I Shouldn't Care	1962	Winn 1917
SENDERS		
Spinning/Pretty Little Pretty	1958	Entra 711/Kent
The Ballad Of Stagger Lee/I Dream Of You	1959	Kent 320
One More Kiss/Everybody Needs To Know	1959	Kent 324
SENIORS (1)		
Evening Shadows Falling (I Think Of You)/I've Got Plenty Of Love	1956	Tetra 4446
Why Did You Leave Me?/Sloo Foot Soo	1958	Excello 2130
SENIORS (2)		
Who's Gonna Know/It's Been A Long Time	1959	Tampa 163
My Soul/Emily (by the Turks)	1960	Ball 001
I've Lived Before/When Will I Fall In Love	1960	Decca 31112
Pitter Patter Heart/Hully Gully	1960	Kent 342
When I Fall In Love/Baby, Say The Word	1961	Decca 31244
SENIORS (3)		
Ah Sweet Mystery Of Love/Rock And Rolly	1960	ESV 1016
SENIORS (4) (DANNY & THE)		
Oh Devil	1966	Panorama 26
SEÑORS		
May I Have This Dance/Searching For Olive Oil	1962	Sue 756
SENSATION-IVIES		
Tell Me/God Bless The Child	1961	Willow 23003
SENSATIONAL DELL-OS (AKA JOHN SHAW & THE DELL-OS)		
So Shy/That's Why I Dream	1958	Mida 106
Lost Love/So Don't Go	1958	Mida 109
Why Did You Leave Me/Why Does It Have To Be Her	1958	U-C 5002/U-C 1031
SENSATIONALS (1) (JIMMY JONES & THE)		
Come On And Go With Me/Walk In The Garden	1959	Savoy 4116
Nobody But The Lord/Before This Time Another Year	1959	Savoy 4126
I Can't Begin To Tell You/In The Storm	1962	Savoy 4174
Lead Me On/So High	1965	Savoy 4234
SENSATIONALS (2)		
Once In A While/Snow White Winter	1960	Candix 306
Wouldn't Be The Same/The City Sleeps	1961	Candix 319
SENSATIONS (1)		
I Can't Change/Mend The Torn Pieces	1964	Junior 1010
SENSATIONS (1) (FB YVONNE BAKER/AKA YVONNE MILLS)		
Yes Sir, That's My Baby/Sympathy	1956	Atco 6056
Please Mr. Disc Jockey/Ain't He Sweet	1956	Atco 6067
My Heart Cries For You/Cry, Baby, Cry	1956	Atco 6075
Little Wallflower/Such A Love	1956	Atco 6083
My Debut To Love/You Made Me Love You	1957	Atco 6090
Romance In The Dark/Kiddy Car Love	1958	Atco 6115
Music, Music, Music/Part Of Me	1961	Argo 5391
Let Me In/Oh Yes, I'll Be True	1961	Argo 5405
We Were Meant To Be/It's Good Enough For Me	1963	Junior 1002
That's What You Gotta Do/You Made A Fool Out Of Me	1963	Junior 1005
Baby/Love Love Love	1963	Junior 1006
You Made A Fool Of Me/That's What You've Gotta Do	1963	Junior 988/Tollie 9009 (64)
I Can't Change/Mend The Torn Pieces	1964	Junior 1010
We Were Meant To Be/It's Good Enough For Me	1964	Junior 1021
SENSATIONS (1) (YVONNE BAKER & THE)		
That's My Desire/Eyes	1962	Argo 5412
No Changes/Party Across The Hall	1962	Argo 5420
When My Lover Comes Home/Father Dear	1963	Argo 5446
SENSATIONS (2) (SONYA & THE)		
Don't Feel Like The Lone Ranger	1963	Gend
SENSATIONS (3)		
The Price Of Love/Don't Take Your Love	1962	River 228
SENTIMENTALS (1)		
I Want To Love You/Teenie, Teenie, Teenager	1957	Mint 801/Checker 875 (57)
Sunday Kind Of Love/Wedding Bells	1957	Mint 802
I'm You Fool, Always/Rock Me, Mama	1958	Mint 803
You're Mine/Danny Boy	1958	Mint 805
Found A New Baby/I'll Miss These Things	1968	Mint 807
This Time/I Want To Love You	1972	Mint 808
SENTIMENTALS (1) (ANN NICHOLS & THE)		
Lover, I'm Waiting For You/I'm Sixteen Years	1958	Tuxedo 926
SENTIMENTALS (1) (JAMES CARTER & THE)		
I Know/Hey, Baby, Hey	1957	Tuxedo 922/Tuxedo 943
SENTIMENTALS (2)		
We Three/Understanding Love	1959	Coral 62100
Love Is A Gamble/If It Isn't For You	1959	Vanity 589
Two Different Worlds/Deep Down In My Heart	1960	Coral 62172
SENTIMENTALS (3) (SYLVESTER JACKSON & THE)		
I'm Your Fool Always/Wild Baby (Vickie Evans & the Sentimentals)	N/A	Playfare 601
SEQUINS & RHYTHM KINGS (JIMMY BURKE WITH THE)		
Ooh! Ooh! Those Eyes/Forbidden Love	1960	Fortune 537
SEQUINS (1)		
Don't Fall In Love/Why Can't You Treat Me Right	1956	Red Robin 140
SEQUINS (2)		
Wedding Bells/Look For A Job (by Little Joe Mosley)	1958	Del-Fi 4107
SEQUINS (3) (JESSIE & THE)		
Hold My Hand/So Weak	1959	Boxer 201/Profile 4008 (59)
SEQUINS (4) (FEMALE)		
To Be Young/The Mountains	1959	Cameo 161
Love Me Forever/They're Dancing Now	1962	Terrace 7511
You Can't Sit Still/Mr. Leader Of The Band	1963	Ascot 2140
Hideaway/I Ain't Gonna Cry (No More)	1963	Terrace 7515
SEQUINS (5) (JANICE RADO & THE) (FEMALE)		
I'm Coming Home/This Feeling	1961	Edsel 782

Artist	Song	Year	Label
SERENADERS (1) (AKA MUSKATEERS/AKA ROYAL JOKERS/AKA ROYALS (2)/AKA SCOOTERS)			
	It's Funny/Confession Is Good For The Soul	1952	Coral 60720
	Misery/But I Forgive You	1952	Coral 65093
	Tomorrow Night/Why Don't You Do Right?	1952	J.V.B. 2001
	Will She Know/I Want To Love You, Baby	1953	Red Robin 115
	Please, Please Forgive Me/Baby	1954	DeLuxe 6022
	M-A-Y-B-E-L-L/Ain't Goin' To Cry No More	1954	Swing Time 347
	Goodbye/Kola (recorded in 1952)	1974	Roadhouse 1017
	My Happiness/Rockin' Man (recorded in 1952)	1974	Roadhouse 1018
	Sunset/My Heart (by the Ontarios)	1974	Roadhouse 1022
SERENADERS (2)			
	Never Let Me Go/I Wrote A Letter	1957	Chock Full O' Hits 101/102/MGM 12623 (58)
	Dance, Darling, Dance/Give Me A Girl	1957	Chock Full O' Hits 103/MGM 12666 (58)
	How Do You Mend A Broken Heart	1959	Cross Country
	My Girl Flip-Flop/Gotta Go To School	1959	Rae-Cox 101
	Adios, My Love/Two Lovers Make One Fool	1963	Riverside 4549
	I'll Cry Tomorrow/If Your Heart Says Yes	1964	V.I.P. 25002
SERENADERS (3)			
	My Last Affair/I Had My Moment	1952	Colony 1000
	Summer Job/Honolulu	1958	Hanover 4507
	Alaska/Where Did You Go 'Out', What Did You Do 'Nothing'	1958	Hanover 4514
	Love Me Now/Gates Of Gold	1958	Teen Life 9
	Goodnight Sweetheart/Come Back My Love	1976	Clifton 16
SERENADERS (4) (GENE MUMFORD & THE)			
	Please Give Me One More Chance/When You're Smiling	1956	Whiz 1500
SERENADERS (5) (LARRY LEE & THE)			
	Dreams Of Heaven	1990	Relic LP 5085
	Too Young	1990	Relic LP 5085
	All Alone	1990	Relic LP 5085
SERENADES			
	A Sinner In Love/The Pajama Song	1957	Chief 7002
SERENADETTS			
	Boyfriend/The Big Night	1961	Enrica 1008
SERVICEMEN			
	My Turn/I Need A Helping Hand	1967	Pathway 102
SESSIONS (1)			
	Girls Go For Guys/Chico	1964	Guyden 2105
SESSIONS (2)			
	Look To The Rainbow (acapella)/For Her (acapella)	1976	Arcade 100
SEVENTEENS (1) (FEMALE)			
	Steady Guy/Bug Out	1958	Golden Crest 503
SEVENTEENS (2) (ROBBY JOHN & THE)			
	Teenage Bill Of Rights/Revolution	1959	Del-Fi 4115
SEVILLES (1) (RICHARD BARRETT & THE)			
	Dream On/I Am Yours	1960	Seville 104
SEVILLES (2)			
	Charlena/Loving You (Is My Desire)	1961	JC 116/Galaxy 721 (64)
	Louella/Salt Mine	1961	JC 118
	Fat Sally/Working Hard	1961	JC 120
	Don't You Know I Care, Pt. 1/Don't You Know I Care, Pt. 2	1962	Cal Gold 172
	Hey Hey Hey/Treat You Right	1964	Galaxy 717
	Baby/Creation	1964	Galaxy 727
SEVILLES (3) (BOBBY MATHIS & THE)			
	Girl In The Drugstore/Going To The City	1960	Sioux 51860
SH-BOOMS (AKA CHORDS (1))			
	Pretty Wild/Could It Be?	1955	Cat 117
	I Don't Want To Set The World On Fire/Lu Lu	1957	Vik 0295
	Blue Moon/Short Skirts	1960	Atlantic 2074
	Sh-Boom/Little Maiden	1961	Atco 6213
SHA-WEEZ			
	Feeling Sad	1953	Aladdin (unreleased)
	You Made Me Love You (Satisfied With My Love)	1953	Aladdin (unreleased)
	No One To Love Me/Early Sunday Morning	1953	Aladdin 3170
SHA-WEEZ (BIG BOY MYLES & THE)			
	Who's Been Fooling You?/That's The Girl I Married	1955	Specialty 564
	Just To Hold My Hand/Hickory Dickory Dock	1956	Specialty 590
SHADES (1)			
	Sun Glasses/Undivided Attention	1958	Big Top 3003
	Wouldn't It Be Nice/The Combination	1962	Joey 6206
	The Chimes/Voodoo Man	1963	Times Square 16/Times Square 93 (64)
	Time Stood Still	N/A	Klik
	So Good	N/A	Klik
SHADES (2)			
	Dear Lori/One Touch Of Heaven	1959	Aladdin 3453/Imperial 5358 (59)
	Strolling After Dark/Splashing	1959	Scottie 1309
SHADES (3) (K.C. GRAND & THE)			
	Lookie Lookie Lookie	1961	Matt 0003
SHADES (4) (JOEY & THE)			
	My Love Is Gone/New York Honky Tonk	N/A	Wild 905
SHADES (5) (ROYAL & THE)			
	Once Upon A Time	N/A	Band Box 358
SHADES OF BROWN			
	Shoo Be Do Wah/Just My Imagination/Whatever Hurts You/Don't Say Goodnight	N/A	Clifton EP 505
SHADOWS (1)			
	Stay/No Use	1953	Decca 28765
	Tell Her/Don't Be Bashful	1953	Decca 48307
	Better Than Gold/Big Mouth Mama	1954	Decca 48322
SHADOWS (2)			
	There Stands The Glass/Bop-Alena	1958	Delta 1509
	I Love You/Looly Lou	1959	El-Gee-Bee 101
	I Wonder Why/Tell This Lonely Heart Goodbye	1961	Dottie 1006
SHADOWS (3)			
	Under The Stars Of Love/Jungle Fever	1958	Del-Fi 4109
SHADOWS (4) (DAVE & THE)			
	At The Fair/Dancing Cheek To Cheek	1962	Checkmate 1016
	Playboy	1964	Fenton 942
SHADOWS (5)			
	The Ten Commandments Of Love (acapella)	1975	Relic LP 102
SHAKERS (1)			
	Fat Mama Twist	1961	Fee Bee 901
	Linda Lee	1961	Fee Bee 907
	Good Luck To You	N/A	Star
SHAKERS (1) (BUDDY SHARPE & THE)			
	Linda Lee/Bald Headed Baby	1958	Fee Bee 230
	I'm Lonely/The Shake	N/A	Rumble
SHAKERS (2) (PEPPER & THE)			
	Need Your Love/For My Baby	1966	Chetwyd 45002
SHALIMARS			
	I Didn't Mean To Hurt You/Baby That's What Love Is	N/A	Mr. Maestro 778
SHALLOWS			
	How Lucky I Am/Wrecking My Life	1961	Rae-Cox 108
	I Wonder/Do The Bug	1962	Forlin 503
	Wonderful Girl/Sunnyside Of The Street	1986	Starlight 49
SHALONS			
	True Love Came My Way/Angel	1977	Ronnie 203

Artist	Song	Year	Label	Artist	Song	Year	Label
SHAM-ETTES					I'll Always Remember/Sock Hop	1959	Ace 133
	You're Welcome Back/He'll			**SHARPTONES (2) (JESSE BELVIN & THE)**			
	Come Back	1967	MGM 13798		Sugar Doll/Let Me Dream	1958	Aladdin 3431
SHAMANS				**SHARPTONES (3) (BILLY SHARP & THE)**			
	Valley Of Tears/Shubby Dubby Doo	1959	Kayham 1/2		Hippity Hop/Stars In My Eyes	1958	Kudo 668
	Southern California/I'll Wait			**SHAW, JOAN (& GROUP)**			
	Forever	1959	Kayham 3/4		Broken Heart/Hand Holdin' Baby	1956	ABC 9724
SHAMROCKS (LITTLE HENRY & THE)				**SHAW, RICKY (& GROUP)**			
	Baby Come To Me/The Ta Ta Song	1961	Kent 398		A Fools Memory/Young And			
SHANNONS					In Love	1962	President 822
	Born Too Late/Don't Ask Me	1958	L&M 1003	**SHAYNES**			
SHANTEERS					Valarie/Let's Go Steady	1961	Pee Vee 5000
	You're Gone/Take Me Back	1962	Rori 708	**SHEIKS (1) (REF PEARLS (1)/REF FIVE PEARLS)**			
SHANTONES					Walk That Walk/The Kissing			
	Come To Me/Little Girl	1956	Trilyte 5001		Song (Sweetie Lover)	1955	Cat 116
SHANTONS					Give Me Another Chance/Baby			
	Triangle Love/Lover's March	1959	Jay-Mar 165		Don't You Cry	1955	Ef-N-De 1000
	To Be In Love With You/Lucille	1959	Jay-Mar 242		So Fine/Sentimental Heart	1955	Federal 12237/Federal 12355 (59)
SHANTONS (SKIP BROWN & THE)					Don't Go To Strangers/Give			
	Why Don't You Believe Me/				Me One More Chance	1975	Monogram 109
	Jenny Lee	59	Pam 112	**SHEIKS (2)**			
SHANTONS (SKIP JACKSON & THE)					Tres Chic	1959	Jamie 1132
	Santa Claus Is Coming To				Song Of Old/Candlestick Cafe	1959	Jamie 1147
	Town/The Christmas Song	60	Jay-Mar 181/Dot-Mar (69)	**SHEIKS (3)**			
	I'm On To You Girl/Promise				Come On Back To Me/Please			
	That You'll Wait	69	Dot-Mar 324		Don't Take Away The Girl I Love	1960	Amy 807
SHARELL, JERRY (& GROUP)				**SHEIKS (4)**			
	Everybody Knows/That's My				Why Should I Dance/What I'd			
	Business	61	Alanna 560		Do For Your Love	1961	Le Grand 1013
SHARKS (AKA FIVE SHARKS)					Cocoanut Woman/Twist			
	Shirley/I'll Be Home	75	Broadcast 1128		That Twist	1961	Le Grand 1016
	Blueberry Hill/I Love You For			**SHEIKS (5) (EDDIE WILLIAMS & THE)**			
	Sentimental Reasons	75	Clifton 10		I Just Can't Help Myself/You			
	You Belong To Me/The Glory				Left Your Happiness	N/A	Coronado 112
	Of Love	76	Broadcast 1132	**SHELLS (1)**			
SHARKS QUINTET					Baby Oh Baby/Angel Eyes	1957	Johnson 104/Candlelite 436 (72)
	I'll Be Home/Shirley	N/A	Broadway		Sippin' Soda/Pretty Little Girl	1958	End 1022/Gone 5103 (61)
SHARMEERS					Pleading No More/Don't Say			
	You're My Lover/A School Girl				Goodbye	1958	Johnson 106/Juanita 106 (58)
	In Love	58	Red Top 109/Clifton 9 (74)		Whispering Wings/Shooma			
SHARMETTES (FEMALE)					Dom Dom	1959	End 1050
	Answer Me/My Dream	62	King 5648		She Wasn't Meant For Me/			
	Wonderful Love/I Gotta Tell It	62	King 5656		The Thief	1959	Roulette 4156
	Tell Me/I Want To Be Loved	62	King 5686		Baby Oh Baby/What's In An			
SHARP CATS (VERNA WILLIAMS & THE)					Angel's Eyes	1960	Johnson 104 (reissue)
	Mine All Mine/Holey Money	N/A	Versailles 865		Explain It To Me/An Island			
SHARP, BOBBY (& GROUP)					Unknown	1961	Johnson 107
	Flowers Mr. Florist, Please/				Better Forget Him/Can't Take It	1961	Johnson 109
	Baby Girl Of Mine	58	Wing 90056		In The Dim Light Of The Dark/			
SHARPETTES (KING & THE)					O-Mi Yum-Mi Yum-Mi	1961	Johnson 110
	How Do I Stand Today/Did				Sweetest One/Baby, Walk On In	1961	Johnson 112
	He Know	64	Aldo 503		Deep In My Heart/(It's A)			
SHARPS (1) (REF CRENSHAWS/REF EBBTIDES (3)/REF FOUR AFTER FIVES/					Happy Holiday	1962	Johnson 119
REF LAMPLIGHTERS/REF RIVINGTONS/REF TENDERFOOTS)					A Toast To Your Birthday/			
	Love Me My Darling/Heaven				The Drive	1962	Johnson 120
	Only Knows (instrumental)	1954	Two Mikes 101		On My Honor/My Royal Love	1963	Johnson 127
	What Will I Gain?/Shufflin'	1957	Aladdin 3401		Our Wedding Day/Deep In			
	Come On/Sweet Sweetheart	1957	Jamie 1040/Vik 0264 (57)/ VDJ 6		My Heart	1963	Josie 912
	Our Love Is Here To Stay/				Sweetest One	1963	Josie LP 4001
	Lock My Heart	1957	Lamp 2007		Baby, Walk On In (a capella)	1963	Josie LP 4001/Candlelite LP 1000 (66)
	6 Months, 3 Weeks, 2 Days,				Ooh, Baby Baby (a capella)	1966	Candlelite LP 1000
	1 Hour/Cha-Cho Hop				Dream (When You're Feeling			
	(by Jack McVea)	1957	Tag 2200/Chess 1690 (58)		Blue) (a capella)	1966	Candlelite LP 1000
	All My Love/Look What				Happy Holiday (a capella)	1966	Candlelite LP 1000
	You've Done To Me	1958	Combo 146/Dot 15806 (58)		Baby Oh Baby (a capella)	1966	Candlelite LP 1000
	Look At Me/Have Love				Fine Little Girl (a capella)	1966	Candlelite LP 1000
	Will Travel	1958	Jamie 1108		Oh, What A Dream (a capella)	1966	Candlelite LP 1000
	Here's My Heart/Gig-A-Lene	1958	Jamie 1114		Bad Girl (a capella)	1966	Candlelite LP 1000
	Teenage Girl/We Three	1958	Win 702		The Closer You Are (a capella)	1966	Candlelite LP 1000
	Double Clutch/If Love Is What				Misty (a capella)	1966	Candlelite LP 1000
	You Want	1960	Star-Hi 10406		So Fine (a capella)	1966	Candlelite LP 1000
	Tapun Tapun	1987	Relic LP 5069		If You Were Gone From Me			
SHARPS (2) (T. PHILLIPS & THE)					(a capella)	1966	Candlelite LP 1000
	Every Star Was Out That Night/				I'm A Happy Man (a capella)	1966	Candlelite LP 1000
	Someone To Love	1960	Firefly 332		Life Is But A Dream (a capella)	1966	Candlelite LP 1000
SHARPSTERS					The Way You Do The Things			
	My Baby Is Gone/Beneath				You Do (a capella)	1966	Candlelite LP 1000
	The Moon	1959	Bella 2208/2209		On The Outside Looking In			
SHARPTONES (1)					(a capella)	1966	Candlelite LP 1000
	Since I Fell For You/Made To							
	Love	1955	Post 2009					

Artist Song	Year	Label
Be Sure My Love (a capella)	1966	Candlelite LP 1000
Oh What A Night/Where Or When (Groups In Choir)	1970	Boardwalk 17
My Cherie/Explain It To Me	1972	Johnson 099 (unreleased)
Will You Miss Me/I'm In The Doghouse	1975	Monogram 108
If You Were Gone For Me/Misty	1976	Clifton 00
Will You Miss/Someone Up There (by Little Nate & the Shells)	1977	Clifton 21
On My Honor/In The Light Of The Dark	1977	Clifton 22
When I'm Blue/Whiplash	N/A	Conlo 879
SHELLS (1) (GM GENE HOLIDAY)		
My Heart Runneth Over (with Love)/Scratch My Name Off The Mail Box	1963	Johnson 125
SHELLS (1) (LITTLE NATE & THE)		
Someone Up There/Will You Miss (by the Shells)	1977	Clifton 21
SHELLS (1) (ROY JONES & THE)		
Satisfied/Made For Lovers	1960	Swirl 101
SHELLS (2)		
Dear One/Same Ol' Thing	1965	Genie 1002
SHELTON, ART (& GROUP)		
Dynaflow	1955	Atlas 1035
SHEPHERD SISTERS (FEMALE)		
Rock & Roll Cha Cha/Gone With The Wind	1954	Capitol 2706/Melba 101 (56)
Alone/Congratulations To Someone	1957	Lance 125
Remember That Crazy Rock 'N Roll Tune/ I Walked Beside The Sea	1957	Melba 108
Gettin' Ready For Freddy/The Best Thing There Is (by the Sheppard Sisters)	1957	Mercury 71244
Heart And Soul/(It's No) Sin	1959	MGM 12766
Here Comes Heaven Again/ I Think It's Time	1959	Warwick 511
Schoen-A, Schoen-A/ Hapsburg Serenade	1961	Big Top 3066
I'm Still Dancin'/Deeply	1961	United Artists 350
Lolita/Ya Ya	1962	United Artists 456
Don't Mention My Name/ What Makes Little Girls Cry	1963	Atlantic 2176
Talk Is Cheap/(Take A Look At My Guy) The Greatest Lover	1963	Atlantic 2195
Alone (original version)/Alone (new version)	1965	York 50002
SHEPHERD, JOHNNIE (& GROUP)		
Rosemarie/I Really Love You	1964	ABC 10548
SHEPHERD, JOHNNIE (BB THE BELMONTS)		
How Blue My Heart/Boom Boom Boomerang	1961	Tilden 3001
SHEPPARD, BUDDY (& GROUP)		
So Many Reasons Why/I'm Hypnotized	1959	Play Me 3517
SHEPPARD, SHANE (BB THE LIMELITES) (AKA SHEP & THE LIMELITES)		
Too Young To Wed/Two Loving Hearts	1959	Apt 25038
SHEPPARDS (1)		
Love/Cool Mambo	1955	Theron 112
Pretty Little Girl	1956	United (unreleased)
Let Me Love You	1956	United (unreleased)
Sherry/Mozelle	1956	United 198/B&F 198 (56)
SHEPPARDS (2)		
Island Of Love/Never Felt Like This Before	1959	Apex 7750
Feel Like Lovin'/Just Like You	1960	Apex 7752
It's Crazy/Meant To Be	1960	Apex 7755
Society Girl/Just When I Needed You Most	1960	Apex 7759
Feel Like Lovin'/Come Home, Come Home	1960	Apex 7760
Just Like You/Tragic	1961	Apex 7762
Never Let Me Go/Give A Hug To Me	1961	Pam 1001
What's The Name Of The Game/Glitter In Your Eyes	1961	Sharp 6039
Every Now And Then/Glitter In Your Eyes	1961	Wes 7750/Vee Jay 406 (61)

Artist Song	Year	Label
Elevator Operator/Loving You	1962	Abner 7006
Tragic/Come To Me	1962	Vee Jay 441
Pretend You're Still Mine/ Walkin'	1963	Okeh 7173
Give A Hug To Me/Island Of Love	1964	Constellation 123
Queen Of Hearts	1964	Constellation LP 4/Collectables LP 5078
I'm Not Wanted	1964	Constellation LP 4/Collectables LP 5078
Forgotten	1964	Constellation LP 4/Collectables LP 5078
Let Yourself Go/Little Girl Lost	1966	ABC 10758
Stubborn Heart/How Do You Like It	1966	Mirwood 5534
Steal Away/Island Of Love	1969	Bunky 7764
Your Love (Has Got A Hole In It)/I'm Not Wanted	1969	Bunky 7766
Queen Of Hearts/So Fine	1974	Owl 330
I Need You So/The Love I Found In You	1976	Robin Hood 135
So In Need For Love	N/A	Collectables LP 5078
SHEPS		
I'm Destroyed (Because Of You)/ I Wonder Why	1996	Early Bird 5002
SHERRY SISTERS		
The Prize/Cinderella It's Midnight	1957	Cindy 3000
SHERWOODS (1)		
Uncle Sam/Three Love Letters Ago	1960	V-Tone 506
SHERWOODS (2)		
The Gang's All Back/Little Big Horn (instrumental)	1961	Johnson 111
Sneakin' Around/Shades Of Summer	1961	Johnson 121
SHERWOODS (2) (TONY RENO & THE)		
I'll Never Stand In Your Way/ Maria Elena	1963	Johnson 123
SHERWOODS (3) (AKA CONCORDS (2)/AKA SNOWMEN)		
Cold And Frosty Morning/True Love Was Born (With Our Last Goodbye)	1963	Dot 16540
SHERWOODS (4)		
Little Heart Take Care/Recipe For Going Steady	1963	Mercury 72042
SHERWOODS (5)		
Happy Holiday/Molly	1964	Magnifico 105
SHERWOODS (6)		
Love You Madly/Moffitt's Mess (instrumental)	1967	Crimson 104/Ray Star
SHERWOODS (7) (JOHNNY SCHILLING & THE)		
King Of The World/Marcelle	1963	C&A 507
SHEVELLES		
Like I Love You/Ooh Poo Pah Doo	1964	World Artists 1023
I Could Conquer The World/ How Would You Like Me To Love You	1964	World Artists 1025
SHIELDS		
You Cheated/That's The Way It's Gonna Be	1958	Tender 513/Dot 15805 (58)
Nature Boy/I'm Sorry Now	1958	Tender 518/Dot 15856 (58)
Play The Game Fair/Fare Thee Well My Love	1958	Tender 521/Dot 15940 (58)
The Girl Around The Corner/ You'll Be Coming Home Soon	1960	Falcon 100/Transcontinental 1013 (60)
You Told Another Lie/Barnyard Dance	1961	Continental 4072
SHIELDS, JOHNNY (& GROUP)		
Out Of Sight, Out Of Mind/ Crying In The Chapel	1963	Armour 4466
SHIRELLES (FEMALE)		
I Met Him On A Sunday/I Want You To Be My Boyfriend	1958	Decca 25506/Decca 30588 (58)/Tiara 6112 (59)
My Love Is A Charm/Slop Time	1958	Decca 30669
I Got The Message/Stop Me	1958	Decca 30761
Dedicated To The One I Love/ Look A Here, Baby	1959	Scepter 1203
A Teardrop And A Lollipop/ Doin' The Ronde	1959	Scepter 1205

Artist	Song	Year	Label
	Please Be My Boyfriend/I Saw A Tear	1960	Scepter 1207
	Tonight's The Night/The Dance Is Over	1960	Scepter 1208
	Tomorrow/Boys	1960	Scepter 1211 (first pressing)
	Will You Still Love Me Tomorrow/Boys	1960	Scepter 1211 (second pressing)
	Mama Said/Blue Holiday	1961	Scepter 1217
	What A Sweet Thing That Was/ A Thing Of The Past	1961	Scepter 1220
	Big John/21	1961	Scepter 1223
	Baby It's You/The Things I Want To Hear (Pretty Words)	1961	Scepter 1227
	Unlucky	1961	Scepter LP 501
	Oh, What A Waste Of Love	1961	Scepter LP 501
	You Don't Want My Love	1961	Scepter LP 501
	Johnny On My Mind	1961	Scepter LP 501
	Tonight At The Prom	1961	Scepter LP 501
	Lower The Flame	1961	Scepter LP 501
	Soldier Boy/Love Is A Swingin' Thing	1962	Scepter 1228
	Welcome Home Baby/Mama, Here Comes The Bride	1962	Scepter 1234
	It's Love That Really Counts/ Stop The Music	1962	Scepter 1237
	Everybody Loves A Lover/ I Don't Think So	1962	Scepter 1243
	Without A Word Of Complaint	1962	Scepter LP 502
	It's Mine	1962	Scepter LP 502
	Rainbow Valley	1962	Scepter LP 502
	I Don't Want To Cry	1962	Scepter LP 502
	The First One	1962	Scepter LP 502
	I'll Do The Same Thing Too	1962	Scepter LP 502
	What's Mine Is Yours	1962	Scepter LP 502
	My Willow Tree	1962	Scepter LP 502
	Foolish Little Girl/Not For All The Money In The World	1963	Scepter 1248
	Don't Say Goodnight And Mean Goodbye/ I Didn't Mean To Hurt You	1963	Scepter 1255
	What Does A Girl Do/Don't Let It Happen To Us	1963	Scepter 1259
	It's A Mad, Mad, Mad, Mad World/31 Flavors	1963	Scepter 1260
	Tonight You're Gonna Fall In Love With Me/Twentieth Century Rock And Roll	1964	Scepter 1264
	Sha-La-La/His Lips Get In The Way	1964	Scepter 1267
	Thank You Baby/Doom's Day	1964	Scepter 1278
	Maybe Tonight/Lost Love	1964	Scepter 1284
	Are You Still My Baby/I Saw A Tear	1964	Scepter 1292
	Everybody's Goin' Mad/March (You'll Be Sorry)	1965	Scepter 12101
	My Heart Belongs To You/ Love That Man	1965	Scepter 12114
	(Mama) My Soldier Boy Is Coming Home/Soldier Boy	1965	Scepter 12123
	I Met Him On A Sunday '66/ Love That Man	1965	Scepter 12132
	Shhh, I'm Watching The Movies/Shhh, I'm Watching The Movies	1965	Scepter 1296
	Que Sera Sera/Till My Baby Comes Home	1966	Scepter 12150
	Shades Of Blue/When The Boys Talk About The Girls	1966	Scepter 12162
	Shades Of Blue/Looking Around	1966	Scepter 12162
	Shades Of Blue/After Midnight	1966	Scepter 12162
	Teasin' Me/Look Away	1967	Scepter 12178
	Don't Go Home (My Little Darlin')/Nobody's Baby After You	1967	Scepter 12185
	Too Much Of a Good Thing/ Shiny Colors	1967	Scepter 12192
	Last Minute Miracle/No Doubt About It	1967	Scepter 12198
SHIRELLES (SHIRLEY & THE)			
	A Most Unusual Boy/Look What You've Done To My Heart	1969	Bell 760
	Playthings/Looking Glass	1969	Bell 787
	Go Away And Find Yourself/ Never Give Up	1969	Bell 815
SHONDELLES			
	Don't Cry My Soldier Boy/ My Love	1962	King 5597
	Special Delivery/Muscle Bound	1962	King 5705
	Ooo Sometimes/Watusi One More Time	1963	King 5755
SHONDELLES (RICKEY LEIGH & THE)			
	To Find An Angel Like You/Why Do Little Girls Hurt Little Boys	1963	Savoy 1620
SHONNIE (& GROUP)			
	Sunset	1954	TNT 113
SHORT STOPS (SHORT & THE)			
	If I Loved Only You	N/A	Fortune LP 8017
SHORT STORIES (LENNY O'HENRY & THE)			
	Billy The Continental Kid/ Cheated Heart	1961	ABC 10222
SHORTCUTS			
	Don't Say He's Gone/I'll Hide My Love	1959	Carlton 513
SHOW STOPPERS			
	When You See Me Hurt/Don't You Know What I Believe	1961	Brent 7021
	Cynthia/But Who Will Pay	1963	Amber 212
SHOWCASES			
	This Love Was Real/Anna, My Love	1964	Galaxy 732
SHOWMEN			
	It Will Stand/Country Fool	1961	Minit 632/Imperial 66033 (64)/Liberty 56166 (67)
	Let Her Feel Your Kiss/Valley Of Love	1963	Airecords 334
SHOWMEN (CARL FROST & THE)			
	I'm Still In Love With You/ Mind Your Mama	1963	Lawn 223
SHOWMEN (TONI & THE)			
	Beware/Try My Love	1965	Ten Star 103
SHOWSTOPPERS (CURTIS & THE)			
	Sad Girl/Let's Workout Baby	1964	Travis 039
SHOWVENISTICS			
	Dream Lover/I Go To Pieces	1993	Clifton 106
SHUFFLERS (1)			
	Ain't Nothin' Wrong With That/ Lovin' On My Mind	1954	Okeh 7040
SHUFFLERS (2) (JAY & THE)			
	Always Be Mine/When The Lights Are Low	1962	Crackerjack 4010
SHUFFLERS (3) (BENNY WILLIAMS & THE)			
	Goodnight My Love/Jackpot	N/A	Champion 103
SHUFFLES			
	Do You Remember My Darling/ Dancin' Little Girl	1963	Rayco 508
SHY GUYS			
	A Love So True/Where You Belong	1966	Palmer 5008
SHY-TONES (AKA HI-TONES/AKA TRENTONS)			
	A Lover's Quarrel/Just For You	1960	1 Goodspin 401/Bruce
	White Bucks/Bandstand Rock	1961	Spot 14
	Annette/White Bucks	1961	Spot 15
SIDEWINDERS (JIM HARRIS & THE)			
	I'm On The Outside Looking In/ Three Chartreuse Buzzards Sittin' On The Fence	1966	Fabar 15564
SIERRAS (1) (AKA FOUR SIERRAS)			
	So Many Sleepless Nights/ Nearer My Heart	1962	Knox 102
	Stormy Weather/Chance	1963	Mail Call 2333/2334
SIERRAS (2) (FEMALE)			
	I'll Believe It When I See It/ I Should Have Loved You	1962	Goldisc G4
	A Plan For Love/Then I'll Still Love You	1963	Cham 101/Dot 16569 (63)
SIGNATURES			
	Someone In Love/Julie Is Her Name	1957	Whippet 210/Gen Norman 210X (57)
SILHOUETTES			
	Wish I Could Be There/Which Way Did She Go	1956	Grand 142
	Get A Job/I Am Lonely	1957	Junior 391/Junior 593 (57)/ Ember 1029 (57)

Artist Song	Year	Label
I Sold My Heart To The Junkman/What Would You Do	1958	Ace 552/Junior 396 (58)
Heading For The Poor House/Miss Thing	1958	Ember 1032
Bing Bong/Voodoo Eyes	1958	Ember 1037
Never/Bull Frog	1961	20th Fox 240
The Push/Which Way Did She Go	1962	Imperial 5899
Your Love/Rent Man	1962	Junior 993
Gaucho Serenade	N/A	Goodway LP 100
Not Me Baby	N/A	Goodway LP 100
SILHOUETTES (BILLY HORTON & THE)		
Evelyn/Never Will Part	1959	Ace 563/Junior 400 (59)
SILKS (CHARLES McCULLOUGH & THE)		
My Girl/Zorro	1961	Dooto 462
You're Not Too Young/That's Alright	1962	Dooto 465
I Cried All Night/Mary's Party	1962	Dooto 467
SILVA-TONES		
That's All I Want From You/ Roses Are Blooming	1957	Monarch 5281/Argo 5281 (57)
SILVER SLIPPERS (BARBARA J. & THE)		
Laughing At Me/Love Is The Thing	1961	Lescay 3001
SILVERTONES (1)		
Hey Good Looking/My Only Love	1960	Elgin 005/006
You Gotta Change Your Ways/ Sentimental Memory	1960	Silver Slipper 1000
SILVERTONES (2)		
Thinking Of You/Canadian Sunset	1962	Joey 302
SILVERTONES (3)		
Get It/Bathsheba	1963	Goliath 1355/Valiant 6045 (64)
Seven Piece Bathing Suit/ Wait For My Gal	1964	Sweet 16
SILVERTONES (4) (RONNIE RICE & THE)		
She's Not Yours/I Want You To Be My Girl	1964	Limelight 3029
SIMMONS, LITTLE MAXINE (& GROUP)		
Since I Lost You/In You Baby, In You Baby	N/A	Varbee 118
SIMMS, LLOYD (& FEMALE GROUP)		
For Sentimental Reasons/ I Want To Know	1961	Atlantic 2078
SINCERES		
I Got A Girl/Joyce	1978	Crystal Ball 126
SINCERES (1)		
You're Too Young/Forbidden Love	1960	Jordan 117
Darling/Do You Remember	1960	Sigma 1003/1004
Please Don't Cheat On Me/ If You Should Leave Me	1961	Richie 545
Our Winter Love/Kookie Ookie	1963	Epic 9583
Sincerely/Snap Your Fingers	1964	Columbia 43110
SINCERES (2)		
The Magic Of Love/Tell Her	1966	Taurus 377
SINCERES (3) (JOHNNY H & THE)		
Why Don't You Write Me/ Crazy Baby	1963	El Zarape 122
SINCLAIRS		
For Your Precious Love/My One And Only Dream	1979	U.G.H.A. 07
For Your Precious Love/My One And Only Dream	1979	UGHA 7
SINGING BELLES (FEMALE)		
The Empty Mailbox/Someone Loves You, Joe	1960	Madison 126
High Noon/Oh Happy Day	1960	Madison 132
SINGING DOVES (CLIFF BUTLER & THE)		
When You Love/People Will Talk	1953	States 123
SINGING WANDERERS (AKA WANDERERS (1))		
Say Hey, Willie Mays/Don't Drop It	1954	Decca 29230
The Wrong Party Again/ Three Roses	1954	Decca 29298
SINGLETON, BEBO (BB THE NOTES)		
Shrine Of The Echo/Feeny Jones	1959	Stentor 101
SINNERS		
Nightmare/Could This Be Love	1962	Eden 1

Artist Song	Year	Label
SINTELLS		
Lundee Dundee (acapella)	1975	Relic LP 105
Please Say It Isn't So (acapella)	1975	Relic LP 105
My Imagination (acapella)	1975	Relic LP 108
SIR NITES (T.L. CLEMONS & THE)		
I Love You So/Who's That Girl	1960	Combo 168
SIRS		
Sixteen Candles/Wow (instrumental)	1968	Charay 33
SIX TEENS		
A Casual Look/Teenage Promise	1956	Flip 315
Afar Into The Night/Send Me Flowers	1956	Flip 317
Only Jim/My Special Guy	1957	Flip 320
Arrow Of Love/Was It A Dream Of Mine?	1957	Flip 322
Baby You're Dynamite/My Surprise	1957	Flip 326
My Secret/Stop Playing Ping Pong (With My Heart)	1957	Flip 329
Danny/Love's Funny That Way	1958	Flip 333
Oh, It's Crazy/Baby-O	1958	Flip 338
Heaven Knows I Love You/ Why Do I Go To School?	1959	Flip 346
So Happy/That Wonderful Secret Of Love	1960	Flip 350
A Little Prayer/Suddenly In Love	1960	Flip 351
SIXTEENS		
Was It A Dream	1964	Regency 626
SKARLETTONES (FEMALE)		
Do You Remember/Will You Dream	1959	Ember 1053
SKIPPER, BUDDY (& GROUP)		
Back On The Beach Again/ Make Believe Baby	1961	Fury 1051
Cancel The Reservation/ Restless Breed	1968	Smash 2173
SKY BOYS (THURL RAVENSCROFT & THE)		
Mad, Baby, Mad/Never Doubt My Love	1955	Fabor 4005
SKYHAWKS		
Love Me Right	N/A	Collectables LP 5039
SKYLARKS (1) (AKA STARLINGS)		
The Glory Of Love/You And I	1951	Decca 48241
SKYLARKS (2)		
Home In Pasadena/I Had The Craziest Dream	1953	RCA 5257
Ol' Man River/There's A Boat Leaving Soon For New York	1957	Verve 10082
SKYLARKS (3) (CHET BARNES & THE)		
Is You Is/Everytime It Rains	1961	Embassy 201
SKYLARKS (4)		
Jeannie/Everybody's Got Somebody	1962	Everlast 5022
SKYLIGHTERS		
How Foolish Am I/That My Man	N/A	Emjay 6152
SKYLINERS (1)		
Since I Don't Have You/One Night, One Night	1959	Calico 103/104/Original Sound 35 (63)
This I Swear/Tomorrow	1959	Calico 106
It Happened Today/Lonely Way	1959	Calico 109
If I Loved You	1959	Calico LP 3000
I Can Dream Can't I	1959	Calico LP 3000
Warm	1959	Calico LP 3000
Tired Of Me	1959	Calico LP 3000
Zing Went The Strings Of My Heart	1959	Calico LP 3000
When I Fall In Love	1959	Calico LP 3000
How Much/Lorraine From Spain	1960	Calico 114
Pennies From Heaven/I'll Be Seeing You	1960	Calico 117/Original Sound 36 (63)
Believe Me/Happy Time	1960	Calico 120
I'll Close My Eyes/The Door Is Still Open	1961	Colpix 188
The End Of A Story/Baion Rhythms	1961	Colpix 607
Close Your Eyes/Our Love Will Last	1961	Colpix 613
Everyone But You/Three Coins In The Fountain	1962	Cameo 215

Artist Song	Year	Label
Tell Me/Comes Love	1962	Viscount 104
Since I Fell For You/I'd Die	1963	Atco 6270/Motown 1046 (63)
This I Swear/It Happened Today	1963	Original Sound 37
The Loser/Everything Is Fine	1965	Jubilee 5506
Who Do You Love?/Get Yourself A Baby	1966	Jubilee 5512
I Run To You/Don't Hurt Me, Baby	1966	Jubilee 5520
Oh How Happy/We've Got Love On OUr Side	1978	Tortoise Int'l 11343
With All My Heart And Soul	1985	Relic LP 5053
I Can't Sleep/Why Should You Taunt Me?	N/A	Doc 496
SKYLINERS (1) (JIMMY BEAUMONT & THE)		
Where Have They Gone/I Could Have Loved You So Well	1974	Capitol 3979
The Day The Clown Cried/ Our Day Is Here	1976	Drive 6520
You're My Christmas Present/ Another Lonely New Year's Eve	1989	Classic Artists 123
SKYLINERS (2)		
Rock N' Roll Ruby/I Do All Right	N/A	Double AA 1045
SKYLITES		
Oh Happy Day/My Only Girl	1961	Ta-Rah 101
SKYTONES		
Mr. Moon	1959	Gaylo 101
SLADES (AKA SPADES (1))		
Baby/You Mean Everything To Me	1957	Domino 200/100/Liberty 55118 (58)
You Cheated/The Waddle	1958	Domino 500
No Time/You Gambled	1958	Domino 800
Summertime/You Must Try	1959	Domino 1000
Just You/It's Better To Love	1961	Domino 901
Take My Heart/It's Your Turn	1961	Domino 906
SLADES (JOYCE HARRIS & THE)		
I Cheated/Do You Know	1961	Domino 903
SLICKS (JIMMY SOMMERS & THE)		
I Love You, You Love Me	N/A	Space
SLIDERS (BYRON GIPSON & THE)		
Honey Dew/The One I Love	1955	Specialty 566
SLIDERS (BYRON "SLICK" GIPSON & THE)		
I Want 'Cha Baby	1956	Specialty
SLIDERS (JOE GORDON & THE)		
Love Is Like A Mountain/ There Is A Great Big Moon	1961	Chevron 012/Chevron 750
SLIDERS (SLICK GIPSON & THE)		
Footloose And Fancy-Free/ Etta Mae	1956	Specialty 587
SMART TONES		
Ginny/Bob-O-Link	1958	Herald 529
SMITH QUARTET, BEN		
Big Fat Lips/The Cadillac Song	1953	Rama 17
SMITH, ARLENE (& FEMALE GROUP)		
Love, Love, Love/He Knows I Love Him Too Much	1961	Big Top 3073
SMITH, ARLENE (& GROUP)		
Mon Cherie Au Revoir/ To Live My Life Again	1963	End 1120
SMITH, HUEY (& GROUP)		
Dearest Darling (You're The One)/Tu-ber-cu-lucas (no group)	1959	Ace 571
SMITH, JIMMIE (& GROUP)		
I'll Cry And Cry Every Night/ Night Time Is The Time	1959	Flip 347
SMITH, KENNY (& GROUP)		
Deep In My Heart/Money Talks	1964	Fraternity 934
SMITH, MELVIN (WITH THE NIGHT RIDERS)		
Zaki Sue/Open The Door, Richard	1958	Cameo 135
SMITH, RICHARD (& GROUP)		
Mama Cried/I Don't Wanna Cry	1958	Hi-Q 5042
SMITH, ROY (& GROUP)		
It's Love	N/A	Adaire 90
SMITH, SAVANNAH (& GROUP)		
Anytime Anyplace Anywhere/ Let It Be	1960	End 1077
SMITH, SHAD (& GROUP)		
Wonderful One/Taxi Cab	1962	Smash 1765
SMITH, WENDELL (& GROUP)		
Tonight's My Night To Cry/ Puddin' Pie	1959	United Artists 166
SMOOTH TONES		
Dear Diary/Crazy Baby	1956	Ember 1001
SMOOTHIES		
Softly/Joanie	1960	Decca 31105
Lonely Boy And Pretty Girl/ Ride, Ride, Ride	1960	Decca 31159
SMOOTHTONES		
Bring Back Your Love (To Me)/ No Doubt About It	1955	Jem 412
Don't Keep Our Love Hidden In The Dark/Little Cupid	1957	Okeh 7078
SNAP SHOTS		
I Need You/That's What I Like	1963	Federal 12496
SNAPPERS		
If There Were/Big Bill	1959	20th Century Fox 148
SNAPS (GINGER DAVIS & THE)		
Love Me The Way I Love You/ Truly	1961	Tore 1008
I'm No Runaround (answer record to "Runaround Sue")/ Laughin'	1962	Swan 4090
Growing Up Is Hard To Do/ Seven Days In September	1965	MGM 13413
SNEAKERS		
You Belong To Me/Mary Lou	N/A	Delta 1868
SNOWMEN (AKA CONCORDS (2)/AKA SHERWOODS (3))		
Cold And Frosty Morning/ You Started It	1964	Herald 597 (second pressing, first is by the Concords)
SO-AND-SOS (ANITA & THE)		
Joey Baby/Rinky Tinky Rhythm	1961	RCA 7974
SOCIALITES (1) (KENNY & THE)		
The King Tut Rock/I'll Have To Decide	1958	Crosstown 001
SOCIALITES (2) (FEMALE)		
Jimmy/The Click	1963	Arrawak 1004
SOCIETY GIRLS (FEMALE)		
SPCLG (Society For The Prevention Of Cruelty To Little Girls)/You Better Stay Home	1963	Vee Jay 524
SOFT TONES (AKA SOFTONES)		
A Moth Around A Flame/ My Mother's Eyes	1955	Samson 103
SOFTONES (AKA SOFT TONES)		
Oh Why/Young Boy	1957	Cee Bee 1062
SOFTWINDS		
Cross My Heart/Oh Baby	1961	Hac 105
SOLDIER BOYS		
I'm Your Soldier Boy/You Picked Me	1962	Scepter 1230
SOLITAIRES		
Wonder Why/Blue Valentine	1954	Old Town 1000
Please Remember My Heart/ South Of The Border	1954	Old Town 1006/1007
Chances I've Taken/Lonely	1954	Old Town 1008
I Don't Stand A Ghost Of A Chance/Girl Of Mine	1955	Old Town 1010
What Did She Say?/My Dear	1955	Old Town 1012
The Wedding/Don't Fall In Love	1955	Old Town 1014
Magic Rose/Later For You, Baby	1955	Old Town 1015
The Honeymoon/Fine Little Girl	1956	Old Town 1019
You've Sinned/You're Back With Me	1956	Old Town 1026 (first pressing)
The Angels Sang/You've Sinned	1956	Old Town 1026 (second pressing)
Give Me One More Chance/ Nothing Like a Little Love	1956	Old Town 1032
Walkin' Along/Please Kiss This Letter	1957	Old Town 1034/Argo 5316 (58)
I Really Love You So (Honey Babe)/Thrill Of Love	1957	Old Town 1044
Walkin' And Talkin'/No More Sorrows	1957	Old Town 1049
Please Remember My Heart/ Big Mary's House	1958	Old Town 1059
Embraceable You/'Round Goes My Heart	1959	Old Town 1066

Artist Song	Year	Label
Helpless/Light A Candle In The Chapel	1959	Old Town 1071
Lonesome Lover/Pretty Thing	1961	Old Town 1096
Honey Babe/The Time Is Here	1963	Old Town 1139
Fool That I Am/Fair Weather Lover	1964	MGM 13221
Chapel Of St. Clair/If I Loved You (recorded in 1954)	1978	Old Town 1003
At Night/Hully Gully	1979	King Tut 178
Silent Grief/Embraceable You	1993	Old Town 1992
SOLOTONES		
Pork And Beans/Front Page Blues	1955	Excello 2060
SONGETTES (FB KATE WEBSTER)		
Sea Of Love/I Feel So Low	1959	Decca 30945
SONGSPINNERS		
Bobbie/Duffy	1958	Leila 1601
SONICS		
As I Live On/Bumble Bee	1955	Groove 0112
Once In A Lifetime/It Ain't True	1958	X-Tra 107/Candlelite 416 (63)/Clifton 12 (75)
This Broken Heart/You Made Me Cry	1959	Harvard 801/Harvard 922 (59)/Checker 922 (59)
Evil Eye/Triangle Love	1959	Nocturne 110/RKO Unique 411 (59)
It's You/Preacher Man	1962	Amco 001
Funny/I Get That Feeling	1962	Armonia 102
Beautiful Brown Eyes/Sugaree	1962	Jamie 1235
Say You'll Be Mine	1987	Relic LP 8011
You Are My Sunshine	1987	Relic LP 8011
Marlene	N/A	Gaiety 114
SONICS (VANCE CHARLES & THE)		
Closer To Me/Let's Fall In Love	1963	Lori 9553
SONNETS		
Why Should We Break Up/ Please Won't You Call Me	1956	Herald 477
Oh Judy/Angel Of My Dreams	1958	Lane 501
Forever For You/I Can't Get Sentimental	1964	Guyden 2112
SONNETTES (FEMALE)		
I've Gotten Over You	1963	Kayo 0001
SONOTONES		
How Do You Speak To An Angel/Sonotone Bounce	1954	Bruce 105
SONOTONES (FB DON GARDNER)		
I Hear A Rhapsody/It's A Sin To Tell A Lie	1955	Bruce 127
SONOTONES (HARRY CARLTON & THE)		
Long Time Baby	N/A	Jarman
SOOTHERS (AKA HARPTONES)		
I Believe In You/The Little White Cloud That Cried	1965	Port 70041
SOPHISTICATES		
I Need You/I Can't Stand It	N/A	Mutt 27318
SOPHOMORES (1)		
Big Joke/After All	1955	Decca 29669
Every Night About This Time/ Cool, Cool Baby	1956	Dawn 216
I Get A Thrill/Linda	1956	Dawn 218
Charades/What Can I Do?	1957	Chord 1302/Epic 9259 (57)
Ocean Blue/I Left My Sugar Standing In The Rain	1957	Dawn 223
Is There A Someone For Me/ Everybody Loves Me	1957	Dawn 225
I Just Can't Keep The Tears From Tumblin' Down/ If I Should Lose Your Love	1957	Dawn 228
Checkers/Each Time I Hold You	1957	Dawn 237
SOPHOMORES (2) (ANTHONY & THE) (AKA TONY & THE TWILIGHTERS (4))		
Gee (But I'd Give The World)/ It Depends On You	1959	ABC 10073
Embraceable You/Beautiful Dreamer (82)	1963	Grand 163/Jason Scott 18
Play Those Oldies Mr. D.J./ Clap Your Hands	1963	Mercury 72103
Better Late Than Never/ Swingin' At Chariot	1963	Mercury 72168
It Depends On You/Gee	1965	ABC 10737
Wild For Her/Get Back To You	1966	ABC 10770

Artist Song	Year	Label
Heartbreak/I'll Go Through Life Loving You	1966	ABC 10844
Workout/Serenade	1966	Jamie 1330
One Summer Night/Workout (instrumental)	1967	Jamie 1340
SORROWS (NICKY DE MATTEO & THE)		
Suddenly/More Than Riches	1960	Guyden 2024
I Wanna Be Lonely/Little Red Kitten	1966	Cameo 407
SOUND MASTERS		
I Want You To Be My Baby/ Lonely Lonely	N/A	Julet 102
SOUNDS (1) (AKA TANGIERS)		
Cold Chills/So Unnecessary	1955	Modern 975
Sweet Sixteen/Anything For You	1956	Modern 981
SOUNDS (2)		
Life/Charlie Chan	1959	Sarg 172
My Pillow Of Dreams/Tell Me Baby	1959	Sarg 181
SOUNDS (3) (VIKKI NELSON & THE)		
Like A Baby/I Was A Fool For Leaving (no group)	1957	Vik 0273
SOUNDS (4) (LEE & THE)		
What Is This Thing Called Love/ Beautiful Romance	1959	Lido 600
SOUNDS (5) (FEATURING FRANK WILLIAMS)		
Little Baby Be Mine/Judy (I Love You So)	1961	Queen 24008
SOUTHWINDS		
Build Me A Cabin/They Call Me Crazy	1958	Fury 1017
SOUVENIRS (1)		
So Long, Daddy/Alene, Sweet Little Texas Queen	1957	Dooto 412
Double Dealing Baby	1957	Dooto LP 224
SOUVENIRS (2)		
I Could Have Danced All Night/It's Too Bad	1967	Inferno 2001
SPACERIDERS (MAI CASSELLE & THE)		
Don't Deceive Me/Do The Dipper	N/A	Half Peach 500
SPADES (1) (AKA SLADES)		
Baby/You Mean Everything To Me	1957	Domino 200/100/Liberty 55118 (58)
SPADES (2)		
I'm On Fire/Close To You	1959	Major 1007
SPADES (3) (DELL RAYS & THE)		
Di Di/Full House (instrumental)	1958	Dice 479
SPANDELLS		
Be My Love/Movements	1977	Robin Hood 146
SPANIELS		
Gerald's Blues	1953	Vee Jay (unreleased)
Sloppy Drunk	1953	Vee Jay (unreleased)
Baby It's You/Bounce (53)	1953	Vee Jay 101/Chance 1141
The Bells Ring Out/House Cleaning	1953	Vee Jay 103
Danny Boy	1954	Vee Jay (unreleased)
Goodnight, Sweetheart, Good- night/You Don't Move Me	1954	Vee Jay 107
Play It Cool/Let's Make Up	1954	Vee Jay 116
False Love	1955	Vee Jay (unreleased)
Do Wah/Don'Cha Go	1955	Vee Jay 131
You Painted Pictures/Hey, Sister Lizzie	1955	Vee Jay 154 (first pressing)
Painted Picture/Hey Sister Lizzie	1955	Vee Jay 154 (second pressing)
Jessie Mae	1956	Vee Jay (unreleased)
False Love/Do You Really?	1956	Vee Jay 178
Dear Heart/Why Don't You Dance	1956	Vee Jay 189
Since I Fell For You/Baby Come Along With Me	1956	Vee Jay 202
You Gave Me Peace Of Mind/ Please Don't Tease	1956	Vee Jay 229
Lucinda	1957	Vee Jay (unreleased)
Everyone's Laughing/I.O.U.	1957	Vee Jay 246
I Need Your Kisses/You're Gonna Cry	1957	Vee Jay 257
I Lost You/Crazee Baby	1957	Vee Jay 264

Artist Song	Year	Label
Lovey Dovey, Baby, Be Mine	1958	Charly LP 1114 (86)
A Stranger In Love	1958	Charly LP 1114 (86)
I'm Gonna Thank Him	1958	Vee Jay (unreleased)
Tina/Great Googley Moo	1958	Vee Jay 278
Stormy Weather/Here Is Why		
I Love You	1958	Vee Jay 290
Heart And Soul/Baby It's You	1958	Vee Jay 301
This Is A Lovely Way To Spend		
An Evening	1958	Vee Jay LP 1002
Automobiles	1959	Charly LP 1021 (81)
Red Sails In The Sunset	1959	Charly LP 1114 (86)
I'll Be Waiting	1959	Solid Smoke LP (84)/Charly LP 1114 (86)
I Like It Like That/Trees	1959	Vee Jay 310
100 Years From Today/These Three Words	1959	Vee Jay 328
People Will Say We're In Love/ The Bells Ring Out	1959	Vee Jay 342
I Know/Bus Fare Home	1960	Vee Jay 350
The Posse	1960	Vee Jay LP 1024
Little Joe	1960	Vee Jay LP 1024
So Deep Within/Baby Sweets	1960	Vee Jay LP 1024/Skylark 582 (79)
I Know, I Know/Jealous Heart (Pookie Hudson bb the Imperials)	1963	Double L 711
For Sentimental Reasons/ Miracles	1964	Double L 720
Maybe/Goodnight Sweetheart	1969	Buddah 153
Fairy Tales/Jealous Heart	1970	North American 001/Calla 172 (70)
Lonely Man/Stand In Line	1970	North American 002
Come Back To These Arms/ Money Blues	1970	North American 3114
Peace Of Mind/She Sang To Me/Danny Boy	1974	Canterbury EP101
Little Joe/The Posse	1974	Owl 328
SPANIELS (POOKIE HUDSON & THE)		
(I Love You) For Sentimental Reasons/Meek Man	1961	Neptune 124
John Brown/Turn Out The Lights	1962	Parkway 839
SPARKELS		
Try Love (One More Time)/ That Boy Of Mine	1964	Old Town 1160
Where There's A Will/We Got It	1963	Poplar 119
SPARKLES (1) (LITTLE ANGEL & THE)		
Come On 'N Rock	1959	Award 126
SPARKLES (1) (LORELEI LYNN & THE)		
Bobby/Rock-A-Bop	1959	Award 128
SPARKLES (2)		
Where There's A Will/We Got It	1963	Poplar 119
SPARKLES (3) (JERRY DIAMOND & THE)		
Lindy-Lou	1958	RCA 7257
SPARKLETONES		
Dear Little Boy/Just One Chance	1963	Pageant 604
SPARKS (1) (CURTIS IRVIN & THE)		
Make A Little Love/Cheatin' On Me	1954	RPM 417
SPARKS (2)		
Mary, Mary Lou/Ol' Man River (instrumental)	1957	Decca 30378
A Cuddle And A Kiss/Roamin' Candle	1957	Decca 30509
Danny Boy/Run, Run, Run	1957	Hull 723
Adreann/The Finger	1957	Hull 724
Robin Red Breast/Something Happened	1958	Arwin 114
The Genie/Gee, That's Bad	1959	Carlton 522
Why Did You Leave/La Macerena	1959	Decca 30974
SPARKS (3) (NATHAN RAY & THE)		
Teen Heart/Hold Me Close	1958	Rocko 510
SPARKS (4)		
Woe, Woe/Cool It	1967	Cub 9151
SPARKS (5)		
Slowly But Surely/Away Over There	1975	Broadcast 1121
SPARKS OF RHYTHM		
Cry On My Shoulder	1989	Relic LP 5080
Somewhere	1989	Relic LP 5080
SPARKS OF RHYTHM (FB JIMMY JONES) (AKA BERLINERS)		
Don't Love You Anymore/ Woman, Woman, Woman	1955	Apollo 479

Artist Song	Year	Label
Stars Are In The Sky/Hurry Home	1955	Apollo 481
Handy Man/Everybody Rock And Go	1960	Apollo 541
SPARKS, MILTON (& GROUP)		
The Voice Of Love/A Certain Smile	1958	Vulcan/Hunt 320 (58)
SPARROWS (1) (AKA BLENDERS (1)/AKA MILLIONAIRES (1))		
Tell My Baby/Why Did You Leave Me?	1953	Jay-Dee 783
I'll Be Lovin' You/Hey!	1954	Jay-Dee 790
Love Me Tender/Come Back To Me	1956	Davis 456/Jay Dee
I'm Gonna Do That Woman In/ Don't Fuck Around With Love (by the Blenders, recorded in 1953)	1971	Kelway 101 (unreleased)
I'm Gonna Hold My Baby Tight	1985	Krazy Kat LP 797
SPARROWS (2) (LITTLE JIMMY & THE)		
Two Hearts Together/Snorin'	1958	Val-Ue 101
SPARROWS QUARTETTE		
Believe Me	N/A	Broadcast 944
SPARROWS QUARTETTE (AKA MEL DARK & THE GIANTS)		
Merry Christmas Baby	1963	Broadcast
Deep In My Heart/Love My Baby	1969	Jet 3000
I Love You So Much I Could Die/Please Come Back To Me	1973	Del Tone 3001
The Christmas Song/He Is My Friend	1974	Jet 3020
We Sing For Fun/The Christmas Song	1975	Jet 3021
It's Written In The Stars	N/A	Broadcast 1000
SPARTANS (1)		
Faith, Hope And Charity/Lost	1954	Capri 7201
SPARTANS (2) (JIMMY & THE)		
You're My Girl/Why Doesn't She Notice Me	1960	Satellite 106
SPARTANS (3)		
One More Chance/Love Is Strange	1961	Audio International 102
SPARTONES		
Well Done Baby/Brother Bill (by the Five Blind Boys)	1972	Vintage 1000
SPEARS (FRANKIE ERVIN & THE)		
Why Did It End?/Try To Care	1961	Don 202
SPEARS, CALVIN (& GROUP)		
Come On Home/Doing The Rock And Roll	1960	Vin 1020
SPECIALS		
I'm Leaving It All Up To You/ Kissin' Like Lovers	1963	Marc 103
SPECTORS THREE (GM PHIL SPECTOR)		
I Really Do/I Know Why	1960	Trey 3001
Mr. Robin/My Heart Stood Still	1960	Trey 3005
SPEIDELS		
Oh Baby/A Lovely One	1960	Monte Carlo 101
SPELLBOUNDS (JOHNNY ADAMS & THE)		
A Part Of Me/Some Day	1963	Watch 6333
SPENCER SISTERS		
Why Did You Lie/Do-Bop-Slam-Boy	1955	Aladdin 3285
SPENCER, CARL (& GROUP)		
Prayer/Tired Of Work	1962	Southside 1007
Cover Girl/Progress	1965	Rust 5104
SPENCER, SONNY (& GROUP)		
Oh Boy/Gilee (no group)	1959	Memo 17984
Hold My Hand/Hey Miss Fine	N/A	Music Hall 24002
SPI-DELLS		
Gee But I Wish/Never Ever	1966	Little Town 575
Take Me As I Am/Over The Weekend	N/A	Tyme 200/Tyme 263
SPICES (1)		
Tell Me Little Girl/Money, Fortune And Fame	1958	Carlton 480
SPICES (2) (SUGAR & THE)		
Bye Bye Baby/Do The Dog	1963	Stacy 968
SPIDELS (AKA SPIEDELS)		
You Know I Need You/Like A Bee	1962	Chavis 1035
Fat Lady/I'll Catch A Rainbow	1963	Minaret 112
SPIDERS		
You're The One/I Didn't Want To Do It	1954	Imperial 5265/Imperial 5618 (59)

Artist	Song	Year	Label
	Tears Began To Flow/I'll Stop Crying	1954	Imperial 5280
	I'm Slippin' In/I'm Searching	1954	Imperial 5291
	Mmm Mmm Baby/The Real Thing	1954	Imperial 5305
	"21"/She Keeps Me Wondering	1954	Imperial 5318
	That's Enough/Lost And Bewildered	1955	Imperial 5331
	Am I The One/Sukey, Sukey, Sukey	1955	Imperial 5344
	For A Thrill/Bells In My Heart	1955	Imperial 5354
	Witchcraft/Is It True?	1955	Imperial 5366
	A-1 In My Heart/Dear Mary	1956	Imperial 5393
	That's The Way To Win My Heart/Goodbye	1956	Imperial 5405
	Honey Bee/That's My Desire	1957	Imperial 5423
	You're The One/Tennessee Slim	1960	Imperial 5714
	Witchcraft/You Don't Love Me (True)	1961	Imperial 5739
	Walking Around In Circles	1961	Imperial LP 9140
	True You Don't Love Me	1961	Imperial LP 9140
	Don't Knock	1961	Imperial LP 9140
	Don't/For Sentimental Reasons (by the Chocolateers)	1974	Owl 334
	You Played The Part	N/A	Imperial (unreleased)
	Why Do I Love You	N/A	Imperial (unreleased)
	Mello Mama	N/A	Imperial (unreleased)
	Love's All I'm Putting Down	N/A	Imperial (unreleased)
SPIDERS (CHUCK CARBO & THE)			
	Don't Pity Me/How I Feel	1956	Imperial 5376
SPIEDELLS			
	Dream Girl	1966	Providence 418
SPIEDELS (AKA SPIDELS)			
	Dear Joan/No	1958	Crosley 201
SPINA, VIC (& GROUP)			
	One Summer Night/We Can Try It Again	N/A	VM
SPINDLES (FRANKIE & THE)			
	My Letter To You/Count To Ten	1968	Roc-Ker 100
	Handwriting On The Wall/Count To Ten	1968	Roc-Ker 101
	For Your Love	1968	Roc-Ker 13314
	Tomorrow/There Is A Beauty	1968	Roc-Ker 575
SPINDLETOPPERS (CARL & THE)			
	It's Written In Your Eyes/Hey Moon	1962	ABC 10346
SPINDRIFTS			
	Belinda/Cha Cha Doo	1958	ABC 9904
SPINNER, ALICE (& GROUP)			
	Good For Me/Sweet Promises	N/A	Hugo 11722
SPINNERS (1)			
	Goofin'/Love's Prayer	1958	Capitol 3955
	Marvella/My Love And Your Love	1958	Rhythm 125
	Bird Watchin'/Richard Pry, Private Eye	1959	End 1045
	Little Otis/Rag Mop	1959	Warner Bros. 5084
SPINNERS (2) (CLAUDINE CLARK & THE)			
	Angel Of Happiness/Teenage Blues	1958	Herald 521
	Party Lights/Disappointed	1962	Chancellor 1113
	Walkin' Through A Cemetery/Telephone Game	1962	Chancellor 1124
	Walk Me Home/Who Will You Hurt	1963	Chancellor 1130
SPIRALS (1)			
	Please Be My Love/Forever And A Day	1961	Smash 1719
SPIRALS (2)			
	Peace Of Mind (acapella)	1975	Relic LP 108
	Adios, My Love (acapella)	1975	Relic LP 108
SPIRALS (3)			
	My Humble Prayer/Lost My Heart	1962	Luxor 1012
SPIRITS (DOUG SAHM & THE)			
	Crazy, Crazy Feeling/Baby What's On Your Mind	1959	Personality 3504
SPITFIRES (TONY CARMEN & THE)			
	Don't Run To Me/Spitfire	1959	Abel 224
SPLENDORS			
	The Golden Years/The Echo Tells Me	1959	Taurus 101
	Who Can It Be/The Golden Years	1959	Taurus 102
	Island Called Romance/Puddin' Tain	1962	Jano 004
	The Dance Is Over/Six Nights A Week	1982	Clifton 69
SPORTSMEN (1)			
	Hot Rod Hop/Ooh Pretty Baby	1955	Key 503
SPORTSMEN (2)			
	Oh Pattie/Please Take My Ring	1959	A 103
	Dreaming/Sandstorm	1959	A 104
SPORTTONES			
	In My Dreams/So Sincere	1959	Munich 101
SPOTLIGHTERS			
	It's Cold/Bam, Jingle, Jingle	1955	Imperial 5342
	Please Be My Girlfriend/Whisper	1958	Aladdin 3436
	This Is My Story/Preachin'	1958	Aladdin 3441
SPOTLITES			
	Travelin'/All Kinds Of Dancin' Going On	1959	Catalina 1001
SPRIGGS, WALTER (& GROUP)			
	I'm Not Your Fool Anymore/Weekend Man	1955	Blue Lake 109
	Everytime/One More Chance	1959	Kaiser 401
SPRINGERS			
	I Know My Baby Loves Me So/I Know Why	1965	Way Out 2699
SPROUTS			
	Goodbye She's Gone/Teen Billy Baby	1957	RCA 7080/Spangle 2002 (57)
	Skinny Minnie	1957	RCA 7172
	Why Did You Go/Twisting On Bandstand	1960	Mercury 71727
SPUTNIKS			
	My Love Is Gone/Hey, Maryann	1957	Pam Mar 602/Class 217
	Johnny's Little Lamb/Wait A Little Longer	1958	Class 222
SPY-DELS			
	We'll Be Together/Boll Weevil Is Back	1962	Crackerjack 4001
SPYDELLS (AKA SPYDELS)			
	We're In Love/Big McGoon	1960	Addit 1220
	In The Night/Hokey Pokey	1963	Beltone 2032
SPYDELS (AKA SPYDELLS)			
	No More Teasing/Wanted Dead Or Alive	1961	MZ 103/MZ 009
	Change Your Mind/Peace Of Mind	1962	Assault 1860
SPYDELS (JOHNNY DOW & THE) (AKA SPYDELLS)			
	You Were An Angel To Me/Talk To Me	1962	Assault 1866
SQUEAKS (BOBBY KNOTTS & THE)			
	Too Young/Oh Yeah	1961	Gee Clef 077
SQUIRES (1)			
	Let's Give Love A Try/Whop	1953	Combo 35
	Oh, Darling/My Little Girl	1953	Combo 42
SQUIRES (2)			
	Sayonara/Mia Bella Donna	1954	Flair 1030
SQUIRES (3) (AKA BLUE JAYS (4)) (GM DON HARRIS/GM DEWEY TERRY)			
	Lucy Lou/A Dream Come True	1954	Kicks 1
	Sindy/Do-Be-Do-Be-Wop-Wop	1955	Mambo 105/Vita 105 (60)
	Me And My Deal/Sweet Girl	1955	Vita 113
	Heavenly Angel/Sweet Girl	1956	Vita 116
	Guiding Angel/You Ought To Be Ashamed (with Effie Smith)	1956	Vita 117
	Venus/Breath Of Air	1956	Vita 128
	Dreamy Eyes/Dangling With My Heart	1957	Aladdin 3360
	Venus/S'Cadillac	1976	Robin Hood 130
SQUIRES (4)			
	Movin' Out/Our Theme	1961	Chan 102/MGM 13044 (61)
SQUIRES (5) (BILLY JONES & THE) (AKA BILLY FORTUNE & GROUP)			
	Every Word Of The Song/Listen To Your Heart (no group)	1958	Deck 478
SQUIRES (6)			
	So Many Tears Ago/Don't Accuse Me	1962	Gee 1082
	Why Should I Suffer/Walkin'	1963	Herald 580
SQUIRES (7)			
	It's Time/Girls	1964	Boss 2120
	Shimmy Stomp/Love Me, Leave Me	N/A	Robway 1

Artist / Song	Year	Label
SQUIRES (8)		
Joyce/Can't Believe That You've Grown Up	1964	Congress 223
SQUIRES (9) (SHIRLEY & THE)		
Drip Drop/I'm In Need	1963	Constellation 107
STACY, CLARENCE (& GROUP)		
Jack The Ripper/If You Love Me	1961	Carol 4114
STAFFORDS		
Come Back To Me/Cry Baby Cry	1956	Decca 29828
STAFFS (CURTIS WILSON & THE)		
My Heart Is Made Of The Blues	1960	Cherry 1014
STAGEHANDS		
Hello Dolly/You Started It	1964	T.A. 101
STAGG, TOMMY (& GROUP)		
Memories Of Love/Four In Love	1961	Bambi 802
STAGS		
Sailor Boy/Cool Capri	1958	M&S 502
STANDARDS		
Tears Bring Heartaches/No No No	1963	Debro 3178/Roulette 4487 (63)
Hello Love/My Heart Belongs To Only You	1963	Magna 1314/Chess 1869 (63)
It Isn't Fair/Everybody Knows	1963	Magna 1315/Glenden 1315 (64)
When You Wish Upon a Star/ When You Wish Upon a Star (instrumental)	1969	Amos 134
STANDARDS (LARRY & THE)		
My Lucky Night/Where Is She	1962	Laurie 3119
STAR DRIFTS		
She's Gone/An Eye For An Eye	1962	Goldisc G3
STAR DUSTERS (ANNA MARIA WITH BLINKY ALLEN'S)		
I'm A Fool To Care/An Angel Cried	1954	Flair 1047
STAR FIRES (AKA STARFIRES (3))		
Each Night At Night/What Good Is Money	1962	Haral 7777/7778
You Done Me Wrong/Like Socks And Shoes	1966	Laurie 3332
STAR LITES (JUNIOR & THE)		
Queen Of My Heart/Tres Suspiros	N/A	Mex Melody 121
STAR MARKS (SAMMY VAUGHN & THE)		
Always Be Mine/Midnight Shuffle	N/A	Stardom 0012
STAR STEPPERS		
The First Signs Of Love/You're Gone	1960	Amy 801
STAR, BOBBY (& GROUP) (FB TONY ALLEN)		
Please Give Me A Chance/ Sweet Man	1959	Radio 120
STAR-TELS		
What More Can I Ask For/ Exterminator Man	N/A	Lamarr 1000
STARBELLS (TERRY STAR & THE)		
My Mama Said It's Alright/Peppi	1963	New-Art 1008
STARDUST		
What Did I Do/Serenade Of The Bells	1982	Clifton 71
STARDUSTERS		
Love Story/Battle Of Bull Run	1958	Edison International 404
STARDUSTERS (BOBBY CHANDLER & HIS)		
I'm Serious/If You Loved Me	1956	O.J. 1000
Me And My Imagination/ Shadows Of Love	1957	O.J. 1005
STARFIRES (1)		
I Have Someone/Three Roses	1958	Decca 30730
Love Is Here To Stay/Tomorrow	1959	Decca 30916
STARFIRES (2) (WAYNE HAMMOND & THE)		
Can't See Why/Carolyn	1959	Gala 105
STARFIRES (3) (AKA STAR FIRES)		
Do-Ko-Icki-No/Yearning For You	1958	Bernice 201
Fender Bender/Camel Walk	1959	Apt 25030
You're The One/So Much	1961	Bargain 5001
Love Will Break Your Heart/ The Dances	1961	Bargain 5003/Atomic 1912 (61)
These Foolish Things/Let's Do The Pony	1961	D&H 200
Chartreuse Caboose/Billy's Blues	1961	Pama 117
Fools Fall In Love/Under The Stars	1962	Duel 518
Hand Full Of Blood/Re-Entry	1963	Sonic 7163
Work Out Fine/Fink	1965	Triumph 61
STARFIRES (3) (FB TOM KING) (AKA STAR FIRES)		
Ring Of Love/Cheating Game	1960	Pama 115
STARFIRES (4) (RAL DONNER & THE)		
Girl Of My Best Friend/It's Been A Long Long Time	1961	Gone 5102
STARFIRES (5)		
Go Chattanooga	1962	Chip 1010
STARGLOWS (FB NATE NELSON)		
Let's Be Lovers/Walk Softly Away	1963	Atco 6272
STARLARKS		
Fountain Of Love/Send Me A Picture Baby	1957	Elm 001/Ember 1013 (57)
Darling, Please Don't Love Me/The Rat	1964	Astra 100
STARLARKS (CHET BARNES & THE)		
Every Time It Rains/Is You Is	1961	Embassy 201
STARLARKS (WES FORBES & THE)		
Heavenly Father/My Dear	1957	Ancho 102/Relic 508 (64)
STARLETS (1) (AKA ANGELS (7))		
P.S. I Love You/Where Is My Love Tonight	1960	Astro 202/203
Romeo And Juliet/Listen For A Lonely Tambourine	1960	Astro 204
STARLETS (1) (JENNY LEE & THE)		
What I Gotta Do/Show Me A Man	1962	Congress 107
STARLETS (2) (FEMALE)		
I'm So Young/He Got It	1960	Lute 5909
Ringo/All Dressed Up	1964	Siana 717
STARLETS (3) (FEMALE)		
Better Tell Him No/You Are The One	1961	Pam 1003
My Last Cry/Money Hungry	1961	Pam 1004
STARLETS (4) (DANETTA & THE) (FEMALE)		
We're Going Steady (You Belong To Me)/Impressions	1962	Okeh 7155
STARLETS (5) (FEMALE)		
Multiply By Three/You Won't Even Know Her Name	1965	Tower 115
You Don't Love Me/I've Had It	1965	Tower 144
STARLETS (6) (ELLA THOMAS & THE) (FEMALE)		
I'm A Stranger/If You Leave Me	1962	Gedinson's 101
STARLETS (7) (HAL DAVIS & THE)		
The Way You Look Tonight/ Way To My Heart	1959	Kelley 105
STARLETTES (FEMALE)		
Jungle Love/Please Ring My Phone	1958	Checker 895
STARLIGHT		
Moonlight And Music/Lonely Teardrops	1989	Clifton 85
STARLIGHTERS (1)		
Love Cry/Last Night	1956	Irma 101
Until You Return/Whomp, Whomp!	1956	Sun Coast 1001
Slipping Out/Rocking Too Much	1957	Lamp 2014
STARLIGHTERS (2)		
It's Twelve O'Clock/The Birdland	1958	End 1031
I Cried/You're The One To Blame	1959	End 1049
A Story Of Love/Let's Take A Stroll (Down Lover's Lane)	1960	End 1072
Betty Jane/Is It Really Love?	1960	Minit 605
Hot Licks/Creepin'	1960	Wheel 1004
STARLIGHTERS (3)		
Zoom/Big Feet	1960	Hi-Q 5016
STARLIGHTERS (4) (JOEY DEE & THE)		
Peppermint Twist, Pt. 1/ Peppermint Twist, Pt. 2	1962	Roulette 4401
STARLIGHTS (1) (JIMMY WITHERSPOON & THE)		
Ain't Nobodys Business/ Who Baby Who	1957	RCA 6977
STARLIGHTS (2) (JOEY & THE)		
The Face Of An Angel/Shimmy Baby	1960	Scepter 1210
STARLIGHTS (3) (BILL PERRY & THE)		
Searching For Love/Count Off Blues	N/A	Premium 101
STARLINGS (AKA SKYLARKS (1))		
The Glory Of Love/You And I	1951	Decca 48241
My Plea For Love/Music, Maestro, Please	1954	Josie 760

Artist Song	Year	Label
I'm Just A Crying Fool/		
Hokey-Smokey Mama	1955	Dawn 212
A-Loo, A-Loo/I Gotta Go Now	1955	Dawn 213
All I Want/That's Me	1959	World Pacific 809
STARLITERS		
Arline/Sweet Sue	1955	Combo 73
STARLITERS (JOEY DEE & THE)		
The Face Of An Angel/		
Shimmy Baby	1960	Scepter 1210
STARLITES (1)		
Missing You/Give Me A Kiss	1957	Peak 5000
My Darling/Sentimental Journey	1960	Queen 5000
Bop Diddlie In The Jungle	N/A	Claremont 959
STARLITES (1) (EDDIE & THE)		
To Make A Long Story Short/		
Pretty Little Girl	1959	Scepter 1202
Come On Home/I Need Some		
Money	1963	Aljon 1260/1261
Three Steps To Go/Nobody		
But You And Me	1972	Bim Bam Boom 102
I Can Dream/You Told Me So	1973	Vintage 1004
STARLITES (1) (KENNY ESQUIRE & THE) (REF DREAMS (1))		
(GM GEORGE TINDLEY)		
They Call Me A Dreamer/		
Pretty Brown Eyes	1957	Ember 1011
Tears Are Just For Fools/		
Boom Chica Boom	1957	Ember 1021
STARLITES (2)		
Valarie/Way Up In The Sky	1960	Fury 1034
Ain't Cha Ever Coming Home/		
Silver Lining	1960	Fury 1045
No More Doggin'/Ain't Cha		
Ever Coming Home	1961	Fury 1045
Vararie (misspelled)/Way Up		
In The Sky	1963	Everlast 5027
Seven Day Fool/Don't Be Afraid	1965	Sphere Sound 705
STARLITES (2) (JACKIE & THE)		
They Laughed At Me/You Put		
One Over On Me	1957	Fire & Fury 1000
I Found Out Too Late/I'm		
Coming Home	1961	Fury 1057
For All We Know/I Heard You	1962	Mascot 128
You Keep Telling Me/Sha		
Pobo Baby	1962	Mascot 130
I'll Burn Your Letters/Walking		
From School	1963	Mascot 131
I Still Remember/I Cried My		
Heart Out	1964	Hull 760
Let Him Go	1991	Relic LP 5090
No More Heart	1991	Relic LP 5090
STARLITES (3)		
Merry Christmas Tonight/Xmas		
In My Heart	1962	Goldband 1151
STARLITES (4)		
Joanie/My Greatest Thrill	1965	Relic 1001
STARNOTES		
This Is It/Say The Word	1962	Caper 101
STARR BROTHERS		
Don Juan/Down On My Knees	1963	Cortland 104
Mr. Auctioneer/Beaufiful Woman	1963	Cortland 106
STARR, ANDY (& GROUP)		
I Know It's True/I Love You Baby	N/A	Arcade 115
STARR, BOBBY (AKA TONY ALLEN) (& GROUP)		
Please Give Me A Chance/		
Sweet Man	1959	Radio 120
STARR, SUZY (& GROUP)		
Lover's Quarrel/One Day	1961	Morgil 711
STARS		
Let's Cuddle Again/When		
You Love	1959	Vega 001
No Letter From You/Night Train	1959	Vega 002
STARTIME KIDS		
The Railroad Song/I Don't Want		
To Walk Without You Baby	1959	Okeh 7111
STARTONES (1) (AKA CARNATIONS (6))		
I Love You So Dearly/Forever		
My Love	1956	Rainbow 341
STARTONES (2)		
Blind Date/No Time For Tears	N/A	Web 1116
STATENS		
Summertime Is Time For Love/		
That Certain Kind	1961	Mark-X 8011

Artist Song	Year	Label
Where Was I/Didn't Mean To		
Fall In Love	1978	Crystal Ball 127
Valentine/Do What You Want	1978	Crystal Ball 115
STATICS (1)		
The Day You Left Me/The Girl		
In My Dreams	1958	Event 4279
STATICS (2) (LYNN & THE)		
Little Girls Dream/Sunday		
Kind Of Love	N/A	Mantis 101
STATLERS		
Vicky/Gone	1962	Little Star 108
STATUES (FB GARY MILES)		
Blue Velvet/Keep The Hall		
Light Burning	1960	Liberty 55245
White Christmas/Jeanie With		
The Light Brown Hair	1960	Liberty 55292
Love At First Sight/The		
Commandments Of Love	1961	Liberty 55363
STATUES (GARY MILES & THE)		
Look For A Star/Afraid Of Love	1960	Liberty 55261
Wishing Well/Dream Girl	1960	Liberty 55279
STEADIES		
Rock To The Philadelphia/		
One Kiss And That's All	1958	Josie 837
Two Lovers In Love/Music		
Goes Round And Round	1959	Tad 0711
STEEL, L.C. (& GROUP)		
Come Back Betty	N/A	K14
STEELERS		
The Flame Remains	N/A	Crash 428
STEINWAYS		
You've Been Leading Me On/		
My Heart Is Not	1966	Oliver 2002
Don't Wonder Why/Call Me	1966	Oliver 2007
STENOTONES (BILLY JAMES & THE)		
Phyllis/My Prayer	1961	Rust 5038
STEPHENS, JIMMY (AKA JIMMY STEVENS) (BB THE SAFARIS)		
Congratulations/Love Dreams	1961	Eldo 112
STEREOPHONICS		
Love Is So Wonderful/No More		
Heartaches	1958	Apt 25003
STEREOS (1) (AKA TAMS (1)/AKA HIPPIES)		
Memory Lane/Teenage Kids	1959	Mink 022/Parkway 863
STEREOS (2)		
A Love For Only You/		
Sweetpea's In Love	1959	Gibraltar 105
I Really Love You/Please		
Come Back To Me	1961	Cub 9095
Sweet Water/The Big Knock	1961	Cub 9103
Echo In My Heart/Tic Tac Toe	1962	Columbia 42626
Unless You Mean It/Do You		
Love Me	1962	Cub 9106
Me Heart/You Left Me Forsaken	1962	Robins Nest 101
Don't Cry Darling/Run Sinner		
Run	1962	Robins Nest 1588
Mumbling Word/Good News	1963	World Artists 1012
Don't Let It Happen To You/		
The Best Thing To Be Is A		
Person	1964	Val 2
Stereo Freeze, Pt. 1/Stereo		
Freeze, Pt. 2	1967	Cadet 5577
I Can't Stop These Tears/		
I Feel Soul A'Coming	1968	Cadet 5626
Walking Along	N/A	unreleased
STEREOS (3) (LITTLE BENNY & THE)		
My Sweetheart/Drinking Wine,		
Spodee-Odee	1959	Spot 106
STEREOS (4) (DAVE & THE)		
This Must Be Love/Roamin'		
Romeo	1961	Pennant 1001
STERIOS		
Life/Sweetpea's In Love	1966	Ideal 110
STEVEDORES (STEVE & THE)		
Honey Bee	1958	Rebel 1314
STEVENS, CAROL ANN (& GROUP)		
A Heart Is A Toy/Lonely Hearted	1961	Carol 4111
STEVENS, JIMMY (AKA JIMMY STEPHENS) (BB THE SAFARIS)		
That's Where The Difference		
Lies/A Funny Thing Happened	1963	Valiant 6049
STEVENS, JULIE (WITH THE PREMIERS (1))		
I Don't Want To Know/Take		
My Heart	1957	Dig 129

Artist / Song	Year	Label
STEVENS, KENNY (& GROUP)		
Echo In My Heart/It Was Love		
At First Sight	1964	Old Town 1158
STEVENS, RANDY (& GROUP)		
All My Love/Sweet Shop	1959	Loma 301
STEWART, DANNY (AKA SLY STONE)		
Long Time Alone/I'm Just A Fool	1961	G&P 901
STEWART, SYLVESTER (AKA SLY STONE) (& GROUP)		
Long Time Away/Help Me With		
My Heart	1962	G&P 901
STIMULATORS		
Warm Summer Nights/(flip is		
instrumental)	N/A	Sound-O-Riffic 2
STINGRAYS		
Let Them Talk/When You Wish		
Upon A Star	1964	Crazytown 101/102
STITES, GARY (& GROUP)		
Don't Wanna Say Goodbye/		
Lawdy Miss Clawdy	1960	Carlton 525
STOMPERS		
Forgive Me/Stompin' Round		
The Christmas Tree	1961	Gone 5120
Foolish One/Quarter To Four		
Stomp	1962	Landa 684
STONE, LAWRENCE (& GROUP)		
Everytime/Until The Real Thing		
Comes Along	1957	Dig 130
STOREY SISTERS (AKA TWINKLES) (FEMALE)		
Cha Cha Boom/Which Way Did		
My Heart Go	1958	Baton 255
Bad Motorcycle/Sweet Daddy	1958	Cameo 126
Lost Love/Lover How I Miss You	1959	Mercury 71457
STORIES (SMITTY & THE)		
Before You Go/Under Your		
Window	1961	Elf 102
STORKS (LENNY & THE)		
My One Sincere	1982	Jason Scott 25
STORM, BILLY (& GROUP)		
Angel Of Mine/The Way To My		
Heart	1958	Barbary Coast 1001
We Knew	N/A	Famous LP 501
STORM, BILLY (BB THE STORMS)		
Sure As You're Born/In The		
Chapel In The Moonlight	1960	Atlantic 2076
Dear One/When You Dance	1961	Atlantic 2098
Honey Love/A Kiss From Your		
Lips	1961	Atlantic 2112
STORMS (1) (WALLY LEE & THE)		
Eeny Meeny/I Never Felt This		
Way	1959	Sundown 123
STORMS (2) (JODY REYNOLDS & THE)		
Beulah Lee	1959	Demon 1515
STORMY WEATHER		
Then You Can Tell Me		
Goodbye/Crazy Love	1976	Catamount 133
Crazy Love/Witchy Woman	1988	Starlight 63
STORYTELLERS (1) (AKA TELLERS FEATURING TIMMY LYMON)		
Hey Baby/You Played Me A Fool	1959	Stack 500
STORYTELLERS (2) (FB STEVE BARRI)		
I Don't Want An Angel/Down		
In The Valley	1963	Capitol 5042
Time Will Tell/When Two People	1963	Dimension 1014/Ramarca 501 (63)
STORYTELLERS (3)		
Please Remember My Love/		
Gee But I Like Your Smile	1990	Classic Artists 118
Heaven's For Real/This Is		
Goodbye	1991	Classic Artists 128
Heart For Heart/The L.A. Shuffle	1991	Classic Artists 133
STRANDS		
How Will I Know/Must You Go		
So Soon	1960	Firefly 331
Old Man River/Never	1962	Triode 101
STRANGERS (1)		
My Friends/I've Got Eyes	1954	King 4697
Blue Flowers/Beg And Steal	1954	King 4709
Hoping You'll Understand/		
Just Don't Care	1954	King 4728
Drop Down To My Place/		
Get It One More Time	1954	King 4745
Dreams Come True/How Long		
Must I Wait?	1955	King 4766
Without A Friend/Think Again	1955	King 4821
It's Too Bad (We Had To Part)	N/A	King (unreleased)
STRANGERS (2)		
We're In Love/J-U-D-Y	1959	Christy 107/108
STRANGERS (3)		
I'm Feeling Sad/You Ain't Too		
Cool	1960	Maske 101
Pa And Billie/Darlin'	1962	Checker 1010
STRANGERS (4)		
Night Winds/These Are The		
Things I Love	1964	Warner Bros. 5438
STRATEGICS		
I Am Looking Too	N/A	Lyndell 773
STRATFORDS (1)		
Never Leave Me	1964	O'Dell 100
Throw Stones	1964	O'Dell 114
STRATFORDS (2)		
Promise Her Anything/Lover's		
Lullabye	1961	Universal Artists 1215
STRAYS (RAY & THE)		
How Will I Know My Love/No,		
No More	1962	Larric 101
STREET CORNER MEMORIES		
Congratulations/Never Let		
You Go	1981	Clifton 64
STREET CORNER SOCIETY		
Barbara Ann/Ronnie I Pizza		
Pie/Rip Van Ronnie	1979	Clifton 35
Hey Senorita/You Belong To Me	1979	UGHA 8
STREET CORNER SYMPHONY		
Earth Angel/I'm Not Ready	1975	Bang 719
Nice Guys/That Love Was Magic	1975	Bang 722
STREET DREAMS		
Hey Boy/Everybody's Got A Home	1986	Starlight 38
You Just Say The Word/		
Bluebird Of Happiness	1986	Starlight 44
STREET SINGERS		
I Was Dreaming/Mambo Love	1955	Dawn 211
Tonight Was Like A Dream/		
Caldonia's Mambo	1956	Tuxedo 899
STREET VOCAL BAND		
Chain Of Broken Hearts/Gee		
Whiz	1980	Clifton 57
STREET-TONES (PATTY & THE)		
I'm So In Love/Wedding Bells	1979	Clifton 37
Rendezvous With You/Oh My		
Angel	1979	U.G.H.A. 09
Let It Please Be You/No, No, No	1980	Clifton 49
Mommy And Daddy/Glory Of		
Love	1981	Clifton 63
Rudolph The Red Nosed		
Reindeer/I'll Stay Home		
(by the Computones)	1981	Clifton 66
Rendezvous With You/Oh My		
Angel	N/A	UGHA 9
STREETCORNER SERENADE		
Goodbye To Love/Mr. Blue	1988	Starlight 65
Last Night I Dreamed/There's		
A Moon Out Tonight	1989	Starlight 68
I Thank The Moon/Suddenly		
There's A Valley	1989	Starlight 70
STREETCORNER SOCIETY		
Hey Senorita/You Belong To Me	1979	U.G.H.A. 08
STRICKLAND, JAN (& GROUP)		
Come To Me My Little Darling/		
Let's	1955	X 0080
STRIDERS		
Rollin'/Come Back To Me		
Tomorrow	1954	Derby 857
I Wonder/Hesitating Fool	1955	Apollo 480
STRIDERS (BETTY McLAURIN & THE)		
My Heart Belongs To Only You/		
I Won't Tell A Soul I Love You	1952	Derby 804
STRIDERS (SAVANNAH CHURCHILL & THE)		
In Spite Of Everything You Do/		
Don't Grieve, Don't Sorrow,		
Don't Cry	1951	RCA 4448
When You Come Back To Me/		
Once There Lived A Fool	1951	Regal 3309/Derby 468
STRIKES		
Baby I'm Sorry/If You Can't		
Rock Me	1956	Lin 5006/Imperial 5433 (57)

Artist	Song	Year	Label	Artist	Song	Year	Label
	I Don't Want To Cry Over You/ Rockin'	1957	Imperial 5446	**STYLES (4)**	Baby You're Alive/I Know You Know That I Know	N/A	Modern 1048
STRINGBEANS	Starlight/Stop Your Crying	1964	Gina 7001	**STYLETTES**	On Fire/Packing Up My Memories	1964	Cameo 337
STRINGS	Love me/Keep It Up	N/A	Mellow Town 1006		My Boy/You'll Go First	1965	Cameo 353
STROGIN, HENRY (& GROUP)	I Wanna Love/Old Folks Boogie While The Young Ones Twist	1962	Ball 1012	**STYLISTS**	One Room/I Wonder	1974	Bim Bam Boom 120
STROLLERS (1)	Bitter Dreams	1957	States (unreleased)	**STYLISTS (1)**	Go, Go Daddy Go/Just Don't Sit There	1955	Crown 145
	In Your Dreams/Go Where Baby Lives	1957	States 163		Mourning/Move It Over, Baby	1959	Jay Wing 5807
STROLLERS (2)	You're The Only One For Me/ Baby Eyes	1957	Zebra 22		I've Been Waiting For You/ Scarey Harry	1960	Sage 317
STROLLERS (3)	Crowded Classroom/We're Strolling	1958	Warner 1018	**STYLISTS (2)**	One Room/I Wonder	1960	Rose 16/17
	Summer Love/King Of All Fools	1960	20th Fox 226	**SUBURBANS (1)**	I Remember/T. V. Baby	1956	Baton 227
	Dee Dee Brown/Favors	1960	Cub 9060		Leave My Gal Alone/My First And Last Romance	1957	Baton 240
	That Look In Your Eye/Nobody But You	1960	Dart 1017	**SUBURBANS (1) (ANN COLE & THE)**	In The Chapel/Each Day	1956	Baton 232
	Ever Since You Kissed Me/ Tangier	1963	Jubilee 5449		Got My Mo-Jo Working (But It Won't Work On You)/ I've Got A Little Boy (no group)	1957	Baton 237
STROLLERS (4)	Come On Over/There's No One But You	1961	Carlton 546	**SUBURBANS (1) (JIMMY RICKS & THE)**	I'm A Fool To Want You/Bad Man Of Missouri	1957	Baton 236
STUART, GLEN (& CHORUS)	Drip Drop/Ruby Baby	1960	Abel 235	**SUBURBANS (2)**	Little Bird/King Of Broken Hearts	1960	Kip 221
STUDEBAKER "7"	Come Go With Me/One Fine Day	N/A	Coulee 142		Love Me/Mississippi Mud	1961	Flamingo 539
STUDENTS (1) (BEVERLY WRIGHT & THE)	Shake Till I'm Shook/Don't Let The Sun Catch You Cryin' (no group)	1956	Groove 0153		Love Me/Lovin' Hands	1961	Gee 1076
STUDENTS (2)	Jenny Lee/Come Back My Love (by the Heartbreakers (1))	1956	Fordham 109		Walk Beside Me/Mary Had A Little Lamb	1963	Shelley 184
	I'm So Young/Every Day Of The Week	1958	Note 10012/Argo 5386 (61)/Checker 902 (61)	**SUBURBANS (3)**	Alphabet Of Love/Sweet Diane Cha Cha	1959	Port 70011
	My Vow To You/That's How I Feel	1958	Note 10019/Checker 1004 (62)	**SUBWAY SERENADE**	That's My Girl/Out Of Sight Out Of Mind	1980	Clifton 53
STUDENTS (3)	Mary/Bye Bye Truly	1958	Red Top		White Christmas/What Are You Doing New Year's Eve	1981	Avenue D 4
	My Heart Is An Open Door/ Mommy And Daddy	1958	Red Top 100		Hello/How Sentimental Can I Be/Secret Love/Count Every Star	N/A	Clifton EP 504
	Philadelphia Girl/Some Saturday	1992	Clifton 103	**SUDDENS (AKA SAFARIS)**	Childish Ways/Garden Of Love	1961	Sudden 103
STUDENTS (4) (BILL STARR & THE)	One Heart/Love For A Year	1960	Applause 1235	**SUEDES (1)**	I Love You So/Don't Blooper	1954	Money 204
STYLE KINGS	Kissing Behind The Moon/ Under The Tropical Sky	1959	Sotoplay 0011	**SUEDES (2)**	Don't Be Shy/Please Be Satisfied	1959	Dart 117
STYLERS	Gentle As A Teardrop/There Were Others	1954	Kicks 2	**SUEDES (3) (ROSIE STEVENS & THE)**	Everybody's Trying To Be My Baby/Wrong Yo Yo	1960	Spinning 6011
	Lost John/Huffin' And Puffin'	1956	Jubilee 5246	**SUGAR BUNS**	Pajama Party/Nails And Snails	1959	Warner Bros. 5046
	Confession Of A Sinner/Gonna Tell 'Em	1956	Jubilee 5253	**SUGAR LUMPS (SUGAR BOY & THE)**	So Long, Goodbye/Mama Won't You Turn Me Loose	1963	Peacock 1925
	You Tell Me/Blues In The Night	1957	Golden Crest 1181/1182	**SUGAR TONES (1) (AKA ENCHANTERS (1))**	You Fool Again/The Sun Shines Once Again	1951	Okeh 6814
	Breaker Of Hearts/Miracle In Milan	1957	Jubilee 5279		Annabelle/Today Is Your Birthday	1951	Onyx 2007
	Kiss And Run Lover/Girlie Girlie Girlie	1958	Golden Crest 1291		They Said It Couldn't Happen	1951	Onyx 2008
	Pushing Up Daisies/Going Steady Anniversary	1963	Gordy 7018		Wishin'/Today Is Your Birthday	1952	Okeh 6877
STYLERS (DICK THOMAS & THE)	Anytime Is Lovin' Time/When Uncle Joe Plays The Rag On His Old Banjo (no group)	1955	Jubilee 5208		I Just Want To Dream/I Know You Gotta Go	1953	Okeh 6992
STYLES (1)	Scarlet Angel/Gotta Go, Go, Go	1961	Serene 1501		Blow The Whistle/Scandal	1954	Benida 5021
	I Love You For Sentimental Reasons/School Bells To Chapel Bells	1964	Josie 920		How Can I Pretend/Hippity Hop Baby/How Can You Forget So Soon	1960	Cannon 391
STYLES (2) (CHUCK MILE & THE)	Be Mine Or Be A Fool/Lovin' Daddy	1962	Dore 630	**SUGAR TONES (2) (CANDY & THE)**	Hurtin' All Over/I-Ay-Ou-Lay-Oo-Ya	1958	Jackpot 48008
STYLES (3) (DONNIE & THE)	Chapel Of Love/Marie	1964	Times Square 106	**SUGARMINTS**	You'll Have Everything/I-I-I Could Love You	1957	Brunswick 55042
				SUGARTONES (JIMMY LANE & THE)	Constantly/Let Your Conscience Be Your Guide	1958	Time 6602

Artist Song	Year	Label
SULTANS (1)		
Lemon Squeezing Daddy/You		
Captured My Heart	1951	Jubilee 5054
Don't Be Angry/Blues At Dawn	1952	Jubilee 5077
Good Thing, Baby/How Deep		
Is The Ocean?	1954	Duke 125
I Cried My Heart Out/Baby,		
Don't Put Me Down	54	Duke 133
What Makes Me Feel This		
Way?/Boppin' With The		
Mambo	1954	Duke 135
If I Could Tell/My Love Is High	1957	Duke 178
SULTANS (2) (BOB OAKES & THE)		
Church Bells My Ring/You		
Gotta Rock And Roll	1956	Regent 7502
SULTANS (3)		
It'll Be Easy/You Got Me Goin'	1961	Tilt 782
Mary, Mary/How Far Does A		
Friendship Go	1962	Jam 107
Christina/Someone You		
Can Trust	1963	Guyden 2079
SULTANS (4)		
A Cottage For Sale/Say Hey Girl	1961	Knowles 105
SULTANS (5) (WARDELL & THE)		
I Need Your Love/I'm Broke	1962	Imperial 5886
SULTANS (6)		
Gloria/I Wanna Know	1965	Ascot 2228
SULTANS FIVE		
Life Is Like A River/Daisy	1964	Raynard 1053
Daisy	1966	Raynard 843
SUMMITS (1)		
Go Back Where You Came		
From/Times Square Stomp		
(instrumental)	1961	Times Square 422
Go Back Where You Came		
From/Times Square Stomp/		
Strollin' At Clifton Music		
(by the House Rockers)	1973	Clifton 1
SUMMITS (2) (FEMALE)		
He's An Angel/Hanky Panky	1963	Harmon 1017/Rust 5072 (63)
SUN-RAYS		
The Lonely Hours/Love Is A		
Stranger	1958	Sun 293
SUN-RAYS (CLIFF & THE)		
Lucky Me/No Treason In My		
Heart	1960	Zil 9002
SUNBEAMS (1)		
Tell Me Why/Come Back, Baby	1955	Herald 451
Please Say You'll Be Mine/		
You've Got To Rock And Roll	1957	Acme 109
SUNBEAMS (2)		
Blue Mountain Waltz/I'm		
Gonna Come Home To Mama	1955	Dot 1271
How About It/Wrap It Up And		
Save	1956	Dot 1280
SUNBEAMS (3) (DONNA RAE & THE)		
Little Fool/Whisper Your Love	1959	Satellite 103
SUNDIALS		
Chapel Of Love/Whether To		
Resist	1962	Guyden 2065
SUNDOWNERS (1)		
Someone To Care/Such A Lovin'	1960	Fargo 1051
Round And Round/Leave Me		
Never	1965	Coed 603
SUNDOWNERS (2) (BIG JIM & THE)		
Poor Little Sad Eyed Sue/Never		
Let Me Go	1962	Chip 1008
SUNGLOWS (1) (SUNNY & THE) (FB SONNY OZUNA)		
Golly Gee/Touring	1959	Sunglow 104/Okeh 7143 (62)
Uptown/Just A Moment	1961	Lynn 511
Talk To Me/Every Week Every		
Month Every Year	1963	Tear Drop 3014/Sunglow 110
Rags To Riches/Not Even		
Judgment Day (by Sunny		
& the Sunliners)	1963	Tear Drop 3022/Sunglow 111
Out Of Sight, Out Of Mind/		
No One Else Will Do (by		
Sunny & the Sunliners)	1964	Tear Drop 3027
It's Too Late/You Gave Me A		
True Love	1964	Tear Drop 3034
You Send Me/His Greatest		
Creation	1964	Tear Drop 3040
Peanuts (La Cacahuta)/Happy		
Hippo (instrumentals)	1965	Sunglow 107/Disco Grande 1021
SUNGLOWS (2)		
Please Say You Love Me/		
If You Don't Want My Love	N/A	Carib 1025
SUNLINERS		
Hully Gully Twist/Sweet Little		
Girl	1962	Hercules 182
So In Love/Little Girl Charm	1962	Hercules 184
SUNLINERS (SUNNY & THE)		
No One Else Will Do/Cheatin'		
Traces	1964	Tear Drop 3123
SUNNY BOYS		
For The Rest Of My Life/		
My Friend Sam	1959	Mr. Maestro 805
Chapel Bells/My Friend Sam	1959	Mr. Maestro 806
For The Rest Of My Life/		
Chapel Bells	1959	Take 3 2001
SUNNY LADS		
That's My Desire/You're In Love	1959	Jax 103
SUNS		
That's My Baby/Dance Girl		
(by the Camelots)	1964	Times Square 32/Relic 541 (65)
SUNSETS (1)		
How Will I Remember?/Sittin'		
And Cryin'	1959	Rae-Cox 102
SUNSETS (2)		
Lonely Surfer Boy/Playmate		
Of The Year	1963	Challenge 9198
My Little Beach Bunny/My		
Little Surfin' Woodie	1963	Challenge 9208
Lydia/Only You, Only Me	1963	Petal 1040
SUNSETS (3) (ADRIAN & THE)		
Cherry Pie/Breakthrough	1963	Sunset 602
SUNSHINE BOYS		
If You Still Want Me/My Love,		
My Love, My Love	1959	Scottie 1307
SUPER HEROES		
Gwendolyn/Fabulous 50's		
(by Little Robert & the K's)	N/A	Dice 100
SUPERBS		
The Fish/Rainbow Of Love	1961	Heritage 103
The Story Book Of Love/Better		
Get Your Own One Buddy	1964	Dore 704
Raindrops, Memories And		
Tears/Baby Baby All The Time	1964	Dore 715
Sad, Sad Day/My Heart Isn't In It	1964	Dore 722
Beans/My Love For You	1964	Melmar 121
Baby's Gone Away/Twine And		
Slide	1965	Dore 731
It Hurts So Much/Live It Up		
(instrumental)	1965	Dore 736
On A Day When It's Raining/		
Spoonful	1966	Dore 753
He Broke A Young Girl's Heart/		
A Million Miles To Paradise	1966	Dore 755
SUPERIOR ANGELS		
Crying In The Chapel	1964	Skylark 0023
SUPERIORS (1)		
Lost Love/Don't Say Goodbye	1957	Atco 6106/Main Line 104 (58)
Eternal Dream/Happy Days		
Are Here Again	1963	Real Fine 837
SUPERIORS (2)		
What Is Love/Flee The Scene	1961	Fal 301
I'm Sorry Baby (I Didn't Mean		
To Do You Wrong)/Dance		
Of Love	1961	Federal 12436
SUPERIORS (3)		
Tell Me To Go/What Would I Do	1965	Verve 10370
Can't Make It Without You/Let		
Me Make You Happy	1966	MGM 13503
Heavenly Angel/I'd Rather Die	1969	Sue 12
SUPERIORS (4) (TONY LAMAR & THE)		
Your Love/Do The Whip	1965	Go Go 1000
SUPERLATIVES		
Forget About Tomorrow/Do		
What You Want To	N/A	Dynamics 1011
Won't You Please/Don't Ever		
Leave Me	N/A	Dynamics 1012
Don't Walk Away/Lonely In A		
Crowd	N/A	Dynamics 1016/Westbound 144

Artist	Song	Year	Label
SUPERPHONICS			
	Teen-Age Partner/My Love		
	For You	1961	Lindy 102
SUPERPHONICS (DAVE KENNEDY & THE)			
	Me Neither/B-L-U-E	1961	Lindy 101
SUPREMES (1)			
	Could This Be You?/Margie	1956	Kitten 6969
	Tonight/She Don't Want Me No		
	More	1956	Old Town 1024 (first pressing)
	Tonight/My Babe	1956	Old Town 1024 (second pressing)
	Zip Boom	1985	Murray Hill LP 000083
SUPREMES (1) (RUTH MCFADDEN & THE) (AKA SOLITAIRES)			
	Darling, Listen To The Words Of This Song/Since My		
	Baby's Been Gone	1956	Old Town 1014
SUPREMES (2)			
	Just For You And I/Honey Honey	1957	Ace 530 (unreleased)
	Just For You And I/Don't Leave Me Here To Cry	1957	Ace 534
	Nobody Can Love You/Snap, Crackle & Pop	1958	Mark 129
	Little Sally Walker/Just Yell	1960	Mascot 126
	Glow/You And Me	N/A	Grog 500
SUPREMES (3) (BILLY THE KID & THE)			
	You Are Mine/Be My Love	1958	Bernice 202
SUPREMES (4) (FB DIANA ROSS) (AKA PRIMETTES)			
	I Want A Guy/Never Again	1961	Tamla 54038
	Buttered Popcorn/Who's Lovin' You?	1961	Tamla 54045
SUPREMES (5) (AKA RUBY NASH & THE ROMANTICS)			
	Another Chance To Love/Fidgety	1961	Apt 25055
SUPREMES FOUR			
	I Lost My Job/I Love You, Patricia	1961	Sara 1032
SURGEONS			
	Don't Tell Me/You Know (by the Electras)	1963	Cee-Jam 100
SURPRISE			
	Denise/Blue Moon	N/A	Kape 102
SWALLOWS (1)			
	Will You Be Mine/Dearest	1951	King 4458
	Wishing For You/Since You've Been Away	1951	King 4466
	Eternally/It Ain't The Meat	1951	King 4501
	Deed I Do	1952	King (unreleased)
	Tell Me Why/Roll, Roll, Pretty Baby	1952	King 4515
	Beside You/You Left Me	1952	King 4525
	I Only Have Eyes For You/You Walked In	1952	King 4533
	Please Baby Please/Where Do I Go From Here	1952	King 4579
	Laugh (Though You Want To Cry)/Our Love Is Dying	1953	King 4612
	Bicycle Tillie/Nobody's Loving Me	1953	King 4632
	Pleading Blues/Trust Me	1953	King 4656
	My Baby/Good Time Girls	1954	After Hours 104/Chariot 104 (54)
	It Feels So Good/I'll Be Waiting	1954	King 4676
	Come Back To Me	1956	Decca 29828
	Angel Baby/Oh Lonesome Me	1958	Federal 12319
	Rock-A-Bye Baby Rock/We Want To Rock	1958	Federal 12328
	Beside You/Laughing Boy	1958	Federal 12329
	Itchy Twitchy Feeling/Who Knows, Do You?	1958	Federal 12333
	Sit And Hold My Hand/When The Swallows Come Back To Capistrano	1986	
	Lover's Question/Oh Lonesome Me	1986	
	Love Bells/Love Bells (acapella)	1986	
	Will You Be Mine/Will You Be Mine	1987	
	Since You've Been Away/Have Mercy Baby	1987	
	Louise/Louise	1987	
	Try To Remember/Ride Eddie Ride	1991	
	Hey Senorita/My Grandmother's Christmas	1991	
	Mother/Let's Talk About Jesus	1991	
	In The Palm Of My Hand	N/A	Federal (unreleased)
SWALLOWS (2) (AKA GUIDES)			
	You Must Try/How Long Must A Fool Go On?	1959	Guyden 2023 (first pressing, second is by the Guides)
SWANKS			
	Little Angel/Keep Walking	1957	Jaguar 3027
SWANN, CLAUDIA (WITH BUDDY GRIFFIN & GROUP)			
	Please Come Back To Me/I Wanna Hug Ya, Kiss Ya (no group)	1954	Chess 1586
SWANS (1)			
	My True Love/(Ain't Like That) No More	1953	Rainbow 233
	For Dreams Come True/Happy	1955	Ballad 1000/1001
	How Sentimental Can I Be/I'm Dressed Up To Cry	1955	Ballad 1004/1005
	It's A Must/Night Train	1955	Ballad 1006
	Happy/Santa Claus Boogie Song	1955	Ballad 1007
	I'll Forever Love You/Mr. Cool Breeze	1955	Fortune 822
	Believe In Me/In The Morning	1956	Steamboat 101
	Why Must I Cry/Just A Little Bit More (by the Idols)	1961	Reveille 1002/Dot 16210 (61)
SWANS (1) (PAUL LEWIS & THE)			
	Little Senorita/Wedding Bells, Oh Wedding Bells	1955	Fortune 813
SWANS (2)			
	I Love You So/Will You Be Mine	1981	Parrot 801/Relic LP 5088 (90)
SWANS (3)			
	If I Could Stop Every Clock/He Wasn't On The Air	1959	Roulette 4213
SWANS (4) (FEMALE)			
	Daydreamin' Of You/The Promise	1963	Parkway 881
	He's Mine/You Better Be A Good Girl Now	1963	Swan 4151
	Please Hurry Home/The Boy With The Beatle Hair	1964	Cameo 302
SWEET & SASSY			
	I Really Love You So/Don't Leave Me	1959	Del Pat 207
SWEET HEARTS (AKA SWEETHEARTS) (FEMALE)			
	My Only You/My Baby	1961	D&H 500
SWEET MARQUEES			
	You Lied/I Love My Baby	1961	Apache 1516
SWEET NUTHINS			
	I Don't Love Him/Nashville, Tennessee	1964	Swan 4195
SWEET SICK TEENS			
	The Pretzel/Agnes, The Teenage Russian Spy	1961	RCA 7940
SWEET TEENS			
	Forever More/Don't Worry About A Thing	1956	Flip 311
	My Valentine/With This Ring	1957	Gee 1030
SWEET TEENS (FAITH TAYLOR & THE) (FEMALE)			
	Your Candy Kisses/Won't Someone Tell Me Why?	1959	Federal 12334
	I Need Him To Love Me/Please Be Mine	1960	Bea & Baby 104
	I Love You, Darling/Paper Route Baby	1960	Bea & Baby 105
SWEET TYMES (AKA TYMES)			
	I Think I Know Her/You Ought To Belong To Me	1967	Epic 10227
SWEETHEARTS (AKA SWEET HEARTS) (FEMALE)			
	Just Got The Feeling/Me Heart	1958	Terrific 151
	Ting-A-Ling-Ling/Sorry Daddy	1961	Ray Star 778
	(He's My) Superman/In Between Kisses	1963	Brunswick 55237
	He's A Yankee/What Did I Do	1963	Brunswick 55240
	Everybody I Know/What Will Mother Say	1963	Brunswick 55255
	No No/Have You Ever Fell In Love	1963	Brunswick 55265
	They Talk Too Much/Puppy Love	1963	H-III 116

Artist	Song	Year	Label
	Summer Days/What Is Love	1963	Hi-III 117
	Eddie My Love/Beauty Is Just Skin Deep	1965	Kent 428
	No More Tears/This Couldn't Be Me	1966	Kent 442
	Come On, Make Love To Me/Sweetheart, Sweetheart	1968	Como 451
SWEETHEARTS (GENE & WENDELL WITH THE)			
	From Me To You/The Roach	1961	Ray Star 777
SWEETHEARTS (VALENTINE & THE)			
	Lipstick And High-Heel Shoes/Romeo Rodriguez	1963	Big Top 3147
SWEETIES			
	After You/Paul's Love	1961	End 1110
SWENSONS			
	Remember Me To My Darling/Golly Boo	1956	X-Tra 100
SWING MASTERS (ANGEL & THE)			
	Listen Baby/What's This Fussin'	1959	DC 0420
SWING TEENS (WAYNE MCGINNIS & THE)			
	Rock, Roll And Rhythm/Lonesome Rhythm Blues	1956	Meteor 5035
SWINGIN' BEARS (BERNADETTE & THE)			
	Crazy Yogi/When You're Dancin' With Me	1961	Beach 1001
SWINGIN' KOOLS (ROYAL EARLS & THE)			
	Forever Dear	1959	Harlem 103
SWINGING EARLS			
	All I Do Is Dream Of You/Yum Yum	1959	Vega 1001
SWINGING HEARTS			
	Please Say It Isn't So/Something Made Me Stop	1960	Lucky Four 1011/Diamond 162 (64)
	How Can I Love You/Spanish Love	1961	620 1002/NRM 1002 (61)
	I've Got It/You Speak Of Love	1964	Magic Touch 2001
SWINGING PHILLIES			
	L-O-V-E/Frankenstein's Party	1958	DeLuxe 6171
SWINGING REEDS (DON REED & THE)			
	Why Don't You Believe Me/Western Union	1958	United 215
SWINGING ROCKS (RUBY & HER)			
	I Cried A Tear Over You	1985	Relic LP 8004
	It's Been A Long Time	1985	Relic LP 8004
SWINGTONES			
	Geraldine/You Know Baby	1958	Rhythm 5001/ABC 9902 (58)
SWISHER, DEBRA (& GROUP)			
	Thank You And Goodnight/You're So Good To Me	1966	Boom 60001
SWORDSMEN			
	Kathi, Please Don't Cry/Lonely Boy, Lonely Girl	1961	Semac 2114
SYCAMORES			
	I'll Be Waiting/Darling, Is It True?	1955	Groove 0121
SYDELLS			
	In The Night/Hokey Pokey	1963	Beltone 2032
SYLLABLES			
	It's You For Me/I've Been Jilted	1959	Imperial 5619
SYMBOLS (1) (MARTY & THE) (AKA DEVOTIONS)			
	You're The One/Rip Van Winkle (by Mr. Bassman)	1963	Graphic Arts 1000
SYMBOLS (2)			
	Last Year About This Time/Better Get Your Own One Buddy	1963	Dore 666
SYMBOLS (3)			
	Canadian Sunset/Gentle Art Of Loving	1966	President 102
	Bye Bye Baby/The Things You Do To Me	1967	Laurie 3401
	The Best Part Of Breaking Up/Again	1968	Laurie 3435
	Bye Bye/I Love You	1973	Vintage 1007
SYMPHONICS			
	Our Love Will Grow/Way Down Low	1963	Tru-Lite 116
	All Roads Lead To Heartbreak/It Won't Be Long	1964	Dee Jon 001
SYMPHONICS (FREDDIE SCOTT & THE)			
	A Blessing To You/Come On Honey	1959	Enrica 1002

Artist	Song	Year	Label
SYNCAPATES			
	Your Tender Lips/Praying For A Miracle	1963	Times Square 7
	The Duke/Do What You're Gonna Do	1965	Mello 552
	Girl Of My Dreams/My Ol' Lady	N/A	Armour 5577
T-BIRDS (1) (GM JESSE BELVIN)			
	Come On, Dance With Me/Green Stamps	1961	Chess 1778
T-BIRDS (2)			
	Nobody But You/Have You Ever Been In Love	1967	Vegas 720
T-BIRDS (3) (DON MIKKELSEN & THE)			
	Chapel Of Love/Where I Came In	1959	Deck 600
TABBYS (1)			
	My Darling/Yes I Do	1959	Time 1008
TABBYS (2)			
	Hong Kong Baby/Physical Fitness Blues	1963	Metro 2
TABS (1)			
	Will We Meet Again/Still Love You Baby	1958	Nasco 6016
	First Star/Avenue Of Tears	1959	Dot 15887
	Rock & Roll Holiday/Never Fo'get	1959	Noble 719/Gardena 110 (60)
	Oops/My Girl Is Gone	1959	Noble 720
	Dance All By Myself/Dance Party	1961	Vee Jay 418
	Mash Dem Taters/But You're My Baby	1962	Vee Jay 446
	Two Stupid Feet/The Wallop	1962	Wand 130
	I'm With You/Take My Love Along With You	1963	Wand 139
TABS (2) (JOANIE TAYLOR & THE)			
	You Lied/Dapper Dan	1961	Herald 568
TADS			
	Your Reason/The Pink Panther	1956	Liberty Bell 9010/Dot 15518 (56)
	Wolf Call/She Is My Dream	1958	Rev 3513
TAFFYS			
	Key To My Heart/Everybody South Street	1963	Fairmount 610
	Peter Cottontail/Can't We Be Sweethearts	1963	Pageant 608
TAGS (JOHNNY NEWTON & THE)			
	Sorry, Sorry/I Ran All The Way Home)/A Teenager In Love	1959	Bell 114
TALENTS (1) (JULIAN BARNETT & THE)			
	Don't Walk Away/Come Back To Me	1958	Herald 519
TALENTS (2)			
	Rockin' The Tease/New Kind Of Gold	1961	Skylark 106
	Three Little Fishes/My Favorite Things	1961	Twink 1215
TALKABOUTS			
	I Don't Seem To Care Anymore/Sweet Lovin' (by the Visuals)	1959	Poplar 117
TAMANEERS			
	Searching/Be Anything But Be Mine	1960	Bramley 102
TAMARAS (LEE DURELL & THE)			
	You Gave Me Love/Party Time	1960	Music City 836
TAMBLYN, LARRY (& GROUP)			
	This Is The Night/Destiny	1965	Faro 612
TAMBLYN, LARRY (BB THE STANDELLS)			
	You'll Be Mine Someday/The Girl In My Heart	1964	Linda 112
TAMS (1) (AKA HIPPIES/AKA STEREOS)			
	Teenage Kids/Memory Lane	1959	Mink 022/Parkway 863 (63)
TAMS (2)			
	Valley Of Love/Sorry	1960	Swan 4055
	Vacation Time/If Love Were Like Rivers	1961	Heritage 101
	Untie Me/Disillusioned	1962	Arlen 711
	My Baby Loves Me/Find Another Love	1962	General American 714
TANGENTS			
	Send Me Something/I Can't Live Alone	1960	Fresh 1
	That Lucky Old Sun/Never Leave Again	1960	Fresh 2274

Artist	Song	Year	Label
	The Wiggle/The Waddle	1960	United Artists 201
TANGERINES (1)			
	The Answer Is Always You/		
	This Is The Way	1961	Wildcat 603
TANGERINES (2)			
	Jim, That's Him/You Know		
	You're Mine	1964	Gina 7002
TANGIERS (1) (AKA HOLLYWOOD FLAMES)			
	I Won't Be Around/Tabarin	1955	Decca 29603
	Remember Me/Oh, Baby!	1956	Decca 29973
	Don't Try/School Days Will		
	Be Over	1958	Class 224
	The Plea/The Waddle	1962	A-J 905
TANGIERS (2)			
	Ping Pong/Don't Stop The Music	1961	Strand 25039
TANNO, MARC (& GROUP)			
	Angel/Dear Baby	1961	Whale 501
TANTONES (1)			
	No Matter/I Love You, Really		
	I Do	1957	Lamp 2002
	So Afraid/Tell Me	1957	Lamp 2008
TANTONES (2) (TRADE & THE)			
	Joanne	N/A	Adam & Eve LP 502
TARGETS			
	It Doesn't Matter/Girls Girls Girls	1961	King 5538
TARTANS			
	Nothing But Love/I Need You	1966	Impact 1010
TASSELLS (FEMALE)			
	Since You Went Away/		
	he Twelfth Of Never	1963	Goldisc G11
TASSELS (FEMALE)			
	To A Soldier Boy/The Boy For Me	1959	Madison 117/Amy 946 (66)
	My Guy And I/To A Young Lover	1959	Madison 121
TATE, PAUL (& GROUP)			
	Everybody But Me/Dance On	1958	Falcon 1012
TATTLETALES			
	Double Trouble/Magic Wand	1959	Warner Bros. 5066
TAYLOR, ADAM (& GROUP)			
	Yvonne/I Need Her	N/A	Le Harve 1028
TAYLOR, ANDREW (& GROUP)			
	That's How I Feel About You/		
	Never Bite Off More Than		
	You Can Chew	1961	Gone 5109
TAYLOR, BERT (& GROUP)			
	Soldier Boy/Tears Of		
	Remember	1955	Essex 396
TAYLOR, BOBBY (& GROUP)			
	You Are My Heart/Pretty Baby	1962	Barbara 62640
TAYLOR, CARMEN (& GROUP)			
	Why Did You Leave Me Alone/		
	So What	1957	King 5085
TAYLOR, JOHNNY (& GROUP)			
	Never Never/Rome Wasn't		
	Built In A Day	1962	Sar 131
TAYLOR, MIKE (& GROUP)			
	Mi-A-Suri Talk/He's A Lover	1963	Dream (no number)
TAYLOR, SAMMY (& GROUP)			
	Don't Lie/Your Precious Love	1964	Enjoy 2028
TAYLOR, TED (& GROUP)			
	Be Ever Wonderful/Since		
	You're Home (no group)	1959	Duke 304
	You Know I Do/Someday		
	(I Know, I Know)	1960	Top Rank 3001
	Anytime, Anyplace, Anywhere/		
	Lost The Best Thing I Ever Had	1961	Suncraft 400
TAYLORTONES			
	A Star/Poor Little Girl	1961	Star Maker 1926
	My Heart Went Zing/Too		
	Young To Love	N/A	C&T 0001
TAYLORTOPS			
	I'll See You Somewhere/		
	I Wanna Be That Way	1959	Alton 2000
TEAM MATES (AKA TEAMATES)			
	Sooner Or Later/I Just Might	1959	Le Cam 701
	Sooner Or Later/If Only I Had		
	Known	1959	Le Cam 706
	Once There Was A Time/		
	Come On Baby	1960	Le Cam 707
	Sylvia/Crazy Baby	1960	Le Cam 709
	Most Of All/Please Believe Me	1965	Soft 104/Paula 220 (65)
	You Must Pay/If Only I Had		
	Known	1966	ABC 10760
TEAMATES (AKA TEAM MATES)			
	We've Believed In Love/		
	Once There Was A Time	1962	Philips 40029
	Calendar Of Love/I Say		
	Goodbye	1964	Le Mans 003
TEAMATES (AKA TEAM MATES) (TANDI & THE)			
	Trampoline Queen/		
	Week-End Lover	1960	Ember 1068
TEARDROPS (1)			
	Come Back To Me/Sweet		
	Lovin' Daddy-O	1952	Sampson 634
TEARDROPS (2)			
	The Stars Are Out Tonight/		
	Oh, Stop It!	1954	Josie 766/Port 70019 (60)
	My Heart/Ooh, Baby	1954	Josie 771
	Al Chiar Di Luna (Porto		
	Fortuna)/We Won't Tell	1958	Josie 856
	You're My Hollywood		
	Star/Cry No More	1959	Josie 862
	Daddy's Little Girl/Always You	1959	Josie 873
TEARDROPS (3)			
	My Inspiration/I Prayed For love	1957	King 5004
	Don't Be Afraid To Love/		
	After School	1957	King 5037
TEARDROPS (4)			
	Jellyfish/Bridge Of Love	1957	Dot 15669
TEARDROPS (5)			
	Sugar Baby/Catch Me,		
	I'm Falling Again	1958	Rendezvous 102
TEARDROPS (6) (BILLY TAYLOR & THE)			
	I'm Young/Wombie Zombie	1959	Felco 101
TEARDROPS (7) (HONEY & THE)			
	You Are The One/Something		
	To Remember You By	1959	Val 202
TEARDROPS (8)			
	Let's Dance/I Know	N/A	Col-Vin 777
TEARS (1) (FEMALE)			
	Nothing But Love/Until The		
	Day I Die	1956	Dig 112
TEARS (2) (LINDA & THE)			
	Good Goodbye/Happy Blues	1965	Challenge 59317
TEARS (3)			
	Hurt/She's Mine	1961	Astronaut 5001
TEARS OF JOY			
	Ready For Your Love/My Girl	1986	Starlight 47
TEASERS (1)			
	How Could You Hurt me So?/		
	I Was A Fool To Love You	1954	Checker 800
TEASERS (2) (JIMMY BRINKLEY & THE)			
	Why Oh Why/Blue Moon	1957	Note 10002
TEASERS (3) (BOBBY & THE)			
	She's A Tease/Harry On A		
	Safari	1960	Fleetwood 1012
TEASERS (4) (SAMMY & THE)			
	As I Remember You/Penny		
	In A Wishing Well	1958	Airport 101
TECHNICS			
	Because I Really Love You/		
	A Mans Confusion	1962	Chex 1012
	Hey Girl Don't Leave Me/I Met		
	Her On The First Of September	1962	Chex 1013
TECHNICS (TONY & THE)			
	Ha Ha He Told Us/		
	Work Out With Your Pretty Girl	1962	Chex 1010
TECHNIQUES			
	Hey! Little Girl/In A Round		
	About Way	1957	Stars 551/Roulette 4030 (57)
	Let Her Go/Marindy	1958	Roulette 4048
	Moon Tan/The Wisest Man In		
	Town	1958	Roulette 4097
TEDDY BEARS			
	To Know Him Is To Love Him/		
	Don't You Worry My Pretty Pet	1958	Dore 503
	Wonderful Loveable You/		
	Till You'll Be Mine	1959	Dore 520
	Oh Why/I Don't Need You		
	Anymore	1959	Imperial 5562
	If You Only Knew/You Said		
	Goodbye	1959	Imperial 5581
	Don't Go Away/Seven Lonely Days	1959	Imperial 5594
TEEN DREAMS (DEBBIE & THE) (AKA DEBBIE & THE DARNELS)			
	The Time/Santa	1962	Vernon 101

Artist	Song	Year	Label
TEEN DREAMS (FEMALE) (AKA DEBBIE & THE DARNELS)			
	The Time/Why Why	1962	Vernon 100
TEEN FIVE			
	Darling I Love You/I'll Never Let You Go (by the Gents) (A capella)	1963	Times Square 2/Times Square 99
	(64/Til The End Of Time/ Island Of Love(by the Gents) (A capella)	1963	Times Square 4/Times Square 98 (64)
TEEN KINGS (1)			
	My Greatest Wish/Don't Just Stand There	1959	Willett 118
TEEN KINGS (2)			
	You Are My Love (You)	N/A	Relic LP 5033
	In The Still Of The Night	N/A	Relic LP 5033
TEEN NOTES			
	Loco In The Coco/My Precious Jewel	1960	Deb 121
	Hi-Fi Sweetie/Big Band Polka	1961	Deb 127
TEEN TONES (1)			
	Gypsy Boogie/Faded Love	1959	Nu-Clear 1
TEEN TONES (2)			
	I'll Never Change/Three Stars	1959	Crest 1057
	Darling I Love You/My Sweet	1959	Dandy Dan 2
	Don't Call Me Baby, I'll Call You/Yes You May	1959	Decca 30895
	My Little Baby/Head Strong Baby	1959	Swan 4040
	Faded Love/Gypsy Boogie	1959	Wynne 107
	Susan Ann/Cuckoo	1960	Deb 132
	I'm So Happy/Shoutin' Twist	1961	Tri Disc 102
	Do You Wanna Dance/Long Cold Winter ahead	1965	T&T 2488
TEEN TONES (3) (JULES BLATTNER & THE)			
	Lover Doll	N/A	K-Ark 612
TEEN-KINGS			
	That's A Teen-Age Love/Tell Me If You Know	1959	Bee 1115
TEENAGE MOONLIGHTERS			
	Sorry Sorry/I Want To Cry	1960	Mark 134
TEENAGERS (FB BY BILLY LOBRANO)			
	Everything To Me/ Flip Flop	1957	Gee 1046
	My Broken Heart/Mama Wanna Rock	1958	Roulette 4086
	Good Lovin'	1986	Murray Hill LP 000148
TEENAGERS (FB BY FRANKIE LYMON)			
	Somewhere/Sweet And Lovely	1964	Columbia 43094
TEENAGERS (FB BY JOE NEGRONI)			
	Jean Of The Ville	1961	Columbia (unreleased)
TEENAGERS (FB BY JOE NEGRONI/KENNY BOBO)			
	Tonight's The Night/Crying	1960	End 1071
TEENAGERS (FB BY JOHNNY HOUSTON)			
	Can You Tell Me?/A Little Wiser Now	1960	End 1076
TEENAGERS (FB JOE NEGRONI)			
	Wild Female/I Hear The Angels Cry	1981	Crystal Ball 142
TEENAGERS (FB SHERMAN GARNES)			
	He's No Lover/Love Me Long (fb Joe Negroni)	1981	Crystal Ball 144
TEENAGERS (FRANKIE LYMON & THE)			
	Why Do Fools Fall In Love/ Please Be Mine	1956	Gee 1002
	I Want You To Be My Girl/ I'm Not A Know It All	1956	Gee 1012
	I Promise To Remember/ Who Can Explain	1956	Gee 1018
	ABC's Of Love/Share	1956	Gee 1022
	I'm Not A Juvenile Delinquent/ Baby, Baby	1956	Gee 1026
	I Was Alone	1957	Gee (unreleased)
	Teenage Love/Paper Castles	1957	Gee 1032
	Love Is A Clown/Am I Fooling Myself Again?	1957	Gee 1035
	Out In The Cold Again/Miracle In The Rain	1957	Gee 1036
	Goody Goody/Creation Of Love	1957	Gee 1039
	Pajama Party	1957	Roulette LP 25021
	Little White Lies	1957	Roulette LP 25021/Forum LP 9006
	Goody Goody Girl/I'm Not Too Young To Dream	1959	Gee 1052
	Fortunate Fellow/Love Put Me Out Of My Head	1977	Robin Hood 155/Murray Hill LP 000148 (86)
	Together	1986	Murray Hill LP 000148
	Begin The Beguine	1986	Murray Hill LP 000148
	You	1986	Murray Hill LP 000148
	It Would Be So Nice	1986	Murray Hill LP 000148
TEENAGERS (JOEY & THE)			
	What's On Your Mind/The Draw (with Sherman)	1961	Columbia 42054
	He's No Lover	N/A	Columbia
	Love Me Long	N/A	Columbia
TEENAIRES (HARLEY DAVIS & THE)			
	My Definition Of You/Mad Lover	1961	Wildcat 0064
TEENANGELS (1) (BUZZ CLIFFORD & THE)			
	Forever/Magic Circle	1962	Columbia 42290
TEENANGELS (2)			
	Tell Me My Love/Ain't Gonna Let You (Break My Heart)	1963	Sun 388
TEENBEATS (1)			
	Nightspot/Only The Stars	1961	Myrl 407
TEENBEATS (2) (GENE & THE)			
	Here I Stand	N/A	Raven 2011
TEENCHORDS (LEWIS LYMON & THE)			
	Too Young/Your Last Chance	1957	End 1003
	I Found Out Why/Tell Me, Love	1957	End 1007/Fury 1007 (57)
	I'm So Happy (Tra-La-La-La)/ Lydia	1957	Fury 1000
	Honey Honey/Please Tell The Angels	1957	Fury 1003
	I'm Not Too Young Too Fall In Love/Falling In Love	1957	Fury 1006
	Dance Girl/Them There Eyes	1958	Juanita 101/Bim Bam Boom 114 (73)
	Too Young/I Found Out Why	1962	End 1113
	Please Tell The Angels/I Want You To Be My Girl	1984	Starlight 21
	Honey Honey/Dance Girl	1984	Starlight 25
	Never Let You Go/I Found Out Why	1994	Park Ave. 9
TEENERS (LULU REED & THE)			
	Say Hey Pretty Baby/It's Easy Child (by Freddy King)	1962	Federal 12477
TEENETTES (1) (FEMALE)			
	Too Young To Fall In Love/ My Lucky Star	1958	Josie 830
	From The Word Go/I Want A Boy With A Hi-Fi Supersonic Stereophonic Bloop Bleep	1959	Brunswick 55125
	Let Me Be The One/Bye Bye Baby	1963	Sandy 250
TEENETTES (2) (BOBBY GRABEAU & THE)			
	Don't Ever Let Me Go/Back To School, Back To You	1959	Crest 1064
TEENETTES (3) (BETTY JAYNE & THE)			
	The Sun Will Rise/Show Your Love	1961	Carellen 101
	Night Angel/Johnny Preacher	1961	Carellen 102
	I'm No Longer Jimmy's Girl/ Tag Along	1961	Carellen 107
	Lonely Teenager/Time Will Tell	1961	Mona Lee 139
	Shoppin' 'Round For Love/ I Would Never Dare	1961	Net 101
TEENOS			
	Love Only One/Alrightee	1958	Dub 2839/Relic 506 (64)
TEENS (1) (LITTLE CLYDE & THE)			
	A Casual Look/Oh Me	1956	RPM 462
TEENS (2) (BARBARA JEAN & THE)			
	Reflection Of You/Marty At The Party	1962	Allison 920
TEENTONES (AKA LEVEE SONGSTERS/AKA MELLO-HARPS)			
	Love Is A Vow/Walkie Talkie Baby	1958	Rego 1004
TEERS (LANCELO & THE)			
	Whispering Bells/It's Not For Me To Say	N/A	Promenade 12
TEJUNS			
	Girl/Nobody Knows	N/A	100 Proof 144
TELEGRAMS			
	Oh Baby Please/Hey Baby	1978	Creole 163

Artist Song	Year	Label	Artist Song	Year	Label
TELLERS (1) (FB TIMMY LYMON) (AKA STORYTELLERS (1))			**TEMPTATIONS (4) (CODY BRENNAN & THE)**		
Hey Baby/You Played Me A Fool	1959	Stack 500	Am I The One/Ruby Baby	1961	Swan 4089
Tears Fell From My Eyes/ I Wanna Run To You	1960	Fire 1038	**TEMPTERS**		
TELLERS (2) (ARTIE BANKS & THE)			I'll See You Next Fall/I'm Sorry Now	1956	Empire 105
Oriental Baby/Spider And The Fly	1961	Imperial 5788	**TEMPTONES (FB DARYL HALL)**		
TEMPESTS (1)			Girl, I Love You/Good-Bye	1966	Arctic 130
Never Let You Go/Falling Like The Rain	1959	Williamette 103	Say Those Words Of Love/ This Could Be The Start Of Something Good	1967	Arctic 136
TEMPESTS (2)			**TENDERFOOTS (REF CRENSHAWS/REF EBBTIDES (3)/REF FOUR AFTER FIVES/REF LAMPLIGHTERS/REF RIVINGTONS/REF SHARPS)**		
My True Story	N/A	Top 6 Hits EP 4	Watussi Wussi Wo/Kissing Bug	1955	Federal 12214
TEMPLES			Save Me Some Kisses/ My Confession	1955	Federal 12219
Whispering Campaign/I Don't Want To Do A Thing But Love You	1958	Date 1004	Those Golden Bells/I'm Yours Anyhow	1955	Federal 12225
TEMPO-MENTALS			Sindy/Sugar Ways	1955	Federal 12228
Burning Desire/Dearest	1957	Ebb 112	**TENDERTONES**		
TEMPO-TONES (FB RICHARD LANHAM)			I Love You So/Just For A Little While	1959	Ducky 713
Get Yourself Another Fool/ Ride Along	1957	Acme 713	**TENNYSON, BILL (& GROUP)**		
In My Dreams/My Boy Sleepy Pete	1957	Acme 715	Even Now/Slow Down	1958	Pet 805
Come Into My Heart/Somewhere There Is Someone	1957	Acme 718	**TERMITES**		
TEMPO-TONES (NANCY LEE & THE)			Give Me Your Heart/Carrie Lou	1964	Bee 1825
So They Say/Meet Me At The Crossroads	1957	Acme 711	**TERRACETONES (REF MONOTONES)**		
TEMPOS (1)			Words Of Wisdom/The Ride Of Paul Revere	1958	Apt 25016
Kingdom Of Love/That's What You Do To Me	1957	Kapp 178	**TERRANS (RENE HARRIS & THE)**		
The Prettiest Girl In School/ Never You Mind	1957	Kapp 199	Moonrise/Soap 'N Water	1963	Graham 801
I Got A Job/Strollin' With My Baby	1958	Kapp 213	**TERRELL, CLYDE (& GROUP)**		
See You In September/Bless You My Love	1959	Climax 102	My One Desire/Poor Folk	1959	Excello 2151
Crossroads Of Love/Whatever Happens	1959	Climax 105	**TERRIFICS (1)**		
Look Homeward Angel/Under Ten Flags	1959	Paris 550	I Don't Care How You Do It/ Bump Ti Dee Ump Bump	1959	Demon 1516
TEMPOS (2) (AKA FOUR ELDORADOS)			**TERRIFICS (2)**		
Promise Me/Never Let Me Go	1958	Rhythm 121	Little Star/De Plu De Pinto De Blue	1958	Bell 88
To Love Again/Patricia (by the Lyrics)	1984	Rhythm 129	**TERRIGAN BROTHERS**		
TEMPOS (3)			Little Love	N/A	Fortune 207
It's Tough/Sham-Rock	1959	Hi-Q 100	**TERRY, GEORGE (& GROUP) (AKA TERRY GEORGE & GROUP)**		
TEMPOS (4)			Dreamy Eyes/Write Me	1965	Sphere Sound 711
Monkey Do/Oh Play That Thing	1963	Fairmount 611	**TERRY, MAUREEN (& GROUP)**		
My Dream Island/My Love Goes Deep	1964	Vee Jay 580	There's A Boy/Whoever You Are	1964	Maria 102
TEMPOS (5)			**TERRYTONES (CLAIRE CHARLES & THE)**		
Why Don't You Write Me/ A Thief In The Night	1964	U.S.A. 810	You're My Ideal/Ah Do Me Kitchie	1961	Wye 1002
My Barbara Ann/When You Loved Me	1965	Ascot 2167	**TERRYTONES (WITH CLAIRE CHARLES & GAYLE FORTUNE)**		
My Barbara Ann/I Wish It Were Summer	1965	Ascot 2173	Teenage Night Theme/ I Cry The Blues	1960	Wye 1003
It Was You/I Gotta Make A Move	1966	Montel 955	I Beg Your Pardon/Three Steps To The Phone	1961	Wye 1010
Let's Stick Together/Don't Act That Way	1966	Riley's 5	**TEXAS MATADORS**		
Don't Leave Me/I Need You	1966	Riley's 8781	Flower Blossom/I Found Her	N/A	IMA 101
Sad Sad Memories	1967	Canterbury 504	**THEMES (1)**		
TEMPS (BOBBY & THE)			The Magic Of You/Yes! That's Love	1959	Excello 2152
Mary Lou, Mary Lou/The Shuffle	1963	ABC 10428	**THEMES (1) (ALVIN GAINES & THE)**		
TEMPTASHUNS			Cross My Heart/Let's Jump The Broomstick	1959	Fidelity 420592
Pretty Ways/Strawberry Man	1964	Federal 12530	**THEMES (2)**		
TEMPTATIONS (1)			Marnie (I Love You)/There's No Moon Out Tonight	1964	Stork 001
Standing Alone/Roach's Rock	1958	King 5118	**THEMES (3)**		
Temptation/Pony Tail	1958	Savoy (unreleased)	Sunday Kind Of Love/I Feel So Funny	N/A	Ideal 21
Mad At Love/Mister Juke Box	1958	Savoy 1532	**THEMES (4) (LANNY HUNT & THE)**		
I Love You, This I Know/Don't You Know	1958	Savoy 1550	I Can't Say I Love You/Over Easy	1964	Sure Star 5001
TEMPTATIONS (2)			**THESE GENTS (REF MARCELS)**		
Birds 'N Bees/Temptations	1959	Parkway 803	Yesterday Standing By (Pt. 1)/ Yesterday Standing By (Pt. 2)	N/A	Western World 55102
TEMPTATIONS (3)			**THIN MEN (DENNIS BINDER & HIS)**		
Barbara/Someday	1960	Goldisc 3001	The Long Man/I'm A Lover	1956	United 194
Letter Of Devotion/Fickle Little Girl	1960	Goldisc 3007	**THINGS TO COME**		
TEMPTATIONS (3) (NEIL STEVENS & THE)			Somewhere/Gypsy Woman	1993	Clifton 107
Ballad Of Love/Tonight My Heart She Is Crying	1961	Goldisc 3019	Java Java/Return To Sender	1993	Clifton 108
			THOMAS, GENE (& GROUP)		
			Down The Road/Crying Inside	1961	Venus 1444
			THOMAS, JERRY (& GROUP)		
			Baby Please/Tell Me	1958	Khoury's 708
			It's So Strange/Someone (no group)	1966	Ascot 2212

Artist Song	Year	Label
THOMAS, RANDY (& GROUP)		
My Heart Cries/Are You Ready		1966Faro 622
THOMAS, VIC (BB THE FOUR-EVERS)		
Marianne/Napoleon Bonaparte	1964	Philips 40183
Village Of Love/Down The		
Stream To The River	1964	Philips 40228
THOMASES (VARETTA & THE)		
Fly By Night/Breaking Hearts	1963	Brent 7040
THOR-ABLES (FB AARON COLLINS)		
Our Love Song/Get That Bread	1962	Titanic 1001
My Reckless Heart/Batman		
And Robin	1962	Titanic 1002
THORNE, ROSCOE (BB THE CAVERLIERS)		
Delores/Peddler Of Dreams	1953	Atlas 1033
THORNS (ANDY ROSE & THE)		
Just For Fun/Love Is Love	1960	Gold Crest 3807
THORNTON SISTERS (FEMALE)		
Watch Your Step/Big City Boy	1964	Bobsan 1000
THORPE, LIONEL (& GROUP) (REF CHORDS)		
More, More, More/Lover		
Lover Lover	1959	Roulette 4144
THRASHERS		
Jeannie/Forever, My Love	1957	Masons 0-1/Candlelite 421 (63)
THREE BEAUS AND A PEEP		
Alibi Baby/The Pal That I		
Loved Stole The Gal That		
I Loved	1954	Columbia 40344
THREE BEAUS AND A PEEP (RICK VALLO & THE)		
If That Would Bring You		
Back To Me/There's No		
You (no group)	1953	MGM 11473
THREE BEAUX AND A PEEP		
For Love/Kent Song (instrumental)	1957	Aladdin 3382
THREE BELLES (FEMALE)		
True Blue Lou/It Makes A		
Difference To Me	1955	Jubilee 5219
THREE CHEERS		
Broken Dream/Teen Talk	1959	Glory 291
THREE CHIMES		
Tears And Pain/Show Me		
The Way	1964	Crossway 444
THREE CHUCKLES (FB TEDDY RANDAZZO)		
Runaround/At Last You		
Understand	1954	Boulevard 100/X 0066 (54)
Foolishly/If You Should Love Again	1955	X 0095
So Long/You Should Have		
Told Me	1955	X 0134
Realize/Blue Lover	1955	X 0150
Times Two, I Love You/Still		
Thinking Of You	1955	X 0162
Anyway/The Funny Little		
Things We Used To Do	1955	X 0186/Vik 0186 (56)
Midnight Til Dawn/Fallen		
Out Of Love	1956	Vik 0232
Won't You Give Me A Chance/		
We're Gonna Rock Tonight	1956	Vik 0244
Solitude	1956	Vik LP 1067
As Time Goes By	1956	Vik LP 1067
In The Still Of The Night	1956	Vik LP 1067
Maybe You'll Be There	1956	Vik LP 1067
I Only Have Eyes For You	1956	Vik LP 1067
Marta	1956	Vik LP 1067
It's Been A Long Long Time	1956	Vik LP 1067
How Deep Is The Ocean	1956	Vik LP 1067
Red Sails In The Sunset	1956	Vik LP 1067
These Foolish Things	1956	Vik LP 1067
Where Or When	1956	Vik LP 1067
To Each His Own	1956	Vik LP 1067/Vik EP 192
And The Angels Sing/Tell Me	1956	X 0194/Vik 0194 (56)
Gypsy In My Soul/We're Still		
Holding Hands	1956	X 0216/Vik 0216 (56)
Runaround/Lonely Traveller		
(by the Chuckles)	1961	ABC 10276
Runaround/You Lied	1966	Cloud 507
THREE COQUETTES (FEMALE)		
I Wonder/Snooty Poo	1960	Hope 1002
THREE D'S		
Tell Me That You Love Me/		
Broken Dreams	1956	Pilgrim 719
Let Me Know/Little Billy Boy	1957	Paris 503
Birth Of An Angel/Never Let		
You Go	1957	Paris 508
Crazy Little Woman/Baby Doll	1958	Paris 511
I Never See My Baby Alone/		
Jumpin' Jack	1958	Paris 514
Nothin' To Wear/Happiest		
Boy And Girl	1959	Brunswick 55152
Broken Hearted/I Love You So	1961	Dean 521
My Fraternity Dance/		
Summertime Sweetheart		
(by Henry Pinard & the		
Three D's)	N/A	Lowell 212
Squeeze/Graveyard Cha-Cha	N/A	Square 502
THREE DOLLS (1) (LARRY STEVENS & THE)		
Wait For Me/A Girl Named Marie	1960	Epic 9358
THREE DOLLS (2) (LA RONDA SUCCEED & THE)		
Aftereffect Of Love/Yes Daddy	1961	Magnificent 111
THREE DOTS		
Window Of Love/Tip Toe	1959	Buzz 104
White Silver Sands/Snow		
Dreams	1960	Rich 1003
THREE DOTS AND A DASH (FB JESSE BELVIN)		
I'll Never Love Again/Let's Do It	1951	Imperial 5164
THREE EMOTIONS		
The Night We Met/The Girl		
I Left Behind	1959	Fury 1026
THREE FRIENDS (1) (AKA HEARTBEATS (2))		
Blanche/Baby I'll Cry	1956	Lido 500/Relic 1021 (73)
I'm Only A Boy/Jinx	1956	Lido 502
Chinese Tea Room/Jinx	1957	Brunswick 55032
Now That You're Gone/		
Chinese Tea Room	1957	Lido 504
THREE FRIENDS (2)		
Walkin' Shoes/Blue Ribbon		
Baby	1961	Cal Gold 169
Dedicated (To The Songs I		
Love)/Happy As A Man		
Can Be	1961	Imperial 5763
Go On To School/You're A		
Square	1961	Imperial 5773
THREE G'S		
Let's Go Steady For The		
Summer/Wild Man	1958	Columbia 41175
Sweet Love/I'd Wait Forever	1958	Columbia 41256
These Are The Little Things/		
Wonder	1958	Columbia 41292
Oh, Suzette/When It's		
Summer Again	1959	Columbia 41383
Barbara/Don't Cry Katy	1959	Columbia 41513
Take That Step/		
Eeny-Meeny-Miny-Moe	1960	Columbia 41584
Love Call/Let's Go Steady		
For The Summer	1960	Columbia 41678
Take My Love/She's Mine	1960	Columbia 41868
Foolish Tears/Blueberry Hill	1961	Columbia 41955
THREE GRACES (FEMALE)		
X Equals Kiss/Jimmy Joe	1959	Golden Crest 515
Lonesome And Sorry/Billy		
Boy's Tune	1959	Golden Crest 528
Missed/7-L	1960	Golden Crest 534
My Hero/Larry Applebaum	1960	Golden Crest 546
THREE HONEYDROPS		
Honeydrop/In The Summer	1957	Music City 813
Rockin' Satellite/You're The		
One For Me	1957	Music City 814
THREE J'S		
Always Stay In Love With		
Me/Oh There She Goes	1957	Glory 253
THREE JAYS (VERA & THE)		
Fire In Your Heart/Be Bop		
Baby Sitter	1957	El-Bee 162
THREE MOODS		
Stop, Look And Listen		
(For The Heart You Save)/		
Never Again	1955	Sarg 124
THREE NATURALS		
Bad Boy/Hang On Baby	N/A	Sin 725
THREE NOTES		
Bertha/Lucy Lucy	1958	Tee Gee 106
THREE PALS (JOHNNY CARDELL & THE)		
Deceived/Rock-A-Billy Yodeler	1957	Rama 227
THREE PALS (ROC LA RUE & THE)		
I'm Not Ashamed/Baby Take		
Me Back	1957	Rama 226

Artist Song	Year	Label
THREE PENNIES		
Why Am I So Shy/A Penny For Your Thoughts	1964	B.T. Puppy 501
THREE PLAYMATES		
Sugah Woogah/Lovey Dovey Pair	1958	Savoy 1528
I Dreamed/Give Your Love To Me	1958	Savoy 1537
THREE QUEENS (GM EDDIE KING)		
Love You Baby/Shakin' Inside	1960	J.O.B. 1122
THREE REASONS		
(I've Got) No Regrets/Kangaroo Twist	1963	JRE 224
THREE VALES		
Blue Lights Down Low/Ay Ay Ay	1957	Cindy 3007
THREE WISHES		
Guiding Light/It's All Said And Done	1963	Dolton 72
THREETEENS (FEMALE)		
X Plus Y Equals Z/For The Love Of Mike	1958	Rev 3522/Todd 1021 (59)
Dear 53310769 (Elvis' U.S. Army Serial #)/Doowaddie	1959	Rev 3516
THRILLERS (1)		
The Drunkard/Mattie, Leave Me Alone	1953	Big Town 109
Lessie Mae/I'm Going To Live My Life Alone	1953	Thriller 3530
'Lizabeth/Please Talk To Me	1954	Herald 432
Take That	N/A	Herald (unreleased)
Long Lasting Love	N/A	Herald (unreleased)
Woman Was Made For Love	N/A	Herald (unreleased)
If You Ever Need A Friend	N/A	Herald (unreleased)
THRILLERS (2) (LITTLE JOE & THE)		
This I Know/Let's Do The Slop	1956	Okeh 7075
Peanuts/Lily Lou	1957	Okeh 7088
The Echoes Keep Calling Me/Lonesome	1957	Okeh 7094
What Happened To Your Halo?/Don't Leave Me Alone	1958	Okeh 7099
Mine/It's Too Bad We Had To Say Goodbye	1958	Okeh 7107/Epic 9293 (58)
Cheery Pt. 1/Cheery Pt. 2	1959	Okeh 7116
I Need Somebody/It's Been A Long Time	1959	Okeh 7121
I'll Never Let You Go/Give Me All Your Love	1959	Okeh 7127
Ev'ry Now And Then/Goodnight, Little Girl	1959	Okeh 7134
Stay/Please Don't Go	1960	Okeh 7136
Run Little Girl/Public Opinion	1960	Okeh 7140/Epic 9431 (61)
I Love You For Sentimental Reasons/One More Time	1961	20th Century 1214
Peanuts/No, No, I Can't Stop	1963	Reprise 20142
How Am I Doing/I'll Do Anything	1963	Rose 835
Peanuts And Popcorn/Chicken Little Boo Boo	1964	Enjoy 2011
Come What May/This I Know, Little Girl	1965	Uptown 715
Someone For Me/Love Me	N/A	Peanuts 85211
THRILLETTES (BETTE RENNE & THE)		
Your Kinda Love/You Ain't So Such A Much	1964	Lawn 246
THRILLS (GEORGE ZIMMERMAN & THE)		
I Ain't Got The Money To Pay For This Drink/Whose Baby Are You	1956	Jab 103
THUNDERBIRDS (1)		
Baby, Let's Play House/Pledging My Love	1955	DeLuxe 6075
Love Is A Problem/Rock Boom Boom	1955	G.G. 518
THUNDERBIRDS (2)		
Blueberries/Ayuh, Ayuh	1955	Era 1000
I'd Be A Fool To Let You Go/Beguino	1955	Era 1004
THUNDERBIRDS (2) (BERT CONVY & THE)		
Hoo Bop De Bow/C'Mon Back	1955	Era 1001
THUNDERBIRDS (3)		
In My Thunderbird/Mary	1957	Holiday 2609
THUNDERBIRDS (4) (BILLY FORD & THE)		
Billy Boy Blow/How Can I Be Sure	1957	Vik 0263
THUNDERBIRDS (5) (RON HOLDEN & THE)		
Love You So/My Babe	1959	Donna 1315/Nite Owl 10 (59)
Gee But I'm Lonesome/Susie Jane	1960	Donna 1324
True Love Can Be/Everything's Gonna Be Alright	1960	Donna 1328
Your Line Is Busy/Who Says There Ain't No Santa Claus?	1960	Donna 1331
Let No One Tell You/The Big Shoe	1961	Donna 1335
So Dearly/Bring Me Happiness (Rosie & Ron)	1961	Donna 1338
I'll Be Happy/I'll Always Have You	1961	Eldo 117
THUNDERBIRDS (6) (RUDY GRAYZELL & THE)		
You'll Be Mine/F.B.I. Story	1959	Award 130
THUNDERBIRDS (7) (JOHNNY & THE)		
They Say/You Are My Sunshine	1959	Clover 1001
THUNDERBIRDS (8) (CHRIS FARLOW & THE)		
Just A Dream/What You Gonna Do	1965	General American 718
THUNDERBOLTS		
Blending/I'm Sorry (instrumental)	1961	Rondack 9768
TIARAS (1) (ROY MILTON & THE)		
Bless Your Heart/Early In The Morning	1960	Lou Wa 1002/Warwick 549 (60)
TIARAS (2) (FEMALE)		
You Told Me/I'm Gonna Forget You	1963	Valiant 6027
Don't Believe A Word/Hey Senor	1963	Valiant 6030
TIBBS, KENNETH (& GROUP)		
Darling I Want Your Love/No More Tears	1958	Federal 12335
TIC TOCS		
Zola/Walking Alone	1957	Back Beat 502
Stop/True By You	1957	Rush 1042
TICK TOCKS (BOBBY MARCHAN & THE)		
Snoopin' And Accusin'/This Is The Life	1960	Fire 1014
TIDAL WAVES		
Booma Shooma Rock/The Clock (Is Ticking My Life Away)	1961	Tide 0020
You Name It/So I Guess	N/A	Strafford 6503
TIDES (1)		
Rock Me Gently/Stoned	1959	Dore 529
Little Carmen/Smoke Signals	1959	Dore 546
Say You're Mine/Follow Me	1961	Dore 579
Ring A Ding Ding/Dear Mr. President	1961	Dore 611
Ring A Ding Ding/Chicken Spaceman	1961	Dore 618
Limbo Rock/Midnight Limbo	1962	Mercury 71990
Banana Boat Song/Patricia	1962	Mercury 72045
TIDES (2)		
Bring It Home To Me/Who Told You	1961	620 1007
Stranger/Would I Still Be Loving You	1961	Warwick 653
TIERS (JIMMY KEMPER & THE)		
I'm Free To Choose/Lonely For Kathy	1964	Le Mans 002
TIFANOS		
It's Raining/Louisiana	1960	Tifco 822
TIFFANIES (AKA TIFFANYS (2)) (FEMALE)		
He's Good For Me/It's Got To Be A Great Song	1967	KR 120
TIFFANYS (1) (MALE)		
The Pleasure Of Love/Atlanta	1962	Swan 4104
I've Got A Girl/I Don't Dig (Western Movies)	1963	Rockin Robin 1
TIFFANYS (2) (AKA TIFFANIES) (FEMALE)		
Love Me/Happiest Girl In The World	1964	Arctic 101
Please Tell Me/Gossip	1964	MRS 777/Atlantic 2240 (64)
I Feel The Same Way Too/I Just Wanna Boy Or Girl	1965	Josie 942
Take Another Look At Me/Heaven On Earth	1966	Josie 952

Artist / Song	Year	Label
He's Good For Me/It's Got To Be A Great Song	1967	RKO 120
TIFFANYS (3) (CINDY GIBSON & THE) (FEMALE)		
(A Lovely) Summer Night/I'll Always Love You	N/A	General 700
TIGERS (1) (LITTLE JULIAN HERRERA & THE)		
Lonely, Lonely Nights/ In Exchange For Your Love	1956	Dig 118
Symbol Of Heaven/Here In My Arms	1957	Dig 137
I Remember Linda/True Fine Mama	1957	Starla 6
TIGERS (2) (DANNY PEIL & THE)		
Jingle Jump	N/A	Raynard 602
TIGERS (3) (AL TIGRO & THE)		
Yvonne/Do The Zombie	N/A	Cuppy 112
TIGRE LILIES		
Love That Melody/Great Mistake	1959	Gone 5047
TILLIS, CLYDE (& GROUP)		
It Makes No Difference Now/ Just Dreaming	1956	Cash 1054
TILLMAN, BERTHA (& GROUP)		
Oh My Angel/Lovin' Time	1962	Brent 7029
I Wish/(I Believe) Something Funny Is Going On	1962	Brent 7032
TILLMAN, LEE		
Here I Go Again/Tarzan	1962	Sonora 211
TILMAN, MICKEY (& GROUP)		
Dear Mom And Dad/I Have Chosen You	1958	Vee Jay 296
TIMBERLANES (1) (DINO & THE) (DION DIMUCCI BEFORE THE BELMONTS)		
The Chosen Few/Out In Colorado (58)	1957	Mohawk 105/Jubilee 5294
TIMBERLANES (2)		
Wedding Bells/Sweet Dreams	1958	Dragon 101
TIMBERS (1) (RONNIE MARTIN & THE)		
Hey Doc/I'm Thankful	1956	Pilgrim 721
TIMBERS (2) (AKA NOBLES (2))		
Oops Oh Lawdy/Stop Crying	1958	Tee Gee 101/Cupid 1002 (58)
TIME SPINNERS (NICK & THE)		
Chapel Of Dreams/In My Younger Days	1974	Kelway 109
TIME-TONES (AKA TIMETONES)		
Here In My Heart/My Love	1961	Times Square 421 (first pressing)/Relic 538 (65)
In My Heart/My Love	1961	Times Square 421 (second pressing)
TIMETONES (AKA TIME-TONES)		
Pretty, Pretty Girl (The New Beat)/I've Got A Feeling	1961	Atco 6201 (Times Square Productions)/Relic 539 (65)
Sunday Kind Of Love (a capella)/Angels In The Sky (a capella)	1963	Times Square 26/Relic 543 (66)
House Where Lovers Dream (a capella)/Get A Hold Of Yourself (a capella)	1963	Times Square 34/Relic 526 (65)
TINDLEY, GEORGE (& GROUP)		
Close Your Eyes/Heart Of Gold	1961	Herald 558
TINGLES		
Tell Me Now/Rain Rain	1961	Era 3040
TINY TIM (& GROUP)		
Face To Face/By My Side	1959	DeLuxe 6184
TIP TOPS (1) (DAVID LASTIE & THE)		
Jack The Ripper, Pt. 1/Jack The Ripper, Pt. 2 (with Little Sonny)	1962	Chess 1800
TIP TOPS (1) (TINY TIP & THE)		
Say It/Matrimony	1962	Chess 1822
I Said A Prayer/I Found My Love	1962	Scarlet 4129
TIP TOPS (2)		
Oo-Kook-A-Boo/He's A Braggin'	1963	Parkway 868
TIP TOPS (3)		
Rama Lama/Super Soul	1965	Kapp 726
TITANS (AKA VITAMINS)		
Sweet Peach/Free And Easy	1957	Specialty 614
So Hard To Laugh, So Easy To Cry/Rhythm And Blues	1957	Vita 148
G'Wan Home Calypso/Look What You're Doing Baby	1957	Vita 158
Don't You Just Know It?/ Can It Be?	1958	Specialty 625

Artist / Song	Year	Label
Arlene/Love Is a Wonderful Thing	1958	Specialty 632
No Time/Tootin' Tutor	1959	Class 244
Everybody Happy/What Have I Done?	1960	Fidelity 3016
A-Rab/Marquette	1961	Nolta 351
TITANS (AKA VITAMINS) (DON & DEWEY & THE)		
Just A Little Lovin'/When The Sun Has Begun To Shine	1957	Specialty 617
TITONES		
Symbol Of Love/The Movies	1959	Scepter 1206
Symbol Of Love/My Movie Queen (The Movies)	1960	Wand 105
TODDS		
Tennessee/May We Always	1961	Todd 1064
Popsicle/Sugar Hill	1961	Todd 1076
TOKAYS (1)		
Fatty-Boom Bi Laddy/Lost And Found	1952	Bonnie 102
TOKAYS (2)		
Hey Senorita/Baby Baby Baby	1967	Brute 001
TOKENS		
Come Dance With Me/Doom Lang	1984	Starlight 24
TOKENS (1)		
Doom-Lang/Come Dance With Me	1957	Gary 1006/Musictone 1113 (59)
TOKENS (2)		
When I Go To Sleep At Night/ Dry Your Eyes	1961	RCA 7896
Sincerely/When The Summer Is Through	1961	RCA 7925
The Lion Sleeps Tonight/Tina	1961	RCA 7954
Tonight I Fell In Love/I'll Always Love You	1961	Warwick 615
B'wa Nina/Weeping River	1962	RCA 7991
The Riddle/The Big Boat	1962	RCA 8018
La Bamba/A Token Of Love	1962	RCA 8052
The Fly Swatter/Bee Side	1962	RCA 8064
Dream Angel Goodnight/I'll Do My Crying Tomorrow	1962	RCA 8089
A Bird Flies Out Of Sight/Wishing Please Write/I'll Always Love You	1962 1963	RCA 8114 Laurie 3180
Tonight I Met An Angel/Hindu Lullaby	1963	RCA 8148
Hear The Bells/ABC-1-2-3	1963	RCA 8210
A Girl Named Arlene/Swing	1964	B.T. Puppy 500/Music Makers 110
He's In Town/Oh Kathy	1964	B.T. Puppy 502
You're My Girl/Havin' Fun	1964	B.T. Puppy 504
Let's Go To The Drag Strip/ Two Cars	1964	RCA 8309
Nobody But You/Mr. Cupid	1965	B.T. Puppy 505
A Message To The World/ Sylvie Sleepin'	1965	B.T. Puppy 507
Only My Friend/Cattle Call	1965	B.T. Puppy 512
The Bells Of St. Mary/Just One Smile	1965	B.T. Puppy 513
The Three Bells/A Message To The World	1966	B.T. Puppy 516
I Hear The Trumpets Blow/ Don't Cry, Sing Along With The Music	1966	B.T. Puppy 518
Breezy/The Greatest Moments Of A Girl's Life	1966	B.T. Puppy 519
Life Is Groovy/Split	1966	B.T. Puppy 524
Please Say You Want Me/ Get A Job	1966	B.T. Puppy 525
Green Plant/Saloogy	1967	B.T. Puppy 552
Portrait Of My Love/She Comes And Goes	1967	Warner Bros. 5900
It's A Happening World/ How Nice	1967	Warner Bros. 7056
Ain't That Peculiar/Bye, Bye, Bye	1967	Warner Bros. 7099
Till/Poor Man	1968	Warner Bros. 7169
Animal/Bathroom Wall	1968	Warner Bros. 7202
Banana Boat Song/Grandfather	1968	Warner Bros. 7233
The World Is Full Of Wonderful Things/Some People Sleep	1968	Warner Bros. 7255
I'll Do My Crying Tomorrow/ A Girl Named Arlene	1969	B.T. Puppy 563

Artist Song	Year	Label
She Lets Her Hair Down/ Oh To Get Away	1969	Buddah 151
Go Away Little Girl-Young Girl/I Want To Love You	1969	Warner Bros. 7280
I Could Be/End Of The World	1969	Warner Bros. 7323
Don't Worry Baby/Some People Sleep	1970	Buddah 159
Both Sides Now/I Can See You Dancing With Me	1970	Buddah 174
Groovin' To The Music-Sesame Street/Listen To The Words, Listen To The Music	1970	Buddah 187
You And Me/I Like To Throw My Head Back And Sing	1972	Bell 190
Penny Whistle Band/The Lord Can't Do A Solo	1974	Atco 7009
Joshua	N/A	RCA LP 2631
A Boy Without A Girl	N/A	RCA LP 2631
Five Hundred Miles	N/A	RCA LP 2631
Shut Down	N/A	RCA LP 2886
Drag City	N/A	RCA LP 2886
Little Deuce Coupe	N/A	RCA LP 2886
My Candy Apple Vette	N/A	RCA LP 2886
(I'll Remember) In The Still Of The Night	N/A	RCA LP 3685
Gee	N/A	RCA LP 3685
Earth Angel	N/A	RCA LP 3685
A Thousand Miles Away	N/A	RCA LP 3685
You're Nothing But A Girl	N/A	RCA LP 3685
Tonight Tonight	N/A	RCA LP 3685
Life Is But A Dream	N/A	RCA LP 3685
"A" You're Adorable	N/A	RCA LP 3685
TOKENS (2) (AKA MARGO, MARGO, MEDRESS & SIEGEL)		
Needles Of Evergreen/Mr. Snail	1968	Warner Bros. 7183
TOKENS (2) (WITH NEIL SEDAKA)		
While I Dream/I Love My Baby	1958	Melba 104
TOKENS (3) (JOHNNY & THE) (AKA JOHNNY & THE KINGS)		
The Taste Of A Tear/ Never Till Now	1961	Warwick 658
TOKENS (4)		
Oh What A Night/(Hey Hey) Juanita	1961	Date 2737
TOLEDOS		
This Is Our Night/John Smith's Body	1961	Down 2003/End 1094 (61)
TOM CATS (TOM RILEY & THE)		
Fools Rush In	N/A	Time 6603
TONE DEAFS (DEAN BARLOW & THE)		
Night Before Last	N/A	Beltone
TONES (1)		
Paula Is Mine/A Love Such As You	1962	Elmar 6001
TONES (2) (LITTLE SAMMY & THE) (AKA LITTLE SAMMY ROZZI & THE GUYS)		
Christine/Over The Rainbow	1962	Pelham 722/Jaclyn 1161 (62)
TONES (3) (W. WILLIAMS & THE)		
A Star/Peanut Man	N/A	Kennedy 5146
TONETTES (AKA CLAREMONTS) (FEMALE)		
Tonight You Belong To Me/ Don't Fall In Love Too Soon	1956	Modern 997
Oh What A Baby/Howie	1958	Doe 101/ABC 9905 (58)
He Loves Me, He Loves Me Not/Uh-Oh	1958	Doe 103
Please Don't Go/No Tears	1962	Volt 101
Stolen Angel/Teardrop Sea	1963	Volt 104
Rockabye Baby	1989	Relic LP 5081
TOP HANDS (JOE DEE & HIS)		
Honky-Tonk Guitar/Blind Heart	1962	Pat Riccio 105
Some Of These Nights/I Thought I Heard You Calling My Name	1962	Pat Riccio 1107
TOP HANDS (JOE DEE & HIS) (WITH THE TREMONTS)		
Believe My Heart/Legend Of Love	1962	Pat Riccio 101
TOP HITS		
Thum-A-Lum-A/Love No One	1961	Norman 504
TOP KICKS		
Don't Break The Heart That Loves You/Boodlya Botten Baby	1954	Guyden 706
TOP NOTES		
Wonderful Time/Walkin' With Love	1960	Atlantic 2066
Say Man/Warm Your Heart	1960	Atlantic 2080
Hearts Of Stone/The Basic Things	1961	Atlantic 2097

Artist Song	Year	Label
Always Late (Why Lead Me On)/ Twist And Shout	1961	Atlantic 2115
Come Back, Cleopatra/Wait For Me Baby	1962	Festival 1021
It's Alright/I Love You So Much	1963	ABC 10399
TOPICS (AKA FRANKIE VALLI & THE FOUR SEASONS)		
The Girl In My Dreams/(no flip)	1962	Perri 1007
TOPICS (BILLY DIXON & THE) (AKA FRANKIE VALLI & THE FOUR SEASONS)		
I Am All Alone/Trance	1960	Topix 6002/Seasons 4 Ever
Lost Lullabye/Trance	1961	Topix 6008
TOPPERS (1) (BOBBY MITCHELL & THE)		
I'm Crying/Rack'Em Back	1953	Imperial 5236
One Friday Morning/4 x 11 = 44	1953	Imperial 5250
Baby's Gone/Sister Lucy	1954	Imperial 5270
Angel Child/School Boy Blues	1954	Imperial 5282
Wedding Bells Are Ringing/ Meant For Me	1954	Imperial 5295
I'm A Young Man/She Couldn't Be Found	1954	Imperial 5309
I Cried/I'm In Love	1955	Imperial 5346
I Tried So Hard/Goin' Round In Circles	1956	Imperial 5392
One Friday Morning/4-11+44	1973	Aladdin 5250
TOPPERS (2)		
I Love You, I Love You/ Bow-Legged Boy	1954	Avalon 63707
Baby Let Me Bang Your Box/ You're Laughing 'Cause I'm Crying	1954	Jubilee 5136
Honey, Honey/George Washington	1956	ABC 9667
Lonely/Three Roads	1956	ABC 9759
TOPPERS (3)		
Tell Me Why/All Around	1962	Stacy 927
TOPPIKS		
Give It A Chance To Grow	N/A	Larsam
TOPPS		
What Do You Do? (To Make Me Love You So)/Tippin'	1954	Red Robin 126
I've Got A Feeling/Won't You Come Home, Baby?	1954	Red Robin 131
Young Girls	N/A	Red Robin (unreleased)
Ain't It Good (Mmm, Baby I Love You So)	N/A	Red Robin (unreleased)
TOPS (1)		
An Innocent Kiss/Walkin' With My Baby	1957	Singular 712
TOPS (2) (LITTLE JIMMY RIVERS & THE)		
Puppy Love/Say You Love Me	1961	Len 1011/Swan 4091 (61)/V-Tone 102 (61)
TOPSIDERS		
Let The Good Times Roll	1963	Josie 907
TOPSY, TINY (BB THE FIVE CHANCES)		
Aw! Shucks Baby/Miss You So	1957	Federal 12303
You Shocked Me/Waterproof Eyes	1958	Federal 12315
TORCHES (AKA DIADEMS)		
Darn Your Love/No I Won't	1965	Ring-O 302
TOREADORS		
Do You Remember/Do You Remember Pt. 2	N/A	Midas 1001
TORKAYS (LITTLE DENNY & THE)		
Rock And Roll Blues	N/A	Perri 1
She's Everybody's Darling/ I'd Love To Take You Walking	N/A	Perri 2
TORMENTORS		
Didn't It Rain	1962	Kerwood 712
TORNADOS (1) (STANLEY MITCHELL & THE)		
Four O'Clock In The Morning/ Would You, Could You	1956	Chess 1649
TORNADOS (2)		
Genie In The Jug/Love In Your Life	1959	Bumble Bee 503
Clap Your Hands And Skate	N/A	Winley 2017
TORNADOS (2) (JOHNNY MANN & THE)		
Breaker Of Dreams/Chick-A-Lou	1958	Donnie 27746
TORNADOS (3) (AARON MCNEIL & THE)		
Without Romance/Carolyn	1960	C.J. 615
TOTS (BARRY & THE)		
I'm A Happy Little Christmas Tree/Christmas Each Day Of The Year	1961	Fury 1058

Artist Song	Year	Label
TOUGHTONES (BOBBY SANDERS & THE)		
It Was You/I'm On My Way	1961	Kaybo 60618
TOWERS (JIMMY & THE)		
One More Chance/The Meaning Of Love	N/A	Debann 102
TOWNSMEN (1)		
It's Time/Little Jeanie	1960	Vanity 579/580
TOWNSMEN (2) (FB LOUIE LYMON)		
I Can't Go/That's All I'll Ever Need	1963	PJ 1340/1341
TOWNSMEN (3)		
Moonlight Was Made For Lovers/ I'm In The Mood For Love	1962	Joey 6202
Is It All Over/Just A Little Bit	1963	Herald 585
Please Don't Say Goodbye/ Gotta Get Moving	1964	Columbia 43207
TOY DOLLS (FEMALE)		
Little Tin Soldier/Fly Away	1962	Era 3093
TR 4		
Never Too Young	1966	Velvet Tone
TRA-VELLES (FEMALE)		
Can't Go For That/Little Bad Wolf	N/A	Debonair 101
TRADEWINDS (RUDY & THE)		
Careless Love/Unemployed	1962	Angle Tone 543
TRADITIONS		
The Wind (acapella)/Once In A While (acapella)	1965	Fellatio 102
Forever And Always/I Gott Go (by the Ditalians)	1996	Savoy 2004
TRAILBLAZERS (SHIRLEE HUNTER & THE)		
Hot Blood/Allentown Jail	1959	Tip Top 720
TRAINS		
We Two/The Plan	1964	Swan 4196
Fourteen And Getting Older/ The Beware Song	1964	Swan 4203
TRAMMELL, BOBBY LEE (& GROUP)		
You Mostest Girl/Uh Oh	1958	Radio 102/Fabor 127 (64)
TRAMPS		
Ride On/You're a Square	1959	Arvee 548
Your Love/Midnight Flyer	1959	Arvee 570
TRANELLS		
Come On And Tell Me/The Music Swayed	1956	Chelten 090
TRAVELERS (1)		
Go Away/Why Darling Why	1953	Okeh 6959
TRAVELERS (2) (FB FRANK LOPEZ)		
Lenora/Betty Jean	1957	Atlas 1086
Love Is All I Crave	1973	Relic LP 5012
TRAVELERS (3)		
I'll Be Home For Christmas/ Katie The Kangaroo	1958	Andex 2011
Why/Teen Age Machine Age	1958	Andex 4006
He's Got The Whole World In His Hands/Green Town Girl	1958	Andex 4012
I'll Always Be In Love With You/ I Go For You	1959	Andex 4033
Rock Me Baby/Girl In The Bikini	1959	MGM 928
June, July, August And September/What A Weekend	1960	ABC 10119
Ivy On The Old School Wall/ Cadwallader	1961	Decca 31215
Oh My Love (Love Me)/White Rose	1961	Decca 31282
Seven Minutes Till Four/Traveler	1962	Don Ray 5965
Tie Me Surfer Board Down, Sport/In The Pines	1963	Gass 1000
She's Got The Blues/Spanish Moon	1963	Princess 52/Vault 911
Windy And Warm/Last Date	1963	Yellow Sand 2
Malibu Sunset/Hang On	1965	Yellow Sand 452
TRAVELERS (4) (ROGER & THE)		
To Be My Love/Smile	1978	Crystal Ball 128
TRAVELERS (4) (ROGER & THE) (AKA PREMIERS (4))		
You're Daddy's Little Girl/ Just Gotta Be That Way	1961	Ember 1079
TRAVELERS (5)		
Too Young/Twist In School	1961	World Wide 8511
TRAVELLERS (1) (FRANKIE VALLEY & THE) (FEATURING FRANKIE VALLI)		
Somebody Else Took Her Home/Forgive And Forget	1954	Mercury 70381
TRAVELLERS (2) (RONNIE CATES & THE)		
Old Man River/Long Time	1962	Terrace 7501
TRAVIS, DANNY (& GROUP)		
Ever Since/Bye-Bye-Baby	1962	Benn-X 54
TREASURERS		
The Story Of Love/I Walk With An Angel	1961	Crown 005
TREASURES (1) (PETE ANDERS & THE) (AKA VIDELS)		
Hold Me Tight/Pete Meets Vinnie (instrumental)	1964	Shirley 500
TREASURES (2) (BONNIE & THE)		
Home Of The Brave/Our Song	1965	Phi-Dan 5005
TREBELAIRES (FEMALE)		
I Gotta/There Goes The Train	1955	Nestor 16
TREBELS		
Oh Darlin'/My Little Girl	1963	Viking 1021
TREBLE CHORDS		
Theresa/My Little Girl	1959	Decca 31015
Without Your Love/Little Louie	N/A	Decca (unreleased)
TRECKLES (AKA TRICKELS)		
With Each Step A Tear/ Outside The Chapel Door	1959	Gone 5078
TRELLS		
I'm Sorry/Bad Weather	N/A	Port City 1112
TREM-LOS		
Walkin' Along/Silly Affair	1961	Nolta 350
TREMAINES		
Jingle, Jingle/Moon Shining Bright	1958	Cash 100/101/Val 100/101 (58)/Old Town 1051(58)
TREMONTS (1) (WITH JOEY DEE & THE TOP HANDS)		
Believe My Heart/Legend Of Love	1961	Brunswick 55217/Pat Riccio 101 (62)
TREMONTS (2)		
Merry-Go-Round Love (a capella)	1975	Relic LP 104
I Hear The Wind (a capella)	1975	Relic LP 104
TREN-DELLS (AKA TREND-ELS)		
Hully Gully Jones/Nite Owl	1962	Jam 1100/Capitol 4852 (62)
Ain't That Funny/Mr. Doughnut Man	1963	Sound Stage 7 2508
Everyday/I'll Be There	1964	Southtown 22001
That's My Desire/Let's Go Steady For The Summer	1965	Boss 9921
TREN-TEENS		
My Baby's Gone/Your Yah Yah Is Gone	1964	Carnival 501
TREND-ELS (AKA TREN-DELLS)		
I'm So Young/Don't You Hear Me Calling, Baby	1961	Tilt 779
I Miss You So/Moments Like This	1962	Tilt 788
TREND-TONES (AKA PARADONS)		
This Is Love/Never Again	1959	Superb 100
TRENDS		
I'll Be True/Class Ring	1959	Argo 5341/Clover 1002
Silly Grin/Once Again	1959	Scope 102
Chug-A-Lug/The Beard	1960	RCA 7733
TRENEY, JOEY (& GROUP)		
Why Walk Alone/This I Declare	1961	Magenta 05
TRENTONS (AKA SHY-TONES/AKA HI-TONES)		
All Alone/Star Bright	1962	Shepherd 2204
TRETONES		
Blind Date/Cool Baby	1960	B-W 604
TREVOR, VAN (BB THE FOUR SEASONS)		
C'Mon Now Baby	1963	Vivid 1004
TREYS		
Come To Me/Sugar Baby	1959	Bella 16
TREYS (WES GRIFFIN & THE)		
It Hurts So Bad/Rockin' Mary	1959	Bella 17
TREYTONES		
Dreamlover	N/A	Sunliner
TRI-DELLS		
Baby I Love You So/Little Do I Know	1960	Eldo 104
TRI-FIVE (JOHN LYTHGOE & THE)		
Jeannie, Joanie, Shirley/ Oh Baby	1961	Varbee 2002
TRI-LADS		
Cherry Pie/Always Be True		58Bullseye 1003
TRI-TONES (1) (AL BARKLE & THE)		
Teenage Angel/The Signal	1957	Vita 171

Artist Song	Year	Label
With This Ring/Sputnik II	1957	Vita 173
TRI-TONES (2)		
Teardrops/Everytime I Think Of You	1964	Miss Julie 6501
TRIADS		
One More Kiss/Nickelodian Tango	1956	Encino 1002
TRIANGLE		
Jacqueline/Your Love Comes Shinin' Through	1970	Paramount 0055
TRIANGLES		
Savin' My Love/'Tis A Pity	1960	Herald 549
Dance The Magoo/Step Up And Go	1962	Fargo 1023
My Oh My/Really I Do	1964	Fifo 107
TRIBUNES		
The Code Of Love/Now That You're Gone	1962	Derrick 502
TRICKELS (AKA TRECKLES)		
With Each Step A Tear/When I Fall In Love	1959	Gone 5078/Power 250 (59)
TRICKS		
My One Desire/Someone Like You	1959	Jane 108
TRIDELS		
Land Of Love/Image Of Love	1964	San-Dee 1009
TRILONS		
I'm The One/Forever	1961	Tag 449
TRINIDADS		
Don't Say Goodbye/On My Happy Way	1959	Formal 1005
One Lonely Night/When We're Together	1959	Formal 1006
TRINITIES (KAYO & THE)		
Kathy Jo/Walking To School With My Love	1960	Souvenir 1004
TRINKETS (1)		
Little Boy/You Can't Be Trusted	1958	Imperial 5497
TRINKETS (2) (AKA VERSALETTES) (FEMALE)		
Fisherman/Nobody But You	1963	Cortland 111
TRIOTONES		
Valerie Jo/Tired Of Being A Little Boy	1959	Intrastate 43
TRIPLETS		
Gently My Love/Bagdad Beat	1960	Dore 574
TRIPPERS		
Charlena/Taking Care Of Business	1967	Ruby-Doo 5
TRITONES (1)		
Sweet And Lovely/Blues In The Closet	1955	Grand 126/Jamie 1035 (57)
TRITONES (2) (TERRY & THE)		
Patty	N/A	Kaybee
TRIUMPHS (TICO & THE) (FB PAUL SIMON)		
I'm Lonely/I Wish I Weren't In Love (by Jerry Landis)	1961	Canadian American 130
Motorcycle/I Don't Believe Them	1961	Madison 169/Amy 835 (61)
Express Train/Wildflower	1962	Amy 845
Cry, Little Boy, Cry/Get Up And Do The Wonder	1962	Amy 860
Cards Of Love/Noise	1963	Amy 876/Jason Scott 14 (81)
TROJANS (1) (AKA FIVE TROJANS)		
As Long As I Have You/I Wanna Make Love To You	1955	RPM 466
Make It Up/The Man I'm Gonna Be	1958	Felsted 8534
Don't Ask Me To Be Lonely/Alone In This World	1958	Tender 516
TROJANS (2)		
All Night Long/I Wanted You So Long	1960	Triangle 51317
Just About Daybreak/Just Got Up	1961	Dodge 804
Medley (Cherry Pie/What's Your Name/A Thousand Miles Away/We Belong Together/Talk To Me)/Diamonds & Pearls	1966	Air Town 003/Air Town 70971
TROJANS (3) (FB HENRY CLEMENT)		
I'll Be Waiting/Trojan's Walls	1961	Zynn 1006
TROOPERS		
My Resolution/Get Out	1957	Lamp 2009

Artist Song	Year	Label
TROOPERS (GEORGE POWELL & THE)		
My Choice For A Mate/In That Order	1959	Lummtone 101
TROPHIES		
Desire/Doggone It	1961	Challenge 9133
Peg O' My Heart/I Laughed So Hard I Cried	1962	Challenge 9149
Felicia/That's All I Want From You	1962	Challenge 9170
Walkin' The Dog/Somethin' Else	N/A	Nork 79907
TROPICALS		
Sweet Sixteen	N/A	Specialty
TROPICS (EDDIE & THE)		
We've Got Something/Don't Monkey With Another Monkey's Monkey	1965	Josie 930
TROUPERS		
Peter, Peter, Pumpkin Eater/Non-Support	1959	Red Top 118/Clifton 8 (74)
Peter, Peter Pumpkin Eater/Non-Support	1974	Clifton 8
TROY, RICKY (& GROUP)		
Linda	1963	Cavetone 511
TROYS		
Ding-A-Ling-A-Ling/The Cling	1959	Okeh 7120
TRU TONES		
Darling I'm Sorry/Surfin' Here We Go	N/A	Tree
Tears In My Eyes/Magic	1957	Chart 634
TRU-TONES (TERRY CLEMENT & THE)		
Teenage Rock/Sugar G	1959	Rocko 517
TRUE LOVES (AKA LOVENOTES (1))		
A Love Like Ours/Never Look Behind	1957	Premium 411
TRUE TONES		
Never Had A Chance/Lovin' From My Baby	1964	Spot 1115
That's Love/He's Got The Nerve	1965	Soulville/Josie 950 (65)/Josie 1003 (69)
Little Hit And Run Darling/La Lala Lala	1965	Spot 1121
TRUELEERS		
Forget About Him/Waiting For You	1963	Checker 1026
TRUETONES		
Honey, Honey/Whirlwind	1958	Monument 4501
Blushing Bride/Singing Waters	1961	Felsted 8625
TU-TONES		
Saccharin Sally/Still In Love With You	1959	Lin 5021
TUCKER, FRANK (& GROUP)		
Nobody But Me/Hey Hester	1956	Baton 234
TUCKER, FRANKIE (& GROUP)		
Fools Will Be Fools/Good Googley Woo	1958	Decca 30707
TUGGLE, BOBBY (& GROUP)		
The $64,000 Question/(flip has no group)	1955	Checker 823
I Wonder/I Know She Loves Me	1956	Checker 840
TUNE BLENDERS		
Oh, Yes, I Know/Shoo-Shoo	1954	Federal 12201
TUNE DROPS		
Rosie Lee/Speak For Yourself	1957	Gone 5003
Smoothie/Jumpin' Jellybeans (instrumental)	1959	Gone 5072
TUNE DROPS (MALCOLM DODDS & THE)		
It Took A Long Time/Beauty And The Beast	1957	End 1000
Fools Rush In/Can't You See	1957	End 1004
Tonight/Unspoken Love	1957	End 1010
Your Voice/The Swingin' Platoon	1958	Decca 30653
TUNE TAILORS		
Beverly/My First Love	1958	Century 4158
TUNE TIMERS		
Thinking/What Have I Got To Dream About	1955	Okeh 7081
TUNE TONES (1)		
Little Sandy/Please Baby, Please	1958	Herald 524
She's Right With Me/Lonesome Soul	1959	Herald 539

Artist Song	Year	Label
TUNE TONES (2) (FB TERRY CLEMENT)		
Jacqueline/French Blues	1961	Zynn 1007
TUNE WEAVERS		
Happy Happy Birthday Baby/		
Ol' Man River	1957	Casa Grande 4037/Checker 872 (57)
I Remember Dear/Pamela Jean	1957	Casa Grande 4038
Happy Happy Birthday Baby/		
Yo Yo Walk (instrumental		
by Paul Gayten)	1957	Checker 872
Ol' Man River/Tough Enough		
(instrumental by Paul Gayten)	1957	Checker 880
Little Boy/Look Down That		
Lonesome Road	1958	Casa Grande 101
There Stands My Love/I'm Cold	1958	Casa Grande 4040
My Congratulations, Baby/		
This Can't Be Love	1960	Casa Grande 3038
Your Skies Of Blue/		
Congratulations On Your		
Birthday	1962	Checker 1007
I Hear Mission Bells	N/A	Casa Grande (unreleased)
Think And Cry	N/A	Casa Grande (unreleased)
TUNE WEAVERS (MARGO SYLVIA & THE)		
Come Back To Me/I've Tried	1988	Classic Artists 104
Merry Merry Christmas Baby/		
What Are You Doing New		
Years Eve	1988	Classic Artists 107
TUNEBLENDERS		
I Thank Heaven/I'm In Love		
With You	1958	Play 1002
TUNEMASTERS (GM ARLENE SMITH)		
Sending This Letter/It's All Over	1957	Mark-X 7002
Tasty Kisses/Once A Heart		
(by the Millionaires)	1990	Mark-X 7010
TUNEMASTERS (WILLIE WILSON & ARLENE SMITH & THE)		
Sending You This Letter/		
I've Lied	1958	End 1011
TUNEROCKERS		
No Stoppin' This Boppin'	1958	Pet 804
TUNES		
The Lie/Only Time Will Tell	1959	Pel 101/Pel 345 (59)
My Heart/Close The Door	1959	Swade 102
TUNESTERS		
Casually/Wykiup	1959	Tiara 6129
TUNISIANS (TERRY & THE)		
The Street/Tom-Tom	1963	Seville 131
TURBANS		
When You Dance/Let Me Show		
You (Around My Heart)	1955	Herald 458
No No Cherry/Tick Tock A-Woo	1955	Money 209
The Nest Is Warm/Tick		
Tock A-Woo	1955	Money 209
When I Return/Emily		
(by the Turks)	1955	Money 211
Sister Sookey/I'll Always		
Watch Over You	1956	Herald 469
I'm Nobody's/B.I.N.G.O. (Bingo)	1956	Herald 478
It Was A Night Like This/All		
Of My Love	1956	Herald 486
Valley Of Tears/Bye And Bye	1957	Herald 495
Congratulations/The Wadda Doo	1957	Herald 510
I Promise You Love/Curfew		
Time	1959	Red Top 115
Diamonds And Pearls/Bad Man	1960	Roulette 4281
Six Questions/The Lament Of		
Silver Gulch	1961	Imperial 5807
When You Dance/Golden Rings	1961	Parkway 820
I'm Not Your Fool Anymore/		
Three Friends (Two Lovers)	1961	Roulette 4326
This Is My Story/Clicky Clicky		
Clack	1962	Imperial 5828
I Wonder/The Damage Is Done	1962	Imperial 5847
TURBO JETS (CLIFF DAVIS & THE)		
Rock & Roll/Back Mountain Rock	1959	Federal 12366
TURKS (AKA HOLLYWOOD FLAMES)		
Emily/When I Return (by the		
Turbans)	1955	Money 211
This Heart Of Mine/Why Did		
You?	1956	Bally 1017
I'm A Fool/I've Been Accused	1956	Money 215
It Can't Be True/Wagon Wheels		
(by the Hollywood Flames)	1957	Cash 1042
Fathertime/Okay	191958	Keen 4016
It Can't Be True/I'm A Fool (61)	1958	Knight 2005/Imperial 5783
Emily/My Soul (by the Seniors)	1959	Ball 001
Hully Gully/Rockville, U.S.A.	1959	Class 256
Emily/Going Back Home	1960	Ball 101
Dianne/Baja	N/A	P.B.D. 112
TURN ONS (TIM TAM & THE)		
Wait A Minute/Opelia	1966	Palmer 5002
Cheryl Ann/Seal It With A Kiss	1966	Palmer 5003
Kimberly/I Leave You In Tears	1966	Palmer 5006
Don't Say Hi/Don't Say Hi		
(instrumental)	1967	Palmer 5014
TURNER, BENNIE (& GROUP)		
I Want To Know	N/A	Skyline 1005
TURNER, IKE (& GROUP)		
My Love/That's All I Need	1959	Sue 722
TUXEDO SLEEPERS (JAMES CARTER & THE)		
I Want To Love You/Jail Wall	1960	Tuxedo 938
TUXEDOS		
Yes It's True/Trouble, Trouble	1960	Forte 1414
TWAINS (TOMMY SAWYER & THE)		
How Deep Is The Ocean/		
15th Row Down	1962	Diamond 112
TWI-LIGHTERS (AKA TWILITERS (1))		
Sittin' In A Corner/It's A Cold,		
Cold, Rainy Day	1956	Groove 0154
TWI-LITES		
Just Can't Let Her Go	N/A	Spenada 101
TWIGGS (HUGH BELL & THE)		
Breaking The Ice	1954	Blaze 109
TWIGGS (MAL HOGAN & THE)		
Till The Sun Stops Shining/		
Pretty Please	1954	Blaze 108
TWIGS (SONNY WOODS & THE)		
Chapel Of Memories/		
Song Of India	1954	Hollywood 1015
Wonderful World/Lover Boy	1954	Hollywood 1026
TWILIGHTERS (1)		
Please Tell Me You're Mine/		
Wondering	1953	Marshall 702
TWILIGHTERS (2) (BUDDY MILTON & THE)		
Please Understand/		
Say Another Word	1954	RPM 418/Cadet
O-O-Wah/I'm The Child	1954	RPM 419
TWILIGHTERS (3)		
Little Did I Dream/Gotta Get		
On The Train	1955	MGM 55011
Lovely Lady/Half Angel	1955	MGM 55014
It's True/Wah-Bop-Sh-Wah	1955	Specialty 548
I Believe/Eternally	1956	Caddy 103/Dot 15526 (56) /Pla-Bac 1113
Pride And Joy/Live Like A King	1957	Ebb 117
How Many Times?/Water-Water	1957	J.V.B. 83
Let There Be Love/Eternally	1958	Cholly 712
She Needs A Guy/Scratchin'	1960	Chess 1803
Yes You Are/A Possibility	1960	Spin 0001
Helene	1960	Spin-It 202
Sit Right Down And Cry/		
Please Come Home	1960	Super 1003
Nothin'/Do You Believe	1961	Eldo 115
To Love In Vain/The Beginning		
Of Love	1961	Fraternity 889/Saxony 2003
Help Me/Rockin' Mule	1961	Ricki 907
My Silent Prayer/Little Bitty		
Bed Bug	1962	Bubble 1334
Sweet Mule/My Beatle Haircut	1964	Roulette 4546
I Need Your Lovin'/Out Of		
My Mind	1968	Vanco 204
TWILIGHTERS (3) (TONY ALLEN & THE)		
Just Like Before/Come-A,		
Come-A, Baby	1961	Bethlehem 3002
It Hurts Me So/The Trakey-Doo	1962	Bethlehem 3004
TWILIGHTERS (4) (TONY & THE) (AKA ANTHONY & THE SOPHOMORES)		
Be My Girl/Did You Make Up		
Your Mind	1960	Jalynne 106/Red Top
Key To My Heart/Yes Or No	1960	Red Top 127/Arcade 1003 (77)
Gee, But I'd Give The World	N/A	Red Top
I Promise To Remember	N/A	Red Top
TWILIGHTERS (5)		
I Wonder Who's Calling/		
Don't Stop Baby	1974	Roadhouse 1014

Artist Song	Year	Label
TWILIGHTS (1) (JAMES CARTER & THE)		
I'm Falling For You/Wild Hog	1956	Tuxedo 917
Get Hep Little Girl/Wild Hog Baby	1959	Tuxedo 932
TWILIGHTS (1) (PHYLLIS BRANCH & THE)		
Calypso Fever/Babalu	1957	Tuxedo 919
TWILIGHTS (2) (AKA EMBERS (9))		
Oh Baby Love/My Heart Belongs To Only You	1959	Finesse 1717
It's Been So Long/For The First Time	1964	Harthon 135
TWILIGHTS (3) (TONY RICHARDS & THE)		
Please Believe In Me/Paper Boy	1960	Colpix 178
Summer's Coming/Shout My Name	1961	Colpix 199
TWILIGHTS (4) (TEDDY & THE)		
Woman Is A Man's Best Friend/Goodbye To Love	1962	Swan 4102
You Gotta Be Alone To Cry/Running Around Town	1962	Swan 4115
I'm Just Your Clown/Bimini Bimbo	1962	Swan 4126
TWILIGHTS (5)		
It Could Be True/Sum'pin Else	1962	Twilight 1028
Bohemian/Little Richard	1963	6 Star 1001/1002
Shipwreck/For The First Time	1967	Parkway 128
TWILIGHTS (5) (HELEN SIMON & THE)		
Believe It Or Not/Living Letter	1963	Felice 713
TWILIGHTS (6)		
I Think I'm Going To Fall In Love With You/I Have The Right	N/A	Select 742
TWILITERS (1) (AKA TWI-LIGHTERS)		
Sittin' In A Corner/It's A Cold, Cold, Rainy Day	1961	Groove 0154
TWILITERS (2)		
Infatuation/Til I Waltz Again With You	1961	Flippin' 106
Hey There/Caused By You	1961	Nix 102
Love Bandit/Back To School	1961	Nix 103
Sweet Lips/You Better Make It	1964	Paloma 100
TWILITERS (3) (RON HOLDEN & THE)		
Ya Got That Lovin' Touch/Things Don't Happen That Way	1962	Baronet 3
TWIN TONES (AKA TWINS)		
He Pretty Girl/How Can I Win Your Love	1955	Atlantic 1064
The Flip-Skip/My Dear	1958	RCA 7148
Joanne's Sister/Who Knows The Secret	1958	RCA 7235
TWIN TUNES		
I'll Make You Mine/Japanese Rhumba	1955	Sound 115
TWINETTES		
Let The People Talk/I'm So Glad	1958	Vee Jay 284
TWINKLE TONES (JIMMIE HOMBS & THE)		
Poor Boys Dream/Joe Cool	1959	Jack Bee 1001
Ask The Stars/Voo Doo Dolly (by the Invictas & Hollywood Rebels with Jimmie Hombs)	1959	Jack Bee 1004
TWINKLES (FEMALE) (AKA STOREY SISTERS)		
Bad Motorcycle/Sweet Daddy	1958	Peak 5001
Fairy Tales/Oh, Little Star	1963	Musicor 1031
TWINKLETONES (ROCKY STORM & THE)		
Should I/My Baby Left Me Swingin'	1958	Josie 847
TWINTONES		
Most Of All/Bumpity Road To Love	1960	Banner 60203
TWISTERS (1) (SAMMY TURNER & THE)		
Thunderbolt/Sweet Annie Laurie	1958	Big Top 3007
TWISTERS (2)		
Count Down 1-2-3/Speed Limit	1959	Felco 103
Come Go With Me/Pretty Little Girl Next Door	1960	Apt 25045
Dancing Little Clown/Turn The Page	1960	Capitol 4451
Elvis Leaves Sorrento/Street Dance	1961	Campus 125
Please Come Back/This Is The End	1961	Sunset 501
TWISTERS (3) (JOEY & THE)		
Peppermint Twist/Silly Chili	1961	Dual 502
Bony Moronie/Mumblin'	1962	Dual 505
Do You Want To Dance/Last Dance	1962	Dual 509
TWO JAYS (JIMMY ALLEN &)		
My Girl Is A Pearl/Forgive Me, My Darling	1959	Al-Brite 1200
TWYLIGHTS		
Darling Let's Fall In Love/I'm Gonna Try	1961	Rock'n 102
TYCE, NAPOLEON (& GROUP)		
Sitting Here/Paper Doll	1960	Norwood 105
TYCOON		
Silent Night/White Christmas	1985	Starlight 27
She Is Mine/Pucker Your Lips	1985	Starlight 28
Your Promise To Me Mine/Together	1985	Starlight 31
Would I Be Crying/Your Love	1986	Starlight 33
TYLER, FRANKIE (REF FRANKIE VALLI & THE FOUR SEASONS)		
I Go Ape/If You Care	N/A	Seasons 4 Ever
TYMES		
The Magic Of Our Summer Love/With All My Heart	1964	Parkway 919
The Twelfth Of Never/Here She Comes	1964	Parkway 933
That Old Black Magic	1964	Parkway LP 7032
Way Beyond Today	1964	Parkway LP 7032
Alone	1964	Parkway LP 7032
Goodnight My Love	1964	Parkway LP 7032
Summer Day	1964	Parkway LP 7032
You Asked Me To Be Yours	1964	Parkway LP 7032
Autumn Leaves	1964	Parkway LP 7032
Let's Make Love Tonight	1964	Parkway LP 7032
Hello Young Lovers	1964	Parkway LP 7038
Chances Are	1964	Parkway LP 7038
Blue Velvet	1964	Parkway LP 7038
I'm Always Chasing Rainbows	1964	Parkway LP 7039
Isle Of Love	1964	Parkway LP 7039
So In Love/Roscoe James McClain	1963	Parkway 871A (first pressing)
So Much In Love/Roscoe James McClain	1963	Parkway 871C (second pressing)
Wonderful! Wonderful!/Come With Me To The Sea	1963	Parkway 884
Somewhere/View From My Window	1963	Parkway 891
To Each His Own/Wonderland Of Love	1964	Parkway 908
Here She Comes/Malibu	1964	Parkway 924
Tyrants (Terry & the)Weep No More/Yea, Yea, Yea, Yea, Yea, Yea	61	Kent 399
TYRONES		
Year Round Love/My Rock 'N' Roll Baby	1956	Mercury 70939
The Campus Rock/(She Wants) Candy And Flowers	1956	Wing 90072
Street Of Memories/Pink Champagne	1957	Mercury 71104
Giggles/Broke Down, Baby	1958	Decca 30559
I'm Shook/Blast Off	1958	Decca 30643
TYSON, ROY (& GROUP)		
Oh What A Night For Love/Not Too Young To Sing The Blues	1963	Double L 723
The Girl I Love/I Want To Be Your Boyfriend	1963	Double L 733
U.S. FOUR		
Make Up Your Mind/Please Don't Stay Away Too Long	1962	Heritage 110
UBANS		
Gloria/On The Bridge	1964	Radiant 102
ULTIMATES (1)		
Lonely Night/I Can Tell You Love Me Too	1961	Envoy 2302
ULTIMATES (2)		
Lost Romance/Foreign Girl (by the Gallant Men)	1962	Ford 117
ULTIMATIONS		
Would I Do It Over	N/A	Marvlus 6020
ULTRATONES		
Restless/Chain Reaction	1960	San Tana 101
Locomotion/Sister Of The Girl I Once Loved	1962	Cary 2001

Artist	Song	Year	Label
UNBELIEVABLES			
	Ring Rang Roe/There's A Little Bit Of Heaven	1965	Era 3155
UNDERBEATS			
	Sweet Words Of Love/Annie Do The Dog	1964	Bangar 00632
	Foot Stompin'/Route 66	1964	Garret 4004
	Book Of Love/Darling Lorraine	1966	Soma 1449
	Shake It For Me/I Can't Stand It	1966	Soma 1458
UNEEKS			
	Look At Me/(flip is instrumental)	1960	Toledo 1501
UNFORGETTABLES			
	Was It All Right/It Hurts	1961	Colpix 192
	Oh Wishing Well/Daddy Must Be A Man	1961	Pamela 204
	He'll Be Sorry/Oh There He Goes	1963	Titanic 5012
UNFORGETTABLES (LITTLE JOHN & THE)			
	Funny What A Little Kiss Can Do/Little Mary	1962	Alan-K 6901
UNIQUE ECHOS			
	Zoom/Italian Twist (instrumental)	1961	Southern Sound 108
UNIQUE TEENS			
	Watcha Know New?/Run Fast	1957	Dynamic 110/Relic 518 (64)
	Jeannie/At The Ball	1958	Ivy 112/Hanover 4510 (58)
UNIQUES (1) (GM EARL KING)			
	Somewhere/Right Now	1957	Peacock 1677
	Mysterious/Picture Of My Baby	1960	Peacock 1695
UNIQUES (10)			
	After New Year's Eve/Kiss, Kiss, Kiss	1981	Clifton 62
UNIQUES (2)			
	Tell The Angels/Hey, Little Cupid	1958	End 1012
	I'm So Unhappy/I'm Confessin'	1960	Bliss 1004/Gone 5113 (61)
	I'm So Unhappy/It's Got To Come From Your Heart	1960	Pride 1018/Gone 5113 (61)/Pride 4
	One Million Miles Away/All At Once	1962	Tee Kay 112
UNIQUES (2) (SABBY LEWIS & THE)			
	Bwana/Sabby	1959	Gone 5074
UNIQUES (3)			
	That's Love/I Cross My Fingers	1959	World Pacific 808
	Fast Way Of Living/Not Too Long Ago	1965	Paula 219
UNIQUES (4)			
	Let Me Weep, Let Me Cry/I've Got A Secret	1959	C-Way 2676
UNIQUES (5)			
	Look At Me/Bossa Nova Cha Cha	1960	Mr. Cee 100
UNIQUES (6)			
	Silvery Moon/Chocolate Bar	1962	Lucky Four 1024
UNIQUES (7)			
	Do You Remember/Come Marry Me	1959	Flippin' 202
	Blue Skies/Loving You	1963	Capitol 4949
	Merry Christmas Darling/Rockin' Rudolph	1963	Demand 2936
	Times Change/Allright Okay You Win	1963	Demand 2940
	Send Him To Me/This Little Boy Of Mine	1963	Roulette 4528
UNIQUES (8)			
	Speedoo (a capella)	1975	Relic LP 105
	Senorita (a capella)	1975	Relic LP 105
	It Was The Night (a capella)	1975	Relic LP 105
	The New Beat (a capella)	1975	Relic LP 108
	Dance (a capella)	1975	Relic LP 109
UNIQUES (9)			
	My Mother's Eyes/Woke Up This Morning	N/A	Dapper 4401
UNISONS (GEORGE JACKSON & THE)			
	Watching The Rainbow/Miss Frankenstein	1961	Lescay 3006
UNITONES			
	Judy/The Sound	1959	Candy 005
UNIVERSALS			
	Again/Teenage Love	1957	Mark-X 7004
	The Picture/He's So Right	1958	Cora-Lee 501
	Prayer Of Love/Have Mercy Baby	1960	Southern 101
	Dear Ruth/Good Lovin'	1960	Southern 102
	Dreaming/Love Bound	1961	Festival 1601
	I'll Just Have To Go On (Dreaming)/Love Bound	1961	Festival 1601/Festival 25001 (62)
	A Love Only You Can Give/I'm In Love	1962	Shepherd 2200
	In My Heart You'll Always Remain/You'll Always Remain	1962	V-Tone 236
	Have Mercy Baby (acappella)	1973	Relic LP 5006
	The Love I Long For (acappella)	1973	Relic LP 5006
	Don't Leave Me This Way (acappella)	1973	Relic LP 5006
	Dear Lord (acappella)	1973	Relic LP 5006
	I'll Be Satisfied (acappella)	1973	Relic LP 5006
	That's My Baby (acappella)	1973	Relic LP 5006
	Money Honey (acappella)	1973	Relic LP 5006
	Love Is A River (acappella)	1973	Relic LP 5006
	Tears In My Eyes (acappella)	1973	Relic LP 5006
	Ebb Tide (acappella)	1973	Relic LP 5006
	Good Loving (acappella)	1973	Relic LP 5006
	Think	1985	Murray Hill LP 000083
UNIVERSALS (SIS WATKINS & THE)			
	Dear Ruth/Gotta Little Girl	1963	Ascot 2124
UNKNOWNS			
	One More Chance/You And Me	1957	Shield 7101/X-Tra 102 (57)
	Oh Summer Love/Cool Wool	1958	Felsted 8535
UNTOUCHABLES (AKA CHAVELLES) (FB BILLY JONES/AKA BILLY STORM)			
	Poor Boy Needs A Preacher/New Fad	1960	Madison 128
	Vicki Lee/Goodnight Sweetheart, Goodnight	1960	Madison 134
	60 Minute Man/Everybody's Laughing	1960	Madison 139
	Lovely Dee/You're On Top	1961	Liberty 55335
	Do Your Best/Raisin' Sugar Cane	1961	Madison 147
	Little Mary/Funny What A Little Kiss Can Do	1962	Alan K 6901
	Medicine Man/Papa	1962	Liberty 55423
UP-TUNES			
	I Wanna Love Just You/Don't Lead Me On	1966	Genie 103
	Lil Blue Tears	1966	Genie 107
UPBEATS (1)			
	I Don't Know/Never In My Life	1957	Prep 119
	The Night We Both Said Goodbye/Oh What It Seemed To Be	1958	Joy 223
	My Last Frontier/Will You Be Mine	1958	Prep 131
	Just Like In The Movies/My Foolish Heart	1958	Swan 4010
	Keep Cool Crazy Heart/You're The One I Care For	1959	Joy 227
	Teenie Weenie Bikini/Satin Shoes	1959	Joy 229
	To Me You're A Song/Unbelievable Love	1959	Joy 233
UPBEATS (2) (RAY ALLEN & THE)			
	Let Them Talk/Sweet Lorraine	1961	Sinclair 1004
	Peggy Sue/La Bamba	1962	Blast 204
UPFRONTS			
	When You Kiss Me/Little Girl	1961	Lummtone 106
	Send Me Someone To Love Who Will Love Me/Baby, For Your Love	1961	Lummtone 107
	I Stopped The Duke Of Earl/B aby, For Your Love	1962	Lummtone 107
	Baby, For Your Love/It Took Time (It Took You)	1962	Lummtone 108
	Most Of The Pretty Young Girls/Do The Beatle	1964	Lummtone 114
UPFRONTS (FB DAVIE "LITTLE CAESAR" JOHNSON)			
	Betty Lou And The Lion/It Took Time (It Took You)	1960	Lummtone 103
	Too Far To Turn Around/Married Jive	1960	Lummtone 104
UPNILONS (FEMALE)			
	Grow Up Romeo/He Fell For Me	1964	Lummtone 115
UPSETS (EDDY & THE)			
	Cry Cry Cry/I Got News	N/A	Dektr 41668

Artist Song	Year	Label	Artist Song	Year	Label
UPSETTERS			**VAL-AIRES**		
Rolling On/Blues	1960	Gee 1055	Launie, My Love/Which One		
UPSTARTS (1)			Will It Be	1959	Willette 114/Coral 62119
Feed Me Baby/Open The					(59)/Coral 62177 (59)
Door Baby	1954	Apollo 468	**VAL-CHORDS**		
UPSTARTS (2) (JERRY MCCAIN & THE)			Candy Store Love/You're		
Courtin' In A Cadillac/That's			Laughing At Me	1957	Gametime 104
What They Want	1956	Excello 2068	**VAL-MONTS (TOMMY SENA & THE)**		
If It Wasn't For My Baby/You			Onions (Remind Me Of You)/		
Don't Love Me No More	1956	Excello 2079	The Wobble	1962	Valmont 905
Run Uncle John Run/Things			**VAL-TONES**		
Ain't Right	1956	Excello 2081	Tender Darling/Siam Sam	1955	DeLuxe 6084
My Next Door Neighbor/			**VALADIERS**		
Trying To Please	1957	Excello 2103	Greetings (This Is Uncle Sam)/		
Listen! Young Girls/Bad Credit	1957	Excello 2111	Take A Chance	1961	Miracle 6
UPSTARTS (3)			While I'm Away/Because I		
Lovely Dream/Get It Together	N/A	Top Ten 2	Love Her	1962	Gordy 7003
UPSTARTS (3) (DON DELL & THE)			I Found A Girl/You'll Be Sorry		
Time/May It Be My Fortune	1961	East Coast 101/102	Someday	1963	Gordy 7013
A Special Love/Someone For			**VALAQUONS**		
Me	1962	East Coast 105/106	Teardrops/Madelaine	1964	Laguna 102
Make Believe Love/I Want You,			Diddy Bop/Jolly Green Giant	1964	Rayco 516
I Need You, I Love You(by			I Wanna Woman/Window		
Don Dell & the Montereys)	1964	Roman 2963	Shopping On Girls Avenue	1965	Tangerine 951
UPTONES (AKA SWALLOWS (3))			**VALCOUNTS (TOMMY SENA & THE)**		
I'll Be There/No More	1962	Lute 6225	I Can't Get Up/Choo Choo Train	1961	Adore 903
Be Mine/Dreamin'	1962	Lute 6229	**VALDOROS**		
Dreaming/Wear My Ring	1963	Watts 1080/Magnum 714 (63)	Don't Open The Grave/		
UPTOWNERS			A Woman, A Man	1957	Silhouette 517
Vicki/You're A Habit	1964	Le Cam 126	**VALENTINES (1)**		
Down By The Riverside/			Tonight Kathleen/Summer Love	1954	Old Town 1009
Hambone	1989	Starlight 67	Lily Maebelle/Falling For You	1955	Rama 171
UPTOWNS			I Love You, Darling/Hand Me		
Here She Comes Again/			Down Love	1955	Rama 181
Asiatic Flu	1963	Laurie 3204	A Christmas Prayer/K-I-S-S Me	1955	Rama 186
UTMOSTS			Woo Woo Train/Why?	1955	Rama 196
I Need You/Big Man	1962	Pan Or 1123	Twenty Minutes (Before The		
UTOPIANS (1) (MIKE (LASMAN) & THE)			Hour)/I'll Never Let You Go	1956	Rama 201
Erlene/I Found A Penny			Nature's Creation/My Story Of		
(And I Made A Wish)	1958	Cee Jay 574 (first pressing)	Love	1956	Rama 208
Erlene/I Wish	1958	Cee Jay 574 (second press-	Don't Say Goodnight/I Cried		
ing)			Oh, Oh	1957	Rama 228
UTOPIANS (2)			Sweetheart Of Mine	1986	Murray Hill LP 000202
Dutch Treat/Ain't No Such			If You Love Me, Pretty Baby	1986	Murray Hill LP 000202
Thing	1962	Imperial 5861	The Joe Smith Theme	1986	Murray Hill LP 000202
Along My Lonely Way/			**VALENTINES (2)**		
Hurry To Your Date	1962	Imperial 5876	That's It Man/Please Don't		
Let Love Come Later/			Leave, Please Don't Go	1960	King 5338
Opera Vs. The Blues	1963	Imperial 5921	That's How I Feel/Hey Ruby	1960	King 5433
UTOPIAS			I'll Forget You/Yes, You Made		
Welcome Back To My Heart/			It That Way	1962	Bethlehem 3055
Sally Bad	1963	Fortune 568	I Have Two Loves/Camping		
Maybe/Good Friends Forever	N/A	Fortune 102X	Out (instrumental)	1963	King 5830
V-8S (AKA V-EIGHTS)			Alone In The Night/Mink Coat		
Pretty Girl/Please Come Back	1959	Most 711/713	And Sneakers	1964	United Artists 764
Chasin' The Blues	N/A	Aura 101	**VALENTINES (3) (LITTLE TOM & THE)**		
V-EIGHTS (AKA V-8S)			School Girl/Letter From My		
My Heart/Papa's Yellow Tie	1960	Vibro 4005/ABC 10201 (61)	Darling	1961	Mr. Big 222
Guess What/Everything That			**VALENTINES (4) (FEMALE)**		
You Said	1961	Vibro 4006	Johnny One Heart/Mama I		
V-EIGHTS (STONEY JACKSON & THE)			Have Come Home	1962	Ludix 102
Let's Take A Chance/Hot Water	1961	Vibro 4007	**VALENTINES (5)**		
V-NOTES			Beautiful/You're Everthin'	1963	Lee 5465
Get A Baby Like Mine/Smashed	1958	Volk 102	**VALENTINOS (REF RADIANTS (1))**		
V.I.P.S (1)			Let Me Be Your Girl/A Kiss		
Strange Little Girl/My Girl Friend	1961	Congress 211	From Your Lips	1960	Brunswick 55171
V.I.P.S (2)			Mr. Magic Moon	1963	Kapp
Fall Guy/Long John	1963	Carmel 44	Whatcha Know New/Easy To		
VACELS			Fall In Love	1982	Clifton 70
You're My Baby/Hey Girl,			Peppermint Stick/Moonglow	1982	Crystal Ball 147
Stop Leading Me On	1965	Kama Sutra 200	I Miei Giorni Felici/On Sunday		
Can You Please Crawl Out Your			Afternoon	1992	Clifton 101
Window/I'm Just A Poor Boy	1965	Kama Sutra 204	**VALETS**		
VACELS (RICKY & THE)			I Need Someone/When I Met You	1958	Jon 4025
Lorraine/Bubble Gum	1962	Express 711	Sherry/You And You Alone	1959	Vulcan/Jon 4219 (59)
His Girl/Don't Want Your			**VALIANT TRIO**		
Love No More	1963	Fargo 1050	You Left Me/I'll Make Her Mine	1965	EV 97500
VAILS			**VALIANTS (1)**		
Great Somewhere/Buy Now,			This Is The Night/Good Golly,		
Pay Later	1960	Belmont 4002	Miss Molly	1957	Keen 34004/Early Bird 001 (95)
There'll Come A Time/She's			Lover, Lover/Walkin' Girl	1957	Keen 34007
Back	1960	Belmont 4004			

Artist Song	Year	Label	Artist Song	Year	Label
Frieda, Frieda/Please Wait,			Come On, Baby/Lambie Baby	1958	Decca 30762
My Love	1958	Keen 4026/Andex 4026 (59)	I Don't Know What To Do/		
Dear Cindy/Surprise	1959	Shar-Dee 703	Better Come Back To Me	1960	Decca 31036
This Is The Night/Walkin' Girl	1961	Keen 82120	**VAN DYKES (2)**		
Please Wait My Love/			The Bells Are Ringing/		
Temptation Of My Heart	1995	Early Bird 003	Meaning Of Love	1958	King 5158/DeLuxe 6193 (61)
VALIANTS (1) (BILLY STORM & THE)			Once Upon A Dream/Dame		
We Knew/Walkin' Girl	1959	Ensign 4035	Tu Corazon	1959	Felsted 8565
Temptation Of My Heart	1969	Famous LP 504	Gift Of Love/Guardian Angel	1960	Spring 1113/Donna 1333 (60)
Love Game	1969	Famous LP 504	**VAN DYKES (3)**		
VALIANTS (2) (SANDY VALE & THE)			King Of Fools/Stupidity	1962	Atlantic 2161
Boppin' On The Beach/			**VAN DYKES (4) (AKA VAN DYKE FIVE)**		
Suntan Tattoo	1959	Decca 30941	Again And Again/Rich Girl	1965	Green Sea 101
VALIANTS (3) (AKA DU DROPPERS/AKA DIXIEAIRES)			Miracle After Miracle/How		
Let Me Go Lover/Let Me Ride	1959	Joy 235	Can I Forget Her	1966	Green Sea 108
VALIANTS (4) (NORMAN SANDS & THE)			Rich Girl/Miracle After Miracle	1967	Co-Op 515
Don't Wanna Leave The			Rock-A-Bye Girl/I'll Be By	1967	Co-Op 516
Congo/Rockin' With Joe	1960	Warwick 598	**VAN LOAN QUARTET (THE JOE VAN LOAN QUARTET)**		
VALIANTS (5)			Until I Fell For You/Trust In Me	1954	Carver 1402
Honky Tonk Joe/Calcutta	1961	Columbia 41931	**VAN-DELLS (MYRON & THE)**		
VALIANTS (6)			Heartaches/Crazy Little Mama	1963	Flo-Roe 15
The Wedding/Velma	1958	Speck 1001	**VANANGOS**		
See-Saw/Blue Jeans And A			A Sad Sad Story/My Girl	1975	Monogram 110
Pony-Tail	1961	Fairlane 21007	**VANCE, SAMMY (& GROUP)**		
You Are Sweeter Than Wine/			Run Run Run/Guilty Of Love	1958	Ebb 134
Love Comes In Many Ways	1962	Imperial 5843	**VANDELLS**		
Living In Paradise/I'm In A			A Small Silver Ring/Bumble Bee	1964	USA 758
World Of My Own	1963	Imperial 5915	**VANDELLS (JOHNNY GRECO & THE)**		
Johnny Lonely/Eternal Triangle	1963	Roulette 4510/Roulette 4551 (64)	Gloria/I Dunno	1963	Far-Mel 1
			VANGUARDS (1)		
Lonely Hours/Come On Let's Go	1964	Cortland 114	So Live/Don't Let It Happen		
VALIANTS (7)			Again	1954	Derby 854
Are You Ready/Frankie's Angel	1962	KC 108	Baby Doll/My Friend Mary Ann	1958	Dot 15791
VALIANTS (8) (PHIL DEMARCO & THE)			Moonlight/I'm Movin'	1958	Ivy 103
Lonely Guy/Be On Your Way	1964	Debby 065	**VANGUARDS (1) (BUDDY GIBSON & THE)**		
VALIDS			Just A Game/The Session	1959	Swingin' 615
Blue Moon (a capella)/Hey			**VANGUARDS (2)**		
Senorita (a capella)	1966	Amber 853	I Love You Darling/Tears Fall	N/A	Regency 743
Barbara Ann (a capella)/			**VANN, JOEY (& GROUP)**		
Congratulations (a capella)	1966	Amber 855	Try To Remember/My Love,		
VALLEYITES (NATHAN MCKINNEY & THE)			My Love	1965	Coed 606
Weep No More/Oh How I			**VANN, TEDDY (& GROUP)**		
Love You	1964	Rayco 526	Young And Pretty Bride/		
VALOR, TONY (& GROUP)			Do You Love Me	1960	Roulette 4300
Story In My Heart/So Tenderly	1963	Musictone 1119	Raindrops/Why Can't You Be		
VALQUINS			True (by the Vernalls)	1958	Rulu 6753
My Dear/Falling Star	1959	Gaity 161/162	**VARNELLS (AKA VERNALLS)**		
VALRAYS			Who Created Love/Strut Time	1961	Arnold 1003
Yo Me Pregunto/Get Aboard	1963	Parkway	Day In Court/All Because	1961	Arnold 1006
Get Aboard/Pee Wee	1963	Parkway 880	**VECTORS**		
I Ask Myself/Honky Tonk	1964	Parkway 904	One Day/Slow, But Sure	1958	Standord 700
I'm Walkin' Proud/It Hurts,			**VEL-AIRES (DONALD WOODS & THE) (AKA DONALD WOODS &**		
Doesn't It Girl	1967	United Artists 50145	**THE BEL-AIRES (3))**		
VALS			This Paradise/Let's Party Awhile	1955	Flip 303 (second pressing, first is by the Bel-Aires)
The Song Of A Lover/					
Compensation Blues	1962	Unique Laboratories (no #)	Death Of An Angel (My Baby's		
Too Late/I'm Stepping Out			Gone)/Man From Utopia	1955	Flip 306/Happy Tiger Era 5065
With My Memories	1964	Ascot 2163	Stay With Me, Always/		
VALTAIRS			My Very Own	1955	Flip 309
Soul/Strangers Away	1964	Selsom 101	Heaven In My Arms/Mighty Joe	1956	Flip 312
The Ko Ko Mo/Moonlight In			You Won't Be Satisfied	N/A	Flip
Vermont	1965	Selsom 106	**VEL-TONES**		
VALTONES			Broken Heart/Please Say		
Have You Ever Met An Angel?/			You'll Be True	1960	Vel 9178
You Belong To My Heart	1956	Gee 1004	Now/I Need You So	1960	Zara 901/Lost Nite 103 (61)
VALUES			I Want To Know/My Dear	1964	Wedge 1013
That's The Way/Return To Me	1962	Invicta 1002	A Fool Was I	N/A	Collectables LP 5037
VALUMES (AKA VOLUMES (3))			Hey Baby/I'll Be	N/A	Del Norte 725
I Love You/Dreams	1962	Chex 1000.2 (correct!) (first pressing, second is by Volumes)	**VELAIRES (1)**		
			Roll Over Beethoven/Frankie		
VAMPIRES (AKA BENTLEYS)			And Johnny	1961	Jamie 1198
Why Didn't I Listen To Mother/			Roll Over Beethoven/Brazil	1961	Jamie 1198
Did Anybody Lose A Tear?	1964	Carroll 104	Dream/Sticks And Stones	1961	Jamie 1203
VAN DELLES			Ubangi Stomp/It's Almost		
Time After Time/I Got The Blues	1962	Bolo 731	Tomorrow	1962	Jamie 1211
VAN DELLOS			Memory Tree/Don't Wake Me Up	1962	Jamie 1223
I Need You/Bring Back	1961	Card 558	Yes, It Was Me/I Could Have		
VAN DYKE FIVE (AKA VAN DYKES (4))			Cried	1965	Hi-Mar 9173
Only If I Had Your Love/Bring			**VELAIRES (2) (DANNY & THE)**		
Back My Life	1967	Corner Closet 101	What Am I Livin' For/Shaggy		
VAN DYKES (1)			Dog	1967	Brent 7072
Run Betty Run/The Fixer	1958	Decca 30654	I Found A Love/It's Over	1967	Ramco 1983

Artist	Song	Year	Label
VELAIRS			
	A Prom And A Promise/Don't Tell Tales Out Of School	1958	MGM 12667
VELLS (1) (LITTLE BUTCHIE & THE)			
	Sometimes Little Girl/Over The Rainbow(by Little Butchie Saunders & His Buddies)	1959	Angletone 535
VELLS (2) (AKA VANDELLAS) (FEMALE)			
	There He Is (At My Door)/You'll Never Cherish A Love So True (Til You Lose It)	1962	Mel-O-Dy 103
VELONS			
	Shelly/From The Chapel	1963	Blast 216
	Summer Love/Why Don't You Write	1968	BJM 6568
	That's What Love Can Do/That's All Right	1968	BJM 6569
VELOURS			
	My Love Come Back/Honey Drop	1956	Onyx 501/Relic 503 (64)
	Romeo/What You Do To Me	1957	Onyx 508/Relic 502 (64)
	Can I Come Over Tonight?/Where There's A Will (There's A Way)	1957	Onyx 512/Gone 5092 (60)/Relic 504 (64)
	This Could Be The Night/Hands Across The Table	1957	Onyx 515/Relic 516 (64)
	I'll Never Smile Again/Crazy Love	1958	Cub 9014
	Can I Walk You Home?/Remember	1958	Onyx 520/Orbit 9001 (58)/Cub 9001 (58)
	Blue Velvet/Tired Of Your Rock & Rolling	1959	Cub 9029
	I Promise/Little Sweetheart	1959	Studio 9902
	Sweet Sixteen/Daddy Warbucks	1960	Goldisc 3012
	Lover, Come Back To Me/The Lonely One	1961	End 1090
	Don't Pity Me/I'm Gonna Change	1967	MGM 13780
	Mio Amore/This Could Be The Night	1984	Starlight 19
	C'Est La Vie/Good Lovin'	1985	Clifton 75
	I Wish You Love/Old Fashioned Christmas	1988	Clifton 82
	C'Est La Vie	1992	Clifton 100
VELPS			
	Little Girl/Korea (recorded in 1957)	1972	Roadhouse 1002
VELS (1)			
	In-Laws/Do The Walk	1963	Amy 881
VELS (2)			
	Please Be Mine/Mysterious Teenage	1957	Trebco 16/Trebco 702 (57)
VELTONES			
	Playboy/Cal's Tune	1959	Coy 101/Kapp 268 (59)
	Take A Ride/Lover's Blues	1959	Jin 107
	I'm Your Fool/Jail Bird	1959	Jin 115
	Someday/Fool In Love	1959	Satellite 100/Mercury 71526 (59)
	Darling/I Do	1966	Goldwax 301
VELVATEENS			
	Please Don't Let Me Go	N/A	Velvet 1001
VELVATONES			
	Real Gone Baby/Feeling Kinda Lonely	1957	Meteor 5042
	Impossible/My Lonely Friend (by the Continentals)	1961	Candlelite 412
VELVATONES (BB LI'L WALTER'S BAND)			
	Impossible/I'm Leaving Home	1959	Nu Kat 110
VELVET ANGELS (AKA DIABLOS)			
	I'm In Love (a capella)/Let Me Come Back (a capella)	1964	Medieval 201
	Since You've Been Gone (a capella)/Baby I Wanna Know (a capella)	1964	Medieval 207
	I'm In Love (a capella)/Baby I Wanna Know (a capella)	1965	Co-Op M102
	Jungle Fever (a cappella)	1972	Relic LP 5004
	I Want To Know Baby (a cappella)	1972	Relic LP 5004
	Old MacDonald (a cappella)	1972	Relic LP 5004
	Your Love (a cappella)	1972	Relic LP 5004
	For Sentimental Reasons (a cappella)	1972	Relic LP 5004
	Mary (Let It All Out) (a cappella)	1972	Relic LP 5004
	When You're Smiling (a cappella)	1972	Relic LP 5004
	Lola (a cappella)	1972	Relic LP 5004/Relic LP 102 (75)
	Mary (a cappella)	1972	Relic LP 5004/Relic LP 102 (75)
	Be Ever Wonderful (a cappella)	1972	Relic LP 5004/Relic LP 108 (75)
	Johnny Johnny (a cappella)/It's Too Soon To Know	1972	Relic LP 5004/Relic LP 109 (75)/Robin Hood 153 (77)
	Fools Rush In	1975	Relic LP 101
	Blue Moon	1975	Relic LP 101
VELVET FIVE			
	Shop Around/Hey Jude	1973	Nostalgia 102
VELVET KEYS			
	Let's Stay After School/My Baby's Gone	1957	King 5090
	Don't Take My Picture, Take Me/The Truth About Youth	1958	King 5109
VELVET SATINS			
	Cherry/An Angel Like You	1964	General American 716
	Up To The Rooftop/Nothing Can Compare To You	1965	General American 006
	Heading For The Rooftop/Angel Adorable	1965	General American 720
VELVET SATINS (BOBBY CAPRI & THE)			
	Charm Bracelet/One Sided Love	1960	Ariste 101/Jason Scott 17 (82)
	You And I/Cleopatra	1963	Johnson 124
	The Night/I'm Gonna Be Another Man	1963	Johnson 126/Clifton 14 (76)
VELVET SOUNDS			
	Silver Star/Devil And The Stocker	N/A	Cosmopolitan 100/101
	Pretty Darling/Who'll Take My Place	N/A	Cosmopolitan 105/106
VELVET TONES			
	Good Lovin'	1965	Velvet Tone 104
VELVET, JIMMY (& GROUP)			
	Young Hearts/It's Almost Tomorrow	1965	Velvet Tone 102
VELVETEENS (1) (FEMALE)			
	Baby Baby/Teen Prayer	1961	Stark 101/102
	Please Holy Father Pt. 1/Please Holy Father Pt. 2	1961	Stark 12591
	I Thank You/Meant To Be	1962	Laurie 3126
	I Feel Sorry For You Baby/Ching Bam Bah	1965	Golden Artist 614
VELVETEENS (2) (TERRI & THE)			
	Bells Of Love/You've Broken My Heart	1962	Kerwood 711
VELVETEERS			
	Tell Me You're Mine/Boo Wacka Boo	1956	Spitfire 15
	Song Of Love	1961	Caprice 101
VELVETIERS			
	Oh, Baby/Feelin' Right Saturday Night	1958	Ric 958
VELVETONES (1)			
	Glory Of Love/I Love Her So	1957	Aladdin 3372/Imperial 5878 (62)
	Melody Of Love/I Found A Love	1957	Aladdin 3391
	Come Back/Penalty Of Love	1959	D 1049/Glad
	Worried Over You/Space Men	1959	D 1072
	Who Took My Girl/Stars Of Wonder	1959	Deb 1008
	My Every Thought/Little Girl, I Love You So	1960	Aladdin 3463
	The Glory Of Love/I Found My Love	1964	Imperial 66020
VELVETONES (2)			
	Starry Eyes/I'm Ashamed	1963	Ascot 2126
VELVETONES (2) (FEMALE)			
	Yes I Will/I Want Him So Bad	1962	Ascot 2117
VELVETONES (3) (BINGO MILLER & THE)			
	Martha Sue/I Know A Valley	N/A	Young Artists 103
VELVETONES (4)			
	Reaching For A Rainbow/In This Whole World	N/A	Vanda 0001
VELVETS (1)			
	They Tried/She's Gotta Grin	1953	Red Robin 120

Artist Song	Year	Label
I/At Last	1953	Red Robin 122/Pilgrim 706 (55)/Event 4285 (55)
I Cried/Tell Her	1954	Red Robin 127/Pilgrim 710 (55)
I-I-I/Dance Honey Dance	1957	Fury 1012
VELVETS (2)		
Happy Days Are Here Again/If I Could Be With You	1959	20th Century Fox 165
Everybody Knows/Hand Jivin' Baby	1959	Plaid 101
That Lucky Old Sun/Time And Again	1961	Monument 435
Tonight (Could Be The Night)/Spring Fever	1961	Monument 441/Monument 515
Laugh/Lana	1961	Monument 448
The Love Express/Don't Let Him Take My Baby	1962	Monument 458
Let The Good Times Roll/The Lights Go On, The Lights Go Off	1962	Monument 464
Crying In The Chapel/Dawn	1963	Monument 810
Here Comes That Song Again/Nightmare	1964	Monument 836
If/Let The Fool Kiss You	1964	Monument 861
Baby, The Magic Is Gone/Let The Fool Kiss You	1966	Monument 961
VELVETS (3) (BOBBY & THE)		
I Promise/Now We Know	1959	Rason 501
VELVETS (4) (RONNIE PRICE & THE)		
White Bucks/Look At Me	N/A	Carousel 1001
VELVETTONES (LEE MARTIN & THE)		
Lover's Plea/Born To Be A Loser	1962	Jin 159
VELVITONES		
Little Girl I Love You/A Prayer At Gettysburg	1959	Milmart 113
VENDORS		
Steppin' Stones/Public Lover No. 1	1963	MGM 13133
Where All Lovers Meet/That's All Right	1963	Victorio 128
VENEERS (FEMALE) (AKA CHANTELS)		
Believe Me (My Angel)/I	1960	Princeton 102
VENETIANS (NICK MARCO & THE)		
Little Boy Lost/Would It Hurt You	1960	Dwain 813
VENTRILLS		
Alone In The Night/Confusion	1967	Ivanhoe 5000/Parkway 141 (67)
VERDICTS (1)		
My Life's Desire/The Mummy's Ball	1961	East Coast 103/104/Relic 507 (64)
VERDICTS (2)		
Never Let Me Go/Now You Did It	1973	Vintage 1009
VERITY (LADY JANE &)		
A Junior At The Senior Prom/Slow Rock	1959	Palette 5031
VERNALLS (AKA VARNELLS)		
Raindrops/Why Can't You Be True	1958	Rulu 6753
VERSA-TONES		
How Long/Cobra	1961	Kenco 5015
VERSAILLES		
Little Girl Of Mine (a capella)/Teenager's Dream (a capella)	1957	Harlequin 401
I'm In The Mood For Love (a capella)/Lorraine (a capella)	1965	Old Timer 607
VERSALETTES (AKA TRINKETS (2)) (FEMALE)		
True Love Is A Treasure/Shining Armor	1963	Witch 116
Don Juan In Town	1963	Witch 120
VERSATILES (1) (SONNY DAY & THE)		
Speedilac/Half Moon	1958	Checker 886
VERSATILES (10) (TOOTSIE & THE)		
I've Got A Feeling/Nobody But You	1962	Elmar 6000
VERSATILES (11)		
My Autumn Love/Heel And Toe	1975	Monogram 114
VERSATILES (2) (AKA MAJORS/AKA PERFORMERS)		
Crying/Passing By	1958	Atlantic 2004
I'll Whisper In Your Ear/Lundee Dundee (by the Majors)	1960	Rocal 1002
White Cliffs Of Dover/Just Words	1962	Peacock 1910
VERSATILES (3) (DEE THOMAS & THE)		
In The Garden Of Love/Don't Know Where I'm Going	1960	Coaster 800
VERSATILES (4)		
Blue Feeling/Just Pretending	1962	Ramco 3717
VERSATILES (5)		
Lonely Boy/Moon Dawg	1964	Sea Crest 6001
VERSATILES (6)		
Easy To Say	1967	Richtone 186
VERSATILES (7)		
Blue Feeling/Just Pretending	1977	Marie 101
VERSATILES (8)		
Lonely Man/Cry Like A Baby	N/A	Staff 210
VERSATILES (9) (JERRY SHELLY & THE)		
Love Only Me/It's All Over	N/A	Star 220
VERSATONES (1)		
Wait For Me/De Obeah Man	1957	RCA 6917
Bikini Baby/Lovely Teenage Girl	1957	RCA 6976
All Around The Bush	1957	RCA LPM-1538/RCA EP 1538
Hold Me Lover/Will She Return	1963	Richie 4081
VERSATONES (2)		
Tight Skirt And Sweater/Bila	1958	All Star 501/Fenway 7001 (60)/Atlantic 2211 (63)
VERSITILES		
Love Me/Don't Go	1962	Amaker 417
VESPERS (AKA FOUR EPICS)		
Mr. Cupid/When I Walk With My Angel	1963	Swan 4156
VESTEE, RUSS (& GROUP)		
Teardrops/Well Alright	1962	Amy 833
VESTELLES (FEMALE)		
Come Home/Ditta-Wa-Do	1958	Decca 30733
VETS		
Wipe The Tears From Your Eyes/Natural Born Lover	1961	Swami 551/552
VI-COUNTS		
Three Months Of Rain/The Loser	1960	Ace 587
VI-KINGS		
Rock A Little Bit/Desert Boots	1960	Del-Mann 545
VI-TONES		
The Storm (So Blue) (acapella)/Fall In Love (acapella)	1964	Times Square 105
VIBES (1) (AKA VIBRANAIRES)		
Stop Torturing Me!/Stop Jibing, Baby	1954	After Hours 105/Chariot 105 (54)
VIBES (2)		
Darling/Come Back, Baby	1957	ABC 9810
VIBES (3)		
What's Her Name?/You Are	1958	Allied 10006
Misunderstood/Let The Old Folks Talk	1959	Allied 10007
VIBES (4)		
Won't You Marry Me	1987	Relic LP 8011
In The Middle Of The Night	1987	Relic LP 8011
Love Me Too	1987	Relic LP 8011
VIBES (5)		
A Killer Comes To Town/You Got Me Crying	N/A	Rayna 103
VIBRA TONES		
Sincerely/Please Tell Me Why	1961	ABC 10218
I'm Begging You Baby/Willie's Dream	1962	Candi 1025
VIBRA-TONES (SABBY LEWIS & THE)		
Forgive Me, My Love/Regretting	1956	ABC 9687
VIBRAHARPS (1) (AKA VIBRA-HARPS)		
Walk Beside Me/Cosy With Rosy	1956	Beech 713
It Must Be Magic/Nosey Neighbors	1959	Atco 6134
The Only Love Of Mine/Be My Dancing Partner	1959	Fury 1022
VIBRAHARPS (2)		
A Friend (a capella)	1975	Relic LP 108
I Hear Bells (a capella)	1975	Relic LP 108
Secret Love (a capella)	1975	Relic LP 108
Talking To My Heart (a capella)	1975	Relic LP 109
VIBRANAIRES (AKA VIBES (1))		
Doll Face/Ooh, I Feel So Good	1954	After Hours 103/Chariot 103 (54)

Artist Song	Year	Label
VIBRATIONS (AKA JAYHAWKS/AKA MARATHONS)		
So Blue/Love Me Like You Should	1960	Bet 001/Checker 954 (60)
Feel So Bad/Cave Man	1960	Checker 961
Doing The Slop/So Little Time	1960	Checker 967
The Watusi/Wallflower	1960	Checker 969
Continental With Me Baby/ The Junkeroo	1960	Checker 974
Stranded In The Jungle/ Don't Say Goodbye	1960	Checker 982
Peanut Butter/Down In New Orleans	1961	Argo 5389
Everlasting Love	1961	Checker (unreleased)
I Still Love You	1961	Checker (unreleased)
Talk That Talk	1961	Checker (unreleased)
All My Love Belongs To You/ Stop Right Now	1961	Checker 987
Let's Pony Again/What Made You Change Your Mind	1961	Checker 990
Time After Time	1961	Checker LP 2978
I Had A Love	1961	Checker LP 2978
People Say	1961	Checker LP 2978
Sweet Slumber/Serenade Of The Bells	1961	Checker LP 2978/Robin Hood 150 (77)
Oh Cindy/Over The Rainbow	1962	Checker 1002
The New Hully Gully/Anytime	1962	Checker 1011
If He Don't/Hamburgers On A Bun	1962	Checker 1022
Between Hello And Goodbye/ Lonesome Little Lonely Girl	1963	Atlantic 2204
Since I Fell For You/May The Best Man Win	1963	Checker 1038
Dancing Danny/Dancing Danny (instrumental)	1963	Checker 1061
My Girl Sloopy/Daddy Woo-Woo	1964	Atlantic 2221
People Say/So Little Time	1977	Robin Hood 149
Time After Time/I'll Never Fall In Love (by the Olympics)	1977	Robin Hood 151
VIBRATIONS (EVELYN DELL & THE)		
Sincerely/Please Tell Me Why	1961	ABC 10218
VICE-ROYS		
Please, Baby, Please/ I'm Yours As Long As I Live	1955	Aladdin 3273
VICEROYS (1)		
I'm So Sorry (It's Ending With You)/Uncle Sam Needs You	1961	Little Star 107/Smash 1716 (61)
Dreamy Eyes/Ball N' Chain	1961	Original Sound 15
I Need Your Love So Bad/ My Heart	1962	Ramco 3715
VICEROYS (1) (JIMMY NORMAN & THE)		
You Crack Me Up/I Know I'm In Love	1963	Little Star 121
VICEROYS (2)		
Until/Bacon Fat	1963	Bolo 750
VICEROYS (3)		
Tears On My Pillow/Not Too Much Twist	1964	Bethlehem 3088
Earth Angel/Death Of An Angel	1964	Imperial 66058
VICTONES		
Two Sides Of Love/Somebody Really Loves You	1959	Front Page 2302
I Need You So/My Baby Changes	N/A	Front Page 1001
VICTORIALS		
I Get That Feeling/Prettiest Girl In The World	1956	Imperial 5398
VICTORIANS (1)		
Heartbreaking Moon/I'm Rollin'	1956	Saxony 103
Wedding Bells/Please Say You Do	1956	Selma 1002
VICTORIANS (2)		
Move In A Little Closer/Lovin'	1963	Arnold 571
Climb Every Mountain/What Makes Little Girls Cry	1963	Liberty 55574
You're Invited To A Party/ The Monkey Stroll	1963	Liberty 55656
Happy Birthday Blue/Oh What A Night For Love	1964	Liberty 55693
If I Love You/Monkey Stroll	1964	Liberty 55728
VICTORIANS (3)		
C'Mon Dream/Catrina	N/A	Hercules 101

Artist Song	Year	Label
VICTORIANS (4)		
Baby Toys	N/A	Reprise 0434
VICTORS (1)		
Slow But Sure	1958	N/A
It Will Happen By And By/ Mi Amor	1959	Jackpot 48015
VICTORS (2) (LITTLE MAN & THE)		
I Need An Angel/King Of The Mountain	1963	Tarheel 064
Smile/My Funny Way Of Looking At You	1964	Roulette 4576
VICTORS (3) (JIMMY VICK & THE)		
I Need Someone	1963	Cherry 7888
VICTORY FIVE		
I Never Knew/Swing Low	1958	Terp 101
VIDALTONES		
Forever/Someone To Love	1961	Josie 900
VIDELS		
I Wish/Blow Winds Blow	1960	Dusty Disc 473/Early 702 (60)
I'll Keep On Waiting/Streets Of Love	1960	Kapp 361
Walking Down The Street/Ya Ya	1964	Fargo 1062
Be My Girl/A Place In My Heart	1959	Rhody 2000/Medieval 203 (61)
Mr. Lonely/I'll Forget You	1960	JDS 5004
Now That Summer Is Here/ She's Not Coming Home	1960	Tic Tac Toe 5005/JDS 5005 (60)
A Letter From Anne/This Year's Mister New	1961	Kapp 405
We Belong Together/It's All Over	1963	Musicnote 117
Hold Me Tight	N/A	Magic Carpet LP 1005
Unlucky Me	N/A	Magic Carpet LP 1005
The Party Starts At Nine	N/A	Magic Carpet LP 1005
Save A Dream	N/A	Magic Carpet LP 1005
VIDEOS		
Trickle Trickle/Moonglow, You Know (58)	1958	Main Line 106/Casino 102
Love Or Infatuation/Shoo-Bee-Doo-Bee Cha Cha Cha	1959	Casino 105
Love Or Infatuation/Shoo Bee Doo	1972	Bim Bam Boom 101
VIDLETTS (FEMALE)		
He's Gone For Good/What Makes The World Go Round	1963	Herald 594
VIKINGS (1) (LEE MARTIN & THE)		
I Lost Again/Change Of Heart	1960	Jin 149
VIKINGS (2) (BARRY & THE)		
I Love You, Yes I Do/Last Night	1964	Jamie 1281
VIKINGS (3) (ERIK & THE)		
Step By Step/Heaven And Paradise	1965	Karate 503
VILLA, JOEY (WITH THE ORIGINAL THREE FRIENDS)		
Blanche/The Oriental	1962	Chevron 500
Blanche/Mona Lisa	1962	MF 101
VILLAGE VOICES		
Too Young To Start/Red Lips	1961	Topix 6000
VILONS		
What Kind Of Fool Am I?/ Let Me In Your Life	1961	Lake 713
Mother Nature/Lone Stranger	1963	Aljon 1259/1260/Relic 524 (64)
Angel Darling/Wish She Was Mine	1972	Bim Bam Boom 104
Tears On My Pillow/Sweetest One	1973	Vintage 1011
VINCENT, STAN (& GROUP)		
Amazon Trail/St. Louis Blues	1962	Poplar 112
VINCENTE, VIN (& GROUP)		
I'm In Your Corner All The Way/Little Cutie	1962	Swingin' 644
VINE, MARTY (& GROUP)		
Cheryl/Rosemary	1961	Mastermade 101
VINES		
I Must See You Again/Love So Sweet	1961	Cee Jay 582
VINTAGE		
Harbor Lights	1966	Catamount 117
VIOLINAIRES		
Another Soldier Gone/Joy In The Beulah Land	1954	Drummond 4000

Artist Song	Year	Label
VIPERS		
Same Old Valarie/Little		
Miss Sweetness	N/A	Duchess 102
VIRGOS		
You're A Stranger/Humpty		
Dumpty	1965	Pioneer 6621
VIRIATIONS		
A Shot Of Love/Tra La La La La	1968	Amy 11006
VISCAYNES		
I Guess I'll Be/Stop What		
You're Doing	1961	Tropo 101
Yellow Moon/Heavenly Angel	1961	VPM 1006
VISCOUNT V		
My Angel/She Doesn't Know	N/A	Lavette 5009
VISCOUNTS (1) (SAMMY HAGEN & THE)		
Out Of Your Heart/Smoochie,		
Poochie	1957	Capitol 3772
Don't Cry/Wild Bird	1957	Capitol 3818
Tail Light/Snuggle Bunny	1958	Capitol 3885
VISCOUNTS (2)		
Raindrop/My Girl	1957	Mercury 71073
Saki Laki Waki/Oo-Oo-Wee	1959	Vega 1003
VISIONS		
Marlene/Darling Dear	1959	Warwick 108
Teenager's Life/Little Moon	1960	Elgey 1003/Lost Nite 102 (61)
All Through The Night/Tell		
Me You're Mine	1961	Big Top 3092
There'll Be No Next Time/		
So Close	1961	Brunswick 55206
Swingin' Wedding/Secret		
World (Of Tears)	1962	Big Top 3119
Tommy's Girl/Oh Boy, What		
A Girl	1962	Mercury 72188
Cigarette/Look At Me Now	1963	Original Sound 32
Down In My Heart/Tell Her Now	1965	Co-Ed 598
VISIONS (CONNIE MCGILL & THE)		
A Million Years/For That		
Great Day	1963	Toy 107
I Wanna Be Yours/Peace Of		
Mind	1963	Triode 115
No I Won't Believe It/		
He Created You For Me	1963	United International 1009
My Love Will Never Change/		
Take It Like A Man	1964	Edge 502
A Million Years/I Want To Be		
Free	N/A	Sugar 502
VISTAS (LITTLE VICTOR & THE)		
No More/Love Marches On	1962	Rendezvous 183
No More/Weeping Eyes	1962	Rendezvous 183
VISUALS		
The Submarine Race/Maybe		
You	1962	Poplar 115
My Juanita/A Boy, A Girl And		
A Dream	1963	Poplar 117
Please Don't Be Mad At Me/		
Blue (Enough To Cry)	1963	Poplar 121/Jason Scott 11 (81)
VITAMINS (AKA TITANS)		
It's So Hard To Laugh, So Easy		
To Cry/Rhythm And Blues	1972	Vita 101
VITELLS		
Shirley/The Dip	1962	Decca 31362
VITONES		
Fall In Love	1989	Relic LP 5079
The Storm (So Blue)	1989	Relic LP 5079
VOCAL LORDS		
Girl Of Mine/At Seventeen	1959	Able (no #)/Taurus (no #)
VOCAL TONES		
Walkin' With My Baby/		
Wanna Lee	1973	Bim Bam Boom 117
VOCAL-TEENS		
Till Then/Be A Slave	1972	Downstairs 1000
VOCAL-TONES		
Walkin' With My Baby/Wanna Lee	1957	Juanita 100
VOCALAIRES (AKA BLUE SONNETS)		
Crying In The Chapel	1962	Herald (unreleased)
Out Of Sight Out Of Mind	1962	Herald (unreleased)
Dance Dance/These Empty Arms	1962	Herald 573
Dream Ship/We Build A Nest		
(by the Actuals)	1976	Ronnie 200
VOCALEERS		
Chittlin Switch/Get Together		
Blues (by Little Esther)	1951	Savoy 824
Be True/Oh! Where	1953	Red Robin 113
Is It A Dream?/Hurry Home	1953	Red Robin 114
I Walk Alone/How Soon?	1953	Red Robin 119
Will You Be True?/Love You	1954	Red Robin 125
Angel Face/Lovin' Baby	1954	Red Robin 132
I Need Your Love So Bad/Have		
You Ever Loved Someone?	1959	Paradise 113
Love And Devotion/This Is		
The Night	1960	Old Town 1089
The Night Is Quiet/Hear My Plea	1960	Vest 832
Cootie Snap/A Golden Tear	1962	Twistime 11
Oh Where/(flip by Mango Jones)	1964	Oldies 45 166
Yes You're Mine/Teardrops		
Fell (by the Scarlets)	1976	Robin Hood 134
If Your Heart Aches	N/A	Relic LP 5094
Yes, You're Mine	N/A	Relic LP 5094
VOCALTONES		
I'm Gonna Get That Gal/My Girl	1956	Apollo 488
Three Kinds Of People/Darling		
(You Know I Love You)	1956	Apollo 492
I'll Never Let You Go/My		
Version Of Love	1956	Apollo 497
Hawaiian Rock 'N Roll/		
Walkin' My Baby	1957	Cindy 3004
My Last Goodbye To You	1989	Relic LP 5082
Please Don't Leave Me	1989	Relic LP 5082
I Ain't Gonna Give Nobody	1989	Relic LP 5082
Come Dance With Me	1989	Relic LP 5082
VOCALTONES (BOBBY HARRIS & THE)		
Don't Do It Baby/Crazy		
Crazy Crazy	1955	Wen-Dee 1933
VOGUES		
Love Is A Funny Little Game/		
Which Witch Doctor	1958	Dot 15798
Try Baby Try/Falling Star	1958	Dot 15859
VOICE MASTERS		
Oops I'm Sorry/Hope And Pray	1959	Anna 101
Needed/Needed (For Lovers Only)	1959	Anna 102
Hit And Runaway Love/		
Advertising For Love	1959	Anna 103
VOICE MASTERS (TY HUNTER & THE)		
Everything About You/		
Orphan Boy	1960	Anna 1114
Everytime/Free	1960	Anna 1123
VOICEMASTERS		
In Love In Vain/Two Lovers	1960	Frisco 15235
VOICES (1) (AKA BOBBY BIRD & THE BIRDS)		
Two Things I Love/Why?	1955	Cash 1011
Hey, Now/My Love Grows Stronger	1955	Cash 1014
Takes Two To Make A		
Home/I Want To Be Ready	1955	Cash 1015
Santa Claus Boogie/		
Santa Claus Baby	1955	Cash 1016
VOICES (2) (RAVON DARNELL & THE)		
I'll Be Back/One Of		
These Mornings	1956	Million 2015
VOICES (3) (FRANKIE BEARSE & THE)		
I Cry/No End To Love	1964	Olimpic 247
VOICES FIVE (BUD JOHNSON & THE) (AKA CHANTERS (2))		
For Sentimental Reasons/		
All Alone	1959	Craft 116
VOICES FIVE (BUDD JOHNSON & THE)		
You're Driving Me Crazy/		
On The Alamo	1959	Stereo Craft 111A
VOL-TONES		
If She Should Call/Don't		
Monkey With A Donkey	1957	Dynamic 108
VOLCANOS		
Gotta Be A False Alarm/		
Movin' And Groovin'	1964	Harthon 138
Take Me Back Again	1965	Harthon 146
Baby/Storm Warning	N/A	Arctic 106
VOLCHORDS		
Bongo Love/Peek-A-Boo Love	1961	Regatta 2004
VOLUMES		
Why/Monkey Hop	1964	Old Town 1154
VOLUMES (1)		
I Won't Tell A Soul/Gotta		
Feed The Ol' Horse Lotta Hay	1954	Jaguar 3004
VOLUMES (1) (LACILLE WATKINS & THE)		
You Left Me Lonely/So		
Disappointed With Love	1954	Jaguar 3006

Artist Song	Year	Label	Artist Song	Year	Label
VOLUMES (2) (JIMMIE LEWIS & THE)			**WAILERS**		
In My Heart/I Saw A Cottage			Hot Love/Stop The Clock	1954	Columbia 40288
In My Dreams	1958	Ivy 104	**WALCOES**		
VOLUMES (3)			Tell Me Why/Moonlight Rock	1959	Drum 011
I Love You/Dreams	1962	Chex 1002 (second press-	**WALKER, CHARLES (WITH THE DAFFODILS)**		
		ing,first is by Valumes)	Slave To Love/Be No Fool		
Come Back Into My Heart/			No More	1959	Champion 1014
The Bell	1962	Chex 1005	**WALKER, WAYNE (& GROUP)**		
Sandra/Teenage Paradise	1963	Jubilee 5446	Whatever You Desire/		
Oh, My Mother-In-Law/Our Song	1963	Jubilee 5454	A Teenage Love Affair	1957	Columbia 40905
Ink Dries Quicker Than Tears/			**WALLACE, JERRY (& GROUP)**		
Why Must We Go To School			Gloria/On A Night When		
(by the Nutmegs)	1963	Times Square 22	Flowers Were Dancing	1956	Mercury 70812
Gotta Give Her Love/I Can't			**WALLACE, JERRY (BB THE JEWELS)**		
Live Without You	1964	American Arts 6	How The Time Flies/With		
I Just Can't Help Myself/One			This Ring	1958	Challenge 59013
Way Lover	1965	American Arts 18	**WANDERERS (1) (AKA SINGING WANDERERS)**		
Trouble I've Seen/That Same			We Could Find Happiness/		
Old Feeling	1966	Impact 1017	Hey, Mae Ethel	1953	Savoy 1109
A Way To Love You/You Got			Mask Off/My Lady Chocaonine	1957	Gone 5005
It Baby	1967	Inferno 2001	Thinking Of You/Great J		
My Road Is The Right Road/			umping Catfish	1957	Onyx 518
My Kind Of Girl	1967	Inferno 2004	Two Hearts On A Window		
Ain't That Lovin' You/I Love			Pane/Collecting Hearts	1958	Cub 9019
You Baby	1968	Inferno 5001	A Teenage Quarrel/My		
I Wanna Be Your Man	N/A	Chex	Shining Hour	1958	Orbit 9003/Cub 9003 (58)
County Jail	N/A	Chex	Please/Shadrach Meshack		
You Put A Spell On Me	N/A	Chex	And Abednego	1959	Cub 9023
Miss Silhouette	N/A	Chex	I'm Not Ashamed/Only When		
La La La Song	N/A	Chex	You're Lonely	1959	Cub 9035
Angel	N/A	Chex	I'm Waiting In Green Pastures/		
Roly Poly	N/A	Chex	I Walked Through A Forest	1959	Cub 9054
VON CARL, JIMMY (BB THE JUNE VOICES)			If I Could Make You Mine/I		
Lonely Night/This Doesn't			Need You More	1960	Cub 9075
Seem Real	1959	Flick 002	For Your Love/Sally Goodheart	1961	Cub 9089
VON GAYELS			I'll Never Smile Again/A Little		
The Twirl/Crazy Dance	1960	Dore 544	Too Long	1961	Cub 9094
The Twirl/Loneliness	1963	USA 1221	Somebody Else's Sweetheart/		
VONDELLS			She Wears My Ring	1961	Cub 9099
Valentino/Errand Boy	1964	Marvello 5003	As Time Goes By/There Is		
Errand Boy/Then I Know	1964	Marvello 5005	No Greater Love	1962	Cub 9109/MGM 13082 (62)
Lenora/Valentino	1964	Marvello 5006	After He Breaks Your Heart/		
VONNS			Run Run Senorita	1962	United Artists 570
Leave Us Alone/So Many			I'll Know/You Can't Run		
Days/So Many Days	1963	King 5793	Away From Me	1963	United Artists 648
VOWELS			How Can I Get Along Without You/		
Your Lovin' Kisses/Bop De			Don't Do Nothing I Wouldn't Do	1975	Savoy 1098 (unreleased)
Do Be Oo Be	N/A	Lebam 157	My First, Last and Only Girl/		
VOWS			What Do I Do	1975	Savoy 1099 (unreleased)
Have You Heard/I Wanna			My Sweetie Pie	N/A	UGHA LP 001
Chance	1962	Markay 103	**WANDERERS (1) (DOLLY COOPER & THE)**		
Girl In Red/Born With Rhythm	1963	Ran-Dee 112	Love Can Be Blind/Be Good		
Dottie/The Things You Do To Me	1963	Tamara 760 (same # used	To Yourself	1954	Savoy 1121
		twice)	**WANDERERS (1) (PEARL WOODS & THE)**		
Say You'll Be Mine/When A			I Can't Wait	N/A	UGHA LP 001
Boy Loves A Girl	1963	Tamara 760 (same # used	**WANDERERS (2)**		
		twice)/Sta-Set 402 (63)	Quiet Night/One Look	1960	Panama 3900
Buttered Popcorn/Tell Me	1965	V.I.P. 25016	**WANDERERS (3) (TONY ALLEN & THE)**		
VOXPOPPERS (1)			Everybody's Somebody's		
Wishing For Your Love/The			Fool/If Love Was Money	1961	Kent 356
Last Drag	1958	Amp-3 1004/Mercury	**WANDERERS (4) (DION & THE)**		
		71282 (58)	Time In My Heart For You/		
Pony Tail/Ping Pong Baby	1958	Mercury 71315	Wake Up Baby	1966	Columbia 43483
Love To Last A Lifetime/			Two Ton Feather/So Much		
Come Back Little Girl	1958	Poplar 107	Younger	1966	Columbia 43692
Why Do You Treat Me This			**WANS (LARRY BURNS & THE)**		
Way/Come Back Little Girl	1958	Poplar 112	Back To School/Ain't No Big Thing	N/A	Voom 17
Can't Understand It/Blessing			**WARBLERS**		
After All	1959	Versailles 200	Is This The Real Thing/It's		
VOXPOPPERS (2) (FREDDIE & THE)			Wrong (by the Ontarios)	1973	Baron 101
Lonely For You/Helen Isn't Tellin'	1960	Warwick 589	Scheming/Love Me Baby		
VOYAGERS			(by the Ontarios)	1973	Baron 106
I Never Loved Anyone/Farewell	1960	Titan 1712	She's Too Tall For Love/		
WADE, EARL (& GROUP)			Lonesome Again	1974	Outhouse 102
You're Still My Baby/Feel So			**WARD, LEE (BB THE CYMBALS)**		
Bad	1961	Seville 111	The Defense Rests/You		
WADE, MORRIS (BB THE FOUR PHARAOHS)			Are My Sunshine	1961	Gait 407
It Was A Night Like This/Is It Too			**WARE, CURTIS (BB THE FOUR-DO-MATICS)**		
Late (by the Four Pharaohs)	1958	Ransom 102	Flame In My Heart/Am I In Love	1961	Kaybee 101
WAGNER, CLIFF (& GROUP)			**WARNER, LITTLE SONNY (& GROUP)**		
When You're Dancin'/Some-			Oh What A Fool/I Love You,		
thing's Got A Hold On Me	1964	Jolum 2509	Oh Darling	1960	Swingin' 627

Artist	Song	Year	Label
WARNER, MERRILL (& GROUP)			
	Don't Let Me Dream Tonight/		
	Sit, Hope And Cry	N/A	Travel 505
WASHINGTON, BABY (& GROUP)			
	The Bells/Why Did My Baby		
	Put Me Down	1959	Neptune 104
	Let's Love In The Moonlight/		
	Work Out	1959	Neptune 107
	Nobody Cares (About Me)/		
	Money's Funny	1961	Neptune 122
WASHINGTON, BABY (BB THE HEARTS)			
	I Hate To See You Go/Knock		
	Yourself Out	1959	J&S 1632/1633
WASHINGTON, DINAH (BB THE DELLS)			
	Am I Blue/I Want To Be Loved		
	(no group)	1962	Mercury 72015
WASHINGTON, ROGER (& GROUP)			
	Unless You Let Me/I Won't		
	Make You Cry	1964	Beacon 563
WATERS, LARRY (& GROUP)			
	I Wonder, Wonder/Wish I Didn't		
	Love You So	1956	Dig 121
WATESIANS			
	I'll Find Myself A Guy/I Told		
	You Baby	1962	Donna 1371
WATKINS, BILLY (& GROUP)			
	Sandman Of Love/Spade		
	Love (no group)	1954	Allied 10000
	Where Is My Love/I Wanna Know	1961	Chess 1786
	Beverly/Just For You	1964	Kent 411
WATKINS, SIS (& GROUP) (AKA UNIVERSALS)			
	Only You Can Give/Here I Stand	1964	Diplomacy 9
WATTS (JIMMY MACK &)			
	I Believe I Love You/True		
	Lover Girl	1960	Gee 1056
WATTS, BETTE (& MALE GROUP)			
	Do Me A Favor/Let It Be Me	1960	Wand 104
WATTS, MAYMIE (& GROUP)			
	Quicksand/There Goes That		
	Train	1955	Groove 0103
WAYMATES			
	Once In A Lifetime	N/A	Skyland
WAYNE, ART (& GROUP)			
	Let Me Make My Own Mistakes/		
	Try And Try Again	1961	Xavier 8890
WAYNE, JAMES (& FEMALE GROUP)			
	It's You/Please Be Mine	1957	Peacock 1672
WAYNE, SCOTTY (& GROUP)			
	Only One/I'm Gonna Leave	1964	Talent 1008
WAYNE, WEE WILLIE (BB THE KIDDS)			
	I Remember/Traveling Mood		
	(no group)	1955	Imperial 5355
WEBER, LEWIS (& GROUP)			
	Judy/Queen Of Rock And Roll	1959	Scottie 1304
WEBS			
	Let Me Take You Home/Do I		
	Have A Chance	1958	Sotoplay 006
	Question/Steamboat	1963	Guyden 2090
	People Sure Act Funny/You		
	Pretty Fool	1966	MGM 13602
	Tomorrow/This Thing Called		
	Love	1967	Popside 4593
	We Belong Together/I Want		
	You Back	1968	Verve 10610
WEBTONES			
	My Lost Love/Walk, Talk		
	And Kiss	1958	MGM 12724
WEEKENDERS (ALAN & THE)			
	Don't Cry No More	1963	Mohawk 140
WELCH, LENNY (& GROUP)			
	My One Sincere/Rocket To		
	The Moon	1958	Decca 30637
	Ebb Tide/Congratulations, Baby	1962	Cadence 1422
WEST RUDY (& GROUP)			
	Just To Be With You (with		
	male group)/You Were		
	Mine (with female group)	1959	King 5276
WEST SIDERS			
	No Tears Left For Crying/		
	Don't You Know	1963	Leopard 5004/United Artists 600 (63)
	Valerie	1963	Leopard 5006
WEST WINDS			
	You Know I'll Miss You/What		
	A Kiss That Was	1964	Enith International 1269
	You're Lookin' At My Guy/Oowee,		
	Oowee, Oowee, Oowee	1964	Kapp 588
WEST, EASTIN (& GROUP)			
	Ring The Telephone/		
	Lazy Woman (no group)	1963	Everest 2028
WESTON, BILLY (& GROUP)			
	It Won't Be This Way/I Need You	1962	Ep-Som 1002
WHALERS (1) (HAL PAIGE & THE)			
	Don't Have To Cry No More/		
	Pour The Corn	1957	Fury 1002/Checker 873 (57)
	Sugar Bird/Thunderbird	1957	J&S 1601
	Going Back To My Hometown/		
	After Hour Blues	1959	Fury 1024
WHALERS (2) (KENNY & THE) (AKA DONNY & THE DREAMERS)			
	Life Is But A Dream/Life Is		
	But A Dream	1961	Whale 504
WHALERS (3) (MOBY DICK & THE)			
	You've Got A Bull	N/A	Forest 2009
WHEELER, ART (& GROUP)			
	Jo Jo/Too Late For Tears	1962	Swingin' 642
WHEELERS			
	Once I Had A Girl/Shine 'Em On	1960	Cenco 107
WHEELETTS (SAMMY & THE)			
	Goodbye My Love/Jackie		
	Please	N/A	Rip Cor 6001
WHEELS (1)			
	My Heart's Desire/Let's Have A Ball	1956	Premium 405
	Teasin' Heart/Loco	1956	Premium 408
	I Can't Forget/How Could I		
	Ever Leave You?	1957	Premium 410
	So Young And So In Love/		
	Where Were You	1958	Time 1003/Early Bird 006 (96)
	Clap Your Hands, Pt. 1/Clap		
	Your Hands, Pt. 2	1959	Folly 800
	No One But You/I've Waited		
	For A Lifetime	1960	Roulette 4271
	I Can't Go On Without You	N/A	Premium
WHEELS (1) (ARTHUR LAKE & THE)			
	May I Count On You?/The		
	Good Earth	1956	Premium 406
WHEELS (1) (RUDY & THE)			
	Copy Cat/It's Not For Me	1959	Curtis 751
WHEELS (2) (FERRIS & THE)			
	Chop Chop/I Want To Dance		
	(Every Night)	1961	Bambi 801
	Moments Like This/He Was A		
	Fortune Teller	1962	United Artists 458
WHEELS (3) (MIDGE OLINDE & THE)			
	Precious Love/Driving Wheel	1962	Viking 1011
WHIPOORWILLS			
	I Want My Love/Kiss A Fool		
	Goodbye	1953	Dooto 1201
	Deep Within/Going To A Party	1961	Josie 892
WHIPPETS			
	I Want To Talk With You/		
	Go Go With Ringo	1964	Josie 921
WHIPS (1) (AKA FLAIRS (1))			
	Pleadin' Heart/She Done Me Wrong	1954	Flair 1025
WHIPS (2)			
	Yes Master/Rosie's Blues	1958	Dore 502
WHIRLAWAYS			
	Smoke! Smoke! Smoke!	1958	Crest 1051
WHIRLERS			
	Magic Mirror/Tonight And Forever	1957	Whirlin' Disc 108/Port 70025 (60)
WHIRLWINDS (1) (JOE WELDEN & THE)			
	Someone/Answer Soon	1959	Khoury's 714
WHIRLWINDS (2)			
	Angel Love/The Mountain	1961	Guyden 2052
	Heartbeat/After The Party	1963	Philips 40139
	Heartbeat/That's My Girl (by		
	De Jan & the Elgins)	1967	Times Square 112
WHIRLWINDS (3) (JAMES LOYD & THE)			
	I Can't Stand Another Broken		
	Heart/I Know About The		
	Boy Next Door	1963	Empala 117
WHIRLWINDS (4) (KENNY BEAU & THE)			
	You're The Right One/Gift Of		
	Love	1959	PL 1015

Artist Song	Year	Label
WHISPERS (1)		
Ever Lovin' Slick/I've Got No Time	1950	Apollo 1156
Don't Fool With Lizzie/Fool Heart	1954	Gotham 309
Are You Sorry?/We're Getting Married	1955	Gotham 312
WHISPERS (2)		
If You Don't Care/Here Comes Summer	1966	Laurie 3344
WHITE, FLOYD (& GROUP)		
Pains Of Love/Hey Theresa	1958	Tee Vee 302
WHITE, RUTH (& GROUP)		
Give Us Your Blessings/Dog Time	1963	Candi 1029
WHOOPING CRANES		
Heart And Soul/Tears And Dreams	N/A	El Rey 1000
WIG TWISTERS		
Wheel Of Love/Baby Wanna Rock	1957	A-Ron 1001
WIGS		
You're Sweeter Than Wine/Chicken Switch	1964	Golden Crest 592
WIL-ETTES		
Summertime Is Gone/One Love Is Lost	1962	Jamie 1234
WIL-SONS		
Let Me Help You/Come On Mama	1961	Highland 1020
WILCO, ROGER (& GROUP)		
So Lonely/I Won't Love Nobody	1961	Milestone 2007
WILDCATS		
Keep Talkin'/Beatin' On A Rug	1955	RCA 6386
WILDE, JIMMY (& GROUP)		
Crazy Eyes For You/Bonnie Bonnie	1962	Chelsea 1006
WILDER BROTHERS		
Party Line/Sick, Sick, Sick	1959	Leeds 781
WILDTONES		
King Cobra/Mendelsohn Rock	1958	Tee Gee 105
WILDWOODS (FB FRED PARRIS)		
When The Swallows Come Back To Capistrano/Heart Of Mine	1960	Caprice 101/102
Golden Sunset/Here Comes Big Ed	1961	May 106
WILLIAMS, ANDRE (& GROUP)		
Just Because Of A Kiss/Bacon Fat	1957	Fortune 831/Epic 9196
WILLIAMS, ANDRE (& GROUP)		
Don't Touch/Please Pass The Biscuits (by Gino Parks)	1957	Fortune 839X
Mrs. Mother U.S.A./Cadillac Jack	1968	Checker 1205
WILLIAMS, BERNIE (& GROUP)		
Don't Tease Me/Why Fool Yourself	1955	Imperial 5360
WILLIAMS, BILLY (& GROUP)		
Ask Me No Questions/I've Got An Invitation To A Dance	1957	Mercury 71187
WILLIAMS, BOBBY (& GROUP)		
Chapel Of Love/You	1958	Deck 142
Just A Fool/So Many Women	1960	Swingin' 619
WILLIAMS, CLARENCE (& GROUP)		
Royal Queen/Love Me	1962	Chancellor 1118
WILLIAMS, COLLY (& GROUP)		
We'll Make It Someday/My Vow	1963	Poplar 118
WILLIAMS, CURLEY (& GROUP)		
This Heart Of Mine/Be Mine	1956	Modern 1004
WILLIAMS, DICKY (& GROUP)		
Te Na Na/What Makes You Think You're In Love	1960	Vin 1021
WILLIAMS, EDDIE (& GROUP)		
Never Too Late/Just One More	1960	R-Dell 114
Have A Heart/Dancing Shoes	1963	Alcor 2013
Should Pretending End/Tears Had Fallen	1964	Corsair 402
WILLIAMS, FLETCHER (& GROUP)		
Stop, Look And Love Me/Mary Lou	1957	Bullseye 1001
WILLIAMS, JIMMY (& GROUP)		
I Knew/Love Only Me	1956	Neil 104
WILLIAMS, JOHNNY (& GROUP)		
Don't Call For Me/My Foolish Pride	1961	Cy 001
WILLIAMS, KAE (& GROUP)		
Everyday Blues/Old Man Mose	1956	Kaiser 385
WILLIAMS, KENNY (& GROUP)		
Old Fashioned Christmas, Pt. 1/Old Fashioned Christmas, Pt. 2	1973	Ben Mor 1001
WILLIAMS, LITTLE CHERYL (& GROUP)		
Jim/Pocket Full Of Money	1962	Elmar 1085/Kapp 500X
WILLIAMS, MARIE (& GROUP)		
Cat Scratching/Come Back To Me	1961	Smart 324
WILLIAMS, MAURICE (& FEMALE GROUP)		
It's Alright/Here I Stand	1961	Herald 572
WILLIAMS, MAURICE (BB THE ZODIACS)		
Lollipop/May I	1965	Vee Jay 678
WILLIAMS, MEL (& GROUP)		
Lonely Heart/Soldier Boy	1955	Federal 12236
Here At My Phone/Talk To Me (no group)	1956	Dig 107
My Love/Don't Cry Baby	1956	Dig 123
All Through The Night/I Cried A Million Tears (no group)	1956	Dig 128
Stay With Me	1957	Capitol EP 940
Stand There, Mountain/I Don't Care If The Sun Don't Shine	1957	Dig 140
WILLIAMS, MEL (BB THE MONTCLAIRS)		
Eternal Love/Roses Never Fade	1955	Decca 29499
God Gave Me You/You're All Right Baby	1955	Decca 29554
You're Alright Baby	1956	Decca EP 2400
WILLIAMS, OTIS (& GROUP)		
It'll Never Happen Again!/It Just Ain't Right	1964	King 5816
WILLIAMS, TONY (& GROUP)		
The Miracle/My Prayer	1961	Reprise 20030
WILLIS, ROBERT (CHICK)		
Pleading/Yes I Do (no group)	1959	Bay-Tone 104
WILLOWS (AKA FIVE WILLOWS)		
This Is The End/Don't Pull, Don't Push, Don't Shove	1956	Club 1014/Michelle 501
Church Bells Are Ringing/Baby Tell Me	1956	Melba 102 (first pressing)
Church Bells May Ring/Baby Tell Me	1956	Melba 102 (second pressing)
Do You Love Me?/My Angel	1956	Melba 106
Little Darlin'/My Angel	1957	Melba 115
Now That I Have You/There's A Dance Goin' On	1961	Four Star 1753
It's Such A Shame/Tears In My Eyes	1964	Heidi 103
Such A Night/Sit By The Fire	1964	Heidi 107
Fooled By Her Kisses/Lazy Daisy	N/A	Mercury
WILLOWS (FB DOTTY MARTIN)		
My Dear, Dearest Darling/You	1960	Warwick 524
WILLOWS (TONY MIDDLETON & THE)		
The First Taste Of Love/Only My Heart	1957	Eldorado 508
Let's Fall In Love/Say Yeah	1958	Gone 5015
WILSON, FAYE (& GROUP)		
I Miss You So/Playing Me For A Fool	1957	Hip 401
WILSON, JIMMY (& GROUP)		
Please Accept My Love/Big Wheel Rolling	1959	Goldband 1074
WILSON, ROBIN (& GROUP)		
Close To Me/Nervous Auctioneer	1960	Monument 426
WILSON, SONNY (& GROUP)		
Lonely Nights/Troubled Times	1961	Plaza 1
WILSON, STEVE (& GROUP)		
Written In The Stars/Oh-Be-Dum	1961	Pamela 205
WILSON, WALLY (& GROUP)		
If You Don't Love Me/The Hunt	1954	Sabre 106
WINCHELL, DANNY (& GROUP)		
I Do, I Do/My Little Tree-House	1957	MGM 12577
WINCHELL, DANNY (BB NINO & THE EBBTIDES)		
Jeannie/Beware You're Falling In Love	1959	Recorte 406
We're Gonna Have A Rockin' Party/Don't Say You're Sorry	1959	Recorte 410

Artist Song	Year	Label	Artist Song	Year	Label
Come Back Baby/I've Chosen You	1959	Recorte 415	Betty Jean/She's My Everything	1955	Rama 175
WINDSONG			I Won't Come To Your Wedding/What Makes You Do The Things That You Do?	1955	Rama 184
Imagination/Canadian Sunset/ Young Wings Can Fly/Lucky Old Sun	N/A	Clifton EP 503	Love's Something That's Made For Two/Beggin' For Love	1955	Rama 53/Rama 157 (55)
WINDSORS (1) (LEE SCOTT & THE)			Come Back My Love/Beggin' For Love	1955	Rama 65
My Gloria/Cool Sea Breeze	1958	Back Beat 506	Come Back My Love/Eleven Roses (And The Twelfth Is You)	1955	Rama 65
WINDSORS (2)			C'Est La Vie/C'Est La Vie (instrumental by Jimmy Wright Orch.)	1956	Rama 194
Carol Ann/Keep Me From Crying	1959	Wig-Wag 203	Wreckless	1986	Rama (unreleased)
WINN, RICKY (& GROUP)			House Of Cards	1986	Rama (unreleased)
Till Eternity	N/A	Campbell 1001	I'm Not The Kind Of Guy/Why Can't You	1991	Classic Artists 131
WINNERS (1)			I Love You Baby	N/A	Casa Grande
My Sin/To Think We're Only Friends	1952	Derby 802	**WRIGHT, BEVERLY (BB THE FOUR STUDENTS)**		
WINNERS (2)			Shake Till I'm Shook/Don't Let The Sun Catch You Cryin' (no group)	1956	Groove 0153
Can This Be Love?/Rockin' And Rollin'	1956	Rainbow 331	**WRIGHT, LEO (& GROUP)**		
WINNERS (3)			I Pretend And Cry/Bops-A-Bops Love	1965	Perico 1257
Dance Romeo Dance/ Lucky Guy	1962	Vee Jay 494	**WRIGHT, MARY (& GROUP)**		
WINSTONS			One Guy/I Was A Fool	1960	Kim 101
Hey Little School Girl/To The Aisle	1957	Cinemascope 8705	**WRIGHT, RUBIN (& GROUP)**		
WINTERS, DAVID (& GROUP)			To You/Bye Bye	1959	Lancer 101
Sunday Kind Of Love/Princess	1959	Addison 5004	**WRIGHT, WILLIE (BB THE SPARKLERS)**		
Dori Anne/Bye Bye	1962	Rori 703	Your Letter/Slowly Losing My Mind	1960	Federal 12372
WISDOMS			I'm Gonna Leave You Baby/ Just Let Me Love You	1961	Federal 12406
Two Hearts Make One Love/ Lost In Dreams	1959	Gaity 169	**WYATT, DON (& GROUP)**		
WIZARDS			I'm In Love/Reason To Love	1961	Brent 7026
I Want To Live/I'm Blind	1965	Era 3161	**WYATT, JOHNNY (& GROUP)**		
Street Corner/A Happier Time	1982	C&J 22650	Once Upon A Time/Bottom Of The Top	1965	Magnum 736
Guardian Angel/What Brought Us Together	1982	C&J 22651	**WYATT, JOHNNY (BB THE CANDLES)**		
WOMBATS (GARY & THE)			One Night With You/Goodnight	1961	Swingin' 643
Summer's Over/Squidgy Bod	1963	Regina 291	**WYNNEWOODS**		
So Tough/Winter Dream	1963	Regina 297	Is That Wrong/You Are The Only One	1959	Wynne 108
WONDERLETTES			**X CLASSMATES (JOE TEX & HIS)**		
How Soon/So Wonderful	N/A	Baja 4506	Charlie Brown Got Expelled/ Blessed Are These Tears	1959	Ace 559
WONDERS (1)			**X-CELLENTS (LITTLE WILLIE & THE)**		
Well Now/Cuttin' Out	1957	Reserve 122	I'll Always Be By Your Side/ Hey Little Willie	1965	Smash 1996
WONDERS (1) (TONY ALLEN & THE)			**YACHTSMEN**		
By My Love, Be My Love/ Tell Me	1958	Forward 601/Tampa 157 (58)	It's So Hard To Be Young/Now	1958	Destiny 402
Looking For My Baby/Loving You	1959	Jamie 1119	Our Future/Strut And Stroll	1961	Har-Glo 420
God Gave Me You/Train Of Love	1959	Jamie 1143	**YELLOW JACKETS (WALTER & THE)**		
WONDERS (2)			Mine Forever More/I Was Wrong	1957	Goldband 1033
I'll Write A Book/Hey Senorita	1959	Ember 1051	**YEOMANS**		
I Wonder/Summer Love	1961	Chesapeake 604	I'm The Guy/Unlucky	1964	Heidi 113
What's The World Comin' To/ One Day At A Time	1961	Manco 1024	**YESTERDAY'S NEWS**		
Please Don't Cry/With These Hands	1962	Bamboo 523	Our Anniversary/Mickey Mouse Chant	1979	U.G.H.A. 06
WONDERS (3)			Old Man River/Babalu's Wedding Day	1980	Clifton 44
Marilyn/Say There	1963	Colpix 699	Stand By Me/Millionaire Hobo	1981	Clifton 60
WOOD, LORI (BB THE BELMONTS)			Countdown To Love/ Countdown To Love	1982	Crystal Ball 148
But That Was Long Ago/The End Of The World For Me	1962	Amy 842	**YESTERDAY'S TODAY**		
WOODS, CORA (& GROUP)			One Mint Julep/Papa Was A Rolling Stone	N/A	Starlight 1
I Don't Want To Cry/Rock In Your Head	1955	Federal 12223	Who's That Knockin'/Ain't No Sunshine	N/A	Starlight 2
Ooh La La/Where Are You	1955	Federal 12229	**YO YO'S**		
WOODS, JASPER (& GROUP) (AKA RICHARD BERRY & GROUP)			Gonna Find A New Love	N/A	Goldwax 310
I'm Coming Home/Hully Gully Papa	1962	VPM 1009	**YO YO'S (DELMA GOGGINS & THE)**		
WOODS, SONNY (& GROUP)			I Thank My Lucky Star/Leave Me If You Want to	1961	Vibro 4008
Together	N/A	Lu Pine	**YORK, PATTI (BB THE SENTIMENTALS)**		
WORLEY-BIRDS (WAYNE WORLEY & THE)			You Walked Away With My Heart/That Old Feeling	1958	Mint 806
To Be Alone/Red Headed Woman	1961	Brent 7024	**YOUNG CHAMPIONS**		
WRENS			Teen Age World/Friday The 13th	1985	Nobletown 822
Eleven Roses (And The Twelfth Is You)/Love's Something That's Made For Two	1955	Rama 110	**YOUNG HEARTS**		
Serenade Of The Bells/Hey, Girl	1955	Rama 174	Do Not Forsake Me/Unwelcome Guest	1961	Infinity 006
Serenade Of The Bells/ Love's Something That's Made For Two	1955	Rama 174			

Artist	Song	Year	Label
YOUNG IDEAS			
	Touchdown/Dream	1959	Swan 4044
YOUNG JESSIE (& GROUP)			
	Make Believe/Shuffle In The Gravel	1957	Atco 6101
YOUNG JESSIE (BB THE FLAIRS (1))			
	I Smell A Rat/Lonesome Desert	1954	Modern 921
YOUNG JESSIE (BB THE JACKS)			
	Mary Lou/Don't Think I Will	1955	Modern 961
YOUNG LADS (1)			
	Moonlight/I'm In Love	1956	Neil 100
YOUNG LADS (2)			
	Night After Night/Graduation Kiss	1963	Felice 909/Felice 712 (63)
YOUNG LIONS			
	Oh Dolly/How Can You Be	1958	Tampa 158
	Summertime With You/Maybe Someday	1959	United Artists 177
	Little Girl/It Would Be	1960	Dot 16172
YOUNG LORDS			
	Peace Of Mind/Oh Stop It (by the Du Woppers)	1970	Kelway 100
YOUNG ONES (AKA YOUNGONES)			
	Marie/Those Precious Love Letters	1963	Yussels 7701
	I'm In The Mood For Love/No No Don't Cry	1963	Yussels 7703
	Diamonds And Pearls (a capella)/Three Coins In The Fountain (a capella)	1963	Yussels 7704
	Sweeter Than/Picture Of Love (by the El Sierros)	1964	Times Square 36/Relic 527 (65)
	I Only Want You (a capella)/Over The Rainbow (a capella)	1965	Times Square 104
	To Make A Long Story Short (acapella)	1975	Relic LP 102
	Mary Ann (a capella)	1975	Relic LP 102/Relic LP 5079 (89)
	Shining Star (a capella)	1975	Relic LP 102/Relic LP 5079 (89)
YOUNG SISTERS			
	My Guy/Casanova Brown	1960	Twirl 2001
	Playgirl/Hello Baby	1961	Twirl 2008
	Jerry Boy/She Took His Love Away	1963	Mala 467
YOUNG, BILLY (& GROUP)			
	Are You For Me/Glendora	1963	Original Sound 29
YOUNG, BOBBY (WITH RICK & THE MASTERS)			
	Only Girl For Me/To Each His Own	1968	Guyden 2087
YOUNG, CECIL (& QUARTETTE)			
	Ooh-Diga-Gow	1954	King
YOUNG, DONNY (& GROUP)			
	From Twelve To Seven/(no flip)	1964	Amcan 407
YOUNG, GEORGE (& GROUP)			
	You Know I Wanna Love You/Wow Wow Wow	1957	Chord 1301
YOUNGONES (AKA YOUNG ONES)			
	Gloria (a capella)/Just Two Kinds Of People (a capella)	1962	Times Square 28/Relic 540 (65)
YOUNGSTERS (1)			
	Shattered Dreams/Rock'n Roll'n Cowboy	1956	Empire 104
	Counterfeit Heart/You're An Angel (With The Devil In Your Eyes)	1956	Empire 107
	Dreamy Eyes/Christmas In Jail	1956	Empire 109
	Dreamy Eyes/I'm Sorry Now	1956	Empire 109
YOUNGSTERS (2)			
	Sweet Talk/Teenager Susan	1958	Apt 25021
	Lucky Sixteen/Piel Canela (by Cinnamon Skin)	1959	Checker 917
YOUNGSTERS (3) (FB SUE BLACK)			
	Take Me/It Doesn't Matter Anymore	1961	Candix 313
YOUNGSTERS (4) (LITTLE PETE & THE)			
	You Told Another Lie/I'll Never Leave You Again	1962	Lesley 1925/Candlelite 428 (63)
YOUNGTONES (1)			
	Bow Legged Baby/Elaine	1958	Brunswick 55083
	Come On Baby/O, Tell Me	1958	Brunswick 55089
YOUNGTONES (2)			
	It's Over Now/You I Adore	1958	X-Tra 104/Candlelite 417 (63)
	Patricia/By The Candleglow (with the Dolls)	1958	X-Tra 110/Times Square 13 (63)
	Can I Come Over?/Gonna Get Together Again	1959	X-Tra 120/121/Candlelite 419 (63)
	I Do/Day Train (by the Blasters)	1964	Times Square 31
Z-DEBS			
	Changing My Life For You/I Would If I Could	1964	Roulette 4544
ZANE, HERB (& GROUP)			
	By You, By You/Let Me In Your Heart	1956	DeLuxe 6099
ZE-MAJESTICS			
	Bobbie Ann/Garlens Mambo	1959	Fox 5014
ZEBULONS			
	Falling Water/Wo-Ho-La-Tee-Da	1960	Cub 9069
ZEE, GINNY (& GROUP)			
	You Can't Imagine/Bobby Baby	1961	Atco 6218
ZEL, RITA (& GROUP)			
	Need You To Help Me/I Don't Understand You No More	1960	J&S 1685
ZELL ROCKS (DANNY ZELLA & HIS)			
	Wicked Ruby/Black Sax	1959	Fox 10057
ZELLA, DANNY (WITH THE LAREDOS)			
	Sapphire/You Made Me Blue	1959	Dial 100
ZEPHYRS			
	There's Something About You/She's Lost You	1965	Rotate 5006
	Let Me Love You Baby	1965	Rotate 5009
ZEPHYRS (BEN JOE ZEPPA & THE) (AKA BENN ZEPPA & THE ZEPHYRS)			
	Baby, I Need (Ting-A-Ling)/A Foolish Fool	1956	Specialty 577
ZEPPA, BEN (BB THE FOUR JACKS)			
	Why Do Fools Fall In Love	1956	Tops 278
	Young Heartaches/Ridin' Herd	1958	Hush 1000
ZEROES			
	Flossie Mae/Twisting With Crazee Babee	1963	Ty-Tex 105
ZEU REVIEW (ZIGGY & THE) (GM ENA ANKA)			
	Come Go With Me/Little Star	N/A	Zeu 5011
	Da Doo Run Run/Sherry	N/A	Zeu 5011
ZIP CODES			
	Your Way/Little Girl Of Mine	1988	Clifton 83
ZIP, DANNY (& GROUP)			
	Hey, Hey, Girl/Please Listen To Me	1964	MGM 13254
ZIPPERS (AKA CONTENDERS/AKA FIVE SCRIPTS/AKA KAPTIONS/AKA LYTATIONS)			
	Let's Forget The Past/Rhythm Train	1963	Long Fiber 202
ZIPPERS (ZIP & THE)			
	Where You Goin', Little Boy/Gig (no group)	1963	Pageant 607
ZIRCONS (1)			
	Only One Love/I Need It	1957	Winston 1020/Dot 15724 (58)
	No Twistin' On Sunday/Mama Wants To Drive	1962	Federal 12452
	Get Up And Go To School/Mr. Jones	1962	Federal 12478
ZIRCONS (2)			
	Lonely Way (a capella)/Your Way (a capella)	1963	Mellomood 1000/Relic 1008 (65)
	(I Hear) Silver Bells/You Are My Sunshine	1964	Cool Sound 1030
	(I Hear) Silver Bells/Traveling Stranger (by the Destinaires)	1964	Old Timer 602
	Stormy Weather (a capella)/Sincerely (a capella)	1964	Siamese 403/Old Timer 603 (64)
	Remember Then/You Baby You	1965	Old Timer 606
	One Summer Night (a capella)/The Lone Stranger (a capella)	1966	Amber 851
ZIRCONS (3)			
	Surfin' In The Sunset/Going Places	1963	Bagdad 1007
ZIRCONS (4)			
	Where There' A Will/Don't Put Off For Tomorrow	1967	Heigh Ho 607

Artist Song	Year	Label
I Couldn't Stop Crying/		
Sit Down Girl	1967	Heigh Ho 608/609
Go On And Cry, Cry/Was It		
Meant To Be This Way	1967	Heigh Ho 645/646
ZIRKONS (JOHNNY PARKER & THE)		
Oongawa/T.V. Commercial	N/A	C T 302
ZODIACS (JOHNNY BALLAD & THE)		
Another Day/My Song	1959	Wildcat 0016
Search For Love/I'll Gamble	1959	Wildcat 0017
ZODIACS (MAURICE WILLIAMS & THE)		
Golly Gee/"T" Town	1959	Cole 100
Lover (Where Are You?)/		
She's Mine	1959	Cole 101
Say Yeah/College Girl	1959	Selwyn 5121
Stay/Do You Remember	1960	Herald 552
Another Little Darling/Lita	1960	Soma 1410
Little Sally Walker/Anything	1960	Soma 1418
I Remember/Always	1961	Herald 556
Come Along/Do I	1961	Herald 559
Come And Get It/Someday	1961	Herald 563
High Blood Pressure/Please	1961	Herald 565
Here I Stand/It's All Right		
(by Maurice Williams)	1962	Herald 572
Funny/Loneliness	1963	Atlantic 2199

Artist Song	Year	Label
Nobody Knows/I Know	1965	Scepter 12113
So Fine/The Winds	1965	Sphere Sound 707
Surely/Don't Ever Leave Me	1966	Dee-Su 309
How To Pick A Winner/Don't		
Be Half Safe	1966	Dee-Su 311
May I/Lollipop	1966	Vee Jay 678
May I/This Feeling	1967	Dee-Su 304
Stay/Dance, Dance, Dance	1967	Dee-Su 318
The Four Corners/My Reason		
For Livin'	1968	Veep 1294
The Nearness Of You	1974	Relic LP 5017
I Love You Baby	1974	Relic LP 5017
But Not For Me	1974	Relic LP 5017
I Got A Woman	1974	Relic LP 5017
We're Lovers	1974	Relic LP 5017/
		Collectables LP 5021
Try/I'd Rather Have A		
Memory Than A Dream	N/A	Plus 4401
Return/My Baby's Gone	N/A	Sea-Horn 503
Little Mama	N/A	Sphere Sound LP 7007
Do You Believe	N/A	Sphere Sound LP 7007
Always	N/A	Sphere Sound LP 7007
Running Around	N/A	Sphere Sound LP 7007

Bibliography

"'Music, Maestro, Please,'" Leroy Kirkland. *Big Town Review*, Issue #2, April-May 1972, p. 41.

"Alan Freed and 7 Others Arrested in Payola Here". *New York Times*, May 20, 1960, 1:2.

"Digital Players Revive Record Industry." *Record Collector's Monthly*, Issue #5, January 1983, p. 1.

"Goldmine's Second Annual One-Hit Wonders: Johnny Cymbal." *Goldmine*, Dec. 1, 1989, p.18.

"OR Disc Jockey Found Fatally Shot in His Car." *Knoxville Sentinel*, Aug. 11, 1976.

"Rarest Record Sells For $3,866." *Record Exchanger*, Issue #26, p. 21.

"Record & Tape Sales Net $4.3 Billion in '84." *Record Collector's Monthly*, Issue #30, May 1985, p. 5.

"Rock 'n' Roll Pied Piper: Alan Freed." *New York Times*, May 20, 1960, p.62.

"The Ravens." *Stormy Weather*, Issue #3, January 1971, p. 4.

Abend, Richard F. "Memories of Those Oldies but Goodies." *Story Untold*, Issue #2, March-April 1978, p. 18.

Aita, Frank. "The Rivieras." *Record Exchanger*, Vol. 4, No. 3.

Anderson, Will. "The Carnations." *Bim Bam Boom*, Issue 8, December 1972.

Arslanian, Jim. "Bruce Patch, the 'Classic' Guy." *Echoes of the Past*, Issue #11, Spring 1990, p. 14.

Baer, Jon. "Peter Tripp & '50s N.Y. Radio." *Record Exchanger*, Issue #23, 1977, p. 22.

Ball, Aimee Lee. "Rock of Ages: WCBS-FM Rides the Crest of an Oldies Revival." *New York Magazine*, Aug. 6, 1990.

Baptista, Todd. *Group Harmony Behind the Rhythm and the Blues*. New Bedford, MA: Hamilton Printing Co., 1996.

Beachley, Chris, "Beach Music: What is it and Where Did it Come From?" *DISCoveries*, May-June 1988, p. 103.

Becker, Bob. "Signs of the Times." *Record Exchanger*, Issue #26, 1978.

Beckman, Jeff, and Feigenbaum, Hank. "Gee, It's the Crows." *Big Town Review*, Vol. 1, No. 2, 1972.

Belniak, Bob. "Hank Ballard: Who Was Annie?" *Echoes of the Past*, Issue #2, Winter 1987, p.8.

Belniak, Bob. "Remembering Jimmy Ricks 1924-1974." *Echoes of the Past*, Issue #8, Summer 1989, p.17.

Bennett, Paul M. "Album Alley." *Bim Bam Boom*, Issue #8, December 1972, p.46.

Bennett, Stephen. "My Radio, Gus Gossert & Me." *From Out of the Past*, Issue #1, Sept.-Oct. 1976, p.14.

Bennett, Stephen M. & Kenneth Cohen. "Then we whispered softly our teenage vows of love." *An Introduction to White and Still All Right!* Scarsdale, N.Y.: Crackerjack Press, 1977.

Betrock, Alan. *Girl Groups: The Story of a Sound*. New York: Delilah Books, 1982.

Bosco, Robert. "Joey/Flips From Bandstand to Obscurity." *Record Collector's Monthly*, Issue #50, Nov.-Dec. 1991.

Bronson, Fred. *Billboard Book of Number One Hits*. New York: Billboard Books, 1985.

Brown, Charles T. *The Rock & Roll Story*. Englewood Cliffs, CA: Prentice-Hall, 1983.

Chapple, Steve & Garofalo, Reebee. *Rock 'n' Roll is Here to Pay*. Chicago, IL: Nelson-Hall, 1977.

Clee, Ken. *The Directory of American 45 R.P.M. Records* (4 Vols). Philadelphia: Stak-O-Wax, 1989.

Coletti, Arlene. The Editor's Viewpoint. *From Out of the Past*, Issue #1, Sept.-Oct. 1976, p. 3.

Cook, Warren Blob. "Paper and Plastic-Part One." *Record Exchanger*, Issue #15, 1973, p. 10.

Cotten, Lee. *Shake Rattle & Roll: The Golden Age of American Rock 'n' Roll*, Vol. 1, 1952-1955. Pierian Press, 1989.

Cox, Herb, and West, Steve. "The Heart and Soul of the Cleftones." *Goldmine*, Feb. 21, 1992.

Davis, Chuck. "Platters," *Chicago Defender*, March 18, 1961.

Davis, Clive. *Clive: Inside the Record Business*. New York: William Morrow, 1975.

Dawson, Jim, and Propes, Steve. *What Was the First Rock 'n' Roll Record?* Boston: Faber and Faber, 1992.

Diskin, Bob. "Brooklyn's Bay Bops Launch White-Group Harmony and Pave the Way for '60s Doo-wop Hitmakers." *Record Collector's Monthly*, Issue #33, Nov.-Dec. 1985.

Doezar, Harold. "Oldies Scene-'59." *Time Barrier Express*, Issue #2, p. 14.

Dunne, Richard W. "The Five Discs." *Goldmine*, Feb. 8, 1991.

Engel, Edward R. *White and Still All Right!* Scarsdale, N.Y.: Crackerjack Press, 1977.

Engel, Ed. "Top 20 White Lead Singers." *Echoes of the Past*, Issue #4, Summer 1988, p. 22.

Ennis, Philip H. *The Seventh Stream: The Emergence of Rock 'n' roll in American Popular Music*. London: Wesleyan University Press, 1992.

Farlekus, Mike. "Memory Lane." *Bim Bam Boom*, Issue #7, September 1972, p. 14.

Feigenbaum, Hank. "The Good Old Days." *Big Town Review*, Issue #1, Feb.-March, 1972.

Ferlingere, Robert. *A Discography of Rhythm & Blues and Rock 'n' Roll Vocal Groups, 1945 to 1965*. Hayward, CA: California Trade School, 1976.

Fileti, Donn. Liner notes from Relic record album 5077: The Golden Groups-Part 47, *The Best of Apollo Records*, Vol. 1.

Fileti, Donn. Liner notes from CD titled, A Lighter Shade of Doo-Wop. Relic Records, August, 1993.

Flam, Steve. "Rock & Roll Revival." *Bim Bam Boom*, Issue #4, Feb.-March 1972, p. 34.

Flam, Steve. "The Classics." *Bim Bam Boom*, Vol. 1, No. 6, 1972.

Fox, Ted. *Showtime At the Apollo*. New York: Holt, Rinehart & Winston, 1983.

Friedwald, Will. *Jazz Singing*. London: Quartet Books, 1990.

Gagnon, Rick & Gnerre, Dave. "Little Caesar & the Romans: Still Singin' Those Oldies But Goodies." *Goldmine*, Aug. 12, 1988.

Garr, Gillian G. *She's A Rebel: The History of Women in Rock & Roll*. Seattle, WA.: Seal Press, 1992.

Gart, Galen. "Sales Figures Show 78s Slipping Away By 1956, Production Curtailments Follow." *Record Collector's Monthly*, Issue #31, June-July 1985, p. 1.

Gart, Galen, ed. *First Pressings: The History of Rhythm & Blues*, Vol. 3: 1953. Milford, NH: Big Nickel Publications, 1989.

Gart, Galen, ed. *First Pressings: The History of Rhythm & Blues*, Vol. 4: 1954. Milford, NH: Big Nickel Publications, 1990.

Gart, Galen, ed. *First Pressings: The History of Rhythm & Blues*, Vol. 5: 1955. Milford, NH: Big Nickel Publications, 1990.

Gart, Galen. *American Record Label Directory and Dating Guide* (4th ed.). Milford, NH: Big Nickel Publications, 1990.

Garvey, Dennis. "Randy and the Rainbows: What's in a Name?" *Goldmine*, Feb. 8, 1991.

Garvey, Dennis. "The Tune Weavers: One-Hit Wonderfuls." *Goldmine*, Feb. 8, 1991.

Garvey, Dennis. "The Bobbettes: Mister Lee's Star Pupils." *Goldmine*, Feb. 21, 1992.

George, Nelson. *The Death of Rhythm & Blues*. New York: E. P. Dutton, 1988.

Gilbert, Bob & Theroux, Gary. *The Top Ten: 1956-Present*. New York: Simon & Schuster, 1982.

Gillett, Charlie. *The Sound of the City: The Rise of Rock and Roll*. New York: Pantheon Books, 1983.

Goldberg, Lenny. "Oldies DJ: Gus Gossert." *Stormy Weather*, Issue #2, Oct./Nov. 1970, p. 5.

Goldberg, Marv. "Toppers, Hurricanes, Memos Are Same Brooklyn R&B Group On Wax." *Record Collector's Monthly*, Issue #43, March-April 1989.

Goldberg, Marvin, "The Midnighters," *Big Town Review*, Issue #3, p. 46, July-August 1972.

Goldberg, Marv, and Redmond, Mike. "The Clovers." *Record Exchanger*, Issue #15, p. 5, June 1973.

Goldberg, Marv and Redmond, Mike. "The Life and Times of the Solitaires." *Record Exchanger*, Issue #16, Fall 1973, p. 4.

Goldberg, Marv, and Redmond, Mike. "Yesterday's Memories: The Blenders." *DISCoveries*, May 1989, p.110-111.

Goldstein, S. & Jacobson, A. *Oldies But Goodies: The Rock & Roll Years*. New York: Mason-Charter, 1977.

Gonzalez, Ferdie and Turco, Art. "It's Not Cherie..." *Record Exchanger*, June 1973.

Gonzales, Fernando L. *Disco-File* (2nd ed.). Flushing, N.Y.: Fernando L. Gonzales, 1977.

Gottlieb, Martin. "The Durability of Doo-Wop." *New York Times*, Jan. 17, 1993, Sec. 2, p. 1.

Gottlieb, Martin. "On the White Side of Crossover Dreams." *New York Times*, Feb. 14, 1993, p. 6.

Greenfield, Jeff. *No Peace, No Place*. Garden City, NY: Doubleday & Co., 1973.

Greig, Charlotte. *Will You Still Love Me Tomorrow?: Girl Groups from the 50s on...*, London: Virago, 1989.

Grendysa, Pete. "Sneakin' Back." *Bim Bam Boom*, Issue #5, April-May, 1972, p. 39.

Grendysa, Peter. "Sneakin' Back." *Big Town Review*, Issue #3, July-Aug. 1972, p. 48.

Grendysa, Pete. "Sneakin' Back." *Bim Bam Boom*, Issue #11, p. 41, 1973.

Grendysa, Peter, Moonoogian, George, and Whitesell, Rick. "The Mills Brothers...Four Boys and a Guitar." *Record Exchanger*, Issue #24, 1977, p. 5.

Grendysa, Peter. "R&B Music on Recycled Shellac: Leon Rene's Exclusive Label." *Record Collector's Monthly*, Issue #6, p. 1, February, 1983.

Grendysa, Peter. "Variable-speed Turntable Makes Old 78s Sing on Key Every Time." *Record Collector's Monthly*, Issue #9, May 1983, p. 1.

Grendysa, Peter. "Fifties (50s) R & B Stars Helped Cheat Themselves By Signing Poorly Negotiated Contracts." *Record Collector's Monthly*, Issue #17, February 1984.

Grendysa, Peter. "The Diablos." *Goldmine*, Jan. 3, 1986.

Grendysa, Peter, "The Coming and Going of the Del Vikings." *Goldmine*, Feb. 21, 1992.

Gribin, Anthony, and Schiff, Matthew. *Doo-wop: The Forgotten Third of Rock 'n' Roll*. Iola, Wis.: Krause Publications, 1992.

Groia, Phil. "The Paul Winley Story." *Bim Bam Boom*, Vol. 2, No. 3, 1974.

Groia, Phil. *They All Sang on the Corner*. Port Jefferson, N.Y.: Phillie Dee Enterprises, 1983.

Guralnick, Peter. *Sweet Soul Music*. New York: Harper & Row, 1986.

Hardy, Phil & Laing, Dave. *Encyclopedia of Rock*. New York: Schirmer Books, 1988.

Heather, Bruce, and Dawson, Jim. "The Pearls: Anatomy of a Doo-Wop Group." *Goldmine*, Feb. 8, 1991.

Heckman, Don. "The Forties." *Record Exchanger*, Issue #3, June 1970, p. 13.

Hibbard, Don J. & Kaleialoha, C. *The Role of Rock*. Englewood Cliffs, CA: Prentice-Hall, 1983.

Hitchcock, H.W. & Sadie, S. (eds.) *The New Grove Dictionary of American Music*. New York: MacMillan, 1986.

Horner, Charlie, and Applebaum, Steve. "The Castelles." *Bim Bam Boom*, Vol. 2, No. 6, 1974.

Horner, Charlie. "Lee Andrews and the Hearts." *Goldmine*, Dec. 28, 1990.

Italiano, Ronnie. "Gus Gossert's Top 40 All-Time Favorite Doo-Wopps." *Time Barrier Express*, Issue #20, Nov.-Dec. 1976, p. 16.

Italiano, Ronnie. "The Nicky Addeo Story, Part One." *Story Untold*, Issue #1, Jan. 1978, p. 30.

Jackson, John A. *Big Beat Heat: Alan Freed and the Early Years of Rock & Roll*. New York: Schirmer Books, 1991.

Jancik, Wayne. "Down the Aisle With the Quin-Tones." *Goldmine*, Dec. 28, 1990.

Jancik, Wayne. "The Dreamlovers: Keeping the Dream Alive." *Goldmine*, Dec. 28, 1990.

Jones, Wayne. "The Five Satins Featuring Fred Parris." *Goldmine*, May 1979.

Keil, Charles. *Urban Blues*. Chicago: University of Chicago Press, 1966.

Keyes, Johnny. *Du-Wop*. Chicago: Vesti Press, 1987.

Krause, Stan. "Gus Gossert-The Man." *Time Barrier Express*, Issue #20, Nov.-Dec. 1976, p. 5.

Kreiter, Jeff. *45 R.P.M. Group Collector's Record Guide*, 4th ed. Bridgeport, OH: Boyd Press, 1992.

Lepri, Paul. *The New Haven Sound: 1946-1976*. New Haven, CT.: by the author, 1977.

Luciani, Tom. "Time Capsule." *Bim Bam Boom*, Issue #4, Feb.-Mar. 1972, p. 17.

Manchester, William. *The Glory and the Dream*, Vol. 1. Boston, MA: Little, Brown & Co., 1973.

Manchester, William. *The Glory and the Dream*, Vol. 2. Boston, MA: Little, Brown & Co., 1974.

Marcus, Greil. "The Girl Groups." In Miller, Jim, Ed. *The Rolling Stone Illustrated History of Rock & Roll*, New York: Rolling Stone Press, 1980.

Mariano, Art. "The Torn Corner." *Big Town Review*, Issue #3, July-August, 1972, p. 43.

Marion, Jean-Charles. "The Aesthetics of Lead Vocals." *Record Exchanger*, Issue #8, 1971, p. 16.

Marion, Jean-Charles. "Early White Arrivals." *Record Exchanger*, Issue #23, p. 26.

Marsh, Dave. *The Heart of Rock & Soul: The 1,001 Greatest Singles Ever Made*. New York: New American Library, 1989.

Marsh, Dave. *Louie Louie*. New York: Hyperion, 1993.

Mawhinney, Paul C. *The Music Master: The 45 RPM Record Directory By Artist* (Vol. I). Pittsburgh, PA: Record-Rama Sound Archives, 1983.

Mawhinney, Paul C. *The Music Master: The 45 RPM Record Directory By Title* (Vol. II). Pittsburgh, PA: Record-Rama Sound Archives, 1983.

McCutcheon, Lynn. "Interview: Sonny Woods." *Record Exchanger*, Issue #4, Aug.-Sep. 1970, p. 20.

McCutcheon, Lynn Ellis. *Rhythm and Blues*. Arlington, VA: Beatty, 1971.

McGowan, James A. *Hear Today, Here To Stay*. Ambler, PA: Akashic Press, 1983.

Mennie, Don. "Digital Audio: Aural Triumph; Archival Disaster." *Record Collector's Monthly*, Issue #5, January 1983, p. 2.

Mennie, Don. "Ducanes Chart With 'I'm So Happy,' Phil Spector Discovers Doo-wop." *Record Collector's Monthly*, Issue #39, Dec. 1987-Jan. 1988.

Mennie, Don. "Don K. Reed Has Made a Home for Doo-Wop on NY Radio With Live and Recorded Music Drawn From Five Decades." *Record Collector's Monthly*, Issue 53, Sept.-Oct. 1993.

Mondrone, Sal et al. "The Cadillacs." *Bim Bam Boom*, Vol. I, Issue 5, April-May 1972.

Mondrone, Sal, Flam, Steve and Newman, Ralph M. "The End of a Legend." *Bim Bam Boom*, Issue #6, July 1972, p. 33.

Moonoogian, G. A. "Wax Fax." *Record Collector's Monthly*, Issue #45, December 1989, p. 12.

Moonoogian, G. A. "Wax Fax." *Record Collector's Monthly*, Issue #49, p. 7, May-June 1991.

Moonoogian, G. A. "Wax Fax." *Record Collector's Monthly*, Issue #51, July-Aug. 1992, p. 23.

Moonoogian, George. "Oh, That Annie." *Record Exchanger*, Issue #23, 1977, p. 20.

Moonoogian, George. "Wax Fax." *Record Collector's Monthly*, Issue #30, May 1985.

Moonoogian, George. "Wax Fax." *Record Collector's Monthly*, Issue #36, Dec.-Jan./1986/87, p. 7.

Moonoogian, George. "Wax Fax." *Record Collector's Monthly*, Issue #50, Nov./Dec. 1991.

Moonoogian, George & Chris Beachley. "Lovin' Dan: A Look Thirty Years Later. Does He Have 59 To Go?" *It Will Stand*, Vol. 3, No. 20, 1981.

Newell, Bill. "Gus Gossert: His early years." *From Out of the Past*, Issue #4, p. 16.

Newman, Ralph. "Tony Passalacqua and the Fascinators." *Bim Bam Boom*, Vol. 1, No. 7, 1972.

Newman, Ralph M. "The Rock & Roll Revival: A Portrait of Richard Nader." *Bim Bam Boom*, Issue #10, p. 34.

Newman, Ralph. "Clear Skies At Last! The Five Sharps Revisited." *Bim Bam Boom*, Issue #13, p. 34.

Newman, Ralph. "The Laurie Story." *Time Barrier Express*, Issue #22, March-April 1977, p. 15.

Norm N. *Rock On*, Vol. I. New York: Thomas Y. Crowell Co., 1974.

Norm N. *Rock On Almanac*. New York: Harper & Row, 1989.

Osborne, Jerry. *Record Collector's Price Guide*, 1st ed. O'Sullivan, Wardside, 1976.

Osborne, Jerry. *Blues, R&B and Soul Price Guide*, 1st ed. O'Sullivan, Wardside, 1980.

Osborne, Jerry. *Rockin' Records: Buyers & Sellers Ref. Book and Price Guide*. Port Townsend, WA: Osborne Enterprises, 1989.

Oxford English Dictionary, 2nd ed. "Doo-Wop." Oxford, GB: Clarendon Press, 1989.

Pavlow, Big Al. *The R & B Book: A Disc-History of Rhythm & Blues*. Providence, R.I.: Music House Publishing, 1983.

Peter, Lawrence. *The Peter Principle*. New York: William Morrow, 1969.

Pollock, Bruce. *When Rock Was Young*. New York: Holt, Reinhardt and Winston, 1981.

Program to The 3rd Annual United in Group Harmony Association Hall of Fame Awards Ceremony, held March 27, 1993, at the Symphony Space Performing Arts Center, New York, N.Y.

Propes, Steve. *Those Oldies But Goodies: A Guide To '50s Record Collecting*. New York: MacMillan, 1973.

Propes, Steve. *Golden Oldies: A Guide To '60s Record Collecting*. New York: Chilton, 1974.

Propes, Steve. "Classic (Doo-Wop) Artists Get the Green Light in LA." *Record Collector's Monthly*, Issue #50, Nov.-Dec. 1991, p. 14.

Propes, Steve and Galen Gart. L.A. *R&B Vocal Groups and Duets, 1945-1965*. To Be Published in 2000.

Pruter, Robert. "Pastels' Promise Eclipsed By Manager's Marital Problems." *Record Collector's Monthly*, Issue #45, December 1989.

Pruter, Robert. "The Five Chances and Their World of Chicago R & B." *Goldmine*, April 6, 1990.

Pruter, Robert. "The Flamingos: The Chicago Years." *Goldmine*, April 6, 1990.

Pruter, Robert. "The Early Dells" *Record Collector's Monthly*, Issue #50, Nov.-Dec. 1991.

Pruter, Robert. *Chicago Soul*. Urbana: Univ. of Illinois Press, 1991.

Pruter, Robert. *Doowop: The Chicago Scene*. Chicago: University of Illinois Press, 1996.

Russo, Chuck. Letters to the Editor. *Stormy Weather*, Issue #3, January 1971.

Santelli, Robert. "Rhino Records remembers doo-wop." *Asbury Park Press*, Asbury Park, N.J.: Feb. 9, 1990, p. 12.

Schoener, Allon (ed.). *Harlem on My Mind: Cultural Capitol of Black America 1900-1968*. New York: Random House, 1968.

Schwartz, Bill. Editorial. *Time Barrier Express*, Issue #20, Nov.-Dec. 1976, p. 3.

Seroff, Doug & Ray Funk. Liner notes to *The Human Orchestra: Rhythm Quartets in The Thirties*, Clanka Lanka Records.

Shaw, Arnold. *Honkers and Shouters: The Golden Years of Rhythm & Blues*. New York: MacMillan, 1978.

Shepherd, John. *Tin Pan Alley*. London: Routledge & Kegan Paul, 1982.

Shore, Michael. *The History of American Bandstand*. New York: Ballantine, 1985.

Sicurella, Joe. "(I Found Out Why) The Lymon Brothers." *Big Town Review*, Vol. 1, No. 3, July-August 1972.

Skadberg, Gordon. Liner notes to *Southern Doo Wop* Vol. 1 & Vol. 2. London: Ace Records, 1996.

Smith, Wes. *The Pied Pipers of Rock 'n' Roll*. Marietta, GA: Longstreet Press, 1989.

Squire. "Off the Wall: A Collector's Memories of Times Square Records." *Echoes of the Past*, Issue #29, Autumn 1994, p. 4.

Stidom, Larry. "Record Report." *Echoes of the Past*, Issue # 23, Spring 1993, p. 20.

Stierle, Wayne. "Just Something I Remember." *Harmony Tymes*, #3, Winter 1987.

Stierle, Wayne. " The Jive Five: A True New York Story." *Goldmine*, Aug. 12, 1988.

Stierle, Wayne. "The Monotones: They Wrote the Book of Love." *Goldmine*, Aug. 12, 1988.

Stilwell, Brian. "What's in a Name?" *Echoes of the Past*, Issue #14, Fall 1990, p. 20.

Sylvani, Lou. "From the Square." *Bim Bam Boom*, Issue #1, Aug.-Sept. 1971, p. 9.

Sylvani, Louie. "From the Square." *Bim Bam Boom*, Issue #7, September 1972, p. 45.

Sylvani, Lou. "Back to the Square." *Time Barrier Express*, September 1974, p. 9.

Tamarkin, Jeff. " The Laddins: A New York Story." *Goldmine*, April 6, 1990.

Tudor, Dean, and Tudor, Nancy. *Black Music*. Littleton, Colorado: Libraries Unlimited Inc., 1979.

Turco, Art et al. "An Interview With Bobby Robinson." *Record Exchanger*, Issue #10, May 1972, p. 4.

Turco, Art. "Interview: 'Little' Anthony Gourdine." *Record Exchanger*, April 1973.

Vance, Marcia, and Groia, Phil. "The Willows." *Bim Bam Boom*, Vol. 1, No. 6, 1972.

Vance, Marcia. "Danny & the Juniors." *Bim Bam Boom*, Vol. 2, No. 6, 1974.

Vera, Billy. "Tracked Down and Identified: The Five Sharps." *Bim Bam Boom*, Issue #6, July 1972, p. 33.

Walsh, Jim. "Polk Miller and His 'Old South' Quartet." *Hobbies*, January 1960, p. 34.

Walsh, Jim. "A Directory of Pioneer Recording Groups." *Hobbies*, p. 32, October 1962.

Ward, Ed. "Italo-American Rock." In Miller, Jim, Ed., *The Rolling Stone Illustrated History of Rock & Roll*. New York: Rolling Stone Press, 1980.

Ward, Ed, et al. *Rock of Ages: The Rolling Stone History of Rock & Roll*. New York: Summit Books, 1986.

Warner, Jay. *American Singing Groups: A History 1940-1990*. New York: Billboard Books, 1992.

Wasserman, Steve. "Buck Ram and the Platters." *Bim Bam Boom*, Vol. 1, No. 6, 1972.

Weinger, Harry. "The Platters' Glory Days." *Goldmine*, Feb. 21, 1992.

Whitburn, Joel. *Pop Memories, 1890-1954*. Menomenee Falls, WI.: Record Research Inc., 1986.

Whitburn, Joel. *Top R&B Singles, 1942-1988*. Memomonee Falls, WI.: Record Research Inc., 1988.

Whitburn, Joel. *The Billboard Book of Top 40 Hits*. New York: Watson-Guptill, 1989.

Whitesell, Rick. "The Early Days of Radio and Vintage Vocal Groups." *Record Exchanger*, Issue #19, 1975, p. 11.

Whitesell, Rick. "The Pipes." *Goldmine*, April 1979.

Williamson, Drew. "Artist Interview: Hank Ballard says there really was an 'Annie'..." *Record Collector's Monthly*, Issue #36, Dec. 1986-Jan. 1987, p. 1.

World Book Encyclopedia. "Transistors." Chicago, IL: World Books, 1987.

Zucker, Mark. "The Saga of Lovin' Dan." *Time Barrier Express*, Issue #2, October 1974, p. 32.

Credits

Photographs:

All photographs in the book have been graciously donated by Bill Himmelman, through his company Music Nostalgia, with the exception of the following:

Chapter 7: The Golden Gate Quartet appeared in Record Exchanger, Vol. 5, No. 1, Issue 23 (on cover).

The Coleman Brothers appeared in Goldmine, #36, p. 31.

The Ravens appeared in Record Exchanger, Vol. 2, No. 4, Issue 9, p. 7.

The Orioles appeared in Record Exchanger, Vol. 2, No. 3, Issue 8 (on cover).

Chapter 9: The Crests appeared in Harmony Tymes, #1, Autumn 1980, p.4.

The Heartbreakers appeared in Time Barrier Express, #22, p. 27.

The Fascinators appeared in Bim Bam Boom, Vol. 1, Issue 7, p.19.

The Devotions appeared in Big Town Review, Vol. 1, No. 2, p.22.

Nino and the Ebbtides appeared in Bim Bam Boom, Vol. 1, Issue 7, p. 11.

Chapter 10: The Six Teens appeared in Big Town Review, Vol. 1, No. 3, p. 67.

The Castelles appeared in Bim Bam Boom, No. 12, p. 26.

Chapter 20: Gus Gossert appeared in Time Barrier Express, Vol. 2, No. 10, Issue 20, Nov.-Dec. 1976 (on cover).

Gus Gossert appeared in Time Barrier Express, Vol. 2, No. 10, Issue 20, Nov.-Dec. 1976, p. 5.

Cover of Record Exchanger, Vol. 2, No. 3, Issue 8.

Cover of Bim Bam Boom, Vol. 1, No. 1, Aug.-Sept. 1971.

Cover of Big Town Review, Vol. 1, Issue 1, Feb.-Mar. 1972.

Cover of Town Barrier Express, Issue 22, Mar.-Apr. 1977.

Cover of Story Untold, Vol. 1, No. 4.

Cover of Harmony Tymes, Issue 1, Autumn 1980.

Chapter 21: The Cadillacs and Esther Navarro (Apollo advertisement) appeared in Bim Bam Boom, Vol. 1, Issue 5, p. 8.

The Cadillacs appeared in Bim Bam Boom, Vol. 1, Issue 5 (on cover).

The Eternals appeared in Big Town Review, Vol. 1, No. 3, p. 6.

Lyrics:

Giving credit to composers, publishers and licensing bodies isn't as easy as it should be. There are two primary sources to track down information of this sort: The record labels themselves or the research departments existing within BMI and American Society of Composers, Authors and Publishers.

Finding information on a record label presumes that one can find the record, and this is not always the case. Some records omit publisher or licensing body. Often the song can be found only on CD and, unfortunately, CDs are generally not well documented. Further, though the research departments of both BMI and ASCAP tried to be helpful, they don't have complete listings of songs, especially obscure songs like some of the ones we were seeking. The same was true of their respective websites. Further, they focus on songs, not artists or lyrics. A search for a title such as "First Kiss" will come up with a number of songs with no artist listings (each with different composers) and one is hard-pressed to narrow them down.

Luckily, we were able to find out most of the relevant information about most of the quoted songs. Any information that will help fill in the blanks for the next edition will be received gratefully.

Chapter 3: "Woo Woo Pretty Girl," by the Indigos. Jan Corbo and Mike Basso (Mayco Music, BMI, 1958).

"Ding Dong" by the Quintones. J. Stein (Arc Music Corp., Myra Music, BMI, 1958).

Chapter 5: "Mr. Bassman" by Johnny Cymbal. Johnny Cymbal (Jalo Music Inc., BMI, 1963).

"I Wonder Why" by Dion & the Belmonts. Ade Olayinka and Ricardo D. Weeks 3 Seas Music Corp., ASCAP, 1958).

"I Remember" by the Five Discs. Paul Abarno (Schwartz Music, Shawn Music, ASCAP, 1958).

"Never Let You Go" by the Five Discs. Five Discs (Original Music Inc., BMI, 1961).

Chapter 7: "Zoom Zoom Zoom" by the Collegians. Donald Hayes and Harlan Jackson (Selma Music, BMI, 1957).

"Blue Moon" by the Marcels. Lorenz Hart and Richard Rogers (Robbins Music Corp. ASCAP, 1934).

Chapter 9: "I Wonder Why" by Dion & the Belmonts. Ade Olayinka and Ricardo D. Weeks (3 Seas Music Corp., ASCAP, 1958).

Chapter 11: "Good Goodbye" by the Bob Knight Four. Zeccola & Sepe (Mick Rick Music Corp., Sepe Music Co., BMI, 1961).

"Pray For Me" by the Four Pharaohs. Robert J. Lowery, W. Morris, Howard R. Ransom,

George Jones and Ronald Lee Wilson (Ransom Music Publishing Corp., BMI, 1957).

Chapter 14: "Charlie Brown" by the Coasters. Jerry Lieber and Mike Stoller (Anne-Rachel Music Corp., Jerry Lieber Music, Mike Stoller Music, ASCAP, 1959).

"Looking For An Echo" by Kenny Vance & the Planetones. Kenny Vance (Warner Brothers Music Corp., ASCAP, 1975).

Chapter 15:"Seven Wonders Of The World" by the Keytones. A. Knight (Embassy Music Corp., BMI, 1957).

"My Beauty My Own" by the Fascinators. J. Potter (1954 on Your Copy 1136)

"My Version Of Love" by the Vocaltones. Rolando Duncan and Robert Robertson (Bess Music, BMI, 1956).

"To Each His Own" by the Ink Spots. Jay Livingston & Ray Evans (Paramount Music Corp., ASCAP, 1946).

"Bye Bye Baby" by Earl Lewis & Channels. Clarence L. Lewis, Earl Lewis and Morgan C. Robinson (Windswept Pacific Songs, Longitude Music, BMI, 1957).

"The Vows Of Love," by the Paragons. Ninny, Ethel Byrd (Ninny-Ethel Byrd, BMI, 1958).

"The Vowels Of Love" by the Poets. D. Andrews-Poets (Reynolds-Andrews Publishing Co., BMI, 1958).

"The Letter" by Vernon Green & the Medallions. Vernon Green (Wixen Music Publishing Inc., BMI, 1954).

"My Reverie" by the Larks. Larry Clinton (Dulcet Music Co., ASCAP, 1938).

"Just To See You Smile Again" by the Four Buddies. John Carroll (Screen Gems-EMI Music Inc., BMI, 1950).

"The Ten Commandments" by the Moonglows. M. Paul (Arc Music, 1958).

"United" by the Love Notes. Hicks, Johnson, Robinson (Pollard-Everlast, BMI, 1957).

"Get Away, Mr. Satan, Get Away" by the Coleman Brothers. Johnny Lange, Hy Heath and Richard Loring (1945).

"Chapel Bells" by the Fascinators. Anthony Passalacqua (Wildcat Music Inc., BMI, 1958).

"The Fabulous Fifties" by Robert Klein & group. Robert Klein (Froben Enterprises Inc., BMI, 1973).

"Mexico" by the Rocketones. Bill Witt, Roland Johnson and Morty Craft (Tenson Music, Selma Music, Craft Music, BMI, 1957)

"Stranded In The Jungle" by the Cadets. James E. Johnson, Ernestine Smith and A. Curry APRS, Shag Publications, BMI, 1956).

"Vines Of Love" by the Del Rios. Morris Muniz and Bert Riley (Glad Music Co., BMI, 1958).

"Peppermint Stick" by the Elchords. Moore and Jimmy Jones (MCA Duchess Music Corp., Jenjillus Music, BMI, 1957).

"Happiness" by the Orchids. Orchids (1955)

"It's Too Soon To Know" by Sonny Til & the Orioles. Deborah Chessler, (Edwin H. Morris & Co., Inc., ASCAP, 1948).

"Tell Me" by the Master-Tones. A. Gray & C. Gray (1954).

"Two Loves Have I" by the Diamonds. J.P. Murray, Barry Trivers & Vincent Scotto (EMI Virgin Music Inc., EMI Miller Catalog Inc., Sacem, ASCAP, 1931).

"Girl In My Dreams" by the Cliques. Joe Josea, Jules Taub, Sam Ling and Maxwell Davis (Carlin Music Corp., BMI, 1956).

"Please Remember My Love" by the Storytellers. Dave Antrell (Autopower Music, Stethoscope Music, BMI, 1990).

"Darling Je Vous Aime Beaucoup" by the Chateaus. Milton DeLugg and Allan Roberts (Music Sales Corp., Summit Music Corp., ASCAP, 1956).

"I Remember" by the Five Discs. Paul Abarno (Schwartz Music, Shawn Music, ASCAP, 1958).

"Those Oldies But Goodies (Remind Me Of You" by Little Caesar & the Romans. Nick Curinga and Paul Politi (Golden Unlimited Music, Maravilla Music, BMI, 1961).

"Great Jumpin' Catfish" by the Wanderers. W. Miller, B. Smith & Y. Patemo (Malver Music, BMI, 1957).

"Let's Go For A Ride" by the Collegians. Harlan Jackson (Sylvia, BMI, 1958).

"Love Doll" by the Scarlets. Larry D. Robinson and Morgan C. Robinson (Arc Music Corp., BMI, 1955).

"Careless Love" by Rudy & the Tradewinds (1960 on Angletone 543)

"Everyone's Laughing" by the Spaniels. Calvin Carter (Conrad Music, BMI, 1957).

"A Night To Remember" by the Five Satins. A. Scott (1958).

"Rama Lama Ding Dong" by the Edsels. George Jones Jr. (Jumbo Music, Twin Music Inc., BMI, 1958).

"Nosy Neighbors" by the Larktones. (1958 on Riki 140).

"Victory" by Gene Pitney with the Embers. Gene Pitney (Pitney Music, BMI, 1958).

"Cora Lee" by Little Bobby Rivera & the Hemlocks. Leroy Jefferson and Morgan C. Robinson (Jonware Music Co., Windswept Pacific Songs, BMI, 1957).

"You Are My Only Love" by the Romans. "Larry" (1958 on Juno 013).

"Love" by the No Names. (1964 on Guyden 2114).

"The Lonely Telephone" by the Quintones. (1955 on Jordan 1601)

"Lonely Nights" by the Hearts. Zelma Sanders (Dare Music Inc., BMI, 1955).

"Willa Bea" by the Ambassadors. John Motley and Louis Van Dyke (Simek Music, BMI, 1953).

"Honey, Honey" by the Trutones. Mills and Henderson (Combine Music, BMI, 1958).

"Story Of A Love Gone Cold" by the Gentlemen (recorded 1954 for Apollo Records).

"My Brother" by the Coolbreezers. Bea Tibbitts (Pamco Music, BMI, 1957).

"Here I Am Broken Hearted" by the Four J's. B.G. De Sylva, Lew Brown and Ray Henderson, (The Songwriters Guild, ASCAP, 1964).

"Double Dealin' Baby" by the Souvenirs. (Dootsie Williams Inc., 1957).

"Little Side Car" by the Larks. Bobby Smith (Bess Music Corp., BMI, 1951).

"I Hate Your Guts" by J.B. & the Sha La La.

"First Kiss" by the El Vireos. (1959 on Revello 1002).

"Pizza Pie" by Norman Fox & the Rob Roys. Norman Fox (Wildcat Music, BMI, 1957).

"Ghost Of My Baby" by the Checkers. Henry Glover (Fort Knox Music Inc., Trio Music Co. Inc., BMI, 1953).

"Way Up" by Lincoln Fig & the Dates. I. Figueroa & M. Mysels (A. & B. Worthy Music Co., BMI, 1958).

"The Freckle Song" by the Four Vagabonds (1947).

"A Little Bit Of Soap" by the Jarmels. Bert Russell (Continental Communications Corp., EMI Music Pub., BMI, 1961).

"Sympathy" by the Cadillacs. Esther Navarro and Jeanne Burns (Jubilee Music Inc., ASCAP, 1955).

"Up Yours" by Tino & the Revlons.

Chapter 21:"Gloria" by the Mills Brothers. Leon Rene (Rene Leon Publications, ASCAP, 1946).

"Gloria" by the Cadillacs. Esther Navarro (Benell Music, BMI, 1954).

"Willa Bea" by the Ambassadors. John Motley and Louis Van Dyke (Simek Music, BMI, 1953).

"I'm Gonna Do That Woman In" by the Sparrows (1953).

"Knock Her Down" by the Orbits. (Eastwick Pub. Co., BMI, 1959).

"Don't Mind Dyin" by the Jayhawks. Curry-Andrews (Reynolds & Andrews, BMI,1956).

"Gonna Feed My Baby Poison" by the Rocketeers. Smith, Jones, Rogers, Harris and Warshaw (Ember Music, BMI, 1953).

"What's That" by the Five Royales. Lowman Pauling (Fort Knox Music Inc., Trio Music Co., Inc., BMI, 1954).

"All Because Of Love" by the Charts. Charts-Johnson (Everlast Publishing, BMI, 1957).

"It Won't Take Long" by the Native Boys. Joe Josea (Powerforce Music, BMI, 1954).

"I'm Gonna Pick Your Teeth With An Ice Pick" by the Mellows (Torchlight Music, BMI).

"Time Takes Care Of Everything" by the Ravens. Cole, Fields and T. Rogers.

"Rubber Biscuit" by the Chips. Nat Epps, Charles Johnson, Shedreck Lincoln and Samuel Strain (Adam R. Levy & Father Enterprises, BMI, 1956).

"Shombalor" by Sheriff & the Ravels. Elmer Sheriff and Aki Aleong (Conrad Music, BMI, 1959).

"Jungle" by the Concepts. Johnnie James and Al Browne (Thornett Music, BMI, 1961).

"Bim Bam Boom" by the El Dorados. Jewel Jones (Conrad Music, BMI, 1956).

"Blind Date" by the Eternals (1961 on Warwick 6111).

"Please Mr. Sun" by Tippie & the Clovermen. Sid Frank and Ray Getzov (Chappell Music Ltd., ASCAP, 1951).

"Mr. Night" by the Motions. M. Kalfin (1961 on Laurie 3112).

"The Decision" by Mr. Lee with the Cherokees (1960).

"I'll Have To Decide" by Kenny & the Socialites. Malou Rene and George Martin Koppel (Nathan Music Corp., 1958).

"Sitting On The Porch" by the Four Peaks.

"Babalu's Wedding Day" by the Eternals. Carlos Girona, William Martin and Alex Miranda (Martin Manor Publishing, BMI, 1959).

"Sixty Minute Man" by the Dominos. Billy Ward & Rose Marks (Fort Knox Music Inc., Trio Music Co. Inc., BMI, 1951).

"Dan, The Backdoor Man" by Georgia White. Jones-Williams (Decca 7269).

"Dapper Dan, The Ladies Man From Dixieland" by Eddie Cantor. Albert Von Tilzer and Lew Brown (Broadway Music Corp., ASCAP, 1921).

"I'm A Sixty Minute Rocket Man" by Ric Harper. Rudolph Toombs (Unichappell Music Inc., BMI, 1951).

"It Ain't The Meat (It's The Motion)" by the Swallows. Henry Glover and Sidney Nathan (Fort Knox Music Inc., Trio Music Co. Inc., BMI, 1951).

"I Can't Do Sixty More" by the Du Droppers. Caleb Ginyard (Bob-Dan Music Co., BMI, 1952).

"Come Up To My Room" by the Majors. Jimmy Beckum (1952 on Derby 779).

"The Last Of The Good Rockin' Men" by the Four Jacks. Ray Robinson, Charles Darnell, Rick Ravon, Mario De Lagarde and Ralph Bass (Fort Knox Music, Trio Music Co. Inc., BMI, 1952).

"Life Of Ease" by the Imperials. Milton Harris and Sax Kari (Kencee Music, BMI).

"Hatchet Man" by the Robins. Jerry Leiber and Mike Stoller (Quintet Music Co., BMI, 1955).

"Don't Knock" by the Spiders. Adolph Smith, Commodore Music, BMI, 1954).